Human Resource Management in Australia

STRATEGY / PEOPLE / PERFORMANCE

THIRD EDITION

McGraw-Hill Irwin

Copyright © 2008 McGraw Hill Australia Pty Limited
Additional owners of copyright are acknowledged on page credits.

Every effort has been made to trace and acknowledge copyrighted material. The authors and publishers tender their apologies should any infringement have occurred.

Reproduction and communication for educational purposes
The Australian *Copyright Act* 1968 (the Act) allows a maximum of one chapter or 10% of the pages of this work, whichever is the greater, to be reproduced and/or communicated by any educational institution for its educational purposes provided that the institution (or the body that administers it) has sent a Statutory Educational notice to Copyright Agency Limited (CAL) and been granted a licence. For details of statutory educational and other copyright licences contact: Copyright Agency Limited, Level 15, 233 Castlereagh Street, Sydney NSW 2000. Telephone: (02) 9394 7600. Website: www.copyright.com.au

Reproduction and communication for other purposes
Apart from any fair dealing for the purposes of study, research, criticism or review, as permitted under the Act, no part of this publication may be reproduced, distributed or transmitted in any form or by any means, or stored in a database or retrieval system, without the written permission of McGraw-Hill Australia including, but not limited to, any network or other electronic storage.

Enquiries should be made to the publisher via www.mcgraw-hill.com.au or marked for the attention of the Permissions Editor at the address below.

National Library of Australia Cataloguing-in-Publication Data

De Cieri, Helen.
Human resource management in Australia : strategy people performance.

3rd ed.
ISBN 9780070135031 (pbk.).

1. Personnel management - Australia. 2. Career development - Australia. 3. Work. I. Kramar, Robin. II. Title.

658.300994

Publisher: Ailsa Brackley du Bois
Developmental Editor: Rosemary Noble
Managing Editor: Kathryn Fairfax
Production Editor: Colette Hoeben
Editor: Alison Moodie
Proofreader: Terry Townsend
Permissions Editor: Philip Millard
Cover and Internal Design: Liz Nicholson
Cover Image: Constantini Michele/photoA/to Agency/Getty Images
Typesetter: Anne McLean, Jobs On Mac
Indexer: Michael Ramsden
Printed on 70 gsm matt art by RR Donnelly in China

Human Resource Management in Australia

STRATEGY / PEOPLE / PERFORMANCE

THIRD EDITION

HELEN DE CIERI
Monash University

ROBIN KRAMAR
Macquarie Graduate School of Management

RAYMOND A. NOE
Ohio State University

JOHN R. HOLLENBECK
Michigan State University

BARRY GERHART
University of Wisconsin

PATRICK M. WRIGHT
Cornell University

McGraw-Hill Irwin

Boston   Burr Ridge, IL   Dubuque, IA   Madison, WI   New York
San Francisco   St. Louis   Bangkok   Bogotá   Caracas   Kuala Lumpur
Lisbon   London   Madrid   Mexico City   Milan   Montreal   New Delhi
Santiago   Seoul   Singapore   Sydney   Taipei   Toronto

CONTENTS IN BRIEF

PART 1 MANAGING THE HUMAN RESOURCE ENVIRONMENT

CHAPTER 1 HUMAN RESOURCE MANAGEMENT IN AUSTRALIA — 2
CHAPTER 2 STRATEGIC HUMAN RESOURCE MANAGEMENT — 52
CHAPTER 3 THE LEGAL CONTEXT FOR HUMAN RESOURCE MANAGEMENT — 90
CHAPTER 4 OCCUPATIONAL HEALTH AND SAFETY — 112
CHAPTER 5 INDUSTRIAL RELATIONS — 148

PART 2 BUILDING HUMAN RESOURCE MANAGEMENT SYSTEMS

CHAPTER 6 ANALYSIS AND DESIGN OF WORK — 176
CHAPTER 7 HUMAN RESOURCE PLANNING AND HUMAN RESOURCE INFORMATION SYSTEMS — 216
CHAPTER 8 RECRUITMENT AND SELECTION — 256

PART 3 DEVELOPING PEOPLE

CHAPTER 9 MANAGING DIVERSITY AND WORK-LIFE BALANCE — 302
CHAPTER 10 PERFORMANCE MANAGEMENT — 340
CHAPTER 11 LEARNING AND DEVELOPMENT — 394
CHAPTER 12 EMPLOYEE DEVELOPMENT AND CAREER MANAGEMENT — 444

PART 4 REWARDING PEOPLE

CHAPTER 13 MANAGING COMPENSATION — 482
CHAPTER 14 PERFORMANCE-RELATED PAY — 526

PART 5 CONTEMPORARY ISSUES FOR HUMAN RESOURCE MANAGEMENT

CHAPTER 15 ETHICS AND HUMAN RESOURCE MANAGEMENT — 562
CHAPTER 16 INTERNATIONAL HUMAN RESOURCE MANAGEMENT — 588
CHAPTER 17 MANAGING EMPLOYEE TURNOVER AND RETENTION — 618
CHAPTER 18 EVALUATING AND IMPROVING THE HUMAN RESOURCE FUNCTION — 656

ENDNOTES — 691
GLOSSARY — 733
INDEX — 743

CONTENTS IN FULL

About this book	xiv	Foreword	xxiv
Highlights of this edition	xvi	About the original authors	xxv
Text at a glance	xviii	About the Australian authors	xxvi
E-Student	xxii	About the contributing authors	xxvii
E-Instructor	xxiii	Acknowledgments	xxix

PART 1   MANAGING THE HUMAN RESOURCE ENVIRONMENT

CHAPTER 1   HUMAN RESOURCE MANAGEMENT IN AUSTRALIA   1

Objectives	2
Introduction	4
The development of theoretical bases for human resource management	6
What activities and roles do HR departments perform?	9
What skills do HR professionals need?	14
Characteristics of the workforce and human resource environment	15
Competitive challenges influencing human resource management	24
Meeting competitive challenges through HRM practices	38
Organisation of this book	41
Chapter summary	44
Web exercises	45
Discussion questions	45
HUMAN RESOURCE EXCELLENCE: THE BEST COMPANIES TO WORK FOR IN AUSTRALIA	3
Managing challenges of globalisation	
HR strategies go global	27
Managing challenges through HR innovation	
Leading organisational change	29
Managing challenges through sustainability	
The human factor	34
Managing challenges through attracting and retaining people	
CEOs lament retention woes	39
Managing people	
Human capital: The state of play in Australia	43
HRM spotlight	
Value added HR	46
Case study	
St George: Banking on the business of HR	48

CHAPTER 2   STRATEGIC HUMAN RESOURCE MANAGEMENT   52

Objectives	52
Introduction	54
What is strategic management?	55
Strategy formulation	61
Strategy implementation	66
Strategic types	72
Strategy evaluation and control	80
Strategy as implementation	82
Strategic human resource executives	83
Chapter summary	87
Web exercises	87
Discussion questions	87
BREAKING IN A NEW CULTURE: VIRGIN BLUE'S STORY	53
Managing challenges of globalisation	
Global leadership: the rise of the GEO	63
HRM spotlight	
Lead vs lag indicators	65
Managing challenges through sustainability	
Finding a better fit	70
Managing challenges through attracting and retaining people	
Topping up on talent	73
Managing challenges of globalisation	
Jobs for sale in a free-trade world	79
Managing challenges through HR innovation	
Measure for measure	81
Managing people	
Asia to outgrow the world	86
Case study	
Planning for the future	88

v

CONTENTS IN FULL

CHAPTER 3 THE LEGAL CONTEXT FOR HUMAN RESOURCE MANAGEMENT   90

Objectives	90
Introduction	92
Chapter map	92
The equal employment opportunity laws	96
Recruitment and selection	102
The termination of employment	103
Occupational health and safety matters	106
Chapter summary	109
Web exercises	109
Discussion questions	109

BULLYING THE NEW BATTLEFIELD	91
Managing challenges through sustainability	
Hard workchoices for HR	94
Managing challenges of globalisation	
Islam in the workplace	98
Managing challenges of attracting and retaining people	
Boss offered sex accuser a hug	102
Managing challenges through HR innovation	
Policing the Internet	104
Managing people	
Virgin Blue treated older candidates differently to younger candidates	107
Case study	
Protecting your path	110

CHAPTER 4 OCCUPATIONAL HEALTH AND SAFETY   112

Objectives	112
Introduction	114
Defining occupational health and safety	115
Occupational health and safety statistics in Australia	117
Australian occupational health and safety law	119
Moving beyond occupational health and safety legal compliance	126
Human resource management strategies for occupational health and safety	134
Occupational health and safety and small businesses	137
Occupational health and safety in the Asia–Pacific region	138
Evaluating occupational health and safety strategies	141
Chapter summary	143
Web exercises	143
Discussion questions	144

DOZENS WILL DIE AT WORK THIS YEAR. INEVITABLE, OR NOT?	113
Managing challenges through attracting and retaining people	
Maximising employee performance while minimising employee stress	116
HRM Spotlight	
Handling drug and alcohol abuse in the workplace	118
Managing challenges through HR innovation	
Firing up workforce health and fitness	129
Managing challenges through sustainability	
Healthy workers get the job done, surveys show	131
Managing challenges of globalisation	
Timewarp: A jump to the left on labour law	140
Managing people	
Lightening the workload	141
Case study	
The Beaconsfield Mine	145

CHAPTER 5 INDUSTRIAL RELATIONS 148

Objectives	148
Introduction	150
From centralisation to decentralisation	150
The emergence of workplace bargaining and conflict resolution	156
The changing nature of employment	159
Declining union density in Australia	162
The growth of employee prerogative	165
Industrial relations challenges for the human resource professional of the future	166
Chapter summary	171
Web exercises	172
Discussion questions	172

HUMAN RESOURCE PROFESSIONALS: NEW ROLES, NEW EXPECTATIONS	149
Managing challenges through HR innovation	
Work in progress	154
Managing challenges through attracting and retaining people	
Commonwealth Bank shuns AWA allegations	161
Managing challenges of globalisation	
Unions in global fight on Alcoa	164
Managing challenges through sustainability	
ANZ and St George lead the way in offshoring jobs	167
Managing people	
Better work deal for youth	170
Case study	
A roster change at Metals	173

PART 2 BUILDING HUMAN RESOURCE MANAGEMENT 175

CHAPTER 6 ANALYSIS AND DESIGN OF WORK 176

Objectives	176
Introduction	179
Work-flow analysis and organisation structure	180
Job analysis	187
Job design	197
The contemporary organisational context for job analysis and job design	203
Chapter summary	211
Web exercises	211
Discussion questions	211

WORDS FROM THE Ys: WE WANT GLOBAL ROAMING	177
Managing challenges through HR innovation	
Work's new rules	187
Managing challenges through sustainability	
Branding the best employer	188
Managing challenges through attracting and retaining people	
Multinational firms send more local Chinese talent overseas	205
Managing challenges of globalisation	
India's young and cool answer call	206
HRM spotlight	
Outsourcing: Making HR more strategic	208
Managing people	
HR in Australia's top companies	208
Case study	
ANZ bank: Breaking out of the mould	212

CONTENTS IN FULL

CHAPTER 7 HUMAN RESOURCE PLANNING AND HUMAN RESOURCE INFORMATION SYSTEMS   216

Objectives	216	SOFTWARE REPLACES CRYSTAL BALL	217
Introduction	218	*HRM spotlight*	
The human resource planning process	219	Coming of age for workforce planning	221
Human resource information systems	232	*Managing challenges of globalisation*	
Information technology used in HRM	235	Up to the job? How India and China risk being stifled by a skills squeeze	233
HRIS: software applications for HRM	240	*Managing challenges through HR innovation*	
Chapter summary	251	Servicing HR's needs	237
Web exercises	251	*HRM spotlight*	
Discussion questions	251	Big brother catches business on hop	241
		Managing challenges through attracting and retaining people	
		Groomed for succession	243
		Managing challenges through sustainability	
		Is HR technology a help or hindrance?	249
		Managing people	
		Hiring hurdles easy with personnel software	250
		Case study	
		The talent game: Three steps to checkmate	253

CHAPTER 8 RECRUITMENT AND SELECTION   256

Objectives	256	GUERRILLA TACTICS IN THE WAR FOR TALENT	257
Introduction	259	*Managing challenges of globalisation*	
The human resource recruitment process	259	Workers of the world take flight	262
Selection	275	*Managing challenges through HR innovation*	
Chapter summary	295	Putting the IT in recruitment	266
Web exercises	297	*Managing challenges through sustainability*	
Discussion questions	297	Staying one step ahead: Graduate recruitment	272
		Managing challenges through attracting and retaining people	
		Living values the Ritz-Calton way	293
		Managing people	
		After BPOs, it is now the turn of RPOs	294
		Case study	
		A look inside the Google talent machine	298

PART 3 DEVELOPING PEOPLE 301

CHAPTER 9 MANAGING DIVERSITY AND WORK–LIFE BALANCE 302

Objectives	302
Introduction	304
A model of diversity management	305
Diversity and equal employment opportunity	308
Role of diversity management in improving organisational performance	310
Initiatives to manage diversity	315
Challenging issues associated with managing diversity	321
Work–life balance	328
Future directions in diversity management	330
Chapter summary	335
Web exercises	335
Discussion questions	335

CULTURAL DIVERSITY, IBM STYLE	303
Managing challenges of globalisation Woods Bagot: Going global	313
HRM spotlight Inside age diversity at Deutsche Bank	315
Managing challenges through sustainability 3M: sustaining our future	318
Managing challenges through HR innovation Diversity in practice: BT	321
Managing challenges through attracting and retaining people Value the differences	331
HRM spotlight Hiring overseas workers	333
Managing people Aging workforce attitudes entrenched management	334
Case study Does diversity pay?	337

CHAPTER 10 PERFORMANCE MANAGEMENT 340

Objectives	340
Introduction	342
An organisational model of performance management	344
Purposes of performance management	347
Performance management criteria	351
Approaches to measuring performance	355
Choosing a source for performance information	374
Rater errors in performance measurement	377
Performance feedback	379
Managing the performance of teams	384
Developing and implementing a system that follows legal guidelines	384
Use of technology for performance management: Electronic monitoring	387
Chapter summary	390
Web exercises	390
Discussion questions	390

HOW INVESTORS RATE HUMAN CAPITAL	341
Managing challenges through attracting and retaining people Fashion stakes	349
Managing challenges of globalisation Outsourcing IT	353
HRM spotlight Chucking the sickies	381
Managing challenges through sustainability HR directions come under APRA gun	386
Managing challenges through HR innovation Finely tuned Sensis	387
Managing people Bridging the performance management gap	388
Case study HR falls short in high performance cultures	392

CONTENTS IN FULL

CHAPTER 11 LEARNING AND DEVELOPMENT — 394

Objectives	394
Introduction to learning and development	396
Training in Australian organisations	399
The National Vocational Training System	402
Designing effective training systems	404
Learning in the workplace	410
Communities of practice	413
Socialisation and orientation	433
Training and pay systems	435
Chapter summary	439
Web exercises	439
Discussion questions	440

SING TEL OPTUS LINKS LEARNING AND DEVELOPMENT TO BUSINESS GOALS — 395

Managing challenges of globalisation
Minerals industry needs 70 000 new workers in next decade — 404

Managing challenges through HR innovation
Blended learning — 424

Managing challenges through sustainability
Ongoing ROI struggles of L&D — 434

Managing challenges through attracting and retaining people
Induction unlocks retention woes — 437

Managing people
Learning and development at OPSM — 438

Case study
Pursuing the intelligent enterprise — 441

CHAPTER 12 EMPLOYEE DEVELOPMENT AND CAREER MANAGEMENT — 444

Objectives	444
Introduction	446
The relationship between learning and development, and careers	447
Approaches to learning and development	449
Career management systems	466
Special issues in learning and development and career management	471
Chapter summary	476
Web exercises	477
Discussion questions	477

TEACH THE STAFF TO STAY — 445

Managing challenges of globalisation
Investment in skills will help meet future challenges — 450

Managing challenges through sustainability
Aboriginal & Torres Islander initiatives at Qantas — 451

Managing challenges through HR innovation
Task to taskmaster — 470

HRM spotlight
Catching and keeping senior women beyond the glass ceiling — 472

Managing challenges through attracting and retaining people
Filling the leader's boots — 474

Managing people
Mentors can help new employees to settle in — 475

Case study
Support from the sidelines — 478

PART 4 REWARDING PEOPLE 481

CHAPTER 13 MANAGING COMPENSATION 482

Objectives	482
Introduction	485
Equity theory and fairness	486
Developing pay levels	488
The importance of process: Participation and communication	501
Current challenges	502
Executive pay	509
Government regulation of compensation	515
Chapter summary	522
Web exercises	523
Discussion questions	523

WHAT ARE YOU WORTH? AHRI REMUNERATION & BENEFITS SURVEY	483
Managing challenges through sustainability $7.8m farewell calls pay deal into question	492
Managing challenges through HR innovation PM's pockets fill with pay rise, tax cuts	503
HRM spotlight Tough times for CEOs: Making do on $5200 a day	510
HRM spotlight Big rewards will stick in the craw, Howard admits	511
Managing challenges through HR innovation Bonus envy—when $500 000 is not enough	513
Managing challenges of globalisation Money can't buy you … Performance	514
Managing challenges through attracting and retaining people Being fair: The new Fair Pay Commission may signal the beginning of broader reforms	520
Managing people Taken to the cleaners	521
Case study Able Management Consultants, Inc.	524

CHAPTER 14 PERFORMANCE-RELATED PAY 526

Objectives	526
Introduction	528
How does pay influence individual employees?	530
How do pay and benefits influence labour force compensation?	534
Programs	535
Managerial and executive pay	547
Process and context issues	552
Organisation strategy and compensation strategy: A question of fit	554
Chapter summary	557
Web exercises	557
Discussion questions	557

A JOB WELL DONE	527
HRM spotlight Recognising highly accomplished teachers or performance/merit pay	531
Managing challenges through attracting and retaining people Crazy brave	533
Managing challenges through sustainability The age of disclosure	544
Managing challenges through HR innovation How can HRM promote organisational innovation?	548
HRM spotlight Executive pay: Reining in the bulls	551
Managing challenges of globalisation The importance of place in the global war for talent	555
Managing people Reputations, risks and rewards	556
Case study Pay role development	559

XI

CONTENTS IN FULL

PART 5 CONTEMPORARY ISSUES FOR HUMAN RESOURCE MANAGEMENT 561

CHAPTER 15 ETHICS AND HUMAN RESOURCE MANAGEMENT 562

Objectives	562
Introduction	564
Why ethics are important in HRM	564
Ethical principles and their actions	567
The rights and responsibilities of employers and employees	571
Issues of justice and fairness in the employment relationship	575
The ethicality of HRM	576
Chapter summary	583
Web exercises	584
Discussion questions	585
NEW RULES FOR ROMANCE	563
Managing challenges through sustainability	
Downshifting: Quitting the rat race	566
Managing challenges of globalisation	
Outsourcing no tail spin for Qantas	574
Managing challenges through attracting and retaining people	
Culture key in anti-corruption	578
Managing challenges through HR innovation	
Security gets under employee's skin	581
Managing people	
Are you making your staff ill?	582
Case study	
The South Blackwater mine	586

CHAPTER 16 INTERNATIONAL HUMAN RESOURCE MANAGEMENT 588

Objectives	588
Introduction	591
Defining international HRM	591
Differences between domestic and international HRM	594
Variables that moderate differences between domestic and international HRM	600
Applying a strategic view of international HRM	607
Chapter summary	613
Web exercises	613
Discussion questions	614
INTERNATIONALLY MOBILE	589
Managing challenges through HR innovation	
Hands across the seas	595
Managing challenges through attracting and retaining people	
What graduates want	599
Managing challenges of globalisation	
Rise of China, India a big plus for world	608
Managing challenges through sustainability	
The global hunt for talent	610
Managing people	
Offshoring still needs management	612
Case study	
Making employees mobile	615

CHAPTER 17 MANAGING EMPLOYEE TURNOVER AND RETENTION — 618

Objectives	618
Introduction	621
Managing involuntary turnover	**622**
Managing voluntary turnover	**630**
Managing employee retention	**640**
Chapter summary	653
Web exercises	653
Discussion questions	653

HR, ANYTIME, ANYWHERE	619
Managing challenges of globalisation Banks keep low profile in outsourcing	623
HRM spotlight Taking the bully by the horns	626
HRM spotlight Frustration grows at staff churn rates of up to 40pc	631
Managing challenges through attracting and retaining people How to keep them keen	641
Managing challenges through sustainability Staying power	643
Managing challenges through HR innovation Taking the pulse	646
Managing people Saturn spins out of control	651
Case study NAB and the art of corporate renewal	654

CHAPTER 18 EVALUATING AND IMPROVING THE HUMAN RESOURCE FUNCTION — 656

Objectives	656
Introduction	658
A strategic approach to measuring HR effectiveness	**659**
Approaches for evaluating effectiveness	**666**
Improving HR effectiveness	**675**
Chapter summary	687
Web exercises	687
Discussion questions	688

DELIVERING ON THE PROMISE OF HR TRANSFORMATION	657
Managing challenges of globalisation Care for staff puts firm a step ahead	661
Managing challenges through sustainability Health hits home in the workplace	663
Managing challenges through HR innovation Lead v Lag indicators: Educating analyst	676
Managing challenges through attracting and retaining people Recruitment innovation: Talent pipelines and supply chains	678
Managing people The future of HR	684
HRM spotlight A puppet, a lie and the HR guy	686
Case study Human resource management in Australia	689

Endnotes	691
Glossary	733
Index	743

ABOUT THIS BOOK

OUR STRATEGIC APPROACH TO HRM

We believe that the way in which people are managed is vital for the sustainability of any organisation. Sustainability relies not only on financial outcomes but also employee wellbeing, customer satisfaction, and social and environmental responsibility. In our view, all human resource management (HRM) activities need to work together in order for the HRM function to help the organisation create and sustain value. Effective HRM is at the core of the three-way linkage between strategy, people and performance. Each chapter of this text discusses the strategic developments in each HR area and emphasises HRM as a means of creating value and helping organisations sustain a competitive advantage.

This is the third Australian adaptation of the international edition which was written by Raymond Noe, John Hollenbeck, Barry Gerhart and Patrick Wright. Those authors did a wonderful job in providing a text that captures the key theoretical, empirical and practical developments and issues in HRM. Their text provides a solid foundation enabling us to develop our book to be relevant to the contemporary HRM scene in Australia and the Asia–Pacific region. We have introduced new themes which capture the challenges pertinent in the local context at the beginning of the twenty-first century. Some of these challenges pose major concerns for organisations.

KEY THEMES IN THIS TEXT

Throughout the text, we address these four key categories of challenges faced by organisations today:

- the challenge of globalisation
- the challenge of attracting and retaining people
- the challenge of HR innovation
- the challenge of sustainability.

As introduced in Chapter 1 and discussed throughout the book, we believe that organisations must successfully deal with these challenges to create and sustain value, and effective HRM is crucial to this process.

FEATURES OF THIS TEXT

- Each chapter reflects the most significant and most recent academic research and organisational practices in HRM. Up-to-date examples are provided throughout each chapter.
- Chapter opening case studies provide examples of practical HRM issues facing organisations in Australia and the Asia–Pacific region. Some of these case studies highlight organisations that have been recognised for their effective HR approaches. Others describe strategies that organisations have developed in order to deal with encountered difficulties.
- Each chapter contains cases featuring practical examples of organisations meeting the four key challenges.
- 'HRM spotlight' cases provide the most current practical examples available of organisations introducing innovative HR strategies, or encountering new and emerging problems.
- At the end of each chapter, a 'Managing People' case and an 'End-of-Chapter' case provide in-depth studies of HRM-related problems or issues encountered by HR professionals and organisations. The case questions require students to critically evaluate problems or issues presented, and to apply the chapter content to analyse the case.
- Web exercises encourage students to use the Internet to explore the latest developments in HRM and to have access to experts in a particular area of HRM.
- Discussion questions at the end of each chapter help students to learn the concepts covered in the chapter and to consider different viewpoints when addressing the HRM issues encountered.

ADDRESSING THE NEEDS OF ACADEMICS, STUDENTS AND MANAGERS

This book aims to provide undergraduate and graduate students with fundamental knowledge about HRM. It will be useful for those who want to become successful HR professionals and for those who have responsibility for managing people. This book identifies effective HRM strategies for managers who have personal responsibility for the design, implementation and maintenance of HRM practices, or who are working with HR professionals. Our intention is to emphasise effective ways to manage people and the issues most likely to be faced in current HR practice.

The text takes a more intellectual and practical approach to HRM than competing books, paying a lot more attention to empirical research and local examples. It addresses the real world complexities and challenges for HRM in Australia and the Asia–Pacific region by providing local examples and the outcomes of current research. Written by experts in their field with strong research, teaching and industry backgrounds, this text successfully explains through illustration, and reinforces the link between concepts and critical thinking.

In the process of preparing this book, we built on our own experience and insights from students, colleagues and professional networks, by seeking input from academics around Australia. This has provided us with invaluable ideas that we have incorporated into the book.

Helen De Cieri
Robin Kramar

THE BOOK CONTAINS THE FOLLOWING FIVE PARTS:	
PART 1	provides an introduction to the field of HRM and the environment faced by employees and employers in Australia. The ways in which HRM can help organisations to meet the key global, stakeholder and work systems challenges are introduced. Key environmental forces include the organisation's strategic approach, legal constraints, and institutional frameworks related to occupational health and safety, and industrial relations.
PART 2	deals with the elements related to building HRM systems—the type of work to be performed, HR planning, HR information systems, and staffing an organisation.
PART 3	covers HR activities related to the development of employees—diversity management and work–life balance, performance management and employee learning, development and career management.
PART 4	addresses issues of rewarding employees, including the design of pay structures and performance-related pay systems.
PART 5	covers contemporary issues for the HRM field, including ethical issues, international HRM, managing employee turnover and retention, and evaluating and improving the HR function.

HIGHLIGHTS OF THIS EDITION

Our intent is to balance our attention on current academic knowledge and practice with discussion of emerging areas for HRM by ensuring that:

- All chapters have been updated and revised, to provide the latest research information and up-to-date examples.
- Contributing authors are active researchers, internationally recognised for their expertise in their respective areas.
- Current and emerging trends and issues that have significant implications for HRM are highlighted throughout the book. These include offshore work, drug testing, workplace bullying, new forms of work and organisation, ethical concerns for HR managers, and the measurement of HR activities.

CONTENTS IN BRIEF

PART 1	MANAGING THE HUMAN RESOURCE ENVIRONMENT	
CHAPTER 1	HUMAN RESOURCE MANAGEMENT IN AUSTRALIA	2
CHAPTER 2	STRATEGIC HUMAN RESOURCE MANAGEMENT	52
CHAPTER 3	THE LEGAL CONTEXT FOR HUMAN RESOURCE MANAGEMENT	90
CHAPTER 4	OCCUPATIONAL HEALTH AND SAFETY	112
CHAPTER 5	INDUSTRIAL RELATIONS	148
PART 2	BUILDING HUMAN RESOURCE MANAGEMENT SYSTEMS	
CHAPTER 6	ANALYSIS AND DESIGN OF WORK	176
CHAPTER 7	HUMAN RESOURCE PLANNING AND HUMAN RESOURCE INFORMATION SYSTEMS	216
CHAPTER 8	RECRUITMENT AND SELECTION	256

1 HUMAN RESOURCE MANAGEMENT IN AUSTRALIA
Includes coverage of theoretical perspectives to provide students with a more comprehensive knowledge base for HRM. This chapter introduces and explains the five challenges that face many HR managers.

2 STRATEGIC HUMAN RESOURCE MANAGEMENT
Provides expanded coverage of strategic HRM and incorporates material addressing strategic linkages for the topics covered in each chapter. In this way, strategic HRM is introduced early and integrated throughout the book.

3 THE LEGAL CONTEXT FOR HUMAN RESOURCE MANAGEMENT
Written by a law academic to address the important legal issues relevant to the Australian HR environment.

4 OCCUPATIONAL HEALTH AND SAFETY
Written to address suggestions by academics that we devote a chapter to this important topic. We have included substantial coverage of OHS concerns such as safety culture, the OHS implications of the ageing workforce, and OHS issues for small businesses. These discussions have been placed within a strategic framework for OHS management.

5 INDUSTRIAL RELATIONS
Thoroughly updated by two of Australia's leading industrial relations academics who discuss changes in Australian industrial relations, such as the emergence of workplace bargaining, changes to dispute resolution processes, and the changing nature of employment relationships.

6 ANALYSIS AND DESIGN OF WORK
Gives a comprehensive discussion of organisational structures and approaches to job design. Recognising that the work context and types of jobs performed have changed dramatically in recent years, we discuss various employment modes used by firms today, such as call centres.

7 HUMAN RESOURCE PLANNING AND HUMAN RESOURCE INFORMATION SYSTEMS
Addresses the increasing importance of information technology. We provide substantial discussion of human resource information systems and issues relating to information technology.

8 RECRUITMENT AND SELECTION
Thoroughly revised to include, for example, more coverage of Internet recruitment.

PART 3	DEVELOPING PEOPLE	
CHAPTER 9	MANAGING DIVERSITY AND WORK-LIFE BALANCE	302
CHAPTER 10	PERFORMANCE MANAGEMENT	340
CHAPTER 11	LEARNING AND DEVELOPMENT	394
CHAPTER 12	EMPLOYEE DEVELOPMENT AND CAREER MANAGEMENT	444
PART 4	REWARDING PEOPLE	
CHAPTER 13	MANAGING COMPENSATION	482
CHAPTER 14	PERFORMANCE-RELATED PAY	526
PART 5	CONTEMPORARY ISSUES FOR HUMAN RESOURCE MANAGEMENT	
CHAPTER 15	ETHICS AND HUMAN RESOURCE MANAGEMENT	562
CHAPTER 16	INTERNATIONAL HUMAN RESOURCE MANAGEMENT	588
CHAPTER 17	MANAGING EMPLOYEE TURNOVER AND RETENTION	618
CHAPTER 18	EVALUATING AND IMPROVING THE HUMAN RESOURCE FUNCTION	656

9 MANAGING DIVERSITY AND WORK-LIFE BALANCE

Focuses on the management of workforce diversity and work–life balance, recognising the importance of these areas in the Australian and Asia–Pacific context.

10 PERFORMANCE MANAGEMENT

Provides discussion of the challenges facing the development and implementation of initiatives designed to manage diversity. Also describes the key features of work–life balance programs and identifies ways in which the costs and benefits of these programs can be determined.

11 LEARNING AND DEVELOPMENT

Written by Australia's leading scholar on training and development, this chapter provides a strong focus on employee learning, often cited as a key knowledge area required for HR professionals. The chapter also discusses how training can help companies gain a competitive advantage.

12 EMPLOYEE DEVELOPMENT AND CAREER MANAGEMENT

Focuses on current trends in formal education, design of successful mentoring and coaching programs, and what companies are doing for management development, including succession planning and helping dysfunctional managers.

13 MANAGING COMPENSATION

Includes discussion of significant issues such as communication in compensation management, new developments in the design of pay structures, and the controversy over executives' pay.

14 PERFORMANCE-RELATED PAY

Presents theoretical bases that explain the dynamics of performance-related pay, identifies types of performance-related pay programs, and discusses the major factors in the development and management of reward strategies.

15 ETHICS AND HUMAN RESOURCE MANAGEMENT

Includes an explanation of basic ethical theories and principles relevant to HRM, discusses rights and responsibilities in the employment relationship, and identifies challenges to the ethicality of HRM.

16 INTERNATIONAL HUMAN RESOURCE MANAGEMENT

Includes an analysis of international HRM issues, extending into the strategic arena, beyond the expatriate focus taken in most IHRM texts.

17 MANAGING EMPLOYEE TURNOVER AND RETENTION

Gives expanded coverage of managing employee turnover and retention, and includes discussion of important HRM issues such as workplace bullying and employee assistance programs.

18 EVALUATING AND IMPROVING THE HUMAN RESOURCE FUNCTION

Explores methods of evaluating and improving the HR function using the most recent research and trends in HR metrics. Discusses concerns related to HRM, such as corporate governance and measuring corporate sustainability, providing a context for measurement.

TEXT AT A GLANCE

Human Resource Management in Australia 3e is a pedagogically rich learning resource. These pages take you on a step-by-step journey through the various features to be found in every chapter. Getting the most out of your text will help you to succeed in your human resource management studies.

LEARNING OBJECTIVES

Every chapter opens with a showcase of the chapter's learning objectives. These tell you what you should be able to do after you have finished reading each chapter. They also **assist with your exam revision**.

CASE STUDIES

Each chapter is launched with **a real business problem** or issue that provides an interesting and meaningful context for the concepts that you are about to explore.

KEY TERMS

To help you learn the language of human resource management, key terms are bolded in the text and defined in the margin. They are also presented in an alphabetical glossary at the end of the text. **Learn the 'lingo' as you go**, and review it before exams.

HRM SPOTLIGHT

What HRM issues are appearing **in the local media**? These short case studies turn the spotlight onto a regionally relevant HRM story that links to the concepts discussed in the text.

XVIII

THE CHALLENGE OF GLOBALISATION

These short cases highlight how companies have gained a competitive advantage through effective human resource management practices **designed to meet global challenges**.

WOODS BAGOT: GOING GLOBAL

Woods Bagot is an architecture, consulting and design studio. Since the company's Adelaide launch in 1869, it has grown its operations with offices in 12 locations around the world, including Australia, Asia, the Middle East and Europe.

A number of years ago, the company had grown to work on larger, more complex projects, and it needed to restructure in order to accommodate further growth. It examined issues such as staffing levels for global projects, how the business could improve sustainability and how it could support international studios from its base in Australia.

A crucial part of the strategy involved global mobility, with a strong focus on workplace culture, and retaining Generation Y are not going to be a sustainable business. We paid a lot of attention to what they were asking for and what they were wanting to do.'

...

A challenge for Pirrello has been teaching managers within the business to think more flexibly when it comes to global mobility and prove that this is more beneficial for them. He was able to do this in the early days by arranging for an employee exchange. The two employees communicated constantly via email and telephone and they shared the differences in their cultural experiences and how the exchange contributed to their learning and development. This process was also shared with other staff via the intranet.

THE CHALLENGE OF ATTRACTING AND RETAINING PEOPLE

These short cases highlight how companies have gained a competitive advantage through effective human resource management practices designed to **attract and retain staff**.

VALUE THE DIFFERENCES

Peter Ward Head of strategy and change SA Water Corporation

At the SA Water Corporation, we are very interested in making sure that we both attract and retain women who may be considering having children—and we are keen to attract them back after maternity leave. In fact, this applies to all staff that want to take leave—for example young people who want to do a sabbatical overseas, not just young mothers.

We are therefore extremely flexible with our leave options. If someone has been here for a while, for example, they can take annual leave or long service

One of the main reasons we want to push the envelope in these areas is that we need a large number of engineers for the future of our business, an increasing number of engineers are young women. At certain stages in their career these workers have different needs to men.

Penny Lovett, general manager, human resources HBA Health Insurance

... Having good policies is only part of the process; it's how you execute them that's really important. Organisations need to offer flexible work practices in a way that values those employees who choose to

THE CHALLENGE OF HR INNOVATION

These short cases highlight how companies have gained a competitive advantage through effective and innovative human resource management practices.

PM'S POCKETS FILL WITH PAY RISE, TAX CUTS

John Howard will score a package of tax cuts, pay rise and inflation driven increases on July 1 worth more than the yearly salary of an Australian on federal minimum wage.

Cuts in tax rates combined with increases in payments to politicians for productivity and inflation will give the Prime Minister and his federal colleagues on both sides of politics, a triple treat in the new financial year.

From July 1, Mr Howard's salary of $288 990 will rise 7 per cent to $309 270 a year. The increase was recommended by the Commonwealth Remuneration Board.

When combined with his personal tax breaks of about $9259—flowing from personal income tax cuts—Mr Howard will have an extra $25 539.

The minimum wage, which two million Australians rely on is currently frozen at $25 188 while the new Fair Pay Commission prepares its first minimum wage decision.

The tribunal was also generous towards the judiciary, with the nation's highest-paid judge now taking home more than $425 580.

Source: Edited from C. Hart & C. Merritt, 2006, 'PM's pockets fill with pay rise, tax cuts', *The Weekend Australian*, June 24–25.

THE CHALLENGE OF SUSTAINABILITY

This boxed feature appears once in every chapter and includes **cutting-edge topics that relate to the broad area of sustainability in organisations**. The focus of these cases goes beyond financial or economic concerns to include social, personal and moral concerns for employers and employees.

3M: SUSTAINING OUR FUTURE

3M believes that active and responsible citizenship can make a successful company even stronger. We vigorously affirm our commitment to sustainable development through environmental protection, social responsibility and economic progress. We are committed to help meet the needs of society today while respecting the ability of future generations to meet their needs.

Our corporate values and sustainability

3M's sustainability policies and practices are directly linked to our fundamental corporate values:

- Act with uncompromising honesty and integrity in every thing

Social Highlights

Bringing Greater Opportunity to Employees Health and Productivity

Health and productivity scorecards have been introduced in US 3M plants. 3M continues to work to reduce preventable health care incidences and optimize productivity worldwide.

Performance-based compensation

3M employee awards are closely linked to the company's growth through employee performance and competitive compensation processes. By linking performance

XIX

TEXT AT A GLANCE

END-OF-CHAPTER MATERIAL

Performance-related Pay **CHAPTER 14**

CHAPTER SUMMARY

Our focus in this chapter has been on the design and administration of programs that recognise employee contributions to the organisation's success. These programs vary as to whether they link pay to individual, group or organisation performance. Often, it is not so much a choice of one program or the other as it is a choice between different combinations of programs that seek to balance individual, group and organisation objectives.

This chapter has examined three theories that can be used as a basis for designing performance-related pay programs. Each theory seeks to explain how desired work performance can be encouraged using different performance pay programs. This carries at least two important implications. First, pay can be a powerful motivator of job performance. An effective pay strategy can have a substantial positive impact on an organisation's success through a number of mechanisms including aligning employee interests with those of the organisation or reinforcing desired job performance immediately, as it occurs. Conversely, a poorly conceived pay strategy can have detrimental effects by not specifying the necessary performance goals for organisational success. Second, the importance of pay means that employees care a great deal about the fairness of the pay process. A recurring theme is that pay programs must be explained and administered in such a way that employees understand their underlying rationale and believe it is fair and equitable. In addition the rewards provided by an organisation need to be rewards that are desired by employees.

The fact that organisations differ in their business and human resource strategies suggests that the most effective compensation strategy may differ from one organisation to another. Although benchmarking programs against the competition is informative, what is successful in some organisations may not be a good idea for others. The balanced scorecard suggests the need for organisations to decide what their key objectives are and use pay to support them.

WEB EXERCISES

Visit BHP Billiton's website at www.bhpbilliton.com and review the approach to rewarding people in BHP Billiton. Suggest ways in which the performance of a recent accounting graduate could be rewarded in a division of BHP Billiton.

Questions
1. Discuss the ways in which pay arrangements influence organisation culture.
2. How does organisational strategy influence pay for performance arrangements?

DISCUSSION QUESTIONS

1. To compete more effectively, your organisation is considering a profit-sharing plan to increase employee effort and to encourage employees to think like owners. What are the potential advantages and disadvantages of such a plan? Would the profit-sharing plan have the same impact on all types of employees? What alternative pay programs should be considered?
2. Gainsharing plans have often been used in manufacturing settings but can also be applied in service organisations. How could performance standards be developed for gainsharing plans in hospitals, banks, insurance companies and so forth?
3. Your organisation has two business units. One unit is a long-established manufacturer of a product that competes on price and has not been subject to many technological innovations. The other business unit is being started. It has no products yet, but it is working on developing a new technology for testing the effects of drugs on individuals via simulation instead of through lengthy clinical trials. Would you recommend that the two business units have the same pay programs for recognising individual contributions? Why or why not?
4. Performance-based pay is merely a way of shifting the risk from the employer to the employee. Discuss.

557

CHAPTER SUMMARIES
The chapter summary **distils the most important concepts** discussed in the chapter and is aligned with the chapter objectives to reinforce your learning. It is clear and succinct for easy reading and understanding.

WEB EXERCISES
Designed to **take your learning further**, Web exercises at the end of every chapter help you understand the value of managing human resources on the Web, and challenge you to examine the online HRM practices of a variety of companies.

DISCUSSION QUESTIONS
These short-answer discussion questions give you **an opportunity to think about and discuss different situations** directly related to the chapter you have read. Discuss the possible solutions to these questions with your peers in a tutorial, or take them home to complete as an independent assignment.

MANAGING PEOPLE

AGEING WORKFORCE ATTITUDES ENTRENCHED MANAGEMENT

Entrenched attitudes towards recruiting, retaining or re-skilling mature-aged workers are the central challenge to engaging their participation in the workforce, according to John Plummer, president of the Recruitment and Consulting Services Association (RCSA).

Speaking at a recent symposium on the ageing workforce, he also said that change is not going to result from policy change alone, as it needs to be led from within an organisation and from the top.

'Age can and does work—age works to benefit the worker and age works to benefit the organisation', he said.

'There are too few examples of organisations successfully and effectively integrating aged workers into their workforces.'

combined industry, union, business and workplace response and a number of actions are required—there is no single policy fix.

Plummer said that choice was key in providing opportunities for the ageing workforce and for business—choice of employment situation, diversity of opportunities for mature-aged workers to develop existing skills or to re-skill, along with choice in superannuation and financial regimes.

'Choice and diversity to allow employers the choice of employment opportunities that make sense to achieve productivity and provide gains for their business', he said. 'The natural ageing of Australia's population will occur—this is inevitable. The role and place of the aged workforce in this ageing process will shape our workplace and our society for decades to come.'

Plummer's comments come on the heels of a recent survey, which found that persistent government and media attention toward the impact of Australia's ageing workforce

MANAGING PEOPLE
It is vital that you can think critically and use the theory you have learned to explain real-world situations. These articles draw from current debates in HRM and challenge you to diagnose specific HRM issues. Discussion questions provide guidance and focus your attention on the key concepts.

CASE STUDY

PAY ROLE DEVELOPMENT

Now is the time for many HR pay specialists to show their mettle. One of the hottest issues at the moment relates to top executives' rewards and the perceived excesses of pay at their level. When the next annual executive review is to be prepared for a company's compensation committee, the HR pay specialist should be pushing for a strong role in its development.

To justify this, HR compensation and benefits specialists need to ensure they are highly skilled and qualified in the broader remuneration field. They should also realise that they are up against the need to dramatically improve the profile and credibility of their profession.

None of Australia's top 50 companies has appointed an

away. The payment of large 'exit parachutes' to CEOs is always controversial, especially if they are leaving under a cloud. The fact is, senior executives know the risks they are taking, and reward for non-performance sets a bad example for everyone. (The practice in the world's second largest economy, Japan, of accepting responsibility for one's performance and suffering the consequences, springs to mind on this point.)

Another important issue for pay specialists to deal with is the pressure to follow what are considered global rates when determining CEO rewards. Global rates tend to be the highest rates—which are those of the United States—rather than a selection of best-practice examples from a range of countries. The local-CEO pay market has largely been overheated by following the practices of other countries, particularly the United States. No HR practice should be applied without taking into account the impact of local market conditions.

Illustrating the importance of this is a recent study showing that expatriates find Australian cities highly desirable locations to live in, while United States cities

END-OF-CHAPTER CASE
The end-of-chapter case explores the chapter topic either in hypothetical or real companies. They are designed to assist in gaining a better understanding of the concepts of that particular chapter. Cases are **drawn from a variety of sources** including the *BRW* and the Australian *Financial Review*. Discussion questions encourage students to critically evaluate the problem and apply the chapter concepts.

XXI

E-STUDENT

The **Online Learning Centre** provides extra resources with this text, comprising of **integrated online product** to assist you in getting the most from your course. This text provides a powerful learning experience beyond the printed page.

The Premium content areas, which are accessed by registering the code at the front of this text, provide you with powerful online resources. After registration, you will have seamless access to the extra resources.

Each component of the Online Learning Centre is described on these pages and can be found in both the student edition and the instructor edition.

POWERPOINT® SLIDES
The student edition contains a set of PowerPoint® slides which distil key concepts from each chapter of the book.

WEBLINKS
Links to management organisations, news services and interesting regional and global companies are provided here. Use these to investigate the management practices of leading organisations and to explore the variety of management resources available to you.

GLOSSARY
Unsure about the meaning of a human resources term? The glossary contains a quick reference to key terms and definitions.

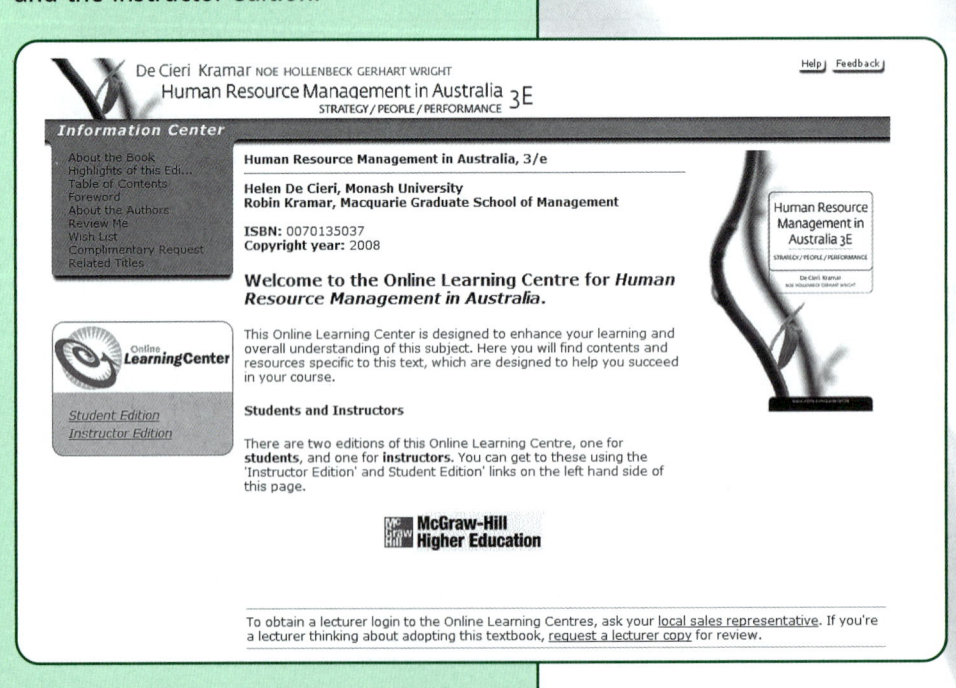

E-INSTRUCTOR

INSTRUCTOR MANUAL
The Instructor manual features comprehensive lecture notes, teaching ideas, additional examples and suggested solutions to discussion questions and case problems. An ideal resource for busy lecturers, the Instructor manual can be used in conjunction with the PowerPoint® slides as part of a powerful teaching package.

POWERPOINT® SLIDES
This text comes with a full suite of colour PowerPoint® slides that distil key concepts from each chapter of the book. Present these slides in lecture theatres to reinforce management principles to your class, and distribute them as lecture notes.

More than 900 multiple-choice questions are available which may be used in WebMCQ's powerful and flexible online quizzing format with tracking and reporting capabilities. Exclusive to McGraw-Hill, WebMCQ allows you to deliver your own online revision quizzes or tests and adapt them to suit your individual or class needs. The Test bank is also available in WebCT or Blackboard format.

COURSE MANAGEMENT SYSTEMS (CMS)
Course Management Systems (CMS) allow you to deliver and manage your course via the Internet. McGraw-Hill can provide online material to accompany this text, formatted for your chosen Course Management System. Ask your McGraw-Hill sales representative for more information.

VIDEO CASES
Five original Australian and Asia–Pacific video clips have been produced as an alternative educational tool to be used in class or during tutorials. These are designed to suit the part themes of the text and are accompanied by explanatory material and discussion questions online. This explanatory material includes discussion questions that aid in prompting debate in tutorials or in the classroom.

www.mhhe.com/au/decieri3e

FOREWORD

I AM VERY PLEASED TO WRITE THE FOREWORD for the third edition of this innovative textbook in Human Resource Management. The text is underpinned by a strategic approach to HRM, focusing on the three-way linkage between strategy, people and performance. As the authors explain, the HRM function can be developed to help the organisation create value and sustain competitive advantage in business. The HR function also plays a major role in initiatives that promote employee wellbeing. Each chapter highlights the strategic achievements that have occurred within each HR topic and addresses four key challenges central to the effective management of people: managing in a globalised context, managing HR innovation, attracting and retaining people, and managing in sustainable ways.

Featuring an Australian and regional focus, the book examines important new areas of HR practice in depth, such as managing workplace relations in the context of changing legislation, outsourcing, work–life balance, ethics and HRM, managing employee turnover and retention, and evaluating the HR function. The book opens with an analysis of the environment for HRM in Australia and then expands upon the intra-organisational aspects of HRM, such as building HRM systems, developing and rewarding people, and identifying new directions of HRM.

This text will appeal to a wide audience. The analysis of current academic knowledge and major areas of HRM practice provides an informed handbook for students, academics and practitioners. The text could easily be used in an undergraduate or graduate HR unit, or as a comprehensive HR handbook for managers. For instructors, the text includes numerous pedagogical features that ensure a sound basis for teaching; and for students, it successfully reinforces the link between theory and critical thinking. All users will be engaged by the real and relevant cases that appear throughout the book, and by the rigorous intellectual and practical approach the authors have taken to the subject, linking key HRM concepts and theories to the outcomes of empirical research.

PETER J DOWLING Life Fellow AHRI
Professor of International Business
Victoria University of Wellington
New Zealand

DEDICATION

To Rowan and Alexandra
HELEN DE CIERI

To Claire and Ingrid
ROBIN KRAMAR

ABOUT THE ORIGINAL AUTHORS

Each member of the US Human Resource Management author team has extensive experience both in the teaching and in the practice of human resources, and their expertise has earned them the respect and acclaim of their peers. Collectively the authors have published scores of articles and books, and served on the editorial boards of leading publications, including the *Academy of Management Journal*, the *Journal of Applied Psychology*, the *Journal of Management*, *Personnel Psychology*, *Organizational Behavior and Human Decision Processes*.

RAYMOND A. NOE is the Robert and Anne Hoyt Professor of Management at The Ohio State University. He is a Fellow of the Society for Industrial and Organizational Psychology, and winner of the 2000 American Society for Training and Development Research Award.

JOHN R. HOLLENBECK is Eli Broad Professor of Management at the Eli Broad Graduate School of Business Administration at Michigan State University, East Lansing. He was the first recipient of the Ernest J. McCormick Award for Distinguished Early Career Contributions to the field of Industrial and Organizational Psychology.

BARRY GERHART holds the Bruce R. Ellig Distinguished Chair in Pay and Organizational Effectiveness and is Director of the Strategic Human Resources Program at the University of Wisconsin-Madison, and has worked for organisations including TRW, Corning, and Bausch and Lomb.

PATRICK M. WRIGHT is Professor and Director of the Center for Advanced Human Resource Studies at Cornell University, and has consulted for such companies as Whirlpool, Amoco, and the government of the state of North Carolina.

ABOUT THE AUSTRALIAN AUTHORS

HELEN DE CIERI (PhD, University of Tasmania) is a Professor in the Department of Management at Monash University and the Director of the Australian Centre for Research in Employment and Work (ACREW). Her teaching experience includes appointments in China, Hong Kong, Malaysia and the USA. Helen teaches undergraduate and graduate students in HRM, strategic HRM and international HRM. Her consulting experience includes projects with private and public sector organisations in Australia and overseas. Helen's research has appeared in leading international academic journals such as the *Journal of Management*, *Human Resource Management*, *International Journal of Human Resource Management*, and *Management International Review*. From 1996 to 2002, Helen was the editor of the *Asia Pacific Journal of Human Resources*. She currently serves on the editorial boards of several international academic journals. Helen's current research interests include strategic HRM in multinational enterprises, work-life management, and the management of global mobility.

ROBIN KRAMAR (PhD, University of Sydney) has been keenly interested in issues associated with people in the workplace for more than thirty years. She is currently Deputy Dean and Professor of Management at Macquarie Graduate School of Management and Director of the Centre of Australasian Human Resource Management. She has held academic positions at a number of universities, including the University of Rennes 1, the University of New South Wales and University of Sydney. Her current role involves lecturing to MBA and Master of Management students in Sydney, Hong Kong and Singapore. Robin's research and consultancy specialities currently focus on strategic human resource management, diversity management, knowledge management and sustainability. She has been funded by the Department of Environment and Water to develop initiatives in the area of 'education for and about sustainability' at MGSM.

Robin's research activities have culminated in the publication of six books and more than twenty articles in refereed journals, almost thirty chapters in books, and numerous refereed conference papers and monographs. Robin is keen to develop links between academic activities and practitioner requirements, and has been actively involved in the development of management education. She was editor of the journal *Asia Pacific Journal of Human Resources* from 2002 to 2007.

ABOUT THE CONTRIBUTING AUTHORS

PETER J. DOWLING (PhD, Flinders University) is Professor of International Business at Victoria University of Wellington, New Zealand and has authored Chapter 16 (International HRM). Previous appointments include The University of Melbourne, Monash University, the University of Tasmania and University of Canberra. Peter has also held visiting appointments at Cornell and Michigan State Universities in the USA and the University of Paderborn and the University of Bayreuth in Germany.

Peter's current research interests are concerned with International HRM, International Management and Strategic Management. He has written or co-authored four books and over seventy journal articles and book chapters and serves on the editorial boards of a number of profesional journals.

Peter is a past National Vice-President of the Australian Human Resources Institute and a Life Fellow of the Australian Human Resources Institute. Currently, he is Vice-President of the Australia & New Zealand International Business Academy, President-Elect of the International Federation of Scholarly Associations of Management (IFSAM) and a Senior Research Affiliate of the Center for Advanced Human Resource Studies at Cornell University.

MICHELLE GREENWOOD (MA, Boston University) has authored Chapter 15 (Ethics and human resource management) especially for this text. Michelle is an academic at the Department of Management at Monash University where she has taught and researched in the area of Business Ethics for twelve years. Her specific fields of interest are ethical issues in HRM, stakeholder theory and social and ethical auditing. Michelle currently serves on the editorial board of *Journal of Business Ethics*.

PETER HOLLAND (PhD, University of Tasmania) has adapted Chapter 13 (Managing compensation) from the international edition on which this book is based. He is a senior lecturer in Human Resource Management and Employee Relations at Monash University. His current research interests are in the areas of reward management, new patterns of work organisation and monitoring and surveillance.

SUZANNE JAMIESON (BA; LLB, University of New South Wales; Grad Dip Pub Sect Mgt, University of Technology, Sydney; LLM; SJD, University of Sydney) has authored Chapter 3 (The legal context for human resource management) from the International Edition on which this book is based. She has taught at the University of Sydney since 1990 after a career as a senior public servant and a trade union official. Since 1991 she has represented the National Pay Equity Coalition in national wage cases before the Australian Industrial Relations Commission and in the extensive litigation around equal pay for women in the New South Wales industrial jurisdiction. Her other principal research interest is in occupational health and safety. Suzanne is a member of the NSW Anti-Discrimination Board and is the Director of the University of Sydney's Celtic Studies Foundation.

ABOUT THE CONTRIBUTING AUTHORS

ANDREW SMITH (MA, Cambridge, MBA, University of Aston, PhD, University of Tasmania) has authored Chapter 11 (Learning and development). He is Professor of Human Resource Management in the Faculty of Business and Director of Research Development at Charles Sturt University. Until recently Andrew was Head of the School of Commerce and previously of the School of Management for a number of years. From 1999–2002 he was General Manager, Research and Evaluation at the National Centre for Vocational Education Research in Adelaide. At CSU Andrew has played a leading role in research development. Andrew has a PhD in the area of enterprise training, which is his particular field of expertise. Andrew has led a number of research projects in the area of workplace training and organisational innovation and change. He is Director of the CSU's Centre for Organisational Performance, Ethics and Leadership (OPEL). Andrew is the author of numerous articles on aspects of employment and training and *Training and Development in Australia* published by Butterworths.

JULIAN TEICHER (PhD, University of Melbourne) has co-authored Chapter 5 (Industrial relations) with Bernadine van Gramberg especially for this text. Julian is the Director of the Graduate School of Business at Monash University. He holds academic qualifications in economics, industrial relations and law. Julian's recent research has spanned privatisation, public sector reform, teamwork and the impact of information and communications technologies on work.

BERNADINE VAN GRAMBERG (PhD, Monash University) has co-authored Chapter 5 (Industrial relations) with Julian Teicher. Bernadine is the Head of School of Management at Victoria University where she also teaches mediation, conciliation and arbitration. She has over twelve years experience in the field of dispute resolution at both corporate and consulting levels, with a professional background in managing equal employment, workplace harassment and bullying disputes. Bernadine has over sixty publications to her credit and has recently written *Managing Workplace Conflict: Alternative Dispute Resolution in Australia*, published by Federation Press.

ACKNOWLEDGMENTS

THE COMPLETION OF THIS EDITION WOULD NOT HAVE BEEN POSSIBLE without the help, patience and encouragement of numerous people who have been generous with their time and assistance.

We would like to thank the American authors for sharing their expertise—Raymond Noe, John Hollenbeck, Barry Gerhart and Patrick Wright. We thank the contributing authors—Peter Dowling, Michelle Greenwood, Peter Holland, Suzanne Jamieson, Julian Teicher, Bernadine Van Gramberg and Andrew Smith—for their fine contributions. We thank Trisha Pettit for her wonderful research assistance, always with great attention to detail and good humour. We are very grateful to our colleagues—particularly Marilyn Fenwick, Catherine Maguire, Susan Mayson, Tui McKeown, and Cathy Sheehan—for sharing their comments on the earlier editions and for their time, wisdom, advice and assistance with various chapters of the book.

We have very much appreciated the efforts of our students, who provided many helpful suggestions and showed great tolerance when we tested the ideas, discussion points and activities in this book. We would also like to thank our families and friends for their help and support. One of the most enjoyable aspects of the preparation of this book has been the opportunity to work with the highly professional and talented team at McGraw-Hill. We thank the McGraw-Hill staff for their great efforts on this book: Publisher Ailsa Brackley du Bois, Managing Editor Jo Munnelly, Developmental Editor Rosemary Noble, Production Editor Colette Hoeben, Permissions Editor Phillip Millard, and Copy editor Alison Moodie.

REVIEWERS

THIS TEXT HAS BENEFITED GREATLY FROM THE THOUGHTFUL CRITICISMS and valuable insights of our Human Resource colleagues around Australia and New Zealand, helping us shape an astute text of which we are proud. We would like to acknowledge the following reviewers for their contribution to this book:

Hudson Bancroft *Curtin University of Technology*
Mary Barrett *University of Wollongong*
Janine Brown *Australian Catholic University*
Ken Burke *Southern Cross University*
Allen Claburgh *Edith Cowan University*
Paul Corcoran *University of the Sunshine Coast*
Doug Davies *University of Canberra*
Elizabeth Ditzel *University of Otago*
Maria Farrell *Charles Sturt University*
Simon Fishwick *University of Tasmania*
Susan Mayson *Monash University*
John Nolan *University of Newcastle*
Apollo Nsubuga-Kyobe *La Trobe University*
Christine O'Connor *University of Ballarat*
Alison Sheridan *University of New England*
Margaret Stovall *Flinders University*
Graham Tonks *University of Tasmania*

ACKNOWLEDGMENTS

INSTRUCTOR RESOURCE AUTHORS

In addition, we would like to acknowledge those who developed the Instructor resource material that accompanies this edition, including Colin Winkler, University of Tasmania for writing the instructor manual and Pinstripe Media, for producing the video cases.

PREVIOUS REVIEWERS

Our appreciation also goes to the reviewers from institutions around Australia and New Zealand who took the time to offer constructive criticism on the previous editions during their development.

Sue Arnison *Northern Territory University*
Richard Ballantyne *Swinburne University*
Nikola Balnave *University of Western Sydney*
Renu Burr *University of Western Australia*
Gary Crone *University of Canberra*
Cherie England *James Cook University*
Luke Faulkner *University of South Australia*
Antonia Girardi *Murdoch University*
Amanda Gudmundsson *Queensland University of Technology*
Linda Hort *Griffith University*
Stacey Jenkins *Charles Sturt University*
Peter Langford *Macquarie University*
Ann Lawrence *Deakin University*
Darren Lee-Ross *James Cook University*
Priscilla Leece *University of Western Sydney*
Renee Malan *University of Southern Queensland*
Paul Nesbit *Macquarie Graduate School of Management*
John Nolan *Newcastle University*
Michael O'Donnell *Australian National University*
Margaret Patrickson *University of South Australia*
Cec Pedersen *University of Southern Queensland*
Michael Pembroke *University of South Australia*
Patty Renfrow *University of Queensland*
James Reveley *University of Wollongong*
Lydia Richards *University of South Australia*
Jie Schen *University of South Australia*
Kate Shacklock *Griffith University*
Cathy Sheehan *University of Tasmania*
Alison Sheridan *University of New England*
Don Smith *University of Southern Queensland*
Meg Smith *University of Western Sydney*
Kim Southey *University of Southern Queensland*
Stephen Teo *University of Technology Sydney*
Natalie van der Waarden *Murdoch University*

PART 1

Managing the Human Resource Environment

1 Human Resource Management in Australia

2 Strategic Human Resource Management

3 The Legal Context for Human Resource Management

4 Occupational Health and Safety

5 Industrial Relations

CHAPTER 1

HUMAN RESOURCE MANAGEMENT IN AUSTRALIA

Objectives

After reading this chapter, you should be able to:

1. Understand the conceptual foundations of human resource management.
2. Discuss the activities and roles of a company's human resource function.
3. Identify the characteristics of the workforce and the human resource environment.
4. Discuss the competitive challenges influencing Australian companies.
5. Provide a brief description of human resource management practices.

Human resource excellence: the best companies to work for in Australia

We have ways of making you stay

Ask not what you can do for your company, but what your company can do for you, advises Siobhan Doran.

MASSAGE ON CALL, a pool table with a city skyline view, free catered lunches and snacks—par for the course in a five-star hotel, but perks of the job? In a labour-short market, some companies are going above and beyond to attract, and retain, the best of the best.

Internet search engine Google recognises this. When it unveiled its new Sydney office in June, the talking point was not just the view over Darling Harbour but the fact that staff would be able to appreciate it while playing pool or sipping a free Nudie juice.

MassMedia Studios is another company opting for the lateral route to employee satisfaction. Company policy dictates 'beer o'clock' at 5pm on a Friday. As well as a pool table, there are a drum kit and a ping-pong table.

Workplace culture is changing as employers invest unprecedented time and resources in finding out just what makes employees tick—and how to keep them.

Roger Collins, professor of management at the Australian Graduate School of Management and chair of the Hewitt Best Employers in Australia and New Zealand judging panel, agrees. 'There certainly has been a power shift', he says. 'Talented employees are sought after and occupy a secure position. Now employers have to be more sensitive as to what is actually required to attract, retain and encourage talent.'

Collins says it's not as simple as copying what good employers have done and hoping for the best. 'What works for some may not work for others', he says.

'Ask any CEO from the best employers [list] and they will ... have strong practices to ensure recognition and linked reward processes are in place.'

And it seems size is also important. The majority of winning companies in the 2005 best employers study have fewer than 1000 employees; many have fewer than 500.

'Local leadership is most clearly prevalent amongst winning best employers', Collins says. 'It should work on two levels. Senior leadership is important and should be visible, accessible and authentic. But more critical are the local leaders.'

American Express, a consistent high achiever on the best employers list, has 2628 employees in Australia and delegates leadership to employees where possible. Human resources head Michelle Thomson says employees are encouraged to build

---

Results of the 2005 Hewitt Best Employers in Australia and New Zealand (ANZ) study

Winner
SalesForce

Best new entrant
ING Direct

Special Commendation for Consistent Improvement
(in alphabetical order)
Seek.com.au
Swiss Re

Hewitt Best Employers (in alphabetical order)
American Express
Bain & Company
Bayer Healthcare ANZ
Blackmores
British American Tobacco
Carson Group
Dell
Golder Associates
Medtronic
Nokia
Select Australasia
Westaff

Source: Hewitt Best Employers in Australia and New Zealand.

PART 1 Managing the Human Resource Environment

Human resource excellence: the best companies to work for in Australia *continued*

their plan and the leaders will ratify it. 'It's a very successful bottom-up approach.'

One example is 'Sunshine Fridays', a scheme that came about as a result of the annual employee survey. 'If an employee is called to a meeting after 4pm [on Friday]', Thompson says, 'they are able to say "that's not a convenient time for me".'

Flexible work arrangements can be great for staff, but they also make good business sense. A US work–family directions study found that for every dollar a company spends on flexible work or family benefits, there is a return of $US2–$6 ($2.60–$7.80) through reduced absenteeism, increased motivation and higher rates of retention.

Being a good employer goes a long way to buffer the effects of any skills shortages. For example, 44 per cent of CEOs in the best employers study say they are experiencing a talent shortage, against 73 per cent in other organisations.

The consensus: it's worth investing in people. Collins says: 'People look for a magic bullet, but a good employer doesn't happen overnight, though the wrong leader will ruin a good employer's reputation overnight. At the end of the day, people's commitment is fragile.'

The stat
42 per cent of CEOs say acquisition and retention of talent is the single most important factor facing their business.

Source: S. Doran, 2006, 'We have ways of making you stay', *The Sydney Morning Herald*, 26 August, p. 1. © 2006 Copyright John Fairfax Holdings Limited. www.smh.com.au

Introduction

The companies judged to be the 'best companies to work for in Australia', as shown on the preceding page, illustrate the key role that human resource management (HRM) plays in determining the effectiveness and competitiveness of Australian businesses. Competitiveness refers to the company's ability to maintain and gain market share in its industry. For example, SalesForce's approach has helped the company gain an advantage over its competitors. That is, SalesForce's human resource practices have helped the company provide services that are valued by its customers. The value of a product or service is determined by its quality and how closely the product fits customer needs.

Competitiveness is related to company effectiveness, which is determined by whether the company satisfies the needs of stakeholders (those groups affected by business practices). Important stakeholders include stockholders, who want a return on their investment; customers, who want a high-quality product or service; and employees, who desire interesting work and reasonable compensation for their services. The community, which wants the company to contribute to activities and projects and minimise pollution of the environment, is also an important stakeholder. Companies that do not meet stakeholders' needs are unlikely to have a competitive advantage over other firms in their industry.

Human resource management refers to the policies, practices and systems that influence employees' behaviour, attitudes and performance. Many companies refer to HRM as involving 'people practices'. To achieve effective outcomes in terms of organisational and individual performance, these practices need to be consistent with the organisational goals, or strategy. Hence, strategic human resource management (SHRM)

Human resource management (HRM)
the policies, practices and systems that influence employees' behaviour, attitudes and performance.

Strategic human resource management (SHRM)
a pattern of planned HR deployments and activities intended to enable an organisation to achieve its goals.

refers to the pattern of planned HR deployments and activities intended to enable an organisation to achieve its goals.[1] In other words, effective HRM practices are developed and used to support business goals and objectives (this is discussed in detail in Chapter 2). As illustrated in Figure 1.1, a strategic approach to human resource management requires the effective management of the HR environment (such as legal compliance), effective management of current issues facing an organisation (such as ethical concerns for HRM), and effective management of a range of important HRM practices. As the figure shows, HRM practices include determining human resource needs (HR planning), attracting potential employees (recruiting), choosing employees (selection), teaching employees how to perform their jobs, preparing them for the future (learning and development), rewarding them (compensation), developing their performance (performance management) and creating a positive work environment (industrial relations and occupational health and safety). Effective HRM practices have been shown to relate to company performance by contributing to employee and customer satisfaction, innovation, productivity and development of a favourable reputation in the firm's community.[2] The potential role of HRM in company performance has only recently been recognised. Many companies have human resource management departments. However, human resource management is not just a functional responsibility! Managers participate in HRM practices on a daily basis. As discussed in Chapter 2, **talent management** is emerging as a new discipline that builds on HRM and encompasses a long-term and integrated approach to managing employees—by attracting them into the organisations, then providing development and engagement opportunities utilising a sophisticated system of HR practices. Throughout the book, we will refer to the emergence of talent management and **human capital management**, although our main focus remains on HRM.[3]

This chapter begins by providing an overview of the development of theory and research on HRM. The second section provides some detail of the development of HRM in Australia. The third section outlines the roles and skills that a human resource management department and/or managers need for any company to be competitive. The fourth section identifies the characteristics of the workforce and the human resource environment that have implications for managing people. The fifth section identifies the competitive challenges that Australian companies are currently facing that influence their ability to meet the needs of shareholders, customers, employees and other stakeholders. We discuss how these competitive challenges are

Talent management
a long-term and integrated approach to managing employees—by attracting them into the organisations, and providing development and engagement opportunities utilising a sophisticated system of HR practices.

Human capital management
a management approach that aims to capture all efforts related to people in an organisation; while human capital management includes HRM, it focuses on measuring the effectiveness of HR activities, with an emphasis on enhancing the fit between those activities and the organisational strategic goals.

FIGURE 1.1 Strategic human resource management

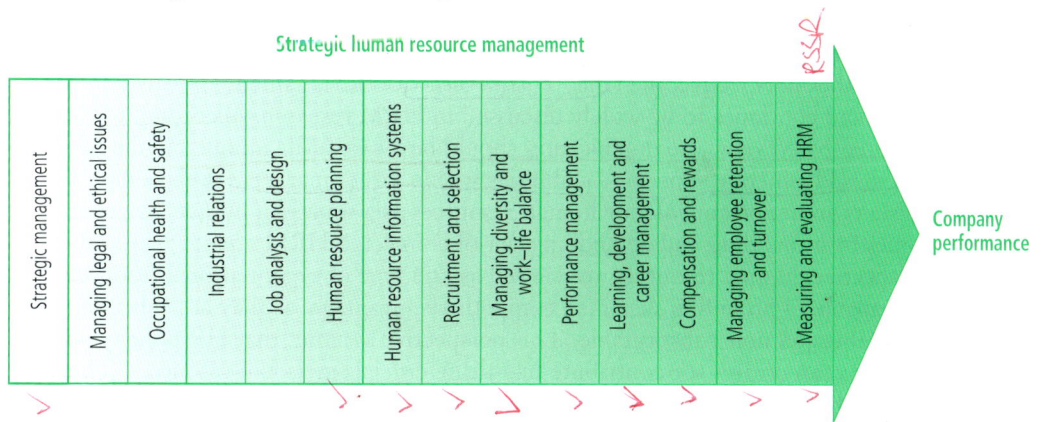

Strategic human resource management

| Strategic management | Managing legal and ethical issues | Occupational health and safety | Industrial relations | Job analysis and design | Human resource planning | Human resource information systems | Recruitment and selection | Managing diversity and work–life balance | Performance management | Learning, development and career management | Compensation and rewards | Managing employee retention and turnover | Measuring and evaluating HRM |

→ Company performance

influencing HRM practices. The chapter concludes by highlighting the HRM practices covered in this book and the ways they help companies deal with the competitive challenges.

The development of theoretical bases for human resource management

HRM recognises the importance of people in relation to financial and physical resources. It is assumed that this recognition will lead to improved utilisation of human resources, congruent with organisational strategy. In turn, this would be expected to lead to improved organisational effectiveness. HRM is based on an understanding of comprehensive policies that govern human resource (HR) programs and practices.

Several factors contributed to the rise of HRM as an organisational function. These include theoretical developments, societal and workforce demographic changes, increasing importance of management strategy, and decline in trade union pressure and economic influences.[4] In the following sections, we discuss the main theoretical and conceptual foundations of HRM and outline the major activities, roles and skills in HRM.

Theoretical perspectives of HRM

HRM functions are focused to some extent on the micro-level of individual behaviour and individual performance. The discipline of psychology has been particularly influential with respect to developments in HRM research. Increasing recognition of the relationships between HRM functions and organisational strategy has led to a more macro-level orientation and the development of the field of strategic HRM (as will be discussed in more detail in Chapter 2).

While much of the research in the HRM field has had an applied and empirical focus, there has been increasing attention to theoretical bases of HRM.[5] Many mainstream HRM developments relate to a *behavioural* perspective of HRM. Research by Miles and Snow[6] shows one of the earliest examples of the behavioural perspective. They identified behaviours necessary for the achievement of various organisational strategic objectives. Schuler and his colleagues developed this approach further as they focused to some extent on the inter-relationships between organisational strategy, HR practices and employee role behaviours.[7] These researchers emphasised the need for HRM practices to be congruent and for them to be linked to the organisational strategy. This perspective assumes that organisational characteristics, such as strategy, lead to HRM practices that elicit certain employee role behaviours, which in turn lead to identifiable outcomes, such as employee attitudes and organisational performance.

Another perspective, the *resource-based view* of HRM, gained popularity in the late 1990s and continues to be widely discussed in HRM research. According to the resource-based view, the organisation should be aware of its unique bundle of assets and should generate superior capabilities within target markets.[8] This perspective presents an important role for human resources as a source of unique advantage that comes from building and defending a set of connected HRM areas.[9] Taking this perspective, human resources are viewed as one type of organisational resources that are capable of providing sustained competitive advantage, as they are valuable, rare, inimitable and non-substitutable. This perspective assumes that HR policies and practices can create—or contribute to—those crucial assets and resources. The most obvious human resources are employees' knowledge, skills and abilities. Similarly, positive employee attitudes or organisational commitment may be important sources of competitive advantage.[10]

Not all theoretical perspectives of HRM can be considered to be strategic. For example, a political-influence perspective is perhaps best considered as a non-strategic perspective, as it examines the effects of political factors on HRM practices. For example, Ferris and colleagues[11] have used a political influence perspective of HRM to systemically investigate several HRM areas. This opposes the dominant 'rational human resources' assumption, which underlies many other perspectives of HRM. A political influence perspective of HRM demonstrates the potential for non-rational and political, rather than strategic or technical, concerns to influence HRM functions—such as performance appraisal. Political influence is defined as '…deliberate attempts to manage and control the meanings shared by others'.[12] This definition reflects the view that political behaviour is part of the area of social influence in the workplace and may have negative, positive or neutral antecedents and outcomes.[13] Some researchers have suggested that, to be an effective and relevant actor, the HR function has to become a political 'influencer' and a critical player in organisation-level choices that impact on global strategic decisions.[14] A necessary part of this process is the willingness of senior managers in an organisation to ensure that the HR function is represented in key policy and decision making fora, such as the board of directors.[15] Access to this level of decision making not only recognises the legitimate power or authority of HR to be a key decision maker but it provides HR with the opportunity to create a 'shared meaning' of what HR can contribute.[16]

These theoretical perspectives are by no means the only approaches to HRM. Numerous theoretical perspectives have been advanced to contribute to the investigation of HRM, although some have received more attention than others. Most HRM theory and research has been microanalytic in level of analysis (focusing on the individual) but unitary in perspective. Several researchers have advocated the development of an integrative approach to HRM that incorporates multiple perspectives. They argue that this would enable more comprehensive and richer understanding of the phenomena under investigation.

Progress in conceptual understanding of HRM over the past two decades can be viewed graphically through conceptual frameworks that have been offered by a number of researchers in order to identify the elements of HRM.

Conceptual foundations of HRM

A conceptual framework of HRM, known as the Harvard framework (because Michael Beer and his colleagues at Harvard University developed it), has provided a foundation for many of the developments made in HRM research.[17] As shown in Figure 1.2, this framework recognises a wide range of stakeholder interests and contextual factors that influence HRM. HR policy choices are identified, relating to employee involvement, reward systems, work systems and HR flows (including recruitment and selection, training and development, and performance management). HR functions and activities are seen as integrated—as a system that is, in turn, integrated with the broader organisational strategy. According to the Harvard framework, HR policy choices result in outcomes of organisational commitment, competence and cost effectiveness and, in turn, have long-term consequences for individuals, enterprises and society.

The Harvard framework has provided a foundation for substantial progress in HRM research and practice. This framework and the concepts included in it have been discussed and debated to some extent, resulting in considerable debate among HRM academics and practitioners.

PART 1 Managing the Human Resource Environment

FIGURE 1.2 The Harvard analytical framework for human resource management

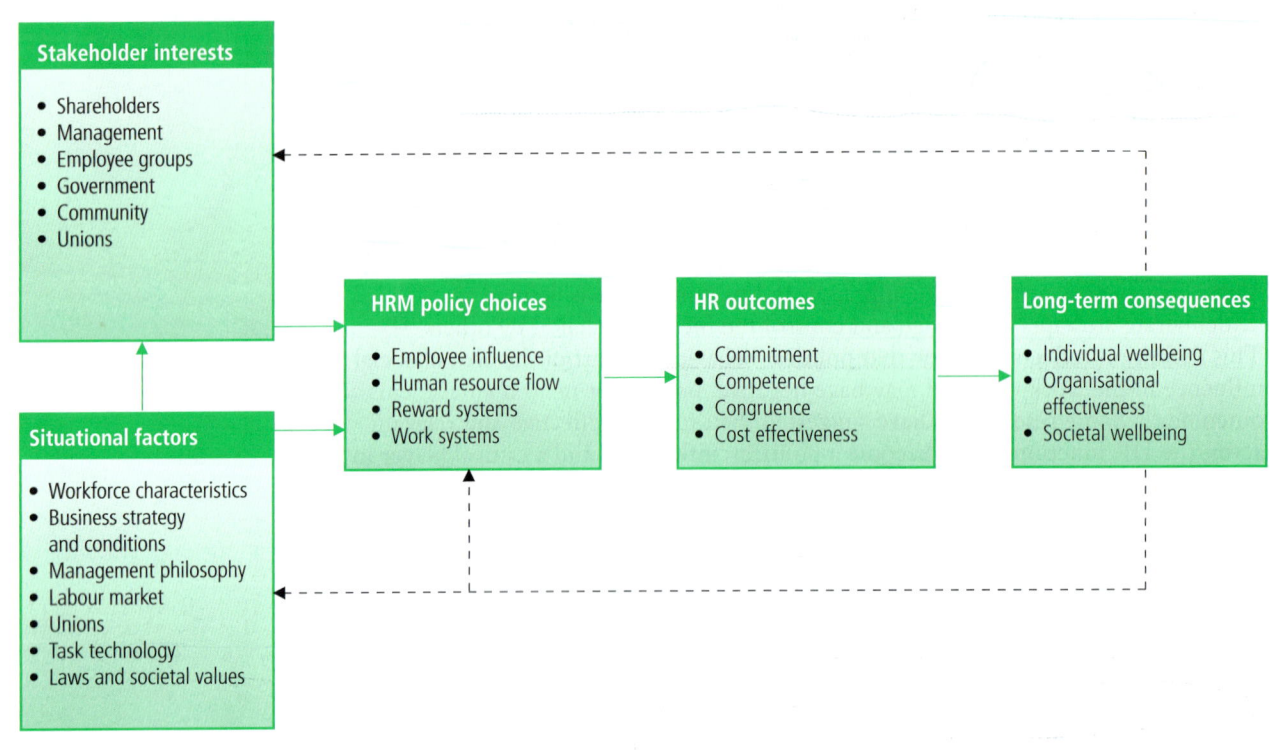

Stakeholder interests
- Shareholders
- Management
- Employee groups
- Government
- Community
- Unions

Situational factors
- Workforce characteristics
- Business strategy and conditions
- Management philosophy
- Labour market
- Unions
- Task technology
- Laws and societal values

HRM policy choices
- Employee influence
- Human resource flow
- Reward systems
- Work systems

HR outcomes
- Commitment
- Competence
- Congruence
- Cost effectiveness

Long-term consequences
- Individual wellbeing
- Organisational effectiveness
- Societal wellbeing

Source: M. Beer, B. Spector, P.R Lawrence, D.Q. Mills & R.E. Walton, 1984, *Managing Human Assets*, Free Press, New York, p. 16.

The dominant approach to HRM that has developed largely from this framework has four main features:

1. The main focus is the enterprise, or firm, as the unit of analysis.
2. People are viewed as social capital. HRM is seen as an investment in human capital.
3. A reciprocal fit between organisational strategy and human resource strategy is seen as crucial. The top level of management integrates HR policy and strategy.
4. HRM is also integrated with general, line management. There is still a role for HR specialists, although all managers are seen as responsible for HRM.[18]

HRM is often described as having developed from personnel administration or personnel management. However, differences between HRM and personnel management have been well-documented, showing HRM to be more complex and strategic. A recent study analysed the responses of 1372 Australian Human Resources Institute (AHRI) members. The results indicate that HR professionals expect to see a more strategic business focus for HR developing in the context of an industrial relations climate that has increased HR's responsibility for employee relations in the workplace. Senior HR professionals are likely to be involved in strategic decision making, as shown in Table 1.1. However, HR professionals at all levels face several challenges including the potential narrowing of their career base; the need for improved HRM metrics; and a broader commitment to attraction and retention initiatives.[19] Empirical studies of the activities undertaken by HR managers indicate a wide range of challenges and issues faced in dealing with organisational strategy, environmental factors and coordinating practices across HRM functional areas.[20]

8

TABLE 1.1 Role of senior HR professionals in strategic decision-making processes (n = 472)

	%
The human resource area **provides operational support**, develops some internal programs to meet specific needs, but is generally viewed as a processor of paperwork and employment activities.	8
The human resource area **reacts to** strategic directions and requests from top management.	7
The human resource area provides **input into and reacts to** strategic directions set by top management, but only on personnel related matters.	36
The human resource area is **actively involved in all types of strategic decisions**, whether or not they directly affect personnel matters.	49

Source: C. Sheehan, P. Holland & H. De Cieri, 2006, 'Current developments in HRM in Australian organisations', *Asia Pacific Journal of Human Resources* 44 (2), pp. 132–52.

The United States approach to HRM generally assumes a unitary frame of reference (see Chapter 5 Industrial Relations and Chapter 15 Ethics and HRM for discussion of **unitarism**) and has emphasised individualistic means of management—labour relations, with consistency of long-term goals between all the various stakeholders. This may stem more from the origins of HRM in a non-union context than from any inherent incompatibility with trade unions or forms of collective bargaining.[21] In contrast, researchers in the United Kingdom have taken rather a different view in suggesting that a unitaristic HRM model that attempts to marginalise the role of trade unions is infeasible and undesirable. It has been suggested that simultaneous handling of both individualistic and collective concerns is an essential requirement for management in the 21st century.[22]

> **Unitarism** assumes that all parties in an organisation share similar goals and interests and, as such, does not acknowledge the potential for conflict between employer and employee.

What activities and roles do HR departments perform?

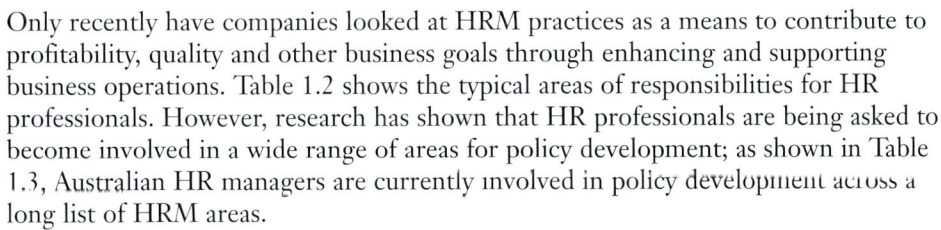

Only recently have companies looked at HRM practices as a means to contribute to profitability, quality and other business goals through enhancing and supporting business operations. Table 1.2 shows the typical areas of responsibilities for HR professionals. However, research has shown that HR professionals are being asked to become involved in a wide range of areas for policy development; as shown in Table 1.3, Australian HR managers are currently involved in policy development across a long list of HRM areas.

Surveys in the United States show that, since 1978, the average ratio of HR department staff to total number of employees has been 1.0 for every 100 employees served by the department. A similar ratio has been reported in Australian organisations. According to Australian national studies, smaller organisations (with fewer than 1000 employees) and larger organisations (greater than 2000 employees) have a larger proportion of clerical staff amongst their HR staff than do medium-sized organisations. In contrast, organisations with between 1000 and 2000 employees have a higher proportion of professional HR staff. This difference may be explained by smaller organisations employing HR clerical staff to attend to administrative functions and larger organisations having more bureaucratic approaches to the HR function than do medium-sized firms.[23]

PART 1   Managing the Human Resource Environment

TABLE 1.2   Typical responsibilities of HR professionals

Strategic management	Strategic planning, strategy formulation and implementation, organisational change, and mergers and acquisitions
Health and safety	Safety inspection, health programs and wellness programs
Employee and community relations	Attitude surveys, industrial relations, reports and publications, labour-law compliance and discipline
Analysis and design of work	Work-flow analysis, and job analysis and design
Human resource planning	Forecasting the supply of and demand for human capital
Human resource information systems	Information systems, databases and employee records
Recruitment and selection	Recruiting, conducting selection tests, interviewing and coordinating temporary labour
Managing diversity and work–life balance	Diversity programs and work–life benefit programs
Learning and development	Orientation, skills training, career management and productivity enhancement
Performance management	Performance appraisals and designing performance management systems
Compensation and reward management	Wage and salary administration (job descriptions, executive compensation, incentive pay and job evaluation) and leave administration (superannuation plans, profit sharing and stock plans)
Employee services	Employee assistance programs, relocation services and outplacement services
International HR	Expatriation management, global mobility programs and global development
Measurement and evaluation	Human resource metrics, employee attitude surveys, and cost–benefit analyses

Source: Adapted from SHRM–BNA Survey No. 60, 1995, *Human Resources Activities, Budgets, and Staffs: 1994–95*, Bulletin to Management, Bureau of National Affairs Policy and Practice Series, 29 June, Bureau of National Affairs, Washington, DC.

Administrative expert
a role performed by HR practitioners, aiming to build an efficient infrastructure by ensuring efficient performance of organisational processes.

Employee champion
a role performed by HR practitioners, aiming to increase employee commitment and capability by listening and responding to employees' concerns.

Change agent
a role performed by HR practitioners, aiming to develop the organisation by managing transformation and change.

Strategic business partner
a role performed by HR practitioners, aiming to execute organisational strategy by aligning HR processes with the organisational strategy.

Activities that the HR department is solely responsible for may include outplacement, labour law compliance, human resource information systems, employee testing for selection, and administration of compensation. The human resource department is most likely to collaborate with other company functions on employment interviewing, performance management and discipline, and efforts to improve quality and productivity. Common specialisations for HR professionals include recruitment, compensation, and training and development.[24]

In leading organisations, the HR function has moved from an administrative function to a strategic leadership role.[25] Ulrich has suggested that there are four roles for HR professionals or departments to fulfill. First, in the 'administrative expert' role, the HR professional aims to build an efficient infrastructure by ensuring efficient performance of organisational processes. Second, in the 'employee champion' role, he or she aims to increase employee commitment and capability by listening and responding to employees' concerns. Third, in the 'change agent' role, the aim is to develop the organisation by managing transformation and change. Fourth is the 'strategic business partner' role, in which the aim is to execute organisational strategy by aligning HR processes with the organisational strategy.[26] These roles are important for HR professionals in Australia. Table 1.4 shows an assessment tool that can be used

TABLE 1.3 Current HRM policy development areas

	n = 1372 %*
Recruitment	76
Performance appraisal (managers)	75
Performance appraisal (non-managers)	69
Selection	67
OHS	57
Work–life balance	55
Training	54
Family friendly policies	49
Values/ethics	48
Grievance procedures	47
Training efforts devoted to skill enhancement	47
Workforce planning	44
Employee discipline	43
Equal employment opportunities	43
Development	42
Performance related pay (managers)	41
Termination management	41
Team building	40
Career management	39
Diversity (e.g. age, ethnicity)	38
Skill development	37
Job analysis	33
Performance related pay (non-managers)	32
Job design	30
Job evaluation	29
Award/union coverage	26
Joint consultation/participation	24
Employee share ownership	13
Skill-based pay	10
Monitoring surveillance	9

*Respondents could select more than one response

Source: C. Sheehan P. Holland & H. De Cieri, 2006, 'Current developments in HRM in Australian organizations', *Asia Pacific Journal of Human Resources* 44 (2), pp. 132–52.

TABLE 1.4 Assessment tool to identify roles performed by HR professionals

Considering the HR professionals and/or function in your organisation, please rate the current quality and level of importance of each of the following HR activities, using a five point scale (1 is low, 5 is high).

	Current quality	Importance
HR helps the organisation:		
1 Accomplish business goals	1 2 3 4 5	1 2 3 4 5
2 Improve operating efficiency	1 2 3 4 5	1 2 3 4 5
3 Take care of employees' needs	1 2 3 4 5	1 2 3 4 5
4 Adapt to change	1 2 3 4 5	1 2 3 4 5
HR participates in:		
5 The process of defining business strategies	1 2 3 4 5	1 2 3 4 5
6 Delivery of HR processes	1 2 3 4 5	1 2 3 4 5
7 Improving employee commitment	1 2 3 4 5	1 2 3 4 5
8 Shaping culture change for renewal and transformation	1 2 3 4 5	1 2 3 4 5
HR makes sure that:		
9 Human resource strategies are aligned with business strategy	1 2 3 4 5	1 2 3 4 5
10 Human resource processes are efficiently administered	1 2 3 4 5	1 2 3 4 5
11 Human resource policies and programs respond to the personal needs of employees	1 2 3 4 5	1 2 3 4 5
12 Human resource processes and programs increase the organisation's ability to change	1 2 3 4 5	1 2 3 4 5
HR effectiveness is measured by its ability to:		
13 Help make strategy happen	1 2 3 4 5	1 2 3 4 5
14 Efficiently deliver HR processes	1 2 3 4 5	1 2 3 4 5
15 Help employees meet personal needs	1 2 3 4 5	1 2 3 4 5
16 Help an organisation anticipate and adapt to future issues	1 2 3 4 5	1 2 3 4 5
HR is seen as:		
17 A business partner	1 2 3 4 5	1 2 3 4 5
18 An administrative expert	1 2 3 4 5	1 2 3 4 5
19 A champion for employees	1 2 3 4 5	1 2 3 4 5
20 A change agent	1 2 3 4 5	1 2 3 4 5
HR spends time on:		
21 Strategic issues	1 2 3 4 5	1 2 3 4 5
22 Operational issues	1 2 3 4 5	1 2 3 4 5
23 Listening and responding to employees	1 2 3 4 5	1 2 3 4 5
24 Supporting new behaviours for keeping the company competitive	1 2 3 4 5	1 2 3 4 5
HR is an active participant in:		
25 Business planning	1 2 3 4 5	1 2 3 4 5
26 Designing and delivering HR processes	1 2 3 4 5	1 2 3 4 5
27 Listening and responding to employees	1 2 3 4 5	1 2 3 4 5
28 Organisational renewal, change or transformation	1 2 3 4 5	1 2 3 4 5
HR works to:		
29 Align HR strategies and business strategies	1 2 3 4 5	1 2 3 4 5
30 Monitor administrative processes	1 2 3 4 5	1 2 3 4 5
31 Offer assistance to help employees meet family and personal needs	1 2 3 4 5	1 2 3 4 5
32 Reshape behaviour for organisational change	1 2 3 4 5	1 2 3 4 5
HR develops processes and programs to:		
33 Link HR strategies to accomplish business strategies	1 2 3 4 5	1 2 3 4 5
34 Efficiently process documents and transactions	1 2 3 4 5	1 2 3 4 5
35 Take care of employees' personal needs	1 2 3 4 5	1 2 3 4 5
36 Help the organisation transform itself	1 2 3 4 5	1 2 3 4 5
HR's credibility comes from:		
37 Helping to fulfill strategic needs	1 2 3 4 5	1 2 3 4 5
38 Increasing productivity	1 2 3 4 5	1 2 3 4 5
39 Helping employees meet their personal needs	1 2 3 4 5	1 2 3 4 5
40 Making change happen	1 2 3 4 5	1 2 3 4 5

Source: Adapted from D. Ulrich, 1997, *Human Resource Champions: The Next Agenda for Adding Value and Delivering Results*, Harvard Business School Press, Boston.

to identify the strength of these roles in an organisation. If these questions have not been considered, it is highly unlikely that, first, the company is prepared to deal with competitive challenges and, second, human resources are being used to help a company gain competitive advantage. Strategic human resource management is discussed in more detail in Chapter 2. We also note that other researchers have suggested additional roles for HR managers, including 'political influencer'[27] (mentioned earlier in this chapter) and 'corporate conscience'[28] (see Chapter 15 Ethics and HRM).

The percentage of time that human resource departments are devoting to administrative roles—such as maintaining records, auditing and controlling, and providing services—has decreased. Advances in technology, such as development of the Intranet, have decreased the role of human resources in maintaining records by allowing HR services to be offered on a self-service basis at substantially less cost than traditional face-to-face services.[29] Self-service refers to giving employees control of HR transactions. Self-service also fits with the changing psychological contract[30]—employees are expected to take greater responsibility for their own careers. Self-service is being used for a wide range of HR services, including training course catalogues and course enrolment, benefits inquiries, and attitude surveys.

Outsourcing of the administrative role has also occurred for several areas of HRM. Outsourcing refers to the practice of having another company (known as a vendor, third-party provider or consultant) provide services. Many companies have outsourced payroll administration. Outsourcing is also being used for training, selection and recruiting employees.

Other roles, such as change leadership and strategic leadership, have increased. One of the most comprehensive studies ever conducted regarding HRM concluded that 'human resources is being transformed from a specialized, stand-alone function to a broad corporate competency in which human resources and line managers build partnerships to gain competitive advantage and achieve overall business goals'.[31] As shown in Table 1.5, comparison between national surveys of HR professionals conducted in 1995 and 2005 indicate that full HR representation on boards of directors has increased, albeit slightly, since 1995 and there is greater recognition of HR's role on senior management committees. Overall, there is an increase in the number of managers in charge of the human resource function being included on high-level committees that are shaping the strategic direction of the company.[32]

Self-service
giving employees control of HR transactions.

Psychological contract
the expectations that employers and employees have about each other.

Outsourcing
an organisation's use of an outside organisation for a broad set of services.

TABLE 1.5 Senior committee representation of HR

	1995 n = 837 %	2005 n = 1146 %
HR representation on the board of directors		
No representation	55	42
HR representative	17	25
Representative with HR as part of their responsibility	28	33
HR representative on the senior management group at the enterprise level	n = 821 %	n = 1372 %
Yes	56	68
No	44	32

Source: C. Sheehan P. Holland & H. De Cieri, 2006, 'Current developments in HRM in Australian organizations', *Asia Pacific Journal of Human Resources* 44 (2), pp. 132–52.

These managers report directly to the CEO, president or board of directors and they are being asked to propose solutions to business problems. For example, as one Australian senior executive has described it, 'proactive HR can deliver enormous value for organisations but achieving this, along with any significant change, requires focus, skills, capabilities and a good understanding of the organisation's broader environment. With this combination, the HR strategy supports and champions the business strategy.'[33]

What skills do HR professionals need?

Figure 1.3 shows the roles and competencies needed by HR professionals. Each of the quadrants corresponds to HR roles listed on the outside of the figure. Within each quadrant, the competencies needed to be successful in the role are included. The roles and examples of the competencies needed to effectively manage human resources in the future are shown on the right-hand side of Figure 1.3. These competencies include providing leadership, vision and ideas to align the HR function with the business strategy and to manage change. These competencies may be particularly relevant to roles such as compensation management and organisational development. Required competencies also include providing guidance and support for individuals and teams, particularly with respect to roles such as diversity management and increasing employees' contributions to the company through employee development.[34] It is important for HR managers to shift their focus from current operations to strategies for the future.[35] Another important requirement is to prepare non-HR managers to develop and implement human resource practices (for example, performance management).

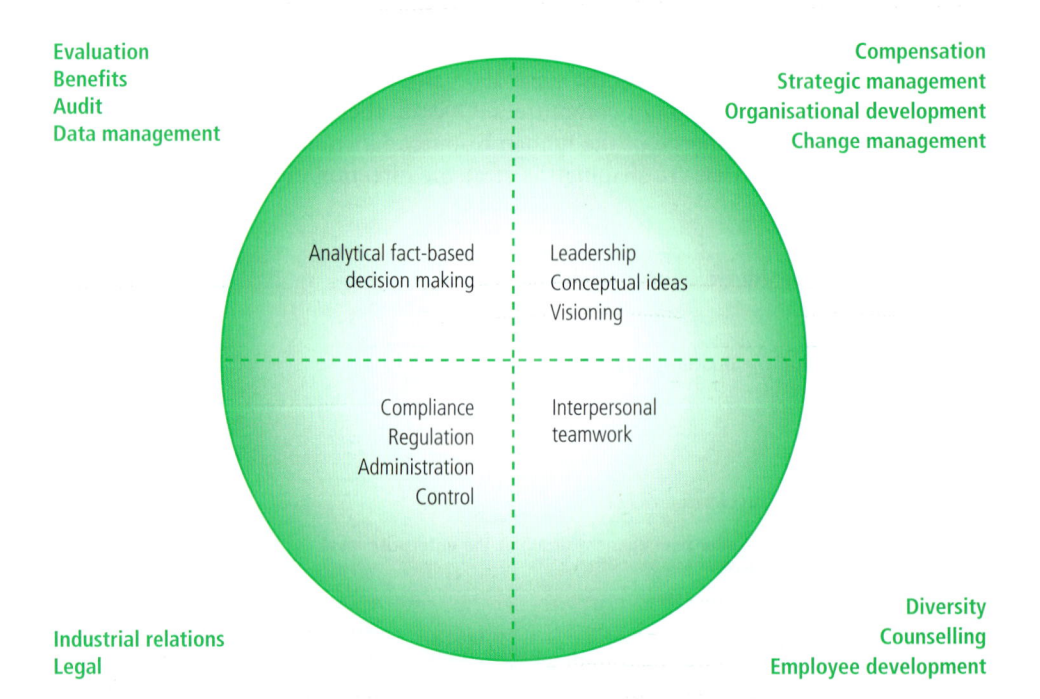

FIGURE 1.3 Human resource roles and competencies

Evaluation
Benefits
Audit
Data management

Compensation
Strategic management
Organisational development
Change management

Analytical fact-based decision making

Leadership
Conceptual ideas
Visioning

Compliance
Regulation
Administration
Control

Interpersonal
teamwork

Industrial relations
Legal

Diversity
Counselling
Employee development

Source: A. Freedman, 1990, *The Changing Human Resource Function*, The Conference Board, p. 11.

The roles and competency related to administration and control are included in the left-hand half of Figure 1.3. The role of HR in administration and control has decreased because technology is being used to manage HR records and provide employees with human resource information systems so they can provide access to information regarding programs and services. However, to effectively manage human resources, analytical skills are needed to measure and evaluate the effectiveness of HR practices.

Characteristics of the workforce and human resource environment

In order to understand the challenges facing HR today, it is necessary to explore the context for the management of people. In this section, we discuss the characteristics of the workforce and the HR environment that have major implications for HRM. To be most effective, HR policy and practices should be developed with an awareness and understanding of these external factors.

Composition of the labour force

Company performance is influenced by the characteristics of its labour force, comprised of current employees. The labour force of current employees is often referred to as the **internal labour force**. Employers identify and select new employees from the external labour market through recruiting and selection practices. The **external labour market** includes persons actively seeking employment. As a result, the skills and motivation of a company's internal labour force are influenced by the composition of the available labour market (the external labour market). The skills and motivation of a company's internal labour force determine the need for training and development practices and the effectiveness of the company's compensation and reward systems.

Competition for talented persons in the external labour market also affects the composition of a company's internal labour market. For example, when unemployment rates are low, many companies are unable to find the employees they need to fill jobs. Many companies and industries are experiencing shortages of available skilled employees. According to a partner with the accounting firm PricewaterhouseCoopers:

> There is a worldwide shortage of skilled people, a long-term [ten years plus] trend that is being exacerbated by the economic boom we are currently experiencing. The worldwide nature of this trend can be seen in the international mobilisation of those [working] at the sharp end, young professionals in accounting, legal, management, information technology and finance, working across home country borders. This skills shortage is not only a problem for those in the new economy. It's an issue for almost any industry where an increase in skills is essential. The most outstanding example of this can be seen in defence force recruitment throughout the developed world. The trend is to recruit a smaller number of more highly skilled service people and [yet] the recruitment shortfall becomes larger each year.[36]

The Australian resident population in June 2004 was 20.1 million people. This is projected to increase to between 24.9 and 33.4 million by 2051, and to between 22.4 and 43.5 million by 2101.[37] In 2004–05, there were 10.4 million people in the Australian labour force. The Australian Bureau of Statistics tracks changes in the composition of the Australian labour force and projects employment trends.[38] The proportion of children in the population aged 14 years or less is projected to decrease

Internal labour force
labour force of current employees.

External labour market
people outside the firm who are actively seeking employment.

from 20 per cent in 2004 to between 13 and 16 per cent in 2051. Over the same period, the proportion of the population aged 65 years and over is projected to increase from 13 per cent to between 26 and 28 percent.[39] The composition of the labour force will change because of shifts in the Australian population. However, overall there will be a slowing of growth in the labour force and an ageing profile.

The ageing workforce

More than 80 per cent of the projected growth in the labour force between 1998 and 2016 will be in the age-group of 45 years and over. In contrast, the teenage labour force (aged 15 to 19 years) is projected to fall by 2016. In 1981, 25 per cent of the labour force was aged 45 years and over; in 2006, the same figure is 36 per cent. The Australian population is ageing due to increased life expectancies and a low level of fertility, which has resulted in proportionally fewer children in the population.[40] An ageing workforce means that employers will increasingly face issues such as career plateauing, retirement planning and retraining of older workers to avoid skill obsolescence. Companies will struggle with how to control the rising costs of benefits and sick leave. Growth in the older labour force suggests that employers will have to find ways to attract, train and retain older employees (see, for example, Chapter 4 Occupational health and safety).

International comparison shows that the age structure of Australia's population in 2000 was similar to that of Canada and the United States of America. In general, European countries and Japan had smaller proportions of children and higher proportions of older people than did Australia. In Italy, Japan and Greece, the number of people aged 65 years and over exceeds the number of children aged 14 years or younger. In contrast, several countries in the Asian region have proportionally more children and fewer older people, reflecting considerably higher fertility rates and lower life expectancies at birth than those in Australia.[41]

Gender issues in the Australian labour force

The Australian workforce is becoming increasingly diverse and one important form of this diversity is related to gender representation. During the last two decades, the overall labour force participation rate has increased slowly, rising from 60.5 per cent in 1984–85 to 64.0 per cent in 2004–05. The main force behind the long-term rise in the labour force participation rate has been an increase in the female participation rate, including an increase in the proportion of women with family responsibilities who are in the workforce.[42] Over the past 20 years, female employment in Australia has increased, while the male rate has fallen. The female participation rate increased from 46 per cent in 1984–85 to 57 per cent in 2004–05. In contrast, the male participation rate fell from 76 per cent to 72 per cent over the same period.[43]

There are large gender differences in occupations. Females are dominant in occupations such as clerical, sales and service work, while males dominate the trade occupations. For example, a higher proportion of males are employed as tradespersons and related workers (20.6 per cent compared to 2.8 per cent for females), while a higher proportion of females are employed as clerical, sales and service workers (27.9 per cent compared to 8.8 per cent for males).[45] Currently, women represent around 25 per cent of managers and administrators in Australian workplaces.[44] However, the higher the level of management, the fewer women to be found: it has been reported that women represent 35 per cent of junior managers in Australian organisations, 24 per cent of middle management, 15 per cent of senior management and only 8 per cent of executive management. Such proportions are even found in those industries dominated by women; for example, women represent 65 per cent of employees in the education industry but hold only 17 per cent of executive management positions.[45] Recent surveys show that only in large organisations (those employing more than 100 staff) have we seen substantial increases in the number of female managers. The more general trend shows that, over the past 10 years, the number of women in management has been relatively stable. Westpac Bank provides an example of an organisation that is committed to increasing the representation of women at all managerial levels, through processes of cultural change and a comprehensive approach to gender equality.[46]

Ethnic diversity in the Australian labour force

Ethnic diversity is another salient characteristic of the Australian population and workforce. Australia has one of the most culturally heterogeneous societies in the world, due to several waves of migration from a broad range of cultural and geographic backgrounds.[47] The social, economic and political implications of this multiculturalism are significant for organisations and Australian society in general.

Indigenous Australians have one of the oldest cultures in the world, with a presence dating back at least 60 000 years. European settlement from 1788 had a dramatic and largely negative impact on Indigenous Australians, who were disadvantaged and marginalised by the social, economic and political policies of European colonists. These disadvantages remain in terms of literacy rates, unemployment, health and housing problems.[48]

Indigenous Australians represent approximately 2 per cent of the national population. Recent research has examined current practices and emerging opportunities for Indigenous Australians in the workforce and noted that significant obstacles remain. For example, the proportion of Indigenous Australians, male or female, who are self-employed is much less than the national average.[49] According to the 2001 census, 52 per cent of Indigenous people aged 15 years and over were participating in the labour force, being either employed at the time of the census (42 per cent employment to population ratio) or unemployed (10 per cent). Forty-eight per cent were not in the labour force.

The employment to population ratio of 42 per cent includes 7 per cent of Indigenous people aged 15 years and over who were reported to be employed in Community Development Employment Projects (CDEP), principally in remote areas of Australia.[50]

National statistics indicate that certain groups of people, such as Indigenous Australians, can experience special difficulties in gaining access to education or training opportunities. Indigenous Australians commonly have had lower levels of participation in post-compulsory education than have the rest of the community.

Prior to the 1960s, the majority of migrants to Australia came from Europe, particularly the United Kingdom. Historically, multiculturalism in Australia was regarded as a governmental social policy problem and attempts were made to reduce cultural heterogeneity by restricting immigration to white Europeans.[51] There has, however, been increasing national awareness of the importance of Australia's Asian geographic positioning vis-à-vis European cultural heritage, with significant demographic change within Australia. In the past few decades, Australian social policy focus shifted significantly to emphasise the benefits and opportunities to be gained in a multicultural society. However, in the current decade, there is intensification of debate around immigration. The dominant view among researchers and policy makers is that immigration yields overall long-term benefits to the economy, although there is recognition of the need for adjustments.[52]

In 2004–05, 25 per cent of people in the Australian workforce were born overseas. The main countries of birth of the population are the United Kingdom, New Zealand, Italy, China, Vietnam, Greece, India and the Philippines. The majority of permanent arrivals in Australia enter under the auspices of the Australian Migration Program. Most permanent arrivals are skilled migrants (46 per cent), 26 per cent arrive under the family migration category, and another 9 per cent arrive under the humanitarian program. Of skilled migrants arriving in 2003–04, 31 per cent came from Europe, 18 per cent from South-East Asia, and 16 per cent from Southern Asia, Sub-Saharan Africa and North-East Asia.[53]

The labour force participation rate for males born overseas is 84 per cent compared with 59 per cent for females born overseas.[54] According to a report by the Australian Federal Race Discrimination Commissioner in 1997, migrants in Australia have come from 160 countries and 40 per cent of people in Australia are migrants or the children of migrants.[55]

Approximately 58 per cent of the immigrant workforce is male. Of those employees born outside Australia, approximately 6 per cent work as managers or administrators, another 32 per cent work as professionals or associate professionals, approximately 12 per cent are tradespeople, 28 per cent work in clerical, sales or service industries, 10 per cent work in production or transport and 11 per cent work as labourers.[56]

The heterogeneous composition of the workforce challenges companies to create HRM practices that ensure the talents, skills and values of all employees are fully utilised to help deliver high quality products and services.

Employee values

Because the workforce is predicted to become more diverse in terms of age, ethnicity and racial background, it is unlikely that one set of values will characterise all employees. For example, it is important to understand generational differences. 'Traditionalists', born between 1925 and 1945, tend to be uncomfortable challenging the status quo and authority. They value income and employment security. 'Baby boomers' (born between 1946 and 1964) have lived through significant social changes, with technological advances and increasing social freedoms. Baby boomers are typically more adaptable and flexible than traditionalists. 'Generation X' (born between 1965 and 1979) typically value unexpected rewards for work accomplishments, opportunities to learn new things, praise, recognition and time with the manager. 'Generation Y' employees (born between 1980 and 1994) are often described as more globally aware, technologically savvy and difficult to retain in one organisation or job. 'Generation Z' (born between 1995 and 2009) are most likely to be children of Generation X; they are already influencing employment via their parents' concerns with work–life flexibility and childcare options.[57]

All employees, however, value several aspects of work regardless of their background. Employees view work as a means to self-fulfilment—that is, a means to more fully use their skills and abilities, meet their interests and allow them to live a desirable lifestyle.[58] Research consistently shows that employees who perceive their work conditions to include aspects such as opportunities to fully use and develop their skills, greater job responsibilities, a fair promotion system, and a trustworthy manager who represents the employee's best interests, are more committed to their companies.[59] Because many employees place more value on the quality of non-work activities and family life than on pay and production, employees will demand more flexible work policies that allow them to choose work hours and locations where work is performed.

Managing diversity involves many different activities (see Chapter 9 Managing diversity and work–life balance for more detail). These include creating an organisational culture that values diversity, ensuring that HRM systems are bias-free, facilitating higher career involvement of women, promoting knowledge and acceptance of differences, ensuring involvement in education both within and outside the company and dealing with employees' resistance to diversity.[60] Table 1.6 presents ways that managing diversity can provide a competitive advantage. To some extent, in many Australian companies, the costs of poorly managing diversity were viewed mainly as increased legal fees associated with discrimination cases. However, as Table 1.6 illustrates, the implications of successfully managing the diverse workforce of the next decade go beyond legal concerns. How diversity issues are managed has implications for creativity, problem solving, retaining good employees and developing markets for the firm's products and services. To successfully manage a diverse workforce, managers must develop a new set of skills, including:

1. Communicating effectively with employees from a wide variety of backgrounds.
2. Coaching and developing employees of different ages, educational backgrounds, ethnicity, physical ability and race.
3. Providing performance feedback based on objective outcomes rather than on values and stereotypes that work against women, minorities and handicapped persons by prejudging their abilities and talents.
4. Creating a work environment that makes it comfortable for employees of all backgrounds to be creative and innovative.[61]

TABLE 1.6	How managing diversity can provide competitive advantage
1 Cost argument	As organisations become more diverse, the cost of a poor job in integrating workers will increase. Those who handle this well will, thus, create cost advantages over those who do not.
2 Resource-acquisition argument	Companies develop reputations on favourability as prospective employers for women and ethnic minorities. Those with the best reputations for managing diversity will win the competition for the best personnel. As the labour pool shrinks and changes composition, this edge will become increasingly important.
3 Marketing argument	For multinational organisations, the insight and cultural sensitivity that members with roots in other countries bring to the marketing effort should improve these efforts in important ways. The same rationale applies to marketing to sub-populations within domestic operations.
4 Creativity argument	Diversity of perspectives and less emphasis on conformity to 'norms' of the past (which characterise the modern approach to management of diversity) should improve the level of creativity.
5 Problem-solving argument	Heterogeneity in decisions and problem solving groups potentially produce better decisions through a wider range of perspectives and more thorough critical analysis of issues.
6 System-flexibility argument	An implication of the multicultural model for managing diversity is that the system will become less determinant, less standardised and, therefore, more fluid. The increased fluidity should create greater flexibility to react to environmental changes (that is, reactions should be faster and cost less).

Source: T.H. Cox & S. Blake, 1991, 'Managing cultural diversity: implications for organizational competitiveness', *Academy of Management Executive*, 5, p. 47. Reproduced with permission of Academy of Management.

A comprehensive example of diversity management is evident in changes in the Australian Public Service (APS).[62] The APS has replaced equal employment opportunity programs with workplace diversity programs. Although these new programs include all of the existing equal employment opportunity provisions of the *Public Service Act*, they focus more on the recognition that diversity can improve organisational effectiveness. Although each APS department is given responsibility for developing its own workplace diversity program, a system of self-evaluation and reporting creates accountability. The Public Service Commissioner assesses the effectiveness and outcomes of workplace diversity programs in each APS agency and the findings are reported annually.[63] Annual Workplace Diversity Awards are presented with the objective of recognising and promoting good employment practices with regard to workplace diversity.

Progress in diversity management is also evident in the private sector. Many companies (for example, Telstra, ANZ Bank and Crown Casino) have utilised diversity-training programs that focus on understanding cultural differences, communication styles and the ways stereotypes influence behaviour towards persons with different characteristics.

The bottom line is that to gain a competitive advantage in the next decade, companies must harness the power of the diverse workforce. These practices are needed, not only to meet employee needs, but to reduce turnover costs and ensure that customers receive the best service possible. The implication of diversity for HR practices will be highlighted throughout this book. For example, from a staffing perspective, it is important to ensure that tests used to select employees are not biased against minority groups. From a work design perspective, employees need flexible schedules that allow them to meet non-work needs. From a training perspective, it is clear that all employees need to be made aware of the potential damaging effects of stereotypes. From a compensation perspective, benefits such as eldercare and daycare need to be included in reward systems to accommodate the needs of a diverse workforce.[64]

Structure of the economy

Competition for labour is affected by the structure of the economy. The structure of the economy, in turn, is influenced by the growth and decline of industries, jobs and occupations.

In the early years of European settlement in Australia, between 1788 and 1850, the country's economic development was led by the pastoral industry. In particular, growth in the wool industry enabled development of other sectors, such as the establishment of local manufacturing industries, to take advantage of emerging market opportunities. In the 1850s and 1860s, gold became Australia's major export earner, leading to rapid expansion of banking and commerce. Manufacturing industries continued to expand from the mid-nineteenth century and by the Second World War the Australian manufacturing sector was sufficiently developed to respond to the demand for war materials and equipment. In the 1950s and 1960s, all Australian economic sectors experienced growth, until the oil crisis in 1973–74 brought worldwide recession. Employment growth between 1968 and 1979 was modest and restricted to service industries.[65]

Since the 1980s there has been a decline in the relative contribution to gross domestic product from goods-producing industries and a rise in the contribution from service industries, although manufacturing remains the most significant industry in terms of its contribution to gross domestic product. In terms of employment, manufacturing has decreased markedly. The contrasting dramatic growth in service-sector employment has culminated in more than 70 per cent of the Australian workforce being employed in various service industries.[66]

Since 1987–88, the industry composition of the Australian labour market has changed considerably. Historically, the manufacturing industry was the dominant employing industry, but its contribution to the number of employed persons has been declining. As recently as 1990–91, the manufacturing industry was the largest employer, but it has fallen from 15 per cent of all employed persons in 1989–90 to 11 per cent in 2004–05. Employment in other traditional commodity-based industries, such as agriculture, forestry, fishing and mining, has also declined over this period.[67]

Manufacturing is now the third biggest employing industry, behind retail trade with 15 per cent of employed persons, and property and business services with 12 per cent of employed persons. Health has risen to 10 per cent and hospitality (accommodation, cafes and restaurants) has risen to 5 per cent.[68]

The growth of jobs in the service sector has important implications for HRM. Research shows that employee perceptions of HRM practices are positively related to customer evaluation of service quality. The more positive the employee perceptions of HRM practices (for example, providing feedback and adequate training), the greater the customers' evaluation of service quality.[69] This suggests that to maximise customer service, companies in the service sector should consider creating both a positive experience for the customer and progressive HRM policies.

Other groups that are growing include executive, administrative and managerial occupations; technical and related support occupations; and marketing and sales occupations. Note that professional specialty, or knowledge work, occupations and service occupations differ on both the amount of education required for the job and expected earnings (as discussed in more detail with regard to the HR innovation challenge later in this chapter). Knowledge work occupations require more education and have greater earnings potential than do service jobs.[70]

Knowledge work usually involves the research and development of new products and/or services; is performed by knowledge workers.

Retail will continue to be a source of jobs for unskilled workers.[71] Technology has made it possible for employees with poor reading and mathematical skills to perform customer transactions by replacing numerical key pads on point-of-sale terminals with pictures of products and menu items.

Skill deficiencies

It is expected that the supply of individuals with the necessary education and training will not meet the job demands of the Australian economy. In Australia at present there are skill shortages in three broad occupational areas. These are professions including accountants and civil engineers, registered nurses, health professionals and some teaching specialisations; trade skills including toolmakers, chefs, hairdressers and sheetmetal workers; and service occupations, including child-care coordinators.[77] Most new jobs created in the next decade will require higher levels of reading and writing skills (for example, skills in reading journals and financial reports as well as writing business letters and reports).

Two problems are evident as we examine skills: new entrants to the workforce who come from diverse backgrounds and the current labour force. New entrants to the labour force often arrive without the skills needed for success. The skills gap has also caused manufacturers to delay adding new businesses. This is especially a problem for small businesses, which tend to rely heavily on the labour market to find skilled employees because they cannot afford to invest in training.

The implications of the changing labour market for managing human resources are far-reaching. Because labour market growth will be primarily based on females and people with English as a second language, Australian companies will have to ensure that employees and human resource management systems are free of bias to capitalise on the perspectives and values that a diverse workforce can contribute to improving product quality, customer service, product development and market share. Increasing levels of employment in the service sector of the economy suggest that HRM practices in these companies need to ensure that customer service is rewarded and improved.

Changes in the employment contract and place of work

Working life in Australia is changing. There are more diverse employment arrangements, more flexible working time patterns, and more people working part-time hours.[73] The contingent workforce, which includes temporary, part-time and self-employed workers, is growing. There are significant changes evident in Australian workplaces, utilising new technologies, widespread multiskilling, new forms of employment and varied hours of work. Recent Australian studies suggest evidence of the common pattern seen in other industrialised countries: employment is moving from the 'traditional' forms of full-time, permanent work towards a wider variety of working arrangements, including part-time work, temporary employment and contract employment.[74]

In 2004–05, 71 per cent of employed people were working in full-time employment. Full-time workers are those who usually work 35 hours or more per week in all jobs or, although usually working less than 35 hours a week, actually worked 35 hours or more during the reference week of the Labour Force Survey. Part-time workers are those who usually work less than 35 hours a week. Part-time employed persons now account for 28 per cent of all employed persons. Women dominate the part-time workforce.[75]

The increase in the number of contingent workers is occurring for several reasons.[76] Erosion of the traditional employment contract—lifetime employment for dedicated service—has occurred. Companies can no longer guarantee job security for their employees. Many companies have reduced the number of full-time employees to lower the associated labour costs and give the organisation the flexibility to contract for skills when needed. Companies that use contingent employees from temporary agencies and contract firms are likely to experience a reduction in the administrative and financial burden associated with human resource management because the agencies take care of selecting, training and compensating the workers.

Contingent work can be attractive from the worker's perspective. Many employees have decided to work on a contingent basis as a result of interests, values and needs. Employees who have lost their jobs may take on temporary work while they are seeking full-time employment. Other employees are contingent workers so they can attend to raising young children or care for a sick family member. Yet other contingent employees use temporary employment as a way to identify potential full-time employers that would satisfy their needs.

The use of contingent employees places a burden on managers to be able to identify when and how many contingent employees are needed—that is, on human resource planning (which is discussed in Chapter 7 HR planning and HR information systems). Managers also have to consider which jobs are critical to the business and may need to be filled by full-time employees. Employee morale may suffer when full-time employees are replaced with contingent workers.

Contingent workforce
temporary, part-time and self-employed workers who are not considered full-time employees.

More work is being done outside the traditional office or factory. Such work is sometimes called distributed work, telework or telecommuting and it includes work done at home, on the road or anywhere a person can connect to the office or peers using information technology.[77] Some estimates suggest that in 2005 about 25 per cent of the labour force was engaged in doing job-related work at home or 'distributed work'. Distributed work has important implications for managing human resources. Employees need to be trained in using information technology to share data, information and ideas with peers, managers and customers. Companies need to adapt types of employee evaluation to fairly and accurately assess performance.[78]

> **Distributed work, telework and telecommuting**
> work done outside of the traditional work environment, including at home, while travelling, or anywhere an employee can interact with managers, peers, customers, products or processes using technology.

Legislation

Several areas in the legal environment have influenced human resource management since the early 1980s. These areas include workplace relations, equal employment opportunity, occupational health and safety, employee pay and benefits, and job security. Employers in Australia must comply with Commonwealth legislation. Further, Australian State and Territory governments have legislated to prescribe minimum conditions of employment, which apply notwithstanding any express provision in an employment contract. Industrial legislation in most jurisdictions (States, Territories and at the federal level) in Australia is undergoing substantial changes.[79] Legislation will continue to have a major impact on HR practices (legal issues are discussed further in Chapter 3; industrial relations are discussed in Chapter 5).

Another area of litigation that will continue to have a major influence on HRM practices involves job security. As companies are forced to close plants and retrench employees because of restructuring, technology changes or financial crisis, the number of cases dealing with the illegal dismissal of employees has increased.[80] Employers' work rules, recruitment practices and performance management systems will need to be revised to ensure that these systems do not falsely communicate employment agreements the company does not intend to honour (for example, long-term employment).

Ethical considerations

Many decisions related to the management of human resources are characterised by uncertainty. Ethics can be considered to cover the fundamental principles by which employees and companies interact, as discussed in detail in Chapter 15 (Ethics and HRM).[81] These principles should be considered in making business decisions and interacting with clients and customers.[82]

As a result of unfavourable perceptions of business practices and an increased concern for better serving the customer, companies are becoming more aware of the need for all representatives of the company to act responsibly.[83] They have an interest in the way their employees behave because customer, government agency and vendor perceptions of the company play an important role in maintaining the relationships necessary to sell products and services.

One way to characterise ethical, successful companies is by identifying four principles.[84] First, in their relationship with employees, customers, vendors and clients, these companies emphasise mutual benefits. Second, employees assume responsibility for the actions of the company. Third, they have a sense of purpose or vision the employees value and use in their day-to-day work. Finally, they emphasise organisational justice and fairness; that is, another person's interests count as much as their own. For example, the company ensures ethical treatment of all stakeholders.

PART 1   Managing the Human Resource Environment

Reputation Index (published between 2000 and 2003) took into account the views of stakeholders and experts, including consumers, investors, employees and activists, about the reputation of companies taken in *Business Review Weekly's* (*BRW's*) list of Australia's top 1000 companies. The model has since been further developed as RepuTex Ratings.

Many leading companies are emphasising ethics as part of their strategy for conducting business. The '**reputation index**'[85] is one research tool that measures the views of stakeholders and experts, including consumers, investors, employees and activists about the reputation of companies taken from the *Business Review Weekly's* (*BRW's*) list of Australia's top 1000 companies. The 'reputation index' assesses these companies on six categories: employee management, environmental performance, social impact, ethics, financial performance and market position. The 'ethical performance' criteria by which companies are measured include whether the company:

- has a code of ethics in place
- has an ethics committee
- is able to demonstrate how the code of ethics informs daily practice
- obtains an independent audit of performance against principles of corporate social responsibility
- has an ethical policy that impacts positively on customers
- ensures that all services are readily available to all consumer groups
- has an ethical and trustworthy approach to marketing and communication.[86]

There are basically three standards that human resource managers must satisfy for these practices to be considered ethical.[87] First, human resource practices must result in the greatest good for the largest number of people. Second, employment practices must respect basic human rights of privacy, due process, consent and free speech. Third, managers must treat employees and customers equitably and fairly. Throughout the book, and particularly in Chapter 15 Ethics and HRM and Chapter 18 Evaluating and improving the human resource function we will highlight ethical dilemmas in human resource management practices.

Why has the importance of human resource management increased over the past two decades? HRM is seen by managers as the most important lever for companies to gain a competitive advantage over both domestic and foreign competitors. We believe this is because HRM practices are directly related to companies' success in meeting competitive challenges. The next section discusses each of these challenges and their implications for HRM.

Competitive challenges influencing human resource management

Four competitive challenges that companies will face in the next decade will increase the importance of human resource management practices. These are: the challenge of globalisation, the challenge of HR innovation, the challenge of sustainability, and the challenge of attracting and retaining people. These four challenges are shown in Figure 1.4.

The challenge of globalisation

We are in the midst of a global restructuring of the world's markets. Over the last three decades, as nations have integrated into the international world economy and markets have internationalised, there has been an unprecedented increase in the number of organisations that have internationalised their operations. Companies are finding that, to survive, they must compete in international markets as well as fend off foreign corporations' attempts to gain ground at home. Concomitant with the expansion of international business has been a remarkable increase in the movement

FIGURE 1.4 Competitive challenges influencing Australian companies

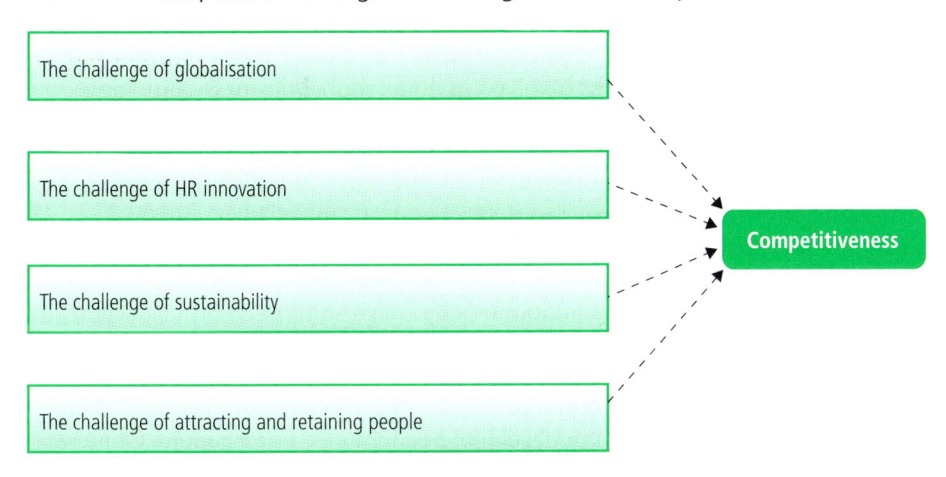

- The challenge of globalisation
- The challenge of HR innovation
- The challenge of sustainability
- The challenge of attracting and retaining people

→ **Competitiveness**

of labour. Australian businesses must develop global markets, use their practices to improve global competitiveness, balance the sometimes competing demands for global integration and local responsiveness, manage global workforce mobility, and better prepare employees for global assignments.

Development of global markets

Anecdotal evidence suggests that the most admired and successful companies in the world have not only created multinational corporations but have created organisations with workforces and corporate cultures that reflect the characteristics of the global markets in which they operate. Examples of these companies include Coca-Cola, Toyota Motors, and Nokia.

These companies' key priorities include traditional business objectives, such as customer focus and innovation. However, a distinguishing characteristic is that these companies believe that people are their most important asset. Believing that employees are the key to success translates into human resource practices, including rewarding employee performance, measuring employee satisfaction, using an intensive employee selection process, promotion from within and investing in employee development.

Many of the former communist nations of Europe and Asia now present enormous opportunities for international business.[88] Under communist rule, these countries were closed to Western businesses. China, with a population of over one billion (one thousand million), represents a huge market for goods and services. China is now one of the largest recipients of foreign direct investment (FDI) in the world. China's transition over the past two and a half decades and its integration into the world economy since its accession to the WTO in 2001 have resulted in significant changes in the context for management practices, and has considerable implications for the management of China's workforce.[89] Taking the political environment as an example, China retains its socialist one-party government system as well as its socialist ideology while moving from a highly centralised command economy to a more market-driven economy;[90] there are numerous implications for HR practices, such as the political influence on staffing and performance management;[91] and the influence of socialist ideology on reward and compensation.[92]

Given the size of its growing economy and its vast population, China has become increasingly significant in international business. Similarly, in Latin America and in countries such as Vietnam, governments are selling State-owned businesses to private investors and foreign investment is welcome. This is not to say that developing these markets is easy. Political instability, poor infrastructure (roads, communications etc.) and poor economies make the risks involved in doing global business quite high.

Many companies are investing in developing economies. They are reacting decisively to global changes and are positioning themselves to be active participants in those areas of the world that are expected to grow most rapidly. For example, many foreign companies have expanded their operations into China, attracted mainly by the fast growth in its economy, the sheer size of its potential market and its abundant labour resources. FDI in China grew from US$4 billion in 1990 to US$40 billion in 2000 and US$70 billion in 2004. According to an official report, by the end of 2004, 90 per cent of the 500 world top companies reported by *Fortune* had invested in China.[93]

Also, over the last decade, there has been substantial growth in outward FDI by companies that are headquartered in developing economies. For example, Chinese multinational enterprises (MNEs) have made a huge amount of outward FDI; China is now one of the world's leading foreign investors.[94] In 2004, China's annual outward investment reached US$5.5 billion, which was a 93 per cent increase over the previous year.[95]

Also, many changes are happening in developed economies. For example, European countries have taken steps to strengthen their competitive positions by adopting a single currency, the euro. It was introduced with the aim of strengthening the competitiveness of European Union countries who adopt this currency. For European businesses, the euro is seen as a way to cut costs and encourage cross-border mergers. On 1 May 2004, the European Union was expanded to bring the total number of member countries to 25 and the EU population to around 455 million people.[96]

While many large firms such as BHP Billiton, News Corporation and Qantas are already multinational corporations that span the globe, many medium-sized and small organisations are becoming increasingly involved in international business. To be successful in the global marketplace, the challenge for all businesses—regardless of size—is to understand cultural differences and to invest in human resources.[97] To compete in the world economy, Australian companies need to put great effort into selecting and retaining talented employees, employee training and development, and dismantling traditional bureaucratic structures that limit employees' ability to be innovative and creative.[98]

Managing global workforce mobility and international assignments
Besides taking steps to ensure that employees are better utilised, Australian companies must ensure effective management of their global workforce. Global mobility management is increasingly recognised as a vital element of human resource management in an international context.[99] Global mobility management encompasses a range of policies and practices that enable knowledge sharing, employee development and achievement of organisational goals and objectives.[100]

Increasing concerns about global risks for MNEs and their employees in uncertain times and difficult locations are leading many MNEs to re-think their approaches to global mobility.[101] MNEs seeking to revise their global mobility management face complex decisions. Possible strategic options to implement include, for example, reducing the use of expatriates; altering the nature of international assignments, relying more on virtual assignments;[102] and or ceasing operations in a location that has become too difficult or risky.

Managing a global workforce also includes preparing and supporting employees and their families with regard to overseas assignments.[103] Companies must carefully select employees to work overseas based on their ability to understand and respect the cultural and business norms of the host country, their language skills and their technical ability. Additionally, companies must be willing to train and develop foreign employees to win foreign business. Several companies (for example, BHP Billiton) bring foreign workers to a learning centre for training and development opportunities and then return them to their home country.[104] They return to their home country with necessary knowledge in such aspects as management competencies and technical knowledge. (These issues are discussed in more detail in Chapter 16 International human resource management.) As discussed in 'Managing challenges of globalisation: HR strategies go global', the complexities of globalisation have many implications for HRM, and for the way in which the HR function is managed in organisations.

HR STRATEGIES GO GLOBAL

MANAGING CHALLENGES OF GLOBALISATION

WITH COMPANIES becoming more global, two-thirds of multinational companies have adopted a HR strategy that is consistent across offices worldwide.

Furthermore, a growing number of multinationals are shifting to more centralised compensation and benefits structures to help ensure that employees and executives around the world share the same incentives.

A recent Watson Wyatt Worldwide survey found that more than half (56 per cent) plan to shift to a more centralised structure over the next two years, up from 42 per cent in 2004. 'A centralised global approach to compensation and benefits is necessary for consistency and alignment with company goals, although multinationals should watch how much emphasis they place on consistency', said Bob Wesselkamper, director of international consulting at Watson Wyatt.

'Local cultures and the availability of resources play a big role, too. The key is finding the right balance, as some programs are best managed globally, while others are best managed locally.'

The Watson Wyatt WorldatWork survey of 275 companies also found most multinational companies manage executive compensation, long- and short-term incentives and performance management globally, largely because these programs are linked to a company's rewards and performance measures.

'Companies are fully centralising programs that drive strategic performance,' said Don Lindner, compensation practice leader at WorldatWork.

'Centrally managing executive compensation programs allows multinationals to strongly link rewards for executives to the results of the total enterprise.'

Part of the push for more centralisation has come from regulatory reporting requirements, such as those in the *Sarbanes-Oxley Act* in the United States. Forty-five per cent of multinationals now have a formal approach to global corporate governance in place, including requiring benefit changes to be approved by global or regional management.

The programs that most frequently require global or regional approval before changes can be implemented are executive compensation (92 per cent) and long-term incentives (73 per cent).

Additionally, 80 per cent of companies are developing clear global policies, and 64 per cent are implementing consistent global tools, processes and technology to strengthen governance procedures for total rewards design and administration around the world.

'Instituting clear policies to support the design and delivery of new rewards programs globally generates benefits beyond simple compliance with regulations', said Laura Sejen, Watson Wyatt's global practice director for strategic rewards.

'It can help companies uncover and address inconsistencies and help them communicate to employees worldwide the value of their total rewards packages.'

Source: C. Donaldson, 2006, 'HR strategies go global', *Human Resources*, 3 October, www.humanresourcesmagazine.com.au.

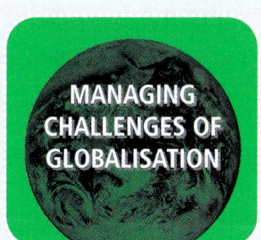

PART 1   Managing the Human Resource Environment

The challenge of HR innovation

Given the many changes in the context of the work and employment, innovations in HR strategies and practices are necessary for the HR system to make a worthwhile contribution to individual employees and to organisational performance. Innovations in HR rely on the effective management of employees, their knowledge and work systems.

The saying 'knowledge is power' has never been more applicable to managers and employees worldwide. It is widely recognised that knowledge is as an essential resource for organisational success and competitive advantage, and should therefore be protected and nurtured within oganisations.[105] Many researchers have written about aspects of knowledge management in recent years and many organisations have sought to develop approaches to knowledge management, which includes processes, techniques, systems and structures that aim to improve the creation, sharing and use of knowledge.[106] The global knowledge economy has emerged as a challenging competitive environment for business and management.[107] The global knowledge economy is defined as having two dimensions: increasingly knowledge-intensive forms of production, and globalisation of economies, communications and cultures.[108] In this context, the management of employees is more important than ever before.

In Australia since the 1970s, successive federal governments have implemented various support schemes for Australian businesses to internationalise and to participate in the global knowledge economy to improve their international competitiveness.[109] These initiatives have been necessary because of Australia's small domestic base and a past focus on commodities-based international operations. Considine and colleagues suggest that, to compete in the global knowledge economy, Australian policy makers and businesses should invest in knowledge, particularly in education, research and development and new technology. These authors argue that failure to become a 'knowledge nation' will lead to Australia being 'increasingly dependent upon others …, leading to further adverse consequences for the trade position, for the level and character of jobs and opportunities, and for the accumulation and distribution of wealth'.[110]

Sveiby[111] differentiates a knowledge paradigm typical of that economy from the more tangible industrial paradigm of the 'old world'. In an industrial paradigm, people are cost generators or resources, the managers' power base is dependent on relative level in the organisation's hierarchy, production is based on physical labourers processing physical resources to create tangible products, and information flows via organisational hierarchy. In contrast, in a knowledge paradigm, people are revenue generators, the managers' power base is dependent on relative level of knowledge, production is based on knowledge workers converting knowledge into intangible structures, and information flows via collegial networks.

As Dodgson[112] and others have suggested, the definition of knowledge is elusive. Critics of the 'knowledge economy' concept[113] argue that several sub-sectors, with differing rates of growth, may be differentiated within the knowledge economy. For example, key growth areas in employment are in low-level service jobs rather than knowledge work, and several authors have argued that the service sector should not be conflated with knowledge work.[114] Throughout this book, we will explore examples of the knowledge economy and knowledge work, and examine the implications for those *not* engaged in these areas (see, for example, Chapter 6 Analysis and design of work and Chapter 15 Ethics and HRM).

The management of knowledge is increasingly tied to the use of technology. Concurrent with the changes in the types of work being done, technological advances

---

Knowledge management processes, techniques, systems and structures that aim to improve the creation, sharing and use of knowledge.

Global knowledge economy increasing knowledge-intensity of production, and globalisation of economies, communications and cultures.

Knowledge workers highly skilled employees whose work utilises theoretical and analytical knowledge, acquired via formal education.

in manufacturing, transportation, telecommunications and microprocessors are changing the way work is performed, managers' and employees' roles, and organisational structure. Technology also has made human resource information systems more available and accessible, and created a need to develop HRM practices that integrate technology with people.

As we noted earlier, for Australian companies to compete in global markets, they will have to learn to better utilise employees' talents and skills and new technology. A key challenge that companies face is how to integrate technology and structure to gain a competitive advantage—that is, competing through technology. One way of combining people and technology is via high-performance work systems (HPWS) that maximise the fit between the company's social system (employees) and its technical system (including information, technology and work).[115]

High-performance work systems involve self-managing work teams. These teams design their own work methods, have high levels of training and share in the organisation's financial results. High-performance work systems rely on flatter, horizontal organisational structures. Organisations often introduce high-performance work systems to help the organisation develop stronger customer orientation and to improve performance and accountability.[116] As discussed in the 'Managing challenges through HR innovation: Leading organisational change', developing and implementing HR innovations include organisational change to support the implementation of new HR initiatives.

High-performance work systems (HPWS)
Work systems that maximise the fit between the company's social system (employees) and its technology (including information, technology and work).

LEADING ORGANISATIONAL CHANGE

MANAGING CHALLENGES THROUGH HR INNOVATION

Alec Bashinsky describes himself as an extremely persistent person. His success at Deloitte as the accounting firm's national partner, people and performance, has led to several awards for human-resources practice, the latest being the JML Australia Human Capital Leadership Award. He has led initiatives such as a staff-referral recruitment program, which is estimated to have saved Deloitte $1.2 million in recruitment fees in the past year.

With adequate resources and a pro-change chief executive, Giam Swiegers, behind him, Bashinsky has been able to orchestrate a new three-year graduate development program. It simply uses the budget previously spent on entertaining prospective graduates. Other learning programs have been introduced—lunchtime seminars have been popular—as well as programs to promote more women into senior ranks.

To make these changes, Bashinsky had to move human resources staff away from their spreadsheets and other mundane tasks to concentrate on more strategic work that will improve the business. 'It is about changing the mandate and structure around HR', he says. 'The company has to change or we will be left behind.'

Bashinsky's next great challenge is centred on developing the leadership capabilities of the firm's partners. Deloitte will invest more in partner development over the next year than it has in the past five.

Tips on leading organisational change include:

- Communicate to the whole group about the desired changes for the business and why they need to be made.
- Rather than thinking of the process of change management as an entire project, break it down into smaller pieces and work on specific areas. Publicise changes as they happen, and then move on to the next stage of the project.
- Bashinsky has had success with what he calls 'tiger teams' within Deloitte. Groups of staff from different walks of life are set up to challenge the ways things are done. 'The group takes something that is existing and tears it to shreds', he says.

Source: E. Ross, 2006, 'HR Innovation', *BRW*, 27 April, p. 69. © 2006 Copyright John Fairfax Holdings Limited. www.brw.com.au

PART 1   Managing the Human Resource Environment

Call centre
also called customer service centre. An organisation (or organisational segment) dedicated to service and/or sales, in which employees interact by telephone or computer with customers to provide a service or to sell a product.

Change in employees' work roles and skill requirements

New technology causes changes in basic skill requirements and work roles and often results in combining jobs. For example, employment in call centres has grown at a rapid rate over recent years. High levels of employee turnover in call centres have pointed to the need to design the jobs to reduce the stress caused by repetitive work, constant performance monitoring by supervisors and continuous contact with customers (by telephone). Many leading corporate call centres have increased salary levels and employee training, in efforts to retain call centre employees and to familiarise employees with sophisticated technology[117] (see Chapter 6 Analysis and design of work).

Computer-integrated manufacturing uses robots and computers to automate the manufacturing process. The computer allows the production of different products that meet market demands simply by reprogramming the computer. As a result, labourer, material handler, operator–assembler and maintenance jobs may be merged into one position. Computer-integrated manufacturing requires employees to monitor equipment and troubleshoot problems with sophisticated equipment, share information with other employees and understand the interaction between components of the manufacturing process. The proliferation and advancement of new information technology in the workplace presents numerous challenges to the way in which work and workforces are organised and managed. HRM is simultaneously driving and being driven by technological changes in the workplace.[118] Many examples of this work are seen in the growth of call centres.[119]

Technology is often a means to achieve product diversification and customisation. As a result, employees need job-specific product knowledge and basic learning skills to keep up with product development and design improvements. To customise products and services, employees must have the ability to listen to, and communicate with, customers. Interpersonal skills, such as negotiation and conflict management, and problem solving skills, are more important than physical strength, coordination and fine motor skills, which were previously required for many manufacturing and service jobs.

The use of teams to perform work

As the information needed to improve product quality and customer service becomes more available to employees at the point of sale (or point of production) because of advances in microprocessing systems, employees are expected to make more decisions concerning how their jobs are performed. One of the most popular methods of increasing employee responsibility and control is work teams. Work teams involve employees, with various skills, who interact to assemble a product or provide a service. Work teams frequently assume many of the activities usually reserved for managers, such as selecting new team members, planning work schedules and coordinating activities with customers and other units within the firm. Work teams also perform inspection and quality control activities while the product or service is being completed—an important component for achieving total quality.

Besides the potential motivational advantages of work teams, labour costs can also be realised for companies adopting teams.[120] Self-managing work teams have two components: the process of self-management and collaborative teamwork. These teams undertake various tasks, including assigning jobs to team members, managing themselves (for example, planning activities, assigning staff to activities), planning and scheduling work, making decisions related to products or services and taking action to remedy problems, such as quality deficiencies.[121] Over the past couple of decades, many companies have reorganised assembly operations—abandoning the assembly line in favour of hybrid operations combining mass production with jobs in which employees perform multiple tasks, use many skills, control the pace of work and assemble the entire final product.

Changes in the nature of managerial work

To gain the maximum benefit from the introduction of new technology in the workplace, managers must be able to move away from the 'military model' of management, which emphasises controlling, planning and coordinating activities, and instead focus on creating work conditions that facilitate employee creativity and innovation. Because of advances in technology, information is more readily accessible to employees at all levels of the company and decision making is increasingly decentralised. Consequently it is difficult, and certainly not effective, for managers to attempt to directly control interactions between work teams or between work teams and customers.

The manager's job is increasingly to empower employees. Empowerment requires a redistribution of power with organisational delayering and devolution of decision making from managers or supervisors to employees. Empowerment means giving employees responsibility and authority to make decisions regarding all aspects of product development or customer service.[122] Employees are then held accountable for products and services and, in return, share in the rewards and failures that result. For empowerment to be successful, managers must serve in a linking and coordinating role.[123] The linking role involves representing employees (or teams) by ensuring that adequate resources are provided to perform the work (external linking), facilitating interactions across departments (informal linking) and ensuring that employees are updated on important issues and cooperate with each other through information- and resource-sharing (internal linking). In addition, managers who successfully perform the internal linking role must be available and willing to help employees deal with problems daily.

Although strong interpersonal and communications skills are required by both managers and employees, managers have to either be able to provide answers to technical issues or, more likely, be able to refer employees to persons within or outside the firm who can provide insight into technical problems. This means that managers have to be more aware of various resources available within the company and the community.

Changes in company structure

The traditional design of many Australian companies emphasised efficiency, decision making by managers, and dissemination of information from the top of the company to lower levels. However, this structure is unlikely to be the most effective in the adaptive work context, in which personal computers give employees immediate access to information needed to complete customer orders or modify product lines. In the adaptive organisational structure, employees are in a constant state of learning and performance improvement. Employees are free to move wherever they are needed in the company. The adaptive organisation is characterised by a core set of values or vital vision that drives all organisational efforts.[124] Previously established boundaries between managers and employees, employees and customers, employees and vendors and the various functions within the company are abandoned. Employees, managers, vendors, customers and suppliers work together to improve service and product quality and to create new products and services. Line employees are trained in multiple jobs, communicate directly with suppliers and customers, and interact frequently with engineers, innovation experts and employees with other functions.

Increased availability of information related to the company's human resources

Improvements in technology related to computers and software have also had a major impact on the use of information for managing human resources. A **human resource information system (HRIS)** is a system used to acquire, store, manipulate, analyse, retrieve and distribute information related to the company's human resources.[125] From the manager's perspective, a HRIS can be used to support strategic decision making, to avoid litigation, to evaluate programs or policies, or to support daily operating concerns. Traditionally, HR software applications were developed in response to record keeping requirements dictated by legislation. As a result, many companies have HRISs that track payroll and benefits information in response to compliance requirements of legislation. In addition, performance management, succession planning and training and employee development applications are becoming increasingly important. For example, changing technology can easily make the skills of technical employees obsolete. To meet internal and external customers' demands, work teams consisting of employees from different functional areas with different skills often have to be assembled. These trends demand that employees' skills and competencies be monitored carefully. Complicating this need for information is the fact that many employees are geographically dispersed across several locations within the same city or country, or even across countries. In response to these needs, many large companies have implemented global human resource management systems. HRIS are discussed in detail in Chapter 7 Human resource planning and human resource information systems

Human resource management practices in high-performance work systems

Unfortunately, many managers have tended to consider technological and structural innovations as independent of each other. That is because, given immediate demands for productivity, service and short-term profitability, many managers tend to implement a new technology (for example, a networked computer system) or a new work design (for example, service teams organised by product) without considering how that new technology might influence the efficiency or effectiveness of the way work is organised.[126] Without integrating technology and structure, maximised production and service will not be attained.

Human resource management practices that support high-performance work systems are shown in Table 1.7. The HR practices involved include employee selection, performance management, training, work design and compensation. These practices are designed to provide employees with skills, incentives, knowledge and autonomy. Research studies suggest that high-performance work practices are usually associated with increases in productivity and long-term financial performance.[127] Research also suggests that it is more effective to improve HR practices as a whole, rather than focus on one or two isolated practices (such as the pay system or the selection system).[128] There may not be a best HR system, but whatever the company does, the practices must be aligned with each other and be consistent with the system if they are to have a positive effect on company performance.[129] This alignment is discussed in more detail in Chapter 2.

The challenge of sustainability

Sustainability has largely been viewed as part of corporate social responsibility, particularly related to the impact a company has on its environment. However, we adopt a broader view of sustainability, as 'the ability of a company to survive and

---

Human resource information system (HRIS)
a system to acquire, store, manipulate, analyse, retrieve and distribute information related to a company's human resources.

TABLE 1.7 — How HR practices support high-performance work systems

- Teams are used to perform work.
- Employees participate in the selection process.
- Employees receive formal performance feedback and they are actively involved in the performance-improvement process.
- Ongoing training is emphasised and rewarded.
- Employees' rewards and compensation relate to the company's financial performance.
- Equipment and work processes are structured to encourage maximum flexibility and interaction among employees.
- Employees participate in planning changes in equipment, layout and work methods.
- Work design allows employees to use a variety of skills.
- Employees understand how their jobs contribute to the finished product or service.

Source: Compiled from Judith A. Neal and Cheryl L. Tromley, 1995, 'From incremental change to retrofit: creating high performance work systems', *Academy of Management Executive*, 9, pp. 42–54; Mark A. Huselid, 1995, 'The impact of human resource management practises on turnover, productivity, and corporate financial performance', *Academy of Management Journal*, 38, pp. 635–72.

succeed in a dynamic competitive environment'.[130] Company effectiveness and competitiveness are determined by whether the company satisfies the needs of stakeholders.[131] Stakeholders include stockholders/shareholders (who want a return on their investment), customers (who want a high-quality product or service) and employees (who desire interesting work and reasonable compensation for their services). The community, which wants the company to contribute to its own activities and projects and to minimise pollution of the environment, is also an important stakeholder. Sustainability includes characteristics such as the ability to deal with economic and social changes, engage in responsible and ethical practices, and to respond to monitoring and evaluation of company practices.[132] Ethical issues are focused in on Chapter 17 Ethics and HRM, and sustainability is discussed with reference to evaluation of HRM in Chapter 18 Evaluating and improving the human resource function. We suggest that sustainability will increasingly be recognised as a driving force, changing the way we work and live. As discussed in 'Managing challenges through sustainability: The human factor' (overleaf), a long-term approach to talent management is required for Australian employers.

Customer service and quality

A major concern for Australian companies seeking to achieve and sustain industry leadership and increase exports relative to their major world competitors is the need to ensure customers' perceptions of the quality of Australian products. But how is quality defined? There is no universal definition of quality. The major differences relate to whether customer, product or manufacturing process is emphasised. For example, quality expert W. Edwards Deming emphasised how well a product or service meets the customer's needs. Another quality expert, Philip Crosby, emphasises how well the service or manufacturing process meets engineering standards.

World competitors such as Japan have emphasised an approach in which quality is designed into a product or service rather than relying on inspection to spot defects or mistakes. This can be considered a 'get it right the first time' approach, a part of the total quality management system. Total quality management (TQM) can be defined as a

Total quality management (TQM)
a cooperative form of doing business that relies on the talents and capabilities of both labour and management to continually improve quality and productivity.

THE HUMAN FACTOR

MANAGING CHALLENGES THROUGH SUSTAINABILITY

The days of managing a workforce with an impersonal attitude to staff are coming to an end.

They litter annual reports like confetti. Those throwaway lines at the end of the chief executive's three or four-page report where he sings the praises of staff—'our most valuable resource'. Typically, so valuable are staff they merit one or two lines; the insult to staff could not be more calculated if the words were preceded by a PS.

What these few words so poignantly symbolise is how management in many companies still only pays lip service to maximising their staff's potential; despite the rhetoric, employees are seen as a cost—not an asset. Anyone who doubts the veracity of this statement need only cast their mind back to how employers bitterly complained—and, in some instances, rorted—the Labor Government's 0.75% training levy; its abolition was one of the Howard Government's first initiatives after winning office in 1996.

But will employers be able to maintain this short-sighted approach into the future? Will inept human-resources management flow to the bottom line as visibly as a bad acquisition? Will a stockmarket that has, until now, largely equated good human-resources management with cost cutting and a 'hard line' towards staff and unions begin to appreciate that highly trained and motivated employees enhance companies' earnings?

There are no clear-cut answers. But one thing that does seem to be changing is that the conventional ratio, whereby about three-quarters of productivity improvements typically come from investment in capital, and only a quarter from investment in people, will be re-aligned. A report by the Boston Consulting Group, titled *2020 Vision—the Manager of the 21st Century*, for Innovation and Business Skills Australia (it is one of 10 Federal Government-sponsored national industry skills councils), argues that employers that fail to invest in their employees will pay the price in the marketplace—in terms of earnings and share price.

The problem is, investment in people is more dangerous than investment in capital. People can walk, plant and equipment cannot. If the emphasis in management is becoming more about getting and retaining skilled knowledge workers, then it will involve very different leadership skills than those normally exhibited by Australian managers. Possessing the ability to understand the motivation and aims of a more mobile, potentially cynical workforce will be paramount. And it will need to be applied to individual workers and the collective workforce, a level of understanding that is largely foreign to the conventional Australian manager.

It is also a foreign way of thinking in the political sphere. When the Howard Government won a Senate majority in 2004, it wasted no time in pushing through the radical WorkChoices legislation, which increased the authority of employers in the workplace. But in many respects it dealt with the issues of yesterday; a heavily regulated system designed for the hierarchical, union-dominated workplaces that were characterised by an us-and-them attitude. The emphasis is on productivity and incremental improvements.

It would be the ultimate irony if employers, having lobbied long and hard for WorkChoices, find the legislation is not the solution to their human-resources needs in the coming years. According to the Boston Consulting Group's report: 'The workplace will increasingly focus on the performance of people as the core company asset ... Greater attention will be given to measuring the performance of people, not just physical and financial assets, and also to developing new techniques for improving performance. Problem-solving and creativity skills will become increasingly important.'

'Executives will need to master a range of new management tools and will be expected to operate efficiently in a highly dynamic environment. They will find themselves assessed on a new range of metrics and will rely much more on output measures to assess their staff. They will require new skills to create more flexible work environments that better accommodate the needs of their employees, including greater numbers of contractors and part-time workers.'

Source: Excerpt from N. Way, 2006, 'The human factor', *BRW*, 4 May, p. 64. © 2006 Copyright John Fairfax Holdings Limited.

'cooperative form of doing business that relies on the talents and capabilities of both labour and management to continually improve quality and productivity using work teams'.[133] Although there are several approaches to TQM (for example, those of internationally recognised TQM experts Deming, Crosby and Joseph Juran), these approaches share some common principles. Table 1.8 illustrates the six basic principles of TQM.

The TQM movement caused a shift in management philosophy: how human-resource issues are handled plays a key role in whether quality is achieved and, ultimately, in the company's success.[134] In companies that have successfully implemented TQM, the corporate climate emphasises collective and cross-functional work, coaching and enabling employees, customer satisfaction and quality, rather than the traditional emphasis on individualism, hierarchy and profit. To ensure the success of TQM, companies need to create an environment that supports innovation, creativity and risk-taking to meet customer demands. Participative problem solving, involving managers, employees and customers, should be used. Finally, communication between managers and employees concerning customer needs, development opportunities and resources, needs to be enhanced.

TABLE 1.8   Principles of total quality management

1	Customer focus
2	Focus on process as well as results
3	Prevention versus inspection
4	Use of employees' expertise
5	Fact-based decision making
6	Feedback

Source: Adapted from Joseph R. Jablonski, 1991, *Implementing Total Quality Management: An Overview*, Pfeiffer and Company, San Diego.

Several rewards have been established to recognise companies for quality, such as the Australian Business Excellence Awards and ISO 9000. ISO 9000 quality standards were developed by the International Organization for Standardization, an organisation in Geneva, Switzerland.[135] These standards were initially developed for companies in the European Community but they have been adopted as national quality standards in nearly 100 countries including Australia, Austria, Switzerland, Norway and Japan. ISO 9000 is the name of a family of standards (ISO 9001, ISO 9002) that includes 20 requirements for dealing with issues such as how to establish quality standards and document work processes. Companies are free to develop their own quality process to meet the standards. ISO 9001 is the most comprehensive standard because it covers product or service design and development, manufacturing, installation and customer service. (ISO 9002 does not include design and development.) ISO 9000 certification is being used as a standard for companies wanting to be competitive both locally and globally. For example, Australian companies hoping to win contracts from European Community customers need to have ISO 9000 certification. United States' automakers, such as Ford, have developed a more rigorous version of ISO 9000 standards (QS-9000) that they are applying to their own operations as well as to those of their suppliers. Suppliers need to meet QS-9000 standards to be major suppliers of parts and services to Ford.

The Australian Business Excellence Awards (formerly Australian Quality Awards) were established in 1987.[136] The Australian Business Excellence Awards evolved from their roots in TQM into a framework for global business excellence. Similar frameworks have been developed in other countries, including the United States (Malcolm Baldridge Award) and Japan (Deming Award); many countries around the world have adopted such frameworks and related awards. To become eligible for an Australian Business Excellence Award, companies must complete a detailed

ISO 9000
a series of quality assurance standards developed by the International Organization for Standardization in Switzerland. ISO 9000 certification is a requirement for doing business in many countries and regions, including Australia, the European community, Iceland, Liechtenstein, Norway, Switzerland, Japan, South America and Africa.

assessment matrix that includes addressing seven categories in which organisations strive to achieve business excellence, namely:

1. leadership
2. strategy and planning
3. knowledge and information
4. people
5. customer and market focus
6. innovation, quality and improvement
7. success and sustainability.[137]

The 'people' category refers to the manner in which an organisation encourages and enables people to make a personally satisfying contribution to achieving organisational goals. This category is comprised of three items, involvement and commitment; effectiveness and development; and health, safety and well-being. Thus, to attain business excellence, while managers must ensure that technological innovations are made and adopted, how the people are managed is more critical.[138] Clearly, to be recognised as leaders in product or service excellence, Australian companies must effectively use their human resources.

Some argue that the popularity of awards, such as the Australian Business Excellence Awards or the Malcolm Baldridge Award in the United States, has caused managers to devote too much time to completing the rigorous evaluation process and too little time to concentrating on promoting quality within the company.[139] Also, along with the recognition of winning the award comes the expectation to devote time speaking to other companies about the organisation's business excellence strategies. However, some companies use the Australian Business Excellence Award application process as a guide for managers to evaluate their own operations rather than as a strict set of rules to follow.

The success of the Australian Business Excellence Awards and Framework has been demonstrated in a study of annual average improvement in key performance indicators measured against companies' scores on the Australian Business Excellence assessment criteria. The research indicates that organisations with higher assessment scores are more likely to be among the best-performing organisations and the assessment score is positively associated with performance of an organisation's business measures.[140]

Apart from winning awards, companies can use an array of measurement tools to gain an indication of their performance. These measurement tools are discussed throughout the book and particularly in Chapter 18. For example, the **balanced scorecard** is an approach that managers can use to obtain an indication of the performance of a company based on the degree to which stakeholder needs are satisfied. The balanced scorecard gives managers the opportunity to look at the company from the perspective of internal and external customers, employees and shareholders.[141] The balanced scorecard can be useful because it brings together most of the features that a company needs to focus on to be competitive. These include being customer-focused, improving quality, emphasising teamwork, reducing new product and service development times, and managing for the long term.

As shown in Table 1.9, the balanced scorecard differs from traditional measures of company performance by emphasising that the critical indicators chosen are based on the company's business strategy and competitive demands. Companies need to customise their balanced scorecard based on different market situations, products and competitive environments.

Communicating the scorecard to employees gives them a framework that helps them see the goals and strategies of the company. It also shows them how these goals

---

Balanced scorecard
a means of performance measurement that gives managers a chance to look at their company from the perspectives of internal and external customers, employees and shareholders.

TABLE 1.9 The balanced scorecard

Perspective	Questions answered	Examples of critical indicators
Customer	How do customers see us?	Time, quality, performance, service and cost
Internal	What must we excel at?	Processes that influence customer satisfaction, availability of information on service and/or manufacturing processes
Innovation and learning	Can we continue to improve and create value?	Improve operating efficiency, launch new products, continuous improvement and empowering of workforce
Financial	How do we look to shareholders?	Profitability, growth and shareholder value

and strategies are measured and how they influence the critical indicators. The balanced scorecard is used by leading larger firms but it can also be useful in small firms. The balanced scorecard may be useful for two reasons: first, to link human resource management activities to the company's business strategy; second, to evaluate the extent to which the human resource function is helping the company meet its strategic objectives. Measures of human resource practices primarily relate to productivity, people and process.[142] Productivity measures involve determining output per employee (such as revenue per employee). Measuring people includes assessing employees' behaviour, attitudes or knowledge. Process measures focus on assessing employees' satisfaction with people-systems within the company. People-systems can include the performance-management system, the compensation and benefits system, and the development system.

The challenge of attracting and retaining people

Australia has recorded unparalleled economic expansion for more than a decade. One of the consequences of this has been an increasing shortage of skilled labour. Similar situations are identifiable in many other countries. This skill shortage places increasing importance on the role of human resource management to attract and retain employees as a source of competitive advantage.[143]

Comprehensive approaches to attracting and retaining employees are based in sound concepts such as 'employer of choice'[144] and employee engagement. As people in the labour market explore new job opportunities, they may be concerned about factors such as an organisation's reputation, organisational leadership, the work environment, support structures and facilities, recognition of employees for their efforts, and availability of a range of opportunities for progression. Employers of choice are those organisations that have implemented approaches to address such concerns; these organisations have been found to have much lower turnover rates and attract many more job applications than other comparable organisations.[145]

Attracting and retaining employees is also reliant on developing and maintaining employee engagement through effective HR practices. Engagement is a state of cognitive, physical and emotional involvement or commitment in their work roles which goes beyond satisfaction. It is measured by examining a set of factors that result in employees who behave in ways that support the business and consistently look for ways to create value.[146] Hence, this is often a key component in organisations seeking to develop high-performance, or high-involvement, work systems.

Employer of choice
an approach to attracting, retaining and motivating employees, based on financial success and factors such as an organisation's reputation, organisational leadership, work environment, support structures and facilities, recognition of employees for their efforts, and availability of a range of opportunities for progression.

Employee engagement
Harnessing of employees to their work roles, including cognitive, physical and emotional engagement.

However, it is also recognised that the expectations of employee engagement may have negative effects, such as work intensification and work-life conflict[147] (for more detail, see Chapter 6 Analysis and design of work and Chapter 9 Managing diversity and work–life balance). One of the challenges faced by employees in high-performance firms is that achieving balance between work and the rest of life is not easy. While there are services available to employees, such as health, personal training and financial advice, the issue remains a fraught one, particularly with an ageing workforce who have family commitments.[148]

Several award programs now operate to provide recognition for organisations who excel at attracting and retaining people. The end-of-chapter case discusses St George Bank, which in 2005 won awards for the best overall use of technology and best HR team categories in the Australian HR Awards, while its executive general manager of human resources, Brett Wright, took out the award for best HR director. Another set of awards that have become well known in the HRM field is the Hewitt Associates Best Employers Awards, as shown in the article at the beginning of this chapter.

Hewitt Associates Best Employers Awards

Hewitt Associates (www.hewitt.com/www.hewittasia.com) is a global human resources outsourcing and consulting firm. Hewitt Associates conduct annual research to conduct 'Best Employers' Awards with various partners in Asia, Canada, Europe, India and Latin America. The Best Employers in Australia and New Zealand research is conducted as a partnership between Hewitt Associates, the Australian Graduate School of Management (AGSM) and John Fairfax Limited (through *AFR BOSS* magazine). The study comprises three survey instruments: an employee engagement survey, collected from a random sample of employees in each organisation; a CEO questionnaire, including the CEO's management philosophies and the alignment of HR practices to the organisation's strategy; and The People Practices Inventory™,[149] a detailed inventory of each organisation's HR practices and policies. The major aim of the Best Employers research is to demonstrate that those organisations that use superior practices for managing people will have the capacity to achieve superior business results.[150]

As discussed in 'Managing challenges through attracting and retaining people: CEOs lament retention woes', achieving excellence in this area is not a simple task; although many employers view attraction and retention of employees as a critical issue, the majority do not have formal employee retention programs.

Meeting competitive challenges through HRM practices

We have discussed the challenges that companies are facing in Australia and worldwide. We have emphasised that management of human resources plays a critical role in determining a company's success in meeting the challenges. HRM practices have not traditionally been seen as providing economic value to the company. Economic value is usually associated with equipment, technology and facilities. However, HRM practices have been shown to be valuable, particularly when managed as a comprehensive and consistent system.[151] Compensation, staffing, training and development, performance management and other HRM practices are investments that directly affect employees' motivation and ability to provide products and services that are valued by customers. Figure 1.5 shows examples of human resource practices that help companies deal with the four challenges.

CEOs LAMENT RETENTION WOES

ALTHOUGH RETENTION is viewed as a critical issue in Australian organisations, two-thirds do not have formal employee retention programs while just 40 per cent employ someone to look after retaining talented staff.

A survey of 282 GMs, CEOs, HR and other line managers found that while more than 80 per cent now rate employee retention of high importance to the business, their companies spend far more on recruitment than they do on retaining the staff they already have.

The TMP Worldwide employee retention survey also found 44 per cent spend more than $100,000 on recruitment costs—mainly advertising and recruitment agency fees—compared with 16 per cent spending in excess of $100,000 on retention. More than a third (36 per cent) spend less than $50,000 annually on employee retention.

In addition, only half the respondents conducted formal follow-ups with new employees in their first three months while less than a third gave feedback to management on the progress of new employees.

Considering the amount of time and resources required to bring a new employee up to speed—about one-and-a-half times the employee's salary—the report found this is clearly inadequate.

'Employee divorce is a lot more expensive than marriage, yet budgets allocated to employee retention would not indicate this', it said.

For HR professionals, the survey's findings point to an urgent need for changes in retention-orientated activities. Companies will remain in transactional recruitment mode and lose the ability to have employees' intellectual property stay with their company if current spending levels on employee retention are maintained.

Formal employee retention programs 'will become an increasingly important part of an HR professional's role,' said Stuart Grenville, TMP managing director, Asia Pacific.

'Those who can demonstrate success in increasing staff retention levels for an employer can confidently lay claim to a contribution to the productivity and hence profitability of that business.'

HR and line management will have to cooperate to make a significant impact on the outcome of any initiatives, he said.

Securing executive support for retention initiatives shouldn't be that difficult, Grenville added.

'There is enough data around to demonstrate the link between effective communications, retention, employee engagement, productivity and profitability', he said.

'It is quite possible that retention will become a key competitive advantage for those who proactively embrace it.'

Source: M. Finch, 2006, 'CEOs lament retention woes', *Human Resources*, 26 July, pp. 1, 15. www.humanresourcesmagazine.com.au

---

HRM practices that help companies deal with the competitive challenges can be grouped into the four dimensions shown in Figure 1.6. These dimensions include the human resource environment, building human resource systems, developing human resources, and rewarding human resources. In addition, many companies face contemporary issues related to managing a global workforce, ethical concerns, employee retention and turnover, and evaluating and improving the human resource function.

Managing the human resource environment

Managing internal and external environmental factors allows employees to make the greatest possible contribution to company productivity and competitiveness. Creating a positive environment for human resources involves:

- linking HRM practices to the company's business objectives—that is, strategic human resource management
- ensuring that HRM practices comply with federal and State or Territory laws
- managing occupational health and safety
- creating an employment relationship and work environment (industrial relations) that benefits both the company and the employee.

PART 1   Managing the Human Resource Environment

FIGURE 1.5 Examples of how HR practices can help companies meet the competitive challenges

```
┌──────────────┐ ┌──────────────┐ ┌──────────────┐ ┌──────────────────┐
│ Challenge of │ │ Challenge of │ │ Challenge of │ │   Challenge of   │
│globalisation │ │HR innovation │ │sustainability│ │attracting and    │
│              │ │              │ │              │ │retaining people  │
└──────┬───────┘ └──────┬───────┘ └──────┬───────┘ └────────┬─────────┘
       ↓                ↓                ↓                  ↓
```

HR Practices

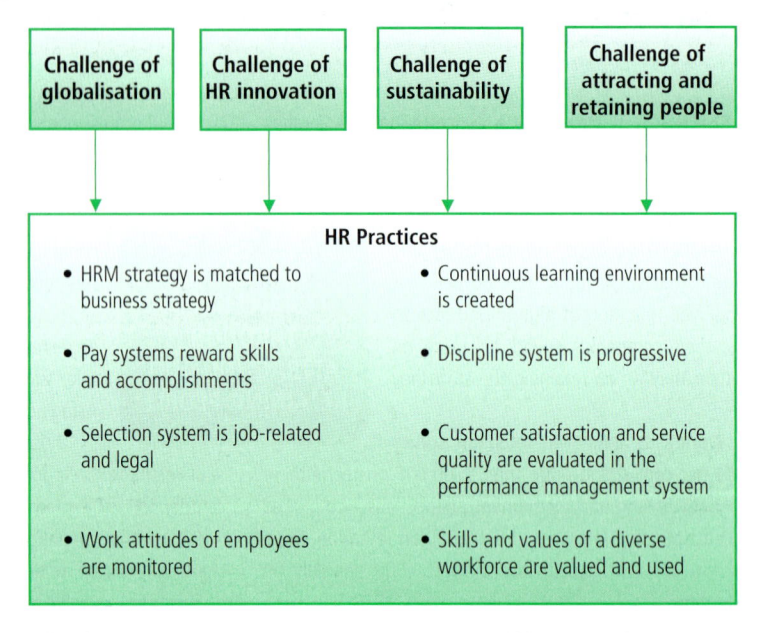

- HRM strategy is matched to business strategy
- Pay systems reward skills and accomplishments
- Selection system is job-related and legal
- Work attitudes of employees are monitored
- Continuous learning environment is created
- Discipline system is progressive
- Customer satisfaction and service quality are evaluated in the performance management system
- Skills and values of a diverse workforce are valued and used

FIGURE 1.6 Major dimensions of HRM practices contributing to company competitiveness

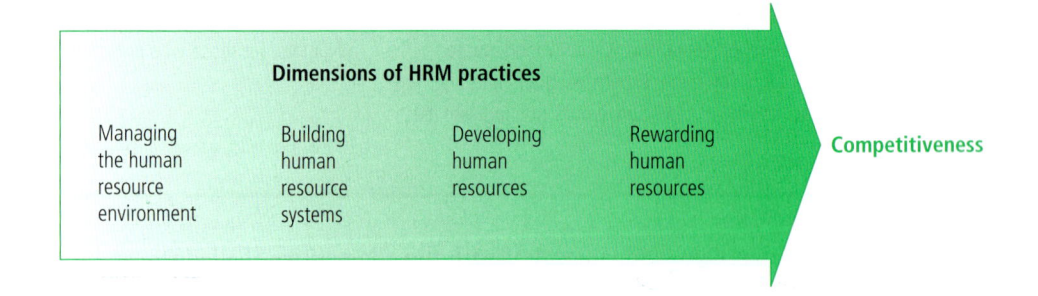

Dimensions of HRM practices

Managing the human resource environment → Building human resource systems → Developing human resources → Rewarding human resources → **Competitiveness**

Building human resource systems

Customer needs for new products or services influence the number and type of employees that businesses need to be successful. Terminations, promotions and retirements also influence human resource requirements. Managers need to develop systems to predict the number and type of employees who are needed to meet customer demands for products and services. Managers must also identify current or potential employees who can successfully deliver products and services. This area of human resource management deals with:

- designing work that is motivational and satisfactory to the employee as well as maximises customer service, quality and productivity
- identifying human resource requirements—that is, human resource planning
- developing effective information systems for human resource management
- recruiting and selecting employees for jobs.

Developing human resources

Managers need to ensure that employees have the necessary skills to perform current and future jobs. As we discussed earlier, because of new technology and the organisational innovations, many companies have redesigned work. As a result, managers and employees may need to develop new skills to be successful in the new environment. Companies need to create a work environment that supports employees' work and non-work activities. This area of human resource management deals with:

- managing diversity and work–life balance
- evaluating and developing employees' performance
- preparing employees and managers for current and future work roles and identifying their work interests, goals, values and other career issues.

Rewarding human resources

Besides having interesting work, pay and benefits are the most important incentives that companies can offer employees in exchange for contributing to productivity, quality and customer service. Also, pay and benefits are used to reward employees' membership in the company and attract new employees. The positive influence of new work designs and new technology on productivity can be damaged if employees are not satisfied with the level of pay and benefits or if they believe pay and benefits are unfairly distributed. This area of human resource management deals with:

- creating pay systems
- rewarding employee contributions

Contemporary issues for human resource management

Many companies are globally expanding their business through joint ventures, mergers and acquisitions, and by establishing new operations. Successful global expansion depends on the extent to which HRM practices are aligned with cultural factors as well as managing employees sent to work in another country.

Human resource management practices of both managers and the human resource function must be aligned and contribute to the company's strategic goals, and facilitate the management of employee retention and turnover. Human resource management practices must contribute to organisational effectiveness.

Contemporary issues for human resource management include:

- managing a global workforce
- managing ethical issues
- managing employee turnover and retention
- evaluating and improving the human resource function.

Organisation of this book

The topics in this book are organised according to the four areas of human resource management and directions for HRM. Table 1.10 lists the chapters covered in the book.

The content of each chapter is based on academic research and examples of effective company practices. Each chapter includes examples of how the human resource management practice covered in the chapter helps a company gain a competitive advantage by addressing global, stakeholder, knowledge economy or employer of choice challenges. Each chapter also discusses future directions for the human resource management practice covered in the chapter.

TABLE 1.10 Topics covered in this book

Chapter number	Chapter title
Part 1:	**Managing the human resource environment**
1	Human resource management in Australia
2	Strategic human resource management
3	The legal context for human resource management
4	Occupational health and safety
5	Industrial relations
Part 2:	**Building human resource management systems**
6	Analysis and design of work
7	Human resource planning and human resource information systems
8	Recruitment and selection
Part 3:	**Developing people**
9	Managing diversity and work–life balance
10	Performance management
11	Learning and development
12	Employment development and career management
Part 4:	**Rewarding people**
13	Managing compensation
14	Performance-related pay
Part 5:	**Contemporary issues for human resource management**
15	Ethics and human resource management
16	International human resource management
17	Managing employee turnover and retention
18	Evaluating and improving the human resource function

MANAGING PEOPLE

HUMAN CAPITAL: THE STATE OF PLAY IN AUSTRALIA

Australian organisations are unique in the way they manage human capital—with both positive and negative outcomes. Craig Donaldson speaks with IBM's Asia–Pacific Leader for Human Capital Management, Bill Farrell, about whether Australian HR processes require a re-think or a move to next generation HR methods.

IBM Business Consulting Services recently conducted its annual Global Human Capital Study, encompassing 320 organisations and 106 chief HR officers worldwide—29 of which were based in the Asia Pacific. It found global organisations in more mature markets risked becoming unresponsive to the needs of their workforce. However, local organisations were generally ahead of the trend in their implementation of human capital management (HCM) processes and practices.

'Yes, we are efficient and ahead of the curve in terms of how we manage the HR transactions, but some of the results show that while we've focused on efficiency, we need to focus next on the effectiveness of the HR function', says Farrell. One particular area where organisations fell down, when compared to the US, was in the area of workforce management. Being able to predict the demand for labour and how to supply it, in terms of both numbers and competency sets of employees, is a newer area for HR functions across the region.

'It's about getting the HR function focused on those issues', Farrell explains. 'If you look at US organisations, over the past two or three years they've really started to focused on the next state of the HR delivery, which is about business transformation outsourcing. Once they've rid themselves of the administrative workload of HR, they move up to the value add around workforce management.'

Farrell said Australian organisations are probably a couple of years away before they really feel comfortable about addressing issues around workforce and talent management. This will be a particular challenge, he predicts. 'There has to be a much more cohesive effort across the business on talent management. It's not HR's job to facilitate and lead it, but it's also the CEO's responsibility to ensure that talent, talent acquisition and retention are key to an organisation's success.'

The turnover downfall

Despite being a leader in efficient HR methods, Australian organisations have real trouble in retaining their best and brightest employees and executives. Current market forces have led to the Asia Pacific region having the highest voluntary turnover at senior and middle management in the world, and Australia closely follows that trend, costing organisations in both dollars and IP.

While Australia rated well in terms of recruitment and management development, Farrell said talent retention was an issue in Australia due to the colliding worlds of skills shortages, double digit growth in the executive search industry, huge gaps in talent availability and sometimes fierce overseas competition for Australian talent.

'I think HR is aware of the whole retention problem, but I'm not sure if organisations are really developing the practices needed to be able to tackle it in the right way. Those organisations which are really very profitable have certain practices which allow them to retain their people', Farrell says. 'This gets into that whole philosophy of the build versus buy issue. Specific organisations do either one or the other, but the study found the challenge is getting the balance right.

HR leadership in mature markets

The IBM study raises a number of key questions. Are current global best practices in HCM simply not sufficient in Australia? Do Australia's unique market forces require a re-think of HR processes or a move up the value chain to next generation HR methods? Are the answers to be found in other mature market economies or the new world?

There is significant room for improvement around the whole concept of workforce management—managing the human capital of an organisation as opposed to managing the human capital function, according to Farrell. Many Australian organisations struggle to effectively quantify the return on their human capital programs.

Repercussions for companies

If HR professionals are unable to focus on delivering business outcomes, there may be a number of consequences for their companies. Particularly amid greater market globalisation. The issue of talent management is one in which Australian companies could suffer significantly not only internally but externally.

'The market will look to those companies and whether they have the talent in the market to grow and be competitive', Farrell says. 'There's examples of that coming up all the time.' He points to instances where the share price of financial services organisations has stalled due to a lack of clarity around chief talent within the organisations.

'We're going to see much more focus on hard measures around succession planning, performance of individuals and the whole issue of performance based pay', Farrell says.

This will require a new way of looking at HR, and the human capital component more specifically, according to Farrell: 'Let's not focus on the HR process for process' sake, but let's focus on how we can improve productivity across our workforce.'

Farrell notes that some of the observations from the study for organisations across Australia and New Zealand are a kind of paradox. On the one hand, Australian companies are in a mature market, but on the other, they're presented with high growth opportunities. Companies have got to manage the balance between the HR function per se and really enabling the business to be more competitive, not only across Australia but across the Asia Pacific. 'The competition for people is becoming global. If we don't get it right now it's going to become more and more difficult in terms of talent management over the next few years.'

Key findings for Asia–Pacific organisations

Asia–Pacific organisations (excluding Japan) have the highest:
- Voluntary turnover at the senior and middle management levels
- Use of reporting number of candidates per position for new hires
- Percentage of companies offering management development programs
- Percentage of companies with a learning strategy
- Flexibility in proactively staffing prior to market demand
- Use of measures of employee satisfaction, attraction/retention of key staff and growth of key staff in leadership compensation.

They are more likely to:
- Evaluate the quality of new joiners as part of the performance measures of recruitment
- Evaluate employee performance on the responsibilities of the role
- Have individual pay arrangements
- Have learning strategy aligned with business objectives.

They are less likely to:
- Have a management leadership development program.

Source: *The IBM Global Human Capital Study* 2005.

Source: Excerpt from C. Donaldson, 2005, 'Human capital: The state of play in Australia', *Human Resources*, 9 August, pp. 14–15. www.humanresourcesmagazine.com.au

QUESTION

1 Does the Australian context require a unique approach to HRM or human capital management?

CHAPTER SUMMARY

In this chapter, we have introduced the field of human resource management and explained its theoretical and conceptual foundations. We have outlined the major human resource management practices, which cover four areas: managing the human resource environment, building human resource systems, developing human resources, and rewarding human resources. We discuss characteristics of the workforce and organisational environment which are important factors for managers to understand. We also present four competitive challenges that companies face: globalisation, HR innovation, sustainability, and attracting and retaining people. We have discussed their implications for human resource management, and will explore these in the following chapters.

WEB EXERCISES

A Visit **www.ahri.com.au**, the *Australian Human Resources Institute* home page.
AHRI is a professional association for human resource management in Australia. AHRI publishes the *Asia Pacific Journal of Human Resources* and *HRMonthly* magazine.

B Visit **www.shrm.org**, the US Society for Human Resource Management (SHRM) home page. SHRM is an important professional society for human resource management, based in the United States. Here you will find current articles related to HR issues. SHRM also publishes *HR Magazine*, a business magazine for human resources. Articles regarding a variety of HR topics are available online at **www.workforceonline.com**.

C Visit the website for the Australian Bureau of Statistics, **www.abs.gov.au**
Here you will find statistical information related to topics including the Australian labour force, economy, employment and population.

D Visit **www.oecd.org**, the website of the Organisation for Economic Co-operation and Development (OECD). The OECD includes 30 countries that share a commitment to democratic government and the market economy, and has active relationships with around 70 other countries, and many non-government organisations. The website includes a range of publications and statistical reports covering economic and social issues.

Questions

1. In this chapter we discuss four competitive challenges that companies face (competing through globalisation, HR innovation, sustainability, and competing by attracting and retaining people.). How are companies dealing with the four competitive challenges? Use web resources such as the websites listed above to find statistics or articles that relate to how a company is dealing with the competitive challenges.
2. Summarise the main topic of the statistical report or article.
3. Identify how it relates to one of the competitive challenges discussed in the chapter.

DISCUSSION QUESTIONS

1. Is HRM becoming more strategic? Explain your answer, with reference to the conceptual and theoretical foundations of HRM.
2. Traditionally, human resource management practices were developed and administered by the company's human resource department. Line managers are now playing a major role in developing and implementing HR practices. Why do you think non-HR managers are becoming more involved in developing and implementing HR practices?
3. Explain the implications of each of the following labour-force trends for HRM:
   (a) an ageing workforce
   (b) a diverse workforce
   (c) skill deficiencies.
4. Staffing, employee development, compensation and performance management are important HRM functions. How can each of these functions help companies deal with global challenges? HR innovation? Sustainability? Attracting and retaining people?
5. This book covers four human resource management practice areas: managing the human resource environment, building human resource systems, developing human resources, and rewarding human resources. Which area do you believe contributes most to helping a company gain a competitive advantage? Which area do you believe contributes the least? Why?
6. What role do HRM practices play in a business decision to expand internationally?
7. What differences do you see between HRM, talent management and human capital management?
8. What disadvantages might result from outsourcing HRM practices? From employee self-service? From increased manager involvement in designing and using HR practices?

VALUE ADDED HR

The new head of human resources at BHP Billiton, Marcus Randolph, does not have a background in salary packaging, occupational health and safety or leadership training. He does not have a degree in human resources management either; rather, he has a science degree and a Master of Business Administration. Randolph's previous role in the company was the president of diamonds and specialty products. In his role as 'chief human capital and excellence officer', Randolph is one of eight members of the inner sanctum of BHP Billiton, known as the office of the chief executive.

Randolph is one of the new breed of human resources director who brings a different set of skills to the executive suite—more generalist line management experience and less (if any) specialist human resources expertise. According to the consultancy Hays Human Resources, average salaries for human resources directors of Australia's top 100 companies are more than $450,000. For that fee they are expected to take an active rather than reactive role and ensure that the company's human resources strategy is linked to overall business strategy. Chief executives are looking for efficiency gains and bottom-line value from these new, commercially focused HR directors.

For a human resources executive to be noticed, they need to demonstrate 'hard-core business outcomes', says Rodney Hanratty, the head of global banking, human resources, for HSBC in Hong Kong. 'Acquisitions can fail if the people aspect is not well thought through. A good human-resources person is essential in that and they can demonstrate added value quickly.'

With people being the key differentiating factor in the knowledge economy, the role of HR has been elevated in progressive companies. Companies including BHP Billiton, St George Bank, Australand, Lion Nathan, Brambles Industries, Foster's Group, Orica, Westpac Banking Corporation and Iluka Resources have invited their most senior human-resources executive into senior management ranks.

'It is about the importance of people in the success of the business and the current and predicted skills shortages', says Robin Kramar, a professor in management at the Macquarie Graduate School of Management. 'What you are seeing in these senior appointments is a different type of HR director.' The new breed of HR director has a strong business knowledge and competencies. They are expected to quickly develop knowledge of the people inside the company and the labour market outside the company, but they are entering the role from a business perspective. 'It's a much more strategic role', says Kramar.

In October 2006, Telstra's chief executive, Sol Trujillo, appointed the former head of human resources at GM Holden, Andrea Grant, as Telstra's new HR director. Grant reports directly to Trujillo and is charged with managing the anticipated staff cuts and dramatic cultural and organisational change in Trujillo's makeover of the telco. Grant's curriculum vitae includes experience in overseeing job cuts at GM Holden.

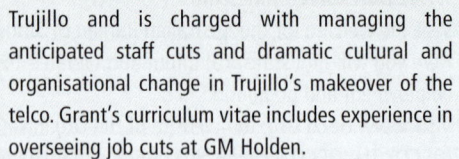

Reshuffles like this go against the prevailing attitude that the HR function is not sufficiently respected by senior management. A recent global survey of 350 human resources directors by the executive recruitment company Egon Zehnder found that tensions remain between the conventional HR department and the rest of the company. Human resources staff felt that they simply took orders, rather than playing an active role in company strategy, with HR still seen as a support function, rather than a strategic or leadership function. The study found that 'unless HR directors step up to the plate and engage with their board colleagues at a different level, HR will remain a subservient function'.

Having to respond and react to so many workplace issues makes it difficult for many HR departments to take on a more strategic role. This dilemma sends some companies to consultants for HR services. Hays Human Resources is working with 20 Australian companies to improve their HR functions. They come to Hays, says director Jacky Carter, 'because they can't be master of all trades'. Carter has seen companies suffer when a company's HR director believes that the answer to everything is one remedy; for example, learning and development. 'Some people who have specialised in certain areas are not comfortable looking at other areas. They will focus on areas they are passionate about, rather than on what is good for the business', she says. That is where a commercially focused eye can stop those bad habits.

The big issues
- Engagement
- Finding ways to make staff more involved and interested in their work
- Link to business strategy
- Making sure that all staff understand how their work affects the company's strategy
- Attraction and retention
- Continuing skills shortages create an environment where finding the right people and keeping them happy is critical
- Measuring the contribution

- Ensuring that human resources practice has real, tangible benefits for the business
- Avoiding marginalisation
- Balancing specialist human-resources skills with more generalist business skills

Source: Excerpt from E. Ross, 2005, 'Value added', *BRW*, 27 October, p. 60. © 2005 Copyright John Fairfax Holdings Limited. www.brw.com.au

Questions:

1 What do you believe are the main challenges facing business and HR in the next five years?
2 What do you see as the most important competencies for senior HR executives to have?
3 In your view, who should have primary responsibility for people management?

PART 1   Managing the Human Resource Environment

CASE STUDY

HUMAN RESOURCE MANAGEMENT IN AUSTRALIA

The importance of a good, strategic HR function has dawned on some of Australia's major banks quicker than others. Given the nature of the business and the players involved, effective change at this level can take a good number of years to effect. But with a supportive CEO and solid understanding of the business, HR can make a major business contribution—one that will give it a potentially significant advantage over competitors.

St George Bank has received a good amount of recognition for such strategies. Last year, for example, it took out the best overall use of technology and best HR team categories in the Australian HR Awards, while its executive general manager of human resources, Brett Wright, took out the award for best HR director.

There were a number of factors that helped St George take out these awards, according to Wright. He believes that having a strong HR team with a strong business focus is one of the most important factors.

All members of the HR team operate with a view to increasing performance and profit in the business, Wright says. 'That's what they're thinking about when they're looking at HR interventions.'

Not having business-focused folk in the HR team can spark a vicious circle which many HR departments get into. Without the right people, Wright knew HR would not have the credibility needed to be invited into the business. 'One of the challenges has been the image and mindset of HR people in general. HR is historically a very traditional function.'

It's a challenge to find professionals with strong HR and business expertise in the current market, and Wright is very particular about who is recruited into the bank's HR team. Additionally, he regularly positions non-traditionalist HR people in senior HR positions, which he says enables a fresh and business oriented perspective on people management.

But he also cautions against a 'one size fits all' approach. 'We've got a mixture of people in HR. There's some traditional people with very good HR expertise, and we've got some non-traditional people who've come from business roles. Others come from very different professions as well. So it's about having the right mix in the team, but the underlying factor is we want HR and business expertise. Without that you just can't build that relationship with a business and you can't talk the language of the business', he says.

A strong relationship with the business

This relationship with the business is also a fundamental part of HR's success within the bank. 'Through a lot of hard work and proving our worth to the business, we've managed to get ourselves to the point where we're very integrated and aligned with it', Wright says. 'It's very seamless. It doesn't really come up as to whether we're HR or business people. We're close to the business and have very strong relationships with the business.'

Being close to the business has also meant HR has been able to anticipate its needs and take a proactive rather than reactive role, according to Wright. Some HR team members also possess specialised skills which enable them to develop quick, innovative solutions with solid outcomes. 'So we're not there to fluff around and say we'll do something, then think about implementing it 12 months later. It's about speed of response and relevant solutions. The business doesn't ask you all the time. Being proactive has been very important in building credibility. This leads to more involvement and respect, which gets you more involved in the business. So it's a continuous cycle.'

Making the business case for soft HR

HR in general has traditionally had a hard time justifying many of its initiatives. Granted, the nature of the function has very often made deliverables hard to define, but Wright says it's not impossible. 'With some of the soft initiatives, I think it's about constructing compelling arguments. You've got to be smart enough and savvy enough to pitch those arguments in a business sense, such as "the business can't afford not to do this"', he says.

At the same time, he cautions against over-promising. 'If you try and contrive an ROI outcome, you're going to get shot down. The business won't believe it, and then your credibility goes', he says. Even when there is some link to ROI on a soft HR initiative, Wright says a prudent approach is best.

He gives the example of an incentive program to increase the productivity of lenders. 'There's a whole range of other things going on. The lenders are being developed, they're being skilled in the product and they're being managed differently. So, is it the incentive program that got the outcome, is it the leadership development or the skill development, or is it a combination of all three? Some of those things you know are going to impact, and like I said, it's about how you construct the argument.'

Justifying the soft side is hard anywhere, according to Wright. All the major banks, for example, are looking at customer service as a means of deepening relationships with customers and building their business at present. 'Each bank's got their own strategy on that. It's all about people, and in some senses that could be regarded as soft, but there's a view out there that it's tangible.'

Balancing business and employee advocacy

Wright says HR should never forget that its core responsibility is to optimise the performance of people. 'You can't do that if you're not looking at the people side and creating the right environment for engagement of those people. One doesn't go without the other; that's the reality of the situation.' He says HR can't expect anyone to do their best work every day if they're working in an environment in which they feel they're not looked after. He says this is a fine balancing act: 'It's about being fair, but not benevolent I suppose. Be business oriented without dismissing the human element.'

HR has a prime role in employee advocacy through engagement, and Wright says it won't be effective if it makes HR decisions in isolation of an understanding of business drivers—or vice versa.

The HR misconceptions of management

HR is often at loggerheads with management for a variety of reasons. HR can be its own worst enemy in some instances, according to Wright, whereby the function is unwilling to even attempt to bridge the gap. 'There's a lot of excuses around the business being too hard to reach, management doesn't understand how important we are and revenues and profits are for others', Wright says.

'You know, we're here to look after the people, and you just can't separate those things. In some respects HR is in a unique position to work with the business to use HR's ability to leverage the people to increase the profit.'

On the other hand, management often perceives HR as a cost and not part of the business machinery. He laments the management mindset which fails to see the potential value HR can add to a business—especially where HR is outsourced completely.

St George Bank's award-winning HR strategies

Brett Wright, group executive of human resources for St George Bank, on taking out three categories at the Australian HR Awards 2005.

Keys to success:
- Position non-traditionalist HR people in senior HR positions to enable a fresh and business oriented perspective on people management
- Successfully build a strong relationship and presence within the business
- Recognise who our customer is—group and individual divisions (businesses)
- Have a proactive, anticipative and innovative approach to solutions for the business
- Be commercially responsive to business needs (speed, quality and on budget).

The challenges along the way:
- Building confidence within the HR team to a level where they believe they can achieve what's required
- Changing the traditional view of HR for themselves and for the customer
- Reading and forecasting the business environment and determining needs
- Actively consolidating HR providers and HR spend across the group
- Marshalling resources, being focused on outcome and being responsive.

Lessons learned in the process:
- Get a very strong management team, with a diverse background and some with business experience
- Employ outstanding people who think like and apply HR practices like a business
- Changing the image and mindset of HR people is not easy
- HR can get a place at the executive table only by performance and not by talk

- Think HR practice and learning in their full sense—long-term implications for culture and organisation rather than short-term policy, process or ad hoc training
- Get in control early.

How HR managers can become CEO:
- Be known for the delivery of commercial outcomes, both group and business
- Bring all HR decisions, including how HR functions, back to business fundamentals. Think and behave like a business
- Focus on outcomes not policy and procedure
- Get the best HR people and demonstrate the power and worth of having the right people in right jobs
- Break outside traditional transactional HR functions and push the boundaries; that is, move from order-taker of training to learning to performance; move from remuneration provider to incentive and packaging modelling to enhance business performance; move from reactionary IR to arguing legislation for flexibility and unleashing people potential.

Source: Excerpt from C. Donaldson, 2006, 'St George: Banking on the business of HR', *Human Resources*, 26 July, pp. 16–17. www.humanresourcesmagazine.com.au.

QUESTIONS

1 Identify and evaluate the HRM characteristics at St George Bank.
2 What do you see as the major HRM issues or challenges at St George Bank?

CHAPTER 2

STRATEGIC HUMAN RESOURCE MANAGEMENT

Objectives

After reading this chapter, you should be able to:

1. Describe the differences between strategy formulation and strategy implementation.
2. List the components of the strategic management process.
3. Discuss the role of the HR function in strategy formulation.
4. Describe the linkages between HR and strategy formulation.
5. Discuss the more popular typologies of generic strategies and the various HR practices associated with each.
6. Describe the different HR issues and practices associated with various directional strategies.
7. List the competencies the HR executive needs in order to become a strategic partner in the company.

Breaking in a new culture: Virgin Blue's story

Virgin Blue was launched with less than 300 employees and today its headcount stands at 2800—and it is still growing. Maintaining a consistent culture through such rapid growth has presented its fair share of challenges for Virgin Blue, but successfully doing so has come with its fair share of rewards as well.

'The culture of the Virgin group is a worldwide phenomenon', says Bruce Highfield, HR director for Virgin Blue. 'The brand itself has a very strong culture and people recognise it for quality, value for money, challenging the establishment and a fun environment, I think.'

Before Virgin Blue's first aircraft ever took off, Highfield says that there was a 94 per cent recognition of the brand.

Establishing the culture

In setting up the airline, Virgin took a number of steps to assist in seeding its unique culture throughout Virgin Blue.

'Many of our senior management team had worked for the Virgin group before and they brought the culture here', says Highfield. 'Having a top team that really works effectively together is really half the battle. Culture starts at the top, and the leadership style of the boss filters down', he says.

Brett Godfrey, Virgin Blue's CEO, feels that the Virgin Blue culture works well in Australia, and acknowledges the work in creating that distinct Virgin culture.

'We're a very different airline to Virgin Express and even Virgin Atlantic. You take some fundamental principles like being family, and you build your local niche around that', he explains.

Richard (Branson) once said that Virgin Blue was more Virgin than Virgin. In Godfrey's opinion, the culture here surpasses those of other Virgin airlines.

'There was an airline in New Zealand for sale and we didn't want to go near it. I felt we had to start our own—our airline wouldn't have been ours if we bought someone else's baggage', he says.

'Unless you get it right, you can't restructure culture. You can restructure your business, but if you've burnt people or if you've killed their enthusiasm or commitment then changing their office spaces or even putting a few more dollars in their pocket will not unduly affect the culture that exists', says Godfrey.

'It's a bit like the *Titanic*—once you've built it and it takes water, it's too late to change direction. That's why it was really important that we got it right from the outset.'

Recruiting for cultural fit

While Virgin Blue has had the benefit of having a cohesive management team to establish its culture, Godfrey says that the airline goes to great lengths to ensure that the culture is supported at all levels.

'Culture is about how you go about doing business with your staff, as opposed to how you do business with your customers, so you've just got to get the recruitment right. We probably spend more money on recruitment than any other company I've been associated with', he states.

Highfield says that the airline looks for people who are optimistic, enthusiastic and humble. While he acknowledges the achievements of Virgin Blue, Highfield says that the airline can't afford to rest on its laurels. 'Most of us are concerned about what's still to be achieved, so I think a good dose of humility is important.'

Despite the global downturn in the aviation industry and the challenges associated with terrorism and the SARS virus, Godfrey says that the high levels of employee engagement have enabled the airline to keep staff motivated and committed.

'Our cost base is superior to our competition, and no doubt they'll all make inroads over the next decade—and sooner rather than later they would probably hope. But the one thing they can never replicate is our corporate culture, and Virgin Blue culture is unique', he says.

PART 1   Managing the Human Resource Environment

Breaking in a new culture: Virgin Blue's story *continued*

'For example, our people still believe—even after two and a half years—that they're on a crusade. This emanates out of the HR department in terms of how we keep people feeling in volunteer mode.'

Godfrey also says that Branson takes a personal approach in dealing with staff: '... he doesn't let a chance go by to say hello to a staff member and shake their hand. It's all about how you treat your people'.

Business model
While people management within Virgin Blue might seem utopian to many organisations, Godfrey says that HR has had to work hard at achieving the successes it has met with. Foremost among these goals is a solid understanding of the business.

'A good HR professional is not just thinking about hiring and firing: they're thinking strategically about how they add value to the business. You can't add that value to the business unless you understand it', Godfrey states.

HR's reporting structures
In recognition of the importance HR plays in Virgin Blue, Highfield reports directly to Godfrey and he is part of Virgin Blue's strategic management team.

'I've never been associated with a company that had HR reporting through the CFO', Highfield states. 'I think that would be a sad day when that occurred. I think it's imperative that the people function reports into the CEO or be part of the executive team—that's pretty well accepted these days.'

Highfield acknowledges that airlines are very much a people business, and he has gained wider business skills in helping set up Virgin Blue. 'In the early days I was involved in marketing and advertising type positions. I used to sit down with the CEO, deputy CEO and management team to consider the environment we were facing, the type of company we wanted to be, how we would employ people and how we'd run the business', he says.

'HR has been involved in designing the people side of the business to match the business model. I've been blessed because HR is intimately involved with the business.'

Source: Based on C. Donaldson, 2003, 'Breaking in a new culture: Virgin Blue's story', *Human Resources*, 24 September, pp. 10–12. www.humanresourcesmagazine.com.au

Introduction

As the preceding Virgin Blue example illustrates, business organisations exist in an environment of competition; and for service organisations like Virgin Blue, organisational culture and people make the difference to customers and the business. Organisations have a number of resources at their disposal that they can use in order to compete with other companies. These resources are physical (for example, plant, equipment, technology, and geographical location); organisational (for example, the structure; planning, controlling and coordinating systems; and group relations); and human (for example, the experience, skill and intelligence of the employees). These resources, under the control of the company, provide the company with competitive advantage.[1]

The goal of strategic management in an organisation is to deploy and allocate resources in a way that provides the organisation with a competitive advantage. As you can see, two of the three classes of resources (organisational and human) are directly tied to the human resource function. As Chapter 1 (Human resource management in Australia) pointed out, the role of human resource management is to ensure that a company's human resources provide it with a competitive advantage. Chapter 1 also pointed out some of the major competitive challenges that companies face today. These challenges require companies to take a proactive, strategic approach in the marketplace.

To be maximally effective, the HRM function must be integrally involved in the company's strategic management process.[2] This means that human resource managers should:

- have input into the strategic plan, both in terms of people-related issues and in terms of the ability of the human-resource pool to implement particular strategic alternatives
- have specific knowledge of the organisation's strategic goals
- know what types of employee skills, behaviours and attitudes are needed to support the strategic plan
- develop programs to ensure that employees have those skills, behaviours and attitudes.

We begin this chapter by discussing the concept of strategy and by depicting the strategic management process. Then we discuss the levels of integration between the HRM function and the strategic management process in strategy formulation. Next we review some of the more common strategic models and, within the context of these models, discuss the various types of employee skills, behaviours and attitudes, and the ways in which human resource practices aid in implementing the strategic plan. Finally, we discuss the new competencies needed by HR executives to fulfil the strategic role of HR.

What is strategic management?

Many authors have noted that, in today's competitive market, organisations must engage in strategic planning to survive and prosper. Strategy comes from the Greek word *strategos*, which has its roots in military language. It refers to a general's grand design behind a war or battle. In fact, the *Shorter Oxford English Dictionary* defines *strategy* as 'the art of a commander-in-chief' and as 'the art of projecting and directing the larger military movements and operations of a campaign'.

Strategic management is a process, an approach that addresses the competitive challenges an organisation faces. It can be thought of as managing the 'pattern or plan that integrates an organisation's major goals, policies and action sequences into a cohesive whole'.[3] These strategies can be either the generic approach to competing or the specific adjustments and actions taken to deal with a particular situation.

First, business organisations engage in generic strategies that often fit into some strategic type. One example is 'cost, differentiation, or focus'.[4] Another is 'defender, analyser, prospector, or reactor'.[5] Different organisations within the same industry often have different generic strategies. These generic strategy types describe the consistent way in which the company attempts to position itself in relation to its competitors.

However, a generic strategy is only a small part of the strategic management process. Thus, the second aspect of strategic management is the process of developing strategies in order to achieve a company's goals—in light of its current environment. Thus, business organisations engage in generic strategies, but they also make choices about such things as how to 'scare off' competitors, how to keep competitors weaker, how to react to and influence pending legislation, how to deal with various

PART 1   Managing the Human Resource Environment

stakeholders and special-interest groups, how to lower production costs, how to raise revenues, what technology to implement, and how many and what types of people to employ. Each of these decisions may present competitive challenges that have to be considered.

Thus, strategic management is more than a collection of strategic types. It is a process for analysing a company's competitive situation, developing a company's strategic goals and devising an action plan and allocating resources (physical, organisational and human) that will increase the likelihood of achieving those goals. This kind of strategic approach should be emphasised in human resource management. Thus, HR managers should be trained to identify the competitive issues a company faces, with regard to human resources, and think strategically about how to respond to these issues.

Strategic human resource management (SHRM) can be thought of as 'the pattern of planned human resource deployments and activities intended to enable an organisation to achieve its goals'.[6] For example, many firms have developed integrated manufacturing systems such as advanced manufacturing technology, just-in-time (JIT) inventory control and total quality management (TQM) in an effort to increase their competitive position. However, these systems must be run by people. Strategic human resource management in these cases entails assessing the employee skills required to run these systems and engaging in HR practices, such as selection and training, that develop these skills in employees.[7] To take a strategic approach to HRM, we must first have an understanding of the role of HRM in the strategic management process.

There are two broad schools of thought that explain SHRM. One school, the external market oriented approach, argues that HR practice choices need to be made so they fit the external market, societal and organisational contexts. According to this view, choices about the particular human resource policies are those which best achieve organisational strategy, goals and outcomes by taking into account the influences of the external factors such as the economy, politics, legislation and the labour market, as well as internal factors such as strategy, workforce characteristics and structure. The second school of thought, which has been developing since the 1990s, is based on the resource-based view (RBV) of the firm. This school argues that organisations need to obtain and utilise their resources, including their people, so they become the best organisation in their sector. The success of an organisation, therefore, depends on building resources—such as people, culture and knowledge—that are difficult to copy and obtain.[8] According to this view, financial, material and technological resources can be copied, but it is the culture, relationships and people that are unable to be copied. If organisations get these right, they provide organisations with a competitive advantage.

Strategic human resource management (SHRM)
the pattern of planned HR deployments and activities intended to enable an organisation to achieve its goals.

Components of the strategic management process

The strategic management process has two distinct yet interdependent phases: strategy formulation and strategy implementation. During **strategy formulation**, the strategic planning group decides on a strategic direction by defining the company's mission and goals, its external opportunities and threats, and its internal strengths and weaknesses. The group then generates various strategic alternatives and compares the ability of those alternatives to achieve the company's mission and goals. During **strategy implementation**, the organisation enacts the strategy that has been chosen. This consists of structuring the organisation, allocating resources, ensuring that the firm has skilled employees in place, and developing reward systems that align employee behaviour with the organisation's strategic goals. Both of these strategic

Strategy formulation
the process of deciding on a strategic direction by defining a company's mission and goals, its external opportunities and threats, and its internal strengths.

Strategy implementation
the process of devising structures and allocating resources to enact the strategy a company has chosen.

56

Strategic Human Resource Management   CHAPTER 2

management phases (strategy formulation and strategy implementation) must be performed effectively. It is important to note that the strategic management process does not happen sequentially. As we will discuss later with regard to emergent strategies, the strategic management process entails a constant cycling of information and decision making. Figure 2.1 opposite presents the two phases of the strategic management process. It indicates how HR practices can be used to achieve HR capability outcomes (such as skills, abilities and knowledge) and also HR actions (such as behaviours and results). These outcomes, in turn, contribute to organisational performance.

Organisations have recognised that the success of the strategic management process depends largely on the extent to which the HR function is involved.[9]

Linkage between HR and the strategic management process

The strategic choice (the organisation's strategy) really consists of answering questions about competition—that is, how the firm will compete to achieve its mission and goals. These decisions consist of addressing the issues of 'where to compete', 'how to compete' and 'with what will we compete', which are described in Table 2.1 (over page). While these decisions are all important, strategic decision makers often give less attention to the 'with what will we compete' issue, resulting in poor strategic decisions. For example, Pepsico in the 1980s acquired the fast-food chains of Kentucky Fried Chicken, Taco Bell and Pizza Hut (that is, 'where to compete'

Strategic choice
the organisation's strategy; the ways in which an organisation will attempt to fulfil its mission and achieve its long-term goals.

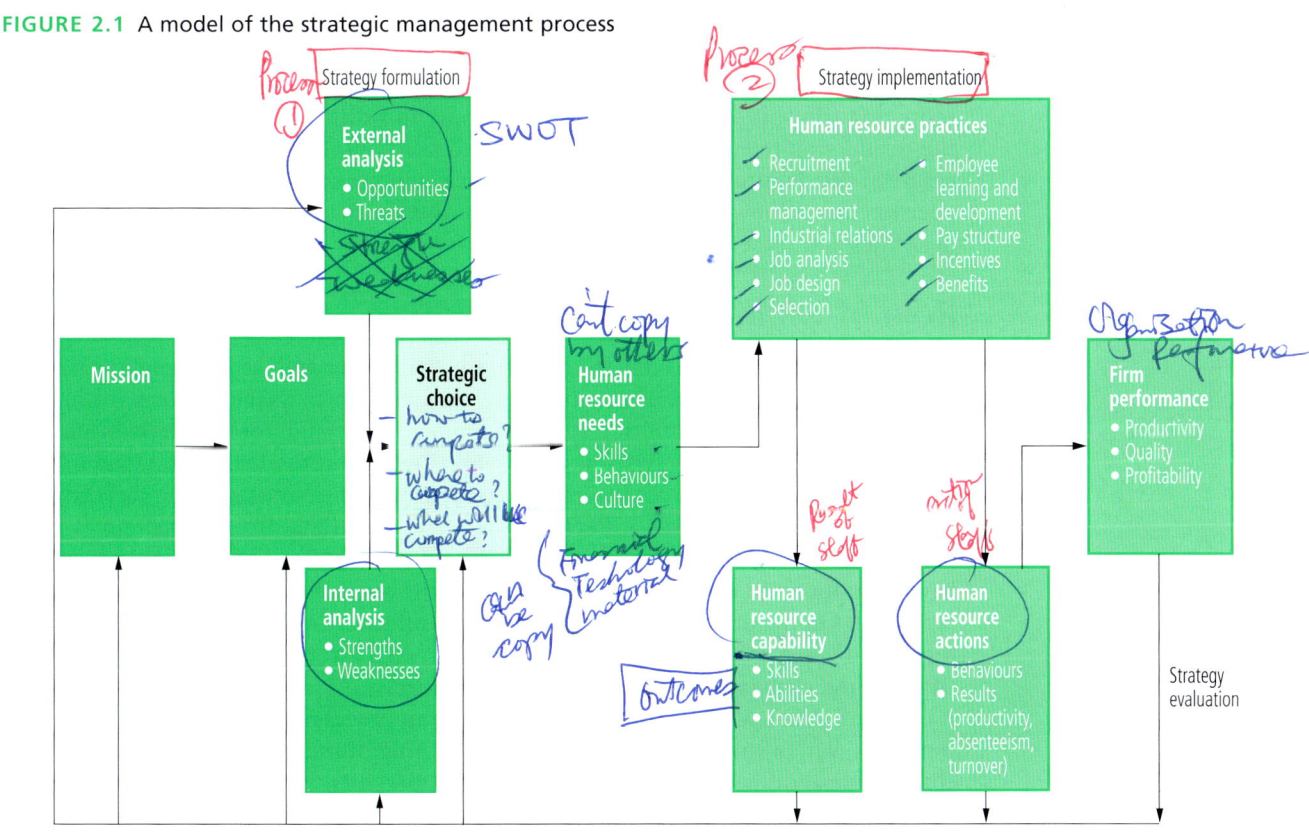

FIGURE 2.1 A model of the strategic management process

TABLE 2.1	Strategy—decisions about competition
1 Where to compete?	In what market or markets (industries, products, etc.) will we compete?
2 How to compete?	On what criterion or differentiating characteristic(s) will we compete? Cost? Quality? Reliability? Delivery?
3 With what will we compete?	What resources will allow us to beat our competition? How will we acquire, develop and deploy those resources to compete?

decisions) in an effort to increase its customer base. However, it failed to adequately recognise the differences between its existing workforce (that is, mostly professionals) and that of the fast-food industry (that is, lower-skilled people and high school students) as well as its ability to manage such a workforce. This was one reason that Pepsico, in 1998, 'spun off' the fast-food chains. In essence, it had made a decision about 'where to compete' without fully understanding what resources it would take to compete in that market (that is, the 'with what will we compete' issue).

Boeing illustrates how failing to address the 'with what will we compete' issue resulted in problems in its 'how to compete' decisions. The aerospace firm's consumer products division was in a 'price war' with Airbus Industries, forcing it to move away from its traditional customer service strategy towards emphasising cost reduction.[10] The strategy was a success at the sales end—as Boeing received large numbers of orders for aircraft from firms such as Singapore, Delta, Continental and Southwest Airlines. It had recently, however, gone through a large workforce reduction (thus, it did not have enough people to fill the orders) and it did not have the production technology to enable the necessary increase in productivity. The result of this failure to address the 'with what will we compete' issue in making a decision about 'how to compete' resulted in the firm's inability to meet delivery deadlines and the ensuing penalties it had to pay to its customers.

Role of HR in strategy formulation

As the preceding examples illustrate, often the 'with what will we compete' questions present ideal avenues for HR to influence the strategic management process. This might be either through limiting strategic options or through forcing thoughtfulness among the executive team regarding how and at what cost the firm might gain or develop the human resources (people) necessary for such a strategy to be successful. For example, HR executives at Pepsico could have noted that the firm had no expertise in managing the workforce of fast-food restaurants. The limiting role would have been for these executives to argue against the acquisition because of this lack of resources. On the other hand, they might have influenced the decision by educating top executives as to the costs (of hiring, training, etc.) associated with gaining people who had the right skills to manage such a workforce.

A firm's strategic management decision making process usually takes place at its top levels, with a strategic planning group consisting of the chief executive officer, the chief financial officer, the president and various directors. Each component of the process, however, involves people-related business issues. Therefore, the HR function needs to be involved in each of those components. One study in the United States of

115 strategic business units within Fortune 500 corporations found that between 49 and 69 per cent of the companies had some link between HRM and the strategic planning process.[11] However, the level of linkage varied; it is important to understand these different levels.

In Australia and Europe, the involvement of HR in strategic development varies considerably. For instance, in Australia, HR is involved in strategic development in 82 per cent of organisations. However, as with the experience in the United States, the level of linkage varies considerably.[12]

Four levels of integration seem to exist between the HR function and the strategic management function: 'administrative linkage', 'one-way linkage', 'two-way linkage' and 'integrative linkage'.[13] These levels of linkage will be discussed in relation to the different components of strategic management. The linkages are illustrated in Figure 2.2 below.

Administrative linkage

In *administrative linkage* (the lowest level of integration), the HR function's attention is focused on day-to-day activities. The HR executive has no time or opportunity to take a strategic outlook towards HR issues. The company's strategic business planning function exists without any input from the HR department. Thus, in this level of integration, the HR department is completely divorced from any component of the strategic management process in both strategy formulation and strategy implementation. The department simply engages in administrative work unrelated to the company's core business needs.

One-way linkage

In *one-way linkage*, the firm's strategic business planning function develops the strategic plan and then informs the HR function of the plan. Many believe this level of integration constitutes strategic HRM—that is, the role of the HR function is to design systems and/or programs that implement the strategic plan. Although one-way linkage does recognise the importance of human resources in implementing the

FIGURE 2.2 Linkages of strategic planning and HRM

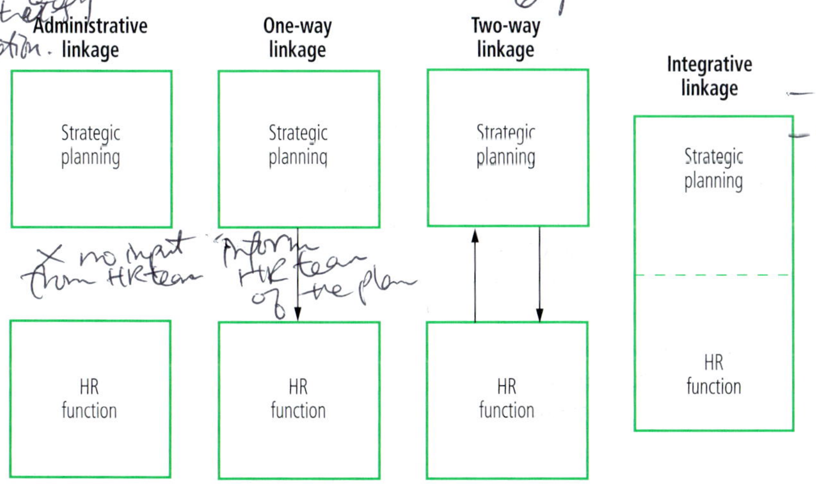

Source: Adapted from K. Golden & V. Ramanujam, 1985, 'Between a dream and a nightmare: on the integration of the human resource function and the strategic business planning process', *Human Resource Management*, 24, pp. 429–51.

strategic plan, it precludes the company from considering human resource issues while formulating the strategic plan. This level of integration often leads to strategic plans that the company cannot successfully implement. A survey of large public and private sector organisations in Australia in 2005 found practices in 7 per cent of organisations in Australia reflected this form of linkage.[14]

Two-way linkage

Two-way linkage does allow for the consideration of human resource issues during the strategy formulation process. This integration occurs in three sequential steps. First, the strategic planning team informs the HR function of the various strategies the company is considering. Then, the HR executives analyse the human resource implications of the various strategies and present the results of this analysis to the strategic planning team. Finally, after the strategic decision has been made, the strategic plan is passed on to the HR executives, who develop programs to implement the plan. The strategic planning function and the HR function are interdependent in the two-way linkage.

Integrative linkage

Integrative linkage is dynamic and multifaceted, and it is based on continuing rather than sequential interaction. In most cases, the HR executive is an integral member of the senior management team. Rather than an iterative process of information exchange, companies with integrative linkage have their HR functions built right into the strategy formulation and implementation processes. It is this role that we will discuss throughout the rest of this chapter.

Human resource managers in many Australian organisations are involved in the Cranet-Macquarie survey[15] on international strategic human resource management. It revealed that, in 2006, almost half of the senior human resource managers were represented on the senior management team. Human resource managers were engaged in the development of corporate strategy from the outset in 51 per cent of organisations and were consulted in 31 per cent of organisations.[16]

Similar findings were reported in another survey [17]. This survey found the HR area was involved in strategic decisions whether or not they affected the personnel area in 49 per cent of organisations. It also found involvement at the various stages of the decision making process, with the highest level of involvement being at the implementation stage.

Thus, in strategic HRM, the HR function is involved in both strategy formulation and strategy implementation. The HR executive provides the strategic planners with information about the company's human resource capabilities, and these capabilities are usually a direct function of the HR practices. This information about human resource capabilities helps 'top' managers choose the 'best' strategy, since they can consider how well each strategic alternative would be implemented. Once the strategic choice has been determined, the role of HR changes to the development and alignment of HR practices that will provide the company with employees having the necessary skills to implement the strategy. In addition, HR practices must be designed to elicit actions from employees in the company. In the next two sections of this chapter, we show how HR can provide a competitive advantage in the strategic management process.

The introductory case about Virgin Blue illustrates how the HR executive is an integral part of the strategic management team. It also illustrates how people, culture and HR management practices are recognised as important influences on the way business is done in Virgin Blue. Employee behaviour, motivation and commitment are recognised as critical to the success of Virgin Blue.

Strategy formulation

Five major components of the strategic management process are relevant to strategy formulation—mission, goals, external analysis, internal analysis and strategic choice.[18] These components are depicted in Figure 2.3. The organisation's mission is a statement of the organisation's reason for being; it usually specifies the customers served, the needs satisfied and/or the values received by the customers, and the technology used. The mission statement is often accompanied by a statement of a company's vision and/or values. For example, Table 2.2 overleaf illustrates the mission, vision and values of Merck & Co.

An organisation's **goals** are what it hopes to achieve in the medium- to long-term future; they reflect how the mission will be operationalised. The overarching goal of most profit-making companies in Australia is to maximise shareholder wealth. Companies have to set other long-term goals though, in order to maximise shareholder wealth. For example, one of Digital Equipment Corporation's goals is to be one of the leading personal computer makers.

External analysis consists of examining the organisation's operating environment to identify the strategic 'opportunities' and 'threats'. Examples of opportunities are customer markets that are not being served, technological advances that can aid the company and labour pools that have not been tapped. Threats include potential labour shortages, new competitors entering the market, pending legislation that might adversely affect the company, and competitors' technological innovations.

Mission
a statement of the organisation's reason for being; it usually specifies the customers served, the needs satisfied and/or the values received by the customers, and the technology used.

Goals
what an organisation hopes to achieve in the medium- to long-term future.

External analysis
consists of examining the organisation's operating environment to identify strategic opportunities and threats.

FIGURE 2.3 Strategy formulation

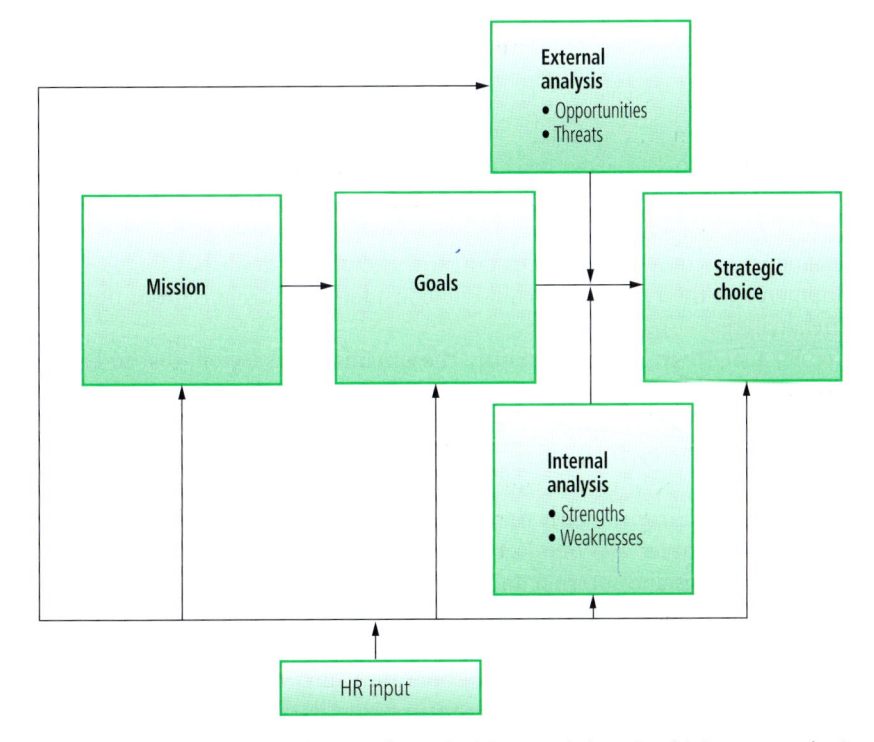

Source: Adapted from K. Golden & V. Ramanujam, 1985, 'Between a dream and a nightmare: on the integration of the human resource function and the strategic business planning process', *Human Resource Management*, 24, pp. 429–51.

PART 1   Managing the Human Resource Environment

> **TABLE 2.2** Merck & Co's mission and values
>
> **MISSION STATEMENT**
> Merck & Co, Inc. is a leading research-driven pharmaceutical products and services company. Merck discovers, develops, manufactures and markets a broad range of innovative products to improve human and animal health. The Merck-Medco Managed Care Division manages pharmacy benefits for more than 40 million Americans, encouraging the appropriate use of medicines and providing disease management programs.
>
> **Our mission**
> The mission of Merck is to provide society with superior products and services—innovations and solutions that improve the quality of life and satisfy customer needs—to provide employees with meaningful work and advancement opportunities and investors with a superior rate of return.
>
> **Our values**
>
> 1. **Our business is preserving and improving human life.** All of our actions must be measured by our success in achieving this goal. We value above all our ability to serve everyone who can benefit from the appropriate use of our products and services, thereby providing lasting consumer satisfaction.
>
> 2. **We are committed to the highest standards of ethics and integrity.** We are responsible to our customers, to Merck employees and their families, to the environments we inhabit, and to the societies we serve worldwide. In discharging our responsibilities, we do not take professional or ethical shortcuts. Our interactions with all segments of society must reflect the high standards we profess.
>
> 3. **We are dedicated to the highest level of scientific excellence and commit our research to improving human and animal health and the quality of life.** We strive to identify the most critical needs of consumers and customers; we devote our resources to meeting those needs.
>
> 4. **We expect profits, but only from work that satisfies customer needs and benefits humanity.** Our ability to meet our responsibilities depends on maintaining a financial position that invites investment in leading-edge research and that makes possible effective delivery of research results.
>
> 5. **We recognize that the ability to excel—to most competitively meet society's and customers' needs—depends on the integrity, knowledge, imagination, skill, diversity, and teamwork of employees, and we value these qualities most highly.** To this end, we strive to create an environment of mutual respect, encouragement, and teamwork—a working environment that rewards commitment and performance and is responsive to the needs of employees and their families
>
> *Source:* www.merck.com/about/mission.html

The Managing People case 'Asia to outgrow the world' describes some of the future developments in the region that could be considered by organisations doing an external analysis.

Internal analysis attempts to identify the organisation's 'strengths' and 'weaknesses'. It focuses on the quantity and quality of resources available to the organisation—financial, capital, technological and human resources. Organisations have to honestly and accurately assess each resource to decide whether it is a strength or a weakness. 'Managing challenges of globalisation: Global leadership: the rise of the GEO' highlights the significant impact that the globalisation of business has on the competencies, attitudes and mindsets required by global organisations.

External analysis and internal analysis combined constitute what has come to be called the SWOT analysis—'strengths', 'weaknesses', 'opportunities' and 'threats'. A **SWOT analysis** involves identifying the organisation's strengths and weaknesses and the opportunities and threats in its external operating environment. After going through SWOT analysis, the strategic planning team has at its disposal all the information it needs to generate a number of strategic alternatives. The strategic managers compare the ability of each of these alternatives to attain the organisation's strategic goals; then

---

Internal analysis
the process of examining an organisation's strengths and weaknesses.

SWOT analysis
involves identifying the organisation's strengths and weaknesses and the opportunities and threats in its external operating environment.

GLOBAL LEADERSHIP: THE RISE OF THE GEO

MANAGING CHALLENGES OF GLOBALISATION

Tomorrow will not be like today. Global business requires global executive officers (GEO) to be like explorers, taking their organisations through unfamiliar and turbulent terrain and preparing their people for the journey and outside-the-square thinking. …

The high-performance organisation of the GEO is becoming what Lynda Gratton, associate professor of organisational behaviour at the London Business School, calls a 'democratic enterprise'. The companies such as BP, BT, HP, Tesco, Sony and AstraZeneca which formed the basis of her research for the democratic enterprise have learnt the benefits of treating employees as individuals, of creating adult-to-adult relationships, of moulding democratic companies.

In part, these GEOs have been responding to three critical forces, which are growing in momentum and will influence companies all over the globe. The first force is demographic and more specifically the expectations and aspirations of Generation X and Generation Y coupled with the Baby Boomers who have new options about retirement and workforce participation. The second is technology, which enables companies to bring choice and information to their employees. And the third is the very real skills and talent shortage.

Global companies want strong, respected cultures to continually attract, engage, retain the best talent from around the world. These global firms understand the desirability and inevitability of diversity and the need to create equal opportunity for all.

Companies that continue to struggle with diversity in the domestic arena will find themselves challenged. Businesses that find themselves at the forefront of international competitiveness should look closely at the inclusiveness of their cultures if they are to prevail in the talent war. Companies need talented people with the mindset, competencies and commitment to execute and devolve global strategy. Clients and other stakeholders rely on it.

Culture shock is the inimitable global experience. Living in another country in itself does not create a true global attitude, particularly if the executive replicates their local way of living and working. In fact, a key reason for failure in an offshore post is the inability to adjust to the foreign culture or to cope with what it feels like to be an outsider. Similarly, when a company uses home country leadership in each of their overseas businesses, not only does that home culture prevail, but the overall mindset tends to be more cloistered than the wider global milieu.

Leading GEOs and their leadership team regard the power of diversity as a way to leverage advantage, performance, growth and talent. Yet, the thought remains, if exposure to the global context is becoming necessary for positions at higher levels in the corporate hierarchy, then more line management expatriate opportunities need to be offered to women or nationals of non-head office countries.

Source: Extract from D. Jacobs, 'Global leadership: te rise of the GEO', *Human Resources,* Issue 105, 30 May 2006, pp. 12–13. www.humanresourcesmagazine.com.au

---

they make their strategic choice. The *strategic choice,* as previously discussed, is the organisation's strategy; it describes the ways in which the organisation will attempt to fulfil its mission and achieve its long-term goals.

Many of the opportunities and threats in the external environment are people-related. With fewer and fewer highly qualified individuals entering the labour market, organisations are beginning to compete not just for customers, but for employees. It is HR's role to keep close tabs on the external environment for human resource-related opportunities and threats, especially those directly related to the HR function: potential labour shortages, competitor wage rates, government regulations affecting employment and so on. For example, projections on the representation of different age groups in the workforce indicate that **older workers** will increase their representation during the first decade of the twenty-first century in Australia, while the representation of workers aged in their late teens and early 20s will decrease.[19] Consequently, organisations will need to re-evaluate their attitudes to older workers, their cultures and many of their human resource policies.[20]

Older workers
variously defined as 55 years of age and over, between 50 and 80 years of age, and as 40-plus years of age.

An analysis of a company's internal strengths and weaknesses also requires input from the HR function. Today, companies are increasingly realising that their human resources are one of their most important assets.[21] Failure to consider the strengths and weaknesses of the company's workforce may result in the company choosing strategies it is not capable of pursuing.[22] However, some research has demonstrated that few companies have achieved this level of linkage.[23] For example, one company chose a strategy of cost reduction through technological improvements. It built a plant designed around a computer-integrated manufacturing system with statistical process controls. Though this choice may seem like a good one, the company soon learnt otherwise. It discovered that its employees could not operate the new equipment because 25 per cent of the workforce was functionally illiterate.[24]

This example illustrates that the company did not know the capabilities of its workforce. It also demonstrates that the value of human capital, that is the people engaged in an organisation, will change as factors, such as technology, change.

When undertaking an analysis of the internal strengths of an organisation, particularly in industries involving knowledge workers, there is a need to value the intangible assets of an organisation. Measuring and valuing human capabilities and human capital has been shown to indicate the potential strength and performance of a company.[25] It has been found that:

> superior human capital management is a leading—rather than lagging—indicator of improved financial success. This finding is more important now, during times of economic uncertainty, than in boom times … If a company's goal is to improve shareholder value, a key priority must be its approach to human capital.[26]

Consequently, it is necessary to use qualitative tools to assess human capital data and it is this data that distinguishes the differences between companies and their potential for future performance. [27]

The 'HRM spotlight: Lead v lag indicators' demonstrates the significance of valuing a company's intangible assets and providing this information in a form suitable for market analysts.

Thus, with an integrative linkage, strategic planners consider all the people-related business issues before making a strategic choice. These issues are identified with regard to the mission, goals, opportunities, threats, strengths and weaknesses, leading the strategic planning team to make a more intelligent strategic choice. While this process does not guarantee success, companies that address these issues are more likely to make a choice that will ultimately succeed. Table 2.3 (p. 66) gives examples of HR's issues in strategic planning.

Research has supported the need to have HR executives integrally involved in strategy formulation. One study of United States petrochemical refineries found that the level of HR involvement was positively related to the refinery manager's evaluation of the effectiveness of the HR function.[28] A second study of manufacturing firms found that HR involvement was highest when top managers viewed employees as a strategic asset and this was associated with reduced turnover.[29] Yet both studies found that HR involvement was unrelated to operating unit financial performance.

However, other research indicates that HR practices that are properly implemented do deliver significant financial benefits to an organisation. These benefits include profitability, shareholder return, stock prices and organisational survival.[30] One of Australia's top publicly listed companies, Boral, attributes increases in operating performance to the consequences of a comprehensive change program and the commitment of employees. Boral introduced a program designed to build the company into a world leader in building and construction materials, as well as a major

LEAD VS LAG INDICATORS

HRM SPOTLIGHT

On the face of it, probably not a lot seems to have changed with the way analysts assess company stocks and the value of intangible assets in recent years. However, a closer inspection reveals significant differences in the way analysts weigh up such factors.

A recent study by Accenture revealed that, in 1980, the book value of a company comprised 80 per cent of its market value. In 1990, this figure decreased to 55 per cent, while intangible assets formed 45 per cent of market value. In 2002, only 25 per cent of a company's book value was reflected in its market value, while the intangibles ballooned to 75 per cent. Despite this, only 22 per cent of investors believe a company's value is tied up in intangible assets.

'There is a large gap between investors' perceptions and reality', according to Dan London, management partner of Accenture's finance and performance management service on line. 'Over the past 25 years, intangible assets have supplanted tangible assets as the key determinate of a company's value, yet traditional accounting methods remain focused on the tangibles, so a significant portion of corporate assets are going undervalued and underreported to investors.'

Analysts are reasonably clear on the effect human capital metrics have on organisations, according to Lyle Potgieter, CEO of IXP3 Human Capital. Rather the issue is more about access to relevant information. In examining the average annual report for Australian listed companies, human capital is lucky to appear as a one line statement, under employee or maybe operational expenses. Given that such expenses are generally 60 per cent of operational expenses, according to Potgieter, he believes important details are missing including net profit per person employed, staff turnover, bonuses paid as a percentage of total staff eligible for a bonus; number of staff who achieved their business objectives; quantum of bonuses paid relative to EBIT; and staff engagement ration.

'In our view, the issue of lead versus lag indicators is not as much of an issue of educating analysts, but rather providing the analysts with adequate information from which they can make sound and educated assessments of organisations', he says.

Source: C. Donaldson, 2006, 'Lead v lag indicators: educating analyst', *Human Resources*, 25 July, p. 12. www.humanresourcesmagazine.com.au

---

force in energy in Australia and the Pacific. Investing in—and securing—the best people were critical components of this program, known as Magna Carta.[31]

Main Roads WA is a public sector organisation that employs 1000 people. It developed a five-year integrated strategy called the 'Dynamic Resourcing Strategy' in 1999. Its objectives were to ensure a strategic and planned approach to organisational change by harnessing people and business management in the corporate direction, assisting to break down functional barriers, facilitating work arrangements in a decentralised structure and increasing people's ability to handle change. The overall strategy consists of three components: preparation, development and placement of employees. It includes many human resource functions, such as planning; attraction and retention; compensation and recognition; labour relations and diversity; organisational learning and development; and employee health, safety and lifestyle. A cost benefit analysis was carried out on the strategy and the predicted outcomes have been achieved. Main Roads WA 'has reduced costs, improved productivity, streamlined operations and increased quality of services, strengthened core business skills, improved and developed overall management expertise and positioned itself to develop a values based organisation'. It has also contributed to a more flexible use of employees, teamwork and decentralisation.[32]

Research has indicated that some companies have fully integrated HR into the strategy formulation process.[33] As we've mentioned before, companies are beginning to recognise that in an intensely competitive environment, strategically managing human resources can provide a competitive advantage. Thus, companies at the

TABLE 2.3 Examples of the role of HR in strategic management

Challenges of HR innovation: People power

Les Cupper from the Commonwealth Bank says:

The thing that occupies me every day is how we use the capability of the people who work for us. So most of our framework is around the way we access capability, and how we create an environment where people can actually use what they've got to contribute. Anything we do has to hang off that, whether it's reviewing performance systems, or recruitment, or looking at the demographics and wondering where we're going to get people in the future. The central question is, what impact does it have on capability?

Question: Is there a particular strand of this issue that has become more difficult?

Cupper replied:

Well, there's the work that we're doing to try to understand labour supplies for an industry that traditionally relies on youth for its main intake. When we look at the demographics and we look at the rates of entry to the labour market going forward, then that mature-age capability is a longer-term challenge for us. So understanding what our employees, who might be approaching traditional retirement ages, feel about staying at work longer or working differently, and looking at where we might be able to get some leverage, is part of the challenge.

Some of the impediments to the way you're able to attract mature age people will require huge systems changes in social infrastructure, superannuation, and taxation. All of those sorts of issues have a long pipeline to get effective change, and so it's not simply what you can do within your own organisation, but what the other systems are that impact on the way people will present themselves as potential employees.

Sam Sheppard from General Electric says:

Our key strategic thrust is growth, and how we can continue to have a strategic competitive advantage through our people.

Andrew Miedler from SC Johnson says:

The main thing is attraction-retention, through what we call our employer brand, which is 'enjoy the difference'. Within that employer brand we have five areas that we want to be good at: leadership, training, career development, employee recognition and work–life balance.

Marg Lennon from Cochlear says:

We have just refined our strategic agenda, and I think our big challenge is implementing this, putting it on the ground, getting people to understand it. What's in it for me? What does this actually mean? It's how do you get everyone on the bus, how do you get them to want to be on the bus, how do you get them to think, oh, I've got some chance of helping the driver steer it?

Source: Based on C. Fox & H. Trinca, 2003, 'Agenda 2003', *Australian Financial Review, Boss* magazine, February, p. 38.

---

administrative-linkage level will either become more integrated or face extinction. In addition, companies will move toward becoming integratively linked in an effort to strategically manage human resources.

It is of utmost importance that all people-related business issues are considered during the strategy formulation process. These issues are identified in the HR function. Mechanisms or structures for integrating the HR function into strategy formulation may help the strategic planning team make the most effective strategic choice. Once that strategic choice is determined, HR must take an active role in its implementation. This role will be discussed in the next section.

Strategy implementation

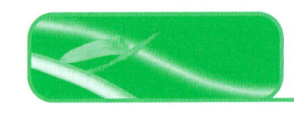

After an organisation has gone through the process of strategy formulation and made its strategic choice, it has to execute that strategy—that is, make it come to life in its day-to-day workings. The strategy a company pursues dictates certain HR needs. For a company to have a good strategy foundation, certain tasks must be accomplished in pursuit of the company's goals, individuals must possess certain skills to perform those tasks and those individuals must be motivated to perform their skills effectively.

The basic premise behind strategy implementation is that 'an organisation has a variety of structural forms and organisational processes to choose from when implementing a given strategy', and these choices make an economic difference.[34] Five important variables determine success in strategy implementation: organisational structure; task design; types of information and information systems; the selection, training and development of people; and reward systems.

As we see in Figure 2.4 below, HRM has primary responsibility for three of the five implementation variables: task design; the selection, training and development of people; and reward systems. In addition, HRM can also directly affect the two remaining variables: organisational structure; and types of information and information systems. First, for the strategy to be successfully implemented, the tasks must be designed and grouped into jobs in a way that is efficient and effective.[35] In Chapter 6, Analysis and design of work, we will examine how this can be done through the processes of job analysis and job design.

Second, the HR function must ensure that the organisation is staffed with people who have the necessary knowledge, skills and abilities to perform their part in implementing the strategy. This goal is achieved primarily through Recruitment and selection (discussed in Chapter 8), Learning and development (discussed in Chapter 11), and Employee development and career management (discussed in Chapter 12).

Third, the HR function must develop performance management and reward systems that lead employees to work for and support the strategic plan. The specific types of performance management systems are covered in Chapter 10 (Performance management) and the many issues involved in developing reward systems are discussed in Chapter 13 (Managing compensation) and Chapter 14 (Performance-related pay). In other words, the role of the HR function becomes one of, first, ensuring that the company has the proper number of employees with the levels and types of skills required by the strategic plan;[36] and, second, developing 'control' systems that ensures those employees are acting in ways that promote the achievement of the goals specified in the strategic plan.[37]

FIGURE 2.4 Variables to be considered in strategy implementation

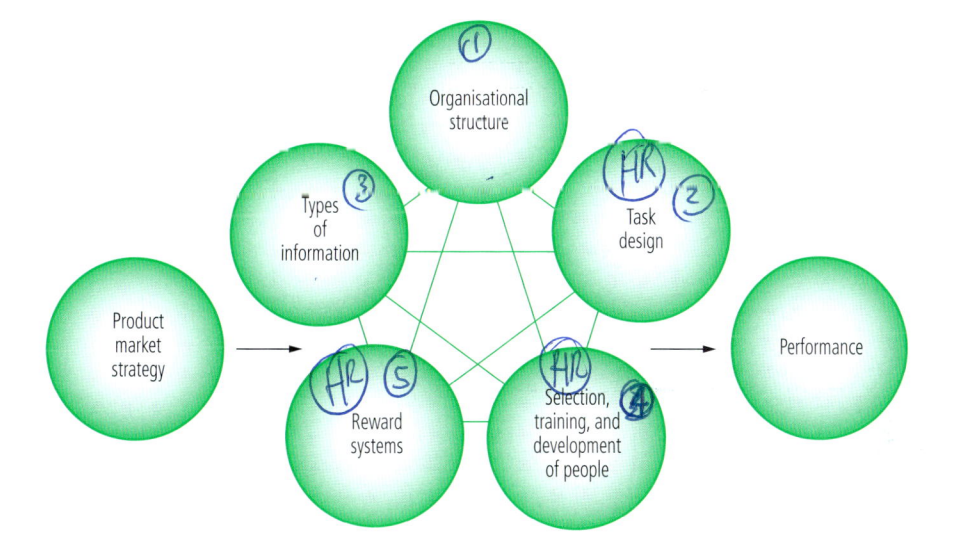

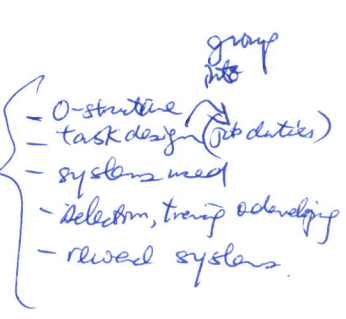

PART 1   Managing the Human Resource Environment

How does the HR function do this? As Figure 2.5 below shows, it is through administering HR practices: job analysis and design, recruitment and selection systems, learning and development programs, performance management systems, reward systems and industrial relations programs. The details of each of these HR practices are the focus of the rest of this book. However, at this point it is important to present a general overview of the HR practices and their roles in strategy implementation. We will then discuss the various strategies companies pursue and the types of HR systems congruent with those strategies. We focus on how the strategic types are implemented and discuss the HR practices associated with various directional strategies.

HR practices

The HR function can be thought of as having six menus of HR practices from which a company can choose the most appropriate to implement its strategy. Each of these menus refers to a particular functional area of HRM: job analysis and design; employee recruitment and selection; employee learning and development; performance management; pay structure, incentives and benefits; and industrial relations.[38] These menus are presented in Table 2.4 on page 69. The table shows that choices need to be made about each of these particular functional areas; for instance, the job analysis and design function requires that choices are made about the complexity and number of tasks, the breadth of skills required and the scope of the job description.

FIGURE 2.5 Strategy implementation

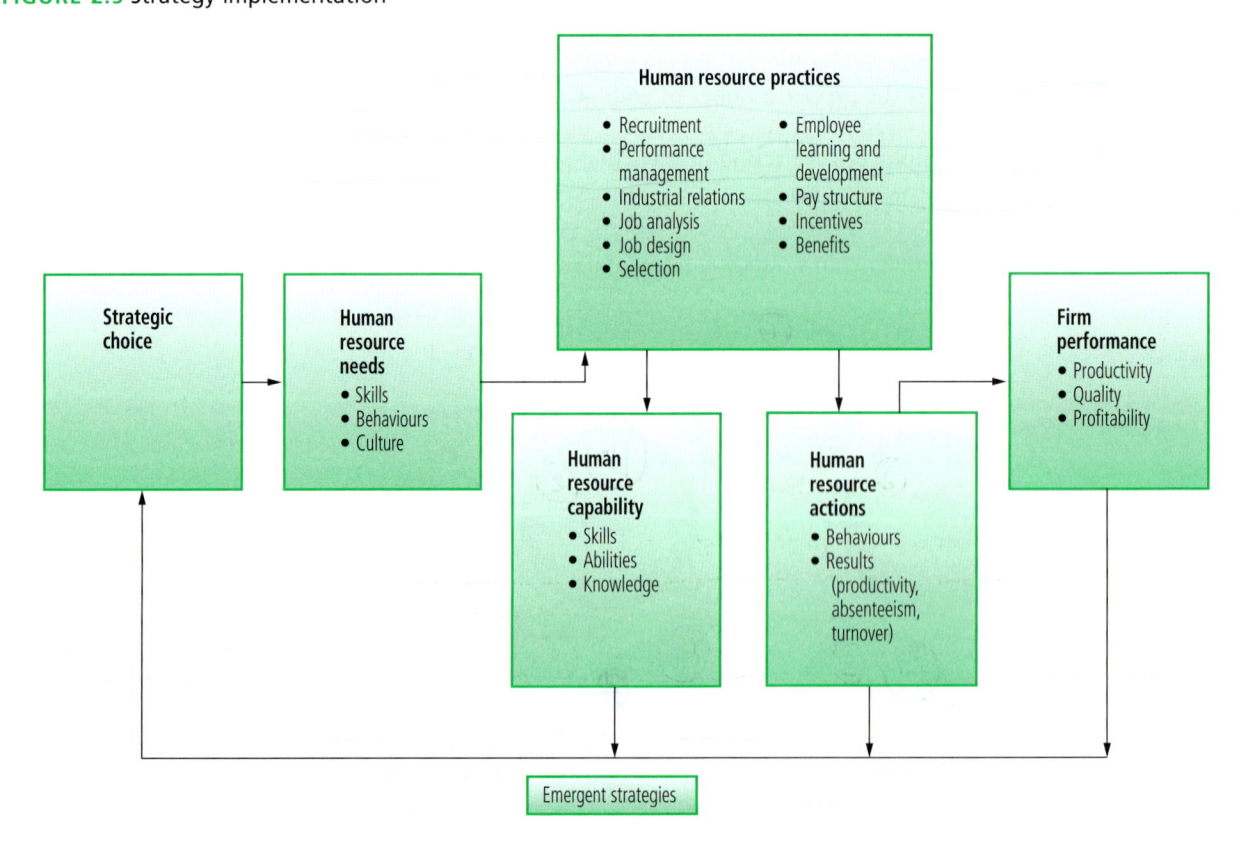

TABLE 2.4 Menu of HR practice options

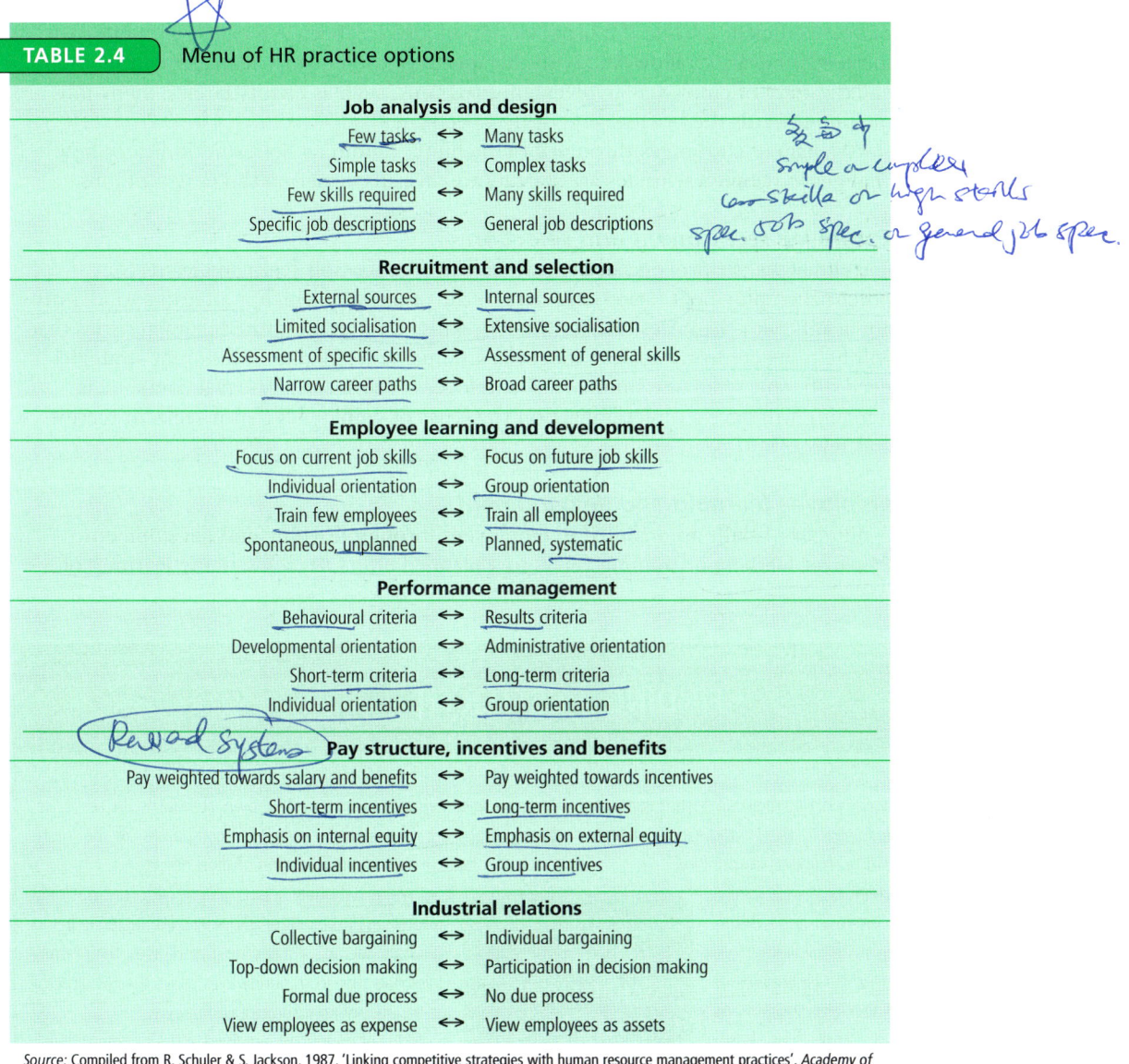

Job analysis and design
Few tasks	↔	Many tasks
Simple tasks	↔	Complex tasks
Few skills required	↔	Many skills required
Specific job descriptions	↔	General job descriptions

Recruitment and selection
External sources	↔	Internal sources
Limited socialisation	↔	Extensive socialisation
Assessment of specific skills	↔	Assessment of general skills
Narrow career paths	↔	Broad career paths

Employee learning and development
Focus on current job skills	↔	Focus on future job skills
Individual orientation	↔	Group orientation
Train few employees	↔	Train all employees
Spontaneous, unplanned	↔	Planned, systematic

Performance management
Behavioural criteria	↔	Results criteria
Developmental orientation	↔	Administrative orientation
Short-term criteria	↔	Long-term criteria
Individual orientation	↔	Group orientation

Pay structure, incentives and benefits
Pay weighted towards salary and benefits	↔	Pay weighted towards incentives
Short-term incentives	↔	Long-term incentives
Emphasis on internal equity	↔	Emphasis on external equity
Individual incentives	↔	Group incentives

Industrial relations
Collective bargaining	↔	Individual bargaining
Top-down decision making	↔	Participation in decision making
Formal due process	↔	No due process
View employees as expense	↔	View employees as assets

Source: Compiled from R. Schuler & S. Jackson, 1987, 'Linking competitive strategies with human resource management practices', *Academy of Management Executive*, Vol. 1, pp. 207–19; C. Fisher, L. Schoenfeldt and B. Shaw, 1992, *Human Resource Management*, 2nd edn, Houghton Mifflin, Boston.

Job analysis and design

Companies produce a given product or service (or set of products or services) and the manufacture of these products requires that a number of tasks are performed. These tasks are grouped together to form jobs. Job analysis is the process of getting detailed information about jobs. Job design deals with making decisions about what tasks should be grouped into a particular job. The way that jobs are designed should have an important tie to the strategy of an organisation, because the strategy requires either new and different tasks or different ways of performing the same tasks. In addition, because many strategies entail the introduction of new technologies, this impacts the way that work is performed.[39]

In general, jobs can vary from having a narrow range of tasks (most of which are simplified and require a limited range of skills) to having a broad array of complex tasks requiring multiple skills. In the past, the narrow design of jobs has been used to

Job analysis
the process of getting detailed information about jobs.

Job design
the process of defining the way work will be performed and the tasks that will be required in a given job.

PART 1   Managing the Human Resource Environment

increase efficiency, while the broad design of jobs has been associated with efforts to increase innovation. However, with the advent of total quality management methods and a variety of employee involvement programs, such as quality circles, many jobs are moving towards the broader end of the spectrum.[40]

'Managing challenges through sustainability: Finding a better fit' indicates how changes in people's attitudes are starting to have an impact on the design of jobs.

Employee recruitment and selection

Recruitment is the process through which the organisation seeks applicants for potential employment. **Selection** refers to the process by which it attempts to identify applicants with the necessary knowledge, skills, abilities and other characteristics that will help the company achieve its goals. Companies engaging in different strategies need different types and numbers of employees. Thus, the strategy a company is pursuing will have a direct impact on the types of employees that it seeks to recruit and select.[41]

Employee learning and development

A number of skills are instilled in employees through learning and development. **Employee learning** or training refers to a planned effort to facilitate the learning of

Recruitment
any practice or activity carried on by the organisation with the primary purpose of identifying and attracting potential employees.

Selection
the process by which an organisation attempts to identify applicants with the necessary knowledge, skills, abilities and other characteristics that will help it achieve its goals.

Employee learning
(training) a planned effort to facilitate the learning of job-related knowledge, skills and behaviour by employees.

FINDING A BETTER FIT

Downshifters want to slow down at work so they can upshift in other areas of their lives. Studies in Australia, the United Kingdom and North America have uncovered a number of primary motivations: a want to spend more time with family, or pursuing hobbies or creative interests, and a desire to live a less materialistic, more sustainable life.

From the corporate perspective, the emergence of downshifting is causing Australian organisations to rethink the very nature of work and work arrangements. For example what is a full-time as opposed to a part-time job? Who defines when and where a job is to be performed? By what measurements should companies remunerate their employees?

From an HR perspective, downshifting can be interpreted as the next level beyond work/life balancing. It requires companies to be even more creative in their understanding of what jobs are, the time it takes to do them, and what it means to integrate corporate needs with employee motivation, talent and the pursuit of individual happiness.

Clearly, if employees are overworked, unhappy and unfulfilled, they can't balance the rest of their lives, irrespective of how attractive their remuneration or how many fringe benefits they receive. Downshifters may not necessarily be cynical, angry or overly critical. They simply do not fit into the traditional fast track mold any more.

MANAGING CHALLENGES THROUGH SUSTAINABILITY

They are measuring success by their own standards. In response, downshifters are increasingly expecting companies to be more flexible and accommodating of their needs.

'We're definitely seeing people who are not only interested in their careers, but also interested in being a whole person—having their work lives, their family lives and their community lives', says the HR director at an Australian insurance company.

'A lot of people are involved in their communities', says another senior HR manager. 'They may have a family or family life, or they may take care of an ageing parent. In any case, they want to make a meaningful contribution to people around them. This is a very important aspect.'

Another HR executive, for a major retailer, says: 'We provide our managers with a lot of flexibility in creating an environment that works for people, rather than trying to fit people into a preset mold. The company optimises its talent focus by not having rigid policies. Rather, we allow managers to work with individuals on helping them succeed. The key issue is access to great talent and the flexibility around how to best access and retain that talent. I am convinced that firm and inflexible policies would be the trigger for that.'

Source: F. Gandolfi, 2006, 'Finding a better fit', *HR Monthly*, April, AHRI, pp. 34–5.

job-related knowledge, skills and behaviour by employees. **Development** involves acquiring knowledge, skills and behaviour that improve employees' ability to meet the challenges of a variety of existing jobs or jobs that do not yet exist. Changes in strategies often require changes in the types, levels and mixes of skills. Thus, the acquisition of strategy-related skills is an essential element of the implementation of strategy.

For example, many companies have emphasised quality in their products, engaging in total quality management (TQM) programs. These programs require extensive training of all employees in the TQM philosophy, methods and often other skills that ensure quality.[42]

Through recruitment, selection, learning and development, companies can obtain a pool of human resources capable of implementing a given strategy.[43]

Performance management

Performance management is used to ensure that employees' activities and outcomes are congruent with the organisation's objectives. It entails specifying those activities and outcomes that will result in the firm successfully implementing the strategy. For example, companies that are 'steady state' (that is, not diversified) tend to have evaluation systems that call for subjective performance assessments of managers. This stems from the fact that those above the first-level managers in the hierarchy have extensive knowledge about how the work should be performed. On the other hand, diversified companies are more likely to use quantitative measures of performance to evaluate managers, because top managers have less knowledge about how work should be performed by those below them in the hierarchy.[44]

Similarly, executives who have extensive knowledge of the behaviours that lead to effective performance use performance management systems that focus on the behaviours of their subordinate managers. However, when executives are unclear about the specific behaviours that lead to effective performance, they tend to focus on evaluating the objective performance results of their subordinate managers.[45]

Pay structure, incentives and benefits

The pay system has an important role in implementing strategies. First, a high level of pay and/or benefits relative to that of competitors can ensure that the company attracts and retains high-quality employees, but this might have a negative impact on the company's overall labour costs.[46] Second, by tying pay to performance, the company can elicit specific activities and levels of performance from employees.

In a study of how compensation practices are tied to strategies, researchers examined 33 high-tech and 72 traditional companies. They classified them by whether they were in a growth stage (greater than 20 per cent inflation-adjusted increases in annual sales) or a maturity stage. They found that high-tech companies in the growth stage used compensation systems that were highly geared towards incentive pay, with a lower percentage of total pay devoted to salary and benefits. On the other hand, compensation systems among mature companies (both high-tech and traditional) devoted a lower percentage of total pay to incentives and a high percentage to benefits.[47]

Industrial relations

Whether companies are unionised or not, the general approach to relations with employees can strongly affect their potential for gaining competitive advantage. The Federal Government's Work Choices legislation provides employers with the opportunity to use Australian Workplace Agreements to provide businesses with

---

Development
(also employee development) the acquisition of knowledge, skills and behaviours that improve an employee's ability to meet changes in job requirements and in client and customer demands.

Performance management
the means through which managers ensure that employees' activities and outputs are congruent with the organisation's goals.

genuine flexibility and the chance to move out of awards. The legislation provides employers with the opportunity to review employment contracts, policies and procedures so they suit the needs of the workplace.[48]

Companies can choose to treat employees as an asset that requires investment of resources or as an expense to be minimised.[49] They have to make choices about how much employees can and should participate in decision making, what rights employees have, and what the company's responsibility is to them. The approach a company takes in making these decisions can result in it either successfully achieving its short- and long-term goals or ceasing to exist.

Research examines how companies develop sets of HR practices that maximise performance and productivity. For example, one study of automobile assembly plants around the world found that plants that exhibited both high productivity and high quality used 'HR best practices', such as a heavy emphasis on recruitment and hiring, compensation tied to performance, low levels of status differentiation, high levels of training for both new and experienced employees, and the use of employee participation through structures such as work teams and problem solving groups.[50] Another study found that HR systems composed of selection testing, training, contingent pay, performance appraisal, attitude surveys, employee participation and information sharing resulted in higher levels of productivity and corporate financial performance, as well as lower employee turnover.[51]

'Managing challenges through attracting and retaining people: Topping up on talent' indicates HR is being recast and repositioned. This will require HR involvement in different ways of thinking and undertaking different activities.

Organisations also need to make decisions about the terms on which they engage people who do its work. It has been suggested[52] that the value and the uniqueness of human capital should be taken into account when deciding whether to engage employees or contractors or to collaborate with partners. The value of human capital, or the people, can be considered in terms of the extent to which they contribute to the core competence or competitive advantage of the organisation. In contrast, the uniqueness of human capital refers to the extent to which the capabilities of the people are specific to the organisation. In the above case, concern with managing talent becomes particularly important when the talent, that is the people, have capabilities that are unique and valuable. In this circumstance Lepak and Snell[53] propose that organisations should engage these people as employees, provide extensive training, career development, broad roles and probably recruit on potential.

Strategic types

As we previously discussed, companies can be classified by the generic strategies they pursue. It is important to note that these generic strategies are not what we mean by a strategic plan. They are merely similarities in the ways companies seek to compete in their industries. Various typologies have been offered, but we will focus on the two generic strategies proposed by Porter: cost and differentiation.[54]

According to Michael Porter of Harvard, competitive advantage stems from a company being able to create value in its production process. Value can be created in one of two ways. First, value can be created by reducing costs. Second, value can be created by differentiating a product or service in such a way that it allows the company to charge a premium price relative to its competitors. This leads to two basic strategies. According to Porter, the 'overall-cost leadership' strategy focuses on becoming the lowest-cost producer in an industry. This strategy is achieved by

TOPPING UP ON TALENT

… Senior executives today are very likely to believe that competitive advantage in knowledge economies comes largely from talent. And so talent management professionals are vital. The opportunity is that CEOs will naturally turn to senior HR professionals to get a talent strategy. …

… [T]here is at long last some momentum for HR actually becoming the strategic business partner it has long wished to be—but leading talent management calls for a more holistic or organisational development-oriented skill set. 'Those HR executives who can't function effectively in this new world, or who continue to only be good at "old world transactional HR" will find themselves out of work', she (Morton) says.

Heads of talent management often report directly to a very senior line executive or the CEO, she adds. 'This is a very different positioning than HR has had. It requires thinking like a line manager, too. HR professionals will I hope, get ready for these changes and realise that they now need to provide real business, not just HR, value.'

In the coming years, Schweyer says a true discipline and science around talent management will begin to take shape, resulting in the formation of talent management departments and the widespread appointment of Chief Talent officers or Chief Human Capital Officers.

'These executives and their teams will oversee the organisaton's integrated efforts to leverage the most value of their investments in human capital and talent', he says.

As a result, traditional HR—payroll, benefits, compliance—will be separate, and in most cases outsourced. Schweyer says there are a number of steps that organisations must take in order to establish a clear advantage through making more intelligent workforce and business decisions, such developing solid employer brands and building talent pools ahead of demand; integrating recruitment, performance management, compensation and learning management; understanding employee motivation and triggers for attrition and being well-schooled in their employees' skills, demographics and retirement profiles, for example.

'Greater use of technology will also enable the rapid development of the discipline as will better managed use of external vendors to whom much transactional work will be outsourced', he adds.

Source: Excerpt from C. Donaldson, 2006, 'Topping up the talent', *Human Resources*, 21 March, p. 14. www.humanresourcesmagazine.com.au

---

constructing efficient large-scale facilities, by reducing costs through capitalising on the experience curve, and by controlling overhead costs and costs in such areas as research and development, service, sales force and advertising. This strategy provides above-average returns within an industry and it tends to bar other firms' entry into the industry, since the firm can lower its prices below competitors' costs. For example, IBM-clone computer manufacturers—like Dell and Compaq—have captured an increased share of the personal-computer market by offering personal computers at a lower cost than IBM and Apple.

The 'differentiation' strategy, according to Porter, attempts to create the impression that the company's product or service is different from that of others in the industry. The perceived differentiation can come from creating a brand image, technology, offering unique features or unique customer service. If a company succeeds in differentiating its product, it will achieve above-average returns and the differentiation may protect it from price sensitivity. For example, IBM has consistently emphasised its brand image and its reputation for superior service while charging a higher price for its computers.

HR needs in strategic types

While all of the strategic types require competent people in a generic sense, each of the strategies also requires different types of employees with different types of behaviours and attitudes. As we noted earlier in Figure 2.1 on page 57, different

PART 1   Managing the Human Resource Environment

Role behaviours
behaviours that are required of an individual in his or her role as a job holder in a social/work environment.

strategies require employees with specific skills and they also require these employees to exhibit different 'role behaviours'.[55] Role behaviours are the behaviours required of an individual in his or her role as a job holder in a social/work environment. These role behaviours vary on a number of dimensions. Additionally, different role behaviours are required by the different strategies. For example, companies engaged in a cost strategy require employees to have a high concern for quantity and a short-term focus, to be comfortable with stability and to be risk averse. These employees are expected to exhibit role behaviours that are relatively repetitive and performed independently or autonomously.

Thus, companies engaged in cost strategies, because of the focus on efficient production, tend to specifically define the skills they require and invest in training employees in these skill areas. They also rely on behavioural performance management systems with a large performance-based compensation component. These companies promote internally and develop internally consistent pay systems with high pay differentials between superiors and subordinates. They seek efficiency through worker participation, and soliciting employees' ideas on how to achieve more efficient production.

On the other hand, employees in companies with a differentiation strategy need to be highly creative and cooperative; to have only a moderate concern for quantity, a long-term focus, a tolerance for ambiguity and to be risk takers. Employees in these companies are expected to exhibit role behaviours that include cooperating with others, developing new ideas and taking a balanced approach to process and results.

Thus, differentiation companies will seek to generate more creativity through broadly defined jobs with general job descriptions. They may recruit more from outside the firm, engage in limited socialisation of newcomers and provide broader career paths. Training and development activities focus on cooperation. The compensation system is geared towards external equity, as it is heavily driven by recruiting needs. These companies develop results-based performance management systems and divisional corporate performance evaluations to encourage risk taking on the part of managers.[56]

A study of HR practice among steel mini-mills in the United States found that mills pursuing different strategies used different systems of HR practices. Mills seeking cost-leadership tended to use control-oriented HR systems that were characterised by high centralisation, low participation, low training, low wages, low benefits and highly contingent pay; whereas differentiator mills used 'commitment' HR systems, characterised as the opposite on each of those dimensions.[57] A later study from the same sample revealed that the mills with the commitment systems had higher productivity, lower scrap rates and lower employee turnover than those with the control systems.

It has been found that the relationship between business strategies and HR strategies is complex in organisations undergoing change. In their studies of Australian services organisations undergoing change, Dunphy and Stace found that the HR strategies were more strongly related to organisational change strategies than to business strategies. Dunphy and Stace state that there is a:

> ... systematic logic that leads from the development of business strategies, to an assessment of the scope of change and leadership style needed to reposition the organisation, and then to the determination of the kind of HRM strategy needed to make the change work.[58]

Dunphy and Stace claim that it is the degree of required organisational repositioning that makes the most powerful impact on the type of HR policies.[59]

They also argue that the degree of repositioning influences the type of leadership required. Leadership plays an essential part in the process of translating strategy and the change associated with this strategy into action. However, different leadership styles are best suited to different circumstances. In situations of extreme turbulence, directive and decisive leaders have been found to be effective.[60] This was recognised at the web portal Yahoo in March 2001, when CEO, Tim Koogle, announced he would step down once a new successor was found. This step was taken in times of a slowing economy, with declining revenues and share prices.[61]

The implementation of policies is complex and shaped by many factors including employee expectations. The Towers Perrin Workplace Index found employees now accept personal responsibility for maintaining their skills and applying these to the most critical areas of their work. However, they see this responsibility as part of an exchange—an exchange in which they receive training, the opportunity for participation, career development and continuing employment. In addition, they were particularly sceptical about management fulfilling their obligations:

> When employees doubt there is reciprocity and fairness, their work ethic and motivation appear to suffer … Over time, negative feelings about the company will erode positive feelings about work itself. And that in turn can adversely affect productivity and performance. Employees who felt they could have a full career with their company were far more motivated to contribute (91 per cent) than those who did not see a future there (48 per cent).[62]

Directional strategies

As discussed earlier in this chapter, strategic typologies are useful for classifying the ways in which different organisations seek to compete within an industry. However, it is also necessary to understand how increasing size (growth) or decreasing it (downsizing) affects the HR function. For example, the top management team might decide that they need to invest more in product development or to diversify as a means for growth. With these types of strategies, it is more useful for the HR function to aid in evaluating the feasibility of the various alternatives and to develop programs that support the strategic choice.

Companies have used four possible categories of directional strategies to meet objectives.[63] Strategies emphasising market share or operating costs are considered 'concentration' strategies. With this type of strategy, a company is attempting to focus on what it does best within its established markets and it can be thought of as 'sticking to its knitting'. Strategies focusing on market development, product development, innovation or joint ventures make up the 'internal growth' strategy. Companies with an internal growth strategy are channelling their resources towards building on existing strengths. Those attempting to integrate vertically or horizontally or to diversify are exhibiting an 'external growth' strategy, usually through mergers or acquisitions. This strategy attempts to expand a company's resources or to strengthen its market position through acquiring or creating new businesses. Finally, a 'divestment', or downsizing, strategy is one made up of retrenchment, divestitures or liquidation. These strategies are observed among companies facing serious economic difficulties and seeking to pare down their operations. The human resource implications of each of these strategies are quite different.

Concentration strategies

A concentration strategy focuses on increasing market share, reducing costs or creating and maintaining a market niche for products and services. Concentration strategies require companies to maintain the current skills that exist in their organisations. Thus,

Concentration strategy
a strategy focusing on increasing market share, reducing costs or creating and maintaining a market niche for products and services.

training programs are provided as a means of keeping those skills sharp among people in the organisation and compensation programs focus on retaining the people who have those skills. Appraisals in this strategy tend to be more behavioural, because the environment is more certain and the behaviours necessary for effective performance tend to be established through extensive experience.

Internal growth strategies

> **Internal growth strategy**
> a focus on new market and product development, innovation and joint ventures.

An internal growth strategy focuses on new market and product development, innovation and joint ventures. Internal growth strategies present unique staffing problems. Growth requires a company to constantly hire, transfer and promote individuals; and expansion into different markets may change the necessary skills that prospective employees must have. In addition, appraisals often consist of a combination of behaviours and results. The behavioural appraisal emphasis stems from the knowledge of effective behaviours in a particular product market, and the results appraisals focus on achieving growth goals. Compensation packages are heavily weighted toward incentives for achieving growth goals. Training needs differ depending on the way the company attempts to grow internally. For example, if the organisation seeks to expand its markets, training will focus on knowledge of each market, particularly when the company is expanding into international markets. On the other hand, when the company is seeking innovation or product development, training will be of a more technical nature, as well as focusing on interpersonal skills such as team building. Joint ventures require extensive training in conflict resolution techniques because of the problems associated with combining people from two distinct organisational cultures.

External growth strategies

> **External growth strategy**
> an emphasis on acquiring vendors and suppliers or buying businesses that allow a company to expand into new markets.

An external growth strategy places an emphasis on acquiring vendors and suppliers or buying businesses that allow a company to expand into new markets.

Increasingly we see external growth strategies, such as consolidation within industries and mergers across industries. For example, British Petroleum's agreement to merge with Amoco Oil represents a consolidation, or reduction, in the number of firms within the industry. On the other hand, Citicorp's merger with Traveller's Group to form Citigroup represents firms from different industries (pure financial services and insurance) combining to change the dynamics within both. Whatever the type, one thing is for sure—mergers and acquisitions are on the increase and HR needs to be involved.

According to a report by the Conference Board, 'people issues' may be one of the major reasons that mergers do not always live up to expectations. Some companies now heavily weigh firm cultures before embarking on a merger or acquisition. For example, prior to acquiring ValueRx, executives at Express Scripts Inc. interviewed senior executives and middle managers at ValueRx in order to get a sense of its culture.[64] In spite of this, less than one-third of the HR executives surveyed said that they had a major influence in how mergers are planned, yet 80 per cent of them said that people issues have a significant impact after the deals are finalised.[65]

In addition to the desirability of HR playing a role in evaluating a merger opportunity, HR certainly has a role in the actual implementation of a merger or acquisition. Training in conflict resolution is also necessary when companies engage in an external growth strategy. All the options for external growth consist of acquiring or developing 'new' businesses and these businesses often have distinct cultures. Thus, many HR programs face problems in integrating and standardising practices across all the company's businesses. The relative value of standardising practices across businesses must be weighed against the unique environmental requirements of each business and the extent of desired integration of the two firms. For example, with regard to pay practices, a company may desire a consistent internal wage structure to maintain employee perceptions of equity in the larger organisation. In a recent 'new' business developed by IBM, the employees pressured the company to maintain the same wage structure as IBM's main operation. However, some businesses may function in environments where pay practices are driven heavily by market forces. Requiring these businesses to adhere to pay practices in other environments may result in an ineffective wage structure.

Communication that is honest and transparent has been found to be critical during the period prior to a merger and during the integration process. When St George Bank and Advance Bank merged in 1997, two hotlines were set up so that HR could answer specific individual questions on one line and anonymous questions could be asked on the other line. In addition, a twice-weekly bulletin that included these questions and answers was published. PricewaterhouseCoopers used a different approach when it was formed, following a merger. Almost 70 per cent of its staff were working off-site, so email was used extensively (as well as telephone surveys and organised focus groups) to explore employee concerns.[66]

It is also necessary for senior management to decide at the beginning of the process of the integration of two organisations whether the change is a merger or a takeover. When it is a merger, senior management must provide leadership regarding the culture and be clear about the skills wanted for the new company and the structure of the new entity, particularly when decisions are made on which staff are to remain. Westacott argues that an organisation's competitive advantage comes from its corporate memory and its staff competency. 'The biggest advantage of blending cultures is it can make a new organisation stronger and have a greater competitive advantage than the two companies prior to the merger.' He argues these advantages can be lost if one of the companies becomes dominant or one has mass staff reductions. This occurred when the pharmaceutical companies Ciba Geigy and Sandoz merged worldwide in 1997–98 to form Novartis, and Sandoz became the dominant firm and culture of the new organisation. There were no senior managers from the old Ciba Geigy within 18 months.[67]

Downsizing

Of increasing importance to organisations in today's competitive environment is HRM's role in downsizing or 'rightsizing'. Downsizing refers to the planned elimination of large numbers of personnel, designed to enhance organisational effectiveness. In Australia, 'downsizing' was the most significant change affecting workplaces during the 1990s. Although it is difficult obtaining data on downsizing it is known that by the mid 1990s, more than one in two organisations—in both the public and private sectors—experienced some form of downsizing.[68] Between 1986–97, there were 3.3 million workers retrenched, of which nearly 2 million were blue-collar males.[69] However, during the 1990s, middle managers experienced the impact of downsizing as organisations focused on core activities, outsourced many other activities and rationalised administrative areas and hierarchies.[70]

The number of organisations undergoing downsizing in the United States also increased significantly. In fact, between 1988–93, there were 1.4 million executives, managers and administrators laid off during downsizing, compared with only 782 000 in the period 1976–81.[71] Figure 2.6 overleaf lists some major company downsizings, as well as statements from the companies' annual reports about the reasons behind the downsizings.

Downsizing
the planned elimination of large numbers of personnel, designed to enhance organisational effectiveness.

PART 1   Managing the Human Resource Environment

FIGURE 2.6 Company downsizings and reasons given

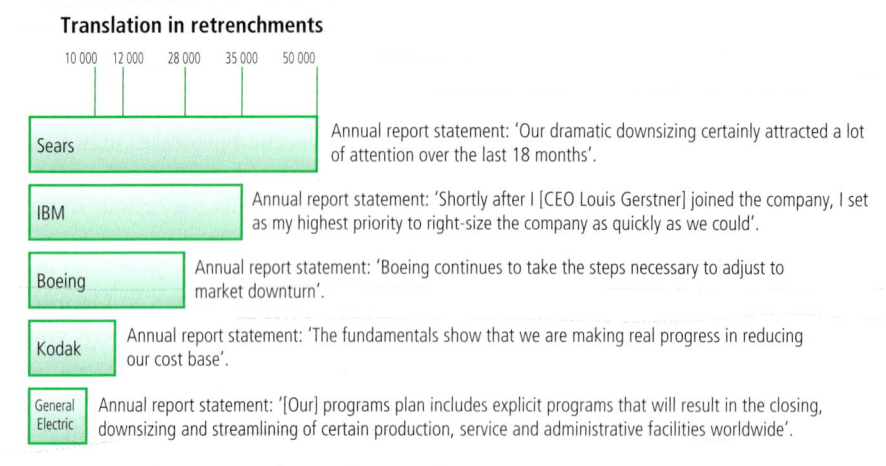

Translation in retrenchments

Company	Retrenchments	Annual report statement
Sears	50 000	'Our dramatic downsizing certainly attracted a lot of attention over the last 18 months'.
IBM	35 000	'Shortly after I [CEO Louis Gerstner] joined the company, I set as my highest priority to right-size the company as quickly as we could'.
Boeing	28 000	'Boeing continues to take the steps necessary to adjust to market downturn'.
Kodak	12 000	'The fundamentals show that we are making real progress in reducing our cost base'.
General Electric	10 000	'[Our] programs plan includes explicit programs that will result in the closing, downsizing and streamlining of certain production, service and administrative facilities worldwide'.

Source: Adapted from 1994, 'Bumstead, you're downsized!', *Time*, 143 (6), 18 April, p. 22.

In spite of the increasing frequency of downsizing, research reveals that it is far from being a universally successful way of achieving the goals of increased productivity and increased profitability. For example, a survey conducted by the American Management Association (AMA), indicated that only about one-third of the companies that went through downsizings actually achieved their goal of increased productivity. Another survey by the AMA found that over two-thirds of the companies that downsize repeat the effort a year later.[72] Research by the American consulting firm Mitchell and Company also found that companies that downsized during the 1980s lagged behind the industry average stock price in 1991.[73]

Similar findings have been made in Australia. Research reveals that organisations do not increase productivity simply by retrenching employees.[74] When downsizing is a consequence of a strategic initiative, such as job redesign, it is possible that performance will increase; however, this is unlikely when downsizing drives job redesign.[75] The 'Managing challenges of globalisation: Jobs for sale in a free-trade world' case illustrates how outsourcing to India has and will continue to be undertaken as a strategic way of downsizing.

Downsizing has an impact on those employees still remaining in the organisation. These employees have been found to develop a 'bunker' mentality, reflected in decreased job satisfaction, decreased staff morale, decreased commitment, decreased motivation, and increased concern about job security and lack of promotion opportunities.[76] Thus, it is important to understand the best ways in which to manage downsizings, particularly from the standpoint of the HR function's role.

Downsizing presents a number of challenges and opportunities for HRM. In terms of challenges, the HR function must 'surgically' reduce the workforce by cutting only the workers who are less valuable in their performance. Achieving this is difficult because the best workers are most able (and often willing) to find alternative employment and may leave voluntarily prior to any layoff.

Early retirement programs, although humane, essentially reduce the workforce with a 'grenade' approach. This type of reduction does not distinguish between good and poor performers; it eliminates an entire group of employees. In fact, recent research indicates that when companies downsize by offering early retirement programs, they usually end up rehiring to replace essential talent within a year. Often the company does not achieve its cost-cutting goals because it spends

JOBS FOR SALE IN A FREE-TRADE WORLD

MANAGING CHALLENGES OF GLOBALISATION

Economic prosperity in recent years had blunted the impact of business process outsourcing—the transfer of a wide range of helpdesk and back-office services to low cost centres, mostly in Asia—but with interest rates rising and fuel prices biting, that is likely to change.

The Organisation for Economic Co-operation and Development last year warned that one in five of Australia's 10 million jobs could be exported if cost alone were the criteria. In the finance sector alone the carnage could amount to 86 per cent of jobs.

Last week unions representing bank workers sounded the alarm that Australia's oldest bank, Westpac, was moving to outsource 485 jobs from a processing centre in western Sydney. The Finance Sector Union warned that by processing customers' confidential financial data offshore, Australian privacy and consumer protection laws would not apply.

But the real concern is jobs. As the business environment becomes ever more competitive, a Who's Who of Australian companies—including Qantas, Woolworths, Telstra and the Commonwealth Bank—have either embarked on or are seriously considering major outsourcing programs. The Finance Sector Union estimates 40 000 to 50 000 jobs could be lost to India and other developing countries, where labour costs are as little as a tenth of those in Australia.

'It's largely a business decision. You would not outsource if it did not make sense.' Call centre work is exposing thousands of young Indians to modern business practices, and paying good salaries by local standards she (Minal Varma) argues.

Outsourcing has been the driver of an economic renaissance in India, currently the world's second-fastest growing economy. In Gurgaon, where Varma's company Genpact, is based, gleaming office blocks, apartment buildings and shopping centres are sprouting up amid dusty bazaars where camels still plod.

… It began a decade ago with big companies subcontracting software engineering to cheaper engineers in India. Now young Indian workers are managing foreigners' bank accounts and completing their tax returns, booking hotel and airline reservations, analysing their medical CAT scans, and even monitoring security camera feeds transmitted over the Internet

Opponents of outsourcing have coined the term 'cyber collie' to describe these Indian workers, evoking images of neo-colonial exploitation akin to 'blackbirding'. Customer service representatives at Genpact adopt foreign accents—even foreign names such as Ralph and Lisa—in order not to alienate their Australian customers.

But to Varma such criticisms ignore the benefits that outsourcing is bringing to a new generation in India, where more than 550 million people are under 25 years of age and desperately want work

And India's winners are aware of new challenges over the horizon. China, Vietnam, the Phillipines, and even former Eastern Bloc countries such as Roumania, hope to steal a slice of global business with enormous growth potential.

Source: C. Kremmer, 2006, 'Jobs for sale in a free-trade world', *The Sydney Morning Herald*, 19–20 August, p. 12.

50–150 per cent of the departing employee's salary in hiring and retraining new workers.[77]

Another HR challenge is to boost the morale of employees who remain after the reduction. This is discussed in greater detail in Chapter 5 Industrial relations. Survivors may feel guilt over keeping their jobs when their friends have been laid off or they may envy their friends who have retired with attractive severance and pension benefits. Their reduced satisfaction with and commitment to the organisation may interfere with work performance. Thus, the HR function must maintain open communication with remaining employees to build their trust and commitment. This means all employees should be informed of the purpose of the downsizing, the costs to be cut, the duration of the downsizing and the strategies to be pursued, rather than withholding information.[78] In addition, companies going through downsizing often develop compensation programs that tie the individual's compensation to the company's success. Employee ownership programs often result from downsizing and gainsharing plans—such as the Scanlon plan (discussed in Chapter 14 Performance-related pay), which originated in companies facing economic difficulties.

In spite of these challenges, downsizing provides opportunities for HRM. First, it often allows the company to 'get rid of dead wood' and make way for fresh ideas. In addition, downsizing is often a unique opportunity to change an organisation's culture. In firms characterised by antagonistic labour-management relations, downsizing can force the parties to cooperate and develop new, positive relationships.[79] Finally, downsizing can demonstrate to top-management decision makers the value of the company's human resources to achieve its ultimate success. The role of HRM is to effectively manage the process in a way that makes this value undeniable. We discuss the implications of downsizing as a labour-force management strategy in Chapter 5 Industrial relations.

Strategy evaluation and control

A final component to the strategic management process is that of strategy evaluation and control. So far we have focused on the planning and implementation of strategy. However, it is extremely important for the firm to constantly monitor the effectiveness of both the strategy and the implementation process. This monitoring makes it possible for the company to identify problem areas and either revise existing structures and strategies or devise new ones. In this process we see emergent strategies appear as well as recognise the critical nature of human resources in competitive advantage.

There is increasing interest in evaluating the contribution of human resource activities to the operation of an organisation. Chapter 18 considers in greater detail the approaches and techniques that can be used to evaluate HR effectiveness. It also suggests ways in which effectiveness could be improved.

'Managing challenges through HR innovation: Measure for measure' provides some insights into ways HR policies can be evaluated.

The role of human resources in providing strategic competitive advantage

Thus far we have presented the strategic management process as including a step-by-step procedure through which HR issues are raised prior to deciding on a strategy and then HR practices are developed to implement that strategy. However, we must note that human resources can provide a strategic competitive advantage in two additional ways: through 'emergent strategies' and through 'enhancing firm competitiveness'.

Emergent strategies

Having discussed the process of strategic management, we also must distinguish between 'intended strategies' and 'emergent strategies'. Most people think of strategies as being proactive, rational decisions aimed towards some predetermined goal. The view of strategy we have presented so far in the chapter focuses on intended strategies. *Intended strategies* are the result of the rational decision-making process used by top-level managers as they develop a strategic plan. This is consistent with the definition of *strategy* as 'the pattern or plan that integrates an organisation's major goals, policies and action sequences into a cohesive whole'.[80] The idea of emergent strategies is evidenced by the feedback loop in Figure 2.1 on page 57.

Most strategies that companies espouse are intended strategies. For example, when Compaq was founded, the company had its strategy summarised in its name, an amalgam of the words computer, compact and quality. Thus, the intended strategy was to build compact portable computers that were completely free of any defects and all

MEASURE FOR MEASURE

MANAGING CHALLENGES THROUGH HR INNOVATION

Question: People tell me it's hard to convince their CEO or executive that they need to get involved in scorecards, number and data. How do you get them to pay attention to that?

In my experience, the first issue is not to position measurement as an HR initiative, but to think about how we execute on the firm's business model, how do we win our future—what kinds of strategic capabilities do we need to win? If we're a pharmaceutical company or make tyres for cars, what's the bundle of resources we need to win in the eyes of our most profitable customers?

Then we begin to ask—given this bundle of logistics, distribution, people, whatever it is—what are the key or 'A' jobs, the strategically critical jobs? Maybe it's an R & D scientist, maybe it's a sales force manager.

Then ask, how does the behaviour of the people differ there? For example, in sales teams, an 80th or 90th percentile salesperson might sell 10 times as much as an average person. That would be a strategically critical job, with a lot of variance in performance. For management, that's a huge opportunity to drive the execution of strategy through the workforce.

In this case, managers should be asking; if there's a lot of variation in the sales force, why is that and how can we improve that?

My next question would be: how do we attract, select, develop, retain, coach and mentor those salespeople so we can move the 50th percentile people to the 75th percentile (or better)? That's a very different kind of story than 'let's measure HR', because its focus is on solving [a] very specific business problem that is directly linked to the performance of the business.

Downstream, it takes you into how to select, develop and retain, but it's a top-down strategy as opposed to bottom-up. In my experience, senior leaders will pay rapt attention to that kind of story because that's how they win.

Source: S. Moore talks to academic consultant M. Huselid about the metrics of proving HR's value, 2006, *HR Monthly*, February, p. 39.

---

of the company's efforts were directed towards implementing that strategy. Following the strategy allowed Compaq to become one of the fastest-growing companies in the world, commanding 20 per cent of the world market in 1991. In 1992, Compaq's performance began to falter again, sparking new CEO, Eckhard Pfieffer, to change Compaq's strategy to focus on being a low-cost producer. This strategic change resulted in Compaq becoming the leading PC maker in the world in 1994.[81]

Emergent strategies, on the other hand, consist of the strategies that evolve from the grassroots of the organisation and can be thought of as what organisations actually do, as opposed to what they intend to do. Strategy can also be thought of as 'a pattern in a stream of decisions or actions'.[82] For example, when Honda Motor Company first entered the United States' market with its 250 cc and 305 cc motorcycles in 1959, it believed that no market existed for its smaller 50 cc bikes. However, the sales on the larger motorcycles were sluggish and Japanese executives running errands around Los Angeles on Honda 50 cc bikes attracted a lot of attention, including that of a buyer with Sears. Honda found a previously undiscovered market as well as a new distribution outlet (general retailers) that it had not planned on. This emergent strategy resulted in Honda having a 50 per cent market share by 1964.[83]

The distinction between intended and emergent strategies has important implications for human resource management. The new focus on strategic HRM has tended to focus primarily on intended strategies. Thus, HRM's role has been seen as identifying, for top management, the people-related business issues relevant to strategy formulation and then developing HR systems that aid in the implementation of the strategic plan.

However, most emergent strategies are identified by those lower in the organisational hierarchy. It is often the 'rank and file' employees who provide ideas for new markets, new products and new strategies. Human resource management plays an important role in facilitating communication throughout the organisation and it is this communication that allows for effective emergent strategies to make their way up to top management. This fact led Philip Caldwell, Ford's chairman in the early 1980s, to state: 'It's stupid to deny yourself the intellectual capability and constructive attitude of tens of thousands of workers'.[84]

Enhancing firm competitiveness

A related way in which human resources can be a source of competitive advantage is through developing a human-capital pool that provides the company with the unique ability to adapt to an ever-changing environment. Recently, managers have become interested in the idea of a 'learning organisation', in which people continually expand their capacity to achieve the results they desire.[85] This requires the company to be in a constant state of learning through monitoring the environment, assimilating information, making decisions and flexibly restructuring to compete in that environment. Characteristics of learning organisations are discussed in Chapter 11 Learning and development. Companies that develop such learning capability have a competitive advantage. Although certain organisational information processing systems can be an aid, ultimately the people (human capital) who make up the company provide the raw materials in a learning organisation.

The human-capital pool—that is, the individual capabilities, knowledge, skills, experience and problem-solving abilities of people in an organisation—can be developed in a variety of ways. At Oticon in Denmark, knowledge workers have no fixed job descriptions, but they work entirely on a project basis; while Buckman Labs has created a knowledge transfer department, with employees gaining both financial rewards and management positions for excelling at knowledge positions. Morgan Bank and the Canadian Imperial Bank of Commerce have reorganised their recruiting and training practices around knowledge competencies, rather than traditional job descriptions. The human-capital pool is one of three important contributors to the intellectual capital of an organisation. With structural capital and customer capital, the human-capital pool is increasingly being recognised as the basis of value creation in organisations.[86]

Thus, the role of human resources in competitive advantage should continue to increase because of the fast-paced change characterising today's business environment. Although United States' automakers have increased the quality of their cars to compete with the Japanese automakers, these competitors have clearly developed such flexible and adaptable manufacturing systems that they can respond to customer needs more quickly.[87] This flexibility of the manufacturing process allows the emergent strategy to come directly from the marketplace by determining and responding to the exact mix of customer desires. It requires, however, that the company has people in place who have the skills to, similarly, adapt quickly.[88] As George Walker, president of Delta Wire, in the United States, stated, 'Anyone can come in and buy machines like I have. The difference is the knowledge of your workers'.[89] This statement exemplifies the increasing importance of human resources in developing and maintaining competitive advantage.[90]

Strategy as implementation

Strategic decisions are important, they involve considerable commitment of resources, they are not easily reversible [91] and they are taken in conditions of uncertainty. The management of strategic change can be very difficult. HR initiatives are able to assist with strategic change, not only through the development of HR policies discussed previously, but also by developing implementation strategies. These strategies can include cultural change strategies, organisational learning strategies[92] and knowledge management theories.

This view of strategy moves HR activities beyond those activities which could be regarded as operational. It places more emphasis on the internal factors of the organisation and examines the processes involved in strategy formulation. These processes include the exercise of power and political processes, the creation and transfer of knowledge and learning and social dynamics between individuals and groups.

Strategic human resource executives

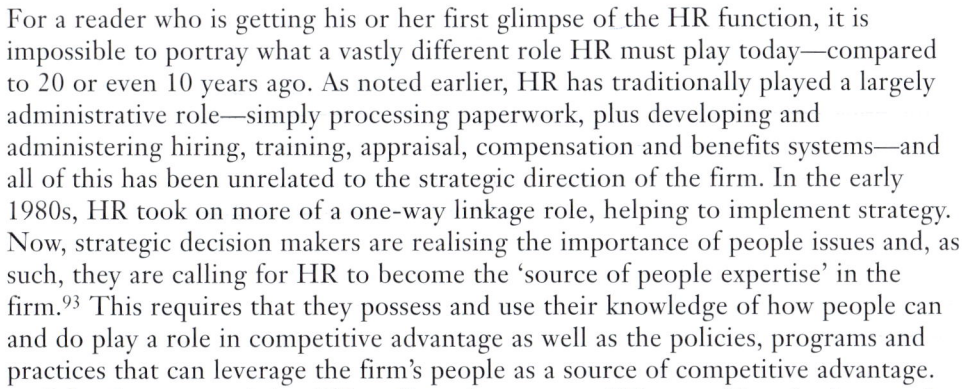

For a reader who is getting his or her first glimpse of the HR function, it is impossible to portray what a vastly different role HR must play today—compared to 20 or even 10 years ago. As noted earlier, HR has traditionally played a largely administrative role—simply processing paperwork, plus developing and administering hiring, training, appraisal, compensation and benefits systems—and all of this has been unrelated to the strategic direction of the firm. In the early 1980s, HR took on more of a one-way linkage role, helping to implement strategy. Now, strategic decision makers are realising the importance of people issues and, as such, they are calling for HR to become the 'source of people expertise' in the firm.[93] This requires that they possess and use their knowledge of how people can and do play a role in competitive advantage as well as the policies, programs and practices that can leverage the firm's people as a source of competitive advantage.

It has been argued that HR staff need to operate HR more like a business and define specific outcomes that they deliver to the business.[94] In order to become like a business, HR will need to have clear strategies, outcomes, products, services and structures so that the HR staff can achieve their goals and deliver the necessary outcomes. Human resource staff can do this by fulfilling four management roles, as we discussed in Chapter 1 Human resource management in Australia. These roles are:

1 strategic human resources role, which aligns HR and business strategy and delivers the execution of strategy
2 management of firm infrastructure role, which reengineers organisation processes and builds an efficient infrastructure
3 management of employee contribution role, which requires listening and responding to employees so that employee commitment and capability is increased
4 transformation and change role, which requires ensuring the organisation has the capacity for change and delivers a renewed organisation.[95]

The availability of technology is facilitating the transformation of the HR function. The Cranet-Macquarie Survey on international strategic human resource management found almost two-thirds of organisations had computerised HR information systems (HRIS) and 29 per cent of the HRIS were primarily interfaced or integrated into a wider management information system. In almost all organisations, the HRIS were used for individual personnel records and payroll.[96]

These developments lead to an entirely new set of competencies for today's strategic HR executive. Human resource executives will increasingly require a range of sophisticated abilities, such as the strategic capabilities of a management consultant, the financial literacy of a business manager, the understandings of operational management that are required of a business services manager and the personal attributes of assertiveness, drive, resilience and a problem solving mentality.[97]

In the future, HR professionals will need four basic competencies to become partners in the strategic-management process[98] (see Figure 2.7 below). First, they will need to have *business competence*—knowing the company's business and understanding its economic and financial capabilities. This calls for making logical decisions that support the company's strategic plan based on the most accurate information possible. In almost all companies the effectiveness of decisions must be evaluated in terms of dollar values; as such, the HR executive must be able to calculate the costs and benefits of each alternative in terms of its dollar impact.[99] In addition, the effectiveness of decisions requires that the non-monetary impact be considered. The HR executive must be fully capable of identifying the social and ethical issues attached to its HR practices. Human resource professionals will need to have a high level of knowledge about the external business world. They will need to know about the marketplace, competitive dynamics, customer requirements, industry shifts, changes in the regulatory environments and so on.[100]

Second, HR professionals will need *professional and technical knowledge* of state-of-the-art HR practices in areas such as staffing, development, rewards, organisational design and communication. New selection techniques, performance appraisal methods, training programs and incentive plans are constantly being developed. Some of these programs can provide value, while others may be no more than the products of today's HR equivalent of snake oil. The HR executive must be able to critically evaluate the new techniques offered as state-of-the-art HR programs and use only those that will benefit the company.

Third, they must be skilled in the *management of change processes*, such as diagnosing problems, implementing organisational changes and evaluating results. Every time a company changes its strategy, even in a minor way, the entire company has to change. These changes result in conflict, resistance and confusion

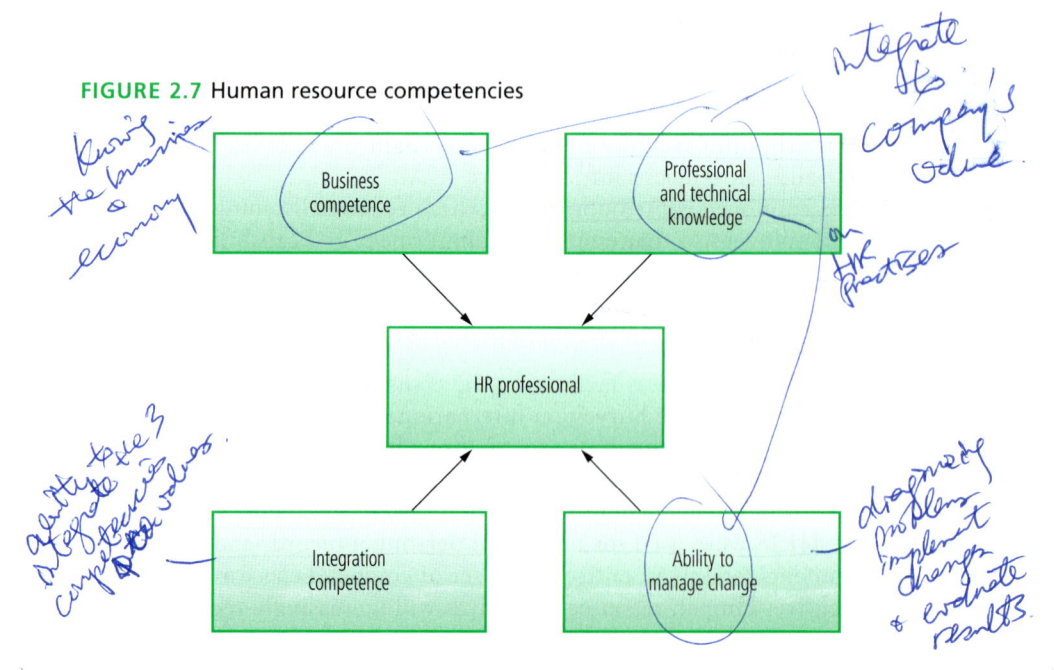

FIGURE 2.7 Human resource competencies

among the people who must implement the new plans or programs. The HR executive must have the skills to oversee the change in a way that ensures its success. In Australia, the management of change was identified by HR executives as the major challenge confronting HR in the first few years of the twenty-first century.[101] In the United States, one survey of Fortune 500 companies found that 87 per cent of the companies had their organisation development/change function as part of the HR department.[102] In Australia, nearly one-third of human resource managers believed change had not been implemented properly in their organisations. Change was more successfully implemented in circumstances where human resource professionals had been involved in developing the vision of the organisation, strategic planning, the change required and where the HR manager was well paid and reported directly to the CEO. Most HR managers, however, still view their role as managing cultures and internal communications.[103]

Finally, these professionals must also have *integration competence*, meaning the ability to integrate the three other competencies to increase the company's value. This requires that, although specialist knowledge is necessary, a generalist perspective must be taken in making decisions. This entails seeing how all the functions within the HR area fit together to be effective and recognising that changes in any one part of the HR package are likely to require changes in other parts of the package. For example, a healthcare company in central Texas was attempting to fill a position in the X-ray department. It was able to identify qualified candidates for the position, but none of the candidates accepted the offer. It was not until the company examined its total package (pay, benefits, promotion opportunities, etc.) and changed the composition of the package that it was able to fill the position. In Australia, this integration has been achieved in ACTEW (Canberra's electricity, water and sewerage authority) by restructuring the HR department and a 'total overhaul of the HR policies and practices'. Human resource practitioners in ACTEW became advisers to line managers with the mission of helping these managers achieve their goals. The overhaul of HR policies and practices involved measures such as improving communication between management and employees, introducing performance management and training, and changing remuneration and benefits by overhauling the competency pay structure and introducing one award to replace the many awards that operated previously.[104]

The new strategic role for HR presents both opportunities and challenges. These include forming a series of partnerships with senior executives, line managers and external providers of HR services.[105] The area of HR has the chance to profoundly impact the way in which organisations compete through people. On the other hand, with this opportunity comes serious responsibility and accountability. Human resource functions of the future must consist of individuals who view themselves as business people who happen to work in a HR function, rather than HR people who happen to work in a business. It has been claimed the 'HR executive is one part management "guru", one part CEO, and one part functional expert'.[106] In order to do this, many HR practitioners will need to move out of their comfort zones and be more comfortable with change.[107]

MANAGING PEOPLE

ASIA TO OUTGROW THE WORLD

In one respect, the future of Asia is clear. It will continue to outgrow the rest of the world and its weight in the world economy will correspondingly rise.

Assuming China grows at eight per cent annually and the United States at four per cent over the next few decades, China will overtake the United States to become the world's largest economy in either less than 20 years or just after mid century, depending upon how you measure gross domestic product (GDP)—at so-called purchasing power parity exchange rates sooner, and at market exchange rates later.

Meanwhile, the share of world GDP produced by Asia as a whole, which has doubled to 30 per cent since World War II, should continue to climb.

What are the grounds for thinking this will happen?

- The enormous potential for technological catch-up.
- Favourable demographics—apart from sheer size of population, China has 2.35 workers for every dependant.
- Vast untapped supplies of rural labour—perhaps 600 million people in China alone.
- Continuing integration of regional economies into global supply chains.

All these factors should turbo-charge growth for at least another 20–23 years.

Trade—within Asia and between Asia and the rest of the world—is likely to undergo greater expansion and transformation than production. Over the 1975–2001 period, East Asia's share of world exports more than tripled to 19 per cent, and over the 1985–2001 period, it doubled. Meanwhile, intra-regional exports (expressed as a share of world trade) went up more sharply, rising six-fold over the 1975–2001 period.

The emergence of China in trade statistics is particularly striking. Its share of world exports has risen from 1.6 per cent in 1985 to 6.5 per cent in 2001. A lot of these exports have been generated from the assembly of parts and components made in other Asian countries. So, as Chinese exports have soared, so have regional exports to China. Over the 1985–2001 period, East Asia's exports to China grew at 11.5 per cent annually, far above the 3.8 per cent annual rate for world trade.

Although the region's growth will probably be rapid, it is unlikely to be smooth. Profound economic transformations are always accompanied by 'gales of creative destruction' in which the structure as well as scale of economies changes out of recognition. Another important structural shift now underway is the 'emergence of the Asian consumer' and a corresponding decline in the traditional export bias of economies.

At least 140 million affluent consumers have emerged in East Asia, according to the Japan External Trade Organisation (JETRO). Their willingness to spend more than their thrifty parents on everything from mobile phones to PCs to home renovations, is fuelling enormous growth in consumer outlays—prompting JETRO to warn Japanese companies to adapt or lose out to overseas competition.

A third structural shift is the relative economic decline of Japan. Japan will remain a major, if not pre-eminent, export market for other Asian economies for decades to come. The slippage, however, in the share of East Asia's exports going to Japan—almost seven percentage points over the 1985–2001 period—is likely to continue as Japan's growth rate lags behind more youthful, less-developed economies.

Setbacks and crises are also quite likely to occur along the path to further development. As the saying goes, 'Those who don't study the past will repeat its error again soon. Those who study it will find other ways to err'.

Source: Based on R. Donnelly, 2003, 'Asia 2004: Asia to outgrow the world', *Asia Today International*, 21 (5), October–November, pp. 12–13.

QUESTIONS

1. Discuss some of the changes—such as economic, social, labour market and political changes—that are predicted to occur in the Asian region in the next 15 years.
2. What are the possible consequences for Australian organisations, particularly organisations doing business in the Asian region?
3. What are some of the consequences of the predicted developments for human resource management in Australia and in organisations doing business in the Asian region?
4. Discuss the impact of these predicted changes on the role of the human resource manager.

CHAPTER SUMMARY

A strategic approach to human resource management seeks to proactively provide a competitive advantage through the company's most important asset: its human resources. The HR function needs to be integrally involved in the formulation of strategy to identify the people-related business issues the company faces. After the strategy has been determined, HRM has a profound impact on the implementation of the plan by developing and aligning HR practices that ensure that the company has motivated employees with the necessary skills. Finally, the emerging strategic role of the HR function requires that HR professionals in the future develop business, professional and technical, change management and integration competencies. As you will see more clearly in later chapters, this strategic approach requires more than simply developing a valid selection procedure or state-of-the-art performance management systems. Only through these competencies can the HR professional take a strategic approach to human resource management.

WEB EXERCISES

This chapter emphasised that for companies to gain a competitive advantage they must integrate HRM into the company's business strategy. Go to Honeywell's home page at www.honeywell.com.

Questions
1. What types of businesses is the company involved in?
2. What is the company's growth and productivity strategy?
3. What are the implications of the company's growth and productivity strategy for how the company manages its human resources? Make sure you describe the implications for recruitment and selection, training, performance management and compensation.

DISCUSSION QUESTIONS

1. Pick one of your favourite sports teams (for example, netball, football or cricket). How would you characterise that team's generic strategy? How does the composition of the team members (in terms of size, speed, ability etc.) relate to that strategy? What are the strengths and weaknesses of the team? How do the strengths and weaknesses dictate the team's generic strategy and its approach to a particular game?
2. Do you think that it is easier to tie human resources to the strategic management process in large or small organisations? Why?
3. Consider some of the organisations you have been affiliated with. What are some examples of human resource practices that were consistent with that organisation's strategy? What are examples of practices that were inconsistent with its strategy?
4. How can strategic management within the HR department ensure that HR plays an effective role in the company's strategic management process?
5. What types of specific skills (for example, knowledge of financial accounting methods) do you think HR professionals will need in order to have the business, professional and technical, change management and integrative competencies necessary in the future? Where can you seek to develop each of these skills?
6. What are some of the key environmental variables that you see changing in the business world today? What impact will those changes have on the HR function in organisations?

CASE STUDY

PLANNING FOR THE FUTURE

In the face of a growing skills shortage, ageing population and changing of the generational guard at work, workforce planning is key to ensuring the long-term success of many organisations. Melissa Yen reports.

How many fully qualified people will you need in the future? What strategies can you implement to attract, retain and motivate your people so that your organisation can fulfil its longer-term strategic growth plan? Such questions are central to workforce planning. However, getting these questions addressed at the executive level is still a challenge for some HR professionals.

Despite such challenges, the current economic environment has pressed many companies to consider workforce planning as a key strategic component of business. A long period of economic growth has presented a range of issues for HR professionals, according to Peter Murphy, principal of Noetic Solutions. The impact of the Federal Government's new industrial relations laws, the rising cost of key commodities such as oil and a less favourable interest rate environment are all taken into account when it comes to the strategic end of workforce planning, he says.

Underlying all this is an increasing awareness of the looming skills shortages and the threat of a rapidly depleting workforce. 'The ageing population has raised the appetite for workforce planning in Australian boardrooms, as directors and C-level executives realise that they have a significant problem looming in the short term. Some organisations are actually actively conducting the process, others considering how to go about it', according to Lyle Potgieter, CEO of IXP3 Human Capital.

The challenges of implementation

Rolling out an integrated and strategic workforce planning initiative is no easy task. 'Achieving alignment with key business needs and issues remains a perennial challenge for HR professionals and organisations trying to get workforce planning initiatives going', says Murphy. 'Being able to get people to think about more than just today's HR problems and think strategically is a challenge.'

One of the greatest challenges HR professionals also face is securing senior management support and ensuring executives understand the need for workforce planning. Detailed analysis of the current workforce status along with a solid understanding of the organisation's strategic plan is critical. Working on solutions before the real problem is properly defined and understood is a mistake that occurs too often, according to Tess Walton and Stacy Chapman, directors of Aruspex. Not doing one's homework in this area leads to problems when it comes to linking business strategy needs and workforce requirements.

Overcoming challenges

It is critical that HR professionals demonstrate a solid knowledge of the business and gain an understanding from the executive level as to how workforce planning strategies will achieve desired business outcomes. 'As with any business problem, you've got to be able to demonstrate the value of what you are doing and how it is going to make the organisation's life better', Murphy says.

A business may find itself floundering and unable to execute its strategy, according to Potgieter, unless the senior executive team understand that workforce planning strategies are needed for dealing with the looming talent exit. He also urges HR professionals and senior managers alike to realise that workforce planning takes a significant time, even years.

'Put in place the infrastructure and tools you will need to implement your strategy. Many of these tools take time to gather the information you require and will also take time to implement. Without these tools, your capability to identify top talent—high potential, high performance individuals—for grooming will be significantly impaired', says Potgieter.

'HR professionals need to note that the ageing workforce issue will affect many roles in the organisation and the capability to implement your strategy without these tools will be seriously diminished.' The Board and senior management should be advised that HR requires access to the strategic plan in order to conduct meaningful workforce planning, he adds.

Establishing ROI [return on investment]

Building a business case for workforce planning has become easier due to looming workforce challenges. It is often more useful to talk to businesses about the risks they face as a result of failing to plan for a critical resource, in the form of workforce skills and competencies, according to Murphy. 'Management find it easier to understand issues when it is presented in terms of risk to the organisation. Organisations plan long term for key inputs—why not people?' he asks.

Walton and Chapman claim they have yet to find a case where ROI cannot be proved. 'Sometimes we've built the case on the basis of a history of retrenchments and rehires; sometimes it's the pain of skill shortages; sometimes it's the cost of being over- or understaffed.'

As long as one can prove that the cost of running a workforce planning initiative will be significantly less than the revenue gain, ROI should be significant, says Potgieter. If this can be backed up by facts and figures, management will appreciate this more.

'For example, let us assume you work for an organisation that employs chartered accountants. Your brief examination of the issue concludes that you will be faced with chronic and sustained shortages of chartered accountants commencing in 2008. You conclude that you expect to be short of 300 employees each year and the shortage in the worst case will be 900 people a year. This translates to a shortage of revenue of between $75 million and $225 million. If HR can put in place strategies to reduce these shortages by 30 per cent, the net gain in revenue is between $22.5 million and $67.5 million', he explains.

'Delaying commencement on this project will be detrimental to your organisation as well as your professional standing in the organisation, as executives will expect you to have the answers when this issue is discussed in the boardroom.'

Source: M. Yen, 2006, 'Planning for the Future', *Human Resources*, 30 May 2006. www.humanresourcemagazine.com.au

QUESTIONS

1 Potgieter argues that workforce planning is essential for the achievement of strategy. Identify some of the benefits of workforce planning.
2 Identify some of the limitations of workforce planning.
3 Discuss the methods and information HR professionals could use to convince the senior management team that workforce planning was a useful tool for strategic management.
4 Discuss the implications of the changing characteristics of the population and the workforce for the issues that will emerge in workforce planning.

CHAPTER 3

THE LEGAL CONTEXT FOR HUMAN RESOURCE MANAGEMENT

Suzanne Jamieson

Objectives

After reading this chapter, you should be able to:

1. Understand the legal context for human resource management (HRM) in Australia.
2. Identify the major equal employment opportunity (EEO) laws in Australia (at a federal and state level).
3. Identify the various types (or heads) of discrimination and how managers might go about preventing their occurrence.
4. Identify the forms of sexual harassment behaviours and the strategies that might be employed to prevent these behaviours.
5. Identify and discuss the essential issues involved in affirmative action laws for women in Australia.

Bullying the new battlefield

Workplace harassment will become the new battleground for sacked employees seeking financial revenge following the Howard Government's abolition of most unfair dismissal claims.

Lawyers expect a wave of claims from workers wanting compensation for alleged mistreatment, including bullying.

The courts, anti-discrimination tribunals and workers' compensation schemes are expected to experience a significant lift in cases linked to sackings.

Jane Seymour, from Australian Business Lawyers, said sacked employees would rush to alternative remedies after the Government's new laws, introduced this week, had exempted employers with fewer than 100 staff from unfair dismissal claims.

'Bullying and sexual harassment are grey areas', she said. 'As unfair dismissal dries up, they will be fertile ground for employees looking for new ways to gain compensation.'

Ms Seymour said a classic case was the awarding of $550 000 to a Queensland woman for a depressive disorder after being verbally abused by her manager. While the payout was overturned on appeal because the woman was found to have a pre-existing disorder, Ms Seymour said similar claims were inevitable, with potentially large settlements.

Last month, a security guard at News Limited, publisher of *The Weekend Australian*, who had been subjected to abusive comments such as 'coconut head' and 'monkey face', was granted $1.9 million by the NSW Supreme Court. By comparison, the maximum payment under the workers compensation scheme for the loss of both eyes is $250 000. A worker who lost a thumb would receive $35 000, plus pain and suffering capped at $50 000.

National president of the Australian Lawyers Alliance Richard Faulks said it was logical that workers denied established rights under unfair dismissal would seek alternative remedies.

Asked about potentially large payouts, he said: 'Courts recognise psychiatric injury as a serious disability.'

With unfair dismissals limited, the Australian Chamber of Commerce and Industry anticipated workers would 'test out' other mechanisms.

ACCI workplace policy director Scott Barklamb said: 'It's a reality we have to face and we would like to see it restricted.' He said employers expected awards for suffering to be 'practical, balanced and consistent with established precedent'.

Ms Seymour advised that employers should avoid bullying behaviour likely to offend or humiliate workers, such as personal abuse, physical contact or performance reviews in front of other staff. Risk factors for harassment included isolating workers, giving them unpleasant tasks or 'persistently asking if they got lucky at the weekend ... when it was made clear they didn't want to speak about it'.

Legal experts advise employers to have a complaints system in place to ensure bullying is reported and cannot be confused with 'performance management'. But some employers are expected to settle rather than go through costly court cases.

Andrew Stewart, professor of industrial law at Flinders University, predicted a big lift in common law, discrimination and unlawful termination claims. A spokesman for Workplace Relations Minister Kevin Andrews said the Government was concerned about potential misuse or legal misrepresentation.

Source: B. Norington, 2006, 'Bullying the new battlefield', *The Australian*, 1 April, p. 5.

PART 1   Managing the Human Resource Environment

Introduction

WorkChoices
the collective name for a series of amendments made to labour law by the Australian Federal Government in 2005.

State
a generic term covering not simply the government of the day, but all the other apparatus as well (including bureaucracy, judiciary, etc.).

Conciliation and arbitration system
a system whereby industrial parties are encouraged to sort out their differences by means of conciliation (with the assistance of the industrial tribunal). However, when this fails to produce a negotiated outcome, the tribunal may impose a binding decision—that is, arbitration. Sometimes this system is called compulsory conciliation and arbitration because the industrial parties must come to conciliation if the other party (or the tribunal) calls for this to happen, and any decision is binding on the parties.

It would not be an act of gross hyperbole to suggest that a seismic shift in the nature of Australian labour regulation has been brought about by the 2005 **WorkChoices** amendments to the principal federal labour legislation. This shift has occurred not just within the detail of the regulation itself but significantly in the relationship between the federal legislation and that of the states. As indicated in the opening case, there are emerging areas of concern and debate related to the legislative changes.

The degree of intervention by the **state** in the Australian workplace has always been a highly contentious matter, no less now than at the time of the adoption of the peculiarly Australasian system of **conciliation and arbitration** which came at the end of a period of huge industrial confrontation and economic downturn in 1904. While much of the debate of a century ago was about the regulation (or not) of collective relations between employers and their employees and those employees' trade unions, the legal regulation of the workplace in relation to its internal functions (that is, human resource management hereafter HRM) continues apace.[1] In an age notable for its debate around deregulation and the cost to business of regulation, there is very little real activity in reducing the levels of workplace regulation and there is no real evidence that this is about to change.[2] The sheer size of the *Workplace Relations Act 1996* after the 2005 amendments bears testimony to this. In fact, when we take into account the development of the human rights/anti-discrimination laws in Australia over the past 30 years at both a state and federal level and the increasingly complex considerations involved in issues of work safety, there is considerably more regulation that must be given more than token acknowledgement.[3] As we see below, involvement in a major anti-discrimination case can cost an organisation not just time and money but can also cost something more valuable but less tangible—the good name of the organisation. Unlike most of the other labour laws operating in the Australian workplace, the human rights laws (apart from the so-called affirmative action laws) operate on the basis of individual complaints, a concept which lends support to the view that there is a move towards individualisation in the regulation of Australian labour.[4] Added to this, we can expect globalisation to have an effect in the development of our labour laws in the future.[5]

Chapter map

Most regulation in the workplace is based on the concept that there is a one-on-one enforceable contract between the worker and the employer. This concept forms the basis of the whole employment relationship, although this has been challenged in recent years. We now see different forms of the employment relationship, including subcontracting and labour hire through so-called temp agencies that were once limited to providing additional secretarial help but now supply labour across a range of industries. Labour law has struggled to keep up with these developments.[6] What we attempt to do in this chapter is to sketch the relationship between the law and the workplace in Australia and in particular to show the way in which the law regulates the recruitment process, the ongoing relationship between the parties to the employment contract (which also includes the obligations on an employer in terms of equal employment opportunity), discrimination matters, sexual harassment issues, the ending of the relationship (whether amicably or not) and the control of the physical environment in which the relationship is played out. In all of this, the role of the

Workplace Relations Act 1996 and the controversial WorkChoices amendments of 2005 are central. In passing, several other areas of law will be alluded to in order to remind us of the complexity of the legal web in which an advanced society governed by the rule of law exists. This chapter will also involve a very short excursus into the law of the constitution and some attention to the issue of who is a worker; because just how this question is answered will dictate all kinds of other matters which are important in the HRM context, such as entitlements to superannuation and workers compensation.

Constitution
a set of rules and principles by which a body (e.g. nation or sports club) may be governed and power relations defined.

The Constitution

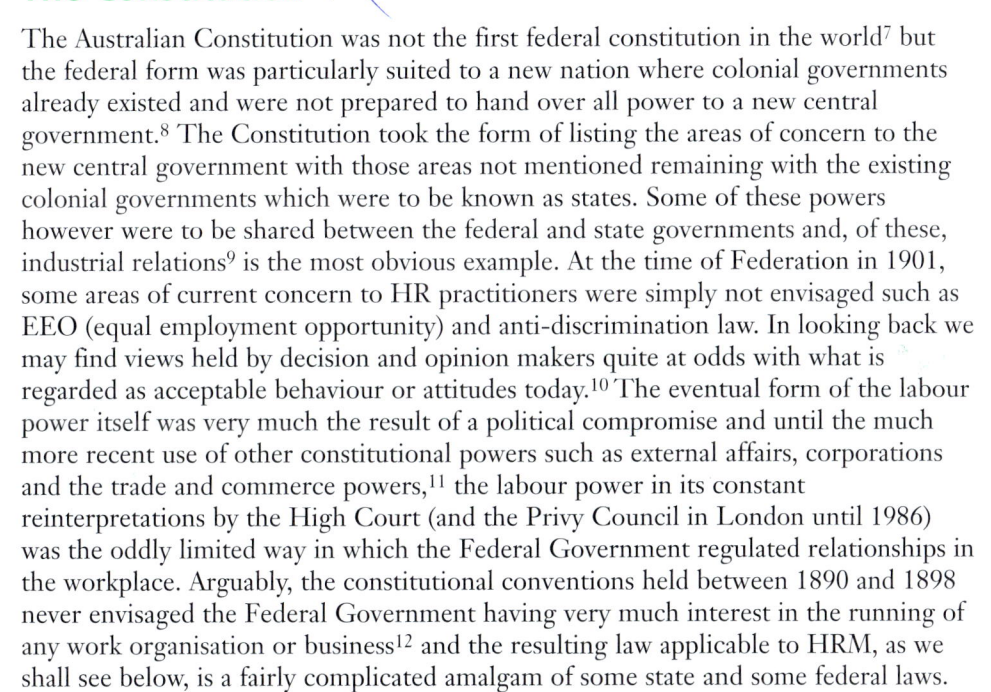

The Australian Constitution was not the first federal constitution in the world[7] but the federal form was particularly suited to a new nation where colonial governments already existed and were not prepared to hand over all power to a new central government.[8] The Constitution took the form of listing the areas of concern to the new central government with those areas not mentioned remaining with the existing colonial governments which were to be known as states. Some of these powers however were to be shared between the federal and state governments and, of these, industrial relations[9] is the most obvious example. At the time of Federation in 1901, some areas of current concern to HR practitioners were simply not envisaged such as EEO (equal employment opportunity) and anti-discrimination law. In looking back we may find views held by decision and opinion makers quite at odds with what is regarded as acceptable behaviour or attitudes today.[10] The eventual form of the labour power itself was very much the result of a political compromise and until the much more recent use of other constitutional powers such as external affairs, corporations and the trade and commerce powers,[11] the labour power in its constant reinterpretations by the High Court (and the Privy Council in London until 1986) was the oddly limited way in which the Federal Government regulated relationships in the workplace. Arguably, the constitutional conventions held between 1890 and 1898 never envisaged the Federal Government having very much interest in the running of any work organisation or business[12] and the resulting law applicable to HRM, as we shall see below, is a fairly complicated amalgam of some state and some federal laws.

While Labor governments were keen to expand the labour regulation field for the Federal Government by means of the external affairs power in particular, the extensive use of the corporations power by the conservative Coalition government in 2005 in its WorkChoices amendments to the 1996 Act, represented the biggest change in the regulation of labour in Australia since Federation. The amendments were challenged in the High Court by five of the Labor governed states and by some unions and a number of peak union bodies. A majority of the court found that the Federal Government could validly use the corporations power in the constitution to support the new workplace laws.[13] The WorkChoices amendments represent a further strengthening of the position of employers generally.

Wages and conditions

Here we must remind ourselves that while the constitutional focus has been on the federal jurisdiction and that that jurisdiction has always received the lion's share of academic attention, the wages and conditions of a very large number of Australian workers have been governed by the industrial relations machinery of the state governments. In some states, like New South Wales for example, that state jurisdiction has a distinctly gendered aspect to it as the highly female dominated occupations of teaching, nursing, clerical and retail work are all covered by state awards and agreements. In the wake of the WorkChoices case the future of the state systems must, at best, be regarded as being under a cloud.

The limited way in which the Federal Government could deal with workplace relations[14] was very largely a collective way of regulating labour and almost from the outset involved the institutional involvement of trade unions which needed to be registered to be a part of the system. Industrial **awards** were the officially recorded outcomes of the resolution of industrial disputes which were legally enforceable and usually laid down the wages and conditions which were the legal entitlements of workers covered by those awards. These entitlements covered workers who were not members of the union as well and in so doing meant that employers who were bound by these comprehensive awards could not be legally undercut by other employers.[15] More recently, certified agreements[16] have replaced awards in most workplaces and these, too, are collective in nature. Like awards they are now a very major source of wages and conditions for many workers and are also legally enforceable.[17] Only the Australian Workplace Agreements created under the *Workplace Relations Act 1996* may be individual in nature[18] and to a large extent represent a major shift in the way in which the regulation of labour is now moving from a collective to an individual model.

Awards
written determinations created by federal or state industrial tribunals, specifying the minimum terms and conditions of employment, such as hours of work, minimum pay and types of leave allowable.

HARD WORKCHOICES FOR HR

With the High Court's dismissal of the states' case against the constitutional validity of WorkChoices, there is no turning back for the Federal Government's national workplace relations system. Australian Workplace Agreements (AWAs) are central to the industrial relations reforms contained in WorkChoices, however, AWAs and their merits have been the subject of much controversy recently.

The Government and most business groups argue there is vast choice and opportunity provided to employees through AWAs. At the other end of the spectrum, unions and most academics see WorkChoices as a tool that will hand over all power to employers by providing them with the ability to effectively cut wages, benefits and dismiss staff without legal ramifications.

Concerns that many entitlements were being stripped from a majority of workplace agreements were confirmed when the Office of the Employment Advocate (OEA) announced findings from a sample analysis of 250 AWAs. Results showed that of the 6263 agreements lodged since the legislation took effect two months beforehand, 64 per cent removed annual leave loadings, 63 per cent cut penalty rates, 52 per cent cut workers' shift loadings and 40 per cent stripped workers of public holidays.

Recent data from the OEA has revealed that 129 678 employees have entered into AWAs, while 308 831 employees have signed up to collective agreements. Some employees who work for a fair-minded employer stand to reap the benefits, while others will be undervalued and undermined. However, with a tightening labour market and the realities of supply and demand, employers need to look seriously at their motives and options around WorkChoices.

Rolling out the changes

With the introduction of WorkChoices, one of the biggest challenges facing employers was assisting and advising employees on workplace agreements under the new laws, and then following through with action.

Nick Aronson, general manager of The Leasing Centre, one of Australia's largest equipment finance companies, says the first issue was in comprehending the obligations and their subsequent impact. 'There was so much negative publicity that just understanding the implications to us was a challenge. We had very carefully drafted employment agreements with all our staff and we'd been advised by our lawyers that these needed replacing with AWAs and we had no idea what that meant.'

Baker's Delight introduced both collective agreements and AWAs since the start of WorkChoices. 'After drawing up the draft of our collective agreement (CA), we sent out letters to all our existing employees clearly stipulating the reasons for introducing a

MANAGING CHALLENGES THROUGH SUSTAINABILITY

The creation of the Australian Fair Pay Commission under the WorkChoices amendments[19] allows some potentially more direct say by the government of the day in the setting of national wage minima and removes that wage setting function from the Australian Industrial Relations Commission which now has almost no wage setting powers at all.[20] These minima are now included among the other Australian Fair Pay and Conditions Standards.[21] Beyond the bare minima, wages are expected to be set/negotiated by the workplace parties. As discussed in Managing challenges through sustainability: Hard workchoices for HR case, there has been substantial controversy around Australian Workplace Agreements since the introduction of WorkChoices.

The contract of employment

While the collective regulation of labour under the conciliation and arbitration system has been the dominant form of labour regulation in Australia for most of the past hundred years or so, all of this is predicated on the existence of an individual contract of employment (which may not even be in writing) between an individual worker and his or her employer without which it is said that no employment relationship exists.[22] Unlike the historical situation in employment, the simple employment relationship of employer and employee is not necessarily the most common form any longer. While

---

new CA, including the benefits and most importantly guaranteeing that their pay and conditions would remain entirely the same', says Rachael Leshinsky, industrial relations manager for Baker's Delight.

For The Leasing Centre, responses to employee queries at the time involved explaining that management themselves were uncertain about what the changes meant and that they were obtaining advice from lawyers—all the while assuring employees that management would do all it could to make things as smooth as possible in day-to-day operations.

Similarly, Jan Gonzalez, managing director of Active Recruitment, sought legal advice to help their boutique recruitment firm handle changes. 'For us, it was very important to have someone understand what our organisation's wants and needs were and how we wanted to convey this to our casual employees', she says.

For Ella Baché, research was important before acting on the legislation. 'We made sure we asked all the questions we needed to before making changes', says Michelle Bakar, human resources, education and training manager for Ella Baché.

Who gets the choice in WorkChoices?
As WorkChoices makes it harder for unions and employees to take industrial action, this may make it easier for employers to offer agreements that seem less generous overall but still meet the Australian Fair Pay and Conditions Standard. However, employers must keep in mind the wider and long-term ramifications of the agreements they negotiate, according to Jason Raftos, solicitor at Minter Ellison Lawyers in Perth.

Unions have drawn attention to their concerns that employers will use the flexibility of WorkChoices to push for a more productive workplace, while placing less focus on employees' entitlements and welfare. Ideally, a balance between these two aspects is what the Federal Government strives for in the success of its legislation.

Keeping communication lines open
While some employers will use WorkChoices as a means of exploiting their staff, other employers have received support from staff by remaining open in their communication. Rachael Leshinsky, industrial relations manager for Baker's Delight, says: 'We had very few problems with our processes. The key was to be as open and honest as possible.'

As Jan Gonzalez, director of Active Recruitment puts it, 'It's not about cutting their benefits, it's about maintaining them and making it easier for them to understand what they are.' The main downside has been a lack of education. If employers produce the facts, then there is less chance of confusion and different perspectives, she says.

Aside from the media hype, it is essential that employers understand their obligation in utilising the benefits of WorkChoices for both the organisation and employee. 'I haven't ever met an employer that has told me an employee won't sign an AWA or collective agreement that gives them more money because they don't support John Howard', Sleeman says.

Source: Excerpt from M. Yen, 2006, 'Hard WorkChoices for HR', *Human Resources,* 28 November. www.humanresourcesmagazine.com.au

subcontracting was historically limited to the building and construction industry, it is much more common across a wider span of industries today.[23] Similarly where once labour hire or agency workers may have been limited to some temporary secretaries in an organisation, today they may be represented amongst accounting, production, nursing, trade and other occupations within an organisation and they may be found in both the public and private sectors. Another large group of workers may be regarded as altogether independent and working in short-term contracts on their own account. In recent cases[24] the High Court of Australia has had to come to terms with new forms of employment and it is not yet clear that they have reached a settled opinion as to who is a worker. This question will often have other issues hanging on for definition. For example, just who is a worker/employee for the purposes of the various state workers compensation statutes will determine how much an employer should pay in insurance premiums for the coverage of workers who may become ill or injured because of the nature of their employment. This is clearly an important question to both employer and the 'worker'. Sometimes persons doing work in an organisation may have some status other than 'employee' to provide flexibility for the employer or because certain costs (like workers compensation premiums) are something the employer wants to shift outside his or her own immediate area of responsibility. Many of these changes in the nature of employment are no doubt driven by increased competition and may eventually be exacerbated by globalisation. It is clear that this area is developing faster than the courts can keep up.

A complex web

The modern organisation exists in a very complex legal matrix which dictates that management also attend to potential legal liability in the areas of taxation, the developing law of corporations, environmental protection and a host of other legal areas dictated by the nature of the enterprise and its wider industry. Here we concentrate solely on the individual aspects of HRM and say nothing of trade union law, bargaining issues or the still developing law of industrial conflict. A general approach to these matters is taken in this chapter because there is significant difference between the states and whether state or federal, change is inevitably part of the picture.[25]

The equal employment opportunity laws

From human rights origins to business case

Equal employment opportunity (EEO)
the government's attempt to ensure that all individuals have an equal opportunity for employment, regardless of characteristics such as race, colour, religion, gender or national origin.

The idea of equal employment opportunity is now more than 20 years old and in this part of the chapter will be used as an organising concept for several different areas of concern (and potential litigation) including discrimination matters, sexual harassment matters and affirmative action issues. Equal employment opportunity means that an organisation will be managed according to a regime where the best person for the job (in terms of promotion, opportunity for training or transfer, etc), irrespective of matters of group identity such as gender, race, colour, religion, age, sexuality or mental or physical disability, will be able to perform in that position according to their intrinsic merit. Merit, of course, is not a word without its own baggage[26] and deserves some thoughtful unpacking in any organisational context. The 'business case' suggests that promoting EEO in a workplace will result in great dividends for the organisation in terms of being able to meet the interests and aspirations of its customers and will promote a harmonious and productive workplace internally.[27] The use of the business case has been particularly popular in Australia when governments have attempted to present EEO matters to sceptical employers

The political inspiration if not the substance of most of our EEO laws is to be found in the struggle against racial discrimination by the black population in the United States of America, culminating in the passage of the *Civil Rights Act 1964*. The end of the Civil War in 1865 did not see an amelioration in the social and economic conditions under which most African Americans lived and the Emancipation Proclamation declared by President Lincoln on 1 January 1863 did not provide for real equality and nor did the Fourteenth Amendment to the Constitution in 1868. This was certainly not assisted by the attitude of the courts which institutionalised segregation in a series of cases[28] that were really not effectively challenged until the landmark school cases of the 1950s.[29] Great social agitation followed in the 1950s and, 1960s—led by the Reverend Dr Martin Luther King Jnr—which eventually saw the passage of the *Civil Rights Act*.

By now there was a conscious realisation arising out of this century-old social and political struggle that the mere creation of legal equality would not remove the reality of social and economic inequality. This debate also underlined the great gulf between equal opportunity and equal outcomes. The *Civil Rights Act* had within it provisions for affirmative action which required workplaces (and especially those in receipt of federal funds like universities) to employ affirmative action programs to assist African Americans into the workplace and into university places in the more difficult to access faculties like law and medicine. Some of these programs were later extended to women and minority groups. Perhaps not surprisingly, a political backlash to these programs developed fuelled partly by the extensive litigation brought by people who missed out on prestigious places in universities and the changing political nature of the times. The presidency of Ronald Reagan in particular saw a diminution in political support for these arrangements which continued even under the presidency of Bill Clinton—a Democrat. At the same time as the concept of affirmative action was under so much pressure in the United States, a very pale form of the concept was introduced in Australia in 1986, as we shall see below.

Simultaneously, an alternative conceptualisation to the problem of inequality and affirmative action and discrimination issues began to develop in the United States when R. Roosevelt Thomas developed what he called **managing diversity**.[30] Managing diversity is said to be about tapping into the potential of all employees and making the greatest use of their differences. It is about acknowledging, understanding and appreciating the differences among a workforce in order to value, utilise and develop the potential of all employees with the additional advantage of creating superior business results. This concept has gathered enormous popularity in the United States and is beginning to gain some traction in Australia and in the United Kingdom.[31] In Australia, however, we will see that managing diversity has not yet received any kind of statutory recognition. It might also be said that the overt managerialist assumptions of managing diversity is light years away from the human-rights oriented civil rights/anti-discrimination approach that came out of the civil rights movement of 45-odd years ago. Whether an anti-discrimination or a diversity management approach is adopted, as discussed in the 'Managing challenges of globalisation: Islam in the workplace', global events can have implications for any workplace.

Managing diversity
(or diversity management) is a process of managing people's similarities and differences; it is built on a set of values that recognises that the differences between people are a potential strength for the organisation; this process of management creates an environment that allows all employees to contribute to organisational goals and experience personal growth. This concept originated from the human-rights oriented civil rights/anti-discrimination approach that came out of the civil rights movement of 45-odd years ago.

ISLAM IN THE WORKPLACE

MANAGING CHALLENGES OF GLOBALISATION

Racial and religious discrimination are certainly not new phenomena, and attitudes and treatment of others have always been influenced by geopolitical events. But the issues faced by a growing number of Muslims in Australian workplaces present new challenges for both employees and HR departments. While discrimination tends to focus on discernible characteristics, the discrimination being felt by some Muslims tends more to be based on the visible aspects of their faith.

Some Muslim leaders and academics blame an ignorance of Islam, the influence of negative political rhetoric and general misinformation, which contribute to an atmosphere of tension. As a result of this, they say, discrimination appears to be seeping further into the workplace.

Monash University lecturer and terrorism expert, Luke Howie, believes there is cause for concern. In his PhD research, which was conducted across a variety of workplaces, it was clear many people feared Muslims and both managers and employees were engaging in discriminatory behaviour of which they were ashamed.

He points out that the discrimination is not necessarily overt abuse or intimidation, and it would often affect both the subject of the discrimination and the perpetrator. 'It was covert, it was not wanting to deal with people, [it was] breaching key performance indicators.' Howie cites the example of a Melbourne retail organisation in which staff weren't greeting patrons who appeared to be Muslim, thus not meeting a 'six-second bracket' for customer welcomes.

Statistics from the NSW Anti-Discrimination Board indicate a decrease in the number of official complaints of discrimination, yet the Human Rights and Equal Opportunity Commission's 2003 study, Isma (Listen), showed that most people interviewed said they wouldn't report incidents of discrimination. This may be due to inadequacy of legislation and the belief that nothing will result from complaints.

While such discrimination may be difficult to prove due to an often covert nature, anecdotal evidence from Muslims, as well as studies such as Howie's, demonstrate that many believe it is occurring and are feeling its effects. Furthermore, the implications—anxiety, intolerance and tension in the office or business—are widespread, with individual prejudices, rather than institutionalised bigotry, shaping the organisational culture.

The Islamic Council of Victoria's (ICV) director, Waleed Aly, agrees it can be difficult to attribute certain behaviour or lack of employment to religious discrimination. 'Often employers are in a position where they can choose between several candidates or whoever would be outstanding. It's in those circumstances that the ability for prejudice to sneak in silently is at its highest, because you're spoilt for choice', he says.

What also emerge are two main types of barriers Muslims may face in the workplace, says Aly. In the white collar sector, it is a problem of 'admission', usually relating to having an unusual surname or because of Islamic dress. 'We get reports of difficulty in getting jobs. But once they're in, there are not many complaints.'

The other barrier lies in the blue collar sector, where Muslims tend to find 'getting the job's not a problem, but they're more likely to experience discrimination or prejudice in the workplace'.

Part of the rising discrimination against Muslims, some observers say, may be attributed to the visibility of the faith, which sees Muslim women donning headscarves, applicants having Islamic names, and staff taking time out to pray—all of which may contribute to difficulties in obtaining or keeping employment.

This can force some to dilute their appearances. 'You hear stories of name-changing, you also hear stories of taking off headscarves. Basically Muslims de-identifying themselves to the greatest extent possible', Aly says.

Howie believes HR are willing to embrace multiculturalism, but indicates that some employees did perceive prayer breaks, for example, as denoting special treatment and see such practices as slightly aberrant. 'There's that comment of why can't they just be like us?'

But it's also important for Muslims to utilise their talents and sell their skills. 'I think if you were an outstanding candidate who offers something truly unique then the fact that you're a Muslim, or have a funny surname ... those factors are not going to hinder you', Aly says.

Source: A. Awad, 2006, 'Islam in the workplace', *Human Resources*, 13 December. www.humanresourcesmagazine.com.au

Anti-discrimination law in the workplace

The Australian anti-discrimination laws are universally built on an individual complaint model that attempts to provide redress for an aggrieved individual who has suffered discrimination on the basis of some group characteristic.[32] Sometimes the legislation will refer to these as grounds or attributes of discrimination. Some of these group characteristics may include:

- gender
- marital status
- pregnancy
- breastfeeding
- sexuality
- race
- colour
- age
- mental or physical disability
- political opinion
- religion
- caring responsibilities
- transgender status
- HIV/AIDS status
- physical features
- trade union activity
- criminal record.

Certain kinds of vilification are also prohibited as is victimisation of persons who make complaints. The various acts make clear where these behaviours are unacceptable; that is, in employment, in the provision of goods and services such as accommodation, etc. All of these grounds do not appear in every jurisdiction and of course as we saw above there is a rather confusing split between state and federal statutes.[33] Often, an individual who is aggrieved will have options as to whether they make a complaint under the local state or the federal legislation. There are many ramifications flowing from this decision including the potential level of damages that might flow from a successful complaint.

It is also very useful to remember that an employer is responsible for the unlawful discriminatory acts of employees in the workplace as well as the employer's own personal unlawful acts. This is called vicarious liability and, as we shall see below, also operates in the area of occupational health and safety (OHS). To some extent, this kind of liability can be reduced (or mitigated as the lawyers would say) by showing that appropriate non-discriminatory policies exist and are known to the staff, that training has occurred and that, in short, the employer has taken reasonable steps to prevent the occurrence of unlawful discriminatory acts in the workplace. An employer needs also to remember that they are not only liable for the behaviour of staff to other staff members but also in employees' dealings with the customers and members of the public.

Two kinds of discrimination are recognised in the various Australian laws in this area. **Direct discrimination** is said to occur when someone is treated less favourably on the basis of a particular characteristic, for example, sex, than someone from the other sex in circumstances which are materially the same. An example of this could be where an employer refuses to promote women into management roles. **Indirect discrimination** occurs where a compulsory requirement is attached to a job, which has

Direct discrimination
when someone is treated less favourably on the basis of a particular characteristic (e.g. gender) than someone with a different characteristic in circumstances that are materially the same.

Indirect discrimination
when a compulsory requirement is attached to a job (which has nothing to do with the real performance of the job) that would prevent substantial proportions of particular groups or individuals from being able to comply and the individual in question cannot comply.

nothing to do with the real performance of the job, and would prevent substantial proportions of particular groups or individuals from complying. An excellent example of this is the common former requirement of Australian police services to insist on certain physical requirements, such as height and weight, among its recruits that saw several different ethnic groups virtually eliminated from consideration.

Of all the types (or heads) of discrimination, disability discrimination appears to be something that continues to attract a growing number of complaints. Whether this is the result of real increases in the rate of discriminatory behaviour towards people with disabilities in the workplace, or that the disabled community is better able to advocate its own issues is not certain. This issue is something that will come to exercise the minds of employers more fully in the next few years as it becomes more widely known that reasonable accommodations (beyond the ubiquitous wheelchair ramps) may need to be made in many more workplaces to enable workers with disabilities to reach their full potential. A growing issue will no doubt be the level of responsibility of employers (and how that might be managed) where mental illness is manifested in the workplace.

Most of the anti-discrimination laws also make clear when exceptions are to occur. For example, while it is generally unlawful to discriminate on the basis of sex, sex may be a genuine occupational qualification in some jobs. Consider the case of when an employer advertises for someone to work in the lingerie department. Female customers may be in a state of undress in this workplace; thus, men will not be welcome and it is inappropriate for them to be employed. Similarly, exemptions from the operation of the laws may be sought in certain circumstances. In NSW an exemption was sought from the Anti-Discrimination Board by a fitness centre proprietor who sought to have some 'women only' times at the gym in order to encourage the large local population of women from a Muslim background to access the facilities. There was significant media discussion around this exemption but the board took the view that there were substantial social gains to be captured by positive steps towards encouraging a fitter lifestyle for this group of women (built on a very small disadvantage for any local male gym users) than by sticking to the strict letter of the law. Often other exemptions are sought by employers to advertise 'Aboriginal only' jobs in order to increase the available pool of employment and training opportunities for a demonstrably disadvantaged group of Australians.

Complaints made within a workplace setting are always much better handled as quickly and professionally as possible. Each organisation needs to have a proper policy on these EEO matters that is clearly articulated to all staff. Training in these areas is often adopted by employers. Designated complaints officers need to be established. Failure to deal effectively with these matters at a local level will see aggrieved parties taking their complaints to the human rights agencies at a state or federal level. Those agencies will generally investigate the complaints and attempt to conciliate between the parties. If this does not work, the complaint may proceed to a hearing in front of a tribunal—with its attendant cost and potential bad publicity. Arising out of this, remedies where the complainant is successful may include various kinds of damages, apologies, promotions or transfers, orders for variations of contracts and orders not to repeat the unlawful act.

Sexual harassment at work

Sexual harassment
behaviour of a sexual nature that is neither welcome nor solicited.

In NSW sexual harassment began life in the courts as a form of sex discrimination[34] because the *Anti-discrimination Act* (NSW) did not specifically mention sexual harassment until 1997. Sexual harassment remains a major problem in the Australian workplace with many potential complainants choosing not to make complaints but to leave the workplace. This constitutes not just an abrogation of an individual worker's human rights but also a great cost to an employer in terms of recruitment, training and other costs. Like all of the other human rights laws at work, the legislation is written in gender-free language so it contemplates the possibility of women harassing women and women harassing men as well as men harassing women or other men. Experience and the statistics produced by the human rights agencies suggest however that the commonest case remains where men harass women. This is probably a reflection of power relations in the workplace and the wider social relations between men and women in our society.

Sexual harassment is said to be behaviour of a sexual nature that is neither welcome nor solicited. This may include the telling of risqué jokes and inappropriate comments, touching or leering, repeated requests for dates or more and more overt acts of a sexual nature that may constitute sexual assault under the criminal laws. Given that large numbers of Australians meet their life partners at work,[35] it does not mean that all forms of sexualised behaviour at work could be characterised as harassment.

One very early case established the fact that the complained of behaviour does not have to be of the most obvious kind (the touching/leering kind) but may be constituted by harassing behaviours that occur because of the complainant's sex. In this case,[36] the complainant was the first woman to work in a particular office and suffered unwanted phone calls, her mail being opened, attacks on the female toilets, advertisements for brothels appearing on the office noticeboard and other offensive behaviours. Because she could not identify the actual perpetrator she brought her action against the employer (who had ignored her many calls for assistance) and the tribunal found the employer liable for the unlawful behaviour of the complainant's co-workers. In a subsequent case (also involving the employment of women in non-traditional workplaces), the tribunal found not just the employer liable for the unlawful acts of the employees but also found the trade union to which the complainant and the alleged harassers belonged to be liable for not assisting the complainants.[37] In both of these cases the very bad publicity was extensive for the respondent companies and organisations. As indicated in the 'Managing challenges through attracting and retaining people: Boss offered sex accuser a hug' case, sexual harassment and harassment of other kinds remain major problems at work.

Affirmative action

Affirmative action programs of the kind where quotas of categories of people who have suffered historical discrimination or wider disadvantage must be employed, promoted or trained have never existed in Australia. The first federal act, the *Affirmative Action (Equal Opportunity for Women) Act 1986*, never called for quotas but instead encouraged larger workplaces to focus on the position and status of women in the organisation. The act only applied to workplaces with more than 100 employees (thus, the vast majority of Australian workplaces were outside its jurisdiction) with the intention of focusing employer attention on the recruitment of women and where they saw those women going in the organisation. No complaint processes were attached to this mechanism and enforcement of the legislation was consciously designed to be weak. The whole process might be called a program approach. In 1999 the act was replaced with the *Equal Opportunity for Women in the Workplace Act*, which weakened the enforcement procedures further.

Affirmative action programs associated with the provision of quotas and other forms of reparation to compensate for past injustices suffered by a class or group of persons. This has most famously occurred in the United States in the case of African American people.

BOSS OFFERED SEX ACCUSER A HUG

When Christina Rich confronted her PricewaterhouseCoopers boss Stuart Edwards about his alleged workplace sexism and discrimination, he offered this solution:

'I just want to give you a big hug to make it better. We just need to go out for dinner with a bottle of wine to nut out the issues and a way forward.'

The accounting multinational's defence of a $10 million sex discrimination case makes these admissions and also reveals Mr Edwards thought it was acceptable to adopt the habit of kissing the highest-paid female partner in the firm.

Mr Edwards believed that since Ms Rich had shared with him matters of a personal nature, they had enjoyed a 'friendly, open and good-humoured relationship'. Therefore, greeting her with a kiss was not out of context, documents filed in the Federal Court this week show.

After Ms Rich objected to the kissing and was also allegedly subjected to sexism, harassment and discrimination from a number of senior partners at the firm, she requested a mediator to resolve the matters.

Mr Edwards's solution to go out to dinner was his way of working through the issues in 'an informal and non-confrontational manner', the response says.

In the nation's biggest workplace sexism claim, Ms Rich says she suffered discrimination, bullying and victimisation and her progress through the organisation was hampered. In its response, PWC confirms a substantial number of the incidents but does not accept that Ms Rich was adversely affected.

Melbourne-based Mr Edwards was the head of the transfer pricing division and Ms Rich, who worked from Sydney, was paid about $1 million a year for her advice in the area, saving clients of the calibre of American Express tens of millions of dollars by moving global profit from one tax jurisdiction to another.

The accounting giant denies that Mr Edwards told Ms Rich that she received a positive performance review because chief executive Tony Harrington 'fancies her'. It admits that partner and board member Tim Cox asked Ms Rich, when watching a corporate video showing a woman sunbaking topless: 'Christina, is that you sunbathing on the beach?' PWC says that comment, too, was made in the context of a 'friendly and good-humoured relationship'.

In justifying Mr Edwards's comments to her that she was emotional, scatty and high-maintenance, the response says these were 'matters of opinion which were reasonably held'.

The firm also claims Mr Edwards's comment to Ms Rich that the pregnancy of another employee was affecting her work did not cause offence to the other woman.

PWC says Ms Rich was uncooperative in mediation from March 2004 and—after making a complaint to the Human Rights and Equal Opportunity Commission—she was placed on restricted duties in August, her pay cut and her access to clients prevented.

'The applicant expressed on a number of occasions her lack of faith and confidence in the firm or its ability to address her concerns', the response says. 'She was operating under intense stress and required real relief from the pressures which she faced' and had 'indicated that she was unwilling or unable to operate as a partner of the firm'.

'In those circumstances the imposition and confirmation of access restrictions in good faith by management and the board respectively was reasonable and in the best interests of the firm.'

Senior partners and board members at all times 'acted in good faith' and took 'all reasonable steps' to reach agreement.

The case follows a landmark settlement of $US54 million paid to several women by Wall Street bank Morgan Stanley in New York in July 2004.

Source: J. Sexton, 2006, 'Boss offered sex accuser a hug', *The Australian*, 29 July, p. 2, Copyright 2006 News Ltd.

Recruitment and selection

Increasing numbers of employers recruit their staff through employment agencies or labour hire companies thereby providing the employer with flexibility and freeing the HR department (where they exist) from the onerous and expensive task of recruitment. Historically, the collective labour law, which has hitherto dominated the regulation of the employment relationship, has had almost nothing to say about recruitment. The old 'closed shop' practices—whereby workers might be drawn from a union list of available labour (called union hall hiring in the USA) or, alternately, promise to join the union as soon as hired—did not operate in all industries in spite of the fact that trade union power was at its peak in the 1950s. Now, of course, this compulsory union membership practice is unlawful in all jurisdictions.

Historically, the public sector has operated according to very strict codes of hiring and at one time used a 'tight' internal labour market approach whereby young recruits (typically without tertiary education) would sit large public exams. The best would be recruited to the public service. Those recruited in this way could expect to move up at least as far as middle management unless they were unlucky enough to be women. Until 1966 women working in the federal public service were required to give up their permanent status on marriage and this would preclude them from any likelihood of advancement. With the removal of the compulsory union membership practices, the principal legal issue surrounding recruitment today is the operation of the human rights laws.

Very few complaints of discrimination at the point of recruitment make it as far as the human rights agencies. Part of this could be explained by the fact that no sensible employer today would tell any potential employee that they have failed to be recruited because of their sex, their colour or their age. Discrimination on the grounds of these three group attributes could lead to successful claims in every jurisdiction except the federal, where age is not a ground. The industrial relations legislation[38] has been used in cases of termination on account of age as an alternative remedy (see below). Discrimination in recruitment highlights one of the most important aspects of whether a potentially aggrieved person will bring an action against an employer. Quite simply, many persons who are discriminated against do not know it has happened[39] and therefore do not complain.

If equal employment opportunity is about protecting the human rights of employees and potential employees, it is also about choosing and keeping the very best available staff for the employer's business. Applying the anti-discrimination laws in a practical sense means that at recruitment the HR staff will not be making assumptions about how a particular group attribute (for example, sex or age) will affect a person's ability to do the job. It would be a clear case of discrimination to ask female candidates how they will juggle work and family commitments as it would be to ask that of men. All workers have families of one kind or another and all workers have non work commitments.[40] The responsibility for keeping within a non-discriminatory framework lies squarely with the employer and the employer's representatives in the HR office. The discrimination laws do not end with hiring and apply equally to decisions concerning promotion, transfer and training. It is these events that do appear more frequently in the statistics of the human rights agencies because, once a person has been recruited and gets to learn the organisational culture and ways of doing things, grievances may occur. One might also speculate about what kind of impact the nature of modern employment has on the preparedness of aggrieved persons to make complaints when no one expects to stay in one organisation for very long and old-fashioned organisational loyalty is a thing of the past.[41]

The termination of employment

In times past, the common law supported employers' rights to hire and fire. However, this previously almost unfettered right is seriously tempered by the anti-discrimination laws and, more recently, by a very complex set of termination laws.[42] The only remedy

PART 1   Managing the Human Resource Environment

known under the common law when a worker alleged they had been unfairly terminated was the remedy of damages. The legislature has developed the newer remedy of 'reinstatement', initially at a state level, but this too has found its way into federal law after a change in views by the High Court in the 1990s. The whole issue of termination and the remedies available remains a volatile and intensely political issue where much debate goes to the question of the appropriate balance to be given to the rights of workers and the rights of employers to determine who will be employed and under what circumstances they will be terminated.[43] The guiding principle governing the unfair dismissal laws is stated to be 'a fair go all round' which is Australian vernacular for the fact that both employers and employees have rights that must be protected in these matter.[44]

The principal changes under the amended federal act include the fact that no application can be brought against an employer with 100 or fewer employees at the date of the termination. Further, no claims will be entertained by the Commission where the dismissal is for genuine operational reasons or for reasons which include genuine operational reasons.[45] Perhaps most significantly, many workers covered by state instruments may find their termination rights governed by federal law because their employer is now regarded as a federal employer.

No one should be terminated on discriminatory grounds or, put more accurately, should this occur the terminated worker will have a good chance of bringing a

Unfair dismissal generally refers to a situation where regard for a fair procedure (i.e. the right to hear of the transgression and be given the opportunity to defend oneself) has been ignored, or where a transgression itself does not reasonably suggest dismissal is an appropriate management response.

POLICING THE INTERNET

MANAGING CHALLENGES THROUGH HR INNOVATION

The growing business importance of internet-based applications such as web surfing, email and instant messaging has also created a new business challenge: setting appropriate policies for those applications and developing suitable ways of monitoring them.

More than 200 workers in Australia have been dismissed and a further 900 suspended as a result of internet misuse since 1998, according to ongoing monitoring by the software company SurfControl. Most of the well-publicised cases have centred on accessing pornographic content via web sites or forwarding inappropriate emails, but concerns over lost productivity through personal use of office technology are also common.

While the scope of the problem is clear, determining who is responsible for setting and enforcing company policy is much more difficult. According to SurfControl's recent white paper on internet policy, 'confusion exists between HR and IT about who should be training employees, while employees are unsure who to turn to about internet misuse'.

Staff can also be touchy about heavy-handed monitoring of personal usage of the internet. One survey of workers by WebSense found that 57 per cent believed that using the web for personal tasks didn't impact their productivity, while 27 per cent argued that it actually improved their overall productivity.

Anecdotal evidence suggests the most effective solution is for IT and HR executives to collaborate on identifying problems and developing policies.

'To deal with internet abuse, IT and HR departments must focus on both the policy and effective technology which will help them to monitor and ensure proper employee internet use', said Saran Gopalakrishnan, senior product manager for WebSense.

The actual deployment of technology is likely to remain a core IT responsibility, and the frequently reactive nature of many businesses to such problems and the nature of the solutions means that ongoing monitoring also often remains an IT role.

However, such strategies will only be effective if the company policy is effectively communicated to all employees. This is where HR has a crucial role to play.

From security to policy

For leading insurance and financial services provider QBE Insurance Group, the initial impetus for implementing a solution to help control incoming email was a simple and pragmatic one—making sure that viruses did not spread across the company network.

successful case against the offending employer. Where this has happened, reinstatement may not be an appropriate remedy as it is very likely that the relationship between the parties has broken down. To use the analogy of a failed marriage, there is not much point in forcing the estranged parties to live together.

Under the common law, an employer always had the right to summarily dismiss someone for misconduct and this has not changed under the statutory arrangements. As most workers[45] have access to industrial tribunals with the jurisdiction to look carefully at these decisions, a prudent employer acts very carefully in these situations. In the case of theft, for example, which is very clearly in the category of misconduct, a sensible employer (or very sensible HR manager) would look very closely at the evidence that links the accused person to the event and make certain that the accused employee had an opportunity to answer the allegations. Some organisations in such circumstances might put the accused person on paid leave until a proper investigation could be carried out. The management of poor performance is another matter altogether and best practice organisations keep careful records of verbal and written warnings given to poor performers. As indicated in 'Managing challenges through HR innovation: Policing the Internet', the use of Internet and emails at work requires effective HR policies to manage concerns about workplace conduct.

'We had good anti-virus solutions running on the desktops and servers, but the biggest threat comes from email', explained group information security manager Murray Laracy.

Malicious computer viruses often spread rapidly via email before the latest updates and patches that protect against them have time to be deployed. To deal with that problem, QBE rolled out a managed service solution from MessageLabs, which scans all incoming email before it arrives at the company and identifies new viruses using predictive techniques to identify virus-like behaviour.

With that problem conquered, Laracy's attention turned to a related area which MessageLabs' technology could help conquer: spam email. 'Currently, QBE blocks around 100 000 unwanted spam messages each week, up from 10 000 a week when the anti-spam component of the solution was first implemented.'

'There are some obvious candidates for things you should block, such as large files and video, but there are also a lot of grey areas', Laracy said. 'Every business is different, and organisations have to decide how intrusive they need to be.'

Coming up with a suitable policy required involvement from multiple areas of the business. 'The discussion needs to happen between IT and HR departments, and you also need to engage within the business so they have input to what is happening and why', Laracy said.

Property and rights

IP Australia's policy towards internet usage in the workplace is summed up very simply by IT security advisor Fred Schelb: 'Zero personal use, plus a bit.'

The company, which manages a range of intellectual property rights across Australia and handles tasks such as granting patents and registering trademarks, has seen its internet policy evolve since the early days of the technology when staff access was unlimited. 'We had to go from a very organic type of culture to one that was more controlled', Schelb explains.

Initially, IP Australia gathered raw data on the sites visited by its employees using a tool called Squid and analysed it using an Excel spreadsheet. Eighteen months ago, IP Australia replaced Squid and WebSpy with a program called ContentKeeper, which automatically analysed and categorised data, providing a detailed picture of the internet usage of all 850 employees and identifying potential areas of concern or patterns that might indicate excessive personal usage. Because patents and trademarks are granted in a wide range of fields, blanket policies blocking entire categories aren't always appropriate.

'Our examiners roam far and wide on the internet, and need to look at a variety of sites for business purposes', Schelb said.

Ensuring staff acceptance was also important. 'We initiated a large-scale awareness program', Schelb said. The process was driven by the IT security team, in line with existing general policies on electronic resource usage. New employees joining the organisation now sign an individual agreement on appropriate usage, in line with the 'zero plus a bit' policy.

Source: Excerpt from A. Kidman, 2005, 'Policing the internet', *Human Resources*, 23 August, pp. 22–3. www.humanresourcesmagazine.com.au

Occupational health and safety matters

The state has been involved in the protection of the physical working environment in the English legal world for more than 200 years.[48] The initial response of the state was to protect children and women (in that order). This was partly based on what was seen as the employers' Christian duty and gradually in response to race fears—the class of factory and other manual workers would not be able to reproduce because the physical working conditions were so bad. Eventually, in this way, women and children were banned from working in coal mines and other obviously dangerous places. The next 100 years saw a shift from industry-specific work safety laws (which tended to leave whole industries free of regulation) that were referred to generically as the factory acts to general duties legislation (often called Robens-style legislation), which does not tell employers exactly what to do and how to do it. Across all of this legislation has been the possibility of investigation by government inspectors and criminal prosecution where employers failed in their duty.[49]

Across all Australian jurisdictions employers have an absolute duty (in some states to the extent practicable)[50] to ensure the health and safety of employees and other persons who may come onto their work premises. These other persons may include consumers in shops, students coming onto a university campus or contracting tradespersons coming in to fix the plumbing. Other duties of a similar nature are owed by designers and manufacturers of equipment and purveyors of workplace chemicals, to mention others. These laws are state laws because of the way in which the Constitution operates, with the only federal OHS laws being those which apply to the Federal Government's own employees and the laws applying to merchant seamen. At this stage, there does not appear to be an intention on the part of the Federal Government to legislate in this area, although it would seem that since WorkChoices came to be, it has the constitutional power to regulate OHS in so-called constitutional corporations.

This form of legislation is often described as self-regulation because the real focus is on the workplace parties. There are provisions in all the statutes for employees to be prosecuted for failure to ensure OHS standards are maintained although prosecutions against workers are relatively rare compared to the number of prosecutions brought against employers. The number of prosecutions brought against employers across Australia annually is very small. While the primary responsibility for OHS remains with the employer, under this legislation there are extensive consultative rights given to workers and their unions and many workplaces must have joint union–management OHS committees at the workplace or other approved consultative mechanisms. Some of these other mechanisms may include appointed or elected OHS representatives chosen from among the employees.

Compensation for injured workers was historically developed by means of the common law, but by the 1870s in the United Kingdom it was clear that the courts were going to devote a lot of creativity in developing ways to deny injured workers any compensation at all. Statutory schemes of workers compensation were developed by the British parliament by the end of the nineteenth century, essentially copying developments in Germany. These schemes were then progressively adopted by the Australian states. Under these schemes, employers must take out compulsory insurance for all their workers. This insurance will be used to pay an amount related to an injured employee's wage/salary if unable to work because of work-related disease or injury. The employee does not need to show that the injury or disease was caused by the negligence of either the employer or another worker. This is referred to as a no-fault scheme. Medical expenses will also be paid where these arise from a work-related injury or disease. In many of these cases, the real question is not about the nature of the disease/injury and the work nexus but about who the employer is and whether the injured worker is actually covered by the legislation. The rapid development of new forms of work relationships presents a constant challenge for courts and legislators alike.

It is now rare in Australia for injured and diseased workers to have access to the form of compensation called 'common law damages'—where negligence at the workplace has led to their injury or disease. Rapidly rising costs have seen this form of compensation very much in retreat.

MANAGING PEOPLE

VIRGIN BLUE TREATED OLDER CANDIDATES DIFFERENTLY TO YOUNGER CANDIDATES

In the case of *Hopper & Others v Virgin Blue Airlines* [2006] QADT 9, the Queensland Anti-Discrimination Tribunal awarded damages to eight women, aged between 36 and 56, who claimed that Virgin Blue discriminated against them on the basis of their age during the recruitment process.

Virgin Blue's recruitment process involved a number of steps. One of the initial stages involved a group assessment process. During this process applicants were assessed against the behavioural competencies of assertiveness, teamwork, communication and 'Virgin Flair'.

The Tribunal accepted that Virgin Blue's 'behavioural competencies' were a legitimate criteria for selection and the methods of testing the competencies were reasonable. However, the Tribunal found that when the assessors subjectively applied the criteria, they did so in a way that was discriminatory. The assessors unconsciously preferred younger people whether or not older people were similarly competent.

The Tribunal also noted that although Virgin Blue was not malicious, it had done nothing to address the concern that its recruitment process had, for a significant period of time, resulted in the airline failing to employ anyone over 36 years of age despite 750 people at or above that age applying for positions.

Statistical evidence showed that although the process was age neutral it had not produced an age neutral result. Virgin Blue did not keep or disclose records of persons that it rejected for employment to refute this evidence.

HR tips

HR personnel conducting behavioural competency assessments should be trained to ensure that the application of the assessment does not produce discriminatory results. Statistical analysis of recruitment results may be an indicator of discrimination in the recruitment process. Employers should be prepared to re-evaluate recruitment policies and practices if the results indicate an over-representation of a particular group of people. Retaining a record of the reasons for not selecting a candidate may be useful evidence to defend a discrimination claim if one is made.

Qantas ordered to reinstate a medically retired employee

In the case of *Kazama v Qantas Airways* (2005) PR969209, the Australian Industrial Relations Commission ordered Qantas to reinstate an employee who was terminated on the grounds that she was medically unfit to work as a flight attendant due to the unacceptable risk of a reoccurrence of Eustachian tube dysfunction and her refusal to accept an offer for other work within Qantas.

Ms Kazama had been employed as a flight attendant since 29 April 1989 until her termination. It was her position that she was, at the time of her dismissal (and since), fit to perform the requirements of her job.

The Commission reviewed extensive medical evidence that was tendered in the form of written reports and expert oral evidence from numerous medical practitioners in order to determine whether Ms Kazama suffered a medical condition that rendered her unfit to work as a long haul flight attendant.

All the doctors agreed that while ever Ms Kazama is not suffering from an incident of Eustachian tube dysfunction, there is no reason why she cannot perform her job. The critical difference between the opinions of the medical practitioners concerned the probability of reoccurrence and the associated risks.

The Commission preferred the evidence of one practitioner over the several others, primarily because the practitioner was a specialist with extensive experience. The Commission found as a matter of fact that a reoccurrence of Eustachian tube dysfunction in Ms Kazama is no more a probability for Ms Kazama than for any other long haul flight attendant.

The Commission was persuaded that Qantas' actions were motivated by a genuine concern for the safety of Ms Kazama and for other in-flight employees and passengers. However, the Commission ordered Qantas to reinstate Ms Kazama on the basis that the termination of her employment was harsh, unjust and unreasonable because Ms Kazama was: not unfit for her employment when she was terminated therefore there was no valid reason for termination; not provided with the views of some of the doctors and that inhibited her ability to respond to the allegation that she was unfit for duty; and terminated without any attempt by Qantas to see how she would handle a return to work on international flights.

HR tips

Employers should ensure that decisions to terminate on medical grounds are objective and accurate. Where medical opinions differ, consideration should be given to which opinion should be preferred (a specialist's opinion may be given more weight than the opinion of a general practitioner). Employers should allow employees an opportunity to respond to the opinions of medical practitioners. Withholding such opinions inhibit the employee's ability to respond and may be viewed as unfair.

Source: S. Wellard, 2006, 'Virgin Blue treated older candidates differently to younger candidates', *Human Resources*, 16 May. www.humanresourcesmagazine.com.au

QUESTIONS

1 What are the main legal issues in the cases outlined regarding Virgin Blue and Qantas?
2 What would you advise the HR function at Virgin Blue and Qantas with regard to these areas?

CHAPTER SUMMARY

The role of law in the Australian workplace remains highly contested. That was the case throughout the first 200 years of European settlement in this country and is clearly continuing. This debate is linked to wider debates about the relative rights of employers and employees and the degree of intervention by outside agents, whether they might be the state or trade unions. The constitutional arrangements in Australia, with its very complex split between state and federal laws, is perhaps more complicated than it needs to be. Single national systems of labour regulation were not politically possible at the time of Federation yet they have crept back onto the agenda 100 years later in the wake of the WorkChoices system.

WEB EXERCISES

The National Library of Australia has a comprehensive area on its website entitled 'Australian Law on the Internet' at www.nla.gov.au/oz/law.html.

Listed on this website is **www.austlii.edu.au** that is another discrete website containing up-to-date versions of all federal and state legislation and a great deal of case law. Pick one area of interest to you (for example, sexual harassment, race discrimination or OHS), locate the relevant statute (remembering there may be more than one) and describe the salient features of the way the legislation works. In addition, name the tribunal where matters under the Act are litigated and analyse one recent case from that jurisdiction—outlining what you think are the core legal issues and how the tribunal came to its final decision. Are there any implications in the decision for the strategic direction of HR in a small Australian company?

DISCUSSION QUESTIONS

1. Why do you think the law of employment is such a 'hotly' contested area for the parties involved, as well as the wider community?
2. Do you foresee a time when this contestation will not occur and some stability in the law will occur? How do you think this will come about?
3. What effect do you think increasing globalisation will have on the national regulation of the employment relationship?
4. Is the employment contract the same as any other contract for the sale of services?

CASE STUDY

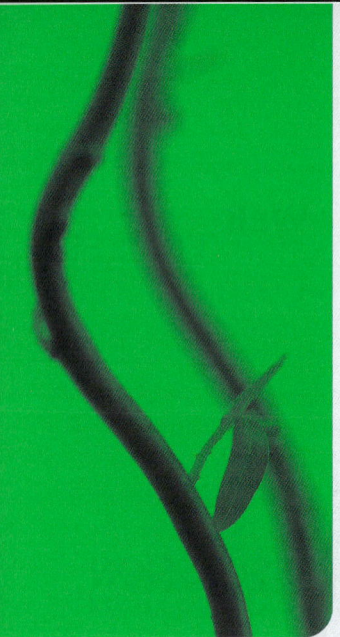

HUMAN RESOURCE MANAGEMENT IN AUSTRALIA

The recent high profile case involving ex-Channel Ten presenter Jessica Rowe has again highlighted the question of how employers can protect themselves against staff being poached and business walking out the door with them. Employers do have the power to take steps to reduce the risk of their business being damaged when a staff member is poached.

The first step is to assess the nature of the risks a business would face if a particular staff member was poached by a competitor. Once these have been identified, an employer can implement a process to reduce specific risks. However, it should never be forgotten that the solution is not solely legal, in the sense of creating an 'iron gate' at the exit.

HR strategies

Employers should also examine the human resource question of what may motivate employees to leave and consider whether a prevention strategy can be implemented, including a remuneration approach that rewards loyalty.

If the exploitation of a customer connection is a real risk, the employer should quickly establish a strategy that ensures each client has several points of contact with employees. The same rule applies with business opportunities the employer is investing in. For example, even if a sales person has most of the contact with a key customer, make sure the sales person regularly reports to the manager on key issues concerning the account and ensure the manger maintains regular contact with the customer.

This will ensure the manager is not in the dark about the customer's plans and requirements. If this strategy is adopted and an employee is poached, the client or potential client will be less likely to consider it has no option but to follow the employee to a competitor.

Confidential information

A careful assessment of the information that exists within the business must also be conducted to identify what is confidential, who has access to it, where it can be accessed and how it could be removed by an employee. Once the assessment has been completed, the employer is best placed to develop practices and policies that will ensure this information is properly managed. Is information that might be held on a laptop used by any employee? Can the information be emailed out or downloaded onto a memory stick? Can the information be removed in any other way by an employee?

In the case of New South Wales, employers should ensure they have a policy on workplace surveillance, including computer surveillance, which complies with the requirements of the *NSW Workplace Surveillance Act 2005*.

The importance of mobile phone numbers should not be forgotten. If customers contact staff members on their mobiles, the employer should ensure it has the right to retain the mobile phone number. Without this right, the employer may find that employees leave but customers continue contacting them on their mobile phones.

Employment contract

The employment contract is a critical tool for employers to use in preventing damage to the business when a staff member is poached. This document will form the basis of any iron gate strategy and provide a legal remedy.

An employer should not rely on a notice period to protect itself against the risks of poaching. Unless they provide 'special services', employees can breach the agreed notice period and a court will not force them to continue working for the employer or stop them from joining a competitor. All an employer can do is claim for damages arising from the breach of the notice period but, in most circumstances, this may not provide the business solution required.

Non-compete clause

The employer must use specifically drafted non-compete clauses in order to deal with the risk of poaching. For a non-compete clause to be enforceable by a court, an employer needs to be careful that its purpose is to protect confidential information or customer connections. It cannot merely attempt to prevent competition or ensure staff stability.

For example, an employee may have confidential information about the terms and conditions of another employee's employment, the business, clients and/or the strategies of the employer. Alternatively, they may have established dealings with customers and some influence over them. In either case, the employer has legitimate reasons to employ a non-compete clause. However, even if there is a legitimate reason, the terms and scope of the clause cannot go further than is reasonably necessary to protect the relevant interests of the employer.

In addition to a non-compete clause, the employer should ensure the employment contract contains a clause that prevents the use and disclosure of confidential information. This clause should address the types of information identified in the assessment. A well-drafted confidentiality clause can create real problems for a competitor and prevent it from exploiting information known by a former employee.

Information and property

An employer should also ensure that its employment contracts contain a provision requiring the employee to return all property. The employer's property should be defined to include all the forms of information and other material that the employee could take from the employer and use against it with a competitor.

Finally, an employer should be prepared to act quickly to enforce its legal rights if it suspects a breach by an employee. Waiting can mean a court will not enforce the non-compete or confidentiality clause, but merely leave the employer with a potential claim for damages.

Top tips: protecting your patch

Don't rely solely on legal remedies. Ensure other strategies are adopted. Furthermore, an employer must conduct a review of its workplace and should consider:
- the type of confidential information an employee may have access to
- the influence that a particular employee may have over specific customers and how to prevent this being exploited
- when and how information is likely to leave with an employee and how best to prevent this.

Employers must also check their employment contracts to ensure they contain:
- an adequate notice clause;
- a specifically drafted non-compete clause that takes into account the circumstances of the individual employee
- a clause which prevents the use and disclosure of confidential information, drafted specifically for the circumstances of the employee.

Source: S. Trew, 2006, 'Protecting your patch', *Human Resources*, 2 May. www.humanresourcesmagazine.com.au

QUESTIONS

1 In your view, what are the major areas of employment law to be considered and understood by HR managers?
2 What are some of the choices involved in designing and implementing HR policies with regard to employment law issues?

CHAPTER 4

OCCUPATIONAL HEALTH AND SAFETY

Objectives

After reading this chapter, you should be able to:

1. Understand the context for occupational health and safety (OHS) in Australia.
2. Understand the major features of the legislative context for OHS.
3. Identify OHS implications of an ageing workforce.
4. Identify the basic features of an OHS management system.
5. Understand the concept of a 'safety culture'.
6. Discuss the relationship of human resource management (HRM) and OHS.

DOZENS WILL DIE AT WORK THIS YEAR. INEVITABLE, OR NOT?

EARLY on Tuesday, a 30-year-old construction worker, a new father, began the first day of the working year.

While many Victorians were still on holidays, the Langwarrin man began unloading an excavator from a trailer at a house site in Narre Warren North.

By about 8am, he was dead, crushed by the excavator when it toppled from the trailer.

Unlike the WorkSafe television advertisement, in which a young boy waits anxiously by the front gate for his father to return from work to play basketball with him, the man's newborn child will not get the same opportunity.

His death follows a worrying increase in the number of workplace deaths last year. Twenty-nine Victorians died at work in 2006, up 60 per cent on 2005.

Despite this mortality figure, and more than 30 000 workplace injuries each year—an average of 82 a day—costing business $1 billion, workplace deaths and injuries receive little publicity. The Langwarrin man's death received only a brief mention in *The Age* the following day.

WorkSafe Victoria deputy director Ross Pilkington said workplace deaths were unacceptable, but, importantly, the annual figure had declined in the past 20 years.

Between 1986 and 1991, the average annual death rate was 41, compared with the most recent five-year average of 27.

Mr Pilkington said that 18 deaths occurred in 2005, but that figure was unusual given that no deaths occurred in the two most dangerous industries, farming and construction.

The reduction in deaths has been partly due to campaigns and safety improvements in those industries, such as fitting roll-over structures to tractors, creating separate paths for pedestrians and forklifts, and safer construction methods.

Mr Pilkington said it was hard to isolate trends in workplace deaths and accidents.

Victorians killed at work	
Year	Number of deaths
2006	29
2005	18
2004	29
2003	27
2002	34
– 5-year average	27
– 2001–1997 average	34
– 1996–1992 average	38
– 1991–1986 average	41

Source: WorkSafe Victoria

There were 17 deaths last year in country Victoria, which could partly be attributed to isolated workers taking on too much, or jobs for which they were not properly trained, and who were a long way from emergency hospitals.

Mr Pilkington said that most deaths could be characterised as 'random events', although most workers, when asked, could identify and fix hazards in their workplace. 'They actually know what the issues are', Mr Pilkington said.

Australian Workers Union national safety representative Yossi Berger described the death and injury statistics as 'a castle of cards', saying the workplace death toll nationally could be closer to 15 000 when taking into account occupational diseases, such as asbestos-related diseases, cardiac heart disease and other stress-related illnesses, and work-related suicides.

> **Dozens will die at work this year. Inevitable, or not?** *continued*
>
> The figures also do not count people killed in traffic accidents while working.
>
> Mr Berger said the real issue to focus on was not fatalities, but the culture of risk-taking in workplaces.
>
> 'It's almost taken by the community that accidents, injuries and fatalities, and fatigue and hours of work problems, are part and parcel of work', he said.
>
> 'Not enough is being done mainly because, culturally, it's regarded to be intrinsic to the business of work.'
>
> Bette Phillips, whose apprentice electrician son was electrocuted, and who counsels relatives through Work-Related Group Support, said most companies' occupational health and safety policies sat unread in filing cabinets.
>
> 'People are taking short cuts even though the company might have policies in place', she said.
>
> The results of such carelessness were grief-stricken families, friends and workmates, with the pain lasting for years.
>
> Ms Phillips said that when she returned to her son's workplace for the 10th anniversary of his death, she was surprised to find the manager in tears.
>
> 'The impact on families and companies is huge', she said.
>
> *Source:* M. Shaw, 2007, 'Dozens will die at work this year. Inevitable, or not?', *The Age*, 6 January, p. 7.

Introduction

In Chapter 3, The legal context for human resource management, we discussed the legal issues for HRM in Australia. For human resource managers, legal issues such as occupational health and safety (OHS) are a major area of concern and activity. In addition to legislative developments, the management of OHS takes place in the context of significant changes affecting the workplace, including globalisation of markets, implementation of new technology, new forms of work organisation and structural changes in the workforce.[1] Overall, workplace and contextual changes have brought challenges and new demands for employers and employees. For example, demands for flexibility and a higher quality of products and services influence organisations and individuals.[2] As the opening article shows, occupational health and safety is an important concern with significant personal and financial implications; failure to ensure the health and safety of employees can have tragic consequences.

We provide this chapter focusing on OHS to demonstrate that managers need to not only be familiar with the relevant legal context, but also to develop a strategic, comprehensive approach to the management of OHS. Managing human resource activities, such as OHS, within legal constraints and in a strategic, proactive and preventive manner is a source of competitive advantage.

Defining occupational health and safety

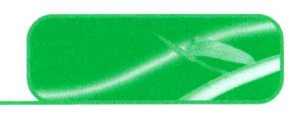

Occupational health and safety (OHS) refers to the physical, physiological and psychosocial conditions of an organisation's workforce, related to aspects of work and the work context.[3] With this broad perspective, effective OHS management relies on improving OHS conditions and preventing hazards (circumstances, procedures or environments that expose individuals to possible injury, illness, damage or loss) in the work context by implementing comprehensive HRM and organisational strategies.[4] The term 'workplace health and safety' is also increasingly used to highlight the fact that OHS issues arise at the workplace or are related to the workplace.

Typical health hazards include toxic and carcinogenic chemicals, physical and biological agents, dust, noise and heat. The ways in which people may be affected are diverse. Illnesses of the respiratory system, particularly chronic bronchitis and emphysema, represent a substantial category of occupational disease. Working in confined spaces and lifting heavy items are associated with many workplace injuries. Sprains and strains of joints and muscles are the injuries accounting for the highest proportion of all workplace injury cases.[5]

Job characteristics and the work environment should also be considered in an analysis of factors linked to work-related illness. For example, **work intensification** (employees working longer hours and working harder than ever before), high psychological demands, low decision latitude and poor social support—in combination—are suggested to be associated with premature development of cardiovascular symptoms and stress-related conditions.[6]

Occupational health and safety also relates to psychosocial factors, which may result in conditions such as stress, dissatisfaction, apathy, inattentiveness and irritability. These include outcomes linked to work-related injury and illness. Occupational stress has become a major area for research in several industrialised countries. A useful and generally applicable definition of *work-related stress* is: 'Occupational stress exists in the person's recognition of their inability to cope with demands relating to work, and in their subsequent experience of discomfort.'[7]

Mendelson offers a definition of the term **stress response** as encompassing 'the total of the individual's emotional and/or physiological response to the event(s) perceived or evaluated as a threat to his or her wellbeing'.[8] The effects of occupational stress can be manifested in a number of ways. First, the effects of stress on productivity and work performance will differ between occupations, but research has consistently indicated that individuals experiencing stress are more likely to develop poor concentration and lack of attentiveness.[9] This may have the combined effect of reducing work rates and increasing the likelihood of accidental injury. Second, the effects of stress may be evident in affective disturbances (such as irritability), behavioural manifestations (such as substance abuse) and psychiatric disorders (such as depressive disorders). Third, the physical effects of stress are seen in cases where, for example, the anxiety response to stress includes both psychological and physiological components. Among the long-term physical health effects of occupational stress, the most frequently cited conditions are: ischaemic heart disease, hypertension, peptic ulceration and diabetes.[10] As discussed in the 'Managing challenges through attracting and retaining people' case, strategies for stress management may be an important and effective aspect of human resource management.

Occupational health and safety (OHS)
the physical, physiological and psychosocial conditions of an organisation's workforce, related to aspects of work and the work context

Hazards
circumstances, procedures or environments that expose individuals to possible injury, illness, damage or loss.

Work intensification
employees working longer hours and working harder than ever before.

Stress response
an individual's emotional and/or physiological response to events perceived or evaluated as a threat to his or her wellbeing.

MAXIMISING EMPLOYEE PERFORMANCE WHILE MINIMISING EMPLOYEE STRESS

Many managers and business owners mistakenly fear that reducing employee stress requires reducing productivity or creating a 'country club' atmosphere, which in today's marketplace could be fatal. In fact, the opposite is true.

When organisations manage in ways that bring out the best in people, they also reduce employee stress. That's why most of *Fortune* magazine's 100 best companies to work for are industry leaders and enjoy high employee productivity. Employees in these companies are both happy and extremely productive.

The key to maximising productivity while minimising stress is understanding the factors that influence whether someone working very hard will feel stressed out and burnt out, or whether they will feel motivated, excited and committed. Scientific research on stress, combined with best practices of high performance companies, offers clear clues about the key factors that determine whether employees will be stressed out or energised by workplace demands.

Maximising employee productivity and performance

Give employees as much control over their jobs as possible. Research shows that control is the biggest factor in whether people feel stressed out or invigorated when facing a challenge. The more control people have over their work, the greater their job satisfaction, the higher their work quality and the lower their stress level. Giving employees control includes giving them the power to make job-related decisions, the flexibility to organise their work in the way they find optimal and the authority to make improvements on how their job is done.

Communicate clearly and often about every thing important. One of the greatest sources of employee stress is not knowing—not knowing about changes taking place in the company, not knowing their supervisor's job and performance expectations and not knowing if they are doing a good job. Communicating clearly in these areas not only reduces employee stress, but also helps them do a far better job.

Talk with your employees about what makes your company great, how you bring value to your customers and how your employees make that possible. People want to feel part of something great and they want to feel that they are making a significant contribution to that greatness. When they feel this way, they not only become energised by challenges, but they're also more able to endure difficulties without becoming burnt out.

Make sure supervisors know how to bring out the best in people. Supervisors play a huge role in employee morale, performance and stress levels. Supervisors who know how to provide guidance, support and encouragement minimise employee stress. Supervisors with poor management skills or personal problems are a tremendous source of stress and can't help employees deal with stressful times.

Encourage employees to talk freely and support one another. An 'all work and no play' environment burns out people quickly. Having a workplace where co-workers can talk without worrying about getting into trouble is especially important in high pressure jobs. Encouraging connections among co-workers also reduces stress, because having social support reduces the negative effects of stressful situations.

Help employees design their jobs to be as rewarding as possible. Although not all jobs are equally rewarding and fulfilling, much can be done to make even the least desirable ones more enjoyable. The more opportunity employees have to make decisions, use their mind and take responsibility, the more fulfilled they will be. To make this work, employees need to be involved in the job enrichment process.

Improve your hiring and orientation process. Because the first few months on the job are often the most stressful, new employees are often the most vulnerable to accidents and injuries. For companies that have a sink or swim approach to new employees, these first few months are also a time of high turnover.

Make sure employees have the resources and training to do their jobs well. When people feel inadequate and ill-equipped to handle a challenge, they get stressed out. If employees don't have the tools, technology, time, staff, or training to do their jobs well, they are going to be stressed out and won't be able to work at their true potential.

Source: Excerpt from D. Lee, 2005, 'Maximising employee performance while minimising employee stress, *Human Resources*, 8 March. www.humanresourcesmagazine.com.au

We suggest that OHS concerns should be viewed as part of an integrated human-resource management strategy. Therefore, job-related stress, and several other workplace issues that are related to OHS, such as workplace bullying, emotional labour, drug testing in the workplace, and employee assistance programs, are discussed in Chapter 17, Managing employee turnover and retention. These issues are complex and encompass a range of human-resource management concerns in addition to occupational health and safety.

As one example, we discuss here briefly the issue of workplace drug and alcohol testing. A national household survey conducted in 2001 found that 4.3 per cent of respondents went to work when they were affected by alcohol during the past 12 months and 2.3 per cent went to work when they were under the influence of other drugs. Also, it has been reported that in 39 per cent of all workplace deaths, the cause was alcohol consumed at work during usual duties or at a work-sponsored function. The issue of alcohol and drugs at work received considerable media attention when Qantas endeavoured to introduce compulsory random drug and alcohol testing for its employees, who represent the largest unionised workforce in Australia.[11] Approaches to alcohol and drug testing have varied across industries. Many industries, such as coal mining, have long carried out routine testing, particularly for blue-collar employees, but more employers are interpreting their legal obligations—to provide a safe workplace—to include testing a broader range of employees for drugs. In the investment banking industry, there have been widespread and enduring rumours of cocaine use. Many major investment banks have policies prohibiting drug use yet do not conduct workplace drug testing.[12] However, as indicated in the 'HRM Spotlight', drug and alcohol abuse can have substantial consequences for individuals, with implications for HR managers dealing with these issues.

Employee representatives and trade unions have pointed to several criticisms of drug tests. First, they do not screen for impairment of the employee's ability, they merely screen for the presence of an illegal substance in the employee's system. Second, workers may view testing as an invasion of privacy. Third, the efficacy of many tests, widely used in some parts of Australian industry, is largely unproved by rigorous research. Also, it has been argued that drug testing ignores other major factors that can impair a worker's productivity and performance, such as stress and fatigue. Yossi Berger, from the Australian Workers Union, says: 'When I say to employers that if you take a sample of drugs off this worker at 3 am to check for your favourite drugs and alcohol, then I want 50 per cent of the sample so I can test for what the workplace is putting into their system for things like fumes and diesel, as well as what the roster may be doing to his hormones, they get very shy about that equity'.[13]

Occupational health and safety statistics in Australia

Work-related injury, illness and death are widely acknowledged to be major social and economic problems in Australia and many other industrialised nations.[14] While substantial improvements in health and safety have been achieved in the past decade or so, recent Australian statistics show the need for OHS to be recognised as an important area for improvement. Two thousand or more Australians die each year from workplace incidents and disease, approximately one in every 20 workers will suffer a work-related injury or disease, and the cost to the Australian economy is around $30 000 million per year.[15] According to preliminary data available, in 2003–04, there were 189 compensated

HANDLING DRUG AND ALCOHOL ABUSE IN THE WORKPLACE

HRM SPOTLIGHT

With an estimated 62 per cent of drug and alcohol abusers in Australia in full-time employment, equating to 300 000 Australian workers, the effects of drugs and alcohol represent a substantial source of hazard in the workplace—not to mention diminished productivity.

Given this, many employers take a proactive approach to drugs and alcohol in the workplace by implementing and enforcing drug and alcohol policies. However, two recent cases suggest enforcement of such policies may not always be upheld by reviewing tribunals.

In a recent unfair dismissal case in New South Wales, the Full Bench upheld a decision of a single judge, ordering the reinstatement of a police officer who was dismissed for a high-range PCA offence.

The officer, while off duty and under the influence of alcohol, lost control of his motor vehicle and ran into two parked cars and two shop fronts. This was the police officer's second drink driving offence in four years.

The Commission was persuaded to reinstate the officer on the basis of a voluntary undertaking the officer had made to abstain from consuming alcohol at any time, whether at work or elsewhere.

Given the undertaking had been made voluntarily, the Commission did not consider it inappropriate to impose the restraint on the officer's private life. The Full Bench did, however, vary the order previously made by the single judge, restricting the ability of the police to administer random breath tests on the officer to the hours in which the officer was on duty.

In ordering reinstatement, the Commission was also influenced by the fact that the officer had while off duty been drinking with colleagues, who had invited him out in an effort to console him over the recent suicide of a close friend; expressed remorse for his actions; suffered significant financial loss for the property damage caused; and undertaken treatment to combat his alcohol abuse.

In a recent decision in Tasmania, the Commission while finding the dismissal of a drug-addicted nurse was fair, recommended the nurse be re-employed at a lower level and be given access to a rehabilitation program. In this case, the nurse had falsified drug records in order to steal and self-administer Panadeine Forte tablets.

The Commission found the nurse had not been dismissed because of his drug dependency, but because he had falsified hospital records and stolen the Panadeine Forte tablets from his employer over an extended period of time.

The Commission indicated that: '[t]o dismiss an individual [because of their drug dependency] without allowing the opportunity for rehabilitation, would in [its] view be contrary to the more enlightened reform and treatment approach reasonably expected in contemporary society'.

Given health professionals are often susceptible to drug dependency issues, a policy for management of such issues would be appropriate.

HR tips

These cases demonstrate that it may be advisable to guide employees towards services to assist with their drug and/or alcohol dependency problems and ensure this issue is addressed in the business's drug and alcohol policy.

The cases also highlight the need for an employee to be clear as to the reason for disciplinary action, including dismissal. The misconduct may be drug or alcohol related; however, the misconduct from which the disciplinary action arose may not always be due to the intoxication of the employee while at work.

These cases also act as useful reminders that drug and/or alcohol dependencies can constitute disabilities. As such, it is important to make carefully considered decisions about disciplining affected employees.

If the employee does not claim a disability, a policy breach may justify disciplinary action. If an employee alleges a disability, it may be necessary to consider whether they can undertake the inherent requirements of their position given the disability.

Source: K. Godfrey, 2006, 'Handling drug and alcohol abuse in the workplace', *Human Resources*, 13 December.
www.humanresourcesmagazine.com.au

---

fatalities in Australia that were a result of workplace activity. It is noteworthy that 177 (94 per cent) of the compensated fatalities were males; only 12 (6 per cent) were female. For compensated cases, the construction industry, with 17 per cent, or 32 fatalities, recorded the highest number of fatalities, followed by the transport and storage industry (30 fatalities).[16] The total preliminary number of workers compensation claims reported in 2003–04 resulting in a fatality, permanent or temporary disability and an absence from work of at least one week was 137 550.

Nationally, the manufacturing industry had the highest number of claims (20 per cent of all claims), followed by health and community services, construction, and retail trade. Twenty-six per cent of all new claims (35 480 claims) were made by employees in the 'labourers and related workers' occupation category.[17]

Australian occupational health and safety law

Occupational health and safety law in Australia has three sources, namely common law duty of care, criminal law and civil statute law (see Chapter 3, The legal context for human resource management).

1. *Common law*. This law (judge-made law, as opposed to acts of parliament) establishes the duties that one individual or group owes to another.[18] Employers, employees, contractors, manufacturers and suppliers all have common law duties with regard to OHS.[19]
2. *Criminal law*. It is possible for OHS incidents to lead to criminal law charges. For example, a workplace death may lead to a charge of manslaughter against individuals and companies involved in the death.[20] On 27 November 2003, the Australian Capital Territory became the first Australian jurisdiction to introduce industrial manslaughter laws. The *Crimes (Industrial Manslaughter) Amendment Act 2003* came into effect on 1 March 2004.[21]
3. *Civil statute law*. This law is also known as legislation. It is made by an act of parliament. Individual statutes are known as 'Acts', such as the *Occupational Health and Safety (Commonwealth Employment) Act 1991*. Occupational health and safety legislation covers a broad range of issues relating to the workplace environment, the work performed and the people involved in or affected by work activities. Occupational health and safety is regulated by the Federal Government, and state and territory governments. However, the responsibility for OHS in Australia rests primarily with the states and territories. Each state or territory has its own legislation and OHS authority, which is responsible for implementing legislation, inspecting workplaces and prosecuting legislation breaches.

In the past two decades, governments have been moving away from prescriptive legislation towards performance-based provisions, which define OHS standards to be met and enable employers to make decisions about how best to implement OHS in their workplace.[22]

The development of regulation and policy with regard to OHS in Australia is indicative of the increasing attention given to OHS across many industrialised nations. Historically in Australia, differences in legislation across the states and territories led to different systems, inadequate information passed between compensation bodies and agencies, and little constructive information about OHS issues was provided to the Australian public.[23] The proclamation of OHS legislation in Australia, as in many other industrialised nations, reflects the emergence of the holistic view that unsafe physical, physiological and psychosocial conditions in the work environment, as well as unsafe actions, need to be eliminated. There is considerable evidence that OHS legislation has played an important role in the reduction of work-related injury, illness and death, although these elements remain significant concerns.[24] Recent developments in OHS legislation and policy parallel developments in industrial relations, particularly the devolution to enterprise bargaining.[25] (See Chapter 5, Industrial relations)

Historically, the need for regulation of OHS was recognised in Europe with the advent of the industrial revolution in the nineteenth century; legislation was required to deal with the increasing risk of injury and illness that arose from the introduction of new machines and workplace processes.[26] Although concern for worker safety would seem to be a universal societal goal, comprehensive legislation regarding OHS did not emerge in this country until the mid 1980s. Australian OHS regulation was strongly influenced by developments in the United Kingdom in the 1970s, in particular the Robens Report.[27] The Robens model had two principal aims: to create a unified approach by bringing together OHS legislation into an umbrella statute containing 'principle-based standards'[28] applying to a range of workplace parties; and to create a more 'effectively self-regulating system'.[29]

Lord Robens, an industrialist, introduced the concept of duty of care by employers to provide safe workplaces. Duty of care underpins OHS laws in all Australian jurisdictions; breaches of this concept are subject to a range of penalties through the courts.[30] **Duty of care** requires everything *reasonably practicable* to be done to protect the health and safety of the workplace. It is requested of all employers, their employees and any others who have an influence on hazards in a workplace. Typical employers' duties under the OHS Acts include: providing workplaces and systems of work that are safe and without risks to health; making arrangements for the safe use, handling, storage and transport of plant and substances at work; and providing adequate information, training and supervision for employees. Typical employees' duties include: not endangering their own or others' safety and health through any act or omission; and cooperating with measures introduced to protect their own and others' safety and health.[31]

Duty of care
the requirement for everything reasonably practicable to be done to protect the health and safety of the workplace.

Australian federal occupational health and safety legislation

The Federal Government introduced the *National Occupational Health and Safety Commission Act* in December 1985. This Act was repealed in 2005 and replaced by the *Australian Workplace Safety Standards Act 2005*.[32]

Table 4.1 above shows the major federal OHS-related legislation in Australia. The *National Occupational Health and Safety Commission Act* established the National Occupational Health and Safety Commission (NOHSC), which comprised 18 members representing employers, unions and government, and employed public service researchers. The NOHSC was established to lead and coordinate national efforts and campaigns to prevent workplace injury, disease and fatality in Australia. It did not have the power to make or enforce legislation. In May 2004, the Federal Government announced that the NOHSC would be replaced by a smaller ministerial advisory group, the Australian Safety and Compensation Council (ASCC). The ASCC membership comprises government, employer and employee representatives. This decision was criticised by employers and unions as a 'cost-cutting measure that could undermine moves towards national health and safety'.[33] A related issue is that funding for Worksafe Australia was reduced—this led to concerns about who will take responsibility for research related to the impact of specific hazards and the development of OHS standards.

As shown on the ASCC website, the *National OHS Strategy 2002–2012* provides a basis for the national approach to OHS; it has set the following targets:

- to sustain a significant, continual reduction in the incidents of work-related fatalities with a reduction of at least 20 per cent by 30 June 2012 (with a reduction of 10 per cent being achieved by 30 June 2007)

| TABLE 4.1 | Principal federal legislation related to OHS |

- The *Commonwealth of Australia Constitution Act 1900* constitutes the Commonwealth of Australia. Section 51 constitutes the basis for federal parliament's legislative power in relation to OHS.
- The *Australian Workplace Safety Standards Act 2005* established the Australian Safety and Compensation Council.
- The *Occupational Health and Safety (Commonwealth Employment) Act 1991* aims to promote the occupational health and safety of persons employed by the Commonwealth and Commonwealth authorities. This legislation has been renamed the *Occupational Health and Safety Act 1991* and amendments due to come into effect in March 2007 will provide a substantial step towards providing a national OHS legislative regime and workers compensation scheme, as self-insurers will then be excluded from state OHS laws.
- The *Occupational Health and Safety (Maritime Industry) Act 1993* provides for the health and safety of persons working on ships and offshore industry mobile units.
- The *Industrial Chemicals (Notification and Assessment) Act 1989* established a national system of notification and assessment of industrial chemicals; information about the properties and effects of the chemicals is obtained from importers and manufacturers of the chemicals.
- The *Federal Court of Australia Act 1976* includes provision for the constitution of an Industrial Branch of the Federal Court of Australia. Part of the jurisdiction of the court is the interpretation of industrial awards and agreements that may contain OHS provisions.
- The *Workplace Relations Act 1996* relates to the prevention and settlement of certain industrial disputes. Part V of the Act deals with inspectors and their powers to investigate matters affecting the safety of employees.

Source: Adapted from *Occupational Health and Safety Commentary and Cases: Legislative Overview*, 2004, CCH Australia Limited, North Ryde. Also see Bart Shanahan and Luke Connolly, 2007, 'OHS goes national', *HR Monthly*, February, pp. 30–31.

- to reduce the incidence of workplace injury by at least 40 per cent by 30 June 2012 (with a reduction of 20 per cent being achieved by 30 June 2007).[34]

Five priorities are identified by the *National OHS Strategy 2002–2012*:

- reduce the impact of risk at work
- improve the capacity of business operators and workers to manage OHS effectively
- prevent occupational disease more effectively
- eliminate hazards at the design state
- strengthen the capacity of government to influence OHS outcomes.[35]

There are five priority industries targeted in the *National OHS Strategy 2002–2012*: agriculture, forestry and fishing; building and construction; health and community services; manufacturing; and transport and storage. These sectors were chosen because national statistics indicate that they have the highest incidence rates and/or high numbers of workers compensation claims, when compared with other industries.[36]

Australian state and territory occupational health and safety legislation

By 1995, each of the Australian state and territory jurisdictions had enacted OHS legislation based, to some extent, on the Robens model.[37] The broad philosophy of state and territory OHS legislation is to improve safety standards to meet the requirements of a dynamic, technologically advanced industrial society. The various OHS Acts place obligations on employers, occupiers of premises, manufacturers, suppliers, employees, self-employed people and the Crown to ensure the safety of employees and others (visitors, contractors, etc.) in their workplaces.[38] The legislation places an obligation on all employers and employees to maintain a secure, healthy and safe working environment, with emphasis placed on duty of care and co-regulation by managers and employees.[39]

The Acts show combinations of preventive, punitive and OHS promotion measures. Legislation enacted in Australian states and territories has become quite consistent, although there are some differences with regard to penalties and varying emphasis on punishment. Some of the features of the principal legislation are outlined below:[40]

- *Australian Capital Territory.* The principal OHS legislation for private sector employees in the Australian Capital Territory is the *Occupational Health and Safety Act 1989*. The Act establishes the OHS Council, sets out the duties of various workplace parties and provides for health and safety representatives and committees. Emergency procedures and the use of improvement and prohibition notices are also covered.
- *New South Wales.* The principal Act covering occupational health and safety in New South Wales is the *Occupational Health and Safety Act 2000*. This replaced the 1983 Act and includes several changes. For example, the absolute duty of employers to provide a safe workplace is more clearly emphasised in the 2000 Act than in the previous 1983 Act. The 2000 Act also emphasises the need for employers to consult with employees on OHS matters and agree on arrangements to maintain ongoing consultation. This may occur through a committee or a safety representative, through other arrangements, or through a combination of these arrangements. The 2000 Act addresses the roles of safety inspectors, including their use of investigation, and improvement and prohibition notices. The 2000 Act contains expanded provisions relating to criminal and other proceedings, and includes sentencing guidelines. In 2005 the NSW government announced the establishment of a five-year statutory review of the *Occupational Health and Safety Act 2000*.
- *Northern Territory.* The principal occupational health statute in the Northern Territory is the *Work Health Act 1986*. In addition to various general provisions relating to OHS, this Act established the Work Health Authority and the Work Health Advisory Council.
- *Queensland.* The *Workplace Health and Safety Act 1995* is the principal OHS law in Queensland. It promotes freedom from, and protects people from, the risk of disease or injury that may be caused or created by workplaces and workplace activities. The Act established an OHS council and industry committees. The Act also covers: OHS representatives, committees and safety officers; the making of OHS standards; imposing OHS obligations on people who may affect the health and safety of others; the appointment and powers of inspectors; and enforcement procedures. Amendments to the Act, effective 1 June 2003, clarify the obligations of all stakeholders, amend the powers of inspectors and increase penalties. The *Workplace Health and Safety and Other Acts Amendment Act 2003* widened the obligations of employers to ensure the safety of all people working from the employer's business or undertaking.[41]
- *South Australia.* The principal Act in South Australia is the *Occupational Health, Safety and Welfare Act 1986*, which aims to: secure the health, safety and welfare of people at work and eliminate risks to their health, safety and welfare; protect the public against risks to their health or safety arising out of, or in connection with, the activities of people at work; involve employees and employers in issues affecting occupational health, safety and welfare; and encourage registered

- *Tasmania.* The Tasmanian *Workplace Health and Safety Act 1995* applies in all workplaces, including mines. It has introduced performance-based legislation to Tasmania and sets out the duty of care of the various workplace parties. Workplaces where hazardous work is carried out may be declared as 'designated workplaces'. Before work begins at a designated workplace, the employer must notify the director of industry safety. The Act provides for the establishment of OHS committees and for the issue of codes of practice. The functions and powers of the chief executive of Tasmania Development and Resources (TDR) and Workplace Safety Tasmania under the Act are also specified. The Act was amended by the *Workplace Health and Safety Amendment Act 2002*, which includes increased penalties.
- *Victoria.* The principal Victorian legislation is the *Occupational Health and Safety Act 2004*. The Act contains, in addition to the general provisions relating to OHS, provisions for OHS representatives and committees, inspections, improvement and prohibition notices, and legal proceedings. In 2004, the Victorian OHS laws were reviewed for the first time in almost 20 years. A report containing wide-ranging recommendations was delivered in April 2004 by Chris Maxwell QC.[42] The *Occupational Health and Safety Act 2004* came into effect on 1 July 2005.[43]
- *Western Australia.* The principal Western Australian OHS statute is the *Occupational Safety and Health Act 1984* (also see *Occupational Safety and Health Legislation Amendment Act 1995*). In addition to the general provisions relating to OHS, this Act established what is now known as the WorkSafe Western Australia Commission, which makes various recommendations to the relevant minister about OHS.

Overall, a wide range of OHS matters are typically covered in OHS state and territory legislation.[44] Common requirements in OHS Acts around Australia include:

- promotion of OHS in the workplace
- provision of safe work systems
- prevention of industrial injuries and disease
- protection of the health and safety of the public in relation to work activities
- specification of penalties for breaches of the Acts
- rehabilitation and maximum recovery from incapacity of injured workers.

Occupational health and safety enforcement authorities

Each OHS Act provides for a regulatory authority to administer OHS law in that state or territory. These authorities comprise an administrative structure and an inspectorate with responsibility for enforcing OHS laws. Occupational health and safety authorities provide both information and assistance, and enforce legal compliance. The emphasis of these authorities is on voluntary compliance with OHS legislation.

Workplace inspectors have powers including:

- entering workplaces to conduct searches, inspections, examinations and tests
- taking samples, photographs and other evidence
- requiring persons on the premises to provide information

- requiring occupiers to provide assistance and facilities to carry out their duties, including the power to stop the use of anything on the premises (as long as notice is given)
- inspecting records and taking copies of records
- serving improvement notices requiring a person to remedy a contravention of an OHS Act (fines may be imposed if there is failure to comply)
- serving prohibition notices preventing an activity from being carried out due to an immediate risk to the health or safety of a person (fines may be imposed if there is failure to comply)
- initiating prosecutions for breach of OHS law in the relevant court.[45]

The OHS authority has the discretionary power to decide whether to prosecute. For example, an authority will prosecute if investigations reveal circumstances such as offences involving risk of death or serious injury, or if prosecution is considered to be in the public interest. The OHS Acts typically include penalty provisions for non-compliance, specifying the maximum fine or prison sentence that can be imposed by the relevant court.

Complementary regulation

In each jurisdiction, the principal statutes are complemented by a number of other Acts and regulations. Despite the trend towards consolidating all the OHS laws, there are many OHS statutes in each state and territory. Specific OHS statutory obligations must be considered in the context of the general statutory duties imposed by OHS legislation.

- *Workers compensation and rehabilitation legislation.* One of the major areas of legislation related to OHS Acts is workers compensation and rehabilitation legislation, which provides compensation to injured employees, regardless of who is responsible for a workplace illness or injury. Prior to the introduction of workers compensation and rehabilitation legislation, injured employees could only bring a common law action against their employer, which required proof of negligence by the employer or a person acting on behalf of the employer. Current workers compensation and rehabilitation legislation in each Australian state and territory has either abolished or severely limited the rights of workers to sue for common law negligence. Hence, the most common OHS legal action by employees is a workers compensation claim.[46] The cost of administering the Australian workers compensation schemes in the 1999–2000 period was $1020 million. Payments made by the schemes on medical and other services in the same year were $1060 million.[47]
- *Vocational rehabilitation.* A key feature of workers compensation regulation and policy in Australia is the encouragement of **vocational rehabilitation** (occupational reintegration for injured workers). The 'return-to-work' policy is based on the joint assumptions that this will be of benefit to individuals and reduce the costs of compensation. Australian jurisdictions have included vocational rehabilitation and return-to-work strategies in the relevant legislation, partly as a means of providing some employment security for injured workers. The incidence of injured workers being dismissed is largely unknown due to a lack of national statistics, but the impact of employment loss is known to be substantial for the individuals, their families and the general social security system.[48] Overall, there is increasing use of rehabilitation facilities to assist in the return of workers to the workforce after

Vocational rehabilitation
occupational reintegration, or return-to-work, for injured workers.

OHS incidents. Hence, there has been substantial growth in the rehabilitation industry and the importance of rehabilitation as part of managing OHS in the workplace.
- *OHS regulations.* Occupational health and safety Acts often set out broad objectives and contain provisions for achieving these objectives. Detailed provisions are often set out in legally binding regulations made under the relevant Act. Occupational health and safety regulations contain provisions relating to, for example, the appointment of safety officers, the election of health and safety committees, workplace inspectors' powers, workplace amenities (such as lunchrooms, toilets and washing facilities), specific processes (such as spray painting), and workplace hazards (such as asbestos).[49]

  When the need arises to change the way in which a specific area or problem is addressed, regulations may be added or amended in a quick and effective manner, thus circumventing the more laborious measure of amending a statute.[50]
- *Codes of practice and national standards.* Codes of practice are issued by the Commonwealth, states and territories to advise employers, and others with obligations under the legislation, how to comply with the legislation. For example, there is a national code of practice for healthcare workers and other people at risk of the transmission of HIV (human immunodeficiency virus) and hepatitis B in the workplace. Where specific technical detail is needed, codes of practice may refer to Australian standards and international standards, such as those of the ISO (International Standards Organization).[51] National standards are regulatory models developed by the ASCC (previously NOHSC). They incorporate nationally agreed minimum standards of OHS to be achieved by the federal, state and territory governments. The ASCC (previously NOHSC) has also developed national codes of practice. Overall, codes of practice and standards provide guidance on setting up safe systems of work.

Occupational health and safety and industrial relations

In each Australian jurisdiction, as has been discussed, there is a principal, wide-ranging OHS Act. These Acts, which aim to increase self-regulation of OHS following the Robens model, are reviewed on a regular basis by tripartite committees (government, employer and union representatives), and unions are often involved in workplace OHS committees. The self-regulatory approach encouraged in OHS legislation is based on the assumption that employers and employees share a common interest in OHS; it also assumes a well-organised trade union movement.[52] However, changes in Australian industrial relations legislation (see Chapter 5, Industrial relations) led these assumptions to flounder. Just as the negotiation of working conditions has been decentralised to the workplace, the participation of unions in negotiating working conditions has been reduced.[53] Under the *Workplace Relations Act 1996 (Cwlth)* and *WorkChoices* amendments (see Chapters 3 and 5), OHS can no longer form part of award deliberations, as OHS is considered a 'further matter' to be decided at the workplace. Hence, although there is widespread recognition of the relationship between OHS and industrial relations, there appears to be a 'disparity between OHS and industrial relations regulatory frameworks. While OHS legislation relies on the involvement of unions and various government bodies in setting and monitoring OHS standards, industrial relations legislation actively discourages third party involvement, particularly union involvement, at the workplace'.[54] (See Chapter 5 for more discussion of industrial relations.)

Moving beyond occupational health and safety legal compliance

Overall, the effective management of OHS demands knowledge of the current legal requirements relevant to one's workplace and/or organisation. Legislation has been unquestionably successful in raising the level of awareness of OHS in Australia. Yet, legislation alone cannot solve all the problems of workplace health and safety. Many industrial injuries are a product of unsafe behaviours, not unsafe working conditions. Major behavioural changes cannot be expected unless employees and employers are convinced of the importance of OHS.[55]

Several governments, including the Victorian State Government, have used advertisements in their efforts to raise awareness and reduce workplace fatalities. To fully maximise the health and safety of workers, employers need to go well beyond the letter of the law and embrace its spirit. National initiatives to raise awareness of OHS include Occupational Health and Safety Week, an annual awareness program that runs in the first week of May each year. This initiative follows the International Day of Mourning—a day to remember those who have been killed at work.

Since conforming to the legislation alone does not necessarily guarantee OHS, many employers go beyond the letter of the law. Effective management of the diverse needs of the workforce and the complex workplace context for OHS requires more than legal compliance. In particular, the challenges related to managing an ageing workforce are particularly relevant to OHS. In the next section, we focus on OHS issues for the ageing workforce. Then, we show how these and other issues can be managed through organisation-based OHS management systems that not only comply with OHS legal requirements but are integrated with a strategic approach to human resource management.

Occupational health and safety and the ageing workforce

Older workers
variously defined as 55 years of age and over, between 50 and 80 years of age, and as 40-plus years of age.

The increasing proportion of **older workers** (variously defined as 55 years of age and over, between 50 and 80 years of age, and 40-plus years of age) has several important implications for OHS management.[56] The increase in the average age of workers is a dominant characteristic of the workforce in Australia and many other industrialised nations. The ageing of the workforce reflects the increase in life expectancy of the population to between 75 and 85 years of age, as well as a sustained low level of fertility, which has resulted in proportionally fewer children in the population.[57] Improvements in medical treatments and technology, and the uptake of healthier dietary habits and lifestyles will continue to contribute to increased numbers of older people who are physically capable of working.[58]

A range of statistics show the need for attention to issues of concern to older workers, and the need for OHS education and management strategies that have the flexibility to address the diverse needs of older workers. The ageing of Australia's population is expected to continue for at least the next 50 years. The proportion of the Australian population aged 65 and over is projected to increase to 24 per cent by 2051. In 1996, the proportions of men and women aged 65 and over were 11 per cent and 14 per cent respectively. By 2051, 22 per cent of men and 26 per cent of women (six million people) are expected to be aged 65 years and over.[59] There has been a decline of older workers in some industries, such as manufacturing, mostly due to a declining labour force of participating males.[60] Female participation has increased over the past 30 years for all age groups—except for those aged 65 years and above.[61] Changes such as the increase in service and information sectors, particularly in part-time employment, have contributed to the gender differences in employment of older workers. This gender difference is also evident in other industrialised nations.[62]

Given the complexity of the data and the diversity in the population of older workers, it is perhaps not surprising that recent research shows that simple conclusions with regard to the relationships between OHS and age are not possible.[63] As discussed below, it is necessary to consider the workplace context, influential factors and differential impacts and outcomes related to OHS for older workers. Numerous misconceptions have led to age discrimination in the workplace.[64] Although older workers are sometimes perceived as slower, less flexible, prone to illness and accidents, more resistant to change, and uninterested in training,[65] there is research evidence that contradicts these perceptions.[66]. Below, we discuss research findings with respect to work-related injury and illness issues that are related to older workers:

- *Work-related injury.* Research findings with regard to the relationship between age and work-related injuries are inconsistent. On one hand, several studies have found no significant relationship between age and work-related injury.[67] On the other hand, complex relationships between age and work-related injury are suggested in research such as that by Ringenbach and Jacobs, who surveyed 209 workers in a nuclear power plant.[68] They found that older workers experienced more days off work (relating to injury) than younger workers. While the older workers did not report having more injuries, they took more days to recover from injury than did younger workers. Australian statistics support the international findings; injury severity increases with age, requiring more time for recovery.[69] James and Brownlea have shown, however, that the severity of impact experienced as a result of work-related injury is not entirely attributable to age.[70] Severity of impact is influenced by a range of factors, including job security, organisational factors, gender role and the provision of various types of support (both instrumental and emotional).
- *Work-related illness.* These illnesses are also a major OHS concern, as there are many and varied sources of occupational disease. While several illnesses are associated with age, an association between work-related illness and age is not clear. As was shown for injuries, job characteristics and the work environment should be considered in an analysis of factors related to work-related illness.[71]
- *Occupational health and safety outcomes and age: the case of absenteeism.* Occupational health and safety issues are often related to outcomes such as absenteeism. There are, however, mixed findings in the research on age and absenteeism.[72] For example, Rhodes found that unavoidable absence among older male workers may be higher than among younger workers, perhaps due to longer recovery periods and health problems associated with age.[73] More recent meta-analytic research, however, has found that older men had fewer short-term absences (that is, less than three days) than did younger men.[74] It is interesting to note that this relationship was not found to apply to women.

The large body of research on shiftwork has raised several important issues related to age and absenteeism, although there are few strong conclusions. On one hand, Härmä, Hakola and Laitinen found that older workers have greater difficulty in making adjustments to shiftwork.[75] On the other hand, Smith, Colligan and Tasto surveyed 660 shiftworkers in the United States food processing industry and found that older workers with longer job tenure had fewer absences due to illness.[76] In their study, it appeared that younger, less-experienced males were the group most influenced by shiftwork in terms of absence.[77]

Overall, this research appears to have two major implications. First, it should not be assumed that older workers are more prone than younger workers to injury or illness. Second, it should be recognised that a diverse workforce will have diverse OHS concerns and comprehensive management approaches are needed. Older workers may face OHS issues that are different from those relevant to younger workers. There is an increasing awareness of the need for comprehensive social policies and OHS management policies to assist older workers and to recognise older people as valuable human resource assets. Organisations as well as employees suffer the effects of work-related injury and illness. If OHS is diminished due to the multitude of influential factors that have been identified in empirical research, neither the employee nor the organisation will benefit. Effective management of OHS requires attention to a range of factors, including general societal factors, organisational factors and individual characteristics. The following section discusses the development of OHS management systems; issues for older workers are highlighted with respect to the HRM strategies that can be implemented for OHS.

The management of occupational health and safety

There are several noteworthy trends in the management of OHS. These trends are found across a range of levels, from social reforms to organisation-specific management approaches. The legislative developments with regard to OHS highlight the need for organisational policies and programs that address the OHS needs of all employees.

Occupational health and safety management should be an integral part of an organisation's strategic planning and management, and strategic planning specifically for OHS management is essential. Occupational health and safety management presents an important challenge for all managers. As we have discussed, there are legal requirements for employers to ensure safe working conditions for employees. Further, there is substantial research and practical evidence to demonstrate that effective management of OHS has benefits for employees, managers and other stakeholders. Stakeholders in OHS management include not only governments, unions, employees, employers and industry associations, but also contractors, suppliers, workplace owners, shareholders, workplace visitors, customers and the general community.

A major trend in OHS management is the increase in attention to prevention, rather than compensation, of work-related injury and illness, for a number of reasons. First, some notable debates over occupational hazards, such as asbestos, have made it clear that preventive actions are essential for the management of OHS. Second, there is widespread acceptance that a system focused on compensation will not effectively reduce occupational ill-health. Third, there is an increase in worker participation and a widening of the definition of occupational health and safety to include all health problems of workers.[78]

Organisational initiatives that seek to improve OHS management vary from simple legislative compliance to OHS management systems that are fully integrated with sophisticated human resource management strategies. Organisations differ in the extent to which they develop techniques, programs and activities to promote safety and prevent accidents. Also, the effectiveness of these techniques and programs varies with the industry type and organisation size. As illutrated in the 'Managing challenges through HR innovation' case, an increasing number of organisations are implementing comprehensive, preventive OHS management systems as part of a

FIRING UP WORKFORCE HEALTH AND FITNESS

A quick glance through Australia's health statistics is a sobering exercise. Some 56 per cent of Australians are overweight or obese. Nearly 80 000 new cases of cancer are diagnosed each year. More than 430 000 Australians are diabetic, with a further 350 000 believed to be suffering from the condition without knowing it. More than 21 per cent of Australians have cardiovascular disease, a condition that claims a life every 10 minutes.

Although these figures are depressing, they needn't be. Many of these illnesses are preventable. More than two-thirds of all cancers could be prevented by lifestyle changes. Not smoking, managing high blood pressure and cholesterol, losing weight and increasing physical activity can also limit the risk of developing cardiovascular disease. Even the onset of osteoporosis (and therefore, fractures in the elderly) can be delayed or prevented by early intervention.

More companies are taking up the challenge to make their workforces fit and healthy. Benefits flow to both the individual and the company when employees are in good physical condition.

Building health at Boral

Boral Ltd, the Australian building resources materials company, employs 10 000 people. Its workforce is mostly blue collar, predominantly male with an average age of 45 years. Eighteen months ago, the company started to roll out free annual health assessments to all employees, making it the largest completed health promotion program in the country to date.

Health seminar topics conducted through Boral in the last 12 months have included nutrition, men's health, exercise and sleep management. The latter is very important to the company from an OHS perspective, as fatigue is a workplace safety issue.

The whole company is undergoing its second round of assessments. Anecdotal evidence to date suggests BWell is a very positive employee engagement tool. 'Employees feel they are being valued by the company, there is a higher health awareness in the organisation and some individuals have had impressive weight loss', says Cate Hathaway, Boral's general manager of workers compensation.

Accor, health and hospitality

Accor is the world's largest hotel, tourism and corporate services group. It has more than 120 hotels in the Pacific region under the brands Sofitel, Novotel, Mercure, All Seasons, Ibis, Formule 1 and Base backpackers. The company employs about 9000 people throughout its properties in Australia and the South Pacific, including 140 in its Sydney regional office.

Darryl Prince, Accor's general manager, human resources for Asia Pacific, says his organisation has been developing its health and wellbeing strategies in consultation with a single provider for the last three to four years. Accor's motivation for introducing a health and fitness program was the physical demands that a career in hospitality puts on its employees. 'You need high energy to work in hospitality. There are demanding customers, demanding hours and you can be around food and alcohol all the time', says Prince.

Prince has approached the issue through annual week-long corporate health expos held at various sites. All employees can have mini health assessments on site, attend lectures on weight control, stress management and nutrition, have skin checks and ergonomic consultations, and participate in yoga or other exercise sessions. Flu vaccinations are available to everyone each year. Accor also sponsors employees who participate in touch football competitions and the *BRW* triathlons.

Items covered by Boral's health assessment:

- Cholesterol
- Diabetes
- Blood pressure
- Body weight
- Physical activity
- Stress, anxiety, depression and loneliness
- Smoking
- Alcohol
- Back care
- Vision and lung function.

The Boral Health Resource Centre provides information to staff and their families on many aspects of the following topics:

- Asthma
- Back care
- Diabetes
- Drugs and alcohol
- Driving
- Exercise
- Financial health
- Gender health
- Heart health
- Winter/Summer health
- Nutrition
- Recipes
- Mental health
- Parenting
- Relationships
- Sleeping/shift work
- Stress management
- Work/life balance.

Source: Excerpt from T. Russell, 2006, 'Firing up workforce health and fitness', *Human Resources*, 20 February, pp. 18–19.
www.humanresourcesmagazine.com.au

OHS management system
organisational policy and programs that cover the planning, implementation, evaluation and improvement of OHS in an organisation.

OHS policy
a written statement approved by top management, typically accompanied by a set of OHS programs, rules and instructions, that identifies OHS accountabilities and sets out the ways in which OHS compliance will be met.

OHS program
a plan designed for policy implementation that identifies the OHS procedures, practices and people necessary to reach policy objectives.

Risk management
the process of identifying all hazards in the work or workplace, followed by an assessment of the associated risks and the implementation of effective measures to control those risks.

Safety climate
the attitudes, beliefs, perceptions and values that employers and employees share in relation to safety, and it is a subset of culture.

Safety culture
results from individual and group values, attitudes, perceptions, competencies and behaviours that determine the commitment to, and the style and effectiveness of, an organisation's OHS management.

strategic approach to human resource management. These often include health assessments such as those described at Boral and Accor.[79]

An **OHS management system** usually involves policy and programs that cover the planning, implementation, evaluation and improvement of OHS in an organisation. The **OHS policy** typically includes OHS goals for the organisation. The written OHS policy, approved by top management, is typically accompanied by a set of OHS programs, rules and instructions that identify OHS accountabilities and set out the ways in which OHS compliance will be met. Most Australian state and territory OHS laws include a provision for employers to prepare and revise, as often as necessary, a written statement of a general OHS policy for employees, and to make arrangements for carrying out that policy, and to bring the policy and any revisions to the notice of all people employed at the workplace.[80]

OHS programs, or plans designed for policy implementation, identify the OHS procedures, practices and people necessary to reach policy objectives.[81]

Fundamental to the performance-based legislative approach and the development of OHS management systems is the management of risk. **Risk management** is a process of identifying all hazards in the work or workplace, followed by an assessment of the associated risks and the implementation of effective measures to control those risks. The steps involved in risk management are discussed in more detail with regard to the conduct of OHS audits.[82]

Fundamental to an OHS management system is an organisational '**safety climate**' or '**safety culture**'.[83] Guldenmund has conducted a comprehensive review of the literature on safety culture and climate.[84] He reports that numerous definitions and models of each have been offered and the relationship between the two concepts has been debated and remains unclear. Similar to the concepts of general organisational culture and climate, the concepts of safety culture and climate have become 'almost interchangeable'.[85] However, it has been suggested that safety culture is more complex, encompassing basic assumptions, artefacts and espoused values about safety in the workplace, while a safety climate is a subset of culture, equating to the attitudes, behaviours and perceptions that employers and employees share in relation to safety.[86]

A definition of safety culture adopted by many researchers is:

the product of individual and group values, attitudes, perceptions, competencies and patterns of behaviour that determine the commitment to, and the style and proficiency of, an organisation's health and safety management … characterised by communications founded on mutual trust, shared perceptions of the importance of safety and by confidence in the efficacy of preventative measures.[87]

Safety cultures include awareness of factors such as:

- OHS practices and procedures
- management of risk
- work pressures
- communication of OHS issues at the workplace
- importance of OHS in training and performance appraisal
- management/supervisory attitudes about OHS
- safety of equipment and facilities
- management/supervisory actions in response to OHS issues
- employee understanding of OHS policies and procedures
- employee participation in activities related to OHS.[88]

As discussed in 'Managing challenges through sustainability: Healthy workers get the job done, surveys show', building awareness and understanding of health and safety issues is important for both individuals and organisations.

HEALTHY WORKERS GET THE JOB DONE, SURVEYS SHOW

TWO wide-ranging Australian studies released in the past six months have raised concerns about the health, and the future health, of the Australian workforce.

The latest National Health Survey by the Australian Bureau of Statistics finds that 62 per cent of Australian men are obese or overweight, a jump of 10 per cent in the past decade. And women are following the trend—more than 45 per cent of women are now overweight or obese, an 8 per cent rise since 1995.

Many Australian studies have focused on health problems among Australian workers but little research has been done to measure the impact of specific health problems on individual or organisational productivity.

One study released late last year suggests the impact is costly.

Consistent with the ABS data, the study found 62 per cent of workers were overweight. It also revealed more than half the respondents were sleep deprived and a fifth had suffered a medical condition in the three months before the survey. Back, neck or spinal problems were the most common complaints, with 29 per cent of people reporting this condition, followed by hayfever, rhinitis or sinusitis (22 per cent), heart disease (21 per cent), migraine (14 per cent) and asthma (13 per cent).

'The health of the Australian workforce was far below what we were expecting', says Anthony Goldman, manager, corporates at Medibank Private. 'We did a comparison with Britain and found we scored lower than the people in Britain, which, when I have talked about this in public forums, has always taken people by surprise.'

Perhaps more worrying for employers, however, was the extent that employees' health is linked to sick days taken and also how effectively they work when suffering from a range of common complaints.

Healthy employees averaged two days sick a year, estimated they worked 143 effective hours per month, and rated their performance 8.5 out of 10. Employees suffering from multiple conditions averaged 18 days sick a year, estimated they worked 49 effective hours and rated their performance at 3.7 out of 10.

Last year, in an effort to start tackling health issues in the workplace, Medibank Private rolled out its Medibank Priority program. Key elements of the corporate program include confidential on-line health assessment tools and on-line health information provided by Vielife, a British provider of health and wellbeing programs. The on-line assessment tools produce anonymous aggregate data identifying the common health conditions prevalent in a specific organisation. Using this information, a health information program can then be targetted.

Medibank Priority has so far been adopted by 39 other large organisations covering 90 000 employees.

At the annual AHRI convention in Melbourne in 2006, Don Iverson, University of Wollongong's Dean of Health and Behavioural Sciences, delivered a keynote address on presenteeism. This is the pervasive problem of people being at work when they are sick or suffering aches and pains but are functioning below full capacity.

A key point in Professor Iverson's address was that people often suffer unnecessarily with many health conditions and that, as a result, the impact of these conditions on their productivity is far greater than it needs to be. 'Employers have to understand that people do not always seek help for their health conditions', he says. 'A US study showed that two out of three people who had all the symptoms of migraine hadn't even gone to the doctor to be diagnosed. In other words, they think it is something that they can tough out', he says.

Health programs that give staff access to information on the health problems specific to their organisation provide simple interventions and a low cost solution to an expensive problem.

Source: Excerpt from W. Taylor, 2006, 'Healthy workers get the job done, surveys show', *The Age*, 10 June, p. 8. © 2006 Copyright John Fairfax Holdings Limited. www.theage.com.au

Elements of OHS management systems

Basic elements of an OHS management system can be categorised into three groups: organisation, responsibility and accountability; consultative arrangements; and specific program elements.[89]

1 *Organisation, responsibility and accountability.* Elements include the involvement of senior managers, line manager/supervisor responsibilities, all managers' accountability for OHS, performance management and the organisation's OHS policy.[90] As with all areas of HRM, responsibility for OHS is shared among HR,

executive, senior and line managers, and employees. Each group will have responsibility and accountability with regard to OHS, although the organisation of OHS responsibilities will vary between organisations. For example, larger organisations are more likely to have a dedicated OHS manager, reporting directly to senior management. An OHS manager's responsibilities may include:
- designing, evaluating and reviewing OHS policy and programs
- checking OHS legal compliance
- conducting or coordinating OHS audits
- providing advice to managers, supervisors and OHS representatives or committees
- communicating OHS information to all stakeholders
- overseeing OHS programs such as training and health promotion.

In many organisations, these activities will be the responsibility of the HR function.[91]

2 *Consultative arrangements*. These include elements such as OHS representatives or committees and broad employee participation.[92] OHS laws require that workplace OHS representatives and committees should provide a link between top management and employees with regard to OHS matters. Occupational health and safety representatives and committees, usually elected by employees, contribute by, for example, making recommendations to the employer about OHS matters.[93] Consultation is a basic requirement for the effective management of OHS, as consultation should enable everyone in the workplace to play a role in ensuring healthy and safe workplaces.[94]

3 *Specific OHS program elements*. These include:
- OHS rules and procedures
- training programs
- workplace inspections
- incident reporting and investigation
- statement of principles for the prevention and control of hazards
- data collection, analysis and record keeping
- OHS promotion and information provision
- emergency procedures
- medical and first-aid facilities and procedures.[95]

Occupational health and safety auditing

Auditing
(of OHS) a systematic examination against established criteria, conducted regularly to identify deviations from the OHS management system and determine whether these deviations can compromise health, safety and productivity.

In addition to the basic elements of the OHS management system, an auditing process is an essential part of managing OHS. **Auditing** (of OHS) is a systematic examination against established criteria, conducted regularly, to identify deviations from the OHS management system, and to determine whether these deviations can compromise health, safety and productivity. The information collected can be used to increase the effectiveness of the OHS management system.[96] The general duties section of each state and territory's OHS laws require employers to provide safe workplaces. While OHS audits may not be explicitly required, there may be requirements to monitor, review and inspect OHS, and regular audits are an effective way of meeting these requirements.

The elements of an OHS management system can be monitored and reviewed through the following steps, which are commonly taken in order to provide an auditing process.[97]

1 *Identification of standards*. Performance standards, or acceptable targets, need to be determined. These targets may include health and safety, budgetary, and production goals.

2 *Allocation of resources.* Appropriate resource allocation is required to ensure it will be possible to meet the targets. Resources may include financial, human and physical resources.

3 *Identification and communication of job hazards.* Using comprehensive OHS data collection, the identification and communication of job hazards is essential. Hazards are circumstances, procedures or environments that expose individuals to possible injury, illness, damage or loss.

Employees, supervisors and other knowledgeable sources need to sit down and discuss potential hazards related to safety. The job hazard analysis technique is one means of accomplishing this.[98] With this technique, each job is broken down into basic elements and each of these is rated for its potential for harm or injury. If there is consensus that some job element has high hazard potential, this element is isolated and potential technological or behavioural changes are considered.

Communication of a hazard and its associated **risk**, which is defined as the potential outcome of injury, illness, damage or loss resulting from a hazard, should take advantage of several media. Direct verbal supervisory contact is important for its saliency and immediacy. Regular staff information sessions can be considerably helpful in communicating OHS information. Written memos are important because they help establish a 'paper trail' that can later document a history of concern regarding the job hazard. Posters, especially those placed near the hazard, serve as a constant reminder, reinforcing other messages. However, it may be necessary to update and change posters regularly; otherwise employees may ignore the 'old' posters.

Risk
the potential outcome of injury, illness, damage or loss resulting from a hazard.

4 *Hazard evaluation and implementation of OHS programs.* Based on the data collected, the severity, risks and costs of OHS hazards and problems can be evaluated and OHS programs can be set up to inspect and monitor, control and eliminate hazards. These programs can then be formulated and implemented, and objectives regarding prevention of hazards may be established.[99]

The extent to which such risk management efforts will actually help to improve OHS depends on the degree of employee acceptance and correct use. If employees are involved in decisions to improve the safety of the work environment, they are more likely to accept the decision. In particular, increased worker participation and widening of the definition of OHS to include all health problems of workers play an important role in preventive OHS.[100]

5 *Analysis and evaluation of results.* The progress of programs should be monitored and evaluated against stated goals and objectives. Rigorous evaluation measures should be applied to OHS programs. Commonly used OHS measures are lost time injury frequency rate (LTIFR), incidents reported (classified by type and severity), near misses (classified by type and potential severity) and cost of accidents. Effectiveness of OHS management strategies may be measured by several indicators such as job performance, workers compensation claims, absenteeism and turnover data, cost effectiveness and productivity data.[101] Less easy to measure are psychological indicators of OHS, such as job satisfaction and job involvement. It is important to ensure that measures are reliable and valid. (See Chapter 18, Evaluating and improving the human resource function, for more discussion of the measurement and evaluation of HR activities.)

Performance assessment against OHS standards is required to ensure individual accountability. In other words, OHS behaviours may be a specific part of an individual's performance appraisal process (see Chapter 12, Employee development and career management). A system for objectively assessing improvements and giving positive feedback for correct safety procedures and behaviours needs to be established.

6. *OHS program and workplace improvement.* Implementation of safer and healthier working conditions and practices, with use of predictive knowledge to promote OHS in the future, is required. An ongoing process of improvement and evaluation will be beneficial to the organisation and employees.[102] The audit cycle should be completed by preparing an audit report, including identification of any corrective actions required, such as revision of existing policies and programs. Occupational health and safety audit reports can be used by line managers as a basis for OHS planning and improvement, and by senior management to confirm that OHS management systems are operating and are regularly reviewed.[103]

There are three main types of OHS audit types: a full-scale 'overview' audit of an operation's OHS management and technical systems; a more focused 'workplace' audit of a specific unit or work area; or a 'procedures' audit to examine a particular workplace hazard and related work practices.[104]

Several auditing tools are available from various OHS authorities and professional organisations. For example, SafetyMAP (Safety Management Achievement Program) is an OHS management system audit tool developed by the Victorian WorkCover Authority.[105] The National Safety Council of Australia uses a Five-star Health and Safety Management System, which is a quality system approach to OHS management. It includes a comprehensive manual and audit standard, including more than 1200 audit criteria, and is available as a computer-based system.[106] The National Safety Council of Australia also conducts an annual national OHS awards program, which recognises people and organisations integrating excellent OHS practices into their mainstream operations.

Human resource management strategies for occupational health and safety

An OHS management system can and should be supported through a wide range of HR strategies, as shown in the following examples. These examples also highlight the OHS implications for an ageing workforce.

Structural strategies

Organisational restructuring in many organisations involves increased use of teams and project-based work arrangements; these changes have implications for OHS and the development of a safety culture. The importance of safety *sub*cultures and safety behaviours among work teams has been identified in several empirical studies.[107] The implementation of teams often, although not always, involves employee empowerment, a redistribution of power with organisational de-layering and devolution of decision making from managers or supervisors to employees. Empowerment is usually undertaken not as a safety initiative, but as a means towards the achievement of organisational effectiveness, productivity, cost reduction and customer satisfaction.[108] Critics of empowerment have suggested that it places more stress on employees and may disrupt traditional career-paths.[109] Hechanova-Alampay and Beehr found that empowerment of employees and an increased span of control were significantly correlated to unsafe behaviours and incidents.[110] These authors suggest, therefore, that the implementation of teams requires consideration of both the competencies of employees and the capacity of managers or supervisors to lead the restructured work group. It should also be noted that work teams can sometimes be disempowering for employees, by reducing an individual's decision making involvement. The development and maintenance of work teams with a positive safety subculture and behaviours may require attention to specific OHS strategies such as training and supervisory responsibilities.[111]

Consideration of OHS with regard to organisational changes such as restructuring strategies, and consultation with workers about such changes, will benefit the organisation and the employee.

Job design

One aspect of altering the work environment to improve OHS is to design the job to be more comfortable and less fatiguing, by taking into consideration the physical, physiological and psychosocial aspects of work. A mismatch between the physical capabilities of employees and the physical demands of jobs can lead to work-related injuries and illness, particularly stress-related illness. Person–job match also applies to the tools required to perform the tasks.[112]

For example, several authors have offered recommendations with regard to older workers and job design. Older workers, such as those in managerial and administrative roles, may be experienced and reliable workers, but may also have quite high expectations with regard to flexibility of work schedules, salary levels, meaningful jobs and continuous learning.[113] Workplace changes such as organisational restructuring may lead to job design concerns: jobs involving experience, knowledge and accuracy may be more appropriate for older workers than jobs requiring speed. While speed in motor skills may decline, older workers can compensate through their experience and knowledge.[114]

With the increase of knowledge-based work and service industries, there is growth in jobs—particularly part-time work—that are not physically demanding. In a study of older workers who had begun new, mostly part-time jobs, Eichar, Norland, Brady and Fortinsky[115] noted that due to the growing number of part-time jobs that are relatively low-skilled, and 'to the extent that older workers in new jobs are influenced most by intrinsically rewarding work, there appears to be a growing mismatch between an occupational niche and those who are being sought to fill it'.[116]

Older workers may compensate for lower physical fitness by having a higher level of safety awareness in the workplace and using appropriately designed tools. Research shows that older workers can perform very effectively with appropriate person–job match and training.[117] Further, OHS policies and practices that are supportive of older workers can influence workers' beliefs about their self-efficacy, in turn affecting their performance.

Health promotion, training and development programs

Occupational health and safety training and development for managers and supervisors should encourage these organisational leaders to develop and maintain concern and commitment to OHS, effective communication about OHS and involvement of employees in OHS. Managerial attitudes and behaviours are an important factor in safety culture and will influence employees' safety attitudes and behaviours.[118] Research has found that safety training increases workers' knowledge and awareness of OHS issues and reduces injuries.[119]

A major area of OHS management focuses on health promotion and training programs. Employee health-promotion programs are defined as: 'ongoing organisational activities designed to promote the adoption of personal behaviours conducive to maintaining and/or improving employee health'.[120] OHS training and

Safety awareness programs
employer programs that attempt to instil symbolic and substantive changes in the organisation's emphasis on safety.

development for employees may include specific communication about their current job tasks and broader organisational OHS issues. **Safety awareness programs** (employer programs that attempt to instil symbolic and substantive changes in the organisation's emphasis on safety) and training programs, along with employee fitness programs, encourage both fitness and safety orientation, and lead to a reduction of work-related injury and illness.[121]

For example, in the Australian mining industry, OHS has been a major concern, largely driven by the trade unions. A substantial amount of research, development and organisational reform has been conducted across the mining industry with regard to roster design, managing fatigue, employee fitness for work, personal wellbeing, lifestyle and sleep management, work and job design, accommodation and facilities (especially in remote locations), and employee assistance programs.[122] However, several commentators have doubted claims of OHS performance improvements in this industry over the past decade. It has been suggested that as the mining industry utilises contractors to a greater extent, OHS incident reports for contractors need to be considered, in addition to those for the mining corporations themselves.

Focusing on the OHS needs of an ageing workforce, it is important to recognise that managing OHS of older workers requires attention to their training and development needs. Paul and Townsend emphasise the need to ensure that employees of all age groups continuously improve their skills in order to work most effectively.[123] The experience and motivation of older workers should be reinforced and encouraged, through provision of training and learning opportunities, to enhance their adaptation to new technology and new forms of work organisation.[124] Friedman argues that 'finding and obtaining work will remain a difficult challenge for many older workers, but, with an effective training system targeted to meeting their needs, the difficulties can become more manageable'.[125] Conversely, he points out that older workers who are more flexible and willing to acquire new skills are those more likely to find employment. Across Australia, increased demand for skilled and experienced labour has positive implications for older workers,[126] and organisations facing labour shortages are more likely to have management policies that accommodate older workers, such as targeted training programs and placement of older workers in special activities.[127]

Diversity management

There is an increasing awareness of the need for comprehensive diversity management strategies related to OHS. For example, as organisations restructure, the contingent workforce is increasing, with more workers employed in non-traditional work arrangements, such as short-term, temporary or fixed-term contracts. For contingent workers, there are particular implications with regard to OHS; precarious employment has been associated with poor safety records. The temporary nature of contingent work may provide few opportunities to develop the working relationships and understanding necessary for the contingent worker to share in the safety culture of the organisation. Strategies to encourage the positive involvement of contingent workers in a safety culture may include: teamwork that encourages and enhances safety awareness and behaviours; supervisory attitudes and actions so that contingent workers are well-informed about OHS; and training to develop safety behaviours.[128] Alternative reward and motivation strategies may be appropriate for contingent workers, such as 'promoting safety as a professional value … rather than assuming that contingent workers will internalise company safety goals'.[129]

Reward management

Reward strategies are also important in the management of OHS. Reward and recognition strategies may include recognition by peers, financial rewards and consultation by management (that is, involvement in decision making).

Reward strategies may also be integrated with strategies to improve the OHS of older workers. Paul and Townsend present a range of reward strategies for managing the OHS of older workers.[130] These include reviewing current HRM policies to accommodate older workers, using flexible benefits and rewarding employees for continuous learning and long tenure.

Overall, these HRM strategies and practices apply equally well to efforts to improve physical, physiological or psychosocial aspects of OHS, and they are likely to be most effective when combined in an integrated approach to OHS and HRM.[131] For example, psychosocial factors related to OHS include the need for flexible OHS programs, including stress counselling. Occupational stress and psychosocial issues may also be addressed through job redesign, involvement of employees in decision making, training opportunities, appropriate pay systems, and effective supervision and leadership.

Occupational health and safety and small businesses

We have discussed a range of OHS strategies that may be applicable in many organisations; however, as Mayhew and others have detailed in a stream of research, it is important to recognise that small businesses have particular OHS concerns.[132] It is evident that there are significant differences between small and large organisations, relating not only to size but to various factors. First, economic and financial instability in small businesses may lead to work pressures and work intensification. Second, small businesses tend to have less access to OHS resources, knowledge and expertise. Third, managerial attitudes and practices differ between large and small businesses. For example, managers in small businesses tend to prefer face-to-face communication and less formal systems of control. Fourth, many regulations tend to be designed for large workplaces with permanent employees and may not be appropriate for small businesses. Such differences have important implications for the management of OHS.[133]

There is increasing evidence that employees in small business have a higher risk of fatality, permanent disability, and temporary disability and illness than employees in larger organisations. For example, outworkers in the clothing manufacturing industry have been found to have an injury incidence rate approximately three times that of factory workers, although these injuries rarely result in workers compensation claims and/or prevention (or treatment) actions.[134] Further, Mayhew reports that there is preliminary evidence of increasing incidence of workplace violence in small business. For example, small retail businesses are at increasing risk of violent hold-ups.[135] It is important to consider the OHS needs of small businesses, as an increasing proportion of the Australian workforce is employed in these organisations (also see Chapter 1, Human resource management in Australia).

There are some characteristics of small business owners that Mayhew suggests have implications for the way in which OHS should be managed in these organisations.[136] For example, small business owners tend to work long hours: according to the

Australian Bureau of Statistics, 44 per cent work between 35 and 50 hours per week, 23 per cent between 52 and 75 hours, and 5 per cent work more than 75 hours per week. Also, small business owners tend to be older than the general workforce: 62 per cent aged between 30 and 50 years of age; 34 per cent aged 50 years or older.[137] It is also interesting to note that a substantial proportion of small businesses are owned by migrants, with at least 30 per cent born outside Australia.[138]

The differences related to organisational size can be dealt with at several levels, from the broad legislative level to the individual level. For example, OHS legislation may be introduced on an incremental basis to allow small business owners time to establish required procedures. When the *Occupational Health and Safety Act 2000* (NSW) was introduced in 2001, medium and large businesses were allowed one year, and small businesses were allowed two years, to establish the required risk management and consultation procedures. Hence, since 1 September 2003, small businesses in New South Wales have been required to comply with all aspects of this Act, including the risk management and consultation provisions of the Act. In addition to such legislative considerations, several strategies at organisational and individual levels have been suggested to improve OHS in small business. Research has shown that mail campaigns are largely ineffective; small business owners and managers prefer face-to-face communication, particularly from peers (not government officials) and industry groups.[139] Cowley, Else and LaMontagne have suggested that social marketing, a tool borrowed from the public health discipline, may be useful to improve OHS risk management, particularly for small business.[140] **Social marketing** refers to the use of commercial marketing strategies to promote behavioural change that will improve the health or wellbeing of the target group, such as a workforce, or of society in general.[141] On-site visits by an OHS inspector have only a short-term effect, although the development of an ongoing relationship with the inspectorate, in addition to the involvement of an industry association, can have a significant positive outcome.[142] Mayhew suggests that OHS clauses should be included in contracts for small businesses, trade educational courses for small business should include OHS information, and industry guidance needs to be provided.[143] Overall, a comprehensive program is advised. For example, in 2003, the Victorian Government provided a step-by-step guide to managing OHS for small to medium workplaces (available on CD-ROM or in booklet form). This guide, promoted as part of a $1 million advertising campaign to improve OHS, was part of WorkSafe Victoria's program to improve OHS in small and medium businesses. The impact of this program remains to be evaluated.[144]

Social marketing
the use of commercial marketing strategies to promote behavioural change that will improve the health or wellbeing of the target group, such as a workforce, or of society in general.

Occupational health and safety in the Asia–Pacific region

Work-related illnesses and injuries are in need of attention across diverse workforces, across organisations of various sizes and types, and across industries, not only in Australia but throughout the Asia–Pacific region.[145] It has been argued that, as an economically advanced country in the Asia–Pacific region, with well-developed approaches to OHS, Australia is able to help regional countries improve their OHS practice.[146] In the 1990s, the Australian Government adopted a strategy and coordination framework to guide Australian OHS activities in the Asia–Pacific region. This strategy involves:

- promotion of a compatible legislative and philosophical framework
- promotion of harmonised standards and technical approaches

- development of relationships between key government and non-government OHS institutions in Australia and Asia–Pacific nations
- facilitation of quality education, training and professional development opportunities
- promotion of Australian commercial and service activities to Asia–Pacific countries
- development of strategic OHS programs in specific nations
- revision of Australia's role with international agencies to complement regional activities
- enhancement of Australian domestic arrangements to ensure an effective OHS role throughout the Asia–Pacific region.[147]

Estimates provided by the United Nations indicate that two-thirds of the world's population growth over the next few decades will be in Asia. If current trends continue, India and the People's Republic of China will account for 70 per cent of urban growth in Asia.[148] Industrialising nations in the Asia–Pacific region are encountering complex challenges with implications for HRM and OHS. The experience of Australian OHS legislation and practice has been suggested as a way of providing useful examples for neighbouring nations.[149]

Developments in Asia–Pacific OHS legislation and social policy have been manifest over the past two decades. For example, the 1994 Labour Law in the People's Republic of China includes OHS as a priority area for attention and improvement.[150] Several Asia–Pacific nations have used the Australian OHS legislation as a guide for developing their own legislative approaches. For example, Australian Government advisors have provided assistance for the development of OHS legislation in Fiji. This project proved the basis for subsequent development of other OHS activities in which Australia has advised Fiji, although there remain a number of areas for improvement, such as the utilisation of worksite inspections. The Malaysian *Occupational Safety and Health Act 1994* was also influenced by Australian legislation. Operating in combination with the provisions of this Act is a system of regulations and approved industry codes of practice designed to maintain or improve the standards of safety and health.

Government plays a role in OHS, not only through legislative processes but also through the development of national standards and enforcement processes. Gunningham discusses the design of national OHS standards, evaluating the options of specifications, performance standards and regulatory system-based standards, recommending that these may be used in combination, in order to achieve 'best practice' in OHS management.[151] However, all regulatory requirements should be evaluated in terms of their effectiveness in achieving social objectives.[152] Performance-based regulation in OHS has been emphasised in regulatory reform in Australia and Malaysia.[153]

There are inevitable dangers in this legislative approach. It has been suggested that any benefits of the self-regulatory emphasis in this OHS legislation may be offset if labour laws are altered in ways that weaken trade unions and inhibit collective bargaining.[154] One criticism of this legislative approach being transferred throughout the region is that there is evidence of weak enforcement of OHS laws in several Asia–Pacific nations.[155] For example, China's labour law establishes an eight-hour workday and a 44-hour work week. Despite this legislation, several studies have reported a much higher number of work hours (averaging 69 hours per week) in China's garment industry, in uncomfortable and unsafe environments. Safety hazards include lack of ventilation and exposure to chemicals without protective clothing or safety devices.[156] There are, however, some interesting developments. For example,

Chen and Chan found that the input of the trade union and Workers' Representative Congress in Chinese factories had a significant, positive impact on the protection of OHS.[157] As discussed in 'Managing challenges of globalisation: Timewarp: a jump to the left on labour law' case, OHS continues to be an important issue for companies operating in China.

Given the increasing focus on international management (discussed in Chapter 16, International human resource management), organisations need to consider how to best ensure the safety of workers regardless of the nation in which they operate. Cultural differences may make this more difficult than it seems. For example, a recent study examined the impact of one standardised corporation-wide safety policy on employees in three different countries: the United States, France and Argentina. The results of this study indicated that the same policy was interpreted differently because of cultural differences. The individualistic, control-oriented culture of the United States stressed the role of top management in ensuring safety in a top-down fashion.

TIMEWARP: A JUMP TO THE LEFT ON LABOUR LAW

CHINA'S workers need stronger union representation and better pay and conditions, and their employers should operate to strict environmental standards and pay higher taxes, while overall economic growth needs to slow.

This is a familiar message from the Australian Industry Group and other manufacturing lobby groups throughout the West. But the novel twist today, is that it's also coming from the Chinese Government.

Talks towards Australia's free trade agreement with China are progressing slowly—and that's just as well, given the shift in priorities in Beijing as the leadership team of President Hu Jintao and Premier Wen Jiabao consolidates its control and starts driving its new agenda.

The ambitious program to create a national welfare system to ensure people have support for pensions, health care and education has taken longer and proven more challenging than even the realists who run Beijing had expected.

In the interim, the dislocation between rising expectations and the reality of daily challenges in China's struggletowns is triggering an unacceptable wave of demonstrations and protests in countryside and cities alike.

One of the answers is simply to go back to the future. In the Mao Zedong years, China's workplaces were expected to provide their employees and their families with basic accommodation, canteens, schools, clinics and pensions. This was the cradle-to-grave security of the iron rice-bowl whose loss many older Chinese still rue.

The draft labour law is part of a trend that might be viewed, a little oddly, as a shift to the left within a state that remains staunchly communist.

One clause says: 'Labour unions or employee representatives have the right, following bargaining conducted on an equal basis, to execute with employers collective contracts on such matters as labour compensation, working hours, rest, leave, work safety and hygiene, insurance, benefits, etc.'

The response of the powerful American Chamber of Commerce in China, with more than 3000 corporate members, testifies to the extent of the concern among foreign investors: 'The serious flaws in the draft, if left uncured, will bring chaos to the labour market, weaken the competitiveness of Chinese enterprises, and bring adverse consequences to the national economy.'

China's chief planning agency, the National Development and Reform Commission (NDRC), recently published its new guidelines for foreign investment under the five-year plan that is just starting.

Jonathan Anderson, the chief Asia economist of UBS, says: 'The driving motivation behind the new guidelines couldn't be more straightforward. Compared to five years ago, China is now awash in investment, awash in industrial capacity and awash in foreign exchange.

The official news agency Xinhua said that the new thrust promoted by the Government comprised a response to 'rampant pollution, growing wealth disparity and complaints about the high costs of education, housing and medical services'.

Source: Excerpt from R. Callick, 2006, 'Timewarp: a jump to the left on labour law', *The Australian*, 4 December, p. 32.

However, this policy failed to work in Argentina, where the collectivist culture made employees feel that safety was everyone's joint concern; therefore, programs needed to be defined from the bottom up.[158]

Evaluating occupational health and safety strategies

As discussed earlier, OHS strategies or practices need to be carefully considered before being selected and implemented. Consultation with OHS experts and resources are recommended ways of gaining information about particular programs. The effectiveness of OHS management and improvement strategies may be measured by several indicators, as discussed earlier with regard to OHS audits. The components of an OHS program should be integrated with the overall organisational policy, to achieve maximum awareness of and improvement in OHS. A comprehensive OHS management system should seek to ensure that the work environment is safe, and that employees are cared for in the event of injury or illness.[159]

MANAGING PEOPLE

LIGHTENING THE WORKLOAD

For all the complications it brings to personal and community health, the cause of obesity is simple: People become overweight when the number of calories they consume exceeds the amount they burn each day. Many work environments contribute to this imbalance, writes Teresa Russell, but some organisations are tackling the problem head on.

In a 2004 telephone survey by MBF Australia of 100 of Australia's top 500 companies, 95 per cent of respondents were either 'very' or 'somewhat concerned' about the potential health impact of obesity on their employees. A similar number agreed that the physical health of employees was important for the overall productivity of the organisation.

However, only 37 per cent of companies had a workplace health program to encourage physical activity and 50 per cent did not believe they were in any way obliged to encourage employees to become physically active.

Not only does obesity increase the risk of developing high blood pressure, heart disease and some cancers, it also results in reduced mobility, less energy, fatigue, breathlessness and sleep apnoea. Recent US research also found that overweight people were subject to discrimination in employment decisions based on body weight, and were stereotyped as emotionally impaired, socially handicapped or possessing negative personality traits.

Australian Taxation Office

David Diment, the Australian Tax Office's assistant commissioner for ATO people and place, says the ATO has a statutory duty of care to take all practical steps to protect the health and safety of its employees. 'Staff play their part by managing their own health and keeping themselves informed about health issues that are relevant to them', he says. 'The Tax Office supports them by providing an active wellbeing program and encouraging them to look after their health.'

The ATO launched the program in 2001. Managing obesity is just a part of the overall program, which gives staff access to yoga, pilates, tai chi, Bollywood dancing classes, relaxation sessions and tenpin bowling.

Two programs introduced to ATO staff that directly target obesity are Weight Watchers at Work and the 10 000-step challenge. Last year, almost 6000 of its 25 000 employees participated in the 10 000-step challenge, a community-based health promotion program that encourages people to add a 30-minute walk into their every day activities (www.10000steps.org.au). Teams of ten staff took the challenge until the combined team result was the equivalent of walking from Port Douglas to Hobart.

Some ATO sites run Weight Watchers at Work on a user pays basis. The combined weight loss of 15 participants at one Victorian site over a recent 13-week period was 100 kg. The participants use meetings to explore the particular challenges of losing weight at work. For example, how to avoid the vending machine, which selections are best from local sandwich shops, how to incorporate exercise into the daily routine, how to manage when you don't get time for lunch and so on.

Victorian Police Force

Being a member of any law enforcement agency brings with it significant health and safety issues. Shift work and high stress situations can have many negative effects on an individual's health. The nature of the job can lead to poor eating habits and weight gain.

For over 15 years, the Victorian Police Force has had an active program to undertake compulsory health assessments and carry out heart disease risk assessments for sworn officers, with the service also available to its civilian workforce.

Duncan Brooks is based in the Dandenong area as one of seven health promotion officers working statewide for the Victorian Police's Fitness and Lifestyle Unit. He says that the results of 160 000 assessments done by Victorian Police shows that the average Victorian police officer is slightly fitter than the normal population, but carries more body fat than average.

The motivation to introduce health and fitness assessments initially came as a result of OH&S concerns. 'People who are fit and healthy have fewer sprains and strains and are less likely to suffer stress-related problems', says Brooks. Alan Veitch, program development officer in the Fitness and Lifestyle Unit, adds that people who have healthier lifestyles enjoy work and provide positive motivation to colleagues.

Brooks says that when the assessments were initially introduced, the workforce response was initially fairly sceptical. 'People worried that their assessment results would be linked to promotions and that the results would not remain confidential. Now most people accept it and do it without question every two years.'

Initiatives beyond the health and fitness assessments now include subsidised Quit Smoking programs, the inclusion of a gym at all new 24-hour police stations, and seminars on men's and women's health by Sally Cockburn (aka Dr Feelgood).

Late last year, a group of employees at the Dandenong Police Centre started a self-funded Weight Watchers at Work program. The group plots its progress, both as a group and individually. Ian Gillespie, acting inspector at Dandenong (see box) says the program has given him a much better understanding of what he is allowed to eat. 'There have been no huge changes in my diet, but I've already lost 7.5 kg in six weeks.' Gillespie thinks it is great that he can get time to go to the meetings at work and says that even those people not involved in the program are taking an interest in weight loss.

Low or no cost initiatives to combat obesity in the workplace

- Provide information to encourage and support staff wanting to lose weight
- Allow employees time to attend self-funded weight loss meetings on site
- Introduce the 10 000 steps program throughout your organisation
- Provide one piece of fresh fruit per day for all staff
- Review food available in staff canteens and subsidise low fat foods
- Encourage exercise by providing bike racks at work or an on-site gym, if your budget stretches that far.

Watching the weight of Victoria's Police

Name: Ian Gillespie
Job: Acting Inspector, Victorian Police (Dandenong)
Age: 45
Weight loss program: Weight Watchers at Work
Reason for participating: Wanted to lose weight and when this option came up, it made life a lot easier
Started losing weight: Mid-December
Exercise: 30 mins on walking machine nightly
Kilos shed: 7.5 kg in six weeks
Goal weight loss: 16 kg (8.5 kg to go)
Feeling: Much better, more energetic
Employer: Gives me time off to attend a meeting at work each Wednesday

Benefits: For every person in the program, and the whole organisation

Colleagues: Everyone is supportive. Even those not on the program take an active interest in progress.

Source: Excerpt from T. Russell, 2006, 'Lightening the workload', *Human Resources,* 6 March, pp. 18–19. www.humanresourcesmagazine.com.au

QUESTION

1 What are some of the key issues involved in introducing and managing a workplace health program?

CHAPTER SUMMARY

One of HRM's major challenges is to perform its function within the legal constraints imposed by the government. Human resource managers and line managers need a good understanding of the legal requirements in order to manage their businesses in ways that are safe. Organisations that do so effectively will definitely have a competitive advantage, particularly in dealing with significant developments such as the ageing of the workforce.

Significant progress has been made with regard to OHS management systems and auditing. The components of an OHS management system should be integrated with organisational policies overall, to achieve maximum awareness of and commitment to improvement in OHS. Human resource management activities such as OHS will continue to be an important concern for organisations and governments in Australia and the Asia–Pacific region.

WEB EXERCISES

A For the latest information about the Australian OHS legislation, the National Library of Australia's website has a section on 'Australian law on the Internet' at **www.nla.gov.au/oz/law.html**. Go to this website to discover more information about the law in Australia.

B For the latest information about Australian OHS such as the national strategy, OHS standards and statistics, including the National OHS Strategy 2002–2012 and the Compendium of Workers' Compensation Statistics Australia, visit **www.ascc.gov.au**.

C For information about OHS and workers compensation at state level, visit one of the following state government websites:
- Victorian Government website for OHS: **www.worksafe.vic.gov.au**
- WorkCover Queensland website: **www.workcover.qld.gov.au**
- WorkCover Western Australia website: **www.workcover.wa.gov.au**.

D Visit the website of the Asia Pacific Occupational Safety and Health Organization (APOSHO) at **www.aposho.org**. The objective of APOSHO is to promote mutual understanding and cooperation among communities in the Asia–Pacific region and to contribute to the enhancement of OHS in these communities through the exchange of information and views.

E Visit the website of the International Commission on Occupational Health (ICOH) at **www.icoh.org.sg**. This commission is an international non-government professional society whose aims are to foster the scientific progress, knowledge and development of OHS.

F The Centre for Sleep Research at the University of South Australia provides a range of research, teaching and consultancy services related to issues such as fatigue, shiftwork and OHS. Visit their website at **www.unisa.edu.au/sleep**.

Questions

1 What are the main features of OHS legislation in your location?
2 Identify some of the current OHS issues in the Asia–Pacific region.
3 What are the major OHS problems and challenges related to employee fatigue?

PART 1   Managing the Human Resource Environment

DISCUSSION QUESTIONS

1. Many have suggested that OHS penalties are too weak and misdirected (that is, aimed at employers rather than employees) to have any significant impact on employee health and safety. Consider the OHS legislation for your state or territory. Do you think that OHS-related sanctions need to be strengthened or are existing penalties sufficient? Defend your answer.
2. What are some of the implications of the ageing workforce for the management of OHS?
3. Suppose you were asked to design an OHS management strategy for an organisation. Identify the basic steps you would take, the important factors to be considered and the elements to be included.
4. Why are OHS concerns for small businesses different from those for large organisations?

CASE STUDY

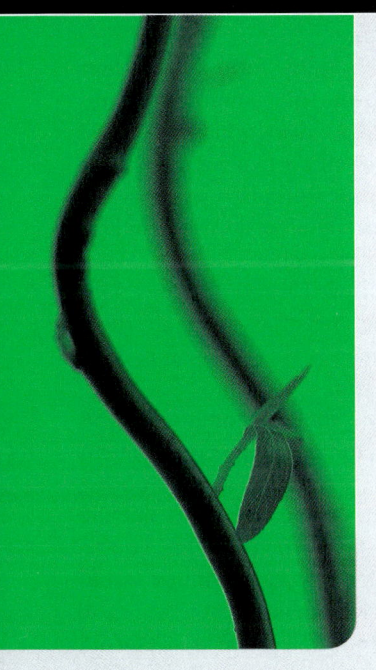

THE BEACONSFIELD MINE

The collapse at a mine in Beaconsfield, Tasmania, on 25 April 2006, killed one miner and trapped two others for 14 days. The case received a lot of media attention and sparked considerable debate about workplace safety, as the following selection of articles indicate.

1. Pressure applied on safety—BEACONSFIELD

BEACONSFIELD mine manager Matthew Gill came under pressure from elements in the joint venture owners to take a less cautious approach to safety.

The Beaconsfield mine in northern Tasmania is 51.5 per cent owned and run by Allstate Explorations, which is in receivership, with the stock market-listed Beaconsfield Gold the junior partner with 48.5 per cent.

Former Beaconsfield Gold director John Miedecke said yesterday Mr Gill was 'a very cautious and conservative mine manager when it came to safety'.

'At times he was criticised for that by various people in both (joint venture) companies', Mr Miedecke said. This began at the reopening of the century-old mine in 1999.

Mr Gill was criticised over his estimates of the capital and operating expenditure required to extract gold safely, he said.

The manager's conservative approach had not been appreciated by the mine's owners, who challenged him over the need for such high expenditure. But Mr Gill got his way after his position was backed by other assessments.

Allstate, which collapsed in 2001, still owes trade creditors 17c of every dollar they lost. But it has paid about $27.5 million in mine profits to Macquarie Bank, which became the biggest creditor when it paid $300 000 for $77 million of inter-company debt.

Allstate chairman Rod Elvish did not deny yesterday that Mr Gill had faced pressure from elements of the joint venture companies over the expenditure needed to extract gold safely.

Such conflicts were a normal part of mining, he said. 'I don't know any mine manager who hasn't had that sort of thing, who hasn't put a proposal up. That's just standard industry practice.'

Mr Miedecke, who quit two years ago because of concerns about the joint venture's structure and management, defended Mr Gill following safety issues raised by miners and unionists.

In his time at the mine, he had never known Mr Gill to succumb to pressure to sacrifice safety to cut costs. 'I would be astounded if he knowingly put people at risk', Mr Miedecke said.

Mr Elvish would not respond to the criticisms of safety from miners and the Australian Workers Union. 'We have a policy that while the guys are still underground we're not going to comment', he said. 'There will be full inquiries and all those matters will be looked at in the proper place.'

Mr Gill has taken a similar position and did not respond to a request for comment.

Source: Excerpt from M. Denholm, 2006, 'Pressure applied on safety—BEACONSFIELD', *The Australian*, 5 May, p. 8.

2. A disaster waiting to happen

Honeycombed mine ripe for collapse—No workers trained in safety

THE Australian Workers Union has opened fire on the Beaconsfield mine, detailing for the first time a succession of safety failures before the rock fall that killed one miner and trapped Brant Webb and Todd Russell for 14 days.

After meeting miners yesterday, the AWU revealed:

- It could not identify a single underground miner who had received occupational health and safety training at the Tasmanian goldmine;
- Miners complained of a reduction in the amount of cement used to harden concrete that backfilled exploited areas of the mine;
- Key 'crown' pillars meant to provide support had been removed from deep workings;

- Steel safety mesh bolted to the walls of the mine—used to stabilise the workings—had failed to contain rocks. The rocks were so active that they were 'blowing out'—that is, blowing the safety protection off the walls.

Mr Russell, Mr Webb and their colleague Larry Knight—who was killed in the rock collapse—had been pinning the mesh to a tunnel 925 metres underground on Anzac Day night when the disaster happened. A representative of Mr Knight's family attended the grim union meeting yesterday, where his former workmates instructed officials to be unyielding in their search for the cause of the tragedy.

Tasmania's Premier, Paul Lennon, said last night the claims should be put before what is expected to be an independent judicial inquiry into the tragedy.

Mr Lennon met the AWU's federal secretary, Bill Shorten, after the union meeting at Beaconsfield. Mr Shorten raised pressure for the independent inquiry, but he held open the possibility that miners could return to parts of the mine declared safe. However, he warned: 'If the current mining methods are sought to be pursued, most of them won't go back down.'

The union also wants scrutiny of Workplace Standards Tasmania, the official regulator, after miners complained it had shown little interest in safety at Beaconsfield. Mr Shorten asked miners if they had any 'constructive interaction' with the regulator, but most 'looked at me fairly blankly, like I was asking a stupid question'.

There had been an unexplained significant 'near miss' at the mine, but Mr Shorten said 'We've heard there was no visit out to the mine, and it was all done by self-regulation. Photos were taken by the mine and posted off to the regulator.'

The regulator's chief inspector, Don Schofield, described the law as 'non-prescriptive, performance legislation' where the onus was on employers to ensure a mine was safe.

The miners' claims were put to the mine's spokesman, Michael Lester, but he said the mine manager, Matthew Gill, was unable to respond. The mine and its majority owner in administration, Allstate, have been virtually silent since the miners were rescued last Tuesday.

Source: Excerpt from A. Darby, 2006, 'A disaster waiting to happen', *The Sydney Morning Herald*, 16 May, p. 1.

3. Mine survivor insists bosses must take rap

BEACONSFIELD mine survivor Brant Webb—whose friend Larry Knight died in the Anzac Day accident—has called for directors to be jailed if their companies are found responsible for workplace deaths.

Mr Webb told a workplace safety forum in Hobart yesterday that a 'breakdown in communications' contributed to the Beaconsfield accident, which entombed him and fellow miner Todd Russell for two weeks.

He said the best way to prevent workplace fatalities was for employers to involve workers in safety decisions and for company directors to be held responsible.

'I think the biggest problem is we have toolbox meetings and staff meetings—all these meetings—and all these minutes are taken ... but ultimately there's not a real lot done out of the meetings', he said.

'Throughout all industry, there's communication breakdown—from the workers to the middle management, to ... top management.'

'I think if they made not the top management but the directors accountable for a life—so if you take a life, you go and sit inside a pen or jail for 15 years—things would change. Someone should be accountable.'

Mr Webb still bears physical and emotional injuries from the April 25 rock fall at the northern Tasmanian goldmine, which had been subject to 'mini earthquakes' linked to mining activity.

Speaking about his experiences at a public forum for the first time, Mr Webb said the mine had seismic monitoring equipment in place and that he would not have worked there had he not believed at the time that it was safe.

However, asked why the mine's safety regime had failed, he said: 'A lack of communication—systems only work if information is passed on.'

Workers' concerns about safety were sometimes not acted on quickly enough. 'By the time the process goes through, it's too late', he said.

Mr Webb said there was also a 'breakdown of communication' between himself and Mr Russell on April 25. Before beginning their shift in a tunnel 925m below ground, the two had spent five minutes listening for movement in the surrounding rock.

'We sat there for about five minutes and took the earplugs out and there was no noise at all ... so we thought this sounds pretty good, there's nothing happening in here, we'll just go in and attack', he said.

In hindsight, he wished they had spent more time listening to the rocks and debating safety. 'We just wanted to finish the job, get back into it', he said.

Mr Webb, who on Monday will launch a book with Mr Russell about their ordeal, also called for a change of culture in heavy industry to reward, rather than intimidate, workers who raise safety concerns.

Employers tended to treat workers' views on safety as 'not credible' and should instead seek to involve workers in work-safety decisions. 'They don't listen to the workers', he said.

Source: Excerpt from M. Denholm, 2006, 'Mine survivor insists bosses must take rap', *The Australian*, 28 October, p. 11.

4. Drilling to deepen Beaconsfield mine

MINING at the Beaconsfield goldmine has moved a step closer after Tasmania's work safety regulator yesterday approved a resumption of blasting and drilling to make the mine deeper.

Workplace Standards Tasmania rescinded a ban on work on the mine's main decline imposed after the Anzac Day rockfall that killed miner Larry Knight just over six months ago.

The decline is a downwards, spiralled road tunnel off which are constructed horizontal drive tunnels to production areas.

Allowing work to resume on the main decline is the first stage toward beginning production in new areas of the mine below 1090m. WST bans remain in place on the construction of drives to production stopes and on the extraction of gold.

A return to gold extraction is expected in the next few months after further approval of safe work plans by WST.

A full return to mining must also pass a financial analysis by mine management.

The Australian Workers Union has vowed to make its own judgment about safety before allowing its members to return to work. AWU national secretary Bill Shorten said he remained to be convinced the mine could be operated safely.

State secretary Ian Wakefield said the union would decide whether decline work could be done safety after receiving a briefing, most likely next week.

Mine joint venture manager Allstate Explorations welcomed the WST approval for resumption of work on the main decline, following a 'rigorous' assessment of a safe work plan prepared by consultants.

Source: Excerpt from M. Denholm, 2006, 'Drilling to deepen Beaconsfield mine', *The Australian*, 3 November, p. 6.

QUESTIONS

1 This case received a lot of media attention. Search Australian newspapers for any recent articles that follow up on this case.

2 What do you think are the major lessons for HR practitioners and managers to learn from this case?

3 How might a strategic approach to HRM help prevent such tragedies in future?

CHAPTER 5   INDUSTRIAL RELATIONS

Julian Teicher
Bernadine van Gramberg

Objectives

After reading this chapter, you should be able to:

1. Discuss the role of human resource management and the Commonwealth Government's pursuit of a neo-liberal industrial relations agenda in bringing about the decentralisation and 'deregulation' of Australian industrial relations.

2. Describe the emergence of workplace bargaining and the changes to dispute resolution processes that have led to a move away from industrial tribunals.

3. Analyse the changing nature of employment relationships including the emergence of individual agreements, non-standard employment arrangements, contracting-out and privatisation.

4. Explain the reasons for the declining membership of Australian unions.

5. Discuss the industrial relations challenges for the HR professional of the future.

Human resource professionals: new roles, new expectations

Human resource professionals are required to fulfil a variety of roles and demonstrate a range of skills in order to meet the objectives of the organisation. They face challenges arising from recent changes in the HR environment; these challenges include a changing employment relationship and the associated opportunities for HR managers to act strategically.

The advertisement below demonstrates several challenges and expectations for HR professionals. Read through this advertisement and refer back to it as you study this chapter. Does this job scenario appeal to you?

Advertisement
HR professional: does this sound like you?

A-Firm
A-Firm is a leading designer of software and programs for use in the office and home. We are looking for an HR professional with a post-tertiary background and relevant experience who can project-manage the implementation of our new pay system.

What we want from you
We are looking for someone who considers themselves the CEO of their own skills, abilities and career path, rather than the employee of an organisation. We are not looking for loyalty or commitment to A-Firm—just results and dedicated work performance. We do not promise you ongoing employment nor do we guarantee that you will see out the project term with us—that is up to you and how we evaluate your performance against the scheduled output targets.

What we are offering
First, we will provide you with all the necessary resources and support you need to deliver this important project in time and on budget. This will include the (negotiable) use of a fully equipped office at A-Firm's prestigious Head Office location, and a pool of staff (which you select yourself).

As your reward, we would like to negotiate a superlative remuneration package with you, which we will provide for the duration of your stay with us, including:
- salary and shares package
- luxury vehicle
- mobile phone
- home office
- full membership of the company gymnasium
- contributions to your private superannuation scheme
- training and professional development support.

We anticipate that your stay with A-Firm will be amply rewarding both financially and through the skills and further training opportunities that you will take with you as you move on with your career to other companies.

For a position description and tendering details, contact www.A-FirmInternational.com

PART 1   Managing the Human Resource Environment

Introduction

Employer associations
organisations that offer a range of services to employers, including industrial relations advice, trade information and financial assistance.

Unions
collections of workers who have joined together in order to better their terms and conditions of employment.

Neo-liberal policies
economic policies including the adoption of free-market principles rather than government regulation, an emphasis on managerial prerogative and a decrease in the role and influence of the AIRC.

While tribunals, **employer associations** and **unions** remain important industrial relations actors in Australia, the gradual decentralisation and 'deregulation' of the industrial relations system has led to some important structural and cultural changes. These developments have been largely underpinned by the growth in human resource management and the rise of **neo-liberal policies**—economic policies including the adoption of free-market principles rather than direct government regulation, an emphasis on managerial prerogative and a decrease in the role and influence of the Australian Industrial Relations Commission (AIRC). Neo-liberal economic principles have been adopted by both Liberal–National and Labor Governments, although the policies of Liberal–National governments have been distinguished by their antipathy toward unions and the AIRC. The implementation of neo-liberal principles has led to a growing focus on the direct parties to the employment relationship and on the way that the relationship is conducted. As a result, there has been a movement away from the formal institutions such as industrial tribunals, unions and, to a lesser extent, employer associations.

This chapter commences with an examination of the decentralisation of Australian industrial relations before turning to the effect of decentralisation on tribunals, unions, employers and employees. First, we describe how the growth of bargaining and dispute resolution in the workplace has led to a decreased emphasis on the role and responsibilities of industrial tribunals. Second, the chapter examines the changing nature of employment in Australia, which is reflected in the increased use of non-standard employment arrangements, such as fixed-term contracts, part-time and casual work. Third, this chapter notes that these changes, along with statutory measures introduced under the rubric of deregulation, are designed to marginalise unions and have been accompanied by decreasing union density in Australia. Fourth, the role and prerogative of employers is described as having been enhanced through the advent of human resource management, the decline of union influence and legislative changes referred to above. The chapter concludes by considering the challenges that lie ahead for the human resource professional in terms of managing industrial relations: an emphasis on strategic assessment of industrial regulation options, contract management skills, rigorous management of participative processes and the management of accurate recruitment and selection procedures.

From centralisation to decentralisation

Australian Industrial Relations Commission (AIRC)
the federal industrial tribunal established to implement section 51(xxxv) of the Australian Constitution, which empowers the Australian Government to legislate for the prevention and settlement of interstate industrial disputes.

Following the passage of the *Conciliation and Arbitration Act 1904*, a federal tribunal (then the Commonwealth Conciliation and Arbitration Court [CCAC] and now the **Australian Industrial Relations Commission [AIRC]**) was established to implement section 51(xxxv) of the Australian Constitution, which empowers the Australian Government to legislate for the prevention and settlement of interstate industrial disputes. In practice, the establishment of the federal tribunal also served to regulate industrial relations through the registration of unions (collections of workers who have joined together in order to better their terms and conditions of employment) and employer associations (organisations that offer ranges of services to employers, including industrial relations advice, trade information and financial assistance). This ensured that employers were compelled to recognise the rights of unions to represent their members and, in turn, unions were compelled to recognise the rights of management. Wages and conditions as well as conflict were dealt with by the industrial tribunal on the basis that if negotiations between these parties failed, a resolution would be imposed through compulsory conciliation and arbitration.

The constitutional provision that gave rise to the federal industrial relations system restricted the tribunal to dealing with interstate industrial disputes. This has meant that a considerable area of employment regulation remained with the states, all of which established their own industrial tribunals following Federation in 1901. Despite the limitation to interstate industrial matters, the federal tribunal became a major player in setting employment standards, although the role of the federal tribunal is now in flux following the enactment of the *WorkChoices* amendments to the *Workplace Relations Act* in 2005. Operating pursuant to the industrial relations power in the Australian Constitution, the practice of creating a 'paper dispute' developed. This practice involved unions making a claim for improved wages or conditions on organisations in different states. In this way the federal industrial tribunal gained interstate jurisdiction to deal with industrial disputes and make awards setting out wages and conditions in ways unlikely to have been anticipated by the framers of the Constitution. Increases to award wages were set by the federal tribunal in test cases, until recently known as national wage cases. While the basis of wage setting in these national wage cases has varied over time, since the 1970s the predominant criteria has been the need to maintain the value of 'real' wages over time, and having regard for the implications of a wage rise for the national economy.

Awards are written determinations created by federal or state industrial tribunals that specify the minimum terms and conditions of employment such as hours of work, minimum pay and types of leave allowable. They contain a series of protections to workers by establishing a floor of minimum labour standards underpinning the wages and conditions of those employees covered by them. In recent years, new award conditions have typically been incorporated in federal awards and have then been applied by state tribunals to employees covered under the corresponding state award. This results in similar terms and conditions for employees undertaking similar work but in different regions of Australia. Consequently, the mainstay of employment regulation in Australia has been the system of industrial awards and the federal tribunal has been regarded as the 'pacesetter' through its award determinations, national wage cases and landmark test cases. It has been argued that the significance of award regulation derives from its role in impeding 'downward' variation in wages and conditions.[1] Such attention to uniformity has reinforced the egalitarian nature of Australian industrial relations. Another feature of the egalitarian nature of tribunal decisions has been observed in the compression of wage differentials, compared with those in the United Kingdom and the United States, where wages have been more dispersed between high- and low-earning professions.[2]

These two defining characteristics of Australian industrial relations, uniformity and egalitarianism, endured until the 1980s. Since then there have been three interrelated developments. (1) decentralisation, (2) deregulation, and (3) the incorporation of neo-liberal policies into employment legislation. **Decentralisation** has seen the lowering of the centre of industrial relations activity from the AIRC to the level of individual workplaces. Strictly, **deregulation** refers to the repeal of laws and regulations that created universal standards of employment, though in practice this has led to a vast increase in the volume of regulation pertaining to industrial relations. For example, the *Workplace Relations Act* now runs to some 1400 pages and it has been augmented by an *Independent Contractors Act 2006*. Deregulation of the labour market has reduced the influence of institutions such as unions and the AIRC; they are considered to be obstacles in the path of free-market relations, as more emphasis is placed on the individual employment relationship. Neo-liberal policies of both the Liberal/National and Labor Governments in Australia drive the free-market agenda and underpin the deregulation and

Awards
written determinations created by federal or state industrial tribunals, specifying the minimum terms and conditions of employment, such as hours of work, minimum pay and types of leave allowable.

Decentralisation
(of industrial relations) lowering of the centre of industrial relations activity from the AIRC to the level of individual workplaces.

Deregulation
(of the labour market) refers to the repeal of laws and regulations that created universal standards of employment.

individualisation of Australian industrial relations. The drivers of these developments, which we discuss next, include economic factors, a strong ideological push from employer and business groups, the adoption of HRM techniques by employers and the acceptance of the neo-liberal agenda by both major political groupings.

In the 1980s the Australian economy was opened up to the forces of international competition and in this environment government policy attention shifted from ensuring the maintenance of real wages (wages adjusted for the effects of inflation) to ensuring business profitability. Underlying the policy shift was the declining share of Australian trade in an increasingly globalised market, which in turn reflected the deteriorating competitiveness of Australian manufactures and falling real prices of agricultural and mineral exports. The lack of competitiveness of Australian companies sparked an extensive series of structural reforms. Macro-economic reform was the first policy response; it included floating the dollar in 1983 and the subsequent deregulation of financial institutions.[3] A key influence advocating labour-market reform was employer groups such as the Business Council of Australia (BCA), National Farmers Federation (NFF) and right-wing 'think tanks' like the HR Nicholls Society. These groups advocated a neo-liberal agenda including the adoption of free-market principles in preference to government regulation; a return to managerial prerogative, particularly through the marginalisation of unions; and a decrease in the role and influence of the AIRC.[4] For instance, the BCA has argued that:

> Any major reform of the industrial relations system would restore the primacy of the relationship of manager and employee at the enterprise level, that it would be directed at improving competitiveness, restore the balance of power and move the system more to capacity to pay and other specific needs at an industry or enterprise level.[5]

By 1986, faced with continued economic turmoil, the federal Labor Government proposed a series of reforms to the industrial relations system. Initially reluctant to take up the more radical proposals of the employer groups, the government focused on a program of micro-economic reform commencing with the weakening of the protective award system, which was seen as harbouring built-in inefficiencies, unnecessary costs and restrictive work practices.

To achieve this objective, the Labor Government instituted a landmark agreement with the Australian Council of Trade Unions (ACTU) in 1983. This agreement, initially labelled the Prices and Incomes Accord (the Accord), consisted of a series of provisions that traded wage restraint and avoidance of industrial action for pro-labour social programs, instituted a centralised wage-fixing system based on adjusting wages in line with productivity and price movements, and implemented a 'restructuring' (removal of restrictive clauses) of awards—a task performed by employer associations and unions, largely though negotiation followed by AIRC ratification. Typical clauses removed from awards during this time were provisions seen to restrict the flexible deployment of workers, such as restrictions on multi-skilling and non-standard forms of employment, such as part-time and casual work. This period of reform has been coined *managed decentralisation* to denote the role played by the AIRC in managing the decentralised bargaining between employer associations and unions.

While the economic imperative for reform was an important driver of decentralisation, another major influence operating during the 1980s was the adoption of human resource management (HRM) policies by employers in Australia. With its focus clearly on employees and employers, HRM was not only a decentralist concept, it was underpinned by a 'unitarist' ideology, which emphasised the importance of cooperation and shared goals between employers and managers and their employees. Such a view had immediate appeal for employers and managers and many employees, and contrasted sharply with the traditional 'pluralist' industrial relations system, with its tendency to adversarialism and its emphasis on third-party resolution of conflict. **Pluralism** is an approach that sees society as comprising a diversity of interest groups with divergent social interests and, as such, this approach accepts conflict between employer and employee as usual. Human resource management strategies that encouraged employee participation and cooperation with and in management were seen as key interventions to either remove unions from the employment relationship or at least to limit their influence.[6]

Pluralism
an approach that sees society as comprising a diversity of interest groups with divergent social interests and, as such, this approach accepts conflict between employer and employee as usual.

The Business Council of Australia called for further decentralisation, particularly in terms of setting wages and conditions at the level of the workplace.[7] Interestingly, its call was supported by sections of the union movement. For instance, in a paper presented to the 1991 ACTU Congress, its then Secretary Bill Kelty disputed the value of centralised wage fixing because it:

> … removes perhaps the main incentive in getting workers active, interested and involved in their workplace. It also reduces the influence of workers in their own workplace and, by implication, workers' self worth.[8]

Under pressure from government, unions and employer associations, the AIRC endorsed the Enterprise Bargaining Principle in 1991, decentralising wages bargaining to the level of the individual workplace.[9] **Enterprise bargaining** (also referred to as workplace bargaining) is negotiations between an employer (or enterprise) and its employees (or their representatives) with a view to deciding terms and conditions of employment. It should be noted that the AIRC decision to endorse enterprise bargaining was by no means straightforward. The AIRC initially rejected the call for enterprise bargaining, stating that the parties 'have still to develop the maturity necessary … the consensus, in our view, is rather superficial'.[10] At this time, the AIRC's concerns included the potential for excessive wage outcomes and the incompleteness of the award restructuring. Once the AIRC endorsed enterprise bargaining, the responsibility for industrial relations shifted to the workplace parties themselves,[11] but with the condition imposed by the AIRC that efficiency and productivity be improved in each case. If the parties to a particular agreement could not demonstrate sufficient productivity improvements, the AIRC would not ratify the proposed enterprise bargaining agreement.

Enterprise bargaining
(also referred to as workplace bargaining) direct negotiations between an employer (or enterprise) and its employees (or their representatives) with a view to deciding terms and conditions of employment.

The primary thrust of the wage fixing principles in recent years has been the encouragement of improved efficiency and productivity and the devolution of prime responsibility for dispute outcomes to the immediate parties involved.[12] Both Liberal–National and Labor governments have continued this movement towards decentralising industrial relations. In 1993, the Labor Government amended the legislation to promote **enterprise agreements** (negotiated between an employer and its employees) as the primary instruments to regulate employment conditions. All agreements were underpinned by an award which provided a safety net of wages and conditions, though the character and role of both agreements and awards have been recast under the *WorkChoices* amendments of 2005. In its current form, the legislation, the *Workplace Relations Act 1996 (Cwlth)* (WRA) (also see Chapter 3), further reduces the role of the AIRC in the prevention and settlement of industrial disputes This is reflected in the objects of the Act with s 3(d) providing for:

Enterprise agreements
negotiated between employers and employees, in conjunction with awards, as the primary instruments to regulate employment conditions.

> (d) ensuring that, as far as possible, the primary responsibility for determining matters affecting the *employment* relationship rests with the *employer* and *employees* at the workplace or enterprise level;[13]

Agreement making, particularly individual agreement making in the form of Australian Workplace Agreements (AWAs) and common law contracts, has been promoted by the Liberal–National Government as the preferred wage-setting mechanism. The WRA now provides for four major forms of employment regulation:

(1) awards, (2) collective union agreements, (3) collective non-union agreements, and (4) individual agreements. Each of these instruments is referred to as a workplace agreement. A **workplace agreement** is a written agreement between an employer and an employee/s (or a union) that is lodged with a government agency, the Office of the Employee Advocate, which is responsible for scrutiny of workplace agreements in order to ensure their conformity with the requirements of the Act. A workplace agreement is a legally enforceable instrument and operates to the exclusion of an awards.

Awards have historically been the basis for terms and conditions for employees at work. They have been the focus of change by the federal Liberal–National Government, which has sought to create a single national system of industrial relations in which, overwhelmingly, employees will have their wages and conditions set by workplace agreements. Notably, the baseline for agreement making is now no longer the underpinning award but the Australian Fair Pay and Conditions Standard which consists of the minimum pay and classification scales and casual loadings, maximum ordinary hours of work, annual leave, personal/carer's leave and parental leave. Over time, awards will be phased out as these minimum five conditions become the basis for negotiations at the workplace. Since the 2006 amendments, awards may contain only 15 allowable matters. Further, s 515 of the WRA specifies that 12 matters are prohibited from being included in an award. These matters include prohibiting clauses that can be used to convert casual employees to another class of employee

> **Workplace agreement**
> a written agreement between an employer and an employee/s (or a union) that is lodged with a government agency.

WORK IN PROGRESS

The jury is still out on the full effect of the federal government's 2005 changes to the *Workplace Relations Act 1996*, known as **WorkChoices**. While the High Court has ruled 5–2 that **WorkChoices** legislation has constitutional validity, there is a high degree of ambivalence within the community about the real nature of the new laws.

Despite the fact that the federal and state governments, industry bodies such as Australian Business Limited, the Australian Industry Group, accountancy and legal firms as well as various union groups have provided courses on the legislation, there seems to be curiously little interest all around.

Every small to medium-size enterprise (SME) in the country has received invitations to training seminars from ABL, a group that sees educating employers about the operation of the WorkChoices legislation as a crucial part of its mandate.

ABL general manager of workplace solutions Greg Pattison says that, for the most part, businesses have been taking a 'wait and see' approach to WorkChoices.

SMEs form the majority of Australian employers and, for them, the new legislation provides an insurance policy. In times of full employment, AWAs are of little consequence to most employers, as many are already paying above the award rates. But the ability to reduce staff (and therefore overheads) quickly when market conditions are poor is a key element, and regardless of political affiliation, most employers who have survived tough times know that this is the difference between trading out of trouble or shutting up shop.

The manufacturer
James Kelman is chief executive of Wax Converters, Australia's largest manufacturer of outdoor and industrial fabrics. Established in 1991, the company has grown rapidly and has plans for expansion. Kelman is something of an oddity in that first, he is in manufacturing; second, he is manufacturing textiles; and third, his business is growing rapidly.

Kelman believes the amendments to the *Workplace Relations Act* are providing benefits to his business and to his employees.

In the past, Wax Converters hired new staff through a labour-hire firm in an attempt to provide the company with some flexibility in staff numbers.

Kelman admits that this process disadvantaged workers because they were not viewed as full-time staff and therefore had difficulty obtaining bank loans or security entitlements.

'It also cost us more to hire staff that way, but because we operate in a volatile sector and because not all people are suited to this industry, we needed the flexibility to make changes', he says.

MANAGING CHALLENGES THROUGH HR INNOVATION

(s 515(b)); prohibiting clauses which specify minimum or maximum work hours (s 515(e)); and prohibiting the provision of paid leave for dispute resolution training (s 515(k)).

The neo-liberal agenda that underlies the successive changes in Australian industrial relations led to re-regulation and individualisation. This has entailed a gradual winding back of AIRC powers and responsibilities, and attempts to curtail union activities.[14] The popular term, 'labour-market deregulation', situates labour as a commodity that can be bought and sold at a price dictated by the market. This has provided a major rationale for reducing the protections from the labour market, which workers were traditionally afforded. Award regulation and the interference of government, tribunals and unions were viewed as distorting market forces by acting to artificially bolster the price of labour.

These trends have not been confined to Australia. For instance, commenting on decentralisation and de-institutionalisation in the United Kingdom, Ferner and Hyman wrote that 'part of the ideological battle has been to *depict* existing institutions as barriers to change that must be systematically destroyed'.[15] Thus, while not removing tribunals or unions, these institutions have been significantly affected by this bipartisan approach to industrial relations reform. The remainder of this chapter examines the impact of these reforms on tribunals, unions, employers and workers. 'Challenges through innovation: Work in progress' discusses the potential impact of the reforms to industrial relations from various perspectives.

'We had up to 10 employees outsourced. It was a more expensive process but it was better in the long run.'

'We are now saving a minimum of $50,000 a year in outsource placement costs so WorkChoices is definitely benefiting our bottom line.'

He says that 50 of the company's 65 employees are on AWAs, 'but it doesn't make much difference because we pay above award anyway'.

Kelman acknowledges that making it in manufacturing in Australia is difficult enough, but to achieve in the textile sector is possible only by applying a flexible workforce model.

Kelman agrees that it is difficult to know the full effect of the new WorkChoices legislation until there is a downturn, when employers will have the ability to reduce staff numbers quickly in order to keep the company viable.

The union
The union debate is somewhat predictable. The unions have announced that as a consequence of the High Court's decision that the WorkChoices legislation is constitutionally valid, they will ramp up their campaign against the laws.

For SMEs, however, the outcome will be positive as they will have the means, through the WorkChoices legislation, to survive to trade another day.

The Act and unfair dismissal
Employers with less than 100 employees are exempt from unfair dismissal laws. Employees excluded from federal unfair dismissal laws include:

- Seasonal workers.
- Employees engaged under a contract of employment for a specified period or a specified task.
- Employees on probation.
- Casual employees engaged for a short period.
- Trainees
- Employees earning $98 200 or above.

Employees who are dismissed for a genuine operational reason are also not allowed to pursue an unfair dismissal claim. But employers should be aware that under WorkChoices, it is still unlawful to dismiss an employee on discriminatory grounds such as:

- Temporary absence from work because of illness or injury.
- Trade union membership or participation in trade union activities.
- Non-membership of a trade union.
- Seeking office as a representative of employees.
- The filing of a complaint, or the participation in proceedings, against an employer.
- Race, colour, sex, sexual preference, age, physical or mental disability, marital status, family responsibilities, pregnancy, religion, political opinion, national extraction or social origin.
- Refusing to negotiate, sign, extend, vary or terminate an Australian Workplace Agreement.
- Absence from work during maternity leave or other parental leave.
- Temporary absence from work because of the carrying out of a voluntary emergency management activity.

Source: Excerpt from T. Blackie, 2006, 'Work in Progress', *BRW*, 23 November, p. 32.

PART 1   Managing the Human Resource Environment

The emergence of workplace bargaining and conflict resolution

In 1996, the Howard-led Liberal–National Government legislated that all industrial awards would be pared back to 20 allowable matters. The process, which was undertaken by the award parties under the supervision of the AIRC, continued through to 2003 although the government originally intended for this task to be completed by mid 1998. This was accompanied by a rationalisation of awards, which was expected to reduce the total number of awards to approximately 1200.[16] As indicated above awards are to become more marginal to the process of regulating the terms and conditions of Australian workers. Reflecting the decreasing reliance on centralised dispute resolution and the shift to agreement making, the number of hearings to certify or otherwise deal with agreements has increased from 6587 in 1997–98 to 8836 in 2005–06 (see Table 5.1 below).

Accompanying the shift to workplace negotiations has been the inevitability that parties in the workplace deal with their own conflicts and disagreements, rather than relying on the AIRC to resolve disputes over claims and existing entitlements—although it is the role of the Federal Court to interpret awards, agreements and other industrial matters. In recognition of the inevitability of grievances arising during the life of an agreement, industrial relations legislation since 1996 has made certification of agreements contingent on the inclusion of a grievance procedure. Part 13 of the WRA provides that all enterprise agreements must contain a dispute resolution procedure and provides a model dispute settlement procedure (DSP) for those agreements that have omitted this clause. We would, therefore, expect that the AIRC would be dealing with fewer industrial disputes as the emphasis is firmly on workplace level dispute resolution.

To some extent this is true. The work of the AIRC shifted away from hearing industrial disputes notified under the provisions of the WRA (s 99 disputes) as can be seen in Table 5.1.[17] Interestingly, at the same time there has been a growth in the number of disputes referred to the AIRC as a result of a failed workplace dispute

TABLE 5.1   Caseload activities of the Australian Industrial Relations Commission (AIRC)

Application	1997–98	1998–99	1999–2000	2000–01	2001–02	2002–03	2003–04	2005–06
Dispute notification (section 99)	3273	2836	2679	2598	2546	2342	2121	1191
Notification under dispute settling procedures of agreements (sections 170LW, 170VG, 293F and 520)	55	288	326	403	556	679	764	956
Agreement (certification, extension, variation, termination and determination of designated award)	6587	9001	6885	10 081	7070	8326	9212	8836
Order relating to industrial action	293	335	425	444	414	451	480	344
Termination of employment	8092	8146	7498	8109	7461	7121	7044	5758
Full bench matters (including appeals)	411	400	434	249	366	534	285	215
Award variations					1493	1715	2054	1538

Source: Compiled from Australian Industrial Relations Commission, 2003, *Annual Report of the Australian Industrial Relations Commission 2002/2003*; Australian Industrial Relations Commission, 2004, *Annual Report of the Australian Industrial Relations Commission 2004*, p. 9.

procedure. One measure of industrial disputation is the level of strike activity. A **strike** occurs when employees refuse to work until their demands (for example, for improved work conditions) are met by their employer. The number of working days lost per 1000 employees has declined from over 200 in 1990 to 60 in 2000,[18] suggesting that disputes are increasingly being resolved without recourse to strike activity. In the September 2006 quarter, working days lost per 1000 employees reached the lowest recorded figure of 2.3 days.[19]

Although dispute notifications and the level of strike activity continue to decline, other dispute matters dealt with by the AIRC have increased. The hearing of unfair dismissal claims by the AIRC grew rapidly when the AIRC gained jurisdiction over this area in 1993. Following the 2005 amendments, the numbers of such disputes coming before the AIRC can be expected to decline dramatically The WRA has now removed the right of employees who work in firms of less than 100 workers to lodge unfair dismissal claims. Also organisations with more than 100 employees that dismiss workers on 'operational grounds' are not subject to the unfair dismissals jurisdiction of the AIRC. The number of s 496 (formally s 127) notifications to stop or prevent industrial action has risen from 293 in 1997–98 to 480 in 2003–04 and flattened out again to 344 in 2005–06. The significance of this development is that, unlike a dispute notification, a section 496 application can initiate a process leading to the imposition of penalties by the Federal Court. Litigation as a form of dispute resolution has increased over this period, leading the President of the AIRC to observe:

> What are the implications of this increase in direct regulation by the Parliament? The first is that there will be a shift towards the Courts—the Federal Court in particular—and away from the Commission in relation to industrial and workplace relations disputes and issues. The reduction in the AIRC's role in providing a forum for the resolution of workplace problems and disputes is likely to lead parties to seek other methods of resolving disputes. Work Choices certainly gives primacy to common law and statutory rights and provides for dispute resolution based on the enforcement of those rights through the judicial system. This effect is a natural consequence of the changes and has been explicitly recognised by the Government which is in the process of appointing, or has appointed, four new Federal Court judges and six new Federal Magistrates to deal with the caseload arising from Work Choices. But litigation, as those attending this conference are particularly aware, is usually expensive and often very expensive.[20]

This is not a desirable outcome for Australian workplaces as litigation is adversarial, fraught with delays and expensive. We can, therefore, expect to see employers and employees looking for alternative means to resolve disputes. Indeed the WRA encourages the use of private dispute resolution consultants in preference to the services of the AIRC. To some extent there has been a small but steady growth in the use of consultants and committees for over 10 years in workplace dispute resolution. Evidence of increased resolution of disputes at the workplace can be observed in the increase in the use of specialist industrial relations (IR) managers, joint consultative committees and formal grievance procedures at Australian workplaces (see Table 5.2).

The WRA promotes the use of private dispute resolution consultants as part of its model DSP in Part 13 of the Act. Research has shown that some organisations had already been using these private players for some time. An examination of the dispute resolution clauses in 1000 federal enterprise agreements ratified in 1999 and another 1000 in 2001[21] found that provision for the use of private third parties (classified here as mediators, but inclusive of facilitators, mediators and arbitrators) increased from 4.5 per cent of agreements in 1999 to 10.1 per cent of agreements in 2001 (see Table 5.3). Although this data is not conclusive, it is a reasonable indication of a growth in the use of private mediators and may presage an emerging trend as Australian industrial relations moves further away from formal institutions such as the AIRC.

Strike
employees' refusal to work until their demands (e.g. for improved work conditions) are met by their employer.

TABLE 5.2 — Changes in dispute resolving mechanisms between 1990 and 1995

	1990	1995
Specialist IR manager	34	46
Joint consultative committee	14	33
Disciplinary procedure	73	92
Grievance procedure	49	71
Formal monitoring	42	46
Training of supervisors in IR	39	72
OHS committee	41	43
EEO/AA policy	58	67

Note: This table shows the changes in workplaces with 20 or more employees.
Source: Compiled from A. Morehead, M. Steele, M. Alexander, K. Stephen & L. Duffin, 1997, *Changes at Work: The 1995 Australian Workplace Industrial Relations Survey*, Longman, Sydney.

TABLE 5.3 — Parties involved in workplace dispute resolution clauses

External party involved in dispute resolution	1999 (n = 1000)	2001 (n = 1000)
Mediator	45	101
AIRC	978	989
Board of reference	4	5

Source: B. van Gramberg, *Exploring Avenues for the Growth of Private Alternative Dispute Resolution in Australian Workplaces*, in I. McAndrew & A. Geare (eds), 2002, *Proceedings of the 16th AIRAANZ Conference*, Association of Industrial Relations Academics of Australia and New Zealand, Queenstown, 6–8 February, pp. 525–35.

The major implication for Australian workers of the increase in private mediation is that the outcomes of mediated disputes are private. There is no public record, no precedents set and, consequently, no behavioural standards are formulated that must be followed in the particular workplace or by industry at large. By contrast, the decisions of the AIRC were based on precedent and, despite the fact that resolutions were arrived at in conciliation, they were within the shadow of relevant precedent. The centralised system of conciliation and arbitration had long been heralded as one that is based on fairness and principles. An early writer on the AIRC, Wooten, highlighted the emphasis on precedent as:

> … a principled approach is necessary throughout the tribunal's jurisdiction to provide reasonable consistency and predictability to the decisions of the tribunal. Without these characteristics decisions will appear arbitrary, capricious and unjust, and will give the parties no guide to regulating their affairs without litigation.[22]

However, the enactment of the WRA has now situated the AIRC's dispute functions in the private realm. Either public hearings or the making of transcripts of proceedings are permitted and the arbitral powers of the AIRC have been pared back to a few situations where parties agree to the tribunal making a recommendation to resolve their dispute.

The changes to the Australian industrial relations system have impacted on the nature of the work of the AIRC. It is no longer the key player in setting wages and conditions; this role now rests with employers and employees and another newly created actor in the Australian industrial relations system, the Australian Fair Pay Commission (see Chapter 3). The AIRC's role in resolving industrial disputes has also been limited to extreme situations. Local agreement making and private resolution of disputes signals the end of the egalitarian or 'fair go' ethos which was embedded in the Australian industrial relations system at its inception.

The changing nature of employment

An interesting feature of the Australian labour market is that at a time when the employment rate is high (61.1 per cent of the employment to population) and unemployment is low (5.1 per cent), the growth in jobs has been overwhelmingly in casual and part-time positions.[23] Certainly the emergence of non-standard forms of employment (such as casual work, part-time and short-term contracts) as mainstream features of working life is not recent and has arguably been one of the significant outcomes of labour-market deregulation in Australia. Non-standard jobs often do not have regular hours or access to holiday and sick leave. Spurred on by the legislatively mandated liberalisation of award clauses regulating casual employment, employers have turned enthusiastically to casual labour.

In theory, casual employees are engaged on an 'as needed' basis and are entitled to receive a loading on their pay in part to compensate them from being excluded from benefits of standard full-time work such as paid annual leave, sick leave, parental leave and redundancy payments. Redundancy payments may arise when an employer declares an employee redundant. **Redundancy** is dismissal based on the elimination of jobs due to organisational restructuring or technological change, which lead to certain jobs or skills being no longer required. Despite the assumption that casual work is made up of short-term employment contracts, in practice it also encompasses long-term, regular employment.[24] The advantages and incentives for employers to use casual labour illustrate the reasons behind its growth. First, the net benefits resulting from not having to pay for non-working time, such as annual leave and public holidays, are significant. Second, there are cost savings such as lower costs of termination, opportunities for work intensification and labour utilisation over non-social hours, which in turn facilitates faster turnover of fixed capital. Employing casual labour may provide benefits in non-cost areas, such as enhancing managerial control and facilitating administrative convenience. It allows management to choose the number and the timing of hours of employment at short notice (and often across non-social hours), providing an avenue of flexible working-time arrangements. A third advantage to employers is that casual labour is excluded from the unfair dismissal laws; thus, there is greater flexibility in recruiting and terminating employees.

Between 1982 and 1990, non-standard employment increased dramatically, with full-time casual employment increasing 90.1 per cent, part-time casual employment by 82.6 per cent and part-time permanent employment by 62.6 per cent. In contrast, standard full-time permanent waged work grew at a much slower rate (14.5 per cent). The proportion of employees who are casual employees in their main job increased from 19.4 per cent in 1990 to 25.8 per cent in 1997.[25] By 2003, this had grown to 28.3 per cent.[26] This represents the highest level of casual employment in the Organisation for Economic Co-operation and Development (OECD) countries—except for Spain. Significantly, the ABS found that, for the decade to 1998, most of the growth in casual work was among men, while the number of males in permanent jobs that entitle them to holiday and sick leave benefits fell significantly. For instance, there has been a contraction of employment in the traditional full-time and male-dominated fields of

Redundancy
dismissal based on the elimination of jobs due to organisational restructuring or technological change, which leads to certain jobs or skills being no longer required.

agriculture, mining and utilities sector.[27] Casualisation of the Australian workforce is particularly widespread in the clerical, sales and services sectors, as well as the basic blue-collar, construction, transport, manufacturing and communications industries.[28]

Another form of non-standard employment was documented in a Productivity Commission report,[29] which provided evidence of a shift towards recruiting workers from labour hire companies, outsourcing and contracting self-employed workers. Indeed, between 1998 and 2002, the number of firms providing labour hire services increased by 30 per cent from 2090 to 2704.[30] A significant feature of this change is that, although nominally self-employed, many of these workers are effectively subordinate, working for one or a small number of quasi employers and subject to detailed direction.[31] These workers are often referred to as 'disguised wage labour' or 'dependent workers'.[32]

While the growth of casual and dependent workers provides employers with considerable benefits, the same cannot be said for many of these workers. Self-employed, fixed-term and casual employees suffer from a lack of entitlements, job insecurity and increased stress. These disadvantages go hand in hand with the almost non-existent career prospects associated with precarious employment.[33]

Introduced under the original 1996 WRA, **Australian Workplace Agreements** allow employers and workers to negotiate directly on an individual basis—as part of the shifting emphasis away from collective bargaining to individualism. The number of AWAs filed with the Office of the Employment Advocate from their inception in March 1997 to December 2004 was 604 989.[34] There is some evidence that the passage of the *WorkChoices* amendments to the WRA has led to an increase in the numbers of AWAs with the Office of the Employment Advocate reporting an 85 per cent increase in both the number of agreements and employees covered by those agreements in the quarter ending September 2006.[35] While this form of individual contract has been increasing, AWAs still represent only 5.4 per cent of the working population.[36] Apart from AWAs, the WRA has facilitated a shift to other types of individual and non-union arrangements. For instance, non-union certified agreements in small businesses with fewer than 20 employees increased from 2.8 per cent of agreements in 1995 to 9.5 per cent in 1999.[37] In addition, employers and employees can agree to opt out of the federal jurisdiction and have their employment, wages and conditions regulated by individual common law agreements; however, since 2006 those agreements must contain the minimum standards provided in the WRA. By May 2002, 38.3 per cent of workers were employed on unregistered individual contracts.[38] There has been some debate related to the use of AWAs, as indicated in 'Managing challenges through attracting and retaining people: Commonwealth Bank shuns AWA allegations'.

While AWAs have been promoted as the Liberal–National Government's preferred form of employment regulation for the Australian workforce, wage rises under AWAs have been found to be significantly lower than those obtained under unionised bargaining. In May 2002, average weekly total earnings for full-time, adult, non-managerial employees employed under award-only conditions were $639. This compares with $914.30 for employees on collective agreements and $836.10 for employees on individual agreements.[39] Other research on AWAs showed that while 79.7 per cent of union agreements provided for a series of further wage increases within the life of the agreement, this occurred in only 29.5 per cent of AWAs (of which 71 per cent specified a three-year duration). Terms and conditions of AWAs were also, generally, less generous than those found in union agreements. Examples include a greater incidence of working time in excess of 38 hours a week in AWAs compared to union agreements (28.8 per cent and 11.8 per cent respectively); and

---

Australian workplace agreements (AWAs) agreements negotiated directly between an employer and employee(s), and introduced under the *Workplace Relations Act 1996 (Cwlth)*.

COMMONWEALTH BANK SHUNS AWA ALLEGATIONS

THE COMMONWEALTH Bank has refuted ACTU and Labor Party claims that it is coercing staff into signing Australian Workplace Agreements (AWAs).

The ACTU claimed that Commonwealth Bank employees do not have a genuine choice when asked to sign one of the new bank-wide AWA individual contracts, and the union challenged the bank to conduct a ballot to determine whether workers want an individual job contract or a collective agreement.

'It is unnecessary and unacceptable that hardworking employees in bank branches as well as in call centres and back-office operations are facing major cuts to their basic job conditions. But that is exactly what big companies are being encouraged to do under the Federal Government's IR laws', said Greg Combet, ACTU secretary.

Unions claimed thousands of bank employees were facing the loss of overtime pay, shift allowances, public holiday pay, rest breaks, RDOs and other basic work conditions under the new AWA.

Under the terms of the AWA, bank employees can be rostered to work at any location any day of the week. Once signed, the AWA individual contract has no guarantee of a pay increase for the five-year life of the contract and this could see workers' pay falling behind cost of living increases, the union claimed.

However, the bank said staff currently employed under the bank's Enterprise Bargaining Agreement (EBA) can remain under the terms of that agreement and will continue to receive overtime, shift allowance, public holiday pay, rest breaks, RDOs and other basic entitlements.

'Our staff can choose to move to an AWA or stay under the enterprise bargaining agreement. No one is being forced', said Commonwealth Bank spokesman Brian Fitzgerald, who added that the bank had been offering AWAs to its staff since 1997.

'Staff on an AWA get a higher salary but they also choose not to have overtime or rostered days or some of the other award-based allowances, so they're getting remuneration in place of some of the allowances they previously received', he said.

Labor Party member Stephen Smith's criticism of the AWAs was also unfounded, according to the Minister for Employment and Workplace Relations, Kevin Andrews.

'Mr Smith failed to mention that five years ago the Financial Sector Union (FSU) agreed on behalf of its members that a range of conditions could be exempted', Minister Andrews said.

He referred to the Commonwealth Bank of Australia Retail Banking Services Enterprise Bargaining Agreement of 2002 which included the bank, the FSU and its members.

The agreement clearly states that where an employee accepts an offer in terms of Clause 12.1, he or she may be exempted from the provisions of the Award and the EBA in relation to rostered days off, overtime and separate allowances, meal allowance, leave in lieu of travelling time, on-call allowances, telephone availability allowance, higher duty allowance and annual leave loading.

'Mr Smith also failed to mention that Commonwealth Bank employees have been entering into AWA arrangements for nearly a decade with in excess of 8000 employees signing AWAs over the past nine years; and five years ago, the Finance Sector Union agreed that AWAs could be offered to employees.'

Minister Andrews also said that employees have been willingly entering into AWA arrangements with the Commonwealth Bank in return for comprehensive salary packages well above the award and collective agreement rates including incentive payments and other flexible conditions negotiated with the bank.

'The Commonwealth Bank has regularly passed on generous wage increases to employees choosing to remain under the Commonwealth Enterprise Agreement; and the employees have a legal right to appoint the union to bargain on their behalf.'

Source: M Yen, 2006, 'Commonwealth Bank shuns AWA allegations', *Human Resources*, 13 December. www.humanresourcesmagazine.com.au

---

AWAs were more likely to contain provisions that reduced payments for non-standard work hours and were less likely to contain provisions for training and staff development.[40] These outcomes demonstrate the neo-liberal proposition that third parties interfere in market processes, such as wages bargaining, and that removing unions from the equation shifts the power balance from employees to employers.

The likely continuing decline in award coverage associated with the changing employment structure of the economy and the impact of the WRA indicates that, in the future, a large proportion of the workforce will receive reduced protections when compared with either the award safety net that was in place previously, which has now been replaced by the safety net of 20 allowable matters provided for in the WRA in 1996.[41] As indicated above, these protections have been further reduced by the legislated safety net of six items (including minimum wages) introduced under the *WorkChoices* amendments. Given that workers affected by these changes are unlikely to be union members, few will have access to the, generally, superior negotiated benefits that apply to unionised sectors.

Declining union density in Australia

For much of the twentieth century, the majority of the Australian workforce belonged to trade unions. This internationally high unionisation rate was punctuated only by periods of recession or war, when rates dropped. The arbitral system with its requirement of union registration has been attributed with encouraging both strong union membership and the proliferation of small unions that have characterised Australian industrial relations.[42] In 1986, union density was still relatively high at 46 per cent.[43] The late 1980s marked the rapid fall of unionisation so that by 1990, 41 per cent of the workforce was unionised and, less than a decade later, in 1999, this had fallen to 26 per cent.[44] Although the decline in trade union membership abated slightly in the early 2000s, by August 2003 it had plummeted to 23 per cent [45] and by 2005 had dropped again to 22.4 per cent. The trend is most marked in the private sector with only 16.8 per cent of employees belonging to unions, compared with 17.4 per cent in August 2004.[46] On one hand, the slowing of the decline has led some to postulate a slight resurgence of interest by Australian employees in unionism.[47] On the other, it has been cited as evidence that unions are increasingly irrelevant to the majority of Australian employees.[48]

The trend away from unionisation in Australia in recent decades has been reflected internationally in other but not all developed Western economies. The reasons for this decline are complex and interrelated. We consider here the role of legislative changes, the decentralisation of industrial relations, the introduction of human resource management practices, the downsizing of the public service and the increased participation of women in the workforce. The WRA has encouraged non-union bargaining and placed greater emphasis on **freedom of association** (the right to join or not to join a trade union). The WRA has significantly altered the role of unions in the workplace. Foremost have been increased restrictions on taking industrial action, union officials entering workplaces, and changes to agreement making processes which marginalise union involvement. These restrictions will make it very difficult for unions to carry out their traditional functions, service their members or advance workers' interests. For instance, to gain access to the workplace to visit a member, a trade union official will have to obtain a certificate that he or she has passed the 'fit and proper person test'. A series of fines is imposed for those who do not follow the bureaucratic requirements in the Act.[49] These changes have also been associated with a conceptual shift from the representation of employees' interests at work to one of 'agency'. In many cases this has reduced union activity to functioning as bargaining agents and providing various services such as discounts on insurance and legal advice.[50]

Apart from the constraints on union activity imposed by the WRA, there has been a contraction of award coverage of employees. The growth in individual agreements and in non-standard forms of employment has created a pool of 41.5 per cent of workers who are not employed under an award.[51] Under the previous industrial framework, in order to regulate wages and conditions in the federal arena, an interstate dispute was

Freedom of association
the right to join or not to join a trade union.

required. Therefore, employees could not access federal awards without belonging to a union, as it has long been held that one person cannot constitute an interstate dispute. As the WRA now draws its constitutional authority from the corporations power and not the industrial relations power, employees do not need to be members of unions in order to enter into any form or workplace agreement, whether it is individual or collective.

Most unions supported the decentralisation of industrial relations in the hope that they would be able to exert industrial pressure at the workplace level; in practice, however, decentralisation has contributed to the decline of unions. In the presence of a hostile federal government—determined to remove union rights—combined with unions' frequently undeveloped organisational capacity at the workplace level, the unions' ability to maintain and improve conditions of work and membership has been impaired. For instance, the Construction, Forestry, Mining and Energy Union (CFMEU)[52] claimed that the logistics of implementing a decentralised bargaining regime that would operate employer by employer, as well as the legal stricture (that each agreement should stand on its own), would spell doom for the union—simply because the 300 CFMEU organisers would each need to negotiate over 300 individual enterprise agreements (representing an average of one enterprise agreement every 1.3 days over a two-year period) in order to adequately cover the industry.

Another important factor that has played a role in the decline of unions is the growth of HRM policies and practices, particularly those practices that encourage employee involvement and participation in decision making at the workplace—such as quality circles, teams and internal communication mechanisms.[53] These mechanisms provide an employee 'voice', which apparently reduces the need to seek advice and assistance from a union.[54] Apart from providing union replacement mechanisms, with the shift to HRM comes a range of practices that tend to focus on the individual in the employment relationship, such as performance-related pay.[55] Thus, it is not surprising that the advent of HRM has been accompanied by the growth of individual contracts. Individualism in the employment relationship highlights the unitarist underpinnings of HRM and, as Townley[56] has argued, it is central to ensuring improved managerial control. Key to this control is the marginalisation or elimination of unions. As we have seen above, in a decentralised bargaining environment, unions may lack the resources and organisational capacity to cater for individual bargaining; thus, they have not thrived.[57] Paradoxically, the rise of HRM has been accompanied by increasing globalisation, and this has provided unions with a means of acting collectively on a much larger scale than was possible at the national level, as 'Managing challenges of globalisation: Unions in global fight on Alcoa' demonstrates.

The restructuring of industry has included privatisation, outsourcing (that is, contracting-out) and downsizing. In the quest for flexibility and efficiency, union membership has been a collateral target. This has been particularly focused in the traditionally highly unionised sectors, such as the public sector and large private companies. In the deregulated telecommunications industry, for example, the number of licensed competitors rose from three in 1996 to 50 in the year 2000.[58] Organisational restructuring aimed at competing in this tight market induced considerable rationalisation, both of staff and other resources.

In March 2000, Telstra announced a $650 million cost-cutting program with an estimated reduction of 10 000 jobs. The announcement came after a period of rapid and intense restructuring following the partial privatisation of the telecommunications company and the deregulation of the industry. In the period from June 1995 to December 1999, one of the union casualties, the Communication, Electrical and Plumbing Union (CEPU), lost 23 per cent of its membership.[59]

UNIONS IN GLOBAL FIGHT ON ALCOA

MANAGING CHALLENGES OF GLOBALISATION

TRADE unions from four nations including Australia are mounting a combined campaign against US aluminium giant Alcoa as part of an emerging pattern of global co-operation among unions.

Union officials from Brazil, the US and Britain met in Melbourne just before Christmas to discuss the campaign with colleagues from the Australian Workers Union and the International Metalworkers Federation.

'Our plan is to start bargaining with Alcoa on a global basis', AWU vice-president Paul Howes said yesterday.

He said that when the AWU sought to discuss the implementation of a new Alcoa policy on working hours, it was told the policy had been decided at the US head office and could not be negotiated locally.

'One of the largest resource-industry employers in Australia has now started telling us a large part of their employment practice is being dictated to them on a global basis', Mr Howes said.

Global links among the unions are developing to strengthen industrial muscle in facing international companies.

The AWU signed a pact with the United Steelworkers Union in the US two years ago, and is concluding another with the key British steel union, Community, next month.

A pact between the largest British, German and US manufacturing unions is expected to be announced this week.

The secretary of the British union Amicus, Derek Simpson, was quoted in British papers yesterday as saying: 'Our aim is to create a powerful single union that can transcend borders to challenge the global forces of capital. I envisage a functioning, if loosely federal, multinational organisation within the next decade.'

Mr Howes said he doubted the potential of a single union because of the disparity in industrial relations regulation around the world.

He said there had been global co-operation for a long time—the AWU has been a member of the International Metalworkers Federation since 1912. But agreements between individual unions to tackle companies on a global basis were new.

Mr Howes said Australian unions were using global unionism to confront increasingly global bargaining by employers. 'The biggest effect will be when they start using their clout in one country to affect an outcome in another.'

He said many global companies had different practices in different parts of the world. In Australia, Alcoa's operations were fully unionised, compared with only half its plants in the US. Conditions in Alcoa's Mexican and Guyana plants were way below Australian standards.

'We sent a number of our rank-and-file members over to look at Alcoa operations in Mexico a couple of months ago, and it shocked them', he said.

Alcoa was unavailable for comment.

Source: D. Uren, 2007, 'Unions in global fight on Alcoa', *The Australian*, 1 January, p. 2.

Finally, the increase in participation rates of women in the workforce was a significant feature of the late twentieth century. While the annual average participation rate for males has been declining more or less continuously over the last 50 years, it was 73 per cent in 2000–01, and it has been increasing for females, reaching 55 per cent in 2000–01.[60] Historically, women have not tended to join unions and, indeed, in the past, unions have prevented women from entering a number of occupations in the interest of protecting male 'breadwinner' jobs.[61] To some extent this has contributed to a culture of union avoidance on the part of many women.

In many industries, unions' responses to workplace changes have been to resort to the 'damage control' measures of negotiating termination packages for their members, or at least to 'hold' pay rates for existing staff. For example, in Victorian local government, faced with massive redundancies, the Australian Service Union's (ASU) efforts to minimise job and salary loss through the negotiation of redundancy packages led to disillusionment for many members, who blamed the union's impotence (rather than the government's privatisation agenda) for their predicament.[62]

The circumstances outlined above do not mean that unions are entirely powerless against the current wave of de-unionisation. A successful recruitment campaign by the

ACTU, *unions@work*, aimed at young workers, has been in place since 1996.[63] The campaign has attracted around 200 000 new members in each year of its operation. The key to the success of *unions@work* has been the strategy of getting young people involved in union activities in their own workplace, particularly where there has been an issue that has needed addressing. In 2003, the ACTU launched *Future Strategies: Unions Working Together for a Fairer Australia*, which aimed to consolidate the success of *unions@work*. *Future Strategies: Unions Working Together for a Fairer Australia* outlined the union movement's vision that comprises three key themes: (1) issues for unions in the wider society, (2) the challenge of organising heartland workplaces, and (3) the challenge of organising new members.[64]

1. *Issues for unions in the wider society*. This theme sets the key values for Australian unions and focuses on both the community and the workplace. In its vision of 'fairness and equality in the community' the ACTU sets out the rights of citizens to a fair share of the nation's wealth, while the policy on 'security and fairness in the workplace' includes the rights to: be paid a decent wage, have a safe workplace, join and be represented by a union, be consulted and have access to affordable childcare.
2. The challenge of organising heartland workplaces. This theme sets out to create 'active, effective and informed' union delegates who are vital to building a resilient Australian union movement. The policy entails increasing union delegate and member numbers, encouraging delegate participation in union and political activities and improving delegate education. These goals form part of the *unions@work* strategy.
3. *The challenge of organising new members*. This theme emerged from the observation that while *unions@work* achieved significant advances in recruitment of new members, less progress was made in areas where jobs are growing. This will entail unions establishing dedicated income streams to finance new recruitment drives, perhaps through a levy on existing members and creating organising teams that draw on the expertise of 'lead organisers' with successful track records in member recruitment.

Clearly, neither *unions@work* nor *Future Strategies: Unions Working Together for a Fairer Australia* have stemmed the flow of members out of unions, but they have provided an innovative start. More recently, union campaigning has turned toward public protest against the WRA with two Australia-wide rallies held in 2006. Whilst the protests received mixed reactions from the media, they served to raise workers' consciousness of the Government's industrial relations agenda.

The growth of employer prerogative

The decline of unions in the face of a political environment shaped by neo-liberal ideology has contributed to the increasing individualisation of the employment relationship, which, in turn, has shifted power towards employers. The turning point in the growth of managerial prerogative occurred in the mid 1980s. This marked the convergence of international influences, such as the Thatcher Government in the United Kingdom and the Reagan Government in the United States, and mounting pressure from Australian employer associations and right-wing think tanks that were critical of government intervention and regulation of industrial relations. Emerging employer activism in industrial relations saw a number of industrial disputes fought out in the courts with the common law proving to be a powerful instrument in support of managerial prerogative.

PART 1   Managing the Human Resource Environment

Corporatism
a formal cooperative agreement between the government and the union movement ensuring union involvement in the reform process.

An early example was the Mudginberri dispute of 1985, which arose over the refusal of the Australasian Meat Industry Employees Union (AMIEU) to accept a piecework payment system, despite its ratification by the AIRC. The employer, with the financial backing of the National Farmers' Federation (NFF), launched legal proceedings in the Australian Federal Court under the *Trade Practices A*ct 1974 in order to prevent picketing by AMIEU members. The court fined the union $1.7 million for trading losses suffered by the employer during the picketing, and the case became a catalyst for a series of similar legally based incidents of employer activism. At one level these decisions demonstrated the power of the common law as an employer instrument to deal with industrial action, but on a deeper level they signalled that employers did not endorse the notion of corporatism (a formal cooperative agreement between the government and the union movement ensuring union involvement in the reform process), which had been the thinking behind the former Labor Government's Accord policy.[65] The corporatist notion of the Hawke Labor Government, which was elected in 1983, included employer groups. Many of the peak business bodies were invited to become formal members of the Accord but declined; some did, however, engage informally in, and support, the Accord process.

Decision making in the workplace operates through four main processes: legal regulation, collective negotiations, individual negotiations and management determination.[66] The distinction between these processes lies in who makes the decisions for the workplace. The current neo-liberal agenda views freedom of contract as the means to strengthen civil liberties and individualism in the workplace.[67] Without tribunals, the employment relationship would be primarily governed by the common law of contract. As the WRA places no requirement on the parties to bargain, indirectly it increases employer control over the employment relationship by broadening managerial prerogative and discretion and, as we have explained above, it also directly increases employer control. Thus, the shift in power in the employment relationship under the WRA provides management with the opportunity to use enterprise bargaining in order to drive down costs by reducing terms and conditions and increasing the use of part-time work and flexible work patterns. For instance, Loudoun and Harley[68] linked the increase in 12-hour shifts to greater employer bargaining power combined with fewer opportunities for the AIRC to supervise bargaining or scrutinise the resulting agreements. In the Australian public sector, outsourcing through competitive tendering has led to lowering of wage rates, increasing the spread of standard weekly working hours, reducing or removing penalty rates and allowances, and cutting training opportunities.[69] Further, savings to organisations through outsourcing services were found to arise through cost shifting (from employers to employees) and through work intensification.[70] Offshoring has also been the subject of considerable debate with regard to job security, as indicated in 'Managing challenges through sustainability: ANZ and St George lead the way in offshoring jobs' case.

Industrial relations challenges for the human resource professional of the future

Three interrelated trends of decentralisation, deregulation and neo-liberalism in industrial relations are the sources of important challenges for the HR professional. The decentralisation and deregulation of the industrial framework provides the HR professional with a range of industrial instruments to utilise: awards, collective agreements (union or non-union), individual agreements and common law contracts

MANAGING CHALLENGES THROUGH SUSTAINABILITY

ANZ AND ST GEORGE LEAD THE WAY IN OFFSHORING JOBS

ANZ and St George are the most aggressive of the major banks in seeking to send back-office jobs offshore, with only the Commonwealth Bank ruling out any immediate likelihood of joining the practice.

Analysis by the *Herald* of the latest statements by the so-called 'four plus one' leading Australian banks as the annual meeting season comes to an end suggests there is a slow but steadily growing movement to transfer processing work done by fully employed staff here to lower-cost countries such as India.

While ANZ, St George, National Australia Bank and Westpac have been sensitive to campaigns being waged by the Finance Sector Union against 'offshoring' by committing to keep their call centres in the country, the equivalent of several hundred jobs across the industry are now, or will soon be, based outside Australia.

Three of the banks have vigorously defended the move, saying that they need to both consider and, if necessary, act upon plans to switch back-office work overseas to remain competitive. NAB, which is due to hold its meeting in Adelaide at the end of next month, is expected to follow suit.

Only the Commonwealth has taken a stand by indicating that, as 'an iconic Australian company', it is committed to maintaining a dedicated and efficient workforce in the country to carry out such work. It has admitted to looking at offshoring in the past, especially given a looming recruitment crisis in the industry, but says it is not on its agenda at present.

ANZ has the most home-grown jobs based overseas, with its biggest presence in the Indian city of Bangalore where it has a long-established IT centre employing about 1400 people. Unlike some of its rivals which have outsourced their work to third parties, ANZ's Bangalore business is a wholly owned subsidiary.

However, ANZ has said that it was looking to use that centre to take on certain back-office and operational functions now undertaken in Australia, which could see it expand substantially over the next one to two years.

St George is following suit with at least 70 processing jobs being sent abroad, and chief executive Gail Kelly has said it would investigate other options for outsourcing that did not involve front-office staff who dealt directly with customers.

NAB has adopted a more low-key approach, successfully trialling the work of 20 staff overseas—but with the expectations that about 150 jobs could be transferred over the next year.

In contrast, Westpac has publicly withdrawn a plan to export 400 transaction processing jobs from its Concord operations centre in NSW because it did not meet projected financial targets. Nonetheless, its BT wealth management business is understood to have based the work of 70 staff abroad and Westpac has made it clear it is looking at other options.

FSU national secretary Paul Schroder said the banks were having to take a careful approach to the issue given the negative response to their plans so far.

'I think they have a major problem over this as their workforces don't like it, their customers don't like it and even some of their shareholders don't like it', he said.

Source: D. John, 2006, 'ANZ and St George lead the way in offshoring jobs', *The Sydney Morning Herald*, 27 December, p. 29.

---

of employment. The HR professional will need strong analytical skills to be able to strategically assess the most appropriate employment instrument to use in order to meet organisational and industrial objectives. For example, which employment instrument best suits an organisation that requires the ability to flexibly respond to fast-changing demands, yet at the same time ensure staff commitment and loyalty?

Much research and debate has surrounded the development of flexible work practices as part of an integrated management strategy in the use of internal and external labour markets.[71] While the clear trend in Australia is to rely on the increasingly common non-standard forms of employment, organisations must be mindful that this may well cut costs but it may also lock them into a low-skill and low-quality strategy.[72] The challenge for the HR professional is to be able to strategically assess the most appropriate form of employment contract, or indeed, whether labour should be hired directly, rather than through a labour hire agency.

The increasingly non-unionised environment has implications for the HR manager. Purcell[73] noted that while managers in non-unionised firms in the United Kingdom reported that they had better employee relations than firms in the union sector, particularly as they had not experienced strikes or other overt forms of industrial conflict, these firms also had higher rates of covert conflict, expressed in increased voluntary labour turnover. These firms also reported higher rates of industrial injuries, a greater use of incentive pay and twice the rate of dismissals as unionised workplaces. The extent to which the HR professional engages with unions needs to be carefully considered.

The rise of managerial prerogative has implications for fairness at work. Unfair decisions imposed on employees are likely to be met with resistance in the form of poor morale, lower productivity or sabotage.[74] The issue of unfairness gains greater saliency from the WRA provisions which exclude up to 90 per cent of the workforce from protection from unfair dismissal and give rise to the prospect of dismissal at will. Increasingly, the role and responsibilities of the HR manager are likely to include ensuring the provision of justice in workplace practices such as hiring, promotions and discipline.

Some organisations appear to be expecting more from employees, but offering less in exchange. For instance, while unitarist ideologies require employees to demonstrate commitment, management practice has emphasised employee disposability. Clearly, the challenge for the HR professional arising from these changes will be to manage recruitment and selection, skills acquisition, employee turnover, employment contracts and participation in an environment that often mitigates against employee commitment and loyalty. (See the advertisement for a HR professional at the beginning of this chapter.)

While traditional tribunal-centred industrial relations operated on a value system with a heavy emphasis on egalitarianism and uniformity, market-based industrial relations place value on employees who possess the skills most in demand at any particular time. The fact that in the contemporary world a particular set of skills may be in demand for only a short period has implications for both employees and managers. The traditional approach has been for organisations to train employees in the skills most needed in-house. However, to the extent that jobs become more casualised, employers will become more reluctant to invest in training and development. The responsibility for skills development, then, will increasingly fall on employees or governments, as only those who possess in-demand skills will be hired. While employees may need to be more proactive and informed regarding their own self-development, organisations will need to adopt strategies to ensure an adequate supply of appropriate skills. The HR professional will need to be well versed in recruitment and selection as well as skills analysis. Targeting employees who possess the relevant skills will be a vital function, particularly in organisations that conduct little or no internal training. Other organisations may combine work and learning, placing some, but not all, the responsibility for skill formation on its employees. Some of these organisations might train employees who then move on to other firms, thus operating as skills exporters.[75]

Managing turnover will also emerge as a key function for the HR professional. The current industrial relations environment is shaped by a labour market that is highly casualised and precarious for many employees. Clearly, the advantage in this scenario is often on the side of the employer, but this may change as labour markets become tighter. Already unemployment is at historically low levels, and in particular labour market segments this is likely to be a long-term phenomenon. Unemployment will fall as the demographically numerous baby boomers (those born from the late 1940s to the late 1950s) leave the workforce. Added to this, workers are becoming more informed regarding which skills are best remunerated; and, as a consequence, they are also likely to be more aggressive in seeking jobs with organisations offering jobs that provide opportunities to develop skills that are in high demand. Many workers will actively seek to move to other firms as they witness new skill mixes rise in demand. Thus, the need to retain good workers will place pressure on HR professionals as well as the systems in use at their firms. Designing employment agreements for those with valued skills may need to take into account explicit training commitments and compensation systems that reward and provide incentives on an individual basis.[76]

Managing the workplace of the future will require the HR professional to adequately deal with the complexities of a contractual environment. Some employees will be sourced through labour hire firms; others will be employed on short-term or fixed-task contracts. Some services will be entirely contracted out to other businesses. Increasing casualisation of the workforce will lead, in turn, to increasing transactions between employers and employees. Each of these transactions represents a different contract and so the HR professional will need to be familiar with processes such as tendering, specifying outputs, service quality and cost in the contract; and monitoring performance and holding providers accountable.[77] Importantly, contract management will be elevated to a key management skill, principally because the financial gains to be made through these arrangements will be almost entirely dependent on managing the contract; and failure will bring serious consequences for service delivery with possible legal ramifications. For instance, during the period of 'compulsory competitive tendering' by local government in Victoria, 50 per cent of a council's operating budget was required to be put out to tender (contracted out). Inexperience with contract management led to problems including contract defaults, cost over-runs, performance failure, contract disputes and inadequate reporting and accountability systems.[78]

Finally, the future HR professional will need to manage employee participation in management in a 'real' and meaningful sense. Workers will be increasingly treated as independent contractors and expected to manage their own professional development and careers. Organisations will be unlikely to offer job tenure; but, instead, they will focus on worker productivity, flexibility and disposability. Thus, the concept of loyalty, on which current organisations base their expectations of employee commitment, will be significantly eroded. The loss of job tenure alone is predictive of a decline in employee loyalty. Instead of relying on employee loyalty in the future, worker participation for the purpose of improving productivity will lie in adequate incentive schemes, training deals and performance-based pay. Management of high-performing teams and maintaining motivation will be key challenges for HR professionals, who will increasingly act as mentors and coaches for a diverse and highly skilled workforce.

PART 1   Managing the Human Resource Environment

MANAGING PEOPLE

BETTER WORK DEAL FOR YOUTH

NSW employers will be required to pay overtime penalties to their under-age employees, and will also have to pay them for training periods and limit their night-time work under new rules relating to child employment.

The principles, laid down by the full bench of the NSW Industrial Relations Commission in a judgement delivered yesterday, chip away at the Federal Government's Work Choices legislation, as they stipulate that no child may be worse off under Work Choices than under the relevant state award.

The full bench held that under the present system, companies 'may now lawfully offer employment to children on terms which are in the corporations' commercial interests, but are to the significant detriment of the child'.

Yesterday's judgement clarified the 'no net detriment' clause of the state *Industrial Relations (Child Employment)* Act, which was created by the State Government last year in response to the federal Work Choices legislation.

Despite the federalisation of the industrial relations system, the states still have jurisdiction over workers under 18.

'There can be no doubt on the evidence that children employed by some corporate employers in this state are presently being exploited in a most unconscionable way,' the commission found.

It heard evidence of children being required to work for no pay during 'training' shifts, as well as being made to work unpaid overtime hours and late, onerous shift hours. The judgement also found a template Australian workplace agreement was being used by some retail chains 'to exploit children by severely undercutting their wages and working conditions compared to what they would otherwise have been entitled to'.

This one-size-fits-all approach belied any suggestion that the agreements were 'the product of genuine negotiations delivering outcomes in the interests of both employers and children', the commission found.

Under the new rules, employers must pay their child workers for all work performed, including for training, probation periods and overtime. They must also limit rostering under-18s to work late at night or early in the morning and give reasonable notice of changes in shift hours. They must pay children the equivalent of what they would have earned under the state award.

The Minister for Industrial Relations, John Della Bosca, welcomed the ruling.

'Due to inexperience many young workers are particularly prone to be exploited under John Howard's Work Choices system ... This is good news for them,' he said.

The federal minister for Workplace Relations, Joe Hockey, said the ruling would confuse employers and possibly discourage them from employing under-18s.

'[The "no detriment"] test is going to further confuse employers and employees about how they go about employing young people,' Mr Hockey said.

Mitchell Bartlett, 17, of Petersham, has left school to pursue his dream of becoming a musician, but in the meantime he needs to support himself, so next week he will start a permanent part-time job at Woolworths in Marrickville.

Mitchell is unsure if he is on an Australian workplace agreement or an award, but he is happy with the conditions. He gets $15 an hour and will be paid for training, although he will not get extra for working Sundays. But he said that even if he did not like his conditions there was probably not much he could do about it.

'I probably wouldn't have the confidence to confront my boss,' he said yesterday. 'When you're young you're at the bottom of the food chain, so you're much easier to exploit. It often happens.'

Source: J. Maley, 2007, 'Better work deal for youth', *The Sydney Morning Herald*, 23 May, p. 8. © 2007 Copyright John Fairfax Holdings Limited. www.smh.com.au

DISCUSSION

Do a media search for news items about youth employment. What are the issues related to employment of workers under the age of 18?

CHAPTER SUMMARY

This chapter has reviewed some of the major developments in Australian industrial relations over recent decades. Since the 1980s there have been three interrelated developments: (1) decentralisation, (2) apparent deregulation (in effect, re-regulation), and (3) the incorporation of neo-liberal ideology into employment legislation. Decentralisation has seen the lowering of the centre of industrial relations activity from the AIRC to the level of the individual workplace. Fewer disputes are being dealt with by the AIRC as workplaces increasingly utilise their workplace dispute resolution procedures or turn to litigation and to private mediators. Workplace bargaining has also shifted the centre of wage determination away from the AIRC to the workplace. Further, decentralisation has seen a shift towards individualising employment agreements with the growth of AWAs and common law contracts of employment, and this is a trend that is likely to continue and accelerate.

The concept of labour market deregulation portrays labour as another commodity. Institutions such as unions and the AIRC are considered to be obstacles to the development of free market relations and legislation has been enacted to pare back the influence of these institutions. Another source of worker protection and a perceived impediment to the operation of the free market is the award system. Since 1986 awards have been restructured to remove restrictive work practices and, now, under the WRA will cease to be the safety net against which workplace agreements are determined. Awards are likely to apply to an ever shrinking number of workers who have not been placed on workplace agreements.

The neo-liberal policies of both Liberal–National and Labor governments in Australia have driven the free-market agenda and have underpinned the deregulation and individualisation of Australian industrial relations. The de-collectivisation resulting from these policies has led to a dramatic fall in union density, an increase in individual employment arrangements and a major growth in non-standard employment. These changes have provided opportunities for employers to strengthen their bargaining power, which in turn has allowed them greater control over the management of production, resulting in increased flexibility and profitability. This has been evidenced by the growth of non-standard employment and the inferior pay and conditions sometimes associated with non-unionised workers when compared to those who are unionised.

These changes are indicative of future employment trends in Australia and elsewhere and have major implications for the role of the HR professional. The HR manager requires the ability to strategically assess the form of employment instrument that best meets organisational and industrial objectives. The management of precariously employed workers will involve considerable attention to recruitment and selection procedures. The rise in managerial prerogative will have implications for workplace justice and maintaining fairness in the workplace will be an increasingly important role for the HR manager. Organisations that invest less in training employees must turn to the market to buy-in those skills that they need. The HR professional must not only rely on the strategic planning of emerging skill sets, but he or she must be fully conversant with skills analysis. In an environment of high staff turnover, old-fashioned notions of commitment and loyalty will need to be replaced by ensuring that performance is maintained through the skilled management of participation and high-performance teams as well as suitable incentive schemes. Finally, the contractual nature of employment will emerge as a key component of the HR professional's work as much of the firm's profitability will arise through the efficient management, monitoring and assessment of employment contracts.

WEB EXERCISES

The AIRC has an informative website at **www.airc.gov.au**, which contains its annual report and a number of links to relevant developments in Australian industrial relations. The following questions refer to the annual report of the AIRC for 2003–04.

Questions

1 Refer to the 'Introduction'. What are the funding issues facing the AIRC in 2005?
2 Refer to 'Significant cases'. Consider the precedent set in the case: *Re Austral Construction Pty Ltd Certified Agreement* where the AIRC refused to certify a non-unionised collective agreement. The employer had changed the wording of s 170LK(4) of the agreement, which allows employees to be represented when meeting with the employer. The employer's new clause stated that if an employee requested representation, it would be the employer who selected the agent for the employee. Do you think this is a fair clause? Why do you think the non-unionised employees who signed this agreement did not object to this clause? Imagine if the AIRC was not bound to check the clauses in a certified agreement. Who would then ensure the fairness of workplace relations?
3 Refer to 'New technology'. How does the AIRC utilise technology in dispensing its workload?

DISCUSSION QUESTIONS

1 Consider the 'job advertisement' for the HR professional at the beginning of this chapter. Do you think what is on offer to the applicant represents a fair exchange? Why or why not? Who bears the business risk—A-Firm or the applicant?
2 With an increasing number of disputes being heard by the courts, and in some cases by private mediators, do you see any future role for the AIRC in settling disputes? Explain.
3 If unionised agreements pay employees more than non-unionised agreements, why do you think that employees are not joining unions?
4 Australian industrial relations is said to have traditionally relied on values such as uniformity and egalitarianism. Are these values relevant in modern times? Why or why not?
5 What do you believe are the main reasons businesses move offshore?

CASE STUDY

A ROSTER CHANGE AT METALS

This case study illustrates a dispute in which an external third party was engaged to resolve a number of matters arising from the planned implementation of a new roster. The parties to the dispute comprised a group of 36 employees and their supervisor. In the four years to 2001, a total of 276 white-collar workers had been retrenched compared to only 10 shop-floor workers. At the time of interview, the downsizing at Metals had still not reached a plateau and the focus of recent closures and redundancies had switched from production to distribution, with all but two distribution centres closing down across New South Wales and Victoria. Metals' north-western plant, where this study was conducted, employed 190 shop-floor and 100 white-collar workers. While the white-collar workers were mostly white Anglo-Australian males, shop-floor employees were all middle-aged males mainly from Greece, Malta and Croatia. This latter group typically had more than 10 years service with the company, they had little formal education and poor to average literacy and numeracy skills. A smaller, more recently employed group emanated from South-East Asia. All the shop-floor workers belonged to the National Union of Workers (NUW). Management, employees and the NUW reported a strong positive working relationship.

The proposed new roster, which was the subject of this dispute, was designed to bring shift work and pay structures into line with other departments within Metals. The result of this would be to reduce working hours (and thus pay) and to rationalise team structures. A further consequence of these changes was that there would be up to 10 redundancies. As the machine operators had developed permanent teams over the years, they became agitated when they realised that, apart from job losses and pay cuts, the new roster would split work teams forcing the operators to work with workers from other teams.

The workers were angered by the roster change, the effect on their pay and on their start and finish times—particularly as the latter would affect their families. The workers also complained that the new team structures stemmed from the supervisor's failure to manage racial abuse and discrimination in the workplace. The shop steward explained that

> ... the whole issue was that one of the supervisor's pals did not want to work with the individual that was being moved out [of a crew] and it was common knowledge ... ... The problem it did create was that it put that individual employee in with another influential individual ... who he'd had a history of racial abuse from (shop steward, 23 March 2001, p. 3).

In the final analysis the management of Metals decided to use a consultant to resolve the roster dispute. The HR manager explained that there were two main reasons for this decision. First, the dispute involved all 36 members of the original three-shift roster, and only a skilled independent consultant would be able to handle such a large group. Second, there were multiple issues of concern, ranging from the effects of the shift changes in both monetary and social terms to allegations of favouritism and mismanagement against the supervisor. The complexity of these issues, according to the shop steward, was the paramount consideration in the hiring of an external third party.

The ADR (Alternative Dispute Resolution) practitioner was chosen principally due to his previous union connections, which gave the HR manager confidence that he would be acceptable to the union. Further, the HR manager had utilised the same practitioner in the past for a similar dispute—but at a different company. As in the previous case, the consultant undertook a private mediation.

The mediation session was conducted at Metals's training room. The consultant had arranged the tables into a U shape and while the employees sat around the U, he stood in the middle. In order to conduct this session the consultant used only a writing pad and pen which he used to note employee responses to his questions.

The employees' comments on the session were instructive. Some of the employees did not raise any issues, but as one explained:

> I didn't say nothing. I am a little bit shy person and especially when I let some people with more experience talk about this. I only have 8 years but some people have over 20 years. So I suppose they know better. In my personal view, you can't make happy everybody at the same time and I agree with a compromise (employee focus group, 28 March 2001, p. 4).

But this employee clearly had some concerns about the process and his own preparedness:

> If I have something to say, I prefer it to be different. Like one thing, everybody receive paper what will be this meeting about, what is the problem and everybody to prepare, just two minutes to have a talk what contribution can I make? Most of us, we are not scientists or something. We are people working … we need little bit of help to make a practical contribution (employee focus group, 28 March 2001, p. 7).

The employees were concerned that the supervisor did not attend. They had thought the dispute would be resolved between themselves and the supervisor. Even though many of them were angry about the supervisor's favouritism toward some team members, they thought his absence was unfair as it denied him the opportunity to air his issues. Clearly, management had hired the consultant only to collect facts which could then be used to make a decision.

QUESTIONS

1 Was the use of an external consultant the only way in which this dispute could have been resolved?
2 The HR manager and the union shop steward both believed the mediator would be suitable because of his union connections. What sort of ethical issues do you believe this raises?
3 The employees did not seem to know what the mediation process involved. What sort of preparation should mediators provide prior to the session?
4 Do issues such as low education levels and poor English language skills provide any special challenges or opportunities for a HR manager?
5 Could the HR manager have acted more strategically in managing this dispute, and indeed in preventing it from escalating into a dispute?

PART 2

BUILDING HUMAN RESOURCE MANAGEMENT SYSTEMS

6 Analysis and Design of Work

7 Human Resource Planning and Human Resource Information Systems

8 Recruitment and Selection

CHAPTER 6
ANALYSIS AND DESIGN OF WORK

Objectives

After reading this chapter, you should be able to:

1. Analyse a work-flow process, identifying the output, activities and inputs in the production of a product or service.
2. Understand the importance of job analysis in human resource management.
3. Choose the right job analysis technique for a variety of human resource activities.
4. Identify the tasks performed and the skills required in a given job.
5. Understand the different approaches to job design.
6. Comprehend the trade-offs among the various approaches to designing jobs.
7. Identify approaches to the management of human capital in various employment modes.

Words from the Ys: We want global roaming

GENERATION Y are the ultimate salespeople. The 3.3 million Australians aged 19 to 31 have learned to package and present their basket of skills to be anything an employer wants them to be, within reason—and their eyes are increasingly turned offshore.

They are the first Australians to see their future as possibly not being within Australia. Their baby boomer parents may have visited Europe on a three month Contiki tour in the early 1980s, but it never occurred to them that their future would lie anywhere but within Australia. As for previous generations, none had the means to travel let alone to contemplate what is becoming known as economic migration.

In the brave new world of the 21st century, young transient and mobile workers are moving between nations in pursuit of economic opportunity and, especially in the case of Generation Y, experiences and relationships.

Generation Y are the children of rich, guilty (because both parents work) and indulgent baby boomer parents.

They are now aged between 14 and 29. They are often a single child in a family; most come from one- or two-kid households.

Loyalty sucks

Add to this the fact that workforce expansion is slowing due to a weakening birth rate effective from the early 1980s and, all of a sudden, the workplace power balance shifts from employer to employee. And especially to young employees who previously were expected to be grateful for a job but who are now calling the shots.

And 'the shots' for Aussie Gen Ys does not necessarily mean working within Australia. There seemed to be a 'break' in workplace culture following the corporate collapses and downsizings of the early 1990s.

The retrenchment of loyal but uncompetitive workers at the peak of the last recession changed the attitudes of Generations X and Y to the corporation. Y's baby-boomer parents then ensconced in middle management were unceremoniously dumped in pursuit of economic rationalism.

The Ys learned the lesson that they should be loyal to none but their own interests. And as they entered the workforce soon after the turn of the century they remained loyal to the corporation only for as long as their job contributed to their commercial capital. Their emotional needs were fostered and supported by coddling boomer parents as well as by a defined group of friends, otherwise known as 'the new family'.

The workplace of the Ys has become a platform for other and later strategic engagements. Their 'single-child syndrome' gives them the confidence to challenge the authority of boomer management. Boomers at the same age were deferential.

How do you hold workers without 'anchors?'

Generation Y is not committed to the 'anchors' that held young boomers in Australia: partner, children, mortgage. The international market for labour has freed up in the last decade. Skilled workers and population is moving more freely into and out of Eastern Europe since the collapse of the USSR and its member states. Hong Kong, China and India have all moved into new economic and political paradigms.

And the centres of world trade, power and influence that interface with this changing world are proving irresistible to bright, young, entrepreneurial—and unconnected—Ys from satellites nations such as Australia and New Zealand. Around one million Australians now live offshore; that's five per cent of the Australian race floating around the globe in pursuit of work or a lifestyle.

In the 21st century workers will be less constrained and confined to national boundaries. This diaspora is already part of the Antipodean demographic profile. It has also infiltrated our culture. We Australians are especially impressed by anyone who 'makes it' overseas. Our media is

What Are You Worth? AHR Remuneration & Benefits Survey *continued*

increasingly littered with 'expat tales'—the bigger the better the more important the international job, the faster our little Aussie hearts beat in reflected pride.

The popular perspective of our expat lionising is that it shows Australians can cut it anywhere. Another perspective is that it sends messages to our kids, to Generation Y, that to truly make it you must do so overseas. Boomer parents now bask—some wallow—in the glory of their Y kids working overseas. It's just so much more glamorous than having your children working in boring Australia.

Having a HECS of a time

And Ys have been only too happy to leave to take up job opportunities in exciting and exotic destinations. And especially because they do not have to repay their HECS debt if working outside the Australian economy.

This debt is repaid only while working within Australia. We have a culture, as well as a debt-repayment scheme, that encourages the brightest Ys to leave this nation, and which later acts as a barrier to re-entry.

It is difficult enough now to retain the best Gen Ys. What will it be like in a decade when representatives of northern hemisphere economies come on recruiting drives to cherry-pick our best graduates?

Australian taxpayers pay good money for 25 years to produce, say, an engineering graduate through various education and health schemes. This is a good investment because that 25-year-old engineering graduate then pays taxes for 35 years. Over the longer term the Aussie taxpayer is in front in this arrangement.

But what a great proposition it is for a stronger economy to attract that engineering graduate to work, and to pay tax, someplace else. Aussie taxpayers invest—and another nation snares the most productive taxpaying years. The worst scenario would be for that engineering graduate to retire back in Australia drawing down on our health system. And the reason why this scenario is a threat right now to the Australian nation is because of the unique values of Generation Y—they are footloose and fancy-free and are predisposed to travelling and working in another country.

Love and hates of a new breed of workers

Generation X and Y employees, whether salespeople or service industry workers, aren't into being told what to do—but they have a thirst for knowledge and are keen to explore new ways of selling. In summary, they:

HATE the older-style 'my way or the highway' command-and-control managers

LOVE bosses who allow them to think creatively to achieve results quickly

HATE hearing about people with the same skills being paid more money than them

LOVE being given constructive feedback rather than carping criticism

HATE spinning their wheels in jobs where they can't reach their full potential

LOVE networking and learning from co-workers—really into collaboration

HATE tokenistic rhetoric. Don't just preach diversity, demonstrate it

LOVE being educated at their boss's expense—it keeps them loyal for a few more months

Source: Excerpt from B. Salt, 2006, 'Words from the Ys: We want global roaming', *The Australian*, 27 May 2006, p. 5.

Introduction

In Chapter 2 Strategic human resource management, we discussed the processes of strategy formulation and strategy implementation. Strategy formulation is the process by which the company decides how it will compete in the marketplace; this is often the energising and guiding force for everything it does. Strategy implementation is the way the strategic plan is carried out in activities of organisational members. We noted that there are five important components in the strategy implementation process; two of which we will discuss in this chapter: the task or job, and organisational structure.[1]

Many of the central aspects of strategy formulation deal with how the work gets done—in terms of both individual job design as well as the design of organisational structures that link individual jobs to each other and the organisation as a whole. The way a firm competes can have a profound impact on the ways in which jobs are designed and how they are linked via organisational structure. In turn, the fit between the company's structure and environment can have a major impact on the firm's competitive success.

For example, if a company wants to compete via a low-cost strategy, it needs to maximise efficiency by breaking jobs down into small, simple components that are executed repetitively by low-wage, low-skilled workers. Efficiency is also enhanced by eliminating any redundancy of support services, so that jobs are structured into functional clusters where everyone in the cluster is performing similar work. (Thus, all marketing people work together in a single unit, all engineering personnel work together in a single unit etc.) People working together within these functional clusters learn a great deal about how the function can be used to leverage their skills into small amounts of increased efficiency via continuous, evolutionary improvements. This type of design can be highly effective in stable, unchanging competitive environments.

On the other hand, if a company wants to compete via an innovation strategy, it needs to maximise flexibility. Flexibility is maximised by aggregating work into larger, holistic pieces that are executed by teams of higher-wage, higher-skilled workers. Flexibility is also enhanced by giving the units their own support systems and decision-making authority to take advantage of local opportunities in regional or specialised product markets. People working together in these cross-functional clusters generate a greater number of creative and novel ideas that can be leveraged into more discontinuous, revolutionary improvements. This is the type of structure and job design that characterises several leading firms, and this type of design can be highly effective in dynamic and changing competitive environments. Clearly, however, there are criticisms that can be levelled at this approach.

Thus, it should be clear from the outset of this chapter that there is no 'one best way' to design jobs and structure organisations. On the one hand, the organisation needs to create a fit between its environment, competitive strategy and philosophy, with its jobs and organisational design on the other.

The changing world of work, including increased global competition, greater use of information and communications technology, and changes in workforce demographics, has led to many changes in the structure of organisations, the way we work and the jobs we do. These changes include growth in contingent work; **work intensification** (employees working longer hours and working harder than ever); job insecurity; **flexible work arrangements** (variations to standard work, which may involve flexible work hours, telework, provision of various leave types, and 'family-friendly' practices such as child-care or elder-care assistance); **telework** (telecommuting, also distributed work—that is, work done outside of the traditional work environment);

Work intensification
employees working longer hours and working harder than ever before.

Flexible work arrangements
variations to standard work; may involve flexible work hours, telework, provision of various leave types, and 'family-friendly' practices such as child-care or elder-care assistance.

Telework
(telecommuting, also distributed work) work done outside of the traditional work environment, including at home, while travelling, or anywhere an employee can interact with managers, peers, customers, products or processes using technology.

global project teams; and new forms of work, such as the growth of service sector jobs (for example, call centre employment, and knowledge work).[2] While many of these changes have brought opportunities for employees and organisations, the changes may also have negative implications. For example, there is evidence of growth in insecure, low-skill, service sector jobs (sometimes referred to as 'McJobs'[3]), and many employees in full-time employment report that they feel less secure and are working harder (work intensification) than ever before. Considering these developments, the way in which job analysis and job design are managed can be an important factor in organisational competitiveness. As discussed in the opening vignette, managers need to understand the diverse needs of their workforce, including the emerging views of Generation Y employees, and design jobs in ways that will attract and retain people in order to enhance organisational competitiveness.

This chapter discusses the analysis and design of work and, in doing so, lays out some considerations that go into making informed decisions about how to create and link jobs. The chapter is divided into four sections, the first of which deals with 'big-picture' issues related to work-flow analysis and organisational structure. The following two sections deal with more specific, lower-level issues related to job analysis and job design. The final section brings together organisational structure, job analysis and job design by considering a contemporary approach to the management of human capital in various employment modes.

The fields of job analysis and job design extensively overlap, yet in the past they have been treated differently.[4] **Job analysis** (the process of getting detailed information about jobs) has focused on analysing existing jobs to gather information for other human resource management practices such as selection, employee development, performance management and compensation.[5] 'Job design', on the other hand, has focused on redesigning existing jobs to make them more efficient or more motivating to jobholders.[6] Thus, job design has had a more proactive orientation towards changing the job, whereas job analysis has had a passive, information-gathering orientation. However, as we will show in this chapter, these two approaches are interrelated.

Job analysis
the process of getting detailed information about jobs.

Work-flow analysis and organisation structure

In the past, HR professionals and line managers have tended to analyse or design a particular job in isolation from the larger organisational context. **Work-flow design** is the process of analysing the tasks necessary for the production of a product or service, prior to allocating and assigning these tasks to a particular job category or person. Only after we have a thorough understanding of work-flow design can we make informed decisions regarding how to initially bundle various tasks into discrete jobs that can be executed by a single person.

Organisation(al) structure refers to the relatively stable and formal network of vertical and horizontal interconnections among jobs that constitute the organisation. Only after we have a thorough understanding of how one job relates to those above (supervisors), below (subordinates) and at the same level in different functional areas (marketing versus production) can we make informed decisions about how to redesign or improve jobs in a way that will benefit the entire organisation.

Finally, both work-flow design and organisation structure have to be understood in the context of how an organisation has decided to compete. Both work-flow design and organisation structure can be leveraged to gain competitive advantage for the firm, but how one does this depends on the firm's strategy and its competitive environment.

Work-flow design
the process of analysing the tasks necessary for the production of a product or service, prior to allocating and assigning these tasks to a particular job category or person.

Organisation(al) structure
the relatively stable and formal network of vertical and horizontal interconnections among jobs that constitute the organisation.

Work-flow analysis

As we noted in Chapter 1, Human resource management in Australia, initiatives such as the institution of national awards have encouraged the development of many business process improvement programs in Australian businesses. A theme common to nearly all such programs is the need to identify clearly the outputs of work, to specify the quality standards for those outputs and to analyse the processes and inputs necessary for producing outputs that meet the quality standards.[7] This conception of the work-flow process is useful because it provides a means for the manager to understand all the tasks required to produce a high-quality product as well as the skills necessary to perform those tasks. This work-flow process is depicted in Figure 6.1 on page 183. In this section, we present an approach for analysing the work process of a department as a means of examining jobs in the context of an organisation.

Analysing work outputs

Every work unit—whether a department, team or individual—seeks to produce some output that others can use. An *output* is the product of a work unit and is often an identifiable thing, such as a completed purchase order, an employment test or a computer. However, an output can also be a service, such as the services provided by an airline that transports you to some destination, a cleaning service that maintains your offices or a baby-sitter who watches your children.

We often picture an organisation only in terms of the product that it produces and then we focus on that product as the output. For example, we could easily identify the output of IBM as computers. However, to produce computers requires many work units, each generating a variety of outputs and each of these work units has a number of individuals who generate some work output. Thus, an important determinant of the effectiveness of any organisation is the efficiency and effectiveness with which it produces the many products within the various work units.

However, merely identifying an output or set of outputs is not sufficient. Once these outputs have been identified, it is necessary to specify the standards for the quantity or quality of these outputs. For example, a productivity improvement technique known as ProMES (productivity measurement and evaluation system) focuses attention on both identifying work-unit outputs and specifying the levels of required performance for different levels of effectiveness.[8] With ProMES, the members of a work unit identify each of the products (outputs) of the work unit for the various customers. They then evaluate the effectiveness of each level of products in the eyes of their customers.

The identification of work outputs has only recently gained attention among HR departments. Many HR executives have strengthened the role of the HR department by developing ways to analyse their customers inside the company and the products that those customers desire from the HR function.[9] This has resulted in HR managers having a clearer understanding of the specific products that they supply to the company and it allows them to focus on producing high-quality products. Without an understanding of the output of a work unit, any attempt at increasing work-unit effectiveness will be futile.

Analysing work processes

Once the outputs of the work unit have been identified, it is possible to examine the work processes used to generate the output. The work processes are the activities that members of a work unit engage in to produce a given output. Every process consists of operating procedures that specify how things should be done at each stage of the development of the product. These procedures include all the tasks that must be performed in the production of the output. The tasks are usually broken down into those performed by each person in the work unit.

Again, to design work systems that maximise efficiency, a manager needs to understand the processes required in the development of the products for that work unit. Often, as workloads increase within a workgroup, the group will grow by adding positions to meet these new requirements. However, many organisations have resisted such growth, and have reduced employee numbers (downsized) with the aim of achieving greater efficiencies. Such aims may not be met, as employees suffer work intensification and may fear that they will lose their jobs (job insecurity), with resultant loss of productivity across the group.[10] In contrast, when the workload lightens, members may take on tasks that do not relate to the work unit's product in an effort to appear busy and retain their jobs. Without a clear understanding of the tasks necessary to the production of an output, it is difficult to determine whether the work unit has become under- or over-staffed. Having a clear understanding of the tasks required allows the manager to specify which tasks are to be carried out by which individuals and eliminate tasks that are not necessary for the desired end. This ensures that the workgroup maintains a high level of productivity.

It is interesting to note that, for example, Microsoft, currently the most successful computer software company in the world, strategically manages the design of the total work-flow process for competitive advantage. To maintain the sense of being an 'underdog', Microsoft deliberately under-staffs its product teams in 'small bands of people with a mission'. This ensures both a lean organisation and high levels of motivation.[11]

Analysing work inputs

The final stage in work-flow analysis is to identify the 'inputs' used in the development of the work unit's product. For example, assume that you were assigned an essay titled 'The importance of human resources to organisational performance'. The output of your work process will be a paper that you will submit to your lecturer. To produce this essay, you must perform a number of tasks, such as conducting research, reading articles and writing the essay. What, however, are the inputs? As shown in Figure 6.1 opposite, these inputs can be broken down into the raw materials, equipment and human skills needed to perform the tasks. Raw materials consist of the materials that will be converted into the work unit's product. Thus, for your assignment, the raw materials would be the information available in the library regarding the various effects of human resources on organisational performance.

Equipment refers to the technology and machinery necessary to transform the raw materials into the product. As you attempt to develop your essay, you may use the library's electronic databases that provide you with recent articles on the relationship between human resources and organisational performance. In addition, once you sit down to write, you will most likely use a computer to 'write' your essay.

The final inputs in the work-flow process are the human skills and efforts necessary to perform the tasks. Many skills are required of you in producing your paper. For example, you need to have some knowledge of how to work the computer-search facilities, you need some typing skill and you definitely need the ability to reason and write. These skills are much more valuable for producing a high-quality essay than are other skills, such as being able to play the saxophone.

It is important to note that a flawed product can be caused by deficiencies at any phase in the production process. For example, if you fail to perform the task of spellchecking your essay before handing it in, you may receive a lower mark. Similarly,

FIGURE 6.1 Developing a work-unit activity analysis

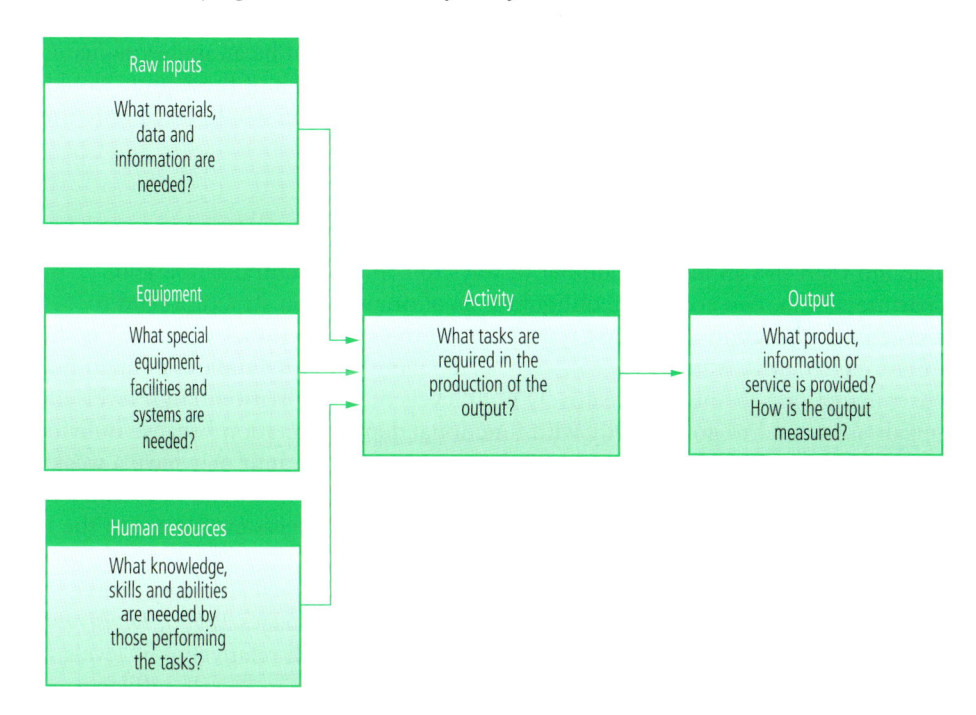

Raw inputs: What materials, data and information are needed?

Equipment: What special equipment, facilities and systems are needed?

Human resources: What knowledge, skills and abilities are needed by those performing the tasks?

Activity: What tasks are required in the production of the output?

Output: What product, information or service is provided? How is the output measured?

if you cannot obtain the best raw materials (that is, you cannot find the right articles), do not use the proper equipment (for example, the computer drive is corrupt) or do not possess the necessary skills (for example, you may find it difficult to express your ideas), your essay will receive less than the maximum mark.

Organisation structure

Whereas work-flow design provides a longitudinal overview of the dynamic relationships by which inputs are converted into outputs, organisation structure provides a cross-sectional overview of the static relationships between individuals and units that create the outputs. Organisation structure is typically displayed via organisational charts that convey both vertical reporting relationships and horizontal functional responsibilities.

Dimensions of structure

Two of the most critical dimensions of organisation structure are centralisation and departmentation. **Centralisation** refers to the degree to which decision-making authority resides at the top of the organisational chart as opposed to being distributed throughout the lower levels (that is, authority is decentralised). **Departmentation** refers to the degree to which work units are grouped based upon functional similarity or on similarity of work flow.

As discussed in the 'Managing people' case at the end of this chapter, many leading Australian companies have centralised their HR function, although there is also merit for some organisations in decentralising the HR function, or developing a hybrid approach.

For example, a school of business could be organised around functional similarity, so that there would be a marketing department, a finance department, an accounting

Centralisation
degree to which decision-making authority resides at the top of the organisational chart.

Departmentation
the degree to which work units are grouped, based on functional similarity or similarity of work flow.

department; and academic staff within these specialised departments would each teach their area of expertise to all kinds of students. Alternatively, one could organise the same school around work-flow similarity, so that there would be an undergraduate unit, a graduate unit and an executive-development unit. Each of these units would have its own marketing, finance and accounting lecturers who would teach only their own respective students and not those of the other units.

Structural configurations

Although there are an infinite number of ways to combine centralisation and departmentation, two common configurations of organisation structure tend to emerge in organisations. The first type, referred to as a 'functional structure', is shown in Figure 6.2 below. A *functional structure*, as the name implies, employs a functional departmentation scheme with relatively high levels of centralisation. High levels of centralisation tend to go naturally with functional departmentation because individual units in the structures are so specialised that members of the unit may have a weak conceptualisation of the overall organisation mission. Thus, they tend to identify with their department and cannot always be relied on to make decisions that are in the best interests of the organisation as a whole.

Alternatively, a second common configuration is a 'divisional structure', three examples of which are shown in Figures 6.3, 6.4 and 6.5 on pages 185–6. *Divisional structures* combine a work-flow departmentation scheme with relatively low levels of centralisation. Units in these structures act almost like separate, self-sufficient,

FIGURE 6.2 The functional structure

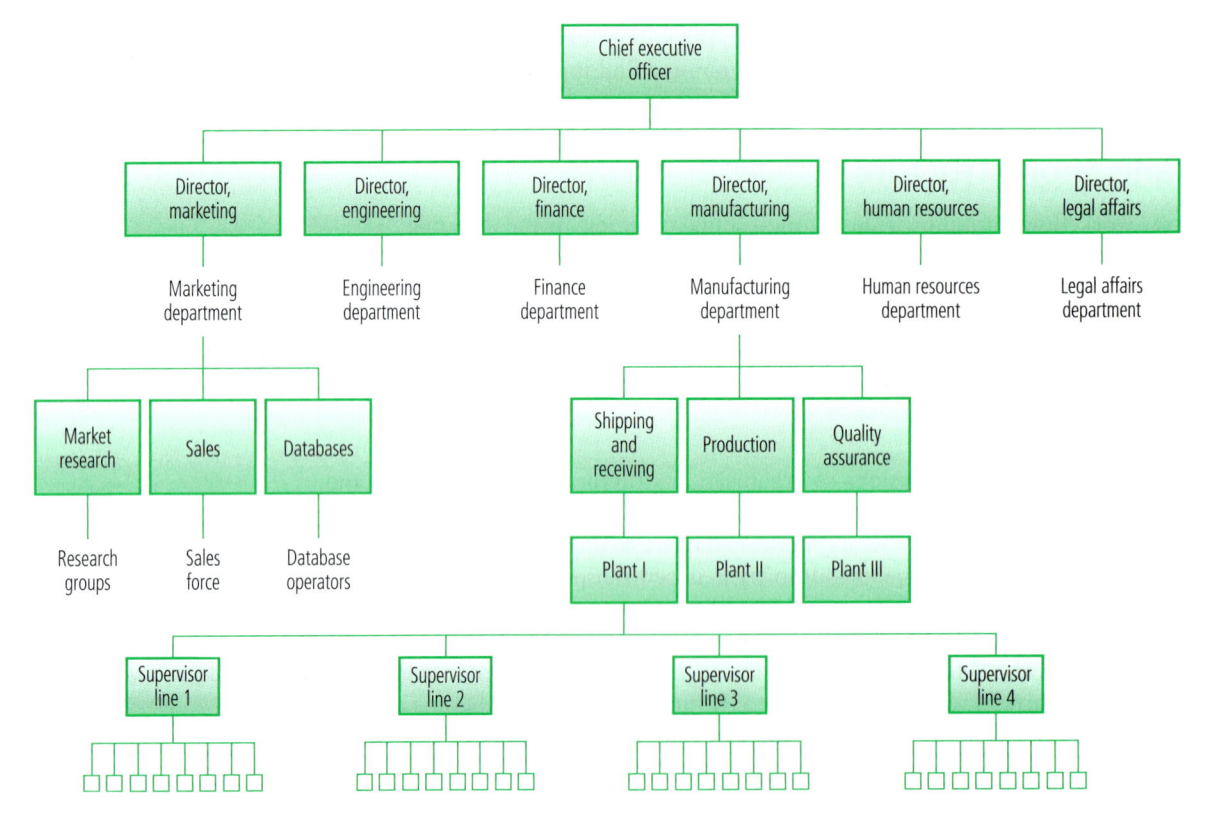

Source: Adapted from J. A. Wagner & J. R. Hollenbeck, 1992, *Organizational Behavior: Securing Competitive Advantage*, 3rd edition, Prentice-Hall, Englewood Cliffs, NJ, p. 291.

FIGURE 6.3 Divisional structure: product structure

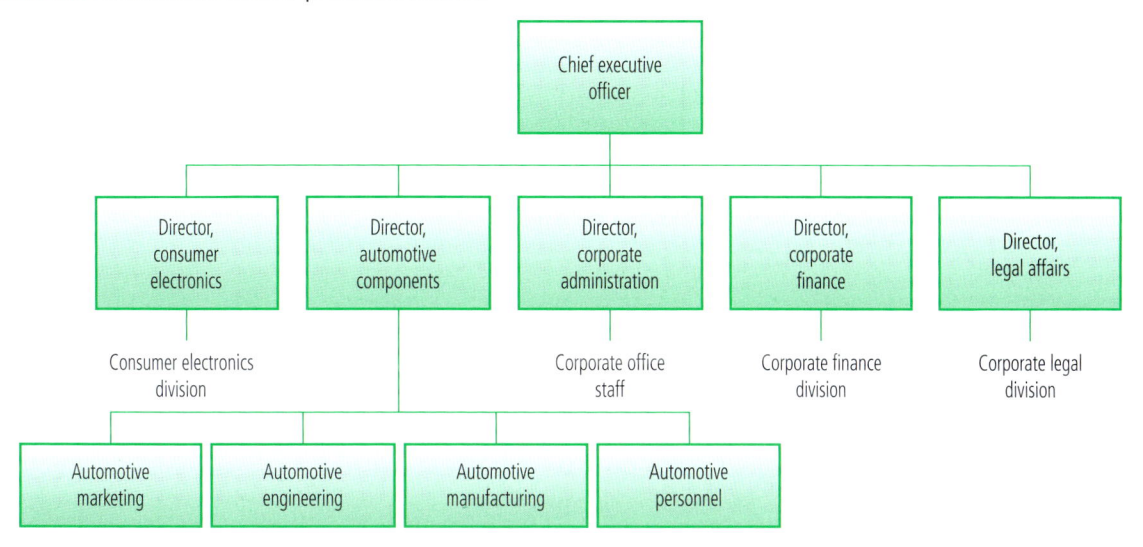

Source: Adapted from J. A. Wagner & J. R. Hollenbeck, 1992, *Organizational Behavior: Securing Competitive Advantage*, 3rd edition, Prentice-Hall, Englewood Cliffs, NJ.

FIGURE 6.4 Divisional structure: geogrphic structure

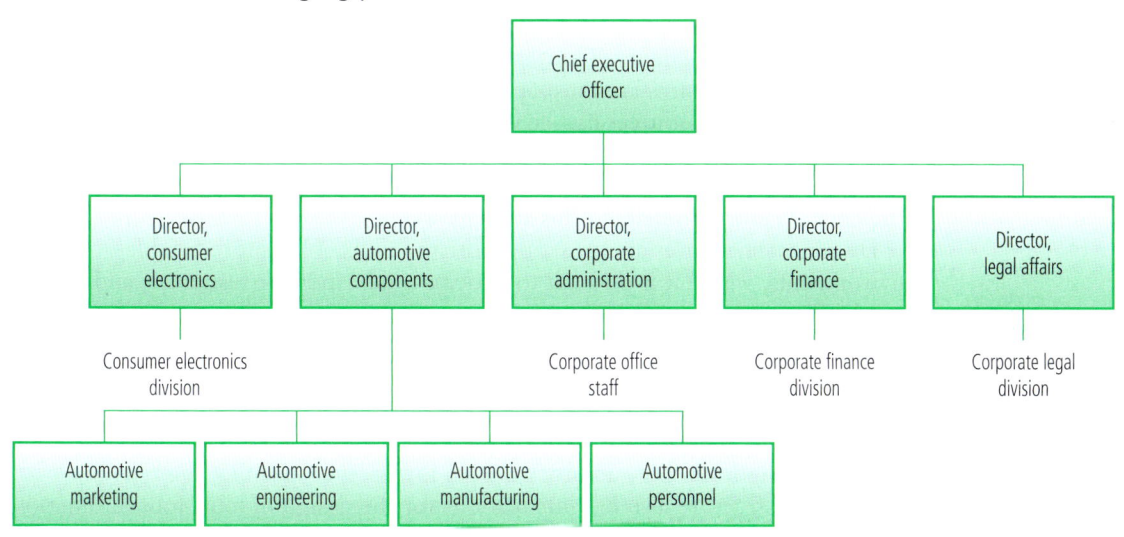

Source: Adapted from J. A. Wagner & J. R. Hollenbeck, 1992, *Organizational Behavior: Securing Competitive Advantage*, 3rd edition, Prentice-Hall, Englewood Cliffs, NJ.

semi-autonomous organisations. The organisation shown in Figure 6.3 is divisionally organised around different products; the organisation shown in Figure 6.4 is divisionally organised around geographic regions; and the organisation shown in Figure 6.5 is divisionally organised around different clients.

Divisional structures tend to be more flexible and innovative because of their work-flow focus, their semi-autonomous nature and their proximity to a homogeneous consumer base. They can detect and exploit opportunities in their respective consumer base faster than the more centralised functionally structured organisations. However, on the downside, divisional structures are not efficient because of the redundancy associated with each group that carries its own functional specialists. Divisional structures can also *self-cannibalise* if the gains achieved in one unit come at

FIGURE 6.5 Divisional structure: client structure

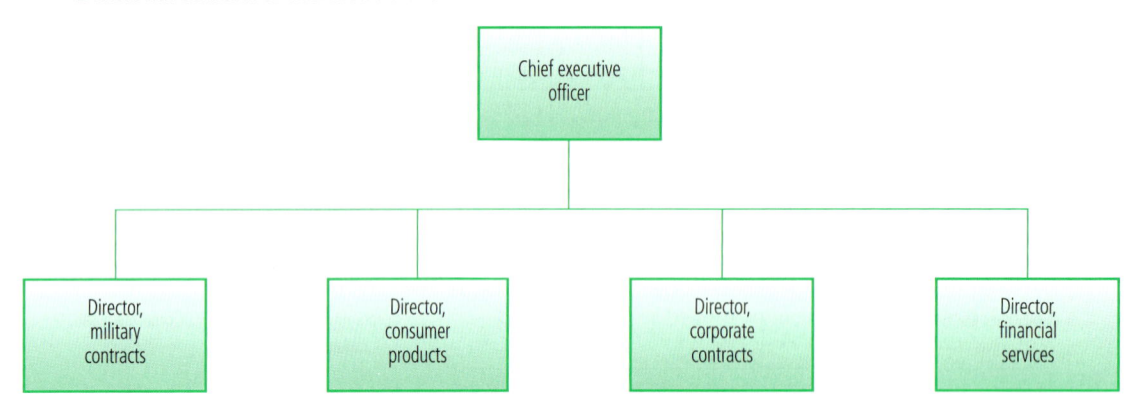

```
                    Chief executive
                       officer
        ┌──────────────┼──────────────┐
   Director,      Director,      Director,      Director,
   military       consumer       corporate      financial
   contracts      products       contracts      services
```

Source: Adapted from J. A. Wagner & J. R. Hollenbeck, 1992, *Organizational Behavior: Securing Competitive Advantage*, 3rd edition, Prentice-Hall, Englewood Cliffs, NJ.

the expense of another unit (for example, if sales in one Coles Group unit, like Coles Supermarkets, come at the expense of another Coles unit, like Bi-Lo supermarkets).

Alternatively, functional structures are considerably efficient, with little redundancy across units, and they provide little opportunity for 'self-cannibalisation'. However, these structures tend to be inflexible and insensitive to subtle differences across products, regions or clients. Thus, in general, no one structure is always the best.

Functional structures are most appropriate in stable, predictable environments, where demand for resources can be well anticipated and coordination requirements between jobs can be refined and standardised over consistent repetitions of activity. This type of structure also helps support organisations that compete on cost, because efficiency is central to making this strategy work.

Divisional structures are most appropriate in unstable, unpredictable environments, where it is difficult to anticipate demands for resources, and coordination requirements between jobs are not consistent over time. This type of structure also helps support organisations that compete on differentiation or innovation, because flexible responsiveness is central to making this strategy work.

Structure and the nature of jobs

Finally, moving from 'big-picture' issues to lower-level specifics, the type of organisation structure also has implications for the design of jobs. Jobs in functional structures need to be narrow and highly specialised, and people need to work alone. Workers in these structures (including middle managers) tend to have little decision-making authority or responsibility for managing coordination between themselves and others. Jobs in divisional structures need to be more holistic, with people working in teams that tend to have greater decision-making authority. As shown in the 'Managing challenges through HR innovation' case, in addition to understanding the organisation structure overall, it is important to recognise that work culture and productivity can be enhanced through physical changes to the work environment.

In our next section, we cover specific approaches for analysing and designing jobs. Whereas all of these approaches are viable, each focuses on a single, isolated job. These approaches do not necessarily consider how that single job fits into the overall work flow or structure of the organisation. Thus, to effectively use these techniques, we have to have a good understanding of the organisation as a whole. Without this 'big-picture' appreciation, we might redesign a job in a way that might be good for

WORK'S NEW RULES

Westpac's human-resources director, Ilana Atlas, says letting go of the desk is the biggest challenge for Westpac employees and managers moving into the bank's new Kent Street headquarters in Sydney.

The bank is progressively moving its offices over this year, undertaking one of Australia's biggest corporate moves by shifting 5000 employees from 11 Sydney business district sites to Kent Street (the bank will retain its office at 60 Martin Place). Atlas says that during the transition the bank will train managers to learn a new style of supervision that does not require a team to be in the same place, and that will free employees to adopt the most productive work styles—including working from home.

In designing the new office space, staff work habits were observed and designers toured innovative workplaces overseas. The staff study found that only about 40 per cent of an employee's work day was spent at a desk; 30 per cent was spent in other places in the building and 25 per cent outside. Portability is a big part of the new work culture.

Atlas says the study also found that the average meeting size was three to four people rather than the previous average of 10, and so smaller rooms were built away from the open-plan desks, all equipped with wireless laptop ports and Internet protocol telephones. A whole floor is devoted to housing semi-permanent project teams.

But the biggest departure from convention is that Westpac will be encouraging employees to use three internal cafes for team and individual work.

Westpac has chosen to use all the available space in the office areas of the building by placing chairs and tables near the employee kitchens and stairs. Atlas hopes the design will encourage staff to bump into each other when moving between floors. Executives are also being encouraged to mix, as only six group executives, including Atlas and chief executive David Morgan, were allocated partitioned offices.

Westpac aims to keep a 5 per cent desk vacancy rate to allow easy mobility within the building. Atlas says new technology, such as Internet video phones used through laptops, will ease the eventual transition of some employees to working from home.

Source: A. Tandukar, 2005, 'Work's new rules', *BRW*, 13 April, p. 60. © Copyright John Fairfax Holdings Limited. www.brw.com.au.

---

that one job, but this may be out of line with the work flow, structure or strategy of the organisation.

Job analysis

Job analysis refers to the process of getting detailed information about jobs.[12] Job analysis has deep historical roots. For example, in his description of the 'just' State, Socrates argued that society needed to recognise three things. First, there are individual differences in aptitudes for work, meaning that individuals differ in their abilities. Second, unique aptitude requirements exist for different occupations. Third, to achieve high-quality performance, society must attempt to place people in occupations that best suit their aptitudes. In other words, for society (or an organisation) to succeed, it must have detailed information about the requirements of jobs (through job analysis) and it must ensure that a match exists between the job requirements and individuals' aptitudes (through selection).[13]

Whereas Socrates was concerned with the larger society, it is even more important for organisations to understand and match job requirements and people to achieve high-quality performance. This is particularly true in today's competitive marketplace. Thus, the information gained through job analysis is of utmost importance; it has great value to both human resource and line managers.

The importance of job analysis to HR managers

Job analysis is such an important activity to HR managers that it has been called the building block of everything that personnel does.[14] This statement refers to the fact that almost every human resource program requires some type of information that is gleaned from job analysis: work redesign, human resource planning, selection, employee learning and development, performance management, career planning and job evaluation.[15] As indicated in the 'Managing challenges through sustainability' case below, an employer's 'brand', based on elements such as the culture, values and work performed in the organisation, can be an important factor in attracting employees and enhancing the company's reputation as an employer.

BRANDING THE BEST EMPLOYER

MANAGING CHALLENGES THROUGH SUSTAINABILITY

THE public sector, ANZ, Virgin, Telstra and Westpac are the most frequently nominated brands for which people would like to work, a survey of more than 600 jobseekers has shown.*

Career opportunities, company reputation and professional development offered are the top reasons given—and nominated ahead of salary or benefits.

This demonstrates the value of creating a strong employment brand, says specialist recruiting firm Hays.

'As candidate shortages continue, forward-looking employers are focusing on what needs to be done to attract talent', says Hays director Jacky Carter. 'Like any consumer brand, an employment brand communicates your identity as a company.'

'It isn't just a statement you adopt because you think it sounds good—it's the essence of what your company stands for', she says.

'It communicates to potential employees what it's like to work for your company.'

Ms Carter says this is clearly not just about the company logo.

'Our survey demonstrates that what most of us perceive as important—the 'look and feel'—is not what we should be primarily focused on. Rather, the message needs to be more complete—the culture, values and environment are of much greater interest to potential employees.'

'A compelling employee-value proposition is also an integral element of employment branding and the recruitment strategy.'

'It sets out who the company is, what is expected from employees and what employees receive from working for the company. In short, it reveals what your company offers that employees value. This includes defining not just the salary or job responsibilities and opportunities, but the company's culture and ambitions.'

'As skills shortages continue to test candidate sourcing and attraction strategies, and competition for the best possible staff remains high, it is no surprise the issue of employment branding continues to gain attention.'

The survey also found:

- A company's reputation as an employer is important in a candidate's decision to work for them in almost 9 out of 10 cases.
- 86 per cent would not work for a company with a bad employer reputation which offered a higher salary than a company with a good reputation.
- In determining a company's reputation as an employer, 68 per cent view treatment and support offered as 'extremely important'.
- Also rated as 'extremely important' were the relationship between management and staff (65 per cent), training and development offered to employees (51 per cent) and quality of products or services (36 per cent).
- 61 per cent would not apply for a job with a company whose vision, values and culture they did not agree with.

Ms Carter says cultural 'fit' with the company and its values is the most important factor in helping candidates associate with the company they work for, closely followed by contributing to decision making and company direction.

But she offers an element of caution. 'Base your branding on truth', she says. 'This is one example where it really does need to "do what it says on the packet".'

* Of 614 responses, the top 10 Australian most frequently named ideal employers were (in order) the public sector, ANZ, Virgin, Telstra, Westpac, IBM, Optus, Microsoft, Vodafone and PricewaterhouseCoopers.

Source: Anonymous, 2006, 'Branding the best employer', *The Adelaide Advertiser*, 25 February, p. 1.

Work redesign
As previously discussed, job analysis and job design are interrelated. Often, a firm will seek to redesign work to make it more efficient or effective. To redesign the work, detailed information about the existing job(s) must be available. In addition, redesigning a job will, in fact, be similar to analysing a job that does not yet exist.

Human resource planning
In human resource planning, planners analyse an organisation's human resource needs in a dynamic environment and develop activities that enable a firm to adapt to change. This planning process requires accurate information about the levels of skill required in various jobs to ensure that enough individuals are available in the organisation to meet the human resource needs of the strategic plan.[16]

Selection
Human resource selection deals with identifying the most qualified applicants for employment. To identify which applicants are most qualified, it is first necessary to determine the tasks that will be performed by the individual hired and the knowledge, skills and abilities that individual must have to effectively perform the job. This information is gained through job analysis.[17]

Employee learning and development
Almost every employee hired by an organisation will require some training in his or her job. Some training programs may be more extensive than others, but all require the trainer to have identified the tasks performed in the job to ensure that the training will prepare individuals to effectively perform the job.[18]

Performance management
Performance management deals with getting information about how well each employee is performing his or her job in order to reward those who are effective, improve the performance of those who are ineffective or provide a written justification for why the poor performer should be disciplined. Through job analysis, the organisation can identify the behaviours and results that distinguish effective performance from ineffective performance.[19]

Career planning
Career planning entails matching an individual's skills and aspirations with opportunities that are, or may become, available in the organisation. This matching process requires that those in charge of career planning know the skill requirements of the various jobs. This allows them to guide individuals into jobs in which they will succeed and be satisfied.

Job evaluation
The process of job evaluation involves assessing the relative dollar-value of each job to the organisation, in order to set up internally equitable pay structures. If pay structures are not equitable, employees will be dissatisfied and quit, or they will not see the benefits of striving for promotions. To put dollar-values on jobs, it is necessary to get information about different jobs to determine which jobs deserve higher pays than others.[20]

The importance of job analysis to line managers

Job analysis is clearly important to the HR department's various activities, but its importance may not be as clear to line managers. There are many reasons. First, managers must have detailed information about all the jobs in their workgroup to understand the work-flow process. Earlier in this chapter, we noted the importance of understanding the work-flow process—specifically, identifying the tasks performed and the knowledge, skills and abilities required to perform them. In addition, an understanding of this work-flow process is essential if a manager chooses to redesign certain aspects to increase efficiency or effectiveness.

Second, managers need to understand the job requirements to make intelligent hiring decisions. Seldom are employees hired by the human resource department without a manager's input. Managers will often interview prospective applicants and recommend who should receive a job offer. However, if the manager does not have a clear understanding of what tasks are performed on the job and the skills necessary to perform them, then the hiring decision may result in selecting candidates that the manager 'likes', but who are not capable of performing the job successfully.

Third, a manager is responsible for ensuring that each individual is performing his or her job satisfactorily (or better). This requires the manager to evaluate how well each person is performing and to provide feedback to those whose performance needs improvement. Again, this requires the manager's clear understanding of the tasks required in every job.

Job analysis information

When preparing for job analysis, it is important to consider the nature (or types) of information required and the potential sources of information that will be used in the job analysis.

Nature of information

Two types of information are most useful in job analysis: job descriptions and job specifications. A **job description** is a list of the tasks, duties and responsibilities (TDRs) that the job entails. Thus, TDRs are observable actions. For example, a clerical job requires the jobholder to type. If you were to observe someone in that position over the course of a day, you would certainly see him or her typing at one time or another. When a manager attempts to evaluate job performance, it is most important to have detailed information about the work performed in the job (that is, the TDRs). This makes it possible to determine how well an individual is meeting each job requirement. Table 6.1 opposite shows a sample job description.

A **job specification** is a list of the knowledge, skills, abilities and other characteristics (KSAOs), also known as **human capital**, that an individual must have to perform the job. **Knowledge** refers to factual or procedural information that is necessary for successfully performing a task. A **skill** is an individual's level of proficiency at performing a particular task. **Ability** refers to a more general enduring capability that an individual possesses. Finally, other characteristics might be personality traits such as one's achievement motivation or persistence. Thus, KSAOs are characteristics about people that are not directly observable; they are observable only when individuals are carrying out the TDRs of the job. Thus, if someone applied for the clerical job discussed earlier, you could not simply look at the individual to determine whether or not he or she possessed word-processing skills. However, if you were to observe that individual type something, you could make an assessment of the level of typing skill the individual had. When a manager is attempting to fill a position, it is important to have accurate information about the characteristics a successful jobholder must have. This requires focusing on the KSAOs of each applicant.[21]

Job description
a list of the tasks, duties and responsibilities (TDRs) that a job entails.

Job specification
a list of the knowledge, skills, abilities and other characteristics (KSAOs) that an individual must have to perform a job.

Human capital
the knowledge, skills, abilities and other characteristics (KSAOs) of individuals.

Knowledge
actual or procedural information that is necessary for successfully performing a task.

Skill
an individual's level of proficiency at performing a particular task.

Ability
an enduring capability that an individual possesses.

TABLE 6.1 A sample job description

Job title: Maintenance mechanic

General description of job: General maintenance and repair of all equipment used in the operations of a particular district. Includes the servicing of company vehicles, shop equipment and machinery used on job sites.

1. *Essential duty (40%):* Maintenance of equipment

   Tasks: Keep a log of all maintenance performed on equipment. Replace parts and fluids according to maintenance schedule. Regularly check gauges and loads for deviances that may indicate problems with equipment. Perform non-routine maintenance as required. May involve limited supervision and training of operators performing maintenance.

2. *Essential duty (40%):* Repair of equipment

   Tasks: Requires inspection of equipment and a recommendation that a piece be scrapped or repaired. If equipment is to be repaired, mechanic will take whatever steps are necessary to return the piece to working order. This may include a partial or total rebuilding of the piece using various hand tools and equipment. Will primarily involve the overhaul and troubleshooting of diesel engines and hydraulic equipment.

3. *Essential duty (10%):* Testing and approval

   Tasks: Ensure that all required maintenance and repair has been performed and that it was performed according to manufacturer specifications. Approve or reject equipment, as being ready for use on a job.

4. *Essential duty (10%):* Maintain stock

   Tasks: Maintain inventory of parts needed for the maintenance and repair of equipment. Responsible for ordering satisfactory parts and supplies at the lowest possible cost.

Non-essential functions

Other duties as assigned.

Sources of job analysis information

In performing the job analysis, one question that often arises is, 'Who should make up the group of incumbents that are responsible for providing the job analysis information?' Whatever job analysis method you choose, the process of job analysis entails obtaining information from people familiar with the job. We refer to these people as subject-matter experts because they are experts in their knowledge of the job.

In general, it will be useful for you to go to the job incumbent to get the most accurate information about what is actually done on the job. This is especially the case when it is difficult to monitor the person who does the job, as may be the case with telework (telecommuting). As noted in Chapter 1 Human resource management in Australia, increasing numbers of employed adults in Australia have an agreement with their employer to work from home on an ongoing basis, using a computer and telephone to perform their work. Critics of telework point out that it can be isolating and sedentary, and it may make it difficult for employees to establish boundaries between their work and home life.[22] Telework does not always deliver the desired benefits for employers or employees. According to Griffith University management lecturer, Dr George Lafferty, teleworkers are in danger of becoming workaholics as the line between work and home becomes blurred. In his research, managers comprised the largest single group of regular teleworkers, followed by IT professionals and administrative and clerical workers. Lafferty suggests that teleworking arrangements should be systematic rather than ad-hoc. However, in his study, more than half of the organisations surveyed had no formal agreement on terms and conditions for their teleworkers. Lafferty's research also identified a lack of systematic analysis of industrial relations, labour processes and regulatory frameworks with regard to teleworking.[23]

Telework also presents challenges for employers seeking to monitor the work being done from home or other locations. Particularly when the job analysis will be used for remuneration purposes, incumbents might have an incentive to exaggerate their duties. Thus, you will also want to ask others familiar with the job, such as supervisors, to look over the information generated by the job incumbent. This serves as a check to determine whether what is being done is congruent with what is supposed to be done in the job. Although job incumbents and supervisors are the most obvious and frequently used sources of job analysis information, other sources can be helpful, particularly for service jobs.

It is important to understand the usefulness of different sources of job analysis information, because this information is only as good as the source. Research has revealed some interesting findings regarding various sources of job analysis information, particularly regarding job incumbents and supervisors.

One question is whether supervisors and incumbents agree in their job analysis ratings. Some research has demonstrated significant differences in the job analysis ratings provided from these two different sources.[24] However, other research has found greater agreement between supervisors and subordinates when rating general job duties than when rating specific tasks.[25] One conclusion that can be drawn from this research is that incumbents may provide the most accurate estimates of the actual time spent performing job tasks. However, supervisors may be a more accurate source of information about the importance of job duties.

Another question is whether a job incumbent's own performance level is related to the job analysis ratings. Although it is intuitively appealing to think that individuals who perform well in a job might give different ratings than individuals who do not perform well, the research has not borne this out. One frequently cited study compared the job analysis ratings of effective and ineffective managers and found that they tended to give the same ratings despite their performance levels.[26] However, more recent research has also examined the relationship between job analysis and employee performance. In this research, no differences were observed between high and low performers regarding the tasks and KSAOs generated, and the ratings made regarding the time spent or the importance of the tasks.[27] However, differences have been observed in the types of critical incidents generated[28] and the ratings of the level of effectiveness of various incidents.[29] Thus, research at present seems inconclusive regarding the relationship between the performance level of the job analyst and the job analysis information he or she provides.

While the relationship between job analysis ratings and job performance is inconclusive, research has strongly demonstrated some demographic differences in job analysis information. One study in the United States found differences between males and females and between African Americans and Caucasians in the importance and time-spent ratings for a variety of tasks.[30] Similarly, another study observed minor differences between males and females and between African Americans and Caucasians in job analysis ratings. However, in this study, larger differences in ratings were the result of the experience level of the job incumbent.[31] These research results imply that when conducting a job analysis, you should take steps to ensure that the incumbent group responsible for generating the job analysis information represents a variety of gender, racial and experience-level categories.

Job analysis methods

There are various methods for analysing jobs and there is no 'one best way'. In this section, we will discuss three methods for analysing jobs: the Position Analysis Questionnaire (PAQ), the task analysis inventory and the job analysis system. Although most managers may not have time to use each of these techniques in the exact manner suggested, the three methods do provide some anchors for thinking about broad approaches, task-focused approaches and person-oriented approaches to conducting job analysis.

Position Analysis Questionnaire (PAQ)

We lead this section with the PAQ, because this is one of the broadest and most well-researched instruments for analysing jobs. Moreover, its emphasis on inputs, processes, relationships and outputs is consistent with the work-flow analysis approach that we used earlier in this chapter (see Figure 6.1 on page 183). The PAQ is a standardised job analysis questionnaire containing 194 items.[32] These items represent work behaviours, work conditions and job characteristics that can be generalised across a wide variety of jobs. They are organised into six sections.

1. Information input. This refers to where and how a worker gets information needed to perform the job.
2. Mental processes. This refers to the reasoning, decision making, planning and information processing activities that are involved in performing the job.
3. Work output. This term refers to the physical activities, tools and devices used by the worker to perform the job.
4. Relationships with other people. This category refers to the relationships with other people required in performing the job.
5. Job context. This relates to the physical and social contexts where the work is performed.
6. Other characteristics. This section refers to the activities, conditions and characteristics other than those previously described that are relevant to the job.

The job analyst is asked to determine whether each item applies to the job being analysed. The analyst then rates the item on six scales: extent of use, amount of time, importance to the job, possibility of occurrence, applicability and special code (special rating scales used with a particular item). These ratings are submitted to the PAQ headquarters, where a computer program generates a report regarding the job's scores on the job dimensions.

Research has indicated that the PAQ measures 32 dimensions and 12 overall dimensions of jobs (listed in Table 6.2 overleaf) and that a given job's scores on these dimensions can be considerably useful. The significant database has linked scores on certain dimensions to scores on subtests of the General Aptitude Test Battery (GATB). Thus, knowing the dimension scores provides some guidance regarding the types of abilities that are necessary to perform the job. Obviously, this technique provides information about the work performed in a format that allows for comparisons across jobs, whether those jobs are similar or dissimilar. Another advantage of the PAQ is that it covers the work context as well as inputs, outputs and processes.

In spite of its widespread use, the PAQ is not without problems. One problem is that to fill out the test, an employee needs the reading level of a university graduate; this disqualifies some job incumbents from the PAQ. In fact, it is recommended that only job analysts trained in how to use the PAQ should complete the questionnaire, rather than job incumbents or supervisors.[33] A second problem associated with the PAQ is that its general and standardised format leads to rather abstract characterisations of jobs. So it does not lend itself well to describing the specific, concrete task activities that comprise the actual job. Thus, it is not ideal for developing job descriptions or redesigning jobs. Methods that do focus on this aspect of the work are needed if this is the goal.

TABLE 6.2	Overall dimensions of the Position Analysis Questionnaire (PAQ)
1	Decision/communication/general responsibilities
2	Clerical/related activities
3	Technical/related activities
4	Service/related activities
5	Regular day schedule versus other work schedules
6	Routine/repetitive work activities
7	Environmental awareness
8	General physical activities
9	Supervising/coordinating other personnel
10	Public/customer/related contact activities
11	Unpleasant/hazardous/demanding environment
12	Non-typical work schedules

Task analysis inventory

Task analysis inventory refers to several different methods, each with slight variations. However, common to these approaches is the focus on analysing all the tasks performed in the focal job. (It is not uncommon to have over 100 tasks.)

For example, the task inventory-CODAP method[34] entails asking 'subject matter' experts to generate a list of the tasks performed in a job. Once this list has been developed, the subject matter experts rate each task on dimensions, such as the relative amount of time spent on the task, the frequency of task performance, the relative importance of the task, the relative difficulty of the task and whether the task can be learned relatively quickly on the job. These ratings are then subjected to the CODAP computer program that organises the tasks into dimensions of similar tasks.

Task inventories focus on providing detailed information about the work performed in a given job. The detail of the information can be helpful in developing both selection exam plans and performance appraisal criteria. Although a task inventory might indirectly suggest the types of KSAOs people might need to perform the job, these KSAOs do not come directly out of the process. Thus, other approaches that do put the focus squarely on the people requirements associated with jobs have been developed.

Fleishman Job Analysis Survey (F-JAS)

Another job analysis technique that elicits information about the worker's characteristics is the Fleishman Job Analysis Survey (F-JAS).[35] This approach defines abilities as enduring attributes of individuals that account for differences in performance. The survey is based on a taxonomy of abilities that adequately represent all the dimensions relevant to work. This taxonomy includes 52 cognitive, psychomotor, physical and sensory abilities. These are listed in Table 6.3 on page 196.[36]

The actual F-JAS scales consist of descriptions of the ability, followed by behavioural benchmark examples of the different levels of the ability along a seven-point scale. An example of the written comprehension ability scale from the F-JAS is presented in Figure 6.6.

FIGURE 6.6 Example of an ability definition and scale from the Fleishman Job Analysis Survey (F-JAS)

Written comprehension
This is the ability to understand written sentences and paragraphs.

How written comprehension is different from other abilities:

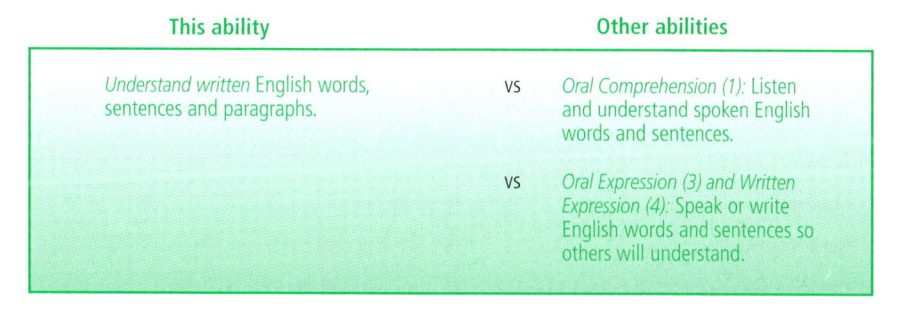

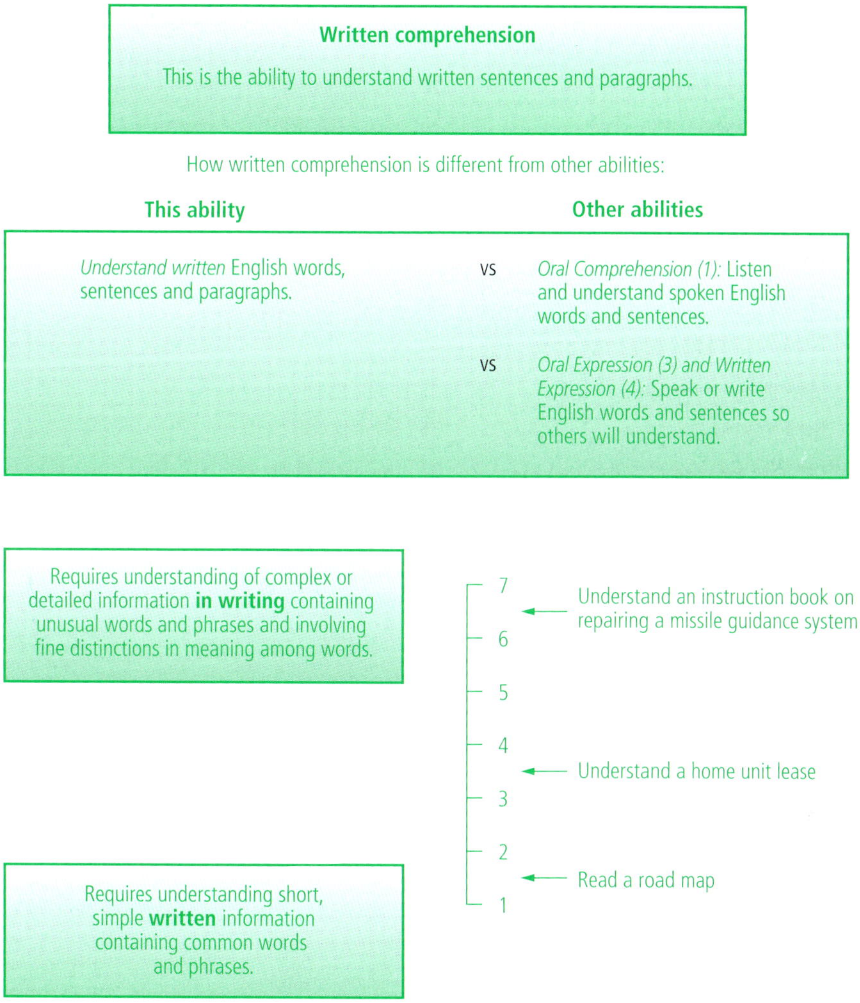

This ability		Other abilities
Understand written English words, sentences and paragraphs.	vs	*Oral Comprehension (1):* Listen and understand spoken English words and sentences.
	vs	*Oral Expression (3) and Written Expression (4):* Speak or write English words and sentences so others will understand.

Requires understanding of complex or detailed information **in writing** containing unusual words and phrases and involving fine distinctions in meaning among words.
— 7
— 6 ← Understand an instruction book on repairing a missile guidance system
— 5
— 4
— 3 ← Understand a home unit lease
— 2
— 1 ← Read a road map

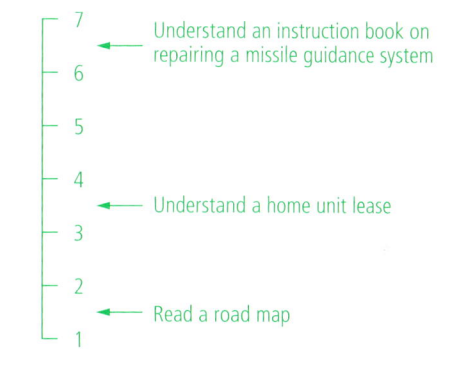

Requires understanding short, simple **written** information containing common words and phrases.

Source: E. A. Fleishman & M. D. Mumford, 1991, 'Evaluating classifications of job behavior: a construct validation of the ability requirements scales', *Personnel Psychology*, 44, pp. 523–76. The complete set of ability requirement scales, along with instructions for their use, may be found in E.A. Fleishman, 1992, *Fleishman Job Analysis Survey* (F-JAS), Management Research Institute, Inc, Potomac, MD. Used with permission.

In using the job-analysis technique, subject matter experts are presented with each of the 52 scales. These experts indicate the point on the scale that best represents the level of that ability required in a particular job. These ratings provide an accurate picture of the ability requirements of the job. Substantial research has shown the value of this general approach for human resource activities, such as career development and selection and training.[37]

Dynamic elements of job analysis

Although we tend to view jobs as static and stable, in fact, jobs tend to change and evolve over time. Those who occupy or manage the jobs often make minor, cumulative adjustments to the job that try to match either changing conditions in the environment or personal preferences for how to conduct the work.[38] Indeed, although

TABLE 6.3 Abilities included in the Fleishman Job Analysis Survey

#	Ability	#	Ability
1	Oral comprehension	27	Arm–hand steadiness
2	Written comprehension	28	Manual dexterity
3	Oral expression	29	Finger dexterity
4	Written expression	30	Wrist–finger speed
5	Fluency of ideas	31	Speed of limb movement
6	Originality	32	Static strength
7	Memorisation	33	Explosive strength
8	Problem sensitivity	34	Dynamic strength
9	Mathematical reasoning	35	Trunk strength
10	Number facility	36	Extent flexibility
11	Deductive reasoning	37	Dynamic flexibility
12	Inductive reasoning	38	Gross body coordination
13	Information ordering	39	Gross body equilibrium
14	Category flexibility	40	Stamina
15	Speed of closure	41	Near vision
16	Flexibility of closure	42	Far vision
17	Spatial orientation	43	Visual colour discrimination
18	Visualisation	44	Night vision
19	Perceptual speed	45	Peripheral vision
20	Selective attention	46	Depth perception
21	Time sharing	47	Glare sensitivity
22	Control precision	48	Hearing sensitivity
23	Multi-limb coordination	49	Auditory attention
24	Response orientation	50	Sound localisation
25	Rate control	51	Speech recognition
26	Reaction time	52	Speech clarity

Source: E. A. Fleishman & M. D. Mumford, 'Ability requirements scales' in Sidney Gael (ed), 1983, *The Job Analysis Handbook for Business, Industry and Government*, John Wiley, New York, pp. 14–29.

there are numerous sources for error in the job analysis process,[39] the fact is that most inaccuracy is likely to result from outdated job descriptions. For this reason, in addition to statically defining the job, the job analysis process must also detect changes in the nature of the job.

For example, in today's world of rapidly changing products and markets, some people have begun to question whether the concept of the job is simply a social artefact that has outlived its usefulness. Indeed, many researchers and practitioners are pointing to a trend referred to as 'dejobbing' in organisations. This practice consists of viewing organisations as a field of work needing to be done rather than a set of discrete jobs held by specific individuals. At Intel, for example, individuals are often first assigned to a project. That project changes over time with corresponding changes in the roles and requirements of the individual. Before that project is complete, the individual is assigned to an additional project or projects. Thus, besides having new responsibilities, the individual is required to work under a variety of team leaders, manage a variety of goals and timetables, and coordinate across various team locations and the schedules of different team members. 'Hot-desking' has been another way in which some organisations have endeavoured to create more flexible work processes. *Hot-desk* workers either work away from the office and rotate through a common office a couple of days a week, or are assigned to a desk each day when they arrive at work. It has been reported that some Australian companies claim to have reduced their property rent by almost a third, by using a mobile and introducing hot-desking, often for a **contingent workforce** (temporary, part-time and self-employed workers who are not considered full-time employees). Critics of hot-desking, such as the Australian Services Union (ASU), have argued that hot-desking contributes to stress, isolation, and causes health problems because employees cannot set up their workspace in ergonomically correct ways.[40]

Contingent workforce
temporary, part-time and self-employed workers who are not considered full-time employees.

To be effective, these practices require that organisations eliminate the traditional hierarchical arrangements in favour of more flexible and fluid structures and processes. These 'project-based' organisational structures require the type of broader understanding that comes from an analysis of work flows. The work can change so rapidly—and it is impossible to rewrite job descriptions every week—thus, it also illustrates the need for much more flexibility in writing job descriptions and specifications. However, legal requirements (as discussed in Chapter 3 The legal context for human resource management) may discourage firms from writing flexible job descriptions. Thus, firms seeking to use their employees as a source of competitive advantage must balance the need for flexibility with the need for legal documentation. This presents one of the major challenges faced by HR departments in the next decade and, rather than taking a passive job analytic approach, these types of changes really require an active approach to job design, such as those discussed in our next section.

Job design

So far we have approached the issue of managing work in a passive way, focusing only on understanding what gets done, the way it gets done and the skills required to get it done. While this is necessary, it is a static view of jobs, in that jobs must already exist and that they are already assumed to be structured in the 'one best way'. However, a manager may often be faced with a situation in which the work unit does not yet exist, requiring jobs within the work unit to be designed from 'scratch'. Sometimes workloads within an existing work unit are increased, or the workgroup size is decreased while the same workload is required—a trend increasingly observed with the movement towards downsizing.[41] Finally, sometimes the work is not being performed in the most efficient manner. In these cases, a manager may decide to change the way that work is done in order for the work unit to perform more effectively and efficiently. This requires redesigning the existing jobs.

Job design is the process of defining the way work will be performed and the tasks that will be required in a given job.[42] **Job redesign** refers to changing the tasks or the way work is performed in an existing job. To effectively design jobs, one must thoroughly understand the job as it exists (through job analysis) and its place in the larger work unit's work-flow process (work-flow analysis). A detailed knowledge of the tasks performed in the work unit and in the job, provides a manager with many alternative ways to design a job. This can be done most effectively through understanding the trade-offs between certain design approaches.

Job redesign
changing the tasks or the way work is performed in an existing job.

Research has identified four basic approaches that have been used among the various disciplines (for example, psychology, management, engineering and ergonomics) that have dealt with job design issues.[43] All jobs can be characterised in terms of how they fare according to each approach; thus, a manager needs to understand the trade-offs between emphasising one approach over another. In the next section we discuss each of these approaches and examine the implications of each for the design of jobs. Table 6.4 below displays how jobs are characterised along each of these dimensions.

TABLE 6.4 Characterising jobs on different dimensions of job design

The motivational job design approach

1	Autonomy	Does the job allow freedom, independence or discretion in work scheduling, sequence, methods, procedures, quality control and other types of decisions?
2	Intrinsic job	Do the work activities themselves provide direct and clear information about the effectiveness feedback (in terms of quality and quantity) of job performance?
3	Extrinsic job	Do other people in the organisation (such as managers and co-workers) provide information feedback about the effectiveness (in terms of quality and quantity) of job performance?
4	Social interaction	Does the job provide for positive social interaction (such as teamwork or co-worker assistance)?
5	Task/goal clarity	Are the job duties, requirements and goals clear and specific?
6	Task variety	Does the job have a variety of duties, tasks and activities?
7	Task identity	Does the job require completion of a whole and identifiable piece of work? Does it give the incumbent a chance to do an entire piece of work from beginning to end?
8	Ability/skill-level requirements	Does the job require a high level of knowledge, skills and abilities?
9	Ability/skill variety	Does the job require a variety of types of knowledge, skills and abilities?
10	Task significance	Is the job significant and important compared with other jobs in the organisation?
11	Growth/learning	Does the job allow opportunities for learning and growth in competence and proficiency?

The mechanistic job design approach

1	Job specialisation	Is the job highly specialised in terms of purpose and/or activity?
2	Specialisation of tools and procedures	Are the tools, procedures, materials etc. used on this job highly specialised in terms of purpose?
3	Task simplification	Are the tasks simple and uncomplicated?
4	Single activities	Does the job require the incumbent to do only one task at a time? Does it not require the incumbent to do multiple activities at one time or in very close succession?
5	Job simplification	Does the job require relatively little skill and training time?
6	Repetition	Does the job require performing the same activity or activities repeatedly?
7	Spare time	Is there very little spare time between activities on this job?
8	Automation	Are many of the activities of this job automated or assisted by automation?

The biological job design approach

1	Strength	Does the job require fairly little muscular strength?
2	Lifting	Does the job require fairly little lifting, and/or is the lifting of very light weights?
3	Endurance	Does the job require fairly little muscular endurance?
4	Seating	Are the seating arrangements on the job adequate (with ample opportunities to sit, comfortable chairs, good postural support etc)?
5	Size difference	Does the workplace allow for all size differences between people in terms of clearance, reach, eye height, leg room etc.?

6	Wrist movement	Does the job allow the wrists to remain straight, without excessive movement?
7	Noise	Is the workplace free from excessive noise?
8	Climate	Is the climate at the workplace comfortable in terms of temperature and humidity and is it free of excessive dust and fumes?
9	Work breaks	Is there adequate time for work breaks given the demands of the job?
10	Shiftwork	Does the job not require shiftwork or excessive overtime?

The perceptual motor job design approach

1	Lighting	Is the lighting in the workplace adequate and free from glare?
2	Displays	Are the displays, gauges, meters and computer equipment used on this job easy to read and understand?
3	Programs	Are the programs in the computer equipment for this job easy to learn and use?
4	Other equipment	Is the other equipment (all types) used on this job easy to learn and use?
5	Printed job materials	Are the printed materials used on this job easy to read and interpret?
6	Workplace layout	Is the workplace laid out so that the employee can see and hear well enough to perform the job?
7	Information-input requirements	Is the amount of attention needed to perform this job fairly minimal?
8	Information-output requirements	Is the amount of information that the employee must output on this job, in terms of both action and communication, fairly minimal?
9	Information-processing requirements	Is the amount of information that must be processed, in terms of thinking and problem solving, fairly minimal?
10	Memory requirements	Is the amount of information that must be remembered on this job fairly minimal?
11	Stress	Is there relatively little stress on this job?
12	Boredom	Are the chances of boredom on this job fairly small?

Source: Reprinted from M. A. Campion & P. W. Thayer, 'Job design: approaches, outcomes, and trade-offs', *Organizational Dynamics*, vol. 15, pp. 66–79. Copyright ©1987, with permission from Elsevier.

Motivational approach

The motivational approach to job design has its roots in the organisational psychology and management literatures. It focuses on the job characteristics that affect the psychological meaning and motivational potential, and it views attitudinal variables (such as satisfaction and intrinsic motivation), job involvement, and behavioural variables (such as attendance and performance) as the most important outcomes of job design. The prescriptions of the motivational approach focus on increasing the complexity of jobs through such interventions as job enlargement, job enrichment and the construction of jobs around socio-technical systems.[44] Accordingly, a study of 213 different jobs found that the motivational attributes of jobs were positively related to the mental-ability requirements of workers in those jobs.[45]

An example of the motivational approach is Herzberg's two-factor theory, which argues that individuals are motivated more by intrinsic aspects of work, such as the meaningfulness of the job content, than by extrinsic characteristics, such as pay.[46] Herzberg argued that the key to motivating employees was not through monetary incentives but through the redesign of jobs to make their work more meaningful.

A more complete model of how job design affects employee reactions is the 'job characteristics model'.[47] According to this model, jobs can be described in terms of five characteristics. *Skill variety* is the extent to which the job requires a variety of skills to be used to carry out the tasks. *Task identity* is the degree to which a job requires completing a 'whole' piece of work from beginning to end. *Task significance* is the extent to which the job has an important impact on the lives of other people.

Autonomy is the degree to which the job allows an individual to make decisions about the way the work will be carried out. *Feedback* is the extent to which a person receives clear information about the effectiveness of his or her performance from the work itself.

These five job characteristics determine the motivating potential of a job by affecting the three critical psychological states of 'experienced meaningfulness', 'responsibility' and 'knowledge of results'. According to the model, when the core job characteristics (and thus the critical psychological states) are high, individuals will have a high level of internal work motivation. This is expected to result in higher quantity and quality of work as well as higher levels of job satisfaction.

Job design interventions emphasising the motivational approach tend to focus on increasing the motivating potential of jobs. Much of the work on *job enlargement* (broadening the types of tasks performed), *job enrichment* (adding more decision-making authority to jobs) and self-managing work teams has its roots in the motivational approach to job design. While most of the research on these interventions has demonstrated that they increase employee satisfaction and performance quality, these interventions do not consistently result in increased quantity of performance.[48]

Mechanistic approach

The mechanistic approach has its roots in classical industrial engineering. The focus of the mechanistic approach is on identifying the simplest way to structure work that maximises efficiency. This most often entails reducing the complexity of the work to provide more human resource efficiency—that is, making the work so simple that anyone can be trained quickly and easily to perform it. This approach focuses on designing jobs around the concepts of 'task specialisation', 'skill simplification' and 'repetition'.

'Scientific management' was one of the earliest and best-known statements of the mechanistic approach.[49] According to this approach, productivity could be maximised by taking a scientific approach to the process of designing jobs. Scientific management first sought to identify the 'one best way' to perform the job. This entailed performing time-and-motion studies to identify the most efficient movements for workers to make. Once the best way to perform the work is identified, workers should be selected based on their ability to do the job, then they should be trained in the standard 'one best way' to perform the job. They should also be offered monetary incentives to motivate them to work at their highest capacity.

The scientific management approach was built on in later years, resulting in a mechanistic approach that calls for jobs to be designed so that they are simple and so that they lack any significant meaningfulness. By designing jobs in this way, the organisation reduces its need for high-ability individuals and, thus, it becomes less dependent on individual workers. Individuals are easy to replace—that is, a new employee can be trained to perform the job quickly and inexpensively.

Biological approach

The biological approach to job design comes primarily from the sciences of *biomechanics* (that is, the study of body movements), work physiology and occupational medicine. It is usually referred to as ergonomics. **Ergonomics** is concerned with examining the interface between individuals' physiological characteristics and the physical work environment. The goal of this approach is to minimise the physical strain on the worker by structuring the physical work environment around the way the human body works. It, thereby, focuses on outcomes such as physical fatigue, aches and pains, and health complaints.

Ergonomics
the interface between individuals' physiological characteristics and the physical work environment.

The biological approach has been applied in redesigning equipment used in jobs that are physically demanding. Such redesign is often aimed at reducing the physical demands of certain jobs so that anyone can perform them. In addition, many biological interventions focus on redesigning machines and technology, such as adjusting the height of the computer keyboard to minimise occupational illnesses (for example, carpal tunnel syndrome). The design of chairs and desks to fit posture requirements is important in many office jobs and is another example of the biological approach to job design. For example, one study found that having employees participate in an ergonomic redesign effort significantly reduced the number and severity of cumulative trauma disorders, lost production time and restricted duty days.[50]

Perceptual-motor approach

The perceptual-motor approach to job design has its roots in the human-factors literature.[51] Whereas, the biological approach focuses on physical capabilities and limitations, the perceptual-motor approach focuses on human mental capabilities and limitations. The goal is to design jobs in a way that ensures they do not exceed people's mental capabilities and limitations. This approach generally tries to improve reliability, safety and user reactions by designing jobs in a way that reduces the information processing requirements of the job. In designing jobs, one looks at the capabilities of the least capable worker and then constructs job requirements that an individual of that ability level could meet. Similar to the mechanistic approach, this approach generally has the effect of decreasing the job's cognitive demands.

Jobs such as air-traffic controller, oil refinery operator and quality control inspector require a large amount of information processing. Many clerical and assembly line jobs, on the other hand, require very little information processing. However, in designing all jobs, managers and employees need to be aware of the information processing requirements and ensure that these requirements do not exceed the capabilities of the least capable person who could potentially be performing the job.

Trade-offs among different approaches to job design

A recent stream of research was aimed at understanding the trade-offs and implications of these different job design strategies. Many authors have called for redesigning jobs according to the motivational approach so that the work becomes more psychologically meaningful. However, one study examined how the various approaches to job design are related to a variety of work outcomes. Table 6.5 overleaf summarises their results. For example, in this study, job incumbents expressed higher satisfaction with jobs scoring high on the motivational approach. Also, jobs scoring high on the biological approach were ones for which incumbents expressed lower physical requirements. Finally, the motivational and mechanistic approaches were negatively related, suggesting that designing jobs to maximise efficiency would, more than likely, result in a lower motivational component to those jobs.

Another study demonstrated that enlarging clerical jobs made workers more satisfied, less bored, more proficient at catching errors and better at providing customer service. However, these enlarged jobs also had costs, such as higher training requirements, higher basic-skill requirements and higher remuneration requirements based on job-evaluation compensable factors.[52] Again, it is important to recognise the trade-off between the motivational value of jobs and the efficiency with which the jobs are performed.

Finally, research has examined how job design approaches relate to pay. Starting from the assumption that *job evaluation* (the process of determining the worth of jobs to organisations) links job design and market forces, researchers examined the relationship between job design approaches and both job evaluation results and pay. They found that jobs that were high on the motivational approach had higher job evaluation scores representing higher skill requirements and that these jobs had higher pay levels. Jobs that were high on the mechanistic and perceptual-motor dimensions had lower skill requirements and, correspondingly, lower wage rates. Finally, jobs that were high on the biological dimension had lower physical requirements and they had a weak positive relationship to wage rates. Thus, it seems reasonable to conclude that jobs redesigned to increase the motivating potential result in higher costs in terms of ability requirements, employee learning and compensation.[53]

To summarise, in designing jobs it is important to understand the trade-offs inherent in focusing on one particular approach to job design. Managers who seek to design jobs in a way that maximises all the outcomes for jobholders and the organisation need to be aware of these different approaches, understand the costs and benefits associated with each and balance them appropriately to provide the organisation with a competitive advantage.

TABLE 6.5 Summary of outcomes from the job design

Job design approach		
Motivational	• Higher job satisfaction • Higher motivation • Greater job involvement • Higher job performance • Lower absenteeism	• Increased training time • Lower utilisation levels • Greater likelihood of error • Greater chance of mental overload and stress
Mechanistic	• Decreased training time • Higher utilisation levels • Lower likelihood of error • Less chance of mental overload and stress	• Lower job satisfaction • Lower motivation • Higher absenteeism
Biological	• Less physical effort • Less physical fatigue • Fewer health complaints • Fewer medical incidents • Lower absenteeism • Higher job satisfaction	• Higher financial costs because of changes in equipment or job environment
Perceptual-motor	• Lower likelihood of error • Lower likelihood of accidents • Less chance of mental overload and stress • Lower training time • Higher utilisation levels	• Lower job satisfaction • Lower motivation

Source: Reprinted from M. A. Campion & P. W. Thayer, 'Job design: approaches, outcomes, and trade-offs', *Organizational Dynamics*, vol. 15, pp. 66–79. Copyright ©1987, with permission from Elsevier.

The contemporary organisational context for job analysis and job design

As noted earlier in this chapter, the work context and the way we work has changed dramatically in recent decades. Bringing together aspects of organisational structure, job analysis and job design, researchers have sought to identify the various employment modes used by firms in today's dynamic environment, recognising that different configurations of HR practices may be appropriate for different employment relationships. Lepak and Snell[54] have developed a typology of four types of human capital, each identifiable by the value and uniqueness brought to the organisation (see Figure 6.7 below). The 'strategic value of human capital refers to its potential to improve the efficiency and effectiveness of the firm, exploit market opportunities and/or neutralise potential threats'.[55] The uniqueness of human capital refers to the degree to which it is 'rare, specialised, and (in the extreme) firm-specific'.[56] As the uniqueness of employees' KSAOs increases, so does the likelihood of the firms investing in employees with HR practices such as ongoing development opportunities and incentives.[57]

Although organisations are becoming less reliant on full-time employees, these core employees remain important, as the employees in quadrant one are both highly unique and of strategic value to the firm; they are the employees most likely to perform **knowledge work**, which often involves the research and development of new products and/or services, performed by a **knowledge worker**, a highly-skilled employee whose work utilises theoretical and analytical knowledge, acquired via formal education.[58] An example of work in this quadrant might be software developers for a vendor of HR information systems.

As Kim and Mauborgne have suggested, '[p]eople possessing knowledge are the key resource for companies pursuing value innovation'.[59] Many people would agree that knowledge is an essential resource for organisational success and competitive advantage.[60] Knowledge workers often possess knowledge that managers do not, and they have autonomy and discretion over their performance. Six major factors have been identified by Drucker[61] as determining knowledge worker productivity. First, the nature of the task must be such that the task does not program the worker. In contrast to manual work—in which, for example, an assembly worker is 'programmed' to

Knowledge work usually involves the research and development of new products and/or services and it is performed by knowledge workers.

Knowledge worker a highly-skilled employee whose work utilises theoretical and analytical knowledge that is acquired via formal education.

FIGURE 6.7 Human capital characteristics and employment modes

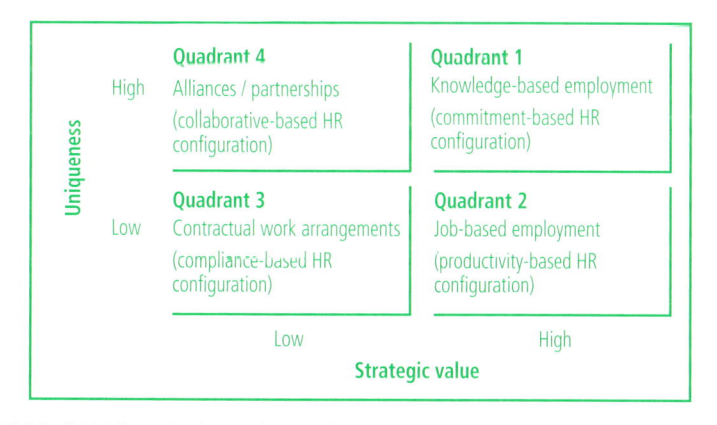

	Low Strategic value	High Strategic value
High Uniqueness	**Quadrant 4** Alliances / partnerships (collaborative-based HR configuration)	**Quadrant 1** Knowledge-based employment (commitment-based HR configuration)
Low Uniqueness	**Quadrant 3** Contractual work arrangements (compliance-based HR configuration)	**Quadrant 2** Job-based employment (productivity-based HR configuration)

Source: D. P. Lepak & S. A. Snell, 2002, 'Examining the HR architecture: the relationships among human capital, employment and HR configurations', *Journal of Management*, 28, p. 520.

perform the required task at his/her point in the production line—knowledge workers define what the task is or should be. An example of this would be seen when doctors diagnose patients in a hospital emergency room. Second, knowledge workers are self-managing; they have autonomy and responsibility for their actions. Third, knowledge workers have responsibility for continuing innovation. Fourth, continuous learning and teaching are intrinsic to knowledge work. Fifth, knowledge worker productivity is measured by quality rather than quantity of output. Finally, knowledge workers must be recognised as assets, rather than costs, to enhance their desire to remain in the organisation.

According to Lepak and Snell's research,[62] the configuration of HR practices suited to knowledge workers encourages organisational commitment, by emphasising opportunities to learn, particularly firm-specific skills, and recognising their entrepreneurial and innovative work efforts with rewards and incentives. As shown in the 'Managing challenges through attracting and retaining people' case, many companies find it difficult to retain professional employees, given the economic growth and skill shortages in the Asia-Pacific region, and are using global assignments to build leadership skills.

Job-based employment (quadrant two) represents human capital that is of strategic value to a firm although it is not unique; the employees' KSAOs, while capable of valuable contributions, are transferable between firms. An example of this work is seen with production workers. The configuration of HR practices suited to these workers is productivity based, emphasising application of their current skills. Compared with quadrant one, organisations are likely to invest less in developmental opportunities or wages for these employees, and the emphasis is more likely to be on short term performance outcomes.[63]

Contract work (quadrant three) represents human capital that is neither of strategic value nor unique to a firm. As Lepak and Snell[64] suggest, work in this category is often 'outsourced'. Hence, the configuration of HR practices is typically compliance-based, meeting legal requirements, but little more. Work is likely to be standardised and simplified, with an emphasis on rules and procedures.

In fact, the largest growth areas in employment are in low level service jobs, rather than knowledge work. One example of this type of work is seen in *call centres* (also called customer service centres—an organisation (or organisational segment) dedicated to service and/or sales, in which employees interact by telephone or computer with customers to provide a service or to sell a product).[65] It has been estimated that almost 3 per cent of the United States' workforce is employed in call centres, and growth in call centre employment in Europe, Asia and Australia has been phenomenal, with an estimated 350 000 to 400 000 call centre workers in Australia. Many jobs are not only being *outsourced* (an organisation's use of an outside organisation for a broad set of services), but are they are also moving outside of Australia—**offshoring**. A recent study by Deloitte Research found that about 275 000 jobs (5 per cent of all jobs in the global communications industry) will go offshore by 2008. Annual savings related to such offshoring are expected to reach AU$19 000 million by 2008.[66] As shown in the 'Managing challenges of globalisation' case, many of these jobs are in India, where a new genre of call centre work is emerging. When Telstra announced that it was outsourcing IT jobs to India, its then chief executive, defended the move by saying that the company was only doing what everyone else was doing. According to Martin Conboy, chief executive of callcentres.net, an Australian provider of research and information on outsourcing in Asia: 'In the US, a call centre costs US$25 an hour per agent. In Australia, it's US$21 and in India it's US$10 per agent per hour'.[67] However, some companies have experienced problems

Offshoring
the movement of jobs to other countries, usually to take advantage of lower costs.

MANAGING CHALLENGES THROUGH ATTRACTING AND RETAINING PEOPLE

MULTINATIONAL FIRMS SEND MORE LOCAL CHINESE TALENT OVERSEAS

Multinationals in China rely on local talent to help them decipher the domestic market and compete with local firms. But will these employees be able to fit into the companies' long-term visions, and some day even enter leadership positions?

It's a question many multinationals are facing. These firms want employees to understand the firms' global vision, acquire leadership skills, and be able to communicate with people in their operations in other regions.

This is why companies such as LG Electronics and General Electric are sending more and more local employees to work either at their headquarters or other regional markets.

In mid-July, the South Korean electronics firm LG decided to send six Chinese employees to work in their operations in the United States, the United Kingdom, Canada, Australia, and the Netherlands. The six stars of the future came from almost all the major functions of LG's units in China: home appliances, telecommunications, home appliance product marketing, human resources, and brand management. LG's employees are expected to stay in a foreign country for six months to learn the local market, build a global vision, and improve their international communication and leadership skills.

In the late 1990s, LG saw explosive growth in China and its brand became a favourite among Chinese consumers. However, since 2000, it has been outshone by its South Korean peer, Samsung Electronics, and some local competitors. LG's decline was due to a slow reaction to the rise of mobile communications and aggressive attacks from local firms.

Since Nam K Woo took over as president of LG Electronics China, he has given himself another title as chief education officer. His plan is to build a strong local management team to bring LG to prominence again.

Now, almost all managers with the South Korean business in China are Koreans, but Woo's goal is to reverse that ratio: he wants 80 per cent of the managers to be Chinese. He also hopes Chinese staff can become heads of business units in the future.

Peter Li, manager of China Engineering Operations with GE Infrastructure Energy, is both a proponent and a product of sending local talent abroad. In 2001, he was assigned the task of leading the biggest project in GE Lighting's new product introduction plan in the United States.

'GE has been sending potential leaders to the headquarters or another regional market for many years', Li says. 'The biggest difference now is that people from China are given more responsibility.'

Formerly, many people were sent to do just engineering projects. Now, some are brought to global headquarters to lead projects, unimaginable five years ago.

The focus of training such employees has shifted away from simple development and marketing skills to building their leadership and communication skills. In China, decisions about projects are often made from statistics and logic alone. In the United States, to get project approval an employee had to sell her or his ideas and hear different opinions based on communication with all stakeholders in the project.

For the technology giant International Business Machines (IBM), it is a different story.

'We are short of hands ourselves, so how can we send people to train them at the headquarters?' says Michael Kwang, talent and learning executive with IBM Greater China Group. 'What we do is ask people from the headquarters to work in China.'

As IBM is expanding in almost every area of its business in China, every year it needs to get hundreds of new staff.

Kwang says that even if IBM China sends some people to work at headquarters, it is for the purpose of replicating the skills of organisations in China quickly. For example, learning the experience of how IBM serves Citibank in the United States so it can do similar business with Bank of China.

Source: Excerpt from Anonymous, 2006, 'Multinational firms send more local Chinese talent overseas', *Industry Updates*, 18 September 2006.

---

and have reversed their off-shoring. For example, Dell Computers stopped sending technical support service calls from the United States to India after complaints from customers.[68]

Service sector employment, such as call centre work, typically involves some degree of **emotional labour**, which Hochschild defined as 'the management of feeling to create a publicly observable facial and bodily display'.[69] This requires employees to utilise both interpersonal and technical skills while adhering to rules regarding the

Emotional labour
jobs in which employees are required to adhere to rules regarding the expression of emotions. This is often evident in front-line customer service jobs.

INDIA'S YOUNG AND COOL ANSWER CALL

MANAGING CHALLENGES OF GLOBALISATION

Bombay's call centre generation challenges India's socially restricted past with its work ethic and partying.

If you have lost your credit card, bought an insurance policy, reported a fault on your mobile phone or tried to book a holiday in the past six years, you have probably spoken to someone like Siddharth Bahl. If you were satisfied with the response, you probably thanked him and noted his courtesy and impeccable English. If not, you may have shouted at him before hanging up in frustration and muttering about how nice it would be to speak to someone who was actually on the same continent.

To consumers on other continents, Bahl and millions like him at business process outsourcing companies (BPOs) across India are faceless voices at the end of a telephone line. But who are they? What motivates them to work long, stressful shifts servicing the whims of demanding, and often rude, customers? Why do they do a job that most of their Western peers consider beneath them?

Bahl, in Bombay, is a 27-year-old accounting and economics graduate from Punjab who has moved quickly from the shop floor working the phones to managing the end-to-end business systems of FTSE 100 and Fortune 100 companies.

'BPO is not a low-end job', Bahl says. 'I get exposure to the best practices of global companies and could go out and get a job in a top bank or telecoms firm because I already know their processes.'

Far from being low-grade, working in a call centre in India offers millions of graduates a ticket to the good life. Besides a starting salary, depending on qualifications, of between 120,000 and 240,000 rupees a year ($3458 and $9617), which is decent by Indian standards and about 25 per cent more than they could expect to earn in other domestic industries.

Hungry, disciplined and highly educated, Bahl is among India's next generation of service sector employees. Earning more in a year than their parents could hope to make in their entire working lives, these 20 somethings are driving their country's growth.

They are worldly, determined to marry for love and unwilling to wait until retirement to enjoy themselves, and will be the most voracious consumers of the next decade.

During the day they put their heads down to forge successful careers in growth sectors such as telecoms, banking, venture capital and engineering.

Some will go to extreme lengths to get the best jobs. Cosmetic surgeons report a spike in liposuction, breast enlargements, tummy-tucking, hair transplants and nose jobs. A third of the patients are men.

After-hours, and in the small hours at that, they are often to be found on the dance floors of Bombay's cosmopolitan club scene.

At the Bombay headquarters of Intelenet, a BPO joint venture between Barclays Bank and HDFC, a leading Indian financial services group, they troop in, sporting the latest fashion accessories before sitting down to an eight-hour shift solving problems for people they will never meet.

The canteen at lunchtime feels like a university campus. Staff, whose average age is 27, tuck into a vast array of Indian food and fresh fruit juices at heavily subsidised prices. A tasty and filling curry costs just 15 rupees (about 40 cents).

Mario Caldeira, 29, a commerce graduate, is playing table tennis. 'Job security doesn't happen very easily in India', he says. 'Before this, getting a cellphone or a DVD player was a luxury. Right now I have my own house. I am proud to be part of this generation.'

His opponent is Ramesh Shukla, a 30-year-old quality analyst, whose very presence at the table is remarkable: he lost both his legs in a train accident and stands on artificial limbs. In the old India he might have been consigned to the streets to beg for a living. His analytical skill, however, means there is a place for him behind a desk in the new economy.

Source: Excerpt from Anonymous, 2006, 'India's young and cool answer call', *The Australian*, 19 September 2006, p. 8.

---

expression of emotions; their ultimate aim is to induce customer satisfaction.[70] Employees engaged in emotional labour, such as call centre employees, are:

> … expected to display emotions that help create a desired 'state of mind' in the customer … employees are often forced to express emotions they do not feel—such as being friendly or happy—or suppress emotions that they genuinely do feel—such as anger or frustration. This can lead to feelings of inauthenticity and emotional dissonance and result in anxiety and burnout.[71]

In call centres, employees may be required to respond to customer inquiries using scripted protocols from which they should not deviate; the work is often repetitive, with little job autonomy or task variety, and employee performance is continuously monitored electronically for customer service, speed and efficiency.[72] These multiple, and sometimes conflicting, work demands may create substantial stresses for call centre employees.[73] Research conducted on almost 500 operators across five call centres in Australia found emotional exhaustion to be associated with high workloads, and pressure from management to emphasise efficiency over customer service.[74] Indeed, critics of call centres have called them 'dark satanic mills of the late 20th century' and 'human battery farms'.[75]

However, call centre work need not be a negative experience. It is possible to design call centre jobs to provide positive outcomes for employees and for the organisation, as was seen in the opening story on page 3 in Chapter 1, showing that a call centre (Salesforce) won the 'Best Employers 2005' award. Indeed, many employers have sought to enhance the appeal of technology-oriented work and to gain concurrent improvements in performance. For example, performance monitoring has been widely criticised for its pervasiveness, and research has shown that excessive use of monitoring causes stress for employees and has ethical implications.[76] It has been suggested that, if used for developmental, rather than punitive, purposes, performance monitoring can be positively associated with employee wellbeing.[77] A study of 223 telecommunications customer service employees found that self managed work teams resulted in improved customer service and sales performance when compared with traditional job design.[78] The author concluded that the autonomous teams provided the opportunity for employees to share knowledge and to learn from each other, to develop more effective sales strategies. Similarly, research has found that the implementation of **high involvement work processes** in call centres, which emphasise employee participation in decision making and systemic relationships between technical, social and other organisational elements, leads to improved employee commitment and job satisfaction.[79] In particular, it has been found that having control over one's work methods and processes, a low level of performance monitoring, and a supportive team leader are the most significant predictors of employee wellbeing in call centres.[80] While research on call centres continues, it appears to date that this is not a radically different form of work; effective call centre management requires a sound understanding of job analysis and job design, in the context of human resource management.

Finally, alliances/partnerships (quadrant four) represent human capital that is unique but not of high strategic value to a firm. Examples include legal or management consultants. The configuration of HR practices, typically, has a collaborative approach, as partnership selection may be based on past relationships, and it may seek to maintain ongoing relationships to apply desired specialised skills.[81]

The development of effective HR configurations across a workforce is possible and it can bring substantial successes to an organisation. For example, Davey is a 70-year-old Australian company that has developed a stream of groundbreaking and award-winning water pumps. It is interesting to note that the organisation is quite small, with 276 employees, as people sometimes assume that such initiatives are only feasible for larger firms. The company has fostered a culture of innovation by supporting supported investment and viewing product development as a priority. The company headquarters and factory moved three years ago to a spacious, purpose-built site in Melbourne's eastern suburbs. This significantly improved the flow and exchange of ideas and feedback between the 170 staff there. The managers emphasise the need to continually share information, raise questions, gather feedback and accept suggestions from staff from different parts of the organisation and from customers and end users.[82]

High involvement work processes
(also see high commitment HRM) a management approach that emphasises employee engagement, participation in decision making, and systemic relationships between technical, social and other organisational elements.

OUTSOURCING: MAKING HR MORE STRATEGIC

Outsourcing is becoming an increasingly mainstream business practice. According to the 2006 National Employee Benefits Trends Survey, 75 per cent of employers outsource at least one HR function no longer restricted to large corporations.

The decision to outsource is based on the organisation's desire to reduce costs, offer improved services and productivity within specific functions, while giving HR time to align itself with the strategic issues of the business.

'Whenever you mention outsourcing there is a common fear reaction: "what does that mean for my job?"', says Catriona Brash, executive partner of human performance at Accenture. 'But in fact it can be a very powerful leader to help refocus HR and to reposition their value add in the context of the business objectives.'

Peter O'Brien, director of ExcellerateHRO Australia and New Zealand, claims that outsourcing HR processes will challenge HR professionals to move from a traditional vertical services organisation to a cross-functional solution that addresses workforce management, talent management, employee engagement, total rewards and HR program costs. Enabled by BPO, HR can have a meaningful impact on the bottom line: 'Over the next five years, CEOs will continue to require HR departments to become comfortable with technology that supports strategic business decisions and human capital management.'

Justyn Sturrock, human capital management partner for IBM Global Business Services believes that as the market continues to realise the limitations of traditional BPO, 'HR will transform to optimise the HR service delivery model. Hence, we see a change in terminology from business process outsourcing to business transformation outsourcing (BTO).'

Potential pitfalls

BTO has seen a fundamental shift in the way HR services are delivered. Sturrock said that HR professionals must be comfortable with relinquishing many traditional elements of their function. 'This will present various degrees of challenge to the HR community', he says.

Sturrock claims that while BTO may not be a new idea, many HR managers may not have been won over by it as, until recently, providers have not been capable of offering the service successfully and on a realistic scale. BTO not only outsources, but transforms HR functions by benchmarking them to best practices, improving reporting with better

MANAGING PEOPLE

HR IN AUSTRALIA'S TOP COMPANIES

Perhaps it's not surprising that nearly half (46 per cent) of the companies in Australia's S&P/ASX 100 involved in a recent study by *Human Resources* magazine describe their HR function as centralised. This structure can offer greater HR expertise and has the potential to be more efficient through economies of scale.

Nor is it surprising that companies with centralised HR functions mostly came from defensive stock market sectors such as financials and information technology. Companies in these groups, like AXA Asia Pacific, Macquarie Bank and Computershare, are relatively unaffected by general fluctuations in the economy. And their tightly packed HR functions are often indicative of their slow, steady, strategic business growth approach.

But there is more to it, of course.

'It's got to do with the extent to which the businesses are or are not related', says Roger Collins, professor of management at The Australian Graduate School of metrics and incorporating better delivery channels, such as enterprise portals and employee service centres, with HR professionals aligning themselves closely with the business and adopting a more operational focus.

According to Andrew Woolf, senior manager of human performance at Accenture, the successful transition will depend on effective relationships.

Another part of the challenge for HR professionals lies in ensuring that the business practice is engineered to match best practice standards before becoming part of an outsourced model. It will be essential for a HR professional to talk straight with the outsourcing company concerning their HR business processes.

Gaining executive support
How can HR best get support from the CEO and CFO level that is critical to their outsourcing program? The key is in proving outsourcing's positive transformational power.

'Start by assessing your current state of operations across three dimensions: people, process and technology. Then define your future state', says O'Brien. 'Build a business case by identifying the business need and quantifying the expected results of outsourcing in terms of cost efficiency and improved functionality.'

Woolf likes to articulate the benefits of BTO to the CEO and CFO and other key executives, in particular superior customer service and the ability for the in-house HR function to refocus on the more strategic aspects of the company.

What to look out for
Ultimately, joint decisions from both organisation and outsourcer are to be made. During the negotiation and contracting process, O'Brien says it is critical to specify the scope of work and the outcomes expected, so an outsourcing partner's service framework and delivery model are engineered to meet your organisation's requirements. 'Both the organisation and service provider must be comfortable with the solutions put on the table.'

Making the return worthwhile
To tackle the critical issue of return on investment (ROI) it is important to ensure that your outsourcing program goes beyond the limitations of traditional BPO by making changes evident as a result of removing various company functions.

Accenture's Brash believes that the outsourcing partnership should be viewed not just as a contract provider but also as a strategic partner in the execution of a core business process.

Source: Excerpt from M. Yen, 2006, 'Outsourcing: Making HR more strategic', *Human Resources*, 11 July 2006, pp. 20–1. www.humanresourcesmagazine.com.au

Question
What are some implications of HR business process outsourcing (HR BPO) for HR professionals?

Management. 'For example, a company like Wesfarmers has a lot of businesses that are unrelated such as Bunnings [hardware] and Lumley's [Insurance]. So with such a diverse group of companies people management practices are largely best determined by the businesses themselves not by head office.

In business units of a company like ANZ, trying to build synergy between similar products, the whole is greater than the sum of the parts, so the centralised HR function rules. Faced with both bear and bull markets, companies find they have to reduce costs and increase the contributions HR makes to the bottom line. A centralised system can allow for its smoother integration into the business as a unit, like any other.

All mixed up and everywhere to go
One of the most surprising findings of the study is that as HR continues to shift from a more administrative function to a strategic operation, a lot of S&P/ASX 100 companies are redesigning their HR structures as well. When combined, the group operating either a decentralised or hybrid HR system accounted for 52 per cent of respondents.

For the 26 per cent of organisations describing their HR functions as decentralised this structure probably offers one very big benefit: speed. 'Some senior managers and boards believe that decentralised HR functions are more adaptive and responsive than centralised models because they're closer to their customers, clients and staff', Collins says.

However, in a decentralised model like this there can be inconsistencies and inertia in people management across a company in everything from remuneration to industrial relations and career development. 'For example, you can't build up an employer brand if everyone is doing their own thing', warns Collins. A coordinated, common message (and messenger) has to come from the top so some form of head office HR is necessary. However, Collins still believes that decentralisation is ultimately more productive.

Meanwhile, combining the centralised and decentralised models must also have its merits because 26 per cent of respondents described their HR functions as hybrids. For obvious reasons, this is the most flexible model and so it remains popular with companies in some of the more volatile stock market sectors such as materials and energy. When material sector firms, like BHP Billiton and Rinker, for example, start to show weak earnings, it can often signal a weakening economy, so a hybrid model can enable faster more proactive responses to those costly people management issues. The result? HR continues to operate strategically as a business unit in itself and doesn't generate overheads.

The financials sector, so dominant on the S&P/ASX 100 (companies in this sector account for 32 per cent), also has its growing share of hybrid HR converts. Companies like AMP and Insurance Australia Group (IAG) have centralised corporate HR responsible for strategic policy and program development. They also operate a decentralised line function that provides HR services and advice within the business. In most cases managers are required to take more responsibility for operational HR activities as part of their role.

Babcock & Brown, with its globally decentralised HR function (coordinated from the Australian headquarters) is a good example of the brave new world of hybrids. 'In building the HR framework and structure, it was expected that HR would function as a central group in each region, with global co-ordination from Australia', says Michelle Seddon, global head of HR.

'Our size [700 employees across 18 countries] also means that a shared central group for each region makes the most sense for now… Central HR management has also meant that we can more easily maintain a big picture view across the multiple businesses in the individual locations and strive for consistency across these.

'However, I am a firm believer that the business cannot and should not be able to delegate responsibility for managing people issues back to HR. We are very clear in communicating to the business that our structure and resourcing levels mean that we will work with them and enable and assist them to manage the people aspects of their business, but will not do it for them', Seddon says.

All things bright and qualified

To say that many of the HR heads in the S&P/ASX 100 group of companies are a clever, educated bunch might be a bit of an understatement. The 57 respondents in our study had between them more than 37 bachelor degrees, at least 16 masters and over 13 certificates, diplomas or graduate diplomas. One respondent alone had two masters and a doctorate.

The perennially popular generalist degrees like arts, commerce and economics are well represented at bachelor level, while business, law and science followed as the next most common amongst the group. There were also bachelors of applied science, engineering, technology and social sciences making for a truly diverse group of qualifications among the nation's top HR professionals.

'I think we'll be seeing a swing towards combined degrees and qualifications among HR professionals, such as HR and employee relations, and HR and IT', says Collins. 'Hybrid degrees will be far more productive in the future. If HR wants to do better work on cost benefit analysis and metrics then disciplines such as accounting and finance will be increasingly necessary.'

Led by such an erudite bunch, no wonder a quick glance at the job ads for mid level HR positions shows that an undergraduate degree in business or human resources is a necessity. In future, HR professionals could be divided into more and more specialised groups such as employment law or industrial relations or IT and need the expertise via relevant education to match.

Already at the most senior levels of the S&P/ASX 100 group, postgraduate qualifications are the norm rather than the exception. Although a Master of Business Administration (MBA) or Master of Science (MSc) in a subject such as psychology may not always guarantee a smooth journey to the top, it can speed things up a bit. Having one of these qualifications on a CV commands the attention of the CEO.

Certificates, graduate diplomas and diplomas were also well represented in the group and reflected the subject mix for any kind of in depth HR study. These include career development, HR management, employment relations, industrial relations and organisational development.

However, it's worth considering a *Personnel Today* report in November 2005 on the results of a UK survey of 135 senior HR practitioners, published by *IRS Employment Review*. *Personnel Today* argued that getting hands-on experience through generalist HR roles is still viewed as more important than gaining qualifications. Certainly gaining experience by working in different business environments can be far more effective than further academic study if HR professionals want to become more business savvy. But whether it would be enough to get the aspiring HR general managers of Australia to where they want to go remains to be seen.

Source: Excerpt from M. Finch, 2006, 'HR in Australia's top companies', *Human Resources*, 6 February 2006, pp. 8–9. www.humanresourcesmagazine.com.au

QUESTION

What are the advantages and disadvantages of a centralised HR function?

CHAPTER SUMMARY

The analysis and design of work is one of the most important components in developing and maintaining a competitive advantage. Strategy implementation is virtually impossible without thorough attention devoted to work-flow analysis, job analysis and job design. Managers need to understand the entire work-flow process in their work unit to ensure that the process maximises efficiency and effectiveness. To understand this process, managers must also have clear, detailed information about the jobs that exist in the work unit, and the way to gain this information is through the job analysis process. Equipped with an understanding of the work-flow process and the existing job, such jobs can be redesigned and configurations of HR practices can be developed. This should ensure that the work unit is able to achieve its goals while individuals within the unit benefit from the various work-outcome dimensions such as motivation, satisfaction, safety, health and achievement.

The work context and types of jobs performed have changed dramatically in recent years. As we have discussed, there are various employment modes used by firms today. While there are numerous challenges in developing effective HR configurations for each employment mode, these modes can bring competitive advantage to an organisation.

WEB EXERCISES

A   Visit www.telcoa.org/. This is the website of the Telework Coalition. What are some of the current issues being reported and discussed on this website?

B   Visit www.cca.org.uk/. This is the website of the Call Centre Association (CCA), which is a professional body for call and contact centres, based in the United Kingdom. The website contains several research publications and surveys of call centres.

C   Visit online.onetcenter.org/. The Occupational Information Network (O*NET) and O*NET OnLine were developed for the United States Department of Labor by the National O*NET Consortium. O*NET OnLine is a web application for job seekers, employment professionals, and others interested in exploring occupations through O*NET. The O*NETTM database has replaced the *Dictionary of Occupational Titles* (DOT) as the United States' primary source of occupational information. The O*NET database and related products helps employers, workers, educators, and students make informed decisions about education, training, career choices, and work.

DISCUSSION QUESTIONS

1   Assume you are the manager of a fast-food restaurant. What are the outputs of your work unit? What are the activities required to produce those outputs? What are the inputs?

2   Now assume you are the manager of a call centre. What are the outputs of your work unit? What are the activities required to produce those outputs? What are the inputs?

3   Compare the two jobs (manager of a fast-food restaurant and manager of a call centre) discussed above. Consider the similarities and differences between the jobs. Compare how these jobs might be valued for compensation and other strategic purposes.

4   Consider the 'job' of a university student. Perform a job analysis on this job. What are the tasks required in the job? What are the knowledge, skills and abilities necessary to perform those tasks? What environmental trends or shocks (for example, computers) might change the job and how would that change the skill requirements?

5   Discuss how the following trends are changing the skill requirements for managerial jobs in Australia:
    (a) increasing global competition
    (b) increasing workforce diversity.

6   Why is it important for a manager to be able to conduct a job analysis? What are the negative outcomes that would result from not understanding the jobs of those reporting to the manager?

7   What are the trade-offs between the different approaches to job design? Which approach do you think should be weighted most heavily when designing jobs?

8   How can we design jobs for maximum efficiency and effectiveness with a diverse workforce?

9   Select a job or employee with whom you are familiar. Categorise the job or employee's human capital into a quadrant of Lepak and Snell's (2002) matrix (see Figure 6.7 on page 203). What configuration of HR practices is appropriate for people in that quadrant?

CASE STUDY

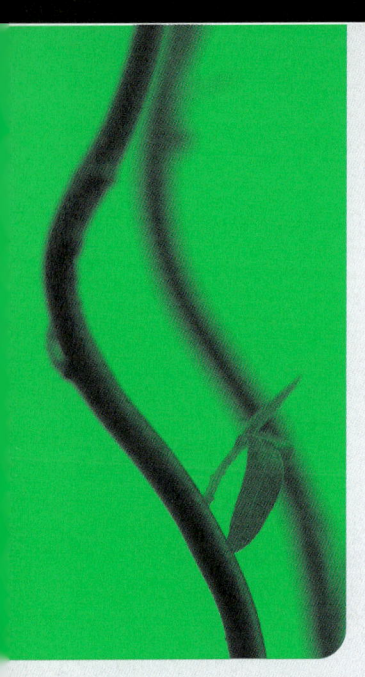

ANZ BANK: BREAKING OUT OF THE MOULD

Australia's major banks operate within a fiercely competitive environment, with intense scrutiny of performance and shareholder returns. But after years of downsizing, streamlining and squeezing efficiencies out of every possible process, Australia's major banks are earnestly looking at the last bastion of competitive advantage—their people. Maximising workforce performance is complex and unchartered territory area for many companies, but arguably one with the greatest returns if they manage to get it right.

ANZ was the first of Australia's big four banks to earnestly undertake organisational transformation in the race to achieve a long-term competitive and sustainable advantage. It is one of the five largest and most successful companies in Australia. With assets of $259 billion, its total shareholder return for the 12 months to 30 September 2005 was 33 per cent. With 1190 worldwide points of representation and 746 branches in Australia, it employs more than 30 000 people across Australia, New Zealand, Asia, the Pacific, UK/Europe, India and the USA.

Following several years of poor performance, ANZ appointed John McFarlane to the role of CEO in the late 1990s. Together with a new management team, the bank realised better financial performance, but McFarlane acknowledged there was widespread ill-will and distrust towards Australia's major banks. After years of branch closures and fee increases, McFarlane says there was a perception that banks were not doing the right thing by the community, their customers or their employees.

First steps of a thousand miles

In 2000, ANZ took the first steps towards organisational transformation. With a mission to transform ANZ into 'the bank with a human face', McFarlane and his leadership team instigated a strategy called Perform (delivering financial performance and shareholder value), Grow (strengthening revenue, leadership and brand) and Breakout (building the foundations for sustainable leadership and long-term success).

Instead of values dreamed up by executives, McFarlane recognised the bank would need to live values based on employee input in order to make decisions using common language and a shared vision of success.

McKinsey also benchmarked the bank against some of Australasia's highest performing organisations. While it performed well in financial and operational areas, it fell down in others, including living its own values. Through this study the bank determined the biggest areas for improvement, and as a result, set up a performance ethic and values assessment survey. Within the performance ethic survey, there are 11 measures where ANZ ranks its position compared to world-class companies. The 11 measures are: mission/aspiration; targets/goals; organisational approach; business unit performance feedback; consequence management; co-ordination and control in terms of people; co-ordination and control in terms of financial; co-ordination and control in terms of operational; motivation in terms of rewards/recognition; motivation in terms of opportunities; and motivation in terms of values.

The studies also provided the bank's leadership team with solid ammunition to earnestly undertake the Perform, Grow and Breakout strategy.

Breaking out of the mould

A foundational element of the strategy is Breakout, which focuses on cultural transformation. McFarlane says Breakout is essentially about creating a fundamentally different experience for the bank's stakeholders, including employees, customers, shareholders and the broader community. It removes bureaucracy in the organisation and gives people a lot more freedom, a lot more responsibility and clear feedback—both positive and negative.

The bank set up a dedicated Breakout and cultural transformation team to drive three major initiatives: Breakout workshops, Breakout charters and Breakout consulting. Breakout workshops focus on emotional and personal development. Breakout charters are a set of

ANZ-wide business projects focused on process changes that support cultural transformation. Breakout consulting provides a range of diagnostic and consulting services to assist business units and teams in living the desired culture.

Performance management

Culture change is a notoriously amorphous concept. In order to achieve any real meaningful change, McFarlane recognised the need to measure and track the success of Breakout. Performance management is integral to this, according to Shane Freeman, group general manager, people capital and Breakout for ANZ.

Performance management is based on a balanced scorecard with very clear key result areas (KRAs) across financial, customer, people and community measures. All staff undergo performance management from divisional managing directors and business unit managing directors, down to front line support and customer facing staff. Rewards are also aligned with performance. Up until 12 months ago the bank paid half yearly bonuses in order to sharpen the focus on performance in the first stages of culture change, but this has now reverted back to yearly bonus payments.

Talent management

ANZ has also set up very rigorous processes that are designed to identify, assess and develop talent. The bank's top 100 people, for example, are assessed externally every two years. From that, the bank puts development plans and actions in place for providing its top talent with new opportunities. To assist in this process across the organisation, line managers are trained to lead the assessment processes at senior management and management levels. Furthermore, internal talent management is backed up by external assessments every two years to ensure quality control. 'It's got some real bite to it and we've replicated that process through the organisation, but in a way that has very strong line management engagement with it', says Freeman.

The bank plots everyone on a curve whereby 20 per cent of staff are at the top, 70 per cent are in the middle and the remaining 10 per cent at the bottom. Compensation is benchmarked accordingly. McFarlane says this demands a philosophy that the bank balance pay for performance. 'In other words, we want them to be more productive but pay them better.'

Building employee engagement

In a bank the size of ANZ, building organisation-wide engagement and support for cultural change is probably one of the biggest challenges faced by McFarlane and his leadership team. Rather than just pushing change down from management, the bank set itself the task of building engagement at top and bottom levels of the organisation. 'We built a lot of trust between me and the senior team as well as the lowest levels of people in the organisation', says McFarlane.

In Hewitt Associates' 2004 best employer study, ANZ achieved equal highest score among other large Australian corporations. The bank achieved an engagement level of 58 per cent in 2004, and in the 2005 study engagement rose to 63 per cent, placing the bank in the high performance best employer's zone. Internal staff surveys have also registered a significant improvement in staff satisfaction. In 1997, this sat at 50 per cent, climbing to 62 per cent in 2001, 78 per cent in 2002 and 85 per cent in 2004. Furthermore, overall knowledge of ANZ values hit 87 per cent in 2004—up from 46 per cent in 2001.

Challenges and lessons learned

As with any major organisational transformation initiative, ANZ has learned some lessons in the process. McFarlane believes that every CEO who retires looks back and wishes they'd been more decisive, particularly when it came to leaving wrong people in roles too long.

Problems around having wrong managers in the job tend to cascade all the way down the organisation, he says, while the gain realised through having the right manager who is passionate about their work is exponential.

In hindsight, McFarlane also says he would have liked a closer relationship with the Finance Sector Union of Australia. In the past, the problem was that the union saw its mission as increasing membership rather than looking after bank employees, but McFarlane says this has now improved.

In looking back, Freeman says the bank should have focused much earlier on having better HR management information for the organisation. For example, making information about the bank readily available to managers on their desktops can improve effectiveness, efficiency and workplace culture issues.

Overall, McFarlane acknowledges that ANZ has learnt from its experience and is able to further refine Breakout as a result. 'Building long-term creativity and competitive advantages inside the company takes time. It's only now that we're getting any form of recognition that these things actually contribute to long-term value.'

The cultural challenge

From bureaucracy and hierarch to meritocracy
- From controlling information to openness and trust
- From silo mentality to collaboration

- From cost reduction to focus on customers and values
- From cost-cutting to growth through innovation (including cost management).

Source: McKinsey & Co.

Keys to ANZ's cultural transformation success
- Leadership of the CEO
- One hundred per cent ownership and commitment from executive management
- Compelling aspiration and meaningful values
- Recognition that transformation is a journey, not a program
- Having the courage to take risks and being prepared to learn from mistakes
- Aligning mindsets, behaviours and the underlying processes and systems
- Recruiting people with the right IQ/EQ mix.

Source: Excerpt from C. Donaldson, 2005, 'ANZ Bank: Breaking out of the mould', *Human Resources*, 29 November. www.humanresourcesmagazine.com.au

QUESTIONS
1 Describe the main features of the organisational transformation at ANZ Bank.
2 What HR practices are used at ANZ Bank to provide meaningful work for their employees?
3 Visit the ANZ Bank's website for more information:
 www.anz.com.au/aus/about/media/default.asp

CHAPTER 7

HUMAN RESOURCE PLANNING AND HUMAN RESOURCE INFORMATION SYSTEMS

Objectives

After reading this chapter, you should be able to:

1. Discuss how to align a company's human resource planning with its strategic direction.
2. Determine the labour demand of workers in various job categories.
3. Discuss the advantages and disadvantages of various ways of eliminating a labour surplus and avoiding a labour shortage.
4. Discuss the types of technologies that can improve the efficiency and effectiveness of HR.
5. Discuss human resource information systems and their various applications for HR activities.

Software replaces crystal ball

The discipline of workforce planning has never been a more complex challenge for human-resources (HR) executives, nor has it been such a critical element in the formulation of corporate strategy.

Many companies find the task of accurately predicting their future labour needs so daunting that they simply ignore it or, at best, approach workforce planning on an ad hoc, short-term basis.

HR professionals agree that organisations that continue to regard workforce planning as either too hard or unnecessary are taking a large commercial risk. But such companies should be encouraged by the recent emergence of innovative workforce planning tools that promise to substantially reduce the complexity of the discipline.

The deputy executive director of the Australian Securities & Investments Commission, Jeremy McNeice, says workforce planning needs to be an integral part of any business strategy. '[It] is an element of management and is fully integrated. You can't say, "We have got a great plan here" and then say, "Oh, now let's start thinking about the people".'

All HR practitioners are clear about the reasons workforce planning has become so critical. In short, the Australian market for skilled and unskilled labour is shrinking. With 14 years of uninterrupted growth in the economy, there is now a severe lack of spare capacity in the labour market.

A report last year by the Australian National Audit Office into workforce planning in the public sector said almost a quarter of all public service employees will be eligible for retirement by 2010, and that situation will worsen within the next 10 years. HR professionals say the position in the private sector is similar. The very fact the audit office conducted a survey into workforce planning in the public service shows how critical the labour market situation has become.

Rilla Moore the executive general manager of property group Stockland, says Australian organisations are only just 'waking up' to workforce planning: 'It's becoming a very complex challenge.' That challenge arises from a dearth of talent available, an ageing workforce and the dramatic difference in work attitudes between baby boomers and generations X and Y—the latter generations being comfortable with 'shopping around' for an employer.

'When you are trying to predict your future workforce based on a good five-year company strategy, it's quite scientific and involves lots of variables,' Moore says. 'How can I predict with some degree of accuracy when there are variables such as what the economy is going to be doing, where our own business is going in terms of growing, shrinking, diversifying, and so on. And you can't approach workforce planning just by saying you are going to have two or three new businesses in a few years so you'll start recruiting right now. That's a cost on your bottom line and will be looked at by shareholders and analysts very critically, because they look much more at the immediate, short term.'

One young Australian company called Aruspex is leading the field in the development of new workforce planning tools. Formed in December 2003 by two HR executives, Tess Walton and Stacey Chapman, Aruspex has produced a new software program, CAPTure, designed to allow organisations to examine their workforce needs up to a decade into the future. Moore is enthusiastic: 'It's an exciting piece of software. It removes the need to do manual scenario planning, which is quite a nightmare.'

CAPTure enables HR executives and chief executives to make quantitative and qualitative decisions about their future workforce. Walton says: 'It used to be the case that workforce planning was just maths, just about numbers. But you can't just talk about workforce planning by saying, 'I'm going to need X number of people to finish this project'. You need to have a look at your own organisational culture, to think about what types of people available in the market are right for you to fulfil

Software replaces crystal ball *continued*

your goals. A lot of money is spent on workforce programs, but it's fired into darkness because companies don't have an accurate, overarching view of exactly which types of employees they should be going after.'

Chapman says: '[HR executives] are concerned how they can position workforce planning with management without being laughed out of the room because they don't have skills as strategic planners. CAPTure gives the heads of human resources the ability to provide insight into the business, because the idea of the product is to present what is going on now with the business and how it's trending to the future.'

According to Walton and Chapman, much education is needed to persuade chief executives and even many HR executives that workforce planning is crucial to the future of any company.

There is a very strong need for an educative process. Where CEOs are sitting around the board table planning their five-year growth strategy—be that incremental revenue growth, new business divisions, whatever—many of them don't know what labour they are going to require for that strategy, and that it might not actually even be available to them or is going to cost them significantly more. The cost of labour is going to rise in coming years and that, of course, has very big implications for pricing, profit margins and market competitiveness.

Trouble ahead: The problem
The Department of Employment last year reported that within five years the shortfall between people leaving and entering the workforce annually would reach 195 000.

That is 15 000 more people than the entire workforce of one of Australia's biggest private-sector employers, Coles Myer.

The emergence of China and India as new economic powers will tighten the global demand for skilled labour, creating an even more critical shortage in Australia.

The solution
A workforce plan is the people element of any strategic organisational plan, and should be considered an essential component of it.

Human-resources staff must develop an effective process for forecasting and evaluating current and future workforce capacity, where there are gaps, and why they exist.

Thereafter they must develop and implement contemporary programs that ensure their organisation can attract and retain a quality workforce.

Source: Excerpt from S. Lloyd, 2006, 'Software replaces crystal ball', *BRW*, 20 April, p. 76. © 2006 Copyright John Fairfax Holdings Limited. www.brw.com.au, *BRW*/Optimum Performance.

Introduction

Employers and employees do not exist in a vacuum. As shown in the opening case, effective workforce planning, or human resource planning, is an aspect of human resource management that is integral to organisational strategic planning. And increasingly, companies are using sophisticated software to facilitate their human resource planning. Developments such as globalisation and changes in society and technology have many implications for human resource management. Two of the major ways that societal trends affect employers are through consumer markets, which affect the demand for goods and services; and through labour markets, which affect the supply of people to produce goods and services. In some cases, a shortage of labour will restrict growth during periods of high demand. In other cases, a surplus of labour will generate costs that cannot be recovered during periods of low product demand. Reconciling these two environmental forces is a challenge. Some organisations will rise to this challenge and others will not—another arena where one organisation can gain a competitive advantage over another.

There are three keys to effectively utilising labour markets to one's competitive advantage. First, organisations must have a clear idea of their current configuration of human resources. In particular, they need to know the strengths and weaknesses of their present employees. Second, organisations must have a plan as to where they are going in the future and be aware of how their present configuration of human resources relates to the configuration that will be needed in the future. Third, where there are discrepancies between the present configuration and the configuration required for the future, organisations need programs that will address these discrepancies. Under conditions of a labour surplus, this may mean creating an effective downsizing intervention. Under conditions of a labour shortage, this may mean waging an effective recruitment campaign and an overhaul of the human resource management approach across the organisation.

The first half of this chapter looks at tools and technologies that can be used to help an organisation develop and implement effective strategies for leveraging labour market 'problems' into opportunities to gain competitive advantage. We set out the actual steps that go into developing and implementing a human resource plan. Through each section, we will focus particularly on recent trends and practices (for example, downsizing and outsourcing) that can have a major impact on an organisation's bottom line results and overall reputation.

It is well recognised that development of information technology has had significant impact on organisations, with specific implications for human resource management. In the second half of the chapter, we focus on the human resource information systems that provide the essential data for planning human resource activities. We examine the types of systems available and specific ways in which these are applied to human resource management activities.

The human resource planning process

Human resource planning (HRP) is the process through which organisational goals are translated into human resource goals concerning staffing levels and allocation. From these human resource goals, an integrated set of policies and programs may be developed. Human resource planning involves forecasting human resource needs for an organisation and planning the necessary steps to meet these needs. The process consists of developing and implementing plans and programs to ensure the right number of employees, with the appropriate skills, is available at the right time and place.

The human resource planning process is directly linked to strategic business planning, as discussed in the 'HRM spotlight' case. Human resource planning helps to ensure that the organisation will fulfil its future business plans in terms of financial objectives, output goals, technologies and resource requirements.[1] By providing a long-term view of developing a staffing plan, human resource planning can be an important contributor to organisational strategic plans. The use of HR planning has been advocated by academics and practitioners alike as a fundamental aspect of a strategic approach to human resource management.[2] A strategic approach to human resource planning means that:

Human resource planning (HRP)
(also workforce planning) the process through which organisational goals are translated into HR goals concerning staffing levels and allocation. Human resource planning involves forecasting HR needs for an organisation and planning the necessary steps to meet these needs.

- There is a focus on planning at the organisational level, not only at an industry or regional level.
- Human resource issues are considered to be part of the organisation's strategic business planning processes.
- The human resource planning process has an emphasis on the organisational 'bottom line', as the human resources are considered to be a part of the overall budgeting and management processes of the organisation.
- Human resource strategies, such as staffing, employee learning and development, managing performance and compensation, are integrated so that the activities in each functional area support and are consistent with those in other human resource areas.
- Human resource managers, senior executives and line managers work together to develop and implement the organisation's strategic business plans.
- Employee needs and wishes for career development are integrated with organisational goals.
- There is adherence to principles of equal opportunity.[3]

An overview of the human resource planning process is depicted in Figure 7.1. The process consists of forecasting, goal setting and strategic planning, followed by program implementation and evaluation. We will now discuss each of these stages.

Forecasting

Forecasting
the attempts to determine the supply of and demand for various types of human resources to predict areas within the organisation where there will be future labour shortages or surpluses.

The first step in the planning process is forecasting, as shown in the top portion of Figure 7.1. In personnel forecasting, the HR manager attempts to ascertain the supply of and demand for various types of human resources. The primary goal is to predict areas within the organisation where there will be future labour shortages or surpluses.

Forecasting, on both the supply and demand sides, can be done using either statistical methods or judgmental methods. Statistical methods are excellent for capturing historic trends in a company's demand for labour and, under the right conditions, they give predictions that are much more precise than those that could be achieved through the subjective judgments of a human forecaster. On the other hand, many important events that occur in the labour market have no historical precedent;

FIGURE 7.1 Overview of the human resource planning process

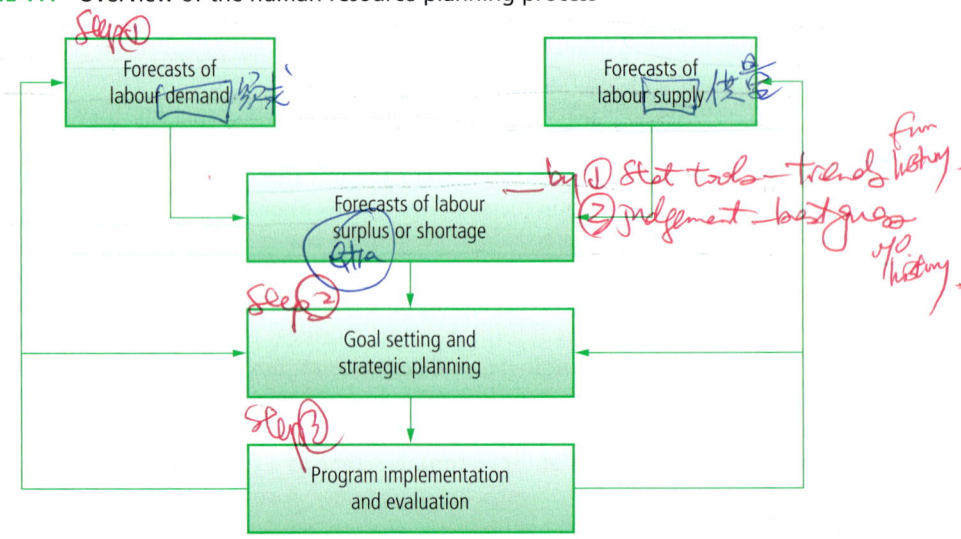

COMING OF AGE FOR WORKFORCE PLANNING

HRM SPOTLIGHT

An ageing workforce and an emerging baby boomer retirement wave are driving more companies toward strategic workforce planning, according to a recent US report. Other forces driving strategic workforce planning include: current movement and projected labour shortages; globalisation; the growing use of contingent, flexible workers; the need to leverage human capital to enhance return; mergers and acquisitions; and the evolution of workplace technology and tools.

Strategic workforce planning involves analysing and forecasting the talent that companies need to execute their business strategy. Strategic workforce planning is aimed at helping companies make sure they have 'the right people in the right place at the right time and at the right price', The Conference Board report found.

This relatively new management process is being used increasingly to help control labour costs, assess talent needs, make informed business decisions such as where to open new facilities or whether it's more cost effective to add full-time employees or contractors, and to assess human-capital needs and risks as part of overall enterprise risk management.

'In many companies, traditional workforce planning was an onerous process that HR imposed on management', said Mary Young, senior research associate for The Conference Board.

Some organisations have enhanced the simple gap analysis (workforce demand versus supply) that constitutes traditional workforce planning by adopting the logic and analytical tools of other corporate functions, such as finance, strategic planning, risk management, and marketing.

But the crux of strategic workforce planning is conversation and a process of enquiry, rather than reliance on spreadsheets crammed with tiny numbers.

To engage senior executives in workforce planning, the process must focus on understanding the strategic business plan and its broad implications for the company's workforce.

Establishing consistent, organisation-wide data is a prerequisite to winning executives' confidence in the results of strategic workforce planning, the *Strategic Workforce Planning: Forecasting Human Capital Needs to Execute Business Strategy* report found.

Other challenges include making the process and tools simple and efficient, developing HR's capabilities and comfort level, establishing a common language to describe jobs and required competencies, integrating workforce planning with business and budget planning, and driving the plan deep into the organisation.

Organisations still in the process of implementing workforce planning already report benefits such as generating insights and knowledge that executives can use to make business decisions, providing a deeper and more nuanced understanding of workforce dynamics than was previously available.

It also enables HR to realise its long-held desire to become a player and a valued contributor to high-level business strategy decisions among other executives.

'Strategic workforce planning enables the organisation to slice and dice its workforce data to discover critical issues, compare different groups, understand patterns and trends, home in on critical segments of the workforce such as mature workers and top performers, and customise its approach to managing different segments of its workforce', said Young.

'While no organisation claims to have achieved it yet, many believe that the ultimate payoff from strategic workforce planning will be a vibrant, internal job market that transcends the boundaries between business units and geographies', said Young.

Hewlett-Packard and IBM are two of the companies described in The Conference Board report as committed to relying on strategic workforce planning, which must be customised to the specific conditions and needs of each company.

In IBM's case, HR and finance departments help senior business leaders plan realistically to execute their business strategy and manage drivers of labour costs. For HP, high-level discussions and a two-way educational process between business leaders and HR emphasises the qualitative over the quantitative.

Source: Excerpt from C. Donaldson, 2006, 'Coming of age for workforce planning', *Human Resources*, 22 August 2006. www.humanresourcesmagazine.com.au

---

hence, statistical methods that work from historical trends are of little use in such cases. In these situations one must rely on the pooled subjective judgments of experts and their 'best guesses' might be the only source from which to make inferences about the future. Typically, because of the complementary strengths and weaknesses of the two methods, companies that engage in human resource planning use a balanced approach that includes both statistical and judgmental components.

Determining labour demand

Typically, demand forecasts are developed around specific job categories and skill areas relevant to the organisation's current and future state. Once the job categories or skills are identified, the planner needs to seek information that will help him or her predict whether the need for people with those skills or people in that job category will increase or decrease in the future. Organisations differ in the sophistication with which such forecasts are derived.

At the most sophisticated level, an organisation might have statistical models that predict labour demand for the next year, given relatively objective statistics on leading indicators from the previous year. A *leading indicator* is an objective measure that accurately predicts future labour demand. Take, for example, a manufacturer of car parts that sells its product primarily to the large car manufacturers, such as Ford and Toyota. It would use several objective statistics on the car manufacturers for one time period to predict how much demand there would be for the company's product at a later time period. As shown in Figure 7.2, inventory levels, sales levels, employment levels and profits at the car manufacturers in one year might predict the demand for labour in the production assembler job category in the next year.

For example, using historical records, one might use multiple regression techniques to assess the best predictive model for estimating demand for production assemblers from information on sales levels, inventory levels, employment levels and profits at the car manufacturers. Since this is not a statistics book, a detailed explanation of regression techniques is beyond our scope. Rather, we will simply note here that this technique will convert information from the four or more leading indicators into a single predicted value for demand for production assemblers that is optimal—at least according to the historical data.

Statistical planning models are useful when there is a long, stable history that can be used to reliably detect relationships among variables. However, these models almost always have to be complemented by subjective judgments of people who have expertise in the area. There are simply too many 'once-in-a-lifetime' changes that have to be considered and that cannot be accurately captured in statistical models. For example, our small-parts manufacturer might learn that the leadership at one of the car manufacturers changed and that the new leadership plans to close 15 plants worldwide over the next 10 years. This event has no historical precedent, so the company might want to consult all its best managers to get their opinions on exactly how much this change would affect the demand for labour in different job categories.

Determining labour supply

Once a company has projected labour demand, it needs to get an indicator of the firm's labour supply. Determining the internal labour supply calls for a detailed analysis of how many people are currently in various job categories (or who have

FIGURE 7.2 Leading indicators of the demand for labour for a hypothetical car parts manufacturer

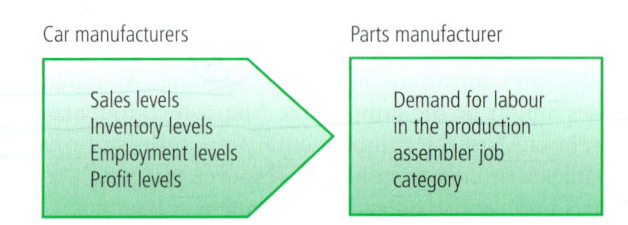

Car manufacturers
- Sales levels
- Inventory levels
- Employment levels
- Profit levels

→

Parts manufacturer
- Demand for labour in the production assembler job category

specific skills) within the company. This analysis is then modified to reflect changes in the near future caused by retirements, promotions, transfers, voluntary turnovers and terminations.

As in the case of labour demand, projections for labour supply can be derived either from historical statistical models or through judgmental techniques. One type of statistical procedure that can be employed for this purpose involves transitional matrices. Transitional matrices show the proportion (or number) of employees in different job categories at different times. Typically, these matrices show how people move in one year from one state (outside the organisation) or job category to another state or job category.[4]

Table 7.1 shows a hypothetical transitional matrix for our car parts manufacturer, focusing on seven job categories. Although these matrices look imposing at first, you will see that they are easy to read and use in determining the internal labour supply. A matrix like the one in this table can be read in two ways. First, we can read the rows to answer the question, 'Where did people in this job category in 2001 go by 2007?' For example, 70 per cent of those in the clerical job category (row seven) in 2001 were still in this job category in 2007 and the remaining 30 per cent had left the organisation. For the production assembler job category (row six), 80 per cent of those in this position in 2001 were still there in 2007. Of the remaining 20 per cent, half (that is, 10 per cent) were promoted to the production manager job category and the other half (the other 10 per cent) left the organisation. Finally, 75 per cent of those in the production manager job category in 2001 were still there in 2007, while 10 per cent were promoted to assistant plant manager and 15 per cent left the organisation.

Reading these kinds of matrices across rows makes it clear that there is a career progression within this firm from production assembler to production manager to assistant plant manager. Although we have not discussed rows one through to three, it might also be noted that there is a similar career progression from sales apprentice to sales representative to sales manager. In this organisation, the clerical category is not part of any career progression. That is, this job category does not feed any other job categories listed in Table 7.1.

A transitional matrix can also be read from top to bottom (that is, the columns) to answer the question, 'Where did the people in this job category in 2007 come from?' (that is, 'where were they in 2001?'). Again, starting with the clerical job (column seven), 70 per cent of the 2007 clerical positions were filled by people who were also

Transitional matrices
matrices showing the proportion or number of employees in different job categories at different times.

TABLE 7.1 — A hypothetical transitional matrix for a car parts manufacturer

			2007							
			1	2	3	4	5	6	7	8
2001	1	Sales manager	0.95							0.05
	2	Sales representative	0.05	0.60						0.35
	3	Sales apprentice		0.20	0.50					0.30
	4	Assistant plant manager				0.90	0.05			0.05
	5	Production manager				0.10	0.75			0.15
	6	Production assembler					0.10	0.80		0.10
	7	Clerical							0.70	0.30
	8	Not in organisation	0.00	0.20	0.50	0.00	0.10	0.20	0.30	

in this position in 2001 and the remaining 30 per cent were external recruits (that is, they were not part of the organisation in 2001). In the production assembler job category (column six), 80 per cent of those occupying this job in 2007 occupied the same job in 2001 and the other 20 per cent were external recruits. The most diversely staffed job category seems to be that of production manager (column five): 75 per cent of those in this position in 2007 held the same position in 2001. However, 10 per cent were former production assemblers who were promoted, 5 per cent were former assistant plant managers who were demoted and 10 per cent were external recruits who were not with the company in 2001.

Matrices such as these are extremely useful for charting historical trends in the company's supply of labour. More important, if conditions remain somewhat constant, they can also be used to plan for the future. For example, if we believe that we are going to have a surplus of labour in the production assembler job category in the next three years, we note that by simply initiating a freeze on external recruiting, the ranks of this position will be depleted by 20 per cent on their own. Similarly, if we believe that we will have a labour shortage in the area of sales representatives, the matrix informs us that we may want to: (1) decrease the amount of voluntary turnover in this position, since 35 per cent of those in this category leave every five years, (2) speed the training of those in the sales apprentice job category so that they can be promoted more quickly than in the past, and/or (3) expand external recruitment of individuals for this job category, since the usual 20 per cent of job incumbents drawn from this source may not be sufficient to meet future needs. As with labour demand, historical precedents for labour supply may not always be reliable indicators of future trends. Thus, statistical forecasts of labour supply also need to be complemented with judgmental methods.

Determining labour surplus or shortage

Once forecasts for labour demand and supply are known, the planner can compare the figures to ascertain whether there will be a labour shortage or labour surplus for the respective job categories. Once this is determined, the organisation can determine what it is going to do about these potential problems.

Goal setting and strategic planning

The second step in the human resource planning process is goal setting and strategic planning, as shown in the middle of Figure 7.1. The purpose of setting specific quantitative goals is to focus attention on the 'problem' and provide a benchmark for determining the relative success of any programs aimed at redressing a pending labour shortage or surplus. The goals should come directly from the analysis of labour supply and demand and should include a specific figure about what should happen with the job category or skill area and a specific timetable for when results should be achieved.

The car parts manufacturer, for instance, might set a goal to reduce the number of individuals in the production assembler job category by 50 per cent over the next three years. Similarly, the firm might set a goal to increase the number of individuals in the sales representative job category by 25 per cent over the next three years.

Once these goals are established, the firm needs to choose from the many different strategies available for redressing labour shortages and surpluses. Table 7.2 shows some of the options for a human resource planner seeking to reduce a labour surplus. Table 7.3 shows some options available to the same planner intent on avoiding a labour shortage.

Human Resource Planning and Human Resource Information Systems   **CHAPTER 7**

TABLE 7.2 Options for reducing an expected labour surplus

Option		Speed	Human suffering
1	Downsizing	Fast	High
2	Pay reductions	Fast	High
3	Demotions	Fast	High
4	Transfers	Fast	Moderate
5	Work sharing	Fast	Moderate
6	Retirement	Slow	Low
7	Natural attrition	Slow	Low
8	Retraining	Slow	Low

TABLE 7.3 Options for avoiding an expected labour shortage

Option		Speed	Revocability
1	Overtime	Fast	High
2	Temporary employees	Fast	High
3	Outsourcing	Fast	High
4	Retrained transfers	Slow	High
5	Turnover reductions	Slow	Moderate
6	New external recruits	Slow	Low
7	Technological innovation	Slow	Low

This stage is critical because the many options available to the planner differ widely in their expense, speed, effectiveness, amount of human suffering and revocability (that is, how easily the change can be undone). In the past decade, the typical organisational response to a surplus of labour has been downsizing, which may be fast but it is high in human suffering. Typical organisational responses to a labour shortage have included hiring temporary employees and outsourcing, responses that are fast and high in revocability. Given the pervasiveness of these choices, we will devote special subsections of this chapter to these options.

Downsizing
We define downsizing as the planned elimination of large numbers of personnel, designed to enhance organisational competitiveness. Three major types of downsizing strategy have been identified.

1. **Workforce reduction.** This is a cost-cutting approach, emphasising short-term results and redundancies.
2. **Organisational redesign.** This involves a restructuring or delayering of the organisation, with elimination of functions, layers and work processes.
3. **Systemic change.** This refers to a program of organisational cultural change involving all staff.[5]

Downsizing
the planned elimination of large numbers of personnel, designed to enhance organisational effectiveness.

Workforce reduction
a type of downsizing strategy, using a cost-cutting approach emphasising short-term results and redundancies.

Organisational redesign
restructuring or delayering of the organisation, with elimination of functions, layers and work processes (often a type of downsizing strategy).

Systemic change
a program of organisational cultural change involving all staff (often a type of downsizing strategy).

Many organisations adopted at least one of these downsizing strategies in the past two decades across industrialised countries, including Australia.[6] There appear to be no signs of this trend abating. The jobs eliminated in these downsizing efforts should not be thought of as temporary losses due to business cycle downturns or a recession, but these jobs should be thought of as permanent losses due to the changing competitive pressures faced by businesses today. As one example shows, the Commonwealth Bank of Australia announced in late 2003 that, as a consequence of process simplification, work redesign and removing unnecessary work, the bank's domestic workforce of 35 000 would be reduced by approximately 3700 between July 2003 and June 2006.[7]

Australian Bureau of Statistics figures show that, although there has been growth in part-time employment and other non-standard types of employment, full-time employment has declined. Part-time employees now represent 28 per cent of all employed people. It is interesting to note that women account for 71 per cent of the part-time workforce.[8] Over one-third of people working part-time report that they would like to work more hours—they are under-employed.[9]

Downsizing and related restructuring is costly for organisations. Rather than trying to stem current losses, the major reasons for most downsizing efforts deal with promoting future competitiveness. Surveys have indicated four major reasons for organisations to engage in downsizing. First, many organisations were looking to reduce costs and, since labour costs represent a big part of an organisation's total costs, this is an attractive place to start. Second, in some organisations, closing outdated plants or introducing technological changes to old plants reduced the need for labour.[10]

The effects of such restructuring can involve substantial change for an organisation and require careful management. For example, the New Zealand Defence Force in 2001 sought professional help for staff having to deal with the 'emotional shock' of redundancy after the decision to eliminate the air combat wing. This decision was anticipated to result in up to 600 job losses in the following four years. After the initial round of redundancies, natural attrition may account for some positions. The New Zealand Defence Force advertised for an organisation experienced at career transition, job search, counselling for emotional shock and referral to professional clinicians. According to deputy chief of air staff, Air Commodore David Bamfield, this was the first time in many decades that the New Zealand Defence Force had a need for downsizing.[11]

A third reason for downsizing was that, for economic reasons, many firms changed the location of where they did business. For Australian companies, at least some of this shift was also due to *offshoring*; that is, jobs moving out of Australia to countries with lower labour and/or production costs. Offshoring is discussed later, with regard to outsourcing (these topics were also discussed in Chapter 6).

A fourth reason for downsizing was that many mergers and acquisitions reduced the need for bureaucratic overheads, displacing many managers and some professional staff members.[12] When an organisation goes through a significant change, such as in a merger or acquisition, it is likely to encounter many human resource planning challenges; downsizing is a common practice in such circumstances. A **merger** is the union of two or more commercial interests or corporations, usually of similar size. An **acquisition**, also often referred to as a takeover, is the process through which one company takes over the controlling interest of another company.[13] There are many reasons why organisations may enter into a merger or acquisition. These include to: increase productive capacity, gain skills of the other firm's workforce, expand into new markets and/or locations, reduce competitors, opportunistic purchase for a cheap price, purchase of valued brands.[14]

Merger
the union of two or more commercial interests or corporations, usually of similar size.

Acquisition
also often referred to as a takeover; the process through which one company takes over the controlling interest of another company.

There are several major steps in the process of managing a merger or acquisition. In the first step, strategic planning should take place, as was discussed in Chapter 2, Strategic human resource management. Second, it is important to have an effective communication plan. Managers should communicate the formal intention of actions. This may include issuing a prospectus and holding a meeting with stakeholders, including staff. Communication is important in order to manage the expectations of stakeholders. The third step is the implementation of the merger or the acquisition. This may include the implementation of tangible changes, such as new systems, and symbolic changes, such as the presentation of the firm's new branding. Marks and Mirvis[15] suggest some roles that may be useful for managers and employees during the transition: the senior leadership group should form a steering committee, transition managers should be selected, and transition task forces should be formed, with clearly identified objectives, guidelines, and resources to achieve their tasks. Finally, stabilisation of the 'new' organisation requires careful management of expectations to ensure that stakeholders see a clear relationship between intentions and implementation.[16] Managing a downsizing program is a complex and challenging task.

Many mergers and acquisitions encounter significant difficulties and many fail.[17] Common problems include: the length of time taken, which leads to frustration and disillusionment; turnover of key managers and employees, which causes loss of valuable human capital; a lack of trust between the parties involved, especially if the takeover is hostile; conflicts between the management style, structure and culture of the organisations; and lack of communication to stakeholders (for example, leading to negative reactions by employees).[18] If a merger or acquisition does involve downsizing, Gutknecht and Keys[19] suggest some key elements to manage the morale of employees who remain in the 'new' organisation: as throughout the process, communication of impending changes is important, management should develop a strategic plan and communicate it to employees; management and employees will inevitably need to be flexible and creative in managing job changes; and the organisation should invest in the re-training and development of employees. While many factors will influence the outcome of such a substantial organisational change, effective management of human resource planning is an important part of the overall process.[20]

Although it is not yet clear whether downsizing efforts have led to enhanced organisational effectiveness, some early indications are that the results have not lived up to expectations.[21]

There seem to be a number of reasons for the failure of most downsizing efforts to live up to expectations in terms of enhancing firm performance. First, although the initial cost savings are a short-term plus, the long-term effects of an improperly managed downsizing effort can be negative.

Second, many downsizing campaigns lead the organisation to lose people who turn out to be irreplaceable assets. In fact, one United States survey indicated that in 80 per cent of the cases, organisations eventually replaced some of the people who were let go, or hired the same people as consultants.[22]

A third reason downsizing efforts often fail is that employees who survive the purges become narrow-minded, self-absorbed and risk-averse. Motivation levels drop off, because any hope of future promotions—or even a future—with the organisation dies out. One survey, reported in 2001, investigating worldwide trends in downsizing, showed that only about one-third of firms have implemented retention plans encouraging staff to stay on through downsizing periods. Another study by Leadership Management Australia showed that, of a cross-section of workers, only

49 per cent expect to have opportunities for career advancement in their workplace, although 80 per cent wish to pursue this.[23]

Many employees also start looking for alternative employment opportunities. The negative publicity associated with a downsizing campaign can also hurt the company's image in the labour market, making it more difficult to recruit employees at a later point in time. The key to avoiding this kind of 'reputational' damage is to ensure that the need for downsizing is well explained and that procedures for implementing downsizing are fair. Although this may seem to reflect commonsense, organisations are often reluctant to provide this kind of information, especially if part of the reason for the downsizing was top-level mismanagement.[24]

Although many of these problems with downsizing efforts can be reduced with better planning, this is hardly a panacea for increasing organisational competitiveness now that we are well into the new millennium. More judicious use of all the other avenues for eliminating a labour surplus (shown in Table 7.2) is needed. A study of the 20 best employers in Asia by Hewitt Associates, a global management consultancy firm, found that these firms either avoided downsizing or minimised redundancies, in spite of the downturn in the global economy. For example, the Portman Ritz-Carlton Hotel in Shanghai, China, which was ranked the best employer, avoided redundancies by asking its employees to find ways of cutting costs.[25] However, because such avenues for eliminating a labour surplus often take effect slowly, without better forecasting, organisations may find downsizing is their only viable option.

Early retirement programs

Another popular means of reducing a labour surplus is to offer an early retirement program. As discussed in Chapter 1, Human resource management in Australia, the average age of the Australian workforce is increasing. Although many 'baby boomers' are approaching the traditional retirement age, the early indications are that this group has no intention of retiring any time soon.[26] Several forces are driving the extension of older workers' careers. First, the improved health of older people, in general, in combination with the decreased physical labour in many jobs has made working longer a viable option. Second, this option is attractive for many workers for financial reasons. Finally, age discrimination legislation has created constraints on organisations' ability to unilaterally deal with an ageing workforce.

Although an older workforce has some clear advantages for employers in terms of experience and stability, it also poses problems. First, older workers are sometimes more costly than younger workers because of their higher seniority. When the value of the experience offsets these costs, then there is not a problem. If experience does not offset these costs, it becomes difficult to pass these costs on to consumers. Second, since older workers typically occupy the best-paid jobs, they sometimes prevent the hiring or block the advancement of younger workers. This is frustrating for the younger workers and leaves the organisation in a perilous position whenever the older workers do decide to retire.

In the face of such demographic pressures, many employers try to induce voluntary attrition among their older workers through early retirement incentive programs. These programs come in an infinite variety. Depending on how lucrative they are, they meet with varied success. Although some research evidence suggests that these programs do induce attrition among lower-performing older workers,[27] to a large extent, such programs' success is contingent upon accurate forecasting. For example, if more employees take up the early retirement offer than were forecast, the organisation may go from having a labour surplus to having a severe labour shortage.[28]

Employing temporary workers

While downsizing was the popular method for reducing a labour surplus, the 1990s also saw hiring temporary workers and outsourcing as means of eliminating a labour shortage. The changing nature of temporary work makes it difficult to determine the number of Australian temporary workers. However, reports from recruitment and management consultancies indicate a 'boom' in temporary and contract work. A survey conducted in the mid-1990s by Morgan & Banks recruitment consultancy found that the number of companies planning to use temporary/contract workers was expected to increase by 10 per cent in the three-month period following the survey.[29] The use of temporary/contract workers has continued to increase over the past decade. It should be noted that temporary workers may operate at any organisational level, including freelance specialists, sub-contractors and independent professionals. For example, temporary general managers comprise the upper strata of Australia's growing temporary workforce. For many companies, temporary workers can entail lower costs, thus providing economic benefits. For many workers, temporary work has advantages of flexibility, particularly for knowledge workers who can negotiate lucrative packages. However, temporary work can also have negative outcomes for the individual in terms of reduced income, mental health and social support[30] (as discussed in Chapter 4, Occupational health and safety).

Temporary employment affords firms the flexibility needed to operate efficiently in the face of swings in the demand for goods and services. Several other advantages with temporary employment arrangements need to be noted as well. In addition to size flexibility, the use of temporary workers frees the firm from many administrative tasks and financial burdens associated with being the 'employer of record'.

Second, small companies that cannot afford their own testing programs often recruit employees who have been tested by a temporary agency.[31] Third, many temporary agencies train employees prior to sending them to employers, which reduces training costs and eases the transition for both the temporary worker and the company.[32]

Finally, because the temporary worker has little experience in the host firm, he or she brings an objective perspective to the organisation's problems and procedures that is sometimes valuable.[33] Also, since the temporary worker may have a great deal of experience in other firms, he or she can sometimes identify solutions to the host organisation's problems that were confronted at a different firm. Thus, temporary employees can sometimes help employers to benchmark and improve their practices.

Certain disadvantages to employing temporary workers need to be overcome to effectively use this source of labour. For example, there is often tension between a firm's temporary employees and its full-time or permanent employees. Surveys indicate that 33 per cent of full-time employees perceive the temporary help as a threat to their own job security. This can lead to low levels of cooperation, and, in some cases, outright sabotage if it is not managed properly.

There are several keys to managing this problem. First, the organisation needs to have plateaued in terms of any downsizing effort before it starts bringing in temporaries. A downsizing effort is almost like a death in the family for those employees who survive, and a decent time interval needs to exist before new temporary workers are introduced into this context. Without this time delay, there will be a perceived association between the downsizing effort (which was a threat) and the new temporary employees (who may be perceived by some as outsiders who have been hired to replace old friends). Any increase in demand for labour after a downsizing effort should probably first be met by an expansion of overtime granted to core full-time employees. If this demand persists over time, one can be more certain that the increase is not temporary and that there will be no need for future downsizing. After this avenue is explored, the full-time employees may then be more receptive to the prospect of hiring temporary employees to help lessen their load.

Second, if the organisation is concerned about the reactions of full-time workers to the temporaries, it may want to go out of its way to hire 'non-threatening' temporaries. For example, while most temporary workers want their temporary assignments to turn into full-time work (75 per cent of those surveyed expressed this hope), not all do. Some prefer the freedom of temporary arrangements. These workers are the ideal temporaries for a firm with fearful full-time workers.

Firms can also create their own non-threatening temporary pool staffed by full-time employees who move from unit to unit, depending on the demand for services. The organisation may use an information system to track each employee's past internal assignments and use this to check on the relevant experience of each such internal transfer.

Of course, in attempting to convince full-time employees that they are valued and not about to be replaced by temporary workers, the organisation must not create the perception that temporary workers are second-class organisational citizens. As with managing the full-time employee concerns, there are several keys to managing the concerns of temporary employees. First, as far as possible, the organisation should treat temporary employees the same way it treats full-time workers. Human resources staff can help to prevent feelings of a two-tiered society by ensuring that the temporary agency provides benefits to the temporaries that are at least minimally comparable with those enjoyed by the full-time workers with whom they interact.

Outsourcing

Whereas a temporary employee can be brought in to manage a single job, in other cases a firm may be interested in getting a broad set of services (such as HR tasks, that would otherwise be performed in-house), performed by an outside organisation—that is, *outsourcing*. Typically, outsourcing involves an organisation entering into a contract with a vendor to perform an activity previously performed by the company. Outsourcing can be distinguished from **procurement**, which refers to situations where a vendor is contracted to perform activities that the organisation has not performed before.[34] Globally, the use of outsourcing for HR activities has grown rapidly. The implications of outsourcing HR activities are discussed in more detail in Chapter 18, Evaluating and improving the human resource function.

Procurement
situations where a vendor is contracted to perform activities that an organisation has not performed before.

Outsourcing is often a strategic decision driven by economies of scale that make it more efficient to hand over work to an outside agent.[35] Outsourcing is a logical choice when the organisation simply does not have certain expertise and is not willing to invest the time and energy to develop this expertise. Outsourcing in the area of manufacturing often involves designing products in one country and then shipping manufacturing responsibilities overseas. In a deal described as the largest of its kind in 2004, Qantas announced that it would transfer its data centre to IBM in a transaction worth $650 million over 10 years, and outsource communications to Telstra in a contract worth $750 million over 10 years. Qantas has retained software support in-house and will keep 700 of its own information technology employees, while outsourcing the work of 192 employees to IBM and Telstra.[36]

Clearly, the labour supplies of countries like China, India, Jamaica and those in Eastern Europe are providing a supply of labour, not only for unskilled and low-skilled work. For example, the ANZ Bank has a large information technology centre in Bangalore (India's 'Silicon Valley'), with more than 400 software developers working on projects there.[37] Technological advancements in computer networking and transmission have sped up the outsourcing process and have also helped it spread beyond manufacturing areas and low-skilled jobs. For example, firms that perform design engineering find that India is fertile ground for outsourcing this type of work. However, as shown in the 'Managing challenges of globalisation: Up to the job? How India and China risk being stifled by a skills squeeze', skill shortages are already evident in India and China, particularly with regard to managers and knowledge workers. There are several challenges for companies seeking to match supply and demand of labour by off-shoring their activities.

Many are concerned that while this type of outsourcing may make good sense in the short term, its long-term implications for Australian firms' competitiveness are negative.[38] Although these firms may be reducing manufacturing costs, eventually they will find it more and more difficult to design and produce products that can take advantage of innovations in technology. It is argued that outsourcing, if left unchecked, starts a downward spiral that prompts more and more outsourcing until the firm itself produces nothing of value.[39] In the meantime, more and more workers in Australia may become displaced. In the end, firms that do the manufacturing soon develop their own design teams and then become direct competitors with a substantial competitive advantage.[40] It is, however, interesting to note that Australia appears to be gaining jobs through global offshore outsourcing by United States' firms; Australia and New Zealand are seen as following India as desirable locations outside the United States.[41]

Overtime and expanding worker hours

Companies facing a shortage of labour may be reluctant to hire new full-time or part-time employees. Under some conditions, these firms may have the option of trying to garner more hours out of the existing labour force by increasing hours of overtime worked.

Despite having to pay workers time-and-a-half for overtime production, employers may see this as preferable to hiring and training new employees—especially if they are afraid that current demand for products or services may not extend to the future. Also, for a short period of time at least, many workers enjoy the added compensation. However, over extended periods of time, employees experience stress and frustration from being overworked in this manner.

Program implementation and evaluation

The programs developed in the strategic-choice stage of the process are put into practice in the program implementation stage, shown at the bottom of Figure 7.1. A critical aspect of program implementation is to make sure that some individual is held accountable for achieving the stated goals and has the necessary authority and resources to accomplish this goal. It is also important to have regular progress reports on the implementation to be sure that all programs are in place by specified times and that the early returns from these programs are in line with projections.

The final step in the planning process is to evaluate the results. Of course, the most obvious evaluation involves checking whether the company has successfully avoided any potential labour shortages or surpluses. Although this bottom-line evaluation is critical, it is also important to go beyond it to see which of the specific parts of the planning process contributed to success or failure.

While the value of human resource planning is generally recognised, it is evident that many organisations do not conduct formal human resource planning. Research has indicated that adoption of formal human resource planning is more likely in organisations that are:

- larger
- have greater overall business planning sophistication
- have top-management support for human resource planning
- have more involvement of human resource managers in the business planning process
- have greater integration across human resource activities.[42]

Human resource information systems

Human resource information system (HRIS)
a system to acquire, store, manipulate, analyse, retrieve and distribute information related to a company's human resources.

An effective human resource planning system relies on reliable and valid information about the organisation's current and potential workforce.[43] **Human resource information systems (HRIS)** allow an organisation to collect, store, maintain, retrieve and analyse data about employees. This may include information gathered across all human resource activities.[44] Hence, HRIS are intended to automate several processes of human resource management.

By providing fundamental information for human resource planning and management, HRIS aid competitive and strategic achievements for organisations. These systems use information technology to allow faster access to information and decision making. Thus, HRIS may lead towards a form of 'virtual human resource management',[45] as the computerisation of human resource activities in organisations may streamline operational aspects of human resource management and reduce much of the administrative burden of this functional area. These systems can support human resource activities in various ways. For example, HRIS may support long-term planning by using information from employee supply and demand forecasts;[46] enable the analysis of outcomes from training programs;[47] support compensation programs with information on pay increases, salary forecasts and pay budgets;[48] and provide information on matters such as employee assistance needs.[49] However, as shown in a report on the use of HRIS in the Australian public service, many HRIS users do not understand what information is needed or how it should be used. The report identifies problems with the HRIS tools being used, the expertise available to use them and the quality of data produced. The report found that executives were unaware of ways HRIS could be used, there was little evidence of consultation with line managers about their information needs to help manage their staff better, and there was a lack of awareness of HRIS capabilities. Further, some organisations did not have the policies and procedures to collect all of their required HR data.[50] Overall, the report recommended that these organisations:

- Have a system for consultation and identifying information to be recorded in HRIS that addresses the strategic and operational HR needs of the executive, HR committee and line managers. This should include the development of key performance indicators to measure HR effectiveness.
- Develop the collecting, recording and maintaining of critical data to support strategic and operational HR needs—where possible, within the one HRIS.
- Review the compliance of HRIS administration manuals with information system security policies, with guidance on managing HRIS security.
- Summarise reporting timeframes, responsibilities, recipients and data sources for HR, and ensure that all staff understand their responsibilities.
- Produce a skills audit, develop a skills inventory for staff extracting HRIS data, and train them to maximise the benefits from investment in HRIS.[51]

UP TO THE JOB? HOW INDIA AND CHINA RISK BEING STIFLED BY A SKILLS SQUEEZE

MANAGING CHALLENGES OF GLOBALISATION

When Ishmael Chawla advertises for software developers in New Delhi, he braces himself for rejection. 'More than half our candidates don't show up for a scheduled interview', says Mr Chawla, 33, who manages the Indian operations of Live-Career, a San Francisco-based provider of online career counselling. 'Even then we probably have one qualified person for every 20 we interview, and by qualified, I essentially mean "trainable".'

'The days when you could put up a job ad and find a graduate prepared to work 18 hours a day for peanuts are gone', says Mr Chawla, who is looking to double his staff of eight over the next two years. 'We have to compromise on levels of education, skills, English. Problems don't end at recruitment—we had one guy who worked here for 10 days then vanished without a trace, presumably to another job.'

In China, the skills shortage is so severe in some sectors that even local Chinese companies are forced to look offshore for suitable staff. The country, unlike many in the developing world, had long been able to meet its own needs for commercial pilots, for instance. Not now.

Huang Mei, an official at United Eagle Airlines, a new private airline in western China, says the carrier could not have got off the ground without foreign pilots. 'Although we need to pay them an annual salary of Rmb800 000 (US$100 000, £55 000), the overall cost is reasonable compared to paying for the training of someone from scratch.'

Many companies question their ability to scale up cost-effectively in both countries. Last month, Apple Computer and Powergen, the UK utility, announced the closure of their Indian support activities. More closures are likely to follow as opportunities for labour cost arbitrage become ever more scarce.

India and China, which represent 40 per cent of the world's supply of labour, have an abundance of unskilled workers and a daunting backlog of unemployed. Over the next five years, according to United Nations predictions, they will respectively contribute an additional 71m and 44m to the global labour pool, the lion's share of demographic growth. During this time the US workforce will expand by 10m, Europe's will not increase and Japan's will decline by 3m.

Although both countries produce millions of graduates annually, the raw numbers are a misleading metric for employable skills. China produces 600 000 university-trained engineers every year, for example, a figure often cited to illustrate the country's inexorable rise as a technology power. But a McKinsey survey of nine occupations including engineers, accountants and doctors found that fewer than one in 10 were employable by multinationals.

Chinese students are the product of an education system built around rote learning. In engineering, a heavily theoretical curriculum leaves them with little experience in problem solving or working in teams. As a result, the pool of engineers suitable to work for multinationals is about 160 000, less than one-third of the graduates or about the same number produced each year by the UK, according to McKinsey.

While 3m students graduate from Indian universities each year, only about 10–15 per cent of general college graduates are considered suitable for direct employment in the offshore information technology and business process outsourcing industries, according to a recent study by India's National Association of Software and Service Companies. The lobby group has warned that the Indian IT sector faces a shortfall of 500 000 professionals by 2010 that threatens the country's dominance of global offshore IT services.

Skilled labour shortages extend far beyond the relatively new professions of IT and IT-enabled services. Sunil Bharti Mittal, the billionaire chief executive of Bharti Airtel, India's leading mobile telecommunications company, has a similar problem to that of United Eagle Airlines: he cannot find enough pilots to fly the two jets he pools with a number of other executives. 'I used to fly in a local flying club where the pilots would be languishing jobless', Mr Mittal says. 'In no time, the monthly salary of a pilot has gone from Rs100 000 to Rs1m–Rs1.2m and, even then, they're not available. We need six pilots but have only found four, and two are expats.'

With India and China both still enjoying spectacular growth, their shallow talent pools have yet to cut into headline GDP numbers. But such shortages are chipping away at their emerging economic strengths. The talent crunch will threaten India's knowledge-based and services-driven growth story. In China's case, it undermines Beijing's aim to re-tool its economic model to build the domestic service sector and wean itself off reliance on manufacturing exports. For both, capturing the demographic dividend may prove far harder than they expected.

Source: Excerpt from R. McGregor, 2006, 'Up to the job? How India and China risk being stifled by a skills squeeze', *Financial Times*, 20 July, p. 15. (c) 2006 The Financial Times Limited. All rights reserved.

Current HRIS have evolved from record-keeping systems for human resource activities. Early record-keeping systems tended to focus on automation of basic HR functions such as payroll administration. When managers sought to retrieve data, the turnaround time for requested information was often long and tedious.[52] This tended to restrict the use of these data other than for administrative and operational purposes.[53]

Several factors led to more sophisticated and integrated HRIS in organisations. First, the development of increasingly complex and comprehensive information technology systems coincided with organisational demands for increased flexibility and access to employee data.[54] Second, the economic pressures in the 1980s and 1990s led to an increased need for measurement, costing and reporting of human resource activities, in order to assess their effectiveness in organisations.[55] Third, the implementation of HRIS in Australian organisations was influenced by increasing demands by federal and state legislation to collect employee data. Areas in which such legislation has been introduced during the past two decades include fringe benefits tax, equal employment opportunity, privacy, occupational health and safety, and the (short-lived) training guarantee levy.

Human resource information systems in organisations today tend to be software-enabled systems that are developed by specialist vendors and promoted to organisations and human resource professionals. Today, there is a wide range of HRIS applications available from consulting firms, software houses and organisations that own HRIS developers.

In many larger organisations, HRIS have been used for three broad HRM functions: transaction processing, reporting and tracking; decision support systems; and expert systems.[56] *Transaction processing* refers to computations and calculations used to review and document HR decisions and practices. This includes documenting relocation, training expenses and course enrolments and filling out government reporting requirements. *Decision support systems* are designed to help managers solve problems. They usually include a 'what if' feature that allows users to see how outcomes change when assumptions or data change. These systems are useful, for example, for helping companies determine the number of new recruits needed based on different turnover rates or the availability of employees with a certain skill in the labour market. *Expert systems* are computer systems incorporating the decision rules of people deemed to have expertise in a certain area. The system recommends actions that the user can take based on the information provided by the user. The recommended actions are those that a human expert would take in a similar situation (for example, a manager interviewing a job candidate).

Expert systems have three elements:

1 a knowledge base that contains facts, figures and rules about a specific subject
2 a decision making capability that draws conclusions from those facts and figures to solve problems and answer questions
3 a user interface that gathers and gives information to the person using the system.

Some companies use expert systems to help employees decide how to allocate their monies for benefits, help managers schedule the labour requirements for projects and assist managers in conducting selection interviews. Expert systems can deliver both high quality and lower costs. By using the decision processes of experts, the system enables many people to arrive at decisions that reflect an expert's knowledge. An expert system helps avoid the errors that can result from fatigue and decision biases. The efficiencies of an expert system can be realised if it can be operated by fewer employees or less-skilled (and likely to be less costly) employees than the company would otherwise require.

Employee self-service

A major trend in HRIS is the increasing use of **employee self-service (ESS) applications**. ESS allows employees to directly enter their personal data into the HRIS. ESS can be used for a variety of applications, such as leave entitlements and pay details. However, ESS typically require investment in infrastructure, such as new software, and effective attention to matters such as data management and information security.[57]

The number of Australian workers using company networks and websites to gain 'self-service' access to HRIS, particularly payroll information, is increasing significantly. This brings several changes in the workload for HR staff. According to Michael Briggs, director of business development at PayConnect Solutions, between 60 and 80 per cent of HR staff time is involved with repetitive administrative tasks, much of which is already computer-based.[58] Employees may also update their personal details, including contact information, qualifications and bank-account details. Managers may access information, including employees' leave accruals and compensation details. Such direct access dramatically reduces the amount of requests placed upon HR staff by managers and employees.[59]

As one example, implementing employee self-service via a company intranet has been an important development for Fujitsu Australia.[60] 'We were really faced with a lot of issues around the human resources technology infrastructure', said Rob Carroll, general manager for human resources at Fujitsu Australia. 'We were a very administration-focused human resources department, and all that administration was becoming a bit of a burden. We wanted to free our HR professionals to work more on strategic issues.' The benefits of an ESS can be significant; Fujitsu estimates that annual savings from the system are more than $250 000. There are also intangible benefits, such as freeing up the time of managers.[61] These issues and benefits, and the need to establish a business case for an investment in HRIS or ESS, are discussed in 'Managing challenges through HR innovation: Servicing HR's needs'.

> **Employee self-service (ESS) systems**
> enable employees to directly enter their personal data into the HRIS and to directly access information, such as leave entitlements or pay details.

Information technology used in HRM

According to the Economist Intelligence Unit and Pyramid Research, Australia is placed second to the United States, and therefore among the 13 countries considered leaders, in the implementation and use of information technology for business purposes (electronic, or e-business).[62] Although the uptake of information technology is high in a global sense, at an operational level, few companies are taking a strategic, holistic approach to HRIS. To be most effective, HRIS need to be integrated into strategic business initiatives and company-wide business processes. Critical to gaining acceptance and use by employees is the management of the change process involved in the implementation of HRIS. Good information technology infra-structure combined with communication and education strategies, such as tutorials, user support and integrated help-desks, are necessary throughout all stages of a HRIS lifecycle.[63]

Technologies being applied to HRM include interactive voice technology, the Internet, networks, client-server architecture, relational databases, imaging, laser disc technology, and groupware and intranets. These technologies improve effectiveness through increasing access to information, improving communications and improving the speed with which HR transactions and information can be gathered. This helps reduce the costs and make it easier to administer HR functions such as recruitment

235

and selection, employee learning and development, compensation and performance management. Technology enables:

- employees to gain complete control over their training and benefits enrolments (self-service)
- the creation of a paperless employment office
- streamlining the HR department's work
- knowledge-based decision support technology, which allows employees and managers to access knowledge on an as-needed basis
- employees and managers to select the type of media they want to use to send and receive information
- work to be completed at any time, any place, day or night
- closer monitoring of employees' work.[64]

Interactive voice technology

Interactive voice technology uses a conventional personal computer to create systems such as an automated phone-response system. For example, a telephone-based assistance system may use interactive voice technology; if the system is unable to 'interpret' the name requested by the caller, the call is redirected to a (human) operator.

The Internet

The Internet has become a widely used tool for communications, a method for sending and receiving communications quickly and inexpensively, and a way to locate and gather resources, such as software and reports.[65] Educational institutions, government agencies and commercial internet service providers provide access to the internet. Employees can communicate with others at their location or across the globe, leave messages or documents and enter 'chatrooms' that are designated for conversation on certain topics. Various newsgroups exist, which are bulletin boards dedicated to areas of interest, where you can read, post and respond to messages and articles. Internet sites can have home pages that identify the person or company and may contain text, images, sounds and video.

The World Wide Web is a user-friendly service on the internet. It provides browser software that enables the user to explore its items (for example, Internet Explorer and Netscape). Every home page on the web has an address, or 'uniform resource locator' (URL). Many organisations have websites to provide financial information to investors, advertise products and services, give the latest news releases about the company and post job openings.[66] The Internet is a valuable source of information on a wide range of HRM topics, available from professional societies, schools and government agencies. In each chapter of this book, we feature Internet addresses related to HRM topics.

Australians have relatively high levels of computer usage. In the week preceding the 2001 Census, 7 881 983 people (42 per cent) had used a personal computer at home. The total number of people who had used the Internet in the week preceding the Census was 6 966 687. Of these, 1 221 430 (17.5 per cent) used the Internet at home and at work.[67]

Networks and client-server architecture

Traditionally, different computer systems (with separate databases) have been used for payroll, recruiting and other human resource functions. A *network* is a combination of desktop computers, computer terminals and servers or minicomputers that share access to databases and a means to transmit information throughout the system. A common

SERVICING HR'S NEEDS

MANAGING CHALLENGES THROUGH HR INNOVATION

Employee Self-Service (ESS) systems are able to eliminate the mundane, routine administration tasks previously required of HR staff. ESS has already evolved beyond the electronic forms model of its infancy and vertical stream HR applications into all areas of business processes, according to Ari Kopoulos, national sales and marketing manager, Employee Connect.

Recent developments

In recent time there has been an increase in demand for 'intelligent' workflows that make managers and employees accountable. These processes have business intelligence built behind them with escalation trigger points and timeouts.

'Typically the new generation workflows "push" tasks to users and require the user to "act". Management can track the task in the process, allowing identification of bottlenecks and inefficiencies. Full history is available for audit purposes. Few HR vendors offer that sort of flexibility and functionality', says French.

There are a number of other emerging trends in ESS that are shaping the way both employers and employees view and use ESS, according to David Page, managing director, Neller. He points to the ability of different departments' ESS applications to come together in one portal.

Another trend Page mentions is the greater adoption of ESS by employees who traditionally have not been users of PCs in the workplace. 'We see this particularly in the manufacturing and logistics (transport) industries, where companies are providing PCs or kiosks in lunchrooms to give their employees access to the intranet and ESS systems.'

Implementation pitfalls

There are a number of key issues that HR managers need to seriously consider before implementing an ESS system. As French points out, the main pitfall is lack of planning 'It is important to start at the top and ensure that senior management understand how ESS will work and to get buy-in.'

There must be a commitment to keeping the organisational structure, particularly reporting lines, up to date, so that all workflows operate as they should, claims Page.

Firstly, Kopoulos suggests clearly defining requirements by engaging key stakeholders and users at the business analysis phase. He recommends that businesses analyse and plan, think about scope, perform an acceptance test and review.

Secondly, Kopoulos suggests ensuring all data is accurate before rollout. An ESS system is only as good as the payroll system it works with.

Effective communication can also be cited as a necessary part of the process. 'Don't just document project issues, communicate them.' To overcome any technophobia he suggests: 'Communicate, educate and reassure them. Offer basic computer skills training to employees as an employee benefit, there are even some government grants available for this type of training.'

Making your ESS site and process as non-threatening as possible will inspire confidence and interest, as well as making the system voluntary. Security is another issue for consideration. 'You'd be surprised how often a HR manager is on leave without any consideration as to who has access to ESS information in their absence', says Page.

Building the business case

Capitalising on the fact that self service technology equals time savings, which are in turn easy to measure, is a must, according to Page.

The best strategy is to seek advice and learn from the experience of others, says French. 'Some vendors will help with ROI (return on investment) proposals. The focus should be on adding value not cost.'

ESS: Justifying ROI

1. Not all business cases are equal. A business case to a CFO will differ from one to a CIO or MD.
2. Quantify the current situation. Analyse transactions, volumes and cycles.
3. Define the vision. Where do you want to go, what are expectations, what are the reporting requirements?
4. Are there any statutory or legislative requirements to be considered?
5. What are the IT/integration requirements?
6. Determine the administrative costs of an ESS.
7. Evaluate the vendors based on scripted demonstration, using real data.
8. Include all assumptions.
9. Present a solid cost benefit analysis.
10. Include a project timetable.
11. Include change management processes.

Data source: Ari Kopoulos, national sales and marketing manager, Employee Connect

Source: Excerpt from M. Yen, 2006, 'Servicing HR's needs', *Human Resources*, 19 September, pp. 16–17.
www.humanresourcesmagazine.com.au

form of network involves client-server architecture. Client-server architecture provides the means of consolidating data and applications into a single system (the client).[68] The data can be accessed by multiple users. Also, software applications can be stored on the server and 'borrowed' by other users. Client-server architecture allows easier access to data, faster response time and maximum use of personal computers.

Relational databases

Databases contain several *data files* (topics), which are made up of *employee information* (records) containing data fields. A *data field* is an element or type of information such as employee name, tax-file number or job classification.

In a relational database, information is stored in separate files, which look like tables. These files can be linked by common elements (fields) such as name, identification number or location. This contrasts with the traditional file structure, in which all data associated with an employee is kept in one file. In the relational database shown in Figure 7.3 below, employees' personal information is located in one file and salary information in another but both topics of information can be accessed via the personnel identification number.

Users of relational databases have the ability to file and retrieve information according to any field or multiple fields across different tables or databases. They provide an easy way to organise data. Also, the number of data fields that can be kept for any employee using a relational database is limitless. The ability to join or merge data from several different tables or to view only a subset of data is especially useful in human resource management. Databases that have been developed to track employee benefit costs, training courses and compensation, for example, contain separate pieces

FIGURE 7.3 Example of a relational database

Personal Information

Last name	First	Gender	Age	Personnel no.	Location
Drake	Raymond	M	34	275-66-3181	Plant
Saucer	Mary	F	28	105-37-6412	HQ
Lui	Tony	M	40	287-97-3783	Plant
Wiggins	Arthur	M	50	173-85-4321	Plant

Relational database links files by common elements

Salary Data

Personnel no.	Salary	Grade level
275-66-3181	$75 000	10
105-37-6412	$29 000	3
287-97-3783	$40 000	6
173-85-4321	$34 750	5

Fields

of employee information that can be accessed and merged as desired by the user. Relational technology also allows databases to be established in several different locations. Users in one plant or division location can access data from any other company location. Consider the example of an oil company. Human resources data—such as the names, salaries and skills of employees working on an oil rig in Bass Strait—can be stored at company headquarters. Databases at the oil-rig site itself might contain employee name, safety equipment issued and appropriate skill certification. Headquarters and oil-rig managers can access information on each database as needed.

Imaging

Imaging (or scanning) refers to scanning documents and storing them electronically so they can be retrieved later.[69] Imaging is particularly useful because paper files take up a large volume of space and are difficult to access. Imaging has been used in applicant tracking and in benefits management. Applicants' resumés can be scanned and stored in a database so they will be available for access at a later date. Some software applications allow the user to scan the resumé based on key items such as job history, education or experience.[70]

Imaging
a process for scanning documents, storing them electronically, and retrieving them.

Laser disc technology

Laser disc technology (for example, compact discs [CDs] and digital versatile discs [DVDs]) has revolutionised training. Using a personal computer, animation, video clips and graphics can be integrated into a training session. Also, the user can interact with the training material through a joystick or touch-screen monitor. Compact discs use a laser to read text, graphics, audio and video from an aluminium disc. Laser disc technology uses a laser to provide high-quality video and sound. It can be used individually (as a source of video on a computer screen) or as part of computer instruction in a classroom setting.

As discussed in Chapter 11 Learning and development, the use of computers in training provides a safe environment for learning how to operate potentially dangerous equipment or tasks in which an error might have grave consequences (such as performing a heart transplant). Use of the computer also allows employees to learn at their own pace, skip or review material and learn when and where material is available. (They do not have to wait for a class to be scheduled, they only need access to the equipment.)

Groupware, intranets and portals

Groupware (or electronic meeting software) is a software application that enables multiple users to track, share and organise information and to work on the same document simultaneously.[71] A groupware system combines such elements as email, document management and an electronic bulletin board. For example, Outlook provides a calendar that enables employees to access each others' calendars and insert meeting times.

Companies have been using groupware to improve business processes such as sales and account management, to improve meeting effectiveness and to identify and share knowledge in the organisation. (See our discussion on creating a learning organisation in Chapter 11 Learning and development.)

Many companies have created their own *intranet*, a private company network that competes with or replaces groupware programs. Intranets are cheaper and simpler to use than groupware programs.72 Many companies are using technology to communicate with their employees, and intranets are central to this revolution in company–employee relations. For many employees in larger organisations, their computers open straight to the company intranet or its portal. Just as Yahoo! is a gateway into the Internet, portals are the employee's point of entry into the organisation's intranet. A portal may guide employees to updates about company developments, resources and often to external sites, such as the *White Pages*. According to Peter Wetenhall, the Melbourne-based e-commerce director of The Boston Consulting Group for Australia and New Zealand, companies may justify the initial, often substantial, costs of establishing an intranet by expected reductions in administration costs and the benefits of improved communication.73

A market research survey commissioned by Corechange, a global provider of e-business software, found that in early 2001, 37 per cent of 157 companies with more than 1000 employees were implementing a portal infrastructure. The majority (73 per cent) said they were implementing a portal for the benefit of their employees.74

Portals enable employee self-service of HR information. For example, PeopleSoft's HRMS provides employees with control over their own personal details, so they can update information such as their bank account details for payroll purposes. Portals are becoming more 'user-centric' because they enable each employee to customise the arrangement and display of content to suit his or her own needs. In addition to providing personalised access, using an Internet architecture enables portability—employees can log in from home or anywhere in the world. Combined with increasing use of broadband technology that enables faster Internet access, information technology is enabling greater geographic flexibility for employees.

Global positioning systems

Global positioning systems are used in a wide variety of applications, ranging from military surveillance to civilian applications, such as automobile navigation. Workplace application of global positioning systems is also being explored across several industries. For example, a media publications company has introduced a new global positioning system to track the progress of people delivering shopping catalogues to household letterboxes for several major Australian retailers. The GPS tracking system is intended to be carried by employees delivering direct marketing materials. The system provides the company with real-time reports on deliveries and is expected to assist in the improvement of delivery times. As shown in 'HRM spotlight: Big brother law catches business on hop', however, there are many issues, including legal considerations, associated with the use of such technology.

HRIS: Software applications for HRM

The technologies through which HR meets stakeholders' needs vary depending on the need being satisfied. Selection systems ensure that applicants selected for employment have the necessary knowledge, skills and abilities to provide value to the organisation. Employee learning and development systems meet the needs of both line managers and employees by providing employees with development opportunities to ensure they are constantly increasing their human capital and, consequently, providing increased value to the company. Performance management systems make clear to employees what is expected of them and ensure line managers and strategic planners know which

BIG BROTHER LAW CATCHES BUSINESS ON HOP

Installing a global positioning system in its fleet of trucks was supposed to be a good business move for a Hunter Valley concreting company. But now it is unsure if it will comply with new laws.

The NSW *Workplace Surveillance Act* comes into force on Friday, making it a criminal offence for employers to secretly monitor staff by using tracking devices in work vehicles, installing video cameras or reading emails without getting approval from a magistrate or giving staff 14 days' notice.

Companies that have already monitored staff should have given them notice on September 23 in order to comply. From Friday, they risk fines of $5500 for every unauthorised act of covert surveillance.

The concreting company, which found out about the legislation only about a week ago, has yet to formally notify staff about tracking devices in trucks.

'We're confused', said a spokeswoman for company, which declined to be named. 'We have GPS in trucks purely to track where the vehicles are … not to see what staff are up to.'

For Australian Business Limited, which has about 28 000 members, confusion over tracking devices in work vehicles is driving most of the calls to its emergency telephone hotline.

ABL senior workplace policy adviser Minna Knight said the organisation believed that companies would not be affected by the law if they simply used tracking devices to monitor vehicles.

'Where it becomes grey is when employers also use that surveillance to detect if an employee is off having a liquid lunch', Ms Knight said.

She said about 80 per cent of ABL members were unlikely to comply with the new laws.

Interstate companies were struggling to draw up policies in NSW that were consistent with other states.

NSW firms also operating in Victoria will soon face the added burden of complying with separate laws there, with a final report and proposed legislation due to be tabled in parliament today.

The two options canvassed by the Victorian Law Reform Commission earlier this year included one similar to the NSW approach, requiring employers to notify staff. A second option would require employers to conform to codes of conduct.

Meanwhile, small businesses in NSW are finding it difficult to draw up computer usage policies that satisfy the act's requirement for adequate notification as long as staff have known of them for at least 14 days.

A partner dealing with investigations and forensic services at PricewaterhouseCoopers, Malcolm Shackell, said companies that did not have computer use policies in place would be restricted by what they could do if they wanted to investigate an allegation, such as fraud or electronic harassment.

Source: R. Lebihan, 2005, 'Big Brother law catches business on hop', *Australian Financial Review*, 5 October, p. 3.

---

employee behaviour will be in line with the company's goals. Finally, reward systems similarly benefit all stakeholders (line managers, strategic planners and employees). These systems ensure managers and employees will use their skills for organisational benefit and they provide strategic planners with ways to ensure all employees are acting in ways that will support the strategic plan. Obviously, reward systems provide employees with an equitable return for their investment of skills and effort.

Today, many personal computer-based human resource applications are available.[75] The wide variety means that several publications that deal exclusively with human resource management (for example, *HRMonthly* and *Human Resources* magazines) devote considerable space to HRIS.

While organisations may utilise integrated HRIS that encompass a range of HRM activities, many companies are still using information systems for only some of their HRM activities. There are specific purposes within HRM activities for which software applications can be particularly useful. In the following sections we review the software applications available for human resource planning, staffing, performance management, employee learning and career development, and compensation and benefits packages.

Human resource planning applications

Succession planning
the identification and tracking of high-potential employees capable of filling higher-level managerial positions.

Two principal computer applications are related to human resource planning: 'succession planning' and 'forecasting'.[76] **Succession planning** (the identification and tracking of high-potential employees capable of filling higher-level managerial positions) ensures that the company has employees who are prepared to move into positions that become available because of retirement, promotion, transfers, terminations or expansion of the business. As shown in 'Managing challenges through attracting and retaining people: Groomed for succession', effective succession planning can bring benefits across many areas of HRM. Forecasting includes predicting the number of employees who have certain skills and the number of qualified individuals in the labour market.

Human resource planning applications usually require more customisation than applications for other human resource functions, because human resource planning involves company-specific calculations involved in determining future employee turnover, growth rates and promotion patterns. They usually contain several data files, including a 'starting-population' file, 'exit-rate' file, 'growth-rate' file and promotion patterns. The starting-population file lists employees by job classification within each job family. These file lists usually include all active, regular, full-time employees. However, starting-population files may include only specific populations of employees. Starting-population data that may be used include job grade, gender, age, service, training and experience information. Starting-population lists that are limited to specific populations of employees are used to identify the mobility patterns of these employee groups. Exit-rate data include promotion patterns, training completion rates, turnover rates and hiring rates. Growth-rate data include the percentage increase in the number of employees within the job or demographic characteristic (for example, females) that are of interest. Promotion patterns include the rate of movement into and out of each position.

Information regarding starting population and exit and growth rates is useful for conducting workforce profile analysis and workforce dynamics analysis.[77]

Workforce profile analysis

To determine future labour supply and demand, it is necessary to identify the characteristics of the current workforce, a process known as a workforce profile review. Software can be used to generate reports that provide information regarding employee demographics, such as: age; the number of employees in each job classification; and the interaction between demographics and company characteristics (for example, the average age of employees within each job classification or division of the company).

Workforce dynamics analysis

A workforce dynamics analysis involves analysing employee movement over time. Promotion, demotion, transfer and turnover data are used. Employee movement data can also be used to forecast the effects of job terminations or hiring on the future workforce. Workforce dynamics analysis provides the following kinds of information:

1. number of new recruits, transfers and promotions by job classification or department
2. the total number of promotions or the number of promotions from a specific job to another job, or from one division to another division
3. the number of employees the company will need in the future
4. the number of employees who will be available to fill future job openings
5. using human resource planning applications for decision making.

GROOMED FOR SUCCESSION

More and more companies are realising they must identify and grow key talent in their organisation or they risk losing them.

Most companies find the process of developing the next generation of leaders a struggle. Last year, the *Hudson Report* surveyed 7688 employers across a range of industries and found that 49 per cent of the managers who responded had not been formally assessed for their leadership skills. Managers were left to figure out their own weaknesses and strengths and set their own development tasks.

According to the report, organisations that do not formally assess their management 'have an incomplete picture of the leadership potential in their ranks, often limited to the top tier of management'. A shift towards more formal assessments is expected as organisations start to see 'the importance of knowledge retention and the strategic value of growing leaders from within'.

Two companies that have successfully put new assessment and development plans in place are BASF Australia, the chemical company, and Victoria's Department of Human Services (VDHS). Both organisations have set up a range of programs to find high-potential staff and mould and 'stretch' them.

Realising a need

BASF Australia's move came after its multinational parent company introduced a 'core competency framework'. The Australian division realised it had nothing in place to identify those who were meeting the core competencies and nothing to help mentor people and develop their skills in the key areas.

'We only had very traditional methods like appraisals to see how well people met the competencies', BASF business division service platform manager David Hawkins says. 'There were a number of things that triggered the decision, but in essence we realised that the region in its entirety hadn't identified high performers particularly well. We realised we needed to get a bit more sophisticated.'

So 18 months ago BASF began setting up a development plan to rectify the situation. The goal was to have local staff at a high enough calibre to be leading processes on the floor at a regional level.

VDHS recently piloted a 'leadership bank' to develop high-potential, first-tier executives and pre-executives. The nine-month program involved everything from networking sessions to facilitating question and answer sessions to mentoring, group coaching around common areas of concern and round-table leadership discussions.

The path to a formalised plan stemmed from a more urgent need to plan for the future. The department had an aged population, and so there was a critical need to develop up and coming talent to make sure that the future needs of the department and its workforce were being targeted.

Getting key stakeholders on board for these sorts of programs can be challenging because often the benefits come in the long-term. Also, news of a problem lurking can be confronting for the management responsible for the way things are going.

Overcoming challenges

When it comes to implementing a program as vast and significant as one to find and develop future leaders, there are sure to be challenges. For the VDHS one was deciding what criteria to use to identify high performers in the first place. Ultimately, they used a mixture of self-assessment and assessment by management and more objective measures such as performance history, ratings against executive capabilities and the department's values, career history and career intention and stakeholder feedback.

But inevitably, people are going to be left out and organisations must address disappointment from those parties and work hard to keep morale up among those who didn't get in the program. That involved offering additional support and advice.

Benefits and rewards

The big pay-off comes in the long run, but there are smaller, more immediate benefits in the meantime. Both BASF and the VDHS are still in the process of assessing the results, so it's too soon to determine the return on investment, but both organisations say the process has been worthwhile and they would do it again.

Source: Excerpt from L. Hoffman, 2005, 'Groomed for succession', *Human Resources*, 23 August, pp. 20–1.
www.humanresourcesmagazine.com.au

The workforce profile review provides managers with information regarding:

1. divisions or departments that have the greatest concentration of employees who are nearing retirement age
2. job classifications in which there are too few employees who are ready for promotion
3. job classifications in which there are few women
4. job classifications or departments that have large groups of employees who lack basic skills.

Managers can use information about employee movement, skills and job openings to make decisions about where employees should be deployed to help the company successfully execute its business strategy. Workforce analytics tools feature in HRIS products from the main enterprise resource planning vendors (Oracle, PeopleSoft and SAP).[78]

Staffing applications

Common software applications used in the area of staffing include applicant tracking, recruitment practices tracking, help in meeting equal employment opportunity reporting requirements and aid in maintaining databases of employee information.

Applicant recruiting and tracking

Applicant tracking helps a company maintain its information on job candidates and identify suitable candidates for particular positions. An effective applicant tracking system does the following:

1. retrieves applications by name or other identifiers
2. tracks all the events in the application process (that is, interviews or tests)
3. allows the user to determine how long an application has remained active
4. contains the information needed to meet equal employment opportunity reporting requirements, such as name, gender, race and date of application
5. tracks data entry (allows for entry of only essential applicant information)
6. simplifies the recruiter's function (provides basic data needed to schedule interviews, generate reports and reduce a list of job candidates)
7. allows an evaluation of recruiting strategy to be made (for example, by identifying which sources of advertising bring in the best candidates or the cost effectiveness of visiting various university campuses)
8. permits customisation (allows additional types of data to be added to the file, such as test results or job offers)
9. increases the applicant pool (potential job candidates can be identified and tracked earlier; qualified candidates can be tracked after a position is filled)
10. increases selection criteria by allowing simultaneous searches based on several types of criteria, such as skills, work history and educational background.[79]

Developing an employee database

Companies usually keep data about employees in one large database. Information in the employee database can be used for many purposes: human resource planning, employee learning and development, administering payroll, and tracking compensation and benefits costs. The master employee database usually includes information such as the employee's name, personnel number, job status (full- or part-time), hiring date, position, title, rate of pay, citizenship status, job history, job location, mailing address, birth date and emergency contacts.

Using staffing applications for decision making

Information related to applicant recruiting and tracking can help managers make recruiting practices more efficient and productive. For example, managers can evaluate the yield of recruiting sources. Those sources that produce the greatest number of applicants who are offered and accept positions are targeted for subsequent recruiting efforts, and low-yield sources are abandoned. Managers can also determine which recruiters are providing the most successful employees.[80]

Performance management applications

Employees' performance ratings, disciplinary actions and work-rule violations can be stored in electronic databases. Personal computers are also increasingly being used for monitoring the actual performance and productivity of service employees.[81] For example, at call centres used by organisations such as airlines, telecommunications and insurance firms, agents answer many telephone inquiries per day. The agents' calls are recorded and reviewed to help the agent improve customer service. Managers can hear what the agents tell customers and see what agents enter on their personal computer screens. One of the disadvantages of monitoring is that employees sometimes find it demoralising, degrading and stressful. To avoid the potential negative effect of performance monitoring, managers must communicate why employees are being monitored. Non-management employees also need to be involved in monitoring and coaching less-experienced employees.[82] As discussed in Chapter 6 Analysis and design of work, if used for developmental, rather than punitive purposes, performance monitoring can be positively associated with employee wellbeing.[83]

There has been considerable debate about whether fully online performance management can be achieved. PeopleSoft spent 27 per cent of revenue on research and development leading up to the market launch of PeopleSoft 8, including their product range, Enterprise Performance Management, which is 'designed to help businesses to carve out a performance score card'.[84] For example, the PeopleSoft Balanced Scorecard displays key performance indicators with assessments against criteria, thus enabling employees to track their own performance against key performance indicators.[85] However, critics of online performance management argue that performance management requires face-to-face communication (or phone or video conferencing at the very least).[86]

Using performance management applications for decision making

Performance management applications are available to help managers tailor performance rating systems to jobs and assist the manager in identifying solutions to performance problems.[87] Software is available to help the manager customise performance rating forms for each job. The manager determines the performance standard for each job and rates each employee according to the appropriate standards. The manager receives a report summarising the employees' strengths and weaknesses. The report also provides information regarding how different an employee's performance was from the established standard.

Performance diagnosis applications ask the manager for information about performance problems (for example, 'Has the employee been trained in the skills that caused the performance problem?') and the work environment (for example, 'Does the employee work under time pressure?'). The software analyses the information and provides the manager with solutions to consider in dealing with the performance problem.

Learning and career development applications

Applications for employee learning and development have been used primarily to track information related to training administration (for example, course enrolments, tuition reimbursement summaries and training costs), employee skills and employees' training activities. Important database elements for training administration include training courses completed, certified skills and educational experience. Training cost information can be used by managers to determine which departments are exceeding their training budgets. This information can be used to reallocate training dollars during the next budget period. Databases are also available that provide professional employees, such as doctors, engineers and lawyers, with access to summaries of journal articles, legal cases and books to help these employees keep up to date.[88]

Career development applications assess the employees' career interests, work values and career goals. The computer provides employees with information about positions in the company that meet their interests and values. Company information systems may also have career development plans for each employee. These may include information such as skill strengths, projected training and development needs, target positions and ratings of readiness for managerial or other positions.

Using learning and career development applications for decision making

Managers can use skills inventories to ensure that they are getting the maximum benefit out of their training budget. Using skills inventories, managers can determine which employees need training and can suggest training programs that are appropriate for their job and skill levels. Skills inventories are also useful for identifying employees who are qualified for promotions and transfers. Finally, they can also be useful for helping managers to quickly build employee teams with the necessary skills to respond to customer needs, product changes, international assignments or work problems.

Career development applications can help managers improve the effectiveness of their career development discussions with employees. They also help employees determine their interests, goals and work values, which is often a difficult and uncomfortable task for managers. By having employees complete a self-assessment of interests, goals and values, managers and employees can have a more efficient and effective career development discussion that focuses on developing career plans and helping employees progress towards their career goals. Career development applications can also help managers advise employees on available development opportunities (for example, new jobs).

Compensation and benefits applications

Applications in compensation and benefits include payroll, job evaluation, salary surveys, salary planning, international compensation and benefits management.[89]

Payroll

Managing a payroll involves calculating and reporting taxes; computing gross pay, deductions and net pay for each pay period; arranging for transfer of monies into appropriate accounts; distributing payments and records to employees; and reporting dollars allocated to payroll and benefits to the accounting function. Several issues have to be considered in designing or choosing a payroll system. The company must decide whether payroll will be administered in-house or by a service bureau (or consulting firm). The company must also decide the extent of integration between payroll and other HRIS.

In many companies, payroll is outsourced to a bureau service or payroll consultancy, a company that provides payroll services to other organisations. One of the advantages of a payroll consultancy is that it ensures that the company's payroll meets legal requirements. It also provides a level of computer expertise that may be unavailable within the company. Many payroll consultancy firms have developed other human resource applications that integrate with their payroll systems. A problem arises when a company wants to use human resource applications that have not been developed by the payroll consultancy. The payroll consultancy may be unable or unwilling to integrate its payroll system with other applications.

Besides deciding whether to have its payroll done by a payroll consultancy, an organisation has to decide whether payroll will be integrated with other human resource data systems. In an integrated payroll system, the information in the payroll system is shared with other databases. In most companies, payroll is not linked to other HRIS. However, the trend is towards integrated systems because of the reduced costs resulting from sharing databases. Another advantage of an integrated payroll is that it cuts down on the storage of redundant information, thus speeding up the computer's processing time.

Job evaluation
Job evaluation involves determining the worth of each job and establishing pay rates. In computerised job evaluation, jobs are given points and the relative worth of each job is determined by the total number of points.[90] Managers and employees complete surveys that ask them to rate their jobs' level of problem solving, interaction with customers and other important compensable factors. The survey data are entered into the computer. A summary of the survey responses is generated and checked for accuracy (for example, jobs high in complexity should also have high ratings of required job knowledge). The computer calculates a point value to assign each job to a salary grade.

Salary surveys
Salary surveys are sent to competing companies to gain information about compensation rates, pay levels or pay structures. The information gathered may include salary ranges, average salary of job incumbents and total compensation of ob incumbents. Software designed specifically for this purpose collects, records, analyses and generates reports comparing company salary ranges with those of competitors.

Salary planning
Salary planning anticipates changes in employees' salaries because of seniority or performance. Salary planning applications calculate merit-increase budgets and allocate salary increases based on merit or seniority. They also allow users to see what effect changes in the amount of money devoted to merit, seniority or cost-of-living wage increases would have on compensation budgets.

International compensation
Software applications also perform Australian and foreign tax calculations necessary to determine the costs of international assignments. Many international compensation applications can also calculate salary levels and cost-of-living differentials between Australian and foreign cities.

Benefits management
Management of benefits (for example, work–life benefits and superannuation) includes tracking coverage for employees and former employees, producing reports on changes in benefits coverage and determining employee eligibility for benefits

programs. Software is available to help administer flexible benefits programs, retirement planning and defined contribution plans. These applications can track the employee's enrolment in each part of the benefits program and determine employee eligibility for coverage. Benefits software applications can reduce the time it takes to process changes in employees' benefits programs. They also allow employers to track current benefits expenses and project future benefits costs.

Using compensation and benefits applications for decision making

The software applications mentioned provide graphic depictions of pay ranges and salary lines. They allow managers to quickly see the effects of changes in compensation rates and policies. Compensation applications can be useful for determining the impact of different percentages of pay increases on total compensation costs. Managers can use job-evaluation data to determine which jobs are over- or under-paid in comparison with other jobs in the company. Hypothetical pay ranges can be constructed based on different compensation strategies. For example, the costs of a 'lead the market' strategy can be determined before the company decides on this compensation approach.

Managers can also use compensation information to make adjustments to an individual employee's compensation. For example, managers can determine whether employee performance ratings are related to merit increases and can identify the employee's position within the pay range.

Overall, HRIS may be useful for any organisation, regardless of industry or size. Although small businesses traditionally operate less formally than larger organisations, increasing government regulation may lead small firms to implement a HRIS—for example, to manage information required in the event of an occupational health and safety issue or unfair dismissal claim. Human resources information, such as letters of employment offers or job descriptions, should be readily accessible. However, in many organisations, including larger companies, HR data may be spread across several systems, ranging from word processing and spreadsheets to databases and accounting/payroll systems, and this data cannot be easily transferred. Moving to a comprehensive, integrated HRIS may entail substantial implementation costs, which need to be considered with regard to the ongoing benefits of a HRIS.[91] As is shown in 'Managing challenges through sustainability: Is HR technology a help or hindrance?', information technology requires careful consideration, to prevent negative outcomes and to maximise benefits.

IS HR TECHNOLOGY A HELP OR HINDRANCE?

MANAGING CHALLENGES THROUGH SUSTAINABILITY

HR professionals have, in recent years, been called upon to prepare their companies for a succession of technological developments—both minor and major.

Business to Employee (B2E) systems, for example, leverage e-business approaches and internet technologies to manage the workforce—and B2E is now widely accepted as a management philosophy. Most HR functions can now be performed by an employee via an internet or intranet-connected PC. Moreover, in Australia there is a surprisingly high degree of HR self-sufficiency, with many employees being able to harness smart systems and software and handle their own HR housekeeping, from performance evaluation to processing leave requests.

The benefits of Employee Self-Service (ESS) systems, which have become popular over the past few years, include cutting the time HR staff need to spend on routine tasks, such as changing employee addresses. ESS also gives staff a greater sense of control and ensures that data entered is more accurate, while the use of a web browser interface generally means training requirements are fairly minimal. Most HR software vendors have added modules for ESS to their packages, so rolling out an ESS system has not been seen as a particularly onerous task.

As web-based ESS systems become commonplace, HR professionals are getting ready to cross the next technological frontier into Management Self-Service (MSS). MSS systems are designed to allow managers to take control of well-documented processes such as salary reviews, training allocations and tracking leave requirements across a large department. Software vendors believe MSS will become a key technology issue for HR professionals over the next 18 months.

Meanwhile, technology has eased the burden of payroll administration and freed up HR and other staff to perform higher value functions. A common approach to handling payroll within an organisation is to outsource it. While this is not a new phenomenon, improvements in technology have made it more compelling for many businesses, making payroll a prominent example of the benefits of outsourcing. 'Over the past five to six years, payroll outsourcing has really grown in popularity', says Jason Low, managing director of The Association for Payroll Specialists (TAPS). 'It's no different to any other sort of outsourcing.'

John Macy, director of Competitive Edge Technology, does not believe there have been any substantial developments in technology over the past five years. He claims that many of the things that are considered contemporary today, such as ESS, MSS and workflow solutions, have been around for a while. The only difference is the term 'human capital management', to describe what we used to call 'human resource management', he says.

According to Macy, the method and expectation of technology 'to support the transformation of HR professionals from administrative slaves into liberated strategic planning analysts' has simply not happened. 'New products have emerged containing workforce analytics tools to support workforce planning functions, but the technology is under-utilised and that has limited its impact', he says. 'The new generation of products about to emerge will transform systems from a closed monolithic, proprietary-based nature, into open and more flexible systems that will be easier to implement, allow simpler integration of multiple third-party products and be capable of being changed later in response to changes in the business operation.'

Source: Excerpt from M Yen, 2006, 'Is HR technology a help or hindrance?', *Human Resources*, 21 March, p. 22. www.humanresourcesmagazine.com.au

MANAGING PEOPLE

HIRING HURDLES EASY WITH PERSONNEL SOFTWARE

HELEN O'LOUGHLIN was given a tough assignment: shave about $5 million off Westpac's recruitment bill and improve the bank's handling of its 27 000 staff.

Ms O'Loughlin, a leader in Westpac's recruitment and retention team, wanted to have staff skill profiles, resumes and performance ratings at her fingertips, but had to look outside the bank for the IT smarts to make it a reality.

Big businesses demand a rapid turnaround of projects and creativity from their workers, but organisations often work at cross-purposes. Ms O'Loughlin turned to software company Taleo to help her counteract the inertia prevalent in the organisation and bring its Oracle HR system into line.

The savings came in seven months. Although Westpac still uses external recruitment firms for some roles, Ms O'Loughlin says 82 per cent of recruiting is done inside the bank. And the implementation time was cut from years to two months.

Taleo specialises in what is known in IT parlance as 'on-demand software'. For a monthly fee, Taleo provides Westpac with software that is accessed by staff through a web browser. Westpac no longer manages software updates, data management, back-ups and infrastructure, and other minutiae associated with IT.

Taleo isn't the only company providing such services. One of the earliest examples is the venerable Hotmail webmail service. Back at the height of the dotcom boom, software-as-a-service was offered by groups calling themselves 'application service providers' (ASP).

Although the demise of the dotcoms destroyed many of those early ASPs, their evolved progeny lives on. And the likes of Taleo and salesforce.com are causing IT buyers to look afresh at their IT infrastructure.

Spruikers claim that on-demand software frees IT departments from housekeeping chores, but detractors point to increased security threats. The customer may also lose some control over the interface and privacy. (Ms O'Loughlin says Westpac's software met 'rigorous standards' for privacy.)

Taleo's system sends an alert to bank staff if there is a vacant job that matches their skills, which may save the company time recruiting from outside. This should send shivers down the spines of recruiters: the bank now knows more about its own skills than the consultants.

But despite the perceived benefits, Ms O'Loughlin says on-demand, hosted services were not in Westpac's IT strategy. So she left the technical arguments behind and played the costs card to get her way.

Ms O'Loughlin says recruitment companies have 'outdated models'—they charge a lot for running advertisements, adding a 'bit of intellectual property in the (talent) database'.

She says she believed a hosted service such as Taleo's could do what recruiters do for a fraction of the price.

Organisations spend big on financial systems and know more about their office furniture than the skills of their staff. They say people are their most important asset, yet they do not have the technology to automate collecting and searching the skills of their staff. Without appropriate technology, staff members who should be considered for roles aren't, and they watch external hiring for jobs they could have done. They become disengaged and may leave unnecessarily. Westpac has reduced this worry.

Changes in corporate structures also cause unnecessary hiring and firing because organisations don't realise their own skills and knowledge—that held in the heads of staff, many of whom are never considered for jobs they can perform.

Westpac can now redeploy staff with Taleo's tools, improving morale and reducing hiring costs.

Westpac's hiring managers are also benefiting from the software. Most companies have intranets listing their available jobs, forcing managers to wade through dozens of inappropriate internal applications.

Taleo technology ensures that only people with appropriate skills are considered, allowing managers to hire faster and to look outside the company only if they need to.

Source: E. Mandla, 2006, 'Hiring hurdles easy with personnel software', *The Age*, 9 May, p. 5. © 2006 Copyright John Fairfax Holdings Limited. www.theage.com.au.

QUESTIONS

1 Identify the main features of the approach to HRIS at Westpac.
2 What are the advantages and disadvantages of using an 'application service provider' (ASP)?

CHAPTER SUMMARY

Human resource planning uses labour supply and demand forecasts to anticipate labour shortages and surpluses. It also entails programs that can be utilised to reduce a labour surplus (for example, downsizing) and eliminate a labour shortage (for example, bringing in temporary workers). When done well, human resource planning can enhance the success of the organisation while minimising difficulties resulting from poorly anticipated labour surpluses or shortages.

To conduct human resource planning in an effective manner, the organisation needs to identify the appropriate goals and then formulate and implement a planning process targeting those goals. Information on available human resources will need to be gathered. Hence, the human resource information system will be of vital importance in this planning process. Certain strategic choices will need to be made in the pursuit of the planning goals. For example, the recruitment and selection strategies discussed in the next chapter, Chapter 8 Recruitment and selection, will be influenced by the human resource planning goals. Finally, the success of these strategies has to be evaluated against the goals established earlier in the process.

Increasingly, organisations will depend on more sophisticated HRIS in order to support human resource activities. Key drivers for this will be the increasing globalisation of business, the development of more flexible, non-traditional organisation structures and the ongoing development of information technology.

WEB EXERCISES

A Visit **www.hrps.org**, the website for the Human Resource Planning Society (HRPS). Identify and discuss one of the current issues reported on this website.

B Visit **www.ihrim.org/**, the website for the International Association for Human Resource Information Management (IHRIM). This website provides information about HR information management, systems issues, trends, and technology. Identify and discuss one of the current issues reported on this website.

DISCUSSION QUESTIONS

1 Discuss the effects that an impending labour shortage might have on the following three areas of human resource management: selection and placement, employee learning and career development, and compensation and benefits. Which area might be most heavily impacted?

2 In what ways might employers (or managers) and employees (or unions) develop joint cooperative programs to avert a labour shortage?

3 Discuss the costs and benefits associated with statistical versus judgmental forecasts for labour demand and labour supply. Under what conditions might either of these techniques be infeasible? Under what conditions might both be feasible, but one more desirable than the other?

4 Some argue that outsourcing an activity is 'bad' because the activity is no longer a means of distinguishing the firm from competitors. (All competitors can buy the same service from the same provider, so it cannot be a source of competitive advantage.) Is this true? If so, why would a firm outsource any activity?

5 What are some of the major issues related to downsizing? What are some ways to improve the process of downsizing for the employer and employees?
6 Identify and discuss some of the advantages and disadvantages of employee self-service systems.
7 In your view, what are the most useful applications of HRIS?
8 What are the likely challenges or problems for Australian organisations that are considering the use of information technology for human resource management purposes?
9 Does information technology enhance or conflict with the role of human resource managers as strategic business partners?

CASE STUDY

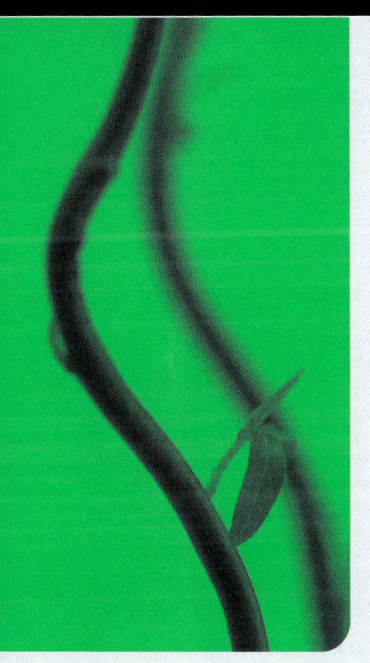

THE TALENT GAME: THREE STEPS TO CHECKMATE

Organisations are increasingly growing the scope of talent management activities in order to handle skill shortages and other changes in the workforce. John Sullivan details three new roles every modern, strategic talent management function must have.

The HR profession is one often perceived by those outside the function as a bureaucratic, compliance-driven, administrative function that is reactive versus proactive and which changes at the speed of a rock.

In most organisations, that perception is well-founded, since most HR processes and policies are developed in response to a significant event and are intended to limit certain behaviours instead of enabling others. HR has become the function known for saying 'you can't do that' as opposed to the function known for saying 'this is how we can accomplish that'. However, a few leading organisations are breaking with tradition—at least when it comes to talent management—establishing new functional structures that account for current labour market realities, and adding proactive initiatives to the stable of HR services.

A growing number of organisations are leveraging the prominence of the impending talent shortage/crisis for corporate leaders. They are growing the scope of talent management activities to include formalised processes, programs and departments focusing on proactive management of employment brand, retention and workforce planning. These groundbreaking organisations are tearing down massive walls that years of political infighting between HR functions have created in order to develop entirely new HR structures. Within these structures all deliverables are integrated to strategically manage the portfolio of talent that the organisation can use to achieve both short- and long-term objectives.

No longer does the training and development function devise and offer training programs for skill sets that can more readily be acquired through recruitment at a lower cost. No longer do key employees leave the organisation because a bad manager kept them from advancing or learning. No longer do offers made to top candidates get rejected because compensation cannot adequately assess the market value of talent. Sounds too good to be true? It isn't, but getting there isn't easy; lots of archaic thinking gets in the way.

Driving change: three new roles defined

While breaking down the barriers between the existing HR functions that impact talent management is in itself a profound success, leading organisations are also formalising a number of proactive activities that add true strategic power to talent management.

By creating a formal workforce planning role, organisations are empowering staffing departments, training departments and operations departments to take the guesswork out of how it will happen. They are managing using robust forecasts that scientifically demonstrate the correlation between workforce utilisation/composition and organisational capability and capacity.

To further support strategic talent management, workforce planning is coming online with two other proactive roles. Employment branding is becoming more mainstream as organisations recognise the need to make themselves more visible and attractive to top talent as well as motivating existing employees. Retention efforts are formalising not just to stave off the need for hard-to-find replacement talent but also to support knowledge management and knowledge transfer between several generations of talent. Each of these new roles is outlined here.

Vice president/director/manager of workforce planning

This role will be responsible for developing systems that ensure the organisation has an adequate supply of talent to support planned business objectives in both existing and

new markets. Note the emphasis here is not to run statistics and create reports, but rather to ensure an adequate supply of talent. Specific responsibilities for this role include:
- Overseeing the creation and management of all strategic HR goals, management practices, organisational policies, and talent management systems to ensure the organisation has the capability and capacity to secure an adequate workforce when needed.
- Participating in organisation-wide strategic planning and operations planning sessions to provide input on workforce-related touch points.
- Projecting the organisation's supply and demand for talent on a moving one, three or five year basis (timing dependent upon industry).
- Identifying gaps in projected supply and demand for talent and developing strategic and tactical plans to acquire the labour needed to meet objectives.
- Marshalling the cooperation and integration of HR deliverables.
- Establishing and maintaining the business case for organisational change needed to retain a position as the employer of choice among key internal and external talent constituencies.
- Analysing data from all internal functions to determine the relationship between talent availability or utilisation and productivity, or the occurrence of 'sentinel events', or unforeseen serious problems.

Vice president/director/manager of employment branding

This role will be responsible for developing systems that identify and manage how the organisation is perceived both internally and externally to ensure that the organisation develops and maintains a dominant position in relevant labour markets as the employer of choice. Note that the emphasis of this new role is not on employment advertising but on understanding and managing perception among key constituents. Specific responsibilities for this role include:
- Developing and implementing an employment branding strategy that ensures key constituents continue to perceive the organisation as an employer of choice, thereby simplifying talent retention, motivation, and attraction.
- Marshalling internal management practices and people programs to ensure that the employment experience delivered is one capable of sustaining projected talent needs.
- Overseeing the creation and integration of employment branding messages in all public relations, media relations, marketing communications, community relations, special events and recruitment advertising campaigns.
- Identifying and developing storylines around company management practices that can be repeated internally and externally through employee referral campaigns and public speeches by executives/managers, news stories and select awards program applications.
- Periodically assessing employment brand internally and externally to ensure alignment between current strategy and labour market conditions.
- Establishing and maintaining the business case for organisational change needed to develop the required employment brand.

Vice president/director/manager of retention

This role will be responsible for developing systems that identify mission-critical talent stores within the organisation and a stable of tools and approaches that can be used on a one-to-one basis to retain them. Note the emphasis here is not to develop organisation-wide approaches that treat employees equally. Rather it is to provide differentiated treatment to top performers in key roles that have been characterised as critical to the success/failure of organisational objectives. Specific responsibilities for this role include:
- Overseeing the development and implementation of talent management methodologies to identify mission-critical roles within the organisation based on objective assessment versus speculation.
- Overseeing the creation and deployment of tools and approaches on a case-by-case basis to ensure the retention of key employees.
- Analysing internal data from all functions to identify relationships between organisational practices/events and turnover.
- Developing and administering knowledge management and transition processes for planned turnover.
- Developing and maintaining systems that monitor and report on managers' abilities to develop and retain top performers.
- Establishing and maintaining the business case for organisational change needed to drive retention efforts.

Conclusion

It's a brave new world—one with few barriers to competition, which is why barriers to strategic talent management must be removed. Existing barriers include isolated HR functions, lack of strategic mindset and lack of infrastructure to power true strategic talent management. Removing these barriers isn't easy, but is a necessity for survival in a global economy. Many professionals in HR are not adequately equipped and will not survive in a modern HR function. Organisations cannot let those incapable of transitioning become barriers themselves.

It is time to step up to the plate. It is time to embrace new proactive activities. It is time to stop talking about being strategic and actually be strategic. Enjoy the future—it's your turn to be the corporate hero.

Source: J. Sullivan, 2006, 'The talent game: three steps to checkmate', *Human Resources*, 16 May, pp. 18–19. www.humanresourcesmagazine.com.au

QUESTION

Do you believe there is a need for organisations to introduce roles such as 'Vice president/director/manager of workforce planning', 'Vice President/director/manager of employment branding', and Vice president/director/manager of retention'. Why?

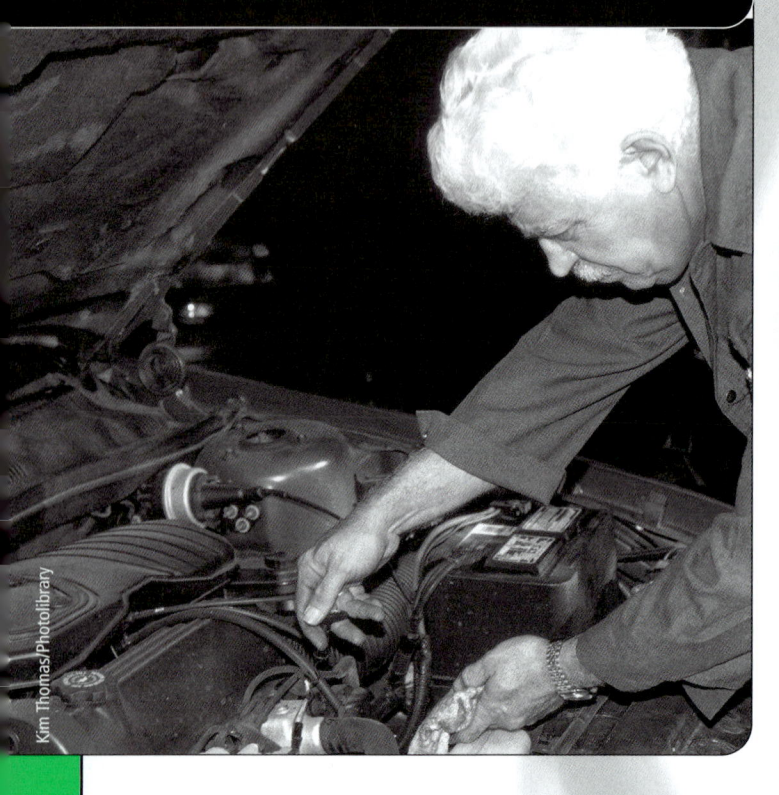

CHAPTER 8
RECRUITMENT AND SELECTION

Objectives

After reading this chapter, you should be able to:

1. Describe the various recruitment policies that organisations adopt to make job vacancies more attractive.

2. List the various sources from which job applicants can be drawn, their relative advantages and disadvantages, and the methods for evaluating them.

3. Explain the recruiter's role in the recruitment process, the limits the recruiter faces and the opportunities available.

4. Establish the basic scientific properties of personnel selection methods, including reliability, validity and generalisability.

5. Discuss how the particular characteristics of a job, organisation or applicant affect the utility of any test.

6. List the common methods used in selecting human resources.

7. Describe the degree to which each of the common methods used in selecting human resources meets the demands of reliability, validity, generalisability, utility and legality.

Guerilla tactics in the war for talent

With good staff hard to find, some companies are getting downright dirty, Fiona Smith writes.

Have you noticed staff contact lists have been removed from company websites? And receptionists are getting cagey when you don't know the name of the person you want to talk to?

This is the first defence against guerilla recruiting—the poaching of staff using underhand or sneaky means.

In the United States this aggressive style of recruiting is well established, with some companies taking the 'war for talent' marketing slogan rather too literally.

Well-publicised examples include one confectionary company invading a competitor's conference by hiring a room across the foyer, putting up a similar banner and getting contact details from all the staff who mistakenly wandered in.

An insurance firm in the US videoed a company's car park and contacted the drivers through a state motor-vehicle database.

IT companies have been involved in frequent skirmishes over staff. In the mid-1990s, Cisco set up shop in Raleigh, North Carolina, across the road from IBM to recruit staff. Nortel and Marconi Communications have had people shoulder sandwich boards to promote their company outside their rivals' premises.

The expert on this style of recruiting is John Sullivan, professor of management at San Francisco State University.

'It is a no-holds style of recruiting where every weakness of a competitor is identified and exploited using minimal, yet highly focused efforts', he wrote in an article last month.

'Guerilla recruiting is about hiring to hurt, about knowingly and purposely inflicting harm on a competitor's ability to do business.'

This kind of approach is frowned upon by the recruitment industry in Australia, but employers and recruiters are certainly having to become more inventive in their attempts to seek out and secure the right sort of talent.

Recruitment companies are going to great lengths to identify good people in skill-short markets, keeping in constant contact in case they can be persuaded to move.

If employers cannot throw enough money to lure someone away from a competitor, they are heading overseas on mass recruiting drives.

On the other hand, companies are also putting in place defensive strategies to keep the people they have—trying to block calls from recruiters, make their workplaces as attractive as possible and bringing their hiring process back in-house using a partnership with a recruitment company.

The president of the Recruitment & Consulting Services Association, Julie Mills, says recruiters are morphing into career consultants, in constant touch with employees they have placed to see whether they are ready to move again or are unhappy with the job.

People are starting to use their recruiter in the same way they might talk to their financial planner on a regular basis.

'Once you've got a person you have put into a role, at a senior end, it is a matter of maintaining that contact so that the minute they feel like shifting, you are the first person they call. Once upon a time, that never happened. The contract was over.

'Because some of those people are a great connection, and people don't stay in a job for 10 years any more, once you have found a really good person, you keep them on your radar.'

The new mobility of the workforce has been a boon for recruitment companies, who can earn 15 to 30 per cent of a person's annual salary each time they place them in a job.

Recruiters are also adopting some headhunter techniques to identify people who may not be looking for a job, but could be persuaded to move.

This involves doing a 'search', which may mean scouring old university graduation lists for leads, trawling through the Internet and newspapers for

Guerilla tactics in the war for talent *continued*

names and getting referrals from others in the industry.

Once, this kind of work was done only for very senior roles with salaries of more than $250 000. Now these searches are being done to fill roles paying $90 000 or more, says the managing director of Chandler Macleod, Stephen Cartwright.

'This may not sound significant, but in the recruitment industry it is a major shift', Cartwright says.

'We are doing searches on an almost daily basis now.'

At Hays Specialist Recruitment, Darren Buchanan, senior regional director, Queensland, says employers who were once content to source staff in Australia are now sending groups of executives overseas 'on spec' to interview people who might be persuaded to come and work for the company in Australia.

About fifty companies in Australia have decided to take back the ownership of their hiring with the help of an outsource recruitment company.

High on their list of priorities is making sure the information gathered about potential hires stays with them and is not passed on to a competitor, says the managing director of Staff & Exec, Sue Healy.

'It would probably be one of the top five considerations for them. Others are better outcomes, getting better quality of hires, better consistency in the recruitment process, and stronger management of the employer brand', she says.

Aside from gathering intelligence through the searching process, Staff & Exec runs in-house referral programs, where clients' staff are offered rewards (anything from a $250 gift voucher to a payment of $4000) for helping recruit a contact.

Specialisation is the way human resources company Hudson tries to keep ahead of the pack. It hires its own staff directly out of the markets it is recruiting for, so, for example, lawyers recruit lawyers.

Hudson executive general manager, Victoria, Andrew Staite, says there is no doubt the ground has shifted, but recruitment companies that have a deep knowledge of their sectors have no need to use guerilla tactics.

'Some of those things are lacking in integrity, bordering on dishonesty', he says. 'I think if you really understand your market, you shouldn't have to undertake those really "out there" attempts to identify people.'

'You will get there by really knowing those markets and the people in the markets.'

'You might be a person who recruits CFOs within a consumer section in Victoria and you need to know every single person who is operating as a CFO or one step off a CFO.'

'So many industries are skills short. If you use the traditional sourcing methods, you are actually only coming up with a small pool of people who are active at any point in the market.'

Battle stations

What to do when a rival poaches your staff:

1. Have your CEO call theirs and ask for co-operation.
2. Counter their spin with stories from their disgruntled former staff.
3. Block access to organisational charts and phone lists.
4. Screen out headhunter calls.
5. Ask staff not to put their business cards in bowls at conferences.
6. Send loyal employees to an interview to see what the rival is offering.
7. Identify your key opinion leaders to talk your company up and the rival down.
8. Encourage weak performers to join the rival.
9. Offer bonuses to those who stay.
10. Offer a bonus if leavers return within three months.

Source: Dr John Sullivan

Source: F. Smith, 2006, 'Guerilla tactics in the war for talent', *Australian Financial Review*, 13 June 2006, p. 68. © 2006 Copyright John Fairfax Holdings Limited. www.afr.com.

Introduction

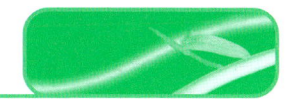

As the preceding article suggests, there are substantial changes and developments in the workplace and in the available technology, and these have significant implications, including ethical concerns, for the way organisations recruit and manage human resources. The developments in globalisation, technology and workforce characteristics present important challenges for human resource management, particularly with regard to staffing, which includes recruiting and selecting employees.

In the first part of this chapter, we familiarise you with the recruitment process, in which individuals find and choose jobs. Personnel recruitment strategies play an important role in enabling employers to reach these individuals and shape their choices. Recruitment serves to create a buffer between planning and actual selection of new employees, which is the topic of the second half of the chapter.

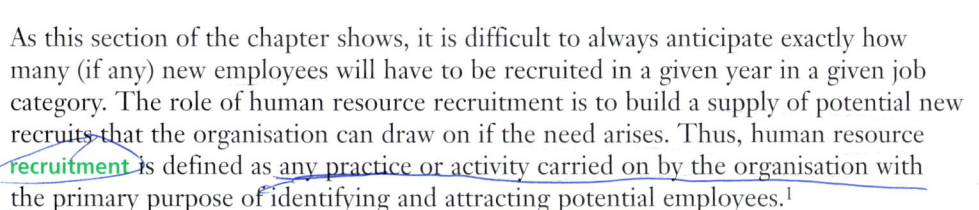

The human resource recruitment process

As this section of the chapter shows, it is difficult to always anticipate exactly how many (if any) new employees will have to be recruited in a given year in a given job category. The role of human resource recruitment is to build a supply of potential new recruits that the organisation can draw on if the need arises. Thus, human resource recruitment is defined as any practice or activity carried on by the organisation with the primary purpose of identifying and attracting potential employees.[1]

Recruitment has many implications for organisations and individuals. Many organisations are dealing with skills shortages and difficulties in attracting and retaining talent. It could be said that every business has some key people, skills or knowledge capital that cannot be easily replaced. In the current environment, individuals are increasingly aware of the expectations they hold of their employment. The advantage is that people are more likely to enter an employment relationship with a clear idea of what is expected of them and what they will gain. However, a disadvantage is that, if employees' expectations are not met, commitment to an organisation, and therefore retention of employment, is unlikely to be sustained (also see Chapter 17).[2]

Recruitment activities are designed to affect: (1) the number of people who apply for vacancies, (2) the type of people who apply for them, and/or (3) the likelihood that those applying for vacancies will accept positions they are offered.[3] The goal of an organisational recruitment program is to ensure that the organisation has a number of reasonably qualified applicants (who would find the job acceptable) to choose from when a vacancy occurs.

The goal of recruiting is not simply to generate large numbers of applicants. If the process generates a sea of unqualified applicants, the organisation will incur great expense in personnel selection (as discussed more fully later in this chapter), but few vacancies will actually be filled.

Further, the goal of recruitment is not to finely discriminate among reasonably qualified applicants. Recruiting new personnel and selecting new personnel are both complex processes. Each task is hard enough to accomplish successfully—even when an individual is well focused. Organisations that explicitly try to do both at the same time, will probably do neither well. For example, research suggests that recruiters provide less information about the company when conducting dual-purpose interviews (interviews focused on both recruiting and selecting applicants).[4]

Recruitment
any practice or activity carried out by the organisation with the primary purpose of identifying and attracting potential employees.

Apparently, applicants also remember less information about the recruiting organisation after dual-purpose interviews.[5]

The importance assigned to recruitment may differ because of strategic differences among companies (see Chapter 2 Strategic human resource management).[6] In general, however, as shown in Figure 8.1 below, all companies have to make decisions in three areas of recruiting: (1) human resource policies that affect the types of jobs the company has to offer, (2) recruitment sources used to solicit applicants, which affect the kinds of people who apply, and (3) the characteristics and behaviours of the recruiter, which affect the perceived fit between the applicant and the job.

Human resource policies

Human resource policies are the organisational decisions that affect the practices and systems that, in turn, influence employees' behaviour, attitudes and performances—thus, affecting the nature of the vacancies for which people are recruited. The research on recruitment makes it clear that characteristics of the vacancy are more important than recruiters or recruiting sources when it comes to predicting job choice.[7]

Human resource policies organisational decisions that affect the practices and systems that, in turn, influence employees' behaviour, attitudes and performances.

Internal versus external recruiting

One desirable feature of a vacancy is that it provides ample opportunity for advancement and promotion. One organisational policy that affects this is the degree to which the company promotes from within—that is, recruits for upper-level vacancies internally rather than externally.

We discuss internal versus external recruiting both here and in 'recruitment sources' later in this chapter, because this policy affects the nature of both the job and the individuals who apply. For now, we will focus on the effects that 'promote-from-within' policies have on job characteristics—noting that such policies make it clear to applicants that there are opportunities for advancement within the company. These opportunities not only spring from the first vacancy, but from the vacancy created when a person in the company fills that vacancy. For example, in a company with three levels of management, a vacancy at the top level that is filled from within may 'trickle down', creating a vacancy at the second level; this, in turn, creates a vacancy at the first level.

FIGURE 8.1 Overview of the individual job choice–organisational recruitment process

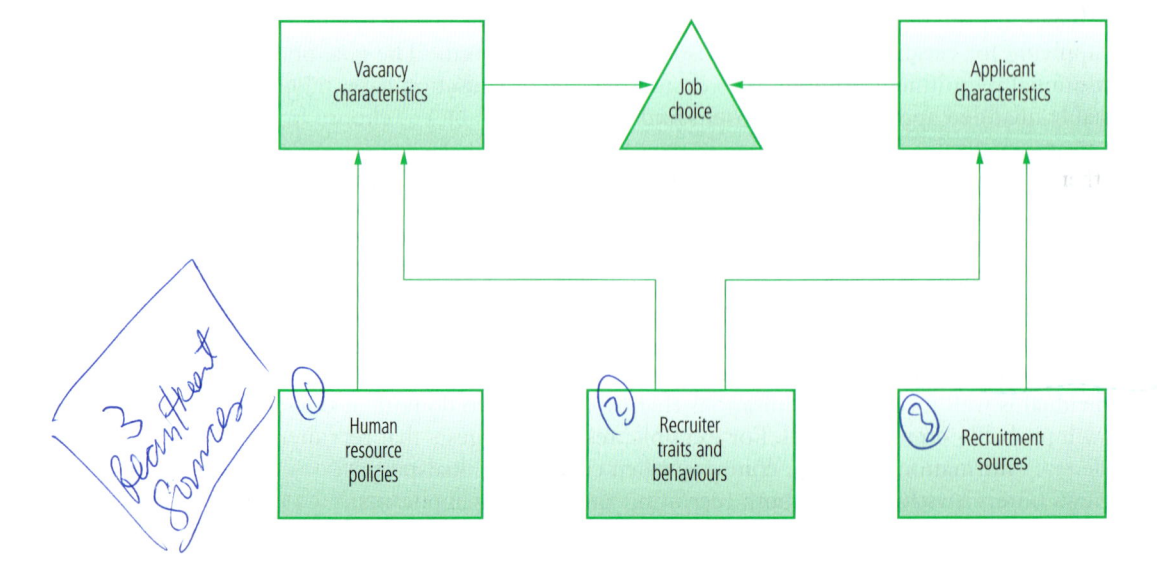

Lead-the-market pay strategies

Companies that take a *lead-the-market approach* to pay—that is, a policy of paying higher-than-current market wages—have a distinct advantage in recruiting, because pay is an important job characteristic for almost all applicants. Pay can also be used to make up for a job's less desirable features—for example, paying higher wages to employees who have to work midnight shifts. These kinds of specific shift differentials and other forms of more generic compensating differentials will be discussed in more detail in later chapters that focus on compensation strategies. We merely note here that 'lead' policies make any given vacancy appear more attractive to applicants.

Organisations that compete for applicants based on pay, increasingly do so using forms of pay other than wages and salaries. For example, employers may use signing bonuses rather than higher wages to attract new recruits, or they may provide lucrative stock option plans.[8] Bonuses and stock options are preferable for many employers because, unlike wages and salaries, they tend not to compound over time and they can be administered more flexibly.

Image advertising

Organisations often advertise specific vacancies—discussed later in 'recruitment sources'. Sometimes, however, organisations advertise in order to promote themselves as a good place to work in general.[9] Image advertising is particularly important for companies in highly competitive labour markets that perceive themselves as having a 'bad' image.[10]

The challenge and responsibility associated with a job is an attractive characteristic for many people. The Australian Army's recent recruitment campaign has pursued this objective. These advertisements focused on the challenge associated with army jobs and positive aspects, such as the opportunity to pursue university studies with the support of your employer.

Although such programs try to promote the employer in the labour market, in general, other image advertising programs target specific groups within the overall labour market.

Emerging recruitment strategies

There is growing recognition that salary is not viewed by HR managers as a highly effective recruitment strategy for talented staff, because job candidates who are motivated only by money are likely to stay with an organisation for only a short time. High turnover can limit the firm's return on their investment in an employee. According to AT Kearney, an executive search consultancy, Australian organisations are following the lead of firms in the United States and exploring new strategies to attract recruits. For example, an emerging trend is for firms to customise, or build, a job to suit the candidate. A recruitment approach used by one Australian company was 'to track a number of outstanding executives on an ongoing basis to establish a relationship with them before offering employment opportunities'.[11] Some organisations maintain 'alumni groups' in order to maintain contact with former employees in case they may wish to return to the firm.[12] As shown in 'Managing challenges of globalisation: Workers of the world take flight', staff shortages present substantial challenges for many organisations, requiring innovative approaches such as international recruitment.

Recruitment sources

The sources from which a company recruits potential employees are a critical aspect of its overall recruitment strategy. The total labour market is expansive; any single organisation needs to draw from only a fraction of that total. The size and nature of

WORKERS OF THE WORLD TAKE FLIGHT

Staff shortages are dire in some professions, and small businesses are being forced to recruit from overseas.

The skills shortage is leaving businesses small and starving. Growth is stalling because there are not enough workers to finish projects; apprenticeships and workers from interstate are not filling the gaps. Bringing workers in from overseas was once considered too expensive for small-business owners. Many now say it is their only choice.

The project manager at the aircraft maintenance company Airflite, Kristian Constantinides, says: 'The shortage is dire. We have been advertising these jobs in Australia for over 12 months. We've just signed a big new seven-year contract, and to complete the work we need another 52 staff. That is just an impossible quota to fill in Australia at the moment.'

Airflite was forced to look for workers overseas. Constantinides spent more than $20 000 interviewing aviation technicians in Britain and Singapore in February and getting approval from the Department of Immigration and Multicultural Affairs (DIMA). He has since sponsored 10 workers and plans to sponsor another 15 over the next two years.

More than 20 per cent of Australian business owners are actively looking for staff overseas, according to a survey released in May by the recruitment firm talent2, and DIMA reports that its skilled migration program has never been so popular. Employer-sponsored migration increased markedly in the last few years.

The labour shortage is expected to worsen as the economy grows and demand rises. With an unemployment rate of 5.1 per cent, Australia is already close to full employment. The problem is particularly acute in Western Australia, where profit-rich resources companies are luring small-business workers from the regions with big money.

Constantinides says: 'If we train people up as apprentices, within three to six months they are approached by one of the big mining firms. They get this spiel from the miners who offer them twice the pay. It is impossible to grow our skill base.'

The scarcity is not restricted to mining and construction. Eighty professions in WA are critically short of workers, according to DIMA. These include hairdressers, chefs and plumbers. Child-care workers, registered nurses, engineers, vehicle tradespeople, electrical tradespeople, food tradespeople and wood tradespeople are also thin on the ground, according to the Department of Employment and Workplace Relations.

George Etrelezis, the managing director of Western Australia's Small Business Development Corporation, says because of the resources boom, most professions are short of workers.

'One owner of a plumbing business in Port Hedland had to fly a worker in from Perth to get a job done. Add the cost of the flight and the worker's accommodation and you get a sense of how desperate people are over here', Etrelezis says.

Assyl Haidar, the chief executive of LIVEINAustralia, a recruitment firm that helps Australian employers find employees overseas, says: 'Recruiting overseas is a new trend, but it is born out of necessity. It is a tough and expensive process.'

It can take employers up to six months to get approval from DIMA, and another three months to sponsor an employee. It is likely to cost more than $30 000 by the time the first employee arrives. 'It is really up to the employer to make the process work', Haidar says.

Getting the paperwork right is the first challenge. Constantinides had three ways of hiring skilled migrants: sponsoring individuals directly; using state government-sponsored migrants; or employing those with working visas already approved.

To get DIMA's support, companies need to prove that they are not offering overseas workers jobs that could be filled by Australians. Constantinides had to show that Airflite had done its best to train an internal employee for the job, that it had spent thousands training apprentices, and that attempts to recruit locally and interstate failed to fill the gap.

So far, most Australian companies have hired workers from culturally similar countries, which has minimised the challenges. But a growing number of employers are turning to countries with huge workforces, such as India or those closer to home in Asia.

Haidar warns that assimilation into the community and the workforce can be difficult. He says employers must be prepared to spend money on human resources and training programs before hiring employees in countries with more extreme cultural differences.

The executive director of the Minerals Council of Australia in Victoria, Chris Fraser, urges employers to spend more on developing training programs that will assist skilled migrants from non-English-speaking countries.

'We have to be smarter about recruitment. We are a part of a global industry; a globalised workforce makes sense. We will face a crisis if we don't embrace this as a possible solution,' Fraser says.

Source: Excerpt from K. Le Mesurier, 2006, 'Workers of the world take flight', *BRW*, 29 June 2006, p. 60. © 2006 Copyright John Fairfax Holdings Limited. www.brw.com.au.

the fraction that applies for an organisation's vacancies will be affected by how (and to whom) the organisation communicates its vacancies.[13] The type of person who is likely to respond to a job advertised on the Internet may be different from the type of person who responds to an advertisement in the classifieds section of the newspaper. In this section, we examine the different sources from which recruits can be drawn, highlighting the advantages and disadvantages of each.

Internal versus external sources

We discussed internal versus external sources of recruits earlier in this chapter and focused on the positive effects that internal recruiting can have on recruits' perceptions of job characteristics. We will now discuss this issue again, but with a focus on how using internal sources affects the kinds of people who are recruited.

In general, relying on internal sources offers a company several advantages.[14] First, it generates a sample of applicants who are well known to the firm. Second, these applicants are relatively knowledgeable about the company's vacancies, which minimises the possibility of inflated expectations about the job. Third, it is generally cheaper and faster to fill vacancies internally.

With all these advantages, you might ask why any organisation would ever employ external recruiting methods. There are several good reasons why organisations might decide to recruit externally.[15] First, for entry-level positions and perhaps for some specialised upper-level positions, there may not be any internal recruits from which to draw. Second, bringing in outsiders may expose the organisation to new ideas or new ways of doing business. Using only internal recruitment can result in a workforce whose members all think alike and who, therefore, may be poorly suited to innovation.[16]

Direct applicants and referrals

Direct applicants are people who apply for a vacancy without prompting from the organisation. **Referrals** are people who are prompted to apply by someone within the organisation. These two sources of recruits share some characteristics that make them excellent sources from which to draw. Many direct applicants are to some extent already 'sold' on the organisation. Most of them have done some homework and concluded that there is enough fit between themselves and the vacancy to warrant their submitting an application. This process is called *self-selection*. When it works effectively, it takes a great deal of pressure off the organisation's recruiting and selection systems. A form of aided self-selection occurs with referrals. Current employees (who are knowledgeable of both the vacancy and the person they are referring) do their homework and conclude that there is a fit between the person and the vacancy; they then sell the person on the job. Indeed, research shows that new recruits who used at least one informal source reported having greater pre-employment knowledge of the organisation than those who relied exclusively on formal recruitment sources. Those who reported having multiple sources were even better, however, in terms of both pre-employment knowledge about the position and subsequent turnover. In fact, the turnover rate for applicants who came from multiple recruiting sources was half that of those recruited via campus interviews or newspaper advertisements.[17]

Factoring into these results the low costs of such sources, they clearly stand out as some of the best sources of new recruits. Indeed, some employers even offer financial incentives to current employees for referring applicants who are accepted and perform satisfactorily on the job (for example, if they stay for at least 180 days).[18] Other companies emphasise their good reputations in the labour market to generate direct applications. Of course, referrals do not necessarily have to come from current

Direct applicants
people who apply for a job vacancy without prompting from the organisation.

Referrals
people who are prompted to apply for a job by someone within the organisation.

employees. The importance of good community relations to recruitment can be seen in the experience of several companies.

Advertisements in newspapers and periodicals

Advertisements to recruit personnel are ubiquitous, although they typically generate less desirable recruits than direct applications or referrals—and do so at greater expense. However, since few employers can fill all their vacancies with direct applications and referrals, some form of advertising is usually needed. Moreover, an employer can take many steps to increase the effectiveness of this recruitment method.

The two most important questions to ask in designing a job advertisement are: 'What do we need to say?' and 'To whom do we need to say it?' With respect to the first question, many organisations fail to adequately communicate the specifics of the vacancy. Ideally, people reading an advertisement should get enough information to evaluate the job and its requirements, allowing them to make a well-informed judgment regarding their qualifications. This could mean running long advertisements, which cost more. However, these additional costs should be evaluated against the costs of processing a huge number of applicants who are not reasonably qualified or who would not find the job acceptable once they learn more about it.

In terms of whom to reach with this message, the organisation placing the advertisement has to decide which medium it will use. The classifieds section of newspapers is the most common medium. It is a relatively inexpensive means of reaching a large number of people within a specified geographic area who are currently looking for work (or at least interested enough to be reading the classifieds). On the downside, this medium does not allow an organisation to target skill levels well. Typically, classified advertisements are read by many people who are either over- or under-qualified for the position. Moreover, people who are not looking for work rarely read the classifieds and, thus, this is not the right medium for luring people away from their current employers. Specially targeted journals and periodicals may be better than general newspapers at reaching a specific part of the overall labour market. In addition, employers are increasingly using television and the Internet as reasonably priced ways of reaching people.[19] The use of Internet recruitment has increased rapidly in the last few years.

Internet recruitment

Internet recruitment may be defined as any method of attracting job applicants that relies on the Internet. It allows employers to conduct searches that are widely distributed geographically, without ever leaving the home office. Within the past few years, the use of the Internet and web-based technology to recruit employees has expanded a great deal, as shown in the examples in 'Managing challenges through HR innovation: Putting the IT in recruitment'). At present, it appears that large firms have some advantage because they are more likely than smaller firms to have their own website and to use Internet recruitment, as the use of the Internet becomes more widespread. However, this gap may be closing.[20]

According to Lievens and Harris,[21] there are five major implications of Internet recruiting. First, it is assumed that the process of persuading candidates to apply for and accept job offers is as important as the employer's selection process. The use of Internet recruitment has increased awareness of recruitment as a marketing exercise for the firm. Second, it is assumed that the Internet makes an individual's job search easier and faster, as submitting one's resumé by email is quicker than a more traditional job search process, such as responding to newspaper advertisements. Third, job searchers can obtain valuable information about potential employers via the Internet, using libraries, chatrooms, or electronic bulletin boards (see www.vault.com).

Internet recruitment any method of attracting job applicants that relies on the Internet.

Fourth, websites are designed with the aim of attracting and retaining the interests of individuals; it is assumed that job searchers will return to the company's website each time they seek a new job. Fifth, it is often assumed that Internet recruitment is cheaper and more effective than traditional recruitment approaches, although there is little evidence to support this assumption.[22] There has been considerable discussion about the advantages and disadvantages of Internet recruitment. For example, advocates of Internet recruitment claim that it attracts a more diverse and highly skilled pool of candidates. However, some research has shown that, while the quantity of applicants may increase, the quality may not.[23] Also, those without access to the Internet will be further disadvantaged.[24]

There is a range of methods for Internet recruitment.[25] For example, many companies include recruitment information on their websites (see www.qantas.com.au or www.bhpbilliton.com). With the introduction of the *Privacy Amendment (Private Sector) Act 2000*, companies that fall under this legislation are unable to retain job applicants' personal information. Therefore, many organisations (for example, The Body Shop) will no longer accept unsolicited electronic applications; they will now only accept applications/resumés for advertised vacancies.[26]

Job boards were one of the first approaches to Internet recruitment. **Job boards** are Internet websites that provide listings of job opportunities and applicants' resumés. For example, News Limited's CareerOne network is a newspaper and website network that includes job advertisements from more than 100 newspapers throughout Australia and lists thousands of jobs online.[27] Some problems have become evident with job boards, due to the sheer volume of material. One disadvantage for recruiters is that many unqualified applicants may submit resumés for a given position, and the processing of these takes time and resources. Such circumstances may reduce the cost savings that might have been anticipated with Internet recruitment.[28]

E-cruitment is an approach that involves the recruiter searching online for job candidates, although the term is often used interchangeably with the more general term, 'Internet recruitment'.[29] However, the ethicality and legality of this approach has been questioned, because the e-cruiter seeks out 'passive' job candidates. Many companies utilise 'firewalls' to prevent outsiders gaining access to lists of their employees.[30] (Also see Chapter 3 The legal context for human resource management.)

Relationship recruitment relies on Internet tools to learn about the interests of individuals who visit a company's website, then the individual is approached regarding a job opportunity.[31] The long-term aim is to develop a relationship with that individual that will lead to a position being filled. For example, Futurestep, www.futurestep.com, is an external recruitment service provider that uses tools such as 'multiple sourcing channels', 'validated cultural assessments', and a 'global database' of over one million professionals, to identify potential job candidates.

Other Internet sites and products, such as www.staff-exec.com.au or www.onetest.com.au, focus more on assisting recruiters. Sites such as these aim to provide objective recruitment, development and retention tools and techniques for employers to utilise when making HR decisions.

Another technological innovation in recruiting that eliminates travel requirements, but allows for a more personal meeting between employer and applicant, is videoconferencing.[32] Used mostly for managerial appointments and sometimes for university recruitment, videoconferencing allows applicants and employers to meet each other using 'face-to-face' technology.

Overall, while the Internet has become a useful tool for recruitment in several ways, its effectiveness remains to be fully tested. Internet recruitment should be used in combination with the overall recruitment strategy of a firm.[33]

Job boards
Internet websites that provide listings of job opportunities and applicants' resumés.

E-recruitment
a method of Internet recruitment that involves the recruiter searching online for job candidates. However, the term is increasingly used to refer to the general process of Internet recruitment.

Relationship recruitment
a recruitment method that relies on Internet tools to learn about the interests of individuals who visit a company's website, then the individual is approached regarding a job opportunity.

PUTTING THE IT IN RECRUITMENT

Recruitment utilises large chunks of time, money and paper in many HR departments. Here are two organisations that have used technology solutions to streamline recruitment.

You'd be hard pressed to find two organisations more different than Lion Nathan and the City of Fremantle. Lion Nathan is a manufacturer of well-known brands such as Tooheys and Hahn beers, and Knappstein and Mitchelton wines. It employs over 3000 people in Australia and New Zealand in diverse areas from brewing to corporate functions.

The City of Fremantle is a traditional local government organisation, employing an average of 750 people through the year, but requiring seasonal increases in staff. It operates in a small, defined geographical area south of Perth in a market that is suffering a severe skills shortage. It employs a diverse workforce, last year hiring 145 new employees through 74 advertised vacancies.

Despite their differences, both organisations have moved to electronic recruitment systems, with the same result. HR has emerged from beneath the administrative burden of manual systems and taken up a more strategic role.

The need

'Our very manual system was time consuming, expensive, laborious and very prone to human error. It was a nightmare', says Denise Ford, HR advisor for the City of Fremantle.

At Lion Nathan, Julie Masnick, HR manager in the people and culture team, says that the manual system they had endured until last year 'didn't provide a best practice hiring experience either internally or externally. The manual system was painful.'

The business case

At Lion Nathan, Masnick formed a steering committee including resourcing, IT, line managers (hiring leaders) and the project sponsor—the organisation's Australian HR division.

'When we presented the business case to the executive team, there was some initial hesitation', says Masnick. After in-depth discussion, they did get the buy-in they felt was necessary for the project's success.

The process at the City of Fremantle was less complex. The HR team wrote a business case and presented it to the management group. Approval was obtained, providing that the system was reviewed in 12 months against the expectations presented in the business case.

Vendor selection and management

Both Lion Nathan and the City of Fremantle created a wishlist of recruitment technology requirements. The City of Fremantle found its vendor through the HR manager's industry knowledge.

Lion Nathan sent requests for proposals to six vendors then asked three of them to present their products to the project team, using a range of hiring scenarios.

The role of IT

Although IT at Lion Nathan did not specify or select the solution, Masnick says they were very involved from the beginning. 'I had an outstanding IT project manager who worked with me, reviewing system compatibility, vendor security and integration with other systems', says Masnick.

In contrast, Ford says IT at the City of Fremantle had very little input, needing just one short meeting with the vendor to sort out what they needed.

What does it do?

Both featured organisations use an externally hosted web-based system that required an upfront capital expenditure and an annual licence fee. Lion Nathan allows its 25–30 preferred recruitment suppliers to link into its system.

Fremantle now has downloadable information packs, which significantly reduce mailing costs. There are seven service centres not attached to the main administration block where the CVs used to be sent, so now those hiring managers can view all the applications from their remote locations.

Any downsides?

Apart from a few minor glitches, Masnick can think of no downsides to the recruitment system at Lion Nathan. It paid for itself in the first six months.

However, 30–40 per cent of candidates at the City of Fremantle are either not computer literate or don't have easy access to a computer to make an online application. They scan any paper CVs into the system and send them directly to the hiring manager. Nevertheless, at the 12 month review, they were meeting or exceeding the expectations in the business case.

Source: BigRedSky

Source: Excerpt from T. Russell, 2006, 'Putting the IT in recruitment,' *Human Resources*, 25 July 2006. www.humanresourcesmagazine.com.au

Public employment agencies

In 1997, the Australian Government privatised Australia's employment services and created the Job Network to replace the Commonwealth Employment Service. The Job Network was intended to provide 'cheaper and more effective employment agency services'.[34] The Job Network system falls under the responsibility of the Department of Employment and Workplace Relations (DEWR, www.dewr.gov.au), although much of the infrastructure is coordinated by Centrelink and the Department of Family and Community Services. Job Network employment agencies must comply with the 'Employment Services Code of Practice'.[35] The system requires all Australians on unemployment benefits, estimated by the government to be around 700 000 people, to attend an interview with a Job Network agency and to post a brief version of their resumé on the government's national database of unemployed people.

The Job Network employment agencies aim to ensure that unemployed individuals eventually move from government aid to employer payrolls. Employers can register their job vacancies with the employment office and the agency will attempt to find someone suitable using its inventory of local unemployed individuals. The agency makes referrals to the organisation and these individuals can be interviewed or tested by the employer for potential vacancies.

However, the Job Network system has not been without problems or criticisms. It has been revealed that thousands of job seekers have failed to attend the compulsory interviews.[36] Also, some incidents have shown embarrassing mistakes in the person–job matching process; for example, it was reported in the media that a Tasmanian man was encouraged to apply for a job as a female prostitute.[37]

Private employment agencies

Unlike public agencies, private employment agencies charge the organisation for referrals. Another difference between private and public employment agencies is that one does not have to be unemployed to use a private employment agency.

One special type of private employment agency is the so-called executive search firm (ESF). These agencies are often referred to as 'headhunters' because, unlike the other sources we have examined, they operate almost exclusively with people who are currently employed. For example, Westpac Banking Group uses ESFs to recruit key executive talent, but they do not do so exclusively.[38] Depending on the role, Westpac might advertise, conduct a search, or use a search firm.[39]

Dealing with executive search firms is sometimes a sensitive process because executives may not want to advertise their availability for fear of their current employer's reaction. Thus, ESFs serve as an important confidentiality buffer between the employer and the recruit. Executive search firms are expensive to employ for both direct and indirect reasons. Directly, ESFs often charge one-third to half of the first year's salary of the executive who is eventually placed.[40] Indirectly, employers who use ESFs may need to lure people not from unemployment, but from jobs with which they may be quite satisfied. A company in a growing industry may have to offer as much as 50 per cent more than the executive's current pay to prompt him or her to take the new job.[41]

Universities

Most universities have placement services that seek to help their graduates obtain employment. Indeed, on-campus interviewing is the most important source of recruits for entry-level professional and managerial vacancies.[42] Organisations tend to focus especially on universities that have strong reputations in areas for which they have critical needs (such as chemical engineering or accounting).[43]

Many employers have found that to effectively compete for the best students, they need to do more than sign prospective graduates up for interview slots. One of the best ways to establish a stronger presence on a campus is with a university internship program. These kinds of programs allow an organisation to get early access to potential applicants and to directly assess their capacities.

The *Graduate Destination Survey*[44] is conducted annually in cooperation with all Australian universities. The survey of graduates in 2005 showed that employment opportunities for new bachelor degree graduates are good, with 80.9 per cent of them in full-time employment within four months of completing their studies. In addition, 12.3 per cent were in part-time or casual employment. It is interesting to note that 22.5 per cent of graduates were undertaking further full-time studies.[45]

The median annual starting salary—for those graduating from bachelor degrees in 2005, in their first full-time employment—was $40 000 ($38 000 in 2004; the highest paid graduates are dentists, with a median salary of $65 000).[46]

Graduates have an employment rate that is much better than the general labour force. Table 8.1 shows the employment activities and median salaries for those bachelor degree graduates available for full-time employment in 2005.

Another way for employers to increase their presence on campuses is to participate in university job fairs. In general, a job fair is a place where many employers gather for a short time to meet large numbers of potential job applicants. Although job fairs can be held anywhere (for example, at a hotel or convention centre), campuses are ideal locations because of the easy access for students. Job fairs are a rather inexpensive means of generating an on-campus presence and can also provide one-on-one dialogue with potential recruits—dialogue that could not be achieved through less interactive media like newspaper advertisements. Organisations often send recent recruits (employees recruited from university in the past three years) to represent the firm at such fairs.

Many managers feel that university campuses are one of the best places to search for *transportable talent*—that is, individuals who will be successful both at home and abroad—which is a growing concern. However, as skills shortages in various professions such as nursing increase, and as more organisations attempt to compete on a global level, the ability to recruit on a global scale is increasingly viewed as important, as noted earlier in the 'challenge of globalisation' article. Graduate recruiters are discerning with respect to the skills they seek in potential employees.[47] Tables 8.2 and 8.3 present the views of 127 graduate employers from various industries across Australia and New Zealand, with regard to the required skills of graduates in the workforce. As shown in the 'Managing challenges through sustainability' examples, there is tough competition amongst firms to attract the best and brightest talent. The challenge of attracting talented employees is evident across many industries and in organisations of all sizes.

Evaluating the quality of a source

As there are few rules about the quality of a given source for a given vacancy, it is generally a good idea for employers to monitor the quality of all their recruitment sources. One means of accomplishing this is to develop and compare yield ratios for each source.[48] Yield ratios express the percentage of applicants who successfully move from one stage of the recruitment and selection process to the next. Comparing yield ratios for different sources helps determine which recruitment source is best or most efficient for the type of vacancy being investigated. Cost-per-recruit data is also useful in establishing the efficiency of a given source.

TABLE 8.1 Breakdown of bachelor degree graduates available for full-time employment, by field of education, 2005 (%)

	In full-time employment (%)	Seeking full-time employment, not working (%)	Seeking full-time employment, working part-time or casual (%)	Further full-time study (%)	Median starting salary ($000)
Agriculture	80.3	6.7	13.0	19.4	37.0
Architecture	86.7	6.5	6.7	29.8	31.5
Building	91.0	4.5	4.5	25.0	35.0
Urban & Regional Planning	91.0	3.0	6.0	20.3	41.0
Humanities	70.7	11.1	18.2	34.4	35.0
Languages	74.9	8.3	16.8	40.2	40.0
Visual & Performing Arts	60.3	13.2	26.5	32.7	32.0
Social Sciences	67.2	11.2	21.5	34.2	38.3
Psychology	70.5	10.8	18.7	44.2	38.5
Social Work	80.2	7.6	12.2	8.1	40.0
Business Studies	81.1	6.9	12.1	15.4	37.0
Accounting	86.9	6.7	6.4	11.1	35.5
Economics	86.1	7.3	6.6	32.1	41.0
Education, Initial	77.9	3.8	18.3	6.4	43.0
Education Post/Other	84.3	3.6	12.0	34.7	39.5
Aeronautical Eng	89.1	5.8	5.1	17.1	45.0
Chemical Eng	83.1	9.6	7.3	18.9	45.7
Civil Engineering	95.7	3.0	1.3	6.3	43.0
Electrical Eng	87.3	8.6	4.0	13.2	45.0
Electron/Comp Eng	78.3	11.7	10.0	14.0	43.0
Mechanical Eng	89.5	4.8	5.8	9.4	44.0
Mining Eng	98.8	1.2	0.0	7.5	63.0
Other Eng	86.9	7.7	5.4	17.7	44.0
Surveying	95.4	2.0	2.6	11.5	40.0
Dentistry	95.0	0.8	4.1	10.2	65.0
Health, Other	81.9	4.3	13.8	26.6	40.0
Nursing, Initial	96.2	1.0	2.8	5.3	38.0
Nursing, Post-initial	94.0	1.3	4.6	4.2	38.0
Pharmacy (pre-reg)	98.7	0.9	0.4	17.7	30.0
Medicine	98.3	0.6	1.1	13.1	48.0
Rehabilitation	90.0	3.1	6.8	13.3	41.2
Law	88.4	6.2	5.4	22.6	41.0
Law, Other	84.6	6.1	9.3	17.4	38.0
Computer Science	73.7	13.6	12.7	17.8	39.9
Life Sciences	71.3	9.9	18.9	46.2	38.0
Mathematics	72.6	14.5	12.9	50.7	42.0
Chemistry	84.7	5.1	10.2	55.3	38.0
Physics	78.9	9.0	12.0	50.9	40.0
Geology	87.4	4.2	8.4	39.2	42.0
Veterinary Science	94.0	3.6	2.4	6.7	37.0
Total %	80.9	6.9	12.3	22.5	40.0
Total N	35 858	3051	5438	14 773	

Source: Graduate Careers Council of Australia, 2005, *The Grad Files*, Graduate Careers Council of Australia, Parkville, Victoria, Australia, (Table 2), www.gradlink.edu.au, viewed 15 September 2006.

TABLE 8.2 Top 10 selection criteria for recruiting graduates

Key selection criteria	%
Interpersonal and communication skills (written and oral)	57.5
Academic qualifications	35.4
Work experience	27.6
Leadership skills	18.1
Passion, knowledge of industry, drive, commitment, attitude	15.7
Teamwork skills	15.7
Critical reasoning and analytical skills/problem solving/lateral thinking/technical skills	15.0
Emotional intelligence (including awareness, strength of character, confidence, motivation)	8.7
Activities—includes both intra and extra curricular	7.9
Cultural alignment/values fit	7.9

Source: Graduate Careers Council of Australia, 2005, *The Grad Files*, Graduate Careers Council of Australia, Parkville, Victoria, Australia, (Table 2), www.gradlink.edu.au, viewed 15 September 2006.

TABLE 8.3 10 least desirable characteristics when recruiting graduates

Least desirable characteristics	%
Lack of interpersonal and communication skills (written, oral, listening), lack of leadership skills	40.2
Lack of drive, motivation, enthusiasm and intitiative	25.2
Arrogance, selfishness, aggression, dominating	18.1
Poor teamwork skills	16.5
Poor or inappropriate academic qualifications or results	15.7
Inflexibility/inability to accept direction, challenge or change	11.8
Other	10.2
Poor attitude/lack of work ethic/approach to work	9.4
Lack of emotional intelligence, self-awareness or self-confidence	9.5
Lack of commitment/high absenteeism/lack of loyalty	9.4

Source: Graduate Careers Council of Australia, 2005, *The Grad Files*, Graduate Careers Council of Australia, Parkville, Victoria, Australia, (Table 2), www.gradlink.edu.au, viewed 15 September 2006.

Table 8.4 shows hypothetical yield ratios and cost-per-hire data for four recruitment sources. For the job vacancies generated by this company, the best two sources of recruits are universities and employee referral programs. Newspaper ads generate the largest number of recruits, but relatively few of these are qualified for the position. Finally, executive search firms generate a small list of highly qualified, interested applicants, but this is an expensive source compared with other alternatives.

Recruiters

The last part of the model presented in Figure 8.1 that we will discuss is the recruiter. We consider the recruiter this late in the chapter to reinforce our earlier observation that the recruiter often gets involved late in the process. In many cases, by the time a

TABLE 8.4 Hypothetical yield ratios for four recruitment sources

	Universities	Employee referrals	Newspaper advertisements	Executive search firms
Resumés generated	200	50	500	20
Interview offers accepted	175	45	400	20
Yield ratio	87%	90%	80%	100%
Applicants judged acceptable	100	40	50	19
Yield ratio	57%	89%	12%	95%
Employment offers accept	90	35	25	15
Yield ratio	90%	88%	50%	79%
Cumulative yield ratio	90/200 45%	35/50 70%	25/500 5%	15/20 75%
Cost	$30 000	$15 000	$20 000	$90 000
Cost per hire	$333	$428	$800	$6000

recruiter meets some applicants, the applicants have already made up their minds about what they desire in a job, what the current job has to offer and their likelihood of receiving a job offer.[49]

Moreover, many applicants approach the recruiter with some degree of scepticism. Knowing that it is the recruiter's job to sell them on a vacancy, some applicants may discount what the recruiter says relative to what they have heard from other sources (for example, friends, magazine articles, the Internet or university lecturers). For these and other reasons, recruiters' characteristics and behaviour seem to have less impact on applicants' job choices than we might expect. Moreover, as shown in Figure 8.2, page 273, whatever impact a recruiter does have on an applicant lessens as we move from reaction criteria (that is, how the applicant felt about the recruiter) towards job choice criteria (that is, whether the applicant takes the job).[50]

Recruiter's functional area

Most organisations must choose whether their recruiters are specialists in human resources or experts at particular jobs (for example, supervisors or job incumbents). Some studies indicate that applicants find a job less attractive and the recruiter less credible when he or she is a HR specialist.[51] This does not completely discount the role of HR specialists in recruiting, but it does indicate that such specialists need to take extra steps to ensure that applicants perceive them as knowledgeable and credible.

Recruiter's traits

Two traits stand out when applicants' reactions to recruiters are examined. The first, which could be called 'warmth', reflects the degree to which the recruiter seems to care about the applicant and is enthusiastic about his or her potential to contribute to the company. The second characteristic could be called 'informativeness'. In general, applicants respond more positively to recruiters who are perceived as warm and informative. These characteristics seem more important than demographic characteristics, such as age, sex or race, which have complex and inconsistent effects on applicant responses.[52]

STAYING ONE STEP AHEAD: GRADUATE RECRUITMENT

What they offer

It's a tough market for both graduate recruiters and graduates themselves at present. The 2005 Australasian Graduate Recruitment Benchmarking study, commissioned by the Australian Association of Graduate Employers, revealed an expected 17 per cent increase in overall graduate intake in 2005, compared to 2004.

The study also revealed employers are spending more time planning and budgeting for recruitment drives and devoting more time over longer periods to promotional activities.

Deloitte, Visy and BlueScope Steel are three companies that have recently set up or revamped their graduate recruitment programs. They are responding in different ways to challenges that graduate recruitment presents.

As a professional services provider, Deloitte's list of services covers commerce, economics, business and law. Twelve months ago they set up D.Academy, a three year blended approach to support graduate growth and development. Beyond technical training, graduates participate in business skills development, networking, breakfasts, a mentoring and peer support program and e-learning.

Packaging and recycling specialist, Visy, established its current graduate program two years ago. It recruits electrical and mechanical engineers and rotates them through roles in its pulp and paper mills, providing graduates with role and location diversity.

BlueScope Steel's graduates are recruited into operational roles and undertake formal training designed to provide them with fundamental leadership competencies. They are offered additional support through mentoring and peer partner programs. BlueScope Steel recruits graduate engineers from a variety of backgrounds. Like Visy, it hires graduates into functional support roles such as accounting, IT, finance, HR, logistics and supply.

All three organisations use a variety of means to attract graduates. Visy focuses more on promotion in specific universities as one tactic. It also advertises its benefits online and in print, particularly in career lift-outs in Sydney and Melbourne.

BlueScope Steel visits careers fairs and builds links with universities. It advertises in graduate publications and personalises the experiences of its graduates using profiles on its websites.

Casting the net early and wide

Deloitte recruits undergraduates for its summer vacancies and the benefits are twofold—the graduates have the opportunity to research their decisions regarding their profession and it gives the company the opportunity to identify talented students.

Visy offers third year engineering students a 'sandwich program' where they work on various projects. 'It's a great source of opportunities for students to come in and feel our culture, and a good way to source talent', says Haggar.

Recruitment and the candidate shortage

All three organisations are feeling the candidate shortage, noting the generation Y change in undergraduate expectations and behaviour.

One associated challenge is keeping graduates engaged in the recruitment process, particularly when that process is stringent and lengthy.

Effectiveness and ROI

Visy, Deloitte and BlueScope Steel see their graduate programs as part of their whole recruitment process.

Visy's current graduate program is too new to effectively measure its return on investment. But they regard the program as an essential contribution to the company's future skill base. Every three or four months they employ a development tracking mechanism to share experiences.

Graduate recruitment has been a long-term practice for Deloitte. It's early days of running D.Academy, but feedback has been positive. Summer vacation hire is also effective with 60 per cent of future graduates recruited from the program.

It's too early for BlueScope Steel to fully measure the impact of their current program, but they regard graduate recruitment and development as critical in securing the company's future leadership and talent pipelines.

Source: Excerpt from K. Brown, 2005, 'Staying one step ahead: graduate recruitment', *Human Resources*, 9 August. www.humanresourcesmagazine.com.au

Recruiter's realism

Perhaps the most well-researched aspect of recruiting deals with the level of realism that the recruiter incorporates into his or her message. Since the recruiter's job is to attract candidates, there is some pressure to exaggerate the positive features of the vacancy while downplaying the negative features. Applicants are highly sensitive to

FIGURE 8.2 Relative impact of the recruiter on various recruitment interview outcomes

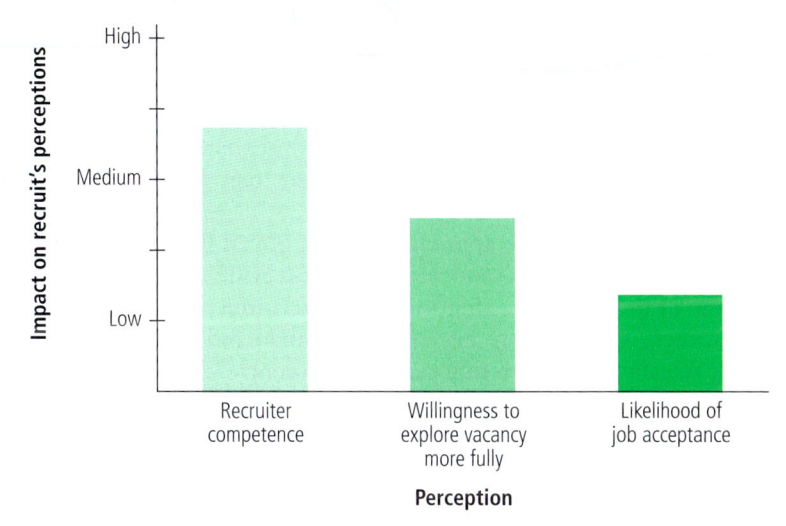

negative information. Research suggests that the highest quality applicants may be less willing to pursue jobs when this type of information is revealed.[53]

On the other hand, if the recruiter goes too far in a positive direction, the candidate can be misled and lured into taking the job under false pretences. This can lead to a serious case of unmet expectations and a high job-turnover rate.[54] In fact, unrealistic descriptions of a job may lead new job incumbents to believe that the employer is deceitful.[55]

Many studies have looked at the capacity of **realistic job previews** (accurate information about the attractive and unattractive aspects of a job, working conditions, company and location, to ensure that potential employees develop appropriate expectations) to circumvent this problem and help minimise early job turnover. On the whole, the research suggests that the effect of realistic job previews on eventual turnover is weak and inconsistent.[56] The idea that one can go overboard in selling a vacancy to a recruit certainly has merit. However, the belief that informing people about the negative characteristics of the job will 'inoculate' them to such characteristics seems unwarranted, based on the research conducted to date.[57] Thus, we return to the conclusion that an organisation's decisions about human resource policies that directly affect the job's attributes (pay, security, advancement opportunities and so on) will probably be more important than recruiter traits and behaviours in affecting job choice.

Enhancing recruiter impact

Although research suggests that recruiters do not have much influence on job choice, this does not mean that recruiters cannot have an impact. While some recruiters are highly skilled, with specialised skills and knowledge, other recruiters receive little training. Recent research has attempted to find conditions in which recruiters do make a difference. Based on this research, an organisation can take several steps to increase the impact that recruiters have on those they recruit.[58]

First, recruiters can provide timely feedback. Applicants react negatively to delays in feedback, often making unwarranted attributions for the delays (for example, the organisation is not interested in my application). Second, recruiters need to avoid behaviours that might convey the wrong organisational impression.[59]

Realistic job preview
accurate information about the attractive and unattractive aspects of a job, working conditions, company and location, to ensure that potential employees develop appropriate expectations.

Table 8.5 below lists quotes from applicants who felt that they had, in the past, extremely 'bad' experiences with recruiters. Third, recruiting can be done in teams rather than by individuals. As we have seen, applicants tend to view line personnel (for example, job incumbents and supervisors) as more credible than HR specialists, so these kinds of recruiters should be part of any team. On the other hand, HR specialists have knowledge that is not shared by line personnel (who may perceive recruiting as a small part of their 'real' job), so they should be included as well.

As an example of an effective approach, IBM, a global firm with over 300 000 employees, has implemented an innovative, business-wide recruitment approach to overcome many of the problems identified with recruitment processes. According to Cheryl Power, recruitment centre manager, Australian and New Zealand staffing, IBM, in order to establish an internal recruitment centre, first developed a business case to convince the IBM leadership team that an internal recruitment centre would improve recruitment processes and remove some of the burden on managers. After gaining commitment from the leadership team, a strategic communications plan was implemented, to inform all managers and employees about the recruitment centre and the introduction of an Internet-based recruitment tool, called 'Best person for the job+' (BPFJ+), for all internal and external candidates seeking employment in IBM. IBM's induction program was also redesigned to ensure a welcome and professional introduction for all new employees. After induction, recruits are allocated mentors and buddies to help them settle into their roles at IBM. A comprehensive graduate recruitment program, which runs for two years, has also been developed. It includes aspects such as mentoring, job rotation, access to skills mentors, and salary reviews. Measurement of results indicate that the new approach has led to a 35 per cent improvement in the time it takes to recruit people into IBM. There has also been a reduction in the company's attrition rate during the first year of employment.[60]

TABLE 8.5 Quotes from recruits who were repelled by recruiters

- 'One firm I didn't think of talking to initially, but they called me and asked me to talk with them. So I did, and then the recruiter was very, very rude. Yes, very rude, and I've run into that a couple of times' (engineering graduate).

- 'I had a very bad campus interview experience ... the person who came was a last-minute fill-in ... I think he had a couple of 'issues' and was very discourteous during the interview. He was one step away from yawning in my face ... The other thing he did was that he kept making these (nothing illegal, mind you) but he kept making these references to the fact that I had been out of my undergraduate and first graduate programs for more than 10 years now' (MBA with 10 years experience).

- '[Company X] has a management training program, which the recruiter had gone through. She was talking about the great presentational skills that [Company X] teaches you, and the woman was barely literate. She was embarrassing. If that was the best they could do, I did not want any part of them. Also, [Company Y] and [Company Z's] recruiters appeared to have real attitude problems. I also thought they were chauvinistic' (arts undergraduate).

- '[Company X] had a set schedule for me which they deviated from regularly. Times overlapped, and one person kept me too long, which pushed the whole day back. They almost seemed to be saying that it was my fault that I was late for the next one! I guess a lot of what they did just wasn't very professional' (industrial relations graduate student).

- 'The guy at the interview made a joke about how nice my nails were and how they were going to ruin them there due to all the tough work' (engineering undergraduate).

Source: Sara L. Rynes, Robert D. Bretz and Barry Gerhart, 1991, 'The importance of recruitment in job choice: a different way of looking', *Personnel Psychology*, 44, pp. 487–522. Used by permission.

Selection

Any organisation that intends to compete through people must take the utmost care with how it chooses organisational members. Employee selection decisions made over the course of an organisation's history are instrumental to its ability to survive, adapt and grow.[61] The competitive aspects of selection decisions become especially critical when organisations are confronted with 'tight' labour markets or when competitors tap the same labour market. If one company systematically skims off the best applicants, the remaining companies must make do with what is left.

The purpose of this section is to familiarise you with ways to minimise errors in employee selection and, in doing so, increase your company's competitive position. First we focus on five standards that should be met by any selection method. We then evaluate several common selection methods according to those standards.

Selection method standards

Employee selection is the process by which companies decide who will or will not be allowed into their organisations. Several generic standards should be met in any selection process. We focus on five: (1) reliability, (2) validity, (3) generalisability, (4) utility and (5) legality. The first four build off each other, in the sense that the preceding standard is often necessary but not sufficient for the one that follows. This is less the case with legal standards. However, a thorough understanding of the first four standards helps us understand the rationale underlying many legal standards.

Reliability

Much of the work in employee selection involves measuring characteristics of people to determine who will be accepted for job openings. For example, we might be interested in applicants' physical characteristics (for example, strength or endurance), their cognitive abilities (for example, mathematical ability or verbal reasoning capacity) or aspects of their personality (for example, their initiative or integrity). Whatever the specific focus, in the end we need to quantify people on these dimensions (that is, assign numbers to them) so we can order them from high to low on the characteristic of interest. Once people are ordered in this way, we can then make decisions about who to recruit and who to reject.

One key standard for any measuring device is its reliability. We define **reliability** as the degree to which a measure is free from random error.[62] If a measure of some supposedly stable characteristic such as intelligence is reliable, then the score a person receives based on that measure will be consistent over time and in different contexts.

- *True scores and the reliability of measurement.* Most of the measuring that occurs in employee selection deals with complex characteristics like intelligence, integrity and leadership ability. However, to appreciate some of the complexities in measuring people, we will consider something concrete in discussing the concepts of true scores and reliability of measurement: the measurement of height. For example, if we were measuring an applicant's height, we might start by using a ruler. Let's say the first person we measure turns out to be 185 cm tall. It would not be surprising to find out that someone else measuring the same person a second time, perhaps an hour later, found this applicant's height to be 184 cm. The same applicant, measured a third time, maybe the next day, might be measured at 186 cm tall.

    As this example makes clear, although the person's height is a stable characteristic, we get slightly different results each time he or she is assessed.

Reliability
the consistency of a performance measure; the degree to which a performance measure is free from random error. One important type of reliability is inter-rater reliability: the consistency among individuals who evaluate the employee's performance.

This means that each time the person is assessed, we must be making slight errors. If a measurement device were perfectly reliable, there would be no errors of measurement. If we used a measure of height that was not as reliable as a ruler—for example, guessing someone's height after seeing that person walk across the room—we might see a great deal of unreliability in the measure. Thus, reliability refers to the measuring instrument (a ruler versus a visual guess), rather than to the characteristic itself.

There is no direct way to capture the 'true' reliability of the measure, because one never really knows the true score for the person being measured. We can estimate reliability in several different ways, however, and since most of these rely on computing a correlation coefficient, we will briefly describe and illustrate this statistic.

The **correlation coefficient** is a measure of the degree to which two sets of numbers are related to each other. The correlation coefficient expresses the strength of the relationship in numerical form. A perfect positive relationship (that is, as one set of numbers goes up, so does the other) equals +1.0; a perfect negative relationship (that is, as one goes up, the other goes down) equals –1.0. When there is no relationship between the sets of numbers, the correlation equals 0.00. Although the actual calculation of this statistic goes beyond the scope of this book (see any introductory statistics book or spreadsheet program), it will be useful for us to conceptually examine the nature of the correlation coefficient and what this means in employee selection contexts.

When assessing the reliability of a measure, for example, we might be interested in knowing how scores on the measure at one time relate to scores on the same measure at another time. Obviously, if the characteristic we are measuring is supposedly stable (like intelligence or integrity) and the time lapse is short, this relationship should be strong. If it were weak, then the measure would be inconsistent—hence, unreliable. This is what is called assessing test–retest reliability.

Plotting the two sets of numbers on a two-dimensional graph often helps us to appreciate the meaning of various levels of the correlation coefficient. Figure 8.3 overleaf, for example, examines the relationship between student scholastic aptitude in one's penultimate year (year 11) and final year (year 12) in secondary school, where aptitude for university may be measured in three ways: (1) via results on assessment tasks, (2) via ratings from a high school counsellor on a one-to-100 scale, and (3) via tossing a dice. In this plot, each X (data point) on the graphs represents a person whose scholastic aptitude is assessed twice (in years 11 and 12), so in Figure 8.3a, X_1 represents a person who obtained a 99 per cent average on assessment tasks in year 11 and a 90 per cent average in year 12; X_{20} represents a person who obtained a 63 per cent average in year 11 and a 68 per cent average in year 12.

Turning first to Figure 8.3a, it is clear that there is a considerably strong relationship between assessment tasks results across the two years. This relationship is not perfect in that the scores changed slightly from one year to the next, but not a great deal. Indeed, if there were a perfect 1.0 correlation, the plot would show a straight line proceeding at a 45-degree angle. The correlation coefficient for this set of data is in the 0.90 range. In this case, this 0.90 is considered the test–retest estimate of reliability.

Turning to Figure 8.3b, we see that the relationship between the secondary school counsellor's ratings across the two years, while still positive, is not as strong. That is, the counsellor's ratings of individual students' aptitudes for university are less consistent over the two years than their test scores. The correlation, and hence test–retest reliability, of this measure of aptitude is in the 0.50 range.

Correlation coefficient
a statistic that measures the degree to which two sets of numbers are related to each other.

Recruitment and Selection CHAPTER 8

Finally, Figure 8.3c shows a worst-case scenario, where the students' aptitudes are assessed by tossing two six-sided dice. As you would expect, the random nature of dice means that there is virtually no relationship between scores taken in one year and scores taken the next. Hence, in this instance, the correlation and

FIGURE 8.3 Measurements of a student's aptitude

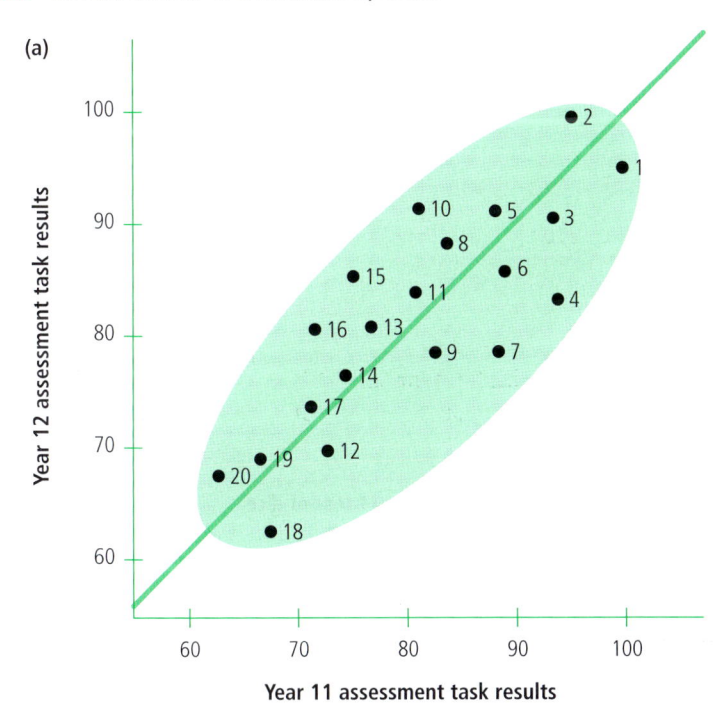

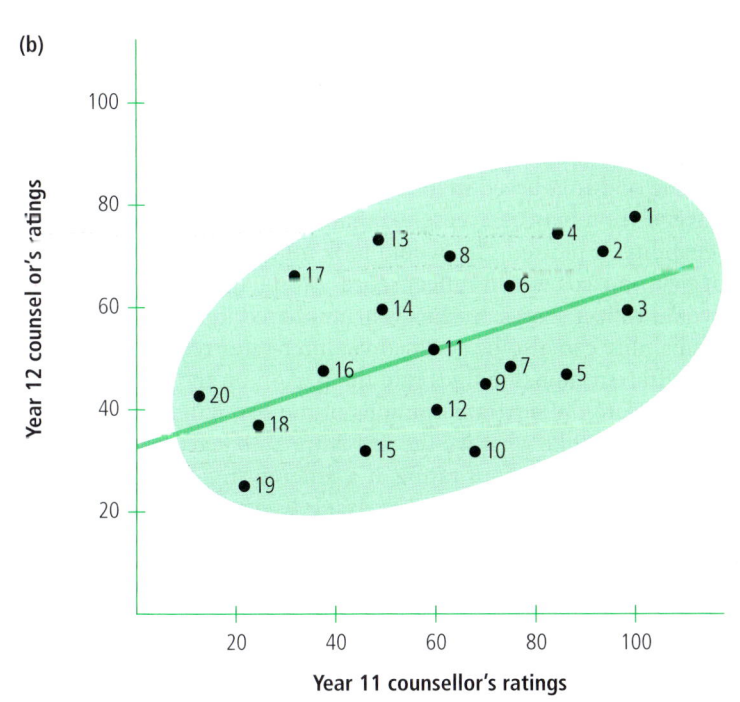

277

FIGURE 8.3 (continued)

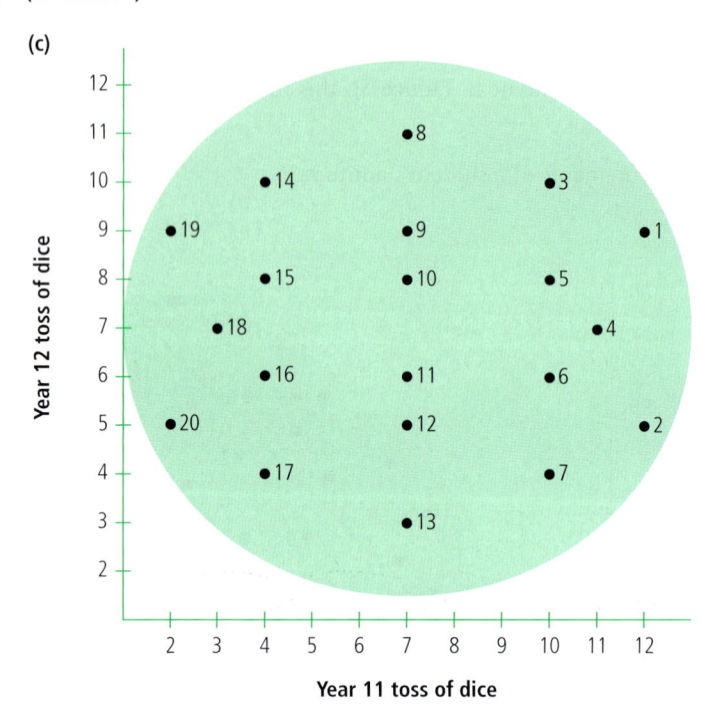

(c)

[Scatter plot showing Year 12 toss of dice (y-axis) vs Year 11 toss of dice (x-axis), with 20 numbered data points scattered randomly within a circular region.]

test–retest estimate of reliability is 0.00. Although no one would seriously consider tossing a dice to be a measure of aptitude, it is worth noting that research shows that overall ratings of job applicants' suitability for jobs based on unstructured interviews is very close to 0.00. Thus, one cannot assume a measure is reliable without actually checking this directly. Novices in measurement are often surprised at exactly how unreliable many human judgments turn out to be.

In addition to test–retest estimates, the consistency of multiple-item tests or scales can be assessed via split-half reliability estimates. For example, the assessment tasks may include a mathematics test that has hundreds of questions. Via this method, one could take this test and break it up into two tests: one consisting of the odd-numbered items and one consisting of the even-numbered items. The correlation between these two halves of the test is referred to as the split-half reliability. If plotted, this would look much like what we see in Figure 8.3a, except that one axis would reflect scores on the odd-numbered items and the other axis would reflect scores on the even-numbered items.

Finally, reliability can also be assessed via inter-rater reliability estimates. In this method, two different human judges rate the person on the dimension of interest and we then correlate the separate opinions of the two judges. If plotted, this would look very much like what we see in Figure 8.3b, except the vertical axis would not reflect the counsellor's rating at a different time. Instead, the vertical axis would reflect a different person's (for example, a teacher's) ratings of the student taken at the same time as the counsellor's rating.

- *Standards for reliability*. Regardless of what characteristic we are measuring, we want highly-reliable measures. Thus, in the previous example, when it comes to measuring students' aptitudes for university, assessment task results are more reliable than counsellor ratings, which in turn are more reliable than tossing a dice.

Although, in an absolute sense, how high is high enough—0.50, 0.70 or 0.90? This is a difficult question to answer specifically, because the required reliability depends in part on the nature of the decision being made about the people being measured.

For example, let us assume that a university admissions officer was considering several students depicted in Figures 8.3a and 8.3b. Turning first to Figure 8.3b, assume the admissions officer was deciding between student 1 (X_1) and student 20 (X_{20}). For this decision, the 0.50 reliability of the ratings is high enough because the difference between the two students is so large that one would make the same decision for admission regardless of the year in which the rating was taken. That is, student 1 (with scores of 100 and 78 in years 11 and 12, respectively) is always admitted and student 20 (with scores of 18 and 42 in years 11 and 12, respectively) is always rejected. Thus, although the ratings in this case are not all that reliable in an absolute sense, their reliability is high enough to make this decision.

On the other hand, let us assume the same university admissions officer was deciding between student 1 (X_1) and student 2 (X_2). Looking at Figure 8.3a, it is clear that even with the highly reliable assessment task results, the difference between these students is so small that one would make a different admission decision depending on what year one obtained the results. Student 1 would be selected over student 2 if the year 11 result was used, but student 2 would be chosen over student 1 if the year 12 result was used. Thus, even though the reliability of the assessment task results is high in an absolute sense, it is not high enough to make this decision. Under these conditions, the admissions officer needs to find some other basis for making the decision regarding these two students (for example, some university medical programs use interviews with potential students as part of the selection process).

Although these two scenarios clearly show that no specific value of reliability is always acceptable, they also demonstrate why, all else being equal, the more reliable a measure is, the better. For example, turning again to Figures 8.3a and 8.3b, consider student 9 (X_9) and student 14 (X_{14}). One would not be able to make a decision between these two students based upon scholastic aptitude results if assessed via counsellor ratings, because the unreliability in the ratings is so large that scores across the two years conflict. That is, student 9 has a higher rating than student 14 in year 11, but student 14 has a higher rating than student 9 in year 12.

On the other hand, one would be able to base the decision on scholastic aptitude results if assessed via the assessment task results, because the unreliability of the assessment task results is so low that results across the two years point to the same conclusion. That is, student 9's scores are always higher than student 14's scores. Clearly, all else being equal, the more reliable the measure, the more likely it is that we can base decisions on the differences that it reveals.

Validity

We define validity (often referred to as content validity) as the extent to which a performance measure assesses all the relevant—and only the relevant—aspects of job performance. A measure must be reliable if it is to have any validity. On the other hand, we can reliably measure many characteristics (for example, height) that may have no relationship to whether someone can perform a job. For this reason, reliability is a necessary but insufficient condition for validity.

> **Validity**
> (often referred to as content validity) the extent to which a performance measure assesses all the relevant—and only the relevant—aspects of job performance.

- *Criterion-related validation.* One way of establishing the validity of a selection method is to show that there is an empirical association between scores on the selection measure and scores for job performance. If there is a substantial correlation between test scores and job-performance scores, criterion-related validity has been established. For example, Figure 8.4 below shows the relationship between 2005 results for year 12 secondary school and 2006 first year university results. In this example, there is roughly a 0.50 correlation between the two years' results. This 0.50 is referred to as a validity coefficient. Note that we have used the correlation coefficient to assess both reliability and validity, which may seem somewhat confusing. The key distinction is that the correlation reflects a reliability estimate when we are attempting to assess the same characteristic twice (e.g. assessment task results in years 11 and 12), but the correlation coefficient reflects a validity coefficient when we are attempting to relate one characteristic (year 12 results) to performance on some task (first-year university results).

Criterion-related validity studies come in two varieties. **Predictive validation** seeks to establish an empirical relationship between test scores taken prior to being recruited and eventual performance on the job. Predictive validation requires one to administer tests to job applicants and then wait for some time after test administration to see how a subset of those applicants (i.e. those who were actually recruited) performed.

Many employers are tempted to use a different design because of the time and effort required to conduct a predictive validation study. **Concurrent validation** assesses the validity of a test by administering it to people already on the job and then correlating test scores with existing measures of each person's performance. The logic behind this strategy is that if the best performers currently on the job perform better on the test than those who are currently struggling on the job, the test has validity. (Figure 8.5 opposite compares the two types of validation study.)

Despite the extra effort and time needed for predictive validation, it is superior to concurrent validation for a number of reasons. First, job applicants (because they are seeking work) are typically more motivated to perform well on the tests than are current employees (who already have jobs). Second, current employees

> **Predictive validation**
> a criterion-related validity study that seeks to establish an empirical relationship between applicants' test scores and their eventual performance on the job.

> **Concurrent validation**
> a criterion-related validity study in which a test is administered to all the people currently in a job and then incumbents' scores are correlated with existing measures of their performance on the job.

FIGURE 8.4 Relationship between students' year 12 school results in 2005 and first-year university results in 2006

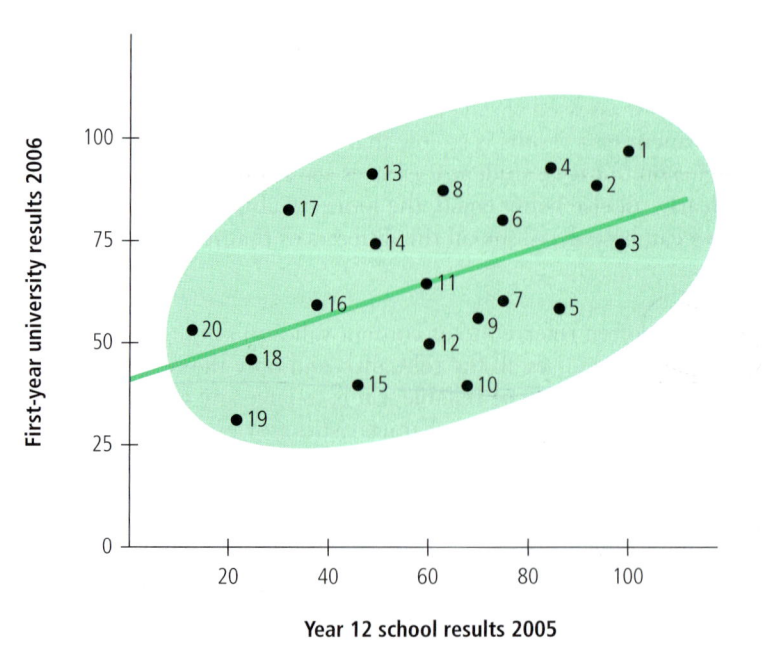

FIGURE 8.5 Graphic depiction of concurrent and predictive validation designs

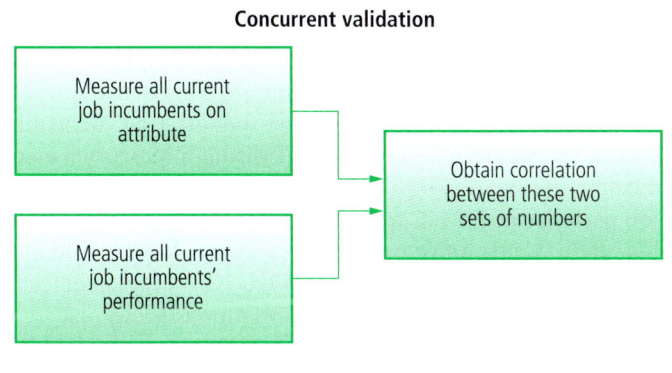

Concurrent validation

- Measure all current job incumbents on attribute
- Measure all current job incumbents' performance
→ Obtain correlation between these two sets of numbers

Predictive validation

- Measure all job applicants on attribute
- ↓
- Recruit some applicants and reject others
- ↓
- Wait for some time period
- ↓
- Measure all newly recruited job incumbents' performance

→ Obtain correlation between these two sets of numbers

have learnt many things on the job that job applicants have not yet learnt. Therefore, the correlation between test scores and job performance for current employees may not be the same as the correlation between test scores and job performance for less-knowledgeable job applicants. Third, current employees tend to be homogeneous—that is, similar to each other on many characteristics.[63] Thus, on many of the characteristics needed for success on the job, most current employees will show a restriction in range. This restricted range makes it hard to detect a relationship between test scores and job-performance scores because few of the current employees will be low on the characteristic you are trying to validate.

For example, if emotional stability is a characteristic required for a nursing career, it is quite likely that most nurses who have amassed five or six years' experience will score high on this characteristic. Yet to validate a test, you need both high test scorers (who should subsequently perform well on the job) and low test scorers (who should perform poorly on the job). Thus, while concurrent studies can sometimes help one anticipate the results of predictive studies, they do not serve as substitutes.[64]

Obviously, we would like our measures to be high in validity but, as with the reliability standard, we must also ask, how high is high enough? When trying to determine how much validity is enough, turning to tests of statistical significance is typical. A test of statistical significance answers the question: 'How likely is it that a correlation of this size could have come about through luck or chance?'

Table 8.6 below shows how big a correlation between a selection measure and a measure of job performance needs to be to achieve statistical significance at a level of 0.05 (that is, there is only a five out of 100 chance that one could get a correlation this big by chance alone). While it is generally true that bigger correlations are better, the size of the sample on which the correlation is based plays a large role as well. Since many of the selection methods we examine in the second half of this chapter generate correlations in the 0.20s and 0.30s, we often need samples of eight to 90 people.[65] A validation study with a small sample (for example, 20 people) is almost doomed to failure from the start. Thus, many companies are too small to use a criterion-related validation strategy for most, if not all, of their jobs.

- *Content validation.* When sample sizes are small, an alternative test-validation strategy, content validation, can be used. **Content validation** is performed by demonstrating that the items, questions or problems posed by the test are a representative sample of the kinds of situations or problems that occur on the job.[66] A test that is content valid exposes the job applicant to situations that are likely to occur on the job and then tests whether the applicant currently has sufficient knowledge, skill or ability to handle such situations.

Content validation
a test-validation strategy performed by demonstrating that the items, questions or problems posed by a test are a representative sample of the kinds of situations or problems that occur on the job.

TABLE 8.6 Required level of correlation to reach statistical significance as a function of sample size

Sample size	Required correlation
5	0.75
10	0.58
20	0.42
40	0.30
80	0.21
100	0.19

For example, a general contracting firm that constructed housing needed to recruit a construction superintendent.[67] This job involved organising, supervising and inspecting the work of many subcontractors involved in the construction process. The tests developed for this position attempted to mirror the job. One test was a scrambled subcontractor test, where the applicant had to take a random list of subcontractors (roofing, plumbing, electrical, fencing, concrete etc.) and put them in the correct order that each should appear on the site. A second test measured construction-error recognition. In this test, the applicant went into a shed that was specially constructed to have 25 common and expensive errors (for example, faulty wiring, upside-down windows etc.) and recorded whatever problems he or she could detect. The content of these tests closely parallels the content of the job; therefore, one can safely make inferences from one to the other.

Although criterion-related validity is established by empirical means, content validity is achieved primarily through a process of expert judgment. One means of quantifying the degree of content validity is to use the content-validation ratio (CVR). To calculate this ratio, various individuals (considered experts on the job) are assembled. These people review each test (or item) and then categorise each test in terms of whether the skill or knowledge that the test assesses is essential to the job. The content-validation ratio is then calculated from the formula:

$$CVR = \frac{n_e - \frac{N}{2}}{\frac{N}{2}}$$

where n_e is the number of judges who rate the item 'essential' and N is the number of judges. (Content-validation ratio) CVR equals 1.0 when all judges believe the item is essential and −1.0 when all judges believe it is non-essential. A CVR of 0.00 means there is complete disagreement on the degree to which the item is essential. Table 8.7 below shows the level of CVR needed to achieve statistical significance as a function of the number of judges.[68]

The ability to use content validation in small sample settings makes it generally more applicable than criterion-related validation. However, content validation has two limitations.[69] First, one assumption behind content validation is that the person who is to be recruited must have the necessary knowledge, skills or abilities at the time he or she is recruited. Thus, it is not appropriate to use content validation in settings where the applicant is expected to learn the job in a formal training program conducted after selection.

Second, since subjective judgment plays such a large role in content validation, it is critical to minimise the amount of inference involved on the part of judges. Thus, the judges' ratings need to be made with respect to relatively concrete and observable behaviours (for example, 'applicant detects common construction errors' or 'arranges optimal subcontractor schedules'). Content validation would be inappropriate for assessing more abstract characteristics such as intelligence, leadership capacity and integrity.

TABLE 8.7 Required level of content-validation ratio to reach statistical significance as a function of the number of judges

Number of judges	Required content-validation ratio (CVR)
5	0.99
8	0.75
10	0.62
15	0.49
30	0.33

Generalisability

Generalisability is defined as the degree to which the validity of a selection method established in one context extends to other contexts. There are three primary 'contexts' over which we might like to generalise: different situations (that is, jobs or organisations), different samples of people and different time periods. Just as reliability

Generalisability
the degree to which the validity of a selection method established in one context extends to other contexts.

is necessary but not sufficient for validity, validity is necessary but not sufficient for generalisability.

In the past, it was believed, for example, that validity coefficients were situationally specific—that is, the level of correlation between test and performance varied as an individual went from one organisation to another, although the jobs studied seemed to be identical. Subsequent research has indicated that this is largely false. Rather, tests tend to show similar levels of correlation across jobs that are only somewhat similar (at least for tests of intelligence and cognitive ability). Correlations with these kinds of tests change as an individual goes across widely different kinds of jobs, however. Specifically, the more complex the job, the higher the validity of many tests.[70]

It was also believed that tests showed differential subgroup validity, which meant that the validity coefficient for any test–job performance pair was different for people of different races or gender. This belief was also refuted by subsequent research and, in general, considerably similar levels of correlations are found across different groups of people.[71]

The evidence suggests that test validity often extends across situations and subgroups; thus, validity generalisation stands as an alternative for validating selection methods for companies that cannot employ criterion-related or content validation. Validity generalisation is a three-step process. First, the company provides evidence from previous criterion-related validity studies conducted in other situations that shows that a specific test (for example, a test of emotional stability) is a valid predictor for a specific job (for example, nurse at a large hospital). Second, the company provides evidence from job analysis to document that the job it is trying to fill (nurse at a small hospital) is similar in all major respects to the job validated elsewhere (nurse at a large hospital). Finally, if the company can show that it uses a test that is the same as or similar to that used in the validated setting, then one can 'generalise' the validity from the first context (large hospital) to the new context (small hospital).[72]

Utility

Utility is the degree to which the information provided by selection methods enhances the bottom-line effectiveness of the organisation.[73] In general, the more reliable, valid and generalisable the selection method is, the more utility it will have. On the other hand, many characteristics of particular selection contexts enhance or detract from the usefulness of given selection methods, including when reliability, validity and generalisability are held constant.

Figures 8.6a and 8.6b overleaf, for example, show two different scenarios where the correlation between a measure of extroversion and the amount of sales revenue generated by a sample of sales representatives is the same for two different companies: company A and company B. Although the correlation between the measure of extroversion and sales is the same, company B derives much more utility or practical benefit from the measure. That is, as indicated by the arrows proceeding out of the boxes (which indicate the people selected), the average sales revenue of the three people selected by company B (Figure 8.6b) is $850 000 compared to $780 000 from the three people selected by company A (Figure 8.6a).

The major difference between these two companies is that company B generated twice as many applicants as company A. This means that the selection ratio (the percentage of people selected relative to the total number of people tested) is quite low for company B (three out of 20) relative to company A (three out of 10). Thus, the people selected by company B have higher amounts of extroversion than those selected by company A; therefore, company B takes better advantage of the relationship between extroversion and sales. Although this might be somewhat offset

---

Utility
the degree to which the information provided by selection methods enhances the effectiveness of selecting personnel in real organisations.

FIGURE 8.6 Relationship between extroversion and sales revenue

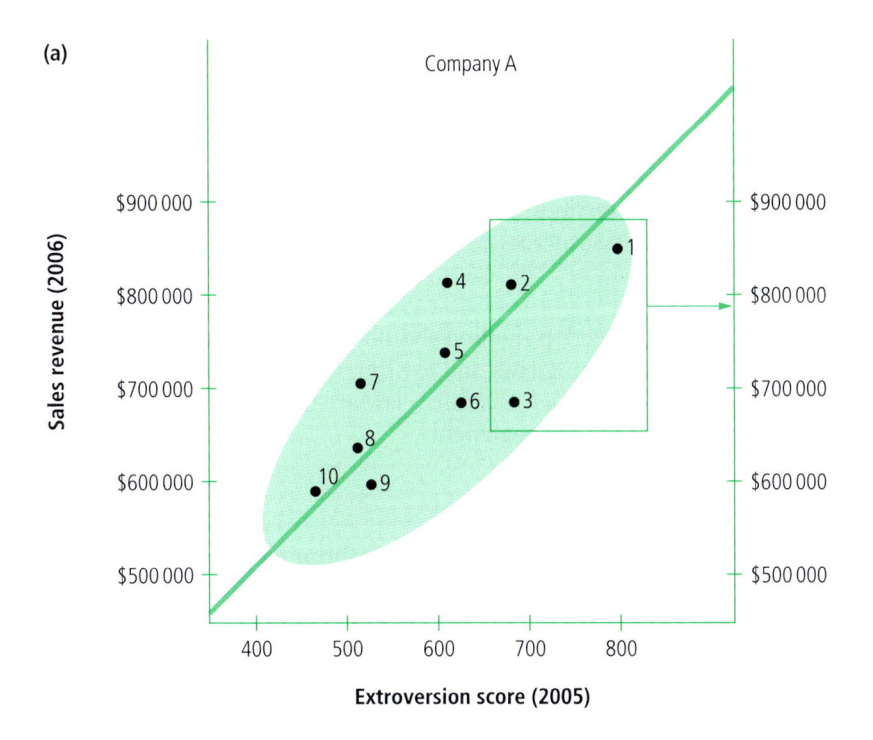

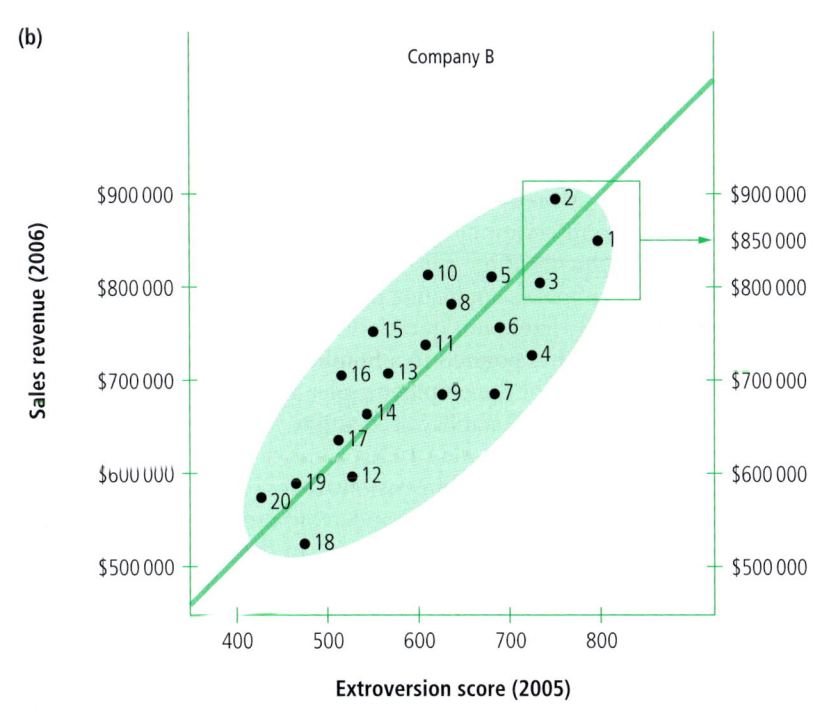

by the cost of recruiting and measuring 10 more people, this added cost is probably trivial relative to the difference in revenue shown in this example ($70 000). Thus, the utility of any test generally increases as the selection ratio gets lower, so long as the additional costs of recruiting and testing are not excessive.

Where the economic consequences to an organisation of failure versus success on the job are great, testing has greater utility. For example, a test of sales ability might have greater utility for a company selling cars than for one selling surfboards. The sales difference between a 'good' car salesperson and an 'average' one might be $100 000 a month, versus a difference of perhaps $2000 a month for a 'good' versus an 'average' surfboard seller.

Finally, the utility of any selection procedure is also a function of how many people are tested and the cost of the testing. Obviously, as the number of people who have to be tested and the cost of the test increase, the utility of the testing process goes down.

Legality

The final standard that any selection method should adhere to is legality. All selection methods should conform to existing laws and existing legal precedents. Many issues relating to selecting employees under Australian law are discussed in Chapter 3 The legal context for human resource management.

Types of selection methods

We have now covered the five standards by which we can judge selection measures. In the next section of this chapter, we examine the common selection methods used in various organisations and discuss their advantages and disadvantages in terms of these standards.

Interviews

Selection interview
a dialogue initiated by one or more persons to gather information and evaluate the qualifications of an applicant for employment.

A selection interview has been defined as: 'a dialogue initiated by one or more persons to gather information and evaluate the qualifications of an applicant for employment'.[74] The selection interview is the most widespread selection method employed in organisations, and remains popular in Australian organisations.[75]

Unfortunately, the long history of research on the employment interview suggests that, without proper care, it can be unreliable, low in validity[76] and biased against a number of different groups.[77] Moreover, interviews are relatively costly because they require at least one person to interview another person and these people have to be brought to the same geographic location. Finally, in terms of legality, the subjectivity embodied in the process often makes applicants upset, particularly if they fail to get a job after being asked apparently irrelevant questions.

Fortunately, recent research has pointed to a number of concrete steps that one can employ to increase the utility of the employee selection interview.[78] First, HR staff should keep the interview structured, standardised and focused on accomplishing a small number of goals. That is, they should plan to come out of each interview with quantitative ratings on a small number of dimensions that are observable (for example, interpersonal style or ability to express oneself) and avoid ratings of abilities that may be better measured by tests (for example, intelligence). In the words of one experienced interviewer for Johnson & Son, Inc. in the United States, 'Gut feelings count but the goal is controlled subjectivity'.[79]

Second, ask questions dealing with specific situations that are likely to arise on the job and use these to determine what the person is likely to do in each situation. These types of situational interview items come in two varieties, as shown in Table 8.8 overleaf. Some items are 'experience-based' and require the applicant to reveal an actual experience he or she had in the past when confronting the situation. Other items are 'future-oriented' and ask what the person is likely to do when confronting a certain hypothetical situation in the future. Research suggests that these types of items

TABLE 8.8 — Examples of experience-based and future-oriented situational interview items

Experience-based

Motivating employees	'Think about an instance when you had to motivate an employee to perform a task that he or she disliked but that you needed to have done. How did you handle that situation?'
Resolving conflict	'What was the biggest difference of opinion you ever had with a co-worker? How did you resolve that situation?'
Overcoming resistance to change	'What was the hardest change you ever had to bring about in a past job, and what did you do to get the people around you to change their thoughts or behaviours?'

Future-oriented

Motivating employees	'Imagine that you and a co-worker disagree about the best way to handle an absenteeism problem with another member of your team. How would you resolve that situation?'
Resolving conflict	'Suppose you were working with an employee who you knew greatly disliked performing a particular task. You needed to get this task completed, however, and this person was the only one available to do it. What would you do to motivate that person?'
Overcoming resistance to change	'Suppose you had an idea for change in work procedures that would enhance quality but some members of your workgroup were hesitant to make the change. What would you do in that situation?'

can both show validity, but that experience-based items often outperform future-oriented items.[80]

Many organisations use these types of situational questions in their interview procedures. Interviewees answer questions that directly relate to past experiences and future behaviours. One director of human resources explained this approach, saying, 'We're looking for specific examples of how they succeeded in previous jobs rather than examining their entire work history'.[81]

It is also important to use multiple interviewers who are trained to avoid many of the subjective errors that can result when one human being is asked to rate another. That is, interviewers need to be made aware of their own biases, prejudices and other personal features that may colour their perceptions of others.[82] A variety of techniques can be used to improve selection methods such as interviews. For example, some employers videotape interviews and then send the tapes (rather than the applicants) from place to place. This is seen by some as a cost-effective means of allowing numerous raters to evaluate the candidate under standard conditions.[83]

References and biographical data

In the same way that few employers would think of hiring someone without an interview, nearly all employers also use some method for getting background information on applicants before an interview.[84] This information can be solicited from the people who know the candidate through reference checks.

The evidence on the reliability and validity of reference checks suggests that these are, at best, weak predictors of future success on the job.[85] The main reason for this low validity is that the evaluations supplied in most reference letters are so positive that it is hard to differentiate applicants.

This problem with reference letters has two causes. First, the applicant usually gets to choose who writes the letter and can, thus, choose only those writers who think the highest of his or her abilities. Second, since letter writers can never be sure who will read the letters, they may fear that supplying damaging information about someone could come back to haunt them, as they may be sued for defamation.

The evidence on the utility of biographical information collected directly from job applicants is much more positive, especially for certain occupational categories such as clerical and sales jobs[86] and for particular outcomes like turnover.[87] The low cost of obtaining such information significantly enhances its utility, especially when the information is used in conjunction with a well-designed follow-up interview that complements, rather than duplicates, the biographical information bank.[88]

The biographical information form also provides a written document that the organisation can verify via outside checks. Indeed, exaggeration may be a substantial challenge for recruiters to detect. It can, however, present significant problems for an organisation.[89] The need to eliminate risk in hiring undesirable applicants has provided a boost to the private investigative services industry, and companies like PeopleWise, which focus on verifying resumés and providing investigative services to corporate clients. One survey found that 20 per cent of job candidates embellish their CVs, and this could be a conservative figure. For example, a job candidate may refer to a previous position as 'management' although the position involved supervising only one person. Many employers, when checking qualifications, will request original documents and cross-reference with universities and employers, to identify fraud.[90]

In terms of legal concerns, selectors should note that asking certain questions is illegal regardless of their impact. There is substantial variation from country to country on what constitutes a legal versus an illegal inquiry. People conducting selection processes should be aware of the legal requirements that pertain to their circumstances (also see Chapter 3 The legal context for human resource management).[91]

Physical ability tests

Although automation and other advances in technology have eliminated or modified many physically demanding occupational tasks, many jobs still require certain physical abilities. In these cases, tests of physical abilities may be relevant not only to predicting performance, but to predicting occupational injuries and disabilities as well.[92] There are seven classes of tests in this area that evaluate: (1) muscular tension, (2) muscular power, (3) muscular endurance, (4) cardiovascular endurance, (5) flexibility, (6) balance, and (7) coordination.[93]

The criterion-related validities for these kinds of tests for certain jobs are quite strong.[94] Unfortunately, these tests, particularly the strength tests, are likely to have an adverse impact on some applicants with disabilities and many female applicants. For example, roughly two-thirds of all males score higher than the highest-scoring female on muscular tension tests.[95]

There are two key questions to ask in deciding whether to use these kinds of tests. First, is the physical ability essential to performing the job and is it mentioned prominently enough in the job description? Second, is there a probability that failure to adequately perform the job would result in some risk to the safety or health of the applicant, co-workers or clients?

Cognitive ability tests

Cognitive ability tests differentiate individuals on their mental rather than physical capacities. Cognitive ability has many different facets, although we will focus only on three dominant facets.[96] 'Verbal comprehension' refers to a person's capacity to understand and use written and spoken language. 'Quantitative ability' concerns the speed and accuracy with which one can solve arithmetic problems of all kinds. 'Reasoning ability', a broader concept, refers to a person's capacity to invent solutions to many diverse problems.

Some jobs require only one or two of these facets of cognitive ability. Under these conditions, maintaining the separation among the facets is appropriate. However, many jobs that are high in complexity require most, if not all, of the facets; hence, one general test is often as good as many tests of separate facets.[97] Highly reliable commercial tests measuring these kinds of abilities are widely available and they are generally valid predictors of job performance. The validity of these kinds of tests is related to the complexity of the job, however, in that one sees higher criterion-related validation for complex jobs than for simple jobs.[98]

Personality inventories

While ability tests attempt to categorise individuals relative to what they can do, personality measures tend to categorise individuals by what they are like. Two reviews of the personality literature independently arrived at five common aspects of personality.[99] We refer to these five major dimensions as the 'Big Five' and they include: (1) extroversion, (2) adjustment, (3) agreeableness, (4) conscientiousness, and (5) inquisitiveness. Table 8.9 opposite lists each of these with a corresponding list of adjectives that fit each dimension.

TABLE 8.9 The five major dimensions of personality inventories

1	Extroversion	Sociable, gregarious, assertive, talkative and expressive
2	Adjustment	Emotionally stable, non-depressed, secure and content
3	Agreeableness	Courteous, trusting, good natured, tolerant, cooperative and forgiving
4	Conscientiousness	Dependable, organised, persevering, thorough and achievement oriented
5	Inquisitiveness	Curious, imaginative, artistically sensitive, broad minded and playful

Although it is possible to find reliable, commercially available measures of each of these traits, the evidence for their validity and generalisability is low. Conscientiousness is one of the few factors that displays any validity across a number of different job categories and many 'real-world' managers rate this as one of the most important characteristics they look for in employees.[100] People who have a high level in conscientiousness show more stamina at work, which is helpful in many occupations. For example, at the highest levels of management, many CEOs of the largest companies report working 80–90 hours a week and get by on as little as five to six hours of sleep each night.[101] Conscientiousness seems to be a particularly good predictor when teamed with tests of mental ability, because there is a stronger relationship between this trait and performance when ability is high.[102] It is also important to note that general mental ability (or intelligence) has been found, in a meta-analytic study, to be better than conscientiousness at predicting job performance. General mental ability was shown to be the best overall predictor of likely job performance.[103]

Although conscientiousness is the only dimension of personality that seems to show predictive validity across all situations, there are contexts where other components of the 'Big Five' relate to job performance.[104] First, extroversion and agreeableness seem to be related to performance in jobs such as sales or management—it is easy to see why these types of attributes would be required for such jobs.[105] These two factors also seem to be predictive of performance in team contexts, although in many cases it is the score of the lowest team member that determines the whole group outcome. That is, one highly disagreeable, introverted or unconscientious member can ruin an entire team.[106]

Finally, the validity for almost all of the 'Big Five' factors in terms of predicting job performance also seems to be higher when the scores are not obtained from the applicant, but are instead taken from other people.[107] The lower validity associated with self-reports of personality can be traced to two factors. First, people sometimes lack insight into what their own personalities are actually like (or how they are perceived by others), so their scores are inaccurate or unreliable. Second, applicants can sometimes fake their responses to personality items, making themselves seem more conscientious, agreeable and extroverted than they really are.[108]

The use of psychometric tests such as personality inventories and cognitive ability tests has been the subject of considerable debate. It appears that the use of these tests for recruitment purposes in Australian organisations is increasing, despite criticism of them as unreliable and unethical. In a recent survey of 8000 people, 44 per cent viewed psychometric tests as too invasive with regard to personal facts and details. In contrast, 69 per cent of human resource directors who were surveyed reported that the tests are extremely valuable in the recruiting process.[109]

According to Robert Spillane, the research evidence shows that personality tests should not be used as a basis for making employment decisions. Their usefulness depends on what is being tested, they may be unethical due to the stress placed on people completing them and the potential for discrimination, and the test results can be faked.[110]

Work samples

Work-sample tests and job-performance tests attempt to simulate the job in miniaturised form. For example, many organisations use an 'in-basket' test when assessing people who are applying for managerial jobs. In this test, job candidates are asked to respond to memos that typify the problems confronted by those who already hold the job. The key in this and other forms of work-sample tests is the behavioural consistency between the requirements of the job and the requirements of the test.[111]

Work-sample tests tend to be job specific—that is, tailored individually to each different job in each organisation. On the positive side, this has resulted in tests that demonstrate a high degree of criterion-related validity. Also, the obvious parallels between the test and the job make content validity high. In general, this reduces the likelihood that rejected applicants will challenge the procedure through litigation. Available evidence also suggests that these tests are low in adverse impact.[112]

Finally, work-sample tests, because they reveal directly the individual's ability to do the job, are particularly useful when recruiting job applicants for whom background information may be hard to collect or interpret.

With all these advantages come two drawbacks. First, by their very nature the tests are job specific, so generalisability is low. Second, partly because a new test has to be developed for each job and partly because of their non-standardised formats, these tests are relatively expensive to develop. It is much more cost effective to purchase a commercially available cognitive ability test that can be used for a number of different job categories within the company, than to develop a test for each job. For this reason, some have rated the utility of cognitive ability tests higher than work-sample tests, despite the latter's higher criterion-related validity.[113]

In the area of managerial selection, work-sample tests are typically the cornerstone in assessment centres. Generically, the term **assessment centre** (a process in which multiple raters evaluate employees' performance on a number of exercises) is used to describe a wide variety of specific selection programs that employ multiple selection methods to rate either applicants or job incumbents on their managerial potential. Someone attending an assessment centre would typically experience work-sample tests such as an in-basket test and several tests of more general abilities and personality. The criterion-related validity of assessment centres tends to be quite high because assessment centres employ multiple selection methods. Indeed, research indicates that one of the best combinations of selection methods includes work-sample tests with a highly structured interview and a measure of general cognitive ability. The validity coefficient expected from such a combined battery often exceeds 0.60.[114]

> **Assessment centre**
> a process in which multiple raters evaluate employees' performance on a number of exercises.

Honesty tests and drug tests

Many problems that confront society also exist within organisations, which has led to two 'new' kinds of tests: honesty tests and drug-use tests. Many companies in the United States formerly employed polygraph tests, or lie detectors, to evaluate job applicants, but this changed with the passage of the *Polygraph Act* in 1988. This United States' Act banned the use of polygraphs in employment screening for most organisations. This move did not eliminate the problem of theft by employees. As a result, the paper-and-pencil honesty testing industry was born.

Paper-and-pencil honesty tests typically ask applicants directly about their attitudes toward theft or their past experiences with theft. Some sample items are shown in Table 8.10 opposite. Given the recent development of these tests, there is not a great deal of independent evidence (that is, evidence not generated by those who publish and sell the tests) on their reliability and validity. A large-scale independent review of validity studies conducted by the publishers of many integrity tests suggests they can be predictive of both theft and other disruptive behaviours.[115] One of the few predictive studies conducted by someone other than a publisher of honesty tests also suggests that these tests predict theft in convenience store settings.[116] Another positive feature of these tests is that one does not see large differences attributable to race or sex, so they are not likely to have an adverse impact on these demographic groups.[117]

TABLE 8.10 Sample items from a typical integrity test

1	It is okay to take something from a company that is making too much profit.
2	Stealing is just a way of getting your fair share.
3	When a store overcharges its customers, it is okay to change price tags on merchandise.
4	If you could get into a movie without paying and not get caught, would you do it?
5	Is it okay to go around the law if you do not actually break it?

Source: Ellyn E. Spragins, 1992, 'True or False? Honesty tests', *Inc. Magazine*, February, p. 104. Copyright 1992 by Goldhirsh Group, Inc.

As is the case with measures of personality, some people are concerned that people confronting an honesty test can fake their way to a passing score. The evidence suggests that people instructed to fake their way to a high score (indicating honesty) can do so. However, it is not clear that this affects the validity of the predictions made using such tests. That is, it seems that despite this built-in bias, scores on the test still predict future theft. Thus, the effect of the faking bias is not large enough to detract from the test's validity.[118]

Although it is always a good rule to locally evaluate the reliability and validity of any selection method, because of the novelty of these kinds of measures this may be more critical with honesty tests.

As with theft, there is a growing perception of the problems caused by drug use among employees. Indeed, some senior executives—more so in larger companies—cite substance abuse as a significant problem in their organisations. Some companies conduct drug testing as a result of such concern.[119] The reliability and validity of drug tests are considerably high because the physical properties of drugs are invariant and subject to highly rigorous chemical testing.

The major controversies surrounding drug tests involve not only their reliability and validity but also whether they represent an invasion of privacy, an unreasonable search and seizure or a violation of due process.[120] Urine analysis and blood tests are invasive procedures and accusing someone of drug use is a serious matter. As with honesty testing, there has not been a great deal of legislation or litigation in this area to date; however, this might not be true in the future.

Employers considering the use of drug tests would be well advised to make sure that their drug-testing programs conform to some general rules. First, these tests should be administered systematically to all applicants applying for the same job. Second, testing seems more defensible for jobs that involve safety hazards associated with failure to perform. Test results should be reported back to the applicant, who should be allowed an avenue of appeal (and perhaps retesting). Tests should be conducted in an environment that is as unintrusive as possible, and results from those tests should be held in strict confidence. Finally, when testing current employees, the program should be part of a wider organisational program that provides rehabilitation counselling or an employee assistance program (for related comments, see Chapter 15 Ethics and human resource management, and Chapter 17 Managing employee turnover and retention).[121]

Overall, the recruitment and selection approaches used by organisations should seek to attract and support the development of a diverse and productive workforce. In particular, many firms and HR managers face challenges with regard to recruiting and selecting older workers. To prevent age discrimination, employers, HR managers and recruitment firms need to overcome prejudices around hiring older workers, and employ staff based on their abilities rather than their age. Recent research conducted by Hudson, which included almost 7500 companies nationally, found that fewer than one in three Australian employers seek to attract mature-age workers. However, according to Hudson CEO Australasia, Anne Hatton, 'With a diminishing pool of talent for employers, mature workers are becoming increasingly important. They are the only remaining segment of the workforce in which participation rates can be increased.'[122] The research also found that almost 70 per cent of Australian managers would like to remain in the workforce on a part-time or casual basis after retiring from full-time work.[123] As shown in 'Managing challenges through attracting and retaining people: Living values the Ritz-Carlton way', the award-winning Portman Ritz-Carlton Hotel in Shanghai has integrated its recruitment approach into a sophisticated system to enhance employee attraction and retention.

LIVING VALUES THE RITZ-CARLTON WAY FOR SUCCESSION

As part of the world renowned Ritz-Carlton chain of luxury hotels, the 578-room Portman Ritz-Carlton in Shanghai has been widely recognised for its high levels of customer service. With 730 employees, the hotel has won multiple industry awards, including Best Business Hotel in Asia and Best Employer in Asia. The management of the Portman Ritz-Carlton in Shanghai put these awards down to their ability to change the culture of their organisation in order to meet guests' needs.

'Understanding what luxury service standards are determines what kind of competencies are required to deliver that level of service. This is then followed by selecting and training people in these competencies', says Lawrence Chi, director of HR at the hotel. A key to building a customer-focused culture has been the hotel's 12 service values, which have essentially weaved their way into the day-to-day operations of the hotel.

Working with values

The Portman Ritz-Carlton's service culture was developed from its beginnings in 1983. A credo was developed at this time, which outlines the service missions of staff to guests and the experience they should strive to offer them.

The gold standards define the Portman Ritz-Carlton's service culture. It incorporates the hotel's credo, its motto ('We are ladies and gentlemen serving ladies and gentlemen') and three steps of service. The first step is the necessary provision of warm and sincere greetings and farewells using the guest's name, followed by the anticipation and fulfilment of each guest's needs. The final step is that the hotel will in turn provide a diverse work environment, quality of life and the fulfilment of individual aspirations by effectively nurturing and maximising talent to the benefit of each individual and the company.

Twelve service values also play a role in the hotel's service culture. Communication is an important part of delivering on the 12 service values. This includes a rollout to senior leaders and middle managers and general sessions to communicate the values to employees, with each division responsible for presenting a different service value to focus on each day. Employees also attend a four-hour training session to better understand the values.

'Every 12 days we rotate one of the service values and so we're focused on one service value a day. When we do our daily line ups and we talk about each day's service value, we talk about things such as opportunities to learn and grow in the hotel and 12 days from then we will talk about it again', says Chi.

While HR may be considered the keeper of the gold standards, culture and philosophy of the organisation, Chi says the living of the values is the responsibility of everyone in the hotel. 'All the executives, whether you are in a finance position or an operations position, your number one priority are your ladies and gentlemen', he says.

Recruitment values

The Portman Ritz-Carlton takes a strict line on recruiting the right people. They select talent and teach staff the technical part of their job, seeking … people who care for and respect the guests and each other, have a high work ethic, are detail oriented and relationship driven.

'You have to make sure that you're selecting for attitudes and values, not for skills and experience. You can't train for attitudes and values, you can train for skills', says Chi. If candidates have the right customer focus, values and a positive attitude, anyone can be trained to do anything in the hotel, Chi says.

Challenges

While the customer service culture of the Portman Ritz-Carlton has been successful, one of the challenges faced by the hotel is in the disconnect between the organisational culture and the national culture. In China, a socialist economic system does not focus on quality of production or work.

The service values have ultimately created a greater sense of loyalty and engagement from employees, according to Chi. With the onus to live out the culture and values of the organisation on each individual, he claims this has provided staff with a greater sense of empowerment and ownership of the guest and the business.

As a result, the hotel has a good retention rate. As the head of HR for the hotel, it is important to keep one's word, Chi adds. 'If you say you're going to implement the employee promise and you say you're going to treat everyone with respect, you just have to do it.'

Source: Excerpt from M. Yen, 2006, 'Living values the Ritz-Carlton way', *Human Resources*, 5 September, pp. 14–15.
www.humanresourcesmagazine.com.au

MANAGING PEOPLE

AFTER BPOs, IT IS NOW THE TURN OF RPOs

With over 22 per cent growth in the job market across industries, India, Inc. will be eyeing executive and specialised talent from overseas.

The employment boom in India is creating a talent shortage. In this changing scenario, a new concept has emerged—Recruitment Process Outsourcing (RPO). The concept aims at taking the burden out of the headhunting business of the corporate sector.

India, Inc. requires R&D talent in the automotive industry, middle and senior level managers, engineers, MBAs, workers in niche industries (such as biotech and IT product development), and English-speaking employees for retail and call center jobs.

In many organisations, recruiters spend a majority of their time sorting through resumes in their inbox or finding candidates from job boards—over 60 per cent of their time is spent in these areas. 'Outsourcing their non-core functions helps save time and increase productivity levels', says M K Khanna, owner of Blue Square, an offshore service provider currently catering to the US market.

Factors driving RPO growth in India include exponential growth in recruitment and employment activity, perceived shortage of talent, changing attitudes at workplace and need to achieve cost savings, efficiencies and recruiting expertise.

An RPO firm, a fast emerging subset of human resource outsourcing (HRO), directly goes to the employers with the right kind of professionals, starting from a fresher to filling up the position of a well-experienced director.

Based on market research, international geographies that are most likely to benefit from this growth are UK (most active RPO market in Europe) with Germany, India, Malaysia and Russia as the fastest emerging markets for RPO, says Sonal Chandole, national sales director, Kelly Services India. The company has a specialized business unit, Kelly HRfirst, which focuses on providing RPO programs for clients worldwide.

The HR Outsourcing worldwide market is estimated by Gartner to touch $75–80 billion by 2008. A Nasscom-McKinsey report has projected that Indian firms' revenues from HRO will increase to $3.5 billion by 2008. Gartner also thinks India can expect to win 10–15 per cent of the US HRO services market. Considering, only 6 per cent of US HR spend is presently off shored, there is a lot of potential in the market.

But the question arises that to what extent is off shoring really possible? 'Strategic RPO works more on a hybrid model where offshore components are complemented with onsite presence which can be short-term for information exchange or long-term for logistics facilitation', tells Kamal Karanth, CEO, Ma Foi, Malaysia. With the advent of new-age technology options it is imminently possible to provide a full-spectrum administrative RPO from a totally different geography, he adds.

But, India's needs are tempered by distrust born from inconsistent pricing and substandard deliverables from past vendors, warns Chandole. The concern over maintaining confidentiality of data and corporate security also is a central issue for companies planning to offshore the services.

The most frequently outsourced HR functions today are 'low-end' transactional duties like payroll, benefits administration, and education.

Few multi-national firms are consolidating their recruitment process by handling the HR functions from a particular base. Keane is currently handling its recruitment processes from India. 'We have small groups of experienced HR personnel in our branches worldwide. These people co-ordinate with our HR department in India giving their specific requirements', says Sukant Srivastava, managing director, Keane's India Operations.

Critics fear that employees in foreign countries may not be able to effectively screen through and route resumes. 'The HR personnel's in every country are required to fill a resource requisition form which gives detailed information about requirements of the job and the needed experience and qualification of the candidates to be reviewed', informs Srivastava.

But, although hard skill assessment of resumes can be undertaken offshore where the profiles are fairly standardized, soft skill assessment which is an important part of an RPO solution can only be done by experts and in countries where the resources are required to be deployed, admits Chandole.

Graduates with the right attitude and aptitude to learn a new process can make a good shot at an entry level position in this industry. People with HR and resource management background have a good career scope in this field. While salaries differ depending on the location of RPO Hub, an individual at the entry level can expect to earn between Rs 1.5–2 lakh annually.

Given the right skills and attitude, a person dedicated to this field for over five years could earn up to Rs 12 lakhs per year, adds the national sales director, Kelly Services, India.

The RPO sector in India is currently at its infant stage. Western expertise combined with Asian diligence, computer literacy, commitment to results and cost effectiveness can lead to a major boom in this segment. The RPO market in India is expected to touch about $30 billion in the next two years. Are we ready to cash in on this opportunity?

Source: Anusri Sahu, 'After BPOs, it is now the turn of RPOs', *The Economic Times,* 20 September 2006. (c) 2006 The Times of India Group.

QUESTION

1 What are the implications for Australian recruiters and employers of the RPO sector in India?

CHAPTER SUMMARY

In the first part of this chapter, we discussed human resource recruiting, a buffer activity that creates an applicant pool—from which the organisation can draw in the event of a labour shortage—that is to be filled with new recruits. Organisational recruitment programs affect the application through HR policies process (for example, promote-from-within policies) that affect the attributes of the vacancies. They can also impact the nature of people who apply for positions by using different recruitment sources (for example, recruiting from universities versus advertising in newspapers). Finally, organisations can use recruiters to influence individuals' perceptions of jobs (for example, eliminating misconceptions and clarifying uncertainties) or perceptions of themselves (for example, changing their valences for various work outcomes).

In the second part of this chapter, we examined the five critical standards with which all employee selection methods should conform: reliability, validity, generalisability, utility and legality. We also looked at nine different selection methods currently used in organisations and evaluated each with respect to these five standards. Table 8.11 overleaf summarises these selection methods and can be used as a guide in deciding which test to use for a specific purpose. Although we discussed each type of test individually, it is important to note in closing that there is no need to use only one type of test for any one job. Indeed, managerial assessment centres use many different forms of tests over a two- or three-day period to learn as much as possible about candidates for important executive positions. As a result, highly accurate predictions are often made and the validity associated with the judicious use of multiple tests is higher than for tests used in isolation.

TABLE 8.11 A summary table evaluating employee selection methods

Method	Reliability	Validity	Generalisability	Utility	Legality
Interviews	Low when unstructured and when assessing non-observable traits	Low if unstructured and non-behavioural	Low	Low, especially because of expense	Low, because of subjectivity and potential interviewer bias; also lack of validity makes job relatedness low
Reference checks	Low, especially when obtained from letters	Low because of lack of range in evaluations	Low	Low, although not expensive to obtain	Those writing letters may be concerned with charges of libel
Biographical information	High test–retest, especially for verifiable information	High criterion-related validity; low in content validity	Usually job specific, but have been successfully developed for many job types	High; inexpensive way to collect vast amounts of potentially relevant data	May have adverse impact; thus, often develop separate scoring keys based on sex or race
Physical ability tests	High	Moderate criterion-related validity; high content validity for some jobs	Low; only pertains to physically demanding jobs	Moderate for some physical jobs; may prevent expensive injuries and disability	Often have adverse impact on women and people with disabilities; need to establish job-relatedness
Cognitive ability tests	High	Moderate criterion-related validity; content validation inappropriate	High; predictive for most jobs, although best for complex jobs	High; low cost and wide application across diverse jobs in companies	Have had adverse impact on race, though decreasing over time
Personality inventories	High	Low criterion-related validity for most traits; content validation inappropriate	Low; few traits predictive for many jobs	Low, although inexpensive for jobs where specific traits are relevant	Low, because of cultural and sex differences on most traits, and low job-relatedness in general
Work-sample tests	High	High criterion and content validity	Usually job specific, but have been successfully developed for many job types	High, despite the relatively high cost to develop	High, because of low adverse impact and high job-relatedness
Honesty tests	Insufficient independent evidence	Insufficient independent evidence	Insufficient independent evidence	Insufficient independent evidence	Insufficient history of litigation, but will undergo scrutiny
Drug tests	High	High	High	Expensive, but may yield high payoffs for health-related costs	May be challenged on invasion-of-privacy grounds

WEB EXERCISES

A In this chapter we discussed how electronic recruiting using the web can be used to identify and attract potential employees. Qantas uses its website to provide potential job candidates with information about the company and about the selection process. Go to **www.qantas.com.au**. Click on 'Employment' and then go to the section for pilot recruitment and selection. See the list of selection tests for pilots shown in the '2007 Cadet Pilot Selection Process Briefing Sheet'. These include skills assessment, psychometric assessment, flight simulation, panel interview, occupational health check and a security check. Why are so many different types of selection tests used for pilots?

B Saville and Holdsworth (SHL) is an international human resource consulting firm headquartered in England and operating across Australia that provides assessment solutions for companies. To learn more about SHL, visit this firm's home page at **www.shlgroup.com**. The firm has a website for students. Go to **www.shldirect.com/shldirect-forstudents/SHL-Direct-2.asp?**

This site provides examples of test questions used by employers in the employee selection process. Click on 'Practice Test and Feedback'. Go to the bottom of the page and click on 'Example Questions'. Review each of the four categories of sample questions by clicking on them (verbal, numerical, diagrammatic and personality).

Questions

1. How would you validate verbal tests? Numerical tests? Diagrammatic tests? Personality tests?
2. Why might job candidates question the validity of personality test items, such as those you reviewed?

DISCUSSION QUESTIONS

1. Discuss the relative merits of internal versus external recruitment. What types of business strategies might best be supported by recruiting externally and what types might call for internal recruitment? What factors might lead a firm to decide to switch from internal to external recruitment or vice versa?
2. Recruiting people for jobs that entail international assignments is increasingly important for many companies. Where might one go to look for individuals interested in these types of assignments? How might recruiting practices aimed at these people differ from those that one might apply to the 'average' recruit?
3. What difficulties might companies need to deal with in using Internet recruitment? Do the roles of the recruiting manager and the HR manager change when Internet recruitment is used? Explain.
4. We examined nine different types of selection methods in this chapter. Assume that you were recently rejected for a job that was based on one of these methods. Obviously, you might be disappointed and angry regardless of what method was used to make this decision, but can you think of two or three selection methods that might leave you the most distressed? In general, why might the acceptability of the test to applicants be an important standard to add to the five we discussed in this chapter?
5. Distinguish between concurrent and predictive validation designs, discussing why the latter is preferred over the former. Examine each of the nine selection methods discussed in this chapter and determine which of these would have their validity most and least affected by the type of validation design employed.
6. Some have speculated that in addition to increasing the validity of decisions, employing rigorous selection methods has symbolic value for organisations. What message is sent to applicants about the organisation through recruiting practices? How might this message be reinforced by recruitment programs that occur before selection and training programs that occur after selection?
7. What does your resumé look like? How truthful is the information provided? Swap your resumé with a classmate and conduct selection interviews with each other to test the truthfulness of the resumé. What type(s) of interview questions will best identify truthfulness in a resumé? What other methods could you suggest to test the truthfulness in a resumé?

CASE STUDY

A LOOK INSIDE THE GOOGLE TALENT MACHINE

Google, through its branding, PR and recruiting efforts, has made itself so well-known and attractive to professionals from every industry and university that they have essentially changed the game of recruiting forever.

The world's first recruiting culture

Google has accomplished something that no other corporation has ever accomplished. In less than a handful of years, they have developed what can only be categorised as a recruiting machine. What they have done better than anyone else is to develop the world's first recruiting culture. What that means is that recruiting and the need for it permeates the entire organisation, from the key leaders on down to the entry-level employees. They have also gone to the extraordinary step of changing the way employees work in order to attract and retain the very best.

Working with 20 per cent time

Many organisations have changed their pay or benefits in order to attract better workers, but none has changed every professional job in the company so that the work itself is the primary attraction and retention tool. Google's founders Larry Page and Sergey Brin, HR director Stacy Sullivan and the leadership team at Google have literally crafted every professional job and workplace element so that all employees are working on interesting projects, learning continuously and constantly challenged.

The key element of changing the work so that the work itself becomes a critical attraction and retention force and driver of innovation and motivation is what Google calls '20 per cent work'. There is no concrete definition of what 20 per cent work means, but generally for professional jobs it means that the employee works the equivalent of one day a week on their own, researching individually selected projects that the company funds and supports. Both the Google Groups and Google News products are reported to have started as a result of personal 20 per cent time projects. In addition to being a phenomenal attraction tool, it also keeps their attrition rate at, as one HR executive put it, 'almost nil', but its greatest value is that it drives innovation and creativity throughout the organisation.

The world's largest recruiting budget

Google recruiting is the best-funded recruiting function in any major product-driven corporation. My own calculations indicate that, at times, Google recruitment has a ratio of one recruiter for every 14 employees (14:1). That ratio surpasses the previous record of 65:1, compared with an average ratio of 100:1 of all HR professionals.

The benefits are breathtaking

Google offers spectacular benefits even though they are not designed just for recruiting purposes. Instead, these benefits are also designed to encourage collaboration, to break down barriers between functions and to stimulate individual creativity and innovation.

These benefits do attract some of the 'wrong people', that is, talented individuals who are seeking benefits rather than an opportunity to do their best work, which creates a screening challenge.

The take away for other firms is that, even if you do match Google's 'non-work' benefits (as firms like SAS have almost done), you are not automatically going to attract the very best and the most innovative.

Recruiting structure

Google has plans to nearly double its workforce, growing from approximately 5000 to 10 000 employees in the near future. The recruitment structure they have designed to enable such growth is, like most successful recruiting organisations, primarily a centralised operations model.

A key tenet of any successful recruiting function is that the function has the capability to handle in-house the most important and visible positions, that is, executive search. At Google, recruiting is responsible for filling both executive leadership and top-level technical positions.

Because Google believes wholeheartedly in sourcing the best talent that is ferociously sought after by competitors, every element of the recruiting function is abundantly staffed with highly focused professionals.

The recruiting model has been broken up into very distinct roles, each requiring specialised expertise. These activities include: recruiting research analysts; candidate developers (sourcers); process coordinators; candidate screeners; specialised recruiters for college; specialised recruiters for technical and leadership executive search; specialised international recruiters to be located in Asia and Europe; recruiting program managers; and recruiting project managers.

Such specialisation enables the function to be managed in a way similar to a supply chain.

Standard recruiting tools

Google has successfully implemented many of the standard best practice tools found at other companies:

Employee referral: Google's referral program relies on its strong brand coupled with its highly enthusiastic workforce.

College recruitment: Google hires a large number of PhDs on the premise that they enjoy exploring areas that no one else has explored. In addition, Google has an outstanding internship program.

Professional networking: Google also effectively uses networking groups like Linkedin and other live professional events.

Recruiter training: Most newly hired recruiters go through extensive recruiter training prior to starting.

'Wow' recruiting tools

Google employs a variety of impressive recruiting tools.

AdWords as a recruiting tool: Because Google is recognised as the master of search, it's not surprising that they utilise their own search tool to find top candidates without active resumes.

Contests as recruiting tools: The Google Code Jam is a global online software writing contest that can attract over 7500 people each year. The top 25 finalists are invited to the Mountain View campus to compete for US$50 000 in prizes as well as a chance to work at Google.

Brain teasers as recruiting tools: Google has placed brainteaser billboards in the Silicon Valley and by Harvard Square. The math puzzles on these billboards challenge mathematics-oriented people and get them thinking. Although they do not specifically mention Google, the billboard puzzle does eventually lead interested participants to the Google site.

Friends of Google: 'Friends of Google' creates an electronic email network of people that are interested in Google and its products but not necessarily interested in working for the company. Thus, Google can build a relationship with thousands of people that like the firm.

Weaknesses in the Google approach

Google recruiting is not without weaknesses. Given the relative youth of the company, none of these weaknesses even reach the level of being considered a threat, but in a company whose slogan is 'great isn't good enough', it's critical that HR and recruitment management spend some time and resources in the following areas:

Employment branding: Although Google is clearly well-known as a great employer, it is clear that much of that recognition has come as a result of programs and ideas that originated outside of HR.

Metrics: Both the HR and the recruiting function have dragged their feet on developing metrics, in particular, Google's inability to track the on-the-job performance of new hires.

Recruiting strategy: Although Google recruiting obviously does great things, those things seem to occur at random and in spite of the fact that there is no formal, well-communicated recruitment strategy.

Speed: Almost everyone who has been a candidate at Google comments on how slow the screening, recruiting, and interview process is.

Contingent labour: The number of temps and contractors in the recruiting function at Google is high. The unwillingness to give permanent jobs immediately to recruiters may reduce Google's ability to get seasoned recruiters.

Emphasis on youth: Google's emphasis on youth culture might hurt its ability to attract more senior and experienced personnel.

Employee benefits at Google

A partial list of Google's 'I-bet-you-don't-have-that-where-you-work' benefits include:

- Flexible hours for nearly every professional employee
- Casual dress everyday (and this goes well beyond business casual)
- Employees can bring their dogs to work, everyday
- Onsite physician and dental care
- Health benefits that begin as soon as an employee reports for work
- Free massage and yoga
- Stock options everywhere
- Free drinks and snacks everywhere (espresso, smoothies, Red Bull, health drinks, kombucha tea, you name it)

- Free meals, including breakfast, lunch and dinner (with multiple locations and world-class chefs)
- Three weeks' vacation during the first year
- Free recreation everywhere, including video games, football, volleyball and pool tables
- Valet parking for employees
- Onsite car wash and detailing
- Maternity and parental leave (plus new moms and dads are able to expense up to US$500 for take-out meals during the first four weeks that they are home with their new baby)
- Employee referral bonus program
- Near site childcare centre
- Backup childcare for parents when their regularly scheduled child care falls through
- Fuel efficiency vehicle incentive program (US$5000 assistance if you buy a hybrid)
- Onsite dry cleaning, plus a coin-free laundry room
- A Friday TGIF all-employee gathering where the founders frequently speak
- A 'no tracking of sick days' policy
- An onsite gym to work off all of the snacks.

Source: Excerpt from J. Sullivan, 2006, 'A look inside the Google talent machine', *Human Resources,* 25 July. www.humanresourcesmagazine.com.au

QUESTIONS

1 What are the features of the attraction and retention strategies at Google?

2 What are the implications of the ageing workforce for Google's approach?

PART 3

DEVELOPING PEOPLE

9 Managing Diversity and Work–Life Balance

10 Performance Management

11 Learning and Development

12 Employee Development and Career Management

CHAPTER 9

MANAGING DIVERSITY AND WORK–LIFE BALANCE

Objectives

After reading this chapter, you should be able to:

1. Describe the differences between diversity management and equal employment opportunity (EEO).
2. Discuss the role of diversity management for organisational performance.
3. Identify the initiatives that can be used to manage diversity.
4. Identify the challenges facing the development and implementation of initiatives designed to manage diversity.
5. Describe the key features of the work–life balance program.
6. Identify the costs and benefits of implementing policies that assist employees to manage their work and non-work.

Cultural diversity, IBM style

The decision to develop a strategy for cultural awareness and acceptance within IBM Australia was driven by corporate values—respect for the individual, legal requirements (*Anti-Discrimination Act* and racial discrimination) and the business case. The organisation's thinking on cultural diversity did not develop in a vacuum. It is a long-term view that by valuing diversity, IBM uncovers new perspectives; taps into different knowledge and experience; and generates innovative ideas, suggestions and methods.

Three pillars are in place to make up IBM's diversity strategy. They are:

1. creating a work–life balance
2. advancing women
3. integrating people with disabilities.

Making the business case for diversity

The organisation's employee opinion survey (EOS) provided the hard data to substantiate the business case for cultural diversity. Modern organisations face a skills quandary. On one hand, their workforce is ageing and skilled workers are increasingly in short supply, while the demands of the clients, driven by globalisation and advanced technology, are becoming more complex. So, any organisation that fails to maximise opportunities for all employees will fall into a talent gap and miss business opportunities.

Part of the business case was about retention, particularly retaining people with languages other than English as their first language. Such employees are crucial to IBM's ability to serve its international clients. For example, an IBM information technology 'helpdesk', based in Brisbane, mainly deals with Japanese clients.

Another part of the business case reflected the global business market in which IBM operates. Employees must recognise and act on global opportunities. They must be able to operate effectively in a variety of cultural and business environments, whether travelling overseas or operating at home.

Establishing that cultural diversity makes good business sense is essential in obtaining the support of business managers. Ironically, it also reduces the need for a large budget to put programs in place.

The diversity team found that once organisational managers understood the rationale for the program and began viewing it as an investment in good commercial practice, they were actually offering to contribute resources in time and incidentals.

Making cultural diversity part of IBM Australia's DNA

Our most effective diversity programs combine 'push and pull' strategies. We have made good headway through company-led, top-down practices such as formalised training or policies like floating cultural holidays (exchanging an Australian public holiday for another significant cultural holiday). However, the truly great progress has come about through the momentum generated by individuals who are passionate about diversity issues and truly want to make diversity happen.

Aside from IBM's diversity team within human resources, three other groups within IBM have formally identified roles in the implementation of the company's overall diversity strategy. These are IBM's diversity council, diversity contact officers and diversity champions.

- *Diversity council*. The organisation's diversity council, chaired by IBM's CEO Philip Bullock, ensures that IBM visibly encourages and values the contributions and differences of employees from various backgrounds. Its key objectives are to heighten employee awareness, increase management awareness, and encourage the effective use of IBM's diverse workforce.
- *Diversity contact officers*. Diversity contact officers are regular permanent employees who volunteer to be conduits of information relating to diversity, are trained as work–life balance

PART 3   Developing People

Cultural diversity, IBM style *continued*

coaches, and help to integrate people with disabilities into the IBM workforce. They include men and women from a variety of ethnic backgrounds, people with disabilities and different sexual preferences, in order to reflect the diversity of the organisation.

- *Diversity champions.* Internal diversity awards recognise and celebrate individuals whose actions encapsulate IBM's diversity principles. They help to raise awareness of the diversity program and establish cultural diversity as the 'norm' within the company.

  The power of internal awards for diversity champions lies in bringing to life the actions of 'real' employees. The diversity team works closely with internal communications and public relations to communicate success stories.

Ensuring that stakeholders outside the company know about the diverse culture within IBM directly supports recruitment efforts, forming commercial relationships and reinforcing the business case.

Cultural awareness and acceptance in action

Cultural diversity education and awareness initiatives at IBM can be grouped into two categories: individual professional development and general staff awareness.

Source: Based on K. Nicolson, 2004, 'Cultural diversity, IBM style', *Human Resources*, 30 June, pp. 10–11. www.humanresourcesmagazine.com.au

Introduction

As discussed in Chapter 2 Strategic human resource management, the people doing the work of an organisation are an important part of the process of creating competitive advantage. These people are not all the same—they have different interests, needs, abilities and aspirations. As discussed by Kylie Nicolson in 'Cultural diversity, IBM style', on the preceding page, the goal of managing diversity in an organisation is to enhance the achievement of an organisation's competitive advantage by managing the similarities and differences between people.

Traditionally, HR policies have been based on assumptions that employees, regardless of their personal characteristics, could be managed in the same way. As a consequence, HR policies have fostered workforce homogenisation; that is, they promote similarity rather than differences among organisational members.[1] This occurs through recruitment and selection policies that emphasise using sources and criteria that have been reliable in the past; also, it occurs through training and development programs that encourage a consistent way of thinking and a tendency to select, promote and evaluate people in terms of the extent to which they reflect the characteristics of the dominant group in the workplace.[2]

Diversity management (or managing diversity) is a process of managing people's similarities and differences; it is built on a set of values that recognises that the differences between people are a potential strength for the organisation; this process of management creates an environment that allows all employees to contribute to organisational goals and experience personal growth. Fundamental to this approach is an

Diversity management (or managing diversity) is a process of managing people's similarities and differences; it is built on a set of values that recognises that the differences between people are a potential strength for the organisation. This process of management creates an environment that allows all employees to contribute to organisational goals and experience personal growth.

304

acknowledgment that a variety of individual characteristics could influence people's experiences at work, shape their perceptions of their environment and their methods and styles of communication.[3] These personal characteristics can be categorised into two dimensions: the primary dimension, which refers to observable characteristics, and the secondary dimension, which refers to underlying or non-observable characteristics.

The concept of diversity in organisations is difficult to define.[4] One way of gaining conceptual clarity about the meaning of diversity is by recognising that there is a diversity of identities based on membership in social and demographic groups. These differences in identities affect social relations in organisations.[5] Thomas[6] states:

> Diversity includes everyone, it is not something that is defined by race or gender. It extends to age, personal and corporate background, education, function, and personality. It includes lifestyle, sexual preference, geographic origin, tenure with organisation, exempt or non-exempt status, and management or non-management.

For a number of years, legislation has required many Australian organisations to provide **equal employment opportunity (EEO)**—the government's attempt to ensure that all individuals have an equal opportunity for employment, regardless of characteristics such as race, colour, religion, gender or national origin.

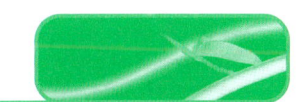

Managing diversity is different to EEO. Equal employment opportunity requires the removal of discrimination from the workplace. Managing diversity is a more wide-ranging process of management. It recognises that the differences between people are a source of strength and competitive advantage for the organisation in the product, service and labour market. A specific example of a program designed to manage diversity is a work–life balance program, which is a set of policies designed to assist employees to be more productive and satisfied in the workplace by providing them with opportunities to balance their work and personal responsibilities. There are, however, a number of issues and challenges associated with the development and implementation of a diversity management program that need to be addressed when such a program is introduced. Managers need to be aware of these issues, particularly when they are designing a program and 'selling' a program to other managers and employees.

In this chapter, we examine a model of diversity management that is used to assist us to understand the purpose and nature of the process. We outline this model in the first section, then we discuss the differences between diversity management and EEO programs. (A more detailed discussion on the role of the legislation providing for anti-discrimination and EEO is provided in Chapter 3 The legal context for human resource management.) We follow on with a discussion of the role of diversity management in providing strategic advantage, a description of some of the initiatives that can be used to manage diversity and a discussion of some of the challenges associated with implementing diversity initiatives. We then outline an example of a specific type of diversity management program and we conclude the chapter with a discussion of future directions for diversity management.

Equal employment opportunity (EEO)
the government's attempt to ensure that all individuals have an equal opportunity for employment, regardless of characteristics such as race, colour, religion, gender or national origin.

A model of diversity management

At various times during the twentieth century, organisations were required to take into account the impact of an individual's personal and domestic needs on their potential performance in the workplace. For instance, during World War II and the 1960s, there was a shortage of labour in Australia and employers recognised that women, and particularly women with children, were potential employees. However, they also saw that the existing employment policies were incompatible with the domestic responsibilities of these women and that they prevented many women from entering the workforce. In an attempt to encourage women into the workplace, these domestic responsibilities were taken into account and policies regarding hours of work were changed. As a result, many manufacturing organisations introduced part-time work during the 1960s so that women with school-aged children would take up jobs.

The principles of EEO and equal treatment for men and women have been regarded as an issue of international concern since 1919. The International Labour Organization (ILO) advocated these principles on the grounds that they were of 'special and urgent importance'. The Declaration of Philadelphia reaffirmed the rights of women and men to material wellbeing and spiritual development in conditions of economic security, freedom and dignity, and equal opportunities.[7]

The ILO seeks to promote the creation of EEO among its member states irrespective of their rate of economic growth or the conditions operating in the labour market. When a member state ratifies a convention, it has a responsibility to undertake legislative and policy measures to promote the principles the ILO embodies. Australia has ratified the following ILO conventions:

- *Equal Remuneration Convention 1951* (no. 100)
- *Discrimination (Employment and Occupation) Convention 1958* (no. 111)
- *Equal Treatment for Men and Women Workers: Workers with Family Responsibilities Convention 1981* (no. 156).

As a consequence, the federal and state governments have undertaken a number of initiatives to implement the principles embodied in these conventions. These include the enactment of anti-discrimination legislation, EEO legislation, government support for equal pay for women, the development of work and family policies, and establishing units within government departments designed to assist employers to write work and family policies.

During the 1970s, 1980s and 1990s, legislation and the decisions of the industrial tribunals required employers to take into account the special needs of some employees. These provisions included maternity, paternity and family leave policies that enabled employees with family responsibilities to take some time away from the workplace. In addition, legislation to provide the creation of EEO required the removal of discrimination from employment policies. However, none of these initiatives systematically linked the policies to organisational strategy, goals, culture and values. The initiatives also failed to acknowledge that in order to effectively manage the special needs of some individuals it was necessary to manage those individuals who did not have that need.

A management process that seeks to achieve its goals and competitive advantage by systematically managing the different needs of individual employees is known as a **diversity management program**. The model outlined in Figure 9.1 opposite indicates that the mission, vision, organisational strategy, goals and values are key influences on the development of diversity management programs. They provide a reference for determining which 'differences' are important to manage and which 'differences' are not as important.

The model also shows that diversity management involves more than managing differences between individuals; it involves managing similarities and differences at the same time. Three aspects of the process of managing the similarities and differences of employees are:

- the need to distinguish between the objective and subjective components
- the need to specify the dimensions of diversity to be managed
- the management of a collective, all-inclusive mixture of differences and similarities along a particular dimension.

Diversity management program
a management process that seeks to achieve its goals and competitive advantage by systematically managing the different needs of individual employees.

FIGURE 9.1 Model of diversity management

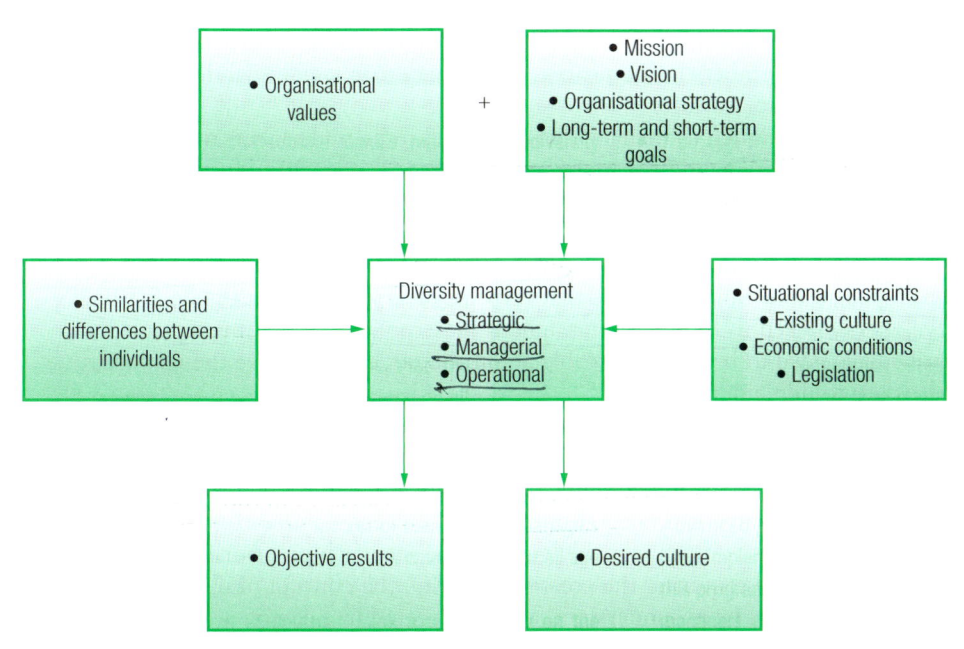

Source: Adapted from R. Kramar, 'Equity and diversity', in J. Teicher, P. Holland & R. Gough (eds), 2002, *Employee Relations Management: Australia in a Global Context*, Pearson Education, Melbourne.

The subjective and objective components of diversity need to be managed. Subjectively, diversity refers to a sense of 'otherness' based on those human qualities that differ from our own. For instance, if you are a person with children, the sense of 'otherness' refers to the feeling you have with those people without children. Objectively, diversity refers to the vast array of personal and cultural differences that constitute the human race. The management of these differences involves managing relationships between individuals with different personal and cultural characteristics. It also involves managing the tensions that often exist between individuals with different personal characteristics.

When programs are developed to manage diversity it is useful to acknowledge two dimensions: the primary and secondary dimensions. The primary dimension includes such immutable characteristics as gender, age, race, physical abilities and qualities, and sexual orientation. The secondary dimension includes characteristics that can change, such as income, religious beliefs, work, functional background, organisational tenure, personality and military experience. These dimensions shape individuals' perceptions of their environment and their method and style of communication.[8] A program designed to manage diversity, therefore, requires identification of the specific dimensions being addressed in the program.

For instance, a diversity management program could identify parental status and geographical location as the particular dimensions being specifically targeted by that program. The process involves acknowledging that all employees, regardless of their personal characteristics, will react to a particular policy. For instance, the management of the dimension of parental status is not only dealing with those employees with preschool-age children, school- and university-age children, but it is also dealing with a collective mixture of employees without these responsibilities. This process involves acknowledging that employees without dependent children could resent the provisions of employment conditions, such as leave without pay, special family leave or childcare facilities for those employees with dependants. Therefore, this process requires the development and operation of mechanisms that allow the effective involvement of all organisational members in the process of diversity management and the development of a new workplace culture.

Initiatives designed to manage diversity need to be undertaken at three levels: strategic, managerial and operational (see Figure 9.1, page 307). Just as other human resource programs should, at the strategic level, specify a culture that reflects the values of the organisation and the organisation's strategy and goals, so too should a diversity management program. At the managerial level, specific policies need to be developed so they build a culture that respects diversity, while at the operational level, people need to be able to implement these policies in the way intended. Individuals need to be knowledgeable about the policies and have the resources necessary to implement them.

Situational factors, such as the existing culture, economic conditions and legislation, are also acknowledged in Figure 9.1 as having an influence on diversity management initiatives. In economic circumstances where skilled labour is in short supply and knowledge is the key differentiator between competitors, managing diversity initiatives is most probably going to be seen as high priority. Similarly, where there is legislation requiring the creation of EEO, the concept of diversity management could be misunderstood and interpreted in a narrow way.

Now we turn to examine the relationship between EEO and diversity management.

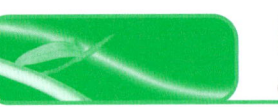

Diversity and equal employment opportunity

The management of diversity should be more than complying with EEO legislation. When managing diversity is understood only in terms of EEO outcomes and the removal of discrimination, it provides a narrow view of diversity management. This approach to diversity management identifies groups with particular personal characteristics, such as gender, race or ethnicity and focuses on issues that arise from discrimination based on these personal characteristics. Policies are then developed to provide for equal treatment of members of different groups by making concessions so that employees with certain personal characteristics or domestic arrangements can assimilate into the prevailing employment patterns.

In Australia, federal and/or state legislation identifies groups in terms of personal characteristics such as gender, race, physical ability, ethnic heritage and family responsibilities. Discrimination and EEO legislation require the removal of policies and the prevention of behaviour that hinder individuals with particular personal characteristics from having fair and equitable access to employment opportunities and the rewards associated with employment.

The *Equal Opportunity for Women in the Workplace Act 1999* (this Act replaces the *Affirmative Action [Equal Opportunity for Women] Act 1986*) adopts this narrow view of diversity. As discussed in more detail in Chapter 3 The legal context for human resource management, this act seeks to promote the principle that employment for women should be dealt with on the basis of merit in relation to employment matters. It also seeks to foster workplace consultation between employers and employees on issues concerning equal opportunity for women in relation to employment.

The *Equal Opportunity for Women in the Workplace Act 1999* is narrow in a number of ways. It emphasises legal compliance and the submission of reports to the Equal

Opportunity in the Workplace Agency. The scope of the Act is also narrow because it only requires employers with 100 or more employees to remove direct and indirect discrimination from their employment policies and practices. The coverage of the Act is restricted to one target group only, that is managerial and non-managerial employees who are women.

The administrative requirements of the *Equal Opportunity for Women in the Workplace Act 1999* sought to further the Coalition Government's policy to build on common interests in the workplace and improve organisational performance. The Act attempts to do this by encouraging the integration of EEO initiatives with organisational objectives and strategy.

The different needs of particular groups in the Australian workforce have been recognised in a limited way. This recognition is reflected in leave provisions for childcare and family responsibilities (for example, maternity, paternity and adoption leave; taking leave for the care of dependants; and management development programs specifically designed for women). In addition, some organisations, such as the Australian Public Service (APS), recognise the need for some groups to take religious holidays that differ from those of Christian members of the community; and the need to provide prayer rooms for some of these groups. The desire to create EEO in Australia has been sought through 'laws and practices that demand similar treatment' for different groups.[9] These policies provide for equal treatment by making concessions so that employees with certain personal or domestic arrangements can assimilate into the prevailing employment pattern. These policies attempt to make it possible for a greater range of people to 'fit in'.[10]

Krautil expresses this idea in a colourful way by making reference to wild animals in the zoo. She says:

> Imagine your organisation is a giraffe house. Equal opportunity has been very effectively widening the door of the giraffe house to let the elephant in, but home won't be best for the elephant unless a number of major modifications are made to the inside of the house. Without these changes the house will remain designed for giraffes and the elephant will not 'feel at home'.[11]

The *Public Service Act 1999* also requires agencies to develop a strategic approach to employment equity and workplace flexibility. However, the approach to EEO is broader. Agencies are required to use workplace diversity programs to develop strategies to attract and retain teams of staff with a diverse range of backgrounds and perspectives. The main objectives of these programs are to build a creative and productive work environment, to improve service delivery and provide a better working environment for employees. Agencies are also required to make progress in eliminating any employment-related disadvantage attributable to Aboriginality, gender, ethnicity, race, or physical or mental disability.[12]

These workplace diversity programs will go beyond the previous requirements to eliminate employment disadvantage and legal compliance by requiring agencies to recognise, value and nurture the different skills and competencies of all people. It is anticipated this will result in the introduction of flexible working practices, agency workforces that reflect the composition of the Australian community and improved agency performance. These programs provide the potential for the adoption of a broad approach to diversity management by explicitly stressing the importance of agencies making the best use of diversity available to them through human resource management processes and by stressing that workplace diversity programs should include EEO legislative requirements, but go beyond this EEO framework.[13] The process of managing diversity is much broader than the creation of EEO and compliance with EEO legislation. The removal of discrimination from employment policies and the workplace is an essential component of the process, but it is not sufficient. In order to achieve its desired outcomes, managing diversity requires the development of a culture and range of supporting policies that contribute to the achievement of the organisation's objectives and strategy. It has been argued that, in a labour market which is becoming increasingly competitive and where knowledge provides an organisation with competitive advantage, managing diversity has become an increasingly important management process for organisations of all sizes.

The results of a survey by Consulting Partners in conjunction with the Australian Human Resources Institute (AHRI) with funding from the Commonwealth Department of Immigration and Multicultural and Indigenous Affairs found that almost 50 per cent of organisations reported having a written diversity management policy, while 21 per cent of organisations claimed to have an informal diversity management policy.[14] However, these policies were concerned with managing specific issues for their workforce. There was an overwhelming focus on providing flexible work and leave policies, with 60 per cent of companies providing flexible work hours and almost 48 per cent providing flexibility with the use of leave arrangements. This narrow approach to diversity management was reflected in the benefits perceived to accrue from diversity management policies. The majority of respondents, 62.1 per cent, identified EEO outcomes as a primary benefit; and 83.6 per cent stated that commitment to EEO was the major reason for implementing diversity management. These responses indicate a desire to achieve legal compliance outcomes rather than a focus of achieving business outcomes, culture change or the creation of an inclusive workplace involving internal and external stakeholders that represent broader views of diversity management. There are, however, examples in Australia of organisations that recognise the importance of diversity management initiatives in contributing to the achievement of organisational outcomes.

More recent surveys conducted in 2003 and 2005 found many organisations with diversity programs argued for diversity as a means to drive employment and reputation, but they did not argue for it as central to bottom-line business benefits.[15] This was reflected in the five top outcomes identified by those in the survey: stature/reputation in the community; retention of employees; to be an employer of choice; recruitment of employees; and maximising the performance of existing staff. However, diversity programs were still narrow as they targeted issues associated with women, harassment, and caring responsibilities, rather than matters associated with religion, nationality and race. Between 2003 and 2005 age diversity emerged as an issue in a greater number of organisations.[16]

Deutsche Bank seeks to achieve industry leadership by fostering an inclusive work environment that enables diverse teams and gives all employees the opportunity to maximise their performance. To this end, age diversity is one of the bank's main global HR initiatives. The age-related initiatives at Deutsche Bank include employability, mentoring, advanced professionals program and training. Central to these initiatives is the process of learning and knowledge transfer.[17]

Role of diversity management in improving organisational performance

Managing diversity can be an important process for improving organisational performance. Four reasons are commonly given for the introduction of a diversity management approach. The reasons are that:

1 there is a 'business case' associated with competing effectively in the labour market
2 it provides a source of competitive advantage
3 the process provides a means of effectively adapting to change
4 there are ideological grounds for its introduction.

Business case

The arguments in terms of the 'business case' focus on the changes expected in the composition of the workforce. A most popular reason given for the implementation of the diversity management approach in Western industrial countries is the expected changes in the demographics of the population and the workforce.[18] Projections of the changes in the population and the workforce indicate women, older workers and workers from a wider variety of ethnic and cultural groups will constitute a larger proportion of the workforce and a larger source of new labour. In Australia, it is predicted that in 2051 the population aged over 65 years will more than double to represent between 24–27 per cent of the workforce.[19]

These changes are similar to those predicted in other Western industrialised countries. For instance, in the United States, it is predicted that over the next 20 years, Hispanic people, African–American people and Asian people will account for about 87 per cent of the growth of the workforce and women will represent almost half the workforce.[20] Similarly, the percentage of the workforce in the age group of over 65 years will increase from the current 12 per cent up to approximately 22 per cent in 2030.[21]

It is argued that these changes will increase competition among employers for skilled labour and consequently these changes will have implications for the ways in which employees will be managed.[22] It will become important that employers be seen as employers of preferred choice. One way of becoming such an employer will be by providing employment conditions that are attractive to prospective employees and by developing and marketing jobs in such a way that they deal with the concerns of these people.

In Australia, we are already seeing a shortage of skilled labour in certain areas. A number of surveys report difficulties in recruiting or retaining some staff, particularly in professional, IT, education, hospital and some trade occupations.[23] There are a number of reasons for this difficulty, including high levels of turnover resulting from increasing competition from employers overseas, a desire on the part of employees for a greater recognition of their need for time for personal and family life, a preference for flexibility in remuneration packages and a demand to know how their work contributes to the strategy and goals of the organisation.[24]

Other arguments for diversity management result from the pressures for international interdependence imposed by globalisation. International corporations were established in many Asian countries by the beginning of the twenty-first century and these organisations were faced with the prospect of having to decide to what extent they adapt their management practices to reflect those of the host country. For instance, the human resource management practices in countries influenced by Confucianism, such as China, Singapore, Taiwan and Hong Kong, can reflect values about gender and about confrontation. These practices can be at odds with those of the international corporation. In addition, many Asian countries have populations consisting of diverse ethnic groups. This is demonstrated in China, which consists of more than 50 recognised ethnic groups, Thailand and many other Asian countries that contain a high proportion of non-indigenous people, and Indonesia where there are more than 200 ethnic groups.[25]

The 'Does diversity pay?' case at the end of the chapter, on page 337, discusses some of the aspects of the business case for diversity management. This case raises a number of interesting issues about the complexity of the business case and its ambiguity. A major point is that the simple argument for diversity management based on what is good for financial business results is based on a view of management that is narrow and difficult to substantiate. The case also indicates the continuing narrow view of diversity discussed later in the chapter.

Competitive advantage

A second reason for implementing a diversity management approach is a recognition that, as markets become increasingly international and as the demography of the population changes, so will the demographic characteristics of customers. Some argue that customer service and products can be more effectively provided if an organisation's workforce mirrors its customers.[26] For instance, in areas with high representations of migrant groups, organisations providing customer services such as real estate agents and bank branches may staff their agencies and/or branches with staff from these migrant groups or with staff who speak the language and understand the culture of these groups. Similarly, companies with global businesses need to acknowledge diversity among their customers and their workforces. When organisations operate in an international environment, the diversity of cultural practices, ethics and employment practices need to be managed. It is often necessary to understand how domestic and international HR practices can complement each other.[27] The 'Managing challenges of globalisation: Woods Bagot: going global' case provides some examples of initiatives undertaken by Woods Bagot to meet the challenges posed by the engagement of a global workforce.

The industry taskforce on leadership and management skills (known as the *Karpin Report*, 1995) acknowledged the value of a less homogeneous managerial workforce as a means of dealing with an increasingly competitive environment. The *Karpin Report* predicted senior managers in 2010 will have more diverse personal characteristics than they did in the 1990s. It predicted that, in 2010, senior managers will be equally likely to be either male or female and come from a wide range of ethnicities and citizenships. This compares to the senior manager in the 1990s, who was usually a male Anglo-Celtic with Australian citizenship. It was also predicted that these senior managers of the future will be required to work in 'non-discriminatory environments' and will require skills to manage customers from diverse cultural backgrounds and have greater cross-cultural awareness.[28] The *Karpin Report* argued for diversity management as a means of improving the competitiveness of Australian business. It made recommendations for action in six areas associated with diversity. These recommendations involved:

1 women in senior and executive management
2 women on boards of publicly listed companies
3 women and management education
4 women and small business
5 the management of cultural diversity
6 indigenous people's labour-market participation and business activity.

Burton[29] demonstrates that a 'managing for diversity' approach is consistent with the *Karpin Report*'s recommendations for effective management in a future competitive environment. For instance, managers need to move from a short-term tactical focus to a longer-term strategic focus. They also need to shift from valuing homogeneity to

WOODS BAGOT: GOING GLOBAL

Woods Bagot is an architecture, consulting and design studio. Since the company's Adelaide launch in 1869, it has grown its operations with offices in 12 locations around the world, including Australia, Asia, the Middle East and Europe.

A number of years ago, the company had grown to work on larger, more complex projects, and it needed to restructure in order to accommodate further growth. It examined issues such as staffing levels for global projects, how the business could improve sustainability and how it could support international studios from its base in Australia.

A crucial part of the strategy involved global mobility, with a strong focus on workplace culture and retaining Generation Y employees as well as attracting further talent from across the globe. Woods Bagot finalised its people and culture strategic plan a year and a half ago.

'We do a lot of consulting with our team to find out what they want because, although our product is designed, it comes from our people, meaning our business literally is our people', says Tasmin McLean, Woods Bagot's human resources manager. 'If they're not on board with us, if we don't understand what they want and make sure our business strategy and what our people want is aligned, then we are not going to be a sustainable business. We paid a lot of attention to what they were asking for and what they were wanting to do.'

...

A challenge for Pirrello has been teaching managers within the business to think more flexibly when it comes to global mobility and prove that this is more beneficial for them. He was able to do this in the early days by arranging for an employee exchange. The two employees communicated constantly via email and telephone and they shared the differences in their cultural experiences and how the exchange contributed to their learning and development. This process was also shared with other staff via the intranet.

'We're working on encouraging the social dynamic to remain, because part of this is about remote teams as well. We're all part of the same team, particularly because we move around so much and people need to maintain their social roots in order to feel like they're still part of the team', says McLean.

Source: M. Yen, 2006, 'Woods Bagot: going global', *Human Resources* magazine, Issue 111, 22 August, pp. 12–13.
www.humanresourcesmagazine.com.au

---

acknowledging diversity as a source of competitive advantage. Training materials have been developed to encourage the development of skills and values consistent with a 'managing for diversity' approach among Australian managers.[30]

Although these claims were made in the 1990s, women are still poorly represented on boards, in senior management positions and in traditional male occupations. The *2006 EOWA Census of Women in Leadership*, produced by the Equal Opportunity Women's Association (EOWA), revealed that in the top 200 companies listed on the Australian Stock Exchange (ASX) at 1 February 2006, 12 per cent of executive management positions were held by women and 3 per cent of CEO positions were held by women.[31]

Managing change

A third reason that is often used for implementing a 'managing for diversity' approach is that it facilitates organisational and cultural change. The continuing major changes in world economies and markets require organisations to be adaptable and flexible in the ways in which they operate, in order to be successful. Adaptability can be achieved in a number of ways, including ensuring that a heterogeneous group of individuals is involved in making business and human resource management decisions. This will limit the influence of 'group-think' and 'cloning'.

Research has shown that policies seeking to manage diversity along the dimension of family status have been effective in managing work performance in times of organisational change.[32] A study at a manufacturing company in the United States found that the provision and use of policies that helped people manage their work and family lives contributed to employees experiencing a greater sense of belonging, improving work performance and accepting organisational change. This was particularly the case when employees were engaged in challenging and non-stressful jobs and had sensitive and supportive supervisors.

It has been found that work teams consisting of people from a variety of backgrounds are more able to contribute to an organisation's competitive advantage. They do this by improving marketing, through enhanced creativity and innovation and through improved problem solving.[33] The expected changes in the age structure of the population has implications for the composition of work teams. Bearing in mind predictions that the percentage of the population—and, therefore, potential customers—aged 65 years and over will increase from the current 12 per cent to 20 per cent in 2026,[34] the importance of including older workers as members of these teams is apparent. In addition, the increasing pressure on individuals to fund their living costs during their later years will no doubt increase the supply of older workers seeking employment. Older workers also have corporate memory, wisdom and longer-term time perspective, which could contribute to organisational effectiveness. (See the 'HRM spotlight' box.)

Ideological reasons

A fourth reason for the development of a managing diversity approach is one that reflects an ideology around the contribution of individuals. Such an approach is consistent with the human resource management approach to managing people, and it is based on the notion of matching the 'needs of the individual to those of the organisation' and integrating human resource decisions with business decisions.[35] Proponents of this approach place emphasis on maximising the potential of individuals who are gifted and creative, an emphasis that is consistent with diversity management. Such an approach requires determining commonly held stereotypes about these groups and it challenges the view that those individuals outside the dominant culture are deficient.

According to this view, the introduction of diversity management initiatives does not solely need to be based on business and efficiency reasons, it is also based on values, such as respect for the individual. Australian organisations such as AMP, NRMA and Alcoa have introduced policies that seek to allow employees to balance their work and home life, not only for business reasons but also because of a belief that demonstrating respect for individuals and their needs is part of the organisation's culture.[36] Similarly, Mobil Oil has introduced a diversity and inclusion program as part of the rebuilding of its company culture.[37]

Westpac operates in the financial services industry and it has taken a much broader view to diversity management by integrating it with corporate social responsibility. It believes:

> [our] future performance is firmly tied to our financial success, but the stark reality is while we must produce results for shareholders, we must also deliver for our customers, and we must meet our responsibilities to our staff and the broader community.[38]

Westpac identifies capabilities, attitudes and behaviours that reflect its values of teamwork, integrity and performance. One of the capabilities all staff need to display is a people capability, and diversity is one of the behaviours identified as reflecting this capability.

> ### INSIDE AGE DIVERSITY AT DEUTSCHE BANK
>
> **HRM SPOTLIGHT**
>
> Age diversity is one of Deutsche Bank's main global diversity initiative issues. This is based on its vision of demonstrating industry leadership by fostering an inclusive work environment in which all employees contribute to their full potential and diverse teams maximise performance. The bank sees this as essential for a true meritocracy, increased shareholder value and greater profitability.
>
> Management of age diversity means that the bank's business and people strategy is focused on all age groups and their individual demands for personal development, career, working practice and job design. Cooperation between different age groups is necessary and an important prerequisite for the success of teams, while managers are responsible for creating an inclusive work environment for all age groups.
>
> Age-related initiatives at Deutsche Bank focus primarily on the following aspects:
>
> - *Employability*. Deutsche Bank is engaged in various activities that focus on learning throughout the work life. This program includes measures that have a special focus on older employees—such as part-time retirement, and new professional perspectives inside and outside the bank as consultants or coaches.
> - *Training*. The needs of older employees, as well as their personal and professional perspectives, are picked out in special training that focuses, for example, on personal and professional orientation at the age of 40, or on preparing for an active retirement.
> - *Mentoring*. The sharing of personal experience and networking are an integral part of a close cooperation between more junior employees and experienced managers. This program has been in operation for more than five years, and it also assists in supporting women in their personal and professional development.
> - *Advanced professionals programs*. 'Know-how' transfer has been implemented in several divisions of the bank. Throughout this program, 'age awareness' training is conducted for HR managers, along with an interview and an Internet-based survey to gauge feedback on the appreciation of experience.
>
> *Source*: Based on U. Drewniak, 2004, 'Inside age diversity at Deutsche Bank', *Human Resources*, 5 May, p. 12. www.humanresourcesmagazine.com.au.

Initiatives to manage diversity

As mentioned previously, the development of initiatives to manage diversity needs to be undertaken at three levels:

1 the strategic level, which recognises diversity as critical for organisational success
2 the managerial level, which is associated with the formulation of management practices and structures that facilitate the effective management of diversity
3 the operational level, in which the practices are implemented in the workplace.

It is necessary to undertake initiatives at these three levels in order to build an organisation that truly manages the similarities and differences of people doing the work.

Strategic initiatives

Action at this level involves specifying and building the desired organisational culture, improving management systems, developing leaders for the future and specifying values that support the business strategy in light of how the population and workforce changes. This section briefly examines some of the processes associated with building a culture that supports values that respect diversity.

Three dimensions of culture need to be addressed when building such a culture. These dimensions are:

1. delineating the nature of the existing culture
2. establishing the dimensions of the desired culture
3. identifying the way in which the 'roots' of the existing culture hinder the development of the desired culture.

The first step involves establishing the dimensions of the existing culture. This can be done through a 'cultural audit'. Such an audit can be done by an outside consultant who can bring a degree of objectivity. Alternatively, in circumstances when trust is high within the organisation, an audit can be undertaken by organisational members, with the assistance of an outside consultant.[39] This audit process can involve in-depth interviews, written surveys, reviews of relevant organisational documents (for example, reports, manuals and memoranda), focus groups and direct observation of organisational members' behaviour. The data collected are used as the basis for drawing inferences about the attitudes of organisational members towards the issue of diversity.

The second step, establishing the dimensions of the desired culture, also involves a number of processes. These include a review of organisational values, so they reflect respect for the needs of individuals, involvement of all contributors in decision making, and processes that facilitate the adaptation of individuals and the organisation to these values. The values should form the basis of the processes used to manage people and the organisational structure. It is important to remember that individuals from a variety of employment relationships, not only employees, contribute to organisational performance and success.[40] Therefore, members of the flexible workforce and outsource providers could also be considered.

The next component of the cultural audit involves assessing formal procedures, such as human resource policies. This assessment provides the means to examine the extent to which the policies support or hinder the desired culture, particularly a culture that values diversity. For instance, policies about hours of work should be based on satisfying the needs of the business as well as the individual. This could be achieved in a variety of ways. It could involve job sharing, telecommuting or contracting the work out. It could also involve scheduling meetings at times that do not conflict with individuals' responsibilities outside the workplace. In the case of older workers, it could suit them to work fewer hours so they could start developing interests they can pursue during retirement.

The company, S.C. Johnson, is a medium-sized family owned business with a focus on innovative household products. It has one aspect of diversity–work–life balance as a core value. It developed a single initiative 'shorter Friday' policy to allow employees to compress their working week, so they can leave at 1 pm on Friday afternoon. The initiative requires that internal and external customer needs are met and it is dependent on results still being achieved. It has been supported by senior management by role-modelling the behaviour and leaving at 1 pm on Fridays.[41]

Esso has explicitly linked diversity management to its business. This has been done through the mission statement and three of its six core values. The mission is to be Australia's most successful petroleum exploration and production company. Diversity management is linked to strategic management, through the two core values, and is a critical success factor for achieving a third core value. The two core values are teamwork and concern for the individual. The critical success factor is maximising the productivity of its people and this is necessary for achieving the third core value, of achieving business excellence.

Esso also conducted a culture audit that assessed the extent to which Esso employees behaved in terms of its six core values, and it evaluated the effectiveness of the formal and informal people-management processes. The culture audit surveyed 27 per cent of the Esso workforce and provided data for the development of priority areas for action at the managerial level.[42]

Hewlett-Packard (HP) also has a core value of 'valuing diversity'. This value is used for performance evaluation. In HP, the behaviours associated with performing according to this value are specified. Such behaviours are exhibited by an employee who:

> Demonstrates a commitment to hiring, developing and retaining a diverse workforce. Creates an environment free of harassment that supports diversity and values individual differences. Actively participates in or supports efforts to recruit and develop minorities and women. Meets workforce diversity goals and/or Affirmative Action goals if appropriate.[43]

The specification of values as a basis for the development of a culture that supports the achievement of the business strategy is an essential foundation for diversity management initiatives. This also provides the basis for a review of human resource policies to ensure they are consistent with, and support, the values and the strategy. The 'Managing challenges through sustainability: 3M: Sustaining our future' case illustrates how 3M has integrated diversity as part of its global strategy.

Managerial initiatives

Once the review of human resource policies has been undertaken, it is necessary to formulate policies that provide for, and support, diversity management. These policies include:

- job analysis, employment structures and working hours
- recruitment and selection procedures and their criteria
- career paths, promotion procedures and their criteria
- performance management systems, particularly performance indicators, training and development procedures and their criteria
- mentoring procedures, communication and difference-management procedures
- the nature of competencies (wisdom, continuity and sense of history)
- reward systems, succession planning and support services, such as eldercare for family members and employee assistance programs

Managerial initiatives in many of these areas can be influenced by the clauses in industrial agreements and awards, which set standards for the above policies.

This stage involves integrating these policies so they support the values promoted by diversity management. This can be done in a variety of ways. For instance, Honeywell uses a Management Practices Index to correlate management styles and perceptions on bias. Four main areas are used to delineate management style. These are building rapport, supporting development, acknowledging value and recognising individuality. These dimensions are included in selection, and appraisal and pay settings; and employees are assessed and rewarded partly in terms of these dimensions.

At Digital, the aim is to make the principle of managing diversity an integrated part of the management practice by making it part of the duties of management and building it into managers' career structures. This is done by Digital's performance appraisal and reward systems, which take account of how managers meet affirmative action and EEO goals.[44] Similar arrangements exist at Westpac, where managers need to meet not only quarterly financial targets, but also EEO targets.[45]

3M: SUSTAINING OUR FUTURE

3M believes that active and responsible citizenship can make a successful company even stronger. We vigorously affirm our commitment to sustainable development through environmental protection, social responsibility and economic progress. We are committed to help meet the needs of society today while respecting the ability of future generations to meet their needs.

Our corporate values and sustainability

3M's sustainability policies and practices are directly linked to our fundamental corporate values:

- Act with uncompromising honesty and integrity in every thing we do
- Satisfy our customers with innovative technology and superior quality, value and service
- Provide our investors an attractive return through sustainable global growth
- Respect our social and physical environment around the world
- Value and develop our employees' diverse talents, initiative and leadership
- Earn the trust and admiration of all those associated with 3M worldwide.

Our sustainability strategies

3M's strategies for sustainability encompass the pursuit of customer satisfaction and commercial success within a framework of environmental, social and economic values.

- Meeting society's and 3M's expectations for environmental improvement:
  - Utilizing 3M's Environmental, Health and Safety Management System
  - Utilizing Life Cycle management to continuously improve the environmental, health and safety impact of our products and processes.
  - Making pollution prevention pay through development of technologies and products.
- Meeting employee and community needs as a socially responsible company:
  - Attracting and retaining a diverse and talented workforce.
  - Supporting continuous learning and knowledge sharing.
  - Supporting communities where we operate.
- Driving 3M's future economic success by satisfying our customers with innovative technology and products and providing our investors an attractive return on their investment.

MANAGING CHALLENGES THROUGH SUSTAINABILITY

Social Highlights

Bringing Greater Opportunity to Employees

Health and Productivity

Health and productivity scorecards have been introduced in US 3M plants. 3M continues to work to reduce preventable health care incidences and optimize productivity worldwide.

Performance-based compensation

3M employee awards are closely linked to the company's growth through employee performance and competitive compensation processes. By linking performance and pay, we are better able to nurture and reward accelerated performance and build on our status as an employer of choice. This, in turn, drives innovation and continues global strength and success.

Leadership development

3M's Leadership Development Institute includes the 3M Accelerated Leadership Development Program, an intense three-week accelerated development experience for some our promising leaders. Participants experience real-life learning by working on 3M business issues and presenting recommendations to senior management.

Career opportunity

3M's reputation as an industry leader and our culture of innovation continue to help attract and retain quality employees around the globe who value the 3M career opportunity.

Equal opportunity and diversity

3M considers a diverse workforce to be essential to the overall success of our company as well as an important social commitment. Diversity at 3M is defined as:

- Respecting differences
- Maximizing our individual potential
- Valuing our uniqueness
- Synergizing our collective talents and experiences for the growth and success of 3M.

As a global company 3M works with diverse customers in diverse markets. The diversity of 3M's global workforce is an indispensable asset and is key to global success.

Source: Extract from www.3M.com/sustainability, accessed on 22 August 2006.

In the early 1990s, following the arrival of Bob Joss at Westpac as CEO, a diversity management strategy was developed as a way of meeting stakeholders' needs. This strategy emphasised that managing diversity would positively impact on a range of stakeholders, including customers (through improved customer service) and shareholders (through better company performance) as well as on male and female employees. To support the strategy, Joss also introduced a measurement process for each business unit. These included statistics on financial, business and people outcomes.

The initiatives designed to promote diversity have developed since the mid 1990s. Initially, merit-based selection procedures were introduced; training and development policies were designed to raise awareness and educate managerial levels about the legislative framework underlying diversity management; core competencies were introduced to review the performance of executives and this became part of the succession planning process. As part of this process, potential candidates for critical positions were identified—with particular attention given to female candidates. The performance management system was reviewed so that it was based on the achievement of defined objectives and competencies.[46] Westpac has developed policies to manage working mothers, employees with disabilities, and more recently Indigenous Australians and mature-age workers, while still encouraging women in management.

The Mature Age strategy developed at Westpac is linked with broader strategy. The strategy was developed after research demonstrated that customers feel more comfortable obtaining advice from someone with similar age and experience. Therefore the mature age strategy seeks to align the composition of the Westpac workforce with the composition of the wider Australian community.[47]

At Esso, the data from the cultural audit provided information for the review of human resource policies. It demonstrated that many policies—including recruitment, training, working conditions, compensation, recruiting, benefits, terminations and transfers, and promotions—needed to be reviewed. The first step taken was to assist supervisors in creating a supportive environment and to make quite clear what behaviour was unacceptable. In addition, a workshop for supervisors was developed that enabled them to understand their managerial style and to develop a style which was consistent with a style that supported diversity. Themes of valuing and managing difference were also integrated into training courses that dealt with people issues for management. In addition, departments, with the assistance of staff in employee relations, developed diversity initiatives that were consistent with their business priorities.[48] Thoughtware Australia Pty Ltd is a small company of eight employees providing software and services to the information and technology and telecommunications, biotechnology and scientific industries. The focus of the business is quality work without regard to hours, starting and finishing times or location. The basis of the employment relationship is that employees are valued for their abilities and these are determined at the time of selection.[49]

A number of organisations in Australia have developed policies to manage a culturally diverse workforce. Qantas Flight Catering has an extremely diverse workforce, made up of people who have different linguistic and cultural backgrounds. A number of initiatives designed to assist staff who have language other than English (LOTE) were developed as part of an internal change program in Qantas Flight Catering. These include:

- a comprehensive induction program that documents all key information and provides for support in other languages
- a system that recognises prior learning so staff skills are documented

- developing a system that assesses qualifications gained in other countries
- developing workplace literacy for both English-speaking and LOTE staff through the Adult Migrant Education Service and supported by volunteer workplace mentors.[50]

At Air International, team structures and team leaders are pivotal for the operation of the plant. This is recognised by involving team members in the selection process. These team members are involved in identifying the qualities they consider desirable in a team leader. One instance of this process occurred in a team where 80 per cent of the team were Indo-Chinese people. Rather than select a leader on the basis of ethnic loyalties, they selected one on the basis of the qualities they had identified. The selected team leader was from another section but because of their involvement in the process, they immediately cooperated with the team leader.

The second phase in the development of a diversity management process is developing human resource policies that reflect the values, strategy, mission and vision of the organisation. Ideally these policies should support each other and be promoted by the senior managers in the organisation.

Operational initiatives

The implementation of human resource policies (see those discussed in the previous section) in the way intended by the policy developers remains one of the most difficult issues in organisations. Managers and supervisors are critical as change agents that are involved in building a culture that values diversity along a number of dimensions. They also play a central role as educator and trainer, and through this they act as change agents. In order to create a culture in which every employee has the opportunity to do his or her best work, a manager or supervisor must implement the policies designed to create an effective diverse workforce. Therefore, it is critical that individuals who understand the nature of diversity are selected for these positions and that behaviour which supports diversity is recognised through performance indicators and rewards.

Effective implementation, therefore, requires that the characteristics of the workforce are acknowledged at the beginning of the planning process that is associated with the implementation of change. Also, the consequences of these characteristics for implementing the policy change need to be assessed. By doing this it would be possible to:

- identify the type of preparation (such as pre-training, communication and developing work relationships) that is necessary before the introduction of change
- establish a realistic time frame and realistic expectations about the speed of change
- assist in the development of realistic milestones against which to measure change
- provide an indication of the resources necessary to make change effective.[51]

Successful diversity programs have been found to communicate the importance of the diversity philosophy in a variety of ways. These include personal intervention by top management, targeting recruitment of non-managers, internal advocacy groups, emphasising EEO statistics and profiles, providing for managing diversity training networks and support groups and providing specific strategies that explicitly seek to manage work and personal needs, such as family needs.[52]

There are many difficulties involved in implementing policy changes that are associated with diversity management initiatives. These are discussed in more detail in the following section. 'Managing challenges through HR innovation: Diversity in practice: BT' discusses some of the ways BT diversity training initiatives have been used with an eye to dealing with some of these challenges, particularly the 'tick box mentality'.

DIVERSITY IN PRACTICE: BT

BT is cited by many diversity experts as a leading example of a company that is taking diversity training seriously, and so achieving results. Caroline Waters, director of people and society explains how they are achieving this.

'We have built it into other types of training so that it is always relevant, timely and interesting.' So, while BT engineers can access specific diversity training courses, they will also encounter it in their general customer service training. For instance when finding out about home visits they will learn how to respect various religious traditions, or how to be sensitive to customers with a disability.

As well as this training, BT has appointed hundreds of diversity coaches. These are peer-group experts who are available to colleagues who want to ask advice about a diversity issue.

Waters says: 'We've got 102 000 employees and each of them learns in a different way, so we look to provide information and training in as many ways as we can. The most important thing to bear in mind is that learning isn't a one-off experience. It continues and people will be much more receptive if they can see how it fits into their day-to-day work.'

BT sees a strong business case for developing a culture which respects diversity, and Waters insists that it represents far more than a pure box-ticking exercise.

'Our business is all about customer service, so to maximise the commercial opportunities presented by an increasingly diverse UK … We need to understand our customers', she says.

MANAGING CHALLENGES THROUGH HR INNOVATION

Diversity and the tick-the-box mentality

… when companies recognise the benefits of true diversity, such as matching the customer base, increased innovation and improved morale, they realise that it delivers tangible financial benefits and better business outcomes. When those in senior management fully and consciously embrace the concept of diversity as a key value underpinning their business, diversity initiatives gain traction, and the organisation is on its way to authentic cultural change.

Sometimes the only way to get the attention of those at the top is by waving the stick of discrimination claims, costly lawsuits and bad publicity …

… authentic diversity is much more. These organisations are aware of current labour market forces and recognise that the way forward to sustainability is authentic inclusion of diversity.'

Source: Diversity@work's S. King & S. MacAdams, 2006, *Human Resources* magazine, Issue 107, 27 June, p. 13.
www.humanresourcesmagazine.com.au

Challenging issues associated with managing diversity

There are a number of challenges associated with managing diversity. These challenges fall into eight categories. They include:

1. the way in which the concept of diversity is understood and informs action
2. implementing techniques to manage diversity
3. demonstrating the improvements arising from diversity management initiatives
4. building a business case for implementing diversity management techniques
5. managing contradictory evidence
6. inexperience with the process
7. the nature of communication and decision making in organisations
8. attitudinal issues.

Concept of diversity

A major challenge associated with managing diversity is the way the concept of diversity is understood, particularly the concept of identity and the level at which identity is understood in organisations. As discussed earlier, when diversity is defined in a very narrow way, the prevailing social, economic and political arrangements are taken as given. Consequently, the approach to managing diversity involves providing policies that prevent discrimination and facilitate the integration of these groups into the existing arrangements. When diversity is conceptualised and managed in this narrow way, it fosters the development of policies that provide for equal treatment and compliance with laws and policies, particularly those providing for EEO. It distracts attention from the need to integrate employment policies with organisational needs and, at the same time, to take into account the different needs of members of different groups.

The broader concept of diversity allows a redesign of the giraffe house referred to by Krautil. Another way of expressing this broader view of diversity is in terms of climbing a ladder.

> Rather than helping people from disadvantaged groups to move up the ladder, managing diversity is more about looking at whether the ladder needs changing. It is less about helping different groups to cope within a dominant male, able-bodied culture; more about valuing the differences which people have.[53]

In Australia, most organisations adopt a narrow view of diversity. Many organisations have widened the door to the giraffe house, but they have not modified the inside of the house, nor have they examined the ladder to see if it needs changing. This is indicated by the tendency for large Australian organisations—previously covered by the *Affirmative Action [Equal Opportunity for Women] Act 1986* and now covered by the *Equal Opportunity for Women Act 1999*—to introduce written EEO policies concerned with some of the employment matters specified in the Act, particularly recruitment, selection, promotion and training. However, organisations have not widely addressed other issues, such as decreasing satisfaction with the balance between family and work life and issues of sexual harassment.[54] Legislation and government policy is critical in establishing expectations about desired standards of behaviour; however, one of the challenges is encouraging organisations to interpret the legislation from a broader perspective.

A further challenge associated with understanding the concept of diversity involves the difficulties of understanding identities in organisations.[55] Individuals have many identities reflecting characteristics such as their gender, ethnicity, function in the organisation, family situation and type of employment. Identities are, therefore, complex and multifaceted. They are also transient as characteristics associated with the secondary dimensions of diversity change. The process of managing diversity involves managing individuals with multiple identities. Associated with this challenge is the issue that there are individual differences within groups. Identities are not homogeneous within social groups. For instance, not all women have the same social identity, because of factors such as the nature of their employment or the role of significant men in their lives.

Identity, therefore, needs to be understood at a number of levels of analysis: individual, group/intergroup, organisational and societal. An understanding of diversity at these four levels recognises that initiatives taken to manage diversity involve actions at all four levels, not only one or two. For instance, if diversity is only understood at the level of the group, those individuals who do not share the 'norms' and values of a group with which they share demographic characteristics will be misunderstood. Although men share the same gender, individual men do not share the same domestic responsibilities. This has been recognised at Esso, where all employees—men and women—have access to 52 weeks parental leave, a variety of flexible working arrangements such as part-time work, adjustable work hours and working from home, and support for dependant care. This dependant care can include care for young children as well as elderly dependants.

Implementation of techniques to manage diversity

Interest in diversity management has been evident for more than a decade in the United States. The three most common techniques used there to manage diversity are 'diversity enlargement', 'cultural audits' and 'diversity sensitivity through training'.[56] A fourth technique often used is the establishment of 'advisory panels'. The following section examines a number of issues associated with implementing these techniques in organisations.

Diversity enlargement

Diversity enlargement refers to increasing the representation of groups with particular personal characteristics such as ethnic or gender backgrounds. The aim of this technique is to change the organisation's demographic composition, but it usually does not involve changing other human resource practices. Commenting on the United States, Kossek and Lobel claim, 'employers seem to assume that increasing diversity and exposure to minority employees will result in improved individual and organisational performance'.[57] They argue that in the United States, many employers implementing these changes do not really support them, but they feel that they are coerced by market demands and the need to appear 'politically correct'. As a result, when a technique of diversity enlargement is viewed as a forced change and is not supported by other policies in the organisation, the effectiveness of the policy is undermined.

In Australia, although the EEO and discrimination legislation in the federal and state jurisdictions does not require forced adherence to quotas, it is possible that some employers would feel coerced by expectations in the labour market and customers to increase the representation of members of particular groups.

Diversity enlargement
a technique aimed at increasing the representation of groups with particular personal characteristics, such as ethnic or gender backgrounds.

Diversity sensitivity through training

Interest in diversity training is quite widespread in the United States, with at least half of all major American companies having signed up for diversity workshops.[58] **Diversity training** is designed to change employee attitudes about diversity and/or develop skills needed in order to work with a diverse workforce. It usually seeks to promote awareness and sensitise people about diversity in order to promote understanding, tolerance and workplace harmony that will ultimately produce a more productive workforce.[59]

However, there is evidence that these workshops do not achieve their objective of improved cohesion between individuals, but, instead, heighten tensions, sharpen differences and increase competition and hostility as members of these groups view themselves as competing for jobs.[60]

Research indicates that people feel most comfortable with people who are similar to themselves in terms of socioeconomic status, gender and attitudes.[61] Group differences can quickly foster prejudice. Although it is not the intention of diversity training, such training can accentuate group differences and fuel prejudice, particularly if it only provides information about the differences between groups.

An instance of this occurred in the California-based grocery chain, Lucky Stores. These stores instituted diversity training sessions designed to teach their employees to acknowledge and cope with their racist and sexist assumptions about women and minority groups. Unfortunately, some employees sued the company for discrimination

Diversity training
is designed to change employee attitudes about diversity and/or develop skills needed in order to work with a diverse workforce.

and used the notes taken during the training as evidence. Lucky Stores was found guilty of discrimination and ordered to pay US$90 million.[62]

Cultural audits

A cultural audit has the potential to assist the process of building a culture that honours diversity. As mentioned earlier, building a culture requires understanding three dimensions of an organisation's culture: the nature of the existing culture, the dimensions of desired culture and the way in which the roots of the existing culture hinder the development of the desired culture. An organisation's culture can be established through a cultural audit.

Thomas[63] suggests this audit can be done by either an outside consultant or, in circumstances where trust is high, by organisational members with the assistance of an outside consultant. This process can involve in-depth interviews, written surveys, reviews of relevant organisational documents, focus groups and direct observation of organisational members' behaviour. The data collected can then be used as a basis for drawing inferences about the attitudes of organisational members towards the issue of diversity. It can identify the major obstacles faced by groups with particular personal characteristics[64] and provide an indication of how these obstacles hinder performance.[65]

Cultural audits are an essential part of managing diversity; however, they are not sufficient to build a culture that allows all members of the organisation to contribute to their fullest potential.[66] For a cultural audit to be effective, it is essential that the formal procedures, such as human resource policies, are assessed. This assessment provides the means to examine the extent to which an organisation's policies support or hinder the desired cultural values.[67]

There is also a danger that a cultural audit will leave the impression that the Caucasian-male culture is the problem and that the Caucasian men in the organisation must bear the burden of most of the change.[68] However, if managing diversity is a mutual process then the process must be inclusive, to allow all members to contribute to their fullest potential. Cultural audits, therefore, need to focus on not only the differences between groups but also the similarities among groups. It is then possible to acknowledge that these similarities and differences need to be managed through human resource policies and practices.

Advisory panels

Advisory panels can be one of two types. They can consist of representatives from all groups of employees in the organisation, with the panel being responsible for enhancing diversity in the organisation to improve organisational performance. Alternatively, these panels can operate as internal advisory groups, consisting of representatives of particular groups, such as women or a particular ethnic group. The representatives meet periodically with senior management to have open dialogue about obvious and subtle barriers impacting on their groups. These panels attempt to create a shared understanding of the challenges and opportunities associated with managing diversity.[69]

A number of organisations in the United States have formed advisory panels. These include Xerox Corporation, Avon, Digital Equipment and US West. Much of the success of these advisory panels came from the common understandings and relationships that were built between senior management and the members of the panels who represented only one specified group.[70]

A study of advisory panels in a large service company located in America's Midwest found both positive and negative effects from having advisory panels. Positive effects included increased sensitivity to diversity issues, improved career advancements and improved relationships within the organisation. More than two-thirds of those interviewed in the study believed the panels raised the sensitivity of senior managers to diversity issues, although only 40 per cent believed the sensitivity of middle managers had been raised. The panels fostered career advancements by encouraging managers to create opportunities through increasing the number of people in these identity groups and through promotion. Relationships in the organisation were improved through the panels by facilitating improved communication on racial and gender issues. This communication contributed to culture change; however, the study indicated that it takes time to create such change. It found members of panels that had been in operation for a greater length of time felt more positive about the results of the panels. The panels also produced negative effects such as increased resentment, limited effect on middle managers and the development of adversarial relationships between members of groups because of a fear of increased competition. As one woman who served on a panel said, 'There's some resentment. It is somewhat quiet. Mid level managers feel that being involved in panels gives women and minorities a power that's not readily available to them'.[71]

Demonstrating improvements

A further challenge associated with managing diversity is demonstrating organisational improvements. There is evidence that there are many benefits to the employer of managing diversity, such as improved employee performance,[72] enhanced workgroup problem solving, creativity and cohesion,[73] a more thorough examination of assumptions and implications of scenarios,[74] a higher level of critical analysis, a lower probability of 'group-think', improved flexibility, innovation and meeting customers' needs.[75] However, it is difficult demonstrating that improvements in individual, group and organisational performance are a consequence of strategies designed to manage diversity. The indirect benefits of managing diversity, such as increased morale, greater job satisfaction, higher productivity and an improved competitive edge are difficult 'if not impossible, to prove'.[76] In the United States it is reported that:

> Despite these reported benefits, their realisation has remained elusive for most firms. This is because traditional HR strategies to manage diversity have largely been introduced piecemeal, lacking integration with other systems. Consequently, they do not change the culture to support the management of heterogeneity; and they end up failing.[77]

It is, however, possible to demonstrate the costs of not valuing and managing diversity in organisations. Some of these costs include absenteeism, turnover, an inability to attract necessary staff, poor morale, increased stress and reduced return on training expenditure. A number of Australian organisations, such as NRMA, Commonwealth Bank, ICI Australia and Pacific Dunlop, have calculated the costs associated with the turnover and absenteeism of staff and realised the importance of limiting these behaviours by identifying the causes of the behaviours that contribute to the costs.[78]

Building a business case

Another challenge involved in managing diversity is the difficulty associated with building a business case that demonstrates that managing diversity adds value to the organisation. Other organisational initiatives 'that present more compelling, factual evidence of payback on investment win out over diversity initiatives, which seem to offer less predictable and tangible benefits'.[79] The most successful business case for managing diversity is one that focuses on attaining an organisation's long-term specific objectives, such as reducing turnover or absenteeism.

For instance, NRMA developed a 'work and family' program as an integral part of its broader strategy, 'improving the way we work'. The major issues associated with building the business case were:

- putting the issue on management's agenda
- building the options through exploration, analysis and development
- getting started through policy decisions, handling opposition and competing perceptions
- keeping the process of development and implementation going by identifying clear responsibilities
- monitoring the implementation against a completion date.

Factors that were critical for the successful management of these issues were the involvement of employees in all stages and a strong HR general manager. She was able to convince the executive of the value of the work and family program by using financial information that described the costs and benefits of introducing the program.[80]

Managing contradictory evidence

In addition, there is evidence that the greater the diversity of observable or primary attributes within a work group or organisational unit, the less integrated the group is likely to be[81] and the higher the level of dissatisfaction and turnover[82]. Negative effects have been found to be greater for the characteristics of race and gender rather than age[83]—thus, indicating the possibility that deep-seated prejudices against people with different racial and gender characteristics could be adversely influencing the management of diversity efforts.

There is also evidence that there are greater coordination costs associated with managing groups with a wide skill base, rather than groups composed of individuals with more homogeneous skills and backgrounds.[84] Similarly, the similarity of the time of entering an organisation can also be important in influencing interaction frequency and attraction between people.[85]

Therefore, one of the challenges of managing diversity is to increase problem solving and creativity within the group; but, at the same time, prevent or manage the dissatisfaction and failure to identify with the group that is associated with group heterogeneity.

Inexperience with the process

Managing diversity requires groups who have not previously worked together to relate as peers. There is evidence that one of the consequences of this is increased sexual harassment.[86] In order to effectively implement policies designed to promote diversity, these barriers will need to be dealt with.

Diversity has always existed in organisations, but individuals have suppressed their diversity —age, lifestyle preference and priorities with respect to families—in order to conform to the stereotype of a 'good employee'. A result of this suppression is that organisations are having trouble dealing with diversity around race and gender issues.[87] As discussed earlier, it can be expected that in the future organisations will also have difficulties managing issues around age and dependant-care responsibilities for aged parents and other family members.

Nature of communication, decision making and skill

The dynamics associated with the selection process of managers can limit the selection of managers from a variety of backgrounds. Managers prefer working with individuals who are similar to themselves because of ease of communication and sense of comfort.[88] This dynamic has been labelled *homosocial reproduction* and could prevent the selection and promotion of employees who are dissimilar to the managers already in organisations.

Galagan lists six barriers that inhibit the effective management of diversity:

- prejudice—equating difference with deficiency
- poor career planning
- a lonely, hostile, unsupportive environment for non-traditional managers
- a lack of organisational 'know-how' by non-traditional managers
- managers being more comfortable with their own kind
- difficulties in balancing family and career.[89]

She also identifies a tendency for managers to reach conclusions without understanding the problems. A pertinent example is the view that high female staff-turnover is related to family commitments. In fact, she found only 7 per cent of female managers leave for family reasons, while 73 per cent leave because they see limited opportunities for women in companies.

Attitudinal issues

In addition to the problems of misdiagnosis, there are major attitudinal barriers to effective management of diversity. These include:

- a denial of the issues
- a lack of awareness
- communicating 'bad' news further up the organisation
- a lack of trust in how others will react to diversity issues
- previous experience with diversity management policies that were unsuccessful
- compulsion to fix 'them not us'
- a need to be in control of all of one's job.

Thomas claims resistance can emanate from a variety of factors associated with perceptions and attitudes in the workplace, and from a lack of strong leadership and direction.[90] He identifies a number of factors involved. These include:

- insufficient motivation resulting from perceptions that diversity management is a legal, moral or social responsibility, rather than a business issue
- moving away from a commitment to assimilation to the prevailing culture
- insufficient understanding of organisational culture
- the presence of attitudes such as racism and sexism
- a detrimental view of affirmative action and a belief that any effort to introduce diversity is an attempt to introduce affirmative action
- lack of a strategic direction
- a desire to avoid risk
- insufficient leadership
- lack of power to succeed
- inadequate change-management skills
- too many other activities
- the way work is done.

Problems can often arise when diversity management programs do not acknowledge the 'other'; for example, the young Caucasian male without family responsibilities. For diversity management to be effective, all groups in the workplace need to perceive that employment policies operate to satisfy their needs as well as those of individuals with different personal characteristics. Therefore, a diversity program that specifically deals with the needs of employees with family responsibilities by introducing paid maternity leave and childcare referral services should also explain how existing policies, such as funding of management education programs and fitness centres, address the needs of many young males without family responsibilities.

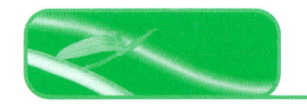

Work–life balance

An important—but singular—aspect of diversity management is enabling employees at different stages of their lives and with different family responsibilities and interests to lead healthy, balanced lives. There is substantial evidence from Australian studies that a large proportion of the workforce feels that the working and non-working parts of their lives are out of balance. This is particularly the case for those employees with family responsibilities. Management is able to implement initiatives that contribute to the achievement of organisational objectives and a competitive advantage in the labour market and, at the same time, satisfy employee needs. The successful implementation of these initiatives requires an acknowledgment of the costs and benefits of these initiatives. There is also a need to manage the perceptions of those employees who do not use the policies.

In Australia, programs known as 'work and family' or **family-friendly programs** include a variety of policy initiatives. The most widely used policies in Australia include flexible hours, part-time work, job sharing, telecommuting or working from home, use of employee sick days to attend to family commitments, employee assistance programs and relocation services.[91] Other policies that are less widely used include paid maternity and paternity leave, childcare information and referral services, eldercare information and referral services, support groups for employees with family issues and paid leave for adoptive parents.

However, many employees lack formal access to any work and family policies because of the nature of their employment relationship and these issues are poorly represented in enterprise agreements. Employees who are engaged on short-term contracts or as casual employees do not have access to these benefits.[92] Casual employees in Australia usually have a loading included in their pay as part compensation for the lack of benefits.[93] Permanent part-time jobs, however, provide the same employment conditions and benefits to their incumbents on a pro-rata basis. Industrial legislation such as the *Workplace Relations Act 1996* seeks to encourage the use of regular part-time work. It is worth noting that part-time workers have low rates of enterprise bargaining.

Many employees are dissatisfied with the balance between the hours they spend at work and the hours they spend with their families. Almost three out of 10 employees say they are dissatisfied with their work–family balance,[94] and more than a quarter of first-line supervisors report their own dissatisfaction.[95] An Australian Council of Trade Union (ACTU) study found that only 44 per cent of respondents to their survey were satisfied with their work and family balance.[96] This is a consequence of a number of factors, including work intensification and the development of a culture of long hours in many workplaces, particularly for professionals, paraprofessionals and managers.[97] It could also be the consequence of formal entitlements to policies such as carers' or

> **Family-friendly programs**
> HR policies such as flexible hours, part-time work, job sharing, telecommuting or working from home, use of employee sick days to attend to family commitments, employee assistance programs and relocation services.

family leave, or flexible hours not actually being used. It has been recognised that the existence of policies designed to improve work–life balance does not automatically create a family-friendly environment,[98] nor does it mean the policies are implemented.[99]

There are a number of consequences from not effectively managing employees' need for a balance between work and family life. Employees who feel work is causing problems in their personal lives are more likely to make mistakes at work.[100] They are more likely to consider resigning and to have unplanned absences from work and they are less likely to experience job satisfaction.[101] On the other hand, in circumstances where employees feel they work in supportive environments that assist them to manage their work and family needs, there is evidence this can lead to increased employee commitment, positive attitudes towards the organisation, improved personal and family lives and improved job satisfaction. These benefits have been found in high-stress work environments, too, where organisations often require more of their employees.[102]

There are a number of issues that need to be dealt with if a work and family policy is going to be effectively implemented. These include:

- getting the issue of work and family onto management's agenda
- building the options through exploration, analysis and development
- getting started through policy decisions and implementation
- handling opposition and competing perceptions
- keeping the process of development and implementation going.[103]

The effective development and implementation of work and family policies requires continuing input from individuals who passionately support the policies. They need to be skilled in demonstrating the benefits of the policies to the organisation and employees; able to organise support among senior staff and other stakeholders (such as trade unions); able to secure resources, manage opposition to the policies, effectively communicate the nature and value of the policies to managers and employees, and effectively use expert advice. The process of implementing work and family policies can be improved by systematically monitoring and evaluating the outcomes of work and family policies.

Alcoa World Alumina Australia operates two mines and three refineries in Western Australia. It adopts the principle that people are the linchpin of the organisation. It seeks to become the best company in the world by attracting and retaining the best people and by recognising and treating employees as individuals with different needs. Alcoa has a number of work and family initiatives including flexible work arrangements, flexible starting and finishing times, paid maternity and paternity leave, assistance with identifying dependant-care facilities and remote on-site childcare facilities.[104]

Many of the challenges raised in the previous section on diversity also apply to the area of work and family. These include the lack of clarity around the concept of work and family; for instance, there is the need to identify the criteria used to define 'family', the need to demonstrate improvements resulting from the introduction of work and family initiatives and the desirability of building a business case. In addition there is the need to manage the perceptions of those employees who are not able to use the work and family policies. There is evidence in Australia, the United Kingdom and the United States that many employees consider the availability of work and family policies for people with children unfair.[105]

One way these perceptions have been managed is to broaden the work and family initiatives into work–life balance programs. These programs provide all employees with some flexibility to manage their work and non-work life. For instance, a work–life balance program could provide employees with the opportunity for career breaks, access to a workplace gym or flexible hours for reasons other than family needs. However, some believe the broadening of work and family balance into work and life balance is premature. Although morale, performance and commitment could improve as a result of these work and life policies, there are not the same social obligations associated with interests as there are with family obligations.[106]

In 2004 the ACTU took a work and family test case before the Australian Industrial Relations Commission (AIRC). The ACTU sought to extend unpaid maternity leave from 12 to 24 months, provide full-time employees with a right to return to work part-time, enable employees to buy up to six weeks extra annual leave through salary sacrifice, request change of work location and start and finishing times after giving birth to a child. Employer groups and the Federal Government oppose the case, claiming it is not the role of business to meet the commitments of the ACTU claims. A consequence of the test case being won is that employers might discriminate against women of childbearing age. 'The Australian Industry Group (AIG) acknowledged the test case would force employers to think twice about employing women of child-bearing age …'[107] The AIRC decided it was necessary to include better provisions in awards. It extended the right to unpaid maternity leave to 24 months and provided employees with the right to return to part-time work.

In addition, work and family issues for men, particularly fathers, have come under increasing scrutiny. In Australia, this scrutiny has come from greater focus in the:

- political arena, particularly around matters of family law, domestic violence and the level of access men have to counselling services
- increasing participation of women in the workforce
- increasing employment insecurity
- increasing competition for talented workers.[108]

'Managing challenges through attracting and retaining people: Value the differences' discusses some of the options offered to employees in HBA Insurance and in the South Australian Water Corporation.

Future directions in diversity management

Managing diversity has not become a high-priority management initiative in Australian organisations. An understanding of the concept has been framed in terms of a narrow view of diversity that has been shaped by anti-discrimination and EEO legislation. Consequently, initiatives in Australia have primarily focused on the two aspects of the primary dimension of diversity: gender and race; and on one aspect of the secondary dimension: family status. Initiatives in Australia have included attempts to attract and retain women, develop existing female staff for senior-management positions and assist them in balancing their family and employment commitments.[109] The initiatives designed to facilitate work–life balance include more flexible working arrangements, holiday care programs and some paid parental leave. In the area of cultural diversity the two most common activities have involved training managers to manage culturally diverse workforces and promoting English literacy and language training in the workplace.

Diversity management in the future will continue to be influenced by legislation. However, it will also be influenced by the changing nature of the workforce and the nature of the relationships that the people doing the work have with the organisation. Just as human resource initiatives are increasingly required to demonstrate the benefits to the organisations, it will become more important for managers to demonstrate the value of diversity initiatives in terms of outcomes that benefit the organisation as well as the individuals within it.

VALUE THE DIFFERENCES

Peter Ward Head of strategy and change SA Water Corporation

At the SA Water Corporation, we are very interested in making sure that we both attract and retain women who may be considering having children—and we are keen to attract them back after maternity leave. In fact, this applies to all staff that want to take leave—for example young people who want to do a sabbatical overseas, not just young mothers.

We are therefore extremely flexible with our leave options. If someone has been here for a while, for example, they can take annual leave or long service leave at half pay. And in several instances, we have organised work for people while they are overseas through secondments with sister utilities. We find that when these workers return to Australia they have much more of a connection with us—and are more likely to return to work with SA Water.

Similarly, while people are overseas, we keep in contact with them by email. We had a major restructuring recently and we ensured that all our staff on leave overseas understood what was going on so they were in the loop when they returned.

We do all the standard things as well, like keeping particular jobs open for people and hiring employees for fixed terms so they know the job they will come back to is similar to the one they left. In addition, we are committed to work/life balance, not only for parents with children, but also for those looking after elderly relatives.

MANAGING CHALLENGES THROUGH ATTRACTING AND RETAINING PEOPLE

One of the main reasons we want to push the envelope in these areas is that we need a large number of engineers for the future of our business, an increasing number of engineers are young women.

At certain stages in their career these workers have different needs to men.

Penny Lovett, general manager, human resources HBA Health Insurance

… Having good policies is only part of the process; it's how you execute them that's really important. Organisations need to offer flexible work practices in a way that values those employees who choose to take them up and encourages them to succeed. Simply offering the policies is not enough. A culture that embraces flexible work practices is critical.

Sometimes this is just a matter of quite simple things: having workplace planning teams; being aware of part-time and job-sharing options; and providing appropriate resources for effective work-from-home (broadband communication). But a culture that values people's output, not just input is also necessary. Performance management systems that measure output can be a good way to recognise people for what they are contributing, rather than just the number of hours they are putting in.

Source: P. Somerville, 2006, 'Value the difference', *HR Monthly*, April, pp. 12–13.

Changing nature of the workforce

During the post-World War II period, the composition of the workforce in Australia became more diverse. The representation of members of a variety of non-Anglo-Saxon cultures, married women, women with children (including preschool-age children) and dual-income families increased. As mentioned earlier, some employers responded by introducing employment policies that enabled women to combine work and domestic responsibilities. During the early 1970s, pressure for government regulation and childcare funding increased and subsequently a number of initiatives were taken, including the *Child Care Act* in 1972. In 1988 the Commonwealth Government announced the first of a series of national childcare strategies that expanded the supply of childcare places.[110] Despite these initiatives, the cost of childcare prohibited women from entering the workforce.

However, it is anticipated that the characteristics of the workforce will change in different ways in the future. Managers are going to need to take into account the various needs of other groups of workers. Labour-force projections indicate that in 2011 the workforce will consist of more people aged over 45 years. The Australian

Bureau of Statistics (ABS) predicts that by 2011, 'Major gains will occur in the 45–54 year age group with a projected increase of 36 per cent for men and 75 per cent for women'.[111] It is also predicted that 'growth rates for 55–64 year olds will result in a 79 per cent increase, with that group becoming 10.8 per cent of the workforce in 2011'.[112] Consequently, as increasing numbers of the workforce belong to these older age groups, we could expect the primary dimension of age to become an important basis for the development of diversity management initiatives.

At a strategic level this could mean that managers would seek to build a culture that explicitly respects people irrespective of their age and, as part of this intent, review their human resource management policies to ensure they reflect this value. At a managerial level it could mean rewriting recruitment, selection, training, performance appraisal, communication and benefits policies and procedures so that they take into account the needs of older employees.[113] The Hertz car rental company, in partnership with the Victorian Government's 45-plus skills initiatives, developed a strategy of recruiting and retaining a more diverse workforce in an attempt to reduce a considerably high turnover rate. The strategy has been successful in increasing the number of employees aged 45 plus—reducing turnover and increasing social benefits to employees. Employees with previous business experience were found to be equipped to work in pressured conditions and employees of different ages learnt from each other on a personal and professional level.[114]

The experience at Hertz highlights another emerging need—the need to manage the different attitudes, expectations and knowledge of different generations. Research indicates employees aged between the mid 40s and late 50s and employees in their 20s have considerably different expectations about how people should be managed and appropriate employment conditions.[115] People born in the 1970s desire flexibility and like to keep their options open, while those born in the immediate post-war period are much more unsettled by constant change. Many of these younger employees are knowledge workers who need to be managed 'as a source of competitive advantage through their commitment, adaptability and high quality skill and performance'.[116] Managers need to accommodate the different expectations of the different generations and, at the same time, develop employment practices that encourage high performance and commitment to organisational outcomes.[117]

The box 'HRM spotlight: Hiring overseas workers' discusses the way in which skill shortages could encourage an even more diverse workforce in Australia. The issuing of '457 visas' to people in occupations in short supply in Australia is further enhancing the racial complexity of workforces.

Employment relationships

Not only will the composition of the workforce change in the future, but the nature of the relationships people have with organisations will also continue to change. The 1990s has been characterised by 'an upward trend in all kinds of non-standard forms of employment which undermine people's job security'.[118] There has been increasing use of casual work, temporary work, outsourcing and the use of agencies and other labour-market intermediaries.[119] Given the predicted changes in the *Workplace Relations Act 1996* and the continuing need for organisations to respond quickly in the marketplace, we could expect these forms of flexible employment to increase.

It, therefore, seems inevitable that employment relationships will become an increasingly important secondary dimension of diversity that needs to be managed. It has been argued that different management styles and expectations are required for different individuals depending on their relationship with the organisation and

HIRING OVERSEAS WORKERS

HRM SPOTLIGHT

In corporate and commercial circles, they call them 'skilled temporary migrants' or 'business long-stay'. To the trade unions and Labor Party, they are 'guest workers'. To the federal government's immigration department they are '457 visas'.

Call them what you will, the people granted entry into Australia as temporary workers [are] part of a new and growing international workplace. But this employment sector is not without controversy. While overseas recruitment is potentially a value tool to meet Australia's skill shortages, there are concerns that it is open to abuse—with grave consequences for the overseas worker, Australia's own workforce and the nation as a whole…

The federal government and other supporters of the program say it is ultimately improving job opportunities for Australians by helping business to expand and compete, and it enhances international knowledge transfer.

But the Labor Party and the union movement say too many employers are abusing the program, it's a poor substitute for long-neglected education and training, and it creates a second class of indentured worker. They say that due to the Howard government's recent industrial 'reforms', the imported workers can sign individual contracts that will drive down wages and conditions for all workers, which is the government's ultimate intention.

The government needed to introduce more stringent checks to ensure employers and migration agents were not docking pay with unreasonable charges for recruitment fees, rent, transport and other costs they made compulsory.

The unions' line of attack has been to expose allegedly exploitative behaviour by specific employers. The employers listed as having skills shortages serious enough to warrant the visas include meat workers, IT professionals, engineers, maritime workers, welders, electricians, bakers and chefs, and the list is growing.

… In early July Toll Holdings was considering importing truck drivers … Vanstone was due to meet industry unions to discuss allegations that abattoir workers on 457 visas were being underpaid and used in unskilled roles. Toll, like many other employers, said it couldn't get the staff it needed to keep on trucking because they were being sucked up by the booming mining sector.

… A Perth heavy engineering company was charging Chinese workers $10 a week for having safety signs interpreted into a language they could understand. In another example, the Liquor, Hospitality and Miscellaneous Union highlighted the plight of six Filipino chefs in Canberra. It said they were being shunted from kitchen to kitchen in a flash café-restaurant scene with a 'simmering culture of racial abuse, worker harassment and wages theft'.

Source: Extract from S. Packer, 2006, 'Welcome?': Hiring overseas workers is proving to be a controversial answer to the skills shortage', *HR Monthly, September,* pp. 16–22.

---

that there will be movement of individuals between different relationships.[120] For instance, an older worker might choose or be required by their employer to move from full-time employment to the role of consultant to the organisation or to part-time work.

Adding value

Management functions are increasingly under pressure to demonstrate the extent to which they add value to the 'business'. This has been reflected in the widespread retrenchments of managers in Australia[121] and the intense debate about the value of managers in areas such as human resource management.[122] Adding value to the organisation can be demonstrated in a number of ways. It can be demonstrated, first, by indicating the impact of the policies on employee behaviour and human resource costs and, second, by outlining the impact of policies in a diversity program on organisational performance indicators, such as stock-market prices.

In the United States, it was found that there was a relationship between announcements regarding the management of a diverse workforce and stock-market evaluations. Announcements of quality affirmative-action programs are associated with positive results on the stock market, while announcements of discrimination settlements against organisations were associated with negative stock price changes.[123]

Similarly, adding value to the organisation can be demonstrated by assessing the impact of particular policies on employee behaviour that are costly to the organisation, and then changing those behaviours. It has been demonstrated that improved maternity leave benefits increase the retention of employees in Australian,[124] British[125] and American[126] organisations. Similarly, it has been demonstrated that the provision of childcare facilities and other benefits that seek to manage individuals' work and family lives can improve employee productivity and change employee behaviour.[127]

MANAGING PEOPLE

AGEING WORKFORCE ATTITUDES ENTRENCHED MANAGEMENT

Entrenched attitudes towards recruiting, retaining or re-skilling mature-aged workers are the central challenge to engaging their participation in the workforce, according to John Plummer, president of the Recruitment and Consulting Services Association (RCSA).

Speaking at a recent symposium on the ageing workforce, he also said that change is not going to result from policy change alone, as it needs to be led from within an organisation and from the top.

'Age can and does work—age works to benefit the worker and age works to benefit the organisation', he said.

'There are too few examples of organisations successfully and effectively integrating aged workers into their workforces.'

He pointed out that mature-aged workers do provide economic and workplace benefits for business, and cited findings from workplace surveys and analysis, which showed productivity increases as well as general benefits for the workplace environment.

The symposium, which brought together policy makers, employers and commentators to identify the solutions to developing the ageing workforce, also found that a combined industry, union, business and workplace response and a number of actions are required—there is no single policy fix.

Plummer said that choice was key in providing opportunities for the ageing workforce and for business—choice of employment situation, diversity of opportunities for mature-aged workers to develop existing skills or to re-skill, along with choice in superannuation and financial regimes.

'Choice and diversity to allow employers the choice of employment opportunities that make sense to achieve productivity and provide gains for their business', he said. 'The natural ageing of Australia's population will occur—this is inevitable. The role and place of the aged workforce in this ageing process will shape our workplace and our society for decades to come.'

Plummer's comments come on the heels of a recent survey, which found that persistent government and media attention toward the impact of Australia's ageing workforce has done little to influence employers, with 62 per cent of companies remaining oblivious to the issue.

The survey was conducted by Catalyst Recruitment and took in 103 Australian companies of various sizes. The survey also found that only 26 per cent of the companies had strategies in place to manage the potentially harmful impact of the ageing workforce on their businesses. It revealed larger companies were more likely to appoint mature-aged employees, but the major obstacles to their employment were their resistance towards change and technologies.

Across the board, knowledge, stability and wisdom were identified as highly-attractive characteristics of mature-aged employees.

Source: Based on 2004, 'Ageing workforce attitudes entrenched', *Human Resources,* 11 August, p. 1, 6. www.humanresourcesmagazine.com.au

QUESTIONS

1 In addition to the reasons stated in this case, why do you think Australian employers are hesitant about employing mature-age employees?
2 What are some of the consequences of people being discriminated against on the basis of age?
3 What are some of the policies that employers could use to effectively manage a diverse workforce that includes mature workers?

CHAPTER SUMMARY

Although the concept of diversity management has not been widely used in Australian organisations, it is likely that increasing attention will be paid to managing employees with different identities based on personal characteristics and on different employment relationships. This will be done in the context of using techniques to ultimately improve the organisational outcomes. Managers intent on introducing initiatives to manage diversity will need to be able to clarify their notion of diversity and the implications of this notion for the policies used to manage the similarities and differences in their organisation. They will also need to demonstrate the value of the initiatives to the organisation and be able to market a case for the introduction of the initiatives.

WEB EXERCISES

Go the Equal Opportunity for Women Agency (EOWA) website at www.eowa.gov.au. This website provides information about the agency, copies of its newsletters and its most recent annual report. Explore the website and answer the following questions.

Questions
1 Describe the initiatives undertaken in three Australian organisations to improve the experience and position of women in their organisations.
2 Describe some of the initiatives undertaken by the agency to assist employers to promote EEO.

DISCUSSION QUESTIONS

1 Identify the differences between an EEO program and a diversity management program.
2 What are some of the advantages and reasons for promoting diversity among the staff of a university or another organisation with which you are familiar? Suggest ways in which diversity among academic staff could be encouraged.
3 A chief executive officer of a large financial institution has asked you to explain the processes involved in developing a diversity program. Outline the steps you would describe.
4 What are some of the difficulties that will need to be dealt with when a diversity program is introduced into an organisation? Suggest ways in which these difficulties could be overcome.
5 What arguments would you use to explain the benefits of policies designed to achieve work–life balance to a senior manager? What are some of the challenges the introduction of such a program could encounter?
6 A retailer with extended shopping hours is experiencing extremely high turnover among its managers and customer-service staff. Of the managers that remain, 60 per cent are expected to retire in the next three years. Suggest ways in which the costs of turnover could be reduced and the expected exodus of managers could be managed using diversity management policies.
7 Do you think most Australian organisations are ready for diversity management policies? When discussing this question you will need to consider the economic, social, legislative and political arrangements influencing organisations, the economy and the labour market. If so, in what circumstances do you think they would be most effective? If not, explain why.
8 Suggest ways in which the results of diversity management could be measured.

PART 3 Developing People

9. The receptionist in your office has come to you and asked if he could change his existing work hours from 9 am to 5 pm, to 11 am to 7 pm. His daughter has taken up rowing and he needs to drive her to rowing training four mornings a week. The office is open all day, from 9 am to 5 pm. What suggestions would you make to the receptionist?

10. You are the chief executive officer of a large women's hospital and have a 'dream' to build a long-day care centre for children that could be used by staff and patients. However, you know the obstetricians will oppose spending money on such a centre. They would prefer to spend money on refurbished consulting rooms. What would you do to try and see your 'dream' realised?

CASE STUDY

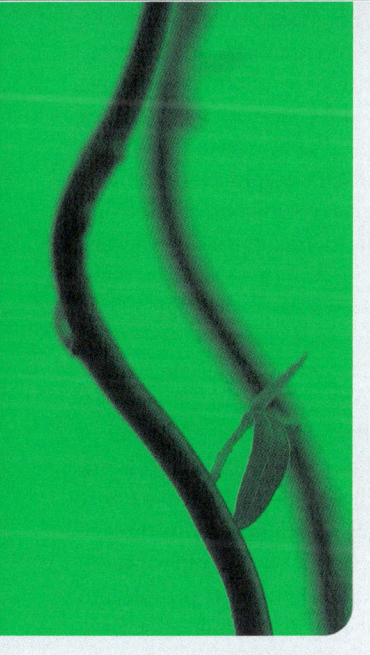

DOES DIVERSITY PAY?

The push for organisations to represent the broader community and make tangible, measurable efforts to improve equality of opportunity helped reshape the Australian workforce in the twentieth century.

By the time the new millennium dawned, executives and HR professionals in the public and private sectors could point to glossy brochures, weighty manuals and impressive web pages spelling out diversity policies and procedures. They could report increased numbers of women in senior roles, improved workplace access for people with disabilities, and training programs to impress on managers and workers that sexual harassment and racial discrimination were definite no-nos.

Many took a leap of faith, arguing that fostering diversity was more than a social and ethical imperative. It made good business sense. How far the rhetoric matched reality often went unquestioned. Neither good-hearted liberals nor harder heads with a sophisticated understanding of the public relations value of the triple bottom line felt any great need to query the assumption that diversity would pay. Those who opposed it often did so on similarly slim empirical grounds.

Now the question is being asked: Would a more rigorous analysis of diversity's impact increase its benefits? Could a more analytical approach help organisations derive greater benefits from diversity?

A new report shows how businesses can use diversity to improve relationships with existing customers and win new customers; forge new market opportunities; maximise workplace productivity; and access new and specialised skills—particularly those in short supply in Australia.

The report, *Making Diversity Work for your Organisation and Australia's Future*, was launched last month by Drake International and the Citizenship and Multicultural Affairs Minister, Gary Hardgrave.

'Australian companies must capitalise on the language skills, cultural experience and personal networks of employees from different backgrounds', says Hardgrave.

He says that embracing cultural diversity will help increase exports and 'create workforces better equipped to meet the challenges of our increasingly competitive market'. Meanwhile a shortage of job candidates may force employers to build more diverse workforces.

Andrew Dingjan, national marketing manager for Drake, says: 'Demand is outweighing supply in the accounting, construction and health fields right now, and while some companies are managing the shortage quite well by drawing on the full potential of the workforce, others are floundering.'

'To find the best possible staff we encourage businesses to recruit from 100 per cent of the talent pool 100 per cent of the time.'

He warns that it is not a numbers game.

'Hiring a bunch of people from different backgrounds will not automatically deliver business benefits', says Dingjan. 'Workplace integration, inclusiveness and effective management are needed to make diversity work.'

American research suggests it is time HR practitioners and others committed to fostering diversity moved beyond rhetoric about an inherent diversity–performance link.

A report by the Diversity Research Network, led by Thomas Kochan and George M. Bunker (professor of management at the Massachusetts Institute of Technology Sloan School of Management) reports that those who want to invoke the business case probably need to reframe the argument. The report explains that they should start by recognising that there is virtually no evidence to support the simple assertion that diversity is inevitably good or bad for business.

The report's views are based on discussion with business and industry leaders and a five-year study of four large organisations with solid records of diversity initiatives.

'It may be that the business case rhetoric has run its course', it concludes. Diversity professionals, industry leaders and researchers might gain more from presenting diversity as a societal expectation and a reality of labour and customer markets.

The research indicated that, to be successful in working with and gaining value from diversity, companies needed to take a sustained, systematic approach and adopt a perspective that considered diversity to be an opportunity, for everyone in the organisation, to learn from each other about how to better accomplish their work. The research also indicated that policies needed to inculcate cultures of mutual learning and cooperation.

It also indicated that human resource practitioners need to take a more sophisticated approach to data collection and analysis of the consequences of diversity and organisational efforts to manage and benefit from it. Otherwise they would be limited in what they could learn about managing diversity, and 'their claims for diversity as a strategic imperative warranting financial investment weakened accordingly'.

Jack Noble, CEO of Diversity@work, a Melbourne-based social enterprise, says that a focus on inclusion can help companies create cultures that do more than tolerate difference, enabling people from all sorts of backgrounds and life experiences to contribute.

Noble believes the desire to be regarded as good corporate citizens and to avoid anti-discrimination claims will continue to drive executive support for diversity programs. 'Reputation is increasingly important. Whether an organisation is looking at how to be an investment of choice, an employer of choice or a business of choice, it is all to do with reputation.

'Managers who visualise their twenty-first century organisations as fiercely competitive, agile and indestructible know they need to have the best people. This will happen only when they have developed a culture of inclusion that fosters innovation, loyalty and productivity.'

'… Meanwhile diversity practitioners are facing up to what may be one of Australia's biggest personnel challenges ever. Older workers will become critical to the survival and success of organisations as the nation's population ages', as Kevin Andrews, federal minister for employment and workplace relations told a symposium in Sydney last year.

Employment and training practices will have to be reviewed to encourage older workers not to opt for early retirement. Human resource staff in the public service have already been briefed on the need for strategies that attract and retain valued older workers. Public service managers have been urged to get familiar with employee retirement intentions, to use learning and development to motivate and equip older workers, and to recognise and reward older staff. They are also looking at how flexible working arrangements and phased retirement can encourage people to keep working longer.

'In the 1982–92 period, 56 per cent of the labour market growth came from the 35–44 age group and 31 per cent from the 45-plus group', says Professor Louise Rolland of Swinburne University of Technology's Centre for Work and Ageing. Expectations for the 2000–10 decade are that only 7 per cent of labour force growth will be in the age group of 35–44 years, with 85 per cent in the older group.

'The shift is fundamentally changing the profile and level of labour supply', says Rolland. 'Companies that have exploited oversupply will have to change their practices to be attractive to the available workers.'

Source: Based on C. Rance, 2004, 'Does Diversity Pay?', *HRMonthly*, April, pp. 22–5. *HRMonthly* is published for the Australian Human Resources Institute, www.ahri.com.au.

QUESTIONS

1 Consider some of the implications for the management style of managers who are younger than the workers they manage.
2 How do you think training, learning, rewards, job designs, hours and leave arrangements would need to change in order to accommodate older workers who want to return to, or remain in, the workforce?
3 Discuss the ways in which employers could assist employees who have responsibilities for their elderly relatives.

CHAPTER 10
PERFORMANCE MANAGEMENT

Objectives

After reading this chapter, you should be able to:

1. Identify the major determinants of individual performance.
2. Discuss the three general purposes of performance management.
3. Identify the five criteria for effective performance management systems.
4. Discuss the six approaches to performance measurement, the specific techniques used in each approach and the ways in which these approaches compare with the criteria for effective performance management systems.
5. Choose the most effective approach to performance measurement for a given situation.
6. Discuss the advantages and disadvantages of the different sources of performance information.
7. Choose the most effective source or sources of performance information for any situation.
8. Distinguish types of rating errors and explain how to minimise each in a performance evaluation.
9. Identify the characteristics of a performance measurement system that follows legal guidelines.
10. Conduct an effective performance-feedback session.

How investors rate human capital

Shareholder demands for 'corporate sustainability' are increasing, and it is little wonder. After the recent company collapses, the information technology and telecommunications (IT&T) sector's decline and the bear market of the last three years, they want evidence that their investments will last the distance. More than half of all Australians own shares, and many of them are increasingly anxious to protect their share-bound retirement savings.

The need to look beyond balance sheets for signs of long-term sustainability is driving slow but powerful market changes. Socially responsible investors are beginning to influence mainstream investment decisions, with high-performing stock indexes such as the Dow Jones Sustainability Index (DJSI) becoming more popular.

Human resource practices constitute or directly influence up to 75 per cent of the DJSI's criteria; this is consistent with recent studies indicating that companies with advanced HRM are more likely to have, or develop, strong share prices. In the 2002 Watson Wyatt study of 750 large public companies, those scoring highly in its human capital index returned 64 per cent over five years. Companies with sophisticated human-capital practices have outperformed the Australian Stock Exchange (ASX) All Ordinaries Accumulation Index by almost three times over 20 years, with a dramatic increase in performance after 1997, according to *The First XI Winning Organisations in Australia* (2002).

Human-capital-measurement specialist, Dr Laurie Bassi, launched an investment management firm in the United States in 2001 with portfolios of companies making 'significant investments in training and learning for their employees'. She was inspired by her study (with Dr Daniel McMurrer) that looked at 500 United States companies over five years. It found that firms making the largest employee development investments returned 137 per cent, compared with 55 per cent for the Standard and Poor's 500 Index. They concluded that a firm's training investment was the single most important statistical predictor of stockholder return.

Some of Australia's biggest institutional investors, the superannuation funds, are beginning to show an interest. After commissioning a review of 2001–02 annual reports, the combined public sector and Commonwealth superannuation schemes and Catholic Superannuation Fund used their considerable leverage to call for companies to disclose more information about the implications of workplace safety.

Hans Kunnen, head of investment markets research at Colonial First State, reinforces the view: 'To the extent that HR issues impinge on overall company earnings and their sustainability, then yes, it's a high priority'.

People are treated as short-term costs rather than as long-term assets, according to Bassi, McMurrer and Karen McGraw in a white paper for their United States-based consultancy, Human Capital Capability. They say that United States' quarterly reporting requirements have led to ignorance of long-term value creation.

Dr Carol Royal of the University of NSW says that while Australian reporting requirements are half-yearly, the trend is evident here too. She says that analysts and fund managers use sophisticated financial analytical tools, but limited qualitative analysis of HR functions, when assessing a company's earnings capacity. Kunnen says, 'HR is a marginal consideration. If you're already worried that earnings growth isn't very robust, something like high executive turnover, could tip the scales'.

So what HR factors do influence Australian investors' decisions? Executive remuneration is an obvious one. 'We want to see adequate benchmarks in place, adequate hurdles they have to overcome, and something other than a very short-term based structure', says Kunnen. While Kunnen wants evidence of equity in executive options, his priority is executive management quality.

> **How investors rate human capital** *continued*
>
> Succession planning is undergoing scrutiny—that is, the quality of the top management layer, rather than the top two or three executives. A stream of executive departures at the Commonwealth Bank and other incidents last year caused concerns for investors.
>
> At Amcor, five HR initiatives are actively promoted to investors, including: succession planning and executive development, blending global strength with local knowledge (utilisation of local talent, not costly expatriate talent), and selecting 'the best of the best' staff during acquisitions and mergers. Peter Wilson, the executive general manager of HR, says that the latter initiative sent a powerful message to the investment community during two recent mergers in which employees of the acquired businesses were selected to run new Amcor business units.
>
> 'We focused on securing the company for the future rather than simply selecting our own', says Wilson.
>
> 'To meet demands for more information on succession planning and management quality, Amcor has recently begun giving analysts more access to its top 50 managers, rather than its top two, as well as more information on executive remuneration and development'.
>
> *Source:* Adapted from F. Sexton, 2003, 'How investors rate human capital', *HRMonthly*, August, pp. 18–22; Leon Gettler, 2000, 'New economy unearths hidden asset : human capital', *The Age*, 2 June, p. 5.

Introduction

Companies that seek to gain competitive advantage through employees must be able to manage the behaviour of all employees—and its subsequent results. The 'How investors rate human capital' case on the preceding page illustrates that some of the most difficult challenges faced by managers are: identifying indicators to measure the value of people; identifying the links between employees' performance and business performance; and how to reward and develop performance. This is particularly the case with knowledge workers.

Performance appraisals are widely used in Australia for many employees and their use increased during the 1990s. Organisations are most likely to use performance appraisals for managers, professionals and technical employees, with about 90 per cent using them for these employees. Although they are not as widely used for clerical and manual employees, 89 per cent of organisations used performance appraisals for clerical staff and more than 60 per cent used them for manual employees.[1]

Traditionally, the formal performance appraisal system has been viewed as the primary means for managing employee performance. Performance appraisal was an administrative duty performed by managers and it was primarily the responsibility of the human resource function. Managers view performance appraisal as an annual ritual—they quickly complete the form and use it to catalogue all the negative information they have collected on an employee over the previous year. Some managers spend as little time as possible giving employees feedback because they may dislike confrontation and do not feel that they know how to give effective evaluations.

Not surprisingly, most managers and employees dislike performance appraisals! The major reasons for this dislike include the lack of ongoing review, employee involvement and recognition for good performance.[2]

Some deficiencies in performance appraisals which are often cited are listed as:

- discouraging teamwork
- assessors are inconsistent or use different criteria and standards
- only valuable for very good or very poor performer
- encourages employees to achieve short-term goals
- too subjective
- produces emotional anguish.

However, these potential problems can be prevented by:

- making collaboration a criterion on which employees are evaluated
- providing training for managers and identifying patterns of performance evaluations that suggest bias or over- or under-evaluation
- evaluate specific behaviours or results to show precisely what employees need to improve
- include long-term and short-term goals in the appraisal process
- managers should be appraised for how they appraise their employees
- evaluate specific behaviours or results
- focus on behaviours, do not criticise employees or comment on their personality, appraise on time.[3]

We believe that performance appraisal is only one part of the broader process of performance management. We define **performance management** as the process through which managers ensure that employees' activities and outputs are congruent with the organisation's goals. Performance management is central to gaining competitive advantage.

Our performance management system has five parts: defining performance, facilitating performance, encouraging performance, measuring performance and feeding back performance information.

The first part of our performance management system specifies which aspects of performance are relevant to the organisation. Job analysis provides the basis for this by establishing the activities and responsibilities required of individuals and teams (discussed in Chapter 6 Analysis and design of work). For instance, in a self-managed team, it is important that team members understand their responsibilities. This can be done by clarifying responsibilities, such as the individual responsibilities regarding particular roles in the team, and clarifying which responsibilities team members will share—such as selecting members of the team, assessing each other's performance and determining how the team members will make decisions. Establishing standards of performance is also an important part of the process of defining performance. This can be done by establishing desired results or outcomes. It can also include establishing the competencies required for effective performance. These competencies are observable on the job and could include skills, knowledge, social role, self-image, trait and motives.[4]

Second, a performance management system facilitates performance by removing obstacles that limit performance. These obstacles could include such factors as outdated equipment, insufficient training and inefficient work practices. Consider the recent finding of the Australian Transport Safety Bureau that showed the performance of Qantas pilots was limited by a lack of training in how to land on wet runways and that this lack of training contributed to an accident.[5] Performance can be facilitated by

Performance management
the process through which managers ensure that employees' activities and outputs are congruent with the organisation's goals.

providing adequate resources such as capital, material and people resources. It has been found that in circumstances where employees lack the tools to achieve the desired performance standards and goals, they become disenchanted and frustrated.[6]

Third, a performance management system needs to encourage maximum performance. This can be done by providing sufficient rewards that are valued by employees. These rewards need to be provided at the right time, usually as soon after the accomplished performance as possible. In addition, the rewards need to be valued by the employees and seen as fair, compared to the rewards provided to other people. It has also been found that there is a strong connection between organisational climate and performance. In situations where managers foster a motivating climate, it is more likely that employees will be enthusiastic and willing to perform.[7]

Fourth, a performance management system needs to measure those aspects of performance that are important for achieving competitive advantage and the organisation's strategy. This is traditionally done through the **performance appraisal**. This is a process that allows for assessing progress towards the achievement of the desired goals or other performance standards. Effective measurement of performance requires careful identification of the performance indicators so that people are clear about the behaviours they need to display. It also requires regular assessment of progress towards these behaviours. Therefore, the annual or six-monthly formal review is only one part of the process of managing employee performance.

Fifth, a performance management system provides feedback to employees through performance feedback sessions, so that employees can adjust their performance to the organisation's goals. The information from the performance appraisal can be used to make a number of human resource decisions. These may include decisions about rewards (for example, merit increases or bonuses) and decisions about development, career management and succession planning.

In this chapter, we examine a variety of approaches to performance management. We begin with a model of the performance management process that helps us examine the system's purposes. Then we discuss specific approaches to one aspect of performance management—the performance appraisal—and the strengths and weaknesses of each. We also look at various sources of performance information. The errors resulting from subjective assessments of performance are presented, as well as the means for reducing those errors. Then we discuss some effective components of **performance feedback**. Finally, we address components of a legally defensible performance management system.

Performance appraisal process that allows for assessing progress towards the achievement of the desired goals or other performance standards.

Performance feedback the process of providing employees with information regarding their performance effectiveness.

An organisational model of performance management

Performance management involves a range of activities, one of which is performance appraisal and feedback. For many years, researchers in the field of HRM and industrial organisational psychology focused on performance appraisal as a measurement technique.[8] The goal of these performance appraisal systems was to measure individual employee performance reliably and validly. This perspective, however, tended to ignore some considerably important influences on the performance management process. Thus, we begin this section by presenting the major purposes of performance management from an organisational perspective, rather than from a measurement perspective. To do this, we need to understand the process of performance. Figure 10.1 on page 346 depicts our process model of performance.

As the figure shows, individuals' attributes—their skills, abilities and so on—are the raw materials of performance. For example, in a sales job, an organisation wants someone who has good interpersonal skills and knowledge of the products. However, it is worth noting that employees make choices about how they use their abilities. They make choices about the level and persistence of the effort they will make. This level of effort is often labelled motivation.

The processes of recruitment and selection influence the level of ability held by people in an organisation. Effective recruitment and selection becomes particularly important in jobs involving high levels of discretion, specialised skills and sales work.[9] As discussed in the chapter on recruitment and selection (Chapter 8) there is a need to adopt 'best practice'—that is, to make selection decisions more valid and reliable. However, the nature of the practices used will be contingent on the nature of the job and the strategy of the organisation.

These raw materials are transformed into objective results through the employee's behaviour. Employees can exhibit behaviours only if they have the necessary knowledge, skills, abilities and other characteristics. Thus, employees with good product knowledge and interpersonal skills can talk about the advantages of various brands and can behave in a friendly, helpful manner (not that they necessarily display those behaviours, but they can display them). On the other hand, employees with little product knowledge or poor interpersonal skills cannot effectively display those behaviours. The objective results are the measurable, tangible outputs of the work, and they are a consequence of the employee's or the workgroup's behaviour. In our example, if a salesperson displays the correct behaviours, he or she will likely make a number of sales.

Another important component in our organisational model of the performance management system is the organisation's strategy. The link between performance management and the organisation's strategies and goals is often neglected. Chapter 2, Strategic human resource management, pointed out that most companies pursue some type of strategy to attain their revenue, profit and market share goals. Divisions, departments, workgroups and individuals within the company must align their activities with these strategies and goals. If they are not aligned, then the likelihood of achieving the goals becomes small. How is this link made in organisations? Primarily by specifying what needs to be accomplished and what behaviours must be exhibited for the company's strategy to be implemented. This link is being recognised as necessary more and more often, through the increasing popularity of **performance planning and evaluation (PPE) systems**. Such systems seek to tie the formal performance appraisal process to the company's strategies by specifying at the beginning of the evaluation period the types and level of performance that must be accomplished to achieve the strategy. Then, at the end of the evaluation period, individuals and groups are evaluated—based on how closely their actual performance matched the performance plan. In an ideal world, performance management systems would ensure that all activities support the organisation's strategic goals.

Finally, our model notes that situational constraints are always at work within the performance management system. As discussed previously, an employee may have the necessary skills and yet not exhibit the necessary behaviours. Sometimes the organisational culture discourages the employee from doing things that might be effective. Workgroup 'norms' often dictate what the group's members do and the results they produce. On the other hand, some people are simply not motivated to exhibit the right behaviours. This often occurs if the employees do not believe that their behaviours will be rewarded with pay raises, promotions and so forth. As mentioned earlier, 'organisational climate'—what it is like to work here—can also

Performance planning and evaluation (PPE) systems
systems that seek to tie the formal performance appraisal process to the company's strategies by specifying at the beginning of the evaluation period the types and level of performance that must be accomplished to achieve the strategy.

FIGURE 10.1 Model of performance management in organisations

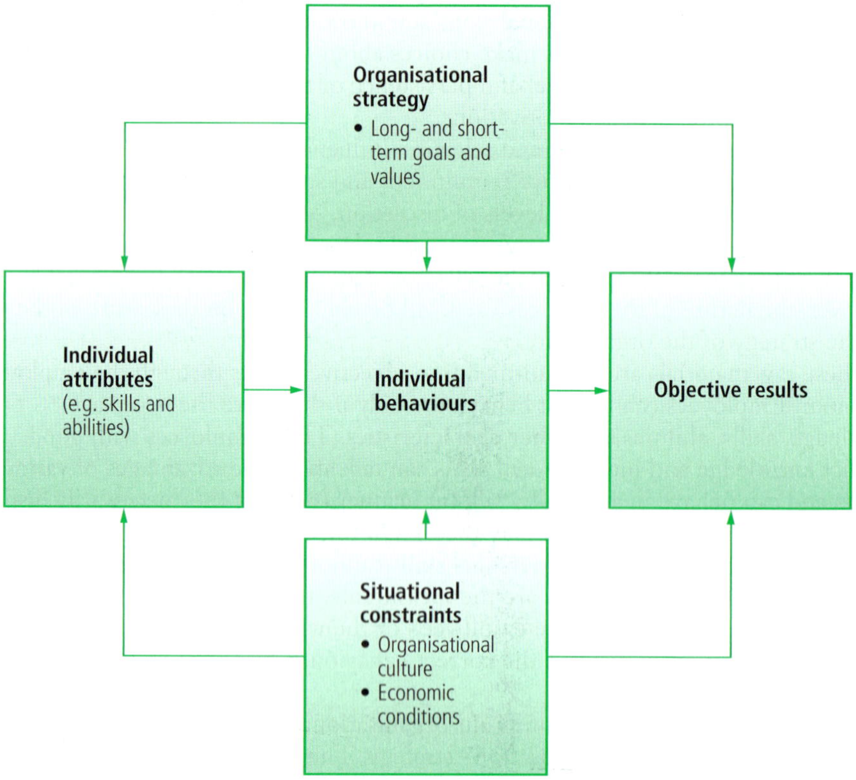

```
                    ┌─────────────────┐
                    │ Organisational  │
                    │ strategy        │
                    │ • Long- and     │
                    │   short-term    │
                    │   goals and     │
                    │   values        │
                    └─────────────────┘
                            │
       ┌────────────────────┼────────────────────┐
       ▼                    ▼                    ▼
┌──────────────┐    ┌──────────────┐    ┌──────────────┐
│ Individual   │    │ Individual   │    │ Objective    │
│ attributes   │───▶│ behaviours   │───▶│ results      │
│ (e.g. skills │    │              │    │              │
│ and          │    │              │    │              │
│ abilities)   │    │              │    │              │
└──────────────┘    └──────────────┘    └──────────────┘
       ▲                    ▲                    ▲
       └────────────────────┼────────────────────┘
                    ┌─────────────────┐
                    │ Situational     │
                    │ constraints     │
                    │ • Organisational│
                    │   culture       │
                    │ • Economic      │
                    │   conditions    │
                    └─────────────────┘
```

influence performance. Managers are able to influence organisational climate by the behaviours they demonstrate, by establishing clear goals and standards and by coaching. Finally, people may be performing effective behaviours yet, the right results do not follow. For example, an outstanding salesperson may not have a large dollar-volume because the economy is 'bad' and people are simply not buying. In many call centres from five to more than 10 calls of each centre agent are monitored per month. Common practices for monitoring the agents' performance include specific, objective performance criteria, scoring systems and immediate feedback. In order to get a fair representation of an agent's handling of calls, call centre coaching should cover a range of situations such as slow periods, busy periods, early in a shift, late in a shift, when a new policy or product is introduced and also include experienced and new agents.[10]

Thus, as you can see in Figure 10.1, employees must have certain attributes to perform a set of behaviours and achieve some results. To gain competitive advantage, the attributes, behaviours and results must be tied to the company's strategy. It is also important to note that constraints exist within the work environment that often preclude employees from performing. Table 10.1 overleaf provides recommendations for an effective performance management system. Regardless of the job or company, effective performance management systems measure performance criteria (for example, behaviours or sales) as precisely as possible. Effective performance management systems also serve a strategic function by linking performance criteria to internal and external customer requirements. Such systems need to include a process for changing the system, based on the effects of situational constraints. We will next examine the purposes of performance management systems.

TABLE 10.1 Recommendations for designing an effective performance management system

- Strive for precision in defining and measuring performance.
- Define performance with a focus on valued outcomes. Use outcomes that can be defined in terms of relative frequencies of behaviour.
- Include performance criteria that incorporate various ways that employees can add value to a product or service (for example, quantity, quality, timeliness, cost effectiveness and interpersonal impact).
- Include measures of work behaviours that add value above and beyond what is necessary to perform the job (for example, assisting co-workers and taking the initiative to repair broken equipment).
- Link performance dimensions to meeting internal and external customer requirements.
- Internal customer definitions of performance should be linked to external customer satisfaction.
- Measure and correct for the impact of situational constraints.
- Monitor actual and perceived constraints through interviews, surveys and observation.

Source: Adapted from Exhibit 2.1 in H.J. Bernardin, C.M. Hagan, J.S. Kane and P. Villanova, 'Effective performance management: a focus on precision, customers, and situational constraints', in J.W. Smither (ed), 1998, *Performance Appraisal: State of the Art in Practice*, Jossey-Bass, San Francisco, p. 56.

Purposes of performance management

The purposes of performance management systems are of three kinds: strategic, developmental and administrative.

Strategic purpose

First and foremost, a performance management system should link employee activities with the organisation's goals. One of the primary ways in which a strategy is implemented is through defining results and behaviours and, to some extent, employee characteristics that are necessary for carrying out that strategy. The next step is to develop measurement and feedback systems that will maximise the extent to which employees exhibit the characteristics, engage in the behaviours and produce the results. To achieve this strategic purpose, the system must be flexible, because when goals and strategies change, the results, behaviours and employee characteristics usually need to change correspondingly.

It has been found that in order to achieve their strategic purpose, effective performance management systems display five characteristics. These are:

1. the alignment of employee performance with organisational objectives
2. a clear articulation of the desired work culture
3. a clear specification of the results and competencies—that is, the 'how the results are to be achieved'
4. the management behaviour and style that encourages discretionary effort
5. the simple processes and documentation that enable line managers and employees to see performance management as part of their daily workplace behaviour.[11]

These five characteristics were developed in a global oil and gas organisation. The organisation faced an urgent need for transformational change so that it could improve its short-term profitability and realise opportunities in the longer term.

Over a 15-month-period, new strategies, culture and structures were implemented. A framework of competencies for leadership was developed in conjunction with a consulting firm and this provided the basis for performance assessment, feedback and development planning. All human resource processes were revised so that they supported the competency-based processes for performance management, selection and succession planning. The performance management system was used as a basis for driving behaviour change and it is reported as being successful.

In addition, as you know from Chapter 2 Strategic human resource management, it is important that other human resource policies and processes are consistent and support the performance management and feedback processes. This characteristic was demonstrated in Australian and New Zealand Direct Line (ANZ DL) in 1998 when it won an Australian Award for Business Excellence. One of the key features of its management approach was the replacement of the annual appraisal with a new two-way process that links individual performance targets to the company's strategic plan. Each person meets their supervisor every month. During this meeting, the individual reviews their performance plan, which includes a key project list, identifies where progress is at and where there are any difficulties. Solutions are then jointly developed and the meeting closes with a joint sign-off on their respective action lists. Managers are held accountable for developing staff. People management issues are looked at each month at the manager's monthly review meeting. This organisation links performance feedback to reward and recognition schemes through merit increases.[12]

However, performance management systems do not commonly achieve their strategic purpose. Surveys in Europe, Australia and the United States reveal organisations typically use the information from the performance appraisal component of a performance management system for administrative purposes, rather than strategic purposes.[13] In Australia, the primary purpose of information from performance appraisals has been found to be for making decisions about improving employee performance in their current job, rather than for making decisions about organisational training needs or future career and organisational training needs.[14] In the United States, only 13 per cent of the companies questioned were using their performance appraisal system to communicate company objectives.[15] Research involving HR practitioners regarding the purposes of performance appraisal suggest that most systems focus on developmental and administrative purposes.[16]

'Managing challenges through attracting and retaining people: Fashion stakes' highlights that a performance management system is used in the Sussan retail stores as one tool to foster the achievement of the strategy.

Developmental purpose

A second purpose of performance management is to develop employees who are effective at their jobs. When employees are not performing as well as they should, performance management seeks to improve their performance. The feedback given during a performance evaluation process often pinpoints the employee's weaknesses. Ideally, however, the performance management system identifies not only any deficient aspects of the employee's performance, but also the causes of these deficiencies—for example, a skill deficiency, a motivational problem or some obstacle holding the employee back.

The Queensland Industry Development Corporation (QIDC) introduced a performance management system that seeks to build a performance culture by establishing processes that encourage performance management each day, rather than once a year. It did this by setting requirements such as quarterly reviews and by

FASHION STAKES

Performance management poses special challenges for a retail organisation with outlets nationwide.

Robyn Batson has been people and development manager at women's fashion retailer Sussan for two years. Before that she worked with Coles Myer, lectured in HR and spent periods in career counselling and project management in the not-for-profit sector.

Batson describes her company's performance review system as participative, simple and forward looking. 'It looks at financial results and key result areas for the previous year, and establishes business and personal goals aligned to the business strategy for the next 12 months.'

Sussan's 210 store managers in Australia and New Zealand report to business managers with responsibility for 15 stores each. Batson says CEO Felicity McGahan is passionate about building a high performance culture. 'She visits stores regularly, connects with staff and engages them so they understand that they are listened to.'

The quality of relationships between managers and employees influences recruitment, performance and retention, says Batson. In retail, employee engagement is critical to providing good service and minimising staff turnover. 'But often managers find it difficult to articulate what an employee is doing well or not so well. They struggle with providing timely and constructive feedback and speaking to employees openly and honestly. Employees expect to be recognised and rewarded, and this is the key to retention.'

MANAGING CHALLENGES THROUGH ATTRACTING AND RETAINING PEOPLE

She acknowledges that managers are a mix of people. 'Some are very task-focused and concerned about getting the stock out and the money in the till. If they were good at having regular discussions with staff, providing feedback, developing people and setting development plans, there would probably be no need for a formal performance review system.'

She knows from her broad experience that dealing with young workers can be confrontational. 'Generation Ys are very good at giving feedback to their manager. They will tell you if they don't like something or disagree with you. If they are not happy, they will leave. A lot comes down to their day to day experience with their manager and team, and whether they feel there are opportunities for on-going growth and development. They are not just thinking about today.'

In an industry short on skilled staff, especially in NSW, it is vital Sussan trains its store managers to deal with people effectively. 'We have to educate them to understand how the expectations of the workforce have changed. Some people might want to be with you six months, others may leave, work in different careers or industries and eventually come back with new skills. It's therefore important that they have a positive experience during their time with us.'

Source: C. Rance, 2006, 'Star Treatment', *HR Monthly*, August, p. 22.

providing managers with the skills to give continuing feedback to their staff. The performance management process begins with planning performance that is based on business plan objectives. Performance plans, development plans and support plans are established. By doing this, training and development activities are planned and clearly linked to what the individual must achieve during that business period.[17]

Recently there has been a shift from the annual performance appraisal to a process which involves coaching. The two major differences between this coaching approach and the traditional performance appraisal are that feedback is continuous and constructive and this feedback and coaching tips are provided by people other than the employee's superior.[18]

Managers are often uncomfortable confronting employees with their performance weaknesses. Such confrontations, although necessary to the effectiveness of the workgroup, often strain everyday working relationships. Giving high ratings to all employees enables a manager to minimise such conflicts, but then the developmental purpose of the performance management system is not fully achieved.[19]

Although the use of performance appraisals for development purposes is common in Australia, the evidence for this use in Asian countries is not clear. Milliman et al. report that the literature suggests that in Korea, Japan and Taiwan there would be a high emphasis on the development purpose; however, their study reveals a low to moderate emphasis on this purpose.[20] In China, development has consistently not been seen as a major purpose of performance appraisals.[21]

Administrative purpose

Performance management information (performance appraisals, in particular) is used to make many administrative decisions: salary administration (pay rises or bonuses), promotions, retention and termination, retrenchment, and recognition of an individual's performance.[22] In Australia, approximately two-thirds of large organisations use information from performance appraisals to assess promotion potential, career development needs and organisational training needs.[23] Few companies, however, are linking performance appraisal systems to performance-related pay decisions.[24]

Despite the importance of these decisions, however, many managers, who are the source of the information, see the performance appraisal process only as a necessary evil they must go through to fulfil their job requirements. They feel uncomfortable evaluating others and feeding those evaluations back to the employees. Thus, they tend to rate everyone highly or at least rate them the same, making the performance appraisal information relatively useless. For example, one manager stated:

> There is really no getting around the fact that whenever I evaluate one of my people, I stop and think about the impact—the ramifications of my decisions on my relationship with the guy and his future here … Call it being politically minded, or using managerial discretion, or fine-tuning the guy's ratings, but in the end, I've got to live with him, and I'm not going to rate a guy without thinking about the fallout.[25]

In cultures, such as Chinese cultures, that value harmony, 'face' and teamwork, it is less likely that organisations will use performance appraisals for administrative purposes such as the determination of pay and promotion. In these collectivist cultures, the maintenance of cohesion in the workplace is important and the use of performance appraisals for these purposes can be regarded as in conflict with the creation of cohesion.[26] However, as organisations in Asian countries become exposed to Western practices, it is possible this could change. For instance, in China some organisations are starting to introduce performance-based compensation and performance-based rewards.[27]

There are difficulties associated with using data from performance appraisals, for both evaluation decisions such as salary increases and promotion, and for development decisions such as career planning and training. There are conflicts for individuals who are seeking valid performance feedback so that they know how well they are performing, they can identify the areas in which they could improve their performance and they can make decisions about training and coaching. However, they are also seeking rewards and to maintain their self-image. This can require individuals to be protective, compared to the open and honest behaviour required to make development decisions.[28]

The purposes of an effective performance management system are to link employee activities with the organisation's strategic goals, to furnish valid and useful information for making administrative decisions about employees and to provide employees with useful developmental feedback. Fulfilling these three purposes is central to gaining competitive advantage through human resources. The tension between serving the purposes of development and evaluation can be managed in a number of different ways.

In circumstances where the purpose of the performance appraisal process is to provide information for development and evaluation, the conflict can be managed by having two appraisal interviews. One can focus on evaluation, while the other one can focus on development. They should be held at different times of the year. These interviews could be done by different people, for instance, the line manager and the HR manager.[29] A vital step in performance management is to develop the measures by which performances are evaluated.

This is particularly important when leaders are evaluated. Leaders are selected and rewarded for achieving tangible results such as financial outcomes, however, increasingly organisations are recognising the value of evaluating the way leaders achieve these results. This is a challenge and it involves measuring a leader's performance in areas such as individual projects, customer service, employee satisfaction, process improvements, learning and development, innovation and business development.[30]

Thus, we next discuss the issues involved in developing and using different measures of performance.

Performance measurement criteria

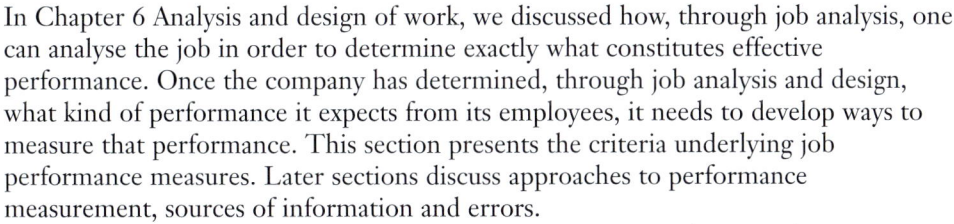

In Chapter 6 Analysis and design of work, we discussed how, through job analysis, one can analyse the job in order to determine exactly what constitutes effective performance. Once the company has determined, through job analysis and design, what kind of performance it expects from its employees, it needs to develop ways to measure that performance. This section presents the criteria underlying job performance measures. Later sections discuss approaches to performance measurement, sources of information and errors.

Although people differ about which criteria they use to evaluate performance management systems, we believe that five criteria stand out: strategic congruence, validity, reliability, acceptability and specificity.

Strategic congruence

Strategic congruence is the extent to which the performance management system elicits job performance that is congruent with the organisation's strategy, goals and culture. If a company emphasises customer service, then its performance management system should assess how well its employees are serving the company's customers. Strategic congruence emphasises the need for the performance management system to provide guidance, so that employees can contribute to the organisation's success. This requires systems that are flexible enough to adapt to changes in the company's strategic posture.

Take, for example, a drug company whose business strategy is to penetrate the North American market for dermatology compounds.[31] To be successful, the company needs to shorten the drug-development cycle, attract and retain research and development talent, and maximise the effectiveness of research teams. These are core competencies of the business. Performance measures are linked directly to the core competencies. These include the quantity of dermatology compound submissions to the Food and Drug Administration (FDA), the quantity of compound approvals by the FDA, the turnover of senior engineers, and team leadership and collaboration. The sources for information regarding these performance measures include FDA decisions, turnover rates and team-member feedback on surveys. Team and individual accountabilities are directly linked to the performance measures. For example, the

Strategic congruence
the extent to which the performance management system elicits job performance that is congruent with the organisation's strategy, goals and culture.

research teams' performance goals include FDA submission and approval of three compounds.

In Australia, BHP (now BHP Billiton) adopted new performance benchmarks for the managers of its business units as a way of developing strategic congruence. The company introduced a measure called 'Performance of relevant peer group companies' in an attempt to encourage these managers to think and behave as mini chief executives reporting to their shareholders and the outside market. It was also an attempt to change the behaviour and attitudes of all employees, so that employees focus on the same sort of issues as the members of the board.[32]

The system, known as a 'balanced scorecard', is a way of developing strategic congruence. It is one way organisations can link their long-term strategy to short-term actions and provide a means for the organisation to continuously improve and learn. This is done by focusing on a number of areas of the organisation, such as financial, internal business processes, learning and growth and translating the vision. The balanced scorecard is one way of signalling to employees what the organisation is attempting to achieve for customers and shareholders. Individual employee performance can be aligned to overall strategy by engaging in three activities. These are communicating and educating, setting goals and linking rewards to performance measures.[33]

The use of the balanced scorecard usually occurs in large organisations; however, it has been used in a few small Australian organisations. Tool-making company AS Tools monitors performance from three dimensions: financial, client and internal business processes, while Shaw Contracting includes a measure of the company's training and development expenditure.[34] When the balanced scorecard is used as a basis for improving employee performance in a small organisation, it is important to determine who will see the results and that the process is seen as a way of improving the performance of the business.

Most companies' appraisal systems remain constant over a long period of time and through a variety of strategic emphases. However, when a company's strategy changes, its employees' behaviour needs to change too.[35] The fact that it often does not change may account for why many managers see performance appraisal systems as having little impact on a firm's effectiveness.

'Managing challenges of globalisation: Outsourcing IT' discusses the increasing use of outsourcing of work to India and China. The process of outsourcing has implications for the process of performance management.

Validity

Validity is the extent to which the performance measure assesses all the relevant—and only the relevant—aspects of performance. This is often referred to as 'content validity'. For a performance measure to be valid, it must not be deficient or contaminated. In Figure 10.2 opposite, the circle on the right represents 'true' job performance—all of those aspects of performance relevant to being successful in the job. On the other hand, companies must use some measure of performance, such as a supervisory rating of performance on a set of dimensions or measures of the objective results on the job. Validity is concerned with maximising the overlap between actual job performance and the measure of job performance (that is, the portion that overlaps in the figure).

A performance measure is deficient if it does not measure all aspects of performance (that is, the lightest portion in the figure). An example is a system at a large university that assesses faculty members based more on their research rather than their teaching—thereby almost ignoring a relevant aspect of performance.

> **Validity**
> (often referred to as content validity) the extent to which the performance measure assesses all the relevant—and only the relevant—aspects of performance.

OUTSOURCING IT

MANAGING CHALLENGES OF GLOBALISATION

It causes political heartburn and unions loathe it. But the outsourcing of information technology services to lower-cost countries has become standard practice. With the 45 per cent cost savings available—according to the most-cited estimates by McKinsey Global Institute—one's commonsense must be questioned if such opportunities are not taken. The real issue is when it works best—and when it is best to stay at home.

'We manufacture shoes and textiles overseas', St George chief information officer John Lobenstein says. 'What's so different about software?'

A survey of 150 companies by IBM Australia's application maintenance division found that half are engaged in talks with overseas suppliers and have already contracted them to do computing work.

'Clients understanding of how India and China can benefit them has come into sharp focus', Korhonen says. 'We're starting to get our minds around fitting into the global fabric—how to take the best of what we've got and the best of what the world has to offer.'

'Certainly, companies looking for continued growth over the next five years and beyond are fearful of competitors taking advantage of global delivery—they fear that they will start losing market share if they themselves don't. The concern is valid, particularly since global brands have a healthy headstart.'

... Penny pinching might be the catalyst for outsourcing overseas, but many of those that have started insist the savings become more significant when service improves too. Of 145 companies surveyed by research company Forrester in 2003, 71 per cent indicated that overseas workers did better work.

... Lehmann Brothers, one of Wall Street's top four investment banks, says retention rates have become so poor at its Indian development centre that it has been forced to give programmers cutting-edge projects just to keep staff motivated. A year ago, Lehman could get six engineers in India for the price of one in the United States. This ratio has dropped to five-to-one as salaries increase.

... Berti says the real issue is maintaining control of a company's brain trust. Building software and maintaining hardware can be done anywhere, but it is likely that business analytics will always be handled at a local level. 'We have a team here focused on understanding what the business are trying to do, translating it into something the technology people offshore can relate to and working with them to develop a solution', he says. 'You need to keep that close to the business.'

Source: Extract from A. King, 2006, 'Home and Away', *BRW*, 21–27 September, pp. 32–3.

FIGURE 10.2 Contamination and deficiency of a job performance measure

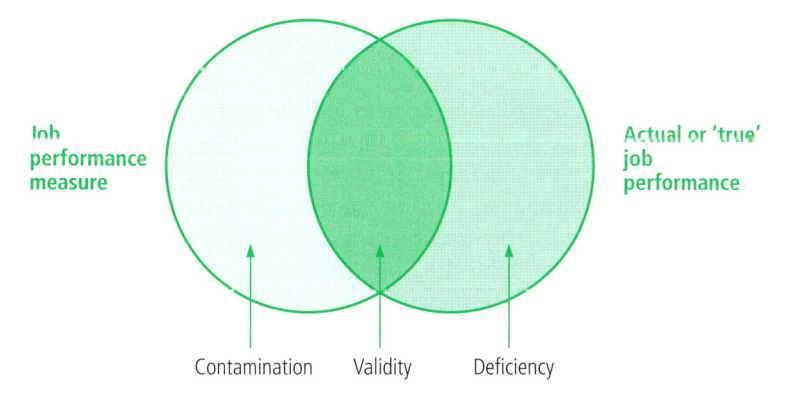

Job performance measure — Actual or 'true' job performance

Contamination | Validity | Deficiency

A contaminated measure evaluates irrelevant aspects of performance or aspects that are not job related (that is, the majority of the circle on the left). The performance measure should seek to minimise contamination, but its complete elimination is seldom possible. An example of a contaminated measure is the use of actual sales figures for evaluating salespeople across very different regional territories. Often sales are highly dependant on the territory (for example, number of potential customers, number of competitors and economic conditions), rather than the actual performance of the salesperson. A salesperson who works harder and better than others might not have the highest sales totals because the territory simply does not have as much sales potential as that of others. Thus, to use these figures alone would be to use a measure that is strongly affected by things beyond the control of the individual employee.

Reliability

Reliability
refers to the consistency of the performance measure; the degree to which a performance measure is free from random error. One important type of reliability is inter-rater reliability: the consistency among the individuals who evaluate the employee's performance.

Reliability refers to the consistency of the performance measure. One important type of reliability is inter-rater reliability—the consistency among the individuals who evaluate the employee's performance. A performance measure has inter-rater reliability if two individuals give the same (or close to the same) evaluations of a person's job performance.

Another type of 'reliability' is internal consistency reliability. This refers to the extent to which a number of items measuring a particular indicator of performance, such as quality, correlate with each other (see Chapter 8 Recruitment and selection, for further discussion on this type of reliability).

Evidence seems to indicate that most subjective supervisory measures of job performance exhibit low reliability.[36] With some measures, the extent to which all the items rated are internally consistent is important (internal consistency reliability).

In addition, the measure should be reliable over time (test–retest reliability). A measure that results in drastically different ratings depending on the time at which the measures are taken lacks test–retest reliability. For example, if salespeople are evaluated based on their actual sales volume during a given month, it would be important to consider their consistency of monthly sales across time. What if an evaluator in a department store examined sales only during May? Employees in the lawn and garden department would have high sales volumes, but those in the men's clothing department would have somewhat low sales volumes. Clothing sales in May are traditionally lower than other months. There is a need to measure performance consistently across time.

Acceptability

Acceptability
refers to whether the people who use the performance measure accept it.

Acceptability refers to whether the people who use the performance measure accept it. Many considerably elaborate performance measures are extremely valid and reliable, but they consume so much of managers' time that they refuse to use them. Alternatively, those being evaluated by a measure may not accept it.

Acceptability is affected by the extent to which employees believe the performance management system is fair. As Table 10.2 opposite shows, there are three categories of perceived fairness: procedural, interpersonal and outcome fairness. The table also shows specifically how the performance management system is developed, how the system is used and how the outcomes linked to it affect perceptions of fairness. In developing and using a performance management system, managers should take the steps shown in the column labelled 'Implications' in Table 10.2 to ensure that the system is perceived as fair. Research suggests that performance management systems which are perceived as unfair are likely to be legally challenged, used incorrectly and they decrease employee motivation to improve.[37]

Some organisations have decided not to continue with formal annual performance appraisals. The Gold Coast City Council negotiated with the union to drop them on

TABLE 10.2 Categories of perceived fairness and implications for performance management systems

Fairness category	Importance for performance management system	Implications
Procedural fairness	Development	• Gives managers and employees opportunity to participate in development of system • Ensures consistent standards when evaluating different employees • Minimises rating errors and biases
Interpersonal fairness	Use	• Provides timely and complete feedback • Allows employees to challenge the evaluation • Provides feedback in an atmosphere of respect and courtesy
Outcome fairness	Outcomes	• Communicates expectations regarding performance evaluations and standards • Communicates expectations regarding rewards

Source: S.W. Gilliland & J.C. Langdon, 'Creating performance management systems that promote perceptions of fairness', in J.W. Smither (ed), 1998, *Performance Appraisal: State of the Art in Practice*, Jossey-Bass, San Francisco, pp. 209–43. Copyright © 1998 by Jossey-Bass Inc. This material is used by permission of John Wiley and Sons, Inc.

the basis that each supervisor records in their diary at least once every six months that they have sat down with each employee and asked them how they feel they are going and if they feel their training is what they require.[38]

Specificity

Specificity is the extent to which the performance measure gives specific guidance to employees about what is expected of them and how they can meet these expectations. Specificity is relevant to both the strategic and developmental purposes of performance management. If a measure does not specify what an employee must do to help the company achieve its strategic goals, it becomes difficult for the measure to achieve its strategic purpose. Additionally, if the measure fails to point out an employee's performance problems, it is almost impossible for the employee to correct his or her performance.

This was a major issue in the New South Wales Police Service in the 1990s. In 1997, in its final report, the Royal Commission into the New South Wales Police Service noted that there were performance management systems in place for the Senior Executive Service (SES) and non-SES to the rank of sergeant, but there were no schemes for constables. Enterprise agreements also provided for performance management systems. However, the effectiveness of these systems was hampered by a number of problems including vagueness surrounding the agreed targets and criteria; the subjective nature of assessment; the unsatisfactory nature of remedial programs; and the disruption to the process because of the high rate of transfers.[39]

Approaches to measuring performance

The model of performance management presented in Figure 10.1 on page 346 shows that we can manage performance by focusing on employee attributes, behaviours or results. In addition, we can measure performance in a relative way, making overall

Specificity
the extent to which the performance measure gives specific guidance to employees about what is expected of them and how they can meet these expectations.

comparisons among individuals' performance. Finally, we can develop a performance measurement system that incorporates some variety of the preceding measures, as evidenced by the quality approach to measuring performance. Various techniques use a combination of these approaches. In this section, we explore these approaches to measuring and managing performance, discuss the techniques that are associated with each approach and evaluate these approaches against the criteria of strategic congruence, validity, reliability, acceptability and specificity.

As with other human resource practices, the particular type of performance appraisal approach that will be most effective is contingent on factors such as the nature of the job, the strategy and the organisation. However, there are challenges about how performance appraisal approaches are implemented. Later sections of this chapter discuss some of these challenges and the ways they can be overcome. In one sense these methods of improving the implementation of performance appraisals represent 'best practice'.

The comparative approach

The comparative approach to performance measurement consists of techniques that require the rater to compare an individual's performance with that of others. This approach usually uses some overall assessment of an individual's performance or worth and seeks to develop some ranking of the individuals within a given workgroup. At least three techniques fall under the comparative approach: ranking, forced distribution and paired comparison.

Ranking

Simple ranking requires managers to rank employees within their departments from highest performer to poorest performer (or best to worst). Alternation ranking, on the other hand, consists of a manager looking at a list of employees, deciding who the best employee is and crossing that person's name off the list. From the remaining names, the manager decides who the worst employee is and crosses that name off the list—and so forth.

Ranking is one method of performance appraisal that has received some specific attention in the courts in the United States. In the Albermarle versus Moody case, the validation of the selection system was conducted using employee rankings as the measure of performance. The court actually stated:

> There is no way of knowing precisely what criteria of job performance that supervisors were considering, whether each supervisor was considering the same criteria—or whether, indeed, any of the supervisors actually applied a focused and stable body of criteria of any kind.[40]

Forced distribution

The forced distribution method also uses a ranking format, but employees are ranked in groups. This technique requires the manager to put certain percentages of employees into predetermined categories, as depicted in Table 10.3 overleaf. The example in the table shows how Merck combines the performance of the division with individual performance to recommend the distributions of employees that should fall into each category. For example, among poorly performing divisions (not acceptable), only 1 per cent of employees should receive the highest rating (TF = top 5 per cent); whereas, among top-performing divisions (exceptional), 8 per cent of employees should receive the highest rating. In some situations, the forced-distribution method forces managers to categorise employees based on distribution rules and not on their performance. For example, although a manager's employees are all above-average performers, the manager is forced to rate some employees as 'not acceptable'.

TABLE 10.3 Proposed guidelines for targeted distribution of performance ratings. Targeted employee rating distribution, by divisional performance

Performance rating for employees	Rating type	Performance rating for divisions				
		EX Exceptional	WD With distinction	HS High standard	RI Room for improvement	NA Not acceptable
TF Top 5%	Relative	8%	6%	5%	2%	1%
TQ Top quintile	Relative	20%	17%	15%	12%	10%
OU Outstanding	Absolute					
VG Very good	Absolute	71%	75%	75%	78%	79%
GD Good	Absolute					
LF Lower 5%	Relative					
NA Not acceptable	Absolute	1%	2%	5%	8%	10%
PR Progressing		Not applicable				

Source: Reprinted with permission of The Conference Board, New York City. Data supplied by Merck and Co.; chart by Kevin J. Murphy, University of Rochester.

Paired comparison

The paired comparison method requires managers to compare every employee with every other employee in the workgroup, giving an employee a score of one every time he or she is considered the higher performer. Once all the pairs have been compared, the manager computes the number of times each employee received the favourable decision (that is, counts up the points) and this becomes the employee's performance score.

The paired comparison method tends to be time consuming for managers and will become more so as organisations become flatter with an increased span of control. For example, a manager with 10 employees must make 45 (that is, 10 × 9/2) comparisons. However, if the group is increased to 15 employees, 105 comparisons must be made.

Evaluating the comparative approach

The comparative approach to performance measurement provides an effective tool when the major purpose of the system is to differentiate employee performance. These techniques virtually eliminate problems of leniency, central tendency and strictness. This is especially valuable if the results of the measures are to be used in making administrative decisions, such as pay rises and promotions. In addition, they are relatively easy to develop and in most cases easy to use; thus, they are often considered acceptable by the users.

One problem with these techniques, however, is their common failure to be linked to the strategic goals of the organisation. While raters can make their ratings based on the extent to which individuals' performances support the strategy, this link is seldom made explicit. In addition, because of the subjective nature of the ratings, their actual validity and reliability depend on the raters themselves. Some firms seek to use multiple evaluators to reduce the biases of any individual, but most do not. At best, we could conclude that their reliability and validity are modest.

These techniques lack 'specificity' for feedback purposes. Based only on their relative rankings, individuals are completely unaware of what they must do differently to improve their ranking. This puts a heavy burden on the manager to provide specific feedback beyond that of the rating instrument itself. Finally, many employees and managers are less likely to accept evaluations based on comparative approaches. Evaluations are dependant on how employees' performance is relative to other employees in a group, team or department (normative standard) rather than to absolute standards of excellent, good, fair and poor performance.

The attribute approach

The attribute approach to performance management focuses on the extent to which individuals have certain attributes (characteristics or traits) believed to be desirable for the company's success. The techniques that use this approach tend to define a set of traits—such as initiative, leadership and competitiveness—and evaluate individuals on these traits.

Graphic rating scales

The most common form that the attribute approach takes is the graphic rating scale. Table 10.4 shows a graphic rating scale used in a manufacturing company. As you can see, a list of traits is evaluated by a five point (or some other number of points) rating scale. The manager considers one employee at a time, circling the number that signifies how much of that trait the individual has. Graphic rating scales can provide the rater with a number of different points (a 'discrete' scale) or with a continuum along which the rater simply places a check mark (a 'continuous' scale).

In the United States, the legal defensibility of graphic rating scales was questioned in the Brito versus Zia (1973) case. In this case, Spanish-speaking employees had been terminated as a result of their performance appraisals. These appraisals consisted of supervisors rating subordinates on a number of undefined dimensions such as volume of work, quantity of work, job knowledge, dependability and cooperation. The court criticised the subjective nature of these appraisals and stated that the company should have presented empirical data demonstrating that the appraisal was significantly related to actual work behaviour.

TABLE 10.4 Example of a graphic rating scale

The following areas of performance are significant to most positions. Indicate your assessment of performance on each dimension by circling the appropriate rating.

Performance dimension	Distinguished	Excellent	Commendable	Adequate	Poor
Knowledge	5	4	3	2	1
Communication	5	4	3	2	1
Judgment	5	4	3	2	1
Managerial skill	5	4	3	2	1
Quality performance	5	4	3	2	1
Teamwork	5	4	3	2	1
Interpersonal skills	5	4	3	2	1
Initiative	5	4	3	2	1
Creativity	5	4	3	2	1
Problem solving	5	4	3	2	1

Mixed standard scales

Mixed standard scales were developed as a means of getting around some of the problems with graphic rating scales. To create a mixed standard scale, we must define the relevant performance dimensions and then develop statements representing good, average and poor performance along each dimension. These statements are then mixed with the statements from other dimensions on the actual rating instrument. An example of a mixed standard scale is presented in Table 10.5, below.

TABLE 10.5 Example of a mixed standard scale

Three traits being assessed:
Initiative (INTV)
Intelligence (INTG)
Relations with others (RWO)

Levels of performance in statements:
High (H)
Medium (M)
Low (L)

Instructions: Please indicate next to each statement whether the employee's performance is above (+) equal to (0) or below (−) the statement.

INTV	H	1	This employee is a real self-starter. The employee always takes the initiative and his or her superior never has to prod this individual.	+
INTG	M	2	While perhaps this employee is not a genius, he or she is a lot more intelligent than many people I know.	+
RWO	L	3	This employee has a tendency to get into unnecessary conflicts with other people.	0
INTV	M	4	While generally this employee shows initiative, occasionally his or her superior must prompt him or her to complete work.	+
INTG	L	5	Although this employee is slower than some in understanding things and may take a bit longer in learning new things, she or he is of average intelligence.	+
RWO	H	6	This employee is on good terms with everyone. He or she can get along with people even when he or she does not agree with them.	−
INTV	L	7	This employee has a bit of a tendency to sit around and wait for directions.	+
INTG	H	8	This employee is extremely intelligent and she or he learns rapidly.	−
RWO	M	9	This employee gets along with most people. Only very occasionally does he or she have conflicts with others on the job and these are likely to be minor.	−

Scoring key:

Statements			
High	Medium	Low	Score
+	+	+	7
0	+	+	6
−	+	+	5
−	0	+	4
−	−	+	3
−	−	0	2
−	−	−	1

Example score from preceding ratings:

	Statements			
	High	Medium	Low	Score
Initiative	+	+	+	7
Intelligence	0	+	+	6
Relations with others	−	−	0	2

As we see in Table 10.5, the rater is asked to complete the rating instrument by indicating whether the employee's performance is above (+), at (0) or below (−) the statement. A special scoring key is then used to score the employee's performance for each dimension. For example, if the employee's performance is above in all three statements, she or he receives a seven. If the employee is below the good statement, at the average statement, and above the poor statement, a score of four is assessed. If the employee is below all three statements, he or she is given a rating of one. This scoring is applied to all the dimensions to determine an overall performance score.

Note that mixed standard scales were originally developed as trait-oriented scales. However, this same technique has been applied to instruments using behavioural rather than trait-oriented statements as a means of reducing rating errors in performance appraisals.[41]

Evaluating the attribute approach

Managers need to be aware that attribute-based performance methods are the most popular methods in organisations. They are quite easy to develop and are generalisable across a variety of jobs, strategies and organisations. In addition, if much attention is devoted to identifying those attributes that are relevant to job performance and carefully defining them on the rating instrument, they can be as reliable and valid as more elaborate measurement techniques.

However, these techniques fall short on several of the criteria for effective performance management. There is usually little strategic congruence between the techniques and the company's strategy. These methods are used because of the ease in developing them and because the same method (for example, list of traits and comparisons) is generalisable across any organisation and any strategy. In addition, these methods usually have considerably vague performance standards that are open to different interpretations by different raters. Thus, different raters often provide extremely different ratings and rankings. The result is that both the validity and reliability of these methods are usually low.

Virtually none of these techniques provides any specific guidance on how an employee can support the company's goals or on what to do to correct performance deficiencies. In addition, when raters give feedback, these techniques tend to elicit defensiveness from employees. For example, how would you feel if you were told that on a five-point scale, you were rated a 'two' in maturity? Certainly you might feel somewhat defensive and unwilling to accept that judgment, as well as any additional feedback; and being told you were rated a 'two' in maturity does not tell you what you need to do to improve your rating.

The behavioural approach

The behavioural approach to performance management attempts to define the behaviours an employee must exhibit to be effective in the job. The various techniques define those behaviours and then require managers to assess the extent to which employees exhibit them. We discuss five techniques that rely on the behavioural approach: critical incidents, behaviourally anchored rating scales, behavioural observations scales, organisational behaviour modification and assessment centres.

Critical incidents

The critical incident approach requires managers to keep a record of specific examples of effective and ineffective performance on the part of each employee. Here's an example of an incident described in the performance evaluation of an appliance repair person:

A customer called in about a refrigerator that was not cooling and was making a clicking noise every few minutes. The technician prediagnosed the cause of the problem and checked his truck for the necessary parts. When he found he did not have them, he checked the parts out from inventory so that the customer's refrigerator would be repaired on his first visit and the customer would be satisfied promptly.

These incidents are used to give specific feedback to employees about what they do well and what they do poorly, and they can be tied to the company's strategy by focusing on incidents that best support that strategy. However, many managers resist having to keep a daily or weekly log of their employees' behaviour. It is also often difficult to make comparisons among employees, since each incident is specific to that individual.

Behaviourally anchored rating scales

A behaviourally anchored rating scale (BARS) builds on the critical incident approach. It is designed to specifically define performance dimensions by developing behavioural anchors associated with different levels of performance.[42] An example of BARS is presented in Figure 10.3 on page 362. As you can see, the performance dimension has a number of examples of behaviours that indicate specific levels of performance along the dimension.

To develop BARS, we first gather a large number of critical incidents that represent effective and ineffective performance on the job. These incidents are classified into performance dimensions and the ones that experts agree clearly represent a particular level of performance are used as behavioural examples (or anchors) to guide the rater. The manager's task is to consider an employee's performance along each dimension and determine where on the dimension the employee's performance fits using the behavioural anchors as guides. This rating becomes the employee's score for that dimension.

Behavioural anchors have advantages and disadvantages. One advantage is that they can increase inter-rater reliability by providing a precise and complete definition of the performance dimension. A disadvantage is that they can bias information recall—that is, behaviour that closely approximates the anchor is more easily recalled than other behaviour.[43] Research has also demonstrated that managers and their subordinates do not make much of a distinction between BARS and trait scales.[44]

Behavioural observation scales

A behavioural observation scale (BOS) is a variation of BARS. Like BARS, a BOS is developed from critical incidents.[45] However, a BOS differs from BARS in two basic ways. First, rather than discarding a large number of the behaviours that exemplify effective or ineffective performance, a BOS uses many of them to define more specifically all the behaviours that are necessary for effective performance (or that would be considered ineffective performance). Instead of using, say, four behaviours to define four levels of performance on a particular dimension, a BOS may use 15 behaviours. An example of a BOS is presented in Table 10.6, page 363.

A second difference is that, rather than assessing which behaviour best reflects an individual's performance, a BOS requires managers to rate the frequency with which the employee has exhibited each behaviour during the rating period. These ratings are then averaged to compute an overall performance rating.

The major drawback of a BOS is that it may require more information than most managers can process or remember. A BOS can have 80 or more behaviours and the manager must remember how frequently an employee exhibited each of these behaviours over a six- or 12-month rating period. This is taxing enough with regard to one employee, but managers often must rate 10 or more employees.

FIGURE 10.3 Task-BARS rating dimension: security officer

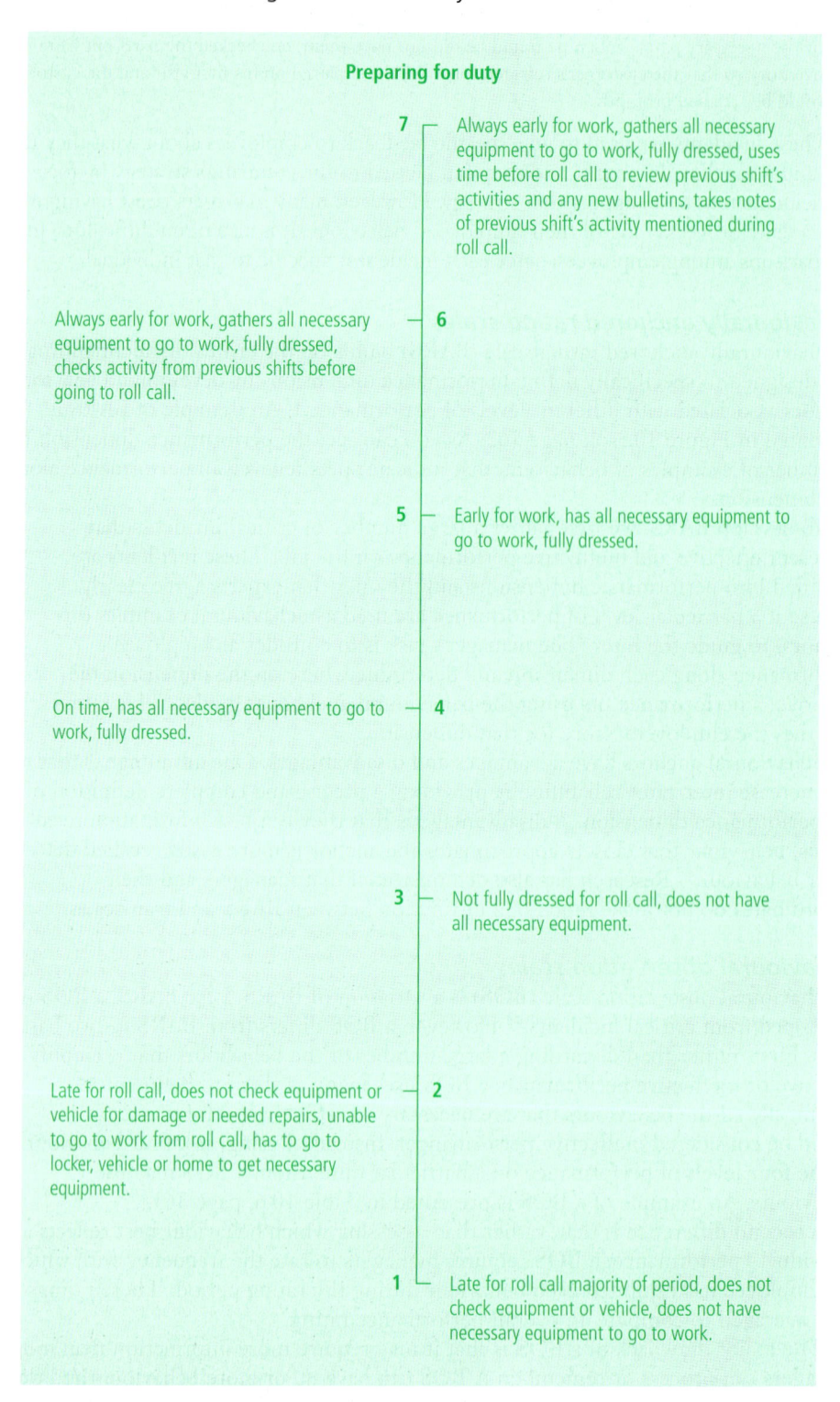

Preparing for duty

7 — Always early for work, gathers all necessary equipment to go to work, fully dressed, uses time before roll call to review previous shift's activities and any new bulletins, takes notes of previous shift's activity mentioned during roll call.

Always early for work, gathers all necessary equipment to go to work, fully dressed, checks activity from previous shifts before going to roll call. — 6

5 — Early for work, has all necessary equipment to go to work, fully dressed.

On time, has all necessary equipment to go to work, fully dressed. — 4

3 — Not fully dressed for roll call, does not have all necessary equipment.

Late for roll call, does not check equipment or vehicle for damage or needed repairs, unable to go to work from roll call, has to go to locker, vehicle or home to get necessary equipment. — 2

1 — Late for roll call majority of period, does not check equipment or vehicle, does not have necessary equipment to go to work.

Source: Adapted from R.J. Harvey, 'Job analysis', in M.D. Dunnette & L.M. Hough (eds), 1991, *Handbook of Industrial and Organizational Psychology*, 2nd edn, Consulting Psychologists Press, Palo Alto, CA, vol. 2, p. 138.

TABLE 10.6 Example of a behavioural observation scale (BOS) for evaluating job performance

Overcoming resistance to change

1. Describes the details of the change to subordinates

   Almost never 1 2 3 4 5 Almost always

2. Explains why the change is necessary

   Almost never 1 2 3 4 5 Almost always

3. Discusses how the change will affect the employee

   Almost never 1 2 3 4 5 Almost always

4. Listens to the employee's concerns

   Almost never 1 2 3 4 5 Almost always

5. Asks the employee for help in making the change work

   Almost never 1 2 3 4 5 Almost always

6. If necessary, specifies the date for a follow-up meeting to respond to the employee's concerns

   Almost never 1 2 3 4 5 Almost always

Total = _____

Below adequate	Adequate	Full	Excellent	Superior
6–10	11–15	16–20	21–25	26–30

Note: Scores are set by management.
Source: Gary Latham and Kenneth Wexley, *Increasing Productivity Through Performance Appraisal*, 1964, 1981, Addison-Wesley, p. 56. Reprinted by permission of Pearson Education, Inc., Upper Saddle River, New Jersey.

A direct comparison of BOS, BARS and graphic rating scales found that both managers and employees prefer BOS for differentiating good from poor performers, maintaining objectivity, providing feedback, suggesting training needs and being easy to use among managers and subordinates.[46]

Organisational behaviour modification

Organisational behaviour modification (OBM) entails managing the behaviour of employees through a formal system of behavioural feedback and reinforcement. This system builds on the behaviourist view of motivation, which holds that individuals' future behaviour is determined by past behaviours that have been positively reinforced. The techniques vary, but most of them have four components. First, they define a set of key behaviours necessary for job performance. Second, they use a measurement system to assess whether these behaviours are exhibited. Third, the manager or consultant informs employees of those behaviours, perhaps setting goals for how often the employees should exhibit those behaviours. Finally, feedback and reinforcement are provided to employees.[47]

Organisational behaviour modification techniques have been used in a variety of settings. One technique, referred to as behaviour management, was used to increase the performance of cleaning people in the hotel industry.[48] Housekeepers were asked to follow a 70-item behavioural checklist—checking off each behaviour as they performed it. By providing feedback and reinforcement, management was able to increase housekeepers' performance, as Figure 10.4 on page 364 shows. Similar results have been observed with respect to the frequency of safety behaviours in a processing plant.[49] However, this method is unlikely to be suitable for some people, such as managers and professionals engaged in open-ended jobs.

FIGURE 10.4 Increases in productivity for housekeepers as a result of behaviour management

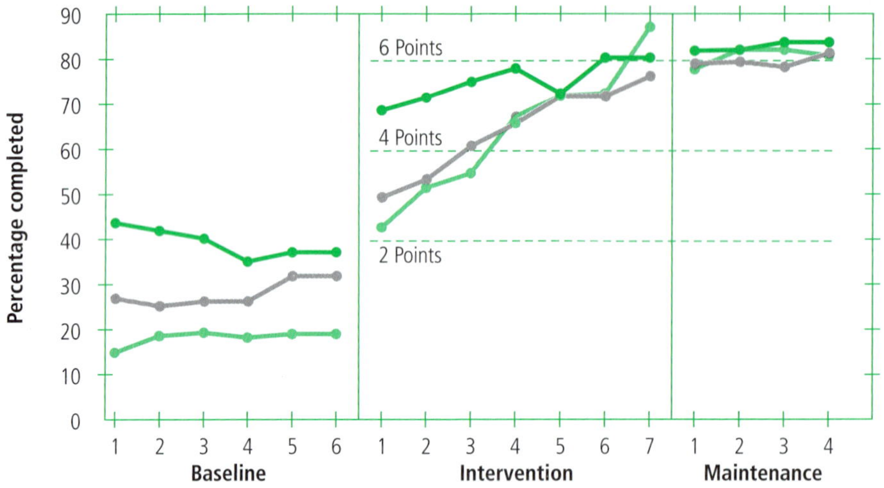

Source: D.C. Anderson, C.R. Crowell, S.S. Sponsel, M. Clarke & J. Brence, 1983, 'Behavior management in the public accommodations industry: a three-project demonstration', *Journal of Organizational Behavior Management*, 4, p. 57. Reproduced by permission of The Haworth Press.

Assessment centres

Although 'assessment centres' are usually used for selection and promotion decisions, they have also been used as a way of measuring managerial performance.[50] At an assessment centre, individuals usually perform a number of simulated tasks, such as leaderless group discussions, in-baskets and role playing. Assessors observe the individuals' behaviour and evaluate their skill or potential as managers. Individual assessment centre programs vary in purpose, length of the assessment process, the ratio of the assessors to the assessed, the extent of assessor training and the number and type of assessment instruments and exercises used.[51]

The advantage of assessment centres is that they provide a somewhat objective measure of an individual's performance at managerial tasks. In addition, they provide specific performance feedback, and individualised developmental plans can be designed. For example, companies such as Cathay Pacific send their managers through assessment centres to identify their individual strengths and weaknesses and to create developmental action plans for each manager.

An interesting public sector application of assessment centres is in the state government of North Carolina in the United States. Managers there can go through an assessment process to become 'certified middle managers'. This process includes an assessment centre at the beginning of the certification program, from which an individualised developmental action plan is created. The developmental plan, implemented over approximately two years, consists of training programs and on-the-job developmental experiences. At the end of the two years, the manager attends the certification assessment centre. Those who successfully meet the criteria set forth in the certification assessment centre then become certified.

Assessment centres are expensive, with costs ranging from US$125 for each candidate to as much as US$3000 for upper-level managers.[52] In addition, it has been shown that assessment centres can be broken down to make them more efficient. For instance, the same basic results are achieved using performance tests and follow-up interviews with trained assessors.[53]

We discuss assessment centres more in Chapter 11 Learning and Development.

Evaluation of the behavioural approach

The behavioural approach can be considerably effective. It can link the company's strategy to the specific types of behaviour necessary for implementing that strategy. It provides specific guidance and feedback for employees about the performance expected of them. Most of the techniques rely on in-depth job analysis, so the behaviours identified and measured are valid. Often, the acceptability is high, because those using the system are involved in developing the measures. Finally, with a substantial investment in training raters, the techniques are reasonably reliable.

The major weaknesses are with the organisational context of the system. Although the behavioural approach can be closely tied to a company's strategy, the behaviours and measures must be constantly monitored and revised—ensuring they are still linked to the strategic focus. This approach also assumes that there is 'one best way' to do the job and that the behaviours that constitute this best way can be identified. One study found that managers seek to control behaviours when they perceive a clear relationship between behaviours and results. When this link is not clear, they tend to rely on managing results.[54] The behavioural approach might be best suited to less complex jobs (where the best way to achieve results is clear) and least suited to complex jobs (where there are multiple ways, or behaviours, to achieve success).

The results approach

The results approach focuses on managing the objective, measurable results of a job or workgroup. This approach assumes that subjectivity can be eliminated from the measurement process and that results are the closest indicator of one's contribution to organisational effectiveness.[55] We will examine two performance management systems that use results: management by objectives, and the productivity measurement and evaluation system (ProMES).

Management by objectives

Management by objectives (MBO) is popular in both private and public organisations.[56] The original concept came from the United States accounting firm of Booz, Allen and Hamilton, and was called a 'manager's letter'. The process consisted of having all the subordinate managers write a letter to their superiors, detailing what their performance goals were for the coming year and how they planned to achieve them. Harold Smiddy applied and expanded this idea at General Electric in the 1950s, and Douglas McGregor has since developed it into a philosophy of management.[57]

In an MBO system, the top management team first defines the company's strategic goals for the coming year. These goals are passed on to the next layer of management, who then define the goals they must achieve for the company to reach its goals. This goal setting process cascades down the organisation so that all managers are setting goals that help the company achieve its goals.[58] These goals are used as the standards by which an individual's performance is evaluated.[59]

There are three components to MBO systems.[60] First, they require specific, difficult and objective goals. (An example of MBO-based goals that were used in a financial service firm is presented in Table 10.7, page 366.) Second, the goals are not usually set unilaterally by management, but they are set with the managers' and subordinates' participation. Third, the managers give objective feedback throughout the rating period in order to monitor progress towards the goals.

Research on MBO has revealed two important findings regarding its effectiveness.[61] Of 70 studies examined, 68 showed productivity gains, while only two showed productivity losses—suggesting that MBO usually increases productivity.

TABLE 10.7	Example of a management by objectives (MBO) measure of job performance		
Key result area	Objective	% complete	Actual performance
Loan portfolio management	Increase portfolio value by 10% over the next 12 months	90	Increased portfolio value by 9% over the past 12 months
Sales	Generate fee income of $30 000 over the next 12 months	150	Generated fee income of $45 000 over the past 12 months

Also, productivity gains tend to be highest when there is substantial commitment to the MBO program from top management: an average increase of 56 per cent when commitment was high, 33 per cent when commitment was moderate and 6 per cent when commitment was low.

Clearly, MBO can have a positive effect on an organisation's performance. Considering the process through which goals are set (that is, involvement of staff in setting objectives), it is also likely that MBO systems effectively link individual employee performance with the firm's strategic goals.

For example, Pier 1 Imports in the United States was able to give store managers and salespeople access to real-time sales totals and analyses, telling them exactly how they were doing compared with, say, the day before or the month before. Instead of creating a 'sweatshop' atmosphere, which worried some critics, employees took the figures as a challenge. 'The more information you give the associates, the more ownership they feel in the store's performance', says Dave Self, a regional manager for 33 Pier 1 stores.

Pier 1 employees agree. 'It adds to the excitement', claims Alicia Winchell, an assistant manager. During the day, clerks at the store rotate their use of a backroom computer that gives them up-to-the-minute sales data. They learn not only how many items were sold and at what price, but also how many people entered the store and the percentage of those who bought something. They know how many items are new and how many were imported from overseas. These figures help managers and sales staff create better value for customers, paying close attention to everyone who walks in the door. Paula Hankins, a store manager, spent a half-hour one day helping an interior designer select some small decorations. The designer had not planned to spend $250 that day, but said that Hankins 'did a great job pointing out what I wanted'.

Pier 1 management makes an important distinction about the data—it is an informational tool, not an instrument of discipline. If a store fails to meet a certain short-term goal, 'it's not like they're blaming us for it', says employee Kim Smith. Results provide valuable insight into the whole performance management picture.[62]

Productivity measurement and evaluation system (ProMES)

The main goal of ProMES is to motivate employees to higher levels of productivity.[63] It is a means of measuring and feeding back productivity information to people.

ProMES consists of four steps. First, people in an organisation identify the products, or the set of activities or objectives, the organisation expects to accomplish. The organisation's productivity depends on how well it produces these products. At a repair shop, for example, a product might be something like 'quality of repair'. Second, the staff define the product indicators. Indicators are measures of how well the products are being generated by the organisation. Quality of repair could be indicated by: (1) the return rate (the percentage of items returned that did not function immediately after repair); and, (2) the percentage of quality-control inspections passed. Third, the staff establish the contingencies between the amount of the indicators and the level of evaluation associated with that amount. Fourth, a feedback system is developed that provides employees and workgroups with information about their specific level of performance on each of the indicators. An overall productivity score can be computed by summing the effectiveness scores across the various indicators.

This technique is somewhat new; hence, it has been applied in only a few situations. However, research thus far[64] strongly suggests it is effective in increasing productivity. (Figure 10.5 below illustrates the productivity gains in the repair shop described previously.) The research also suggests the system is an effective feedback mechanism. However, users found it time-consuming to develop the initial system. Future research on ProMES needs to be conducted before drawing any firm conclusions, but the existing research indicates that this may be a useful performance management tool.

Evaluation of the results approach

One advantage of the results approach is that it minimises subjectivity, relying on objective, quantifiable indicators of performance. Thus, it is usually highly acceptable to both managers and employees. Another advantage is that it links an individual's results with the organisation's strategies and goals.

A disadvantage is that objective measurements can be both contaminated and deficient—contaminated because they are affected by things that are not under the employee's control, such as economic recessions; and deficient because not all the

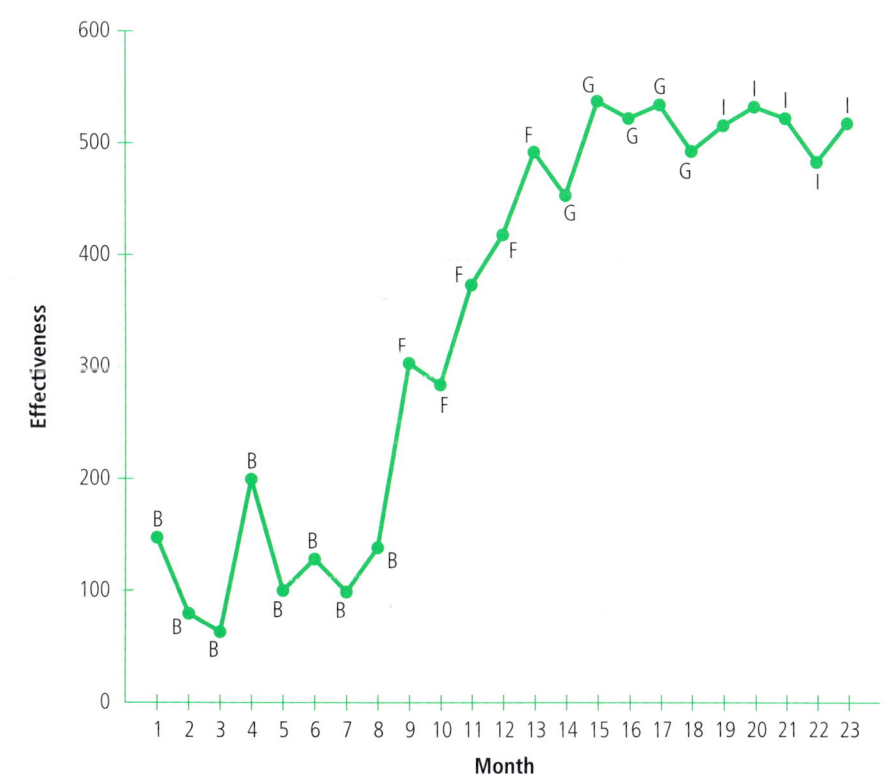

FIGURE 10.5 Increases in productivity for a repair shop using ProMES

Source: R.D. Pritchard, S.D. Jones, P.L. Roth, K.K. Stuebing & S.E. Ekeberg, 1989, 'The evaluation of an integrated approach to measuring organizational productivity', *Personnel Psychology*, 42, pp. 69–115. Used by permission.

important aspects of job performance are amenable to objective measurement. Another disadvantage of the results approach is that individuals may focus only on aspects of their performance that are measured, neglecting those that are not. For example, if the large majority of employees' goals relate to productivity, it is unlikely they will be concerned with customer service. One study found that objective performance goals led to higher performance, but that they also led to less helping of co-workers.[65] A further disadvantage is that, although results measures provide objective feedback, the feedback may not help employees learn how they need to change their behaviour to increase their performance. If cricket players are in a hitting slump, simply telling them that their batting average is low may not motivate them to raise it. Feedback focusing on the exact behaviour (for example, taking one's eye off the ball and dropping one's shoulder) that needs to change would be more helpful.[66] Other limitations of the MBO approach include the ingenious ways employees seek to make easy goals look more difficult than they are. In addition, a focus on bottom line measures provides little assistance in planning development initiatives.[67]

The quality approach

Thus far, we have examined the traditional approaches to measuring and evaluating employee performance. Two fundamental characteristics of the quality approach are a customer orientation and a prevention approach to errors. Improving customer satisfaction is the primary goal of the quality approach. Customers can be internal or external to the organisation. A performance management system designed with a strong quality orientation can be expected to:

- emphasise an assessment of both people and system factors in the measurement system
- emphasise that managers and employees work together to solve performance problems
- involve both internal and external customers in setting standards and measuring performance
- use multiple sources to evaluate persons and system factors.[68]

Based on this chapter's earlier discussion of the characteristics of an effective performance management system, it should be apparent that these characteristics are not just unique to the quality approach, but they are characteristics of an effective appraisal system.

Advocates of the quality approach believe that most United States companies' performance management systems are incompatible with the quality philosophy for a number of reasons:

1. most existing systems measure performance in terms of quantity, not quality
2. employees are held accountable for 'good' or 'bad' results to which they contribute, but do not completely control
3. companies do not share the financial rewards of successes with employees in accordance with how much those employees have contributed to the successes
4. rewards are not connected to business results.[69]

Sales, profit margins and behavioural ratings are often collected by managers to evaluate employees' performance. These are people-based outcomes. An assumption of using these types of outcomes is that the employee completely controls them. However, according to the quality approach, these types of outcomes should not be used to evaluate employees' performance because they do not have complete control over them (that is, they are contaminated). For example, for salespeople, performance evaluations (and salary increases) are often based on attainment of a sales quota. It is assumed that salespeople's abilities and motivation are directly responsible for their performance. However, quality approach advocates argue that better determinants of whether a salesperson reaches the quota are 'systems factors' (such as competitors' product price changes) and economic conditions (which are not under the salesperson's control).[70] Holding employees accountable for outcomes affected by systems factors is believed to result in dysfunctional behaviour, such as falsifying sales reports, budgets, expense accounts and other performance measures, as well as lowering employees' motivation for continuous improvement.

Quality advocates suggest that the major focus of performance evaluations should be to provide employees with feedback about areas in which they can improve. Two types of feedback are necessary: (1) subjective feedback from managers, peers and customers about the personal qualities of the employee and (2) objective feedback based on the work process itself and using statistical quality-control methods.

Performance evaluation should include a discussion of the employee's career plans. The quality approach also strongly emphasises that performance appraisal systems should avoid providing overall evaluations of employees (for example, ratings such as excellent, good and poor). Categorising employees is believed to encourage them to behave in ways that are expected, based on their ratings. For example, 'average' performers may not be motivated to improve their performance; rather, they may continue to perform at the expected level. Also, because employees do not have control over the quality of the system in which they work, employee performance evaluations should not be linked to compensation. Compensation rates should be based on prevailing market rates of pay, seniority and business results, which are distributed equitably to all employees.

Statistical process control techniques are considerably important in the quality approach. These techniques provide employees with an objective tool to identify causes of problems and potential solutions. These techniques include process-flow analysis, cause-and-effect diagrams, Pareto charts, control charts, histograms and scattergrams.

Process-flow analysis involves identifying each action and decision necessary to complete work, such as waiting on a customer or assembling a television set. Process-flow analysis is useful for identifying redundancy in processes that increase manufacturing or service time. For example, one business unit at Owens-Corning, an international company that operates in the advanced glass and building material systems industries, was able to confirm that customer orders were error-free only about 25 per cent of the time (an unacceptable level of service). To improve the service level, the unit mapped out the process to identify 'bottlenecks' and problem areas. As a result of the mapping process, one simple change (installing a free-call number for the facsimile machine) increased the overall accuracy of orders as well as the speed of transactions.[71]

In cause-and-effect diagrams, events or causes that result in undesirable outcomes are identified. Employees try to identify all possible causes of a problem. The feasibility of the causes is not evaluated and, as a result, cause-and-effect diagrams produce a large list of possible causes.

A Pareto chart is used to highlight the most important cause of a problem. In a Pareto chart, causes are listed in decreasing order of importance, where importance is usually defined as the frequency with which the cause resulted in a problem. The assumption of Pareto analysis is that the majority of problems are the result of a small number of causes. Figure 10.6, page 370 shows a Pareto chart listing the reasons managers give for not selecting current employees for a job vacancy.

PART 3 Developing People

FIGURE 10.6 Pareto chart

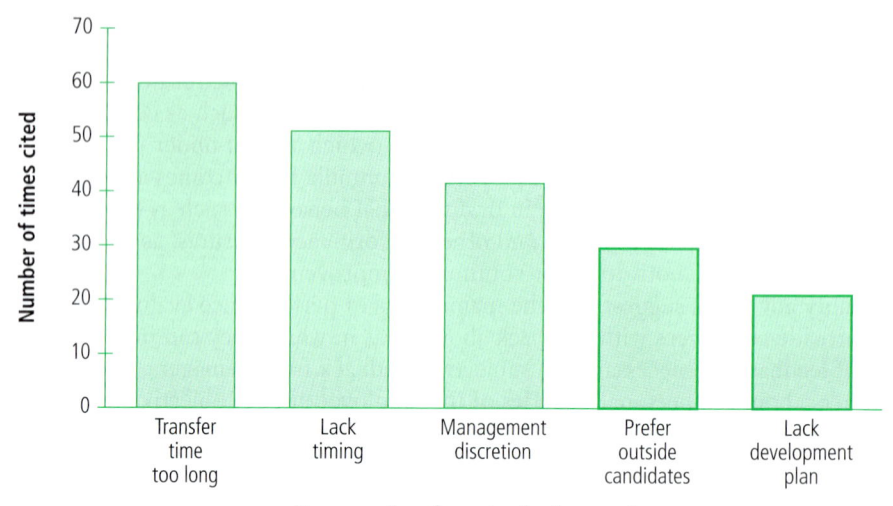

Source: C. Carter, 1992, 'Seven basic quality tools', *HR Magazine*, January, p. 83. Reprinted with permission of *HR Magazine*. Published by the Society for Human Resource Management, Alexandria, VA.

FIGURE 10.7 Control chart

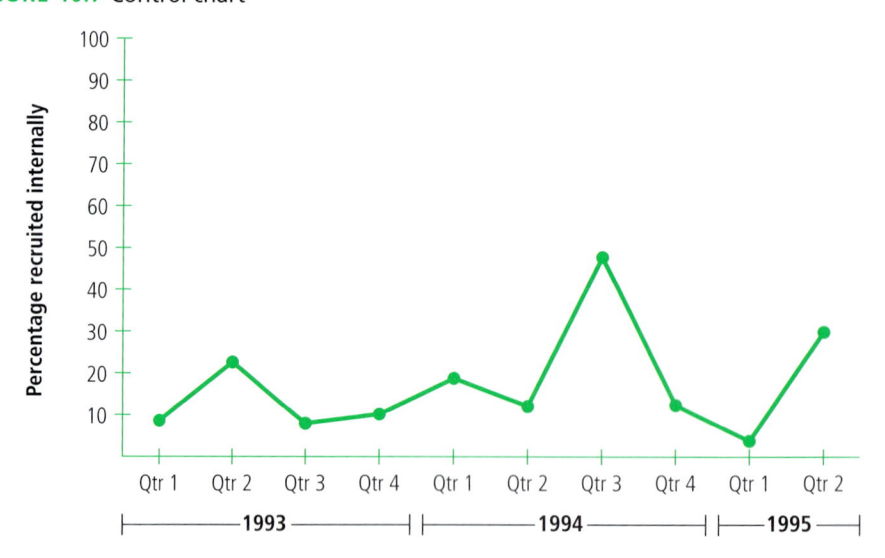

Source: C. Carter, 1992, 'Seven basic quality tools', *HR Magazine*, January, p. 82. Reprinted with permission of *HR Magazine*. Published by the Society for Human Resource Management, Alexandria, VA.

Control charts involve collecting data at multiple points in time. By collecting data at different times, employees can identify what factors contribute to an outcome and when they tend to occur. Figure 10.7 shows the percentage of employees recruited internally for a company for each quarter between 1993 and 1995. Internal recruiting increased dramatically during the third quarter of 1994. The use of control charts helps employees understand the number of internal candidates who can be expected to be recruited each year. Also, the control chart shows that the amount of internal recruiting conducted during the third quarter of 1994 was much larger than usual.

FIGURE 10.8 Histogram

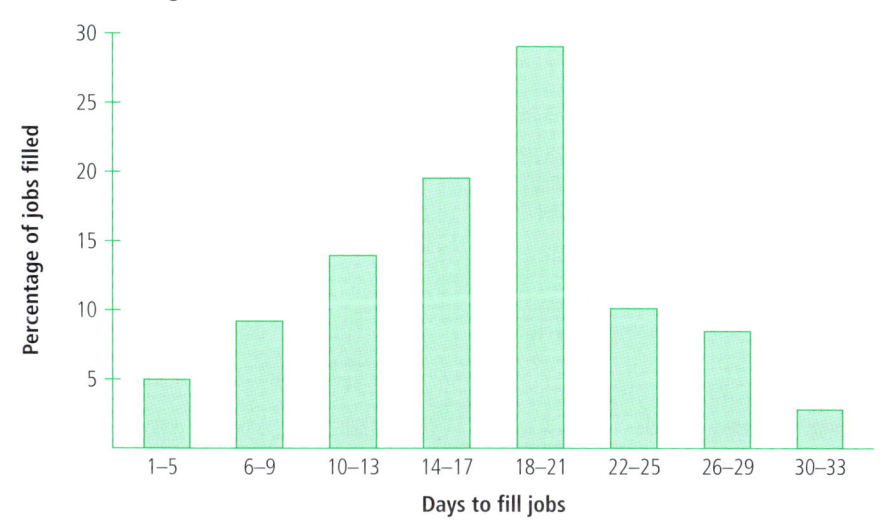

```
Percentage of jobs filled vs Days to fill jobs

30 |
25 |
20 |                      ▓
15 |              ▓       ▓
10 |      ▓       ▓       ▓   ▓   ▓
 5 |  ▓   ▓       ▓       ▓   ▓   ▓   ▓
    1-5  6-9 10-13 14-17 18-21 22-25 26-29 30-33
```

Source: C. Carter, 1992, 'Seven basic quality tools', *HR Magazine*, January, p. 83. Reprinted with permission of *HR Magazine*. Published by the Society for Human Resource Management, Alexandria, VA.

Histograms are used for displaying distributions of large sets of data. Data are grouped into a smaller number of categories or classes. Histograms are useful for understanding the amount of variance between an outcome and the expected value or average outcome. Figure 10.8 is a histogram that shows the number of days it took a company to fill job vacancies. The histogram shows that most jobs took from 18 to 21 days to fill, and the amount of time to fill jobs ranged from one to 33 days. If a HR manager relied simply on data from personnel files on the number of days it took to fill positions, it would be extremely difficult to understand the variation and average tendency in the amount of time to fill the positions.

Scattergrams show the relationship between two variables, events or different pieces of data. They can help employees determine whether the relationship between two variables or events is positive, negative or zero.

Evaluation of the quality approach

The quality approach relies primarily on a combination of the attribute and results approaches to performance measurement. However, traditional performance appraisal systems focus more on individual employee performance, while the quality approach adopts a systems oriented focus.[72] Many companies may be unwilling to completely abandon their traditional performance management system because it serves as the basis for personnel selection validation, identification of training needs or compensation decisions. Also, the quality approach advocates evaluation of personal traits (for example, cooperation), which are difficult to relate to job performance unless the company has been structured into work teams.

In summary, organisations can take five approaches to measuring performance output: comparative, attribute, behavioural, results and quality. Table 10.8 overleaf summarises the various approaches to measuring performance based on the criteria we set out earlier (that is, strategic congruence, validity, reliability, acceptability and specificity) and illustrates that each approach has strengths and weaknesses. As the quality approach illustrates, often the most effective way of measuring performance is to rely on a combination of two or more alternatives. For example, performance

TABLE 10.8 Evaluation of approaches to performance measurement

Approach	Strategic congruence	Validity	Reliability	Acceptability	Specificity
Comparative	Poor, unless manager takes time to make link	Can be high if ratings are done carefully	Depends on rater, but usually no measure of agreement used	Moderate; easy to develop and use but resistance to normative standard	Very low
Attribute	Usually low; requires manager to make link	Usually low; can be fine if developed carefully	Usually low; can be improved by specific definitions of attributes	High; easy to develop and use	Very low
Behavioural	Can be quite high	Usually high; Minimises contamination and deficiency	Usually high	Moderate; difficult to develop, but accepted well for use	Very high
Results	Very high	Usually high; can be both contaminated and deficient	High; main problem can be test–retest—depends on timing of measure	High; usually developed with input from those to be evaluated	High regarding results, but low regarding behaviours necessary to achieve them
Quality	Very high	High, but can be both contaminated and deficient	High	High; usually developed with input from those to be evaluated	High regarding results, but low regarding behaviours necessary to achieve them

management systems in many companies evaluate the extent to which managers reach specific performance goals as well as evaluate their behaviour. Organisations can also take an approach that measures the process—or means—by which performance is achieved.

The means-based approach

The means-based approach to performance assessment focuses on the way in which performance outcomes and results are achieved. This approach provides a way of determining the extent to which performance outcomes are the result of the behaviours of an individual rather than the behaviours of other people or aspects of the organisation's environment. This approach also acknowledges that there could be a tension associated with achieving results in the short term and building a successful organisation in the longer term.[73]

During the late 1980s and 1990s, concern about the focus on results began to emerge in Australia. There was increasing concern that this focus was short term and that it tended to reinforce poor management behaviours that neglected the processes associated with achieving the results.[74] At the same time, the competency movement emerged in Australia as part of a move to try and make employees, particularly managers, more internationally competitive.[75] This approach acknowledged that organisational performance could be improved by recognising existing competencies and encouraging the development of further individual and collective competencies.[76] During the 1990s, increasing interest was shown in using competencies as an integral part of performance management by making it an integral part of job evaluation, performance evaluation and competency-based pay systems.[77]

Competency models of assessment identify distinguishing characteristics of superior performers in a particular job. These distinguishing characteristics are represented as a number of groups or units of competencies—for instance conceptual, technical, interpersonal (this latter unit includes two types of skills: developing and motivating others, and negotiating and influencing skills)—which are described in terms of three to six behavioural indicators. Table 10.9 below provides a framework developed to describe managerial competencies. This framework includes five units of competency and many behaviours associated with these competencies.

It has been suggested that these behaviourally based frameworks could be improved by also measuring an individual's emotional intelligence.[78] Emotional intelligence refers to an individual's ability to recognise and understand their own feelings and those of others, and then use this information to maximise their own performance. Emotional intelligence is reflected in the ability to motivate yourself, the ability to manage stress and emotions and the ability to influence others and build effective relationships. It involves the competencies of self-awareness, emotional management, empathy, self-motivation, social effectiveness, relationships, personal style and communication. Freeman[79] argues that combining a behaviourally based competence system and an emotional intelligence questionnaire provides feedback that gives insight into personal motivators and feelings as well as how the actual behaviour of individuals is perceived by others.

A performance management system can combine both output-based and means-based approaches. Such a model can assess and reward employees for both the results

TABLE 10.9 A proposed framework for managerial competencies

Competency unit	Examples of competency elements
1 Personal management	Professionalism and self-confidence, personal integrity, commitment and enthusiasm, attendance and punctuality, achievement orientation, self-awareness, personal time management and ability to learn from past failures.
2 Strategic and change management	Development of organisation-wide strategies, awareness of organisational mission, environmental awareness, coordinating across internal boundaries, vision for organisation's future, change agent, and designing and reviewing organisational units.
3 Leadership and teambuilding	Building teams, building team morale, awareness of interpersonal differences, coaching and developing others, evaluating staff performance, facilitating group interaction, delegating effectively, participating in teams, and leading and conducting meetings.
4 Problem solving and decision making	Creative and innovative thinking, analytical–conceptual ability, evaluating alternatives, flexibility in decisions, judgment and perception, problem-solving ability, accurate problem diagnosis, making spontaneous decisions and identifying urgencies in decisions.
5 Administrative and operations management	Inventory administrations, operational scheduling, purchasing, cost accounting, productivity monitoring, job analysis, recruitment and selection, and product and service marketing.

Source: J. Hunt & J. Wallace, 1997, 'A competency-based approach to assessing managerial performance in the Australian context', *Asia Pacific Journal of Human Resources*, 35 (2), p. 63. © Sage Publications, 1997. Reprinted by permission.

and the way the results are delivered. These mixed models are often used to make compensation decisions, while competency assessment alone is more long term and is used for employee development and career planning.[80]

In most cases, the performance measures consist of some kind of ratings. These ratings must come from some source. The next section discusses the various sources of performance information.

Choosing a source for performance information

Whatever approach to performance management is used, it is necessary to decide who to use as the source of the performance measures. Each source has specific strengths and weaknesses. We discuss five primary sources: managers, peers, subordinates, self and customers.

Managers

Managers are the most frequently used source of performance information. Surveys in Australia demonstrate that managers or immediate supervisors provide information for performance feedback in almost all organisations that have a performance management system.[81] It is usually safe to assume that supervisors have extensive knowledge of the job requirements and they have had adequate opportunity to observe their employees—in other words, they have the ability to rate their employees. In addition, because supervisors have something to gain from the employees' high performance and something to lose from their low performance, supervisors have the motivation to make accurate ratings.[82] Finally, feedback from supervisors is strongly related to performance.[83]

Problems with using supervisors as the source of performance information can occur in particular situations. In some jobs, for example, the supervisor does not have an adequate opportunity to observe the employee performing his or her job duties. For example, in an outside sales job, the supervisor does not have the opportunity to see the salesperson at work most of the time. This usually requires that the manager occasionally spends a day accompanying the salesperson on sales calls. However, on those occasions the employee will be on his or her best behaviour, so there is no assurance that the employee's performance on that day accurately reflects her or his performance when the manager is not around. In some situations, supervisors might also not understand what the employee is doing, because the work is very complex and/or varied. There may be other circumstances where the supervisor has a large span of control.

Also, some supervisors may be so biased against a particular employee that to use him or her as the sole source of information would result in less-than-accurate measures for that individual. Favouritism is a fact of organisational life, but it is one that must be minimised as much as possible in the performance management process.[84] Thus, the performance evaluation system should seek to minimise the opportunities for favouritism to affect ratings. One way to do this is not to rely on only a supervisor's evaluation of an employee's performance.

While managers are the most frequently used source of performance information, it is ironic that upper-level managers or chief executive officers, whose decisions affect all the company's shareholders, rarely receive performance evaluation. This situation is beginning to change.

Peers

Another source of performance information is the employee's co-workers. Peers are an excellent source of information in a job such as law enforcement, where the supervisor does not always have the opportunity to observe the employee. Peers have expert knowledge of job requirements and they often have the most opportunity to observe the employee in day-to-day activities. Peers also bring a different perspective to the evaluation process, which can be valuable in gaining an overall picture of the individual's performance. In fact, peers have been found to provide extremely valid assessments of performance in several different settings.[85]

Peer assessment is considerably important in the context of managing the performance of teams. In circumstances where team members are usually not given very much supervision, other team members are more likely to be familiar with individuals' performance. At Digital Equipment Corporation (DEC), manufacturing employees are organised into teams and a three-step assessment process operates. First, when it is performance assessment time, a committee is established. The committee consists of a chairperson chosen by the team member, two randomly chosen team members, the person being assessed (the ratee) and the 'consultant' to the team. Second, information about performance is collected in a number of ways. The ratee prepares a summary of achievements during the year and the committee collects additional information and provides this to the ratee. The ratee then prepares a performance appraisal document. Third, the committee reviews the document, meets with the ratee, provides a formal rating, sets goals for next year and reviews the written summary of the meeting prepared by the chairperson. The document is sent to the human resources department.[86]

One disadvantage of using peer ratings is the potential for personal feelings to bias ratings.[87] Little empirical evidence suggests that this is often a problem, however. Another disadvantage is that when the evaluations are made for administrative decisions, peers often find the situation of being both rater and ratee uncomfortable. When these ratings are used only for developmental purposes, however, peers react favourably.[88]

Subordinates

Subordinates are an especially valuable source of performance information when managers are being evaluated. Subordinates often have the best opportunity to evaluate how well a manager treats employees. One study found that managers viewed receiving upward feedback more positively when receiving feedback from subordinates who were identified, but subordinates preferred to provide anonymous feedback. When subordinates were identified, they inflated their ratings of the manager.[89]

One problem with subordinate evaluations is that they give subordinates power over their managers, thus putting the manager in a difficult situation.[90] This can lead to managers emphasising employee satisfaction over productivity. However, this happens only when administrative decisions are made from these evaluations. As with peer evaluations, it is a good idea to use subordinate evaluations only for developmental purposes. To assure subordinates that they need not fear retribution from their managers, it is necessary to use anonymous evaluations and use at least three subordinates for each manager.

Self

Although self-ratings are not often used as the sole source of performance information, they can still be valuable.[91] Obviously, individuals have extensive opportunities to observe their own behaviour and they usually have access to information regarding their results on the job.

One problem with self-ratings, however, is a tendency toward inflated assessments. This stems from two sources. One, if the ratings are going to be used for administrative decisions (for example, pay rises), it is in the employees' interests to inflate their ratings. Two, there is ample evidence in the social psychology literature that individuals attribute their poor performance to external causes, such as a co-worker who they think has not provided them with timely information. Although self-ratings are less inflated when supervisors provide frequent performance feedback, it is not advisable to use them for administrative purposes.[92] The best use of self-ratings is as a prelude to the performance feedback session to get employees thinking about their performance and to focus discussion on areas of disagreement.

Customers

Service industries accounted for virtually all job growth between 1996 and 2006.[93] As a result, we would expect many companies to be moving towards involving customers in their evaluation systems. One writer has defined services this way: '… something which can be bought and sold but which you cannot drop on your foot'.[94] The unique nature of services—the product is often produced and consumed on the spot—means that supervisors, peers and subordinates often do not have the opportunity to observe employee behaviour. Instead, the customer is often the only person present to observe the employee's performance and, thus, is the best source of performance information.

Many companies in service industries have moved towards customer evaluations of employee performance. Marriott Corporation provides a customer satisfaction card in every room and sends mail surveys to a random sample of customers after their stay in a Marriott hotel. Whirlpool's Consumer Services Division conducts both mail and telephone surveys of customers after factory service technicians have serviced their appliances. These surveys allow the company to evaluate an individual technician's customer-service behaviours while in the customer's home.

There are two situations in which using customer evaluations of employee performance is appropriate.[95] The first is when employees' jobs require them to directly provide a service to the customer or link the customer to other services within the company. Second, customer evaluations are appropriate when the company is interested in gathering information to determine what products and services the customer wants. That is, customer evaluations serve a strategic goal by integrating marketing strategies with human resource activities and policies. Customer evaluations collected for this purpose are useful for both evaluating the employee and helping to determine whether changes in other HR activities (for example, training and compensation systems) are needed to improve customer service. The transfer of knowledge from customers facilitates the adaptation of the organisation to changing expectations, and it is a feature of a 'learning organisation'.

The weakness of customer surveys is their expense. Printing, postage, telephone and labour can add up to hundreds of dollars for the evaluation of one individual. Thus, many companies conduct such evaluations only once a year for a short period of time.

In conclusion, the best source of performance information often depends on the particular job. One should choose the source or sources that provide the best opportunity to observe employee behaviour and results. Table 10.10 opposite summarises this information for most jobs. Often, eliciting performance information from a variety of sources results in a performance management process that is accurate

| TABLE 10.10 | Frequency of observation for various sources of performance information |

	Source				
	Supervisor	**Peers**	**Subordinates**	**Self**	**Customers**
Task					
Behaviours	Occasional	Frequent	Rare	Always	Frequent
Results	Frequent	Frequent	Occasional	Frequent	Frequent
Interpersonal					
Behaviours	Occasional	Frequent	Frequent	Always	Frequent
Results	Occasional	Frequent	Frequent	Frequent	Frequent

Source: Adapted from K.R. Murphy & J.N. Cleveland, 1991, *Performance Appraisal: An Organizational Perspective*, Allyn and Bacon, Boston.

and effective. In fact, one recent popular trend in organisations is called '360-degree appraisals'.[96] This technique consists of having multiple raters (bosses, peers, subordinates and customers) provide input into a manager's evaluation. The major advantage of the technique is that it provides a means for minimising bias in an otherwise subjective evaluation technique. It also provides greater reliability in the feedback and it opens communication within the workplace.[97]

However, there are also a number of disadvantages, including the interpretation of differences between rater groups, raters' fear of being identified and the cost of a 360-degree system. Such 360-degree instruments have been used primarily for strategic and developmental purposes[98] and their use has increased in Australia during the last 10 years.[99] This system is also discussed in Chapter 11 Learning and development.

Rater errors in performance measurement

Research consistently reveals that humans have tremendous limitations in processing information. Thus, we often use 'heuristics', or simplifying mechanisms, to make judgments, whether they are judgments about investments or about people.[100] These heuristics, which often appear in subjective measures of performance, can lead to rater errors. Performance evaluations may also be purposefully distorted. We discuss rater errors and appraisal politics next.

Similar to me

'Similar to me' is the error we make when we judge those who are similar to us more highly than those who are not. Research has demonstrated that this effect is strong and, when similarity is based on demographic characteristics such as race or sex, it can result in discriminatory decisions.[101] Most of us tend to think of ourselves as effective; so if others are like us—in race, gender, background, attitudes or beliefs—we assume that they too are effective.

Contrast

Contrast error occurs when we compare individuals with one another instead of against an objective standard. Consider a completely competent performer who works with a number of peers who are outstanding. If the competent employee receives lower-than-deserved ratings because of his outstanding colleagues, that is contrast error.

Distributional errors

Distributional errors are the result of a rater's tendency to use only one part of the rating scale. Leniency occurs when a rater assigns high (lenient) ratings to all employees. Strictness occurs when a manager gives low ratings to all employees—that is, holds all employees to unreasonably high standards. Central tendency reflects that a manager rates all employees in the middle of the scale. These errors pose two problems. First, they make it difficult to distinguish among employees rated by the same rater. Second, they create problems in comparing the performance of individuals rated by different raters. If one rater is lenient and the other is strict, employees of the strict rater will receive significantly fewer rewards than those rated by the lenient rater.

Halo and horns

These errors refer to a failure to distinguish among different aspects of performance. 'Halo error' occurs when one positive performance aspect causes the rater to rate all other aspects of performance positively—for example, professors who are rated as outstanding researchers because they are known to be outstanding teachers. 'Horns error' works in the opposite direction: one negative aspect results in the rater assigning low ratings to all the other aspects.

Halo and horns errors are a problem in that they preclude making the necessary distinctions between strong and weak performance. Halo error leads to employees believing that no aspects of their performance need improvement. Horns error leads to employees becoming frustrated and defensive.

Reducing rater errors

Two approaches to reducing rating errors have been offered.[102] Rater error training attempts to make managers aware of rating errors and helps them develop strategies for minimising those errors.[103] These programs consist of having the participants view videotaped vignettes designed to elicit rating errors such as 'contrast'. They then make their ratings and discuss how the error influenced their ratings. Finally, they are given learning points regarding ways to avoid committing those errors. This approach has been shown to be effective for reducing errors, but there is evidence that reducing rating errors can also reduce accuracy.[104]

Rater accuracy training, also called frame-of-reference training, attempts to emphasise the multidimensional nature of performance and thoroughly familiarise raters with the actual content of various performance dimensions. This involves providing examples of performance for each dimension and then discussing the actual or 'correct' level of performance that the example represents.[105] Accuracy training does seem to increase accuracy, provided that the training allows raters to practise making ratings and the training offers feedback about their accuracy.[106]

Appraisal politics

Appraisal politics refers to evaluators purposefully distorting a rating to achieve personal or company goals. Research suggests that several factors promote appraisal politics. These factors are inherent in the appraisal system and the company culture. Appraisal politics are most likely to occur when raters are accountable to the employee being rated, there are competing rating goals and a direct link exists between performance appraisal and highly desirable rewards. Also, appraisal politics are likely to occur if top executives tolerate distortion or are complacent towards it and if

---

Appraisal politics refers to evaluators purposefully distorting a rating to achieve personal or company goals.

distortion strategies are part of 'company folklore' and are passed down from senior employees to new employees.

It is unlikely that appraisal politics can be completely eliminated. Unfortunately, there is little research on the best methods to eliminate appraisal politics. To minimise appraisal politics, managers should keep in mind the characteristics of a fair appraisal system, as shown in Table 10.2 on page 355. In addition, managers should:

- train raters on the appropriate use of the process as discussed previously
- build top management support for the appraisal system and actively discourage distortion
- give raters some latitude to customise performance objectives and criteria for their ratees
- recognise employee accomplishments that are not self-promoted
- make sure constraints, such as a budget, do not drive the process
- make sure that appraisal processes are consistent across the company
- foster a climate of openness to encourage employees to be honest about weaknesses.[107]

Even though many organisations are vying with each other to attract and retain employees, workplace bullying is alleged to be a widespread serious issue. Excessive performance monitoring and poor management processes can contribute to employees experiencing stress and bullying from other employees. If these allegations of bullying are not dealt with promptly there is the risk of high employee turnover, low morale and sick leave absences.[108]

Performance feedback

The **performance feedback process** is a process whereby the defined expected performance information and the measured performance information is fed back to the employee, so that he or she can correct any deficiencies. The performance feedback process is complex and provokes anxiety for both the manager and the employee. Table 10.11 below, provides examples of feedback that managers have given employees. You be the judge as to these statements' effectiveness in improving employees' performance!

Performance feedback process a process whereby the defined expected performance information and the measured performance information is fed back to the employee.

TABLE 10.11 Examples of performance feedback

- Since my last report, this employee has reached rock bottom and has started to dig.
- His men would follow him anywhere, but only out of morbid curiosity.
- I would not allow this employee to breed.
- This associate is really not so much of a 'has-been', but more of a 'definitely won't-be'.
- Works well when under constant supervision and cornered like a rat in a trap.
- When she opens her mouth, it seems that this is only to change whichever foot was previously in there.
- He would be out of his depth in a parking-lot puddle.
- This young lady has delusions of adequacy.
- He sets low personal standards, then consistently fails to achieve them.
- This employee should go far—and the sooner he starts, the better.
- This employee is depriving a village somewhere of an idiot.

Source: Y. Harari, 1997, 'The daily dose', www.thedailydose.com, 22 July.

Few of us feel comfortable sitting in judgment of others. The thought of confronting others with what we perceive to be their deficiencies causes most of us to shake in our shoes. If giving negative feedback is painful, receiving it can be excruciating—thus, the importance of the performance feedback process.

'HRM spotlight: Chucking the sickies' discusses the issue of absenteeism in Australia. It raises the issue implicitly of whether absenteeism is a performance issue.

Characteristics of an effective performance feedback process

If employees are not made aware of how their performance is not meeting expectations, their performance will almost certainly not improve. In fact, it may get worse. Effective managers provide specific performance feedback to employees in a way that elicits positive behavioural responses. The following process increases the potential for a successful performance feedback session.

Feedback should be given frequently, not once a year

There are two reasons for this. First, managers have a responsibility to correct performance deficiencies immediately on becoming aware of them. If performance is sub-par in January, waiting until December to appraise the performance could mean an 11-month productivity loss. Second, a major determinant of how effectively a feedback session goes is the extent to which the subordinate is not surprised by the evaluation. An easy rule to follow is that employees should receive such frequent performance feedback that they already know almost exactly what their formal evaluation will include.

Create the right context for the discussion

Managers should choose a neutral location for the feedback session. The manager's office may not be the best place for a constructive feedback session because the employee may associate the office with unpleasant conversations. Managers should describe the meeting as an opportunity to discuss the role of the employee, the role of the manager and the relationship between them. Managers should also acknowledge that they would like the meeting to be an open dialogue.

Ask the employee to rate his or her performance before the session

Having employees complete a self-assessment before the feedback session can be considerably productive. It requires employees to think about their performance over the past rating period and it encourages them to think about their weaknesses. Although self-ratings used for administrative decisions are often inflated, there is evidence that they may actually be lower than supervisors' ratings, when they are provided for developmental purposes. Another reason a self-assessment can be productive is that it can make the session go more smoothly by focusing discussion on areas where disagreement exists, resulting in a more efficient session. Finally, employees who have thought about past performance are more able to participate fully in the feedback session.

Encourage the subordinate to participate in the session

Managers can take one of three approaches in performance feedback sessions. In the 'tell-and-sell' approach, managers tell the employees how they have rated them and then justify these ratings. In the 'tell-and-listen' approach, managers tell employees how they have rated them and then let the employees explain their side of the story. In the 'problem solving' approach, managers and employees work together to solve

CHUCKING THE SICKIES

HRM SPOTLIGHT

Many workers view the sickie as an Aussie tradition, but absenteeism is costing the country $7 billion each year.

A new survey has revealed Australians on average take 8.5 sick days a year, costing more than $2500 an employee.

Physical and mental health reasons accounted for 71 per cent of absences, and more than 90 per cent of sick leave was for two days or less, for illnesses such as cold and flu, headache and gastro.

Drug and alcohol related issues were responsible for 4 per cent of absent work days, while 29 percent of workers reported missing work in the past three months for personal problems.

The Direct Health Solutions national survey of managers and employees also found 98 per cent of workers admitted going to work unwell, while 43 per cent believed their manager didn't encourage them to take days off when ill.

Most managers and employees agreed that medical certificates were no longer a useful or reliable tool.

More than half the managers surveyed said they received inaccurate medical certificates and 35 per cent of workers confessed to submitting fake certificates.

Direct Health Solutions' managing director Paul Dundon said the number of annual sick days was 'the same if not higher than five years ago'.

Mr Dundon said a 2003 study found workers took an average of 8.2 days.

He said although mental-health-related conditions were on the rise, workers were still reluctant to tell their bosses the true nature of their time off.

'It's difficult for people to communicate to their employer that they've got a mental health problem', Mr Dundon said.

Results from the survey showed 40 per cent of respondents rated their health around the average mark.

The new Work Choices legislation has also put sick days under the spotlight, with the Australian Medical Association saying it makes it easier for workers to 'chuck a sickie'.

Under the changes, employers can request a medical certificate for one day off work but employees don't have to rely on doctors.

The legislation allows them to obtain a certificate from more than 300 000 registered health practitioners, including osteopaths, chiropractors and Chinese medicine practitioners.

Health Check

Australians take an average of 8.5 days absence each year, costing the economy $2 billion annually

- 98 per cent of workers admitted going to work despite feeling unwell
- 58 per cent took sickies in the past year because of cold and flu, followed by headaches (54 per cent) and gastro (29 per cent)
- 43 per cent of workers felt their manager didn't encourage them to take time off when ill.

Source: M. Wood, 2006, 'Chucking sickies has ill effect on economy', *The Sun Herald*, 2 April, p. 9.

---

performance problems in an atmosphere of respect and encouragement. In spite of the research demonstrating the superiority of the problem-solving approach, most managers still rely on the tell-and-sell approach.[109]

When employees participate in the feedback session, they are consistently satisfied with the process. (Recall our discussion of fairness earlier in this chapter.) Participation includes allowing employees to voice their opinions of the evaluation and also to discuss performance goals.[110] One study found that, other than satisfaction with one's supervisor, participation was the single most important predictor of satisfaction with the feedback session.[111]

Recognise effective performance through praise

One usually thinks of performance feedback sessions as focusing on the employee's performance problems. This should never be the case. The purpose of the session is to give accurate performance feedback, which entails recognising effective performance as well as poor performance. Praising effective performance provides reinforcement for that behaviour. It also adds credibility to the feedback by making it clear that the manager is not just identifying performance problems.

Focus on solving problems

A common mistake that managers make in providing performance feedback is to try to use the session as a chance to punish poor performing employees by telling them how utterly lousy their performance is. This only reduces the employees' self-esteem and increases their defensiveness, neither of which will improve performance.

To improve poor performance, a manager must attempt to solve the problems that are causing poor performance. This entails working with the employee to determine the actual cause of the problems and then agreeing on how to solve the problems. For example, a salesperson's failure to meet a sales goal may be the result of his or her lack of a proper sales pitch, lack of product knowledge or stolen sales by another salesperson. Each of these problems requires a different solution. Without a problem solving approach, however, the correct solution might never be identified.

Focus feedback on behaviour or results, not on the person

One of the most important things to do when giving negative feedback is to avoid questioning the employee's worth as a person. This is best accomplished by focusing the discussion on the employee's behaviours or results, not on the employee. To say, 'You're screwing up! You're just not motivated!' will bring about more defensiveness and ill feelings than stating, 'You did not meet the deadline that you agreed to because you spent too much time on another project.'

Minimise criticism

Obviously, if an individual's performance is below standard, some criticism must take place. However, an effective manager should resist the temptation to reel off a litany of offences. Having been confronted with the performance problem, an employee often agrees that a change is in order. However, if the manager continues to come up with more and more examples of low performance, the employee may get defensive.

In some countries, for instance in those countries in which Confucian values operate, the giving of feedback, particularly negative feedback, needs to be managed in a sensitive manner. It has been suggested that the Western-style appraisal approach of giving top-down feedback to an individual is inappropriate in this context.[112]

Agree to specific goals and set a date to review progress

The importance of goal setting cannot be overemphasised. It is one of the most effective motivators of performance.[113] Research has demonstrated that it results in increased satisfaction, motivation to improve and performance improvement.[114] Besides setting goals, the manager must also set a specific follow-up date to review the employee's performance towards the goal. This provides an added incentive for the employee to take the goal seriously and work towards achieving it.

Managing the performance of marginal performers

As we emphasised in the previous discussion, employees need performance feedback to take actions to improve their current job performance. As we will discuss in Chapter 11 Learning and development, performance feedback is also needed for employees to develop their knowledge and skills for the future. In addition to understanding how to effectively give employees performance feedback, managers need to be aware of what types of actions are likely to improve and maintain that performance. For example, giving performance feedback to marginal employees or unsatisfactory employees may not be sufficient for improving their performance. **Marginal employees** are those employees who are performing at a bare-minimum level due to a lack of ability and/or motivation to perform well.[115]

Figure 10.9 below shows actions for the manager to take with four different types of employees. As the table highlights, managers need to take into account whether employees lack ability and/or motivation, when considering ways in which to improve employees' performance. To determine an employee's level of ability, a manager should consider if the employee has the knowledge, skills and abilities needed to perform effectively. Lack of ability may be an issue if an employee is 'new' in a job or the job has recently changed. To determine employees' levels of motivation, managers need to consider if employees are doing the jobs they want to do and if they feel they are being appropriately paid or rewarded. A sudden negative change in an employee's performance may indicate that he or she is experiencing personal problems.

Employees with high abilities and motivation are likely to be good performers (solid performers). Figure 10.9 emphasises that managers should not ignore such employees. Managers should provide development opportunities to keep them satisfied and effective. Poor performance resulting from lack of ability but not motivation (that is, misdirected effort) may be improved by skill development activities, such as training or temporary assignments. Managers with employees who have the ability but lack motivation (under-utilisers) need to consider actions that focus on interpersonal problems or incentives. These actions include making sure that incentives or rewards that the employee values are linked to performance and making counselling available to help employees deal with personal problems or career or job dissatisfaction. Chronic poor performance by employees with low ability and motivation (deadwood) indicates that outplacement or firing may be the best solution.

> **Marginal employees**
> those employees who are performing at a bare-minimum level due to a lack of ability and/or motivation to perform well.

FIGURE 10.9 Ways to manage employees' performance

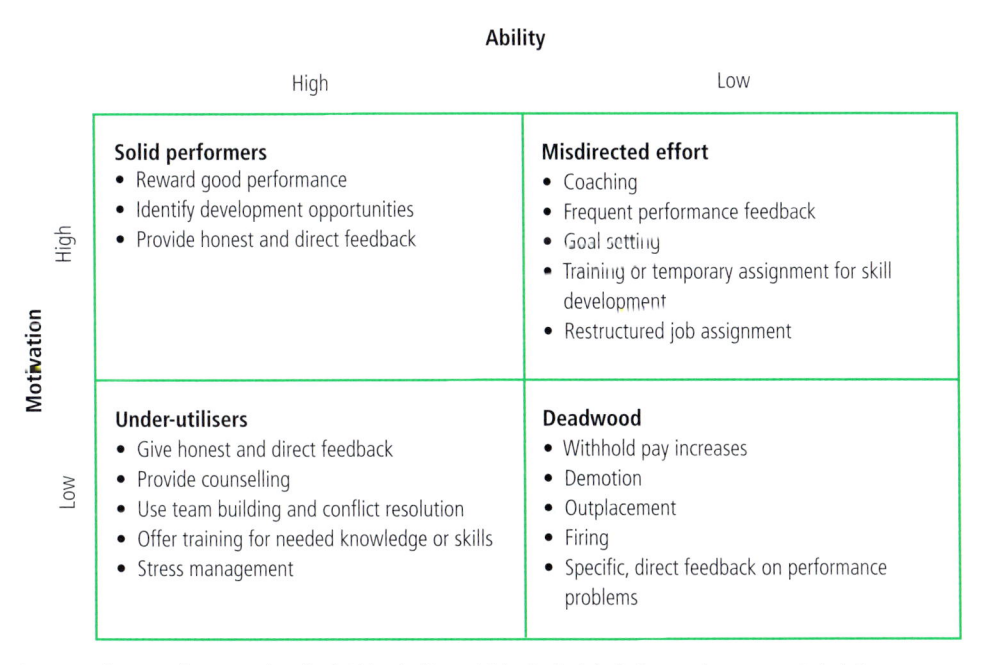

	Ability: High	Ability: Low
Motivation: High	**Solid performers** • Reward good performance • Identify development opportunities • Provide honest and direct feedback	**Misdirected effort** • Coaching • Frequent performance feedback • Goal setting • Training or temporary assignment for skill development • Restructured job assignment
Motivation: Low	**Under-utilisers** • Give honest and direct feedback • Provide counselling • Use team building and conflict resolution • Offer training for needed knowledge or skills • Stress management	**Deadwood** • Withhold pay increases • Demotion • Outplacement • Firing • Specific, direct feedback on performance problems

Source: Based on M. London, 2003, *Job Feedback: Giving, Seeking, and Using Feedback for Performance Improvement*, 2nd edn, Lawrence Erlbaum Associates, Mahwah, NJ, pp. 96–7. Used by permission.

PART 3   Developing People

Managing the performance of teams

Many of the same factors involved in managing the performance of individuals are involved in managing teams. Organisations need to ensure the following processes are undertaken so that teams perform in ways that provide competitive advantages. First, senior management must provide clear support and demonstrate how their activities contribute to the vision and strategy of the organisation.[116] In circumstances where an organisation believes teams are important to the organisation, it is advisable to assign a top manager or group to continually develop and monitor each team's actions. This action provides a clear message to all individuals in the organisation—that is, contributions to team efforts are important and that if the performances of individuals are to be successful, they will need to behave as effective team members. Second, it is essential that efforts to promote teamwork are regarded as important and rewarded. Teamwork can be rewarded by making sure performance indicators allow managers to demonstrate their effectiveness in building teams; it can also be rewarded by making sure resources are available for building teams and these teams are rewarded for work that contributes to the organisation's performance. Third, the performance of a team can be enhanced by ensuring that time is made available for teambuilding and that people understand what teambuilding is and what it is not. Teambuilding is about assisting people to work together to accomplish results for the organisation, to identify factors that limit the performance of the team and to enhance any actions that improve teamwork.[117]

As with individuals, teams need to be clear about the goals and results required of them. Individuals in the team need to understand the roles they must assume and there needs to be an organisational climate of trust in which individuals are prepared to share information. People also need to be able to participate in decision making so that decisions are implemented with commitment. As mentioned previously, managers need to be supportive of team members.

Developing and implementing a system that follows legal guidelines

In Australia there are six legal issues associated with the conduct and use of performance appraisal information. They involve:

1 documentation for legal protection
2 possibility of condoning poor performance by inaction
3 employer's duty to the poor performer
4 adequate warning before dismissal
5 effects of equal employment opportunity (EEO)
6 termination.

Performance appraisal records can be used by dismissed employees to challenge the decision to terminate their employment. It is important to include all material relating to performance in a formal record, particularly information relating to poor performance and counselling. A series of good performance assessments could mean an employee is entitled to a substantial amount of time to rectify their performance inadequacies.

Employers also run the risk of unfair dismissal actions in circumstances where they put up with poor performance for a long period of time without starting formal review procedures. An employee can argue that the employer could be seen to have condoned the poor performance as adequate. This situation is likely to occur where the performance assessment procedure is poorly designed and implemented and when it shows an adequate level of performance.

According to unfair dismissal laws, employers have a duty to poor performers. These laws prohibit employers from forcing an employee to resign or making work conditions unpleasant enough to resign—these actions would be interpreted as dismissal. For poor performers, employers are required to take the following actions: introduce a review process separate from the usual performance appraisal; ensure the review process is formal and documented; give the employee notice that their performance is inadequate; and focus on improving performance in a specified area, in a fixed time frame that is balanced and reasonable (at least three months).

Although there is no standard warning that applies in all circumstances, it is suggested that employers provide clear, written and recorded notice of the deficiencies of performance and give an explicit warning that failure to remove these deficiencies in a reasonable period of time will carry the risk of termination.

As discussed in Chapter 3 The legal context for human resource management, discrimination and EEO legislation prohibits discrimination on a number of grounds. Therefore, any decisions based on a performance assessment that was judged to be discriminatory would be unlawful. This discrimination does not have to be conscious or intentional and it may result from a manager's attitudes or beliefs. However, an organisation can be held accountable for decisions such as promotion based on performance assessments. For instance, in the D. Harrison versus Department of TAFE case, it was found that a female TAFE teacher had been discriminated against because of her gender when performance assessments were made. This discrimination prevented her from being placed on promotion lists. The Anti-Discrimination Board found Ms Harrison was 'somewhat forceful and aggressive but not unduly so and certainly no more than was acceptable in male applicants'. The board found the discrimination was the result of 'subconscious assumptions, which translated into behaviour, which became unlawful'.[118]

Organisations can avoid this type of action by ensuring: appraisal criteria are job-related, appraisal criteria have been checked, appraising managers and supervisors are trained in appraisal, and there is no direct or indirect use of outlawed grounds of choice.

The *Workplace Amendment (Work Choices) Act 2005* provides the opportunity for the development of individual based working arrangements. This will require managers to conduct effective performance assessments in order to formulate individual contracts. The legislation also requires employers with more than 100 employees to conduct and document regular performance assessments. These requirements prohibit an employer from dismissing an employee without valid reason. They require an employer to give an employee an opportunity to defend any allegations as well as give adequate notice to the employee.

Employees are entitled to procedural and substantive fairness whenever any action is taken in response to a negative assessment of performance. These actions could include a warning, direction, suspension, transfer, demotion or removal of benefits. Legal obligations regarding fairness can be met by ensuring the:

- development of a transparent performance appraisal system that can be consistently applied
- review of performance is made against clearly specified criteria (for example, a position description and performance goals)
- results of previous performance assessments are taken into account
- systems to deal with counselling and warnings are in place

- nature and duration of the actions are clear and the reasons as to why the actions have been taken are clear
- duration of the actions and the reasons as to why the actions have been taken are clearly explained to the employee
- employee understands how their performance could be improved and how this improvement would be assessed
- employee is informed of the consequences of not improving performance and the procedures to be followed if this occurs.[119]

Performance of an organisation is also influenced by the decisions of directors and senior managers. 'Managing challenges through sustainability: HR directors come under APRA gun' discusses recent federal government legislation that seeks to shape the performance of company directors and senior managers.

HR DIRECTORS COME UNDER APRA GUN

The Australian Prudential Regulation Authority's (APRA's) new prudential standards for banks will place heads of HR who report to their CEO directly in the regulatory firing line.

The standards are designed to establish a minimum benchmark for acceptable practice in the appointment of Board directors, senior management, and certain auditors and actuaries.

The community expects such executives to have the appropriate skills, experience and knowledge for their roles, and act with honesty and integrity, according to APRA chairman, John Laker.

APRA defined responsible persons as 'those whose conduct is most likely to have a significant impact on its sound and prudent management'.

'Under the standards it is up to the regulated institution to determine who they deem to be key "responsible persons" that manage and oversee their institution', an APRA spokesperson said.

'Ordinarily that would include the directors, CEO, CEO's direct reports, auditors, actuaries, and those responsible for key aspects of risk management.'

APRA said the onus is on regulated institutions to ensure that their boards, senior management and other responsible persons are fit and proper.

'APRA will not be vetting appointments and we see our powers as reserve powers—to be used when an institution is unable or unwilling to take action itself', Laker said.

From 1 October this year, regulated institutions must have their own policies to ensure that responsible persons are fit and proper. This must be assessed ahead of the initial appointment and reassessed annually.

Furthermore, additional criteria must be met for the appointment of certain auditors and actuaries. The standards involve only minimal reporting requirement, according to APRA.

'In terms of fit and proper, the board has to now establish a fit and proper test for responsible persons', said Fred Hawke, and insurance specialist at Clayton Utz.

'No one expects a lot of people to suddenly be disqualified from working in the insurance industry, but they recognise it as an additional level of HR in assessing fitness and propriety.'

'What they're looking for is detail in the guidance notes about how far they have to drill down into assessments and what will be a good policy', he said.

If a bad apple got through, Hawke said, a company would not have necessarily breached the rules. In such cases, APRA will look to ensure an appropriate policy was in place and whether that policy was pursued.

Hawke said there was a good basis for APRA's guidelines, citing cases in the past where people have achieved significant positions in insurance companies.

'In the early 90s a director of a life insurance company nearly bought the company with its own statutory funds and nearly got away with it', he said. 'A few years earlier a fellow got control of a local subsidiary of an overseas company. He was managing director and chairman and walked out the door with the investment portfolio under his arm in a leather satchel one afternoon. That kind of thing just can't happen.'

Laker said APRA's new prudential standards will strengthen protection for depositors and policyholders against the risks of incompetence, mismanagement and fraud and will more generally, 'help to underpin public confidence in regulated institutions'.

Source: C. Donaldson, 2006, 'HR directors come under APRA gun', *Human Resources*, Issue 100, 21 March, p. 1 and p. 8.
www.humanresourcesmagazine.com.au

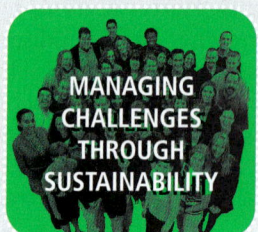

FINELY TUNED SENSIS

At the advertising and searching company Sensis, when feedback indicated that the employees' approach to performance management was insufficiently forward looking, the tailor made on-line system My Progress was used to rectify matters. Employees now rate their own performance prior to performance reviews.

'We think it's a fairly novel approach', says Sean Curtain, group manager for HR. 'It used to be very top down. Every six months the manager would give something of a monologue, telling the employee what they needed to have done over the past six months and whether they had done it. Now it's more of a two way conversation about roles, objectives, targets and contribution.'

Sensis, which employs 3500 people including a sales force of 1500, won an AHRI award last year for excellence in people management.

Formal reviews are held at least twice-yearly, and more often if either the manager or employee requires it. 'That may be in a remedial situation, when a person moves jobs or just as a part of positive career development', says Curtain. 'It's important that people don't operate in a vacuum—that they understand how their work contributes.'

Sensis's performance management is linked to remuneration and career prospects through its emphasis on development. 'It links into retention both informally—you are more likely to keep people if they can see that the business is taking an interest in them and knows the work they have done—and formally because it plans a path for the employee over the next year or two.'

The system helps HR and senior management identify talent. 'It's a tangible sign of how a person is doing—an internal reference check—that should confirm something we already know. In addition to performance management we plot people on a talent matrix and identify high performers.'

'Companies set themselves up for criticism if they manage performance badly', says Curtain. 'If they pay it lipservice, or even have embarrassing situations where reviews are done on employees who actually haven't been present, people will see it as a governance exercise, not something that benefits them.'

Getting managers on board is vital. Sensis ran the usual education program when the system was launched, but Curtain says discussions with individual managers are often needed.

'You have to explain why performance reviewing is helpful. Some managers will do it because it's the right thing to do, some see that it will lighten their workload later on and some see that they will be more successful managers by doing it.' Sometimes it is necessary to spell out the line management involves responsibility and not just a nice title on a business card.

Source: C. Rance, 2006, 'Managers can get tied up on the day-to-day and not look to the long term', Star Treatment, *HR Monthly*, August, p. 21.

MANAGING CHALLENGES THROUGH HR INNOVATION

Use of technology for performance management: Electronic monitoring

An area in which use is made of electronic monitoring of performance is that of monitoring the use of the internet and email. The use of such monitoring is increasing each year in companies worldwide as companies seek to defend themselves against diminished productivity, potential legal liability and information theft.[120] Three Australian organisations, Westpac, Telstra and National Australia Bank, have installed monitoring software, but they use the software only when a specific complaint is lodged by a staff member. On the other hand, Colonial and Australia and New Zealand Banking Corporation have each sacked staff for distributing pornography and they take a more proactive approach by searching for predetermined keywords.[121]

Two other applications of technology involve use of global positioning systems (GPS) and 'Headtrax'. When GPS/internet tracking systems are installed in vehicles it enables the vehicle to be tracked and contacted at anytime. This enables monitoring of the use of the vehicle, the amount of time taken for breaks and whether the vehicle is used for personal use. In addition, technology is also used to collate and analyse data about employees and their performance. Microsoft uses a system known as 'Headtrax' which has the facility to record performance information, as well as a range of other information. The Headtrax tool has a module called 'key people' which identifies people who have been rated as high potentials, that is, as an A or a B, and then provides this information to senior managers.[122] 'Managing challenges through HR innovation: Finely tuned Sensis' (page 387) provides an example of the way Sensis has used technology as part of a performance management process.

MANAGING PEOPLE

BRIDGING THE PERFORMANCE MANAGEMENT GAP

Defence Housing Authority (DHA) is the third largest government business enterprise in Australia, behind Telstra and Australia Post. It was established in 1988 to manage the 7000 houses owned by the Department of Defence. In 2000, it started managing housing allocations and subsequently took over the total business of relocating defence-force staff and their families. This large government business enterprise has tripled in size in the past three years and it now employs 800 staff across its 16 housing management centres and in its Canberra head office. The learning and development (L&D) department of five people is now one year old.

Ericsson is a world leader in mobile and broadband Internet communications. Its Australian and New Zealand business, established in 1951, provides hardware, software and services to many of the Asia–Pacific region's biggest telecommunications carriers. Ericsson's 1480 employees are mostly sales and service personnel, as its manufacturing arm closed in the 1990s. The telecommunications market has been under pressure in the past few years, with all players contracting in size in the face of a broader range of competitors.

Performance management tools

In 1994, Ericsson's headquarters in Sweden initiated a company-wide focus on performance management, which resulted in Ericsson Australia and New Zealand introducing a performance management system called CaPeR (competence and performance equals reward). There had been a number of previous systems used throughout the business until then. Consultants were contracted to streamline them all into the CaPeR system.

Judy Edsall, Ericsson's director of people and organisations, Australia and New Zealand, describes the original CaPeR system as a 'highly sophisticated, paper-based competency tool that was not universally embraced because of its complexity'.

Then last year, Ericsson spent a further $35 000 on technical development to convert CaPeR into a more streamlined, intranet-based tool. This state of the art system allows assessment, feedback and comments to be recorded electronically. It also includes a series of 33 video clips on performance management that range from 30 seconds to 17.5 minutes duration. Subjects covered include customer focus, teamwork, poor performance, dealing with inappropriate behaviour, preparing for a performance review, feedback and hints for managers. Human resource managers regularly audit the content and quality of each performance review, including competence development needs analysis.

Defence Housing Authority, on the other hand, has a paper-based performance management form, which it developed. Debbie Burns, DHA's learning and development manager, describes the document as a work in progress. 'Down the track, we'd like to get to the stage where we can develop it in electronic form, but due to all the other changes happening in the organisation, it's not the highest priority in L&D', she says.

Competency modelling

The key to developing an appropriate L&D strategy is correctly identifying both human and business competencies for every role or team within an organisation. When Judy Edsall was working on assignment at Ericsson headquarters in Sweden in the mid 1990s, she was part of the team that defined the corporation's global competency model. This model excluded technical competence for Ericsson engineers who use a system called PECS (professional engineering competencies system).

The local CaPeR system features a 'competence dictionary' that is based on the global model, but with modifications. It includes 10 human competencies (for example, building relationships, influencing others, communication etc.), 16 business competencies (for example, customer focus, project management and computer literacy) and two compulsory compliance competencies (for example, OHS and managing difference).

As it is a much younger organisation that has recently experienced a major shift in traditional business, DHA's core competencies are now under review. 'We have defined new competencies and are currently testing the competency framework', says Debbie Burns.

Measuring effectiveness

'Performance management is a fundamental part of every manager's job', says Edsall. When the new managing director, Barry Borzillo, was appointed in mid 2002, he wanted to improve the quality of leadership across the organisation, as well as ensure that every employee understood the impact that his/her performance has on the company.

Edsall says, 'you'd like to think that you could measure the effectiveness of CaPeR in the company's bottom line, but that's difficult. The tool is just a record of discussion that occurs—it is the quality of the performance that's important'.

Reviews occur at a minimum of every six months, but quarterly is the preferred time frame within Ericsson. According to Edsall, effectiveness of the whole process is reflected in three ways: employees should exhibit expected behaviour; employees should continue to grow and develop, even if they choose to stay in the same job; and the HR audits of the system should continue to show high-quality reviews with meaningful input from both the manager and employee.

Defence Housing Authority measures the effectiveness of its performance management and L&D through its annual staff survey, initiated in March 2002. Seventy-five per cent of all defence-force relocations occur between November and February, meaning that most training and development can only occur during the other eight months.

'The results of our first staff survey were scathing', explains Burns. 'Employees had just come off the busy posting period and were deeply unhappy about the lack of support they were getting in the form of training and development.'

This resulted in an immediate response from management, which committed the next eight months to improving business systems and processes, opening lines of communication across the business and building an L&D department of five within HR, replacing the previous positions of a part-time training manager and a training coordinator.

The staff survey conducted in March 2003 showed an increase in staff satisfaction levels from 'below 49 per cent in the previous year to 76 per cent this year', says Burns. 'The other measure we use is staff turnover and we have gone from 21 per cent last year to 16 per cent this year, with a target of 12.5 per cent for next year.'

Communication

The critical factors in any performance management process are 'defining clear objectives and providing honest feedback', Edsall affirms. 'The toughest job in an organisation is deciding when the gap between actual and required performance is too large to be bridged by training and development. If the performance management process is working well, that conversation will be no surprise to the employee.'

'A real commitment by the whole organisation to open communication in the last year has been critical in improving staff satisfaction levels', says Burns. The organisation listened to the issues surrounding the training and development of its staff and responded accordingly.

Neither Ericsson nor the Defence Housing Authority has performance management or learning and development programs set in stone. They are reviewed regularly and modified to suit the business environments in which they operate. Although one is high-tech and the other is more traditional in nature, they are both aligned to organisational objectives and fulfilling internal customers' needs.

Source: Based on 2003, 'Building the performance management gap', *Human Resources,* 13 August, pp. 18–19. www.humanresourcesmagazine.com.au

QUESTIONS

1 The case describes some aspects of performance management in two organisations. Discuss some of the competencies managers and employees need to effectively participate in these two systems.

2 Explore the ways a performance management system can influence staff satisfaction.

PART 3   Developing People

CHAPTER SUMMARY

Measuring and managing performance is a challenging enterprise and one of the keys to gaining competitive advantage. Performance management systems serve strategic, administrative and developmental purposes—their importance cannot be overestimated. A performance measurement system should be evaluated against the criteria of strategic congruence, validity, reliability, acceptability and specificity. Measured against these criteria, the comparative, attribute, behavioural, results and quality approaches have different strengths and weaknesses. Thus, deciding which approach and which source of performance information are the best depends on the job in question. Effective managers need to be aware of the issues involved in determining the best method or combination of methods for their particular situations. In addition, once performance has been measured, a major component of a manager's job is to feed that performance information back to employees in a way that results in improved performance rather than defensiveness and decreased motivation. Managers should take action based on the causes for poor performance: ability and/or motivation. Managers must be sure that their performance management system can meet legal scrutiny, especially if it is used to discipline or fire poor performers.

WEB EXERCISES

Go to the Griffith University website at **www.griffith.edu.au/hrm/performance_management/home.html** and review the information about the performance management process for general staff.

Questions
1 Assess the procedures and criteria used at Griffith University to manage the performance of general staff.
2 Suggest any possible weaknesses of the processes.
3 Suggest ways in which the process of performance management of general staff could be improved.

DISCUSSION QUESTIONS

1 What are examples of administrative decisions that might be made in managing the performance of office staff? What are examples of decisions that might be made for developmental purposes?
2 What reasons would you give to argue for the implementation of a performance management system? What reasons would you use against establishing a performance management system?
3 If you were developing a performance measurement system for sales assistants, what types of attributes would you seek to measure? What types of behaviours? What types of results?
4 What sources of performance information would you use to evaluate the performance of general staff in a business school at a university?
5 The performance of students is usually evaluated with an overall results measure for each subject. How is this measure contaminated? How is it deficient? What other measures might you use to more adequately evaluate student performance?
6 Think of the last time that you had a conflict with another person, either at work or at university. Using the guidelines for performance feedback, how would you provide feedback to that person regarding his or her performance in a way that is effective?
7 Explain what fairness has to do with performance management.
8 Why might a manager intentionally distort appraisal results? What would you recommend to minimise this problem?
9 Can computer monitoring of performance ever be acceptable to employees? Explain.
10 You have a friend who owns a cleaning company that services offices and homes. In this company, teams of three staff from a variety of countries such as Australia, Hong Kong, Singapore, Korea and Thailand are engaged to clean each site. The company employs almost 100 people. A supervisor is responsible for managing six teams working in a particular area. Your friend knows you are studying HRM and has asked you about the performance tools that could be used to manage the performance of the employees, the techniques for giving feedback and the uses made of the performance appraisal information. Your friend wants to know about these issues because she is

planning to grow the company and there will be career opportunities developing and she is aware that there is some tension between people in some of the teams. You have decided to discuss your friend's request with a number of your colleagues in the subject you are studying.

11 'Performance appraisals as we know them will disappear in the next five years in Australia.' Discuss. In your answer you could consider contextual factors that could influence performance appraisals such as the industrial structure, the size of organisations, the location of the work, the personal characteristics of people doing the work, the nature of the work and the structure of the work.

CASE STUDY

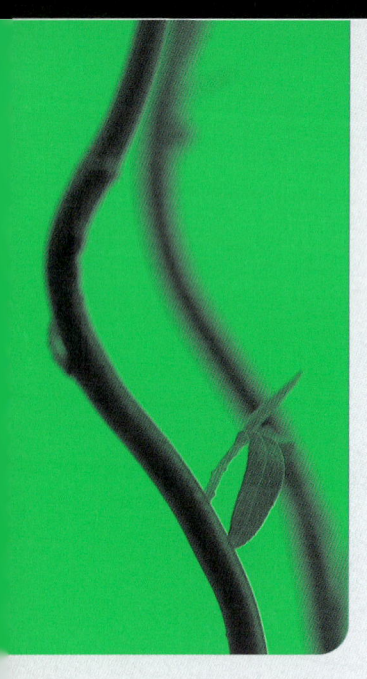

HR FALLS SHORT IN HIGH PERFORMANCE CULTURES

A lack of individual support from HR departments along with underspending on the formal development of employees are the biggest problems when it comes to developing individual careers for professionals in Australian organisations.

As a result, organisations that fail to develop and maintain a high performance culture are at risk of having higher staff turnover, as employees seek more progressive and dynamic companies to learn and grow.

These are the findings from a recent Australian Institute of Management (AIM) survey of nearly 2000 professionals, which revealed a startling disparity between the attitudes of staff who operate in a high performance culture, and those who do not.

Professionals who work in high performance cultures are more positive about their workplace and are more likely to remain loyal to their employers, according to AIM chief executive officer (CEO) Jennifer Alexander.

'On the flipside, those professionals who believe they do not operate in a high performance organisation are unhappy with where they work and are already thinking about moving on from their position', she said.

While survey respondents were split on whether they believed their organisation encouraged a high performance culture, 40 per cent would not hesitate in accepting an offer of employment from a competing firm due to lack of progress or opportunity to develop with their current employer.

'This result is a sharper reminder to CEOs and managers that commercially savvy organisations which encourage innovation are more likely to retain the best and brightest employees', said Alexander.

While 73 per cent received ongoing education and training from their workplace to develop their skills, the survey found that 60 per cent of professionals believe their organisation is not doing enough to develop individual careers or potential.

However, 66 per cent thought their managers did a good job of encouraging individuals to be innovative in seeking new ways to improve their performance.

'Overall achieving characteristics that define a high performance culture is something even a small company can achieve, but managers must be prepared to invest time and effort before they can be rewarded with committed, high performing staff', said Alexander.

The survey found that there were a number of characteristics in common with high performing cultures, including: an environment that encourages open discussion; a positive 'can do' attitude towards getting the task done; rewarding employees for good work; a solid definable goal that can be achieved; and staff that work well independently.

Additionally, 47 per cent of professionals work in organisations with processes in place to build stronger staff loyalty and commitment, while the remainder are currently working on addressing these issues.

Seventy per cent of survey respondents were employed as professionals, while 10 per cent were in practice support roles and 20 per cent did not define their role.

Source: Based on, 2004, 'HR falls short in high performance cultures', *Human Resources*, 25 August, p. 4. www.humanresourcesmagazine.com.au

QUESTIONS

1 Discuss the actions that organisations could take to encourage a 'high performance' culture.
2 Discuss the difficulties that could occur in attempting to create such a culture.

CHAPTER 11

LEARNING AND DEVELOPMENT

Andrew Smith

Objectives

After reading this chapter, you should be able to:

1 Discuss how training can help companies gain a competitive advantage.
2 Discuss the development of learning and development in Australia.
3 Recognise the different elements of the Australian national training system.
4 Conduct a needs assessment.
5 Evaluate employees' readiness for training.
6 Discuss the strengths and weaknesses of presentation, and hands-on and group training methods.
7 Explain the potential advantages of new technologies for training.
8 Design a training session to maximise learning.
9 Choose an appropriate evaluation design based on training objectives and analysis of constraints.

Sing Tel Optus links learning and development to business goals

Sing Tel Optus is Australia's second largest telecommunications carrier. It has developed a significant learning and development policy that provides a blend of training and career development for all its 11 000 employees. The company believes that its learning and development program not only helps to skill their employees but also make them an attractive employer in a tight labour market.

The learning and development policy of the company is described on the company's website:

> At Optus we believe that the learning and development programs and benefits we provide are important in differentiating ourselves in the market place.
>
> We are committed to providing continued career development in order to realise and maximise the full potential of every employee.
>
> All new employees who join Optus are invited to 'Begin the Journey' via an intranet based induction program which develops and reinforces the importance of shared and continual learning…

A major and increasingly important part of the learning and development function at Sing Tel Optus is the Registered Training Organisation (RTO). The RTO, known as Optus College, was first formed in 1999 and is located in the corporate Learning and Develop-ment function and has a remit to provide qualifications based training across the entire organisation. The motivation for the company to establish the RTO was to provide basic training for the ever increasing numbers of staff that were being hired to staff the call centre businesses in the various divisions.

Of the qualifications offered by Optus, the Certificate III in Telecommunications is the largest single program. It is offered to all new Customer Service Representatives (CSRs) when they join one of the company's call centres. Although the program is not mandatory, nearly all new employees undertake and complete the qualification which takes 12 months. The company feels that nationally recognised training is not only important from the point of view of increasing the skills of their call centre staff but also offers a significant level of reward and also employability to the employees who complete the qualification. As the RTO Manager says:

> A lot of people really do value it (the qualification). We actually have a graduation ceremony three times a year and quite often we get a rep to speak about what the qualification has meant to them. Quite often we have had mature age students get up and say 'this is the first qualification I've ever had and I can go home and say I'm really proud of this qualification'.

The training is based on a 4 week off-the-job induction program, although this varies from 2 to 6 weeks depending on the call centre. This training is mandatory for all new employees and is run by training staff from the learning and development function. In this induction new staff learn the basics of how to deal with different types of customers and queries on the phone. The training includes role plays as well as product knowledge and is guided towards the competencies in the qualification. On successful completion of the induction, the trainees are moved to an off-line call centre team, known as a Development Team.

At this stage, the training shifts into an on-the-job mode. The call centre teams are managed through a rigorous performance management system. The performance management system sets tight standards for the time that CSRs spend on an individual query and the way in which the query was handled. Every month, Team Leaders hold 'one on ones' with each of the dozen members of their team. The CSRs are rated on a four step scale from poor performance to highly commendable and the Team Leader discusses the performance feedback from quality assurance with each CSR. From these performance management meetings, the Team Leaders decide whether the CSR needs additional training. This training is delivered in the form of on-the-job coaching. The embedded nature of the training in the performance management system creates an atmosphere of continual training. As one CSR put it:

> There's more ongoing training. Every week they have new things up that we are learning … I think that is a really important thing, the fact that they are always giving us

PART 3 Developing People

Sing Tel Optus links learning and development to business goals *continued*

refreshers, like we get training folders every week. Two sometimes three folders a week.

Although the training for CSRs is the largest single program run by Optus, the company has extended the use of nationally recognised training to other groups. All members of the Learning and Development function (some 80 staff) have completed the Certificate IV in Assessment and Workplace Training. The other major area for nationally accredited training was for Team Leaders who undertake the Certificate IV in Business (Frontline Management). As with the Certificate III in Telecommunications, the Frontline Management qualification is delivered primarily on-the-job with a number of activities that are designed to increase the supervisory experience of a CSR.

The provision of nationally recognised training has enabled Sing Tel Optus to develop a reputation as an employer of choice in a tightening labour market and it also helped to develop visible career pathways for employees in the organisation. Thus, since its inception at the company, nationally recognised training has become increasingly central to the human resource strategy of the company. As the General Manager for Learning and Development explains it:

> In the broader sense, the learning and development function within the business is an enabler of continuous performance improvement. So that is around the development of fundamental skills that are required for the individual to be able to do their job.

Sing Tel Optus is developing the strategic importance of nationally recognised training in the company still further by utilising the competencies in Training Packages to underpin the performance management system. The company developed a Success Profile based on the Training Package competency standards. This process is being underwritten by the development of Success Profiles for groups of jobs in the organisation. As the Organisation Development manager describes it:

> The success profile is a competency model that covers behaviours required for high performance, skills and knowledge, job challenges and experiences and some personal attributes.

In this way, the competencies contained in the Training Package can be used not only to build the basis of the Success Profile for a job but also ensure that the appropriate qualification is tailored to fulfilling the requirements of individuals to gain the skills necessary to move into the job or simply perform at a higher standard.

Source: E. Smith, R. Pickersgill, A. Smith & P. Rushbrook, 2005, *Enterprises' commitment to nationally recognised training for existing workers*, National Centre for Vocational Education Research, Adelaide.

Introduction to learning and development

Learning and development (also employee development) the acquisition of knowledge, skills and behaviours that improve an employee's ability to meet changes in job requirements and in client and customer demands.

Training focuses on the development of the skills of the workforce and, although it may be job oriented, training is related primarily to meeting the skills needs of the organisation.

The term 'learning and development' has emerged in recent years in Australia to describe the activities associated with the development of people in organisations. It is very closely related to training, HRD and to VET but has its own emphasis. In essence, learning and development borrows something from all three of the other fields.

Training

Training has a rather narrow connotation. It is focused on the development of the skills of the workforce and, although it may be job oriented, training is related primarily to meeting the skills needs of the organisation.

Human resource development

Human resource development (HRD), especially in the sense developed by the ASTD (American Society for Training and Development) in the USA, is a far broader concept embracing all aspects of development that may happen in the organisation – individual, career and organisational. It forms a major part of the entire human resource management systems of organisations.

Vocational education and training

Vocational education and training (VET) is a more externally focused concept than training. Like training, it is concerned with meeting the skills needs of the organisation but VET is essentially focused on meeting the skills needs of individuals so that they can find employment in the labour market. This involves gaining nationally recognised qualifications that may or may not meet an organisation's needs.

In Australia, the concept of learning and development has developed from all these fields. As shown in Figure 11.1 learning and development is concerned with aspects of training, HRD (human resource development) and VET (vocational and educational training).[1] Thus, the learning and development practitioner will be focused on meeting the skills needs of the organisation through training and development, will be involved in the wider aspects of HRD such as performance management and organisational development, and will also be involved with the organisation's interactions with the national VET system.

Evidence of the emergence of the learning and development field has come from the USA. In the late 1990s, the American Society for Training and Development sponsored a study of the development of the field of HRD since their *Models for HRD Practice*[2] in the late 1980s which had led to the concept of the HR Wheel. The origins of the study lay in the growing realisation in the ASTD that training and HRD practitioners were moving away from traditional models of training based on formal, classroom-based activities to more workplace centred concepts of learning. At the same time, it was clear that enterprises were increasingly concerned with the performance of their employees rather than the general notion of development. The ASTD described these moves in the following terms:

> ... traditional human resource development practitioners are moving their focus away from formal training events and toward various types of learning experience that can solve performance problems and increase business results. The term workplace learning reflects the broader array of

FIGURE 11.1 Learning and development

Sidebar:

Human resource development (HRD)
especially in the sense developed by the ASTD in the USA, refers to a wide range of organisational strategies, policies, plans, practices and organised activities that aim to improve personal growth and/or performance, in order to improve the job, the individual, and/or the organisation. It forms a major part of the entire human resource management systems of organisations.

Vocational education and training
VET is a more externally focused concept than training. Like training, it is concerned with meeting the skills needs of the organisation but VET is essentially focused on meeting the skills needs of individuals so that they can find employment in the labour market. This involves gaining nationally recognised qualifications that may or may not meet the needs of the employing organisation.

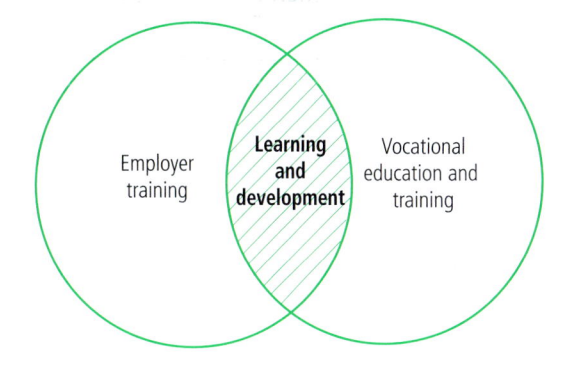

learning solutions that practitioners are now using. Today's HRD practitioners are also shifting their energies toward analyzing the root causes for gaps in productivity and finding the best solution that will close these gaps whilst increasing corporate profitability. This new focus is called improving performance … Workplace learning and performance (WLP) is the integrated use of learning and other interventions for the purpose of improving individual and organizational performance.[3]

The ASTD concept of workplace learning and performance is very close to the emerging Australian concept of learning and development. Adapting the workplace learning and performance notion in this way.

Table 11.1 contrasts and emphasises the differences between training and development, HRD and learning and development. Learning and development builds on the notion of integration between different development activities in the organisation but goes further by linking it to the specific performance issues whether individual or organisational.

TABLE 11.1 Comparison of training, HRD and learning and development

Issue	Training	Human resource development	Learning and development
Definition	Through planned learning interventions, training focuses on identifying and developing competencies that enable employees to perform their current jobs.	HRD is the integrated use of training, organisational development and career development to improve individual, group and organisational effectiveness.	Learning and development is the integrated use of learning and other interventions for the purpose of improving individual and organisational performance.
Assumptions about human nature	To be productive people want and need to be instructed about their jobs.	People should be considered to be self-actualising. Learning is the key to self-actualisation.	People want to learn and develop. People seek to achieve their potential. Learning and performance go hand in hand by helping organisations and employees reach their goals.
Goal	The major goal is improved knowledge, skills and attitudes about the job.	The major goal is the integration of training, organisational development and career development for the purpose of achieving improved performance through planned learning.	The major goals are: • Improving human performance • Balancing individual and organisational needs • Building knowledge capital within the organisation • Improving financial return.
Nature of learning in organisations	Learning should be focused on the job performed by the individual. The results of training should be immediate and their relationship to the job should be readily apparent.	Increased skill and knowledge about a particular set of tasks will lead to greater organisational effectiveness. Pairing an individually focused intervention with other interventions best facilitates learning.	1 Learning interventions may or may not be appropriate for solving specific performance problems. 2 Continuous learning is an important organisational strategy because it builds the intellectual capital that is crucial to individual and organisational performance.

Source: Based on W.J. Rothwell, E.S. Sanders & J.G. Soper, 1999, *ASTD Models for Workplace Learning and Performance: Roles, Competencies and Outputs*, ASTD, Alexandria, VA, p. 9.

Training in Australian organisations

Although learning and development goes well beyond traditional notions of training, training is still a key element in the learning and development portfolio. It represents the specific strategy of managers to improve the skills base of their organisations.

In comparison to many countries, Australia keeps good statistical information on the extent and nature of training carried out by Australian employers. Since 1989 the Australian Bureau of Statistics (ABS) has conducted five surveys of employer training expenditure. The original survey conducted as a pilot in 1989 indicated that only 22 per cent of Australian employers carried out any form of training for their employees and that an average of 2.2 per cent of payroll costs was invested in training activities with employees receiving, on average, 22 hours of training per annum.[4]

This data, together with the results from some international comparisons of incentive schemes to promote higher levels of enterprise investment in training, provided a significant part of the case for the then federal Labor government enacting the Training Guarantee Scheme in 1990. This scheme operated from 1990 to 1996 (although it was technically suspended in 1994) and required Australian enterprises with payroll costs of over A$200 000 to spend at least 1.5 per cent of their payroll on the provision of 'structured' training for their employees or pay an equivalent levy to the Australian Taxation Office. Assessments of the effectiveness of the Training Guarantee in raising the level of training expenditure in Australia vary but it is generally accepted that the scheme failed to lift training provision for the majority of employees in any significant or lasting fashion.[5] Subsequent iterations of the Employer Training Expenditure (TES) survey have tended to confirm the original rather gloomy assessment of the state of enterprise training in Australia. Table 11.2 summarises the data from the first four TES surveys and shows that although training expenditure appeared to increase to 1993, it had retreated by 1996.

Employer size correlates closely with the incidence of training in enterprises. In 1996, 88.3 per cent of large enterprises (100 or more employees) provided structured training compared to only 13.4 per cent of small enterprises (less than 20 employees). The 2002 data indicates an increase in the incidence of training in all size categories with 98 per cent of large organisations, 70 per cent of medium sized and 39 per cent of small organisations reporting the provision of structured training.[6] Spending on training also varies considerably by sector and industry. In 1996, public sector organisations

TABLE 11.2 Employer training expenditure (July–September 1989–96)

	1989	1990	1993	1996
% Employers reporting training expenditure	22	24	25	18
% Payroll spent				
Private sector	1.7	2.2	2.6	2.3
Public sector	3.3	3.2	3.4	3.2
Total	**2.2**	**2.6**	**2.9**	**2.5**
Average expenditure per employee (A$)	133	163	191	186
Average training hours per employee	5.5	5.9	5.6	4.9

Source: Australian Bureau of Statistics (unpublished data)

spent 3.2 per cent of payroll on training compared with their private sector counterparts who spent 2.3 per cent. However, the increase from 1989 to 1996 was almost entirely accounted for by the private sector, which improved its performance by over 30 per cent, whilst public sector on training spending as a percentage of payroll remained fairly static. Variation across industry sectors is also apparent, with air transport, mining and communications spending well over the average whilst manufacturing, retail and recreation and personal services spent considerably less than the average.

The ABS conducts two other surveys which present data on industry training—the Employer Training Practices Survey and the Survey of Education and Training Experience. The Survey of Education and Training Experience (SET) (and its forerunners) is a household survey sampling some 20 000 dwellings and collecting data on all individuals aged from 15 to 64 years for the previous year. The results from the 1997 SET show that in 1997, 80.2 per cent of workers received some form of training. On-the-job training was the most common form of training with 71.6 per cent of workers receiving this type of training.[7] The incidence of in-house training in organisations was far less with only 33 per cent of workers receiving this form of training. About 16 per cent of workers were studying for an educational qualification. However, like the figures on training expenditure, there is considerable variation between industries on the type of training received by employees. Employees in the utilities, communications or service industries were more likely to receive training than those in transport, manufacturing or agriculture. The results of the three surveys for employee training to 1997 are summarised in Table 11.3.

The data from SET display some interesting contrasts with the TES data. The most obvious difference is that the experience of training for individual workers is far higher than the TES data might lead one to expect. Over the 1990s, 80 per cent or more of workers undertook some training. Although the most common experience is of on-the-job training, over 30 per cent of workers have received in-house training— very similar to the 'structured' training definition used in the TES. Also, the pattern of provision has changed during the period 1989–97 in different ways to the pattern of training expenditure from the TES. Whereas the overall incidence of training and of on-the-job training rose in the early 1990s and fell away later in the decade, in-house or structured training increased since 1993 and participation in external training courses almost doubled during the period.

Data from the 2001 SET shows that the incidence of employer sponsored training appears to be increasing.[8] The proportion of Australian workers undertaking work related training grew from 30 per cent of the workforce in 1993 to 45 per cent in 2001. Thirty-seven per cent of workers completed at least one work related training course

TABLE 11.3 Individuals' experience of training, 1989–97

Activity	1989 %	1993 %	1997 %
Some training undertaken	79.0	85.8	80.2
Studied in previous calendar year	16.8	18.6	15.8
In-house training course	34.9	31.3	33.0
External training course	9.8	11.8	20.0
On-the-job training	71.8	81.8	71.6

Source: Australian Bureau of Statistics.

in 2001 and the proportion of workers completing on-the-job training grew from 65 per cent in 1996 to 69 per cent in 2000. Despite the apparent decline in employer training expenditure since the mid 1990s, the majority of Australian workers claim they are receiving some form of training from their employers and many are undertaking formal, off-the-job training in their firms.

More evidence of the widespread provision of industry training can be gained from the Employer Training Practices Survey (TPS). The TPS is a qualitative survey that gathers information on the type and extent of training provided by enterprises to their employees. Data is collected for a full year rather than for three months as is the case for the TES. Two Training Practices surveys have been carried out covering the years 1993 and 1996. In 2002, the Training Practices Survey was carried out in combination with the Training Expenditure Survey in a new survey—the Training Expenditure and Practices Survey.[9] However, the data from the 2002 survey is not fully comparable with the previous years.

The results from the 1997 TPS show that 61 per cent of all employers provided training to their employees during 1996. This increased to 81 per cent in the 2002 survey. Thirty-five per cent provided structured training whilst 53 per cent provided unstructured training in 1996, increasing to 41 per cent and 79 per cent respectively in 2002. As with training expenditure, the incidence of enterprise training in the TPS varies considerably with size. In 1996, 99 per cent of large enterprises provided training whilst 57 per cent of small employers provided training for their employees. The provision of structured training follows the same pattern with 93 per cent of large enterprises providing structured training and 30 per cent of small enterprises. By 2002, this had increased to 98 per cent of large enterprises and 39 per cent of small enterprises. The TPS data also shows that the low incidence of training provision amongst small enterprises is concentrated in the micro-business end of the spectrum— those enterprises employing fewer than five people, including those businesses that have no employees and represent about half of all small businesses. The figures for small business from the 1996 survey are summarised in Table 11.4.

Despite the similarity in the pattern of training provision, however, there is a remarkable difference in the incidence of training provided by the TES and the TPS. In almost every case, the incidence of structured training detected by the TPS appears to be about double that detected by the TES. Thirty-five per cent of enterprises report providing structured training to their employees in the TPS compared to only 17.7 per cent of enterprises in the TES. Thirty per cent of all small enterprises provided structured training in the TPS compared to 13.4 per cent in the TES. For larger enterprises, the figures are more comparable. Nevertheless, 99 per cent of enterprises provided structured training in the TPS compared with 88.3 per cent in the TES.

How do Australian enterprises fare in comparison to other developed countries? In recent years, data showing an apparent decline in training expenditure and in the hours

TABLE 11.4 Percentage of small business enterprises providing training, 1996

Type of training	1–4 employees %	5–9 employees %	10–19 employees %	All small business %
Structured training	20	43	60	30
Unstructured training	38	65	78	49
All training	45	74	86	57

Source: Australian Bureau of Statistics (unpublished data)

of training provided to employees of Australian enterprises in the wake of the abolition of the Training Guarantee Scheme has led to charges that employers are reducing their commitment to training and that policies need to devised to compel them to increase their investments in training.[10] Similar calls have also been heard in the UK where employers have been blamed for that country's apparent poor record on training.[11]

However, it is by no means clear that Australian employers spend so much less than many counterparts in other developed nations as is often implied. Figures from the European Union's Continuing Vocational Training Survey (CVTS II) show that Australia lies towards the top end of the normal range of employer training expenditure of about 0.5 to 1.7 per cent of payroll costs. Table 11.5 displays data from the most recent Training Expenditure and Practices Survey with data from CVTS II. Whilst not strictly comparable, the data are very consistent in that they measure the direct, net training costs borne by employers.

Although these figures are only broadly comparable, it is nevertheless clear that assumptions that Australia lags well behind other developed nations in employer training expenditure are at least highly questionable and probably inaccurate. The data suggests that Australia lies towards the upper end of the normal range of employer expenditure on training of existing workers of between 0.5 and 1.7 per cent of payroll costs. It is interesting to note from this data that countries such as Germany that have been held up in the past as models for the Australian training system, fare less well when comparisons are based on the continuous training provided by employers than on the training provided for young people through the apprenticeship system. Also, the comparison with France with its well-known training levy system is most noteworthy.

In summary, it appears that a significant amount of training is being provided by Australian employers. Some 80 per cent of Australian workers report receiving some form of training from their employers. Over 80 per cent of Australian employers claim to be providing some form of training for their employees. Between one third and one half of Australian workers are taking part in formal, structured training in the workplace with 70 per cent of workers taking part in on-the-job training. Over 40 per cent of Australian employers claim to provide structured training.

The National Vocational Training System

The vocational education and training (VET) system is one of the three major sectors of education in Australia, together with school education and higher (university) education. The VET system is a largely publicly funded education system that is intended to develop the vocational skills of the Australian workforce. The VET

TABLE 11.5 Percentage of wages and salaries spent by employers on employee training: Australia (2002) and selected EU countries (1999)

Country	% payroll	Country	% payroll
Australia (2002)*	1.3	France	1.3
Denmark	1.7	Finland	1.3
Netherlands	1.7	Germany	0.9
Norway	1.6	Austria	0.8
Ireland	1.5	Spain	0.5

Source: All figures derived from the Eurostat CVTSII database except those marked with an asterisk*; ABS, 2003

system sprang out of the apprenticeship system that was imported into Australia during the colonial period from Britain and the movement in the late nineteenth century towards education for working men and women embodied in the Mechanics' Institutes. Since the early twentieth century the VET system has grown into the second largest of the three education sectors—there are twice as many students in the VET system as in universities. In 2005 there were over 1.6 million students studying towards a VET qualification in Australia representing a 70 per cent increase since 1992 when the total number of students in VET stood at 1 million.[12]

The VET system is organised around a series of vocational qualifications known as the Australian Qualifications Framework. The qualifications range from a Certificate 1 to a Diploma. Most occupations in the economy now have a VET qualification attached to them—often a series of qualifications ranging from the Certificate I at the lower end of the skills spectrum to the Diploma at the highest level. These qualifications are contained in 80 or more Training Packages which define the qualifications for occupations and industries and the competency standards on which they are based. Training Packages comprise sets of qualifications, competency standards and assessment guidelines for qualifications relating to particular industries and occupations. They describe the qualifications that are appropriate to the industry or occupation and set out the competencies that have to be passed in order to gain the qualifications. In all, there are some 80 Training Packages that have been developed through tri-partite industry and occupational bodies, usually the Industry Training Advisory Bodies. Although subject to much criticism in their early days for their apparently rather narrow approach to vocational education,[13] Training Packages have become successfully embedded as the basis for most accredited training in the country. Since the early 1990s, the VET system has been founded on competency-based training (CBT). In the CBT system of teaching and learning, students have to meet the competency standards that have been defined for the occupation and are usually assessed in a workplace setting, emphasising the strong industrial and vocational orientation of VET.

Much of the training in the VET system is carried out through the state-based Technical and Further Education (TAFE) institutes. TAFE institutes are large, publicly funded vocational training colleges. Most students attend TAFE on a part-time basis as they are usually employed whilst they are studying for a vocational qualification. Since the early 1990s, other private training providers have entered the VET market so that TAFE now accounts for approximately 80 per cent of all students in the VET system.[14]

A major component of the new VET system is the apprenticeship and traineeship system. Apprenticeship is a very old concept in VET, dating back to the Middle Ages in Europe when young men were apprenticed to a master craftsman to learn their trade. These apprenticeships often involved many years working as a low paid assistant to the craftsman after which the apprentice became a skilled artisan and was able to set up independently. The modern apprenticeship and traineeship system is based on the original concept of combining work and learning. Apprenticeships are normally four years in duration and apply to a defined set of traditional skilled trades such as plumbing, fitting or hairdressing. They involve a combination of off-the-job training, usually at a TAFE institute, and work for the employer. Traineeships were introduced in the mid-1980s as a shorter form of apprenticeship attached to the non-traditional occupations. Traineeships are usually one or two years in duration but share a common off and on-the-job training method. Traineeships were slow to develop in the early years of their introduction but since the mid-1990s, the number of trainees has grown dramatically under the stimulus of government subsidies for training. In 2006 there were over 400 000 apprentices and trainees in Australia in training, more

MINERALS INDUSTRY NEEDS 70 000 NEW WORKERS IN NEXT DECADE

MANAGING CHALLENGES OF GLOBALISATION

Australia's booming minerals sector will need 70 000 more workers by 2015 with the largest shortages projected to be tradespeople (26 983) and the semi-skilled (22 059), a new Minerals Council of Australia report has warned. Of the 70 000 workers needed, 42 000 will be required in WA, 15 000 in Qld and 5000 in both New South Wales and South Australia. Fastest growth is expected to be between now and 2010 with the 'most dramatic' need for workers in copper, nickel and bauxite. 'There is the potential for a rapid onset of significant labour shortages', the report says. But it's not just unskilled and semi-skilled workers who are in demand. Over the next 10 years, 7659 extra professionals will be needed, posing a challenge to all stakeholders associated with the professions in the minerals sector. This is particularly so in regard to the attraction and retention of students in the mining engineering and science programs at tertiary level, the report says. We are not just looking at a skills shortage but in fact a people shortage', Western Australia Chamber of Minerals and Energy president Dr David Smith said following the release of the report 'Industry must continue to be enterprising to attract, train and retain workers.' One industry initiative included setting up a technical college in the Pilbara in partnership with the Federal and Western Australia governments, Smith said. Given that the projected gaps are largest in occupations that require low skill levels, the labour shortage problem is not one that training policy could easily address, the report says. 'It's more a matter of attracting people to the industry.' Women are identified as an 'alternative labour pool' that can be tapped. 'Crucial' challenges here were likely to include providing child care in remote locations, designing family-friendly policies and changing the 'blokey' culture associated with mining.

Source: 2006, *HR Report*, Issue 380, 18 October.

than three times the number in 1995.[15] Australia now has the largest per capita number of apprentices and trainees than any country in the world.

The training of workers in vocational, work-related skills is a major element of the development of human resources in most enterprises in the Australian economy. Most organisations, and nearly all medium or large organisations, employ people with a VET qualification and are often involved in their training.

Designing effective training systems

One of the key characteristics of training systems that contributes to competitiveness is that training systems are designed according to the instructional design process.[16] *Instructional design process* refers to a systematic approach for developing training programs. Table 11.6 opposite presents the six steps of this process, which emphasises that effective training practices involve more than choosing the most popular and colourful training method.

Step one is to conduct a 'needs assessment', which is necessary to determine if training is needed. Step two involves ensuring that employees have the motivation and basic skills to master the training content. Step three involves ensuring that the training session (or the learning environment) has the factors necessary for learning to occur. Step four involves ensuring that trainees apply the content of training to their jobs. This also involves support from managers and peers for the use of training content on the job as well as helping the employees to gain an understanding of how to take personal responsibility for skill improvement. Step five involves choosing a training method. As we shall see in this chapter, a variety of training methods is available, ranging from traditional on-the-job training (OJT) to use of new technologies such as the internet. The key is to choose a training

Learning and Development **CHAPTER 11**

TABLE 11.6 Components of instructional design

1 Conducting needs assessment
- Organisational analysis
- Person analysis
- Task analysis

2 Ensuring employees' readiness for training
- Attitudes and motivation
- Basic skills

3 Creating a learning environment
- Identification of learning objectives and training outcomes
- Meaningful material
- Practice
- Feedback
- Observation of others
- Administering and coordinating program

4 Ensuring transfer of training
- Climate for transfer
- Manager and peer support
- Opportunity to use learned capabilities
- Technological support
- Self-management skills

5 Selecting training methods
- Presentational methods
- Hands-on methods
- Group-building methods

6 Evaluating training programs
- Identification of training outcomes
- Evaluation designs
- Determining return on investment

method that will provide the appropriate learning environment in order to achieve the training objectives. Step six involves evaluation—that is, determining whether training achieved the desired learning outcomes and/or financial objectives.

Conducting a needs assessment

The first step in the instructional design process—**needs assessment**—refers to the process used to determine if training is necessary. Figure 11.2 overleaf shows the causes and outcomes resulting from a needs assessment. As we see, there are many different reasons or 'pressure points' which suggest that training is necessary. These pressure points include: performance problems, new technology, internal or external customer requests for training, job redesign, new legislation, changes in customer preferences, new products or employees' lack of basic skills. Note that these pressure points do not guarantee that training is the correct solution. Consider, for example, a delivery truck driver whose job is to deliver anaesthetic gases to medical facilities. The driver mistakenly hooked-up the supply line of a mild anaesthetic to a hospital's oxygen system, contaminating the hospital's oxygen supply. Why did the

Needs assessment
the process used to determine if training is necessary.

405

driver make this mistake, which is clearly a performance problem? The driver may have made this mistake because of a lack of knowledge about the appropriate line hook-up for the anaesthetic, anger over a requested salary increase that his manager recently denied or the valves for connecting the gas supply were mislabelled. Only the lack of knowledge can be addressed by training. The other pressure points require dealing with issues related to the consequence of good performance (pay system) or the design of the work environment.

Needs assessment typically involves organisational analysis, person analysis and task analysis.[17] *Organisational analysis* involves considering the context in which training will occur. That is, organisational analysis involves determining the appropriateness of training—given the company's business strategy, its resources available for training and support by managers and peers for training activities.

Person analysis helps to identify who needs training. Person analysis involves:

- determining whether performance deficiencies result from a lack of knowledge, skills or abilities (a training issue), or from a motivational or work-design problem
- identifying who needs training
- determining employees' readiness for training.

Task analysis includes identifying the important tasks and knowledge, skills and behaviours that need to be emphasised in training for employees to complete their tasks.

In practice, organisational analysis, person analysis and task analysis are usually not conducted in any specific order. However, because organisational analysis is concerned with identifying whether training fits with the company's strategic objectives and whether the company wants to devote time and money to training, it is usually conducted first. Person analysis and task analysis are often conducted at the same time because it is often difficult to determine whether performance deficiencies are a training problem without understanding the tasks and the work environment.

What outcomes result from a needs assessment? As shown in Figure 11.2, the needs assessment process results in information related to who needs training and what trainees need to learn, including the tasks in which they need to be trained, plus knowledge, skills, behaviours or other job requirements. A needs assessment helps to determine whether the company will purchase training from a vendor or consultant, or else develop training using internal resources.

FIGURE 11.2 The needs assessment process

What is the context?

Reasons or 'pressure points'
- Legislation
- Lack of basic skills
- Poor performance
- New technology
- Customer requests
- New products
- Higher performance standards
- New jobs

Organisational analysis

Task analysis

Person analysis

In what do they need training?

Outcomes
- What trainees need to learn
- Who receives training
- Type of training
- Frequency of training
- Buy-versus-build training decision
- Training versus other HR options such as selection or job redesign

Who needs training?

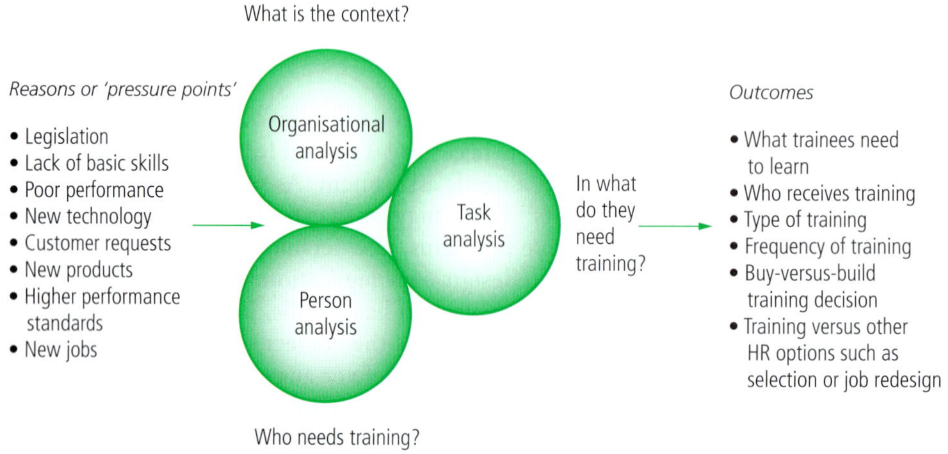

Organisational analysis

Managers need to consider three factors before choosing training as the solution to any pressure point: support of managers and peers for training activities, the company's strategic direction and the training resources available.

1 *Support of managers and peers.* Various studies have found that peer and manager support for training is critical. The key factors to success are:
   - a positive attitude among peers and managers about participation in training activities
   - managers' and peers' willingness to provide information to trainees about how they can more effectively use knowledge, skills or behaviours learned in training on the job
   - the availability of opportunities for the trainees to use training content in their job.[18]

   If peers' and managers' attitudes and behaviours are not supportive, employees are not likely to apply training content to their jobs.

2 *Company strategy.* In Chapter 2 Strategic human resource management, we discussed the importance of business strategy for a company to gain a competitive advantage. The plan or goal that the company chooses to achieve strategic objectives has a major impact on whether resources (money, trainers' time and program development) should be devoted to addressing a training pressure point.

   There are four major business strategies—concentration, internal growth, external growth and disinvestment.[19] Each strategy differs based on the goal of the business. A concentration strategy focuses on increasing market share, reducing costs or creating and maintaining a market niche for products and services. An internal growth strategy focuses on new market and product development, innovation and joint ventures. For example, the merger between BHP and Billiton created one company with strengths across international markets. An external growth strategy emphasises acquiring vendors and suppliers or buying businesses that allow the company to expand into new markets. A disinvestment strategy emphasises liquidation and divestiture of businesses.

   It is important to identify the prevailing business strategy to ensure that: (1) the company is allocating enough of its budget to training activities; (2) employees are receiving training on relevant topics; and (3) employees are receiving the right amount of training.[20]

   A good example of how a training function can contribute to a business strategy is evident in the launch of Australia's first corporate university in April 1999: the Coles Institute, developed by Coles supermarkets and Deakin University. The Coles Institute provides employees of Coles supermarkets with education and training ranging from training programs for electronic scanning to PhDs in marketing. According to Coles' managing director, Alan Williams:

   > Coles' move towards a more permanent workforce, combined with greater emphasis on training and higher education, will ensure highly skilled and motivated employees. The Coles Institute will give employees more career opportunities and enable them to be better at their jobs. Customers will get better service and the business as a whole will benefit.[21]

   Other large organisations such as Unisys, Ford Australia and Telstra have developed in-house 'corporate universities', with courses ranging from job-specific technical courses to general skills like communication and leadership. Dr Dallas Isaacs, manager of Telstra's education services, says: 'The only sustained competitive advantage is the ability to learn smarter. It allows you to learn from your successes and failures and move quickly on opportunities'.[22]

3. *Training resources.* It is necessary to identify whether the company has the budget, time and expertise for training. In terms of financial support, according to an Australian Bureau of Statistics (ABS) survey, the most common form of support provided by employers during 2001–02 was payment of employees' wages and salaries while they attended training (89 per cent of all employers that provided structured training to employees). More than three-quarters of employers (77 per cent) paid their employees' structured training fees, and half paid for employees' training materials. Large employers were more likely to provide each form of support than were smaller employers.[23] Of course, financial resources are not the only important resources to consider.

For example, if the company is installing computer-based manufacturing equipment in one of its plants, it has three possible strategies for dealing with the need to have computer literate employees. First, the company can decide that given its staff expertise and budget, it can use internal consultants to train all affected employees. Second, the company may decide that it is more cost effective to identify employees who are computer literate by using tests and work samples. Employees who fail the test or perform below standards on the work sample can be reassigned to other jobs. Choosing this strategy suggests that the company has decided to devote resources to selection and placement rather than training. Third, because it lacks time or expertise, the company may decide to purchase training from a consultant.

Many companies identify vendors and consultants who can provide training services by using tenders or requests for proposals.[24] A request for proposal (RFP) is a document that outlines for potential vendors and consultants the type of service the company is seeking, the type and number of references needed, the number of employees who need to be trained, funding for the project, the follow-up process used to determine level of satisfaction and service, expected date of completion of the project and the date by which proposals must be received by the company. The RFP may be mailed to potential consultants and vendors or posted on the company's website. The RFP is valuable because it provides a standard set of criteria against which all consultants will be evaluated. The RFP also helps eliminate the need to evaluate outside vendors who cannot provide the needed services.

Person analysis

Person analysis helps the manager identify whether training is appropriate and which employees need training. In certain situations, such as the introduction of a new technology or service, all employees may need training. However, when managers, customers or employees identify a problem (usually as a result of a performance deficiency), it is often unclear whether training is the solution.

A major pressure point for training is poor or substandard performance—that is, there is a gap between employees' current performance and their expected performance. Poor performance is indicated by customer complaints, low performance ratings or on-the-job incidents, such as accidents and unsafe behaviour. Another potential indicator of the need for training may be given when the job changes—such that current performance levels need to be improved or employees must be able to complete new tasks.

Figure 11.3 opposite shows the factors that influence employees' performance and learning. These factors include person characteristics, input, output, consequences and

FIGURE 11.3 Factors that influence employee performance and learning

Person characteristics
- Ability and skill
- Attitudes and motivation

Input
- Understand need to perform
- Necessary resources (equipment etc.)
- Interference from other job demands
- Opportunity to perform

Output
- Standard to judge successful performers

Consequences
- Positive consequences/incentives to perform
- Few negative consequences to perform

Feedback
- Frequent and specific feedback about how
- the job is performed

} Performance and learning

Source: G. Rummler, 1996, 'In search of the holy performance grail', *Training and Development*, April. Reprinted with permission.

feedback.[25] **Person characteristics** refer to an employees' knowledge, skills, abilities and attitudes. **Input** relates to the instructions that tell employees what, how and when to perform. Input also refers to the support they are given to help them perform. This support includes resources such as equipment, time and budget. Support also includes feedback and reinforcement from managers and peers. **Output** refers to a job's performance standards. **Consequences** refer to the type of incentives that employees receive for performing well. **Feedback** refers to the information that employees receive while they are performing, concerning how well they are meeting objectives.

From a manager's perspective, in order to determine if training is needed for any performance problem, you need to analyse: characteristics of the performer, input, output, consequences and feedback. How might this be done? Based on the model in Figure 11.3, you should ask several questions to determine if training is the likely solution to a performance problem.[26] Assess whether:

1. The performance problem is important and has the potential to cost the company a significant amount of money from lost productivity or lost customers.
2. Employees do not know how to perform effectively. Perhaps they received little or no previous training or the training was ineffective. (This problem is a characteristic of the person.)
3. Employees cannot demonstrate the correct knowledge or behaviour. Perhaps they were trained but they infrequently or never used the training content (knowledge, skills etc.) on the job. (This is an input problem.)
4. Performance expectations are clear (input) and there are no obstacles to performance, such as faulty tools or equipment.
5. There are positive consequences for good performance, while poor performance is not rewarded. For example, if employees are dissatisfied with their compensation, their peers or a union may encourage them to slow down their pace of work. (This involves consequences.)
6. Employees receive timely, relevant, accurate, constructive and specific feedback about their performance (a feedback issue).
7. Other solutions, such as job redesign or transferring employees to other jobs, are too expensive or unrealistic.

Person characteristics
an employee's knowledge, skills, abilities and attitudes.

Input
instructions that tell employees what, how and when to perform; also the support they are given to help them perform.

Output
a job's performance standards.

Consequences
the type of incentives that employees receive for performing well.

Feedback
information that employees receive while they are performing, concerning how well they are meeting objectives.

If employees lack the knowledge and skills to perform and the other factors are satisfactory, training is needed. If employees have the knowledge and skills to perform but input, output, consequences or feedback are inadequate, training may not be the best solution. For example, if poor performance results from faulty equipment, training cannot solve this problem but repairing the equipment will. If poor performance results from lack of feedback, then the employees may not need training, but their managers may need training on how to give performance feedback.

Task analysis

Task analysis results in a description of work activities, including tasks performed by the employee and the knowledge, skills and abilities required to successfully complete the tasks. A *task* is a statement of an employee's work activity in a specific job. There are four steps in task analysis:

1. Select the job(s) to be analysed.
2. Develop a preliminary list of tasks performed on the job by interviewing and observing expert employees and their managers and talking with others who have performed a task analysis.
3. Validate or confirm the preliminary list of tasks. This involves having a group of subject matter experts (job incumbents, managers etc.) answer, in a meeting or on a written survey, several questions regarding the tasks. The types of questions that may be asked include: 'How frequently is the task performed? How much time is spent performing each task? How important or critical is the task for successful performance of the job? How difficult is the task to learn? Is performance of the task expected of entry-level employees?'[27]

    Table 11.7 opposite presents a sample task analysis statement questionnaire. This information is used to determine which tasks will be focused on in the training program. The person or committee conducting the needs assessment must decide the level of ratings across dimensions that will determine whether a task should be included in the training program. Tasks that are important, frequently performed and of moderate-to-high levels of difficulty should be included in training. Tasks that are not important and are infrequently performed will not be included in training. It is difficult for managers and trainers to decide whether tasks that are important, performed infrequently and of minimal difficulty should be included in training. Managers and trainers must determine whether important tasks—regardless of how frequently they are performed or their level of difficulty—will be included in training.
4. Once the tasks are identified, it is important to identify the knowledge, skills or abilities necessary to perform each task successfully. This information can be collected using interviews and questionnaires. Information concerning basic skills and cognitive ability requirements is critical for determining whether certain levels of knowledge, skills and abilities are prerequisites for entrance to the training program (or job) or whether supplementary training in underlying skills is needed. For training purposes, information concerning how difficult it is to learn the knowledge, skills or abilities is important—as is whether the knowledge, skills or abilities are expected to be acquired by the employee before taking the job.[28]

Learning in the workplace

The workplace has become the central focus for the debate about improving the way we learn. Learning and development has become viewed as a key strategy for improving the economic performance of Australian organisations, and organisations

Learning and Development CH.

TABLE 11.7 Sample task statement questionnaire

Name: Date:

Position:

Please rate each of the task statements according to three factors:

1 the importance of the task for effective performance
2 how frequently the task is performed
3 the degree of difficulty required to become effective in the task.

Use the following scales to make your ratings.

Importance	Frequency
4 = Task is critical for effective performance	4 = Task is performed once a day
3 = Task is important but not critical for effective performance	3 = Task is performed once a week
2 = Task is of some importance for effective performance	2 = Task is performed once every few months
1 = Task is of no importance for effective performance	1 = Task is performed once or twice a year
0 = Task is not performed	0 = Task is not performed

Difficulty

4 = Effective performance of the task requires extensive prior experience and/or training (12–18 months or longer).
3 = Effective performance of the task requires minimal prior experience and training (6–12 months).
2 = Effective performance of the task requires a brief period of prior training and experience (1–6 months).
1 = Effective performance of the task does not require specific prior training and/or experience.
0 = This task is not performed.

	Task	Importance	Frequency	Difficulty
1	Ensuring maintenance on equipment, tools, and safety controls			
2	Monitoring employee performance			
3	Scheduling employees			
4	Using statistical software on the computer			
5	Monitoring changes made in processes using statistical methods			

themselves have introduced significant changes into their workplaces which demand considerable investmddents in training and development with an increasing emphasis on the development of behavioural skills.

But not all learning that occurs in the workplace is the result of a training intervention. Much of the learning that occurs has been called 'informal and incidental'.[29] This means that people are learning at work all the time. Training programs provide an opportunity for more formal or structured learning but much of what employees learn is done outside the formal training system.

Also, employees are adults. They have a lot of experiences that they bring with them into the workplace and these experiences colour the way they learn. Adult learning theory[30] describes the way that employees learn at work. A key strand in modern thinking on how employees learn at work has been the learning theory of constructivism. Constructivism is based on the theories of a number of cogni psychologists, in particular the work of Jean Piaget and Lev Vygotsky. Both Piaget and Vygotsky were concerned with the psychological development of children but their theories have been used extensively to account for adult learning. Constructivism acknowledges that the individual can only apprehend the world through the medium of their senses and that therefore individuals will derive their own 'constructs' about the world in order to make sense of it. This process of making sense of the world is learning. The constructs that individuals create to explain the world will be fashioned not only by their senses but also by the experiences and ideas they bring to their own learning. In the constructivist view, individuals' learning does not result in an accurate representation of reality, this is impossible in an interpretivist framework but rather a personal way of making sense of the world. Doolittle and Camp[31] use the notion of cognition to describe the constructivist view of learning in terms of four principles:

1 Knowledge is not passively accumulated but is rather the result of active cognising by the individual.
2 Cognition is an adaptive process that functions to make an individual's behaviour more viable in a given environment.
3 Cognition organises and makes sense of one's experience and is not a process to render an accurate representation of reality.
4 Knowing has roots both in biological/neurological construction, and in social, cultural and language interactions.

These principles stress the role of the individual in actively constructing their own world view. This will, perforce, be different from the world views that others construct, even if they have undergone the same learning experiences.

Doolittle and Camp[32] describe eight lessons for trainers and teachers that follow from a constructivist view of learning:

1 **Learning should take place in an authentic and real world.** Experience is the main catalyst for learning and all learning should be built on experience.
2 **Learning should involve social negotiation and mediation.** Social interaction provides the basis for learning socially relevant skills and knowledge. Some knowledge can only be gained in a social setting; for example, cultural knowledge etc.
3 **Content and skills should be made relevant to the learner.** Constructivism emphasises the use of knowledge for social adaptation. If the learner is attempting to use knowledge to adapt to new social settings then the knowledge has to be relevant. Relevance will increase the motivation of the learner.
4 **C... nd skill should be understood within the framework of the ...rior knowledge.** All learning has to take into account the learner's ...ledge. Learners build on that proper knowledge.
   ...ould be assessed formatively, serving to inform future learning ... Since a learner's prior knowledge is not visible, assessment needs to ... knowledge in order to inform the learning experience.
   ...uld be encouraged to become self-regulatory, self-mediated and ... he basis of constructivism is that learners are active in their own ...ners therefore need to know how to regulate their own learning
   ...eachers serve primarily as guides and facilitators of learning, ...s. This is very close to Rogers's concepts of facilitation for adult ...ers do not transmit knowledge, learners construct it for themselves.
   ...eachers should provide for and encourage multiple ...d representations of content.** Since constructivism holds that

there is no such thing as verifiable 'truth', learners need to develop complex understandings of reality. Multiple perspectives will help learners develop complex and more rounded understanding.

If workplace learning is such an important part of the learning experience for people, it is important to understand how the workplace can be improved to encourage learning to take place. As Billett[33] has observed, in the modern workplace learning and work are often indistinguishable.

Learning and work are interdependent. We learn constantly through engaging in goal-directed everyday activities—indeed, as we think and act, we learn. However, the quality of this learning is likely to depend on: (a) the kinds of activities that individuals engage in: (b) their access to the contribution of situational factors including support and guidance; and (c) how individuals engage, interact and interpretatively construct knowledge from these situations.[34]

Billett identifies both routine and non-routine activities at work as providing opportunities for learning. Routine tasks, often associated with the almost automated response of the skilled person, helps to embed skills and knowledge through repeated practice. Through a process of compilation and chunking of knowledge, learners come to know routine tasks so well that they can carry them out without having to think. The learner who has not yet automated these tasks will need to pay great attention to what they are doing. Whilst routines can provide for learning to smoothly apply skills and knowledge to predictable situations, it can also have a downside. When things change and the routine is no longer appropriate or has to be modified, the skilled person can find that they unlearn their previous skills and knowledge as well as learn new things.

Non-routine tasks at work provide the opportunity to develop the higher order problem solving skills that are necessary to deal with unpredictable situations. Thus Billett provides the example of driving a car. The mechanics of starting the car and using the gears to progress is an example of routine learning. Once mastered, the techniques of driving become automatic to the point where the driver does not have think about how to drive the car. But driving around an unfamiliar city to get to a destination can be a major problem for a driver. This is an example of a non-routine activity. The driver has not been in this part of town before and has to think very carefully about what he or she is doing in order to get to the destination.

TABLE 11.8 Learning through everyday activity

	Routine activities	**Non-routine activities**
Activities and outcomes	Reinforces what we have already learned through:	Creates new knowledge through:
Problem solving	Routine problem solving	Non-routine problem solving.

Source: S. Billett, 2001, *Learning in the workplace: strategies for effective practice*, Allen and Unwin, Sydney, p. 30.

Communities of practice

In a development of constructivism in the workplace, Jean Lave and Etienne Wenger developed the influential notion of communities of practice. Lave and Wenger looked at the way that employee learning is often done in groups—social learning. The concept of social learning is very like that of constructivism in that it posits that employees will learn under the influence of what others around them think. Theses groups have been called 'communities of practice'.

The concept of communities of practice came from Lave and Wenger's seminal study of a number of different communities all over the world. Included in these groups were tailors in West Africa.[35] In this study Lave and Wenger found that the learning that young apprentice tailors undertook was embedded in the community of tailors of which they were a part. The tailors lived together on a street of tailors and the apprentices lived with them. Their learning of the trade of tailoring was structured through their life in this community. In their learning processes the apprentice tailors aspired to become experts in tailoring, although this status of an expert might never be reached because the nature of trade moved and changed as they learnt.[36] The apprentice tailors went through a process of watching and observing the expert tailors and gradually taking a greater degree of responsibility under the guidance of the expert tailors. Lave and Wenger referred to the apprentices and their masters as 'newcomers' and 'old timers' respectively. In Lave and Wenger's view, the difference between this process and the normal process of apprenticeship was that the apprentice tailors were part of a living community of tailors, a community of practice. However, as Smith[37] has pointed out, this is very similar to the nature of pre-industrial apprenticeships when apprentices commonly lived with their masters for a number of years before reaching their goal of being a journeyman.

Wenger[38] has described the principles of social learning that underpin the notion of communities of practice.

- We are social beings. Far from being trivially true, this is a central aspect of learning.
- Knowledge is a matter of competence with respect to valued enterprises—such as singing in tune, discovering scientific facts, writing poetry, being convivial, growing up as a boy or girl and so forth.
- Knowing is a matter of participating in the pursuit of such enterprises, that is, of active engagement with the world.
- Meaning—our ability to experience the world and our engagement with it as meaningful—is ultimately what learning is to produce.

Thus, for Wenger, learning takes place as a social activity and cannot be viewed as a purely personal and individual activity. Clearly, the notion of the community of practice is very much an extension of social constructivism into workplace learning. Lave and Wenger's notion of the social relations of learning is illustrated in Figure 11.4.

In this diagram Wenger identifies four components of learning:

1. **Community.** Participation in a community is a recognisable competence.
2. **Identity.** The personal history of the individual in the content of the community.
3. **Meaning.** The way in which we experience the world.
4. **Practice.** Engagement in the activities of the communities and the resources that underpin these.

Each of these components is learned in the community of practice. Lave and Wenger's notion of the community of practice is very attractive and corresponds to many of the practices of learning and development that we can observe in enterprises. However, it is not without its critics. Smith[39] has commented that the model lacks a sense of dynamism. The communities that Lave and Wenger investigated were quite exotic and very traditional. The West African tailors had handed down the traditional skills of tailoring over many generations and theses skills have remained largely

FIGURE 11.4 Components of a social theory of learning: an initial inventory

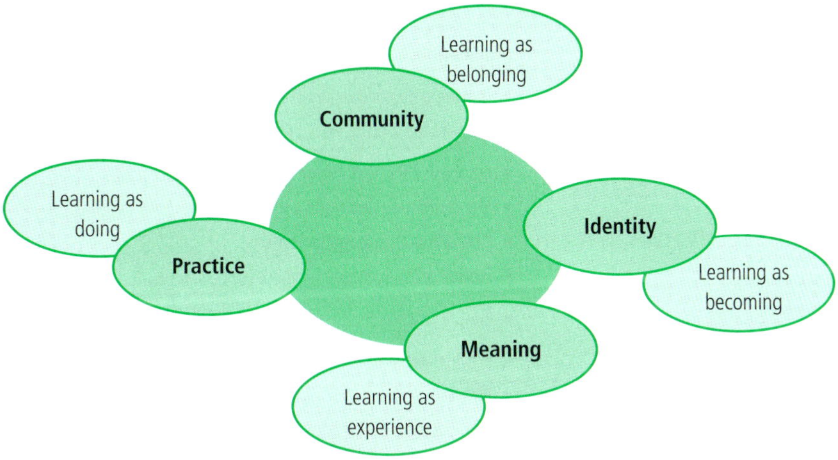

Source: E. Wenger, (1998), *Communities of practice: learning, meaning and identity.* Cambridge University Press, p. 5.

unchanged over that time. Few modern workplaces would resemble such a traditional and unchanging situation. The pace of change in contemporary organisations means that communities of practice may have to be focused on change rather than the passing down of traditional ways of working.

Moreover, in modern society people do not belong only to one community of practice. People may belong to a number of such communities—some based in the workplace, others in the broader profession and others outside work altogether. Thus, people may play a variety of roles in a number of different and overlapping communities of practice.

Creating a learning environment

Learning involves a permanent change in behaviour. For employees to acquire knowledge and skills in the training program and apply this information in their jobs, the training program needs to include specific learning principles. Educational and industrial psychologists and instructional design specialists have identified several conditions under which employees learn best.[40] Table 11.9 overleaf shows the events that need to take place for learning to occur in the training program and their implications for instruction.

Employees need to know why they should learn

Employees learn best when they understand the objective of the training program. The *objective* refers to the purpose and expected outcome of training activities. There may be objectives for each training session as well as overall objectives for the program. Training objectives, based on the training needs analysis, help employees understand why they need training. Objectives are also useful for identifying the types of training outcomes that should be measured to evaluate a training program's effectiveness.

A training objective has three components:

1. statement of what the employee is expected to do (performance)
2. statement of the quality or level of performance that is acceptable (criterion)
3. statement of the conditions under which the trainee is expected to perform the desired outcome (conditions).[41]

TABLE 11.9 Instructional events and their implications for the learning environment

Instructional events	Implications
Informing the learner of the lesson objective	• Provide a demonstration of the performance to be expected. • Indicate the kind of verbal question to be answered.
Presenting stimuli with distinctive features	• Emphasise the features of the subject to be perceived. • Use formatting and figures in text to emphasise features.
Limiting the amount to be learned	• Chunk together lengthier material. • Provide a visual image of material to be learned. • Provide practice and over-learning to aid the attainment of automatisation.
Providing learning guidance	• Provide verbal cues to proper combining sequence. • Provide verbal links to a larger meaningful context. • Use diagrams and models to show relationships among concepts.
Elaborating the amount to be learned	• Vary the context and setting for presentation and recall of material. • Relate newly learned material to previously learned information. • Provide a variety of contexts and situations during practice.
Providing cues that are used in recall	• Suggest cues that elicit the recall of material. • Use familiar sounds or rhymes as cues.
Enhancing retention and learning transfer	• Design the learning situation to share elements with the situation of use. • Provide verbal links to additional complexes of information.
Providing feedback about performance correctness	• Provide feedback on the degree of accuracy and timing of performance. • Confirm that original expectancies were met.

Source: Adapted from R.M. Gagne, 1995–96, 'Learning processes and instruction', *Training Research Journal*, pp. 17–28.

For example, a training objective for a customer service training program for retail salespersons might be:

> After training, the employee will be able to express concern [performance] to all irate customers by a brief (fewer than 10 words) apology, only after the customer has stopped talking [criteria] and no matter how upset the customer is [conditions].

Good training objectives provide a clear idea of what the trainees are expected to do at the end of training. Standards of satisfactory performance (for example, speed, time constraints, products and reactions) that can be measured or evaluated should be included. Any resources (equipment and tools) that the trainees need to perform the action or behaviour specified in the objective need to be described. The conditions under which performance of the objective is expected to occur also need to be described. These conditions can relate to the physical work setting (for example, at night), mental stresses (for example, an angry customer), or equipment failure (for example, malfunctioning landing gear on an aircraft).

Employees need to use their own experiences as a basis for learning

Employees are more likely to learn when the training is linked to their current job experiences and tasks—that is, when it is meaningful to them.[42] To enhance the meaningfulness of training content, the message should be presented using concepts, terms and examples familiar to the trainees. For example, in the Coles supermarket customer service training program, the meaningfulness of the material is enhanced by using scenarios of unhappy customers actually encountered by salespersons in stores. Recent research indicates that besides linking training to current job experiences, learning can be enhanced by providing trainees with the opportunity to choose their practice strategy and other characteristics of the learning environment.[43]

Employees need to have opportunities to practise

Practice involves having the employee demonstrate the learned capability (for example, cognitive strategy and verbal information) emphasised in the training objectives under the conditions and performance standards specified by the objective. For practice to be effective, it needs to actively involve the trainee, include over-learning (repeated practice), take the appropriate amount of time and include the appropriate unit of learning (amount of material). Practice also needs to be relevant to the training objectives.

Learning will not occur if employees practise only by talking about what they are expected to do. For example, using the objective of the customer service course previously discussed, practice would involve having trainees participate in role playing with unhappy customers (that is, customers upset with poor service, poor merchandise or exchange policies). Trainees need to continue to practise, although they have been able to perform the objective several times (over-learning). Over-learning helps the trainee become more comfortable using new knowledge and skills and increases the length of time the trainee will retain the knowledge, skill or behaviour.

Trainers need to be sure that instruction does not exceed employees' short-term and long-term memory capacities. Research suggests that no more than four to five items can be attended to at one time. If a lengthy procedure or process is to be taught, instruction needs to be delivered in shorter sessions or chunks in order not to exceed memory limits.[44] Visual images are another way to reduce demands on memory. Finally, *automatising* (making performance of a task so automatic that it requires little thought or attention to be performed) is another way to reduce memory demands. For example, it would be difficult for a jet engine mechanic to perform some of the later parts of a maintenance procedure unless the earlier steps (such as removing the cover of the turbines) have been automatised. The more automatisation of a procedure that occurs, the more memory is freed up to concentrate on other learning and thinking. Automatisation occurs through over-learning—that is, learners are provided with extra learning opportunities, including after they have demonstrated that they can perform adequately.

It is also important to consider whether to have only one practice session or to use distributed (multiple) practice sessions. Distributed practice sessions have been shown to result in more efficient learning of skills than continuous practice.[45] With factual information, the less meaningful the material and the greater its length or difficulty, the better distributed the practice sessions are for learning.

A final issue related to practice is how much of the training should be practised at one time. One option is that all tasks or objectives should be practised at the same time (whole practice). Another option is that an objective or task should be practised individually as soon as it is introduced in the training program (part practice). It is probably best to employ both whole and part practice in a training session. Trainees should have the opportunity to practise individual skills or behaviours. If the skills or behaviours introduced in training are related to one another, the trainee should demonstrate all of them in a practice session after they are practised individually.

For practice to be relevant to the training objectives, several conditions must be met.[46] Practice must be related to the training objectives. The trainer should identify what trainees will be doing when they are practising the objectives (performance), the criteria for attainment of the objectives and the conditions under which they may perform. These conditions should be present in the practice session. Next, the trainer needs to consider the adequacy of the trainees' performance. That is, how will trainees know whether their performance meets performance standards? Will they see a model of desired performance? Will they be provided with a checklist or description of desired performance? Can the trainees decide if their performance meets standards or will the trainer or a piece of equipment compare their performance with standards?

If trainees' performance does not meet standards, the trainer must also decide if he or she will understand what is wrong and how to fix it. That is, trainers need to consider if trainees can diagnose their performance and take corrective action, or if they will need help from the trainer or a fellow trainee.

Employees need feedback

Feedback is information about how well people are meeting the training objectives. To be effective, feedback should focus on specific behaviours and be provided to a trainee as soon as possible after that trainee's behaviour occurs.[47] Also, positive trainee behaviour should be verbally praised or reinforced. Videotapes made of trainees and played back at a later time are a powerful tool for giving feedback. Trainers should view the videotape with trainees, provide specific information about how behaviours need to be modified and praise trainee behaviours that meet objectives.

Employees learn by observing and interacting with others

According to social learning theory, people learn by observing and imitating the actions of models. For the model to be effective, the desired behaviours or skills need to be clearly specified and the model should have characteristics (such as age or position) similar to the target audience.[48] After observing the model, trainees should have the opportunity to reproduce the skills or behaviour shown by the model in practice sessions.

The idea of communities of practice discussed above suggests that learning occurs on the job as a result of social interaction. Every company has naturally occurring communities of practice that evolve as a result of relationships that employees develop to accomplish work. For example, Xerox needed to train service representatives as a result of merging three separate service departments into a single unit. They trained the service representatives by bringing them together in shared work spaces where they were in constant contact with each other. In this environment, the service representatives taught each other how to do their jobs and practised their skills on customer calls. One representative described the experience as involving continuous learning through sharing information with other representatives and hearing how other representatives have dealt with different types of service calls.

Employees need the training program to be properly coordinated and arranged

Training coordination is one of several aspects of training administration. *Training administration* refers to coordinating activities before, during and after the program.[49] Training administration involves:

1. communicating courses and programs to employees
2. enrolling employees in courses and programs
3. preparing and processing any pre-training materials (for example, readings or tests)
4. preparing materials that will be used in instruction (for example, copies of overhead computer slides)

5   arrangements for the training facility and room
6   testing equipment that will be used in instruction
7   having backup equipment (for example, Textas) should equipment fail
8   providing support during instruction
9   distributing evaluation materials (for example, tests, reaction measures and surveys)
10 facilitating communications between trainer and trainees during and after training (for example, coordinating exchange of email addresses)
11 recording course completion in the trainees' training records or personnel files.

Good coordination ensures that trainees are not distracted by events (such as an uncomfortable room or poorly organised materials) that could interfere with learning. Activities before the program include communicating to trainees: the purpose of the program, the place it will be held, the name of a person to contact if they have questions and any preprogram work they are supposed to complete. Books, speakers, handouts and videotapes need to be prepared. Any necessary arrangements to secure rooms and equipment (such as a DVD player) should be made. The physical arrangement of the training room should complement the training technique. For example, it would be difficult for a team-building session to be effective if the seats could not be moved for group activities. If visual aids are going to be used, all trainees should be able to see them. Make sure that the room is physically comfortable, with adequate lighting and ventilation. Trainees should be informed of starting and finishing times, break times and the location of bathrooms. Minimise distractions such as phone messages. If trainees are asked to evaluate the program or take tests to determine what they have learned, allot time for such an activity at the end of the program. Following the program, any credits or recording of the names of trainees who have completed the program should be completed. Handouts and other training materials should be stored or returned to the consultant. The end of the program is also a good time to consider how the program could be improved and whether it will be offered again.

Ensuring transfer of training

Transfer of training refers to the use of knowledge, skills and behaviours learned in training on the job. As Figure 11.5 below shows, transfer of training is influenced by the climate for transfer, manager support, peer support, opportunity to use learned capabilities, technological support and self-management skills. As we discussed earlier,

Transfer of training refers to the use of knowledge, skills and behaviours learned in training on the job.

FIGURE 11.5 Work environment characteristics influencing transfer of training

TABLE 11.10	Characteristics of a positive climate for transfer of training
1	Supervisors and co-workers encourage and set goals for trainees to use new skills and behaviours acquired in training: • task cues—characteristics of a trainee's job are used to prompt or remind him or her to use new skills and behaviours acquired in training • feedback consequences—supervisors support the application of new skills and behaviours acquired in training • lack of punishment—trainees are not openly discouraged from using new skills and behaviours acquired in training • extrinsic reinforcement consequences—trainees receive extrinsic rewards for using new skills and behaviours acquired in training • intrinsic reinforcement consequences—trainees receive intrinsic rewards for using new skills and behaviours acquired in training.
2	Newly trained managers discuss how to apply their training on the job with their supervisors and other managers.
3	The job of a newly trained manager is designed in such a way as to allow the manager to use the skills taught in training.
4	Supervisors notice newly trained managers who use their training.
5	When newly trained managers fail to use their training, they are not reprimanded.
6	Newly trained managers who successfully use their training will receive a salary increase.
7	Supervisors and other managers appreciate newly trained managers who perform their job as taught in training.

Source: Adapted from J.B. Tracey, S.I. Tannenbaum & M.J. Kavanagh, 1995, 'Applying trained skills on the job: the importance of the work environment', *Journal of Applied Psychology*, 80.

learning is influenced by the learning environment (for example, meaningfulness of the material, opportunities for practice, and feedback) and employees' readiness for training (for example, self-efficacy and basic-skills level). If learning does not occur in the training program, transfer is unlikely.

Climate for transfer

One way to think about the work environment's influence on transfer of training is to consider the overall 'climate for transfer'. *Climate for transfer* refers to trainees' perceptions about a wide variety of characteristics of the work environment that facilitate or inhibit use of trained skills or behaviour. These characteristics include manager and peer support, opportunity to use skills and the consequences for using learned capabilities.[50] Table 11.10 above shows characteristics of a positive climate for transfer of training. Research has shown that transfer of training climate is significantly related to positive changes in managers' administrative and interpersonal behaviours following training.

Manager support

Manager support refers to the degree to which trainees' managers: (1) emphasise the importance of attending training programs; and (2) stress the application of training content to the job. For example, Kmart Australia shows the importance of support and coaching for new and less-experienced or less-skilled employees. In the competitive retail environment in which Kmart operates, it is recognised that the focus on quality products and superior customer service depends on fostering the development of all employees and providing career path opportunities for them. Kmart has established a retail traineeship, which provides a full-time entry-level position with a link to career paths. The traineeship is delivered in accordance with national retail industry standards and leads to the award of a nationally recognised qualification (Certificate II in Retail Operations). Kmart also established, within each participating store, a position for a workplace coach to provide on-the-job learning support to trainees.

Each workplace coach receives further professional/career development and nationally recognised qualifications in workplace training and assessing. Through this program, Kmart has made a substantial investment in its traineeship program and in the skill base of existing staff.[51]

The greater the level of manager support, the more likely it is that transfer of training will occur.[52] The basic level of support that a manager can provide is acceptance in allowing trainees to attend training. The highest level of support is to participate in training as an instructor (teaching in the program). Managers who serve as instructors are more likely to provide many of the lower-level support functions, such as reinforcing use of newly learned capabilities, discussing progress with trainees and providing opportunities to practise. To maximise transfer of training, trainers need to achieve the highest level of support possible. Managers can also facilitate transfer through reinforcement (use of action plans). An *action plan* is a written document that includes the steps that the trainee and manager will take to ensure that training transfers to the job. The action plan identifies: (1) specific projects or problems that the trainee will work on; and (2) equipment or other resources that the manager will provide to help the trainee. The action plan includes a schedule of specific dates and times that the manager and trainee agree on, in order to meet and discuss the progress being made by using learned capabilities on the job.
At a minimum, special sessions should be scheduled with managers to explain the purpose of the training and to set expectations that they will encourage attendance at the training session. These sessions should also be used to provide practice opportunities, reinforce use of training and follow-up with employees to determine the progress in using newly acquired capabilities.

Peer support

Transfer of training can also be enhanced by creating a support network among the trainees.[53] A *support network* is a group of two or more trainees who agree to meet and discuss their progress in using learned capabilities on the job. This could involve face-to-face meetings or communications via email. Trainees could share successful experiences in using training content on the job. They can also discuss how they obtained the resources that were needed to use training content or how they coped with a work environment that interfered with the use of training content.

A newsletter might be written to show how trainees are dealing with 'transfer of training' issues. The newsletter would be distributed to all trainees, and it might feature interviews with trainees who were successful in using new skills. Managers may also provide trainees with a 'mentor' — a more experienced employee who previously attended the same training program. The mentor may be a peer. The mentor can provide advice and support related to transfer of training issues (for example, how to find opportunities to use the learned capabilities).

Opportunity to use learned capabilities

Opportunity to use learned capabilities (opportunity to perform) refers to the extent to which the trainee is provided with or actively seeks experience with newly learned knowledge, skills and behaviours from the training program. The opportunity to perform is influenced by both the work environment and trainee motivation. One way in which trainees have the opportunity to use learned capabilities is through assigned work experiences (for example, problems and tasks) that require their use. The trainee's manager usually plays a key role in determining work assignments. The opportunity to perform is also influenced by the degree to which trainees take personal responsibility to actively seek out assignments that allow them to use newly acquired capabilities.

The opportunity to perform includes breadth, activity level and task type.[54] *Breadth* includes the number of trained tasks performed on the job. *Activity level* refers to the number of times or the frequency with which trained tasks are performed on the job. *Task type* refers to the difficulty or criticality of the trained tasks that are actually performed on the job. Trainees who are given opportunities to use training content on the job are more likely to maintain learned capabilities than trainees given few opportunities.[55]

The opportunity to perform can be measured by asking former trainees to indicate: (1) whether they perform a task, (2) how often they perform the task, and (3) the extent to which they perform difficult and challenging tasks. Individuals who report low levels of opportunity to perform may be prime candidates for *refresher courses* (courses designed to let trainees practise and review training content). Refresher courses are necessary, because people attending these courses are likely to have experienced a decay in learned capabilities, since they have not had opportunities to perform. Low levels of opportunity to perform may also indicate that the work environment is interfering with using new skills. For example, the manager may not support training activities or give the employee the opportunity to perform tasks using skills emphasised in training. Finally, low levels of opportunity to perform may indicate that training content is not important for the employee's job.

Technological support
Electronic performance support systems (EPSS) are computer applications that can provide, as requested, skills training, information access and expert advice.[56] These systems may be used to enhance 'transfer of training' by providing trainees with an electronic information source that they can refer to on an as-needed basis, as they attempt to apply learned capabilities on the job.

Self-management skills
Training programs should prepare employees to self-manage their use of new skills and behaviours on the job.[57] Specifically, within the training program, trainees should be given the opportunity to set goals for using skills or behaviours on the job, identify conditions under which they might fail to use them, identify the positive and negative consequences of using them and monitor their use of them. Also, trainees need to understand that it is natural to encounter difficulty in trying to use skills on the job; relapses into old behaviour and skill patterns do not indicate that trainees should give up. Finally, because peers and supervisors on the job may be unable to provide rewards for using new behaviours or provide feedback automatically, trainees need to create their own reward system and ask peers and managers for feedback.

Selecting training methods

A number of different methods can be used to help employees acquire new knowledge, skills and behaviours. According to the Australian Bureau of Statistics Training Expenditure and Practices survey in 2001–02, the training arrangements most commonly used to deliver structured training were external workshops, lectures and so on (76 per cent of employers that provided structured training used these training arrangements); followed by structured on-the-job training (55 per cent), attendance at internal workshops, lectures and so forth (42 per cent); and computer-assisted structured training (33 per cent).[58] The data show that the amount of all types of training conducted increases with organisational size.

Technology is having a major impact on the delivery of training programs. It is forecast that between 25 and 40 per cent of all corporate learning in Australia will soon use online and internet technology.[59] New technology is also influencing training administration and training support. Multimedia training (such as CDs) and virtual reality enable training environments to almost perfectly mimic the 'real' work setting. New technologies also allow trainees to see, feel and hear how equipment as well as other people respond to their behaviours. Interactive voice response and imaging systems make it possible to have paperless enrolment in training and tracking of training records. Software is available to facilitate storage and sharing of intellectual capital (information and learned capabilities) between employees. Electronic performance support systems (EPSS) give employees access to information from experts on an as-needed basis.

New training technologies can result in lower delivery costs and greater flexibility in delivery.[60] For example, training delivered by an instructor at a central location requires employees to spend time away from their regular job and requires the company to incur travel costs for bringing employees to a central location. Lower delivery costs can be realised by using satellite-based training or distance learning in which training programs are transmitted via satellite to several locations. Use of a CD-ROM or e-learning also gives an employee the flexibility to participate in training on a 24-hour basis at home or work, through the use of a personal computer. Linking training to personal computers also gives employees more responsibility for their own training. Such technology includes characteristics that can enhance learning, which are not often found in traditional instructor-led programs (for example, immediate feedback, multiple practice opportunities and opportunities for employees to learn at their own pace).

However, having state-of-the-art instructional technology should not be the guiding force in choosing a training method. The specific instructional method used should be based on the training objectives. Instructional methods can be crudely grouped into three broad categories: (1) presentation methods; (2) hands-on methods; and (3) group-building methods.[61]

Presentation methods

Presentation methods refer to methods in which trainees are passive recipients of information. Presentation methods include traditional classroom instruction, distance learning, audiovisual techniques and blended learning. These are ideal for presenting new facts, information, different philosophies and alternative problem solving solutions or processes.

- *Classroom instruction.* This type of instruction typically involves having the trainer lecture a group. In many cases, the lecture is supplemented with question-and-answer periods, discussions or case studies. Classroom instruction remains a popular training method despite new technologies such as interactive video and computer-assisted instruction. Traditional classroom instruction is one of the least expensive, least time-consuming ways to present information on a specific topic to a large number of trainees. Also, the more active participation, job-related examples and exercises that the instructor can build into traditional classroom instruction, the more likely trainees will learn and use the information presented on the job.
- *Audiovisual techniques.* Audiovisual instruction includes computer-based presentations with software such as overheads, slides and video. Video has been used for improving communications skills, interviewing skills and customer-service skills and for illustrating how procedures (for example, welding) should be followed.[62] Video is, however, rarely used alone. It is usually used in

conjunction with lectures to show trainees 'real-life' experiences and examples. Video is also a major component of behaviour modelling and, naturally, interactive video instruction.

The use of video in training has a number of advantages. First, the trainer can review, slow down or speed up the lesson, which gives the trainer flexibility in customising the session—depending on the expertise of trainees. Second, trainees can be exposed to equipment problems and events that are not easily demonstrated, such as equipment malfunctions, angry customers or emergencies. Third, trainees are provided with consistent instruction. The interests and goals of a particular trainer do not affect program content. Fourth, videotaping trainees allows them to see and hear their own performance without the interpretation of the trainer. As a result, trainees cannot attribute poor performance to the bias of external evaluators such as the trainer or peers.

Most problems in video training result from the creative approach used.[63] These problems include too much content for the trainee to learn, poor dialogue between the actors (which hinders the credibility and clarity of the message),

BLENDED LEARNING

MANAGING CHALLENGES THROUGH HR INNOVATION

Broadly defined, blended learning refers to the use of multiple solutions and training techniques within the same learning program. Effective blended learning is far more than a few different learning mediums bundled together.

Blended learning is a variant of distance education that uses technology (hi-tech, such as TV or the internet; or low-tech, such as voice mail or conference calls), combined with traditional face-to-face education or training.

Bersin & Associates' 2002–03 US study, *Blended Learning: What Works*, found: the prospect of a global recession triggered development of large, highly effective blended learning programs, some with a return on investment (ROI) of more than 700 per cent; blended learning was 'the highest impact way to deliver corporate training on mission critical business initiatives'; and the cost of blended learning programs varied greatly, depending on audience size, media and infrastructure.

Rebel Sport

Scott Ford, Rebel Sport's national training manager, takes a practical approach to media selection. He starts the design of all training programs with the end-users and asks them what they want and how they want it delivered. Ford is a big believer in giving responsibility to the end-users.

All employees at Rebel's national chain of 50 stores can access the company's online training modules at 'Rebel University'—part of a blended approach that also incorporates face-to-face instruction and training as well as in-store coaching and practical assessment.

Ford says that the best way to measure ROI is to see changed behaviour, following training, reflected in the bottom line.

Australian Kitchen Industries

Steven Bosley, CEO of Australian Kitchen Industries, says that there is no difficulty when it comes to measuring the ROI of training. Five out of seven of his top retail stores also ranked highest in uptake of learning programs. He sees no coincidence in these results. The company has 30 retail stores and employs 450 people in its four divisions of design, manufacturing, sales and installation. Bosley measures the ratio of training costs to revenue, total number of modules completed and costs per employee. 'We implemented the blended learning program 18 months ago, but it will be another 12 months before it will be performing at its peak', he says.

Bosley wanted a centralised approach to training and first considered a blended approach when he 'stumbled across an online policies and procedures package' a few years ago. He wanted to encourage learning across the company and to develop and retain staff. Preferring to promote from within, Bosley felt a centralised training approach was a much fairer way of allocating a training budget. All job specifications, including competencies and required skill levels, are available to all staff. Employees can prepare themselves for promotions utilising some of the learning modules on the company's web-hosted site.

overuse of humour or music, and drama that makes it confusing for the trainee to understand the important learning points emphasised in the video.
- *Blended learning*. As discussed in the 'Managing challenges through HR innovation: Blended learning' case, blended learning programs can bring substantial benefits to employees and the organisation. **Blended learning** uses multiple presentation methods within the same training program. It combines the use of technology (for example, internet) with more traditional face-to-face education (for example, classroom sessions).

Blended learning
the use of multiple presentation methods within the same training program.

Hands-on methods

Hands-on training methods require the trainee to be actively involved in learning. Hands-on methods include on-the-job training (self-directed learning and apprenticeships), simulations, business games and case studies, behaviour modelling, interactive video and electronic or e-learning, including web-based training. These methods are ideal for developing specific skills, understanding how skills and behaviours can be transferred to the job, experiencing all aspects of completing a task, and dealing with interpersonal issues that arise on the job.

St George Bank

St George Bank's manager of design and technology, Bob Spence, says that the bank's media choices were determined by the instructional design process. 'We defined the learning objectives, then developed test items for these objectives. We then decided what was the best way to teach the material and choose appropriate media', explained Spence. St George, which won the 2003 Australian HR Awards e-learning category, rolled out e-learning in October 2001 (using its system called 'e-luminate') starting with its orientation program. It followed this with a management development program and now hosts 120 online modules.

New customer service officers are trained using three different media: e-luminate; a purpose-built simulated branch; and on-the-job supervision. Spence says, 'e-learning is good for recall, remembering and stating facts and works best for a lot of our compliance requirements, such as EEO, OHS, emergency evacuation procedures and complying with the *Financial Services Reform Act* (FSRA). We use our simulated branch as a classroom and apply the knowledge learned through e-luminate, as well as practising with security systems, cash systems etc. We then use on-the-job supervision to test performance.'

Management development programs seem to lend themselves perfectly to a blended approach. St George uses e-luminate to teach the principles of management through self-paced learning, ensuring participants arrive in the classroom with the same level of knowledge. It has classroom sessions to discuss case studies and observe group dynamics, and it follows this with practical projects to be carried out in the workplace.

Spence says that the business case for blended learning is compelling. If you count the costs of accommodation, transport and marking tests in a traditional face-to-face approach, blended learning is not only cost effective, but also considerably efficient, because it automates a lot of the administration.

IBM

This company's e-learning system, Global Campus, has been operating for around seven years; and it is also a provider of e-learning solutions. Robert Orth, HR director Australia and New Zealand, was involved in its development and testing at a global level. 'We had to determine what training was needed across the organisation, to whom it should be given, what were the priority areas and how much we needed to spend', says Orth.

Some training can be delivered through technology and some requires high-value face-to-face learning. The management development program has become an example of truly blended learning, replacing a two-week class course. Participants now complete web-based factual learning via Global Campus. They are provided with an online tutor and allocated a 'learning space', which they share with other course participants. The tutor supervises class discussions and online simulations. At the six-month mark, one week of high-value face-to-face learning is scheduled, and the last six months is dedicated to reinforcement, again with supervision by the online tutor.

Orth says that 40 per cent of IBM's training is done by e-learning. He measures the quality and effectiveness of all training programs through class satisfaction surveys, assessments and observed cultural or behavioural change. To build a business case, delivery cost, development of content and travel and living expenses have to be assessed. When using a blended approach that incorporates e-learning, much of the content is reusable. 'The other advantage in our business is the speed with which new information can be disseminated', continues Orth. 'We call it "just-in-time learning".'

Source: Based on T. Russell, 2004, 'Blended learning: does it stack up?', *Human Resources*, 25 February, pp. 14–15.
www.humanresourcesmagazine.com.au

- *On-the-job training (OJT)*. This process can be useful for training newly hired employees, upgrading the skills of experienced employees when new technology is introduced, cross-training employees within a department or work unit, and orienting transferred or promoted employees to their new jobs. The basic philosophy of OJT is that employees learn through observing peers or managers performing the job and trying to imitate their behaviour.

    On-the-job training takes various forms, self-directed training programs and apprenticeships. Regardless of the specific type, effective OJT programs include the following characteristics:

    1. A policy statement that describes the purpose of OJT and emphasises the company's support for it.
    2. A clear specification of who is accountable for conducting OJT. If managers conduct it, this is mentioned in their job descriptions and it forms part of their performance evaluation.
    3. A thorough review of OJT practices (program content, types of jobs, length of program and cost savings) at other companies in similar industries.
    4. Training managers and peers in the principles of structured OJT.
    5. Availability of lesson plans, checklists, procedure manuals, training manuals, learning contracts and progress report forms for use by employees who conduct OJT.
    6. Evaluation of employees' levels of basic skills (reading, computation and writing) before OJT.[64]

- *Simulations*. This training method represents a 'real-life' situation, with a trainee's decisions resulting in outcomes that mirror what would happen if the trainee were on the job. Simulations, which allow trainees to see the impact of their decisions in an artificial, risk-free environment are used to teach production and process skills as well as management and interpersonal skills.

    Simulators need to have identical elements to those found in the work environment. The simulator needs to respond exactly like the equipment would under the conditions and response given by the trainee. For this reason, simulators are expensive to develop and need constant updating, as new information about the work environment is obtained.

    Simulators replicate the physical equipment that employees use on the job or for educational and training purposes. For example, at Monash Medical Centre in Melbourne, the 'anaesthetic patient simulator' is a state-of-the-art, hands-on simulator that represents the 'real' clinical environment and the patient. A specially instrumented, adult-size, full-body mannequin stands in for the patient, and the trainee can use existing anaesthesia and patient monitoring equipment, without modification, to make up the work environment. There is also a speaker in the mannequin's head to provide it with a 'voice' and a twitch response in one of its thumbs, which will respond appropriately to stimulation. Similar simulators are used in several countries for education, training and research. From basic skills to crisis management, simulator-based learning is increasingly used in many areas of anaesthesia education.[65]

    Simulations are also used to develop managerial skills. Looking Glass® is a simulation designed to develop both teamwork and individual management skills.[66] In this program, participants are assigned different roles in a glass company. On the basis of memos and correspondence, each participant interacts with other members of the management team over the course of six hours. Participants' behaviour and interactions in solving the problems described in correspondence are recorded and evaluated. At the conclusion of the simulation, participants are given feedback regarding their performance.

A recent development in simulations is the use of virtual reality technology. Virtual reality is a computer-based technology that provides trainees with a three-dimensional learning experience. Using specialised equipment or viewing the virtual model on the computer screen, trainees move through the simulated environment and interact with its components.[67] For example, Motorola uses virtual reality in its advanced manufacturing courses for employees learning to run the Pager Robotic Assembly facility. Employees are fitted with a head-mount display that allows them to view the virtual world, which includes the actual laboratory space, robots, tools and the assembly operation. The trainees hear and see the actual sounds and sights as if they were using the 'real' equipment. The equipment responds to the employees' actions (for example, turning on a switch or dial).

- *Business games and case studies*. Business games in which trainees must gather information, analyse it and make decisions, and situations that trainees study and discuss (case studies) are primarily used for management skill development. Games stimulate learning because participants are actively involved and they mimic the competitive nature of business. The types of decisions that participants make in games include all aspects of management practice, including industrial relations (for example, agreement in contract negotiations), marketing (for example, the price to charge for a new product), and finance (for example, financing the purchase of new technology).[68] Documentation on learning from games is anecdotal.[69] Games may give team members a quick start at developing a framework of information and help develop cohesive groups. For some groups (such as senior executives), games may be more meaningful training activities (because the game is realistic) than presentation techniques, such as classroom instruction.

    Case studies may be especially appropriate for developing higher-order intellectual skills such as analysis, synthesis and evaluation. Managers, doctors and other professional employees often require these skills. Cases also help trainees develop the willingness to take risks given uncertain outcomes, based on their analysis of the situation. To use cases effectively, the learning environment must give trainees the opportunity to prepare and discuss their case analyses. Also, face-to-face or electronic communication among trainees must be arranged. Learners must be willing and able to analyse the case and then communicate and defend their positions, because trainee involvement is critical for the effectiveness of the case method.

    There are a number of available sources for pre-existing cases. It is especially important to review pre-existing cases to determine how meaningful they will be to the trainee. Pre-existing cases on a wide variety of problems in business management (for example, human resource management, operations, marketing and advertising) are available from Harvard Business School, Melbourne Business School, McGraw-Hill publishing company and various other sources.

- *Behaviour modelling*. Research suggests that behaviour modelling is one of the most effective techniques for teaching interpersonal skills.[70] Each training session, which typically lasts four hours, focuses on one interpersonal skill, such as coaching or communicating ideas. Each session includes a presentation of the rationale behind the key behaviours, a videotape of a model performing the key behaviours, practice opportunities using role playing, evaluation of a model's performance in the videotape and a planning session devoted to understanding how the key behaviours can be used on the job. In the practice sessions, trainees are provided with feedback regarding how closely their behaviours match the key behaviours demonstrated by the model. The role playing and modelled performance are based on actual incidents in the employment setting in which trainees need to demonstrate success.

- *Interactive video*. This term refers to the combination of the advantages of video and computer-based instruction. Instruction is provided one-on-one to trainees via a monitor connected to a keyboard. Trainees use the keyboard or touch the monitor in order to interact with the program. Interactive video is used to teach technical procedures and interpersonal skills. The training program may be stored on a videodisc or CD-ROM.

- *E-learning*. Electronic learning methods (often referred to as e-learning) include *web-based training*, which refers to training that is delivered on public (internet) or private (intranet) computer networks and displayed by a web browser.[71] Web-based training supports virtual reality, animation, interactions, communications between trainees and 'real-time' audio and video. The sophistication of web-based training varies. The simplest level facilitates communications between trainers and trainees. More complex uses of the internet involve actual delivery of training. At the highest level, the internet (or intranet) is used for both training and storage of intellectual capital, and trainees are actively involved in e-learning. Sound, automation and video are used in e-learning. In addition, for web-based training, trainees are linked to other resources on the web. They are required to share information with other trainees and to deposit knowledge and insights gained from the training (such as potential applications of the training content) in a database that is accessible to other employees. For example, Qantas is using e-learning in its e-university, Qantas College Online. Courses range from management and supervisor development programs to hospitality skills courses. Trainees may choose whether to spend 12 days in a classroom, or spend only one day in the classroom and complete the rest of the course online. The courses use learner-centred simulations, in which trainees are confronted with all sorts of predicaments—for example, what happens if they are on a Melbourne-to-Hawaii flight and discover that the first-class meals have been left behind. Trainees must decide upon the most appropriate and best strategies for informing passengers, handling complaints, dealing with the media and ensuring it never happens again.[72]

Group-building methods

Group-building methods help trainees share ideas and experiences, build group or team identity, understand the dynamics of interpersonal relationships and get to know their own strengths and weaknesses and those of their co-workers. Various training techniques are available to improve workgroup or team performance, to establish a new team and to improve interactions among different teams. All involve examining feelings, perceptions and beliefs about the functioning of the team, discussion, and development of plans to apply what was learned in training to the team's performance in the work setting.

- *Adventure learning*. This method of learning focuses on the development of teamwork and leadership skills by using structured outdoor activities.[73] Adventure learning appears to be best suited for developing skills related to group effectiveness such as self-awareness, problem solving, conflict management and risk taking. Adventure learning may involve strenuous, challenging physical activities such as abseiling or white-water rafting.

  It may also use structured individual and group outdoor activities such as climbing walls, going through rope courses, making *trust falls* (in which each trainee stands on a table and falls backwards into the arms of fellow group members), climbing ladders and travelling from one tower to another using a device attached to a wire (flying fox) that connects the two towers.

For adventure learning programs to be successful, the exercises should be related to the types of skills that participants are expected to develop. Also, after the exercises, a skilled facilitator should lead a discussion about what happened in the exercise, what was learned, how what happened in the exercise relates to the job situation and how to set goals and apply what was learned on the job.[74]

Does adventure learning work? Rigorous evaluations of the impact of adventure learning on productivity and performance have not been conducted. However, participants often report that they gained a greater understanding of themselves and the ways in which they interact with their co-workers. One of the keys to the success of an adventure learning program may be the insistence that whole workgroups participate together so that group dynamics that inhibit effectiveness can emerge and be discussed.

The physically demanding nature of adventure learning and the requirement that trainees often have to touch each other during the exercises may increase the company's risk for negligence claims due to personal injury, intentional infliction of emotional distress and invasion of privacy.[75]

- *Team training.* Training in teams involves coordinating the performances of individuals who work together to achieve a common goal. Such training is an important issue when information must be shared and individuals affect the overall performance of the group. For example, in the military as well as the private sector (such as air force and commercial airlines), much of the work is performed by crews, groups or teams. Successful performance depends on the coordination of individual activities to make decisions, team performance and the readiness to deal with potentially dangerous situations (for example an over-heating nuclear reactor).

    Team training strategies include cross-training and coordination training.[76] *Cross-training* involves team members understanding and practising each other's skills so that members are prepared to step in and take another member's place should that member temporarily or permanently leave the team. Coordination training involves training the team in how to share information and decision-making responsibilities, to maximise team performance. Coordination training is especially important for commercial aviation and surgical teams who are in charge of monitoring different aspects of equipment and the environment, but must share information to make the most effective decision regarding patient care or aircraft safety and performance. *Team leader training* refers to training that the team manager or facilitator receives. This may involve training the manager in resolving conflict within the team or helping the team coordinate activities or other team skills.

    Team training usually involves multiple methods. For example, a lecture or video may be used to disseminate knowledge regarding communication skills to trainees. Role plays or simulations may be used to give trainees the opportunity to put the communication skills emphasised in the lecture into practice. Boeing utilised team training to improve the effectiveness of teams used to design the Boeing 777.[77] At Boeing, 250 teams with eight to 15 members each worked on the design of the aircraft. Team members included engineers with different specialties (for example, design engineers and production engineers), reliability specialists, quality experts and marketing professionals. This type of team is known as a 'concurrent engineering team', because employees from all the business functions (that are needed to design the aircraft) work together at the same time. For concurrent engineering teams to be successful, team members must understand how the process or product they are working on fits with the finished product; because each 777 aircraft contains millions of parts, it is important that they fit together!

Boeing's team training approach began with an extensive orientation for team members. The orientation emphasised how team members were supposed to work together. Following orientation, the teams were given their work assignments. Trainers helped the team work through issues and problems on an as-needed basis. That is, trainers were available to help if the teams requested help. Trainers provided training in communication skills, conflict resolution and leadership.

Research suggests that teams that are effective in training develop procedures to identify and resolve errors, coordinate information gathering and reinforce each other.[78]

- *Action learning*. This type of learning involves giving teams or workgroups an actual problem, having them work on solving it and commit to an action plan, and holding them accountable for carrying out the plan.[79] Typically, action learning involves between six and 30 employees. It may also include customers and vendors. There are several variations on the composition of the group. In one variation, the group includes a single customer for the problem being dealt with. Sometimes the groups include cross-functional team members (that is, members from different company departments) who all have a stake in the problem. Or the group may involve employees from multiple functions who all focus on their own functional problems, each contributing to help solve the problems identified.

    Action learning is a widespread training practice in Europe, but it is not as well known in Australia. Although action learning has not been formally evaluated, the process appears to maximise learning and transfer of training, because it involves 'real-time' problems that employees are facing. Also, action learning can be useful for identifying dysfunctional team dynamics that can get in the way of effective problem solving.

Evaluating training programs

Examining the outcomes of a program helps in evaluating its effectiveness. These outcomes should be related to the program objectives (discussed earlier), which help trainees understand the purpose of the program.

Identification of training outcomes

Training outcomes can be placed into five categories: cognitive outcomes, skill-based outcomes, affective outcomes, results and return on investment.[80]

1 *Cognitive outcomes*. These outcomes are used to determine the degree to which trainees are familiar with principles, facts, techniques, procedures or processes emphasised in the training program. Cognitive outcomes measure what knowledge trainees learned in the program. Typically, paper-and-pencil tests are used to assess cognitive outcomes.
2 *Skill-based outcomes*. Such outcomes are used to assess the level of technical or motor skills and behaviours. They include acquisition or learning of skills (skill learning) and use of skills on the job (skill transfer). The extent to which trainees have learned skills can be evaluated by observing their performance in work situations such as simulators. Skill transfer is usually determined by observation. For example, a resident medical student may perform surgery while the surgeon carefully observes, gives advice and assists as needed. Peers and managers may also be asked to rate trainees' behaviours or skills, based on their observations.

3 *Affective outcomes.* These outcomes include attitudes and motivation. One type of affective outcome is trainees' reactions towards the training program. Reaction outcomes refer to trainees' perceptions of the program, including the facilities, trainers and content. (Reaction outcomes are often referred to as a measure of 'creature comfort'.) This information is typically collected at the program's conclusion. Reactions are useful for identifying what trainees thought was successful and what inhibited learning.

   Reaction outcomes are typically collected via a questionnaire completed by trainees. The questionnaire usually asks questions like the following: 'How satisfied are you with the training program?', 'Did the session meet your personal expectations?' or 'How comfortable did you find the classroom?' Keep in mind that while reactions provide useful information, they usually only weakly relate to learning or transfer of training.

   Other affective outcomes that might be collected in an evaluation include tolerance for diversity, motivation to learn, safety attitudes and customer-service orientation. Affective outcomes can be measured using surveys. The specific attitude of interest depends on the program's objectives. For example, attitudes towards equal employment opportunity laws might be an appropriate outcome to use to evaluate a diversity training program.

4 *Results.* The results outcomes are used to determine the training program's payoff for the company. Examples of results outcomes include reduced costs related to employee turnover or accidents, increased production and improvements in product quality or customer service. For example, to evaluate a program designed to teach delivery truck drivers safe driving practices, Federal Express monitored drivers' accidents and injuries over a 90-day period after they had completed the training program.[81]

5 *Return on investment* (ROI). This term refers to comparing the training's monetary benefits with the cost of the training. Training costs include direct and indirect costs.[82] *Direct costs* include: salaries and benefits for all employees involved in training, including trainees, instructors, consultants and employees who design the program; program material and supplies; equipment or classroom rentals or purchases; and travel costs. *Indirect costs* are not related directly to the design, development or delivery of the training program. They include: general office supplies, facilities, equipment and related expenses; travel and expenses not directly billed to one program; training department management and staff salaries not related to any one program, and administrative and staff support salaries. Benefits refer to the value the company gains from the training program.

Chapter 18 Evaluating and improving the human resource function, shows a detailed example of training evaluation designs and methods to determine the costs, benefits and return on investment from a training program.

Which training outcomes measure is best? The answer depends on the training objectives. For example, if the instructional objectives identified business-related outcomes—such as increased customer service or product quality—then results outcomes should be included in the evaluation. Both reactive and cognitive outcomes are usually collected before the trainees leave the training site. As a result, these measures do not help determine the extent to which trainees actually use the training content in their jobs (transfer of training). Skill-based, affective and results outcomes that are measured following training can be used to determine transfer of training—that is, the extent to which training has resulted in a change in behaviours, skills or attitudes, or has directly influenced objective measures that are related to company effectiveness (for example, sales).

Reasons for evaluating training

Many companies are beginning to invest millions of dollars in training programs to help gain a competitive advantage. Firms with high-leverage training practices not only invest large sums of money into developing and administering training programs but they also evaluate training programs. Why should training programs be evaluated? Several reasons include:

1. Identifying the program's strengths and weaknesses. This includes determining whether the program is meeting the learning objectives, the quality of the learning environment and whether transfer of training to the job is occurring.
2. Assessing whether the content, organisation and administration of the program (including the schedule, accommodation, trainers and materials) contribute to learning and the use of training content on the job.
3. Identifying which trainees benefited the most or least from the program.
4. Gathering data to assist in marketing programs through collecting information from participants about whether they would recommend the program to others, why they attended the program and their level of satisfaction with the program.
5. Determining the financial benefits and costs of the program.
6. Comparing the costs and benefits of training versus non-training investments (such as work redesign or a better employee selection system).
7. Comparing the costs and benefits of different training programs to choose the best program.

Evaluation designs

A number of different evaluation designs can be applied to training programs.

1. *Pre-test/post-test with comparison group*. In this method, a group of employees who receive training and a group who do not are compared. Outcome measures are collected from both groups before and after training. If improvement is greater for the training group than the comparison group, this provides evidence that training is responsible for the change.
2. *Pre-test/post-test*. This method is similar to the 'pre-test/post-test comparison group' design but it has one major difference: no comparison group is used. The lack of a comparison group makes it difficult to rule out the effects of business conditions or other factors as explanations for changes. This design is often used by companies that want to evaluate a training program but are uncomfortable with excluding certain employees, or only intend to train a small group of employees.
3. *Post-test only*. In this method, only training outcomes are collected. This design can be strengthened by adding a comparison group (which helps to rule out alternative explanations for changes). The post-test-only design is appropriate when trainees (and the comparison group, if one is used) can be expected to have similar levels of knowledge, behaviour or results outcomes (for example, same number of sales, and equal awareness of how to close a sale) prior to training.
4. *Time series*. In the time-series method, training outcomes are collected at periodic intervals before and after training. (In the other evaluation designs we have discussed, training outcomes are collected once each, before and after training.) A comparison group can also be used with a time-series design. One advantage of the time-series design is that it allows an analysis of the stability of training outcomes over time. This type of design is frequently used to evaluate training programs that focus on improving readily observable outcomes (such as accident rates, productivity and absenteeism) that vary over time. For example, a time-series design was used to evaluate the extent to which a training program helped improve the number of safe work behaviours in a food-manufacturing plant.[83] Observations of

safe work behaviour were made over a 25-week period. Training that was directed at increasing the number of safe behaviours was introduced after approximately five weeks. The number of safe acts observed varied across the observation period. However, the number of safe behaviours increased after the training program was conducted and remained stable throughout the observation period.

There is no one appropriate evaluation design. Several factors need to be considered in choosing an evaluation design:[84]

1. size of the training program
2. purpose of training
3. implications if a training program does not work
4. company 'norms' regarding evaluation
5. costs of designing and conducting an evaluation
6. need for speed in obtaining program effectiveness information.

For example, if a manager is interested in determining how much employees' communications skills have changed as a result of participating in a behaviour modelling training program, a pre-test/post-test comparison group design is necessary. Trainees should be randomly assigned to training and no-training conditions. These evaluation design features give the manager a high degree of confidence that any communication skill change is the result of participating in the training program.[85] This type of evaluation design is also necessary if the manager wants to compare the effectiveness of two training programs.

Evaluation designs without pre-testing or comparison groups are most appropriate in situations where the manager is interested in identifying whether a specific level of performance has been achieved (for example, can employees who participated in behaviour-modelling training adequately communicate their ideas?). In this situation the manager is not interested in determining how much change has occurred.

Determining return on investment

Cost–benefit analysis is the process of determining the economic benefits of a training program using accounting methods. Determining the economic benefits of training involves determining training costs and benefits. This is discussed in more detail in Chapter 18. As discussed in the 'Managing challenges through sustainability: Ongoing ROI struggles of L&D' case, many organisations are struggling with the challenge of showing the business impact of their learning and development investment.

Socialisation and orientation

Organisational socialisation is the process by which new employees are transformed into effective members of the company. 'Effective socialisation' involves being prepared to perform the job well, learning about the organisation and establishing work relationships. 'Socialisation' involves three phases: anticipatory socialisation, encounter and settling in.[86]

Organisational socialisation
the process by which new employees are transformed into effective members of a company.

Anticipatory socialisation

Anticipatory socialisation occurs before the individual joins the company. Through anticipatory socialisation, expectations about the company, job, working conditions and interpersonal relationships are developed. These expectations are developed through interactions with representatives of the company (for example, recruiters, prospective peers and managers) during the recruitment and selection process. The expectations are also based on prior work experiences in similar jobs.

Anticipatory socialisation
socialisation that occurs before an individual joins a company. Includes expectations about the company, job, working conditions and interpersonal relationships.

ONGOING ROI STRUGGLES OF L&D

MANAGING CHALLENGES THROUGH SUSTAINABILITY

While the biggest challenge for learning and development managers is to prove the business impact of their learning organisations to senior management, only a small number of learning organisations are delivering measurable value in terms of productivity gains, revenue growth, net income growth and overall industry recognition.

A survey of learning executives at 285 cross-industry organisations in the Unites States found that while chief learning officers (CLOs) are increasingly being measured in terms of the business impact of their learning organisations, this is not being done in terms that can be translated into meaningful business metrics, such as increased revenues or decreased employee turnover and costs.

Sponsored by Accenture Learning, the report also found that only 2 per cent of CLOs are measured on how successfully they align the learning function to corporate strategic goals.

However, a small number of learning organisations are providing measurable business impact to their companies by excelling at certain key capabilities: aligning learning initiatives to business goals; measuring overall business impact of the learning function; extending learning to customers, suppliers and business partners; supporting their organisations' most critical competencies and jobs; integrating learning with functions such as knowledge and talent management; using technology to deliver learning; and delivering leadership development courses.

According to the report, these high performance organisations, representing approximately 10 per cent of the organisations surveyed, exceeded their peers in productivity (as measured by sales per employee), which was 27 per cent greater than their competitors'; revenue growth (40 per cent higher); and net income growth (50 per cent higher).

'These high performance learning organisations contribute to the overall performance of their enterprises, finding distinctive ways to do more with less and ensuring that those in control of budgets understand the value that their learning organisation is producing', said Hap Brakeley, president of Accenture Learning.

In addition, the report found that these leading organisations manage the learning department as a business, aligned to the organisation's business goals. The vast majority (88 per cent) of the leaders identified 'the business of the company' as a critical competency for learning executives, compared with 72 per cent of other respondents.

Source: Based on 2004, 'Ongoing ROI struggles of L&D', *Human Resources,* 29 November. www.humanresourcesmagazine.com.au

---

Potential employees need to be provided with realistic job information. A realistic job preview provides accurate information about the attractive and unattractive aspects of the job, work conditions, company and location, in order to ensure that employees develop appropriate expectations. This information needs to be provided early in the recruiting and selection process. It is usually given in brochures, in videos or by the company recruiter during an interview. Although research specifically investigating the influence of realistic job previews on employee turnover is weak and inconsistent, we do know that unmet expectations resulting from the recruitment and selection process have been shown to relate to dissatisfaction and turnover.[87] As we will see, employees' expectations about a job and a company may be formed by interactions with managers, peers and recruiters, rather than from specific messages about the job.

Encounter

The encounter phase occurs when an employee begins a new job. No matter how realistic the information was that they were provided with during interviews and site visits, individuals beginning new jobs will experience shock and surprise.[88] Employees need to become familiar with job tasks, receive appropriate training and understand company practices and procedures.

Challenging work plus cooperative and helpful managers and peers have been shown to enhance employees' learning of a new job.[89] New employees view managers as an important source of information about their job and the company. Research evidence suggests that the nature and quality of the new employee's relationship with the manager has a significant impact on socialisation.[90] In fact, the negative effects of unmet expectations can be reduced by the new employee having a high quality relationship with his or her manager! Managers can help create a high quality work relationship by helping the new employee understand his or her role; by providing information about the company; and by being understanding regarding the stresses and issues that the new employee is experiencing.

Settling in

In the settling-in phase, employees begin to feel comfortable with their job demands and social relationships. They begin to work on resolving work conflicts (for example, too much work to do and conflicting demands of the job) and conflicts between work and non-work activities. Employees are interested in the company's evaluation of their performance and in learning about potential career opportunities within the company.

Employees need to complete all three phases of the socialisation process to contribute to the company fully. For example, employees who do not feel that they have established good working relationships with co-workers will likely spend time and energy worrying about relationships with other employees rather than being concerned with product development or customer service. Employees who experience successful socialisation are more motivated, more committed to the company and more satisfied with their jobs.[91]

Orientation programs play an important role in socialising employees. Orientation involves familiarising new employees with company rules, policies and procedures. Table 11.11 overleaf shows the content of orientation programs. Typically, a program includes information about the company, the department in which the employee will be working and the workplace community.

While the content of orientation programs is important, the process of orientation cannot be ignored. Too often, orientation programs consist of completing payroll forms and reviewing personnel policies with managers or human resource representatives. The new employee is a passive recipient of information. New employees have little opportunity to ask questions or interact with peers and their managers.

Effective orientation programs include active involvement of the new employee. Table 11.12 overleaf shows the characteristics of effective orientation programs. An important characteristic of effective orientation programs is that peers, managers and senior co-workers are actively involved in helping new employees adjust to the workgroup.[92]

Training and pay systems

Training is increasingly being linked to employees' compensation through the use of skill-based pay systems. (The characteristics of skill-based pay systems are discussed in detail in Chapter 13 Managing compensation.) In skill-based pay systems, employees' pay is based primarily on the knowledge and skills they possess, rather than the knowledge and skills necessary to successfully perform their current job.

Skill-based pay systems have several implications for training systems. Since pay is directly tied to the amount of knowledge and skills that employees have obtained, they will be motivated to attend training programs. This means that the volume of training conducted, as well as the training costs, will increase. Skill-based pay systems require continual evaluation of employees' skills and knowledge to ensure that employees are competent in the skills acquired in training programs.

TABLE 11.11 — Content of orientation programs

1 Company-level information:
- Company overview (for example, values, history and mission)
- Key policies and procedures
- Compensation
- Employee benefits and services
- Safety and accident prevention
- Employee and union relations
- Physical facilities
- Economic factors
- Customer relations

2 Department-level information:
- Department functions and philosophy
- Job duties and responsibilities
- Policies, procedures, rules and regulations
- Performance expectations
- Tour of department
- Introduction to department employees

3 Miscellaneous:
- Community
- Housing
- Family adjustment

Source: J.L. Schwarz & M.A. Weslowski, 1995, 'Employee orientation: what employers should know', *Journal of Contemporary Business Issues*, no. 3, Fall, p. 48.

TABLE 11.12 — Characteristics of effective orientation programs

- Employees are encouraged to ask questions.
- Program includes information on both technical and social aspects of the job.
- Orientation is the responsibility of the new employee's manager.
- Avoid debasement and embarrassment of new employees.
- Formal and informal interactions with managers and peers occur.
- Programs involve relocation assistance (for example, house hunting, information session on the community for employees and their spouses).
- Employees are provided with information about the company's products, services and customers.

INDUCTION UNLOCKS RETENTION WOES

MANAGING CHALLENGES THROUGH ATTRACTING AND RETAINING PEOPLE

Getting the induction process right might seem like a big investment at the time, but with the skills shortage intensifying it's simply too big a risk for an employer to ignore, warns Chandler Macleod Recruitment Solutions GM Lorraine Christopher. 'Employers can get the job description right and get a person on board, but then not enough thought goes into induction', Christopher told HR Report. 'The cost of losing an employee in their first year of employment is estimated at three times their annual salary, plus hire costs of 25 per cent to 30 per cent. For an employee on $50 000, that's a $165 000 loss. If you multiply that by the number of staff you lost last year the figures are alarming.' Surveys by Recruitment Solutions show organisations with solid induction processes in place had a turnover that was 'next to zero' in the first 90 days, Christopher said. That compares to 47 per cent of staff turnover that occurs when there is no formal 'on-boarding' process. 'What's shocking is that there is no line on a balance sheet that indicates the high cost of turnover', Christopher said. 'Where this process has been taken seriously, organisations that had turnover of 30 per cent or higher have reduced it to 20 per cent over a 12-month period. In an organisation of 400 to 500 people that's an extraordinary saving.' Christopher stressed that these types of initiatives have to be driven from the boardroom. 'As less and less people are available in the market place, organisations that aren't clear about their employee value proposition (EVP) and hiring processes will have difficulty meeting their business objectives', she said. While it can take days to develop a business strategy and budgets, aligning a HR strategy to achieve it is almost an afterthought, Christopher said. 'But where are the gaps and what do we need to do to fill them? It's your intellectual capital and what you do to retain them that will keep you ahead of your competitors,' Christopher said.

Key techniques for ensuring employee satisfaction and long-term commitment should start at the beginning of the recruitment process, advises Christopher. 'How you describe the job and your culture is very important', Christopher told *HR Report*. 'Is it accurate? A lot of companies have trouble describing their culture. You also need to have very clear performance indicators, a clear profile of the person required for the role and honest communication throughout the interview.'

Once on board, a creative and structured induction process should include:

- A session on corporate values and history.
- An overview of the CEO's strategy and financial goals.
- A meet-and-greet session with senior managers.
- An explanation and example of a performance review.
- A tailored coaching and mentoring program.
- Skills development and training.
- Regular two-way feedback to assess progress.

'You're appealing to different types of people and you need all of them in an organisation', Christopher said. 'What are their motivations? What makes them feel comfortable and productive in their workplace? You need to look at individual needs, it's not a blanket approach.' A couple of the major banks and oil companies were getting it right, Christopher said. 'Advertising by the banks has changed', Christopher said. 'They're using a different philosophy that focuses on what's in it for the people considering joining the company. They understand the need for balancing work with lifestyle and are attracting working mothers by subsidising childcare.'

Source: 2006, *HR Report*, Issue 376, 23 August.

PART 3   Developing People

MANAGING PEOPLE

LEARNING AND DEVELOPMENT AT OPSM

OPSM has undergone change of almost biblical proportions in the last three and a half years. The cornerstone of this corporate change has been its learning and development (L&D) driven people strategy which provides meaningful career development for employees with high potential.

At the beginning of this century, OPSM's corporate culture 'was like the 1960s', according to Chris Georgiou, group general manager human resources.

The beginning of rapid change in the organisation commenced in 2001, as the once conservative, publicly-listed company went into an aggressive acquisition phase.

With this rapid change came the need to change the culture of the organisation. 'We were losing market share and although customers appreciated the warm patient care culture that prevailed, market research showed us that they wanted a positive fashion experience as well', Georgiou explains. 'The culture did not encourage anyone to challenge poor performance. We were failing to meet the full retail needs of our customers.'

In 2001, the board appointed Jonathon Pinshaw, a new CEO with a strong people focus, and a management shake-up ensued. Georgiou describes the HR challenge as starting with a virtual blank slate. A new OPSM brand was launched in new stores, and the balance between patient care and meeting customers' retail needs had to be struck. 'We needed tools to facilitate and accelerate cultural change, fully supported by the CEO and his leadership team', he says.

Laying the foundations

The first thing Georgiou did was to hire Cheryl Walters, the current group L&D manager. She now oversees a team of eight people, who focus on operational training as well as the implementation of the cultural strategies. Before developing a high potential program, they set about laying the foundations. Walter says, 'There was no succession planning and no talent identification processes in place, so the first thing we did was introduce these processes back in July 2001.' She says that they started with a management feedback tool that was used on managers in senior and critical positions in the organisation.

Both Walters and Georgiou had experience with the feedback tool in other organisations. Walters describes the feedback tool as 'a simple to use, yet powerful program that lets people understand the areas they need to develop and how to build on strengths'.

High potentials

The next layer of career development was the introduction of a training program that provided managers with tools to address development gaps identified through the feedback tool. A group of 15 people from the leadership team were identified as 'high potentials' and they embarked on a 12-month leadership development program.

As part of the program, the 15 participants were given two business problems to solve. These problems were selected in consultation with OPSM's CEO and Georgiou. Using what they learned from the program, the participants had to solve the twin challenges of how OPSM should respond to new entrants in the market and how the organisation should retain its leadership talent. 'We have seen quantum leaps in performance and results in the business as a direct result', says Georgiou.

Once this first program is completed, the graduates will be involved in special projects and mentoring programs and take an active role in creating a high performance environment at OPSM.

Challenges

Building the first level of management development with the feedback program also presented various problems. Walters explains that current leadership behaviours had to be exposed, and once awareness was raised, a high performance career program could be introduced. 'Almost all managers rose to the challenge, but a few left the organisation. The result is that we now have a committed team of leaders embracing new learning and challenges', Walters affirms.

Stakeholders and ROI

The key stakeholders for the career development initiatives at OPSM were the leadership team, the CEO and the board of directors. 'Nothing ever went to the board without first getting 100 per cent commitment from the entire senior leadership team', Georgiou asserts. Although the board was characterised as conservative, he says that it understood the value of people initiatives.

'We've never had a request from the senior leadership team to justify the costs or present return on investment information on our career development initiatives because they were fully integrated with the overall business strategy. They made good business sense. We were required to help improve the culture and we measure this through our employee opinion surveys. I don't think it's possible to demonstrate the value of a single program, in any case', Georgiou points out.

Career development program advice

When asked what advice he would give to other HR professionals looking to set up a career development program, Georgiou strongly advises practitioners not to do it. 'Look at what your organisational strategy is and develop a people strategy that's integrated with it. Don't start with the career development program', he cautions.

View from the top

Chief operating officer Chris Beer has been with OPSM for 20 years. He characterises OPSM's previous corporate culture, board and management team as 'conservative, but very caring'. Despite this, some of the businesses it bought were much more staid and conservative and viewed OPSM as 'the enemy'. The acquisitions were run as three separate businesses until just 12 months ago. 'We brought three brands together under one shared service and these parts of the business entered a new phase of enlightenment. Parochialism disappeared, people were empowered and this calendar year has seen phenomenal improvement in results', Beer enthuses.

Beer is highly optimistic that OPSM will be able to retain its identified high-potential employees while it is working on identifying their next career moves within the business.

Source: Based on T. Russell, 2004, '20/20 vision: L&D OPSM style', *Human Resources*, 20 September, www.humanresourcesmagazine.com.au

QUESTIONS

1. Identify and discuss the main features of OPSM's learning and development approach.
2. What are some of the barriers to winning support for such programs in organisations?

CHAPTER SUMMARY

Many companies are using new technology to give employees control of their learning and career development. Technological innovations, new product markets and a diverse workforce have increased the need for companies to re-examine how their training practices contribute to learning. In this chapter, we discussed a systematic approach to training, including: needs assessment, design of the learning environment, consideration of employee readiness for training and transfer of-training issues. We reviewed numerous training methods and stressed that the key to successful training is to choose a method that best accomplishes the objectives of training. We also emphasised how training can contribute to effectiveness through establishing a link with the company's strategic direction and demonstrating return on investment (also see Chapter 18 Evaluating and improving the human resource function).

WEB EXERCISES

The national vocational training system is coordinated through the federal Department of Education Science and Training. The department's website www.dest.gov.au houses the National Training Information Service. This database contains all the details of the 80 or so Training Packages that contain the competency standards and qualifications for most occupations in Australia. The database also contains information on all the Registered Training Organisations that deliver nationally recognised training. Go to the website and browse through the national training system.

PART 3 Developing People

DISCUSSION QUESTIONS

1. Assume you are general manager of a small hotel. Most training is unstructured and occurs on the job. Currently, the more senior employees are responsible for teaching new employees how to perform the job. Your company has been profitable, but recently customers have been complaining about the poor quality of service, particularly in the restaurant and in housekeeping. You have decided to change the OJT provided to restaurant and housekeeping staff. How will you modify the OJT to improve the quality of the services provided to customers?

2. A training needs analysis indicates that managers' productivity is inhibited because they are reluctant to delegate tasks to their subordinates. Suppose you had to decide between using adventure learning and interactive video for your training program. What are the strengths and weaknesses of each technique? Which would you choose? Why? What factors would influence your decision?

3. To improve product quality, a company is introducing a computer-assisted manufacturing process into one of its assembly plants. The new technology is likely to result in substantial modification of jobs. Employees will also be required to learn statistical process control techniques. The new technology and push for quality will require employees to attend numerous training sessions. More than 50 per cent of the employees who will be affected by the new technology completed their formal education over 10 years ago. How should management maximise employees' readiness for training?

4. How could assessment be used to create a productive work team?

CASE STUDY

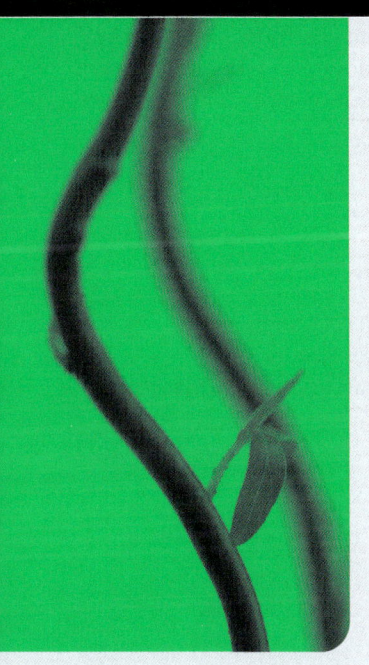

PURSUING THE INTELLIGENT ENTERPRISE

Enterprise learning is fast being recognised as a popular and cost-effective means of developing an organisation's workforce.

Five years ago, St. George Bank was investing approximately 2 per cent of its salary budget (equating to $13 million per year) in staff development. Training was generally restricted to entry-level induction. Only two of the bank's seven business divisions operated formal training programs. Incredibly, a complex web of 770 external training organisations were on St. George Bank's payroll.

Some may say that, back then, the bank's approach to learning and development was decentralised, inconsistent and hugely inefficient.

In 2000, Colin Pitt was appointed head of the bank's Corporate Performance Centre (CPC). Two of his immediate priorities were the rationalisation of St. George's outsourced training providers (using a competitive tender to reduce the 770 external training organisations to 30) and the development of an online learning strategy. The driver at the time was cost reduction, and the initial imperative was to halve training costs.

A learning management system (LMS) was selected in early 2001, christened 'e-luminate' and was operational by the end of that year.

A few years on, St. George boasts one of the most admired HR teams in the country and is generating enviable results in the learning and development arena. Colin Pitt reports that the bank has realised a 20-fold increase in training output with 25 per cent less cost. For St. George, the bottom-line saving is about $3 million annually.

According to Bob Spence, the bank's manager of learning design and delivery, the success of the enterprise learning strategy is due to the close relationship the CPC enjoys with the business. This intimacy ensures all learning programs are relevant and meet the needs of the stakeholders.

'We have people who are operating, in essence, as relationship managers for the CPC. They work within the business day-by-day, understanding what the business requirements actually are and then bringing back to the CPC recommendations for various interventions to overcome problems and meet their demands—whether they're training demands or some other sort of HR requirement', says Spence.

St. George has resisted the urge to extract the largest possible cost savings from its enterprise learning strategy. Its approach does not revolve around e-learning or the learning management system. Instead, it has opted for a blended model, although this model does not achieve as dramatic a saving as pure e-learning.

Systems training and lending courses are conducted in conventional classrooms, along with St. George's induction program, which (for customer service staff) runs for a full four weeks.

Conversely, the bank's management development program takes nine months to complete and consists of three components: around 25 hours of online content, followed by four one-day workshops and then consolidation of learning through on-the-job as well as individual and group projects.

'We also have other courses where online learning is completed prior to coming into the classroom. The whole idea of that is to make sure everyone is up to speed so the cost of getting people together in the classroom is more effective. We can jump in and do case studies or role plays and make use of the group dynamics, as opposed to wasting time on tutorial type activities', Spence explains.

Finally, there are courses that are 100 per cent online, such as the *Financial Services Reform Act* (FSRA) compliance training. Around 20 per cent of St. George's total training is compliance-based.

The bank commenced FSRA compliance training in September 2003, only six months out from the March 2004 deadline. Using the learning management system, it delivered more than 100 000 courses at a completion rate of up to 18 000 courses per month. The curriculum was determined by each employee's role within the bank, but it contained an average of 11 courses.

The cost of delivering the FSRA compliance training electronically was only 10 to 15 per cent of the cost of conventional training. This one program easily paid for the entire learning management system.

'The return on investment was easy to measure because we knew the precise cost of developing and deploying the program online. The bank is very satisfied with the system and the progress we've made', Spence says.

The CPC has many more projects on its to-do list, including extending training to its brokers and agents network. The bank is also building a new training centre that will include 10 classrooms and a sophisticated telephone simulation facility. Virtual classrooms are another technology that Spence would like to investigate over the next 12 months.

'We're continually looking at new and improved ways of introducing innovation into the courses we run, and introducing technology into the classroom. There's a real thirst in our organisation to innovate and it's certainly very clear within the Corporate Performance Centre why we need to do that', Spence says.

Source: Based on J. Burns, 2004, 'Pursuing the intelligent enterprise', *Human Resources*, 21 November, pp. 16–17, www.humanresourcesmagazine.com.au

QUESTIONS

1 Identify and discuss the main features of the learning and development approaches at St George Bank.
2 In what ways can HR professionals win support for such programs in organisations?

CHAPTER 12

EMPLOYEE DEVELOPMENT AND CAREER MANAGEMENT

Objectives

After reading this chapter, you should be able to:

1 Discuss current trends in using formal education for learning and development.

2 Explain how assessment of personality types, work behaviours and job performances can be used for employees' learning and development.

3 Explain important concepts in career management.

4 Develop successful mentoring programs.

5 Explain how job experiences can be used for skills development.

6 Explain how to help managers coach employees.

7 Discuss the steps in the career management system.

8 Discuss what companies are doing for management development issues, including succession planning and helping dysfunctional managers.

Teach the staff to stay

MANY organisations now believe that offering abundant training and career development opportunities is the key to attracting and retaining ambitious and often impatient graduates and young professionals. One organisation, however, believes it's not just generation Y that laps up training opportunities and welcomes a challenge.

Not-for-profit community agency MECWA has found that since it adopted a more strategic approach to learning and development about two years ago, staff of all ages and levels have embraced expanded opportunities to learn and take on new work. As well, the return for the organisation has extended well beyond a drop in staff turnover.

Last month, MECWA, which employs 750 paid staff and 450 volunteers, was named winner of the Employer Achievement in Creating a Learning Culture award at the 2006 community services and health industry training awards.

Now in its 46th year, MECWA provides housekeeping, personal care and nursing care in the home; community housing and nursing home accommodation; activity programs; life skills training and meals on wheels to more than 5000 elderly and disabled people in Melbourne and the Mornington Peninsula.

MECWA's manager of learning and development, Trish Gerritsen, who has driven the changes, joined nearly three years ago when the chief executive and board decided staff development must become a top priority. Ms Gerritsen holds a masters of professional education and training and moved from training manager at Victoria's Court Network.

Her first challenge was to devise a learning and development program for the demographics of the organisation. More than 90 per cent of MECWA staff are women, 50 per cent are aged over 50 and most are either permanent part-timers or casuals, with many working weekends and shiftwork.

After a year of consultations and a needs analysis, Ms Gerritsen produced a multifaceted and co-ordinated framework called the Support Through Education Program, known as the STEP program.

The program includes New STEP, a comprehensive orientation program; STEP Ahead, an in-house training program; STEP Up, which pays staff to gain qualifications through external training programs; STEP Together, a peer support program: Safe STEP, where trained staff mentor and assess their peers in safe work practices; and Wise STEP which includes a resource library, newsletter and handbooks.

'One of my main aims when I came here was that people would be participants in learning rather than just recipients of learning', Ms Gerritsen says. 'So one of the first things we did was with our first-aid training. We brought that in-house and we used skilled nurses within the organisation to be the first-aid trainers. We have an agreement with Swinburne Hawthorn and we got them (selected MECWA nurses) to do Level II First-Aid, Level III First-Aid and Certificate IV in workplace training and assessment training, so they became licensed to teach first-aid. So they got a certificate from Swinburne and we gave them a professional development opportunity.'

She says another part of the STEP program which has proved particularly successful has been the STEP Up program, which has resulted in staff winning promotions and having greater mobility within the organisation. 'All we had when I started was a couple of CPR classes and a couple of food-handling classes.'

'We did train people in the Certificate II in Aged Care but we had a very big attrition rate.'

'I changed the traineeships so they were a dual qualification. First I got an RTO (registered training organisation) to run a combined Certificate III in Aged Care and Certificate III in Home Care so people would walk away with two qualifications. And when that was such a big success, I organised a triple qualification. So by doing extra units staff walked out with a Certificate III in Aged Care, a Certificate III

Teach the staff to stay *continued*

in Home Care and a Certificate III in disability. We were one of the first to do that in Victoria.'

It was a move that has given staff the option of moving from working in home care to residential care, which is better paid and less isolating for some workers.

The take-up rate for the certificate programs has been encouragingly high. More than 130 staff have gained qualifications and a further 58 employees are undertaking certificate courses.

Ms Gerritsen says teaming up with training organisations specialising in aged care and disability and building relationships with such RTOs over time has led to the drop-out rates in such courses falling to almost zero. 'For many people these are the first qualifications they are getting, so we have picked the RTOs to run these programs that will really nurture them ... For some people it is quite daunting if they haven't been to school for, say, 30 years', she says.

HR Manager Anna Pannuzzo says that while learning and development is separate to HR, the STEP program complements MECWA's other initiatives aimed at becoming an employer of choice.

The investment in staff development is being reflected in many HR statistics, including Workcover statistics. MECWA's Workcover claims halved between 2002–03 and last financial year, the days lost due to Workcover injuries were slashed by 75 per cent, while the average cost per claim has been reduced 75 per cent.

Source: W. Taylor, 2006, Teach the staff to stay. *The Age*, 19 August, p. 11. © 2006 Copyright John Fairfax Holdings Limited. www.theage.com.au

Introduction

As the preceding case study illustrates, and as discussed in Chapter 11, learning and development activities are a key component of a company's human resource management efforts. Traditionally, more strategic types of development have been provided to management level employees, while line employees have received training designed to improve a specific set of skills needed for their current job. However, with the greater use of work teams and increased involvement of employees in all aspects of business, development is becoming more important for all employees. Why? Learning and development is a necessary component of a company's efforts to improve quality, to meet the challenges of global competition and social change, and to incorporate technological advances and changes in work design. Increased globalisation of product markets compels companies to help their employees understand cultures and customs that affect business practices. Employees need to develop a broader range of technical and interpersonal skills, because more of an employee's responsibilities are organised on a project or customer basis (rather than on a functional basis), and because of an increased use of work teams. Employees must also be able to perform roles that are traditionally reserved for managers. Legislation, labour market forces and company social responsibility dictate that employers provide women and minority groups with access to learning and development activities that will prepare them for managerial positions. The emphasis placed on both training, and learning and development has increased because companies (and their employees) must constantly learn and change

Employee Development and Career Management CHAPTER 12

to meet customer needs and compete in new markets. For many employees, taking the next career step and moving to a new job can present many challenges. To deal with such challenges, employees across a wide variety of industries and occupations will benefit from personal development and life-long learning. Despite the necessity of learning and development, it is recognised that the pressures of globalisation and competition have negative implications in many workplaces, leading to a changing workplace culture, with declining levels of loyalty and greater individualisation of workers. Any employee's learning and development, and indeed career development, needs to be understood in the context of an increasingly confronting picture.

We begin this chapter by discussing the relationship between learning and development, and careers. While Chapter 11 examined areas such as vocational education and training, we look at development approaches including formal education, assessment, job experiences and interpersonal relationships. We emphasise the types of skills, knowledge and behaviours that are strengthened by each development method. Choosing a development approach is one part of the career management system. Before one or multiple developmental approaches are used, the employee and the company must have an idea of the employee's development needs and the purpose of development. Identifying the needs for and purposes of development is another important part of the career management system. Then, an overview of the steps of the career management system is provided. Employee and company responsibilities at each step of the system are emphasised. We conclude with a discussion of special issues including succession planning and dealing with managers who exhibit dysfunctional behaviours in the workplace.

The relationship between learning and development, and careers

Learning and development

Learning and development (also employee development) refers to the acquisition of knowledge, skills and behaviours that improve an employee's ability to meet changes in job requirements and in client and customer demands. Formal education, job experiences, relationships, and assessment of personality and abilities help employees to prepare for the future. Learning and development are future-oriented; thus, the concept involves learning that is not necessarily related to the employee's current job.[1] As discussed in Chapter 11, traditionally, training is focused on helping employees' performance in their current jobs. Learning and development helps prepare them for other positions in the company and increases their ability to move into jobs that may not yet exist.[2] Learning and development also helps employees prepare for changes in their current job that may result from new technology, work designs, new customers, or new-product markets. In Chapter 11, we emphasised the strategic role of training. It is important to note that as training continues to become more strategic (that is, related to business goals), the distinction between training, and learning and development will blur.

Learning and development
(also employee development) the acquisition of knowledge, skills and behaviours that improve an employee's ability to meet changes in job requirements and in client and customer demands.

Development and careers

Traditionally, careers have been described in various ways.[3] Careers have been described as a sequence of positions held within an occupation. For example, a university faculty member can hold assistant, associate and full professor positions. A career has also been

Careers
a sequence of positions held within an occupation.

447

PART 3   Developing People

described in the context of mobility within an organisation. For example, an engineer may begin her career as a staff engineer. As her expertise, experience and performance increase, she may move through advisory engineering, senior engineering and senior technical positions.[4] Finally, a career has been described as a characteristic of the employee. Each employee's career consists of different jobs, positions and experiences.

The new concept of the career is often referred to as a protean career.[5] A **protean career** is a career that is frequently changing due to both changes in the person's interests, abilities and values, and changes in the work environment. Compared to the traditional career, employees here take major responsibility for managing their careers. For example, an engineering employee may decide to take a sabbatical from his engineering position to work in management for a year. The purpose of this assignment could be to develop his managerial skills as well as help him personally evaluate if he likes managerial work more than engineering.

> **Protean career**
> a career that is frequently changing due to both changes in the person's interests, abilities and values, and changes in the work environment.

Changes in the psychological contract between employees and companies have influenced the development of the protean career.[6] A **psychological contract** is the expectations that employers and employees have about each other. Traditionally, the psychological contract emphasised that the company would provide continued employment (job security) and advancement opportunities if the employee remained with the company and maintained a high level of job performance. Pay increases and status were linked directly to vertical movement in the company (that is, promotions).

> **Psychological contract**
> the expectations that employers and employees have about each other.

The protean career has several implications for employee development. The goal of the new career is psychological success. **Psychological success** is the feeling of pride and accomplishment that comes from achieving life goals that are not limited to achievements at work (for example, raising a family and good physical health). Psychological success is controlled by the employee—in contrast to traditional career goals, which were not only influenced by employee effort, but were controlled by the availability of positions in the company. Psychological success is self-determined rather than solely determined through signals the employee receives from the company (for example, salary increases and promotions). Psychological success appears to be especially prevalent among the groups of people in their twenties and those entering the workforce. These groups, often called generation X and generation Y, are often unimpressed with status symbols—they want flexibility in doing job tasks and they desire meaning from their work.[7]

> **Psychological success**
> the feeling of pride and accomplishment that comes from achieving life goals.

Employees need to develop new skills rather than rely on a static knowledge base. This has resulted from companies' need to be more responsive to customers' service and product demands. The types of knowledge that an employee needs to be successful have changed.[8] In the traditional career, *knowing how* (having the appropriate skills and knowledge to provide a service or produce a product) was critical. Although knowing how remains important, employees need to 'know why' and 'know whom'. *Knowing why* refers to understanding the company's business and culture so that the employee can develop and apply knowledge and skills that can contribute to the business. *Knowing whom* refers to relationships that the employee may develop in order to contribute to the company's success. These relationships may include networking with vendors, suppliers, community members, customers or industry experts. Learning to 'know whom' and to 'know why' requires more than formal courses and training programs. Learning and development in the protean career are increasingly likely to involve relationships and job experiences, rather than formal courses. The emphasis on continuous learning as well as changes in the psychological contract are altering the direction and frequency of movement within careers—*career pattern*.[9] As discussed in Chapter 11, learning should be carried out as part of an overall framework or systematic approach to learning and development.

448

Traditional career patterns consisted of a series of steps arranged in a linear hierarchy, with higher steps in the hierarchy related to increased authority, responsibility and compensation. Expert career patterns involve a life-long commitment to a field or specialisation (for example, law, medicine and management). These types of career patterns will not disappear. Rather, career patterns involving movement across specialisations or disciplines (a spiral career pattern) will become more prevalent. Thus, companies that want to develop employees (as well as employees who want to take control of their own careers) will need to provide their employees with the opportunity to: (1) determine their interests, skill strengths and weaknesses; and (2) based on this information, seek out appropriate development experiences that will likely involve job experiences and relationships, as well as formal courses.

The most appropriate view of a career is that it is 'boundaryless'.[10] It may include movement across several employers or different occupations. A career may also involve identifying more with a job or profession, than with the present employer. A career can also be considered boundaryless in the sense that personal or family demands and values influence career plans or goals. Finally, *boundaryless* may refer to the fact that career success may not be tied to promotions. Career success may be related to achieving goals that are personally meaningful to the employee—rather than those set by parents, peers or the company.

As this discussion shows, to retain and motivate employees, companies need to provide systems that identify and meet employees' development needs. This is especially important to retain good performers and employees who have potential for managerial positions. This system is often known as a career management or development planning system. We will discuss this system in detail later in the chapter.

As noted in Chapter 11, the three areas of training, learning and development, and career management can be considered in combination as **human resource development** (HRD).[11] HRD has been defined as 'organised learning activities arranged within an organisation in order to improve performance and/or personal growth for the purpose of improving the job, the individual, and/or the organisation'.[12] We suggest that HRD refers not only to the operational activities or practices, but also to a wide range of organisational strategies, policies, plans and practices.[13] Research has shown that HRD provides important benefits for individuals and organisations. Effective HRD practices can lead to outcomes such as enhanced individual and organisational competencies.[14] In turn, these outcomes can contribute to performance outcomes such as higher performance and sustained competitive advantage for the organisation.[15] Further, as shown in the 'Managing challenges of globalisation: Investment in skills will help meet future challenges' article, according to Neil Coulson, chief executive of the Victorian Employers' Chamber of Commerce and Industry, it is vital for employers to adopt innovative approaches to training and development, in order to compete in the global marketplace.

Human resource development (HRD)

especially in the sense developed by the American Society for Training & Development (ASTD) in the USA, refers to a wide range of organisational strategies, policies, plans, practices and organised activities that aim to improve personal growth and/or performance, in order to improve the job, the individual, and/or the organisation. It forms a major part of the entire human resource management systems of organisations.

Approaches to learning and development

Four approaches are typically used to develop employees: (1) formal education, (2) assessment, (3) job experiences and (4) interpersonal relationships.[16] Many companies use a combination of these approaches. Continuing the discussion begun in Chapter 11, in the following sections, we explore each type of development approach.

Keep in mind that although the large majority of development activity is targeted at managers, all levels of employees may be involved in one, or more, development activities. For example, retail sales assistants usually receive performance appraisal feedback (a development activity related to assessment). As part of the appraisal process they may be asked to complete an individual development plan that outlines:

449

INVESTMENT IN SKILLS WILL HELP MEET FUTURE CHALLENGES

A MORE innovative approach to education and training is required for Victorian industry to maximise its potential in the competitive world marketplace.

The challenges facing industry and policymakers include how world competition has become more intensive, a tightening economy, an ageing population and workforce, difficulties in attracting new entrants to traditional trades, and broad-based labour and skill shortages.

In such an environment, we believe there needs to be a significantly increased focus on an investment in skills and knowledge development, and attracting and retaining skilled people.

Victorian skill shortages mirror national trends and continue to limit business growth in several industry sectors. There are statewide recruitment difficulties in many trades and professions, and in many regional areas skill shortages and problems recruiting and retaining staff are significant barriers to further growth.

Several other factors are working to constrain Victoria's long-term stock of skills. They include:

- The ageing of the existing workforce.
- Falling numbers of new entrants to the workforce.
- Current superannuation arrangements encouraging early retirement.

The key to tackling these issues lies in a more innovative approach to education and training by federal, state and territory governments and the private sector, and a change in community perceptions towards study, training and work. This is the central finding of VECCI's federal-state relations taskforce, chaired by Sutton Tools chief executive Michael Grogan.

In tackling these issues, the taskforce called for the following reforms.

Preparation of young people

A new, targeted marketing campaign aimed at parents, young people and educators promoting the value of apprenticeship and traineeship opportunities.

The introduction of modified new apprenticeships for year 10 students providing enhanced access to alternative curriculum options as well as improved standards of literacy and numeracy support.

Expanded funding of school enterprise skill centres. These models leverage existing school infrastructure in close partnership with employers, schools and training providers.

Maximising workforce participation

Welfare to Work reforms must tackle the risk issues for industry as well as the provision of work-readiness programs for recipients to manage their effective transition to work.

The training system must recognise the legitimacy of, and focus on, the challenge of retraining and reskilling older workers.

Given current labour and skill shortages, the Victorian share of national migration should be increased from the current 25 per cent to 30 per cent to meet skills and labour gaps over the short to medium term.

Improving the training system

The federal and state governments need to review the additional funding required for the Victorian training system (embodied in the Government Funded Training Program). Such funding to be increased by a minimum of $25 million a year over the next three years. This will help ensure the state's training system can meet accelerating demand ahead of worsening skill and labour shortages.

Structural reform of apprenticeships must occur to focus on competence attainment rather than fixed duration. Additional financial support should expand VET programs in schools with stronger articulation arrangements to subsequent apprenticeship take-up.

A skilled workforce provides a competitive edge, improving productivity, economic growth and living standards. Taken together, these reforms will help deliver these outcomes.

Source: Excerpt from N. Coulson, 2005, 'Investment in skills will help meet future challenges', *The Age*, 16 December, p. 10. Neil Coulson is the chief executive of the Victorian Employers' Chamber of Commerce and Industry.

---

how they plan to change their weaknesses; and their future plans (including positions or locations desired, and education or experience needed). It may also be appropriate for an organisation to maintain an employee training and development program that aims to assist a particular segment of its workforce, as shown in 'Managing challenges through sustainability: Aboriginal & Torres Strait Islander initiatives at Qantas'.

ABORIGINAL & TORRES STRAIT ISLANDER INITIATIVES AT QANTAS

[Qantas] are committed to working in partnership with Aboriginal and Torres Strait Islander communities, through a range of initiatives including employment and training programs, community involvement and sponsorships.

Qantas' Aboriginal and Torres Strait Islander Program has been in place for more than 10 years and employs a dedicated program coordinator. Currently, between 1 and 2 per cent of the airline's workforce is of Aboriginal or Torres Strait Islander descent.

Employment and training program

[Qantas] have a comprehensive Aboriginal and Torres Strait Islander employment and training program.

Introduced in 1988, it aims to have an overall representation of Aboriginal and Torres Strait Islander people across all occupations and levels to reflect the broader community, its customers and its commitment to Equal Employment Opportunity legislative and reporting requirements.

Qantas employs a full-time Diversity Coordinator who is responsible for the airline's Aboriginal and Torres Strait Islander Program Unit.

This role includes offering assistance to Indigenous employees of Qantas with regard to career and training development, and monitoring and developing employment strategies, whilst ensuring the program is effectively integrated into the airline's divisions, subsidiaries, regions and ports.

In 2002, [Qantas] developed an Indigenous staff pin as a symbol of the airline's ongoing commitment to strengthening relationships between non-Indigenous and Indigenous Australians.

Source: Aboriginal & Torres Strait Islanders Initiatives at Qantas, www.qantas.com.au/info/about/employment/aboriginalInit, accessed 30 October 2006.

Formal education

Formal education programs include: off-site and on-site programs that are designed specifically for the company's employees, short courses that are offered by consultants or universities, executive programs, and university programs in which participants actually live at the university while taking classes. These programs may involve lectures by business experts, business games and simulations, adventure learning and meetings with customers. In Chapter 11, we discussed **vocational education and training**, which is one of the major systems for formal education in Australia. Here, we will focus on other types of formal education, such as university education and executive education. Many professionals, including HR professionals, have undertaken a university program such as a masters degree in HRM or a Master of Business Administration (MBA). Each type of program has benefits for individuals, depending on their interests and career aspirations. Specialist programs such as a masters degree in HRM can provide a depth of knowledge about the HRM field; an MBA can provide broader business knowledge and perhaps lead to broader career prospects. There is a wide variety of programs available. In Australia, more than 40 universities offer over 80 types of MBAs to over 25 000 students. However, the qualification will not guarantee employment or a successful career. As explained by Tim Trumper, managing director of publishing company Time Inc. South Pacific: 'I see an MBA degree as the beginning of learning, not the end of it. When I'm hiring someone, I look at the whole package—work experience plus any formal education. People must have well-developed careers first. If all else is equal, an MBA on a CV probably shows that the candidate has gumption, a strong work ethic and is open to learning'.[17]

There are several important trends in executive education. More and more companies and universities are using distance learning to reach executive audiences.

Formal education programs include off-site and on-site programs that are designed specifically for the company's employees, short courses that are offered by consultants or universities, executive programs, and university programs in which participants actually live at the university while taking classes.

Vocational education and training
VET is a more externally focused concept than training. Like training, it is concerned with meeting the skills needs of the organisation but VET is essentially focused on meeting the skills needs of individuals so that they can find employment in the labour market. This involves gaining nationally recognised qualifications that may or may not meet the needs of the employing organisation.

For example, Deakin University in Victoria offers an MBA program by distance education. Using their personal computers, students 'attend' CD-ROM video lectures as well as traditional face-to-face lectures. They can download study aids and additional videos and audio programs. Students discuss lectures and work on team projects using computer bulletin boards, email and live 'chat rooms'. They use the Internet to research specific companies and class topics.

Another trend in executive education is for companies and the education provider (business school or other educational institution) to create short, customised courses with the content designed specifically to meet the needs of the audience. Many companies (for example, BHP Billiton, Coles Myer and Ford) have training and development centres that offer one- or two-day seminars as well as week-long programs. Also, in recent years, corporate universities have emerged as an increasingly significant aspect of contemporary corporate training and development.[18] For example, Motorola University China has been established to develop and grow young Chinese managers.[19]

A final important trend in executive education is to supplement formal courses from consultants or a university faculty with other types of development activities. AVON Products' 'passport program' is targeted at employees that the company thinks can become general managers.[20] To learn AVON's global strategy, these employees meet for each session in a different country. The program brings a team of employees together for six one-week periods that are spread over 18 months. Participants are provided with the general background of a functional area by a university faculty and consultants. The team then works with senior executives on a country project, such as how to penetrate a new market. The team projects are presented to AVON's top managers.

Most companies consider the primary purpose of education programs as providing the employee with job-specific skills.[21] There is increasing research on the effectiveness of formal education programs. In a study of Harvard University's Advanced Management Program, participants reported that they acquired valuable knowledge from the program (for example, how globalisation affects a company's structure). They said the program broadened their perspectives on issues facing their companies, increased their self-confidence and helped them learn new ways of thinking and looking at problems.[22]

Of course, employees may also take the initiative to seek out a formal educational program that suits their own interests and aspirations. Useful websites with information about study courses include: Department of Education, Science and Training: www.dest.gov.au; Open Learning Australia: www.ola.edu.au; and The Good Guides: www.thegoodguides.com.au.

Assessment

Assessment
collecting information and providing feedback to employees about their behaviour, communication style or skills.

Assessment involves collecting information and providing feedback to employees about their behaviour, communication style or skills.[23] The employees, their peers, managers and customers may be asked to provide information. Assessment is most frequently used to identify employees with managerial potential and to measure current managers' strengths and weaknesses. Assessment is also used to identify managers with the potential to move into higher-level executive positions and it can be used with work teams to identify the strengths and weaknesses of individual team members and the decision processes or communication styles that inhibit the team's productivity.

Companies vary in the methods and the sources of information they use in developmental assessment. Many companies provide employees with performance

Employee Development and Career Management   CHAPTER 12

appraisal information. Companies with sophisticated development systems use personality assessments to measure employees' skills, personality types and communication styles. Self, peer and managers' ratings of employees' interpersonal styles and behaviours may also be collected. Popular assessment tools include the: Myers-Briggs Type Indicator® instrument (MBTI® instrument), assessment centre, Benchmarks®, performance appraisal and 360-degree feedback system.

Myers-Briggs Type Indicator® Personality Instrument

The **Myers-Briggs Type Indicator® Instrument (MBTI® Instrument)** is a personality assessment used for team building and leadership development that identifies employees' preferences for directing and receiving energy, information gathering, decision making and lifestyle. It is the most popular personality assessment for employee development. The assessment consists of more than 100 questions about how the person feels or prefers to behave in different situations (for example, 'are you usually a good "mixer" or rather quiet and reserved'). The MBTI® Instrument is based on the work of Carl Jung, a psychologist who believed that differences in individuals? behaviour resulted from preferences in decision making, interpersonal communication and information gathering. The MBTI® Instrument identifies individuals' preferences for directing and receiving energy (Introversion [I] versus Extraversion [E]), information gathering (Sensing [S] versus Intuition [N]), decision making (Thinking [T] versus Feeling [F]) and lifestyle (Judging [J] versus Perceiving [P]).[24] The *energy dimension* determines where individuals gain interpersonal strength and vitality. Extraverted types (E) gain energy through interpersonal relationships. Introverted types (I) gain energy by focusing on personal thoughts and feelings. The *information gathering* preference relates to the actions individuals take when making decisions. Individuals with a Sensing (S) preference tend to gather facts and details. Intuitive types (N) tend to focus less on facts and more on possibilities and relationships between ideas. *Decision-making style* preferences differ, based on the amount of consideration the person gives to others' feelings in making a decision. Individuals with a Thinking (T) preference tend to be objective in making decisions. Individuals with a Feeling (F) preference tend to evaluate the impact of potential decisions on others and be more subjective in making a decision. The *lifestyle* preference reflects an individual's tendency to be flexible and adaptable. Individuals with a Judging (J) preference focus on goals, establish deadlines and prefer to be conclusive. Individuals with a Perceiving (P) preference tend to enjoy surprises, like to change decisions and dislike deadlines.

Sixteen unique personality types result from the combination of the four MBTI® Instrument preferences (see Table 12.1 overleaf). Each person has developed strengths and weaknesses as a result of using his or her preferences. For example, individuals who are Introverted (I) types and have Sensing (S), Thinking (T) and Judging (J) preferences—known as ISTJs—tend to be serious, quiet, practical, orderly and logical. These people are likely to organise tasks, be decisive and follow through on plans and goals. These ISTJs may display the need for development in the areas opposite their preferences: Extraversion (E), Intuition (N), Feeling (F) and Perceiving (P). Potential weaknesses for ISTJs include problems dealing with unexpected opportunities, appearing too task-oriented or impersonal to colleagues, and making overly quick decisions.

The MBTI® Instrument is used for understanding such things as communication, motivation, teamwork, work styles and leadership. For example, it can be used by salespeople or executives who want to become more effective at interpersonal communication by learning things about their own personality styles and the way they

> **Myers-Briggs Type Indicator® Instrument (MBTI® Instrument)**
> a personality assessment used for team building and leadership development that identifies employees' preferences for directing and receiving energy, information gathering, decision making and lifestyle.

453

PART 3   Developing People

> **TABLE 12.1** The 16 personality types used in the Myers-Briggs Type Indicator® Instrument

	Sensing types (S)		Intuitive types (N)	
	Thinking (T)	**Feeling (F)**	**Feeling (F)**	**Thinking (T)**
Introverts (I) and Judging (J) types	**ISTJ** Serious, quiet, and earn success by concentration and thoroughness. Practical, orderly, matter-of-fact, logical, realistic and dependable. Take responsibility.	**ISFJ** Quiet, friendly, responsible and conscientious. Work devotedly to meet obligations. Thorough, painstaking and accurate. Loyal and considerate.	**INFJ** Succeed by perseverance, originality and desire to do whatever is needed or wanted. Quietly forceful, conscientious, and concerned for others. Respected for their firm principles.	**INTJ** Usually have original minds and great drive for their own ideas and purposes. Sceptical, critical, independent, determined, and often stubborn.
Perceiving (P) types	**ISTP** Cool onlookers—quiet, reserved and analytical. Usually interested in impersonal principles, how and why mechanical things work. Flashes of original humour.	**ISFP** Retiring, quietly friendly, sensitive, kind, and modest about their abilities. Shun disagreements. Loyal followers. Often relaxed about getting things done.	**INFP** Care about learning, ideas, language and independent projects of their own. Tend to undertake too much, then somehow get it done. Friendly, but often too absorbed.	**INTP** Quiet, reserved, impersonal. Enjoy theoretical or scientific subjects. Usually interested mainly in ideas; little liking for parties or small talk. Sharply defined interests.
Extroverts (E) and Perceiving (P) types	**ESTP** Matter-of-fact, do not worry or hurry, enjoy whatever comes along. May be a bit blunt or insensitive. Best with real things that can be taken apart or put together.	**ESFP** Outgoing, easy going, accepting, friendly, make things more fun for others by their enjoyment. Like sports and making things. Find remembering facts easier than mastering theories.	**ENFP** Warmly enthusiastic, high-spirited, ingenious, imaginative. Able to do almost anything that interests them. Quick with a solution and to help with a problem.	**ENTP** Quick, ingenious, good at many things. May argue either side of a question for fun. Resourceful in solving challenging problems but may neglect routine assignments.
Judging (J) types	**ESTJ** Practical, realistic, matter-of-fact, with a natural head for business or mechanics. Not interested in subjects they see no use for. Like to organise and run activities.	**ESFJ** Warm-hearted, talkative, popular, conscientious, born cooperators. Need harmony. Work best with encouragement. Little interest in abstract thinking or technical subjects.	**ENFJ** Responsive and responsible. Generally feel real concern for what others think or want. Sociable and popular. Sensitive to praise and criticism.	**ENTJ** Hearty, frank, decisive and leaders. Usually good at anything that requires reasoning and intelligent talk. May sometimes be more positive than their experience in an area warrants.

Source: Reproduced with special permission of the publisher, CPP, Inc., 1055 Joaquin Road, Suite 200, Mountain View, CA 94043, Fax 6502 623-9273 from *Manual: A Guide to the Development and Use of the Myers-Briggs Type Indicator®* by Isabel Briggs-Myers and Mary H. McCaulley. Copyright 1985 by Peter Briggs-Myers and Katharine D. Myers. All rights reserved. MBTI, Myers-Briggs Indicator are registered trademarks of of the Myers-Briggs Type Indicator Trust in the United States and other countries. Further reproduction is prohibited without the publisher's consent.

are perceived by others. The MBTI® Instrument can help develop teams by matching team members with assignments that allow them to capitalise on their preferences and helping employees understand how the different preferences of team members can lead to useful problem solving.[25] For example, consider assigning brainstorming tasks to employees with an Intuitive (I) preference. Employees with a Sensing (S) preference are likely to enjoy the responsibility of evaluating ideas.

Research on the validity, reliability and effectiveness of the MBTI® Instrument is extensive and varied.[26] The most recent revision of the MBTI® Instrument, based on item-response theory, demonstrated a high degree of internal consistency with coefficient alphas ranging from 0.85 to 0.95 for the four preference scales across a number of samples. The results from the most recent revision of the instrument are also stable over time. Studies in which the MBTI® Instrument was administered at two different times found that 55 to 80 per cent of those assessed were classified as exactly the same type the second time. The test-retest correlations on the four preference scales across the two administrations ranged from 0.83 to 0.97. People who take this personality assessment find it a positive experience and say that it helps them to change their behaviour. The results from this instrument seem to be related to an individual's occupation, as well as other important behaviours such as creativity, coping with stress, ideal work environment, job satisfaction, relationship satisfaction, academic achievement, and leadership.

The MBTI® Instrument is a valuable tool for understanding communication styles and the ways in which people prefer to interact with others. The MBTI® Instrument does not measure how well employees perform their preferred functions; thus, it should not be used to appraise performance or evaluate employees' promotion potential. Indeed, the MBTI® Instrument measures preferences rather than competencies and is best used in the context of developing individuals in a range of settings such as psychotherapy, education, career counselling, and organisational development.

Assessment centre

The **assessment centre** is a process in which multiple raters or evaluators (also known as assessors) evaluate employees' performance on a number of exercises.[27] An assessment centre is usually held at an off-site location such as a conference centre. From six to 12 employees usually participate at one time. Assessment centres are primarily used to identify whether employees have the personality characteristics, administrative skills and interpersonal skills needed for managerial jobs. They are also increasingly being used to determine if employees have the necessary skills to work in teams.

The types of exercises used in assessment centres include leaderless group discussions, interviews, in-baskets and role plays.[28] In a **leaderless group discussion**, a team of five to seven employees is assigned a problem and must work together to solve it within a certain time period. The problem may involve buying and selling supplies, nominating a subordinate for an award or assembling a product. In the **interview** situation, employees may be asked to answer questions about their work and personal experiences, skill strengths and weaknesses, and career plans. An **in-basket** is a simulation of the administrative tasks of a manager's job. The exercise includes a variety of documents that may appear in the in-basket on a manager's desk. The participants are asked to read the materials and decide how to respond to them. Responses might include delegating tasks, scheduling meetings, writing replies or completely ignoring the memo! **Role plays** refer to the participant taking the part or role of a manager or other employee. For example, an assessment centre participant may be asked to take the role of a manager who has to give a negative performance review to a subordinate. The participant is provided with information regarding the subordinate's performance. The participant is asked to prepare for and actually hold a 45-minute meeting with the subordinate in order to discuss the performance problems. The role of the subordinate is played by a manager or a member of the assessment centre design team or company. The assessment centre might also include testing. Interest and aptitude tests may be used to evaluate an employee's vocabulary,

Assessment centre
a process in which multiple raters evaluate employees' performance on a number of exercises.

Leaderless group discussion
a team of five to seven employees assigned a problem to solve together within a certain time period.

Interview
situation in which employees may be asked questions about their work and personal experiences, strengths and weaknesses, and career plans.

In-basket
a simulation of the administrative tasks of a manager's job.

Role play
a participant taking the part or role of a manager or other employee.

general mental ability and reasoning skills. Personality assessments may be used to determine if employees can get along with others, their tolerance for ambiguity and other traits related to success as a manager.

The exercises in the assessment centre are designed to measure employees' administrative and interpersonal skills. Skills that are typically measured include leadership, oral communication, written communication, judgment, organisational ability and stress tolerance. Table 12.2 below shows an example of the skills measured by the assessment centre. As you can see, each exercise gives participating employees the opportunity to demonstrate several different skills. For example, the exercise requiring scheduling to meet production demands evaluates employees' administrative and problem-solving ability. The leaderless group discussion measures interpersonal skills such as sensitivity towards others, stress tolerance and oral communication.

Managers are usually used as assessors. The managers are trained to look for employee behaviours that are related to the skills that will be assessed. Typically, each assessor is assigned to observe and record one or two employees' behaviours in each exercise. The assessors review their notes and rate each employee's level of skills (for example, five equals a high level of leadership skills and one equals a low level of leadership skills). After all employees have completed the exercises, the assessors meet to discuss their observations of each employee. They compare their ratings and try to agree on each employee's rating for each of the skills.

As we mentioned in Chapter 8 Recruitment and selection, research suggests that assessment centre ratings are related to performance, salary level and career advancement.[29] Assessment centres may also be useful for development purposes, because employees who participate in the process receive feedback regarding their attitudes, skill strengths and weaknesses.[30] In some organisations, such as Shell, training courses and development activities (that are related to the skills that are evaluated at the assessment centre) are available to employees.

Benchmarks®

Benchmarks®
an instrument designed to measure the factors that are important in order to be a successful manager.

Benchmarks® is an instrument designed to measure the factors that are important in order to be a successful manager. The items measured by Benchmarks® are based on research that examines the lessons executives learn at critical events in their careers.[31]

TABLE 12.2 Examples of skills measured by assessment centre exercises

Skills	In-basket	Scheduling exercise	Leaderless group discussion	Personality test	Role play
Leadership (dominance, coaching, influence, and resourcefulness)	X		X	X	X
Problem solving (judgment)	X	X	X		X
Interpersonal (sensitivity, conflict resolution, cooperation and oral communication)			X	X	X
Administrative (organising, planning and written communications)	X	X	X		
Personal (stress tolerance and confidence)			X	X	X

Note: X indicates skill measured by exercise.

This includes items that measure managers' skills in dealing with subordinates, acquiring resources and creating a productive work climate. Table 12.3 below shows the 16 skills and perspectives that are believed to be important for becoming a successful manager. These skills and perspectives have been shown to be related to performance evaluations, ratings of promotability by bosses and actual promotions received.[32] To get a complete picture of managers' skills, managers' supervisors, their peers and the managers themselves all complete the instrument. A summary report presenting the self-ratings and ratings by others is provided to the managers, along with information about how the ratings compare with those of other managers. A development guide that provides examples of experiences that enhance each of the skills, and shows how successful managers use the skills, is also available.

Performance appraisal and 360-degree feedback system

As discussed in Chapter 10 Performance management, 'performance appraisal' is the process of measuring employees' performance. Performance appraisal information can be useful for employee development under certain conditions.[33] The appraisal system must provide specific information to employees about their performance problems and ways in which they can improve their performance. This includes providing a

TABLE 12.3 Skills related to managerial success

1	Resourcefulness	Can think strategically, engage in flexible problem-solving behaviour and work effectively with higher management.
2	Doing whatever it takes	Has perseverance and focus in the face of obstacles.
3	Being a quick studier	Quickly masters new technical and business knowledge.
4	Building and mending relationships	Knows how to build and maintain working relationships with co-workers and external parties.
5	Leading subordinates	Delegates to subordinates effectively, broadens their opportunities and acts with fairness toward them.
6	Compassion and sensitivity	Shows genuine interest in others and sensitivity to subordinates' needs.
7	Straight forwardness and composure	Is honourable and steadfast.
8	Setting a developmental climate	Provides a challenging climate to encourage subordinates' development.
9	Confronting problem subordinates	Acts decisively and fairly when dealing with problem subordinates.
10	Team orientation	Accomplishes tasks through managing others.
11	Balance between personal life and work	Balances work priorities with personal life so that neither is neglected.
12	Decisiveness	Prefers quick and approximate actions, rather than slow and precise actions, in many management situations.
13	Self-awareness	Has an accurate picture of strengths and weaknesses and is willing to improve.
14	Hiring talented staff	Hires talented people for his or her team.
15	Putting people at ease	Displays warmth and a good sense of humour.
16	Acting with flexibility	Can behave in ways that are often seen as opposites.

Source: Adapted with permission from C.D. McCauley, M.M. Lombardo & C.J. Usher, 1989, 'Diagnosing management development needs: an instrument based on how managers develop', *Journal of Management*, 15, pp. 389–403.

PART 3   Developing People

clear understanding of the differences between current performance and expected performance, identifying causes of the performance discrepancy and developing 'action plans' to improve performance. Managers must be trained in providing performance feedback and they must provide that feedback often. Managers also need to monitor employees' progress in carrying out their 'action plans'.

Over the past decade or so, many organisations have increased their use of performance appraisals for management development including the upward feedback and 360-degree feedback process. **Upward feedback** refers to the performance appraisal process for managers, which involves collecting subordinates' evaluations of managers' behaviours or skills. The **360-degree feedback system** is a special case of the upward feedback process. It is a performance appraisal process for managers, which includes evaluations from a wide range of people who interact with the manager. The process includes self-evaluations as well as evaluations from the manager's boss, subordinates, peers and customers. The raters complete a questionnaire asking them to rate the person on a number of different dimensions. Table 12.4 below provides an example of the type of skills and items used in a questionnaire designed for a 360-degree feedback system. In this table, 'communicating information and ideas' is the dimension of the manager's behaviour that is being evaluated. Each one of the five items relates to specific aspects of written and oral communications (for example, clarity of messages). Typically, raters are asked to rate the degree to which each particular item is a strength or whether development is needed.

The results of a 360-degree feedback system show the manager how he or she was rated on each item. The results also show how self-evaluations differ from evaluations from the other raters. Typically, managers are asked to review their results, seek clarification from the raters and participate in development planning designed to set specific development goals that are based on the strengths and weaknesses identified.[34] Table 12.5 opposite shows the type of activities involved in development planning—using the 360-degree feedback process.[35]

The benefits of 360-degree feedback include: collecting multiple perspectives of managers' performance; allowing the employee to compare his or her personal evaluation with the views of others; and formalising communications about behaviours and skills rated between employees and their internal and external customers. Several studies have shown that performance improvement and behaviour change occur as a result of participating in upward feedback and 360-degree feedback systems.[36]

Potential limitations of 360-degree feedback systems include: the time demands placed on the raters to complete the evaluation; managers seeking to identify and punish raters who provided negative information; the need to have a facilitator in order to help interpret results; and companies' failure to provide ways in which managers can act on the feedback they receive (for example, development planning, meeting with raters and taking courses).

Upward feedback
a performance appraisal process for managers, which involves collecting subordinates' evaluations of managers' behaviours or skills.

360-degree feedback system
a performance appraisal process for managers that includes evaluations from a wide range of people who interact with the manager. The process includes self-evaluations as well as evaluations from the manager's boss, subordinates, peers and customers.

TABLE 12.4   Sample dimension and items from a 360-degree feedback instrument

Communicating information and ideas

1	Person makes points effectively to a resistant audience.
2	Person is skilled at public speaking.
3	Person is good at disseminating information to others.
4	Person has good writing skills.
5	Person writes understandable, easy-to-read memos.

TABLE 12.5 Activities in development planning

1. Understand strengths and weaknesses.
   - Review ratings for strengths and weaknesses.
   - Identify skills or behaviours where self and others' (manager, peer and customer) ratings agree and disagree.
2. Identify a development goal.
   - Choose a skill or behaviour to develop.
   - Set a clear, specific goal with a specified outcome.
3. Identify a process for recognising goal accomplishment.
4. Identify strategies for reaching the development goal.
   - Establish strategies such as reading, job experiences, courses and relationships.
   - Establish strategies for receiving feedback on your progress.
   - Establish strategies for receiving reinforcement for new skill or behaviour.

In the case of effective 360-degree feedback systems, reliable or consistent ratings are provided, raters' confidentiality is maintained, the behaviours or skills assessed are job-related (that is, valid), the system is easy to use and managers receive and act on the feedback.[37]

Information technology allows 360-degree feedback questionnaires to be delivered electronically to the raters via their personal computers. This helps to increase the number of completed questionnaires returned, makes it easier to process the information and makes it quicker to provide feedback reports to managers.

Regardless of the assessment method used, the information must be shared with the employee for development to occur. Along with the assessment information, the employee needs suggestions for correcting skill weaknesses and using skills already learned. These suggestions may include participating in training courses or developing skills through new job experiences. Based on the assessment information and available development opportunities, employees should develop an action plan to guide their self-improvement efforts.

Job experiences

Most employee development occurs through job experiences.[30] **Job experiences** refer to relationships, problems, demands, tasks or other features that employees face in their jobs. A major assumption of using job experiences for employee development is that development is most likely to occur when there is a mismatch between the employee's skills and past experiences and the skills required for the job. To be successful in their jobs, employees must stretch their skills—that is, they are 'forced' to learn new skills, apply their skills and knowledge in a new way and master new experiences.[39] To prepare employees to grow overseas business markets, many companies are using international job experiences.

Most of what we know about development through job experiences comes from a series of studies conducted by the Centre for Creative Leadership (CCL).[40] Executives were asked to identify key events in their careers that made a difference in their managerial styles and the lessons they learned from these experiences. The key events included: those involving the job assignment (for example, fix a failing operation); those involving interpersonal relationships (for example, getting along with supervisors); and the specific type of transition required (for example, situations in

Job experiences
the relationships, problems, demands, tasks and other features that employees face in their jobs.

which the executive did not have the necessary background). The job demands and what employees can learn from these demands are shown in Table 12.6 below.

One concern in the use of demanding job experiences for employee development is whether they are viewed as positive or negative stressors. Job experiences that are seen as positive stressors challenge employees to stimulate learning. Job challenges viewed as negative stressors create high levels of harmful stress for employees exposed to them. Recent research findings suggest that all the job demands, with the exception of obstacles, are related to learning.[41] Managers reported that obstacles and job demands that were related to creating change were more likely to lead to negative stress than the other job demands.

This suggests that companies should carefully weigh the potential for negative consequences, before placing employees in development assignments involving obstacles or creating change.

TABLE 12.6 Job demands and the lessons employees learn from them

Making transitions
- Unfamiliar responsibilities: the manager must handle responsibilities that are new, considerably different or much broader than previous responsibilities.
- Proving yourself: the manager has added pressure to show others he or she can handle the job.

Creating change
- Developing new directions: the manager is responsible for starting something new in the organisation, making strategic changes in the business, carrying out a re-organisation or responding to rapid changes in the business environment.
- Inherited problems: the manager has to fix problems created by a former incumbent, or take on problem employees.
- Reduction decisions: decisions about shutting down operations or staff reductions have to be made.
- Problems with employees: some employees lack adequate experience, are incompetent or are resistant.

Having a high level of responsibility
- High stakes: clear deadlines, pressure from senior managers, high visibility and responsibility for key decisions make success, or failure, in this job clearly evident.
- Managing business diversity: the scope of the job is large, with responsibilities for multiple functions, groups, products and customers or markets.
- Job overload: the sheer size of the job requires a large investment of time and energy.
- Handling external pressure: external factors that affect the business (for example, negotiating with unions or government agencies, working in a foreign culture and coping with serious community problems) must be dealt with.

Being involved in non-authority relationships
- Influencing without authority: getting the job done requires influencing peers, higher-level management, external parties or other key people over whom the manager has no direct authority.

Facing obstacles
- Adverse business conditions: the business unit or product line faces financial problems or difficult economic conditions.
- Lack of top management support: senior management is reluctant to provide direction, support or resources for current work or new projects.
- Lack of personal support: the manager is excluded from key networks and gets little support and encouragement from others.
- Difficult boss: the manager's opinions or management styles differ from those of the boss, or the boss has major shortcomings.

Source: C.D. McCauley, L.J. Eastman & P.J. Ohlott, 1995, 'Linking management selection and development through stretch assignments', *Human Resource Management*, 34, pp. 93–115. ©1995 Wiley Periodicals, a John Wiley Company.

Employee Development and Career Management   **CHAPTER 12**

Although the research on development through job experiences has focused on executives and managers, line employees can also learn from job experiences. As we noted earlier, for a work team to be successful, its members now need the kinds of skills that only managers were once thought to need (for example, dealing directly with customers, analysing data to determine product quality and resolving conflict among team members). Besides the development that occurs when a team is formed, employees can further develop their skills by switching work roles within the team.

Figure 12.1 below shows the various ways that job experiences can be used for employee development. These include enlarging the current job, job rotation, transfers, promotions, downward moves and temporary assignments with other companies.

Enlarging the current job

Job enlargement refers to adding challenges or new responsibilities to an employee's current job. This could include such activities as special project assignments, switching roles within a work team or researching new ways to serve clients and customers. For example, an engineering employee may be asked to join a taskforce charged with developing new career paths for technical employees. Through this project work, she may be asked to take leadership for certain aspects of career-path development (such as reviewing the company's career development process). As a result, she has the opportunity not only to learn about the company's career development system, but to use leadership and organisational skills to help the taskforce reach its goals.

Job enlargement
adding challenges or new responsibilities to an employee's current job.

Job rotation

Job rotation involves systematically moving a single individual from one job to another over the course of time. The job assignments may be in various functional areas of the company or the movement may occur between jobs in a single functional area or department.

Job rotation
the process of systematically moving a single individual from one job to another over the course of time. The job assignments may be in various functional areas of the company or movement between jobs in a single functional area or department.

FIGURE 12.1 How job experiences are used for employee development

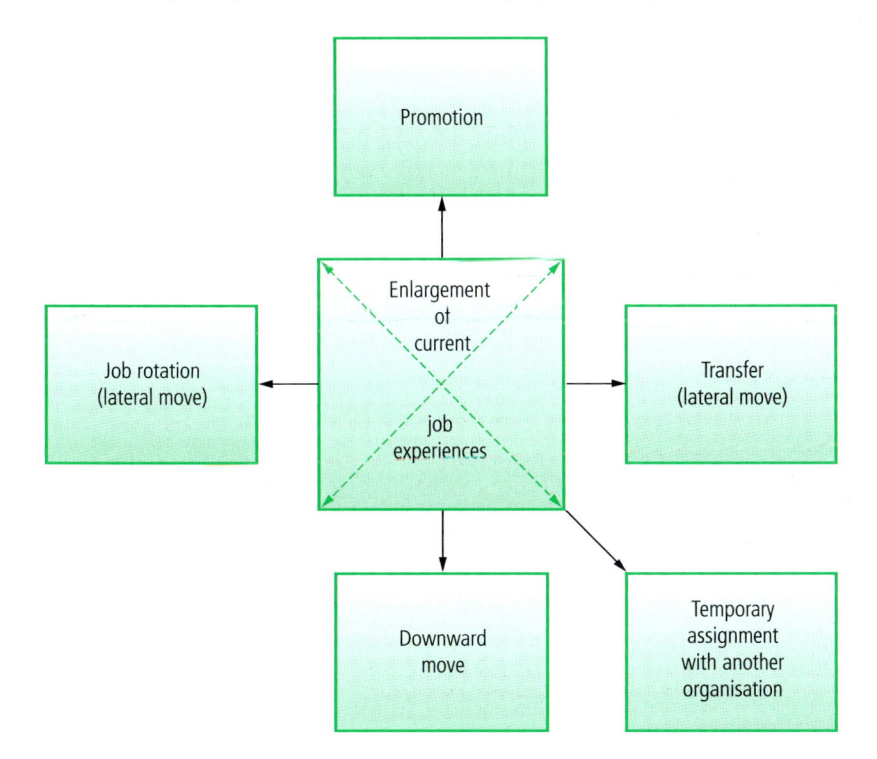

- Promotion
- Job rotation (lateral move)
- Enlargement of current job experiences
- Transfer (lateral move)
- Downward move
- Temporary assignment with another organisation

461

Job rotation helps employees gain an overall appreciation of the company's goals, increases their understanding of different company functions, develops a network of contacts and improves their problem solving and decision making skills.[42] Job rotation has also been shown to be related to skill acquisition, salary growth and promotion rates. There are several potential problems with job rotation though, for both the employee and the work unit. The rotation may create a short-term perspective on problems and solutions for employees and their peers. Employees' satisfaction and motivation may be adversely affected because they find it difficult to develop functional specialties and they do not spend enough time in one position to receive a challenging assignment. Productivity losses and workload increases may be experienced by both the department gaining a rotating employee and the department losing the employee due to training demands and loss of a resource.

The characteristics of effective job rotation systems are shown in Table 12.7 below. As we see, effective job rotation systems are linked to the company's training, development and career management systems. Job rotation is also used for all types of employees, not only those with managerial potential.

Transfers, promotions and downward moves

Upward, lateral and downward mobility is available for development purposes in most companies.[43] In a **transfer**, an employee is given a job assignment in a different area of the company. Transfers do not necessarily involve increased job responsibilities or increased compensation. They are likely to be lateral moves (a move to a job with similar responsibilities). A **promotion** is advancement into a position with greater challenges, more responsibilities and more authority, than in the previous job. Promotions usually include pay increases.

Transfers may involve relocation within Australia or to another country. A transfer can be stressful not only because the employee's work role changes, but if the employee is in a two-career family, the spouse must also find new employment. Also, the family has to join a new community. Transfers disrupt employees' daily lives, interpersonal relationships and work habits.[44] People have to find new housing, shopping, health care and leisure facilities, and they may be far away from the emotional support of friends and family. They also have to learn a new set of work 'norms' and procedures, they must develop interpersonal relationships with their new managers and peers and they are expected to be as productive in their new jobs as they were in their old jobs—although they may know little about the products, services, processes or employees for whom they are responsible.

Transfer
the movement of an employee to a different job assignment in a different area of the company.

Promotion
advancement into a position with greater challenge, more responsibilities, and more authority than the employee's previous job.

TABLE 12.7 Characteristics of effective job rotation systems

1	Job rotation is used to develop skills as well as give employees experience needed for managerial positions.
2	Employees understand specific skills that will be developed by rotation.
3	Job rotation is used for all levels and types of employees.
4	Job rotation is linked with the career management process so employees know the development needs addressed by each job assignment.
5	Benefits of rotation are maximised and costs are minimised through managing the timing of rotations in order to reduce workload costs and help employees understand job rotation's role in their development plans.
6	All employees have equal opportunities for job rotation assignments, regardless of their demographic group.

Source: Based on L. Cheraskin & M.A. Campion, 1996, 'Study clarifies job rotation benefits', *Personnel Journal*, November, pp. 31–8.

Many companies have difficulty getting employees to accept transfers, because they can provoke anxiety. Research has identified the employee characteristics associated with a willingness to accept transfers[45]: high career ambitions, a belief that his or her future with the company is promising, and a belief that accepting a transfer is necessary for success in the company. Employees who are not in long-term relationships and not active in the community are, generally, most willing to accept transfers. Among employees who are married or in long-term relationships, the willingness of partners to move is the most important influence on whether these employees accept transfers.

A **downward move** occurs when an employee is given a job change involving a reduced level of responsibility and authority.[46] This may involve a move to another position at the same level, but with less authority and responsibility (lateral demotion); a temporary cross-functional move; or a demotion because of poor performance. Temporary cross-functional moves to lower-level positions, which give employees experience working in different functional areas, are most frequently used for employee development. For example, engineers who want to move into management often take lower-level positions (for example, shift supervisor) to develop their management skills.

Downward move
a job change involving a reduction in an employee's level of responsibility and authority.

Employees are more willing to accept promotions than they are to accept lateral or downward moves because of the psychological and tangible rewards of promotions (for example, increased salary, status in the company and feelings of self-worth). Promotions are more readily available when a company is profitable and growing. When a company is restructuring and/or experiencing stable or declining profits—especially if numerous employees are interested in promotions and the company tends to rely on the external labour market to staff higher-level positions—promotion opportunities may be limited.[47]

Unfortunately, many employees have difficulty associating transfers and downward moves with development. They see them as punishments rather than as opportunities to develop skills that will help them achieve long-term success with the company. Many employees decide to leave a company rather than accept a transfer. Companies need to successfully manage transfers, not only because of the costs of replacing employees, but because of the costs directly associated with transfers. One challenge that companies face is learning how to use transfers and downward moves as development opportunities—convincing employees that accepting these opportunities will result in long-term benefits for them.

To encourage the employee to accept a transfer, promotion or downward move as a development opportunity, the company may provide:

- information about the content, challenges and potential benefits of the new job and location
- involvement in the transfer decision by sending the employees to preview the new location and giving that employee information about the community
- clear performance objectives and early feedback about his or her job performance
- a host at the new location, to help the employee adjust to the new community and workplace
- information about how the job opportunity will affect the employee's income, tax, mortgage payments and other expenses
- reimbursement and assistance in selling and purchasing or renting a place to live
- an orientation program for the new location and job
- information on how the new job experiences will support the employee's career plans

- assistance for dependent family members, including identifying schools and childcare and eldercare options
- help for the spouse in identifying and marketing his or her skills and finding employment.[48]

It is well worth noting that career management steps may be affected by many factors that are beyond an individual's control. External factors may have a significant influence over an individual's career development opportunities—particularly international transfers or expatriate assignments (discussed in Chapter 16 International human resource management, in more detail). After the attack on the World Trade Center on September 11, 2001, prospects for executives seeking jobs overseas have been more affected by the prospect of a global recession and political uncertainty. In the weeks and months following September 11, corporate reaction to these events included recalling expatriate executives and banning overseas travel. Several multinational firms have reduced executives' career development programs, for reasons including concerns about global uncertainties and costs. While some analysts have suggested that the reduction in the expatriate recruitment market may be as much as 30 per cent, overall, the use of expatriate assignment and other forms of international work continues in multinational firms.[49]

Temporary assignments with other organisations

> **Sabbatical**
> a leave of absence from the company to renew or develop skills.

Two companies can agree to exchange employees. Temporary assignments can include a **sabbatical** (a leave of absence from the company to renew or develop skills). Employees on sabbatical often receive full pay and benefits. Sabbaticals provide employees with the opportunity to get away from the day-to-day stresses of their jobs and acquire new skills and perspectives. Sabbaticals also allow employees more time for personal pursuits such as writing a book or spending more time with young children. Sabbaticals are common in a variety of industries ranging from consulting firms to the fast-food industry.[50] For example, McDonald's Corporation in the United States offers an eight-week sabbatical to employees with 10 years of service; and they offer a 16-week sabbatical to those with 20 years of service. How employees spend their sabbaticals varies from company to company. Some employees may work for a non-profit service agency, others may study at a college or university, or travel and work on special projects in overseas subsidiaries of the company.

Interpersonal relationships

Employees can also develop skills and increase their knowledge about the company and its customers by interacting with a more experienced organisational member. Mentoring and coaching are two types of interpersonal relationships that are used to develop employees.

Mentoring

> **Mentor**
> an experienced, productive senior employee who helps develop a less experienced employee.

A **mentor** is an experienced, productive senior employee who helps develop a less experienced employee (the protégé). Most mentoring relationships develop informally as a result of interests or values shared by the mentor and protégé. Research suggests that employees with certain personality characteristics (for example, emotional stability, the ability to adapt their behaviour based on the situation, high needs for power and achievement) are most likely to seek a mentor and be an attractive protégé for a mentor.[51]

Mentoring relationships can also develop as part of a planned company effort to bring together successful senior employees with less experienced employees.

- *Developing successful mentoring programs.* Although many mentoring relationships develop informally, one major advantage of formalised mentoring programs is that they ensure access to mentors for all employees, regardless of gender or race. An additional advantage is that participants in the mentoring relationship know what is expected of them.[52] One limitation of formal mentoring programs is that mentors may not be able to provide counselling and coaching in a relationship that has been artificially created.[53] Table 12.8 below presents the characteristics of a successful formal mentoring program. Mentors should be chosen based on interpersonal and technical skills. They also need to be trained.
- *Benefits of mentoring relationships.* Both mentors and protégés can benefit from a mentoring relationship. Research suggests that mentors provide career and psychosocial support to their protégés. Career support includes coaching, protection, sponsorship and providing challenging assignments, exposure and visibility. Psychosocial support includes serving as a friend and a role model, providing positive regard and acceptance, and creating an outlet for the protégé to talk about their anxieties and fears. Additional benefits for the protégé include higher rates of promotion, higher salaries and greater organisational influence.[54] Mentoring relationships provide opportunities for mentors to develop their interpersonal skills and increase their feelings of self-esteem and worth to the organisation.
- *Purposes of mentoring programs.* Mentoring programs are used to socialise new employees, to increase the likelihood of skills transfer from training to the work setting and to provide opportunities for women and those people in minority groups to gain the exposure and skills needed to evolve into managerial positions.

Some companies have initiated group mentoring programs, because of the lack of potential mentors, a formal reward system supporting mentoring, and a belief that the quality of mentorships developed in a formal program is poorer than informal mentoring relationships. In group mentoring programs, a successful senior employee is paired with a group of four to six less experienced protégés. One potential advantage of the mentoring group is that protégés can learn from

Career support
coaching, protection, sponsorship and providing challenging assignments, exposure and visibility.

Psychosocial support
serving as a friend and role model, providing positive regard and acceptance, and creating an outlet for a protégé to talk about their anxieties and fears.

TABLE 12.8 Characteristics of successful formal mentoring programs

1	Mentor and protégé participation is voluntary. The relationship can be ended at any time without fear of punishment.
2	The process of mentor–protégé matching does not limit the development of informal relationships. For example, a mentor pool can be established to allow protégés to choose from a variety of qualified mentors.
3	Mentors are chosen on the basis of: their past record in developing employees; their willingness to serve as a mentor; and evidence of positive coaching, communication and listening skills.
4	The purpose of the program is clearly understood. Projects and activities that the mentor and protégé are expected to complete are specified.
5	The length of the program is specified. Mentor and protégé are encouraged to pursue the relationship beyond the formal time period.
6	A minimum level of contact between the mentor and protégé is specified.
7	Protégés are encouraged to contact one another to discuss problems and share successes.
8	The mentor program is evaluated. Interviews with mentors and protégés are used to obtain immediate feedback regarding specific areas of dissatisfaction. Surveys are used to gather more detailed information regarding benefits received from participating in the program.
9	Employee development is rewarded, which signals to managers that mentoring and other development activities are worth their time and effort.

each other as well as from a more experienced senior employee. The leader helps protégés understand the organisation, guides them in analysing their experiences and helps them clarify career directions. Each member of the group may have specific assignments to complete or the group may work together on a problem or issue.[55]

Coaching

Coach
a peer or manager who works with an employee to motivate him or her, help in skills development and provide reinforcement and feedback.

A **coach** is a peer or manager who works with an employee to motivate him or her, help in skills development and provide reinforcement and feedback. There are three roles that a coach can play.[56] Part of coaching may be one-on-one with an employee (for example, giving the employee feedback). Another role is to help employees to learn for themselves. This involves helping them find experts who can assist them with their concerns and teaching them how to obtain feedback from others. Also, coaching may involve providing resources such as mentors, courses or job experiences that the employee may not be able to gain access to without the coach's help. For example, at National Semiconductor in the United States, managers participate in a 360-degree feedback program. Each manager selects another manager as a coach. Both attend a coaching workshop that focuses on skills such as active listening. The workshop presents a coaching process that includes creating a contract outlining members' roles and expectations, discussing 360-degree feedback, and identifying specific improvement goals and a plan for achieving them. After each pair works alone for six to eight months, they evaluate their progress.

To develop coaching skills, training programs need to focus on four issues related to managers' reluctance to provide coaching.[57] First, managers may be reluctant to discuss performance issues (although they are with a competent employee) because they want to avoid confrontation. This is especially an issue when the manager is less of an expert than the employee. Second, managers may be better at identifying performance problems than they are at helping employees solve them. Third, managers may also feel that the employee interprets coaching as criticism. Fourth, as companies downsize and operate with fewer employees, managers may feel that there is not enough time for coaching.

Career management systems

Career management system
used in an organisation to identify employees' development needs and to enable employees to progress through a sequence of positions, developing their knowledge, skills and abilities.

Many organisations are recognising the strategic value of implementing career management systems for their employees. A **career management system** is used in an organisation to identify employees' development needs and to enable employees to progress through a sequence of positions, developing their knowledge, skills and abilities. For example, KPMG Australia implemented a sophisticated competency framework for career management. This framework covers all 4500 employees in Australia. The Australian operation is one of seven KPMG locations using this global competency framework (the others are the United States, the United Kingdom, Germany, France, the Netherlands and Canada). According to the head of human resources at KPMG Australia, Jeffrey Pearse:

> The idea is to link our business goals with individual 'smart' goals so that everyone, from partners to people who work in the kitchens, can realise their full potential. Different behaviours are expected to be demonstrated at different levels through what we call 'interventions'. These are designed to encourage employees to set goals and move to the next level.[58]

At KPMG, an employee drives his or her own career management, with the HR function providing the framework and line managers providing guidance where needed. The support services provided by HR include briefing sessions, goal-setting, training on performance feedback and information about performance management for new employees.[59]

Companies' career management systems vary in the level of sophistication and the emphasis they place on the different components of the process. Steps and responsibilities that may be included in a career management system are shown in Figure 12.2 below.

Self-assessment

Self-assessment helps employees determine their interests, values, aptitudes and behavioural tendencies. It often involves personality assessments such as the Myers-Briggs Type Indicator® Instrument (described earlier in this chapter); and psychological tests such as the Campbell™ Interest and Skill Survey (CISS)®, a registered trademark of the Centre for Creative Leadership; and the Self-Directed Search®, a registered trademark of Psychological Assessment Resources, Inc. The CISS helps employees identify their occupational and job interests; the Self-Directed Search identifies employees' preferences for working in different types of environments (for example, sales, counselling or landscaping). Assessments may also help employees identify the relative values they place on work and leisure activities. Self-assessment can help employees to consider where they are now in their careers, identify future plans and gauge how their careers fit with their current situations and available resources. In some companies, counsellors assist employees in the self-assessment process and interpret the results of personality assessments.

Through the assessment, a development need can be identified. This need can result from gaps between current skills and/or interests and the type of work or position the employee wants.

Reality check

Employees receive information about how the company evaluates their skills and knowledge and where they fit into the company's plans (for example, potential promotion opportunities and lateral moves). Usually, this information is provided by the employee's manager as part of the performance appraisal process. It is not uncommon in well developed career management systems for the manager to hold separate performance appraisals and career development discussions.

FIGURE 12.2 Steps and responsibilities in the career management process

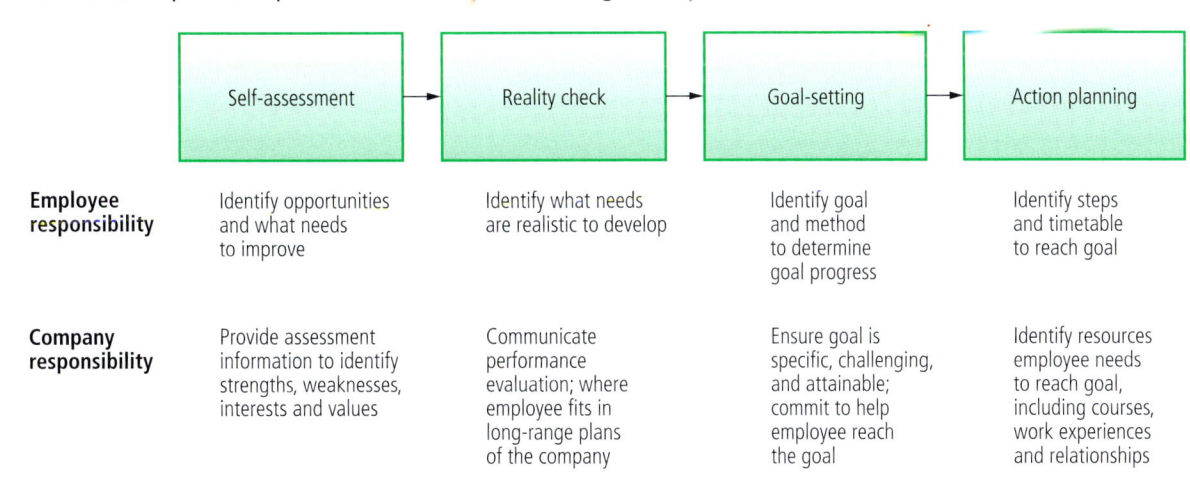

	Self-assessment	Reality check	Goal-setting	Action planning
Employee responsibility	Identify opportunities and what needs to improve	Identify what needs are realistic to develop	Identify goal and method to determine goal progress	Identify steps and timetable to reach goal
Company responsibility	Provide assessment information to identify strengths, weaknesses, interests and values	Communicate performance evaluation; where employee fits in long-range plans of the company	Ensure goal is specific, challenging, and attainable; commit to help employee reach the goal	Identify resources employee needs to reach goal, including courses, work experiences and relationships

Goal-setting

Employees determine their short- and long-term career goals during this phase of the career-planning process. These goals usually relate to desired positions (for example, to become a sales manager within three years), level of skill application (for example, to use an individual's budgeting skills to improve the unit's cash-flow problems), work setting (for example, to move to corporate marketing within two years) or skill acquisition (for example, to learn how to use the company's human resource information system). These goals are usually discussed with the manager and written into a development plan. A career development plan is shown in Figure 12.3 opposite.

Action planning

During this phase, employees determine how they will achieve their short- and long-term career goals. An **action plan** is a written document that includes the steps that the trainee and manager will take to ensure that training transfers to the job. Action plans may involve any one development approach or a combination of development approaches discussed in this chapter (for example, enrolling in courses and seminars, getting additional assessment, obtaining new job experiences or finding a mentor or coach).[60] It is important to note that the development approach used is dependent on the needs and developmental goal.

Several important design factors should be considered in the process of developing a career management system (see Table 12.9 below). Tying the development of the system to the business objectives and needs; top management support; and having managers and employees participate in building the system are especially important to help overcome resistance to using the system.

Employees may also seek to explore websites that offer career development and management advice and links to sites with related information. These websites include:

- mycareer.com.au
- www.seek.com.au
- www.careersonline.com.au
- www.aacc.org.au

As discussed, a career management system may include a range of elements to provide employee development opportunities. Many organisations are recognising the benefits of such systems and introducing programs for career management.

> **Action plan**
> a written document that includes the steps that the trainee and manager will take to ensure that training transfers to the job.

TABLE 12.9 Design factors of effective career management systems

1	System is positioned as a response to a business need.
2	Employees and managers participate in development of the system.
3	Employees are encouraged to take an active role in career management.
4	Evaluation is ongoing and used to improve the system.
5	Business units can customise the system for their own purposes (with some constraints).
6	Employees need access to career information sources (including advisors and positions available).
7	Senior management supports the career system.
8	Career management is linked to other human resource practices such as performance management, training and recruiting systems.

Source: Based on B. Baumann, J. Duncan, S.E. Forrer and Z. Leibowitz, 1996, 'Amoco primes the talent pump', *Personnel Journal*, vol. 75, February, pp. 79–84.

FIGURE 12.3 Career development plan

Development needs—current position
Specific knowledge and skills needed to improve or maintain satisfactory performance:

Development needs—future position
Specific knowledge and skills to get ready for next position:

Target job:

Development activities
Manager and employee will work together to implement the following actions:

Development objectives
Behaviour or results demonstrating development needs are being met:

Results:

Date:

Employee's signature:

Manager's signature:

Leadership development is also an area of particular interest for many organisations.[61] For example, Rio Tinto, the global mining corporation, partnered with leading business schools in Australia, England and the USA to introduce the Senior Leadership Programme, a development program for the company's present and future leaders.[62] As discussed in 'Managing challenges through HR innovation: Task to taskmaster' (overleaf), developing leaders is no easy task.

TASK TO TASKMASTER

There is no guarantee that a person who is good at technical tasks will be good at the new role. It is particularly a problem in professional firms, partly because they have a partnership structure that is inherently oriented towards performing tasks, rather than managerial results.

Developing leaders involves several transitions. The most difficult is the first: from technical expert to 'people manager'. The shift required is to move away from performing a set of tasks to being responsible for results, which in turn means being able to manage the people who perform the tasks.

Australian companies are generally not confident that they are developing the range of leaders needed to manage their businesses in the future, according to the Development Dimensions International (DDI) Leadership Forecast 2005–06. When organisations select new internal leaders they often base their decisions on the candidates' technical expertise or past performance, even though the new position requires different skills. Company systems often reward technical rather than interpersonal skills. He says companies must develop a higher success rate for that first transition if they are to develop enough leaders from a workforce within an ageing population.

Guy Templeton worked as an engineer and a management consultant before joining the law firm Minter Ellison as chief executive. A focus on business results for clients is pushing Templeton's campaign to widen lawyers' and partners' skills beyond technical training to close the gap between what is technically correct and the best solution to a business problem.

An acute shortage of lawyers with three to five years' experience is threatening firm succession planning. The solution to the problem is in improving partners' skills so they are able to form better relationships with their direct reports and co-ordinate development opportunities.

The first task is to inspire people to want to improve their skills. Minter Ellison provides career planning to discover the aspirations and options for young lawyers.

A clear expectation for leaders in the firm is the second element in staff development. A survey designed to understand who were the most valuable partners in the firm found that those who developed people skills and client relationships in addition to billing hours for legal work came out on top.

Templeton then worked with the partners to define nine competencies that encapsulated the skills each partner needed to ensure the success of the firm. The first competency was technical expertise. 'You really can't be a great lawyer if you are not good at the law', he says. 'But it is also [about] business opportunities, thought leadership, business planning, taking responsibility, persuasive arguments, client focus, generating a collaborative environment and developing employees.'

Coaching busy partners

Robyn Campbell was the human-resources director of another national law firm, Clayton Utz, for 11 years and now works as a consultant. Busy partners do not have time to do the MBAs favoured by management consultants and professional managers, and they often cancel seminars held during work hours because of client commitments. Coaching after hours is the favoured method of management development.

Coaching high-achieving partners can be difficult because they are very demanding and may be dismissive early in the process so using management theory gives them a framework in an unfamiliar area of study.

The national partner for people and performance at accounting firm Deloitte, Alec Bashinsky, strengthened the firm's management development program by adding more interpersonal skills training at partner and graduate level when he joined the firm 2 years ago.

He also introduced Deloitte's employee engagement survey, which not only ranks the firm's engagement as a whole but also the engagement of teams under individual partners. The results are used with the revenue figures as part of the performance management process.

Deloitte also runs an annual survey of employees to find out which of the partners are the best mentors and the most inspirational leaders. The top 30 out of 300 partners are recognised at the annual partner event.

A helping hand
- Find out the career aspirations and motivations of younger staff.
- Define the behaviour expected of the firm's leaders.
- Provide candid and detailed feedback.
- Supply basic management theory as an intellectual framework.
- Coaching is useful for time-poor professionals.
- Create a learning environment where some mistakes are tolerated.
- Recognise small wins to build confidence.

Source: Excerpt from A. Tandukar, 2006, 'Task to taskmaster', *BRW*, 8 June, p. 60. © 2006 Copyright John Fairfax Holdings Limited. www.brw.com.au

MANAGING CHALLENGES THROUGH HR INNOVATION

Special issues in learning and development and career management

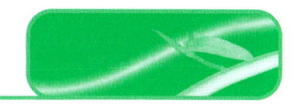

Employee development and career management involve a range of activities that are important for both individuals and the organisation. In several ways, employee development and career management have implications for the long-term success of individuals' careers and organisational development. In this section, we focus on two areas that are widely practised in larger firms, yet still under-utilised in many organisations. First, succession planning can be used as part of a strategy to develop the 'next generation' of leaders. Second, development strategies for management with dysfunctional behaviours are increasingly being included as part of the HR tool box. For example, concerns about workplace bullying have led to increasing awareness of the need for effective HR strategies to prevent and address dysfunctional behaviours.

Succession planning

Succession planning primarily involves the identification and tracking of high-potential employees. *High-potential employees* are those employees the company believes are capable of being successful in higher-level managerial positions, such as general manager of a strategic business unit, functional director (for example, director of marketing) or chief executive officer (CEO).[63] High-potential employees typically participate in fast-track development programs that involve education, executive mentoring and coaching, and rotation through job assignments.[64] Job assignments are based on the successful career paths of the managers whom the high-potential employees are being prepared to replace. High-potential employees may also receive special assignments, such as making presentations and serving on committees and taskforces. As shown in 'HRM spotlight: Catching and keeping senior women beyond the glass ceiling', the failure to retain high-potential employees is an important and potentially costly issue.

The objectives of fast-track development programs are:

- developing future managers for middle management and executive positions
- providing companies with a competitive advantage in attracting and recruiting talented employees
- helping to retain managerial talent within the company.[65]

Research suggests that the development of high-potential employees involves three stages.[66] A large pool of employees may initially be identified as high-potential employees, but the numbers are reduced over time because of turnover, poor performance or a personal choice not to strive for a higher-level position. In stage one, high-potential employees are selected. Those who have completed elite academic programs (for example, an MBA) or who have been outstanding performers are identified. Psychological assessments such as psychometric assessment and assessment centres may also be used.[67]

In stage two, high-potential employees receive development experiences. Those who succeed are the ones who continue to demonstrate good performance. A willingness to make sacrifices for the company is also necessary (for example, accepting new assignments or relocating to a different region). Good oral and written communication skills, an ease in interpersonal relationships and a talent for leadership are a must. High-potential employees who meet their senior managers' expectations in what is known as a tournament model of job transitions, are given the opportunity to advance to the next stage of the process.[68] Employees who do not meet the expectations are ineligible for higher-level managerial positions in the company.

Succession planning
the identification and tracking of high-potential employees capable of filling higher level managerial positions.

CATCHING AND KEEPING SENIOR WOMEN BEYOND THE GLASS CEILING

In recent years, many more businesses have increased the number of women filling very senior posts. This reflects more enlightened recruitment and promotion policies, a genuine desire for equality of opportunity and a need to show that boardrooms are no longer ghettos for white, middle-aged men. While there is still a long way to go before women have fully open access to the most senior roles, many observers believe that we are approaching a tipping point on the path to true meritocracy.

However, it is important to confront another issue that threatens to undermine the positive progress that has been made. Getting a more balanced representation of women in top jobs is only worthwhile if these women are also able to deliver high quality work when they get there and if they are motivated to stay once they arrive.

So what can businesses do to ensure that their high-flying female executives can thrive, succeed and stay in their jobs once they've made it to the top? How do the top employers tackle this problem and what lessons do their experiences have for other firms?

A globally successful investment bank had, to its credit, significantly increased the number of women in senior posts. There was concern, however, that once they had broken through the glass ceiling, they received little or no support to establish themselves in their roles or to develop their careers still further. Indeed, the early warning signs of strain and attrition were beginning to show.

An anonymous online questionnaire, administered to the top 250 women in the business, came up with a number of disturbing findings (see box). These suggested that a significant proportion of the senior women who had advanced up the career ladder in the business were unsure about whether they would stay and were concerned about whether their continuing career progression would be satisfactory.

A number of career progression diagrams showed that the chances of getting appointed to a vacant post at director level were 63 per cent for men and 10 per cent for women. Indeed, women were twice as likely to leave as get promoted.

The findings sent shockwaves through the company. To its credit, the business responded with a number of imaginative initiatives aimed at improving things, including a formal career mentoring process for senior women, opening up opportunities for cross-functional career moves to allow broadening of experience and exposure, and a series of measures to promote work–life balance. When the exercise was repeated for the company a year later, the picture had improved considerably.

There are lessons that can be drawn. Improving the numerical representation of women at the top of organisations is not an end in itself.

Simple analysis of recent patterns of promotion, retention and job movement can reveal a lot about how well an organisation's 'internal labour market' is operating—and how equitable it is.

We can't assume that women who make it to the top are unambiguously delighted once they get there. For many, the pressure to perform better than their male peers can be intense. Unless they continue to feel supported in their new roles, companies can find themselves with an uncomfortable retention problem which can make life at the top look far less appealing for the next generation of high-flying women.

Retention stats in the investment bank

— 72 per cent had thought seriously of leaving
— 53 per cent expected to stay with the firm for at least another five years
— Most important factors influencing retention (in rank order):

1. Job satisfaction/job interest
2. Recognition/feeling valued
3. Scope to extend job responsibilities
4. Working environment
5. Bonus opportunities

Those most likely to leave within five years were:

1. Less likely to have a career sponsor/mentor
2. More likely to be childless
3. More likely to be the main earner

— 34 per cent rated their career progression as slower or much slower than they expected when they joined the firm
— 55 per cent viewed career prospects with the firm as essential in keeping them
— 41 per cent disagreed that the firm actively supported their professional development

Source: The Work Foundation

Source: Excerpt from S. Bevan, 2006, 'Catching and keeping senior women beyond the glass ceiling', *Human Resources*, 1 November. www.humanresourcesmagazine.com.au

To reach stage three, high-potential employees usually have to be seen by top management as fitting into the company's culture and having the personality characteristics needed to successfully represent the company. These employees have the potential to occupy the company's top positions. In stage three, the CEO becomes actively involved in developing the employees who are exposed to the company's key personnel and given a greater understanding of the company's culture. It is important to note that the development of high-potential employees is a slow process. Reaching stage three may take 15–20 years.

Some companies' succession planning systems identify a small number of potential managers for each position. While this approach allows developed activities to be targeted at a select few highly talented managers, it also limits the company's ability to staff future managerial positions and may cause a talent drain. That is, high-potential employees who are not slotted into the short list for managerial positions may leave the company. Overall, in many Australian organisations, succession planning is increasingly viewed as an important part of effective HRM. As shown in 'Managing challenges through attracting and retaining people: Filling the leader's boots', effective succession planning can provide benefits to employees and to the organisation.

Development for managers with dysfunctional behaviours

A number of studies have identified managerial behaviours that can cause an otherwise competent manager to be ineffective. These behaviours include: insensitivity to others, inability to be a team player, arrogance, poor conflict management skills, inability to meet business objectives and inability to change or adapt during a transition.[69] For example, a skilled manager who is interpersonally abrasive, aggressive and an autocratic leader may find it difficult to motivate subordinates, may alienate internal and external customers and may have trouble having his or her ideas accepted by superiors. These managers are in jeopardy of losing their jobs and have little chance of future advancement because of their dysfunctional behaviours. Typically, a combination of assessment, training and counselling are used to help managers change dysfunctional behaviours.

One example of a program designed specifically to develop managers with dysfunctional behaviours is the individual coaching for effectiveness (ICE) program at Rutgers University.[70] Although such programs' effectiveness needs to be further investigated, research suggests that managers' participation in them results in skill improvement and reduced likelihood of termination.[71] The ICE program includes diagnosis, coaching and support activities. The program is tailored to the manager's needs. Clinical counselling or industrial organisational psychologists are involved in all phases of the ICE program. They conduct the diagnosis, coach and counsel the manager, and develop action plans for implementing new skills on the job.

The first step in the ICE program diagnosis involves collecting information about the manager's personality, skills and interests. Interviews with the manager, his or her supervisor and colleagues, as well as psychological assessments, are used to collect this information in order to determine whether the manager can actually change the dysfunctional behaviours. For example, personality traits such as extreme defensiveness may make it difficult for the manager to change his or her behaviours. If it is determined that the manager can benefit from the program, then specific developmental objectives tailored to his or her needs are set. The manager and his or her supervisor are typically involved in this process.

FILLING THE LEADER'S BOOTS

Succession planning plays a key role in developing future leaders in any organisation, although many still struggle to identify and develop those potential leaders. Furthermore, factors such as skills shortages, changing generational expectations, shorter careers with individual companies and the ageing of the workforce make good succession planning vital if some companies are simply to survive in the future.

Over the next few years, around the world, more employees will leave the workforce than enter it, according to Helen Scotts, general manager of Hay Group. 'Current senior leaders are disproportionately represented in those numbers that will exit. Those employees who enter the workforce in the same period will not necessarily seek a career pathway ending inevitably in a leadership role. They will seek other options and make other choices', she says.

The growing interest in succession planning is fuelled by demographic changes such as an ageing but increasingly mobile workforce. The fact that the job for life notion no longer exists or appeals, combined with Generation Y showing limited interest in the long-term career path, has resulted in a stark realisation that many critical roles within companies may not have a successor, she says.

Succession planning gaps

There are a number of common pitfalls that occur when engaging in succession planning. Some organisations are more reactive whereby they become aware of a potential 'critical role flight', or unscheduled resignation from a critical role, according to Sarah Kearney, managing director of SHL Australia.

'They then scour the organisation for the person who seems to be most ready to take on the role. The risks are many associated with this approach, for both the organisation and the individual. In fact, it can be decisions such as this that can seriously damage a potential high-performing individual's career and create an even higher level of exposure for the organisation.'

Another common pitfall is identifying critical roles based on the incumbent's attributes, rather than the actual role requirements. Another mistake many organisations make is in carrying out 'replacement' planning rather than succession planning.

By identifying groups of high performers within the organisation and developing them so that they could take on a variety of roles if necessary, Coleman says the organisation will have a number of appropriate people to select from and high performers will be retained as the range of possible future roles for them is broader.

Many organisations adopt an acquisition approach to succession planning, where they consistently seek external experts and leaders to fill their critical vacancies. 'This is not only extremely costly, but also quite high risk. The risk relates to the potential fit between the acquired employee and the role, culture and values of the organisation', she says.

Succession planning's season

There are a number of demographic factors at play that will make succession planning more vital for organisations than ever before. As it becomes harder to recruit the right talent from outside the organisation, businesses will find more success by developing their own talent internally for key senior positions.

A window for HR

This presents a unique opportunity for HR in being able to step up to this challenge and deliver initiatives that genuinely add value to the business and contribute to its sustainability.

The first step is to learn as much as you can about how leading organisations are approaching succession planning. The next is to encourage the leadership team to see succession planning as something that should be owned and driven by them with support from HR (rather than the other way around).

Kearney also highlights the importance of working with the executive or leadership team, and the CEO, to determine a strategy for sustained retention and succession management and ensure that full commitment to this strategy is secured.

Critical roles should be identified and accurately profiled against role requirements, and not the individual in the role.

Once the capabilities for the critical roles have been determined, Kearney says the next step is to execute the talent management component of the strategy. 'That involves identifying high performers in the organisation and assessing their potential to succeed in more senior and complex roles. The biggest pitfall here is that people assume high performance means high potential—and it doesn't.'

Securing executive support

One of the most powerful ways to encourage executives to commit to a holistic approach to succession planning, including a strong focus on development, is to highlight the risks involved in not effectively planning for future leadership needs.

Source: Excerpt from C. Donaldson, 2006, 'Filling the leader's boots', *Human Resources*, 5 September. www.humanresourcesmagazine.com.au

The coaching phase of the program first involves presenting the manager with information about the targeted skills or behaviours. This may include information about principles of effective communication or teamwork, tolerance of individual differences in the workplace or conducting effective meetings. The second step is for the manager to participate in behaviour modelling training. The manager also receives psychological counselling to overcome beliefs that may inhibit learning the desired behaviours.

The support phase of the program involves creating conditions to ensure that the manager is able to use the new behaviours and skills acquired in the ICE program on the job. The supervisor is asked to provide feedback to the manager and the psychologist about progress made in using the new skills and behaviours. The psychologist and manager identify situations in which the manager may tend to rely on dysfunctional behaviours. The coach and manager also develop action plans that outline how the manager should try to use 'new' behaviours in daily work activities.

MANAGING PEOPLE

MENTORS CAN HELP NEW EMPLOYEES TO SETTLE IN

Adrian Jenkins has been helping unemployed people find work for the past 22 years. He started on the front desk at a CES office, later moved to Employment National, the agency formed to manage the first contracts with private and not-for-profit employment agencies, and today is the Victorian manager of Sarina Russo Job Access, a private Job Network provider with eight offices in Melbourne.

According to Mr Jenkins, the caseloads of employment consultants have become increasingly challenging over the past decade as they face a higher proportion of clients for whom a lack of work is only one of their problems.

More clients, he says, now struggle with substance abuse or undiagnosed mental health problems, are in transitional housing or are dealing with other complex problems.

The implication for employment agencies is that even though a buoyant economy means employers are more willing to take on job seekers they would have overlooked a decade ago, the traditional case-management model of placing job seekers and maintaining phone contact is often inadequate to stop a placement failing. 'We found we were placing people, but they weren't staying', he says.

So to more effectively help clients needing more intense and individualised support and monitoring, the company introduced mentors. 'If we can get a job seeker past that first dangerous three-month period, then we have far greater chance of them staying in employment', says Mr Jenkins.

Jo Langhorne has been contracted to act as a mentor since November last year and supports 20 to 30 Sarina Russo Job Access clients.

Ms Langhorne had worked for eight years at Flight Centre. She started as a consultant, moved into training and finished as an area manager.

'In my Flight Centre background I was used to working with young, motivated, pumped-up salespeople who really wanted to achieve something', she says. 'So this is very different for me. But what I have learnt is that it is not that people don't want to achieve, it's that they don't know what's possible.'

She cites many examples of job seekers she's successfully worked with, including a young woman who, although new in a job, was taking regular sick days. 'Once a week she would be phoning in sick and she was really jeopardising her job', Ms Langhorne says.

'Meeting with her, however, I realised that she had nothing really to look forward to. She didn't have any goals and she had no incentive to work because she lived at home, so if she didn't work it didn't really matter because her parents would help her out.'

'But then we worked out that she did really want to buy her own home. I was then able to link this to why she should go to work. So how much deposit she would need, how much she needed to earn each week, and how much she needed to put aside. She was someone who hadn't held a job for more than eight to 10 weeks, but she is still in her job now.'

How Ms Langhorne supports other clients depends on what they need to stick at a job. 'Most of my work is in the middle of the afternoon to early evening. I usually speak to employers in the afternoon and then call people after they have returned home from work.'

For others it involves more hands-on assistance, coaching on handling interviews or sitting down with a client and his or her employer to clarify expectations.

Ms Langhorne says her main focus is on helping people readjust to work and teaching them workplace etiquette.

'I work with people who have been unemployed from six weeks to three, four or six years. If someone has been unemployed for three or four years-plus, their routine may be that they can sleep in and they don't have to be anywhere on time.'

'So I make sure they turn up on time and that their life supports them going to work. That is, that they're not out 'til four in the morning if they have to go to work at 7am.'

'Sometimes it is just educating the job seekers about the workforce. That you don't make a doctor's appointment during the day, that you make it before work or after work. Or if it is one that you absolutely have to have during the day, then you ask your employer first, you don't say to them, "I'm not coming in tomorrow because I have an appointment"', she says. Ms Langhorne says the approach hasn't worked for everyone but it has helped dozens of job seekers to hold down jobs and has given them hope for the future.

Source: W. Taylor, 2006, 'Mentors can help new employees to settle in', *The Age*, 1 July, p. 19. © 2006 Copyright John Fairfax Holdings Limited. www.theage.com.au

QUESTIONS

1 What do you see as the main issues and requirements for mentors in this mentoring program?
2 What do you see as the main issues and requirements for mentees in this mentoring program?

CHAPTER SUMMARY

In this chapter, we have emphasised the various learning and development methods that companies use to support career management: formal education, assessment, job experiences and interpersonal relationships. Most companies use one or more of these approaches to develop employees. Formal education involves enrolling employees in courses or seminars offered by the company or educational institutions. Assessment involves measuring the employee's performance, behaviour, skills or personality characteristics. Job experiences include job enlargement, rotating to a new job, promotions or transfers. A more experienced, senior employee (a mentor) can be used to help employees better understand the company and gain exposure and visibility to key people in the organisation. Part of a manager's job responsibility may be to coach employees. Regardless of the development approaches used for effective career management, employees should have a career development plan to identify: (1) the type of development needed, (2) development goals, (3) the best approach for development, and (4) whether development goals have been reached. For career development plans to be effective, both the employee and the company have responsibilities that need to be completed.

WEB EXERCISES

A The Australian Women's Mentoring Network offers women from any professional, personal or ethnic background access to a mentor who can offer advice and support concerning career and work–life balance issues, based on their own professional and life experiences, and skills. Visit its website at www.womensmentoring.com.au.

B The Growth Connection is a Sydney-based consultancy specialising in mentoring. Visit its website at www.growconnect.com.au to view newsletters, mentoring links, discussion papers, and a live case study of a mentoring program involving nearly 2000 employees in a public-sector organisation.

Questions

1 What types of benefits can companies expect from mentoring programs designed for career development?

2 What types of benefits can individuals expect from mentoring programs designed for career development?

DISCUSSION QUESTIONS

1 List and explain the characteristics of effective formal education programs.

2 Why do companies develop formal mentoring programs? What are the potential benefits for the mentor? For the protégé?

3 Your boss is interested in hiring a consultant to help identify potential managers among current employees of a fast-food restaurant. The manager's job is to help wait on customers and prepare food during busy times, oversee all aspects of restaurant operations (including scheduling, maintenance, on-the-job training and the purchase of food) and help motivate employees to provide high-quality service. The manager is also responsible for resolving disputes that might occur between employees. The position involves working under stress and coordinating several activities at one time. Your boss asks you to outline the type of assessment program you believe would do the best job of identifying employees who will be successful managers. What will you say?

4 What is coaching? What roles may coaches play? Explain.

5 Why should companies be interested in helping employees plan their careers? What benefits can companies gain? What are the risks?

6 What is the manager's role in a career management system? Which role do you think is most difficult for the typical manager? Which is the easiest role? List the reasons why managers might resist involvement in career management.

CASE STUDY

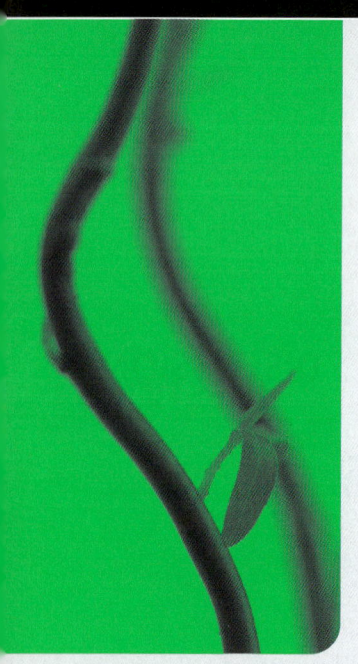

SUPPORT FROM THE SIDELINES

Most organisations understand the value of having effective leaders, but hiring them in from outside is an expensive exercise. Teresa Russell talks with two organisations that have invested in coaching to get the most of their senior people and up-and-coming leaders.

A GREAT football coach can turn a team of players that won the wooden spoon one year into a team of champions holding the trophy at the grand final the next. The team members don't change, it's just that the new coach is able to bring the best out in the players. They may learn a few new skills from the coach, but mostly, the coach just gets all the previously untapped talent to shine. The same principle applies to business coaches.

Carolyn Barker, the CEO of the Australian Institute of Management for Queensland and the Northern Territory, says that a good coach should be an objective sounding board, able to provide honest feedback and support. So what does that look like in real terms?

Stockland

As one of Australia's top 30 companies, Stockland employs around 1400 people throughout its 40 shopping centres and in its Saville hotel business. Rilla Moore, executive general manager of human resources, says the company has experienced 400 per cent growth in the five years leading up to 2005, resulting in a huge influx of new people.

'Despite the fact that we have a very young staff (80 per cent are 40 or under) and our oldest senior leader is 43, the group has fantastic business skills. The organisation believes in the power of effective leadership and its positive impact on business results', says Moore. Coaching is a key element in Stockland's succession management, talent management and leadership development—three areas the company has identified as key to its successful leadership.

Many organisations employ external coaches for senior management teams, but Stockland has gone one step further. Its 40 top leaders have attended an advanced skills coaching program to become better coaches of their own people.

Moore has three coaching vendors which were selected because of her knowledge of the market. 'Good coaching providers do extensive interviewing and match individuals with a coach based on requirements and style. It's critical when selecting the coach to get the chemistry right. The individual must also be ready to accept coaching. It's very expensive—if you push people into it too soon, you won't maximise your investment', she says.

Coaching topics covered by the external consultants include effectively leading your own team, working effectively with your peers, working effectively with your boss and understanding the organisational dynamics (culture) and working within them. 'Of course, none of this works unless you have an MD who is committed and demonstrates the leadership attributes you want in the organisation', says Moore.

Coaching outcomes are measured in both qualitative and quantitative ways at Stockland. The company undertakes an annual employee survey measuring, among other things, people leadership and employee engagement—key drivers of productivity and retention. Moore says that the organisation rates highly on both these measures and that turnover at Stockland is below the industry average. Exit surveys show that 90 per cent of departing employees would be happy to work for Stockland again. She also uses 360-degree surveys and observation of behaviour, as well as feedback from an employee's manager.

HR professionals need to be the architects of an organisation's leadership development and people strategy, clearly positioning the coaching as part of the strategy and not just as an ad hoc addition to the program. Also, says Moore, 'you must monitor and measure results and make sure that people understand why they are being coached. They have to understand whether it is to help them do their current job, or to skill them up for their next role.'

Moore also believes it is vital for HR professionals to be good coaches themselves. She coaches a few of the top people at Stockland, who chose her over an external coach.

NSW Independent Pricing and Regulatory Tribunal

Operating as a statutory authority with 73 full-time and part-time staff, the NSW Independent Pricing and Regulatory Tribunal (IPART) is an independent economic regulator of electricity, gas, water and transport.

Marianne Guy, IPART's human resources manager, describes the organisation as a young agency with enthusiastic, passionate and professional staff who are, for the most part, analysts with economic, engineering, legal or financial training. 'All managers are coaches—whether they know it or not. Leaders are responsible for getting the best possible performance from their staff. Calling it coaching makes it more personal', says Guy.

IPART started a formal coaching program two years ago, initially motivated by a need for succession planning. It was called an executive development program, starting with 360-degree feedback and followed by four one-hour coaching sessions. Guy says that the results were powerful because most people had never been involved in 360-degree feedback before and now everyone was involved.

'The coaching was like a rebirth for some managers who were prepared to have high disclosure. Every manager who went through got something out of it,' says Guy.

She believes that HR's role should be to facilitate the learning experience for managers and to encourage their full participation. 'If you are ever offered coaching, you should grab it. It's like attending a classroom lecture, multiplied by one thousand in just one hour.' She sees another part of her role as matching the correct provider with the organisation and providing feedback to them during the process.

After canvassing six external providers, she chose one that not only had a good cultural fit with IPART, but also had extensive experience with other agencies. 'We wanted the coaching to be a fun journey that would not bog managers down. It had to be personal and enjoyable—almost contagious', she says.

The effectiveness of the coaching is measured through feedback, and some of the best feedback Guy received was from the CEO. The progress made by one of his direct reports was extraordinary and greatly contributed to the CEO's continuing support of the program over time.

Phase two of the program is currently under discussion, but will involve face-to-face training with managers about how to coach members of their teams, followed by more individual coaching.

How to pick a coach and what to ask

Look at previous coaching experience
- How long have you worked as a coach?
- In what kinds of organisations and industry sectors have you worked?
- What kinds of issues/problems have you coached individuals on?

Ask for references
- Are you able to provide references/contact details from previous clients?
- Are they members of a professional body?
- Are you a member of any professional bodies? If so, at what level?
- Do you adhere to a code of ethics/conduct as part of your membership?

Check out professional indemnity insurance
- Do you hold professional indemnity insurance?
- If yes, with whom and at what level?

Look at supervision issues
- How do you maintain your objectivity and perspective during coaching?
- Do you have your own coach/supervisor?

Assess their method
- How do you suggest we evaluate the success/impact of the coaching?
- Can you describe the theoretical framework you use for your coaching?
- What tools and models do you like to use?

Source: AIM, QLD and NT

Source: T. Russell, 2006, 'Support from the sidelines', *Human Resources*, 6 March, pp. 16–17. www.humanresourcesmagazine.com.au

QUESTIONS

1 Outline the main features of the approach to coaching described in this case.
2 How could coaching be measured and evaluated?

PART 4

REWARDING PEOPLE

13 Managing Compensation

14 Performance-related Pay

CHAPTER 13: MANAGING COMPENSATION

Peter Holland

Objectives

After reading this chapter, you should be able to:

1. List the major decision areas and concepts in employee compensation management.
2. Describe the major administrative tools used to manage employee compensation.
3. Explain the importance of competitive labour-market and product-market forces in compensation decisions.
4. Discuss the significance of process issues such as communication in compensation management.
5. Describe new developments in the design of pay structures.
6. Explain the reasons for the controversy over executive pay.
7. Describe the regulatory framework for pay in Australia.

What Are You Worth? AHRI Remuneration & Benefits Survey

A shortage of HR practitioners for mid-level to senior generalist positions and some specialists is becoming critical, leading to longer recruitment periods and a tendency to bigger starting packages for job candidates.

While there is no evidence of an explosion in salaries, a survey by the Australian Human Resource Institute (AHRI) members has found base salaries across all disciplines increased by 5.5 per cent last year, outstripping CPI (3 per cent) but coming in under Australian Bureau of Statistics Average Weekly Ordinary Time Earnings (AWOTE) index of 6.2 per cent.

The annual AHRI Remunerations and Benefits survey recorded larger increases across the board in the private sector, although public sector HR administrators reported the biggest single average increase for the year of 6.8 per cent. In the private sector, the highest increase went to HR advisors (6.2 per cent), technical experts (6.0 per cent), middle management (5.9 per cent) and senior management (5.9 per cent).

Employers and recruiters contacted by *HR Monthly* variously blame the shortage of practitioners on industry sector-specific issues such as the resources boom, new legislation (WorkChoices, super choice and amendments to OHS law); and, to some extent the failure by organisations to train and mentor practitioners to allow them to take on more senior, strategic roles. A recent forecast by Hays Human Resource adds that a number of recent restructures have led to a demand for HR generalists who are 'commercially aware and can operate at a higher strategic level'.

The Olivier Internet Job Index shows that, while the 42.1 per cent increase in the number of job ads for HR practitioners in the past 12 months hasn't been as high as in some professions (such as engineering and in some financial service sectors), it is significantly above the average of 34.6 per cent. Western Australia and Queensland recorded the highest increase in the number of ads (57.2 per cent and 56.5 per cent), thanks to the resources boom in WA says Robert Olivier of the Olivier Group, and the maturing of the economy in Queensland. Olivier says a large part of the increase in HR job ads is down to growth in size of SMEs coupled with a raft of new employment laws leading to a need for practitioners.

The shortage of HR job candidates is 'the most dramatic I've seen in four years', says HR practice leader for Hudson, Emma Wright. She confirms 'significant increase' in remuneration for mid-level HR generalists and some specialists. Headhunting candidates is also becoming more common at lower levels of seniority, with one recruiter commenting that searching for candidates at the $60 000 level is no longer unusual.

Among the generalists, those winning the jobs and commanding the highest packages are the 'commercially astute operators who can link HR strategy to the business objectives and therefore have a direct impact on the bottom line', says Wright.

It's a theme repeated again and again by employers and recruiters.

Noting the 'huge demand' for 'middle senior level' practitioners, Melanie Laing, regional HR director at Unisys Asia Pacific, says those with the appropriate skills are 'thin on the ground'.

The introduction of improved attraction and retention strategies is also driving demand for compensation and benefits experts who have achieved average salary increases of 7.2 per cent according to the AHRI survey.

In a candidates' market, HR practitioners are not only asking for bigger salaries, they are also becoming more choosy about their working conditions. Gabrielle Riddington from Hamilton James & Bruce says flexible hours are increasingly sought by candidates and granted by employers.

Candidates very much know their value in the market and they're definitely looking for flexibility

What Are You Worth? AHRI Remuneration & Benefits Survey *continued*

and being able to really balance their lifestyle and their work more says Nicole Issacs, regional director of Hays Human Resources.

Issacs says she has just recruited for an organisation with a minimal turnover and where many of the staff have been employed for more than 10 years. 'I asked the client what it is about the organisation that made people stay. He said it is the culture. Nobody puts in for overtime, even though they have the right, because they know if they need to take time off or work different hours for a period their pay won't be docked.'

The non-financial elements of reward and recognition are as important to candidates as the financial ones, says Laing for Unisys. While more people are demanding flexibility, others want to nail down their career paths.

'We've really had to seriously look at HR and treat it—as we should be doing—as we would any other part of the organisation', says Laing. 'That's meant career development programs, identifying the high performers and looking for those who can be included in the talent management program.'

Source: Adapted from T. Evan, 2006, *HR Monthly*, April, pp. 18–25.

TABLE A Average base salary movement

Position	%
Consultant—general	4.9
Consultant—HR specific	5.2
Non-HR executive	4.2
HR administrator	5.7
HR advisor	5.8
HR middle management	5.5
Manager—operations	4.9
Manager—other	5.9
Professional/technical expert	5.2
Senior HR management	5.8
Non-HR senior management	5.0
Other	4.0

TABLE B HR administrator

	Private	Public
BASE SALARY ($)	54 226*	54 903**
Annual leave loading	765	672
Entertainment allowance	–	6 000
Car allowance	4 500	–
TOTAL CASH ($)	54 576	55 537
Original cost of vehicle provided	36 500	–
Parking	1 000	–
Other benefits subject to FBT	24 804	900
Other benefits not subject to FBT	–	–
Employer superannuation	5 026	6 437
TOTAL REMUNERATION ($)	62 240	62 021
Fringe benefit tax	14 298	848
TOTAL EMPLOYMENT COST ($)	64 164	62 066
Performance bonus	5 244	2 944
TOTAL PACKAGE ($)	65 576	62 686

* Annual percentage movement in base salary 5.4%
** Annual percentage movement in base salary 6.8%

What Are You Worth? AHRI Remuneration & Benefits Survey *continued*

TABLE C Middle management

	Private	Public
BASE SALARY ($)	79 832*	77 895**
Annual leave loading	910	980
Entertainment allowance	–	3 000
Car allowance	13 437	11 500
TOTAL CASH ($)	81 731	78 871
Original cost of vehicle provided	32 989	32 508
Parking	3 772	1 500
Other benefits subject to FBT	3 377	11 420
Other benefits not subject to FBT	3 626	10 606
Employer superannuation	7 709	8 940
TOTAL REMUNERATION ($)	92 322	91 933
Fringe benefit tax	5 323	7 039
TOTAL EMPLOYMENT COST ($)	93 627	94 117
Performance bonus	10 364	9 990
TOTAL PACKAGE ($)	98 369	96 529

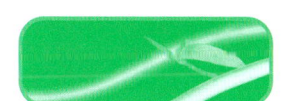

* Annual percentage movement in base salary 5.9%
** Annual percentage movement in base salary 4.5%

TABLE D Senior HR manager

	Private	Public
BASE SALARY ($)	119 106*	99 371**
Annual leave loading	1 381	1 243
Entertainment allowance	3 863	3 333
Car allowance	18 080	11 260
TOTAL CASH ($)	123 348	101 193
Original cost of vehicle provided	41 790	34 045
Parking	3 778	3 278
Other benefits subject to FBT	10 403	10 226
Other benefits not subject to FBT	5 195	3 960
Employer superannuation	12 236	11 311
TOTAL REMUNERATION ($)	140 890	116 983
Fringe benefit tax	8 691	7 140
TOTAL EMPLOYMENT COST ($)	144 702	120 256
Performance bonus	25 641	9 464
TOTAL PACKAGE ($)	160 275	123 411

* Annual percentage movement in base salary 5.9%
** Annual percentage movement in base salary 5.4%

Introduction

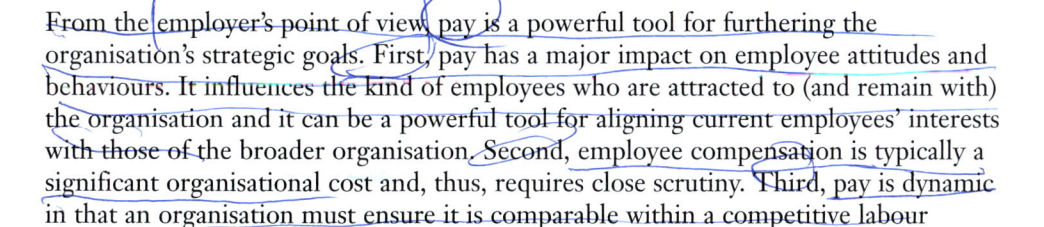

From the employer's point of view, pay is a powerful tool for furthering the organisation's strategic goals. First, pay has a major impact on employee attitudes and behaviours. It influences the kind of employees who are attracted to (and remain with) the organisation and it can be a powerful tool for aligning current employees' interests with those of the broader organisation. Second, employee compensation is typically a significant organisational cost and, thus, requires close scrutiny. Third, pay is dynamic in that an organisation must ensure it is comparable within a competitive labour market (as the opening case study illustrates).

From the employees' point of view, policies having to do with wages, salaries and other earnings have a major impact on their overall income and, therefore, their standard of living (for example see tables A, B and C). In addition, both the level of pay and its seeming fairness compared with others' pay is important. In Australia this has become an increasingly important issue as successive federal governments continue to deregulate the labour-market structures and wage-determining mechanisms, integrating us further into the global labour market. Pay is also often considered a sign of status and success. In a labour market where skill shortages are becoming a major issue, employees attach great importance to pay decisions when they evaluate their relationship with the organisation. Therefore, pay decisions must be carefully managed and communicated.

Pay decisions can be broken into two major areas: pay structure (the relative pay of different jobs and how much they are paid) and individual pay. In this chapter, we focus on pay structure, which, in turn, entails a consideration of pay level and job structure. Pay level is defined here as the average pay (including wages, salaries and bonuses) of jobs in an organisation. Job structure refers to the relative pay of jobs in an organisation. Consider the same two jobs in two different organisations. In organisation one, jobs A and B are paid an annual average compensation of $40 000 and $60 000, respectively. In organisation two, the pay rates are $45 000 and $55 000, respectively. Organisations one and two have the same pay level ($50 000) but the job structures (relative rates of pay) differ.

Both pay level and job structures are characteristics of organisations and reflect decisions about jobs rather than about individual employees. This chapter's focus is on why and how organisations attach pay policies to jobs. In the next chapter (Chapter 14 Performance-related pay), we look within jobs to discuss the different approaches that can be used to determine the pay of individual employees as well as the advantages and disadvantages of these different approaches.

Why focus on developing a pay structure for jobs? As the number of employees in an organisation increases, so too does the number of human resource management decisions. In determining compensation, for example, each employee must be assigned a rate of pay that is acceptable in terms of external, internal and individual equity and in terms of the employer's cost. Although each employee is unique—and thus requires some degree of individualised treatment—standardising the treatment of similar employees (for example, those with similar jobs) can help greatly to make compensation administration and decision making more manageable and more equitable. Thus, pay policies are often attached to particular jobs rather than tailored entirely to individual employees.

Pay structure
the relative pay of different jobs (job structure) and how much they are paid (pay level).

Pay level
the average pay, including wages, salaries and bonuses, of jobs in an organisation.

Job structure
the relative pay of jobs in an organisation.

Equity theory and fairness

In discussing the consequences of pay decisions, it is useful to keep in mind that employees often evaluate their pay relative to that of other employees. Equity theory suggests that people evaluate the fairness of their situations by comparing them with those of other people.[1]

According to the theory, a person, P, compares his or her own ratio of perceived outcomes, O (for example, pay, benefits, working conditions) to perceived inputs, I (for example, effort, ability and experience) to the ratio of a comparison other, o.

$$O_p/I_p <, >, \text{ or } = O_o/I_o$$

If P's ratio (O_p/I_p) is smaller than the comparison other's ratio (O_o/I_o), under-reward inequity results. If P's ratio is larger, over-reward inequity results, although evidence suggests that this type of inequity is less likely to occur and less likely to be sustained because P may rationalise the situation by re-evaluating his or her outcomes less favourably or inputs (that is, self-worth) more favourably.[2]

The consequences of *P*'s comparisons depend on whether equity is perceived. If equity is perceived, no change is expected in *P*'s attitudes or behaviour. In contrast, perceived inequity may cause *P* to restore equity. Some ways of restoring equity are counterproductive, including:

- reducing one's own inputs (for example, not working as hard)
- increasing one's outcomes (for example, theft)
- leaving the situation that generates perceived inequity (for example, leaving the organisation or refusing to work or cooperate with employees who are perceived as over-rewarded).

As noted, equity theory's main implication for managing employee compensation is that to an important extent, employees evaluate their pay by comparing it with what others get paid, and their work attitudes and behaviours are influenced by such comparisons. Another implication is that employee perceptions are what determine their evaluation. The fact that management believes its employees are paid well compared with those of other companies does not necessarily translate into employees' beliefs. Employees may have different information or make different comparisons than management. The way management communicates these benefits can also be a factor.

(See the 'Managing challenges through HR innovation: Bonus envy—when $500 000 is not enough' case on page 513 and 'HRM spotlight: Big Rewards can stick in craw, Howard admits' on page 511.)

Three types of employee social comparisons of pay are especially relevant in making pay-level and job-structure decisions (see Table 13.1 overleaf). First, external equity pay comparisons focus on what employees in other organisations are paid for doing the same general job. Such comparisons are likely to influence the decisions of applicants to accept job offers as well as the attitudes and decisions of employees about whether to stay with an organisation or take a job elsewhere (see Chapter 6 Analysis and design of work, and Chapter 15 Ethics and human resource management). The organisation's choice of pay level influences its employees' external pay comparisons and their consequences. A market pay survey is the major administrative tool that organisations use in choosing a pay level. Second, internal equity pay comparisons focus on what employees within the same organisation, but in different jobs, are paid. Employees make comparisons with lower-level jobs, jobs at the same level (but perhaps in different skill areas or product divisions) and jobs at higher levels. In Australia a common issue is where one group or level of employees win substantial increases in terms and conditions; this 'wage drift' subsequently causes wage compression with higher level groups within the organisation and may be a source of conflict for management as they attempt to re-establish comparative work values (also see Chapter 5 Industrial relations). This point illustrates the perceptions of fairness[3] in the workplace, which assumes:

- there is an unrecognised comparative standard of fair payment for all levels within the organisation
- an unconscious or tacit knowledge of the standards exists and is shared throughout the workforce
- equitable pay is only achieved when it is perceived to match the level of work or effort and the individual's ability to undertake it.[4]

These comparisons may influence general attitudes of employees; their willingness to transfer to other jobs within the organisation; their willingness to accept promotions; their inclination to cooperate across jobs, functional areas or product

TABLE 13.1 Pay structure concepts and consequences

Pay structure decision area	Administrative tools	Focus of employee pay comparisons	Consequences of equity perceptions
Pay level	Market pay surveys	External equity	External employee movement (attraction and retention of quality employees); labour costs; and employee attitudes
Job structure	Job evaluation	Internal equity	Internal employee movement (promotion and job rotation); cooperation among employees; and employee attitudes

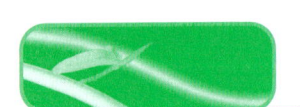

groups; and their commitment to the organisation. The organisation's choice of job structure influences its employees' internal comparisons and their consequences. **Job evaluation** is the major administrative tool organisations use to design job structures.

Third, employees make internal equity pay comparisons with others performing the same job. Such comparisons are most relevant to the following chapter (Chapter 14 Performance-related pay), which focuses on using pay to recognise individual contributions and differences.

It is clear that equity and consistency are the main aims of pay structure decisions, while the dynamic nature of the internal and external environment will continually distort this relationship. In addressing the issues of fairness and equity, organisations should be seen to be acting in accordance with the principles of distributive and procedural justice ideals. **Distributive justice** refers to the perception that rewards are distributed in relation to contribution—an issue that has raised considerable debate in the area of executive pay. **Procedural justice** (also procedural fairness)—a concept of justice focusing on the methods used to determine the outcomes received—refers to the process and policies that govern pay decisions. We now turn to ways to choose and develop pay levels and pay structures, the consequences of such choices and the ways in which two administrative tools—market pay surveys and job evaluation—help in making pay decisions. (See 'Managing challenges through sustainability: $7.8m farewell calls pay deals into question' on page 492).

Job evaluation
an administrative procedure used to measure job worth.

Distributive justice
(also distributive fairness) the perception that rewards are distributed in relation to contribution.

Procedural justice
(also procedural fairness) a concept of justice focusing on the methods used to determine the outcomes received.

Developing pay levels

In developing pay levels within the organisation, several key criteria need to be taken into account such as external or market factors and internal organisational issues. Market factors in particular are becoming an increasingly important aspect of attracting quality human resources in countries like Australia that are experiencing significant skill shortages across a variety of sectors.

Market pressures

Any organisation faces two important competitive market challenges in deciding what to pay its employees: product-market competition and labour-market competition.

Product-market competition
First, organisations must compete effectively in the product market. In other words, they must be able to sell their goods and services at a quantity and price that will

bring a sufficient return on their investment. Organisations compete on multiple dimensions (for example, quality and service) and price is one of the most important dimensions. An important influence on price is the cost of production.

An organisation that has higher labour costs than its product-market competitors will have to charge higher average prices for products of similar quality. Thus, for example, if labour costs are 30 per cent of revenues at company A and company B, but company A has labour costs that are 20 per cent higher than those of company B, we would expect company A to have product prices that are higher by (0.30 × 0.20) = 6%. At some point, the higher price charged by company A will contribute to a loss of its business to competing companies with lower prices (like company B). One study in the United States, for example, found that in the early 1990s the wage and benefit cost to produce a small car was approximately US$1700 for Ford Motor Co., US$1800 for Chrysler and US$2400 for General Motors.[5] Thus, if all other costs were equal, General Motors would have to sell the same quality car for US$600 to US$700 more than would Ford or Chrysler.

Therefore, product-market competition places an upper boundary on labour costs and compensation. This upper boundary is more constrictive when labour costs are a larger share of total costs and when demand for the product is affected by changes in price (that is, demand is elastic). Although costs are only one part of the competitive equation (productivity is just as important), higher costs may result in a loss of business. In the absence of clear evidence on productivity differences, costs need to be closely monitored.

What components make up labour costs? A major component is the average cost per employee. This is made up of both direct payments (such as wages, salaries and bonuses) and indirect payments (such as health insurance, social security and unemployment compensation). A second major component of labour costs is the staffing level (number of employees). Not surprisingly, financially troubled organisations often seek to cut costs by focusing on one or both components. Staff reductions, hiring freezes, wage and salary freezes, and sharing benefits costs with employees are several ways of enhancing the organisation's competitive position in the product market.

Labour-market competition

A second important competitive market challenge is labour-market competition. Essentially, labour-market competition is the amount an organisation must pay to compete against other companies that hire similar employees. These labour-market competitors typically include not only companies that have similar products but also those in different product markets that hire similar types of employees. If an organisation is not competitive in the labour market, it will fail to attract and retain employees of sufficient numbers and quality. For example, even if a computer manufacturer offers newly graduated electrical engineers the same pay as other computer manufacturers, if automobile manufacturers and other labour-market competitors offer salaries $10 000 higher, the computer company may not be able to hire enough qualified electrical engineers. Labour-market competition places a lower boundary on pay levels.

Employees as a resource

Organisations have to compete in the labour market; therefore, they should consider their employees not only as a cost, but as a resource in which the organisation has invested and from which it expects valuable returns (also see Chapter 18 Evaluating and improving the human resource function). Although controlling costs has a direct effect on an organisation's ability to compete in the product market, the organisation's competitive position can be compromised if costs are kept low at the expense of employee productivity and quality. Having higher labour costs than your competitors is not necessarily 'bad' if you also have the best and most effective workforce—one that produces more products of better quality. (See 'Managing challenges of globalisation: Money can't buy you … Performance' case on page 514).

Pay policies and programs are some of the most important human resource tools for encouraging desired employee behaviours and discouraging undesired behaviours. Therefore, they must be evaluated, not just in terms of costs, but in terms of the returns they generate—how they attract, retain and motivate a high-quality workforce. For example, if the average revenue per employee in company A is 20 per cent higher than in company B, it may not be important that the average pay in company A is 10 per cent higher than in company B.

Deciding what to pay

Although organisations face important external labour- and product-market pressures in setting their pay levels, a range of discretion remains.[6] How large the range is depends on the particular competitive environment the organisation faces. Where the range is broad, an important strategic decision is whether to pay above, or below, the market average. The advantage of paying above the market average is the ability to attract and retain the top talent available, which can translate into a highly effective and productive workforce. The disadvantage, however, is the added cost.

So, under what circumstances do the benefits of higher pay outweigh the higher costs? According to efficiency wage theory, one circumstance is when organisations have technologies or structures that depend on highly skilled employees. For example, organisations that emphasise decentralised decision making may need higher calibre employees. Another circumstance where higher pay may be warranted is when an organisation has difficulties observing and monitoring its employees' performance. It may, therefore, wish to provide an above-market pay rate to ensure there is an incentive to put forth maximum effort. The theory is that employees who are paid more than they would be paid elsewhere will be reluctant to 'bludge' (that is, not work hard) because they wish to retain their good job.[7]

Market pay surveys

As mentioned in Chapter 1 (Human resource management in Australia), total quality management emphasises the key importance of benchmarking, a procedure in which an organisation compares its own practices against those of the competition. This notion is relevant in compensation management. Benchmarking against product-market and labour-market competitors is typically accomplished through the use of one or more pay surveys, which provide information about the going rates of pay among competing organisations. The amount and type of benchmarking will be dependent on the size and complexity of the organisation and the nature of the external environment, industry and characteristics of the jobs. The use of pay surveys requires answers to several important questions:[8]

1. Which employers should be included in the survey? Ideally, they would be the key labour-market and product-market competitors.
2. Which jobs are included in the survey? Only a sample of jobs is ordinarily used; therefore care must be taken that the jobs are representative in terms

of level, functional area and product market. Also, the job content must be sufficiently similar.
3. If multiple surveys are used, how are all the rates of pay weighted and combined? Organisations often have to weight and combine pay rates because different surveys are often tailored towards particular employee groups (labour markets) or product markets. The organisation must decide how much relative weight to give to its labour- and product-market competitors in setting pay.

In addition, the contents of the jobs should be clearly defined, understood, and relatively stable and have the agreement of all employees involved. Several factors come into play when deciding how to combine surveys.[9] Product-market comparisons that focus on labour costs are likely to deserve greater weight when:

- labour costs represent a large share of total costs
- product demand is elastic (that is, it changes in response to product price changes)
- the supply of labour is inelastic
- employee skills are specific to the product market (and will remain so).

In contrast, labour-market comparisons may be more important when:

- attracting and retaining qualified employees is difficult
- the costs (administrative, disruption etc.) of recruiting replacements are high.

As this discussion suggests, knowing what other organisations are paying is only one part of the story. It is also necessary to know what those organisations are getting in return for their investment in employees (also see Chapter 18 Evaluating and improving the human resource function). To find that out, some organisations examine ratios such as *revenues:employees* and *revenues:labour* cost. The first ratio includes the staffing component of employee cost, but not the average cost per employee. The second ratio, however, includes both. Note that comparing these ratios across organisations requires caution. For example, different industries rely on different resources (for example, labour and capital). So, comparing the ratio of revenues to labour costs of a petroleum company (that is, capital intensive and high ratio) to a bank (that is, labour intensive and low ratio) would be like comparing apples and oranges. Such comparisons can, however, be useful. Besides revenues, other return-on-investment (ROI) data might include product quality, customer satisfaction and potential workforce quality (for example, average education levels).

Rate ranges

As the preceding discussion suggests, obtaining a single 'going rate' of market pay is a complex task that involves a number of subjective decisions — it is both an art and a science. Once a market rate has been chosen, how is it incorporated into the pay structure? Typically—especially for white-collar jobs—it is used for setting the midpoint of pay-rate ranges for either jobs or pay grades. Market survey data are also often collected on minimum and maximum rates of pay as well. The use of ranges permits a company to recognise differences in employee performance, seniority, training and so forth in setting individual pay (covered in the next chapter, Performance-related pay). In Australia, the changes in the regulation of the labour market since the late 1980s have been important catalysts in the development of pay ranges. The Structural Efficiency Principle (better known as **award restructuring**) established guidelines for the restructuring of industrial awards (which is the basis for the terms and conditions for the many employees in Australia) to incorporate a link between financial rewards and skill acquisition to create appropriate relativities both between and within jobs.

Award restructuring
(or the Structural Efficiency Principle) a reform of the Australian wages system aimed at developing a more highly skilled workplace; for example, by the reduction of job classifications, the establishment of skill-related career paths linked to pay scales, and multi-skilling to enhance workforce flexibility.

$7.8M FAREWELL CALLS PAY DEAL INTO QUESTION

Tony D'Aloisio's generous $7.8 million consolation prize for losing his job as the boss of the Australian Stock Exchange has thrown the spotlight back on executive remuneration.

The Australian Shareholders Association has expressed its concern at the ASX not embracing the practice of rolling contracts, which can keep the termination payments down.

'It does appear that ASX has not adopted the practice current with a lot of companies on a rolling 12-month contracts, rather they have locked him into a three-year contract', said ASX deputy chairman John Curry. 'As a result, they have to pay it all out. If they are on a rolling contract they only have to pay out 12 months.' Mr Curry is concerned that Mr D'Aloisio's successor, Robert Elstone, has the same fixed-term contract.

Corporate governance specialist ISS Australia said companies had swung away from long fixed-term contracts unless there were mitigating circumstances. 'It is out of step with investor expectations', said ISS director Dean Paatsch.

Mr Curry acknowledged that Mr D'Aloisio 'has worked very hard and he has done everything the ASX wanted from him and then got the prize taken away, so I feel a little sympathy with him'.

'(The payment) is high, but there are some definite reasons—it's not like he was moved sideways by the board for non-performance', he said.

In the US debate on executive remuneration has been sparked by companies being caught backdating options to enable executives to collect at notably low share prices.

In Australia, the corporate regulator is investigating claims that some companies are allowing executives to hedge their options without telling shareholders.

Remuneration was a focus for shareholders last year after Federal Government-initiated changes gave them a non-binding vote on executive pay. The Australian Council of Superannuation Investors recommended it members vote against 35 separate remuneration packages during the annual meeting season, including on the grounds of excessive termination payments.

TOP 20 PAYOUTS 1999–2005

Name	Company	Payment ($) millions	Year
Chris Cuffe	Commonwealth Bank (Colonial First State)	26.54	2003
David Murray	Commonwealth Bank	17.50	2005
Brian Gilbertson	BHP Billiton	9.99	2002
Paul Anderson	BHP Billiton	9.13	2002
Peter MacDonald	James Hardie	8.24	2004
Sheryl Pressler	Lend Lease	7.99	2001
John Fletcher	Brambles	7.71	2001
David Higgins	Lend Lease	6.67	2003
Frank Cicutto	NAB	6.61	2004
Peter Yates	PBL	6.54	2004
Michael Chaney	Wesfarmers	5.37	2005
Len Bleasel	AGL	4.81	2001
Dennis Eck	Coles Myer	4.71	2001
Tom Fraser	AMP	4.68	2002
Fred Hilmer	Fairfax	4.50	2005
Peter Shafron	James Hardie	4.41	2004
Keith Lambert	Southcorp	4.37	2003
John Akehurst	Woodside Petroleum	3.55	2003

Source: ISS Australia
Some amounts consist partly of accrued bonuses and other payments

Source: Cartoon by Andrew Weldon, 2006, 'Levels of Compensation', *The Age*, 27 July, Business, p. 1.

Source: Based on Kirsty Simpson, 2006, '$7.8m farewell calls pay deal into question', *The Age*, 27 July, Business, p. 1.

Key jobs and non-key jobs

In using pay surveys, it is necessary to make a distinction between two general types of jobs: 'key jobs' (or benchmark jobs) and 'non-key jobs'. Key jobs have relatively stable content and—perhaps most importantly—are common to many organisations. Therefore, it is possible to obtain market pay survey data on them. Note, however, that to avoid too much of an administrative burden, organisations may not gather market pay data on all such jobs. In contrast to key jobs, non-key jobs are, to an important extent, unique to organisations; thus, by definition, they cannot be directly valued or compared through the use of market surveys. Therefore, they are treated differently in the pay-setting process.

Developing a job structure

Although external comparisons of the sort we have been discussing are important, employees also evaluate their pay using internal comparisons. For example, a director of marketing may expect to be paid roughly the same amount as a director of information systems because they are at the same organisational level, with similar levels of responsibility and similar impacts on the organisation's performance. A job structure can be defined as the relative worth of various jobs in the organisation, based on these types of internal comparisons. We now turn to a discussion of how such decisions are made.

Job evaluation

One typical way of measuring job worth is to perform an administrative procedure called job evaluation. Evaluations can be generated in a variety of ways but they typically include input from a number of people. A job evaluation committee is commonly used to generate ratings. There are numerous ways to evaluate jobs. These can generally be categorised as non-analytical and analytical schemes. Non-analytical schemes simply compare whole jobs and make no allowance for specific job-related factors. The most common is the job-ranking method. The job-ranking method compares each job within the organisations and ranks them in a hierarchy of importance to the organisations. The benefits of this method are its simplicity and ease of understanding as well as being relatively inexpensive to maintain. However, the rankings are likely to be somewhat arbitrary and while there might not be problems with 'vertical' comparison, the method may present difficulties with 'horizontal' evaluations, which involve determining comparable worth across the organisation. To overcome this, basic paired comparisons can be introduced. This involves a point system, which evaluates pairs on a basis of 'win, lose or draw'.

The most widely used approach is the analytical approach. The most popular methods include the point-factor or point-rating system, which yields job evaluation points for each compensable factor (the characteristics of jobs that an organisation values and chooses to pay for) and factor comparison, which compares jobs against a number of factors.[10] The point-factor system generates scores for each compensable factor of each job. Job evaluators often apply a weighting scheme to account for the differing importance of the compensable factors to the organisation. Weights can be generated in two ways. First, 'a priori' weights can be assigned, which means factors are weighted using expert judgments about the importance of each compensable factor. Second, weights can be derived empirically based on how important each factor seems to be in determining pay in the labour market. (Statistical methods such as multiple regression can be used for this purpose.) For the sake of simplicity, we assume in the following example that equal 'a priori' weights are chosen, which means that the scores on the compensable factors can be simply summed.

Key jobs
benchmark jobs, used in pay surveys, that have relatively stable content and are common to many organisations.

Non-key jobs
unique to organisations, and cannot be directly valued or compared through the use of market surveys.

Compensable factors
the characteristics of jobs that an organisation values and chooses to pay for.

Table 13.2 below shows an example of a three-factor job evaluation system applied to three jobs. Note that the jobs differ in the levels of experience, education and complexity required. Summing the scores on the three compensable factors provides an internally oriented assessment of relative job worth in the organisation. In a sense, the computer programmer job is worth 41 per cent (155/110 – 1) more than the computer operator job and the systems analyst job is worth 91 per cent (210/110 – 1) more than the computer operator job. Whatever pay level is chosen (based on benchmarking and competitive strategy), we would expect the pay differentials to be somewhat similar to these percentages. The internal job evaluation and external survey-based measures of worth can, however, diverge. The advantages of this method include increased reliability and objectivity because it is based on a series of criteria that have been weighted in terms of their importance to the organisation. By evaluating key criteria they are more acceptable for horizontal comparison of work value. However, this method is time consuming to develop and maintain and assumes that all aspects of the job can be quantified in the same way. In addition, the nature of the weighting, no matter how systematic, will always be a subjective interpretation. It also assumes that this weighting will not change.[11]

Factor comparison in principle is an analytical method as it uses a comparative approach to jobs on the basis of a number of factors. Typical factors could include:

- mental requirements
- skill requirements
- physical requirements
- responsibilities
- working conditions.

The major advantage of this method is that factors are compared job by job. This provides the opportunity to evaluate each job on its individual merits within the organisation. However, this method has the drawbacks of being complex and time consuming to undertake and maintain.[12]

Developing a pay structure

In the example provided in Table 13.3 opposite, there are 15 jobs, 10 of which are key jobs. For these key jobs, both pay survey and job evaluation data are available. For the five non-key jobs, by definition, no survey data are available, only job evaluation information. Note that, for simplicity's sake, we work with data from only two pay surveys and we use a weighted average that gives twice as much weight to the first survey. Also, our example works with a single structure. Many organisations have multiple structures that correspond to different job families (for example, clerical, technical and professional) or product divisions.

TABLE 13.2 Example of a three-factor job evaluation system

	Compensable factors			
Job title	Experience	Education	Complexity	Total
Computer operator	40	30	40	110
Computer programmer	40	50	65	155
Systems analyst	65	60	85	210

How are the data in Table 13.3 combined to develop a pay structure? First, it is important to note that both internal and external comparisons must be considered in making compensation decisions. However, because the pay structures suggested by internal and external comparisons do not necessarily converge, employers must carefully balance them. Studies suggest that employers may differ significantly in the degree to which they place priority on internal- or external-comparison data in developing pay structures.[13]

At least three pay setting approaches, which differ according to their relative emphasis on external or internal comparisons, can be identified.[14]

Market survey data

The approach with the greatest emphasis on external comparisons (that is, market survey data) is achieved by directly basing pay on market surveys that cover as many key jobs as possible. For example, the fortnightly rate of pay for job A in Table 13.4, on page 497, would be $1919; for job B, $2106; and for job C, $2807. For non-key jobs (jobs D, E, H, M and O), however, pay survey information is not available, and we must proceed differently. Basically, we develop a market **pay-policy line** based on the key jobs (for which there are both job evaluation and market pay survey data available). As Figure 13.1 overleaf shows, the data can be plotted with a line of best fit estimated. This line can be generated using a statistical procedure (regression analysis). In other words, the predicted monthly salary (based on fitting a line to the key job data) is obtained by plugging the number of job evaluation points into this equation. Thus, for example, job D, a non-key job, would have a predicted monthly salary of $3083.

Pay-policy line
a mathematical expression that describes the relationship between a job's pay and its job evaluation points.

TABLE 13.3 Job evaluation and pay survey data

Job	Key job?	Job title	Job evaluation	Survey 1 (S1)	Survey 2 (S2)	Survey composite (2/3 × S1 + 1/3 × S2)
A	y	Computer operator	110	$2012	$1731	$1919
B	y	Engineering tech I	115	2206	1908	2106
C	y	Computer programmer	155	2916	2589	2807
D	n	Engineering tech II	165	—	—	—
E	n	Compensation analyst	170	—	—	—
F	y	Accountant	190	3613	3099	3442
G	y	Systems analyst	210	4275	3854	4134
H	n	Computer programmer—senior	225	—	—	—
I	y	Director of personnel	245	4982	4506	4823
J	y	Accountant—senior	255	5205	4270	4893
K	y	Systems analyst—senior	270	5868	5652	5796
L	y	Industrial engineer	275	5496	4794	5262
M	n	Chief accountant	315	—	—	—
N	y	Senior engineer	320	7026	6572	6875
O	n	Senior scientist	330	—	—	—

Source: Adapted from S. Rynes, B. Gerhart, G.T. Milkovich & J. Boudreau, 1988, *Current Compensation Professional Institute*, American Compensation Association, Scottsdale, AZ. Used with permission.

As Figure 13.1 also indicates, it is not necessary to fit a straight line to the job evaluation and pay survey data. In some cases, a pay structure that provides increasing monetary rewards to higher level jobs may be more consistent with the organisation's goals or with the external market. For example, non-linearity may be more appropriate if higher level jobs are especially valuable to organisations and the talent to perform such jobs is rare—for example, executive positions.

Pay policy line

A second pay setting approach that combines information from external and internal comparisons is to use the pay policy line to derive pay rates for both key and non-key jobs. This approach differs from the first approach in that actual market rates are no longer used for key jobs. This introduces a greater degree of internal consistency into the structure because the pay for all the jobs is directly linked to the number of job evaluation points.

Pay grades

Pay grades
jobs of similar worth or content grouped together for pay administration purposes.

A third approach is to group jobs into a smaller number of pay classes or **pay grades** (jobs of similar worth or content grouped together for pay administration purposes). Table 13.5 opposite (see also Table 13.4 opposite, last column), for example, demonstrates one possibility: a five-grade structure. Each job within a grade would have the same rate range (that is, be assigned the same midpoint, minimum and maximum). The advantage of this approach is that the administrative burden of setting separate rates of pay for hundreds (or thousands) of different jobs is reduced. It also permits greater flexibility in moving employees from job to job without raising concerns about, for example, going from a job having 230 job evaluation points to a job with 215 job evaluation points. What might look like a demotion in a completely job-based system is often a non-issue in a grade-based system. Note that the **range spread** (the distance between the minimum and maximum) is larger at higher levels, in recognition of the fact that performance differences are likely to have more impact on the organisation at higher job levels (see Figure 13.2, page 498). Generally, the overlap should not exceed 50 points of the range.

Range spread
the distance between the minimum and maximum amounts in a pay grade.

FIGURE 13.1 Pay policy lines, linear and natural logarithmic functions

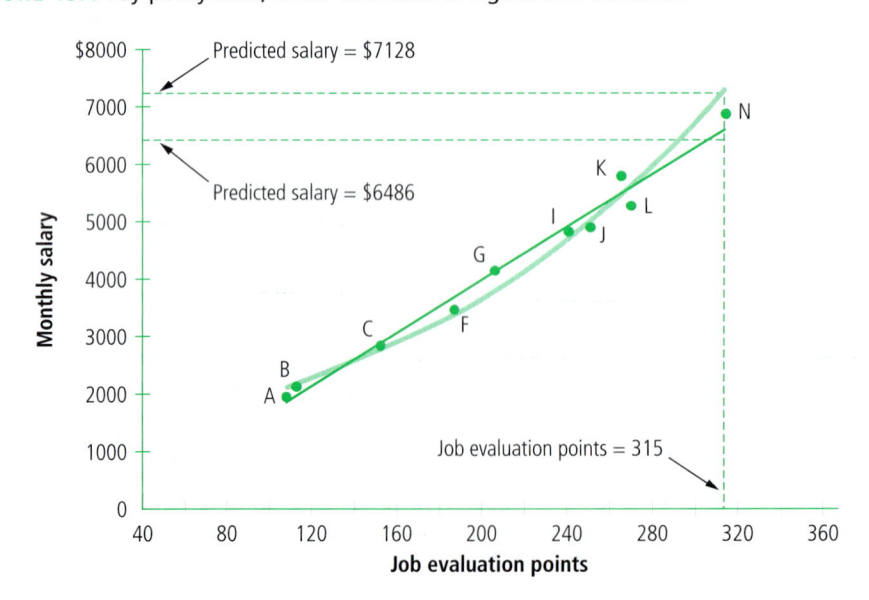

TABLE 13.4 Pay midpoints under different approaches

Job	Key job?	Job title	Job evaluation	(1) Survey + policy	(2) Pay midpoints policy	(3) Grades
A	y	Computer operator	110	$1919	$1835	$2175
B	y	Engineering tech I	115	2106	1948	2175
C	y	Computer programmer	155	2807	2856	3310
D	n	Engineering tech II	165	3083	3083	3310
E	n	Compensation analyst	170	3196	3196	3310
F	y	Accountant	190	3442	3650	3310
G	y	Systems analyst	210	4134	4104	4444
H	n	Computer programmer—senior	225	4444	4444	4444
I	y	Director of personnel	245	4823	4898	4444
J	y	Accountant—senior	255	4893	5125	5579
K	y	Systems analyst—senior	270	5796	5465	5579
L	y	Industrial engineer	275	5262	5579	5579
M	n	Chief accountant	315	6486	6486	6713
N	y	Senior engineer	320	6875	6600	6713
O	n	Senior scientist	330	6826	6826	6713

Source: Adapted from S. Rynes, B. Gerhart, G.T. Milkovich and J. Boudreau, 1988, *Current Compensation Professional Institute*, American Compensation Association, Scottsdale, AZ. Used with permission.

TABLE 13.5 Sample pay grade structure

Pay grade	Job evaluation points range Minimum	Job evaluation points range Maximum	Fortnightly pay rate range Minimum	Fortnightly pay rate range Midpoint	Fortnightly pay rate range Maximum
1	100	150	$1740	$2175	$2610
2	150	200	2648	3310	3971
3	200	250	3555	4444	5333
4	250	300	4463	5579	6694
5	300	350	5370	6713	8056

The disadvantage of using grades is that some jobs will be underpaid and others overpaid. For example, job C and job F both fall within the same grade. The midpoint for job C under a grade system is $3310 per fortnight, or about $400 or so more than under the two alternative pay setting approaches. Obviously, this will contribute to higher labour costs and potential difficulties in competing in the product market. Unless there is an expected return to this increased cost, the approach is questionable. Job F, on the other hand, is paid between $130 and $340 less per fortnight under the grades system than it would be otherwise. Therefore, the company may find it more difficult to compete in the labour market.

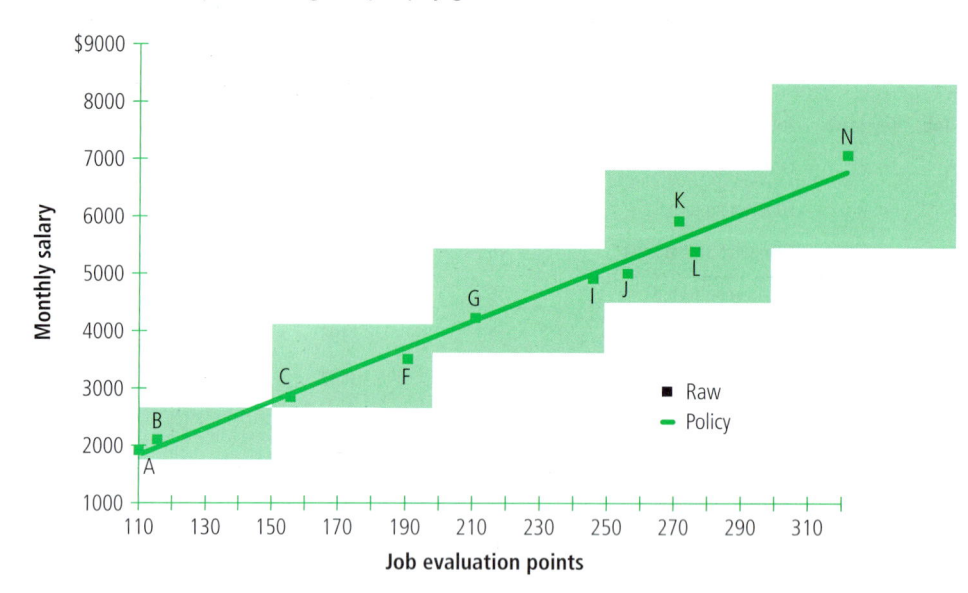

FIGURE 13.2 Graph showing sample pay grade structure

Conflicts between market pay surveys and job evaluation

An examination of Table 13.4 (page 497) suggests that the relative worth of jobs is quite similar overall, whether based on job evaluation or pay survey data. However, some inconsistencies typically arise and these are usually indicated by jobs whose average survey pay is significantly below or above the pay policy line. The closest case in Table 13.4 is job L, for which the average pay falls significantly below the policy line. One possible explanation is that a relatively plentiful supply of people in the labour market are capable of performing this job, so the pay needed to attract and retain them is lower than would be expected given the job evaluation points. Another kind of inconsistency occurs when market surveys show that a job is paid higher than the policy line (for example, job K). Again, this may be a reflection of relative supply and demand, in this case resulting in pay being driven higher.

How are conflicts between external and internal equity resolved, and what are the consequences? The following example of the directors of marketing and information processing may help illustrate the type of choice faced. The marketing director's job may receive the same number of job evaluation points but market survey data may indicate that it typically pays less than the information processing director's job, perhaps because of tighter supply for the latter. Does the organisation pay based on the market survey (external comparison) or on the job evaluation points (internal comparison)? (See the 'Managing challenges through HR innovation: PM's pockets fill with pay rise, tax cuts on page 503).

Emphasising the internal comparison would suggest paying the two directors the same. In doing so, however, either the director of marketing would be 'overpaid' or the director of information processing would be 'underpaid'. The former drives up labour costs (product-market problems); the latter may make it difficult to attract and retain a quality director of information processing (labour-market problems).

Another consideration has to do with the strategy of the organisation. In some organisations (for example, Pepsi and Nike), the marketing function is critical to success. Thus, although the market for marketing directors is lower than that for information technology directors, an organisation may choose to be a pay leader for the marketing position (for example, pay at the 90th percentile) but only meet the market for the information systems position (for example, pay at the 50th percentile). In other words, designing a pay structure requires careful consideration of which positions are most central to dealing with critical environmental challenges and opportunities in reaching the organisation's goals.[15]

What about emphasising external comparisons? Two potential problems arise. First, the director of marketing may be dissatisfied because she expects a job of similar rank and responsibility to that of the information technology director to be paid similarly. Second, it becomes difficult to rotate people through different director positions (for example, as a training and development tool), because going to the marketing director position might appear as a demotion to the director of information processing.

There is no one right solution to such dilemmas. Each organisation must decide which objectives are most essential and choose the appropriate strategy. However, there seems to be a growing sentiment that external comparisons deserve greater weight because organisations are finding it increasingly difficult to ignore market competitive pressures.[16]

Monitoring compensation costs

Pay structure influences compensation costs in a number of ways. Most obviously, the pay level at which the structure is pegged has an influence on these costs. However, this is only part of the story. The pay structure represents the organisation's intended policy, but the actual practice may not coincide with it. Take, for example, the pay-grade structure presented earlier. The midpoint for grade one is $2175, and the midpoint for grade two is $3310. Now consider the data on a group of individual employees in Table 13.6, below. One frequently used index of the correspondence between actual and intended pay is the **compa-ratio**, computed as follows:

$$\text{grade compa-ratio} = \frac{\text{actual average pay for grade}}{\text{pay midpoint for grade}}$$

Compa-ratio
an index of the correspondence between actual and intended pay.

The compa-ratio provides a direct assessment of the degree to which actual pay is consistent with the pay policy. A compa-ratio less than 1.00 suggests that actual pay is

TABLE 13.6 Compa-ratios for two grades

Employee	Job	Pay	Midpoint	Employee compa-ratios
Grade 1				
1	Engineering tech I	$2306	$2175	1.06
2	Computer programmer	2066	2175	0.95
3	Engineering tech I	2523	2175	1.16
4	Engineering tech I	2414	2175	1.11
				1.07
Grade 2				
5	Computer programmer	3906	3310	1.18
6	Accountant	3773	3310	1.14
7	Accountant	3674	3310	1.11
				1.14

lagging behind the policy, whereas a compa-ratio greater than 1.00 indicates that pay (and costs) exceeds that of the policy. Although there may be good reasons for compa-ratios to differ from 1.00, managers should also consider whether the pay structure is allowing costs to get out of control.

Globalisation, geographic region, and pay structures

Market pay structures can differ substantially across countries both in terms of their level and in terms of the relative worth of jobs. Compared with the labour market in Frankfurt, markets in Budapest and Bangalore provide much lower levels of pay overall and much lower payoffs to skill, education and advancement. These differences create a dilemma for global companies (also see Chapter 16 International human resource management).

For example, should an Australian software engineer posted to Bangalore be paid according to the standard in Sydney or Bangalore? Organisations generally have two options when considering the structure of international compensation, these are the market rate and balance sheet approaches. Market rate compensation is linked to the levels and structures of the host country. The advantages of this approach include simplicity in determining and understanding equity at a local level. However, disadvantages can occur with expatriates doing similar jobs in different locations. Such variations can make it difficult to recruit the right person for the job. In our example therefore, if the Bangalore market standard is used, it may be all but impossible to find an Australian software engineer willing to accept an assignment in Bangalore. The balance sheet approach is the more widely used approach. This method focuses on maintaining relativities with the home country and compensating for the costs (both financial and social) in undertaking the assignment. The advantage of this method is that the cost of an overseas assignment is neutralised. However, this method is more complex to manage when relativities such as exchange rates and tax systems are taken into account (for example, the introduction of the GST in 2000). In addition, this method can create problems in terms of differential pay for people doing similar jobs from different countries and locals. Typically, expatriate pay and benefits (for example, housing allowance and tax equalisation) continue to be linked more closely to the home country. However, this link appears to be slowly weakening and now depends more on the nature (for example, developmental) and length of the assignment.[17]

Within the United States, Runzheimer International reports that 56 per cent of companies have either a formal (30 per cent) or informal (26 per cent) policy that provides for pay differentials based on geographic location.[18] These differentials are intended to prevent inequitable treatment of employees who work in more expensive parts of the country. For example, the Cost of Living Index for New York City is 22 per cent higher than in the average metropolitan area of other parts of the United States, whereas it is 7 per cent lower than average in Nashville. Therefore, an employee receiving an annual pay of US$50 000 in Nashville would require an annual pay of US$65 600 in New York City to retain the same purchasing power. The most common approach (74 per cent of companies) is to move an employee higher in the pay structure to compensate for higher living costs. However, the drawback of this approach is that it may be difficult to adjust the salary downward if costs in that location fall or the employee moves to a lower-cost area. Thus, 22 per cent of companies choose to pay an ongoing supplement that changes or disappears in the event of such changes. Differences in the cost of living require similar pay differentials in Australia. For example, the cost of living in Sydney is higher than in Adelaide or Hobart.

The importance of process: Participation and communication

Compensation management has been criticised for following the simplistic belief that 'if the right technology can be developed, the right answers will be found'.[19] In reality, however, any given pay decision is rarely obvious to the diverse groups that make up organisations, regardless of the decision's technical merit or basis in theory. Of course, it is important when changing pay practices to decide which program or combination of programs make most sense, but it also matters how such decisions are made and how they are communicated.[20]

Participation

Employee participation in compensation decision making can take many forms. For example, employees may serve on taskforces that are charged with recommending and designing a pay program. They may also be asked to help communicate and explain the program's rationale. This is particularly true in the case of job evaluation as well as many of the programs discussed in the next chapter (Chapter 14 Performance-related pay). To date, for what are perhaps obvious reasons, employee participation in pay-level decisions remains fairly rare.

It is important to distinguish between participation by those affected by policies and those who must actually implement the policies. Managers are in the latter group (and often in the former group at the same time). As in other areas of human resource management, line managers are typically responsible for making policies work. Their intimate involvement in any change to existing pay practices is, of course, necessary.

Communication

A dramatic example of the importance of communication was found in a study of how an organisation communicated pay cuts to its employees and the effects on theft rates and perceived equity.[21] Two organisation units received 15 per cent across-the-board pay cuts. A third unit received no pay cut and served as a control group. The reasons for the pay cuts were communicated in different ways to the two pay-cut groups. In the 'adequate explanation' pay-cut group, management provided a significant amount of information to explain its reasons for the pay cut and also expressed significant remorse. In contrast, the 'inadequate explanation' group received much less information and no indication of remorse. The control group received no pay cut (and, thus, no explanation).

The control group and the two pay-cut groups began with the same theft rates and equity perceptions. After the pay cut, the theft rate was 54 per cent higher in the 'adequate explanation' group than it was in the control group. In the 'inadequate explanation' scenario, however, the theft rate was 141 per cent higher than it was in the control group. In this case, communication had a large, independent effect on employees' attitudes and behaviours.

Communication is likely to have other important effects. We know, for example, that not only actual pay but the comparison standard influences employee attitudes.[22] Under two-tier wage plans, employees doing the same jobs are paid two different rates, depending on when they were hired. Moreover, the lower paid employees do not ordinarily move into the higher paying tier. Commonsense might suggest that the lower paid employees would be less satisfied. Not necessarily. In fact, a study by Peter

Cappelli and Peter Sherer found that the lower paid employees were more satisfied on average.[23] Apparently, those in the lower tier used different (lower) comparison standards than those in the higher tier. The lower tier employees compared their jobs with unemployment or lower paying jobs they had managed to avoid. As a result, they were more satisfied, despite being paid less money for the same work. This finding does not mean that two-tier wage plans are necessarily a good idea. Rather, consistent with equity theory, it shows that the way employees compare their pay with other jobs matters, and managers need to take this into consideration. Employees increasingly have access to salary survey information, which is likely to result in more comparisons and, thus, a greater need for effective communication.

The move towards leaner, flatter organisational structures emphasising a more participative work environment through team building and joint effort[24] (as discussed in Chapter 6 Analysis and design of work) has also affected the reward systems and structures, as organisations seek to develop congruence with a more collaborative work culture.[25] Reward systems are central to facilitating and reinforcing these organisational values.[26] The use of a two-tier compensation system, when the effort or success is the result of many, can work against the organisation's strategies, goals and cultural values.[27] The significant part that teamwork plays in achieving organisational success in the new, delayered organisation has directed attention to how employee reward systems can contribute to team effectiveness.[28] Managers play the most crucial communication role in this respect because of their day-to-day interactions with their employees. Therefore, they must be prepared to explain why the pay structure is designed as it is and to judge whether employee concerns about the structure need to be addressed with changes to the structure. One common issue is deciding when a job needs to be reclassified because of substantial changes in its content. If an employee takes on more responsibility, he or she will often ask the manager for assistance in making the case for increased pay for the job. It is also important, therefore, to have feedback mechanisms and in particular appeal processes to provide employees with the opportunity to put their case. The fact that the internal and external environment (and, therefore, comparable factors) are changing continuously provides the organisation with the opportunity to reassess compensation in a proactive rather than a reactive way. This process can be accommodated within the remit of the job evaluation committee.

Current challenges

Despite the effort organisations put into creating a reliable and valid job-based structure, problems will arise from time to time for a variety of reasons. Human resource managers need to understand these issues and how to address them.

Problems with job-based pay structures

The approach taken in this chapter, that of defining pay structures in terms of jobs and their associated responsibilities, remains the most widely used in practice.[29] However, job-based pay structures have a number of potential limitations.[30] First, they may encourage bureaucracy. The job description sets out specific tasks and activities for which the incumbent is responsible and, by implication, those for which the incumbent is not responsible. Although this facilitates performance evaluation and control by the manager, it can also encourage a lack of flexibility and a lack of initiative on the part of employees: 'Why should I do that? It's not in my job description.' Second, the structure's hierarchical nature reinforces a top-down decision making and information flow as well as status differentials, which do not lend

MANAGING CHALLENGES THROUGH HR INNOVATION

PM'S POCKETS FILL WITH PAY RISE, TAX CUTS

John Howard will score a package of tax cuts, pay rise and inflation-driven increases on July 1 worth more than the yearly salary of an Australian on federal minimum wage.

Cuts in tax rates combined with increases in payments to politicians for productivity and inflation will give the Prime Minister and his federal colleagues on both sides of politics, a triple treat in the new financial year.

From July 1, Mr Howard's salary of $288 990 will rise 7 per cent to $309 270 a year. The increase was recommended by the Commonwealth Remuneration Board.

When combined with his personal tax breaks of about $9259—flowing from personal income tax cuts—Mr Howard will have an extra $25 539.

The minimum wage, which two million Australians rely on is currently frozen at $25 188 while the new Fair Pay Commission prepares its first minimum wage decision.

The tribunal was also generous towards the judiciary, with the nation's highest-paid judge now taking home more than $425 580.

Source: Edited from C. Hart & C. Merritt, 2006, 'PM's pockets fill with pay rise, tax cuts', *The Weekend Australian*, June 24–25.

ON THE RISE

Pay rises for judges and politicians

	Rise ($)		Rise ($)
Chief Justice, High Court	16 820	Prime Minister	20 280
High Court Judge	15 260	Deputy Prime Minister	15 990
Chief Justice, Federal and Family	14 240	Treasurer	14 625
Deputy Chief Justice, Family Court	13 330	Cabinet Minister	13 455
Federal, Family Court Judges	12 940	Other Ministers	12 645
Chief Federal Magistrate	11 900	Opposition Leader	14 430
Federal Magistrate	10 000	MPs	7 800

themselves to taking advantage of the skills and knowledge of those closest to production. Third, the bureaucracy required to generate and update job descriptions and job evaluations can become a barrier to change because wholesale changes to job descriptions can involve a tremendous amount of time and cost. Fourth, the job-based pay structure may not reward desired behaviours, particularly in a rapidly changing environment where the knowledge, skills and abilities needed yesterday may not be very helpful today and tomorrow. Fifth, the emphasis on job levels and status differentials encourages promotion-seeking behaviour, but it may discourage lateral employee movement because employees are reluctant to accept jobs that are not promotions or that appear to be steps down.

Responses to problems with job-based pay structures

Whilst problems will inevitably arise with such a dynamic issue, in an increasingly knowledge-based global economy it is important to look at more contemporary ways to develop and overcome issues.

PART 4   Rewarding People

Delayering and banding

Delayer
reduce the number of job levels within an organisation.

As noted, in response to the problems caused by job-based pay structures and the rigidity of the Australian labour market, organisations have used award restructuring to delayer or reduce the number of job levels to achieve more flexibility in job assignments and in assigning merit increases. The Williamstown Naval Dockyards in Victoria, for example, changed from having pay based on 390 work classifications and 180 allowances to one enterprise-based agreement, which included two work classifications and 12 pay grades.[31]

The focus of this restructuring in Australia has been the development of a more highly skilled workforce, which can contribute to increasing organisational efficiency and competitiveness. The scope of changes in award restructuring have included the development of career paths and multi-skilling with a focus on enhancing flexibility.[32] This has entailed the development of new job classifications to provide a mechanism for a structured development of the skill levels within an organisation. As research indicates, the key reforms undertaken through the principle of award restructuring have focused on the reduction of job classifications, the establishment of skill-related career paths and variations in terms and conditions of employment[33] (also see Chapter 5 Industrial relations).

Table 13.7 below shows how banding might work for a small sample of jobs. IBM's change to 'broadbands' was accompanied by a change away from a point-factor job evaluation system to a more streamlined approach to evaluating jobs, as Figure 13.3 opposite shows.

One possible consequence of delayering and banding is a reduced opportunity for promotion. However, systematic planning can minimise problems. Therefore, organisations need to consider what they will offer employees instead. In addition, to the extent that there are separate ranges within bands, the new structure may not represent as dramatic a change as it might appear. These distinctions can easily become just as entrenched as they were under the old system. 'Broadbands', with their greater spread between pay minimums and maximums, can also lead to weaker budgetary control and rising labour costs. Alternatively, the greater spread can permit managers to better recognise high performers with high pay. It can also permit the organisation to reward employees for learning.

Paying the person: pay for skill, knowledge and competency

A second, related response to job-based pay structure problems has been to move away from linking pay to jobs and towards building structures based on individual characteristics such as skill or knowledge.[34] This financial flexibility provides the

TABLE 13.7   Example of pay bands

Grade	Traditional structure Title	Band	Banded structure Title
14	Senior accountant	6	Senior accountant
12	Accountant III		
10	Accountant II	5	Accountant
8	Accountant I		

Source: P. LeBlanc, 1992, *Perspectives in Total Compensation*, 3 (3), March, pp. 1–6. Reprinted with permission from Sibson Consulting, a division of the Segal Company, www.sibson.com.

Managing Compensation CHAPTER 13

FIGURE 13.3 IBM's job evaluation approach

Below is an abbreviated schematic illustration of the IBM job evaluation approach:

Position reference guide

Band	Skills required	Leadership/contribution	Scope/impact
1			
2			
3			
4			
5			
6			
7			
8			
9			
10			

Factors: Leadership/contribution
- Band 6: Understand the mission of the professional group and vision in own area of competence.
- Band 7: Understand the departmental mission and vision.
- Band 8: Understand departmental/functional mission and vision.
- Band 9: Has vision of functional or unit mission.
- Band 10: Has vision of overall strategies.

Both the bands and the approach are global. In the United States, bands 1–5 are non-managerial; bands 6–10 are managerial. Each cell in the table contains descriptive language about key job characteristics. Position descriptions are compared to the chart and assigned to bands on a 'best fit' basis. There are no points or scoring mechanisms. Managers assign employees to bands by selecting a position description that most closely resembles the work being done by an employee using an online position description library. That's it!

Source: A.S. Richter, 1988, 'Paying the people in black at Big Blue', *Compensation and Benefits Review*, May–June, pp. 51–9. Copyright © 1998 by Sage Publications, Inc. Reprinted by permission of Sage Publications, Inc.

incentive for employees to increase their skill base. Competency-based pay is similar but usually refers to a plan that covers exempt employees (for example, managers). The basic idea is that if you want employees to learn more skills and become more flexible in the jobs they perform, you should pay them to do it. (See Chapter 11 Learning and development, for a discussion of the implications of skill-based pay systems on training.) According to Gerald Ledford, however, it is 'a fundamental departure' because employees are now 'paid for the skills they are capable of using, not for the job they are performing at a particular point in time'.[35] As Table 13.8 overleaf—showing the skill levels determining pay rates for a shipbuilder—indicates, employees have the opportunity to develop their skills and ability in a variety of areas.

Skill-based pay refers to pay that is based on the skills employees acquire and are capable of using. Skill-based pay systems seem to fit well with the increased breadth and depth of skill that changing technology continues to bring.[36] For example, in a production environment, workers might be expected not only to operate machines but

Skill-based pay
pay based on the skills employees acquire and are capable of using.

505

also to take responsibility for maintenance and troubleshooting, quality control, or modifying computer programs.[37] Toyota concluded years ago that:

> … none of the specialists [for example, quality inspectors, many managers and foremen] beyond the assembly worker was actually adding any value to the car. What's more … assembly workers could probably do most of the functions of specialists much better because of their direct acquaintance with conditions on the line.[38]

In other words, an important potential advantage of skill-based pay is its contribution to increased worker flexibility, which in turn facilitates the decentralisation of decision making to those who are most knowledgeable. It also provides the opportunity for

TABLE 13.8 Skill levels determining pay rates for a shipbuilder

Level	Skill proficiency
1	Highest level—team leader AA
	Team leaders shall be appointed by the company. Employees must have completed all required training programs to enable selection for this level. It is usually expected that it will take an employee about 48 months to achieve the required training, necessary work experience and demonstrated competency in work for this level. The accumulation of 560 points—80 points from level 1, 80 points from level 2, 80 points from level 3, 80 points from level 4, 80 points from level 5, plus credits gained from having trade qualification.
2	Multi-skilled—leadership capability
	The accumulation of 480 points—80 points from level 2, 80 points from level 3, 80 points from level 4, 80 points from level 5, plus credits gained from having trade qualification. It is usually expected that it will take an employee about 24 months to achieve the required training, necessary work experience and demonstrated competency in work to enable selection for this level.
3	Shipbuilding skills
	The accumulation of 400 points—80 points from level 5, 80 points from level 4, 80 points from level 3, plus credit gained from trade qualification. It is usually expected that it will take an employee about 12 months to achieve the required training, necessary work experience and demonstrated competency in work to enable selection for this level.
4	Trade-equivalent skills—team leader A
	Non-trades employees appointed as team leaders by the company will be required to complete the specified leadership training programs and gain relevant experience. It is usually expected that it will take an employee about 48 months to achieve the required training, necessary work experience and demonstrated competency in work to enable selection for this level. Level 4 shall require the accumulation of 320 points—80 points level 7; 80 points level 6; 80 points level 5 and 80 points level 4. Trade equivalent skills at level 4 requires the accumulation of 320 points. All non-trade points shall be credited resulting in the employee requiring 80 points from level 5 and 80 points from level 4. It is usually expected to take up to six months to achieve the required training and necessary work experience to enable selection to this level.
5	Special skills—entry level 2
	Non-trade specialist skills and trade entry level 2 requirements. Employees will have completed the equvalent of 24 modules for ASF level 3. Trades employees will complete the required induction and familiarisation program, which will take three months. Level 5 shall require the accumulation of 240 points—80 points level 7; 80 points level 6 and 80 points level 5. Trades entrants will gain the required points by completion of the induction program, i.e. they shall be credited 240 points upon completion of the required familiarisation program.
6	Semi-skilled
	Employees would expect to take about 18 months to complete the required training and relevant necessary work experience. The accumulation of 160 points—80 points from level 6 and 80 points from level 7.
7	Basic skills
	Up to six months experience and the accumulation of 80 points from the training matrix.
8	Entry level—1
	Employees categorised at entry level 1 will complete mandatory induction requirements including occupational health and safety and site familiarisation. Employees will remain on this level for three months, which is required to complete the familiarisation program.

Source: Based on Tenix Defence Pty Ltd, 2004, *Certified Agreement Industrial Award 2004–2007*, attributed to Dr John Varnum AM, Tenix's group general manager, corporate and industrial affairs, pp. 16–17.

leaner staffing levels because current employees who are multi-skilled can now cover employee turnover or absenteeism.[39] In addition, multi-skilled employees are important in cases where different products require different manufacturing processes or where supply shortages or other problems call for adaptive or flexible responses—characteristics typical, for example, of many newer so-called advanced manufacturing environments (for example, flexible manufacturing and 'just-in-time' systems).[40] More generally, it has been suggested that skill-based plans also contribute to a climate of learning and adaptability and give employees a broader view of how the organisation functions. Both changes should contribute to better use of employees' know-how and ideas. Consistent with the advantages just noted, a field study found that a change to a skill-based plan led to better quality and lower labour costs in a manufacturing plant.[41]

As noted, skill-based and competency-based approaches also have potential disadvantages.[42] First, although the plan will likely enhance skill acquisition, the organisation may find it a challenge to use the new skills effectively. If it has not been carefully planned, it may find itself with large new labour costs but little payoff. In other words, if skills change, work design must change as quickly, to take full advantage. Second, if pay growth is based entirely on skills, problems may arise if employees 'top out' by acquiring all the skills too quickly, leaving no room for further pay growth. (Of course, this problem can also afflict job-based systems.) Third, and somewhat ironically, skill-based plans may generate a large bureaucracy—usually a criticism of job-based systems. Training programs need to be developed. Skills must be described, measured and assigned monetary values. Certification tests must be developed to determine whether an employee has acquired a certain skill. Finally, as if the challenges in obtaining market rates under a job-based system were not enough, there is almost no body of knowledge regarding how to price combinations of skills (versus jobs) in the marketplace. Obtaining comparison data from other organisations will be difficult until skill-based plans become more widely used.

Can the Australian labour force compete?

We often hear that the Australian labour costs are simply too high to allow Australian companies to compete effectively, particularly with companies in other countries in our region (see Table 13.9 overleaf). The ratio of average hourly labour costs (cash and benefits) for production workers in manufacturing in Australia and in other advanced industrialised countries compared to newly industrialised countries can be as high as 10 to one.[43]

Increasingly this argument is being used in the service sector as these jobs (such as jobs in call centres) are increasingly outsourced or 'offshored' to countries such as India. Based solely on a cost approach, it would perhaps make sense to try to shift many types of production from industrialised countries like Australia to newly industrialised countries. Would this be a good idea? Not necessarily. There are several factors to consider: instability of country differences in labour costs, skill levels, productivity, and non-labour considerations.

Instability of country differences in labour costs

First, note that relative labour costs are considerably unstable over time. Changes in currency exchange rates have an important influence on such comparisons and these exchange rates often fluctuate significantly from year to year. This point is well illustrated by the changes between two major industrial countries, Germany and the United States. For example, in 1985, when German labour costs were 74 per cent of those in the United States, the US-dollar was worth 2.94 German marks. But in 1990,

PART 4   Rewarding People

TABLE 13.9 International comparisons of hourly compensation costs for production workers in manufacturing

Country	Labour cost US$ 2002	Labour cost adjusted for current US rate 2002	Index US = 100
Australia	15.55	22.17	103.94
Austria	23.59	28.23	132.34
Belgium	25.50	30.52	143.08
Brazil	2.57	2.56	12.02
Canada	16.03	18.92	88.69
Denmark	24.23	32.66	153.12
Finland	24.13	28.87	135.37
France	19.48	23.32	109.31
Germany 2	28.06	33.58	157.44
Germany (former West)	29.30	35.06	164.38
Hong Kong	5.83	5.86	27.46
Ireland	16.88	20.20	94.71
Israel	12.14	12.89	60.43
Italy	16.70	19.99	93.71
Japan	18.83	22.30	104.56
Korea	9.16	9.82	46.05
Mexico	2.38	2.07	9.70
Netherlands	24.32	29.10	136.43
Norway	27.40	32.01	150.08
Singapore	7.28	7.74	36.31
Spain	13.48	16.13	75.61
Sweden	20.19	27.27	127.85
Switzerland	24.11	30.37	142.39
Taiwan	5.41	5.63	26.38
United Kingdom	17.48	21.63	101.40
United States	21.33	21.33	100.00

Source: Robi Bendorf, CPM, 2004, 'International comparisons of hourly compensation costs for production workers in manufacturing', Bendorf and Associates, viewed in June, 2004, at www.bendorf.com/articles/ilr022804.html.

the US-dollar was worth 1.62 German marks. If the exchange rate in 1990 were still one to 2.94, the average German hourly wage (in US-dollars) would have been US$11.80 or about 80 per cent of the United States' average. In any event, relative to countries like Germany, United States' labour costs are now a bargain; this explains, in part, decisions by companies such as BMW and Mercedes–Benz to locate production facilities in South Carolina and Alabama, respectively, where labour costs are lower than Germany's labour costs by 30 per cent or more.

Skill levels

Second, the quality and productivity of national labour forces can vary dramatically. This is an especially important consideration when comparisons are drawn between labour costs in industrialised countries like Australia and developing countries like Mexico. For example, the secondary school graduation rate in Australia is over 80 per cent, versus 26 per cent in Mexico.[44] Thus, lower labour costs may reflect the lower average skill level of the workforce. As a consequence, certain types of skilled labour may be less available in low labour cost countries. On the other hand, any given company needs only enough skilled employees for its own operations.

Productivity

Third, and most directly relevant, are data on comparative productivity and unit labour costs, essentially meaning labour cost per hour divided by productivity per hour worked. One indicator of productivity is *gross domestic product* (or total output of the economy) per person, adjusted for differences in purchasing power. On this measure, the combination of lower labour costs and higher productivity translates into lower unit labour costs.[45]

Non-labour considerations

Fourth, any consideration of where to locate production cannot be based on labour considerations alone. For example, although the average hourly labour cost in country A may be $15 versus $10 in country B, if labour costs are 30 per cent of total operating costs and non-labour operating costs are roughly the same, then the total operating costs might be $65 (50 + 15) in country A and $60 (50 + 10) in country B. Thus, although labour costs in country B are 33 per cent less, total operating costs are only 7.7 per cent less. This may not be enough to compensate for differences in skills and productivity, transportation costs, taxes and so on. Further, the direct labour component of many products, particularly high-tech products (for example, electronic components), may often be 5 per cent or less. Thus, the effect on product price competitiveness may be insignificant.[46]

In fact, an increasing number of organisations have decided that it is more important to focus on non-labour-related factors in deciding where to locate production.[47] Product development speed may be greater when manufacturing is physically close to the design group. Quick response to customers (for example, making a custom replacement product) is difficult when production facilities are on the other side of the world. Inventory levels can be dramatically reduced through the use of manufacturing methods like 'just-in-time' production; but suppliers need to be in close physical proximity. Intangible issues such as quality, service and security must also be considered as well as the benefits Australia has in terms of political stability and high-quality corporate governance systems. These factors can make Australia an increasingly attractive destination for high-quality skilled work from Europe, the US and North Asia.

Executive pay

The issue of executive pay has been given widespread attention in the media from a variety of sources including politicians, trade union leaders, shareholders and academics (see the 'HRM spotlight: Tough times for CEOs: Making do on $5200 a day' overleaf).

On the one hand, the topic has received more coverage than it deserves because there are few top executives and their compensation accounts for only a small share of an organisation's total labour costs. On the other hand, top executives have a disproportionate ability to influence organisation performance, so decisions about their compensation are critical. Top executives also help to set the tone or culture of the organisation. If, for example, the top executive's pay seems unrelated to the organisation's performance, staying high although business performance is poor, employees may not understand why some of their pay should be at risk and why their pay should depend on how the organisation is performing.

Executive pay in Australia

In Australia, the public visibility of top executive pay has highlighted the perceived inequities of the widening gap between top executives and employee compensation. This is reflected in Australian data, which indicated that in the period 1992–2002, executive remuneration rose from 22 times average weekly earnings to 74 times average weekly earnings.[48] However, in an international context, top executive pay in Australia is considered relatively modest.[49] Research indicates that Australia lies mid-table on a world ranking of major Western market economies.[50] Countries including

TOUGH TIMES FOR CEOs: MAKING DO ON $5200 A DAY

HRM SPOTLIGHT

Australia's corporate high-flyers are doing it hard—just ask them.

When the *Australian Financial Review* issued its annual survey showing another leap in chief executives' pay, it passed almost without comment.

The survey showed that, in 2004, the average total remuneration of a chief executive of Australia's largest 300 listed companies rose 16 per cent to $1.9 million ($5200 a day). This was 34 times the average earnings of an adult full-time employee.

Fair enough. What else is new? Perhaps we've finally learnt to see things from the viewpoint of the much put-upon CEOs. As Don Argus, Chairman of BHP Billiton and Brambles, explained to the *Review*, the debate about executive pay is often unfairly simplified, ignoring the components of executive pay packages.

Good point. Did you realise, for instance that the base salary of those 300 chief executives' averages less than $700 000? That's a mere 13 times employees' average ordinary-time earnings. And chief executives base salaries increased by just 6 per cent, which was the same as the increase in employees' average earnings.

The point is that this guaranteed portion of chief executives' incomes accounted for only about 40 per cent of their total remuneration. If you set aside about 10 per cent to cover perks and other benefits, such as retention payments (money to discourage executives from leaving the company), the remaining half is 'at risk'.

On average, 'short-term incentives' annual bonuses were worth about $600 000 up 22 per cent on the previous year. What more proof do you need that chief executives were working their butts off last year?

The last component of executives' packages is 'long-term incentives', otherwise known as options to buy the company's shares at a discount price. The practice of issuing options got a bad rap after the bursting of the dotcom bubble but, fortunately, it's coming back. According to John Egan, of remuneration consultants Egan Associates, at the 2005 annual meeting season about 40 of the top 100 companies took proposals to shareholders to issue options to executive directors. Long-term incentives account for the remaining $400 000 of the average 1.9 million package, but chief executives are anxious for the public to understand that such amounts aren't received in cash.

Chief executive salaries in Australia are still well behind those paid in the United States. And as Michael Chaney, president of the Business Council of Australia, told the *Review*, 'If we don't offer world-class remuneration we have to accept that there will be a much smaller pool of talent available to run our companies'. Chaney explained that chief executives' remuneration reflected a world market and the higher the level of public scrutiny.

But don't reserve all your sympathy for chief execs. Although average director's fees have risen to about $120 000 a year, independent company directors are also doing it tough. Argus of BHP Billiton noted that its directors had to attend seven meetings a year. If they were coming from the US, 'they are not going to do that unless it's worthwhile'.

Source: Excerpt from 'Ross Gittins Tough times for CEOs: making do on $5200 a day', *The Age*, 23 November, p. 23.

Argentina, Brazil, Mexico and Singapore are ahead of Australia. However top executive pay remains a contentious issue. In response to the perceived inequities and the 'performance gap' (see the 'HRM spotlight' and 'Managing challenges through sustainability'), changes are starting to occur in the way top executive pay is structured in an effort to increase accountability.

The fact that the differential between top-executive pay and that of an average manufacturing worker has been described as creating a 'trust gap'—that is, in employees' minds, a 'frame of mind that mistrusts senior management's intentions, doubts its competence and resents its self-congratulatory pay' (See the 'HRM spotlight: Tough times for CEOs: Making do on $5200 a day on page 510). The issue becomes even more salient at a time when so many of the same companies with high executive pay are simultaneously engaging in downsizing or other forms of employment reduction. A good example of this in Australia is the financial sector where the last decade has seen substantial reduction in staff and branch closures, while research identifies that the CEOs of the four major banks average 188 times the pay of front-line customer service staff.[51]

Employees might ask, therefore, if the banks need to cut costs to remain competitive, 'why not cut executives' pay, rather than our jobs?' The issue is one of perceived fairness in difficult economic times. One study, in fact, reported that business units with higher pay differentials between executives and 'rank-and-file'

BIG REWARDS CAN STICK IN THE CRAW, HOWARD ADMITS

Prime Minister John Howard, whose salary is 3.5 per cent of Telstra boss Sol Trujillo's, says it is surprising that some chief executives get bonuses even if the companies are not doing well.

Asked about Mr Trujillo's $2.6 million bonus, announced this week, Mr Howard said some people thought corporate salaries were a bit rich.

Mr Howard and Treasurer Peter Costello run a $800 billion-plus economy, yet get a comparative pittance.

Former Miss Universe Jennifer Hawkins is paid more than the Prime Minister. Ms Hawkins will receive $400 000 for her work as the face of Myer.

Mr Howard received a pay rise in June, pushing his salary to $309 000, which is about $90 000 less than the salaries of the head of his own department Ken Henry and Defence Department head Ric Smith.

Based on his total package of $8.7 million, Telstra is paying Mr Trujillo $24 000 a day to run the telco, compared with Mr Howard's $846 a day.

At least Mr Howard beats Opposition leader Kim Beazley who earns only $220 000 a year—and has to commute from Perth.

This week Telstra reported a 26 per cent slump in its annual net profit to $3.2 billion.

It was the lowest since 1999 and the biggest annual percentage fall since listing.

Mr Howard was guarded in his criticism. 'But I believe in competitive capitalism and I always loath to get into the business of saying, well he gets paid too much', he said on 3AW radio in Melbourne.

'You have got to have a society where some people, because of their responsibilities and the financial acumen they have and the risks that they take, are paid more than others.'

Nevertheless Mr Howard admitted there were some circumstances where executive salaries and remuneration did 'stick in the craw'.

'But, as for Mr Trujillo, I don't particularly want to single him out', Mr Howard said.

Several other Australian chief executives outrank Mr Trujillo in terms of pay packets.

Macquarie Bank chief executive Alan Moss earned $21.2 million according to the company's past annual report.

Leighton Holdings' Wal King is second at $12.8 million, while Babcock & Brown's Phillip Green gets $12.18 million.

Source: Based on F. Anderson, 2006, 'Big rewards can stick in the craw, Howard admits', *Weekend Australian Financial Review*, 12–13 August, p. 3.

employees had lower customer satisfaction, which was speculated to result from employees' perceptions of inequity coming through in customer relations.[52] Perhaps more important than how much top executives are paid, is how they are paid and what changes are occurring. (See 'Managing challenges of globalisation: Money can't buy you … Performance', page 514). This is an issue we turn to in the next section and discuss in more detail in Chapter 14 Performance-related pay.

Trends and issues in executive pay

The rise in interest in the topic of executive pay has developed from a perceived need to increase accountability and its relationship to organisational performance. In an increasingly complex environment, a range of issues need to be considered when determining an organisation's success and how this can be translated into the design, structure and governance of executive pay. Over the past decade or so there have been moves towards aligning executive pay and organisational performance.[53] This section introduces evolving trends in the development of performance-related pay for executives.[54]

Governance

The United Kingdom and the United States have been leaders in the field of corporate governance and accountability in senior management pay, requiring clear guidelines and transparency in the formulation, design and structure.[55] The influence of this in Australia has been highlighted by a report on Australian organisations, which found deficiencies, ambiguity and variance in remuneration disclosure, making it difficult to compare and contrast organisational performance and senior management rewards.[56] As a prerequisite to attracting and retaining investments, it is likely that Australian organisations will increasingly be required to meet higher standards of remuneration disclosure and show a relationship to performance.

Design and structure

The labour market for executives and, in particular, CEOs, is increasingly being seen as an international market, as organisations worldwide cope with the same competitive pressures.[57] Although the extent and nature of this internationalisation will vary from sector to sector, the pressure for performance accountability is being reflected in the make-up of executive pay. The increasing use of short-term indicators (STIs) and long-term indicators (LTIs) reflects what has generally been termed the 'US model' of pay.[58] In the United States, a strong relationship between firm performance and CEO pay has been identified over the past 15 years as the use of STIs and LTIs has increased, although the empirical evidence is not conclusive.[59] Notwithstanding, Japanese and European organisations have increasingly taken up this model. In Australia the trend is similar.

However, because of the strong growth in world share markets in the 1990s, several researchers have argued that the growing proportion of stock options has resulted in senior managements being rewarded, although their organisations have under-performed.[60] See 'Managing challenges through HR innovation: Bonus envy—When $500 000 is not enough' opposite and 'Managing challenges of globalisation: Money Can't Buy You … performance', on page 514. It has been said that: 'The ultimate goal of providing superior total returns to the shareholders can be better accomplished by rewarding top managers only when they out-perform the competition.'[61] In this context, CEO compensation should be linked to a 'Benchmark Index' of firms in the same industry or sector of the market.

BONUS ENVY—WHEN $500 000 IS NOT ENOUGH

MANAGING CHALLENGES THROUGH HR INNOVATION

It is bonus time at the big investment banks, but the financial wizards who have been burning the midnight oil during a bumper year of corporate activity are not happy.

In the heart of Sydney's financial district and along Melbourne's Collins Street, investment bankers are complaining that top-tier managers have hogged this year's bonus pool.

Bankers who have been in the game for about nine years received bonuses of up to $500 000, while more senior executives pocketed as much as $900 000.

Many corporate advisers from UBS and Deutsche Bank were particularly unhappy with the size of their bonuses, having dominated advisory work on takeovers last year. Between them they notched up US$29 000 million ($36 600 million) in deals.

They are not griping because their bonuses are down on last year, but they are griping because they are not as big as many had expected in a year when the value of corporate deals leapt 66 per cent to US$69 900 million, just shy of the record levels set during the 'dot-com' boom.

The value of new floats, such as Virgin Blue and Multiplex, topped $8000 million—a dramatic turnaround from the previous two years, when the share market slumped and the death of deals shrank bonus pools and triggered the biggest round of job cuts for more than two decades.

At UBS, it is understood, the bonus pool for the outperforming Australian division grew by a meagre 5 per cent in a year when the firm advised on 51 deals worth US$14 710 million.

The other bank that revelled in a blockbuster year, but did not distribute the spoils, was Deutsche Bank.

Local advisers have also been hit by the soaring Australian dollar, which has destroyed the added bonus that many in the big European and Wall Street investment banks received when they converted their US dollar and euro bonuses into the weaker local cash.

As one chief executive of a major firm put it: 'The bonuses looked all right, but when they were translated back into Aussie dollars, they weren't so good.' That is hardly solace for many bankers who regularly work 14 hours a day, sometimes seven days a week.

Merrill Lynch Investment Managers and Credit Suisse Asset Management are facing similar complaints from some of their London-based employees whose bonuses have been hit by the slide in the US dollar.

It seems the biggest winners this season were on Wall Street itself, where the bonuses paid by the major firms were expected to be more than 25 per cent up on the lowly returns of the 2002 calendar year.

The disappointment among the locals has sparked speculation that more senior-level bankers will move to rival banks this year—a far cry from 12 months ago, when most felt lucky to still have a job.

In good times, top-flight analysts and senior corporate advisers at the European and Wall Street investment banks earned base pays of as much as $400 000 to $450 000 each, with bonuses of up to four times that. In some cases, bonuses can make up as much as 80 per cent of a corporate adviser's overall remuneration.

For senior executives on stockbroking dealing desks, annual salaries can range between $175 000 and $250 000 each, and they can double that payment in bonuses.

On average, first-year investment bank analysts last year received bonuses of about $25 000 to $40 000 each. A vice-president, who had been in the game for about nine years, would get as much as $500 000 and a director would pocket up to $900 000.

At the top of the pecking order, sources say that bonuses for the head of an investment bank have reached about $4.5 million.

On the stockbroking side of some firms, separated from the investment banking and equity capital markets operations by so-called Chinese walls, reactions to bonuses appeared muted despite the Australian stock exchange All Ordinaries Index rising 25.3 per cent last year, and trading volumes rising on the share market.

Despite the lower than expected pay cheques, sales of luxury items are holding up well. Sydney's biggest Porsche dealer says that finance industry people are still valued clients and business overall is roaring along.

Source: Excerpt from T. Harcourt, 2004, 'Bonus envy: when $500k is not enough', *Australian Financial Review*, 20 February, p. 1.

The demand for a link between organisational performance and CEO pay raises the question: what are the most appropriate measures of performance? Given the complexity of the role of CEO and other senior executives and divergent stakeholder interests, multiple criteria are required in order to align these two variables.[62] The search for more appropriate measures has seen the emergence of several alternatives.

From a financial perspective, measures such as economic value added (EVA), cash-flow returns on investments and discounted cash-flows have been suggested.[63]

MONEY CAN'T BUY YOU … PERFORMANCE

Recent research by international adviser Proxy Australia shows that Australian Chief Executives are enjoying windfall gains on stock options, far above the value disclosed to shareholders. The study has prompted shareholder calls for greater disclosure of executive remuneration arrangements, including disclosing option gains and valuation methods.

Internationally, executive remuneration has become the most contentious aspect of contemporary corporate governance. As US legal scholar Ima Anabtawi recently wrote: 'Few recent issues have drawn more ire from the public or more bewilderment from scholars than the compensation of public company CEOs.' What has been of particular concern is the 'decoupling' of executive pay from company performance. That is CEO remuneration continues to skyrocket even as the companies they manage enjoy modest growth, no growth or negative growth.

US law professors Lucian Bebchuck and Jesse Fried point out that in the US between 1991 and 2003 the average large-company CEO's total remuneration increased from 140 times the pay of the average worker to 500 times average pay. Similarly in Australia between 1992 and 2002 CEO remuneration increased from about 22 times average weekly earnings to 74 times average earnings.

Bebchuck and Fried do not in any way question the legitimacy of using 'pay for performance' as the principal methodology for determining executive pay, and indeed contend that appealing to the hip pocket of executives is the best way to motivate them to perform and to satisfy their personal objectives. Pay executives as much as they can dream of, they contend, so long as there is a demonstrable correlation between higher pay and better company performance.

Source: Based on J. McConvill, 2005, 'Money Can't Buy You … Performance', *The Age*, 10 June, p. 5.

However, because of the focus on financial indicators, their value remains limited, as Figure 13.4 opposite illustrates. The 'balanced scorecard', developed in the United States, attempts to address the more divergent aspects of organisational performance and strategy.[64] Arguing that no single measure can provide a clear assessment of overall organisational performance,[65] and that multiple measures need to focus on the range of critical business areas, the *balanced scorecard* is a means of performance measurement that gives managers a chance to look at their company from the perspectives of internal and external customers, employees and shareholders (as was introduced in Chapter 1 Human resource management in Australia). The balanced scorecard can include:

- *Financial.* The financial perspective in terms of traditional measures of profit and returns for shareholders.
- *Internal business process.* The internal business perspective, including measures of operational efficiency, such as asset utilisation.
- *Growth and learning.* Measures of learning and innovation, as an indication of future strategic prospects.
- *Customer.* The customer perspective in respect of measures of service and market stance.

The balanced scorecard is useful in determining the success of the organisation in both financial and non-financial areas of the business, and it is increasingly being used in United States[66] and European companies.[67] While the balanced scorecard has a role to play in determining remuneration, it is important to get the 'right measures on the scorecard' to ensure that no unexpected or unintended consequences result from the way the targets for the measures are achieved.[68]

The pay of CEOs remain a contentious aspect of the performance/reward nexus. The trend towards internationalisation of the global economy will see the issue of

FIGURE 13.4 A comparison of CEO pay and stock-market-based indicators

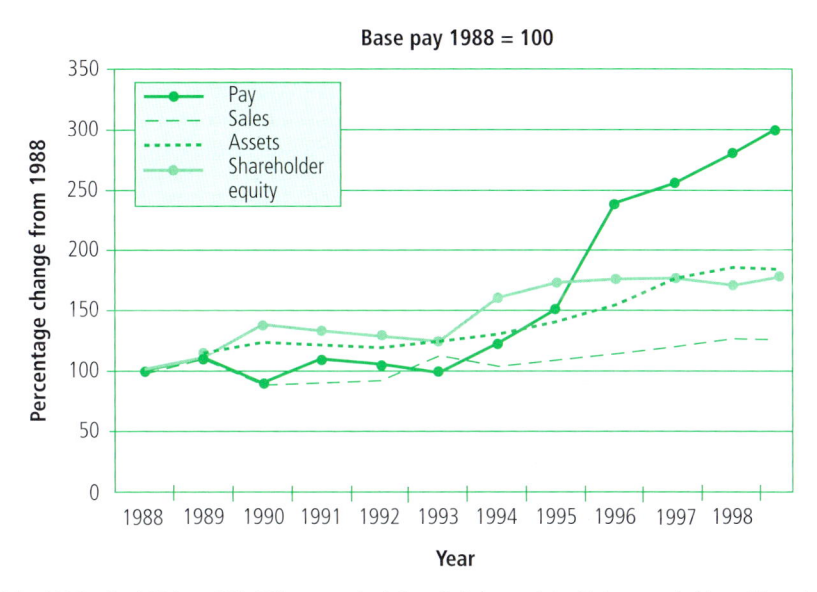

Source: P.J. Holland, P.J. Dowling & P.A. Innes, 2001, 'CEO compensation in Australia: is there a relationship between principles, policies and practices?', *Asia Pacific Journal of Human Resources*, 39 (3), p. 50. Reprinted by permission of Sage Publications Ltd.

developing appropriate reward structures become more complex, as organisations seek to attract, retain and motivate key employees, while ensuring that the reward is performance orientated, fair, equitable and linked to the strategic objectives of the organisation. The imperative is growing for rewards for CEOs to take account of the complexities of organisational performance over a longer period of time, to reflect the dynamic and changing nature of the organisation, its stakeholders and markets.

While it is clear that Australian CEO compensation is following the trends set in the United Kingdom and the United States, the increasing use of more sensitive indicators may help to more clearly identify the dynamic relationship between CEO compensation and organisational performance, especially in such a small but highly visible market.

Government regulation of compensation

Throughout most of the twentieth century in Australia, there has been a model of centralised wage determination where both federal and state governments have had a history of intervention. Over the last two decades, however, governments have undertaken significant programs of deregulation of the labour market and wage determination mechanisms, with the recent development of the Australian Fair Pay Commission (AFPC) arguably the most significant change to the principles of (minimum) wage determination since Federation.

The development of minimum wage and prevailing wage laws

Industry protection was a foundation principle of the Federation of Australia in 1901. The fundamental tenet of the protectionist framework was to ensure the development of Australia's fledgling economy. This instrument of capital protection enacted through tariff policies provided a mechanism for these benefits to be passed on to the labour force through wage determination and was instrumental in developing and consolidating the Federation, as Kelly points out:

> It was a device that tied both capital and labour to the post-Federation consensus. The Commonwealth Arbitration Court, later the Conciliation and Arbitration Commission, then the Industrial Relations Commission, became the forum for its entrenchment.[69]

The system of wage determination was unique in that wage rates were not determined by market forces or an employer's ability to pay, but by what was deemed to be a 'fair and reasonable wage'.[70] The determination of what was considered a fair 'living' wage was resolved in the Commonwealth Arbitration Court in the landmark test case—the Sunshine Harvester Judgment in 1907. In this case, Justice Higgins, under the excise tariff legislation, determined a fair and equitable **minimum wage** (the lowest amount that employers are legally allowed to pay) based on the requirements of an average family with one wage earner.[71]

What ensured the binding of capital and labour under this judgment was that under the 'new protection' policy, tariff protection was conditional on the adherence to a 'fair and equitable' wage, determined by the courts.[72] This judgment, thus, established a distinctly Australian pattern of centralised wage determination.[73] It also ensured that tariff protection and wage determination were inseparable. While protection yielded a lower per capita income than would free trade, it increased the demand for labour and, therefore, the size of the population that could be supported at a given real wage, such as that laid down in the Harvester Judgment. More generally, this point may be restated as saying that protection of a labour-intensive industry leads to an increase in the equilibrium real wage.[74]

In undertaking to determine wage rates, the Australian Conciliation and Arbitration Court (ACAC)—now the Australian Industrial Relations Commission (AIRC)—through industrial awards became the regulator of wages, through what has become known as the National Wage Case. As Hill, Howard and Lansbury explain:

> In the National Wage Case, the Commission considers the entire award structure and decides whether there are factors within the economy which suggest that wages as a whole should be varied. The Commission does not have the constitutional power to initiate and undertake such a review, so the National Wage Case must be placed in the context of dispute settlement. Labour and management, via representative organisations, contrive a dispute, within the meaning of the Conciliation and Arbitration Act, over critical elements of the award wage structure, and the Commission hears this synthetic dispute and determines what, if any, variation in award wages is appropriate.[75]

The wage fixation system was enshrined in the Australian regulatory framework and remained the central wage fixing mechanism until 1967, when over-award payments had, to a large extent, marginalised this process.[76] In direct response to this, 'wage indexation' was introduced. Wage indexation was initially conceived as part of an incomes policy whereby both wage and non-wage forms of income would be regulated.[77] As Gardner and Palmer point out, 'The system, introduced and modified over time, comprised an integrated set of wage-fixing principles, the core of which was the regular adjustment of wages to changes, in a price index.'[78] Wage indexation allowed the commission to regain control over regulating wage determination. During this period, the Equal Pay Case broadened the concept of equal pay for work of equal value. As with the philosophy underpinning the National Wage Case, the system was geared to provide the highest wages the economy could afford.[79] However, this further entrenched inefficiency within the systems, as this form of wage determination

Minimum wage the lowest amount that employers are legally allowed to pay.

did not apply costs associated with inefficiency. The effect of this policy on a relatively labour-scarce, high-wage economy was, of course, to protect the most labour-intensive manufacturing industries.[80]

However, the post-war period to 1975 was characterised by stable economic conditions and market expansion. In this environment, these (protectionist) policies artificially sustained the Australian economy, leaving it ill-prepared for changes in economic conditions. With the advent of the oil shocks of the 1970s and the subsequent economic instability, the structural environment in place in Australia, both at macro- and micro-economic levels, was exceptionally vulnerable to the new 'post-Keynesian' economic environment, characterised by economic instability, deregulation and international competition.

The reconstruction of wage determination

From April 1975, wage indexation became quarterly to constrain wage costs. However, the system remained under pressure from work-value anomalies and other inequities and in 1981, wage indexation was abandoned.

The incoming Hawke Federal Labor Government introduced the Prices and Incomes Accord ('the Accord') after its election in 1983. The Accord was an agreement between the federal government and the trade union movement that was to provide the framework for restructuring and deregulating various parts of the economy including labour markets and wage determination. While essentially a reworking of the wage indexation process, the Accord provided an adaptable platform to develop a more flexible and closer relationship between wage policy and productivity. The Accord (1983–96) was an anti-inflationary, broad-based national incomes policy modelled on the British social contract of the late 1970s. Through its various stages over its 13-year lifespan, it provided the framework for negotiating progressive economic and structural reforms to enhance economic performance, with wage determination reform a key feature.

The structural changes to facilitate a micro-economic reform agenda had been initiated with the reduction of tariffs in the 1970s and financial deregulation in the mid 1980s. However, reform of the highly regulated labour market and wage determination structures and processes had, to a large extent, remained unchanged since the *Conciliation and Arbitration Act 1904* and the Harvester Judgment (1907). These areas were seen as key issues in developing increasing competitiveness.[81] The Accord proved to be an ideal vehicle for the Hawke Federal Labor Government's micro-economic reform agenda, focusing specifically on the labour market and industrial relations and wage determination.

The Restructuring and Efficiency Principle

The Restructuring and Efficiency Principle was an innovative 'two-tier' wage system introduced as part of the National Wage Case in 1987. The first tier operated in the tradition of the former centralised wage-fixing system, in which a flat wage adjustment was uniformly granted. For the second-tier, a wage increase of up to 4 per cent was available but had to be achieved through productivity trade-offs or cost savings through labour-market reforms.[82] The paradigm shift in this process was the move from a pure entitlement principle of wage adjustment to one requiring productivity offsets.[83]

The initial focus of micro-economic reform was the removal of excessive costs and restrictive work and management practices, while introducing elements of multi-skilling. The development of this framework was envisaged as the catalyst for enhanced industrial efficiency. For the workforce, the opportunity for increased remuneration completed the 'win–win' scenario. The key element in this policy was the development of labour flexibility, which had emerged as a major theme in workplace reform debates in the 1980s.[84] Research indicates that second-tier agreements produced genuine change in efficiency and competitive practices.[85]

The Structural Efficiency Principle: award restructuring

In 1988 ACAC stated that the usefulness of the Restructuring and Efficiency Principle had been exhausted, but it had laid the foundation for further workplace reform.[86] This reform came as a new wage system linked to the reform of the industrial award system. Wage increases were to be paid in accordance with a new principle—**Structural Efficiency Principle**—which came to be more commonly known as 'award restructuring'.[87]

The focus of award restructuring was the development of a more highly skilled workplace to contribute to increasing organisational efficiency and competitiveness. The scope of changes in award restructuring included the development of career paths and multi-skilling with a focus on enhancing flexibility.[88] This entailed the development of new classification structures to provide a mechanism for a structured development of the skill levels within an organisation.[89] Award restructuring focused on the reduction of job classifications and the establishment of skill-related career paths linked to pay scales.

Award restructuring facilitated the process of limited or 'managed decentralised' productivity bargaining between the parties to awards.[90] While the results of award restructuring were mixed,[91] in retrospect it provided the platform for further workplace reforms through enterprise-based agreements, particularly in the manufacturing and public sectors.[92] Award restructuring also provided the foundation for the further decentralisation of workplace reform or what has been described as coordinated flexibility.[93] This new industrial relations framework facilitated rather than impeded change, by allowing more flexibility, innovation processes and agreements and trade-offs between pay and productivity.[94]

The Enterprise Bargaining Principle

The Enterprise Bargaining Principle introduced in the 1991 National Wage Case continued the momentum of deregulation by providing the framework for enterprise-specific agreements to become the main vehicle in the determination of working conditions and rates of pay.[95] However, the framework of the Structural Efficiency Principle was maintained, with wage increases having to be based on improved productivity and efficiency. A key procedural reform undertaken by the Commission under this principle was the reduction in its role as arbitrator over total wage outcomes, preferring the role of conciliation between the parties to ensure minimal safety net provisions. This development placed the responsibility for enterprise bargaining firmly in the hands of the negotiating parties.[96]

Further reforms followed the establishment of the Enterprise Bargaining Principle. This was primarily driven by the Keating Federal Labor Government, which considered that the pace of reform needed to be increased. The legislation that followed included Certified Workplace Agreements in 1992, the Enterprise Awards Principle[97] in October 1993 and the *Industrial Relations Reform Act 1993 (Cwlth)*, which consolidated these changes. The thrust of these changes maintained the progressive shift of responsibility for the substance of agreements firmly to the workplace, while further reducing the role of third parties in negotiations.

Structural Efficiency Principle (or award restructuring) a reform of the Australian wages system aimed at developing a more highly skilled workplace; for example, by the reduction of job classifications, the establishment of skill-related career paths linked to pay scales and multi-skilling to enhance workforce flexibility.

The election of the Howard Federal Coalition Government in 1996 provided further impetus to the decentralisation of labour regulation and workplace reform. A key aim of the *Workplace Relations Act 1996 (Cwlth)* was:

> providing the means for wages and conditions of employment to be determined as far as possible by agreement of employers and employees at the workplace or enterprise level, upon a foundation of minimum standards.[98]

This continued deregulation or 'fragmented flexibility' has created a substantial change in the regulatory environment of the labour market[99] and wage determination, with the commission's powers to arbitrate now restricted to approximately 20 issues. These changes have been predicated on the philosophy that a more dynamic and competitive economic environment can best be enhanced by increasingly decentralising responsibility for pay determination to the workplace, as it is the management and the workforce that understand the needs and constraints within an enterprise.[100] (Also see Chapter 3 The legal context for human resource management, and Chapter 5 Industrial relations).

The Australian Fair Pay Commission (AFPC)

After the 2004 Federal election, it became clear that not only had the Howard Federal coalition won a fourth term in government, it had also won control of the Senate. This was the first time in 25 years that both houses of parliament were controlled by the governing party. The significance for the government has been the ability to develop new polices (and review previous polices stymied by the Senate) with the expectation they would pass through. This has been the case with industrial relations and within this the founding principles and practices of wage determination. The detail and focus of this change is to be through the newly established Australian Fair Pay Commission (AFPC). The details and features of the AFPC are dealt with in more detail in Chapter 5 Industrial Relations. Here the focus will be on it role regarding wage determination.

The AFPC is based on the UK Low Pay Commission (LPC). The role of the LRC was initially to establish a national minimum wage in Britain[101] (90 years after Australia). The establishment of the AFPC was announced in May 2005, to in effect, replace the Australian Industrial Relations Commission as the arbiter of federal wage rates including the minimum wage. The Commission is made up of one chairperson who has a five-year fixed term and four part-time commissioners on four year fixed terms. According to the then Workplace Relations Minister Kevin Andrew, the AFPC would also determine the timing, scope, conduct and frequency of wage reviews[102]. At the time of writing, the AFPC has yet to make its first decision.

As well as reading 'Managing challenges through attracting and retaining people: Being fair: The new Fair Pay Commission may signal the beginning of broader reforms' case below and Chapter 5, students interested in further information on the AFPC are encouraged to go to the websites of the Federal Government and the Australian Council of Trade Unions (ACTU) for current analysis and debate surrounding the AFPC.

BEING FAIR: THE NEW FAIR PAY COMMISSION MAY SIGNAL THE BEGINNING OF BROADER REFORMS

The establishment of the Australian Fair Pay Commission as part of the Work Choices package has divided opinion. Critics may argue that it will reduce minimum wages but it begs the question of what 'fairness' exactly is in the minimum wage setting.

The commission's role is to set and adjust minimum and award classifications, wages and casual loadings, as well as minimum wages for juniors, trainees, apprentices and disabled employees. Rather than cutting minimum wages, it is likely that it will be more closely aligned to movements in the economy.

Work Choices prohibits the commission from adjusting the rate below that announced in the last safety net review, and it is unlikely to be set below that level in 'real' terms due to political and economic pressures.

It is more likely that the commission will set levels below in 'relative' terms, meaning that there could be greater wage disparity in the labour market between workers on minimum wages and those at the top of the income spectrum.

As a result, some economists advocate the need for a more co-coordinated approach—through reforming taxation and the social security systems, along with IR—in order to raise the living standards of the low-paid and the unemployed.

The chairman of the commission, Professor Ian Harper, wants to examine the link between social security benefits and tax credits with minimum wages in Australia. He has signalled his intention to explore how changes in the minimum wage affect the disposable incomes net of income tax and social security payments for low-paid workers. In an article in *The Australian* (20 October 2005) he said: 'Informing itself of the spectrum of views on this question, and gathering and analysing evidence must be a priority for the commission.'

Professor Harper also wants to commission members to go out to workplaces and consult those affected by its decisions. This approach is based upon the UK's Low Pay Commission approach, which according to LPC commissioner professor William Brown (*The Age* 24 November 2005) 'is widely appreciated, and is invaluable in giving early insights into labour market change'. Not that this is new to the Australian Industrial Relations Commission. Until recent times, the AIRC regularly visited workplaces through 'work value cases' to ascertain the experience and skill a worker needed to perform their job.

However, critics suggest that the new Australian Fair Pay Commission will not be independent because commissioners do not have tenure and they will therefore be likely to be subservient to Howard government policy.

While governments in many comparable countries already set minimum wages—including the UK where the LPC only recommends minimum wage levels—the experience in Australia would suggest that this is an incorrect assumption.

Fair Pay commissioners will be appointed on a part-time basis (unlike AIRC members), and will be able to continue their employment and careers outside the commission.

The experience to date of statutory appointments also provides little evidence that such appointees are servants of government policy. In fact some appointees on fixed-term contracts have been the most vocal critics of current government policy, such as federal Sex Discrimination Commissioner Pru Goward and Professor Alan Fels, the former chairman of the Australian Competition and Consumer Commission.

Critics have also suggested that the Australian Fair Pay Commission will only represent an employer agenda. It is significant that Professor Harper has indicated his desire for union and employee interests to be represented on the panel, as well as independent experts. However, one would expect that all commissioners serve in an individual capacity—as occurs at the Low Pay Commission in the UK—and not as representatives of the organisations to which they belong.

Minimum wages need to be set according to certain principles underpinned by equality, fairness for the employed and unemployed, and a capacity for workers and employers to create value and worth.

To further Australia's skill base and workforce participation levels, we need an integrated approach that uses a combination of tax, skills training and welfare reform with IR reform. This would maintain high levels of productivity as well as increase living standards for those in employment and those underutilised in the labour market.

Source: Based on P.J Gollan, 2006, 'Being Fair', *HR Monthly* June, p. 30.

MANAGING PEOPLE

TAKEN TO THE CLEANERS

Other people would shrink from the prospect but Brisbane man Stephen Ward likes nothing better than working the graveyard shift. Ward, 39, starts work at three in the morning.

He cleans office buildings in the city. Unless there's a complaint, and he says there are hardly ever complaints, no one seems to notice he has been and gone.

He works for a contract cleaning company for three to five hours a night. Ward has been a cleaner for more than 20 years. These days though, he can't get the hours he wants and he can't do his job as he would like—there's never enough time.

There are more than 90 000 contract cleaners in Australia dusting, mopping and vacuuming offices, shopping centres and schools as most of us sleep. But this invisible army of cleaners is under pressure from what their union, the Liquor, Hospitality and Miscellaneous Union, calls a 'race to the bottom'.

While employment in the fast-growing industry has more than doubled since the late 1990s, the ferocious competition for cleaning contracts means property managers for some of the largest corporations in the country can pressure contract cleaning companies to undercut each other.

'What is already a highly competitive industry could devour itself in a dog-eat-dog environment', says Alan Hardcastle, editor and publisher of the industry publication *Inclean*.

Hardcastle says the typical tactic from some property owners and managers to tell the cleaning company it has won the contract, then demand it drop the per-hour cleaning rate from $25 an hour to $19 or $20 (which isn't enough to pay award wages as well as superannuation and workers compensation).

'The contractor is then left to give up that contract or fall in line', Hardcastle says. 'The person who suffers is the cleaner, who is expected to do more in less time.'

After finishing his shift at 8am, Ward tells *Inquirer* the problem is that the owners of many commercial buildings 'need more cleaning than they're willing to pay for'.

The LHMU says the result is that cleaners and security officers can't get enough work to sustain them. Research by the union reveals the average income for cleaners in Australia is $14 300. That's almost $1000 a year less than the poverty-level wage for an individual, LMHU national secretary Jeff Lawrence says.

Fearful that standards will drop further as the Work Choices legislation emboldens employers to find ways to cut cleaners' pay and conditions, the LHMU—together with New Zealand's Services and Food Workers Union—is launching the Clean Start campaign. The union hopes to persuade building owners and tenants that it is in their best interest to give contracts to responsible employers who treat employees fairly and guarantee occupational health and safety standards.

Under the present system, according to the union's brochure on the subject, 'the standard of cleaning … In commercial office buildings is at an all-time low'.

Companies bidding at competitive rates—$20 an hour—may resort to a sort of subterfuge tacitly understood by all sides.

'The fact that everyone understands but no one acknowledges is that the quality of cleaning will not meet the standards set out in the tender document', Hardcastle says.

But some companies make such unreasonable demands and reputable contractors avoid them, he says. 'It is commonplace in the industry for reputable cleaning contractors to state that they will not deal with … Property owner-managers [who] have unreasonable expectations of what can be done for the price they offer', he says.

In the NSW parliament in 2002, Ian West, a member of the Legislative Council—and a former LHMU official—criticised Westfield after a union organiser found that some cleaners at Westfield shopping centre at Parramatta, in the western suburbs of Sydney, hadn't been paid for four weeks.

'Westfield management appears to have adopted a strategy of increasing profits by engaging the cheapest tenderer, who in turn makes his profit off the backs of underpaid cleaners', West told Parliament at the time.

Whatever the truth or otherwise of that claim, Julia Clarke, manager of corporate affairs at the Westfield Group, says it would not happen now. 'We have a good relationship with the union for cleaners, here and in the US, and have met with them on several occasions in recent times', she says. 'We work with them closely on specific issues that need to be resolved. We require all our contractors to meet their legal obligations, and we'd want to know about it if they weren't.'

Inquirer has previously reported that big corporations in Australia have successfully insulated themselves from responsibility for cleaners at the bottom of the heap by using procurement companies to hire contract cleaning companies, while turning a blind eye to the subcontracting that is starting to undermine the industry.

If anything has changed since, says the owner of one contract cleaning company, it is that the cutthroat competition has resulted in increasing numbers of contractors and subcontractors ignoring their legal obligations and paying $10 an hour cash in hand.

'Companies that weren't paying cash in hand a few years ago are doing it now', the owner says. 'The property owners don't care. It doesn't win you work to have good occupational health and safety standards and a good reputation. The prices being quoted on jobs make it obvious this is what is happening.'

Despite consultation with the union, the Building Service Contractors Association of Australia, the body that represents the larger contract cleaning companies, still hasn't decided where it stands.

Asked if his organisation supports the union initiative to stop the downward spiral, BSCAA chief executive Rick MacKenzie says, 'We haven't actually developed a policy on it just yet. We still have to sit down as an industry association and look at it. We need to do a release for the media but we haven't done it yet'

Source: Based on E. Wynhausen, 2006, 'Taken to the cleaners', *Inquirer Weekend Australian,* April, 15–16, p. 26

QUESTIONS

1 What are the direct and indirect ramifications for organisations that choose to undercut standard rates?
2 In a competitive global environment and a highly deregulated economy is this just a case of labour market forces at work? Discuss.

CHAPTER SUMMARY

In this chapter, we have discussed the nature of the pay structure and its component parts, the pay level and the job structure. Equity theory suggests that social comparisons are an important influence on how employees evaluate their pay. Employees make external comparisons between their pay and the pay they believe is received by employees in other organisations. Such comparisons may have consequences for employee attitudes and retention. Employees also make internal comparisons between what they receive and what they perceive others within the organisation are paid. These types of comparisons may have consequences for internal movement, cooperation and attitudes (for example, organisation commitment). Such comparisons play an important role in the controversy over executive pay, as illustrated by the focus of critics on the ratio of executive pay to that of lower-paid workers.

Pay benchmarking surveys and job evaluation are two administrative tools widely used in managing the pay-level and job-structure components of the pay structure, which influence employee social comparisons. Pay surveys also permit organisations to benchmark their labour costs against other organisations. Globalisation is increasing the need for organisations to be competitive in both their labour costs and productivity. The nature of pay structures is undergoing a fundamental change in many organisations. One change is the move to fewer pay levels to reduce labour costs and bureaucracy. Second, some employers are shifting from paying employees for narrow jobs to giving them broader responsibilities and paying them to learn the necessary skills. Finally, the chapter provides an overview of the development of the Australian wage system,

including the recent development of the Australian Fair Pay Commission.
A theme that runs through this chapter and the next is the importance of process in managing employee compensation. How a new program is designed, decided on, implemented and communicated is, perhaps, just as important as its core characteristics.

WEB EXERCISES

Several websites provide salary surveys for clerical, professional and managerial jobs. One of these sites is Job Smart. Go to www.jobsmart.org. Click on 'Salary Surveys' then on 'Profession-specific salary surveys'. From the list of professions presented choose one that interests you. Review the information provided and answer the following questions.

Questions
1 What is the value of this website for employers? For employees?
2 From a HRM perspective, what are the advantages of using websites such as this one to establish salary ranges and adjust the current salary structure? What are the disadvantages?

DISCUSSION QUESTIONS

1 What are the potential consequences of having a pay structure that is out of line with your competitors? How would you go about finding out whether your organisation remuneration is competitive?
2 Top management has realised that in an era of increasing skill shortages it will be harder to attract and retain key talent. You have been asked to suggest innovative alternatives to the traditional 'job-based' approach to employee compensation that will attract and retain current and potential employees. List the advantages and disadvantages of these new approaches.
3 If major changes of the type mentioned in the previous question are to be made, what types of so-called process issues need to be considered? Of what relevance is equity theory in helping to understand how employees might react to changes in the pay structure?
4 (a) Are executive pay levels unreasonable? Why or why not? (Use examples to illustrate.)
   (b) What measures are available to make them more accountable?
5 What is the AFPC? What is the role of the AFPC?

CASE STUDY

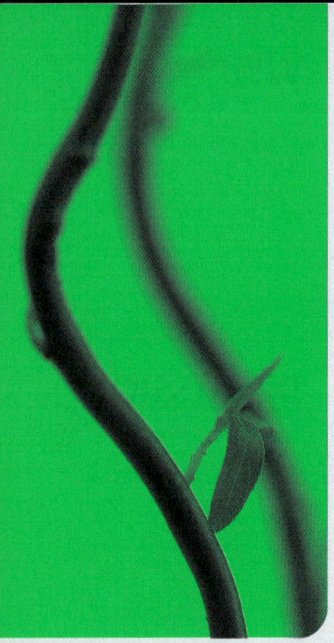

ABLE MANAGEMENT CONSULTANTS, INC.

Able Management Consultants, Inc. (AMC) is a successful established management consulting firm with offices around Australia and it is part of a worldwide network of consultants. The head office of AMC is in London, England. The firm specialises in four major areas of consulting: change management, recruitment and selection, job analysis and remuneration systems.

The Australian division was established in 1990 and has grown rapidly in the last few years as Australian managers have come to recognise the importance of human resource management issues to sustained competitive advantage. The shift to enterprise bargaining has also aided the growth of the Australian operation as organisations experiment with a range of HRM techniques. At present AMC employs 60 staff across Australia: 37 as consultants and 23 in various support and administrative roles.

One of AMC's objectives is to maintain its role as a market leader in human resource and change management consulting in the Asia–Pacific region. It sees its competitive advantage in terms of being able to supply its clients with innovative ideas and solutions to a broad range of organisational problems. In the highly competitive business of management consulting it is imperative that AMC provides a high quality service to organisations in both the private and public sectors.

Consider the following scenario.

You have been with the organisation for a few years now and are considering your future with the company. Maybe you should move on? In your time with AMC you have rotated through each of the four sections of the company, so you feel that you have had a chance to truly experience the range of opportunities for a young consultant.

As you reflect on your experiences with AMC, you become uncomfortable with the highly competitive nature of your work environment. You feel that you must work long hours in order to be seen to be 'committed to AMC', despite the fact that you can get your work done in an efficient manner. You are dismayed by the effects of the performance management system. The performance management system provides for merit pay on the basis of a complex formula which includes three main components: measures of client satisfaction, the number of clients and the amount of revenue generated. This means that most of your colleagues are unwilling to help out when things get tough, as each employee is only rewarded for the achievement of their individual objectives. When you raised this as an issue at your last evaluation, your manager told you that this is the pay system that operates throughout the worldwide operations of AMC and it was not designed to respond to the wishes of a junior employee.

At your last performance evaluation, you also raised a question about your future prospects with AMC. What would you need to do to get ahead in the firm? Your manager said that you just have to work hard and hope that someone will die or retire!

The workload is high, so there is little time for training and professional development, despite the fact that (as a management consultant) it is your job to develop new products and find innovative solutions to clients' problems. You see little opportunity for advancement within AMC. There is a large group of senior consultants who have established reputations, and they are unlikely to leave. You could go to one of the overseas divisions but you like being in Australia and it would be difficult for your partner to get a job elsewhere, so you feel that this is not really an option.

Source: Dr M. Brown, University of Melbourne & Professor H. De Cieri, Monash University.

QUESTIONS

1 How would you describe the approach to HRM within Able Management Consultants? Identify and discuss the HRM problems at AMC.
2 Identify and critically evaluate any inconsistencies between the internal HRM practices of AMC and the overall strategic objectives of the consulting firm. What are the implications of any inconsistencies at AMC for organisational performance?

CHAPTER 14

PERFORMANCE-RELATED PAY

Objectives

After reading this chapter, you should be able to:

1. Describe three theories that explain the dynamics of performance-related pay.
2. Identify a number of performance-related pay programs.
3. List the major factors to consider in matching the pay strategy to the organisation's strategy.
4. Describe the way the rewards of managers and executives can be tied to company performance.
5. Explain the importance of process issues, such as communication, in compensation management.

A job well done

Many areas of HR are coming under more scrutiny, with a view to greater cost effectiveness. Reward and recognition programs are one such area, with companies reviewing links to the bottom line and best to tailor such programs.

Some leading organisations are investing considerably more—approximately 1 to 2 per cent—of their payroll on non-cash rewards for recognition-based programs, according to Adrian Finlayson, CEO of Wishlist Holdings. While there is no industry-wide, fact-based research on the actual spend on employee gifts and rewards, he estimates that spend on such initiatives probably represents about 0.5 per cent of payroll across all sectors.

'In recent years we have seen a significant expansion in the range of products and services that are being offered to employees as part of their incentive and recognition programs. Once well-known branded products were being offered but now more inspirational choices are being offered such as unforgettable experiences such as a NASCAR drive, a weekend getaway, swimming with the whales and much more', says Finlayson.

… 'Ideally the rewards delivery should be no more than a few days to a week (after great performance is achieved) but this is not always possible, so a strong customer service ethic is required to ensure if this can't be achieved then the participant is contacted and provided with advice and options.'

Tailoring rewards

The starting point for tailoring an employee rewards program is to start with the end in mind …

Once the business objectives are agreed among the key stakeholders a program can be designed that will deliver the results. The program design needs to define business outcomes, the value placed on each behaviour and reward, and way participation and communication will be encouraged.

The type of incentive offered will depend on various factors such as the demographics and needs of the employees. For instance engineers might rather be rewarded with an investment in their training and education, than receive a gold watch.

In addition successful reward and recognition programs require consultation or focus groups with the management team and also with employee stakeholders.

Common pitfalls

'Recognition programs should be consistently applied across the company. Otherwise staff can often feel alienated if they didn't receive an incentive and other staff did or vice versa,' says Louise Carmody (national sales and marketing manager, EzyBite—Accor Services).

Cash incentives can often be forgotten as an incentive, however, they can create a feeling of competition between employees, she says.

'It is important that the rewards don't just become an expected part of the job, just for doing the job they are already paid to do. If this happens then the program will have very little credibility in the eyes of the participants and will not deliver the returns that management expect,' says Finslayson.

A good incentive program evolves overtime as the challenges to the business change. It must be rigorously reviewed and refined to ensure it is performing at an optimum level.

Measuring ROI

Measuring return on investment (ROI) of employee benefit programs is difficult because improved staff morale is often an intangible element of the workplace, says Carmody. Looking at aspects such as improved sales, lower absenteeism than past years and lower staff turnover are areas that can prove that your incentive program is working. 'These factors are not always indicators of a successful retention program as other external and internal influences could be making these changes.'

Staff surveys and consistent communication are other ways in which upper managers can monitor the results of the gift and incentive programs, she adds.

PART 4   Rewarding People

A job well done *continued*

There is a growing trend towards much greater accountability and the need to deliver results, according to Finlayson. 'The key to proving an ROI is extensive analysis of the current situation and then rewarding behavioural changes which lead to the desired business outcomes that can be tracked and measured by the program', he says.

'Most organisations generally implement a range of initiatives that complement each other and therefore it is difficult to fully attribute the results to just one program. However, with a solid business case and firm objectives it is possible to create a strong link between the outcomes and the various initiatives which lead to the results.'

Alberto Culver

Alberto Culver is a global company which produces hair and beauty products. In Australia, the company has recently taken a more strategic approach to reward and recognition.

The senior management team wants to acknowledge and reward people in a more consistent manner, according to Neil Perrett, HR Director for Alberto Culver Australia. 'It's more than just the emails that go out from time to time or recognition from managers. Quite often a manager might be more aware of these issues than others, so their department might be getting more regular recognition than others because of this. Our management team has discussed this and they want to recognise and reward performance in a way that ensures consistency and equality across the organisation', he says.

Perrett says it's important to have executive support in place for such initiatives, which also reinforces employees' perceptions of the importance of reward and recognition programs. 'The way we used to do things was to focus on business benefits from an HR point of view. The HR function is not the first to be expendable. As such, the programs and policies and systems we put in place need to be directly related to a core part of the business as well as top down support.'

Source: Adapted from 2006, 'A job well done', *Human Resources*, 19 September, p. 22–3. www.humanresourcesmagazine.com.au

Introduction

The opening case study illustrates some of the developments and complexities in using the employee incentive scheme to motivate employee behaviour. One of the issues is that the compensation system's power is sometimes misdirected, so it motivates the wrong behaviours. The pay system must encourage behaviours that both contribute to profits in the short run and build customer satisfaction for long-term success. In other situations, changing economic circumstances may lead to employee-relation problems if employees believe they are being penalised for factors beyond their control.

In the preceding chapter, we focused on setting pay for jobs. In this chapter, we focus on using pay to recognise and reward employees' contributions to the organisation's success. An employee's pay does not depend solely on the job she or he holds. Instead, differences in performance (individual, group or organisation), seniority, skills and so forth, are used as a basis for differentiating pay levels among employees.[1]

Several key questions arise in evaluating different pay programs for recognising contributions. First, what are the costs of the program? Second, what is the expected return (for example, in terms of influences on attitudes and behaviours) from such investments? Third, does the program fit with the organisation's human resource strategy and its overall business strategy?

Organisations have a relatively large degree of discretion in deciding how to pay, especially compared with the pay-level decisions discussed in the previous chapter. The same organisational pay level or 'compensation pie' can be distributed or 'sliced' among employees in many ways. Whether each employee's share is based on individual performance, profits, seniority or other factors, the size of the pie (and, thus, the cost to the organisation) can remain the same.

Regardless of cost differences, different pay programs can have considerably different consequences for productivity and return on investment. Indeed, a study of how—and how much—150 organisations paid found not only that the largest differences between organisations had to do with how they paid, but that these differences resulted in different levels of profitability.[2]

The approach to remuneration structure changed in Australia during the twentieth century. The centralised wage system developed to become a complex system involving contracts such as awards, over-award payments and minimum wages, and then, in the 1970s the Federal Government 'sought to promote performance related remuneration practices to boost productivity in the manufacturing industry'.[3] During the 1980s and 1990s the remuneration practices of multinationals; greater global competition; desire for efficiencies and cost savings; and the shift to enterprise bargaining and then individualised contracts further encouraged changes in remuneration practices, including the growth in the use of performance-based pay. It is noteworthy these pressures led to the adoption of performance-based pay for non-managerial employees as well as managerial staff. O'Neill reports that:

> … the early 90s saw a very significant shift from discretionary bonuses to target-based incentive plans based on the 'do this-get that' principle of plan design. This was accompanied by a rapid spread of performance pay plans to cover almost all supervisory and management positions. This in turn prompted the HR function to re-engineer performance planning to ensure the integrity of performance plans and their link with pay.[4]

Australia also witnessed an increase in the use of performance-based pay for non-managerial employees during the 1990s and in the first decade of the twenty-first century.[5] It has been predicted that the *Workplace Amendment (Work Choices) Act 2005* will provide greater opportunity for the performance pay schemes.[6]

The interest and implementation of performance-based pay for employees is based on the assumption that pay can influence behaviour, employee performance and consequently organisational performance, outcomes and effectiveness. Theories, such as expectancy, equity, agency and reinforcement theory, explain the different dynamics that influence employee behaviour in the workplace. Research indicates that pay based on performance can improve employee performance[7] and the investment in such schemes results in returns for shareholders. However, despite some evidence for the effectiveness of performance-based pay systems, there are also significant problems involved in the implementation of these schemes.[8] As highlighted in Chapter 2, any human resource initiative, such as performance-based pay, needs to be consistent and reinforce other human resource policies. For instance, for performance-based pay to be effective, it is important to have a performance appraisal process that is and is also perceived as fair. Performance-based pay can be one element in creating a performance-based culture.[9]

This chapter focuses on pay in a narrow way. It focuses on providing monetary rewards for performance. However, this does not mean that other rewards should not be considered as rewards for exceptional performance. Many of these other rewards can be costed (for example, a weekend away at a luxury resort or a dinner for two at a special restaurant does have a monetary value). Other rewards could include attendance at a company conference that provides networking, learning and pleasure activities.

The use of pay-for-performance schemes in many circumstances is controversial. 'HRM spotlight: Recognising highly accomplished teachers or performance/merit pay', opposite, discusses the issue of performance-based pay for teachers.

How does pay influence individual employees?

Pay plans are typically used to energise, direct or control employee behaviour. Interest in the use of pay as a way of influencing behaviour has been acknowledged for many years[10] and was popularised by Taylor when he developed his principles of 'Scientific Management'[11]. In addition, a range of motivation and behavioural theories provide different explanations for the factors that influence behaviour generally and in the workplace. Equity theory, described in the previous chapter, is relevant here as well. Most employees compare their own pay with that of others, especially those in the same job. Perceptions of inequity may cause employees to take actions to restore equity. Unfortunately some of these actions (for example, quitting or lack of cooperation) may not be helpful to the organisation.

Three additional theories also help explain compensation's effects: reinforcement, expectancy and agency theories.

Reinforcement theory

The 'Law of effect' by E.L. Thorndike states that a response followed by a reward is more likely to recur in the future. The implication for compensation management is that high employee performance followed by a monetary reward will make future high performance more likely. By the same token, high performance not followed by a reward will make it less likely in the future. The theory emphasises the importance of a person's actual experience of a reward. Recognition programs that reward employees, who have performed exceptionally, immediately or soon after their achievement, are an example of the application of **reinforcement theory**.

Reinforcement theory claims that a response followed by a reward is more likely to reoccur in the future

Expectancy theory says that the attractiveness of any job is a function of valence, instrumentality and expectancy. .

Expectancy theory

Expectancy theory refers to the theory that says the attractiveness of any job is a function of valence (the desirability of the reward to a person), instrumentality (performance is perceived as securing the reward), and expectancy (the belief that his efforts will affect performance). This explains behaviours (job performance) at work in terms of the expectations people have in the workplace. Expectancy theory of motivation argues that the effort people make at work is based on the availability of a desired reward and the expectation that successful job performance will result in the achievement of this reward. Their job performance is then influenced by three factors: their ability to perform to this standard, a clear perception of their role, and the necessary organisational resources and support to perform their role. It follows, therefore, that good job performance could be motivated by providing rewards that are desired by people and by rewarding behaviours that contribute to organisational success. The achievement of desired rewards, however, is not sufficient to provide job satisfaction. Job satisfaction depends on the extent to which people believe the rewards they achieve are equitable. In circumstances

RECOGNISING HIGHLY ACCOMPLISHED TEACHERS OR PERFORANCE/MERIT PAY

HRM SPOTLIGHT

Recent opportunistic statements in the Australian media have again focused attention on the question of 'performance or merit pay' to teachers. These have included statements by the Federal Education Minister proposing a federal government funded 'incentive fund' to reward high achieving teachers, but notably in the context of an accusatory stance arguing 'complacency in accepting low standards' (*The Australian*, 15 July 2006) with commentary from Jennifer Buckingham, Centre for Independent Studies, stating that 'teacher unions will not consider any policy that would differentiate between teachers' and that 'union representatives should get out of the way' (*The Courier Mail*, 19 July 2006).

In a further elaboration of the federal government's position, the *Daily Telegraph* newspaper in Sydney on 9 August 2006 reported that Minister Bishop would be 'pushing ahead' with a scheme to pay cash bonuses to teachers of high performing students and that 'the scheme would form part of the next round of funding negotiations with the states and territories next year'.

In a report to Teaching Australia, Lawrence Ingvarson has once again trundled out his recommendation to 'extend the teacher pay scale to reward long serving teachers who excel in their field … recognise professional development and performance in the classroom. Taking results into account would, however, be problematic' (*The Courier Mail*, 19 July 2006).

In a commentary on the renewed debate Cheryl O'Connor, Australian College of Educators, said that: 'Whatever the obstacles in Australia, the idea of providing greater rewards for great teachers is worthy and well overdue' (*Adelaide Advertiser* and *Canberra Times*). Yet the few obstacles that she identifies are substantial.

O'Connor notes in her article that 'great teachers rarely say their successful teaching is the result of their individual effort. Whatever the skills of particular teachers, they say, much of what occurs in classrooms depends to a considerable extent on the talents and professionalism of a team of people who teaches students'.

The August 2005 DEST report 'Performance-based rewards for teachers' provides an alleged overview of teacher reward systems internationally and in particular OECD countries. The report focuses on 15 countries and their performance pay models, including USA, UK, Israel, Singapore, Denmark, Mexico, Korea, Germany, France and New Zealand.

The report concludes simply that '… it is clear that performance-based rewards systems can work' (DEST report August 2005, p. 30).

The Australian newspaper article (15 July) states that 'The Association of Independent Schools of NSW is looking at introducing merit-based pay to replace the current system of incremental rises.'

Against this backdrop one might be misled to believe that there is no history of engagement with, or consideration of, let alone implementation of any systemic approach to recognising highly accomplished teachers in Australia. One might mistakenly consider that such an 'initiative' is the domain of employers, including government and indeed that there is little question about the appropriateness or 'workability' of such a scheme.

Experience in both Australia and overseas paints quite a different picture.

What becomes apparent is that some interest groups are seeking to overlay accountability measures arising from populist opinion guised as a commitment to improving teacher quality and remuneration. Much of the performance pay agenda fails to acknowledge either breadth and depth of teachers' work or the genuine need for commitment, including financial, to supporting an integrated career package for the teaching profession.

Frighteningly the idea of a popularity contest to recognise 'talented' teachers was promoted by Minister Bishop when she launched the 2006 National Science Week (AAP, 9 August) by stating: 'People say to me, how can you possibly judge who is a good teacher or a bad teacher. You go into any school and you say, who are the good teachers and the bad teachers, and they'll tell you. Students can tell you, parents can tell you.'

There is a gulf between the rhetoric and historic implementation of performance or merit pay and a genuine engagement by employers and governments with teacher unions in recognising highly accomplished teachers.

Source: Independent Education Union, 2006, *Recognising highly accomplished teachers or performance pay?*, Independent Education Union, August.

where rewards are not regarded as equitable and job satisfaction is adversely affected, employees' efforts could be reduced.

Although expectancy theory implies that linking an increased amount of rewards to performance will increase motivation and performance, some authors have questioned this assumption, arguing that monetary rewards may increase extrinsic motivation but decrease intrinsic motivation. Extrinsic motivation depends on rewards (for example, pay and benefits) controlled by an external source; whereas, intrinsic motivation depends on rewards that flow naturally from work itself (for example, performing interesting work).[12] In other words, paying a child to read books may diminish the child's natural interest in reading and the child may, in the future, be less likely to read books unless there are monetary incentives. Although monetary incentives may reduce intrinsic motivation in some settings (for example, education), the evidence suggests that such effects are small and isolated in work settings. Therefore, while it is important to keep in mind that money is not the only effective way to motivate behaviour and that monetary rewards will not always be the answer to motivation problems, it does not appear that monetary rewards run much risk of compromising intrinsic motivation in most work settings.[13] (See 'Managing challenges through attracting and retaining people: Crazy brave'.)

Agency theory

This theory focuses on the divergent interests and goals of the organisation's stakeholders and the ways in which employee compensation can be used to align these interests and goals. We cover agency theory in some depth because it provides especially relevant implications for compensation design.

An important characteristic of the modern corporation is the separation of ownership from management (or control). Unlike the early stages of capitalism, where owner and manager were often the same, today, with some exceptions (mostly smaller companies), most stockholders are far removed from the day-to-day operation of companies. Although this separation has important advantages (for example, mobility of financial capital and diversification of investment risk), it also creates agency costs—the interests of the **principals** (that is, owners) and their **agents** (that is, managers) may no longer converge. What is best for the agent, or manager, may not be best for the owner.

Three types of agency costs arise in managerial compensation.[14] First, although shareholders seek to maximise their wealth, management may be spending money on things such as perquisites (for example, 'superfluous' corporate jets) or 'empire building' (for example, making acquisitions that do not add value to the company but may enhance the manager's prestige or pay). Second, managers and shareholders may differ in their attitudes towards risk. Shareholders can diversify their investments (and, thus, their risks) more easily than managers (whose only major source of income may be their job), so managers are typically more averse to risk. Thus, they may be less likely to pursue projects or acquisitions that have a high potential payoff. It also suggests a preference on the part of managers for relatively little risk in their pay (for example, a high emphasis on base salary and a low emphasis on uncertain bonuses or incentives). Indeed, research shows that managerial compensation in manager-controlled firms is more often designed in this manner.[15] Third, decision-making horizons may differ. For example, if managers change companies more than owners change ownership, managers may be more likely to maximise short-run performance (and pay), perhaps at the expense of long-term success.

Agency theory is also of value in the analysis and design of non-managers' compensation. In this case, the divergence of interests may exist between managers (now in the role of principals) and their employees (who take on the role of agents).

In designing either managerial or non-managerial compensation, the key question is: 'How can such agency costs be minimised?' Agency theory says that the principal must choose a contracting scheme that helps align the interests of the agent with the

Principal
in agency theory, the owner of a business; in HR management, may refer to a manager.

Agent
in agency theory, a manager or one who acts on behalf of an owner (principal); in HR management, may refer to an employee.

CRAZY BRAVE

'My experience working for a big company was that I was never given the freedom, I was never rewarded or appreciated', John Ilhan says. 'I learnt from that experience that people should be given a go. It is a simple thing, but most companies don't do it. How can you get people to really commit and care about your business like they would their own business. That's the trick.'

These days, delegation, rewards and flexibility are the 'tricks' he uses at Crazy John's to hold onto staff. His turnover rate is very low 25 per cent for retail staff and 15 per cent in his core management group.

'I don't believe in controlling people', he says. 'Everyone should be allowed to try their own style. There are these key principles or values (in our business) but anything outside those—do what you want. I don't care what you do as long as you can demonstrate you are growing the business and the numbers stack up.'

Sitting in the boardroom, which is decorated with sporting memorabilia, in his South Melbourne head office, Ilhan turns and points through the glass to the staff on the floor. 'These are some of the best people you will ever meet in the world', he says, 'You go through the tough times, the good times, with loyalty and dedication, I think I am very fortunate.'

They are hardly salubrious surrounds for the head office of a national company. Windows are scarce, some workers queue to use the sandwich maker in the cramped kitchen, and files are piled high in the corners. But people (some 600 nationwide) seem prepared to work for 'Crazy' John Ilhan.

'What we are finding now that the company has grown is people now want to work for us', he says. 'We are getting top people saying, I want to work for you, and these are people from bigger companies. You get managing directors of global companies asking the same question.'

Ilhan uses his secretary to reinforce the point: 'My PA is a young girl. She is not qualified, but she has been trained. Sure she could learn a lot more, but we are sending her to a school and we are paying for it. But she is so dedicated and committed and has such a great work ethic—why wouldn't you work on someone like that and develop them?'

Ilhan made headlines this year when he rewarded 100 of his staff with an all-expenses paid, $500 000 Hawaiian holiday. Some of the younger staff on the trip had never travelled overseas and didn't even have a passport.

In other years, Crazy John's top 100 salespeople have lived it up in Fiji, Bali and Queensland. Just before Christmas, Ilhan hosts 50 people and their partners at the Palazzo Versace on the Gold Coast. The company now wants to make the Hawaiian experience an annual event for staff as an incentive for good performance.

Source: 2006, D. Kitney, 'Crazy Brave', *Australian Financial Review, Boss magazine,* September, pp. 32–3.

---

principal's own interests (that is, reduces agency costs). These contracts can be classified as either behaviour-oriented (for example, merit pay) or outcome-oriented (for example, stock options, profit sharing and commissions).[16]

At first glance, outcome-oriented contracts seem to be the obvious solution. If profits are high, compensation goes up. If profits go down, compensation goes down. The interests of 'the company' and employees are aligned. An important drawback, however, is that such contracts increase the agent's risk; and, because agents are averse to risk, they may require higher pay (a compensating wage differential) to make up for the exposure to risk.[17]

Behaviour-based contracts, on the other hand, do not transfer risk to the agent; and, thus, they do not require a compensating wage differential. However, the principal must be able to monitor, with little cost, what the agent has done. Otherwise, the principal must either invest in monitoring and information, or structure the contract so that pay is linked at least partly to outcomes.[18]

Which type of contract should an organisation use? It depends partly on the following factors:[19]

- *Risk aversion.* This aversion among agents makes outcome-oriented contracts less likely.

- *Outcome uncertainty*. Profit is an example of an outcome. Agents are less willing to have their pay linked to profits to the extent that there is a risk of low profits. They would, therefore, prefer a behaviour-oriented contract.
- *Job programmability*. As jobs become less programmable (that is, less routine), outcome-oriented contracts become more likely because monitoring becomes more difficult.[20]
- *Measurable job outcomes*. When outcomes are more measurable, outcome-oriented contracts are more likely.
- *Ability to pay*. Outcome-oriented contracts contribute to higher compensation costs because of the risk premium.
- *Tradition*. A tradition or custom of using (or not using) outcome-oriented contracts will make such contracts more (or less) likely.

In summary

In summary, the reinforcement, expectancy and agency theories all focus on the fact that behaviour–reward contingencies can shape behaviours. However, agency theory is of particular value in compensation management because of its emphasis on the risk–reward trade-off, an issue that needs close attention when companies consider variable pay plans, which can carry significant risk. However, when considering the broad issue of reward for performance, it is important to remember from Chapter 6 Analysis and design of work, that supporting and reinforcing employee performance might not be all about pay. Motivation theories that focus on employee needs—such as those of Maslow[21], Herzberg[22] and McClelland[23]—indicate that employee performance can be stimulated by a variety of factors other than financial ones. For instance, people who have a strong need to achieve will be more motivated by interesting, stimulating work[24] rather than power or more money. Research[25] on 2300 executives, managers and employees indicates that all three types of employees wanted a better balance between work and family life. The study found more than 30 per cent of these people would take a pay cut for a shorter working week of 35 hours, while 70 per cent believed productivity would be unaffected or improved by working shorter hours.

Other research indicates that employees at all levels, from CEOs to shopfloor employees, say that an excellent workplace is one in which 'the atmosphere of mutual respect was overwhelming'. In these workplaces, there was mutual respect, recognition and trust and colleagues supported each other and helped each other to get their jobs done.[26]

How do pay and benefits influence labour force composition?

Traditionally, using pay to recognise employee contributions has been thought of as a way in which to influence the behaviours and attitudes of current employees; whereas pay level and benefits have been seen as a way in which to influence 'so-called' membership behaviours—decisions about whether to join or remain with the organisation. However, there is increasing recognition that individual pay programs may also affect the nature and composition of an organisation's workforce.[27] For example, it is possible that an organisation that links pay to performance may attract more high performers than an organisation that does not link the two. There may be a similar effect with respect to job retention.[28]

Continuing the analysis, different pay systems appear to attract people with different personality traits and values.[29] Organisations that link pay to individual performance may be more likely to attract individualistic employees, while organisations relying more heavily on team rewards are more likely to attract team-oriented employees.

Companies increasingly need to acknowledge that employees at different life stages will be attracted and retained by different rewards, and benefits are playing an important role in achieving this. For instance, in Australia, people in the information technology (IT) industry aged 20–35 years have been found to want career-development opportunities[30] and lifestyle benefits, such as gymnasium memberships and company-sponsored leisure courses.[31]

As discussed in Chapter 13 Managing compensation, the design of compensation programs needs to be carefully coordinated with the business and human resource strategy. Increasingly, both in Australia and overseas, employers are seeking to establish stronger links between pay, benefits and performance. In Australia, the use of performance-related pay increased dramatically during the mid 1990s to mid 2000s. Large organisations increased their use of variable pay and non-monetary benefits.[32] See 'Managing challenges of globalisation: The importance of place in the global war for talent' case on page 555.

In addition companies are making decisions about where they get the work done, based on relative wage rates in different countries. Many organisations are competing in a global product or service market and they are also competing in a global labour market. Pay decisions are, therefore, influenced by the availability of labour supplies in other countries or the need to attract people from these other countries to Australia.

Programs

When rewarding employees' performance, an organisation does not have to choose one program over another. Instead, a combination of programs is often the best solution. For example, one program may foster teamwork and cooperation but not enough individual initiative. Another may do the opposite. When a number of programs are used, a balance may be attained.[33]

Table 14.1 overleaf provides an overview of the programs that are used for recognising employee contributions. Each program shares a focus on paying for performance. These programs differ according to four design features: payment method, frequency of payout, ways of measuring performance, and choice of which employees are covered.

In a perhaps more speculative vein, Table 14.1 overleaf also suggests the potential consequences of such programs for: performance motivation of employees, attraction of employees, organisation culture, and costs.

Finally, there are three contingencies that may influence whether each pay program fits the situation: organisation structure, management style, and type of work.

We now discuss the different programs and some of their potential consequences in more depth.

Merit pay

Merit pay is linked to outstanding past performance. In merit pay programs, annual pay increases are usually linked to performance appraisal ratings (see Chapter 10 Performance management). Research indicates that more than half of all non-management workers in large companies have a component of their pay linked to individual performance that is measured against specified performance criteria. Four

PART 4   Rewarding People

TABLE 14.1 Programs that are used for recognising individual employee contributions

	Merit pay	Incentive pay	Profit sharing	Ownership	Gainsharing	Skill-based
Design features						
Payment method	Change in base pay	Bonus	Bonus	Equity changes	Bonus	Change in base pay
Frequency of payout	Annually	Weekly	Semi-annually or annually	When stock sold	Monthly or quarterly	When skill or competency acquired
Performance measures	Supervisor's appraisal	Output, productivity, sales	Profit	Stock value	Production or controllable costs	Skill or competency acquisition
Coverage	All employees	Employees with direct influence on performance measures	Total organisation	Total organisation	Production or service unit	All employees
Consequences						
Performance motivation	Little relationship between pay and performance	Clear performance and reward connection	Little pay and performance relationship	Very little pay and performance relationship	Some impacts in small units	Encourages learning
Attraction	Over time, pays better performers more	Pays higher performers more	Helps with all employees	Can help lock in employees	Helps with all employees	Attracts learning-oriented employees
Culture	Competition within work groups	Encourages individual competition	Knowledge of business	Sense of ownership	Supports cooperation and problem solving	Learning and flexible organisation
Costs	Requires well-developed performance	Maintenance high	Relates costs to ability to pay	Cost not variable with performance	Ongoing maintenance needed; and variable operating costs	Can be high
Contingencies						
Organisation structure	Helped by measurable jobs and work units	Many independent jobs	Fits any company	Fits most companies	Fits small stand-alone work units	Fits most companies
Management style	Some participation desirable	Control	Works best with participation	Works best with participation	Fits participation	Works best with participation
Type of work	Individual unless group appraisals done	Stable, individual easily measurable	All types	All types	All types	All types

Source: Adapted and modified from Edward Emmet Lawler III, 'Pay for performance: a strategic analysis', in L.R. Gomez-Mejia, George T. Milkovich and Ray Olsen (eds), 1989, *Compensation and Benefits*, BNA Books, Washington, DC, pp. 136–81.

out of five managers have a component of performance-related pay and it accounts for more than 11 per cent of their total pay. Approximately 30 per cent of certified agreements include an element of performance pay and objective criteria for determining performance.[34] Indeed, given the pervasiveness of merit pay programs, we devote a good deal of attention to them here.

Merit increase grid
a grid that combines an employee's performance rating with that employee's position in a pay range to determine the size and frequency of his or her pay increases.

Basic features

The size and frequency of pay increases are determined by two factors. The first factor is the individual's performance rating (because better performers should receive higher pay). The second factor is their position in their salary range. A **merit increase grid** combines an employee's performance rating with that employee's position in a pay range to determine the size and frequency of his or her pay increases. Let's take an organisation where ratings for performance are given between one (low performance) and five (high performance) and where people are paid a salary at a point within a salary range. An employee being paid at the high end of the salary range and rated as an excellent performer would receive a merit pay increase that represented a lower percentage of their salary, than another employee who was also rated as an excellent performer, but being paid at a lower salary within the same salary range. One reason for this is to control compensation costs and maintain the integrity of the pay structure.

In controlling compensation costs, another factor that requires close attention is the distribution of performance ratings (see Chapter 10 Performance management). In many organisations, 60–70 per cent of employees fall into the top two (out of four or five) performance-rating categories.[35] This means tremendous growth in compensation costs because most employees will eventually be above the midpoint of the pay range, resulting in 'compa-ratios' well over 100. To avoid this, some organisations provide guidelines regarding the percentage of employees who should fall into each performance category, usually limiting the percentage that can be placed in the top two categories. These guidelines are enforced differently, ranging from true guidelines to strict forced-distribution requirements.

In general, merit pay programs have the following characteristics. First, there is a focus on identifying individual differences in performance. These are assumed to reflect differences in ability or motivation. By implication, system constraints on performance are not seen as significant. Second, the majority of information on individual performance is collected from the immediate supervisor. Peer and subordinate ratings are rare and, where they do exist, they tend to receive less weight than supervisory ratings.[36] Third, there is a policy of linking pay increases to performance appraisal results.[37] Fourth, the feedback under such systems tends to occur infrequently, often once per year at the formal performance-review session. Fifth, the flow of feedback tends to be largely unidirectional, from supervisor to subordinate.

Criticisms of traditional merit pay programs

Criticisms of this process have been raised. For example, W. Edwards Deming, a leader of the total quality management (TQM) movement, argued that it is unfair to rate individual performance because 'apparent differences between people arise almost entirely from the system that they work in, not from the people themselves'.[38] System factors include co-workers, the job, materials, equipment, customers, management, supervision and environmental conditions. These are believed to be largely outside the worker's control, instead falling under management's responsibility. Deming argued that the performance rating is essentially 'the result of a lottery'.[39] He also argued that the individual focus of merit pay discourages teamwork: 'Everyone propels himself forward, or tries to, for his own good, on his own life preserver. The organisation is the loser'.[40] As an example, if people in the purchasing department are evaluated based on the number of contracts they have negotiated, they may have little interest in materials quality, although manufacturing is having quality problems.

Deming's solution was to eliminate the link between individual performance and pay. This approach reflects a desire to move away from recognising individual contributions. What are the consequences of such a move? It is possible that fewer employees with individual achievement orientations would be attracted to, and remain with, the organisation. One study of job retention found that the relationship between pay growth and individual performance over time was weaker at higher performance levels. As a consequence, the organisation lost a disproportionate share of its top performers.[41] That is, too little emphasis on individual performance may leave the organisation with average and poor performers.

Thus, although Deming's concerns about too much emphasis on individual performance are well taken, one must be careful not to replace one set of problems with another. Instead, there needs to be an appropriate balance between individual and group objectives. Ranking and forced-distribution performance-rating systems need to be considered with caution, lest they contribute to behaviour that is too individualistic and competitive.

Another criticism of merit pay programs is the way they measure performance. If the performance measure is not perceived as fair and accurate, the entire merit pay program can break down. One potential impediment to accuracy is the almost exclusive reliance on the supervisor for providing performance ratings, although peers, subordinates and customers (internal and external) often have information on a person's performance that is as good as, or better than, that of the supervisor. A 360-degree performance feedback approach (discussed in Chapter 10 Performance management) gathers feedback from each of these sources.

In general, process issues appear to be important in administering merit pay. In any situation where rewards are distributed, employees appear to assess fairness along two dimensions: distributive (based on how much they receive) and procedural (what process was used to decide how much they receive).[42] Some of the most important aspects of procedural fairness, or justice, appear in Table 14.2 below. These items suggest that employees desire clear and consistent performance standards, as well as opportunities to provide input, discuss their performance and appeal any decision they believe to be incorrect.

TABLE 14.2 Aspects of procedural justice in pay-rise decisions

Indicate the extent to which your supervisor did each of the following:

1	Was honest and ethical in dealing with you.
2	Gave you an opportunity to express your side.
3	Used consistent standards in evaluating your performance.
4	Considered your views regarding your performance.
5	Gave you feedback that helped you learn how well you were doing.
6	Was completely candid and frank with you.
7	Showed a real interest in trying to be fair.
8	Became thoroughly familiar with your performance.
9	Took into account factors beyond your control.
10	Obtained input from you before a recommendation.
11	Made clear what was expected of you.

Indicate how much of an opportunity existed, after the last pay-rise decision, for you to do each of the following things:

1	Make an appeal about the size of a raise.
2	Express your feelings to your supervisor about the salary decision.
3	Discuss, with your supervisor, how your performance was evaluated.
4	Develop, with your supervisor, an action plan for future performance.

Source: R. Folger & M.A. Konovsky, 1989, 'Effects of procedural and distributive justice on reactions to pay raise decisions', *Academy of Management Journal*, vol. 32, p. 115. Reproduced with permission of Academy of Management.

Perhaps the most basic criticism is that merit pay does not really exist. High performers are not paid significantly more than mediocre or poor performers in most cases.[43] For example, in the late 1980s and early 1990s, merit-increase budgets often did not exceed 4–5 per cent. Thus, high performers might receive 6 per cent rises, versus 3.5–4 per cent rises for average performers. On a salary of $40 000 per year, the difference in take-home pay would not be more than about $300 per year, or about $6 per week. Critics of merit pay point out that this difference is probably not significant enough to influence employee behaviours or attitudes. Indeed, as Figure 14.1 below indicates, many employees do not believe that there is any payoff to higher levels of performance.

Of course, small differences in pay can accumulate into large differences over time. The present value of the salary advantage would be $29 489 (based on a discount rate of 5 per cent). For example, over the course of a 30-year career, an initial annual salary difference of $740 with equal merit increases thereafter of 7 per cent would accumulate into a career salary advantage of $75 738.[44] Whether employees think in these terms, however, is open to question; and in terms of expectancy theory, a low merit increase for an outstanding performer could result in reduced job satisfaction and subsequent effort. If they do not think in these terms, however, nothing prevents an organisation from developing a communication program that makes it clear to employees that what may appear to be small differences in pay can add up to large differences over time. It should also be kept in mind that merit ratings are often closely linked to promotions, which, in turn, are closely linked to salary. Thus, in merit pay settings where performance differences are not recognised in the short run, high performers are likely to have significantly higher career earnings.

Finally, the accumulation effect, described above, can also be seen as a drawback if it contributes to an entitlement mentality. Here, the concern is that a big merit increase given early in an employee's career remains part of base salary 'forever'. It does not have to be re-earned each year and the cost to the organisation grows over time, perhaps more than either the employee's performance or the organisation's profitability would always warrant. Merit bonuses (payouts that do not become part of base salary) that are in lieu of traditional merit increases are, thus, used by some organisations instead.

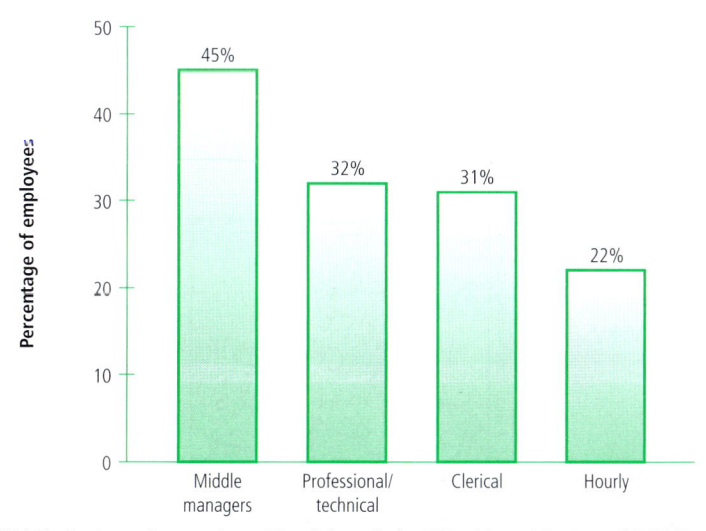

FIGURE 14.1 Percentage of employees who agreed that better performers get better increases

Category	Percentage
Middle managers	45%
Professional/technical	32%
Clerical	31%
Hourly	22%

Source: Hay Group, 1994, *The Hay Report: Compensation and Benefit Strategies for 1995 and Beyond*, Hay Group, Philadelphia. Reprinted with permission.

Individual incentives

Like merit pay, individual incentives reward individual performance, but with two important differences. First, payments are not rolled into base pay. They must be continuously earned and re-earned. Second, performance is usually measured as physical output (for example, number of saucepans produced) rather than by subjective ratings. Individual incentives have the potential to significantly increase performance. Locke and his colleagues found that monetary incentives increased production output by a median of 30 per cent—more than any other motivational device studied.[45]

Nevertheless, individual incentives are relatively rare for a variety of reasons.[46] First, most jobs (for example, those of managers and professionals) have no physical output measure. Instead, they involve what might be described as 'knowledge work'. Second, there are many potential administrative problems (for example, setting and maintaining acceptable standards) that often prove intractable. Third, individual incentives may do such a good job of motivating employees that they do whatever they get paid for and nothing else (see Figure 14.2 below). Fourth, as the name implies, individual incentives typically do not fit well with a team approach. Fifth, they may be inconsistent with the goals of acquiring multiple skills and proactive problem solving. Learning new skills often requires employees to slow or stop production. If the employees are paid based on production volume, they may not want to slow down or stop. Sixth, some incentive plans reward output volume at the expense of quality or customer service. Therefore, although individual incentives carry potential advantages, they are not likely to contribute to a flexible, proactive, problem-solving workforce. In addition, such programs may not be particularly helpful in the pursuit of TQM objectives. Another difficulty with individual incentives is that, as with merit pay, results can reflect events outside the control of the managers and employees.

Profit sharing and ownership

At the other end of the individual–group continuum are profit sharing and stock ownership plans. The use of profit sharing and stock ownership schemes increased in Australia during the 1990s and it is reported that the top 150 companies in Australia have some sort of plan.[47] These plans seek to align the interests of employees and managers with those of the organisation

FIGURE 14.2 How incentives sometimes 'work'

Source: Scott Adams, 'Dilbert', copyright United Feature Syndicate Inc. Reprinted by permission.

Profit sharing

Under **profit sharing**, payments are based on a measure of organisation performance (profits) and the payments do not become part of an employee's base salary. Profit sharing has two potential advantages. First, it may encourage employees to think more like owners, taking a broad view of what needs to be done to make the organisation more effective. These schemes, therefore, represent the application of agency theory. Thus, the sort of narrow self-interest encouraged by individual incentive plans (and perhaps also by merit pay) is, presumably, less of an issue. Instead, increased cooperation and citizenship are expected. Second, because payments do not become part of base pay, labour costs are automatically reduced during difficult economic times and wealth is shared during good times. Consequently, organisations may not need to rely on retrenchments as much to reduce costs during tough times.[48]

Does profit sharing contribute to better organisation performance? The evidence is not yet clear. Although there is consistent support for a correlation between profit sharing payments and profits, questions have been raised about the direction of causality.[49] For example, although organisations can have similar profit sharing schemes, the profitability of these organisations can vary considerably, suggesting that other factors have more influence on profitability.

This illustrates the fundamental drawback of profit sharing. Why should automobile workers at one organisation receive profit sharing payments that are only a fraction the size received by those doing the same type of work at another organisation? Is it because the workers at the more profitable organisation performed 15 times better than their counterparts at the less profitable organisation that year? Probably not. Rather, workers are likely to view top management decisions regarding products, engineering, pricing and marketing as more important. As a result, with the exception of top (and perhaps some middle) managers, most employees are unlikely to see a considerably strong connection between what they do and what they earn under profit sharing. This means that performance motivation is likely to change very little under profit sharing. Consistent with expectancy theory, motivation depends on a strong link between behaviours and valued consequences such as pay (instrumentality perceptions).

Not only may profit sharing fail to increase performance motivation, employees may also react negatively when they learn that such plans do not pay out during business downturns.[50] First, they may not feel they are to blame, because they have been performing their jobs well. Other factors are beyond their control, so why should they be penalised? Second, what seems like a 'small' amount of risked pay for a manager earning $160 000 per year, can be very painful to someone earning $30 000 or $40 000.

Consider the case of the Du Pont Fibers Division, in the United States, which had a plan that linked a portion of employees' pay to division profits.[51] After the plan's implementation, employees' base salary was about 4 per cent lower than similar employees' in other divisions unless 100 per cent of the profit goal (a 4 per cent increase over the previous year's profits) was reached. Thus, there was what might be called downside risk. However, there was also considerable upside opportunity: if 100 per cent of the profit goal was exceeded, employees would earn more than similar employees in other divisions. For example, if the division reached 150 per cent of the profit goal (that is, 6 per cent growth in profits), employees would receive 13 per cent more than comparable employees in other divisions.

How did the plan work? Initially, it worked fine. The profit goal was exceeded and employees earned slightly more than employees in other divisions. In the following year, however, profits were down 26 per cent and the profit goal was not met.

> **Profit sharing**
> a group compensation plan in which payments are based on a measure of organisation performance (profits) and do not become part of an employee's base salary.

Employees received no profit sharing bonus. Instead, they earned 4 per cent less than comparable employees in other divisions. Profit sharing was no longer seen as a very good idea. Du Pont management responded to employee concerns by eliminating the plan and returning to a system of fixed base salaries with no variable (or risk) component. This outcome is perhaps not surprising from an agency theory perspective, which suggests that employees must somehow be compensated before they will be willing to assume increased risk.

One solution some organisations choose is to design plans that have upside but not downside risk. In such cases, when a profit sharing plan is introduced, base pay is not reduced. Thus, when profits are high, employees share in the gain; but, when profits are low, they are not penalised. Such plans largely eliminate what is purported to be a major advantage of profit sharing: reducing labour costs during business downturns. During business upturns, labour costs will increase. Given that the performance benefits of such plans are suspect, an organisation runs the risk under such plans of increasing its labour costs with little return on its investment.

In summary, although profit sharing may be useful as one component of a compensation system (for example, to enhance identification with broad organisational goals), it may need to be complemented with other pay programs that more closely link pay to outcomes that individuals or teams can control (or 'own'). In addition, profit sharing runs the risk of contributing to employee resistance and higher labour costs, depending on how it is designed.

Ownership

Employee ownership is similar to profit sharing in some key respects, such as encouraging employees to focus on the success of the organisation as a whole. In fact, with ownership, this focus may be stronger. Also, like profit sharing, ownership may not result in motivation for considerably high individual performance; and, because employees may not realise any financial gain until they actually sell their stock—typically on leaving the organisation—the link between pay and performance may be less obvious than under profit sharing. Thus, from a reinforcement theory standpoint—with its emphasis on actually experiencing rewards—performance motivation may be especially low.

One way of achieving employee ownership is through **stock options**, which give employees the opportunity to buy stock at a fixed price. Say that the employees receive options to purchase stock at $10 per share in 1995 and the stock price reaches $30 per share in 2000. They have the option of purchasing stock (that is, 'exercising' their stock options) at $10 per share in 2000, thus, making a tidy return on investment if the shares are then sold. If the stock price goes down to $8 per share in the year 2000, however, there will be no financial gain. Therefore, employees are encouraged to act in ways that will benefit the organisation.

Stock options have typically been reserved for executives. More recently, there seems to be a trend toward pushing eligibility farther down in the organisation.[52] In fact, many companies, particularly in the IT industry, now grant stock options to employees at all levels. In Australia, Cisco Systems, a high-tech North Sydney-based company, issues stock options to all employees.[53] However, only about 5 per cent of Australian employees contribute to employee share ownership plans. A federal government inquiry is examining ways of making these plans more attractive and strengthening the regulation of these schemes.[54] Some studies suggest that organisation performance is higher when a large percentage of top- and middle-level managers are eligible for long-term incentives, such as stock options; which is consistent with agency theory's focus on the problem of encouraging managers to

Stock option
an employee ownership plan that gives employees the opportunity to buy the company's stock at a previously fixed price.

think like owners.[55] However, it is not clear whether these findings would hold up for lower-level employees, who may see much less opportunity to influence overall organisation performance.

An employee stock ownership plan (ESOP), which provides employers with certain tax and financial advantages when stock is granted to employees, is the most common form of employee ownership. The use of these schemes is less widespread in Australia than in other countries.[56] In the United States, the number of employees in such plans increased from four million in 1980 to over 10 million in 1999.[57] In Japan, 91 per cent of listed companies have an ESOP and these companies appear to have higher average productivity than non-ESOP companies.[58]

In Australia, it appears the existence of an ESOP in a company does not by itself improve organisational performance. There are reports that employee commitment and productivity improve in some companies. For instance, Qantas reports that anecdotal evidence suggests employees are taking a broader interest in the long-term financial performance of the group, while at the Commonwealth Bank, it is reported the ESOP (introduced in 1996) increased employee motivation and created a stronger link between shareholder value and employee rewards. In companies that have used ESOPs for a number of years (for example, Lend Lease, Coca-Cola Amatil, Cadbury Schweppes and Esso), it is reported the ESOPs create a greater sense of community.[59]

A number of unique issues are raised by ESOPs. On the negative side, they can carry significant risk for employees. This was evidenced following the adjustment in the stock market in early 2000 in Australia when an analysis of the ESOPs of listed companies showed many of the shares issued under the schemes were trading below their weighted average issue price.[60] Employee stock ownership plans can be attractive to organisations because they have tax and financing advantages and can serve as a takeover defence (under the assumption that employee owners will be 'friendly' to management). These plans give employees the right to vote on their securities (if registered on a national exchange).[61] As such, some degree of participation in a select number of decisions is mandatory, but overall participation in decision making appears to vary significantly across organisations with ESOPs. Some studies suggest that the positive effects of ownership are larger in cases where employees have greater participation,[62] perhaps because the 'employee–owner comes to psychologically experience his/her ownership in the organisation'.[63]

Finally, what are the monetary costs of ownership plans? In the case of options, a company does not realise an expense on its income statement until the option is exercised as long as the option price equals the market price at the time the option is issued. As such, companies may lose sight of their real cost. Briefly, one can compare the issuing of stock options to the government printing money. The more money that is printed, the less valuable a dollar becomes. Similarly, if stock, in the form of either options or ESOPs, is distributed, but the real value of the company remains the same, then shareholder value is diluted.[64]

'Managing challenges through sustainability: The age of disclosure' discusses the increasing pressure to impose performance hurdles on the variable component of pay and the use of share plans as a way of improving retention.

Gainsharing, group incentives and team awards

As mentioned previously, attempts have been made to overcome the limitations of rewards that encourage individual performance at the expense of organisational, group or team performance. Plans such as gainsharing, group incentives and team awards are used in some organisations to overcome these limitations.

Employee stock ownership plan (ESOP)
an employee ownership plan that provides employers certain tax and financial advantages when stock is granted to employees.

PART 4   Rewarding People

THE AGE OF DISCLOSURE

Constant pressure from stakeholder activist groups to increase performance hurdles for the variable component of Australian executives' pay package is pushing up the level of bonuses being demanded, a recent study has found.

Revealed at a boardroom lunch put on by specialist financial advice and investment management company ipac, the findings were part of a preview of the results of the annual review by Equity Strategies of share plans in the Top 200 ASX listed companies. Of the Top 200, there were 40 new or amended plans approved by shareholders in calendar 2005.

According to Equity Strategies director Edward Wright, performance hurdles have again proven contentious, with a good deal of indecision evident among Australian boards as to the best method of share plans to utilise as well as how to expense them.

Nineteen companies adopted options plans, 15 adopted performance rights and 15 adopted other types of plans (including five restricted share/deferred bonus plans).

Of the 40 plans approved, 37 adopted performance hurdles. By far the most popular performance measure has been Total Shareholder Returns (TSR) rather than earnings per share (EPS), despite, as Wright pointed out, that EPS has always been the first question on analysts' lips. Of those using TSR, 28 companies used a relative measure compared with an index of comparable companies, while the remaining five used an absolute value.

EPS has proven less popular, according to Wright, because of suspicion surrounding share price manipulation. However, he contends that there is no evidence of share price or capital manipulation to meet EPS targets.

He also points out that the oft-quoted Enron example was not subject to any performance hurdles. However, there is clear evidence that as hurdles become more difficult to achieve, their value to the executive is diminished.

One of the main reasons for approving share plans cited by Australian boards in 2005 was their being used as a retention strategy. This has proven particularly prevalent in the mining and financial services sectors. The ageing workforce is being mentioned increasingly regularly as a factor likely to exacerbate the skill shortage.

However, despite their use in this manner, share plans have not proven to be particularly successful. Instead, if an organisation targets a specific individual, if that person has a share plan with another company, it just raises the bar as to how much money is required to lure them into a new role.

In other words, if you stand to make an additional million by simply sticking around your existing employer, then before you would go those wooing you, the first thing you'll settle is getting that million, ideally up front.

Allocating value is becoming an increasingly important aspect of all share plan holders.

There is an incentive for companies to minimise the valuation to reduce the reported cost of the valuation. In 2005 there was a mixture of approaches to valuation.

Source: D. Hovenden, 2006, 'Equity proving obtuse in age of disclosure', *Human Resources*, Issue 100, 21 March, p. 5.
www.humanresourcesmagazine.com.au

Gainsharing

Gainsharing
a form of group compensation based on group or plant performance (rather than organisation-wide profits) that does not become part of the employee's base salary.

Gainsharing programs offer a means of sharing productivity gains with employees. Gainsharing is a form of group compensation that is based on group or plant performance and it does not become part of the employee's base salary. Although sometimes confused with profit sharing plans, gainsharing differs in two key respects. First, instead of using an organisation-level performance measure (profits), the programs measure group or plant performance, which is likely to be seen as more controllable by employees. Second, payouts are distributed more frequently and not deferred. In a sense, gainsharing programs represent an effort to pull out the best features of organisation-oriented plans like profit sharing, and individual-oriented plans like merit pay and individual incentives. Like profit sharing, gainsharing encourages the pursuit of broader goals more so than individual-oriented plans. Unlike profit sharing, however, gainsharing can motivate employees as much as individual plans do because of the more controllable nature of the performance measure and the frequency of payouts. Indeed, studies indicate that gainsharing has a positive impact on performance.[65]

Table 14.3 overleaf shows the workings of one type of gainsharing, the Scanlon plan—developed in the 1930s by Joseph N. Scanlon, president of a local union at Empire Steel and Tin Plant in Mansfield, Ohio, in the United States. The Scanlon plan provides a monetary bonus to employees (and the organisation) if the ratio of labour costs to the sales value of production is kept below a certain standard, $240 000 (20 per cent of $1.2 million) in this example. There is a saving of $30 000 because actual labour costs were $210 000. The organisation receives 50 per cent of the savings and the employees receive the other 50 per cent, although part of the employees' share is set aside in the event that actual labour costs exceed the standard in upcoming months.

Gainsharing plans like the Scanlon plan and pay-for-performance plans in general often encompass more than just a monetary component. As Table 14.4 overleaf indicates, there is often a strong emphasis on taking advantage of employee 'know-how' in order to improve the production process through teams and suggestion systems. In a related issue, a number of recommendations have been made about the organisation conditions that should be in place for gainsharing to be successful. Commonly mentioned factors include:

- management commitment
- a need to change or a strong commitment to continuous improvement
- management's acceptance and encouragement of employee input
- high levels of cooperation and interaction
- employment security
- information sharing on productivity and costs
- goal setting
- commitment of all involved parties to the process of change and improvement
- agreement on a performance standard and calculation that is understandable, seen as fair and closely related to managerial objectives.[66]

Group incentives and team awards

Whereas gainsharing plans are often plant-wide, group incentives and team awards typically pertain to a smaller workgroup.[67] Group incentives (like individual incentives) tend to measure performance in terms of physical output; whereas team award plans may use a broader range of performance measures (for example, cost savings, successful completion of product design and meeting deadlines). As with individual incentive plans, these plans have a number of potential drawbacks. Competition between individuals may be reduced but it may be replaced by competition between groups or teams. Also, as with any incentive plan, a standard-setting process must be developed that is seen as fair by employees and these standards must not exclude important dimensions such as quality.

Balanced scorecard

As the preceding discussion indicates, every pay program has advantages and disadvantages. Therefore, rather than choosing one program, some companies find it useful to design a mix of pay programs, one that has the right chemistry for the situation at hand. Relying exclusively on merit pay or individual incentives may result in high levels of work motivation but unacceptable levels of individualistic and competitive behaviour and too little concern for broader plant or organisation goals. Relying too heavily on profit sharing and gainsharing plans may improve the degree of cooperation and concern for the welfare of the entire plant or organisation, but it may reduce individual work motivation to unacceptable levels. However, a particular mix of merit pay, gainsharing and profit sharing could contribute to acceptable performance on all these performance dimensions.

TABLE 14.3 Example of gainsharing (Scanlon plan)

Single ratio Scanlon monthly report

	$
Sales	1 100 000
Less sales returns, allowances, discounts	25 000
Net sales	1 075 000
Add: increase in inventory (at cost or selling price)	125 000
Value of production	1 200 000
Allowed payroll costs (20% of value of production)	240 000
Actual payroll costs	210 000
Bonus pool	30 000
Company share (50%)	15 000
Subtotal	
Reserve for deficit months (25%)	3 750
Employee share—immediate distribution	11 250

Source: B. Graham-Moore & T. L. Rose, 1990, *Gainsharing: Plans for Improving Performance*, BNA Books, Washington, DC, p. 57, Copyright © 1990, the Bureau of National Affairs, Inc., Washington, DC. Reprinted with permission.

TABLE 14.4 Employee involvement plans for non-management employees

Type of employee involvement program	Percentage using program	Median percentage of employees participating	Median number of hours spent per participating employee per year
Individual suggestion plans	42	20	5
Ad-hoc problem solving groups	44	20	22
Team group suggestion plans	28	25	10
Employee–management teams	19	15	40
Quality circles	26	16	50
Percentage of all plans using any type of employee involvement program	66		

Source: Jerry L. McAdams, 1995, 'Design, implementation, and results: employee involvement and performance reward plans', *Compensation and Benefits Review*, March–April, pp. 45–55. Reprinted by permission of Sage Publications Ltd.

One approach that seeks to balance multiple objectives is the *balanced scorecard* (a means of performance measurement that gives managers a chance to look at their company from the perspectives of internal and external customers, employees and shareholders, see Chapters 1 and 13). Kaplan and Norton describe the balanced scorecard as a way for companies to 'track financial results while simultaneously monitoring progress in building the capabilities and acquiring the intangible assets they would need for future growth'.[68]

A mix of measures might be used by a manufacturing firm looking for a way to motivate improvements in a balanced set of key business drivers. The four performance measures used in this situation could be financial, return on capital employed, customer satisfaction and product returns. The performance-based pay received by an employee will depend on the extent to which they achieve agreed targets in each of these four performance measures. The total performance payment will represent the sum of the amount earned in achieving in each of these measures.

Not only are there advantages and disadvantages of different forms of pay-for-performance schemes, but 'Managing challenges through HR innovation: How can HRM promote organisational innovation' reports on research in the UK that cautions against using pay-for-performance.

In addition to the drawbacks discussed above, other difficulties and limitations have been highlighted regarding the use of performance-based pay policies. There are difficulties associated with the implementation of these policies. It has been found that pay for performance has a destructive impact on self-esteem, intrinsic motivation, teamwork and creativity. In addition, these policies encourage employees to focus on short-term outcomes and link rewards with political skills. Other complexities involved in implementing pay-for-performance schemes involve the difficulties associated with measuring and assessing performance, the impact and lack of control over external conditions and the influence of budgets.[69]

Managerial and executive pay

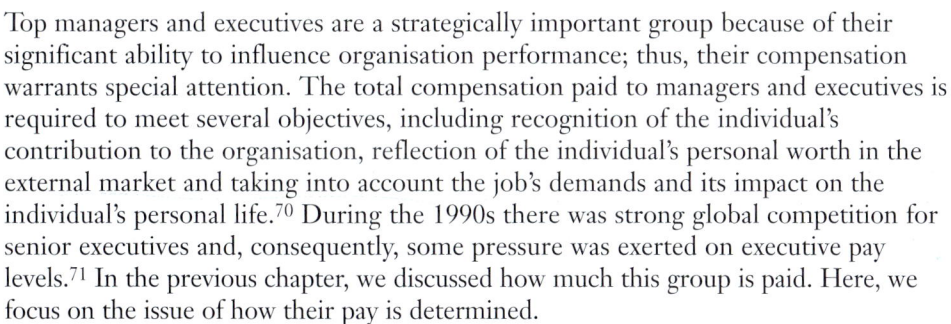

Top managers and executives are a strategically important group because of their significant ability to influence organisation performance; thus, their compensation warrants special attention. The total compensation paid to managers and executives is required to meet several objectives, including recognition of the individual's contribution to the organisation, reflection of the individual's personal worth in the external market and taking into account the job's demands and its impact on the individual's personal life.[70] During the 1990s there was strong global competition for senior executives and, consequently, some pressure was exerted on executive pay levels.[71] In the previous chapter, we discussed how much this group is paid. Here, we focus on the issue of how their pay is determined.

In Australia and the United States, the compensation of top executives is virtually independent of corporate performance.[72] There are numerous examples of chief executive officers receiving compensation increases even when the company is performing poorly. Research[73] in the United States indicates that there is no significant link between company performance and the size of the annual bonus of CEOs. Similar results have been found in Australia where it was reported that 'remuneration increases are sometimes associated with a decline in company performance'.[74]

How can executive pay be linked to organisation performance? From an agency theory perspective, the goal of owners (shareholders) is to encourage the agents (managers and executives) to act in the best interests of the owners. This may mean less emphasis on non-contingent pay, such as base salary, and more emphasis on outcome-oriented 'contracts' that make some portion of executive pay contingent on the organisation's profitability or stock performance.[75] However, Gomez-Mejia and Wiseman claim 'hundreds of studies' fail to demonstrate that there is a consistent relationship between executive remuneration and performance.[76] There are also concerns about the assumptions regarding the alignment of executives' interests and those of the organisation.[77] Executives could be more interested in pursuing outcomes most beneficial to their self-interest.

Among middle- and top-level managers, it is becoming more common in Australia to use both short-term bonus and long-term incentive plans to encourage the pursuit of both short- and long-term organisation performance objectives.

HOW CAN HRM PROMOTE ORGANISATIONAL INNOVATION?

MANAGING CHALLENGES THROUGH HR INNOVATION

Our work investigating managerial practices in UK manufacturing organisations has shown that people management practices play an important role in promoting innovation.

Having developed an instrument to analyse innovation (defined by West and Farr in 1990) as 'the intentional introduction and application in a job, work team or organisation of ideas, processes, products or procedures which are new, and designed to benefit the job, the work team or the organisation', we were able to give each of the 30 organisations in our sample a score of between one and seven to capture innovation in a range of domains. This instrument took into account the magnitude of the innovation in terms of people involved in its implementation, and how new and different it was.

We found that much innovation involves relatively minor, ongoing improvements, rather than major change. To achieve sustained innovation, organisations must be able to draw upon the skills and knowledge of employees at all levels of the business.

So which HRM practices are most likely to promote a positive learning environment? We developed a scale to take into account three facets of HRM that shape the learning environment and predict the extent to which individuals gain the skills to promote innovation. First, organisations should have a vision statement capturing their approach to learning and development and communicating to staff the importance that they attach to these processes. Second, they must implement and endorse mentoring schemes. Last, they should consider offering staff the opportunity to have regular career development meetings. Where a positive learning climate exists, organisations tend to be more innovative.

The results also show that organisations that make explicit the link between appraisal and remuneration perform relatively less well in innovation terms than those whose appraisal systems have no relationship with pay. Many have argued (for example, Lawler 1995) that pay-for-performance schemes provide a 'line of sight' between performance and reward, thereby enabling individuals to make appropriate decisions about where best to direct the effort. Our findings do not imply that performance-related pay is ill advised in all circumstances, but we suggest that organisations should exercise caution before introducing such schemes.

People are central to innovation, and this study suggests that high innovation can be achieved when people are empowered to make changes at local levels. HRM has an important, perhaps crucial role to play in creating an environment that enables people to develop the skills and confidence necessary to affect change.

Key points

- Organisational innovation is an important determinant of competitive performance and advancement, enabling organisations to anticipate and respond to the challenges of globalisation.
- HRM has an important, perhaps crucial role to play in promoting organisational innovation—to the extent that it creates a positive environment for learning and removes barriers that may inhibit creative performance (for example, linking pay to performance).

Source: J. Dawson, H. Shipton & M. West, 2005, 'How can HRM promote organisational innovation?', *People Management*, 21 April, p. 52, Personnel Publications Ltd.

To what extent do organisations use such pay-for-performance plans and what are their consequences? A recent study in the United States suggests that organisations vary substantially in the extent to which they use both long-term and short-term incentive programs. The study further found that greater use of such plans among top- and middle-level managers was associated with higher subsequent levels of profitability. As Table 14.5 opposite indicates, greater reliance on short-term bonuses and long-term incentives (relative to base pay) resulted in substantial improvements in return on assets.[78] This was also confirmed in the Cranfield-Macquarie survey in 1996, 1999 and 2005.[79]

In Australia there is increasing pressure to tie senior executives' compensation to company performance. Surveys show that a majority of large organisations include variable rewards, such as bonuses, incentive pay and stock options.[80] Since the late 1980s there has been a significant change in the structure of CEO and executive remuneration. There has been greater use made of long-term and short-term incentive schemes and, consequently, a reduction in the importance of fixed pay. Figure 14.3 below indicates that the percentage of the total remuneration of CEOs in Australia paid as fixed annual reward decreased from 90.5 per cent in 1987 to 50.4 per cent in 1998.[81] Telstra and John Fairfax Holdings are two Australian companies that have restructured the compensation of executives so that it is more closely tied to the performance of the company. The compensation program for Telstra executives seeks to provide performance incentives for the long term and the short term by using measures of customer service, employee attitudes and performance relative to their specific business plan. In addition, executive compensation will be linked to the performance of Telstra shares relative to the performance of the benchmark ASX All Ordinaries Index.[82]

During 2003–04 the remuneration of executives in Australia's listed companies underwent a substantial change. A report by Ernst and Young found that the formulation of executive strategies and practices was challenging because 'companies need to formulate their remuneration strategy appropriately but they must be seen to do so—shareholder and public perception is vital'.

TABLE 14.5 The relationship between managerial pay and organisation return on assets

Bonus/base ratio %	Long-term incentive eligibility %	Predicted return on assets %	Predicted return on assets $[a]
10	28	5.2	250 million
20	28	5.6	269 million
10	48	5.9	283 million
20	48	7.1	341 million

a Based on the assets of the average Fortune 500 company in 1990.

Source: B. Gerhart & G.T. Milkovich, 1990, 'Organizational differences in managerial compensation and financial performance', *Academy of Management Journal*, vol. 33, pp. 663–91. Reproduced with the permission of the Academy of Management.

FIGURE 14.3 How incentives sometimes 'work' (percentage of total annual reward)

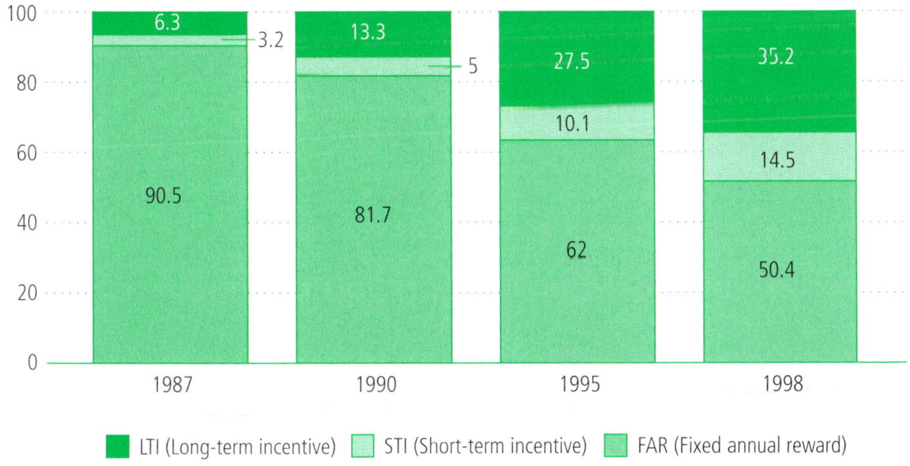

Year	FAR	STI	LTI
1987	90.5	3.2	6.3
1990	81.7	5	13.3
1995	62	10.1	27.5
1998	50.4	14.5	35.2

■ LTI (Long-term incentive) ■ STI (Short-term incentive) ■ FAR (Fixed annual reward)

Source: G. O'Neill, 2000, 'Lies, damned lies, statistics ... and CEO pay', *HRMonthly*, February, p. 31. *HRMonthly* is published for the Australian Human Resources Institute, www.ahri.com.au.

The report found that:

- Long-term incentives continued to play a key role in executive remuneration, particularly in larger companies.
- Generally, the larger the company and the more senior the role, the greater proportion of pay was at risk.
- Managing directors had the highest proportion of total remuneration delivered through long-term incentives.
- Share options continued to be the most common long-term incentive plan type—however, more so in the ASX 100 to 200 companies than the top 100.
- Total Shareholder Return (TSR) was the most common performance measure for executive long-term incentive plans.
- Performance re-testing in executive long-term incentive plans was more prevalent in larger companies.[83]

Concerns are frequently expressed about the relationship between the executive remuneration and average weekly earnings. The *Australian Financial Review* found the median total remuneration (including salary, benefits, bonuses and equity-based rewards) of the top 100 CEOs was $2 143 249 compared to average weekly ordinary time earnings amounting $49 381 per annum.[84]

The Federal Government has developed a corporate reform package that gives shareholders the right to vote against executive pay packages they believe are too rich. The votes of the shareholders will be non-binding and they will not formally compel boards to back down. In effect their votes will constitute a vote of no confidence in the board's proposals. (See 'HRM spotlight: Executive pay: reining in the bulls'.)

Earlier, we saw how the balanced scorecard approach could be applied to paying manufacturing employees. It is also useful in designing executive pay. Table 14.6 below shows how the choice of performance measures can be guided by a desire to balance shareholder-, customer- and employee-related objectives. Arthur Martinez of Sears refers to financial results as a lagging indicator that tells the company how it has done in the past; whereas, customer and employee satisfaction are leading indicators that tell the company how its financial results will be in the future. Thus, Sears ties

TABLE 14.6 Whirlpool's three-stakeholder scorecard

Stakeholder	Measures
Shareholder value	• Economic value added
	• Earnings per share
	• Cash flow
	• Total cost productivity
Customer value	• Quality
	• Market share
	• Customer satisfaction
Employee value	• High performance culture index
	• High performance culture deployment
	• Training and development diversity

Source: E.L. Gubman, 1988, *The Talent Solution*, McGraw-Hill, New York.

EXECUTIVE PAY: REINING IN THE BULLS

HRM SPOTLIGHT

The remuneration of top company executives is likely to remain a contentious issue as more and more Australians dabble in the surging stock market.

More than half of the Australian population owns shares either directly or indirectly through a managed fund or self-managed superannuation fund, according to the most recent figures from the Australian Stock Exchange (ASX).

In 2004, 55 per cent of Australia's adult population, or approximately 8 million people owned shares (up from 51 per cent in 2003).

The ASX is yet to release 2005 figures, but there are indications that Australia is becoming a nation of shareholder capitalists who will demand tighter measures to curb corporate greed and avert corporate collapses. And top of the list is reigning in fat cat salaries.

There have been deeply held, and often founded, suspicions among shareholders that company executives receive large pay packets at the expense of shareholder returns. Well-publicised payouts for executives who fail to deliver have also done little to quell concerns.

According to Fiona Balzer, corporate information officer of the Australian Shareholders Association, retail investors tend to be justifiably concerned with executive salaries as areas of 'wastage' in the business.

'There is a lot of attention paid to executive salary compared to other issues, but we feel that it is at an appropriate level ... Excess remuneration is more than about wastage as the remuneration policy is designed to motivate executives and a poorly designed scheme rewards inappropriate behaviour.'

Greater scrutiny of the way businesses conduct themselves and the salaries paid to their executives has benefited from new requirements in the Corporations Act, which put the adoption of the company's remuneration report to a non-binding vote at the company's annual general meeting.

The regime was introduced as part of CLERP9 and applied to most listed companies for the first time in the late 2005 AGM season.

'Prior to the adoption of this initiative we had started to see a decline in the huge payouts for poor performance and a move away from NED (non-executive director) retirement schemes', Balzer said.

'The increase in transparency required now the remuneration report is debated at the AGM has commenced an improvement in effective remuneration policy and practice.'

Retail investors have benefited from the growth of accessible and affordable over-the-phone and on-line share trading services such as those offered by Commonwealth Securities (CommSec).

In 2004 the ASX found that share ownership appeared to have broadened to include more Australians on average incomes and non-tertiary education attainment level.

Combined with the non-binding vote on executive remuneration the ramifications of this growth on the interactions between company boards and shareholders are significant.

Source: M. Finch, 2006, 'Executive pay: reining in the bulls', *Human Resources*, Issue 103, 2 May, p. 1 & 6.
www.humanresourcesmagazine.com.au

---

compensation to each type of objective. Eastman Kodak follows a similar approach. In 1996, its CEO, George Fisher, had his annual bonus reduced by $290 000 from its 1995 level. Why? The bonus was based on three components: shareholder satisfaction, customer satisfaction and employee satisfaction. Relative to 1995, only shareholder satisfaction was 'strong'. Therefore, the bonus was reduced. In 1997, Mr Fisher agreed to a new contract that tied even more of his bonus to these criteria. So, Kodak does not reward only financial results. Nevertheless, George Fisher's total compensation for 1996 was still $5.5 million, the majority of which was based on stock plans. So, results continue to be the main driver of executive pay at Kodak.

In Australia, the 1998 *Company Law Review Act* requires that information about the compensation packages of directors and senior executives is given in the company's annual report. Companies are required to give an explanation of the link between company performance and executive compensation, provide details of the components of the directors' remuneration as well as details for the five highest-paid executives.[85]

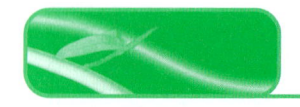

Process and context issues

In Chapter 13 Managing compensation, we discussed the importance of process issues such as communication and employee participation. Significant differences in how such issues are handled can be found both across and within organisations, suggesting that organisations have considerable discretion in this aspect of compensation management.[86] As such, it represents another strategic opportunity to distinguish one's organisation from the competition.

Employee participation in decision making

Consider employee participation in decision making and its potential consequences. Involvement in the design and implementation of pay policies has been linked to higher pay satisfaction and job satisfaction, presumably because employees have a better understanding of and greater commitment to the policy when they are involved.[87]

What about the effects on productivity? Agency theory provides some insight. The delegation of decision making by a principal to an agent creates agency costs, because employees may not act in the best interests of top management. In addition, the more agents there are, the higher the monitoring costs.[88] Together, these suggest that delegation of decision making can be costly.

On the other hand, agency theory suggests that monitoring would be less costly and more effective if it were performed by employees, because they have knowledge about the workplace and behaviour of fellow employees that managers do not have. As such, the right compensation system might encourage self-monitoring and peer monitoring.[89]

Researchers have suggested that two general factors are critical to encouraging such monitoring: monetary incentives (outcome-oriented contracts in agency theory) and an environment that fosters trust and cooperation. This environment, in turn, is a function of employment security, group cohesiveness and individual rights for employees—in other words, respect for and commitment to employees.[90]

Communication

Another important process issue is communication. Earlier, we spoke of its importance in the administration of merit pay, both from the perspective of procedural fairness and as a means of obtaining the maximum impact from a merit pay program. More generally, a change in any part of the compensation system is likely to give rise to employee concerns. Rumours and assumptions based on poor or incomplete information are always an issue in administering compensation, partly because of its importance to employee economic security and wellbeing. Therefore, in making any changes, it is crucial to determine how best to communicate reasons for the changes to employees. Some organisations now rely heavily on videotaped messages from the chief executive officer to communicate the rationale for major changes. Brochures that include scenarios for typical employees are also used, as are focus-group sessions where small groups of employees are interviewed to obtain feedback about concerns that can be addressed in later communication programs.

Pay and process: intertwined effects

The preceding discussion treats process issues, such as participation, as factors that may facilitate the success of pay programs. At least one commentator, however, has described a more important role for process factors in determining employee performance:

> Worker participation apparently helps make alternative compensation plans … work better—and also has beneficial effects of its own … It appears that changing the way workers are treated may boost productivity more than changing the way they are paid.[91]

This suggestion raises a broader question: How important are pay decisions, per se, relative to other human resource practices? Although it may not be terribly useful to attempt to disentangle closely intertwined programs, it is important to reinforce the notion that human resource programs, even those as powerful as compensation systems, do not work alone.

It has been shown that companies require a suite of human resource practices that fit together and are consistent. For instance, organisations that use instrumental policies such as process, measurement and incentives as control mechanisms (hard control levers) tended not to use strategy, networks and culture as a means of control (soft control levers)[92]. The GLOBE project examined the way large global corporations sought to coordinate worldwide and maintain local flexibility. This study suggested that it might be better to adopt either a 'soft' or a 'hard' approach rather than a mix of practices.[93]

Consider gainsharing programs. As described earlier, pay is often only one component of such programs (see Table 14.4 on page 546). How important are the non-pay components?[94] On the one hand, there is ample evidence that gainsharing programs that rely almost exclusively on the monetary component can have substantial effects on productivity.[95] On the other hand, a study of an automotive parts plant found that adding a participation component (monthly meetings with management to discuss the gainsharing plan and ways to increase productivity) to a gainsharing pay-incentive plan raised productivity. In a related study, employees were asked about the factors that motivated them to engage in active participation (for example, suggestion systems). Employees reported that the desire to earn a monetary bonus was much less important than a number of non-pay factors, particularly the desire for influence and control in how their work was done.[96] A third study reported that both productivity and profitability were enhanced by the addition of employee participation in decisions, beyond the improvement derived from monetary incentives such as gainsharing.[97]

It has been shown that performance-based pay is difficult to implement.[98] Their study in 13 organisational units in Hewlett-Packard demonstrated that the costs of pay for performance programs outweighed the benefits. The costs included not only the time and money involved in designing and redesigning the schemes, but also low morale, loss of flexibility, loss of teamwork and a focus on pay rather than the task. They attributed these results to three things:

1 the unit managers' lack of knowledge about how to design and implement pay for performance programs
2 the culture of Hewlett-Packard traditionally opposed instrumental incentive schemes and the tightly coupled individual and group incentives did not fit this high commitment culture
3 the local unit managers' did not involve employees in the decision to adopt pay for performance, or its design or in the resolution of problems that emerged during its implementation.[99]

It has also been found that pay-for-performance programs deteriorate over time.[100] As a result these programs need to be redesigned and implemented repeatedly.

PART 4   Rewarding People

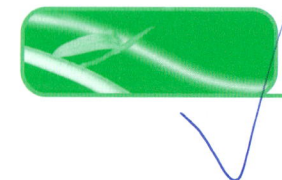

Organisation strategy and compensation strategy: A question of fit

Although much of our focus has been on the general, or average, effects of different pay programs, it is also useful to think in terms of matching pay strategies to organisation strategies. To take an example from medicine, using the same medical treatment regardless of the symptoms and diagnosis would be foolish. In choosing a pay strategy, one must consider how effectively it will further the organisation's overall business strategy. Consider again the findings reported in Table 14.5 on page 549. The average effect of moving from a pay strategy with below-average variability in pay to one with above-average variability is an increase in return on assets of almost two percentage points (from 5.2 per cent to 7.1 per cent). In some organisations, however, the increase could be smaller. In fact, greater variability in pay could contribute to a lower return on assets in some organisations. In other organisations, greater variability in pay could contribute to increases in return on assets of greater than two percentage points. Obviously, being able to tell where variable pay works and where it does not could have substantial consequences.

In Chapter 2 Strategic human resource management, we discussed directional business strategies, two of which were growth (internal or external) and concentration ('sticking to the knitting'). How should compensation strategies differ according to whether an organisation follows a growth strategy or a concentration strategy? Table 14.7 opposite provides some suggested matches. Basically, a growth strategy's emphasis on innovation, risk taking and new markets is linked to a pay strategy that shares risk with employees but also provides them with the opportunity for high future earnings by having them share in whatever success the organisation has. This means relatively low levels of fixed compensation in the short run, but the use of bonuses and stock options, for example, pay off handsomely in the long run. Stock options have been described as the pay program 'that built *Silicon Valley*', a concentrated IT-industry area in the United States, having been used by companies such as Apple, Sun Microsystems and others.[101] When such companies become successful, everyone from top managers to secretaries can become millionaires if they own stock. Growth organisations are also thought to benefit from a less bureaucratic orientation, in the sense of having more decentralisation and flexibility in pay decisions and in recognising individual skills, rather than being constrained by job or grade-classification systems. On the other hand, concentration-oriented organisations are thought to require a considerably different set of pay practices by virtue of their lower rate of growth, more stable workforce and greater need for consistency and standardisation in pay decisions.

This chapter discussed the nature and ways in which various performance-based pay initiatives could be used to shape employee performance. 'Managing challenges of globalisation: The importance of place in the global war for talent' highlights that performance-based pay is not enough to secure the people and performance required by an organisation. It indicates that in order to attract, retain and motivate talented people it will be just as important for the organisation to be located in a desirable city.

TABLE 14.7 Matching pay strategy and organisation strategy

Pay strategy dimensions	Organisation strategy	
	Concentration	Growth
Risk sharing (variable pay)	Low	High
Time orientation	Short term	Long term
Pay level (short run)	Above market	Below market
Pay level (long-run potential)	Below market	Above market
Benefits level	Above market	Below market
Centralisation of pay decisions	Centralised	Decentralised
Pay unit of analysis	Job	Skills

Source: Adapted from L.R. Gomez-Mejia & D.B. Balkin, 1992, *Compensation, Organisational Strategy, and Firm Performance*, South-Western, Cincinnati, OH, appendix 4b.

THE IMPORTANCE OF PLACE IN THE GLOBAL WAR FOR TALENT

MANAGING CHALLENGES OF GLOBALISATION

The demand for talent has reached pandemic levels across the world. To illustrate, consider knowledge workers (commonly defined as those with bachelor degrees or better) in the United States. Today unemployment among this group is around 2 per cent, essentially meaning that anyone who wants a job can get one. Even during the last US recession, roughly between 2001–2005, unemployment in this group never went above 4 per cent, which is the rate economists consider full employment.

Without a doubt, the countries, and more to the point, the city regions that can develop, attract, mobilise and retain talent will be the 'places to be' in the future—for workers and businesses.

In this regard, the work of Dr Richard Florida is among the best known and most cited. Florida ranks cities worldwide against a variety of factors, mainly centring on their diversity, openness and share of 'creative jobs' in their economies. Florida believes that the combination of these things makes them magnets for talent.

Globally, Florida's top 10 list includes cities in Canada, Australia, New Zealand, Europe and Scandinavia. Florida and others have identified migration patterns towards 'cool' cities. In the US, Florida says:

Talented, educated immigrants and smart, ambitious young Americans congregated, during the 1980s and 1990s, in and around a dozen US city-regions. These areas become hothouses of innovation, and modern-day equivalents of renaissance city-states, where scientists, artists, designers, engineers, financiers, marketers, and sundry entrepreneurs fed off each other's knowledge, energy, and capital to make new products, new services, and whole new industries—cutting edge entertainment in Southern California, new financial instruments in New York, computer products in northern California and Austin, satellites and telecommunications in Washington, DC, software and innovation retail in Seattle, biotechnology in Boston.

Just like organisations, cities and countries will thrive or stagnate in the 21st century based on the quality of their talent. Due in part to globalisation, we are in the most competitive economic environment in history. The talent that will drive the future for a city—create new ideas, even whole new industries (the next Microsoft, Ikea, Dell, Google or TATA)—will be conceived and built by talented people.

As urbanisation accelerates worldwide, a handful of cities in each continent will be the winners. They will succeed based on the choices of talented workers who will discriminate based on a city region's creative outlets, its tolerance, its diversity and the degree to which it is globally integrated.

Source: A. Schweyer, 2006, 'The importance of place in the global war for talent', *Human Resources*, Issue 113, 19 September, pp. 12–13. www.humanresourcemagazine.com.au

MANAGING PEOPLE

REPUTATONS, RISKS AND REWARDS

Despite part-time hours, company directors claim that the risks they take and the experience they bring more than outweigh their hefty earnings.

A part-time job where you can earn more than $400 000 a year? Welcome to the world of the professional company director, where those in the club can collect a handful of these jobs despite being in virtual semi-retirement.

At the top of the profession are the likes of Brambles and BHP Billiton chairman Don Argus, AMP and Mayne chairman Peter Wilcox, ANZ and Woodside chairman Charles Goode and Insurance Australia Group and Woolworths chairman James Strong.

A Korn/Ferry study last year found the average non-executive chairman of a company with revenue of more than $5000 million (mostly top-20 companies) receives $273 000 in total fees, including base fees, retainers, committee fees, super and other benefits). Non-executive directors (large company boards usually have at least eight directors) average $110 590.

This may seem excessive to the public, but in a survey last month of 57 members of the Australian Institute of Company Directors (AIDC), 24 of which are on the boards of the top-200 companies, nearly two-thirds thought they were not adequately compensated for the role. This, according to the survey, is due to perceived risks, among which is the loss of reputation if things go wrong.

Take AMP, for example. The company overhauled its board (for the second time) earlier this year when it was reporting a series of multi-million dollar losses from its United Kingdom operations.

In these circumstances, how does AMP attract the 'best' directorial material? Incoming directors, if we are to use history as a guide, must be taking on the job with a sense of trepidation

Trans-Tasman life insurer Tower has had a similar experience to AMP. Tower's non-executive chairman, Olaf O'Duill, who was thrust into the job earlier this year with the company fighting for survival, says that it is difficult to balance the risks that directors run and their rewards.

'It varies from company to company. In general, my view is that directors these days are underpaid', O'Duill says. 'I don't know how much money will compensate people for running the risks.'

The woes of Tower—which included having to recapitalise the company, appoint a new chief executive and outline a new corporate strategy to investors—saw O'Duill's workload increase markedly above that of a similar company's counterpart. The usual workload is perhaps a few days a month, including one full board meeting and committee meetings. O'Duill's workload increased to two to three days a week, once Tower's problems started to intensify.

'A non-executive directorship is not a full-time job. It's not meant to be a full-time job. When things are going ok, it's fine', he says.

O'Duill says that the two fundamental jobs of non-executive directors are to get the right chief executive and, with management, work out the company's strategic direction.

'Everything else falls out of that', he says. You are paid for presumably whatever wealth of business experience you have got, to consider issues and hopefully develop some semblance of cohesion with your colleagues.

'If you want the right calibre of people with the thinking power and experience to sit on the board and challenge the CEO, for goodness sake, pay a reasonable price.'

O'Duill agrees that the best way for non-executive directors to keep accountable is for them to own shares in the company.

Source: Based on A. Hughes, 2003, 'Reputations, risks and rewards', *The Sydney Morning Herald*, 5 November, p. 12.

QUESTIONS

1 What are the risks of non-executive directors who are on the board of a company?
2 Do you agree with O'Duill—the best way to keep non-executive directors accountable is for them to own shares in the company?
3 Would you take up a position of non-executive director on the board of a company?

CHAPTER SUMMARY

Our focus in this chapter has been on the design and administration of programs that recognise employee contributions to the organisation's success. These programs vary as to whether they link pay to individual, group or organisation performance. Often, it is not so much a choice of one program or the other as it is a choice between different combinations of programs that seek to balance individual, group and organisation objectives.

This chapter has examined three theories that can be used as a basis for designing performance-related pay programs. Each theory seeks to explain how desired work performance can be encouraged using different performance pay programs. This carries at least two important implications. First, pay can be a powerful motivator of job performance. An effective pay strategy can have a substantial positive impact on an organisation's success through a number of mechanisms including aligning employee interests with those of the organisation or reinforcing desired job performance immediately, as it occurs. Conversely, a poorly conceived pay strategy can have detrimental effects by not specifying the necessary performance goals for organisational success. Second, the importance of pay means that employees care a great deal about the fairness of the pay process. A recurring theme is that pay programs must be explained and administered in such a way that employees understand their underlying rationale and believe it is fair and equitable. In addition the rewards provided by an organisation need to be rewards that are desired by employees.

The fact that organisations differ in their business and human resource strategies suggests that the most effective compensation strategy may differ from one organisation to another. Although benchmarking programs against the competition is informative, what is successful in some organisations may not be a good idea for others. The balanced scorecard suggests the need for organisations to decide what their key objectives are and use pay to support them.

WEB EXERCISES

Visit BHP Billiton's website at **www.bhpbilliton.com** and review the approach to rewarding people in BHP Billiton. Suggest ways in which the performance of a recent accounting graduate could be rewarded in a division of BHP Billiton.

Questions

1. Discuss the ways in which pay arrangements influence organisation culture.
2. How does organisational strategy influence pay for performance arrangements?

DISCUSSION QUESTIONS

1. To compete more effectively, your organisation is considering a profit-sharing plan to increase employee effort and to encourage employees to think like owners. What are the potential advantages and disadvantages of such a plan? Would the profit-sharing plan have the same impact on all types of employees? What alternative pay programs should be considered?
2. Gainsharing plans have often been used in manufacturing settings but can also be applied in service organisations. How could performance standards be developed for gainsharing plans in hospitals, banks, insurance companies and so forth?
3. Your organisation has two business units. One unit is a long-established manufacturer of a product that competes on price and has not been subject to many technological innovations. The other business unit is being started. It has no products yet, but it is working on developing a new technology for testing the effects of drugs on individuals via simulation instead of through lengthy clinical trials. Would you recommend that the two business units have the same pay programs for recognising individual contributions? Why or why not?
4. Performance-based pay is merely a way of shifting the risk from the employer to the employee. Discuss.

5 Managers' and executives' performance is increasingly tied to organisational performance. Discuss the benefits and limitations of this approach.
6 Employees' expectations and desires about rewards will vary over time. Discuss the ways in which these changes could be effectively taken into account in designing a reward system and in the communication and administration of a reward system.
7 Discuss the arguments for and against of using performance based pay as one of the methods for encouraging innovation.

CASE STUDY

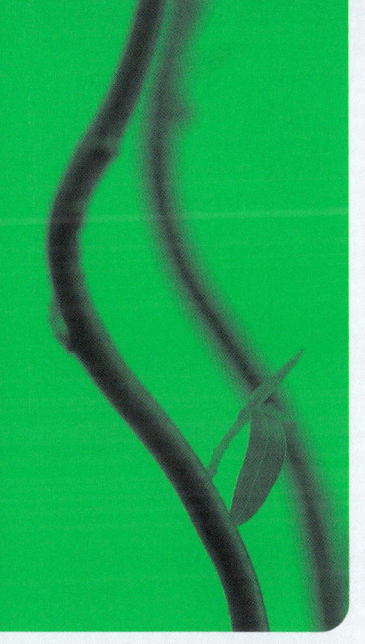

PAY ROLE DEVELOPMENT

Now is the time for many HR pay specialists to show their mettle. One of the hottest issues at the moment relates to top executives' rewards and the perceived excesses of pay at their level. When the next annual executive review is to be prepared for a company's compensation committee, the HR pay specialist should be pushing for a strong role in its development.

To justify this, HR compensation and benefits specialists need to ensure they are highly skilled and qualified in the broader remuneration field. They should also realise that they are up against the need to dramatically improve the profile and credibility of their profession.

None of Australia's top 50 companies has appointed an HR director to its board, a recent study showed. Some may attend meetings, but they do not have regular mainstream involvement. Human resource compensation and benefits specialists are going to have to put it right.

To do so, they should start by working towards a strong correlation between rewards and company performance. Performance measurement is extremely challenging and currently it is not being done well. Try to find a simple methodology that takes into account a range of relevant factors—beyond return on investment or the share price. A share price index, which may be subject to the fluctuations on the share market over which company executives have no control, is not suitable as the sole measurement of success.

Along with the range of performance factors to be taken into account, specialists should be taken into account. Specialists should encourage a change away from the focus on short-term delivery to include longer-term targets. The current short-term-tenure trends of CEOs could be detrimental to their companies.

While keeping this in mind, HR pay specialists should strive to see the 'golden parachutes' of redundancy fall away. The payment of large 'exit parachutes' to CEOs is always controversial, especially if they are leaving under a cloud. The fact is, senior executives know the risks they are taking, and reward for non-performance sets a bad example for everyone. (The practice in the world's second largest economy, Japan, of accepting responsibility for one's performance and suffering the consequences, springs to mind on this point.)

Another important issue for pay specialists to deal with is the pressure to follow what are considered global rates when determining CEO rewards. Global rates tend to be the highest rates—which are those of the United States—rather than a selection of best-practice examples from a range of countries. The local-CEO pay market has largely been overheated by following the practices of other countries, particularly the United States. No HR practice should be applied without taking into account the impact of local market conditions.

Illustrating the importance of this is a recent study showing that expatriates find Australian cities highly desirable locations to live in, while United States cities were well down on the list of expatriate preferences.

There are also the many cultural differences between the two countries. It has been well publicised that high-profile United States executives employed in Australia have not had a good track record. The one thing that is really global about CEO pay is the universal outcry against its excess. It has been argued that executive search consultants may have used the argument of the global nature of CEO pay to their advantage. Their commissions are high and directly linked to executive compensation. A million dollar package brings in a considerably large fee, and you would think a compensation committee would see the potential for conflict of interest in this system.

Have board members sufficiently accessed advice from consultants with training and experience to gauge local and external market conditions in order to make recommendations on compensation? Such consultants can also provide the independent advice needed to appease vocal shareholders.

While a small number of influential consultants may have been considered to have unduly influenced executive remuneration levels, they are not representative of this niche area.

There are clearly opportunities for in-company HR compensation and benefits specialists to improve their profile and impact on their employers. To start, they can do a number of things to boost their skills and qualifications in the broader remuneration field.

They can become members of World at Work (formerly the American Compensation Association), attending its annual conferences and studying for its examinations.

They can familiarise themselves with shares/stocks. The development and management of stock plans has become something of a science in the United States, made all the more complicated by the legislation that must be complied with. They should obtain some understanding of this for its relevance locally—and Australia does have a few specialists in this field.

Subscribing to local remuneration and benefits surveys of executive remuneration can help in becoming familiar with local pay trends for local executives and those employed by international companies. Only half the picture is revealed when buying compensation summaries compiled from selected annual reports.

Ultimately, delivering professional results to a compensation committee can only lead to being better recognised as an effective specialist. Human resource specialists can expect directors and other managers to consult with them more in future. Many compensation committees comprise company directors with little specialised knowledge, and HR specialists have the advantage of being able to present pay for the company as a whole. Treating senior executives separately has been shown to be impractical and inequitable.

Source: Based on Peter Barton, 2004, 'Pay role development', *HRMonthly*, March, pp. 28–9. *HRMonthly* is published for the Australian Human Resources Institute, www.ahri.com.au.

QUESTIONS

1 Assess the suggestions of the ways in which in-house remuneration specialists could increase their profiles.
2 Discuss the impact of global pressures on executive pay rates, packages and benefits.
3 Identify some of the difficulties associated with these global pressures.

PART 5

CONTEMPORARY ISSUES FOR HUMAN RESOURCE MANAGEMENT

15 Ethics and Human Resource Management

16 International Human Resource Management

17 Managing Employee Turnover and Retention

18 Evaluating and Improving the Human Resource Function

CHAPTER 15

ETHICS AND HUMAN RESOURCE MANAGEMENT

Michelle Greenwood*

Objectives

After reading this chapter, you should be able to:

1. Identify factors in the emergence of the debate on ethical issues in HRM.
2. Describe and discuss basic ethical theories and principles.
3. Understand issues involved in the consideration of rights and responsibilities in the employment relationship.
4. Understand issues involved in the consideration of fairness and justice in the employment relationship.
5. Identify challenges to the ethicality of HRM.

* Michelle Greenwood would like to thank Tracy Wilcox, University of New South Wales, for her contribution to the development of ideas in this chapter.

New rules for romance

British companies are increasingly drawing up formal codes of conduct for employees whose work interests spill over into a sexual relationship.

A survey of leading employers reveals that the proportion of firms who have written guidelines for office romances has more than doubled in the last two years. The study found 10 per cent of companies now expect enamoured co-workers to declare their relationship if their private and professional lives could lead to a 'real or perceived' conflict of interest.

Britain's long-work-hours culture means an estimated 30 per cent of people will meet their life partner at work. The consequent growth in office romances has led to human resource managers now trying to formalise flirting, in a bid to minimise reprisals against employers if a relationship ends.

According to the survey of 43 companies and institutions—including British Telecom, the Foreign Office, five National Health Service trusts and four finance houses—some 28 per cent of employers are considering bringing in formal guidelines.

The study, carried out for a specialist journal, *IRS Employment Review*, said:

> If dealt with appropriately and conducted sensibly, workplace romances should not present any problem to employers. But get it wrong, and the consequences can be far reaching—potential claims for sexual harassment, charges of favouritism, decreased productivity and fear of reprisal or retaliation.

The result is increasing boardroom 'twitchiness' about how to balance the privacy of workers and an employer's need to ensure a sexual relationship does not lead to unfair pay rises or promotions. While most companies (40 per cent) still prefer to solve any potential difficulties by having an 'informal chat' with the people involved, 10 per cent said they would seek to generate a workplace culture which would make office romances unacceptable. None had introduced so-called 'love contracts', a device now commonplace in America under which an office couple undertake not to sue their employer for sexual harassment should their relationship end. At least one United Kingdom company in the survey made it clear that all office relationships were to be declared, saying: 'Any employee who is working with a person with whom they have a personal relationship should inform the personnel manager.'

Other employers believed office romances can only be disruptive. Speaking anonymously, one said: 'We have a large number of workplace relationships, and I believe they often undermine core issues such as productivity, teamwork and motivation.' Experts said that far from causing disruption, relationships between people sharing the same work experiences could help to combat stress and provide support.

A spokesman for Liberty, the human-rights group, said:

> Companies have a right to protect themselves against extreme behaviour such as people getting pay rises for sexual favours. But it is wrong to impose these sort of reporting requirements on people just because they work for the same company. Any healthy, normal office will have a reasonable proportion of office romances.

Professor Cary Cooper, an occupational psychologist at the University of Manchester Institute of Science and Technology, said that when a relationship developed between a boss and a subordinate, it was fair for companies to move one of the couple to a different department. He also said that employers had to be careful. 'I think UK employers would be wise to draw a line beyond which they do not pry into their employees' private lives.'

Source: Based on Cahal Milmo, 2002, 'New rules forcing workers to declare office romances', *The Independent,* London, 11 December, p. 6.

PART 5   Contemporary Issues for Human Resource Management

Introduction

Critical reflection on the way in which organisations are managed is important. There is significant debate about the moral role that business organisations have in society.[1] Business ethics is a field of study that addresses this debate. It has been argued that an essential foundation of business ethics is the idea that the organisation must be seen as a moral entity.[2] This chapter discusses basic ethical theories and principles relevant to HRM, identifies ethical issues related to HRM and identifies challenges to the ethicality of HRM.

Why ethics are important in HRM

The study of ethics in the HRM context is important because of dynamic and interrelated shifts in the organisation of work: changes in international economies; changes at the national level in policy and institutional structures; and changes at an enterprise level in the policies, systems and practices of employment. **Ethics** is a general term commonly used to refer to both moral beliefs and ethical theory.[3] **Ethical theory**, in contrast, suggests more specific reflections on the nature and justification of right actions in a manner that introduces clarity, substance and precision of argument.[4]

The activities of HRM do not take place in isolation from other organisational activities. Within each organisation, HRM decisions and practices influence other organisational decisions and practices, which in turn influence HRM. These organisational activities also interact with the external environment in which the organisation operates. Hence, external environmental issues like globalisation and the increasing power of corporations are of relevance to HRM practices in organisations. The significance of ethical theory for critically evaluating management practices can, thus, be linked to a number of issues. Underpinning these issues is the current predominance of **economic rationalist frameworks** (the general term for neo-liberal or neo-classical economic systems within Western society) and the resulting change in the way organisations are viewed, both internally and within society at large.

Internationalisation of economies

The dominance of neo-classical (or neo-liberal) economic systems within Western society has been noted by theorists across disciplines.[5] A **neo-classical (or neo-liberal) paradigm**—the view, often in economics, that human behaviour is driven by the relationship between scarce means and alternative ends—is described by Etzioni as a 'utilitarian, rationalist and individualist paradigm' in which individuals seek to 'maximise their utility, rationally choosing the best means to serve their goals'.[6] Wilcox and Lowry have observed that it is common for human activity in organisations to be seen as economic activity.[7] The classical argument that pursuit of economic self-interest is in the interest of the common good has found a return to favour. According to Kamoche, we can expect businesses to make decisions based on a 'putative rational assessment of the most efficient utilisation of available resources to generate "added value"'. Thus, the question of utilising humans as resources to generate and retain this value needs to be addressed by HRM.[8]

The increasingly global economy has significant implications for the functioning of corporations. Multinational corporations (MNCs) are the 'dominant actors on the global stage'.[9] In many cases, MNCs own the media that promote their products,

---

Ethics
general term commonly used to refer to both moral beliefs and ethical theory.

Ethical theory
specific reflections on the nature and justification of right actions in a manner that introduces clarity, substance and precision of argument.

Economic rationalist frameworks
general term for neo-liberal or neo-classical economic systems within Western society.

Neo-classical (or neo-liberal) paradigm
the view, often in economics, that human behaviour is driven by the relationship between scarce means and alternative ends, such that individuals act in a rational self-serving manner to maximise their own utility.

invest in the companies that provide them with services and pay much of the taxes that keep the governments running. Many MNCs are economically more powerful than many governments—for example, the turnover of General Motors is about the same as the gross domestic product of Denmark.[10] Despite their increase in power, these corporations have not necessarily increased their level of responsibility towards society. Unfortunately, there are numerous examples of where the actions of MNCs have led to the decline and devastation of economic, social and environmental conditions in Third World nations.[11]

The implications of globalisation for the Australian workplace are profound (also see Chapter 16 International human resource management). For example, the reduction of trade protection tariffs has resulted in many jobs moving offshore, particularly in the manufacturing sector. This loss of jobs has only been partly compensated for by increases in service-sector employment. However, most of the newly created jobs are temporary in nature and, thus, insecure and without career development.[12] There has been a dramatic increase in the number of part-time and casual jobs, and the amount of work being performed outside traditional working hours. There are also emerging trends in work patterns, such as downshifting, as discussed in 'Managing challenges through sustainability: Downshifting: Quitting the rat race'. Increasingly, there is a mismatch between the demands on labour and the desires of the workers, with many full-time workers wanting to work less and many casual workers and many under-employed workers wanting to work more.[13]

Changing employment relations

In response to global demands, successive governments since the 1990s have made significant changes to the industrial system in Australia. There has been deregulation of the labour market, reform of workplace legislation and a lessening of the role of industrial relations institutions such as the Australian Industrial Relations Commission (AIRC) and trade unions (also see Chapter 5 Industrial relations). Legislative reform has removed much of the independent or third-party involvement in the employment relationship (for example, the Federal Government's *Workplace Relations Act 1996*). In many cases, employment contracts have shifted towards **transactional psychological contracts** (expectations between employers and employees that are focused on a specific economic exchange with little flexibility and narrowly defined terms) and away from **relational psychological contracts** (expectations between employers and employees that tend to focus on open-ended relationships with emotional involvement as well as economic exchange), and are of limited duration.[14] (Also see Chapter 12 Employee development and career management, for a discussion of psychological contracts.) Together with increasing responsibility for industrial relations, these changes have led to increasingly complex employment relationships at the enterprise level. These momentous shifts are of great significance to HRM. Removal of the previous checks and balances has resulted in very different assumptions about social and employment relationships and, as such, dramatic changes in the role of managers and management prerogative.

Transactional psychological contracts expectations between employers and employees that are focused on a specific economic exchange with little flexibility and narrowly defined terms.

Relational psychological contracts expectations between employers and employees that tend to focus on open-ended relationships with emotional involvement as well as economic exchange.

HRM as the locus of employment ethics

The activities of HRM are particularly open to ethical critique.[15] The policies and practices of HRM are frequently designed to elicit employees' commitment and loyalty to the company while at the same time expecting organisational members to accept 'increased uncertainty and insecurity'.[16] It has been noted that the primary activities of HR practitioners 'have a direct impact on society' and have the potential to help or harm people, affecting the quality of life of employees and their families.[17]

DOWNSHIFTING: QUITTING THE RAT RACE

In a society filled with conflicting responsibilities and commitments, work/life balance has become a predominant issue in the workplace. An increasing number of professionals around the world are opting to pursue a more balanced lifestyle. Work/life balance initiatives per se are not new. In fact, it was Rosabeth Moss Kanter's seminal book *Work and Family in the United States: A critical review and agenda for research and policy* in 1977 that brought the issue of work/life balance to the forefront of research and organisations. In the 1980s and 1990s, companies slowly began to introduce work/life programs. Not surprisingly, a new management buzzword has emerged—downshifting.

What drives downshifting? Downshifters tend to place less value on money and individual possessions and instead focus more on time, health, and peace of mind. A number of key drivers of downshifting have been identified by the Australian Institute in 2003. They include a desire for a more balanced life, a clash of personal values in the workplace, a more fulfilled lifestyle, and poor health as a result of excessive stress at work.

A recent survey conducted in the United States showed that 19 per cent of adult Americans had voluntarily decided to reduce their income and consumption levels in the past five years. Similarly, the Australian Institute reported in 2003 that 23 per cent of adult Australians have chosen to downshift to a simpler lifestyle on less income over the past ten years. Similar findings have been reported in New Zealand and Canada. A November 2004 poll conducted by the *US News and World Report* found that 48 per cent of Americans have done at least one of the following in the past five years: cut back their hours at work, declined or did not seek a promotion, lowered their expectations for what they need out of life, reduced their work commitments, or moved to a community with a less hectic way of life.

Anecdotal evidence of prominent downshifters abounds. Australian Gabriela Mouson, 41, is a downshifter. A former HR director of a large bank, Mouson recently downshifted from a secure corporate job, to being a work-at-home mother. 'I always found HR to be a meaningful career, but, I would spend half my day doing what I loved to do and the other half of my day doing what my job description required me to do', says Mouson. Increasingly, what she found was that she loved the coaching and mentoring parts of HR, but not everything else that went with it. A little more than six months ago, she left to establish a coaching and consulting firm that helps individuals reach personal and business successes.

A corporate view of downshifting

The emergence of downshifting is causing organisations to rethink the very nature of work and work arrangements: What is a full-time job? What is a part-time job? Who defines when and where a job is to be performed? What are the measurements by which companies remunerate for work? From a HR perspective, downshifting can be interpreted as the next level beyond work-life balancing. It requires companies to be even more creative in their understanding of what jobs are, the time it takes to do them, and what it means to integrate business needs with employee motivation, talent, and the pursuit of individual happiness.

Clearly, if employees are overworked, they are not able to balance the rest of their lives, irrespective of how attractive their remuneration is and no matter how many perks they receive. Downshifters may not necessarily be cynical, angry, or overly critical. They simply do not fit into the traditional fast-track mould anymore. They are also measuring 'success' by their own standards. In response, downshifters are expecting companies to be more flexible and accommodating in their endeavours.

Corporate Australia already has made some concessions toward work–life balancing by providing telecommuting, job-sharing, part-time work, flextime, and sabbaticals. However, downshifters are increasingly expecting more innovative solutions to modern life's dilemmas.

Is HR ready for downshifting?

Flexibility obviously creates staffing challenges for management. In some companies and departments, flexibility is clearly limited. Blue-collar plant workers, for instance, will not be able to telecommute, so there are certain functions and environments that are more inclined toward certain formats of flexibility.

Source: Excerpt from Anonymous, 2005, 'Downshifting: Quitting the rat race', http://www.humanresourcesmagazine.com.au/articles/56/0C036F56.asp, 1 November.

Human resource professionals have more discretionary power over employment matters than in the past. This is a result of employment relations becoming more enterprise focused; less institutionalisation and standardisation of employment matters; and a decline in union representation. One outcome of this is that HR professionals now face an increased responsibility for dealing with ethical issues in the workplace. Writers now refer to the 'centrality of ethics in HRM'.[18] In many ways HR professionals are now expected to act as ethical stewards[19], or the 'conscience' of organisations[20]. Some have stressed the role of HRM in raising awareness about ethical issues, promoting ethical behaviour and disseminating ethical practices. According to the Australian Human Resource Institute (AHRI): 'Together with line management, it is HR's responsibility to communicate and ensure that sound ethical practice underpins and is intrinsic to the culture of the organisation.'[21]

Ethical principles and their application

Business ethicists have argued that any attempts to understand ethical issues in business need to be based on a framework of theories for assessing whether something is right or wrong—worthy or unworthy.[22] There are a number of possible approaches within the field of ethics that can make up this framework. Ethical theories assist in the understanding of decision making, and in the development of analytical and reasoning skills. They can provide a common language to debate and evaluate ethical issues, and to reflect critically on the way organisations are managed.

In determining whether a course of action is right or wrong, people engage in some sort of moral reasoning, whether or not they are aware of their doing so. This reasoning typically draws on one or more ethical frameworks or theories. The following sections will look briefly at five types of ethical theories: deontological theory, which is principle-based; teleological theory, which is outcome-based; and virtue ethics, justice ethics and ethical relativism, which are contingency-based. Further, the notion of ethical pluralism, that moral reasoning in applied situations is often based on a number of ethical principles, is considered. As an example of applied ethical pluralism, the stakeholder theory of the firm provides a framework for discussion of the organisation–employee relationship.

Deontology

Deontological theory (from the Greek word *deon*, meaning 'duty') is an ethical view based on the concept of the inherent rightness or wrongness of actions, independent of their consequences. Deontological approaches are based on principles of duties and obligations. The ethical theories of the philosopher Immanuel Kant (1724–1804) are the most well-known examples of deontological ethics. Kantianism or Kantian ethics is based on several principles, including his categorical imperative—that we should only act in the manner in which we would want others to act. Another important deontological rule or imperative is that we should treat others with dignity and respect. Kant argued that persons should be treated as ends in themselves, and never only as means to ends. Respect for human beings is essential because human beings possess an intrinsic moral dignity; and, therefore, they cannot be treated merely in an instrumental manner.

Deontological constraints or rules are typically framed in ways that direct individual behaviour. As such, if a person does something bad (for example, harming someone), it is seen far more harshly than if a person fails to do something good (for example, not preventing someone from coming to harm). Individuals are seen as responsible for the things they intend rather than for the consequences of their actions. Most religious approaches to ethics are deontological in nature, including Judaism, Islam, Christianity and Confucianism.[23]

There are two major criticisms of deontology.[24] First, how do we know what sorts of things are wrong and why they are wrong? We do not know exactly what the

Deontological theory
an ethical theory based on the specific principle that actions have inherent rightness or wrongness dependent on whether they correspond to a duty but independent of their consequences.

principles by which we should live are, and from where these principles come. Responses to this criticism include: the constraints are based on common moral intuition 'seasoned with a bit of tradition'[25] (in the main from Judeo-Christian teachings); the constraints are derived from fundamental principles such as the Kantian imperatives; and the constraints can be understood from the wrong action itself (if murder is wrong, why is it so?). Second, there is the problem of what to do if the principles conflict with each other. The controversial issue of drug testing in the workplace is often posed as a conflict between an employee's right to privacy and another employee's right to a safe work environment. If conflicting principles are not negotiable, then it is impossible to not do wrong. However, deontologists believe that these are exceptional conditions and that they do not undermine an otherwise credible moral theory.

Consequentialism

Teleological theory
an outcome-based ethical theory that considers the rightness or wrongness of our acts to be determined by a comparative assessment of their consequences.

Teleological theory (from the Greek word *telos*, meaning 'goal') differs from deontological views in that it does not hold that there are special kinds of acts that are right or wrong. For teleologists (sometimes called consequentialists) the rightness or wrongness of our acts is determined by a comparative assessment of their consequences.[26] Fundamentally, consequentialism maintains that morality is decided solely by the consequences of actions. As such, the good is defined independently from the right.

Utilitarianism
an ethical theory that defines an action as right if it maximises the common or collective good.

The best-known form of consequentialism is utilitarianism. **Utilitarianism** is an ethical theory that defines an action as right if it maximises the common or collective good—for example, the greatest good for the greatest number.[27] Utilitarianism is based on the writings of Jeremy Bentham (1748–1832) and John Stuart Mill (1806–1873). Utilitarianism is based on the maximisation of good and the minimisation of harm and evil,[28] and as such resembles a cost–benefit analysis.[29] Teleological approaches are particularly relevant to HR practices such as promotion and remuneration, where the parties involved are concerned with fair and equitable outcomes.

Consequentialist approaches have also been subject to critique. The most significant concern is that it is possible to argue, using a utilitarian analysis, that certain actions are morally right, even if they violate human rights. Supporters of consequentialism suggest that this is acceptable as it occurs only in exceptional circumstances. Nevertheless, it is argued that such a view allows the general habit of contemplating such deeds, thus making nothing 'unthinkable'.[30] In the employment context, retrenchment of loyal workers or plant closures that affect entire communities are often justified by utilitarian claims, despite the impact of such actions on the rights of individual employees. In addition, there is the problem that it is difficult to evaluate the good or harm involved in particular actions, or the worth of, for example, a human life or a natural environment.

Virtue ethics

Virtue ethics
focuses on the person who performs the action rather than the principles or the outcome of an action. Virtue ethics is concerned with the character or character traits of the actor as expressed in his or her actions.

Unlike the focus of deontology on the principles of action, or the focus of utilitarianism on the outcomes of an action, the focus of **virtue ethics** is not on the action but on the person who performs the action. More specifically, virtue ethics is concerned with the character or character traits of the actor as expressed in his or her actions. A moderate form of the theory suggests that virtue ethics is a necessary complement to deontological and consequentialist theories. A radical form of the theory undermines those other theories and suggests that they are morally bankrupt.[31]

Virtues that make human activity possible and human society harmonious tend to be valued by all societies, across all time periods. The shared needs of society, namely to cooperate and live together, supply members with the necessities of life, protect against intruders and natural disasters, and communicate, require universal virtues such as courage, honesty, generosity and congeniality. What is considered virtuous, however, does seem to differ from one society or situation to another. In addition, virtues can become outmoded. For example, a shift to a more conciliatory and cooperative industrial relations environment, may bring about a corresponding shift in the virtues valued in human resource managers. Thus, there does appear to be some non-universal or relative aspects of what is considered virtuous (see sections on ethical relativism). Most societies, however, consider the virtues of cooperation, honesty and trustworthiness as essential for business activities.

Justice ethics

What a person deserves, or is entitled to, is often decided by specific rules and laws. These rules are commonly subject to evaluation and revision against principles such as equality, non-discrimination, fairness and retribution. Employment laws and practices are heavily reliant on such rules. **Justice ethics** are based on the duty to treat all parties fairly and to distribute risks and benefits equitably. The word 'justice' is used broadly to cover both these principles and the specific rules derived from these principles.[32]

John Rawls' theory of justice[33] holds that all economic goods and services should be distributed equally, except when an unequal distribution will work to everyone's advantage. In direct contrast to utilitarianism, this notion rejects the greater good that allows for some to be disadvantaged. Rawls' position requires that the worst-off in society be advantaged by just distribution and demands that we use a conceptual device called the **veil of ignorance** to uphold a 'Kantian conception of equality'. Each person should imagine they are ignorant of his of her particular characteristics such as race, gender, intelligence, family background—that is, each person should put him or herself in the *original position*. In doing so, people would adopt principles based on fairness and would not favour their particular condition. Rawls' theory is primarily focused on distributive justice.

Ethical relativism

Ethical relativism is at the other end of the spectrum to the **universalism** (or absolutism), which refers to the belief that there is a single truth, such as that assumed by deontology and consequentialism. As we look around us, it is apparent that moral standards appear to vary from place to place, and that different cultures hold different views on the morality of particular acts. The theory of **ethical relativism** is based on the notion that there is not a single ethical truth, but that ethical beliefs are contingency-based, for example whatever a culture thinks is right or wrong is really right or wrong for the members of that culture.[34] This implies that there are no independent principles or standards for determining if a practice is right or wrong, and, therefore, no moral belief or set of beliefs is more correct than another.

There are many critiques and criticisms of ethical relativism.[35] First, by accepting the thesis of ethical relativism we are accepting the idea that a practice, no matter how morally objectionable it may be to us, is allowable merely because others believe in it. This would mean that one belief or behaviour (for example, torture) is not more right or wrong than another (for example, respecting human dignity).

Justice ethics
based on the duty to treat all parties fairly and to distribute risks and benefits equitably. 'Justice' is used broadly to cover both these principles and the specific rules derived from these principles.

Veil of ignorance
a conceptual device that requires each person to put him or herself in the original position, that is, to imagine he or she is ignorant of his of her particular characteristics such as race, gender, intelligence and family background.

Universalism
(or absolutism) the belief that there is a single truth. In ethics, universalism implies a single perspective as to what is right and wrong and it is in contrast to relativism.

Ethical relativism
the concept that there is not a single ethical truth but that ethical beliefs are contingency based (some forms hold that whatever a culture thinks is right or wrong is really right or wrong for the members of that culture).

Second, conflicts between different cultures or groups would be impossible to resolve. In many cases, individuals belong to more than one group, each with distinct moral frameworks. For example, an individual could be a member of a profession; employee of an organisation; citizen of a country; and affiliated with a religion. In the case of a conflict, how would an individual decide which moral framework should take precedence?

Third, under relativist frameworks, moral reform and progress would not be possible. Without an independent set of criteria, there is no way to argue that a belief is morally defective and should be improved or replaced. Ethical relativism is at risk of deteriorating into **subjectivism** (the view that individuals are the sole authority over their ethical principles) because it can provide no principled way of choosing between moral frameworks.[36]

Fourth, it is plausible that despite obvious differences, cultures often agree on ethical standards. In many cases cultures agree about the basic moral principles, but they show differences in how they enact those principles. Thus, culturally-specific HR practices, such as the Japanese commitment to lifelong employment, should not be assumed to be based on distinct ethical principles; but they may well be a different way of implementing a shared principle, such as respect for human dignity (see Chapter 16 International human resource management, for a discussion of the distinction between **emic** and **etic**).

Subjectivism
the view that individuals are the sole authority over their ethical principles.

Emic (also see etic)
culture-specific aspects of concepts or behaviour.

Etic (also see emic)
culture-common aspects of concepts or behaviour.

Ethical pluralism and applied ethics

Ethical pluralism (the idea that moral reasoning in applied situations is often based on a variety of ethical principles accepting a pluralistic approach to ethical decision making) is gaining popularity in areas of applied ethics. The attraction of **pluralism** (an approach that sees society as comprising a diversity of pressure groups with divergent social interests and, as such, this approach accepts conflict between employer and employee as usual) in ethical theory is easy to understand.[37] Appeal can be made to the fact that human beings are complex, multifaceted creatures. It has been shown that not one theory or set of theories presents an entirely comprehensive understanding of human behaviour.[38] Bowie notes that an advantage of pragmatic pluralism is that the pluralist does not have to address any of the inadequacies of any one ethical theory nor defend any one foundation principle.[39] Goodpaster suggests that forming the habits of **moral insight** (the capacity of an individual to determine whether a person or action is moral in terms of being right, good, virtuous and/or just) may be more important than dogmatic adherence to a single set of principles.[40]

Ethical decisions are often a case of balancing various demands. This means accepting a pluralistic approach to ethical decision making that 'permits several basic methods or principles to be in tension or conflict with one another'.[41] The decision-making processes in organisations need to take into account the needs and desires of many parties. Ethical HRM decisions are likely to reflect fundamental human rights, issues of equity and fairness and positive outcomes for those concerned. Codes of conduct of multinational corporations commonly reflect a variety of ethical principles.

It must be emphasised that ethical pluralism in no way equates to ethical relativism. The pluralist is not suggesting that ethical 'norms' are constructed by each actor or set of actors, but rather that each actor will use a variety of different (absolute) principles to guide their behaviour. Pluralism and relativism are not the same, either conceptually or practically.[42] Yet, as with ethical relativism, the traditionalist ethicists are highly critical of the philosophical inconsistencies of the ethical pluralism approach.

Ethical pluralism
the idea that moral reasoning in applied situations is often based on a variety of ethical principles accepting a pluralistic approach to ethical decision making. Supporters suggest that moral insight is more important than adherence to ethical dogma.

Pluralism
an approach that sees society as comprising a diversity of interest groups with divergent social interests and, as such, this approach accepts conflict between employer and employee as usual.

Moral insight
the capacity of an individual to determine whether a person or action is moral in terms of being right, good, virtuous and/or just.

The stakeholder concept as applied ethical pluralism

The notion that the organisation has a moral relationship with a number of non-owner stakeholders was first elaborated by Freeman as a **stakeholder theory** of the firm.[43] This conception of responsibilities of the corporation draws unashamedly from Kantian ethics, the principle that 'the corporation and its managers may not violate the legitimate rights of others to determine their own future',[44] and utilitarian ethics, the principle that 'the corporation and its managers are responsible for the effects of their actions on others'[45]. In addition, there are notions of procedural justice in the suggestions that stakeholders should participate in decisions that directly affect them, and that organisations should show accountability to their stakeholders. Indeed, it has been argued that fairness provides the normative core to stakeholder theory.[46] Stakeholder theory also appeals to the ethical virtue of managers, particularly their honesty and trustworthiness. As a theory of multi-constituency relationships, stakeholder theory assists our understanding of the organisation–employee relationship. Employees are seen as unique stakeholders by virtue of their investment of physical, intellectual and emotional labour in the firm and the risks involved in making such investments. Stakeholder theory is based on the assumption that the various stakeholder groups will have different interests in the firm and that these interests will sometimes conflict. Thus, it is in keeping with a *pluralist* industrial relations view of the firm.

Stakeholder theory
a theory of the firm that holds that the organisation has a moral relationship with a number of non-owner stakeholders based on the notion that these stakeholders have a stake or claim in the firm.

The rights and responsibilities of employers and employees

Ethical debate in HRM has traditionally focused on the rights and responsibilities of employees and employers, and issues of justice and fairness in the employment relationship. This section presents the theoretical background and the practical implications of both the rights and justice approaches to HRM.

Rights ethics

The discussion of **human rights** (the right of people, particularly vulnerable people, to moral protection) has proliferated in the twentieth century. The moral protection of vulnerable people has become a major focus of business ethics.[47] The protection of employees in the workplace from practices that violate human dignity and self-respect has translated into the promotion of employees' rights for safety, non-discrimination and freedom of speech, among others. According to Nozick:

Human rights
the right of people, particularly vulnerable people, to moral protection.

> All persons have a right to be free to do as they choose. The moral obligation not to interfere with a person follows from this right. That the obligation follows from the right is a clear indication of the priority of rights over obligations; that is, in this theory the obligation is derived from the right not the other way around.[48]

The ethical theories discussed earlier, including deontology and consequentialism, are commonly understood as theories of obligation. Some theorists argue for a theory of rights that is not reducible to a theory of obligations and as such is independent of the ethical theories of obligation and virtue. In contrast, Beauchamp and Bowie claim that rights theorists have failed to show that rights are absolute moral demands rather than prima facie claims.[49] There is no doubt, however, that current theories of employees' and other stakeholders' rights provide valuable frameworks for debate.

Fundamental rights of employees

Rights and duties of employees suggests that employees are seen to have rights and duties that not only encompass basic human rights and duties but also take into account the particular demands of the work setting.

Traditionally, ethical considerations in the employment relationship, within the domain of business ethics, have been concerned with upholding the **rights and duties of employees**—employees are seen to have rights that encompass basic human rights and take into account the particular demands of the work setting. These rights include the right to fair and safe work conditions, the right to freedom of speech and freedom of association, and the right to collective bargaining and representation (see Table 15.1 below). Lists of such rights can be found in many texts[50] and have been institutionalised in several forums such as the International Labour Organization.

TABLE 15.1 Rights and responsibilities of employees and issues related to these

Employee rights	Issues of fairness and justice
Right to freedom from discrimination:	• Equal opportunity • Affirmative action • Sexual and racial harassment
Right to privacy:	• Health and drug testing • Work–life balance • Presenteeism • Electronic privacy and data protection
Right to due process:	• Selection, promotion and firing • Disciplinary proceedings • Grievance proceedings
Right to collective bargaining and association and the right to strike:	• Organisation of workers in trade unions • Industrial action
Right to participation:	• Participation in company's decisions
Right to healthy and safe working conditions:	• Working conditions • Occupational health and safety
Right to fair wages:	• Pay • New forms of work
Right to freedom of conscience and speech:	• Whistleblowing • Cultural control
Right to work:	• Fair treatment in recruitment and selection • Non-discriminatory rules in recruitment and selection
Employee duties	**Issues of fairness and justice**
Duty to comply with labour contract:	• Acceptable level of performance (health and drug testing, and industrial action) • Work quality • Loyalty to the firm (whistleblowing)
Duty to comply with the law:	• Bribery
Duty to respect the employer's property:	• Working time (presenteeism) • Unauthorised use of company resources for private purposes • Fraud, theft, embezzlement

Source: Adapted from A. Crane & D. Matten, 2004, *Business Ethics*, Oxford University Press, Oxford.

In many industrialised countries, employees' rights are enshrined through legal mechanisms: common law, statutes, statutory agreements and awards, and employment contracts (see Chapter 3 The legal context for human resource management). This may not be the case for employees of MNCs. In many cases MNCs based in developed countries employ (either directly or indirectly) employees in the Third World and developing countries. The basic rights of these employees are unlikely to be protected by law in the MNC's parent country or the host country. Despite the fact that many developed countries are signatories to international protocols on labour rights, laws in the parent country of MNCs are unlikely to explicitly cover offshore operations of corporations (exceptions are the United States' *Foreign Corrupt Practices Act* and the Organisation for Economic Cooperation and Development's (OECD's) convention on bribery). As indicated in 'Managing challenges of globalisation: Outsourcing no tail spin for Qantas', offshoring raises many concerns for stakeholders, including employers, unions, employees, and government. The host country is unlikely to ensure labour rights. This may be due to deficiencies in legislation or legislative institutions, or the inability or unwillingness to enforce any such legislation.[51] This is particularly the case when MNCs operate in *free trade zones*—that is, zones within developing countries where regulations in certain areas, for example taxation, are suspended in order to encourage MNCs to operate in the country in question.[52]

Beyond basic rights

We are cautioned against reliance on simplistic lists of employees' rights as these can be ambiguous and, as such, open to a variety of interpretations and applications.[53] More sophisticated arguments about employees' rights have been developed recently, including the *right to meaningful work*[54] and the *right to employability*[55]. According to Bowie, individuals have a right to *meaningful work*; that is, work that:

- is freely entered into
- allows the worker to exercise his/her autonomy and independence
- enables the worker to develop his/her rational capacities
- provides a wage sufficient for physical welfare
- supports the moral development of employees
- is not paternalistic in the sense of interfering with the worker's conception of how she/he wishes to obtain happiness.[56]

This definition of meaningful work is based on the Kantian imperative that one should always treat a person as an end and never merely as a means. Bowie argues 'that at this point in human history within the context of business the possession of meaningful work is necessary for respecting humanity as an end in itself'.[57] In addition, Bowie claims that meaningful work provisions are not utopian in that they enhance quality and productivity and as such are 'buttressed' by a practical case of economic necessity.

It has been argued that all employees have a right to employability and, therefore, a right to training and development.[58] Rowan suggests that it is of greater value to consider the principles underpinning these rights. According to Rowan, the moral foundations of employee rights are:[59]

- fair pay based on concepts of equity, distributive justice, autonomy and respect
- safety in the workplace based on the principles of respect and avoiding harm
- due process in the workplace based on concepts of respect, fairness and honesty
- privacy based on concepts of respect, freedom and autonomy.

OUTSOURCING NO TAIL SPIN FOR QANTAS

MANAGING CHALLENGES OF GLOBALISATION

Speaking before the annual conference of the Australian Human Resources Institute in Melbourne, Qantas's executive general manager, Kevin Brown, revealed that the airline began massaging public opinion some 18 months before it began sending Australian jobs offshore.

Brown said, 'When you've got the "Spirit of Australia" as a tag line, brand is a very big consideration. When you've got somebody like union leader Bill Shorten saying it's the "Spirit of Panda" airlines … it's a very emotive issue.'

'What will the brand sustain? What does the brand stand for? And can you get both customers and the public to understand our choices?'

Brown's speech addressed perhaps the touchiest issue in Australian corporate life and the peculiar place Qantas occupies in it.

It also underlined the shift in workplace strategy under WorkChoices. As unions face more constraints, they have moved from reliance on industrial relations law to the court of public opinion, so business confronts an increasingly sophisticated campaign based on polling and use of focus groups.

The airline's chief executive, Geoff Dixon, a one-time journalist, is perhaps the canniest business player of politics and the media in Australia. One who is able to successfully lobby Canberra for protection from competition on the lucrative trans-Pacific route for the national carrier, but who can also argue that international pressures mean that options such as offshoring have to be explored.

Brown sang from the same songsheet as his boss, citing the loss of about 490 000 jobs in the global airline industry since 2000. Qantas expects its fuel bill this financial year to be about $2.9 billion, up $1 billion (after hedging) from 2004–05.

People manager Brown said the airline had used these pressures as a backdrop when it 'launched the debate into the community about where we source our work from'. He argued it would have been 'delinquent' not to consider labour alternatives given the state of the global airline sector and the effects of globalisation, although it appears that Qantas began sowing the seeds for the changes well before the more recent blow-out in fuel costs.

Brown criticised the media for taking a simplistic view ['You're going to China because they're low-paid—that's a bad thing'].

He said offshoring involved broader issues dealing with productivity and overhead savings, along with judgements relating to the 'footprint' of the business.

He said the debate 'could be described as scratching the xenophobic nature of Australia', and raised a 'lot of emotional issues about what people believe and think'.

'The nature of outsourcing tends to evoke an emotional response in its own right.'

He reckoned that the question of skills—who's got them and who can sustain them—would become increasingly important in the debate in Australia. Qantas was considering whether to offshore some of its 126 information technology platforms in the main airline and a key question was 'where you can get the skills'.

He said the decision to base 400 cabin crew in London was producing savings of about $20 million a year through less hotel costs and less downtime.

A slide shown during Brown's speech said no cabin crew jobs had been lost over setting up the London base.

But that sits oddly with the Flight Attendants Association of Australia, which says it was briefed the day before about 325 voluntary redundancies being offered to long-haul cabin crew.

In any case, Brown said a 'more emotive' issue concerned a review of the airline's 6000 maintenance staff, who were and are overwhelmingly based in Australia.

Brown conceded that shifting a slab of those jobs offshore would have had a 'knock-on effect' for the Australian defence sector, putting a dent in the critical mass required for aviation work.

In the end, Qantas decided to shut down its Sydney heavy maintenance operation but kept maintenance elsewhere in Australia, resulting in a net loss of 340 jobs, while keeping more than 2900 other maintenance jobs in Sydney.

Brown argued that it was the 'right decision for Australia', although difficult for the individuals involved.

Qantas is viewed by the public with a proprietary air. About 14 000 of the 38 000 Qantas employees interact with customers—making for an operational intensity faced by few businesses.

'It's a large business made up of small transactions and, of course, the iconic brand of Qantas means that people have an expectation that, once they pay for their ticket, they own a share in the company.'

Source: Excerpt from M. Skulley, 2006, 'Outsourcing no tailspin for Qantas', *Australian Financial Review*, First, 6 June, p. 53. © 2006 Copyright John Fairfax Holdings Limited. Not available for re-distribution.

The likelihood of conflicting employee rights—and, therefore, employer responsibilities (see the earlier discussion of conflicting deontological constraints)—also presents a concern. The case of drug testing at the South Blackwater mine provides an example of such an ethical problem (see the case, 'The South Blackwater mine', at the end of the chapter, page 586).

Employee duties

Whenever an individual has a right, there exists a corresponding duty or obligation.[60] **Whistleblowing** (that is, reporting outside an organisation, on activities within an organisation, that have the potential to cause serious harm to the public) has often been used as the hallmark issue in the debate about employees' obligations to the firm. Traditionally, whistleblowing was seen as a conflict between the employee's commitments of loyalty to the organisation and to their work colleagues versus the employee's duties to the public or society at large. Theorists have taken sides in the debate. On one side, Bok has argued that employees face potentially conflicting duties and, as such, must give serious consideration to which of these duties is the greater imperative.[61] On the other side, Duska has argued that employees owe no obligation of loyalty to the firm and, therefore, there is no conflict of duty.[62] More recently, Larmer has suggested that whistleblowing is not a breach of an employee's organisational loyalty, but in fact it is an employee's act of responsibility towards the organisation—possibly an obligation of the employee.[63]

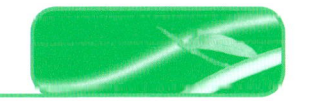

Whistleblowing
reporting outside an organisation on activities, within an organisation, that have the potential to cause serious harm to the public.

It is evident that less attention is given to the employers' rights than to the employees' rights in the employment ethics debate.[64] This occurs despite claims that the organisation–employee relationship is based on mutual obligations[65] and it is a two-sided relationship[66]. Although the vexed question of whether an employee is obliged to be loyal to the firm within a whistleblowing scenario—an issue that is often cited as the litmus test of employee obligation—may be interpreted not as an employer's right to loyalty, but as an employee's right to dissent.[67] It has been noted earlier that companies have become increasingly powerful and influential, and that the position of many employees has become increasingly marginalised. Beauchamp and Bowie conclude that the moral grounds for employee loyalty have been destroyed due to the collapse of the social contract between a company and its employees.[68] In such an environment, protecting the interest of the employees becomes a much greater ethical priority.

Issues of justice and fairness in the employment relationship

The focus of ethical concern within the field of HRM has tended towards the equity and fairness implications of employment practices. Balancing employment practices with ethical concerns dates back to the advent of industrialisation, with the fair and proper treatment of employees being a controversial issue right from the beginning of the industrial revolution.[69] The questions of how employees should be treated, how they should be paid, how they should be trained, under what conditions they should be expected to work, how hard they should work, how they should be disciplined, and how their employment should be terminated, are fundamental to HRM. Responding to these questions is the crux of both the practice and the study of HRM. Issues that are widely noted to be of ethical potency include discrimination, sexual harassment, equal employment opportunity (EEO) and whistleblowing (see Table 15.1 on page 572). More recently, this list has been extended to include drug testing, electronic surveillance and freedom of speech (see the case, 'The South Blackwater mine', at the end of the chapter on page 586). Hence, it is not surprising that organisational justice is a significant area of ethical concern in HRM.

Organisational justice reflects individual or group perceptions of fairness within an organisation and behavioural reactions to such perceptions.[70] Organisational justice subsumes issues of equity in the distribution of resources, or **distributive justice** (the perception that rewards are distributed in relation to contribution); perceived fairness of decision-making processes, or **procedural justice** (also procedural fairness—a concept of justice focusing on the methods used to determine the outcomes received); and the quality of interpersonal treatment in processes, or **interactional justice**.[71] (These concepts are also discussed in Chapter 13 Managing compensation, and Chapter 17 Managing employee turnover and retention.) In essence, each aspect of justice raises a particular question in relation to ethical treatment within the employment relationship. Distributive justice focuses on employee views as to: Did I get what I deserved? Procedural justice raises the question: Are the rules and procedures used to reach these decisions equitable? Interactional justice asks: Do those who apply these procedures listen to my views and treat me with respect?[72]

In industrialised countries, many of the practices that are vulnerable to justice concerns are regulated through legislation (see Chapter 3 The legal context for human resource management). In most cases this legislation is aimed at achieving procedural justice, for example a fair and non-discriminatory recruitment process, rather than distributive justice, for example, 50 per cent of women should be employed. While there is an increasing amount of legislation setting the rules of workplace practice, there is also an increasing amount of autonomy in the individual workplace in the interpretation and implementation of these rules. According to Winstanley and Woodall, procedural justice remains an abiding ethical concern in the areas of recruitment and remuneration.[73] Given the growth of workplace law and litigation (especially EEO considerations), the agenda of HRM is increasingly becoming one of 'showing justice is being done'.[74]

Beyond rights and issues

The limitations of a rights approach to ethical issues, in general, have been noted (see the earlier section on deontology). Ciulla expresses concern at the problem-based and legalistic nature of the rights approach to work within business ethics texts.[75] There is a tendency to focus on the overt problems at the expense of the broader ethical questions related to work. Business ethics scholars should examine some of the basic assumptions about the employment relationship and how that relationship affects employees. According to Ciulla:

> Business ethics is about more than problem solving; it is a field of critical study that should help people think in new ways about business and its responsibilities towards employees, society and other stakeholders. The present and future questions about work require a reassessment of the relationship of employees to the corporation.[76]

The ethicality of HRM

Sidebar definitions:

Organisational justice reflects individual or group perceptions of fairness within an organisation and behavioural reactions to such perceptions.

Distributive justice (also distributive fairness) the perception that rewards are distributed in relation to contribution.

Procedural justice (also procedural fairness) a concept of justice focusing on the methods used to determine the outcomes received.

Interactional justice (also interpersonal fairness) refers to the quality of interpersonal treatment in processes.

Ethicality of HRM refers to the ethical endowment or quality of HRM—that is, the extent to which HRM possesses such qualities.

Current debate on the **ethicality of HRM** identifies a number of challenges to the extent that HRM and the HR manager can be ethical. Previously, these issues have been depicted at two levels: the micro level that considers individual or 'bundles' of HR practices, and the macro level that considers HRM as a whole.[77] Extending this thinking, it is posited that the macro-level debate can be delineated further to consider the ethicality of HRM at the particular business or enterprise level, and at the ethicality of HRM at a societal level. Wilcox and Lowry have noted that the impact of human resource strategies is 'not confined solely to the level of the firm; rather, HRM strategies affect individuals within organisations and throughout society'.[78] Hence, the analysis that follows will consider the limitations on the ethicality of HRM at three levels: at the level of the HR manager and HR function, at the level of the enterprise and at the societal level.

The HR manager and HR function

At the micro level, the ethical nature of HRM practice relates to the moral development of HR practitioners; the existence of moral 'rules' of those implementing HR; and any conflicts of roles or interest that these practitioners may face.

The moral development of managers

The ethicality of HR managers may be promoted or limited by a number of factors. In his theory of **cognitive moral development**, Kohlberg posited that some individuals are more developed in their moral capacities than others.[79] The theory suggested that there are stages of moral development that individuals move through as they reach adulthood and that individuals vary according to their progression through this developmental continuum. As individuals progress in their moral development, the principles on which they base their behaviour are internalised and become intrinsic to their being. This is irrespective of the specific nature of these principles (for example, deontological or justice-based). A number of business ethics researchers have used this theory of moral reasoning to explain the moral behaviour of individuals in organisations, particularly managers. Trevino, however, cautioned that in order to more fully understand ethical behaviour in an organisational context, other factors beyond cognitive moral development such as personality variables (for example, locus of control, self-monitoring and ego strength) and situational influences (for example, reward systems) must be considered, as indicated in the 'Managing challenges through attracting and retaining people: Culture key in anti-corruption' case on the next page.[80]

> **Cognitive moral development** refers to the development of moral judgment, the formation of a system of values or moral ideas from organised patterns of thought.

'Rules' for a moral manager

Guidance as to what makes a more decent HR manager can be interpreted directly from moral philosophers such as Kant[81] and Heller[82]. In his development of a Kantian theory of leadership, Bowie claims that leaders should enhance the autonomy of their followers.[83] Such leaders will insist on more participation on the part of the followers, be protective of the interests of dissenting voices and never sacrifice the humanity of one set of stakeholders, not even for the sake of another set of stakeholders.[84] According to Heller, the decision to commit oneself to act decently is a fundamental choice that people make on a day to day basis. Thus, she presents a theory of morality based on the 'existential choice of decency' that is 'embedded in historical and communal shared meanings'.[85] Macklin has derived a set of principles from Heller's philosophy to guide human resource managers on how to make 'just' judgments, deal with moral conflicts, determine whether a particular goal is morally permissible, and determine how best to pursue a moral goal.

Duality of roles or conflict of interest

It has been argued that HR managers are compromised, and face moral dissonance, by virtue of their dual role of employer representative and employee activist. This ambiguity

CULTURE KEY IN ANTI-CORRUPTION

The commitment of senior leaders and personal convictions are the most important drivers in company decisions to strengthen anti-corruption programs, according to a US report.

Companies rarely cited a business case, like the cost of doing business or brand equity, as the key reason for establishing or enhancing the scope of their anti-corruption systems.

Instead, they believe that it is part of a larger effort to build a culture of compliance within the company—'one that is rooted as much in the company's system of values and beliefs as in the need to respond to the developing global legal and regulatory regime that is transferring much of the anti-corruption prevention, detection, and enforcement burden to the companies', said Ronald Berenbeim, principal researcher at The Conference Board, which released the report.

The report, based on a survey of 165 multinational companies, found that one-third said senior management leadership and conviction is the single most important factor in their company's decision to develop an anti-corruption program.

The most common rationale for anti-corruption programs are legal. For example, general home country prohibitions were the single most important factor by 27 per cent, while 7 per cent said Sarbanes-Oxley was a priority and 13 per cent cited ethical considerations as justifications for investing in anti-corruption initiatives.

'Company anti-corruption practices and procedures have become significantly more widespread, detailed and sophisticated since the 2000 report', said Berenbeim.

'In some companies, reported incidents of corrupt activity have actually increased, but this is attributed to better reporting systems rather than an increase in corruption. And there is a growing recognition among US companies of the need to adopt an ethics-based approach that emphasises adherence to broad principles rather than narrow compliance to specific rules.'

Anti-corruption programs are subject to high levels of review. More than three-quarters of the survey participants report, or in some cases have dual reporting relationships, to a C-Suite executive, board member or board committee.

In addition, companies are now more likely to seek outside assistance in some aspect of their anti-corruption program. Nearly one-third (32 per cent) use outside counsel and 18 per cent use a consultant.

More than 40 per cent of survey participants do business in China, Brazil, Mexico and India—countries that are at high risk for corrupt practices in business. According to 36 per cent of the companies active in China, that country poses 'the greatest overall challenge to the company's operations because of the level of corruption'.

Source: C. Donaldson, 2006, 'Culture key in anti-corruption', *Human Resources*, 13 December. www.humanresourcesmagazine.com.au

---

has 'sharpened' as organisations respond to increased competitive pressures.[86] In addition, it has been suggested that HR managers are limited by unrealistic expectations, deficiencies in training and lack of professional identity. It has been proposed that, in order to fulfil the responsibilities of the role as a HR manager, an individual would need to be an intelligent, articulate and ethical persuader, and a respected and trusted negotiator/conflict resolver who is capable of inspiring people by invoking a clear vision of the best an organisation can achieve; building an ethical culture; and monitoring the fairness of the organisation's social and environmental behaviour.[87] This is certainly a tall order for an individual who may not be specifically trained in HR, or who may not have a university degree at all. The professional status of HR managers is equivocal and in its developmental stages. HR managers are not accorded the same status as well established professional groups such as medical practitioners or psychologists. In Australia, specific guidelines for ethical conduct and professional development were established by the Australian Human Resources Institute as recently as August 2006.[88] Furthermore, there are no mandatory registration requirements and a HR professional may choose whether to affiliate with the Australian Human Resources Institute.[89] In many cases, HR activities are undertaken by managers working in functions other than HR.

HRM within the enterprise

At the macro level, the ethical nature of HRM in the enterprise will vary with ethical leadership and culture; the extent to which HRM is used as a strategic tool; and the development of high commitment HRM practices in the organisation.

Ethical leadership and culture

The ethical behaviour of a HR manager is necessarily limited by the ethicality of senior management and organisational culture. Empirical work by Wiley found that 'regardless of gender, position or company size, employment managers' ethical behaviour is influenced most by the behaviour of senior managers and their immediate supervisors'.[90] Human resource managers who continue to take an ethical stance in an unsupportive organisational environment are risking negative personal and professional consequences. When an ethical conflict becomes too great, it is likely to be resolved by the HR manager resigning.[91] A feature of this is the level of influence that HRM has in the organisation, the level of relevance and power attributed to the HR manager and the HR function. Foote and Robinson found that 'the extent to which HR professionals were able to influence organisational ethics was highly contingent upon the culture and structure of the organisation'.[92]

Strategic HRM or HRM as a strategic tool?

In a bid to overcome the perceived low relevance and power of HRM in many organisations, the function is increasingly being positioned as *strategic human resource management (SHRM)*, where the aim is to become a strategic aspect of the business and reinforce broader organisational goals. Human resource practitioners are under pressure to eschew their traditional role as employee champions in order to become accepted by their management colleagues as business partners.[93] According to Wilcox and Lowry, the reframing of HRM to become 'strategic' provides a backdrop for the acceptance of the use of individuals as a means to an economic end. Human resource strategies such as large-scale downsizing, that would once have been considered radical, are now seen as mainstream strategic choices.[94] Similarly, the practice of contracting-out manufacturing work to plants in the so-called 'developing world' is now widely established.[95] Wilcox and Lowry have noted that what was once labelled **'hard' HRM** (that is, performance-oriented HRM where employees are viewed instrumentally as a means to achieve an organisation's economic goals) has become common HRM practice and is now framed as SHRM.[96] They note that '"strategic" choices such as these can lead to the subordination of fundamental human rights, such as the right to a safe workplace, just remuneration [and] freedom of association'.[97]

'Hard' HRM
performance-oriented HRM where employees are viewed instrumentally as a means to achieve an organisation's economic goals.

High commitment HRM

One approach to HRM emphasises the 'humanness' of employees; however, this approach remains available only to some employees. So-called 'core' or *knowledge workers* (highly skilled employees whose work utilises theoretical and analytical knowledge, acquired via formal education) are often the subject of employee-centred or **high commitment HRM**—a management approach that emphasises employee engagement, participation in decision making, and systemic relationships between technical, social and other organisational elements. (See 'Managing challenges through attracting and retaining people'.) These workers are distinguished from their 'periphery' or second-tier counterparts by having access to job security (if they so wish), high remuneration, training and development, and extensive consultation and empowerment. They are valued because their job or

High commitment HRM
a management approach that emphasises employee engagement, participation in decision making, and systemic relationships between technical, social and other organisational elements.

organisational knowledge is seen as essential to organisational effectiveness. High commitment HR practices are designed to generate employee commitment and involvement.

High commitment practices 'empower' employees by giving them autonomy together with suitable learning and involvement in decision making. Such practices purport to encourage risk taking, develop democratic processes and open the organisation to critical scrutiny. Claydon and Doyle have observed that, from a deontological perspective, the empowerment of employees can be endorsed on the basis of employee rights to self-determination and personal growth at work. However, they go on to caution that self-interest, on behalf of the individual or the group, may play a large part in such HRM practices. The HRM discourse 'slides between deontology and ethical egoism (pursuit of self-interest)'.[98] The other side of a double-edged sword has been identified whereby such practices can lead to work intensification, excessive emotional labour and the shouldering of responsibilities that were previously borne by appropriately compensated managers.[99] In addition, these forms of **'soft' HRM** (commitment orientated HRM that emphasises mutuality—mutual goal, mutual influences, mutual benefits—between employees and the organisation) may be insidious forms of control aiming to achieve employee compliance through the manipulation of organisational culture.[100] Gandz and Bird identified an 'empowerment paradox' where empowerment is used to disempower people through their co-option into a group that represses dissent.[101]

'Soft' HRM
commitment-oriented HRM that emphasises mutuality—mutual goal, mutual influences, mutual benefits—between employees and the organisation.

HRM within society

The commodification of labour

At the societal level, HRM has ethical implications by virtue of the commodification of humans for their labour and the suppression of pluralism and collectivism.

Radical industrial relations has long been concerned with the treatment of workers as objects to be exploited in order to achieve organisational goals and the corresponding lack of respect and dignity this affords them. According to Ciulla, such critique is fundamental to debate on the ethical tensions in the employer–employee relationship, particularly issues around exploitation and power[102] and, as such, its apparent demise is to be lamented. According to Wilcox and Lowry, the notion of employees constituting the **human capital** (referring to the knowledge, skills, abilities and capacities of individuals) of an organisation, attenuates Keenoy's concern that people become valued for their 'resourcefulness' (and what that costs) rather than their 'humanness' (and what that might deserve).[103] This instrumental focus on using humans to maximise competitive advantage has been regarded as an acceptable price to pay for the recognition of HRM as fundamental to corporate strategy.[104]

Human capital
the knowledge, skills, abilities and other characteristics (KSAOs) of individuals.

This inherent action of turning something or someone into, or treating something or someone as, a mere commodity—the **commodification** of individuals—in employment relationships has been analysed by Walsh through the application of Kantian principles.[105] According to Kant, it is an imperative that persons are ends in themselves and possess a worthiness or dignity. In addition, persons cannot be ascribed price as this 'evacuates' their intrinsic value or dignity. However, treating someone as a means is not incompatible with treating him or her as an end. What is not allowed is that they should be treated as mere means. Likewise, in order to treat someone with dignity, that is to treat them as if they are intrinsically valuable, they should not be treated as mere commodities. According to this analysis, the only HRM that is ethically permissible is employee-centred HRM, and this would be

Commodification
the action of turning something or someone into, or treating something or someone as, a mere commodity.

SECURITY GETS UNDER EMPLOYEE'S SKIN

Workers have chip implanted to access restricted areas

At the Ohio security firm CityWatcher.com, a few employees don't have chips on their shoulder about their work—their chips are embedded under their skin.

To enter the data center housing servers at the company that provides video surveillance, monitoring and storage for government and businesses, CEO/founder Sean Darks and two employees swipe their forearms across a device that reads the microchip embedded under their skin.

The microchips, about the size of a grain of rice, are made by Florida-based VeriChip, which makes wearable, attachable—and implantable—radio frequency identification (RFID) chips. The company claims to have the first and only such patented, FDA-cleared RFID implantable microchip and the only one with skin-sensing capabilities. The implantable 'smart tags' can be injected through a syringe. The tags fulfilled Darks' need for a unique, cutting-edge security measure that goes beyond his firm's keycard access system and alarm system to secure the expensive servers and the valuable information they contain, he told CNN.

CityWatcher.com is believed to be the first employer in the United States where employees have had chips embedded under their skin.

The news is stirring debate over privacy, ethical and legal issues, and concern that employees' jobs could be at risk if they refuse to have an employer's chip implanted.

Darks said wearing the microchip does not violate his personal privacy. '[The chips] do not put out any signal that can be tracked', he said in a CNN video clip. The chip does not contain personal information.

Darks said in various news accounts, which also note that the employees with the personal chip volunteered for the process, 'The only thing a chip will be able to do is tell you when I went in that door; it won't tell you what I ate for lunch or where I was at', he said.

However, RFID chips operate on a spectrum that is 'broadcasting whatever information is contained on them constantly', noted Lillie Coney, associate director for the Washington, D.C.-based Electronic Privacy Information Center.

'You can't disengage it. Wherever you are you are broadcasting that you are affiliated with this company, and that's more information than people need to know', she said. 'You've turned them into a target, and you've put their personal security at risk.'

Source: K. Gurchieck, 2006, 'Security gets under employee's skin', *HR News*, April, p. 32.

---

only when there are safeguards to ensure that it is genuinely implemented.[106] In addition, Guest and Conway provide evidence to suggest that employees generally prefer high commitment HRM practices to many of the 'harder' alternatives.[107]

The suppression of pluralism and collectivism

The **managerialist view** looks at organisational behaviour and theory from the exclusive point of view of managers, the functional agents of an administered society. **Unitarism** assumes that all parties in an organisation share similar goals and interests and, as such, it does not acknowledge the potential for conflict between employer and employee. The managerialist and unitarist underpinnings of HRM have been clearly identified.[108] The development of HRM has coincided with changes in the management of the employment relationship—not just at the enterprise level, but also at the societal level. At the enterprise level, the lack of opportunity for employees to pursue their interests separate to those of the organisation, through practices such as cultural control and alternative dispute resolution, has been noted. At a societal level, there have been institutional changes in the way wages and conditions are determined, disputes are resolved and workers are represented and protected. The last decade has seen both legislative reform and the decrease of **collectivism**—the tendency to emphasise the interests and wellbeing of the group over those of each individual—through unionisation (see the section on Changing employment relations, p. 565). There is a trend for individuals to no longer identify as union members or see

Managerialist view
looks at organisational behaviour and theory from the exclusive point of view of managers, the functional agents of an administered society.

Unitarism
assumes that all parties in an organisation share similar goals and interests and, as such, does not acknowledge the potential for conflict between employer and employee.

Collectivism
the tendency to emphasise the interests and wellbeing of the group over those of each individual.

themselves as members of a collective of workers. The reduced importance of unions has led to a demise in the voice and autonomy of employees.[109] As noted earlier, the labour market has become increasingly casual and there has been an increase in contract employment arrangements.[110] Such changes in standard employment arrangements may further promote individualisation and mitigate collective identification. The emphasis on individualisation of HRM has spread beyond particular enterprises to have an impact on the workforce in general. In the past, the lives of workers were shaped by the state and union movement, institutions in which they held a democratic vote. Now it is business that determines how employees should live.

MANAGING PEOPLE

ARE YOU MAKING YOUR STAFF ILL?

There are some jobs that obviously carry a health risk. Bullfighter or bomb disposal expert, for example. But, according to the latest Health and Safety Executive (HSE) figures, every job carries some element of risk. The HSE's statistics show that two million employees are suffering from an illness they believe was either caused or exacerbated by their job.

And while working on a construction site is clearly an occupation that requires a hard hat, it is office life that is making most of us hide under the duvet—whether the direct cause is unrealistic deadlines, incompetent line managers or poor seating. Despite all the rhetoric, work is still making us sick.

Under pressure

But why is this? Dr Les Smith, head of clinical governance for health programme provider First Assist, says many employees feel trapped in the workplace.

'The biggest issue for staff is mental health—pressure and demands, and a lack of physical activity. On one level, we are just too cooped up', he says.

'We spend our time stuck in traffic jams, sitting down all day, drinking coffee for a caffeine hit, then feeling dehydrated, getting home too late to exercise, then eating late and having disturbed sleep', adds Smith.

'Employers would still do well to revisit the HSE website and measure their practices against the checklists', she says. 'Even stress is covered by management regulations. You can do a lot just by making sure you are compliant with all the legislation.'

Positive thinking

As for the catch-all concept of 'wellbeing', Dr Jenny Leeser, clinical director of occupational health at Bupa Wellness, believes this is just a matter of common sense.

'It's both physical and mental, and it's about feeling positive, and having enough energy to be productive at work, and to enjoy your non-working life', she says.

Achieving this balance means treating your employees with respect, argues professor Frank Bond of the department of psychology at Goldsmiths College, University of London.

'The most important factor is the degree of control people have over how they do their jobs', he says. 'The more repetition there is, the more stressful it is; the more variety there is, the more engaged they are.'

'And knowing they are contributing something worthwhile is also important—not necessarily in ethical terms, but in the sense that they can see how what they do fits into the overall scheme of things.'

Just a small increase in the amount of autonomy people have can have a disproportionate effect on their satisfaction at work, says Bond. For example, call centre employers could institute daily rather than hourly targets, so that employees make more calls in the afternoon if that is a better time for them.

Open all hours

This message has yet to get through to some employers, however. Many still respond to the pressure of market competition by putting equal pressure on staff, with potentially disastrous results.

One HR manager, who prefers to remain anonymous, left his job in professional services because he was so stressed by the company culture.

'The drive was to employ people as cheaply as possible, and then get them to work flat out, arriving early and leaving late. Anyone who packed up before 6.30pm was frowned upon, and at appraisal time it was the ones who put in the longest hours who got the biggest promotions', he says.

In this situation, employees experience stress, low morale, poor motivation and cynicism about their role: the precise opposite of wellbeing.

Collaboration culture

The message from experts is that getting out of this pattern means both changing management styles, and making it easier for staff to make healthy choices about how they live their lives.

'The first step for a healthy workplace is inclusivity; you need to gain everyone's trust', says Pauline Crawford, founder and director of management consultancy Corporate Heart. 'You need staff engagement; they need to buy in. People don't always use free gyms because they don't feel they have invested anything in them. Pharmaceuticals giant GlaxoSmithKline sells pedometers to staff at cost price because they are more likely to use them than if they are free.'

Management style is the key. There's more to it than providing facilities; it's about the way people treat each other. Which means that HR cannot manage alone', says Crawford. 'Collaboration between HR, occupational health and senior management is vital. The danger is that everyone passes the buck', she says. 'It's about the overall culture of the organisation. It's not necessarily a health issue.'

Case study: Oracle

Vance Kearney, vice-president for HR (Europe, Middle East and Africa) at business software company Oracle, believes that healthy messages for staff have to be part of a comprehensive management attitude.

'You can't impose wellbeing on people', he says. 'But what you can do is raise awareness of the issues, and give people the tools to be healthy. Work is only one element in stress levels. If things are pressurised at work, and not going well at home either, then you have the opposite of work–life balance.'

Making these tools easily accessible and attractive is important, says Kearney. 'If you look at our restaurant, it looks like the restaurant at [health farm] Champneys. There's a huge variety of salads, but we always have an unhealthy option.' Staff can also use company bikes to get into town from Oracle's office on the Thames, and there is a range of health assessments available to all staff as part of the flexible benefits scheme. These include EPT scans, which can give an early warning about a range of cancers.

Source: Courtesy of *Personnel Today* magazine, www.personneltoday.com, www.humanresourcesmagazine.com.au/articles/E2/0C0422E2.asp, 11 July 2006.

QUESTIONS

1 According to Dr Lesser, the current focus on wellbeing in the workplace may 'lull some HR professionals into thinking they have all angles covered' and that 'quick fixes can be counter-productive'. What does she mean by this?

2 What are suggested to be the real causes of illness in the workplace?

3 What are some of the solutions identified to address these problems?

CHAPTER SUMMARY

This chapter deliberates on the ethical issues involved in the employment relationship in general and specifically in HRM. The chapter provides a context for ethical issues in HRM today and reasons why these issues are vital for the future. Fundamental ethical theories and the principles that arise from these theories are explained, including the pragmatic notion of ethical pluralism. The traditional view of the rights and responsibilities of employers and employees is summarised. This includes essential employee rights such as the right to receive fair pay, the right to a safe work environment and the right to freedom of speech and action. Corresponding issues of justice and fairness are reviewed. Attention, then, is turned to the ethicality of HRM. The limitations of the ethicality of HRM are considered at three levels ranging from the

PART 5   Contemporary Issues for Human Resource Management

micro to the macro. First, ethical challenges faced by HR managers and the HRM function are examined. This includes some discussion on the role of the professionalisation of HRM. Second, HRM within the enterprise is considered. Two emerging trends, the development of strategic HRM and the development of high commitment HRM for knowledge workers, are discussed. Third, the societal level concerns raised by HRM, the commodification of labour and the suppression of the employees' voice are noted.

WEB EXERCISES

A Visit the Gap website www.gapinc.com/, UNITE www.uniteunion.org/ and Behind the Label www.behindthelabel.org/.

Questions
1 What actions does the Gap say it has undertaken to address its critics such as the Union of Needletrades, Industrial and Textile Employees?
2 Do you think these actions are appropriate?
3 Are there any other actions you think the Gap should take?

B All Australian states have some whistleblower protection legislation. The first whistleblower protection legislation was enacted in South Australia in 1993, the *Whistleblowers Protection Act*, followed in 1994 by the Queensland *Whistleblowers Protection Act*, the Australian Capital Territory's *Public Interest Disclosure Act* in 1994 and New South Wales' *Protected Disclosures Act* in 1994. Victoria enacted the *Whistleblowers Protection Act* in 2001, followed by the Tasmanian *Public Interest Disclosures Act* in 2002 and the Western Australian *Public Interest Disclosure Act* in 2003. The *Whistleblowers Protection Act 2001* became law in Victoria on 1 January 2002. The Northern Territory has drafted, but not enacted, the *Public Interest Disclosure Bill 2005*.

Questions
1 What organisations does this legislation cover?
2 What are the protections provided by the Acts?
3 What are the principles behind the Acts?
4 In your opinion, should the Acts be changed to include more or different types of organisations?

For further information, see the following websites:
- Victorian Legislation and Parliamentary Documents www.dms.dpc.vic.gov.au/
- Office of Queensland Parliamentary Council
  www.legislation.qld.gov.au/LEGISLTN/CURRENT/W/WhistleblowProR99_01_.pdf
- South Australia Consolidated Acts www.austlii.edu.au/au/legis/sa/consol_act/wpa1993322/
- Northern Territory
  www.nt.gov.au/justice/docs/lawmake/whistleblower_legislation_disc_paper_040611.pdf
- Whistleblowers Australia www.whistleblowers.org.au/

C Large Australian organisations have followed the lead of multinational corporations like Nike and produced social reports as part of their annual report or as stand-alone reports. Westpac's social impact report emphasises its 'commitment to take greater account of our impact on society and treat it as a business basic'. (Visit www.westpac.com.au/internet/publish.nsf/Content/WI+Social+accountability.)

Look at the reports provided on the websites of some Australian companies (for example, Western Mining Corporation www.wmc.com/sustainability/index.htm and British American Tobacco Australia www.bata.com.au).

Questions

1 What sort of social issues do they report on?
2 What sort of employee- and HRM-related issues do they report on?
3 How many pages are given to employee issues compared with the overall number of pages in the company report (if you are looking at a stand-alone report, remember to include page totals from the other reports as well)?
4 What style or form do the employee-related sections of the reports take and how do these compare with other sections, such as the financial and environmental sections?
5 What are you able to say, if anything, about the ethicality of the company's HRM policies and practices?

DISCUSSION QUESTIONS

1 The very nature of office work is making employees sick. Consider the opinions presented in 'Are you making your staff ill?'. Not only are the jobs themselves problematic due to long hours with no breaks, lack of physical activity, high pressure and demands, but organisational cultures are to blame for not allowing individuals sufficient control over their work and autonomy in their lives. Consider the opinions presented in 'Downshifting: Quitting the rat race'. Some employees are rejecting demands to work longer and harder by sacrificing income and career opportunities, and reducing their material comfort and consumption, in pursuit of a more fulfilling life. What has changed/is changing in the nature of work that is causing employees to be sick? What solutions are being proposed in some companies to deal with this problem? Are workplace-based solutions adequate, or does there need to be a larger rethink of the work within society?

2 'Ask not what you can do for your company but what your company can do for you' advises Siobhan Doran in 'We have ways of making you stay' (see the opening case in Chapter 1). The best employers use high commitment HRM practices to attract and retain staff. What justifications might be made for such HRM practices? What ethical principles, if any, are these justifications based upon? Are there ethical concerns about such practices either for the targeted employees or for others?

3 In 2006, the Australian Institute of Human Resource Management introduced a code of ethics and professional conduct[111] and continuing professional development as part of their membership accreditation.[112] According to AHRI, the introduction of the code 'represents the desire of members of the Australian Human Resources Institute (AHRI) to establish the ethical and professional conduct expected to lead and elevate the human resources profession'.[113] Thus, this code represents a move towards the professionalisation of HRM in Australia. What are the implications of this move for the HR function and HR managers? What are the implications for HRM within the enterprise? What are the implications of the ethical treatment of employees and ethicality of HRM?

CASE STUDY

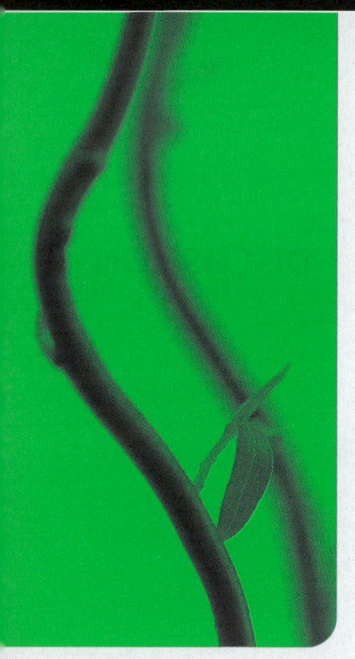

THE SOUTH BLACKWATER MINE

Background

South Blackwater Coal Ltd (SBCL), located in Queensland, employs 400 workers. As part of policy development to ensure a safer working environment, management and trade unions were in the process of negotiating policies and procedures for drug testing at the mine (in line with other mines in the region). Previously, testing only took place if staff were involved in an accident. During this process, management found a used syringe on site and took this as prima facie evidence of illicit drug use in the workplace. Management immediately moved to install drug-testing procedures at the mine. Trade unions advised their members to refuse this blanket testing for drugs, at which point they were stood-down by the company. After one week and three visits to the Australian Industrial Relations Commission (AIRC), the case was (theoretically) resolved. The following analysis illustrates the problems and issues associated with the implementation of these procedures.

The company's perspective

South Blackwater Coal Ltd's management had been negotiating with the Construction, Forestry, Mining and Energy Union (CFMEU) and the Communication, Electrical, Electronic, Energy, Information, Postal, Plumbing and Allied Service Union (CEPU) for approximately 10 months, in an attempt to implement a company 'drugs and alcohol' policy at the South Blackwater coal mine. From management's perspective, the rationale for such a drug policy was to:
- identify drug problems that might exist in the workforce and incorporate results into education
- ensure the drug-testing scheme operates effectively, and consider changes that may be required in future anti-drug efforts
- ensure the company provides a 'safe workplace' and that 'safe systems of work' are not jeopardised by individuals under the influence of illicit substances.

In August 2000 a needle-stick injury, caused by a used syringe on site, was reported. The general manager, Jim Randall, noted that: 'After we had our experts look at it, it was obvious it had been used for some kind of drug injection on site.'

Management took this as prima facie evidence of drug abuse in the workplace. Due to its responsibility to maintain a safe work environment, and its frustration regarding the negotiation process to date, SBCL management informed the unions in July 2000 that it was implementing its drugs and alcohol policy in August of that year. The first stage introduced 'blind' drug tests for all employees (as a precursor to random drug testing). These tests required each employee, contractor and visitor to provide a urine sample for testing, but no specific records were to be kept. Senior SBCL management indicated that the company believed it had the right, if not the obligation, to test for illicit drugs and alcohol abuse, claiming the concern for employee safety and the vicarious liability of the company for employee actions and citing a requirement under law to provide both a safe workplace and safe systems of work.

Management stated that the introduction of such testing was consistent with industry standards, and SBCL's competitors had undertaken similar substance tests for some time. It argued that 'blind' testing would merely provide the company with useful statistical data, which it could act on should the need arise.

The unions' perspective

Representatives from the CFMEU and CEPU cited two important issues behind their decision not to 'allow' their members to provide samples. First, the union rejected managerial arguments concerning the need for a 'safer workplace'. The unions argued that the employer's concern was not so much safety, but rather an attempt to increase the ability to rid themselves of 'trouble employees'. Union representatives were concerned that management were interested to know whether employees were using illicit substances, not why they were using them. As the state secretary of the CFMEU, Andrew Vickers, stated:

> ... the miners were not against drug-testing but did not want a half-baked scheme put up as part of a feelgood exercise by management. Peeing in a cup and submitting that for drug testing will not tell you if you're stressed or fatigued. We want proper procedures and protocols used and genuine safety measures, not just more arrows in the company's quiver of punitive measures.

The second issue identified was the inability of substance testing to accurately gauge the level of employee impairment while on duty. It was the contention of the unions that substance testing may be inherently flawed. In addition, union representatives noted that if the issue was OHS, then measures of impairment and chemical ingestion relating to the work itself should also be included in these safety procedures. As Steve Pierce of the CFMEU stated:

> ... The union wanted pupil dilation tests and psychmotor tests (which measure average reaction times), and protocols including anonymity, protection from legal action and proven validity attached to urine testing. It also wanted increasing use of 12-hour shifts examined in tandem with fatigue and stress tests. Finding out down the line that you've dangerous practices is too late ... I believe tests for impairment are probably more accurate than just a test for presence of substance ... We're not condoning the use of illegal substances, but a person could be measured to have it in his system when in fact there is no impairment.

Representatives of the CFMEU maintained this argument—while agreeing that drug-testing procedures were consistent with the company's 'fitness for duty' policy, these procedures needed to form part of a 'proper set of comprehensive procedures' aimed at the detection of fatigue and stress levels as well as illicit substance abuse and subsequent employee rehabilitation. The CFMEU's counter position focused on four points:

1. The union will refuse to allow members to submit for drug testing if the employees are collectively unhappy with the intrusion into their personal lives.
2. The testing of urine samples does not reveal the extent of impairment, with some drugs staying in the human body long after any significant effects have 'worn off'.
3. The drug-testing policy discounts any analysis of why the employee is taking illicit substances, focusing only on the question as to whether they are taking drugs. Such a lack of analysis fails to indicate whether working conditions may be partly responsible for employee dependence upon illicit substances (for example, 12-hour shifts, work stress levels, poor job satisfaction and unrealistic deadlines).
4. The drug-testing policy fails to test for chemicals that may enter the bloodstream of an employee via their work duties (for example, carbon dioxide levels and excessive dust particles). These may be harmful and adversely affect their performance.

Source: Based on P. Holland, 2003, 'Case study: drug testing in the Australian mining industry', *Surveillance and Society*, 1 (2), 2003, pp. 204–9, www.surveillance-and-society.org.

QUESTIONS

1. Is drug testing more important than employee privacy?
2. Senior management at SBCL argue that it needs to implement drug testing in order to ensure the safety of employees and visitors at their mine site. Union representatives have argued that such drug testing would result in an inappropriate invasion of employees' privacy. Summarise the arguments for and against drug testing.
3. What ethical principles underlie these arguments?
4. Which arguments do you find most convincing?

CHAPTER 16
INTERNATIONAL HUMAN RESOURCE MANAGEMENT

Peter J. Dowling

Objectives

After reading this chapter, you should be able to:

1 Understand the historically significant issue of expatriate assignment management and review the evolution of these assignments to reflect the increasing diversity with regard to what constitutes international work and the type and length of international assignments.

2 Outline the differences between domestic and international human resource management, and detail a model which summarises the variables that moderate these differences.

3 Understand the complexity of international HRM, the increasing potential for challenges to existing international HRM practices and current models, and an increasing awareness of the wide number of choices within international HRM practices due to increased transparency and faster and more detailed diffusion of these practices across organisational units and firms.

Internationally mobile

The easiest part of any international assignment is catching the plane from one country to another. The hardest part starts with the HR department, well before take-off. Teresa Russell talks with two HR professionals who successfully manage a large and diverse number of employees on international assignments.

In the past, the role of HR in international assignments was to manage the processes involved in getting an employee from one country to another. This ranged from drafting employment contracts for the period of expatriation, ensuring salaries and expenses were paid in the right currencies, into the right accounts in the right countries, and liaising with removalists, travel agents and real estate agents to get the person, their family and their belongings moved.

Although all these things still need to occur, a level of sophistication has now developed around international assignments. Other issues such as security, global talent management and managing the needs of a wide range of international assignees (age, experience, life stage, skill sets) are relatively recent challenges.

Two companies that have well-developed international assignment strategies, policies and procedures are Unisys and Fonterra. Unisys is a worldwide technology services and solutions company, providing expertise in consulting, systems integration, outsourcing, infrastructure, and server technology. Melanie Laing is its Sydney-based regional human resources director, Asia Pacific, responsible for 4500 employees in 13 countries. She is therefore also responsible for all international assignees in the region.

Fonterra Co-operative Group Ltd collects milk from its 11 600 New Zealand-based shareholders (dairy farmers), processes it into a range of products and markets those products globally in 140 countries. With annual revenue of NZ$12.3 ($11.2) billion, Fonterra is the fourth-largest dairy company in the world by revenue, and second in the volume of milk processed annually. It employs 20 000 people globally. Deborah de Cerff is Fonterra's Auckland-based global mobility centre manager, responsible for the administration of the company's 148 short- and long-term international assignees who are currently posted in 40 countries.

Profile of assignees

There used to be a typical profile of an expatriate in many companies: male, aged between 30 and 40, moving up the ladder and getting an overseas appointment to round out their company experience on the way to a top job. These days, both Unisys and Fonterra see a wide variety of employees on international assignment.

'The employee we choose depends on the commercial imperative, which always comes first. It includes top talent, but may just be those who possess a wide variety of competencies. We transfer people both ways to and from head office, and we already have a diverse working population, locally recruited, in Australia', explains Laing.

Fonterra defines six different types of mobile employees. 'The business need determines who actually goes where, but the plan is to ensure that a skills transfer and development of local expertise occurs as a result of an international assignment', says de Cerff. She says that the globally mobile workforce today differs from the traditional expatriate of 18 years ago, when she started working as a consultant in the international transfer market.' There are a growing number of employees travelling on extended business trips, as well as a wide range of assignees. Those from Generation X and Y have different needs and motivations compared to baby boomers. This wide variety of expectations need to be accommodated in each employee's contract', says de Cerff.

All in the family

The hardest things to get right are usually the personal issues involved in the transfer of the assignee's family, according to Laing at Unisys. These include whether the partner can work, what schooling

Internationally mobile *continued*

options are available and whether for example, a son or daughter with special needs can be provided with the right resources in the posting country. 'You must spend time with the employee up front and ensure transparency from them so these issues can be solved and dealt with. Manage the issues sensitively and offer some flexibility', suggests Laing.

De Cerff agrees, although she has special challenges because of the large numbers of countries she deals with, having just a few assignees in each. 'It is difficult to stay in touch with the housing market and schooling system in the back blocks of Venezuela, for example, so we rely heavily on our joint venture partners or destination service companies to provide up-to-date information. You must recognise the individual personal needs of each family', she says.

Proven systems

Both companies were asked what they did well when it came to international assignments. Each said it was the way they managed the whole term of the contract.

Fonterra created its global mobility centre four years ago, acknowledging the importance of a consistent, fair and equitable approach across what were once all different businesses. A centralised approach also allows de Cerff and her team to track spending, achieve better returns and apply good ideas across the global business.

Unisys believes it is very organised around the important issues of legal, tax, housing and schooling, as it has chosen the right partners in these areas. According to Laing, the assignee has always had previous exposure to the country they are going to be living in, because of frequent shorter business trips in the past.

Where to next?

Both Fonterra and Unisys promise overseas assignees that they will be repatriated at company expense, but there is no guarantee of any, or any particular job at the end of an assignment. 'We start planning six to eight months before the end of an assignment and do our best to find them a position that suits. We have a lot of back-to-back international assignments, because of the technical competencies people have and the fact that our objective is to transfer knowledge to local markets', says de Cerff.

Attraction or retention?

Laing believes that Unisys' international mobility strategy has a part to play as a retention mechanism for some of its employees. She says strategies have to be customised, especially to appeal to Generation Xs and Ys.

De Cerff believes overseas assignments are an integral part of Fonterra's attraction and retention strategies. 'However, we don't market them in those terms. They depend on the business needs and a certain person's skill set at a particular point in time.'

Unisys' internationally mobile tips

- Know what is happening with competitors
- Talk to professional providers
- Don't underestimate the costs or challenges
- Have all systems, policies and programs in place, but allow flexibility
- Be organised

Source: M. Laing, regional human resources director, Asia Pacific, Unisys.

Fonterra's internationally mobile tips

- **Understand your business**
- **Identify future talent requirements (skill vs knowledge based)**
- **Be flexible to reflect changes in political and business environments**
- **Have clear objectives for sending someone on assignment**
- **Get specialist advice—especially on tax, immigration and government legislation**
- **Security—know where employee population is and keep them informed**
- **Logistics—ensure everything is covered before departure**
- **Immigration—know what passport your assignee holds**
- **Health cover—make sure emergency evacuation plans are included**
- **Cultural briefings—either outsource this or use internal mentors**

Source: Deborah de Cerff, global mobility centre manager, Fonterra.

Source: T. Russell, 2006, 'Internationally mobile', *Human Resources*, 6 February, pp. 18–19.
www.humanresourcesmagazine.com.au

Introduction

As shown by the examples in the opening case study, the globalisation of business is forcing managers to grapple with complex issues as they seek to gain or sustain a competitive advantage. Globalisation has impacted significantly on many organisations, with various implications for human resource management. Faced with unprecedented levels of foreign competition at home and overseas, firms are beginning to recognise that not only is international business high on the list of priorities for top management, but they are also beginning to recognise that finding and nurturing the human resources required to implement an international or global strategy is of critical importance.[1]

The field of **international HRM** has been characterised by three broad approaches.[2] The first[3] emphasises cross-cultural management: examining human behaviour within organisations from an international perspective. A second approach developed from the comparative industrial relations and HRM literature[4] and seeks to describe, compare and analyse HRM systems in various countries. A third approach seeks to focus on aspects of HRM in **multinational enterprises**.[5] These approaches are depicted in Figure 16.1. In this chapter, we take the third approach. Our objective is to explore the implications that the process of internationalisation has for the activities and policies of HRM. In particular, we are interested in how HRM is practised in multinationals.

As Figure 16.1 demonstrates, there is an inevitable overlap between the three approaches when one is attempting to provide an accurate view of the global realities of operating in the international business environment. Obviously, cross-cultural management issues are important when dealing with the cultural aspects of foreign operations as are the contextual issues of industrial relations and legal requirements of a local national jurisdiction. While the focus of much of this chapter is on the established multinational enterprise (MNE)—a firm which owns or controls business activities in more than one foreign country—it is also important to note that small, internationalising firms which are yet to reach multinational firm status, and family-owned firms, also face international HRM issues.[6]

International HRM (IHRM)
the field of study related to the interplay among human resource activities, types of employees and countries of operation.

Multinational enterprise (MNE)
an enterprise that conducts transactions in or between two countries, with a system of decision making that permits influence over resources and capabilities, where the transactions are subject to influence by factors external to the parent country of the enterprise.

Defining international HRM

Before we can offer a definition of international HRM, we should first define the general field of HRM. Typically, HRM refers to those activities undertaken by an organisation to effectively utilise its human resources. These activities would include at least the following:

1. human resource planning
2. staffing (recruitment, selection, placement)
3. performance management
4. training and development
5. compensation (remuneration) and benefits
6. industrial relations.

The question is, of course, which activities change when HRM goes international. A model (shown in Figure 16.2 overleaf) developed by Morgan, is helpful. He presents IHRM on three dimensions:

PART 5   Contemporary Issues for Human Resource Management

FIGURE 16.1 Inter-relationships between approaches to the field

Cross-cultural management — a — IHRM in the multinational context — b — Comparative HR and IR sysems

1 The broad human resource activities of procurement, allocation and utilisation. (These three broad activities can be easily expanded into the six HR activities listed above).
2 The national or country categories involved in international HRM activities:
   - the **host-country** where a subsidiary may be located
   - the home-country where the firm is headquartered
   - 'other' countries that may be the source of labour, finance and other inputs
3 The three categories of employees of an international firm:
   - **Host-country nationals (HCNs)**
   - **Parent-country nationals (PCNs)**
   - **Third-country nationals (TCNs).**

Host country the country in which the parent-country organisation seeks to locate or has already located a facility.

Host-country nationals (HCNs) employees born and raised in a host country.

Parent-country nationals (PCNs) employees who were born and live in a parent country.

Third-country nationals (TCNs) employees born in a country other than a parent or host country.

Thus, for example, the US multinational IBM employs Australian citizens in its Australian operations (HCNs), often sends US citizens (PCNs) to Asia-Pacific countries on assignment, and may send some of its Singaporean employees on an assignment to its Japanese operations (as TCNs). The nationality of the employee is a major factor in determining the person's 'category' which in turn is frequently a major driver of the employee's compensation.

Morgan defines international HRM as 'the interplay among these three dimensions in Figure 16.2 — human resource activities, type of employees, and countries of operation'. We can see that in broad terms international HRM involves the same activities as domestic HRM (for example, procurement refers to HR planning and staffing). However, domestic HRM is involved with employees *within*

FIGURE 16.2 A model of IHRM

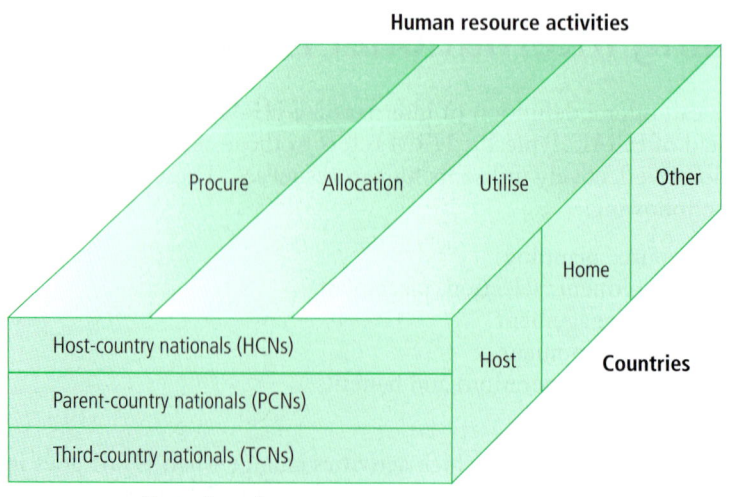

Human resource activities: Procure, Allocation, Utilise, Other

Countries: Home, Host

Type of employees: Host-country nationals (HCNs), Parent-country nationals (PCNs), Third-country nationals (TCNs)

Source: Adapted from P.V. Morgan, 1986, 'International Human Resource Management: Fact or Fiction', *Personnel Administrator*, 31(9), p. 44.

only one national boundary. Increasingly, domestic HRM is taking on some of the flavour of international HRM as it deals more and more with a multicultural workforce. Thus, some of the current focus of domestic HRM on issues of managing workforce diversity may prove to be beneficial to the practice of international HRM. However, it must be remembered that the way in which diversity is managed within a single national context may not necessarily transfer to a multinational context without some modification.

What is an expatriate?

One obvious difference between domestic and international HRM is that staff are moved across national boundaries into various roles within the international firm's foreign operations—these employees have traditionally been called '**expatriates**'. An expatriate is an employee who is working and temporarily residing in a foreign country. Some firms prefer to call such employees 'international assignees'. While it is clear in the literature that PCNs are always expatriates, it is often overlooked that TCNs are expatriates, as are HCNs who are transferred into **parent-country** operations outside their home country.[8] Figure 16.3 illustrates how all three categories may become expatriates.

Lately, the term '*inpatriate*' has come into vogue to signify the transfer of subsidiary staff into the parent country (headquarters) operations.[9] Its use has added a level of confusion surrounding the definition of an expatriate. For example, the *International Human Resource Management Reference Guide*, published by the Institute for International Human Resources (a division of the US Society for Human Resource Management), defines an inpatriate as a 'foreign manager in the US'. A 'foreign manager in the US' is then defined as 'an expatriate in the US where the US is the host-country and the manager's home-country is outside of the US'.[10] In other words, an inpatriate is also defined as an expatriate. A further indication of the confusion created by the use of the term 'inpatriate' is that some writers in international management define a HCN as an inpatriate. HCNs only become 'inpatriates' when they are transferred into the parent country operations as expatriates, as illustrated in Figure 16.3.

Given the substantial amount of jargon in international HRM, it is questionable as to whether the term 'inpatriate' adds enough value to justify its use. However, companies now use the term. For example, the Finnish multinational Nokia uses 'expatriate' to signify staff who are transferred out of, and 'inpatriate' to signify staff

Expatriates
employees sent by their company in one country to work in a different country.

parent country
(also known as the home country) the country in which a company's corporate headquarters is located.

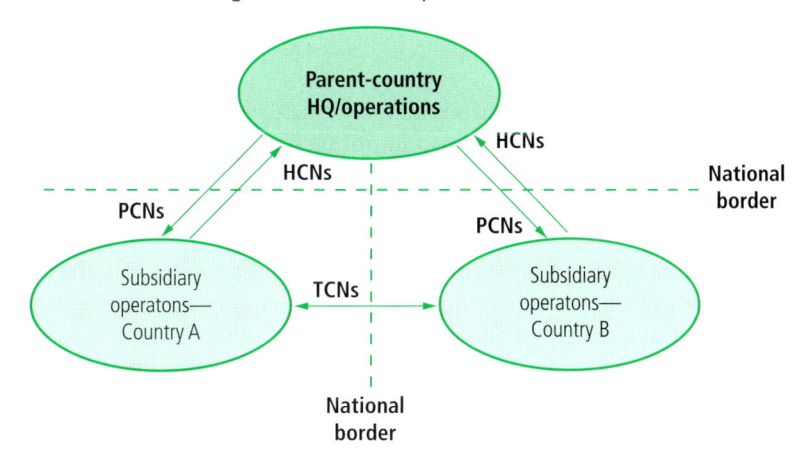

FIGURE 16.3 International assignments create expatriates

transferred into, a particular country. These terms are regarded as a constant reminder to all managers that there are movements of staff that need to be managed, and not all are PCNs. For clarity, we will use the term expatriate to refer to employees who are transferred out of their home base into some other area of the firm's international operations, unless we are directly quoting from another source. In doing so, we recognise that there is increasing diversity with regard to what constitutes international work and the type and length of international assignments and the increasingly strategic role of the HR function in many organisations which in turn influences the nature of some expatriate roles. As discussed in 'Managing challenges through HR innovation: Hands across the seas', there continue to be new roles emerging in international management.

Stahl and Björkman have recognised this expansion in the scope of the field of IHRM in their recently published *Handbook of Research in International Human Resource Management* where they define the field of IHRM in the following way:

> ... we define the field of IHRM broadly to cover all issues related to the management of people in an international context. Hence our definition of IHRM covers a wide range of human resource issues facing MNCs in different parts of their organizations. Additionally, we include comparative analyses of HRM in different countries.[11]

Differences between domestic and international HRM

In our view, the *complexity* of operating in different countries and employing different national categories of workers is a key variable that differentiates domestic and international HRM, rather than any major differences between the HRM activities performed. Dowling[12] argues that the complexity of international HR can be attributed to six factors:

1. more HR activities
2. the need for a broader perspective
3. more involvement in employees' personal lives
4. changes in emphasis as the workforce mix of expatriates and locals varies
5. risk exposure
6. broader external influences.

Each of these factors is now discussed in detail to illustrate its characteristics.

More HR activities

To operate in an international environment, a human resources department must engage in a number of activities that would not be necessary in a domestic environment: international taxation; international relocation and orientation; administrative services for expatriates; host-government relations; and language translation services.

Expatriates are subject to international taxation, and often have both domestic (that is, home country) and host country tax liabilities. Therefore, tax equalisation policies must be designed to ensure that there is no tax incentive or disincentive associated with any particular international assignment.[13] The administration of tax equalisation policies is complicated by the wide variations in tax laws across host countries and by the possible time lag between the completion of an expatriate assignment and the

HANDS ACROSS THE SEAS

Working efficiently and profitably in virtual teams spread around the globe requires more than the usual competencies and organisational processes. Siemens' Monika Altmaier investigates what is involved in transforming global, virtual business and what the role of HR should be.

Employees in Melbourne and Perth, customers in Madrid, suppliers in Dubai, partners in Bangalore, London and Shanghai, the HR department in Brisbane. Nowadays, relationships like these tend to be the rule rather than the exception. Tough global forces, such as international competitiveness, cost pressure, tighter deadlines, customer focus, fast product cycles, innovation demands and increasing globalisation, are driving companies to do business in project-based trans-national virtual teams. Global business time is 24 hours a day, 365 days per year. That is why companies such as IBM, EADS and Siemens have made virtual team skills one of the core competencies for their managers and employees running their global business.

MANAGING CHALLENGES THROUGH HR INNOVATION

Global transformation in Siemens

Like any global company, Siemens, which has 450 000 employees in 190 countries, needs to respond to these new forces in business. We also recognised new business models for outsourcing, insourcing, off-shoring, cost-cutting, sales initiatives, the diminishing availability of resources and the global acceleration of commercial activity.

We saw that one crucial means of making these transformations was through virtual teaming. We needed to create the environment and processes so that our people could work together closely across geographic and organisational boundaries, communicating electronically rather than travelling.

HR as a driving force for global success through virtual teaming

Who else, if not HR professionals, should drive organisation-wide, systemic transformational initiatives? Here is how Siemens' HR organisational departments were involved.

Our success would not have been possible without the involvement of top management ensuring immediate and high-level leadership communication between headquarters and the relevant countries and also ensuring the concept was endorsed locally.

New incentive and reward systems, new career paths and new promotion criteria were defined together with HR so that virtual managers did not feel they were losing promotion opportunities because they were not as visible as other managers.

We saw that constant accessibility, even on the road and during leisure time, makes it possible to delocalise the workplace. HR supported the change towards more remote ways of working by offering flexible working times, agreements and contracts.

We enhanced innovation and creativity by ensuring team diversity and by empowering the team members with the help of change agents. Resistance to change was overcome by communicating frequently, honestly, consistently and continuously.

HR helped us with the analysis and design of organisational and virtual team components, and defined virtual team values and boundaries. In kick-off face-to-face workshops with newly forming virtual teams we defined a clear vision, binding mission and shared purpose. The responsibilities, roles and accountabilities were clearly fixed and recorded in a charter. Building trust-based personal relationships was crucial at this stage and that is why we started with face-to-face workshops.

Personal lessons learned

I would advise any organisation embarking on virtual teaming as a systemic initiative to put the following into practice:

- Set up virtual teams as a company-wide project hand in hand with business transformation while standardising virtual teaming process across the organisation.
- Establish the right balance between rules and freedom to encourage creativity and innovation (the global/local dimension).
- Expand virtual teaming competencies in the organisation by letting inexperienced people work together with experienced people.

Organisational benefits achieved through 'going virtual'

At Siemens we are increasing productivity, cost-effectiveness and efficiency through virtual teaming. Going virtual shortens product development cycles by up to 50 per cent. We are able to reduce travel expenses and make better use of time by minimising the cost of arranging and supporting face-to-face meetings.

Five key points

1. Tough global forces, such as international competitiveness, are driving companies to do business in trans-national virtual project teams.
2. Some companies anticipate that in five years time, employees will do 50 per cent of their work virtually.
3. Working virtually can, in some cases, shorten product development cycles by up to 50 per cent.
4. The challenges posed by working in global, virtual teams include not just technological issues but also business process, management and cultural issues.
5. Remote working has a social impact—for example, on leisure time—but HR can support employees by offering flexible working times and contracts.

Source: Excerpt from M. Altmaier, 2006, 'Hands across the seas', *Human Resources*, 24 January. www.humanresourcesmagazine.com.au

settlement of domestic and international tax liabilities. In recognition of these difficulties, many multinational firms retain the services of a major accounting firm for international taxation advice.

International relocation and orientation involves arranging for predeparture training; providing immigration and travel details; providing housing, shopping, medical care, recreation, and schooling information; and finalising compensation details such as delivery of salary overseas, determination of various overseas allowances, and taxation treatment. Many of these factors may be a source of anxiety for the expatriate and require considerable time and attention to successfully resolve potential problems—certainly much more time than would be involved in a domestic transfer/relocation such as London to Glasgow, Frankfurt to Munich, New York to Dallas, Sydney to Melbourne, or Beijing to Shanghai.

A multinational firm also needs to provide administrative services for expatriates in the host countries in which it operates. Providing these can often be a time-consuming and complex activity because policies and procedures are not always clear-cut and may conflict with local conditions. For example, ethical questions can arise when a practice that is legal and accepted in the host country may be at best unethical and at worst illegal in the home country. For example, a situation may arise in which a host country requires an AIDS test for a work permit for an employee whose parent firm is headquartered in the United States, where employment-related AIDS testing remains a controversial issue. How does the corporate HR manager deal with the potential expatriate employee who refuses to meet this requirement for an AIDS test and the overseas affiliate which needs the services of a specialist expatriate from headquarters? These issues add to the complexity of providing administrative services to expatriates.

Host-government relations represent an important activity for a HR department, particularly in developing countries where work permits and other important certificates are often more easily obtained when a personal relationship exists between the relevant government officials and multinational managers. Maintaining such relationships helps resolve potential problems that can be caused by ambiguous eligibility and/or compliance criteria for documentation such as work permits. US-based multinationals, however, must be careful in how they deal with relevant government officials, as payment or payment-in-kind, such as dinners and gifts, may violate the US *Foreign Corrupt Practices Act*.[14] Provision of language translation services for internal and external correspondence is an additional international activity for the HR department. Morgan[15] notes that if the HR department is the major user of language translation services, the role of this translation group is often expanded to provide translation services to all foreign operation departments within the multinational.

The need for a broader perspective

HR managers working in a domestic environment generally administer programs for a single national group of employees who are covered by a uniform compensation policy and taxed by one national government. Because HR managers working in an international environment face the problem of designing and administering programs for more than one national group of employees (example, PCN, HCN and TCN employees who may work together in Zurich at the European regional headquarters of a US-based multinational), they need to take a broader view of issues. For example, a broader, more international perspective on expatriate benefits would endorse the view that all expatriate employees, regardless of nationality, should receive a foreign service or expatriate premium when working in a foreign location. Yet some multinationals which routinely pay such premiums to their PCN employees on overseas assignment (even if the assignments are to desirable locations) are reluctant to pay premiums to foreign nationals assigned to the home country of the firm. Such a policy confirms the traditional perception of many HCN and TCN employees that PCN employees (particularly US and European PCNs) are given preferential treatment.[16] Complex equity issues arise when employees of various nationalities work together, and the resolution of these issues remains one of the major challenges in the international HRM field.

More involvement in employees' personal lives

A greater degree of involvement in employees' personal lives is necessary for the selection, training and effective management of both PCN and TCN employees. The HR department or HR professional needs to ensure that the expatriate employee understands housing arrangements, health care, and all aspects of the compensation package provided for the assignment (cost-of-living allowances, premiums, taxes and so on). Many multinationals have an 'International HR Services' section that coordinates administration of the above programs and provides services for PCNs and TCNs such as handling their banking, investments, home rental while on assignment, coordinating home visits and final repatriation.

Repatriation
the preparation of expatriates for return to the parent company and country from a foreign assignment.

In the domestic setting, the HR department's involvement with an employee's family is limited. The firm may, for example, provide employee health insurance programs. Or, if a domestic transfer is involved, the HR department may provide some assistance in relocating the employee and family. In the international setting, however, the HR department must be much more involved in order to provide the level of support required and will need to know more about the employee's personal life. For example, some governments require the presentation of a marriage certificate before granting a visa to an accompanying spouse. Thus, marital status could become an aspect of the selection process, regardless of the best intentions of the firm to avoid using a potentially discriminatory selection criterion. In such a situation, the HR department should advise all candidates being considered for the position of the host country's visa requirements with regard to marital status and allow candidates to decide whether they wish to remain in the selection process. Apart from providing suitable housing and schooling in the assignment location, the HR department may also need to assist children left behind at boarding schools in the home country.[17] In more remote or less hospitable assignment locations, the HR department may be required to develop, and even run, recreational programs. For a domestic assignment, most of these matters either would not arise or would be primarily the responsibility of the employee rather than the HR department.

Changes in emphasis as the workforce mix of PCNs and HCNs varies

As foreign operations mature, the emphases put on various human resource activities change. For example, as the need for PCNs and TCNs declines and more trained locals become available, resources previously allocated to areas such as expatriate taxation, relocation and orientation are transferred to activities such as local staff selection, training and management development. The latter activity may require establishment of a program to bring high-potential local staff to corporate headquarters for developmental assignments. The need to change emphasis in HR operations as a foreign subsidiary matures is clearly a factor that would broaden the responsibilities of local HR activities such as human resource planning, staffing, training and development, and compensation.

Risk exposure

Expatriate failure (also premature termination) the premature return of an expatriate from an international assignment.

Frequently, the human and financial consequences of failure in the international arena are more severe than in domestic business. For example, **expatriate failure** (the premature return of an expatriate from an international assignment) and underperformance while on international assignment, is a potentially high-cost problem for international companies. Direct costs (salary, training costs, and travel and relocation expenses) per failure to the parent firm may be as high as three times the domestic salary plus relocation expenses, depending on currency exchange rates and location of assignments. Indirect costs such as loss of foreign market share and damage to key host country relationships may be considerable.

Another aspect of risk exposure that is relevant to international HRM is terrorism, particularly in the current political climate since the tragic 9/11 event in New York in 2001. Most major multinationals must now consider political risk and terrorism when planning international meetings and assignments, and spending on protection against terrorism is increasing. Terrorism has also clearly had an effect on the way in which employees assess potential international assignment locations.[18] The HR department may also need to devise emergency evacuation procedures for highly volatile assignment locations subject to political or terrorist violence or major epidemic or pandemic crises such as severe acute respiratory syndrome (SARS) and avian influenza.[19] For a comprehensive analysis of the impact of SARS on human resource management in the Hong Kong service sector, see Lee and Warner.[20]

Broader external influences

The major external factors that influence international HRM are the type of government, the state of the economy, and the generally accepted practices of doing business in each of the various host countries in which the multinational operates. A host government can, for example, dictate hiring procedures, as has been the case until recently in Malaysia. The Malaysian government during the 1970s introduced a requirement that foreign firms comply with an extensive set of affirmative action rules designed to provide additional employment opportunities for the indigenous Malays who constitute the majority of the population but tend to be underrepresented in business and professional employment groups relative to Chinese Malays and Indian Malays. Various statistics showing employment levels of indigenous Malays throughout the firm were required to be forwarded to the relevant government department. Many foreign investors regarded these requirements as a major reason for complaints about bureaucracy and inflexibility in Malaysia and these complaints are one significant reason for the revision of these requirements.

In developed countries, labour is more expensive and better organised than in less-developed countries, and governments require compliance with guidelines on issues such as labour relations, taxation, and health and safety. These factors shape the activities of the subsidiary HR manager to a considerable extent. In less-developed countries, labour tends to be cheaper and less organised, and government regulation is less pervasive, so these factors take less time. The subsidiary HR manager must spend more time, however, learning and interpreting the local ways of doing business and the general code of conduct regarding activities such as gift giving. It is also likely that the subsidiary HR manager will become more involved in administering benefits either provided or financed by the multinational such as housing, education, and other facilities not readily available in the local economy.

Also, as discussed in 'Managing challenges through attracting and retaining people: What graduates want', there are significant developments in many countries, such as China, and these have implications for the expectations held by employees and employers with regard to HR practices.

WHAT GRADUATES WANT

MANAGING CHALLENGES THROUGH ATTRACTING AND RETAINING PEOPLE

Finding a job is similar to looking for Mr or Miss Right, and the resulting relationship hinges greatly on mutual respect and compromise.

At least that's how Wang Yingmin, a director with Headquarters Human Resources (HR) Department of Haier Group, sees it.

The search for a healthy marriage between employer and employee is especially important for recent graduates, who will get their first jobs and know little about work environment, says Wang.

'Companies or employers should offer chances for fresh blood and create opportunities for their career development', he says.

Haier and 49 other foreign and domestic enterprises were ranked among the Best Employers in Chinese Undergraduates' Eyes 2006, an annual HR award conducted by ChinaHR.com, a domestic professional human resources website.

Company requirements

Jason Zhang, president of ChinaHR.com, indicates that both Chinese and multinational companies are focusing on university students, the main force for the nation's future development, and have taken active steps to reach them.

Some of the companies voted among the Best Employers, such as IBM, Proctor & Gamble (P&G), Microsoft Corporation and Haier Group, hold regular campus job briefing conferences and fairs regularly to compete for the qualified recent graduates.

Some, including chain retailing conglomerate Wal-Mart, transnational elevator producer Otis Elevator Company and Motorola, have collaborated with universities to set up specific schools to train people for their companies or the industries they are engaged in.

IBM started its Undergraduate Summer Holiday Internship Programme three years ago, which allows hundreds of undergraduates to get hands-on experience in IBM's various departments. This helps them learn about the company's operation mechanism and corporate culture.

Around 60 per cent to 70 per cent of the interns enter IBM as employees after graduation, says Kuang Haodong, talent and study managing director of IBM Greater China's HR department. About 30 to 50 per cent of IBM China's new employees come straight out of university each year.

ChinaHR.com's Zhang points out that those voted Best Employers emphasise the comprehensive qualities of graduates and are interested in those with clear targets who know exactly what they want and can do.

'Sunny guys with open minds and team-work spirit are favoured', says Zhang. 'Additionally, they should boast basic knowledge about the company.'

Compensation, including competitive salary, training opportunities, promotion space, working conditions and flexible working time are the most crucial elements influencing graduates' choices, according to the ChinaHR.com survey.

The corporate brand, which includes reputation and inter-sector influential ability, market prospects and the personality of corporate leader, is next on the priority list.

Most graduates are indifferent about corporate culture, a factor determined by employer-to-employee relations, HR ideology and human relations.

Vice-chairman of Beijing HR Service Industrial Association, Zhang Yuquan, believes that the government should encourage the establishment of qualified HR service agencies to build bridges between job seekers and employers.

'In universities, similar facilities should be set up to not only provide information but also offer guidance and consultant services for students', he adds.

ChinaHR.com's survey reveals that more than 90 per cent of undergraduates access networking websites when looking for a job.

Job fairs come in second place, with 78.6 per cent of interviewees saying they have attended one in the hunt for work.

About half of the surveyed students get job information from their university job guidance centres and posters around campuses.

'Intermediary agencies can build bridges between enterprises and undergraduates to avoid imbalanced information supply and acquisition', says Haier's Wang, adding that it will be common sense that a good matchmaker is helpful in creating a successful marriage.

Source: Excerpt from Anonymous, 2006, 'What graduates want', *Industry Updates*, 31 July. Copyright 2006 China Daily Information Company. All Rights Reserved.

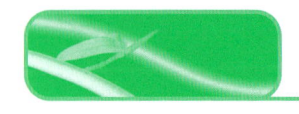

Variables that moderate differences between domestic and international HRM

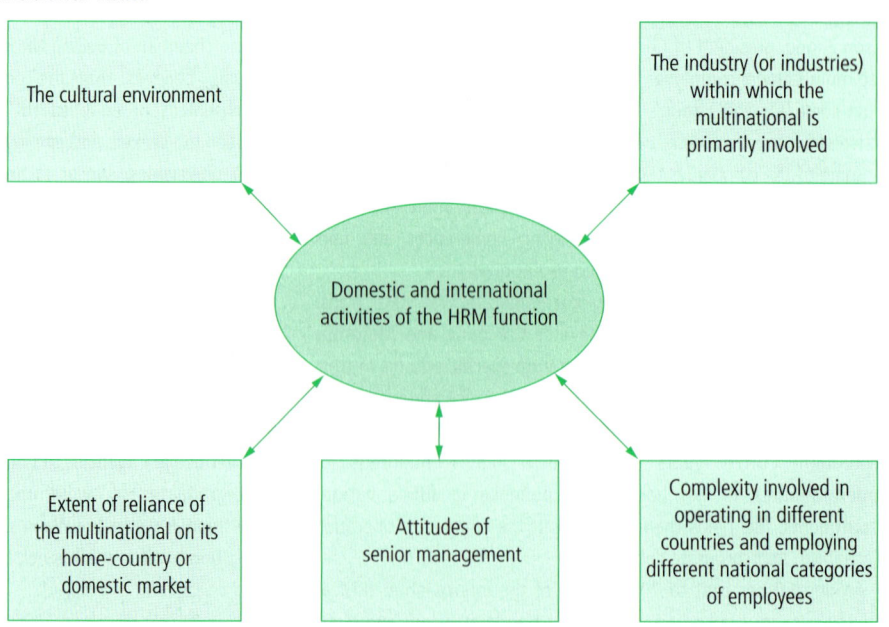

Earlier in this chapter it was argued that the *complexity involved in operating in different countries and employing different national categories of employees* is a key variable that differentiates domestic and international HRM, rather than any major differences between the HRM activities performed. Many firms underestimate the complexities involved in international operations, and there has been consistent evidence to suggest that business failures in the international arena are often linked to poor management of human resources. In addition to complexity, there are four other variables that moderate (that is, either diminish or accentuate) differences between domestic and international HRM. These four additional moderators are:

1. the cultural environment
2. the industry (or industries) with which the multinational is primarily involved
3. the extent of reliance of the multinational on its home-country domestic market
4. the attitudes of senior management.

Together with the complexity involved in operating in different countries, these five variables constitute a model which explains the differences between domestic and international HRM (see Figure 16.4).

The cultural environment

There are many definitions of *culture*, but the term is usually used to describe a shaping process over time. This process generates relative stability, reflecting a shared knowledge structure that attenuates (that is, reduces) variability in values, behavioural

FIGURE 16.4 A model of the variables that moderate differences between domestic and international HRM

Source: P.J. Dowling, 1999, 'Completing the Puzzle: Issues in the Development of the Field of International Human Resource Management', *Management International Review*, Special Issue No. 3, p. 31. Reproduced with permission.

norms and patterns of behaviour.[21] An important characteristic of culture is that it is so subtle a process that one is not always conscious of its effect on values, attitudes, and behaviours. One usually has to be confronted with a different culture in order to fully appreciate this effect. Anyone travelling abroad, either as a tourist or on business, experiences situations that demonstrate cultural differences in language, food, dress, hygiene and attitude to time. While the traveller can perceive these differences as novel, even enjoyable, for people required to live and work in a new country, such differences can prove difficult. They may experience **culture shock**—a phenomenon experienced by people who move across cultures. The new environment requires many adjustments in a relatively short period of time, challenging people's frames of reference to such an extent that their sense of self, especially in terms of nationality, comes into question. People, in effect, experience a shock reaction to new cultural experiences that cause psychological disorientation because they misunderstand or do not recognise important cues. Culture shock can lead to negative feelings about the host country and its people and a longing to return home.[22]

Because international business involves the interaction and movement of people across national boundaries, an appreciation of cultural differences and when these differences are important is essential. Research into these aspects has assisted in furthering our understanding of the cultural environment as an important variable that moderates differences between domestic and international HRM. However, while cross-cultural and comparative research attempts to explore and explain similarities and differences, there are problems associated with such research. A major problem is that there is little agreement on either an exact definition of culture or on the operationalisation of this concept. For many researchers, culture has become an omnibus variable, representing a range of social, historic, economic and political factors that are invoked *post hoc* to explain similarity or dissimilarity in the results of a study. As Bhagat and McQuaid[23] have noted:

> Culture has often served simply as a synonym for nation without any further conceptual grounding. In effect, national differences found in the characteristics of organizations or their members have been interpreted as cultural differences.

To reduce these difficulties, culture needs to be defined *a priori* rather than *post hoc* and it should not be assumed that national differences necessarily represent cultural differences.

Another issue in cross-cultural research concerns the *emic–etic* distinction.[24] **Emic** refers to culture-specific aspects of concepts or behaviour, and **etic** refers to culture-common aspects. These terms have been borrowed from linguistics: A phon*emic* system documents meaningful sounds specific to a given language, and a phon*etic* system organises all sounds that have meaning in any language.[25] Both the emic and etic approaches are legitimate research orientations. A major problem may arise, however, if a researcher imposes an etic approach (that is, assumes universality across cultures) when there is little or no evidence for doing so. A well-known example of an imposed etic approach is the **convergence hypothesis** that dominated much of US and European management research in the 1950s and 1960s. This approach was based on two key assumptions.[26] The first assumption was that there were principles of sound management that held regardless of national environments. Thus, the existence of local or national practices that deviated from these principles simply indicated a need to change these local practices. The second assumption was that the universality of sound management practices would lead to societies becoming more and more alike in the future. Given that the United States was the leading industrial economy at that time, the point of convergence was the US model.

Culture shock
a phenomenon experienced by people who move across cultures. People, in effect, experience a shock reaction to new cultural experiences that cause psychological disorientation because they misunderstand or do not recognise important cues.

Emic
(also see etic) culture-specific aspects of concepts or behaviour.

Etic
(also see emic) culture-common aspects of concepts or behaviour.

Convergence hypothesis
the hypothesis that management practices around the world would converge, based on two assumptions. First, that there were principles of sound management that held regardless of national environments. Second, that the universality of sound management practices would lead to societies becoming more and more alike in the future.

Divergence hypothesis
in opposition to the convergence hypothesis, the notion that societies and management practices around the world will remain, or become more, dissimilar.

To use Kuhn's[27] terminology, the convergence hypothesis became an established paradigm that many researchers found difficult to give up, despite a growing body of evidence supporting a **divergence hypothesis**. In an important paper reviewing the convergence/divergence debate, Child[28] made the point that there is evidence for both convergence and divergence. The majority of the convergence studies, however, focus on macro-level variables (for example, organisational structure and technology used by firms across cultures), and the majority of the divergence studies focus on micro-level variables (for example, the behaviour of people within firms). His conclusion was that although firms in different countries are becoming more alike (an etic or convergence approach), the behaviour of individuals within these firms is maintaining its cultural specificity (an emic or divergence approach). As noted above, both emic and etic approaches are legitimate research orientations, but methodological difficulties may arise if the distinction between these two approaches is ignored or if unwarranted universality assumptions are made.[29] The debate on assumptions of universality is not limited to the literature in international management as this issue has also become a topic of debate in the field of international relations and strategic studies where international management research is cited.[30] For a recent review of the convergence/divergence question, see Brewster.[31]

The importance of cultural awareness

Despite the methodological concerns about cross-cultural research, it is now generally recognised that culturally insensitive attitudes and behaviours stemming from ignorance or from misguided beliefs ('my way is best', or 'what works at home will work here') not only are inappropriate but often cause international business failure. Therefore, an awareness of cultural differences is essential for the HR manager at corporate headquarters as well as in the host location.[32] Activities such as hiring, promoting, rewarding and dismissal will be determined by the practices of the host country and often are based on a value system peculiar to that country's culture. A firm may decide to head up a new overseas operation with an expatriate general manager but appoint as the HR department manager a local, a person who is familiar with the host country's HR practices. This practice can assist in avoiding problems but can still lead to dilemmas for senior managers. For example, in a number of developing countries (Indonesia is one such example) local employees feel an obligation to employ their extended family if they are in a position to do so. This may lead to a situation where staff are hired who do not possess the required technical competence. While this could be seen as a successful example of adapting to local expectations and customs, from a Western perspective this practice would be seen as nepotism, a negative practice which is not in the best interests of the enterprise because the best people have not been hired for the job.

Wyatt[33] recounts a good example of the fallacy of assuming 'what works at home will work here' when dealing with work situations in another culture. HR department staff of a large firm in Papua New Guinea were concerned over a number of accidents involving operators of very large, expensive, earthmoving vehicles. The expatriate managers investigating the accidents found that local drivers involved in the accidents were chewing betel nut, a common habit for most of the coastal peoples of Papua New Guinea and other Pacific islands. Associating the betel nut with depressants such as alcohol, the expatriate managers banned the chewing of betel nut during work hours. In another move to reduce the number of accidents, free coffee was provided at loading points, and drivers were required to alight from their vehicles at these locations. What the managers did not realise was that betel nut, like their culturally acceptable coffee, is, in fact, a stimulant, though some of the drivers were chewing it to cover up the fact that they drank beer before commencing work. As Wyatt points out, many indigenous workers used betel nut as a pick-me-up in much the same way as the expatriates used coffee.

Coping with cultural differences, and recognising how and when these differences are relevant, is a constant challenge for international firms. Helping to prepare staff and their families for working and living in a new cultural environment has become a key activity for HR departments in those multinationals that appreciate (or have been forced, through experience, to appreciate) the impact that the cultural environment can have on staff performance and wellbeing.

Hofstede's framework of national culture

Before leaving the issue of culture and cultural differences, it is appropriate to acknowledge the important contribution to the international management literature of the cultural typologies proposed over 25 years ago by Hofstede in his classic book *Culture's Consequences: International Differences in Work-Related Values* which proposed that national culture can be set out as a measurable set of constructs.[34] While a more detailed discussion is beyond the scope of this chapter, a very considerable literature has been generated since the initial publication of Hofstede's book, much of it examining the methodological limitations of the cultural dimensions proposed by Hofstede (Individualism/Collectivism; Power Distance; Masculinity/Femininity; and Uncertainty Avoidance).[35] Part of this literature includes conceptual critiques of Hofstede's work with a relatively recent paper by McSweeney generating a considerable amount of debate.[36] For a broader review of the contribution of Hofstede's work to the field of international management, see Hoppe,[37] Gerhart and Fang,[38] and Leung et al.[39]

Industry type

Porter[40] suggests that the industry (or industries if the firm is a conglomerate) in which a multinational firm is involved is of considerable importance because patterns of international competition vary widely from one industry to another. At one end of the continuum of international competition is the **multidomestic industry**, one in which competition in each country is essentially independent of competition in other countries. Traditional examples include retailing, distribution and insurance. At the other end of the continuum is the **global industry**, one in which a firm's competitive position in one country is significantly influenced by its position in other countries. Examples include commercial aircraft, semiconductors and copiers. The key distinction between a multidomestic industry and a global industry is described by Porter as follows:

> The global industry is not merely a collection of domestic industries but a series of linked domestic industries in which the rivals compete against each other on a truly worldwide basis … In a multi-domestic industry, then, international strategy collapses to a series of domestic strategies. The issues that are uniquely international revolve around how to do business abroad, how to select good countries in which to compete (or assess country risk), and mechanisms to achieve the one-time transfer of know-how. These are questions that are relatively well developed in the literature. In a global industry, however, managing international activities like a portfolio will undermine the possibility of achieving competitive advantage. In a global industry, a firm must in some way integrate its activities on a worldwide basis to capture the linkages among countries.

The role of the HRM function in multidomestic and global industries can be analysed using Porter's value-chain model.[41] In Porter's model, HRM is seen as one of

Multidomestic industry
an industry in which competition in each country is essentially independent of competition in other countries.

Global industry
an industry in which a firm's competitive position in one country is significantly influenced by its postion in other countries.

four support activities for the five primary activities of the firm. Since human resources are involved in each of the primary and support activities, the HRM function is seen as cutting across the entire value chain of a firm. If the firm is in a multidomestic industry, the role of the HR department will most likely be more domestic in structure and orientation. At times there may be considerable demand for international services from the HRM function (for example, when a new plant or office is established in a foreign location and the need for expatriate employees arises), but these activities would not be pivotal—indeed, many of these services may be provided via consultants and/or temporary employees. The main role for the HRM function would be to support the primary activities of the firm in each domestic market to achieve a competitive advantage through either cost/efficiency or product/service differentiation. If the multinational is in a global industry, however, the 'imperative for coordination' described by Porter would require a HRM function structured to deliver the international support required by the primary activities of the multinational.

The need to develop coordination raises complex problems for any multinational. As Laurent[42] has noted:

> In order to build, maintain, and develop their corporate identity, multinational organizations need to strive for consistency in their ways of managing people on a worldwide basis. Yet, and in order to be effective locally, they also need to adapt those ways to the specific cultural requirements of different societies. While the global nature of the business may call for increased consistency, the variety of cultural environments may be calling for differentiation.

Laurent proposes that a truly international conception of human resource management would require the following steps:

1 an explicit recognition by the parent organisation that its own peculiar ways of managing human resources reflect some assumptions and values of its home culture
2 an explicit recognition by the parent organisation that its peculiar ways are neither universally better nor worse than others but are different and likely to exhibit strengths and weaknesses, particularly abroad
3 an explicit recognition by the parent organisation that its foreign subsidiaries may have other preferred ways of managing people that are neither intrinsically better nor worse, but could possibly be more effective locally
4 a willingness from headquarters to not only acknowledge cultural differences, but also to take active steps in order to make them discussable and therefore usable
5 the building of a genuine belief by all parties involved that more creative and effective ways of managing people could be developed as a result of cross-cultural learning.

In offering this proposal, Laurent acknowledges that these are difficult steps that few firms have taken:

> They have more to do with states of mind and mindsets than with behaviors. As such, these processes can only be facilitated and this may represent a primary mission for executives in charge of international human resource management.[43]

Implicit in Laurent's analysis is the idea that by taking the steps he describes, a multinational attempting to implement a global strategy via coordination of activities would be better able to work through the difficulties and complex trade-offs inherent in such a strategy. Increasingly, multinationals are taking a more strategic approach to the role of HRM and are using staff transfers and training programs to assist in coordination of activities.

Reliance of the multinational on its home-country domestic market

A pervasive but often ignored factor which influences the behaviour of multinationals and resultant HR practices is the extent of reliance of the multinational on its home-country domestic market. When for example, we look through lists of very large firms (such as those that appear in *Fortune* and other business magazines), it is frequently assumed that a global market perspective would be dominant in the firm's culture and thinking. However, size is not the only key variable when looking at a multinational—the extent of reliance of the multinational on its home-country domestic market is also very important. In fact, for many firms, a small home market is one of the key drivers for seeking new international markets.

The United Nations Conference on Trade and Development (UNCTAD), in its annual survey of foreign direct investment, calculates what it refers to as an 'index of transnationality' which is an average of ratios of foreign assets to total assets; foreign sales to total sales; and foreign employment to total employment.[44] The 'top ten' multinationals are shown in Table 16.1. Based on this index of transnationality, the most foreign-oriented multinational is Thomson Corporation (Canada), with an average of 98 per cent of the three ratios (foreign assets to total assets, foreign sales to total sales, and foreign employment to total employment) located outside of Canada.

The only US firm in the first 20 multinationals ranked by the Transnational Index is the AES Corporation (electricity, gas and water), which the McDonald's Corporation is ranked 38th.[45] The reason for this lower ranking of US firms in terms of the Transnational Index is as obvious as it is important—*the size of the domestic market* for US firms. A very large domestic market (for US firms this is in effect the North American Free Trade Agreement [NAFTA] market) influences all aspects of

TABLE 16.1 World top 10 non-financial transnational corporations, ranked by transnational index

Transnational index	Ranking by foreign assets	Company name	Home economy	Industry
1	65	Thomson Corporation	Canada	Media
2	86	CRH Plc	Ireland	Lumber and other building materials
3	22	News Corporation	Australia	Media
4	27	Roche Group (Umoe AS)	Switzerland	Pharmaceuticals
5	92	Cadbury Schweppes Plc	United Kingdom	Food and beverage
6	44	Philips Electronics	The Netherlands	Electrical & electronic equipment
7	2	Vodaphone Group Plc	United Kingdom	Telecommunications
8	54	Alcan Inc.	Canada	Metal & metal products
9	89	Publicis Groupe SA	France	Business services
10	5	British Petroleum Company Plc	United Kingdom	Petroleum exploration, refining and distribution

Source: The data in this table is based on the World Investment Report, 2005, *TNCs and the Internationalisation of R&D*, United Nations Conference on Trade and Development (UNCTAD), September.

how a multinational organises its activities. For example, it will be more likely to use an international division as the way it organises its international activities and even if it uses a global product structure, the importance of the domestic market will be pervasive. A large domestic market will also influence the attitudes of senior managers towards their international activities and will generate a large number of managers with an experience base of predominantly or even exclusively domestic market experience. Thus, multinationals from small advanced economies like Switzerland (population 7.5 million), Ireland (4 million), Australia (20 million) and The Netherlands (16.5 million) and medium-size advanced economies like Canada (33 million), the United Kingdom (60 million) and France (61 million) are in a quite different position to multinationals based in the United States which is the largest advanced economy in the world with a population of 298 million. US multinationals also enjoy the advantage of a dominant position in the NAFTA market (the US, Canada and Mexico) which has a total market population of 438 million.

If the UNCTAD data is rank ordered only on the ratio of foreign assets to total assets (that is, excluding the ratios of foreign sales to total sales, and foreign employment to total employment) the listing shown in Table 16.2 demonstrates the effect of large-scale domestic sales and domestic employment on the Transnational Index ranking in Table 16.1, with four US firms listed and only two firms from the Transnational Index (the British companies Vodafone Group and British Petroleum) remaining. In other words, the removal of domestic sales from the Transnational Index significantly reinterprets the data which is presented in Table 16.1. It is therefore worth keeping in mind that the frequent criticism of US companies, US senior managers and US business schools as inward-looking and ethnocentric may perhaps be true to some extent, but it is equally true that a focus on domestic US sales

TABLE 16.2 World top 10 non-financial transnational corporations, ranked only by foreign assets

Transnational index	Ranking by foreign assets	Company name	Home economy	Industry
1	77	General Electric	United States	Electrical and electronic equipment
2	7	Vodafone Group Plc	United Kingdom	Telecommunications
3	72	Ford Motor Company	United States	Motor vehicles
4	90	General Motors	United States	Motor vehicles
5	10	British Petroleum	United Kingdom Company Plc	Petroleum exploration, refining and distribution
6	31	ExxonMobil Corporation	United States	Petroleum exploration, refining and distribution
7	22	Royal Dutch/Shell Group	United Kingdom/ The Netherlands	Petroleum exploration, refining and distribution
8	68	Toyota Motor Corporation	Japan	Motor vehicles
9	16	Total	France	Petroleum exploration, refining and distribution
10	62	France Telecom	France	Telecommunications

Source: The data in this Table is based on the World Investment Report, 2005, *TNCs and the Internationalisation of R&D*, United Nations Conference on Trade and Development (UNCTAD), September.

and revenue is also an entirely rational response to the overwhelming importance of the North American market for many of these businesses. The demands of a large domestic market present a challenge to the globalisation efforts of many US firms. As Cavusgil[46] has noted in an important book on internationalising business education, the task of internationalising business education in the United States is a large one. So, too, is the task facing many US firms in terms of developing global managers.

Attitudes of senior management to international operations

The point made by Laurent earlier in this chapter that some of the changes required to truly internationalise the HR function 'have more to do with states of mind and mindsets than with behaviors' illustrates the importance of a final variable that may moderate differences between international and domestic HRM: the attitudes of senior management to international operations. It is likely that if senior management does not have a strong international orientation, the importance of international operations may be underemphasised (or possibly even ignored) in terms of corporate goals and objectives. In such situations, managers may tend to focus on domestic issues and minimise differences between international and domestic environments.

Not surprisingly, senior managers with little international experience (and successful careers built on domestic experience) may assume that there is a great deal of transferability between domestic and international HRM practices. This failure to recognise differences in managing human resources in foreign environments—regardless of whether it is because of **ethnocentrism**, inadequate information or a lack of international perspective—frequently results in major difficulties in international operations. The challenge for the corporate HR manager who wishes to contribute to the internationalisation of their firm is to work with top management in fostering the desired 'global mindset'. This goal requires, of course, a HR manager who is able to think globally and to formulate and implement HR policies that facilitate the development of globally oriented staff.[47] 'Managing challenges of globalisation: Rise of China, India a big plus for world' gives some indication of emerging issues for senior managers to consider with regard to global changes brought by the rise of industrialising nations such as India and China.

Ethnocentrism
the assumption that one's own cultural approach is superior to any other. An ethnocentric approach to international staffing typically results in all key management positions being held by PCNs. Also, international HRM activities are typically developed and administered by PCNs.

Applying a strategic view of international HRM

Our discussion up to this point has suggested that a broader or more strategic view of IHRM is required to better explain the complexity and challenges of managing IHRM issues. An example of a theoretical framework that has been derived from a strategic approach using a multiple methodological approach is that of De Cieri and Dowling.[48] Their framework is depicted in Figure 16.5 and assumes that multinational firms operate in the context of worldwide conditions, including the external contexts of industry, nation, region and inter-organisational networks and alliances. An example of the latter would be the impact of the removal of internal trade barriers and integration of national markets following the recent expansion of the membership of the European Union. These external factors exert direct influence on internal organisational factors, HRM strategy and practices, and multinational concerns and goals.

The internal organisational factors are shown in order of most 'tangible' to most 'intangible'. MNE structure refers to both the structure of international operations,

RISE OF CHINA, INDIA A BIG PLUS FOR WORLD

MANAGING CHALLENGES OF GLOBALISATION

FORBES magazine editor-in-chief Steve Forbes, who is also president and chief executive of Forbes Inc, talks about the effect that global tensions and the rise of China and India will have on the world economy.

How successful has the present administration in Washington been in strengthening economic links with Asia?
I think the ties are deepening, not so much because of Washington, but because entrepreneurs, investors and companies are seeing opportunities there. This is often what happens—politicians can talk but others make things happen.

Do the current security issues in the Middle East and North Korea seriously affect global economic growth?
These issues psychologically affect the prices of oil and other commodities. It makes people more hesitant about investing. But the global economy has done very well in the last three years, despite the war in the Middle East and the friction with North Korea.

What are the new drivers for economic growth?
Broadband technology, which is altering the traditional balance between telephony, TV, radio and cable. That is going to change existing industries. But a lot of new ways of doing old things will also emerge. A lot of traditional industries will do things in new ways and have great opportunities for growth.

What kind of impact will the rise of China and India have on the world economy and on other Asian economies?
If both countries continue to pursue proper economic policies, their growth will bring tremendous benefit. Having two-plus billion people becoming part of the global economy and wanting to improve their standard of living is a major positive.

How can an economy like Singapore compete with the likes of China and India?
The key is focusing on value-added. If you have cutting-edge technologies and an environment that is favourable for business, that can be a great asset. Singapore is known for its rule of law and stability.

What do you make of worries here that China's economy will overtake that of the US?
To put things into perspective, the growth in the US economy over the past few years in absolute terms exceeds the size of the Chinese economy. China still has a long way to go and it will take constant reforms to make that possible.

What are the challenges that could derail China's economic growth?
You could come up with all kinds of scenarios: internal dissension, especially in the rural areas where they feel that local officials are still tyrannical; a perception that the environment is hostile to local entrepreneurs; corruption could be a flashpoint. There are all sorts of things, but this is what political leaders get paid for.

Source: Excerpt from Anonymous, 2006, 'Rise of China, India a big plus for world', *Straits Times*, 5 August. (c) 2006 Singapore Press Holdings Limited.

intra-organisational networks and mechanisms of coordination. The life cycle stage of the firm and the industry in which it operates are important influences on HRM strategy and practices in multinationals as are the various international modes of operation and levels of firm strategy. The most intangible organisational factors are experience in international business and headquarter's international orientation. Following developments in the literature, such as that of Taylor, Beechler and Napier,[49] who take an integration of resource dependence and resource-based perspective, the model suggests that there are reciprocal relationships between organisational factors, strategic HRM, and multinational concerns and goals.

With regard to HR strategy and practices, reciprocal relationships between strategic issues and HRM strategy and practices have been highlighted by research taking a resource-based perspective.[50] In addition, several studies have shown that HR activities such as expatriate management are influenced by both external and internal factors.[51] A more strategic approach to HRM is expected to assist the firm in achieving its goals and objectives. This view is influenced by the emerging body of strategic HRM literature that examines the relationships between endogenous

FIGURE 16.5 A model of strategic HRM in multinational enterprise

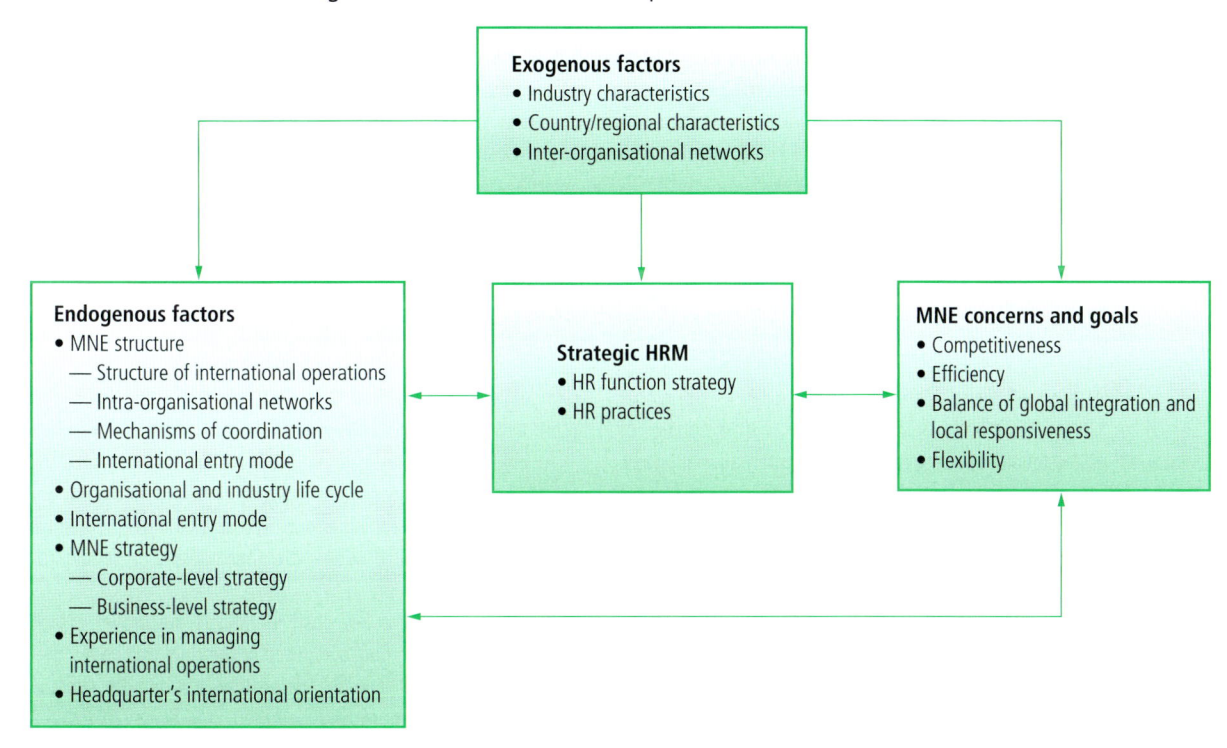

Exogenous factors
- Industry characteristics
- Country/regional characteristics
- Inter-organisational networks

Endogenous factors
- MNE structure
  — Structure of international operations
  — Intra-organisational networks
  — Mechanisms of coordination
  — International entry mode
- Organisational and industry life cycle
- International entry mode
- MNE strategy
  — Corporate-level strategy
  — Business-level strategy
- Experience in managing international operations
- Headquarter's international orientation

Strategic HRM
- HR function strategy
- HR practices

MNE concerns and goals
- Competitiveness
- Efficiency
- Balance of global integration and local responsiveness
- Flexibility

Source: Adapted from H. De Cieri and P. J. Dowling, 1999, 'Strategic Human Resource Management in Multinational Enterprises: theoretical and empirical developments', in P.M. Wright et al. (eds), *Research in Personnel and Human Resource Management: Strategic Human Resources in the 21st Century,* Supplement 4, Stamford, CT, JAI Press.

characteristics, HRM strategy and practices and firm performance or competitive advantage.[52] While some research has suggested that multinationals will gain by utilising and integrating appropriate HRM strategy and practices, to enhance firm performance,[53] the evidence is inconclusive and important questions remain about the nature of this relationship.[54] The model offered by De Cieri and Dowling aims to assist in the cross-fertilisation of ideas to further develop theory and empirical research in strategic HRM in multinational firms.

The enduring context of IHRM

As Figures 16.4 and 16.5 show, international firms compete in an increasingly complex environment where the level of challenge of doing business can be highly variable. Internationalising firms rely on having the right people to manage and operate their businesses and good IHRM practices that are appropriate to the context in which they occur. This combination of appropriate people and HR practices has been a constant critical success factor in international business ventures. For example, the following quotation is taken from a detailed case study of a large US multinational, where the authors, Desatnick and Bennett,[55] concluded:

> The primary causes of failure in multinational ventures stem from a lack of understanding of the essential differences in managing human resources, at all levels, in foreign environments. Certain management philosophies and techniques have proved successful in the domestic environment: their application in a foreign environment too often leads to frustration, failure and under-achievement. These 'human' considerations are as important as the financial and marketing criteria upon which so many decisions to undertake multinational ventures depend.

The study was reported in 1978 but many international managers today would concur with the sentiments expressed in this quote. 'Managing challenges through sustainability: The importance of place in the global war for talent' provides some suggestions for future directions and emerging issues for managers of international HRM. In this chapter we attempt to demonstrate some ways in which an appreciation of the international dimensions of HRM can assist in the process of international management.

THE GLOBAL HUNT FOR TALENT

Opportunities to work overseas are increasing rapidly as the global search for talent rises. Carole Goldsmith speaks with a number of seasoned professionals about trends in the international talent marketplace and their experiences working overseas.

Asian conglomerate, Jardine Matheson Limited (Jardines) employs 239 000 employees globally. Its diverse group of businesses includes engineering, construction, transport services, motor trading, property, retailing, restaurants, hotels, financial services and insurance broking.

Twelve and a half years ago, Geoffrey Brown and his wife, left the sunny shores of Brisbane, to travel to Hong Kong (HK), where he had accepted a position as assistant treasurer at Jardines Corporate Treasury.

After ten years working in accounting and finance at Mount Isa Mines in Brisbane and completing an MBA, Brown was ready for international challenges. He was approached by PriceWaterhouseCoopers and recruited to join Jardines. The recruitment process took four months and included interviews with the country chairman of Jardines Australia and Jardines' group finance director in Hong Kong.

'Jardines is very good at moving people on assignment from country to country', Brown says. 'They flew us to HK and transported our furniture and possessions there. Our housing in HK is included in my package. In 2000 we were also transported back to Sydney with our children and housed when I was Colliers Jardines' regional group finance director in Sydney for two years.'

Now Brown is finance director of Hongkong Land, one of Jardines major listed companies. This is his fifth position at Jardines, and he travels extensively across Asia as part of his job. 'One of the many benefits of working for a conglomerate like Jardines is the opportunity to change jobs and areas of work', he says.

Recruiting international talent

Ritchie Bent, group head of human resources at Jardines, says: 'We are very active in recruiting international talent, but because we are such a large organisation, with 239 000 employees, we have a huge internal talent pool which we can draw from', he says.

'At holding company level, in 2007, we are currently focusing on 211 key position holders, identified during our annual HR planning process conducted from September to February, where the findings are presented to the chairman.'

These key position holders are drawn essentially from a pool comprised of the chief executives, the two levels beneath this position, the finance stream, the HR stream, and identified 'high-flyers'. In some cases they will be the same people.

'Of this group of 211, around 50 per cent are transferable around the group; that is to say, their skills can be deployed in different industries. More than 80 per cent of key senior positions are filled internally', Bent says.

'However, when we recruit for senior key positions, we will benchmark against the international market. To illustrate this, in the case of Geoff Brown's current role, finance director of Hongkong Land, we used one of the major search firms to identify three external candidates who could do the job.'

The company identified three internal candidates, who were then compared and Geoff ultimately emerged as the favoured candidate. In the process, however, the firm identified a particularly good candidate who, while not suitable for the Hongkong Land job, was eminently suitable for another role and was subsequently hired.

Brown's former position was taken by an internal candidate from the group audit function, with the audit role filled by someone from the Mandarin Oriental Hotel Group, and Mandarin identified someone from the open market, Bent says.

Developing and managing talent

Brown was selected to participate in the company's executive leadership development plan and found it very beneficial to his management and career progress. As a key component of this plan, CEOs of each of the group's companies discuss the 'promotability rating' of key managerial staff with their direct managers annually. They are then assessed and promoted if suitable for the position.

'I participated in the group's general managers program in 1997, held at a UK management college. After that we worked on projects, applying the skills we had learnt to the businesses we were working in. The direct development initiative is another program I joined. Director-level people from Jardines' businesses visit corporations globally and examine organisational change and their business operations. For example, we went to Ireland and the UK, visited BP and British Airways, and learnt from their CEOs and senior directors', Brown says.

Jardines also offers reciprocal arrangements, where they welcome senior managers from other companies to speak with the CEOs of their different businesses.

Pros and cons of Hong Kong

'I enjoy working with Jardines and across Asia. We love the diversity of culture here and HK is a very fast exciting and dynamic place to live', Brown says.

'As an Australian living in HK, it is quite easy and close to return to Brisbane for the weekend when we get homesick or have a family celebration. Also, we have a house on the Sunshine Coast and we love spending holidays there.'

'A downside of living in HK is the pollution. One of the biggest challenges for HK to remain competitive, and continue to attract new international businesses and talent, is to clean up the environment and to drastically reduce the high air pollution levels.'

US and UK for Australian lawyer

An Australian female lawyer, (who prefers to remain anonymous) recently returned to Australia after almost ten years working both in New York and London. She is now employed as a solicitor in advocacy and practice at the Law Institute of Victoria in Melbourne.

Following the completion of a master of laws degree at New York University, she worked as a lawyer for two years in a large New York law firm that employed around 400 people. She then moved to London to start a new position as a staff lawyer for a non-government organisation (NGO) that had around 15 employees. Three years later she was promoted to acting director.

'I was paid market rate as a US attorney and the salary at the time was higher than I would have earned in Australia. My experience of working for an Australian law firm for over two years assisted me to get the New York job.'

She loved working in New York and says the local people, including work colleagues, were very friendly and helpful. 'I worked together with highly qualified law professionals and they were very client and business focused. As a young woman, I was fully respected for what I could do and I really thrived in that environment.'

The NY law firm also encouraged pro bono work. During her New York posting, she undertook pro bono work for asylum seekers and for an organisation that helped abused women.

'I went to London to take up the opportunity to work on international environment and human rights law and policy in the not-for-profit sector. These are areas of great concern for me. The salary was lower than for the NY job, however, the work was very rewarding', she says.

Australian lawyers sought after

'I know that Australian lawyers are highly regarded in the USA and UK, and are actively sought by law firms there', says the lawyer.

She says the only negatives of working internationally are being away from your family. 'Living and working internationally opens your eyes to all sorts of opportunities and new ways of living. This enhances your understanding of people and of the world.'

Expats over compensated?

Thirty-eight per cent of companies believe that international assignees are over compensated; according to KPMG's 2006 Global Assignment Policy and Practices, Tax survey. Furthermore, 48 per cent of organisations feel that too much time is spent administering assignees; while there was a 54 per cent increase in short term assignments compared to last year, said Achim Mossmann, national director, global mobility advisory services, KPMG International Executive Services. At least 900 organisations have participated in some of the surveys since its inception eight years ago.

Source: C. Goldsmith, 2007, 'The global hunt for talent', *Human Resources*, 3 April. www.humanresourcesmagazine.com.au

PART 5   Contemporary Issues for Human Resource Management

MANAGING PEOPLE

OFFSHORING STILL NEEDS MANAGEMENT

Despite the significant savings achievable by offshoring and outsourcing business processes, executives and HR divisions need to ensure their management is fully integrated with the company's operations if it is to avoid the risks inherent in transferring work overseas, a recent study has warned. In offshoring, companies face 'a wide range of people management issues both overseas and at home', according to the report, developed by US-based global research organisation, The Conference Board.

'Does cheaper also mean riskier?' the study asks. 'As labour demand rises in offshoring markets, offshorers and potential offshorers would be right to wonder how long the arbitrage opportunity will last. Will labour supply continue to meet growing demand?' The offshoring landscape has already begun to change—in India, for example, increasing demand for IT skills is driving up pay levels.

'The ongoing trend towards offshoring and outsourcing, and the reliance business have on external suppliers to run their own business could also be an emerging risk issue', said Ross Castle, risk services provider Aon's national manager, client research and development. 'Many companies have followed the trend towards concentrating on their core business—outsourcing and offshoring for cost and efficiency reasons. But have they considered all their risks and dependencies and are the implications of interruption factored into these business decisions?'

More traditional complications associated with offshoring include the reaction of workers in the 'home' country who lose their jobs to outsourced labour. Companies are, however, learning they can quell discontent by designing plans to aid employees who lose their jobs, overcoming resistance from disgruntled workers and maintaining morale among remaining employees, according to The Conference Board.

'All of these groups must be considered if a company wants to protect its image as an employer of choice', said Ton Heijmen, senior advisor to the Board on offshoring and outsourcing. 'Meeting these and other challenges calls for innovative approaches and developing specific leadership qualities.'

Leaders of offshoring projects require project management skills; interpersonal, networking persuasion and technical skills; and should be able to manage relationships with empathy, according to the Board. They also need to be good integrators and capable of managing conflict and inspiring group and individual cooperation.

'While manufacturing has a long history of being managed from afar as a discrete process, business processes and other services that touch many integral parts of a company's operations involve a higher degree of coordination and integration with different parts of the organisation', said Heijmen. 'In addition to operational issues, executives should consider the special processes they'll need to institute to manage people and projects, drive behaviour, and resolve conflicts half a world and many time zones away—regardless of the offshoring structure they choose.'

Before embarking on a major offshoring project, ensure you are familiar with:
- the essentials of local employment law
- the requirements and obligations regarding termination
- the standard contractual terms that apply
- the costs of hiring and firing
- the procedures prospective vendors follow to screen employees, including background checks and references

Source: The Conference Board

Source: Anonymous, 2006, 'Offshoring still needs management', *Human Resources,* 24 January, pp. 1, 6. www.humanresourcesmagazine.com.au

QUESTIONS
1 What are the major HR management issues related to offshoring?
2 What strategies would you suggest to address these issues?

CHAPTER SUMMARY

The purpose of this chapter has been to provide an overview of the emerging field of international HRM. We did this by:

- defining key terms in IHRM and considering several definitions of IHRM
- introducing the historically significant issue of expatriate assignment management and reviewing the evolution of these assignments to reflect the increasing diversity with regard to what constitutes international work and the type and length of international assignments
- outlining the differences between domestic and international human resource management by looking at six factors which differentiate international and domestic HR (more HR activities; the need for a broader perspective; more involvement in employees' personal lives; changes in emphasis as the workforce mix of expatriates and locals varies; risk exposure; and more external influences) and detailing a model which summarises the variables that moderate these differences
- presenting the complexity of IHRM, the increasing potential for challenges to existing IHRM practices and current models, and an increasing awareness of the wide number of choices within IHRM practices due to increased transparency and faster and more detailed diffusion of these practices across organisational units and firms.

We concluded that the complexity involved in operating in different countries and employing different national categories of employees is a key variable differentiating domestic and international HRM, rather than any major differences between the HR activities performed. We also discussed four other variables that moderate differences between domestic and international HRM: the cultural environment; the industry (or industries) with which the multinational is primarily involved; the extent of reliance of the multinational on its home-country domestic market; and the attitudes of senior management. These five variables are shown in Figure 16.4. Finally, we discussed a model of strategic HRM in multinational enterprises (Figure 16.5) which draws together a number of external environment and internal organisational factors which impact on IHRM strategy and practice and in turn on MNE goals.

In our discussion of the international dimensions of HRM in this book, we shall be drawing on the HRM literature. Subsequent chapters will examine the context for IHRM and the international dimensions of the major activities of HRM: HR planning and business operations, recruitment and selection, performance management, training and development, compensation, and labour relations. We will provide comparative data on HRM practices in different countries, but our major emphasis is on the international dimensions of HRM confronting multinational firms, whether large or small, when facing the challenge of managing people in an international context.

WEB EXERCISES

A GMAC Global Relocation Services is a consulting firm that provides services for expatriate management. Its website provides information about international relocation and expatriate management. Go to its home page at www.windhamint.com/ and locate the latest *Global Relocation Trends Survey*. Identify three trends reported in this survey and discuss their implications for international HRM.

B The www.expatworld.com website includes information and links to many services and sources for expatriates. Select a country and build a profile of living and working information that would be useful for an expatriate being assigned to that location.

DISCUSSION QUESTIONS

1. What are the main similarities and differences between domestic and international HRM?
2. Define these terms: international HRM, PCN, HCN and TCN.
3. Discuss two HR activities in which a multinational firm must engage that would not be required in a domestic environment.
4. Why is a greater degree of involvement in employees' personal lives inevitable in many international HRM activities?
5. Discuss at least two of the variables that moderate differences between domestic and international HR practices.

CASE STUDY

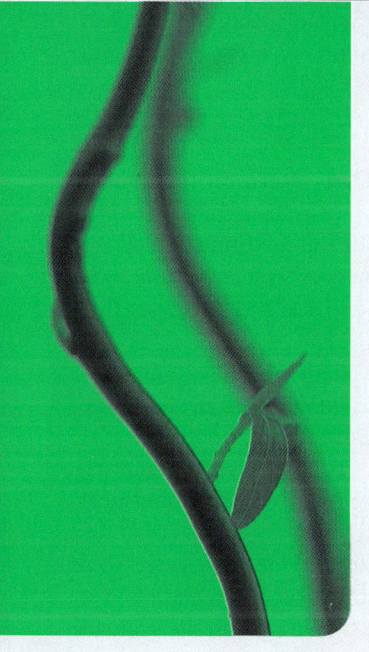

MAKING EMPLOYEES MOBILE

Overseas assignments can present a considerable headache for HR professionals. Melissa Yen looks at some of the latest developments in the area, strategies for lightening HR's load and how a leading organisation approaches the issue of international mobility.

As the war for talent intensifies and employees' company loyalty decreases, global relocation programs are becoming an increasingly popular method of recruiting and rewarding high achieving staff. But as HR professionals know, the success of any global mobility program depends upon the fulfilment of employees' professional and personal needs.

How the objectives of the organisation impact upon its relocation program, how to select the most suitable candidates for international assignments, how to determine the success of each program and how they can be completed in the most cost-effective manner are questions that must be answered by HR.

Latest developments

According to Charlotte Furness of Toll Transitions, the relocation industry is experiencing a boom. To employees, first class relocation services and proactive support before, during and after a move do more to command loyalty than the equivalent in a salary increase.

'HR professionals are recognising that to attract top global talent to their organisation they need to be offering more than a good salary. Companies have to "sell" the destination location almost as much as the position', Furness says. As a result of this, she believes there has been greater emphasis on providing 'settling in' services, which can include local orientation programs and cross-cultural training as well as networking opportunities, especially for spouses.

As Sarah Cuthbertson, Ernst & Young's manager of mobility explains, international moves are becoming an increasingly common part of recruitment and resourcing as the candidate-short market in Australia demands that searches be extended offshore. Ernst & Young encourages the sharing of its people across borders to assist with more effective resource management, skill advancement and, most importantly, strengthening of its strategic markets such as China and India.

'As part of our People First strategy', Cuthbertson says, 'Ernst & Young look to create an environment where people can grow and our global mobility policies facilitate both personal and professional development. Our annual mobility programs also encourage the exchange of our staff worldwide and assist us to reward and retain our best people.'

Sandra Cittadini, director of global mobility for KPMG, adds that organisations are tending to move away from some of the more severe cost-saving initiatives, such as reducing the core elements that make up their 'standard' or 'long term' international assignment policies, in order to keep with their long term competitive strategy. Cittadini has also observed that companies are starting to review those policy elements which in the past may have been left to management discretion and not been supported by cost containment parameters. They are also starting to look at the level of non-compliance, or exceptions to policy where significant, particularly where there is no one individual in the company appointed as the 'gatekeeper' to administer the international mobility program and monitor the policy.

'In addition, the introduction of short term, project-based rotational assignments of between three and 12 months, and local "plus" packages have become more popular, addressing the company's requirement to be flexible when sending employees overseas or when trying to hire people on local conditions', says Cittadini.

Meanwhile, as employee loyalty diminishes and company jumping increases, Shani Alexander, director of Relocations Made Easy, believes that 'HR is looking to a range of integrated, cost-effective and even self-service solutions, as the traditional relocation package doesn't suit every single assignment into the future.'

Challenges

HR must communicate with payroll and finance in order to deliver a successful outcome for both the assigned employee and the organisation. In turn, it is essential that HR become involved with any international mobility program at its earliest stages. Having a seat at the planning table and being heard is a challenge Cittadini says will be faced by most HR professionals.

'Managing assignees is not just about policy terms and conditions, but about the organisation's compliance as well. The risks associated with sending employees into a foreign environment, without addressing migration, tax, payroll and local employment conditions can be high, not only for the company but for the individual as well.'

In order to overcome scenarios where the HR manager has been advised just days prior to departure, or even worse, after the fact, that several individuals have been or will be assigned to a particular country, Cittadini stresses the importance of educating the business about the potential risks involved with inadequate planning: 'HR have to be involved at the planning stage of these discussions. They cannot be bought in after the fact', she says.

Not least because it is not just the welfare of the employee that is at stake, but also, potentially, the welfare of their family. Spouses who do not have the social framework of the company to rely on quickly feel isolated after an international move: 'HR professionals should be conscious of this and pay particular attention to the emotional wellbeing of international recruits. Many organisations overlook the need for post-relocation support, which is readily available', says Furness.

Another challenge commonly faced by HR professionals, says Shani Alexander, is the initial difficulty of sourcing good candidates who go on to complete the relocation and assimilate smoothly into the new city and workplace and move onto permanent residency.

The greatest challenge for HR at Ernst & Young, meanwhile, is in managing the continual demand for mobility. 'Recruitment remains both locally and internationally focused. However, there is room for growth on the international side. The challenge is to secure high calibre candidates and to have them arrive in Australia within the shortest of timeframes. Our labour agreement with the Department of Immigration and Multicultural Affairs facilitates our international resourcing, but we are still hindered by the worldwide skills shortage', says Cuthbertson.

A dedicated mobility team made up of assignment services managers, migration agents and tax advisors is also used to ensure the movement of people is seamless throughout the pre-assignment, on-assignment and repatriation phases.

Establishing ROI

When attempting to demonstrate return on investment for international assignments, it is essential that HR communicate the importance of the investment they are making to the rest of the business as well as demonstrate the benefits the program will provide and the costs that will be incurred.

'We strongly encourage our clients to prepare detailed cost projections, to ensure they understand up front the full cost of the assignment. This includes the compensation methodology to be used, benefits, net/gross allowances, social security and home and host country tax', says KPMG's Cittadini.

Furness also suggests building a business case from internal data by looking at both the successes and failures of international recruitments. 'Failure of an assignment will be even more expensive. Research suggests somewhere in the range of two to three times an employee's salary. Close to 50 per cent of relocations fail because of cultural difficulties and family issues', she says.

For Ernst & Young, taking into account the main aims of the international assignment, whether it be to develop new business, strengthen markets, advance skills and industry experience or retain and reward high calibre staff is a must. 'The return will vary and, therefore, the business case must capture the overall assignment objectives from the outset. This is done through selection, career management and repatriation planning to ensure the right people are placed in the right place, at the right time', says Cuthbertson. 'Career management is a priority and whilst our global mobility policies provide the 'how to' around this, an international secondment is a two-way commitment. Both the assignee and the firm have a responsibility to make it a success so that the return on investment is realised.'

According to Alexander, preparation is the key. She stresses the need to have well conceived HR policies in place rather than acting in an ad hoc way. Gaining access to resources and knowledge that will enable HR consultants to respond efficiently to the myriad of compliance issues such as tax, health and visas is a first step.

'Help the candidate prepare and set proper expectations of the new city so they don't turn around and go home soon after arrival [forcing] the company to bear the extreme cost of a failed relocation', says Alexander. 'Failed assignments because a candidate has unmet expectations of the new city can cost the company $100 000 and they then have to do it all again.

Source: M. Yen, 2006, 'Making employees mobile', *Human Resources*, 28 June, pp. 20–1. www.humanresourcesmagazine.com.au

QUESTIONS

1 What are the major challenges related to a strategic approach to expatriate management?
2 How would you measure the return on investment (ROI) of expatriate assignments?

CHAPTER 17

MANAGING EMPLOYEE TURNOVER AND RETENTION

Objectives

After reading this chapter, you should be able to:

1. Distinguish between involuntary and voluntary turnover and discuss how each of these forms of turnover can be leveraged for competitive advantage.

2. List the major elements that contribute to perceptions of justice and how to apply these in organisational contexts involving employee assistance, discipline and dismissal.

3. Specify the relationship between job satisfaction and various forms of job withdrawal and identify the major sources of job satisfaction in work contexts.

4. Design a survey feedback intervention program and use this to promote the retention of key organisational personnel.

HR, anytime, anywhere

FedEx is a global shipping, logistics and supply chain management company. With annual revenues of US$31 ($40) billion, FedEx operates in about 220 countries and territories around the world and employs more than 260 000 employees and contractors globally.

For the ninth straight year, FedEx has been ranked among the 100 best companies to work for by *Fortune* magazine and the US-based Great Place to Work Institute. FedEx has also been among the leaders of *Fortune's* World's Most Admired Companies list for the past few years and one of the 50 Best Companies in America for Asians, Blacks and Hispanics.

People service profit

In the fiercely competitive air express cargo transportation industry, FedEx attributes much of its success to its corporate 'people service profit' philosophy. Under the founder of FedEx, Frederick Smith, employees were an integral part of the decision-making process, due to his belief that 'when people are placed first they will provide the highest possible service, and profits will follow'.

This philosophy is a value chain that suggests that, by taking care of employees, they will deliver the high levels of service demanded by customers, who will in turn reward the company with continued patronage and profitability.

The 'people service profit' philosophy forms the basis for all business decisions, according to John Allison, vice president of HR for FedEx Asia Pacific. 'This is our number one philosophy. We believe in it and we promote it. The focus we have on developing our people inside the organisation is critical, and HR is responsible for making sure that we provide the right programs and that we deliver them', he says.

Surveying the workforce

FedEx has a number of initiatives in place to support its 'people service profit' philosophy. FedEx runs an annual employee survey, 'survey feedback action', which rates management's commitment to the philosophy and forms a basis for improvement. This survey is conducted each April, and every employee is asked 32 questions about the company in general and management performance.

The survey is seen as a problem-solving tool that operates both horizontally and vertically throughout FedEx. The first ten items on the survey serve as a review of management by subordinates. The scores on these ten items become the numerical measurement that determines whether the company's annual people goal within the 'people service profit' goal structure is being met.

Managers hold feedback sessions with their employees to discuss the survey findings and identify problems within and outside of their department. As a group, they develop formal, written action plans for solving these problems. Groups usually review plans throughout the year to determine whether problems are being solved satisfactorily.

'It's a dialogue, not a one way street', says Allison. 'It's an opportunity for the manager and employees to talk as a group, to understand what the issues are. Once they develop an action plan to solve these issues, this becomes the responsibility of all the employees in the workgroup. It's not just the manager trying to resolve the issues, but it's the employees and the manager working together to resolve whatever those issues may be. It's a means of engaging all of our employees so that they can participate in expressing concerns about issues and at the same time participate in solving any problems that might arise.'

Guaranteed fair treatment

Another process in FedEx that supports the 'people service profit' philosophy is the guaranteed fair treatment procedure. This allows employees to escalate complaints all the way up

Internationally mobile continued

the company if they feel they have been treated unfairly—something of an employee appeal process for having complaints or grievances heard.

Issues could include disputed performance reviews, disciplinary actions, terminations, and job postings for which employees feel they should have been seriously considered, yet were not.

Employees must attempt to resolve the grievance with their manager or supervisor before initiating the procedure. 'For example, if an employee got a warning letter for their poor performance, or disagreed with their performance appraisal rating, then they can have this addressed through the guaranteed fair treatment procedure if they feel they have been treated so', according to Allison.

The employee's manager, their senior manager and managing director as a group can examine the employee's complaint and make a judgement as to whether or not management acted according to the company's 'people service profit' philosophy.

HR as counsellor

The 'grow your own' philosophy also applies to HR positions within FedEx. The majority of HR practitioners have come through the ranks and most often worked in frontline positions. This allows HR to play both a management and counselling role within FedEx.

The automation of administrative HR processes is creating opportunities for HR to be redeployed in the business to create extra value, according to Allison. 'If you are removing administrative processes, the best way to make use of HR is to redeploy your HR resources as business counsellors—talking about people issues, resolving people issues, solving people conflicts and being a participant in the business.'

Since its foundation, FedEx has had a chief people officer who reports to the chief executive, Allison says. 'So HR is engaged in all aspects of the business. Promoting the "people service profit" philosophy is a part of our job, but it's not just our job—it's everybody's job in the business.'

Manager as HR

There is a misconception in business that HR needs to do everything in terms of people, according to Ross. 'They're seen as the ones that need to discipline, motivate, keep records of employees, look after health and safety—everything. That's not true. HR are not there to be the keepers alone.'

Most people see HR as problem solvers for all people problems, he says, when in fact they should act as a support role for line managers in equipping them to handle appropriate situations. 'Managers think, "I have this problem now, let's give it to HR." I would anticipate that HR is simply a back office function in some organisations, that they don't need to go out and be part of the business. But it's all about teamwork, it's all about understanding, it's all about communication—particularly in a service industry', Ross says.

Growing FedEx's own

FedEx has a strong philosophy of growing its own management talent, according to John Allison, vice president of HR for FedEx Asia Pacific. Ninety-one per cent of the company's management has been promoted from within, and FedEx typically only hires from the outside for frontline positions or entry-level professional management positions. 'From the frontline manager to the senior managers, all those jobs are made available in the company', he says.

Source: Excerpt from C. Donaldson, 2006, 'HR anytime, anywhere', *Human Resources*, 16 May 2006, pp. 12–13.
www.humanresourcesmagazine.com.au

Introduction

Every manager recognises the need for satisfied, loyal customers. If the firm is publicly listed, it is also safe to assume that every manager appreciates the need to have satisfied, loyal investors. Customers and investors provide the financial resources that allow the organisation to survive. Not every manager understands the need to generate satisfaction and loyalty among employees, however. Yet retention rates among employees are related to retention rates among both customers[1] and investors,[2] as discussed in the FedEx example at the beginning of this chapter. Research indicates that the necessary conditions for this linkage between employees and organisational performance are:

- when employees possess knowledge and skills the managers lack
- when employees are motivated to apply these skills and knowledge through discretionary effort
- when the firm's business or production strategy can only be achieved when employees contribute such discretionary effort.[3]

Since managers in many organisations have been slow to pick up on this linkage, this provides yet another area where one firm can gain a competitive advantage over others in the market. That is, successful firms like FedEx are able to convert employee satisfaction and loyalty, on the one hand, into customer and investor satisfaction and loyalty on the other. Considering the demographic shifts discussed in Chapter 1, such as the ageing population, globalisation, and shortages of skills and talent, the attraction and retention of talent becomes a vital concern for employers.[4] This may be more important in service industries, where customer service is a key element in competitive advantage. In a case that has become well known, Sears department stores in the United States demonstrated an employee–customer–profit chain, in which a five-unit increase in positive employee attitudes, about their jobs and the company, led to a 1.5-unit increase in the customers' impressions of the company (that is, helpful service and merchandise value). In turn, this led to increased customer retention and recommendations to others, resulting in a 0.5 per cent increase in revenue growth.[5]

In addition to retaining key personnel, another hallmark of successful firms is their ability and willingness to dismiss employees who are engaging in counterproductive behaviour. Indeed, it is somewhat ironic that one of the keys to retaining productive employees is ensuring that they are not being made miserable by supervisors or co-workers who are engaging in unproductive, disruptive or dangerous behaviour.

Thus, to compete effectively, organisations must take steps to ensure that good performers are motivated to stay with the organisation, whereas chronically low performers are allowed, encouraged or, if necessary, required to leave. Retaining top performers is not always easy, however. Recent developments have made this more difficult than ever. For example, retrenchments and downsizings have reduced company loyalty.[6] Couple this general attitude of mistrust with the 'tight' labour markets characterising the 2000s and we have a workforce that is both willing and able to leave at a moment's notice. Similarly, the increased willingness of people to sue their employer, combined with an unprecedented level of violence in the workplace, has made discharging employees legally complicated and personally dangerous.

The purpose of this chapter is to focus on employee turnover and retention. The material presented in previous chapters (such as those on Performance management and Learning and development—Chapters 10 and 11, respectively) can be used to help establish who the current effective performers are, and who is likely to respond well to future developmental opportunities. This chapter discusses what to do to retain high-performing employees who warrant further development, and it discusses managing the separation process for low-performing employees who have not responded well to developmental opportunities.

The chapter first examines involuntary turnover—that is, turnover initiated by the organisation (often among people who would prefer to stay). The chapter then deals with voluntary turnover—that is, turnover initiated by employees (often those the company would prefer to keep). Although both types of turnover reflect employee separation, they are clearly different phenomena that need to be examined separately.[7] The chapter then examines the strategies and interventions that may be used to enhance retention of employees.

Managing involuntary turnover

Involuntary turnover reflects a separation initiated by the organisation, often when the individual would prefer to stay a member of that organisation. Despite a company's best efforts in the areas of employee selection, training and design of compensation systems, some employees will occasionally fail to meet performance requirements or will violate company policies while on the job. When this happens, organisations need to invoke a discipline program that could ultimately lead to the individual's discharge. In some cases, organisational changes, such as restructuring or economic changes, will lead to job losses. For a number of reasons, discharging employees can be a considerably difficult task that needs to be handled with the utmost care and attention to detail.

First, there are legal aspects to this decision that can have important repercussions for the organisation, as discussed in Chapter 3, The legal context for human resource management. Termination decisions must follow the legislation.

There have been cases where an employee responded to a termination decision with violence directed at the employer. Although any number of organisational actions or decisions may incite violence among employees, the 'nothing else to lose' aspect of employee dismissal cases makes for a dangerous situation. Indeed, although the needs of investors, co-workers and customers may dictate discharging a given employee, the person actually implementing the dismissal needs to consider their own safety as well. The development of a standardised, systematic approach to discipline and discharge is critical in all organisations. These decisions should not be left solely to the discretion of individual managers or supervisors.

Termination of employment may not be due to any issues of individual performance, but it may be due to broader organisational changes, such as a plant closure, redundancy decision, or decision to move jobs off-shore, as discussed in 'Managing challenges of globalisation: Banks keep a low profile in outsourcing'. Whatever the factors leading to the loss of employment, there are critical financial and personal risks associated with employee dismissal and job losses. For example, in late 2004, around 600 workers lost their jobs when Kodak closed its plant in Coburg, Victoria. The company blamed the rise of digital photography for the closure, although union representatives claimed that they had urged Kodak in recent years to investigate ways of keeping the plant open. Kodak Australia's chairperson, John Allen, said 'These closures have been caused by the fundamental change in consumer behaviour driven by the increasing popularity of digital photography in Australia and

Involuntary turnover reflects a separation initiated by the organisation, often when the individual would prefer to stay a member of the organisation.

worldwide', he said. 'It's a very sad day but I think on site here it's understood that this is a technology-driven change.' Earlier in 2004, the United States parent company, Eastman Kodak, announced plans to cut up to 15 000 jobs worldwide by 2006. The Victorian workers were told at a staff meeting in mid-September that the plant would close around six weeks later. Kodak offered counselling and career advice to help employees find new jobs, and the state and federal governments offered to assist with training.[8]

Even where a company continues to trade or a plant remains in operation, job losses can be a very challenging matter for managers and employees. For example, in late 2006, Ford Australia announced about 640 job losses at its Victorian operations. This represents a reduction in car production at the Broadmeadows plant by 20 per cent: from 450 to 360 per day. Ford spokesperson Sinead McAlary said the company would offer a voluntary separation package for both hourly and salaried employees, which

BANKS KEEP LOW PROFILE IN OUTSOURCING

MANAGING CHALLENGES OF GLOBALISATION

Banks looking to outsource thousands of jobs to low-cost countries such as India are being threatened by state Labor governments with the loss of lucrative contracts if they go ahead.

But the banks say they are responding to the inevitable effects of globalisation and should not be penalised by state governments.

Westpac head of business and consumer banking Mike Pratt said it was a matter of survival for his bank as it battled new market entrants, many of which were subsidiaries of multi-national companies with significant back-office operations in countries such as India.

'We live in a global world of financial services and a lot of those global players ... are looking at returns in this market and think they are pretty healthy and so are attacking the incumbents such as Westpac and others.'

'The reality is that from a cost base point of view a number of new entrants in this market have a significant advantage. You simply can't ignore that if you are an incumbent player', he said.

'In a market like the mortgage market, which is absolutely a commodity market, it is all about cost. You have got to get your cost down or you will not survive.'

Each of the top five banks, except for Commonwealth Bank of Australia, has, or is considering shifting jobs offshore.

ANZ Banking Group has the biggest operation with about 1300 staff working in a fully owned subsidiary in Bangalore in India.

Some analysts have accused the banks of being laggards in the speed at which they have addressed opportunities to move jobs overseas, saying they could boost industry profits by more than $2 billion if they matched the endeavours of some overseas rivals. A joint study prepared by Credit Suisse and Swamy and Associates said that up to 40 per cent of a bank's cost base was 'amenable to offshoring'.

'We assess Australian banks to be laggards in the global banking industry in terms of their response to the offshoring phenomenon', it said.

Some bankers agree they could move most of their technology requirements offshore, such are the cost advantages of countries like India, but say they have to balance that with the risks and sensitivities of such a move.

CBA says that after weighing the positives and negatives, it has no plans to explore significant opportunities in this area.

But the other major banks seem to be looking to exploit opportunities to move jobs overseas in a step-by-step process aimed at minimising disruption and public outcry over such a move. They say they have no intention of including jobs that interact directly with customers.

Westpac's Mr Pratt said the expertise on offer in India would 'blow away' any doubters.

He said overseas studies had found that customer service was enhanced by outsourcing offshore, which could boost a bank's competitive position in its home market.

But bodies such as the Finance Sector Union say outsourcing overseas represents a major threat to 370 000 employees of the country's financial services sector. The FSU wants the federal government to introduce legislation requiring banks to tell customers when they are being serviced from outside Australia.

FSU national secretary Paul Schroder said the trend would be a major battleground for the banks and their staff.

Source: Excerpt from S. Oldfield, 2006, 'Banks keep low profile in outsourcing', *Australian Financial Review*, 22 September, p. 67.

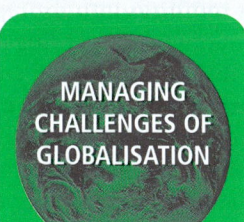

would include all employee entitlements. Ms McAlary said the job cuts were based on a 'long-term decline of the large car segment and we are essentially aligning production to meet current market demand'. According to a spokesperson from the Australian Manufacturing Workers Union, the Ford job losses were a major blow, as 2000 jobs were already lost in the automotive components industry in the previous 12 months.[9]

Principles of justice

In Chapter 10 Performance management, we touched on the notion of fairness (or 'justice'), particularly as this relates to the notions of distributive fairness, procedural fairness and interpersonal fairness.[10] There we noted that employees are more likely to respond positively to negative feedback regarding their performance if they perceive the appraisal process as being fair on these three dimensions. Obviously, if fairness is important with respect to ongoing feedback, it is more critical in the context of a final termination decision. Therefore, we will explore the three types of fairness perceptions in greater detail here, with an emphasis on how these need to be operationalised in effective discipline and discharge policies.[11]

As we noted in Chapter 15 Ethics ande human resource management, distributive fairness refers to the judgment that people make with respect to the outcomes received in relation to contribution (also known as outcome 'fairness'). Clearly, a situation where one person is losing his or her job, while others are not, is conducive to perceptions of outcome unfairness on the part of the discharged employee. The degree to which this potentially unfair act translates into the type of anger and resentment that might spawn retaliation in the form of violence or litigation, however, depends on perceptions of 'procedural justice', 'distributive justice' and 'interactional justice'.[12]

Whereas 'distributive justice' focuses on the ends, procedural justice and interactional justice focus on the means. If methods and procedures (used to arrive at and implement decisions that negatively impact on the employee) are seen as fair, the reaction is likely to be much more positive, than if this is not the case. **Procedural justice** focuses specifically on the methods used to determine the outcomes received. Table 17.1 opposite details six key principles that determine whether people perceive procedures as being fair. Although the person is given all the negative ramifications of being dismissed from his or her job, the person being dismissed may accept the decision with minimum anger if the procedures used for arriving at the decision are consistent, unbiased, accurate, correctable, representative and ethical.

Whereas procedural justice deals with how a decision was made, **interactional justice** refers to the quality of interpersonal treatment in processes. Table 17.2 opposite lists the four key determinants of interactional justice. When the decision is explained well and implemented in a fashion that is socially sensitive, considerate and empathetic, this helps diffuse some of the resentment that might arise from a decision to discharge an employee.

The issue of workplace surveillance and employee privacy provides an example of the importance of workplace justice. Several writers have reported that procedural justice concerns that are related to privacy have increased, particularly with regard to the use of modern technology for surveillance of employees in the workplace. Many employers supervise and monitor employee performance, and this is not a new management practice. Many employers perceive electronic monitoring as important—for example, to ensure workplace security or to reduce legal liability caused by employee misconduct.[13] However, the increasing use of electronic technology for workplace surveillance has raised concerns about privacy and employees' rights (also see Chapter 15 Ethics and human resource management). Computer monitoring in

Procedural justice (also procedural fairness) a concept of justice focusing on the methods used to determine the outcomes received.

Interactional justice (also interpersonal fairness) refers to the quality of interpersonal treatment in processes.

TABLE 17.1 Six determinants of procedural justice

1	Consistency	The procedures are applied consistently across time and other persons.
2	Bias suppression	The procedures are applied by a person who has no vested interest in the outcome or no prior prejudices regarding the individual.
3	Information accuracy	The procedure is based upon information that is perceived to be true.
4	Correctability	The procedure has built-in safeguards that allow one to appeal mistakes or bad decisions.
5	Representativeness	The procedure is informed by the concerns of all groups or stakeholders (co-workers, customers and owners) affected by the decision, including the individual being dismissed.
6	Ethicality	The procedure is consistent with prevailing moral standards as they pertain to issues like invasion of privacy or deception.

TABLE 17.2 Four determinants of interactional justice

1	Explanation	Emphasises aspects of procedural fairness that justify the decision.
2	Social sensitivity	Treats the person with dignity and respect.
3	Consideration	Listens to the person's concerns.
4	Empathy	Identifies with the person's feelings.

workplaces, for example, on assembly lines and in call centres, is common; however, several writers have raised concerns about work intensification in these 'electronic sweatshops'.[14] As employer demands continually increase, in order to improve efficiency, this leads to unrealistically high expectations of staff and stressful outcomes for employees. Hence, it is important for justice principles to be managed in the workplace. An understanding of justice principles helps to explain why many organisations have enacted various policies regarding matters such as workplace bullying, drug testing, employee assistance programs (EAPs), redundancy and outplacement. Development of effective HR policies and practices to address such issues will not only assist with the management of involuntary turnover, but it will also help to prevent problems arising in the workplace—thus, supporting efforts for employee retention.

Workplace bullying

An alarming issue that has received increasing attention is **workplace bullying**, defined as repeated and persistent negative acts by one employee, or a group of employees, against others, which creates a hostile work environment.[15] Bullying may lead to significant problems for individuals and their organisations. It has been estimated, based on proportionate statistics gathered in the United Kingdom, that one in four Australians are affected by workplace bullying; and bullying costs employers up to $12 000 million a year, for matters such as workers compensation claims.[16]

The emotional, physical, legal, reputational and financial costs make workplace bullying a serious issue for individuals, unions and employers. The ACTU launched a campaign against workplace bullying in October 2000, aiming to raise awareness about the dangers and effects of workplace bullying on individuals and employers.[17]

Workplace bullying
repeated and persistent negative acts by one employee, or a group of employees, against others, which create a hostile work environment.

Worldwide, over the past decade, the incidence of workplace violence appears to have been increasing, with concerns raised across diverse industries, ranging from the maritime industry to tertiary education.[18] Workplace bullying has received increasing attention from academic researchers.[19] The effects of bullying are alarming for both individuals and employers. Research has shown that, for individuals, the impact of bullying includes decreased job satisfaction, increased illness, and loss of employment. Bullying is also associated with higher employee turnover and absenteeism, and decreased organisational commitment and productivity.

Policies and practices to address workplace bullying, as for many other problems in the workplace, require a comprehensive approach, including identification of current or potential issues, articulation of the organisation's stance on preventing and eliminating bullying, development and maintenance of HR processes to support this stance, and encouragement of a workplace culture that enables employees to speak up about bullying.[20] (See 'HRM spotlight: Taking the bully by the horns'.)

Drug testing in the workplace

Drug and alcohol abuse are recognised as social concerns that may arise within the employment context. In the United States, workplace drug testing has become a fairly common workplace experience, a multi-million-dollar industry and a major issue for HRM and industrial relations. The prevailing approach by employers is to identify and remove illicit drug users from the workforce.[21] The United States National Safety Council has reported that 80 per cent of employees injured in serious drug-related incidents in the workplace were innocent co-workers and others.[22] However, workplace drug-testing programs have met with substantial criticism from employee representatives (as noted in Chapter 8 Recruitment and selection), based on concerns

TAKING THE BULLY BY THE HORNS

Workplace bullying is a subject many employers ignore until someone steps out of line. When a complaint is made, they may deal with it effectively so the victim feels supported and the bully is reprimanded. Or they might let it spiral out of control so the victim takes time off and lodges a Workcover claim and HR is left to defuse widespread ill feeling.

The latter is all too common, according to an Australian psychologist and international authority on bullying, Evelyn Field. There are several reasons why many managers and HR staff are failing to tackle bullying, but she believes that most often it is because they don't understand how widespread the problem is, the lasting damage it can cause people or how costly unchecked workplace bullying is to organisations and the community.

A study by Griffith University in 2001 estimated workplace bullying could be costing the Australian economy as much as $36 billion. Ms Field believes such costs could be slashed if more organisations established, communicated and enforced clear anti-bullying policies and procedures and invested in training their staff in effective communication.

In Australia Ms Field is best known for her work in preventing bullying in schools and teaching children social survival skills. She only branched into workplace bullying in response to the success of her book Bully Busting (Finch, 1999), which sold 21 000 copies and was translated into Italian, Croatian and Arabic. In her book she focused on school behaviour but she kept hearing from adults that they were relying on the book to help them tackle bullies at work. Since then, along with running corporate seminars on preventing and dealing with workplace bullying, she has run support groups for victims.

According to Ms Field, when a person has been bullied and the matter hasn't been resolved effectively, the victim often leaves the organisation but the trauma remains with them. As a result, when they

about employee privacy rights and 'a lack of rigorous evidence regarding effectiveness'.[23] As Oleson[24] has detailed, employee and union responses to workplace drug-testing programs may emphasise justice principles, such as: 'fair treatment for all workers, respect for the dignity of the individual, and enforcement of safety standards'. At present, most workplaces do not have anti-drug policies or programs and do not perform drug-testing. However, in Australia, as we noted in Chapter 4 Occupational health and safety, debate has grown about this issue. There are important implications not only for individuals and employers, but also for the development of social policy.[25]

Employee assistance programs

To assist employees with dependencies and to provide services to meet the diverse needs of their workforce, many employers are turning to **employee assistance programs (EAPs)** that attempt to ameliorate problems encountered by workers who are drug dependent, alcoholics or psychologically troubled. An EAP is a referral service that supervisors or employees can use to seek professional treatment for various problems. Employee assistance programs began in the 1950s with a focus on treating alcoholism, but in the 1980s they expanded into drug treatment as well. In the 1990s, more companies broadened their EAPs to include services such as counselling and health care, including mental health. These programs continue to evolve and many are now fully integrated into companies' overall health promotion and employee benefits programs.[26] Australian organisations with EAPs include Zoos Victoria and Telstra.[27] According to the United States Department of Labor, every $1 invested in an EAP saves employers $14 in employee costs. Dr John Lang, director of preventative health at HealthCorp Group (HCG), estimates that Australian employers receive a return of between three and seven times their EAP investment.[28]

Employee assistance programs (EAPs)
employer programs that attempt to ameliorate problems encountered by workers who are drug dependent, alcoholic or psychologically troubled.

join a new organisation, even if they have landed a better-paid job, bigger office and more comfortable conditions, their past experiences may affect how they assimilate and perform in the new role.

'If a person is asked in a job interview why they left their last job, they will say something like, "I wanted to get ahead". I don't think most people could say "because I was bullied at work", because they would feel embarrassed and ashamed, as though it was their fault', she says. 'But once they are in the job, some of the difficulties may show themselves. 'They are hyper-alert and can be extra sensitive because of what they have gone through and because it wasn't dealt with in their last place. They may feel people are having a go at them when they are just laughing … and their confidence will be down.'

'Another thing is that people can be cautious to try their hardest. They will give you 60 per cent rather than 95 per cent in terms of their wisdom, time and other things.'

Ms Field says the key to preventing bullying and stamping out bad behaviour is to ensure all staff understand what constitutes bullying and that such behaviour is unacceptable. When organisations have in place and spell out their policies to new staff in induction programs, staff understand that 'this new organisation is very different to their last one', she says.

She also suggests knowledge of policies be included in training and development for all supervisors and managers. The key to successful prevention is that everyone in the organisation hears the same message. 'That we respect people in this workplace, that we understand that people will have differences of opinion and that we have structures by which we resolve them. If there are issues around bullying, then the workplace will take steps to deal with it.'

Ms Field also suggests that all new staff be given communication skills training to reinforce the message that healthy communication between staff is important in the organisation.

'I think whether people have come into an organisation with their communication skills intact or not that they benefit from being given training and skills.'

Finally, to stamp out bullying all staff need to know what will happen if an incident is reported. 'People have to know that if they treat other people badly, there will be a consequence such as there will be three warnings and they will be out, or that they will not be promoted. Once the structures are there, people tend to fit in with the structures.'

Source: W. Taylor, 2006, 'Taking the bully by the horns', *The Age*, 30 September, p. 11.

Employee assistance programs vary widely, but most share some basic elements. First, the programs are usually identified in official documents published by the employer (for example, employee handbooks). Supervisors (and union representatives, where relevant) are trained to use the referral service for employees whom they suspect of having health-related problems. Employees are also trained to use the system to make self-referrals when necessary. For example, AMP provides an EAP offering a confidential counselling service for employees.[29] This service is part of AMP's comprehensive range of human resource strategies aimed at employee retention. Finally, costs and benefits of the programs (as measured in positive employee outcomes such as return-to-work rates) are evaluated on an annual basis—typically.

Given EAPs' wide range of options and evolving nature, we need to constantly analyse their effectiveness. For example, there is a current debate about the desirability of costly, intensive, inpatient alcoholism and substance abuse services over less costly outpatient care. Some fear that the lower initial costs of outpatient treatment might be offset by higher long-term costs, because of relapse or other forms of failure. Although both employers (for cost reasons) and employees (for convenience reasons) may be attracted to short-term, low-cost treatments, everyone might be better served by focusing on long-term costs and wellbeing.

Another controversy surrounding EAPs is whether to establish an in-house EAP staffed with professionals who work for the company or employ an outside agency. The in-house approach is usually more cost-effective and offers employees rapid, convenient access to services. However, in-house plans run the risk of a loss of confidentiality. Indeed, employees who alleged that they suffered harm in the course of obtaining services from in-house EAPs[30] have filed lawsuits.

By adhering to certain guidelines, employers can minimise their liability while still benefiting from EAPs. First, the company should retain the services of qualified, experienced professionals and be able to objectively document their qualifications. Second, the company should not use coercive tactics in securing employees' participation in the EAP. This is easier said than done and supervisors will likely require training in how to confront troubled employees in a manner that makes them willing to seek help, rather than becoming defensive. Third, companies should ensure confidentiality for employees using EAPs. For example, it is a good idea to strictly limit access to the EAP data in the human resource information system. Fourth, employers should ensure that employees have the opportunity to provide feedback on the services received through their EAP. This allows the company to catch any problems while they are still isolated events.[31]

Outplacement counselling

As companies restructure, rationalise operations and reduce or 'downsize' staffing levels, many Australian workers experience retrenchment.[32] According to Ted Davis, managing director of a prominent Australian outplacement specialist firm: 'Close to 100 per cent of people in professional or managerial positions are now likely to face retrenchment at some point in their career'.[33] Research conducted at Queensland University of Technology shows that the four major Australian banks retrenched 25 000 employees in the 1990s.[34] Between 1996 and 2000, Telstra cut 26 000 jobs. In March 2000, Telstra announced that over the following two years another 16 000 jobs would be removed from its total workforce of 51 700 people.[35]

Whether involuntary unemployment is the result of dismissal or redundancy, it may be a difficult process for any individual. The terminal nature of an employee discharge may not only leave the person angry, it may also lead to confusion as to how to react and leave the person in a quandary regarding what happens next. Therefore, many organisations provide **outplacement counselling**, which refers to counselling that tries to help displaced employees manage the transition from one job to another.

Some organisations have their own in-house staff to conduct this counselling. In other companies, outside consultants are kept on a retainer basis, to help with individual cases. Whether in-house staff or outside consultants provide outplacement counselling, the goals remain the same—that is, outplacement programs are in place to help former employees deal with the psychological issues (for example, grief, depression, fear and anger) associated with losing their jobs, while at the same time helping them find new employment.[36] Many companies, particularly larger firms, now utilise outplacement specialists. Many employers pay for outplacement programs of three months or longer to help employees find new employment.

According to the consulting firm DBM Australia, in a survey conducted in 1999 with 450 managers and executives in outplacement programs, 39 per cent were from the finance sector and only half of these remained in the finance sector when they found new employment. The survey showed that the 'typical' client of outplacement services was male, aged 46, had worked for his previous firm for 10 years and had been earning around $115 000 a year. On average, it took these clients five months to find new employment.[37]

Of course, not all retrenchments are involuntary. Downsizing programs will often include voluntary retrenchments, which some employees view as positive opportunities to explore new career directions. In cases of involuntary retrenchment, too, despite the initial trauma, many employees do in fact view involuntary retrenchment as an opportunity and go on to develop in new directions.

There are several reasons for the increased use of outplacement services. The manner in which a dismissal or retrenchment is managed can have significant implications for the individual and the organisation. First, provision of outplacement services may be a way to provide some comfort, respect and dignity for individuals who are dismissed. Second, employers realise that the morale of employees remaining with their organisation will be affected by the way in which they observe the treatment of departing employees. Third, companies seek to protect their image and credibility in the broader community. Fourth, outplacement services may also be regarded as a way to reduce a firm's exposure to legal action.[38]

Outplacement specialist firms in Australia typically provide senior executives with an 'office' so those clients may use computers, a research library and other services. Clients are encouraged to bring their spouses into the 'office' so that they can share in the program and develop an awareness of the processes involved in the outplacement program. Outplacement counsellors work with clients to develop personalised strategies in order to find suitable employment.[39]

Outplacement counselling and services are aimed at helping people realise that losing a job is not the end of the world and that other opportunities exist. Indeed, for many people, losing a job can be a critical learning experience that plants the seed for future success. For example, Kevin Davis accepted a redundancy package at ANZ Banking Group in the mid 1990s. He moved on to operate a business that provides training to managers and other staff, to help them to develop mentoring skills. He also conducts 'career-planning courses at schools and teaches redundant workers about taking responsibility for their careers and lives'.[40]

While dismissal or retrenchment may be inevitable in some circumstances, outplacement services can provide valuable assistance, provided it is done in an effective way.[41] It is also recognised that retaining people who can make contributions is a key to gaining and maintaining competitive advantage. The next section of this chapter discusses the management of voluntary turnover.

Outplacement counselling
refers to counselling that tries to help displaced employees manage the transition from one job to another.

Managing voluntary turnover

Employers are more concerned than ever about employee retention and many firms are implementing strategies to manage turnover and retention. For example, in 1998, Ernst & Young created an 'office of retention', which had its own separate budget and was charged with identifying a subset of people at all levels of the organisation who were central to Ernst & Young's future and doing what was necessary to keep these people happy.[42] More recently, many organisations have developed a strong focus on the retention of talent.

Voluntary turnover reflects a separation initiated by the individual, often when the organisation would prefer that the person stay a member of the organisation.[43] Reasons for voluntary turnover vary among individuals, but the issue is a widespread and costly concern for organisations. As discussed in 'HRM spotlight: Frustration grows at staff churn rates of up to 40 per cent', turnover can be very dysfunctional for an organisation. Also, employee turnover carries some risks for individuals: some achieve benefits through turnover, yet others can have negative experiences.[44] In this section of the chapter, we examine the 'job withdrawal process' that characterises voluntary employee turnover and illustrate the central role that job satisfaction plays in this process. We also discuss what aspects of job satisfaction seem most critical to retention and how to measure these facets. For example, surveys have shown that, in many workplaces, job flexibility and lifestyle choices are seen as vital factors in retaining skilled employees, and career development and salary are reported as particularly important for the retention of middle managers. According to Rosemary Foxcroft, managing director of management consultancy firm DBM: 'for senior managers, however, what appears to be important is a broader range of strategies, including remuneration, lifestyle and career development'.[45] Finally, we show how survey feedback interventions, designed around these measures, can be used to strategically manage the voluntary turnover process so that high performers are retained, while marginal performers are allowed to leave. One reason as to why it is important for managers to understand the factors that influence turnover decisions is that, on average, companies lose about A$1 million for every 10 professional and managerial employees who resign.[46]

> **Voluntary turnover** reflects a separation initiated by the individual, often when the organisation would prefer that the person stay a member of the organisation.

Process of job withdrawal

Job withdrawal is a set of behaviours that dissatisfied individuals enact to avoid the work situation. The right side of Figure 17.1 below shows a model grouping the overall set of behaviours into three categories: behaviour change, physical job withdrawal and psychological job withdrawal.

> **Job withdrawal** a set of behaviours that dissatisfied individuals enact to avoid the work situation.

FIGURE 17.1 An overall model of the job dissatisfaction–job withdrawal process

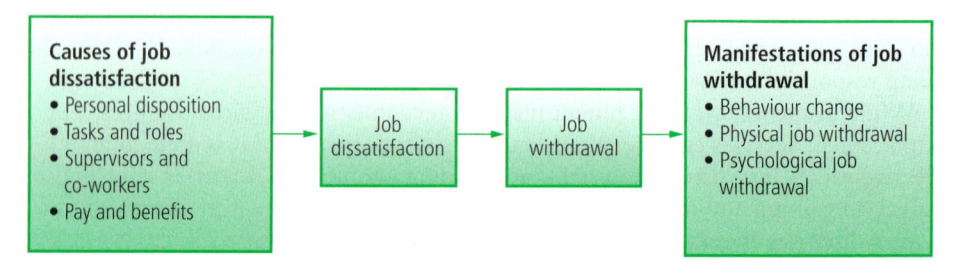

Causes of job dissatisfaction
- Personal disposition
- Tasks and roles
- Supervisors and co-workers
- Pay and benefits

→ Job dissatisfaction → Job withdrawal →

Manifestations of job withdrawal
- Behaviour change
- Physical job withdrawal
- Psychological job withdrawal

FRUSTRATION GROWS AT STAFF CHURN RATES OF UP TO 40pc

Australian law firms are becoming used to annual staff turnover rates of at least 20 per cent, but that doesn't mean they're happy about it.

One firm, which did not wish to be named, said its turnover was costing it more than $100 000 for each person that left and, in total, $3 million a year.

There's a growing sense of frustration that higher salaries, flexible workplaces, mentoring and other perks are doing little to stem the flood out of firms' doors of generation X and Y lawyers with three to six years post-qualification experience.

In some firms, the turnover rate is reaching alarming proportions: rates of 30–40 per cent among early career lawyers are now not unusual.

A survey released last week by the Law Institute of Victoria on flexible work practices reported anecdotal evidence of employee churn rates of between 20 and 40 per cent.

And in the US, a survey of 175 firms released last month by Wachovia Wealth Management reported an average lawyer attrition rate of 24.9 per cent for firms with more than 300 lawyers. 'The velocity of attorney turnover is astounding', it concluded.

While no firm interviewed by *The Australian Financial Review* admitted to losing 40 per cent of its staff annually, most said their turnover was 'in the low 20s'.

'Most of the top level is around 20 per cent', says John Denton, the managing partner of Corrs Chambers Westgarth. 'And everyone is working hard to bring it down.'

He said an average of 20 per cent would be unacceptably high for most businesses, which might expect annual staff turnover of 5–10 per cent. 'Even though we're operating on industry norms, we consider those norms to be too high', said Mr Denton, who described Corrs' turnover rate as 'down towards 20 per cent'.

At just under 20 per cent, Baker & McKenzie is doing better than many of its competitors, but national managing partner Mark Chapple would like to see turnover fall to 10–12 per cent. 'Realistically, that's as low as you could hope to go', he said.

Most of the departures are not to competitors, but to overseas work and travel, in-house roles and other careers such as investment banking.

Baker & McKenzie's most recent exit survey of people leaving the firm showed 30 per cent were heading overseas, 20 per cent were going to in-house roles and only 5 per cent were defecting to rival law firms.

Freehills reports a similar pattern, with many of its younger lawyers heading off to London, contributing to a turnover rate slightly over 20 per cent. But managing partner Peter Butler says retention rates at fifth year and above improve quite significantly.

Source: L. Schmidt. 2006, 'Frustration grows at staff churn rates of up to 40pc', *Australian Financial Review*, 21 July, p. 57. © 2006 Copyright John Fairfax Holdings Limited. www.afr.com Not available for re-distribution.

We present the various forms of withdrawal in a progression—as if individuals try the next category only if the preceding is either unsuccessful or impossible to implement. This theory of progression of withdrawal has a long history and many adherents.[17] Others have suggested that there is no tight progression in that any one of the categories can compensate for another, and people choose the category that is most likely to redress the specific source of dissatisfaction.[48] Either way, the withdrawal behaviours are clearly related to one another and they are all at least partially caused by job dissatisfaction.[49]

Behaviour change

One might expect that an employee's first response to dissatisfaction would be to try to change the conditions that generate the dissatisfaction. This can lead to supervisor–subordinate confrontation, perhaps conflict, as dissatisfied workers try to bring about changes in policy or upper-level personnel. Where employees are unionised, it may lead to an increased number of grievances being filed.[50] Where employees are not unionised, dissatisfaction can lead to the formation of a union. Research indicates that there is a considerably strong relationship between dissatisfaction with economic aspects of work and unionisation activity[51] (see Chapter 5 Industrial relations).

In organisations without unions, employees can also initiate change through **whistleblowing** (that is, reporting outside an organisation on activities within an organisation that have the potential to cause serious harm to the public).[52] Employees can also take legal action against their employers when disputed policies relate to race, gender, safe working conditions or any other aspect of employment regulated by laws. Such lawsuits are costly, both financially and in terms of the firm's image, regardless of whether the firm wins or loses. Most employers would prefer to avoid litigation altogether. Keeping a majority of their employees happy is one means of achieving this.

Whistleblowing reporting outside an organisation on activities within an organisation that have the potential to cause serious harm to the public.

Physical job withdrawal

If the job conditions cannot be changed, a dissatisfied worker may be able to solve his or her problem by leaving the job. This could take the form of an internal transfer if the dissatisfaction is job-specific (for example, the result of an unfair supervisor or unpleasant working conditions). On the other hand, if the source of the dissatisfaction relates to organisation-wide policies (for example, lack of job security or below-market pay levels), organisational turnover is likely. It is interesting to note that recent research by Sandra Trudgett has shown that women and men resign from organisations for essentially the same reasons—related to their personal career advancement.[53]

Many employees who would like to quit their jobs have to stay on if they have no other employment opportunities. Another way of physically removing oneself from the dissatisfying work is to be absent.[54] Like turnover, absenteeism is disruptive and costly to an organisation. Absenteeism is a substantial problem in many organisations. Turnover, absenteeism and workplace inefficiencies may all be symptoms of workplace cultures and practices that are less than ideal. Organisations that seek to increase employee morale, commitment and satisfaction, and reduce sources of stress and problems at work, will improve their ability to recruit and retain talented and valued employees.[55]

A survey conducted in 1999 estimated that absenteeism costs Australian businesses $2560 million each year. The same survey found that 12.4 per cent of respondents admitted that none of their absenteeism in the previous year had been genuine. Sixty-seven per cent preferred to take a 'sickie' on a Monday and 25 per cent chose a Friday, in order to have an extended weekend. The most popular 'reasons' for absenteeism were the flu (54 per cent), stomach upsets (21 per cent), migraines (12.2 per cent), diarrhoea (6.4 per cent) and food poisoning (5.7 per cent).[56]

Another survey, commissioned by the Australian Industry Group (AIG), was conducted with over 200 manufacturing firms. This survey found that as few as one in nine days taken off from work were due to illness. This survey also showed that businesses could save $1000 per employee each year if absenteeism rates could be reduced by 1 per cent.[57] Due to the complex range of factors that may contribute to absenteeism, developing strategies to reduce absenteeism may be challenging.

A dissatisfied employee may be late for work; thus, not absent for a whole day. This may not be as disruptive as absenteeism; however, tardiness can be costly and it is related to job satisfaction.[58] Tardiness can be especially costly when companies are organised around teams, because the tardy individual often creates difficulties that spill over and affect the other team members.

Psychological withdrawal

When dissatisfied employees are unable to change their situation or remove themselves physically from their jobs, they may psychologically disengage themselves from their jobs. Although they are physically on the job, their minds may be somewhere else.

This psychological disengagement can take several forms. First, if the primary dissatisfaction has to do with the job itself, the employee may display a considerably low level of **job involvement**—that is, the degree to which people identify themselves with their jobs. People who are uninvolved with their jobs consider their work an unimportant aspect of their lives. For them, performing well or poorly on the job does not really affect their self-concept, which makes them harder to motivate.[59] Over time, job dissatisfaction leads to low job involvement.

> **Job involvement**
> the degree to which people identify themselves with their jobs.

A second form of psychological disengagement, which can occur when the dissatisfaction is with the employer as a whole, is a low level of **organisational commitment**—that is, the degree to which an employee identifies with the organisation and is willing to put forth effort on its behalf.[60] Individuals who have low organisational commitment are often only waiting for the first good opportunity to quit their jobs. In other words, they have developed a strong intention to leave their organisations. In the meantime, like individuals with low job involvement, they are often difficult to motivate. Like job involvement, organisational commitment is strongly related to job satisfaction.[61] Organisational commitment has been attracting a great deal of attention recently. Many employers feel that the staffing policies of recent decades may have killed company loyalty.[62] To cope with global competition, deregulation, hostile takeovers and unprecedented levels of corporate debt, many companies were 'forced' to slash their labour costs through massive retrenchments.

> **Organisational commitment**
> the degree to which an employee identifies with the organisation and is willing to put forth effort on its behalf.

Job satisfaction and job withdrawal

As shown in Figure 17.1, the key driving force behind all the different forms of job withdrawal is job satisfaction. We will define **job satisfaction** as a pleasurable feeling that results from the perception that a person's job fulfils or allows for the fulfilment of that person's important job values.[63] This definition reflects three important aspects of job satisfaction. First, job satisfaction is a function of values, defined as: 'what a person consciously or unconsciously desires to obtain'. Second, the definition of job satisfaction emphasises that different employees have different views about which values are important, and this is critical in determining the nature and degree of their job satisfaction. One person may value high pay above all else, another may value the opportunity to travel. Yet another may value staying within a specific geographic region. The third important aspect of job satisfaction is perception. It is a person's perception of his or her present situation, relative to his or her values, that matters. An individual's perceptions may not be a completely accurate reflection of reality and different people may view the same situation differently.

> **Job satisfaction**
> a pleasurable feeling that results from the perception that a person's job fulfils or allows for the fulfilment of that person's important job values.

In particular, people's perceptions are often strongly influenced by their frame of reference. A **frame of reference** is a standard point that serves as a comparison for other points and, thus, provides meaning. For example, an upper-level executive who offers a 6 per cent salary increase to a lower-level manager might expect this to make the manager happy, because inflation (the executive's frame of reference) is only 3 per cent. The manager, on the other hand, might find the pay rise quite unsatisfactory, because it is less than the 9 per cent rise received by one of her colleagues who does similar work (the manager's frame of reference). A person's frame of reference often reflects his or her average past experience.[64] It may also reflect his or her perceptions of other people's experience (that is, his reference group).[65] Thus, values, perceptions and importance are the three components of job satisfaction. People will be satisfied with their jobs as long as they perceive that their jobs meet their important values.

> **Frame of reference**
> a standard point that serves as a comparison for other points and, thus, provides meaning.

Sources of job dissatisfaction

Many aspects of people and organisations can cause dissatisfaction among employees. We will focus on the categories shown on the left side of Figure 17.1.

Personal dispositions

Dissatisfaction is an emotion that ultimately resides within the person; thus, it is not surprising that many who have studied these outcomes have focused on individual differences. **Negative affectivity** is a term used to describe a dispositional dimension that reflects pervasive individual differences in satisfaction with any and all aspects of life. Individuals who are high in negative affectivity report higher levels of aversive mood states, including anger, contempt, disgust, guilt, fear and nervousness across all contexts (that is, work and non-work).[66]

> **Negative affectivity**
> a dispositional dimension that reflects pervasive individual differences in satisfaction with any and all aspects of life.

People who are high in negative affectivity tend to focus extensively on the negative aspects of themselves and others.[67] They are also more likely, in a given situation, to experience significantly higher levels of distress than others—which implies that some people bring dissatisfaction with them to work. Research has shown that negative affectivity in early adolescence is predictive of overall job dissatisfaction in adulthood. Research has also shown significant relationships between work attitudes measured over five-year[68] and 10-year[69] periods, including workers who changed employers and/or occupations. Thus, these people may be relatively dissatisfied regardless of what steps the organisation or the manager takes.

Although those low in negative affectivity generally report more job satisfaction than those who are high in it, when people who are generally low in negative affectivity do decide they are dissatisfied with their work, their behavioural reaction is much stronger. That is, research on nurses has shown that the relationship between job satisfaction and turnover is especially high for those low in negative affectivity. Relative to those with a positive outlook on life, people high in negative affectivity are more used to being dissatisfied and hold out less hope that finding a new job will lead to any better results.[70]

Although the causes of negative affectivity are not completely known, research that examined identical twins who were raised apart suggests that there may be a genetic component.[71] Thirty-four pairs of twins were measured for their general job satisfaction and their satisfaction with intrinsic and extrinsic aspects of the job. The researchers found a significant relationship between the ratings for each member of a pair, despite the fact that the twins were raised apart and worked at different jobs. Other research on genetic twins reared apart has shown similar effects on perceptions of the degree to which an individual's organisation provides a supportive climate.[72]

This suggests the importance of personnel selection as a way of raising overall levels of employee satisfaction. Interviews should assess the degree to which any job applicant has a history of chronic dissatisfaction with his or her employment. If an applicant states that he was dissatisfied with his past six jobs, what makes the employer think he will not be dissatisfied with this one? Although the focus here is on the workplace context, we must recognise that dissatisfaction with other facets of life can spill over into the workplace. That is, a worker who is having problems with a spouse or family may attribute some of this negative affect to the job or organisation.

As many as one in 10 workers suffer from depression, anxiety, stress and burnout, according to a worldwide study conducted by the International Labour Organization, headquartered in Geneva, Switzerland, focusing on mental health in the workplace. Mental health problems among the work-age population are rising in all the countries studied, as are the costs of mental health disabilities (also see Chapter 4 Occupational health and safety).[73]

In Australia, workplace stress is widespread, expensive and increasing. Nationally, the total cost of workers compensation claims for stress-related conditions is estimated at over $200 million every year.[74] Total financial costs have been estimated to be between three and six times this figure, in addition to the personal costs suffered. Numerous surveys of workers and workplaces have found that the most frequently cited causes of stress in the workplace include lack of communication, increased workload, job insecurity, organisational change and poor work organisation. Clearly, these issues relate to the health of the organisation, not the individual, and must be addressed by comprehensive changes in organisational culture, HRM strategies and practices. At Westpac Banking Corporation, employees are offered health maintenance and stress management programs and the bank involves individuals and groups in decision-making processes. Westpac is doing this to not only maintain employees' health, but it is convinced that it results in better service delivery; and happy employees mean satisfied customers.[75]

Although managers cannot be expected to become clinical psychologists, in their attempt to diagnose some work-related performance problems, they should be aware of the possibility of illnesses such as depression. Employees can be advised to seek help from qualified professionals via a company-sponsored employee assistance program (EAP).

Tasks and roles

As a predictor of job dissatisfaction, nothing surpasses the nature of the task itself.[76] Many aspects of a task have been linked to dissatisfaction. Several elaborate theories relating task characteristics to worker reactions have been formulated and extensively tested. We discussed several of these in Chapter 4 Occupational health and safety. In this section, we will focus on three primary aspects of tasks that affect job satisfaction: the complexity of the task, the degree of physical strain and exertion of the job, and the value the employee puts on the task.[77]

With a few exceptions, there is a strong positive relationship between task complexity and job satisfaction. That is, the boredom generated by simple, repetitive jobs that do not mentally challenge the worker leads to frustration and dissatisfaction.[78] Moreover, monotony at work has been shown to have a particularly strong negative effect on women, relative to men. For example, one study of blue-collar workers in 32 manufacturing plants showed that increased repetitive activity at work led to absenteeism rates among women that were three times those for men.[79]

One intervention that employees themselves often introduce to low-complexity situations is to bring personal stereo headsets to work. Many supervisors disapprove of this practice, which can be understood in situations where employees need to interact with customers. However, in simple jobs with minimal customer contact (for example, processing paperwork or data entry) the research actually suggests that personal stereo headsets can improve performance. For example, one study examined stereo headset use among workers in 32 jobs within a large retail organisation. The results indicated the stereo group outperformed a non-stereo control group on simple jobs (for example, invoice processing), but performed worse than the controls for jobs that were high in complexity (for example, accounting).[80]

The second primary aspect of a task that affects job satisfaction is the degree to which the job involves physical strain and exertion.[81] This aspect is sometimes overlooked at a time when automation has removed much of the physical strain associated with jobs. Indeed, the fact that technology has aimed to lessen work-related physical exertion indicates that such exertion is almost universally considered undesirable. Nevertheless, many jobs can still be characterised as physically demanding.

The third primary aspect is whether the object of the work promotes something valued by the worker. Many volunteer workers perform their jobs almost exclusively because of the meaning they attach to the work. Although some of these jobs are low in complexity and high in physical exertion, these volunteers view themselves as performing a worthwhile service. Thus, this overrides the other two factors and increases satisfaction with the job.

One of the major interventions aimed at reducing job dissatisfaction is job enrichment, which explicitly focuses on the task as a source of dissatisfaction. **Job enrichment** refers to specific ways in which to add complexity and meaningfulness to a person's work. As the term suggests, this intervention is directed at jobs that are 'impoverished' or boring because of their repetitive nature or low scope. Many job-enrichment programs are based on the job characteristics theory discussed earlier in Chapter 4 Occupational health and safety.

For example, in many organisations, work has for several decades been structured along four large functional units: manufacturing, research, marketing and finance. Segmenting the work this way reduces the meaningfulness of many jobs. It also isolates workers from each other and distances them from customers. Thus, restructuring the organisation into separate product divisions—so that each does its own manufacturing, research, marketing and finance—can provide employees with a better understanding of not only their own specialisation, but also the organisation and its customers overall.

Job design characteristics, such as meaningful, varied work, rather than tedious, exhausting work, have been well documented as being influential in employee motivation, organisational commitment, job satisfaction and job performance[82] (also see Chapter 6 Analysis and design of work). Organising work around projects can be an effective form of developing organisational commitment and performance. When employees feel a sense of ownership over their tasks, and if their tasks comprise a complete project, they have greater commitment to high performance. Team-based projects can further reinforce employee commitment and performance. If the team members are accountable for their performance, and rewards are based on team performance, employee commitment has been shown to increase.

For example, at the Fisher and Paykel range and dishwasher manufacturing division in New Zealand, employees were organised into semi-autonomous 'everyday work teams'. Team-building activities and skill development training were provided. The teams were given authority to make changes in production or other work procedures. Several improvements were achieved with no costs involved. One team achieved a saving of $900 per annum by recycling polystyrene packaging. Another team saved $7000 per annum by bringing in-house an activity previously provided by a vendor. While these particular gains are small, in terms of overall improvements and organisational climate, the implementation of teams is considered to be successful.[83]

Another task-based intervention is **job rotation**—the process of systematically moving a single individual from one job to another over the course of time. Although employees may not feel capable of putting up with the dissatisfying aspects of a particular job indefinitely, they often feel they can do so on a temporary basis. Job rotation can do more than simply spread out the dissatisfying aspects of a particular job. It can increase work complexity for employees and provide valuable cross-training in jobs so that employees eventually understand many different jobs. This makes for a more flexible workforce and increases workers' appreciation of the other tasks that have to be accomplished for the organisation to complete its mission.[84]

Person–job match (also known as job customisation) programs allow employees to assess their own interests, skills and values, and encourage managers to tailor rewards and assignments to suit the needs of individuals. There are several issues to consider in such programs. First, these programs require careful management of fairness and equity issues, to ensure **distributive justice**—the perception that rewards are distributed in relation to contribution. Second, the form of reward must be considered. If programs are selective, legal issues and the effects on morale must be determined.[85]

In addition to the specific task performed by an individual, in the broader scheme of work, each person also has a 'role' in the organisation.[86] The person's role in the organisation can be defined as the set of expected behaviours that both the person and other people who make up the social environment have for the person in that job. These expected behaviours include all the formal aspects of the job and usually much more as well. That is, co-workers, supervisors and clients or customers have expectations for the person that go beyond what is formally described as the person's job. Expectations have a large impact on how the person responds to the work.

Three aspects of organisational roles stand out as significant influences on job satisfaction: role ambiguity, role conflict and role overload. **Role ambiguity** refers to the level of uncertainty about what an organisation expects from an employee in terms of what to do or how to do it. Ambiguity associated with work methods and scheduling are two of the most problematic forms of ambiguity. By far the most critical dimension in terms of predicting job satisfaction, however, is ambiguity relating to performance criteria. Employees have a strong need to know precisely how they are going to be evaluated on the job—and when this is unclear, job satisfaction suffers.[87]

A second source of dissatisfaction is **role conflict**—recognition of incompatible or contradictory demands by the person who occupies a role. Role conflict occurs in many different forms. For example, a member of a cross-functional project team might have a project manager as well as a manager in his or her functional area who holds mutually exclusive expectations for the employee. Another form of role conflict occurs when the employee may be occupying more than one role at a time and the roles have incompatible expectations. Conflict between work roles and family roles, for example, is common in organisations (also see Chapter 9 Managing diversity and work–life balance).

This is especially a problem when an employee is asked to accept an assignment overseas that is highly disruptive to other members of the family. Research shows that the inability to effectively manage this type of role conflict is the single biggest cause of expatriate turnover (see Chapter 16 International human resource management, for more details about expatriate management).[88] Many organisations try to minimise work–family conflict for both domestically and internationally placed employees through various forms of family-friendly benefits (for example, company-sponsored daycare or flexitime).[89] This type of conflict creates dissatisfaction among employees and can lead to problems in retention.

Dissatisfaction can also arise from **role overload**, a state in which too many expectations or demands are placed on a person (whereas role underload refers to the opposite problem). There can be either too much or too little task scope. Research on job stress has focused primarily on high-scope jobs (that is, jobs that require the person to manage too many things). As we have noted, role overload seems to be an increasingly prevalent problem in today's organisations, because of their emphasis on downsizing and cost cutting.[90]

Interventions that are aimed directly at role elements have been created because role problems are ranked slightly behind job problems in creating job dissatisfaction. One such intervention is the **role analysis technique**—a method that enables a role occupant and other members of the role occupant's role-set to specify and examine their expectations for a specific employee. As shown in Figure 17.2, role analysis is

Distributive justice
(also distributive fairness) the perception that rewards are distributed in relation to contribution.

Role ambiguity
the level of uncertainty about what an organisation expects from an employee in terms of what to do and how to do it.

Role conflict
recognition of incompatible or contradictory demands by the person occupying a role.

Role overload
a state in which too many expectations or demands are placed on a person.

Role analysis technique
a method that enables a role occupant and other members of the role occupant's role-set to specify and examine their expectations for the role occupant.

designed to increase the communication and understanding of the various sets of role expectations that exist for a specific employee.[91]

In the role analysis technique, the role occupant and each member of the role occupant's role-set (for example, supervisors, co-workers and subordinates) are asked to write down their expectations for the role occupant. Then everybody is gathered together and each person goes through his or her list. All the expectations are written out so that ambiguities can be removed and conflicts identified. Where there are conflicts, the group as a whole tries to decide how they should be resolved. When this is done throughout an organisation, instances of overload and underload may be discovered and role requirements may be traded off so that more balanced roles are developed.

Supervisors and co-workers

The two primary sets of people in an organisation who affect job satisfaction are co-workers and supervisors. A person may be satisfied with her or his supervisor and co-workers for one or more of the following three reasons. First, she or he may have many of the same values, attitudes and philosophies as the co-workers and supervisors. Most individuals find this considerably important. Indeed, many organisations try to foster a culture of shared values among employees. If individuals cannot generate a unifying culture throughout an entire organisation, it is worth noting that increases in job satisfaction can be derived simply from congruence among supervisors and subordinates at each level.[92]

Second, a person may be satisfied with his or her supervisor and co-workers because they provide social support. Social support is the degree to which the person is surrounded by other people who are sympathetic and caring. Considerable research indicates that social support is a strong predictor of job satisfaction, whether the

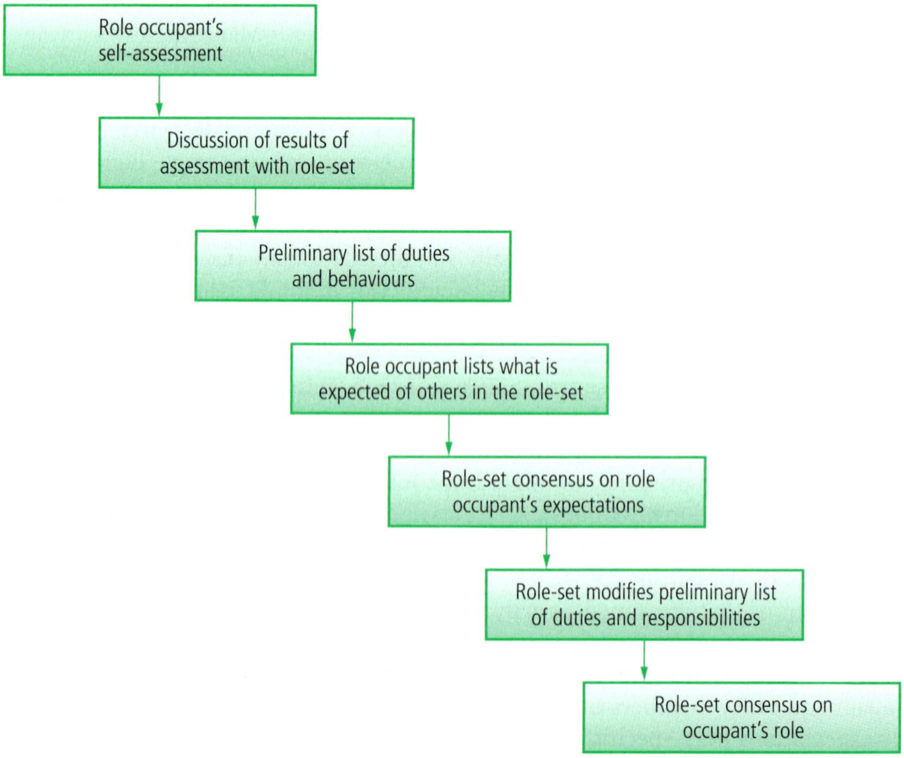

FIGURE 17.2 A schematic representation of the role analysis technique

support comes from supervisors or co-workers.[93] Also, as we indicated earlier, fair interpersonal treatment in terms of interactional justice is also a strong predictor of job satisfaction and turnover.[94]

Third, a person's supervisor or co-workers may help that person attain some valued outcome. For example, a new employee may be uncertain about what goals to pursue or what paths to take in order to achieve those goals. He or she will likely be satisfied with a supervisor or with co-workers who can help clarify those goals and paths.[95]

Many organisations foster team building, both on and off the job (for example, via sports teams or social activities), because a supportive environment reduces dissatisfaction. The idea is that group cohesiveness and support for individual group members will be increased through exposure and joint efforts. Although management certainly cannot ensure that each stressed employee develops friends, it can make it easier for employees to interact—a necessary condition for developing friendship and rapport.

Pay and benefits

While we should not discount the influence of the job incumbent, the job itself and the surrounding people in terms of influencing job satisfaction, for most people work is their primary source of income and financial security. Pay is also seen as an indicator of status within the organisation and in society at large. Thus, for some people, pay is a reflection of self-worth, so pay satisfaction takes on critical significance when it comes to retention.

One of the main dimensions of satisfaction with pay deals with pay levels—that is, the absolute amount of income associated with the job. Indeed, when it comes to retention, employees being recruited away from one organisation by another are often lured with promises of higher pay levels. Satisfaction with benefits is another important dimension of overall pay satisfaction.

Whereas satisfaction with pay levels reflects an interest in the absolute value of these dimensions, two other important aspects of pay satisfaction take on a more relative nature. Satisfaction with pay structure deals with how happy the person is with the manner in which pay within the organisation is ranked or ordered across different job categories. A manager of a salesforce, for example, might be satisfied with his or her overall pay, but if he or she discovers that, due to sales commissions, some subordinate actually has a higher pay, then dissatisfaction with the structure of pay may result. Finally, relative to changes over time, satisfaction with pay rises also needs to be considered. People generally expect that their pay will increase over time and to the extent that this expectation is not met, they may become dissatisfied with pay increases.

It is interesting to note that a recent Australian Government parliamentary inquiry found that employees who buy shares in their company are less likely to be absent. The report shows that companies with share ownership plans have a 2.2 per cent absenteeism rate compared to a 2.5 per cent absenteeism rate for companies without such a plan.[96]

Bonuses and/or incentives are common human resource practices that are intended to increase the retention of employees. These may include signing bonuses, performance-related pay, premium payments for highly valued skills and payment of incentives. However, a criticism of these practices is that it is relatively easy for competitors to 'match' remuneration packages. Lucrative packages may, in effect, contribute more to wage inflation than to long-term retention.[97]

Considering the criticism of financial rewards, it may be wise to include non-financial rewards into remuneration programs. These may include activities such as giving employees more control over their work schedule, involving employees in project teams to solve business problems, and recognition of employees in several ways—informally, personally and frequently.

Like non-financial rewards, loyalty programs such as the social function of the work environment, particularly employee loyalty to colleagues, are (it has been argued) an important factor in employee retention. Social ties that bind employees to their work colleagues and current employment can be created and reinforced via company-sponsored social activities. Creating teams (as previously discussed) also reinforces social ties at work.

Managing employee retention

It is well recognised that human resource management strategies are able to influence the development and retention of employees.[98] Retention and development of 'intellectual capital' or knowledge possessed by employees represents a 'key source of sustainable competitive advantage for organisations,'[99] as discussed in 'Managing challenges of attracting and retaining people: How to keep them keen'..

For example, AMP has a comprehensive range of employee retention strategies in addition to its EAP. The company's flexible work practices include part-time work with pro rata benefits, job sharing, working from home and flexible hours. There are also programs for employees on parental leave to maintain contact with the organisation and a range of options to help women return to work after having children. The company has individual development programs for all employees, study assistance, a bonus scheme, a share-option program and an annual employee opinion survey.[100]

The issue of employee retention has become a 'hot' topic among HR researchers and practitioners. Two major reasons for the growing importance of retention have been identified: the ongoing rise in employee turnover rates in many industries and the increasing costs associated with employee turnover.[101] It should be acknowledged, however, that long-term retention of all employees might be neither desirable nor possible. It is inevitable that some employees will be attracted by opportunities outside an organisation and lured by aggressive recruiting strategies in other organisations. Peter Cappelli argues that: 'the old goal of HR management—to minimise overall employee turnover—needs to be replaced by a new goal: to influence who leaves and when'.[102]

Many employee retention strategies have been documented in the HR research literature. Some may be more suitable for a given organisation than others. It is necessary to place retention strategies in the context of an overall approach to knowledge development and organisational performance.[103] Conceptual HRM literature strongly argues for the importance of developing a strategic partnership role for HRM, incorporating consistent HR strategies and practices; and the empirical results point to significant economic returns to the organisation for doing so.[104]

The 'war for talent' is a phrase coined by the management consultancy McKinsey and Company in a 1998 article in the *McKinsey Quarterly*. The phrase reflects the fierce competition for skilled employees, particularly knowledge workers. For these workers, many companies have developed retention strategies to enhance employee views of their remuneration, share schemes, training, career paths and workplace flexibility. It should be noted that the focus of much of this activity is on knowledge workers. Most workers do not enjoy such favoured status.[105]

David Smith, human resources manager at NRMA, says:

> The competition for talent is certainly a reality in Australia. I believe senior management now is well aware of this and that is why we're seeing people management and leadership emerge as key performance areas, along with the traditional financial, customer and efficiency performance measures. Attraction and retention are the key to successful people management, but so is developing and growing internal talent.[106]

HOW TO KEEP THEM KEEN

Talent retention is top of mind for HR at present. Five HR directors reveal their approach to keeping the best performers—UK style.

Brian Fitzgerald, director of HR development, Atkins

'For engineering consultancy Atkins, which has about 14 000 staff, keeping talented people happy is a business imperative. To this end we have set up a Management Development Centre (MDC), which uses several evaluation techniques including 360-degree surveys, rigorous self-assessment interviews and psychometric testing.'

'In our experience, what marks out a contented person from a restless one is the feeling that their company treats them as an individual, and considers their careers on a long-term basis.'

'In essence, Atkins engages and examines with delegates their current capabilities and potential future contribution. Agreeing appropriate development plans has helped to create a culture in which people tend to stay and thrive.'

Chris Thomas, people and customers director, FirstAssist Group

'Talent management starts with a clear business strategy, enlightened senior managers and sound reward policies.'

'We give our best people objectives that will stretch them, and seek to unlock their talent and prepare them for the future. We give them space, in the form of freedom to think and act, and opportunity, in the form of new and varied accountabilities.'

'We find the more space and the more opportunity we give them, the better they perform and the longer they stay.'

Susana Berlevy, head of human resources Europe, HSBC Private Bank

'A good, structured recruitment process, which thoroughly assesses candidates, has to be the starting point. People who are carefully selected against criteria which predict high performance in a job, are more likely to be successful, and successful people stay longer.'

'Creating realistic mutual expectations pre-employment has the effect of increasing the likelihood of candidates accepting the job offer, and dramatically aiding retention in the first year.'

'Accelerated early development is essential to get people up to speed quickly. Provide real work in the first week of the new job—work which plays to their strengths—which will set them up to succeed. As well as creating value sooner, they build self-respect and a positive reputation, and stay longer.'

Mark Wilcox, director of people and organisational development, HR Europe, Sony

'The key to keeping good people is to ensure that they know their strengths, and can be placed somewhere they can be best utilised. Any amount of pay and benefits will not keep people doing things they don't like and things that play to their weaknesses.'

'If you do nothing else, assess and feedback to talented people how they are seen by others in the business. Then make an effort to match their talents to the key roles in your organisation.'

Terry McDougall, assistant chief executive HR, London Borough of Hackney

'My experience has taught me to lead by example, model good practice, and to be straightforward and honest with people about their abilities.'

'I think staff need to be encouraged and praised when they are doing a good job, and coached and supported when they are under pressure. No magical solution, just being hands-on and having good formal communication channels such as regular one-to-ones.'

'My best staff say they stay because they are valued.'

Source: Excerpt from an article that first appeared in *Personnel Today* magazine, www.personneltoday.com. Anonymous, 2006, 'How to keep them keen', Human Resources. 26 July, pp. 28–9.
www.humanresourcesmagazine.com.au

One factor that has increased the competition for knowledge workers is that these employees demonstrate increasing job mobility. Ten years ago, professionals and executives typically changed jobs twice during their working lives. Today, they will change jobs five times over their career span. According to a recent Australian report, 39 per cent of managers move jobs every three years. The negative financial impact of high staff turnover on Australian employers is substantial, and exacerbated by the loss of intellectual property and experience, disruption to work teams, and impact on the morale of other employees.[107]

Some suggested employee retention strategies include:

- Employers must provide a clear and exciting strategic vision and communicate this effectively to employees.
- Employers must maintain ongoing and regular communication with staff and a commitment throughout the organisation to address workplace issues.
- Employers must demonstrate integrity and ethical behaviour, managing in ways that are sustainable and socially responsible.
- Employers must understand and manage the diversity of their workforce and the challenge of operating in a globalised economy.
- A company's leaders need to demonstrate strong business skills and relevant industry competencies.

For example, the brewing group, Lion Nathan, offers talented people 'long-term opportunities to meet their potential, to personally grow. We believe people are looking for diversity, for rewarding work and work that rewards'.[108] Lion Nathan, to give employees a stake in the company, offers free shares worth up to $1000. It also promotes talented people ahead of the usual time it would take.[109]

For organisations striving to improve employee attraction and retention, it is important to recognise that the leadership team, and broad organisational characteristics such as strategy, culture and reputation, are key influences on employee attitudes, as discussed in 'Managing challenges through sustainability: Staying power'.

Selection and orientation programs

Eileen Garger claims that an effective retention strategy starts at the earliest stages of staffing the organisation.[110] She emphasises the importance of 'employee–organisation fit', with employee selection focused on employee attitude and organisational culture factors.

Orientation of new employees should not be aimed at inundating them with information. Rather, the aim should be to promote a sense of membership and to build a long-term relationship. Some specific strategies include:

- involvement of new employees in social activities
- involvement of employees' families in social activities
- involvement of senior managers in orientation for new employees
- use of 'mentors' to assist new employees
- accountability of line managers for the orientation of new employees.

Employee development and career management

Several writers advocate the design and promotion of long-term career paths for all employees, with heavy investment in employee development (also see Chapter 12 Employment development and career management).[111] For employee development to become a high priority in the organisation, senior executives must be involved in promoting the benefits of development, and line managers must work with employees to establish goals and offer assistance for employees to attain their goals.

Specific strategies to encourage career development include:

- Career counselling based on the 'concept of employees taking primary ownership of their career direction, with support from the organisation'.[112]
- Providing supportive resources, such as information about careers provided through the company website; career seminars; email broadcasts; high-profile (easily accessible) career counsellors; and orientation programs for new employees.

STAYING POWER

Retaining talented staff is often a case of providing and maintaining a positive and desirable workplace culture.

When Jetstar's chief executive, Alan Joyce, was to return to Ireland to take charge at Aer Lingus, his former employer, the story was splashed all over the Irish press and Joyce knew he had to tell his boss, Qantas chief executive Geoff Dixon, about the offer. Dixon's response was to outline what Joyce would lose by leaving. 'Geoff did a very good selling job', Joyce says. He had good reason to stay put, as a candidate for more senior roles within Qantas when Dixon retires, and the likelihood of a leading role in developing a low-cost, long-haul international carrier.

Joyce knows he is not the only one in Jetstar that headhunters are interested in luring away and he likes the fact that his staff are sought after.

BRW asked 10 senior Australian executives, who had switched jobs in 2005, why they had moved. Lack of career opportunity with their existing employer was the main reason cited for moving. The market position and reputation of the new employer were also drawcards. The biggest criticisms of former employers related to lack of recognition and lacklustre workplaces (one likened theirs to a morgue). Only one executive mentioned money.

The executives also discussed their cynicism about companies that talk about 'being a team', 'promoting work-life balance' and 'treating everybody equally', but do nothing about it; or harping on about their cultural vision, then ditching that vision to achieve a certain business objective.

A national survey by recruiter Hudson confirms a disconnect between employers' perceptions of their workplace and the views of employees and prospective employees. Sixty three per cent of job seekers say that employers are not meeting their expectations.

Although the idea of changing culture appears relatively straightforward, the process is hard work—'because we are human', Di Stefano says. Realistically assessing a company's culture and developing an employment brand around this (as separate from the products or services the company offers) is a challenge for employers.

Best-practice companies

It is easier to place talented executives in companies that have a good story to tell. Companies such as ANZ Banking Group, Lion Nathan, Unilever, McDonald's, Mars, Sara Lee Household & Bodycare, Citigroup, IBM and Golder Associates are consistently highly ranked on Australian employer-of-choice surveys, but there is always room for improvement.

The controversy surrounding comments by Allens Arthur Robinson's managing partner, Tom Poulton, 'that managers don't have a right to free time', is still echoing throughout the business community. The managing director Australia for Michael Page International, Stephen Moir, says: 'That is a complete cultural clash with generations X and Y. There is no point in offering talent free parking and training if there is a feeling that you are going to be flogged to death.'

But it is pointless to have a chief executive who is charming, ethical, and has a good work-life balance if other managers are not enforcing the appropriate culture. To ensure this does not happen, Westpac provides regular training for the 2500 managers among its 27 000 staff. The bank's recruitment and retention department leads the program and monitors its progress, measuring turnover of staff, turnover among high performers and turnover in specific groups.

Jetstar's Melbourne head office has a start-up buzz about it. Joyce sits alongside his colleagues in an open-plan office and knows all the staff that work on his floor and what they are doing. Managers take part in a program that has them spending one day each month on the business's front lines. Joyce's last experience was as a check-in attendant at Avalon Airport, near Melbourne. Joyce also keeps in contact with all 1200 staff through a one-minute voice message to staff every week on their mobile phones, updating them on business performance. Performance reviews are held regularly throughout the year.

The managing partner of the executive search and leadership development services company Heidrick & Struggles, Ron Graham, says: 'The boss needs to understand a talented employee's "hot buttons".' By this he means what the bargaining chips are: time, a sabbatical, salary, their domestic situation, their partner's employment. These are the things that headhunters want to know—what it will take to move them; the current boss needs to know what will make the person stay. 'You have got to know that stuff about high performers so you can meet their needs', he says.

Source: Excerpt from E. Ross, 2005, 'Staying power', *BRW*, 29 September, p. 64.© 2005 Copyright John Fairfax Holdings Limited. www.brw.com.au

- Changing the image and perception of long-term (managerial) careers in the organisation. If casual employees do not view themselves as a good 'match' for the managerial roles in the organisation, it may be due to inaccurate perceptions or a poor image of current management.

Measuring and monitoring job satisfaction

Most attempts to measure job satisfaction rely on workers' self-reports. There is a vast amount of data on the reliability and validity of many existing scales, as well as a wealth of data from companies that have used these scales—allowing for comparisons across firms. Established scales are excellent places to begin if employers wish to assess the satisfaction levels of their employees. An employer would be foolish to 'reinvent the wheel' by generating its own versions of measures of these broad constructs. Of course, in some cases, organisations want to measure their employees' satisfaction with aspects of their work that are specific to that organisation (for example, satisfaction with one particular pay practice versus another). In these situations, the organisation may need to create its own scales, but this will be the exception rather than the rule.

One standardised, widely used measure of job satisfaction is the Job Descriptive Index (JDI). The copyright for this instrument is held by Bowling Green State University in the US. The JDI emphasises various facets of satisfaction: pay, the work itself, supervision, co-workers and promotions. Table 17.3 presents several items from the JDI scale. Other standardised scales emphasise overall satisfaction. Table 17.4 opposite presents sample items from one of these measures. Finally, some scales avoid language altogether, relying on pictures. The faces scale in Figure 17.3 opposite is an example of this type of measure.

Other scales exist for those who want to get more specific about different facets of satisfaction. For example, although the JDI we just examined assesses satisfaction with pay, it does not break up pay into different dimensions.[113] The Pay Satisfaction Questionnaire (PSQ) focuses on these more specific dimensions (that is, pay levels,

TABLE 17.3 Sample items from a standardised job satisfaction scale (the JDI)

Instructions: Think of your present work. What is it like most of the time? In the blank beside each word given below, write:

Y for 'yes', if it describes your work
N for 'no', if it does not describe your work
? if you cannot decide.

Work itself	Pay	Promotion opportunities
___ Routine	___ Less than I deserve	___ Dead-end job
___ Satisfying	___ Highly paid	___ Unfair policies
___ Good	___ Insecure	___ Based on ability

Supervision	Co-workers	
___ Impolite	___ Intelligent	
___ Praises good work	___ Responsible	
___ Does not supervise enough	___ Boring	

Source: W. K. Balzar, P. Cain Smith, D.A. Kravitz, S.E. Lovell, K.B. Paul, B.A. Reilly and C.E. Reilly, 1990, *User's Manual for the Job Descriptive Index (JDI) and the Job in General (JIG) Scales*, Bowling Green State University, Bowling Green, OH.

TABLE 17.4 Sample items from a standardised scale that measures overall job satisfaction

Instructions: Put a tick beside the answer that you feel is most appropriate regarding your present job.

All in all, how satisfied are you with your job?
_____ Very satisfied
_____ Somewhat satisfied
_____ Not too satisfied
_____ Not at all satisfied

If a good friend of yours told you that he or she was interested in working in a job like yours for your employer, would you recommend it to him or her?
_____ Strongly recommend this job
_____ Would have doubts about recommending this job
_____ Strongly advise against taking this job

Knowing what you know now, if you had to decide all over again to take the job you have now, what would you decide?
_____ Decide without hesitation to take the same job
_____ Would have some second thoughts about taking the same job
_____ Definitely decide not to take the same job

Source: Robert P. Quinn and Graham L. Staines, 1979, *The 1977 Quality of Employment Survey*, Survey Research Center, Institute for Social Research, University of Michigan, Ann Arbor, MI. Reprinted with permission.

FIGURE 17.3 Example of a simplified, non-verbal measure of job satisfaction

Job satisfaction from the faces scale
Consider all aspects of your job. Circle the face that best describes your feelings about your job in general.

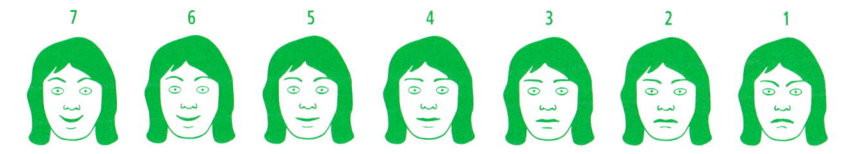

7   6   5   4   3   2   1

Source: The faces were adapted from R.B. Dunham & J.B. Herman, 1975, 'Development of a female faces scale for measuring job satisfaction', *Journal of Applied Psychology*, 60, pp. 629–31. © 1975 by the American Psychological Association. Adapted by permission.

benefits, pay structure and pay increases). Thus, this measure gives a more detailed view of exactly what aspects of pay are most or least satisfying.[114] Taking this further, we can find scales that take only one of the JDI's dimensions—pay level—and then break it down further into multiple facets of satisfaction with pay level.

Clearly, there is no end to the number of satisfaction facets that we might want to measure, but the key in operational contexts, where the main concern is retention, is making sure that scores, on whatever measures are taken, truly relate to voluntary turnover among valued people. For example, satisfaction with co-workers might be low, but if this aspect of satisfaction is not central to employees, it may not translate into voluntary turnover. Similarly, in an organisation that bases pay rises on performance, low performers might report being dissatisfied with pay rises, but this may not reflect any operational problem. Indeed, the whole strategic purpose of many pay-for-performance plans is to create this type of dissatisfaction among low performers, to motivate them to higher levels of performance.

Survey-feedback interventions

Employee survey research
a process of monitoring employees' job satisfaction and organisational and other important job attitudes using questionnaires, interviews or focus groups.

Regardless of what measures are used or how many facets of satisfaction are assessed, a systematic, ongoing program of **employee survey research** (a process of monitoring employees' job satisfaction and organisational and other important job attitudes using questionnaires, interviews or focus groups) should be a prominent part of any human resource strategy for a number of reasons, as discussed in 'Managing challenges through HR innovation: Taking the pulse'. First, it allows the company to monitor trends over time and, thus, prevent problems in the area of voluntary turnover before they happen. For example, Figure 17.4 opposite shows the average profile for different facets of satisfaction for a hypothetical company in 2002, 2004 and 2006. As the figure makes clear, the level of satisfaction with promotion opportunities in this company has eroded over time, whereas the satisfaction with co-workers has improved. If there was a strong relationship between satisfaction with promotion opportunities and voluntary turnover among high performers, this would constitute a threat that the organisation might need to address via some of the techniques discussed in Chapter 10 Performance management, and Chapter 11 Learning and development.

A second reason for engaging in an ongoing program of employee satisfaction surveys is that such a program provides a means of empirically assessing the impact of changes in policy (for example, introduction of a new performance appraisal system) or personnel (for example, introduction of a new CEO) on worker attitudes. For

TAKING THE PULSE

MANAGING CHALLENGES THROUGH HR INNOVATION

Employee surveys have become an increasingly popular tool with large companies in the past few years. From the basic employee opinion surveys through to more sophisticated cultural and organisational surveys, such tools are growing in complexity as well as in the kind of data they make available.

Most organisations now recognise that traditional employee surveys have no positive impact on organisational performance, according to Andrew Beveridge, business manager at Hay Group. 'For years most employee surveys focused on employee satisfaction and basically involved dumping a lot of data on companies without any business context or recommendations for action. It turns out that satisfied employees can produce poor results, and dissatisfied employees can actually prove to be reasonably productive in the short to medium term. Employee satisfaction simply isn't the right measure', he says.

The traditional employee survey's lack of impact has led to a greater focus on employee engagement, says Beveridge, along with the ability of an organisation's leaders to increase the discretionary effort of employees.

As such, there is a move towards a more integrated view of employee and organisational surveys, according to Brigit Douglas-Raper, project manager, Hewitt Best Employers. 'Not only are organisations measuring employee engagement, they are now starting to integrate engagement surveys with organisational culture or values surveys', she says. 'Organisations are seeking to better understand how their culture and their people interact and how the organisation can effectively leverage these components to deliver on the strategic objectives of the organisation.'

Steve Ewin, vice president for Gallup, says culture varies within an organisation more widely than across organisations, and thus the single biggest development is that companies now realise that engagement must be measured at the work group level. 'Individual teams are now taking responsibility for improving their own engagement levels. Engagement surveys are linked to key business outcomes and now have a high degree of focus from CEOs and executive teams', he says.

Surveying the challenges

While HR plays an instrumental role in the survey process, the degree to which organisational change is successful is the responsibility of an organisation's leaders. The CEO and executive team's commitment are key to taking action on survey results and driving change.

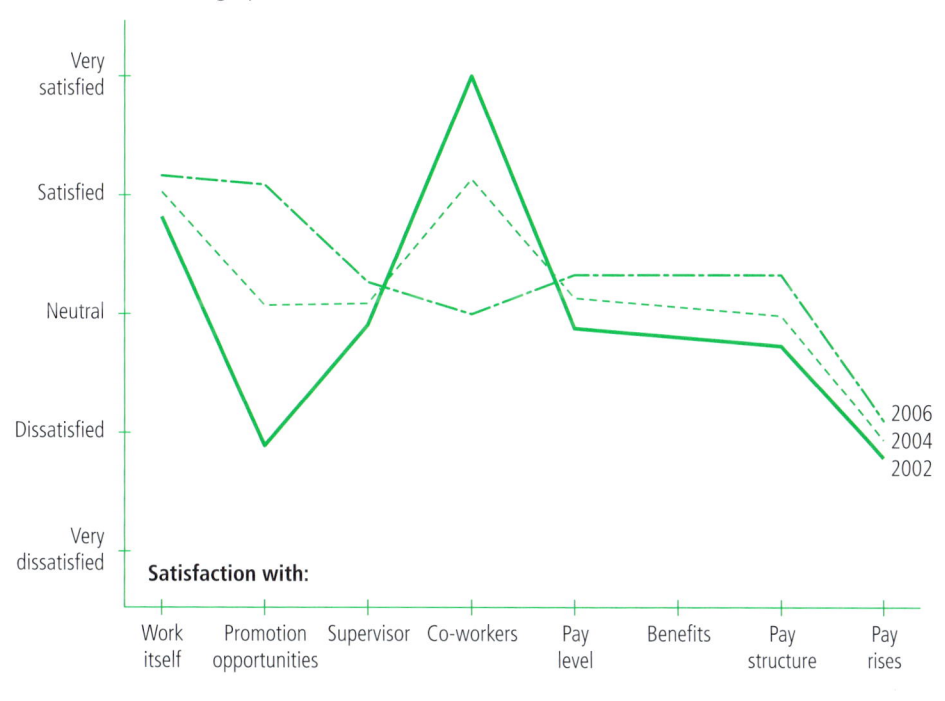

FIGURE 17.4 Average profile for different facets of satisfaction over time

[Line graph showing satisfaction levels (Very dissatisfied, Dissatisfied, Neutral, Satisfied, Very satisfied) across facets: Work itself, Promotion opportunities, Supervisor, Co-workers, Pay level, Benefits, Pay structure, Pay rises, for years 2006, 2004, 2002]

'Following the announcement of results, we often see HR professionals struggling to attract the commitment of senior leaders to acting on the engagement results and taking personal accountability for achieving long-term increases in employee engagement. Without senior leaders acting as champions of the change process, organisations are unable to sustain momentum and often find their engagement levels plateau over time.'

Dealing with 'the too hard basket'

While many executive teams can be happy enough to support the initial rollout of a survey, this enthusiasm can sometimes quickly wane when less than positive results come back. In such cases, results are often swept under the carpet as executives prefer to focus on issues that involve less personal and organisational change.

Such organisations will often be selective in their communication to employees, choosing to communicate the good news but avoiding openly addressing the organisation's key challenges.

Dealing with executive and line resistance

The ability to influence executives and line managers is an increasingly important skill for HR professionals. When it comes to organisational surveys and cultural change, the ability to influence becomes critical as change often becomes personal for leaders.

The most effective HR professionals are also great leaders and know exactly how to frame communications in a way that inspires action. The alternative is to shun the leadership role and act as the company 'police'—'detecting and punishing the failure to adhere to company HR procedures. Not only is this a boring role, it also removes any ability of HR to have a meaningful impact on an organisation', he says.

Additionally, it is important for line managers and leaders within the organisation to be held accountable for engaging their people. She adds that HR professionals can drive accountability for change by integrating key behaviours required to increase engagement with individual managers' performance measures.

Building the business case

HR professionals need to link engagement to measures that are important in the business and continue to measure engagement over time to assess impact. There is a correlation between action planning and execution and increased engagement scores, she says. For example, a large multinational measured not only engagement, but implementation of actions across the business. It found that where the percentage of actions implemented score increased from one survey cycle to the next, so too did engagement.

Source: Excerpt from C. Donaldson, 2006, 'Taking the pulse', *Human Resources*, 30 May, pp. 18–19. www.humanresourcesmagazine.com.au

example, Figure 17.5 below shows the average profile for different satisfaction facets for a hypothetical organisation one year before and one year after a merger. An examination of the profile makes it clear that since the merger, satisfaction with supervision and pay structure have gone down dramatically and this has not been offset by any increase in satisfaction along other dimensions. Again, this might point to the need for training programs for supervisors (such as those discussed in Chapter 11 Learning and development) or changes in the job evaluation system (like those discussed in Chapter 13 Managing compensation).

Third, when these surveys incorporate standardised scales like the JDI or PSQ, they often allow the company to compare itself with others in the same industry along these dimensions. For example, Figure 17.6 opposite shows the average profile for different satisfaction facets for a hypothetical organisation and compares this to the industry average. Again, if we detect major differences between one organisation and the industry as a whole (for example, on overall pay levels), this might allow the company to react and change its policies before there is a mass exodus of people moving to the competition. Indeed, this kind of mass migration not only threatens firms but can destabilise an entire nation if the exodus is in a vital industry. For example, according to Figure 17.6, the satisfaction with pay levels is low relative to the industry, but this is offset by higher-than-industry-average satisfaction with benefits and the work itself.

As we showed in Chapter 8 Recruitment and selection, the organisation might want to use this information to systematically screen people. That is, the fit between the person and the organisation would be best if the company selected applicants who reported being most interested in the nature of the work itself and benefits, and rejected those applicants whose sole concern was with pay levels.

Within the organisation, a systematic survey program also allows the company to check for differences between units and, hence, benchmark 'best practices' that might be generalised across units. For example, Figure 17.7 opposite shows the average

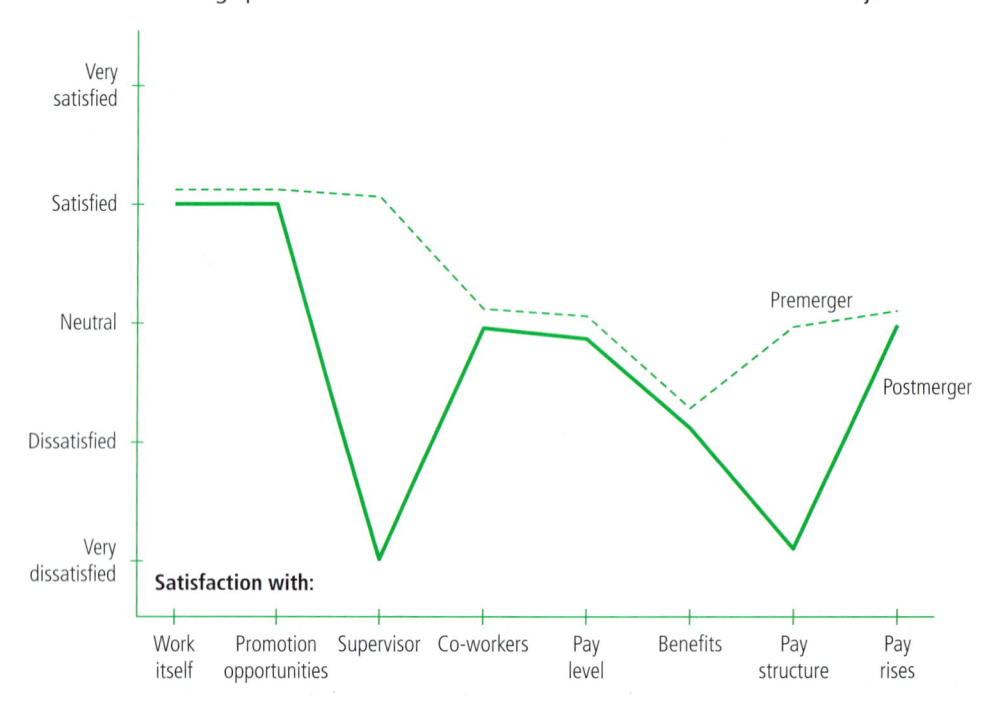

FIGURE 17.5 Average profile for different facets of satisfaction before and after a major event

FIGURE 17.6 Average profile for different facets of satisfaction versus the industry average

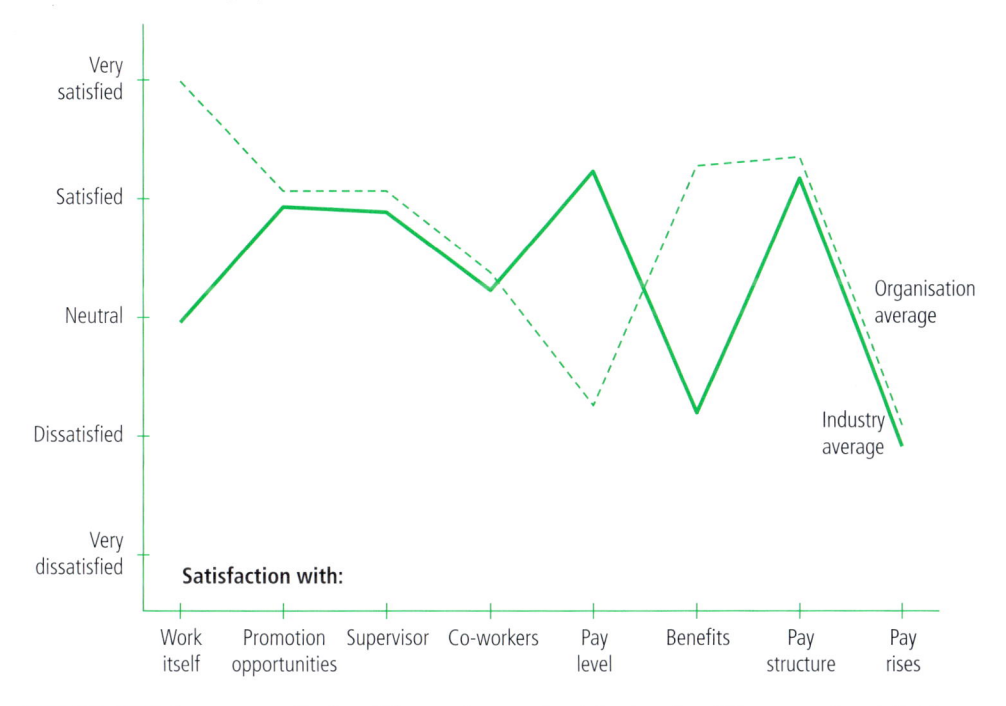

FIGURE 17.7 Average profile for different facets of satisfaction for different regional divisions

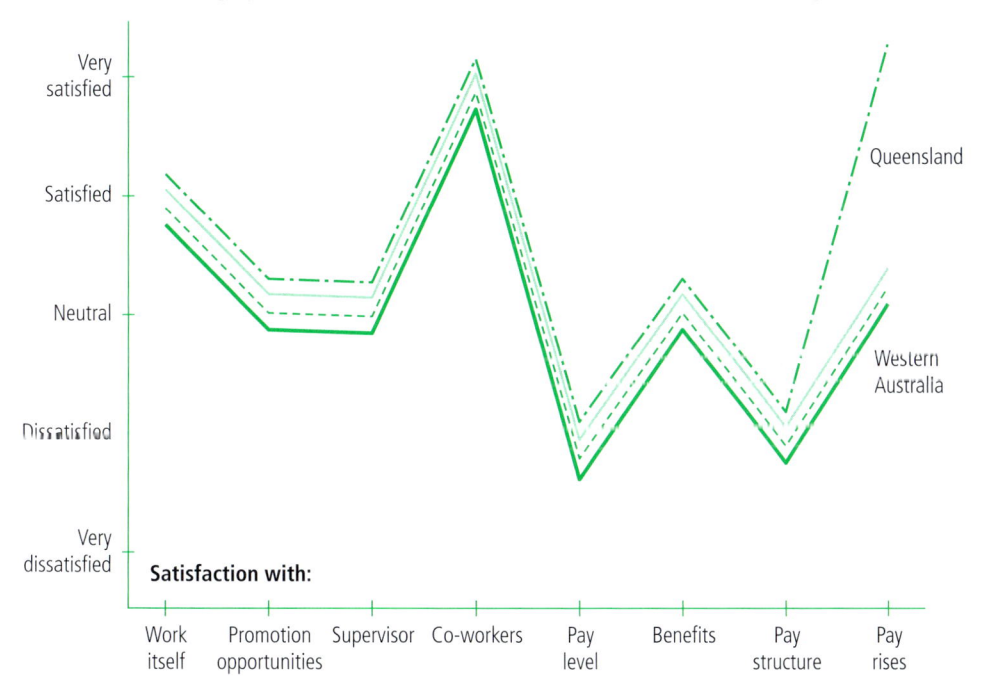

profile for four different regional divisions of a hypothetical company. The figure shows that satisfaction with pay increases is much higher in one of the regions (Queensland), relative to the other regions. If the overall amount of money allocated to pay increases was equal through the entire company, this implies that the manner in which pay increases are allocated or communicated in the Queensland region might be something that the other regions should look into. Of course, there may be alternative explanations for regional variations. For example, the higher costs of living in Victoria or New South Wales may lead to a need for interstate differences in pay increases.

Finally, yearly surveys give employees a constructive outlet for voicing their concerns and frustrations. Employees' ability to handle dissatisfying work experiences is enhanced when they feel they have an opportunity to air their problems. Individuals' formalised opportunities to state complaints about work situations have been referred to as **employee voice**.[115] Research has shown that voicing provides employees an active, constructive outlet for their work frustrations.[116] For example, a study of nurses indicated that providing voicing mechanisms, such as an employee attitude survey and question-and-answer sessions between employees and management, enhanced worker attitudes and reduced turnover.[117]

> **Employee voice**
> an individual's formal opportunity to complain about his or her work situation.

Reliable and valid data on employee turnover and retention are necessary for decisions to be made about future HRM strategies. Attitude surveys of employees may provide some useful data about current employees. It is also valuable for managers to know why employees may choose to leave an organisation. A common method for gathering data about the nature and causes of employee turnover is the use of exit interviews with employees. Exit interviews may be formal or informal, structured or relatively unstructured information-gathering sessions held with employees when they leave the organisation (or six months later).[118] Exit interviews gather information about the employee's impressions and experiences during his or her time in the organisation.[119] The aim of exit interviews is usually not to encourage the employee to remain in the organisation; it is more likely intended to maintain positive relations with the departing employee or to identify poor HRM and management practices that may have led to job dissatisfaction.

Research has shown, however, that the effectiveness of exit interviews is often limited by flaws in their design and implementation.[120] Managers conducting exit interviews should be trained to conduct these interviews in an objective manner, to reduce perceptual bias about the employee's comments. Also, departing employees may be reluctant to be open about their views, because they will not wish to jeopardise possible future relations with the manager or the organisation. For these reasons, HR specialists are more likely to conduct effective exit interviews than the managers who have been in direct reporting relationships with the departing employee.[121] Exit interviews conducted by consultants outside the organisation have been shown to elicit more accurate and detailed information than those conducted by managers.[122]

Exit interviews are often time consuming, especially where there is high employee turnover. Hence, some organisations use exit surveys, comprising simple questions that can be scanned and analysed more quickly. Obviously, the data obtained via these surveys will be less detailed than that obtained in interviews. Biased responses may still occur in exit surveys, as employees may not be motivated to provide the organisation with accurate and detailed feedback.[123] Employees are more likely to disclose their reasons for departure when: (1) the exit interview or survey data are treated confidentially and handled only in aggregated, not individual form; (2) employees are protected from possible retaliation by supervisors; and (3) the organisation has demonstrated action to address problems raised in exit interviews or surveys by departing employees.[124]

Obviously a great deal can be learned from employee satisfaction surveys. It is surprising that many companies conducting regular customer satisfaction surveys fail to show the same concern for employee satisfaction. Retention is an issue involving both customers and employees, however, and—as we noted at the outset of this chapter—the two types of retention are substantially related.

Although findings such as these are leading more and more companies to do such surveys, conducting an organisational opinion survey is not something that should be taken lightly. Especially in the beginning, surveys such as this often raise expectations. It is critical that the organisation conducting the survey is ready to act on the results.

Retention strategies should be varied according to factors such as skill levels, amount of training required and relative rareness of skills. Employee retention strategies should be evaluated for effectiveness and impact. For example, at Sun Microsystems, all projects require an estimated return on investment in advance of implementation.[125] Strategies to measure the effectiveness of HR programs are discussed in more detail in Chapter 18 Evaluating and improving the human resource function.

MANAGING PEOPLE

SATURN SPINS OUT OF CONTROL

Fictional case study

A dot-com survivor's recovery is being stifled by unmotivated and unhappy staff, and there is no money to offer incentives.

The chief executive of the technology provider Saturn did not need to read the latest employee satisfaction survey to know. It was obvious: poor morale was holding the company back. A survivor of the 2001 dot-com crash, Saturn had managed to revive the business but the shareholders would demand a lot more than that, and Mike, the chief executive, knew he could not afford anything to be below standard.

Saturn had undertaken five years of reduced technology spending and made some redundancies. The market had been improving gradually but that was not being reflected in the financial figures.

When Mike questioned the senior management team each month about what was wrong, the answer was always 'poor implementation'. Senior managers assured him the employees had the right skills but the teams lacked the motivation to achieve their targets. In particular, a chance conversation with a middle manager was disconcerting. Instead of suggestions on how to pitch new business following the optimistic forecasts, he said employees were simply overworked and could not take on new tasks.

The annual satisfaction survey of employees had worse news. They were not happy with their pay and conditions despite the company awarding small increases across the board in line with the improved market conditions. They complained that even though the hiring and wage freezes had ended, they were not better off than before the dot-com crash five years previously. Mike knew the company was still under financial pressure but staff did not appreciate that, or care for that matter. Mike could not understand why the company's message of recovery had not got through to, and buoyed, employees. He addressed them once a month at a staff meeting, at 5pm on Fridays, to report on the sales growth and targets he expected for the next month. Most employees nodded their heads and did not ask questions when prompted.

Mike knew he had to do something fast. He could not use financial rewards to improve morale, so it had to be some other approach. It was also worrying that staff turnover was running at 25 per cent. How could he keep the skilled employees he needed to win business? How could he stop competitors, which had taken an aggressive approach to the market opening, hiring his staff on lucrative contracts?

Response 1

David Jenkinson, human resources manager, EDS Australia

Mike is in a tough spot. He will shortly lose most of his intellectual property if he stays on this path so he needs to think about what to do. Mike's items for action:

- He must ensure he has the right people in the right roles and get his leaders focused on human capital as well as business matters.
- Mike needs managers to select who Saturn needs to retain, based on key skills, and have conversations with these employees to let them know they are needed and understand what Saturn can do to retain them.
- Mike must put coaching and mentoring programs in place, accessible at all levels. He must set up career development and succession planning for all employees, especially the leadership team. Internal personal training and external courses should be offered.
- Introduce performance-based pay and reward outstanding achievements. Be creative and timely with rewards. If the budget is tight, there are inexpensive ways to reward people.
- Create compensation packages for new and existing employees that could include flexible working practices, study assistance, time off in lieu, health programs, group discounts and public recognition of achievements.
- Introduce an employee scorecard for 'engagement'. Look beyond turnover and retention of key individuals, absenteeism and measuring internal promotion against external offers.
- Mike must understand employee turnover. If exit interview data is not being collected, he should introduce the practice immediately. He needs to review the data and understand why people leave.
- He must implement more frequent and more consistent communication: use the leadership team to spread messages regularly and consistently throughout the organisation.

If Mike adopts a more focused approach on his people, he will see his figures improve dramatically. It is all about being respected and trusted as a leader to guide the company. He needs to back it up with good people skills and practices to ensure he rebuilds any trust that may have been lost.

Response 2
Kylie Hammond, managing director, Amazing Results, executive search and coaching

Managing employee morale is one of the truest tests of leadership capability. Mike has acknowledged that he has a problem and there are many ways to improve the situation, including:

- Managers. Employees look to managers as a barometer for how the company is really doing. Regular communication with employees is required, combined with honest feedback about how the company is doing and what needs to happen to turn the company around. Enthusiasm and passion for a business is contagious. Managers who genuinely demonstrate enthusiasm for the business are the front line of defence against morale issues.
- Communication. Managers should walk the floor, visit projects, speak with employees one-on-one and have regular team meetings. Do not shy away from concerns—bring them out in the open. When employees stop talking, it is the first sign of trouble. Involve employees in the solutions, asking them for suggestions to improve the morale of the company. Consistency in the message is important.
- Training. Skilled employees are highly valued by your competitors. When salary increases are not feasible, do not limit training opportunities. Training is an excellent tool to help retain employees and show them they are valued. Be open about the fact that employees will be headhunted from time to time.
- Fun. Staff meetings on Fridays at 5pm are not the ideal way to motivate employees after a long week, unless the boss is providing drinks and pizza. Conduct meetings earlier in the week and make the meetings fun and informative—and ask for employee concerns to be submitted beforehand so matters can be aired in an open forum. Make the workplace an enjoyable place to work, and remember that happy employees can produce extraordinary results.

Source: A. Tandukar, 2006, 'Saturn spins out of control', *BRW*, 9 March, p. 86. © 2006 Copyright John Fairfax Holdings Limited. www.brw.com.au

QUESTION
1. How would you suggest Mike keep the skilled employees he needed to win business?
2. How would you suggest he could stop competitors, which had taken an aggressive approach to the market opening, hiring his staff on lucrative contracts?

CHAPTER SUMMARY

This chapter has examined issues relating to employee turnover and retention, which have become important strategic and HRM issues in many organisations. Involuntary turnover reflects a separation initiated by the organisation, often when the individual would prefer to stay a member of the organisation. Voluntary turnover reflects a separation initiated by the individual, often when the organisation would prefer that the person stay a member of the organisation. Organisations can gain competitive advantage by strategically managing the separation process so that involuntary turnover is implemented in a manner that minimises or prevents negative outcomes and voluntary turnover among high performers is kept to a minimum. Voluntary turnover can be minimised by a range of employee retention strategies and interventions, measuring and monitoring employee levels of satisfaction with critical facets of job and organisation, and addressing any problems identified by such surveys.

WEB EXERCISES

A Visit www.expertss.com. This is the website for Expert Survey Systems Inc, a company that provides employee attitude survey services to various firms. This website provides information and resources on organisational surveys. Use this website to answer the following questions.

Questions
1 Review the demonstration version of the 89-item employee opinion survey. What aspects of the work environment are measured by this survey? What suggestions do you have for improving this survey?
2 What are some of the methods used to share survey results with employees? Identify strengths and weaknesses for each method.

B Visit www.betterhealth.vic.gov.au/. The Better Health Channel (BHC) was established in May 1999 by the Victorian Government. The site aims to provide information and to help improve the health and wellbeing of the Victorian community. The website has fact sheets about a wide range of topics, including healthy living, weight management, physical activity, pregnancy, nutrition, children's health, and a wide range of information on the symptoms, care and treatment of numerous health conditions.

Questions
1 Do you think HR managers should be responsible for providing information and resources such as this, to benefit the health and wellbeing of employees?

DISCUSSION QUESTIONS

1 Organisational turnover is generally considered a negative outcome and many organisations spend a great deal of time and money trying to reduce it. What situations would indicate that an increase in turnover might be what an organisation needs?
2 Given the difficulty of terminating employees, what organisational policies might promote the retention of high-performing workers, but voluntary turnover among low performers?
3 Three popular interventions for enhancing worker satisfaction are job enrichment, job rotation and role analysis. What are the critical differences between these interventions, and under what conditions might one be preferable to the others?
4 If off-the-job stress and dissatisfaction begin to create on-the-job problems, what are the rights and responsibilities of the human resource manager in helping the employee to overcome these problems? Are intrusions into such areas an invasion of privacy, a benevolent and altruistic employer practice or simply a prudent financial step to be taken to protect the firm's investment?
5 Discuss the advantages of using published, standardised measures in employee attitude surveys. Do employers ever need to develop their own measures for such surveys? Where would a person turn in order to learn how to do this?

NAB AND THE ART OF CORPORATE RENEWAL

The reputation of National Australia Bank among customers, analysts, shareholders and staff has taken a serious beating in recent years. Melinda Finch talks with Elizabeth Hunter, head of people & culture, about the ambitious transformation program designed to redevelop and revitalise Australia's largest bank.

NAB lost more than $360 million in the foreign currency scandal of January 2004. What were NAB's main people management and related issues at the time?
Following the foreign exchange losses, we quickly recognised that we had a number of broadly based issues that needed to be tackled.

Firstly, we were too bureaucratic and cumbersome—our business structure was complex and we tended to over-engineer the way we did things. Management lacked ownership and accountability for costs.

Secondly, we were inward-looking and not customer-focused—we operated in silos and there was a lack of divisional cooperation.

Thirdly, we had a weak compliance framework—our people did not have sufficient awareness of our policies, and in some cases policies and procedures were not well developed. Our processes for monitoring compliance were complex and did not allow issues of substance to be identified and escalated.

Finally, we had major gaps in our cultural framework—while we had a set of values, people were not held accountable and values were not reflected in the way people were assessed. Culture change programs were voluntary and there was a lack of visible and consistent leadership in this area.

The Australian Prudential Regulation Authority's March 2004 review of NAB found that some of the 'people & culture' policies—including codes of conduct, structured performance management systems and formal systems for resolving disputes—weren't respected or applied by some individuals or management. In such cases, did HR fail to implement or maintain these policies? Was this an organisation-wide problem?
We had a lot of policies already in place, but they weren't necessarily integrated with what we were saying was important. To help realign these areas, we introduced a set of corporate principles that outline the expected behaviour of all our employees. The principles are embedded across our whole business and reinforce the importance of having a culture that not only values great performance but also the right behaviours. 'How' we achieve our results is just as important as 'what' we achieve.

In the Macquarie Research Equities review of NAB in September 2005, low levels of employee engagement were cited as reasons for downgrading the bank's earnings forecast and reducing the stock recommendation to neutral. Were there internal indicators of employee disengagement prior to this analysis? And, if so, what was being done to address them?
We were very aware of the key issues that were adversely affecting our performance. Unfortunately, there were no quick fixes for these underlying problems and it was going to take time to rebuild the organisation.

Our 2005 employee opinion survey results strongly reinforced that our people are committed to our customers, but they also highlighted our biggest challenge—how to get our people to engage with the organisation as well as the customer. In other words, how to rebuild their connection with NAB.

Organisational transformation is nothing new among Australian banks—what's so different about NAB's culture and people agenda?
Cultural transformation is seen by all parts of the business as integral to delivering on the organisation's strategy and mitigating business risk. Leadership teams within each of

the regions we operate in view cultural transformation as a top business priority, and identified it as such by making it a part of this year's strategic planning process.

A good example of how we have aligned the behaviour we want to see and our formal systems and processes is our new Enterprise Agreement. The agreement supports the cultural transformation of our business through increased flexibility, simplicity, reward for performance, and recognising we are a diverse workforce with different needs.

Another important driver of cultural transformation is having a compelling vision that employees can commit to and believe in. We have done a lot of work to communicate our organisation's aspirations and goals, and ensure employees understand what they mean and how they can contribute to achieving them.

To bring our new brand to life, we introduced a set of 'brand behaviours' that strongly reflect and reinforce our corporate principles. They also helped to demonstrate that our brand is much more than a logo—it is our people and the customer experience that sets us apart from our competitors. Living our brand every day means delivering on our promises, being real, easy to do business with, and backing our customers.

APRA's March 2004 review argued that cultural change had to be driven from the top—is this happening?

I would agree that most models of culture change emphasise the importance of top leaders role modelling the right behaviours and helping to drive change through the organisation. All of our leaders are responsible for bringing our people along with us on the change journey.

How is the people & culture division ensuring that the organisational culture that is being talked about is the same as the one that is being acted upon?

First and foremost, we have spent time understanding what's going on in our culture and continually checking to see that people are working on the right things. Measurement is a critical ingredient—you need people working on things that will address your cultural issues.

A good example of this is around one of the cultural issues we needed to address—our people were scared to escalate problems and issues. We have since done a lot of work in this area to ensure we have a number of 'safe' channels in place. Some of these include:

- A confidential alert line—a telephone-based channel that is staffed by specially trained operators who handle any concerns raised with care and discretion. An employee can remain anonymous if they choose. The alert line has been extremely valuable as a channel, as the quality of some of the disclosures received have alerted us to the emerging risks in a timely manner and have enabled us to address them.
- Concern online—an online channel available to our employees for raising issues and concerns. Once again an employee can remain anonymous.
- CEO and executive feedback lines—our Australian CEO and executive general managers have their own feedback email addresses. Since September 2004, over 1500 emails from employees have been sent to the Australian CEO's feedback line. Since May 2005, around 600 emails (about 15 per week) have been sent through this channel. Although this channel can be used to raise a serious issue or concern, it is mostly used to provide general comments and suggestions or ask questions.
- Within people & culture, we have a people advisory centre—a call centre available to all employees for people-related queries and concerns. We also have a case management team that provides employees and people leaders with guidance, advice and support on the resolution of workplace issues.

How important is employee engagement?

'We weren't surprised with the results of our last employee opinion survey, and in particular the responses we received on questions such as "I have thought about leaving", which are part of the subset of questions that contribute to the engagement score', says NAB's head of people & culture, Elizabeth Hunter.

'However, focusing only on the subset of questions related to engagement during our period of stabilisation did not provide an insightful construct. We have found the alternative "satisfaction" measure to be a broader and more appropriate measure for our organisation at this point in time. We have focused on identifying the root causes of the issues underpinning engagement and satisfaction, which has helped us better align our solutions.'

Source: Excerpt from M. Finch, 2006, 'NAB and the art of corporate renewal', *Human Resources*, 16 May, pp. 10–11. www.humanresourcesmagazine.com.au

QUESTIONS

1 What do you see as the major issues or challenges for HRM at NAB?
2 Outline and evaluate the current HRM strategies at NAB.
3 What HRM strategies would you suggest for NAB? Explain and justify your recommendations.

CHAPTER 18

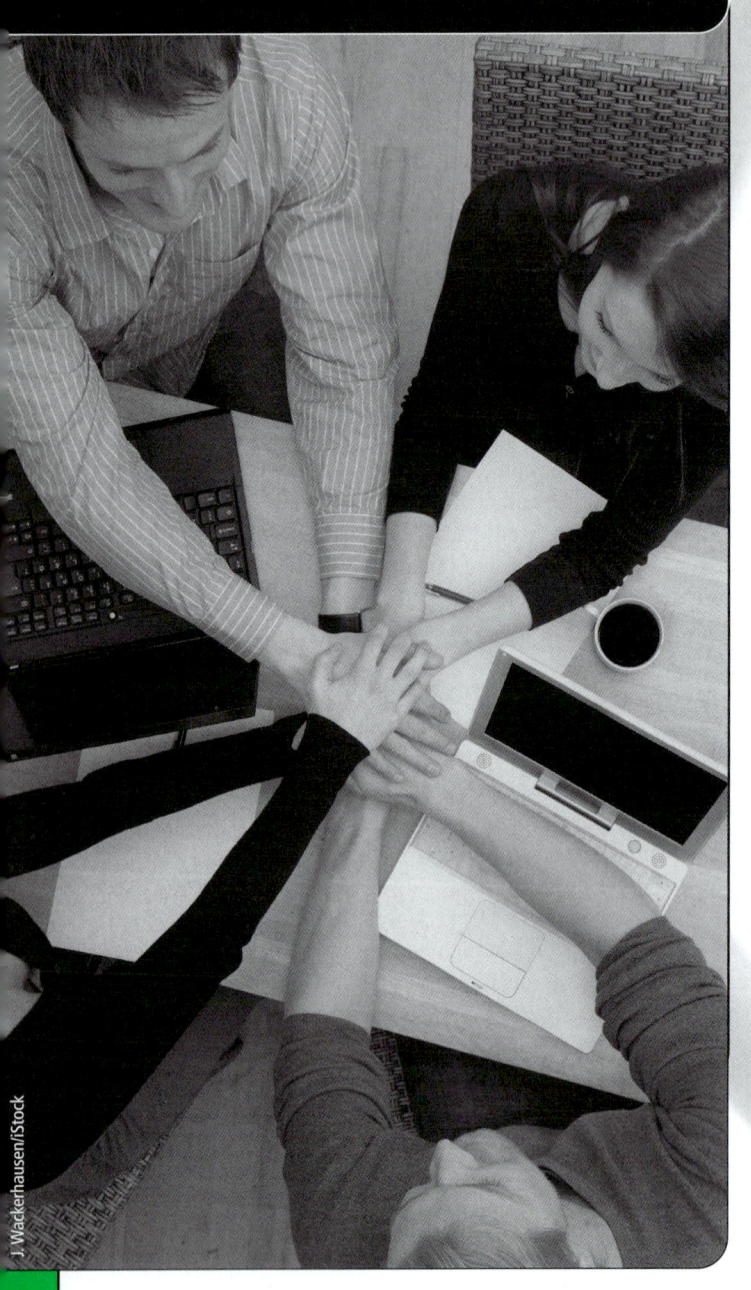

EVALUATING AND IMPROVING THE HUMAN RESOURCE FUNCTION

Objectives

After reading this chapter, you should be able to:

1. Understand the reasons why many companies are trying to measure HR.
2. Explain the approaches to evaluating the effectiveness of HR practices.
3. Discuss the issues related to measuring and evaluating the HR function.
4. Discuss how outsourcing HR activities may improve service delivery efficiency and effectiveness.
5. Relate how process reengineering is used to review and redesign HR practices.
6. Consider future directions for the HR function.

Nearly 80 per cent of companies globally have completed, or are in the process of completing, HR transformation, but many HR departments have yet to deliver improvements from the transformation process. There remains a significant gap between what is expected of HR leaders and what they deliver.

An 18-month Mercer Human Resource Consulting study involving 1100 organisations found that companies are being driven by the need to align the HR function more closely with business objectives and by the desire to offer more strategic support to the organisation.

However, HR functions are yet to be credited with driving business outcomes. Recent Mercer research suggests that nearly 60 per cent of finance executives still view HR as more of a cost centre than a strategic partner. Data from Mercer's regional HR transformation studies reveal that HR has a very different view, and some executives perceive that they are spending more time on strategic activities. Nonetheless, there is no escaping the fact that the incremental gains and demonstrable impact on business performance do not reflect two decades worth of effort. The HR function is still primarily an administrative and compliance-based function, with almost 50 per cent of its time being spent in these areas. Less than 15 per cent of its time is spent on strategic, value-based interventions.

The 18-month study shows that although the HR function has strong competence in professional knowledge, and team, interpersonal and leadership skills, it lacks competence in financial management, data management and technology. In short, it lacks the skills that are required to deliver the business credibility that HR transformation is seeking to address.

Indeed, the skills of the HR function are seen as one of the major barriers to effective HR transformation. Together with inappropriate skills, the inability of the function to use technology effectively has often meant that significant business investments have been under-utilised.

The function has also observed a general lack of business commitment for HR transformation, both in terms of the need for HR to play a more strategic role and the confidence in its capacity to do so. In short, the function has neither the skills nor the infrastructure to deliver effective transformation; and the business leadership is not always convinced of the need.

In filling the gap between traditional and strategic skills, the primary solution adopted by 95 per cent of organisations is to train and develop existing employees. Less than half would rely on new recruits or transferring skills, while around 40 per cent would depend on outsourcing to close the gap.

Training is of major importance and has a big part to play in transformation, but it is unlikely to be the only action that a function needs to take. The links between traditional skills and the knowledge now required are being stretched. Administrators may not be effective at planning, strategy and design, while HR generalists are not always the best strategic business partners. The increasing complexity and scope of today's functional strategies demand skills and competencies that were not needed 10 or 15 years ago and are not available through traditional training. Effective transformation has often resulted in a 35–50 per cent turnover of existing staff, to obtain the requisite skills and competencies to drive business performance.

Globally, the most respected HR leaders in organisations are business executives first and HR specialists second. They partner with and are confidants of their CEOs and leadership teams; and they often find themselves at the epicentre of corporate change, and being given credit for bringing about the toughest of business transformations.

These HR leaders are also being recruited by progressive domestic and global boards. Responding to the intense focus on complying with new corporate governance legislation and increasing investor scrutiny, boards are retooling to ensure they have the right mix of highly qualified specialists, including HR experts. The price of failing to make the connection between overall business strategy and HR strategy is high. There will be a temptation for the organisation to hand over the HR services to an outsourcing organisation who will claim to transform the function and make it work at considerably less cost.

However, HR functions that grab the nettle—those that can convince the business of the value of transformation; can recognise that skills and capabilities in HR can change if needed; and can harness technology—thus becoming effective strategic partners and making a positive contribution to the continuing success of the organisation.

Source: Based on P. Vernon, 2004, 'Delivering on the promise of HR transformation', *Human Resources*, 29 November. www.humanresourcesmagazine.com.au This case was originally published in *Strategic HR Review*, 3 (6), September–October.

Introduction

Throughout this book we have emphasised how human resource practices can help companies gain a competitive advantage and improve the experience of work for employees. We have identified specific practices related to: managing the internal and external environment; designing work and measuring work outcomes; and acquiring, developing and rewarding human resources. We have also discussed the best of current research and practice in order to show how HR may contribute to a company's competitive advantage.

As discussed in Chapter 1 Human resource management in Australia, the role of the HR function has been evolving over time. This chapter's opening article discusses some of the key challenges facing the HR function in its efforts to demonstrate its contribution to the organisation's performance or bottom line. Although the HR function began as an administrative function, most HR managers now see the function's major role as being much more strategic. However, this evolution has resulted in a misalignment between the skills and capabilities of the function's members and the new requirements of the function. Virtually every HR function in top companies is going through a transformation process in order to create a function that can play this new strategic role, while successfully fulfilling its other roles. In many successful organisations, the HR budget is viewed as an investment rather than an expense. As Peter Chaffe, director of organisational development with the South Sydney City Council (SSCC), has said:

> What we do in HR develops more than the individual, it contributes to the development of the organisation as a whole. Over the last few years, we have come to recognise that our people are a real and tangible asset, and as such require an ongoing investment in order to ensure not only their development but that of the organisation.[1]

While some managers accept that the contribution of the HR function may be difficult to measure in terms of the bottom line, some HR professionals argue that empirical measurements are essential when evaluating the contribution of the HR department. For example, Mr Col Peebles, HR director with KONE Elevators, says: 'In terms of our budget, each item such as training is reviewed in relation to a benchmark and there has to be a justification for more expenditure.'[2] The first focus of this chapter is understanding the organisational context for measuring HR's effectiveness. Second, we explore measurement approaches for assessing the effectiveness of the HR function and, third, we discuss approaches to improving the HR function in an organisation.

A strategic approach to measuring HR effectiveness

A strategic approach to HRM involves designing and implementing a set of internally consistent policies and practices to ensure that a firm's human capital is enhanced via an increasing capacity to learn and apply new knowledge—thus, contributing to the achievement of business objectives and sustainable competitive advantage.[3] Many managers recognise that financial performance alone is not sufficient to retain employees and customers.[4] Before we can understand how to measure HR's contribution to the firm, we need to understand some important concepts that are currently being debated about the assessment of corporate management and performance.

HRM and corporate sustainability

Following revelations of corporate 'wrongdoing' in companies like Enron, HIH Insurance and James Hardie, companies are under increasing pressure to establish and maintain high standards of **corporate governance**, which is defined as the way in which decisions are made about the deployment of an organisation's resources and the resolution of conflicts among an organisation's stakeholders.[5] The traditional focus of corporate governance is on financial performance, reporting to shareholders, and protecting shareholders' interests. However, as society in general, and employees and customers in particular, expect executives and managers to demonstrate the highest standards of ethics, transparency and responsiveness, there is increasing pressure for the focus of corporate governance to broaden, to address the concerns of all stakeholders (also see Chapter 15 Ethics and human resource management). 'Effective corporate governance depends on access to relevant, high-quality information that enables performance tracking and invites new forms of stakeholder engagement.'[6] In order to measure and report on corporate performance, many companies refer to the **triple bottom line**, the combination of economic, social and environmental performance indicators for an organisation.[7]

Related to corporate governance and the triple bottom line are the important concepts of **corporate social responsibility (CSR)** (and corporate sustainability), which are now considered by many as synonyms,[8] referring to the continuing, voluntary commitment by companies to establish and maintain a systematic approach to the management of environmental, social, economic and governance issues. This requires companies and managers to behave in ethical ways and to contribute to economic development while improving quality of life for employees, their families, the local community and society in general.[9] It is suggested that sustainability will, increasingly, be recognised as a driving force—changing the way we work and live.[10]

Corporate governance
the way in which decisions are made about the deployment of an organisation's resources and the resolution of conflicts among an organisation's stakeholders.

Triple bottom line
the combination of economic, social and environmental performance indicators for an organisation.

Corporate social responsibility (CSR)
(and corporate sustainability) the continuing, voluntary commitment by companies to establish and maintain a systematic approach to the management of environmental, social, economic and governance issues. This requires companies and managers to behave in ethical ways and to contribute to economic development while improving quality of life for employees, their families, the local community and society in general.

Sustainability report
a company report presenting information on the economic, environmental and social dimensions of its activities, products and services. (It is synonymous with social report, citizenship report, triple bottom line report, corporate social responsibility report.) Where it includes governance issues, it may be referred to as a quadruple bottom line report.

Companies including Shell, BP and Westpac have invested huge resources in developing their approaches to corporate sustainability and many companies now provide regular sustainability reports.[11] A **sustainability report** is a company report presenting information on the economic, environmental and social dimensions of its activities, products and services. (This is synonymous with a social report, citizenship report, triple bottom line report or a corporate social responsibility report.) Where it includes governance issues, it may be referred to as a quadruple bottom line report.

For example, Telstra released its first corporate social responsibility report in November 2003. The report includes specific performance figures related to issues such as Telstra's philanthropic activities and contributions during natural disasters.[12] Some companies have taken action in response (at least partly) to scandal or widespread criticism. The National Australia Bank (NAB) had a difficult year in 2004. In addition to the *2004 Annual Financial Report*, the NAB released a *Corporate Social Responsibility Report* for the first time. This report is a stand-alone, externally audited report of the NAB's performance against non-financial indicators—including environmental and social impact indicators (such as customer, community and employee relations). 'The message from our stakeholders is clear—they have asked us for greater transparency and accountability, and have told us we need to rebuild trust with them', said Mr Stewart, NAB's chief executive officer.[13] Similarly, with regard to Shell's actions taken after criticism of its environmental management and human rights policies in the 1990s, John Simpson, director of Shell Australia, said:

> In response to rising community concern, we listened to the 100 000 people we employed and created an environment in which we could talk to the public about issues of concern and provide them with information. By being transparent and publicly addressing those concerns, we closed the gaps between our policy and the personal values of our employees.[14]

As shown in 'Managing challenges of globalisation: Care for staff puts firm a step ahead' opposite, awareness of corporate sustainability has grown in societies and companies throughout the Asia–Pacific region[15], and discussion about corporate sustainability is not confined to large organisations.[16] However, it is recognised that it is difficult to define and measure corporate sustainability or corporate social responsibility, as there is a wide array of related concepts, numerous views and substantial critique.[17] Further, the purpose and application of these concepts has been hotly debated. For example, triple bottom line reporting has been criticised for providing a 'smokescreen behind which firms can avoid truly effective social and environmental reporting and performance'.[18]

Issues related to corporate sustainability and incorporating ethical principles and values into business practice have become increasingly important for HR managers, yet these issues are fraught with challenges. For example, HR managers may be required to play important roles in corporate governance, such as the design, implementation and maintenance of corporate codes of conduct,[19] but training in and enforcement of codes of conduct may be difficult, especially across the complex operations of a multinational enterprise (see Chapter 16 International human resource management).[20]

Measuring corporate sustainability

Despite the controversy, many investors are seeking socially responsible investment (SRI) or 'ethical' investment portfolios.[21] According to a past director of investment strategy at Deutsche Bank Australia, Don Stammer, SRIs in Australia, now totalling about $2000 million, are forecast to increase to $35 000–40 000 million over the next 10 years.[22] However, there is confusion in this area, as investors vary in their ideas

CARE FOR STAFF PUTS FIRM A STEP AHEAD

MANAGING CHALLENGES OF GLOBALISATION

Shoe manufacturer Yue Yuen Industrial (Holdings) places a premium on the welfare of its employees. That's good news because the company employs 250 000 people in Asia and Latin America.

That global scope, which has seen it become the largest branded athletic and casual footwear manufacturer in the world, brings the company an International Certificate of Excellence in this year's DHL/SCMP Business Awards.

The company takes great pride in its ability to compete at the highest level, while looking after the interests of its workers in Hong Kong, the mainland, Indonesia, Mexico and Vietnam.

Yue Yuen executive director Steve Li said the company had two major guiding principles: serving the customer to provide the best quality product and looking after the interests of the employees, who last year assembled some 158 million pairs of shoes for international brands such as Nike, Adidas, Reebok, New Balance, Asics, Puma, Timberland and Rockport.

Under what Mr Li described as a corporate social responsibility program, the listed company places emphasis on workers' welfare, benefits, safety, health and environmental protection.

'We are looking for long-term development of the staff and more than 300 people are enrolled in our evening high school funded by Yue Yuen', he said.

The company is also into community help. In Vietnam, for example, 'we built some residential houses for the poor people', Mr Li said, adding that Yue Yuen had also helped flood victims and provided social welfare in the countries where it operates. Last year, it contributed $500 000 towards controlling the SARS outbreak in Hong Kong.

It all makes good economic sense. If you have a happy workforce, you are likely to have a productive workforce. And Yue Yuen has had some productive years, with a compound average growth rate of 18 per cent over the past decade, according to Mr Li.

In layman's terms, that means that sales rocketed to US$2.5 billion last year from US$405 million in 1992.

Over the same period, net profit rose to US$308 million from US$56 million.

Mr Li said the company now had a 17 per cent share in the global market in athletic and casual footwear. About 42 per cent of its customers are in the United States, with about 30 per cent in Europe and 23 per cent in Asia, according to company statements.

The company's founders in Taiwan, the Tsai family, probably never dreamt of such riches. The parent company, Pou Chen, used to make simple footwear in factories in Taiwan. But as Taiwan's workforce became more expensive, clients looked for cheaper sources. Not wanting to be left behind, the Tsai family set up Yue Yuen in 1988 and began moving manufacturing facilities into the mainland.

'We started a small-scale manufacturing plant in Zhuhai [in 1987] and then expanded to Dongguan in [1988]', Mr Li said. Two more factories were opened in the southern towns of Zhongshan and Huangjiang as the company began picking up brand-name business.

Yue Yuen was listed in Hong Kong in 1992.

A marked recent characteristic of Yue Yuen's business has been closer cooperation with clients.

'I would say [that now] more of the business is ODM [original design manufacture]—that means we jointly develop and design the new product,' said Mr Li.

Other recent developments have included Yue Yuen's diversification into retailing. It is a licensee in the mainland for the sale of brands such as Hush Puppies, Converse and Asics. It has also started branching out into the manufacture of sports apparel and accessories.

'We have factories in Mexico, China and Vietnam making apparel for brands like North Face and Columbia as well as several joint ventures producing Nike and adidas sportswear', Mr Li said.

The company is now involved in upstream business—sourcing shoe-making materials such as leather and sole units. Yue Yuen has stakes in tanning factories in China, Taiwan and Vietnam.

'For the future we will continue to expand our footwear manufacture', Mr Li said, while adding that the company would also place a greater focus on the retail business in the mainland and its burgeoning apparels unit.

Yue Yuen also sees the Beijing Olympics in 2008 as an opportunity to strike gold.

'I think the Olympics in China will be a very big event and since we are a sports shoe and apparel maker we look forward to a big market in China', Mr Li said.

Source: L. Dobbs, 2004, 'Care for staff puts firm a step ahead: the world's largest branded footwear maker takes pride in its employee relations and strong customer service', *South China Morning Post*, 3 December, p. 2.

about what constitutes an ethical investment. Consultancies that conduct research into a company's degree of social responsibility might consider a range of factors including environmental records, industrial relations records and human rights. Information may be obtained from company reports, as well as government and media reports and court decisions, and consultation with representatives of government agencies, environmentalists and trade unions. Research firms must constantly monitor companies and update their reports.[23]

Three main methods are used to assess an SRI. The first is negative screening, in which companies are assessed as non-SRIs for a variety of reasons, including their environmental records, their products or their company policies. In contrast, the second method is positive screening, in which companies are identified as SRIs based on factors such as a good environmental or social record. The third method is the best-of-sector approach, which allows SRI investors to invest in, for example, mining stocks by selecting the 'least-worst' performer in that industry. While many research consultants use SRI ratings, and some use a 'Reputation Index' (see Chapter 1 Human resource management in Australia), the use of ratings or rankings is a controversial issue, as some argue that the information on which researchers base their company assessments is too complex to 'force' into a simple numerical rating, and concerns have been raised about methodology and conflicts of interests.[24]

Over 2000 companies around the world disclose social and environmental data using the *Global Reporting Initiative Guidelines*, which are a framework for reporting on an organisation's economic, environmental and social performance.[25] The Global Reporting Initiative was established in 1997 as a joint initiative between a United States non-governmental organisation (CERES) and the United Nations Environment Programme. The aim of the Global Reporting Initiative is to improve the 'quality, rigour and utility of sustainability reporting'.[26]

The International Organization for Standardization (ISO) is currently developing new international guidelines aimed at improving corporate sustainability. It is anticipated that Standards Australia, as the Australian chapter of the ISO, will adopt the guidelines as an Australian standard. The proposed standard will include issues such as the role of management in managing social impacts, and measuring, improving and reporting performance on financial, social and environmental measures.[27]

Corporate social responsibility/sustainability has implications for HRM. At the moment HRM is playing a negligible role, however, as CSR becomes an accepted way of doing business HR will need to be able to demonstrate the benefits of workplace practices that reflect CSR. HR will be required to integrate CSR through its roles as business partner, employee advocate, administrative expert and change agent.[28]

Links between the HR function and organisational performance, or sustainability, are often difficult to demonstrate, as the assessment of HR performance and its relationship with organisational performance is a complex and often difficult task. A simple indicator may not adequately measure performance, as organisations have different goals relating to effectiveness and efficiency. A recent survey of 249 executives worldwide, conducted on behalf of Deloitte Touche Tohmatsu by the Economist Intelligence Unit (EIU), found that the majority of board directors and senior executives considered factors such as customer satisfaction, innovation, supplier relations and employee commitment as critical to corporate success, although they recognised that these factors are difficult to measure. When they were asked why board members and senior managers lacked information on intangible assets, such as the contribution of HR, respondents identified two main barriers: the absence of developed tools for analysing non-financial measures, and scepticism that such measures would directly impact the bottom line. Despite such difficulties, three-quarters of the

HEALTH HITS HOME IN THE WORKPLACE

MANAGING CHALLENGES THROUGH SUSTAINABILITY

The inactive nature of working behind a desk, along with all the added health problems of stress, poor nutrition, and longer working hours has seen increases in developing many life-threatening illnesses. As a result, it has become essential for organisations to consider taking all necessary measures to ensure they do all they can to help maintain and improve the physical and even mental health of their employees.

Traditionally, company health promotion programs have often been seen as a privilege reserved for senior management. But now, large corporations are making health a priority for their entire staff. As a result, other companies that operated with the 'exec only' mindset are taking a new look at the market, says John Lang, managing director of Good Health Solutions.

'A lot of employers have embraced employee wellbeing, because it's seen as a good thing to do around corporate citizenship and responsibility. These days we're finding the more progressive companies are saying we want outcomes, such as reductions in WorkCover claims, reductions in illness and absence, improvements in productivity and so forth', he says. 'It's not something our industry has traditionally measured. I'd venture to say that out of maybe 500–600 corporate health promotion programs going on around Australia, there's probably only two that track and validate the hard core business metrics.'

There has also been increased use of the online medium to provide health-related information, according to Lang. Individualised online health profiles based on age, gender, lifestyle, risks, likes and dislikes, can boost staff engagement in corporate health programs to up to 90 per cent—'especially if you can push content out to people, rather than relying on them having a bit of discretionary time at their disposal to browse a website looking for more information. That's definitely been a significant development', he says.

According to research conducted in 2005 by Medibank Private, Australian workers with poor health take up to nine times more annual sick days than workers with good health while the healthiest employees are nearly three times more productive while at work than the least healthy.'

For HR professionals, health can no longer be thought of as a government and society issue—it's a critical business issue', says Clive Pinder, managing director of wellbeing consultancy vielife Group Limited. The research demonstrates the monetary link between employee health issues and critical business drivers like productivity and absence, he says, and reflects US and European research which has found employees in good health are up to 23 per cent more productive than those in poor health.

Source: M. Yen, 2006, 'Health hits home in the workplace', *Human Resources*, Issue 100, 21 March, p. 20.
www.humanresourcesmagazine.com.au

---

respondents reported that their companies were under increasing pressure to monitor non-financial performance indicators.[29] A well-thought-out measurement system needs to act as a guide for evaluating HR's contribution to strategy implementation[30] and provide a valid and systematic justification for resource allocation decisions. A measurement system should provide the HR function with the opportunity to demonstrate its contribution not only to business success and employee satisfaction and performance, but also to corporate sustainability. In the following sections, we will discuss HR activities and systematic approaches for the measurement of HR effectiveness. 'Managing challenges through sustainability: Health hits home in the workplace' discusses some of the benefits of employee wellbeing programs and some measures that can be used to assess the outcomes of the programs.

Activities of HR

It is important to understand the activities in which HR engages in terms of their strategic value. One way of classifying these activities is depicted in Figure 18.1 overleaf. *Transactional* activities (the day-to-day transactions such as pay administration, maintaining human resource information systems and employee services) are often low in their strategic value. *Traditional* activities such as performance management, learning, recruiting, selection, compensation and industrial relations are the nuts and bolts of HR. These activities typically have moderate strategic value, since they often form the practices and systems to ensure strategy execution. These activities can provide valuable contributions to the organisation's bottom line. As discussed in the opening case for this chapter, *transformational* activities create long-term capability and adaptability for the firm. These activities include knowledge management, management development, cultural change and strategic redirection and renewal. Obviously, these activities comprise the greatest strategic value for the firm.

As we see in Figure 18.1 below, most HR functions spend the vast majority of their time on transactional activities and traditional activities, and little on transformational activities. Often, HR functions that have focused more on transactional and operational activities for a long time tend to lack the systems, processes and skills for delivering state-of-the-art HR activities; and they are thoroughly unable to contribute in the transformational arena. However, virtually all HR functions, in order to add value to the firm, must increase their efforts in the traditional and transformational activities. Professor Roger Collins, from the Australian Graduate School of Management, says that the first step towards improving the position of the HR function is to be excellent at traditional, or operational, HR. He says:

> Unless you can get the day-to-day stuff right, you have no credibility. If you can't get the payroll and training programs right, senior management won't even consider that you can add value at a higher level. Once you have the basics right, then you have to understand what drives the performance of the business.[31]

FIGURE 18.1 Categories of HR activities

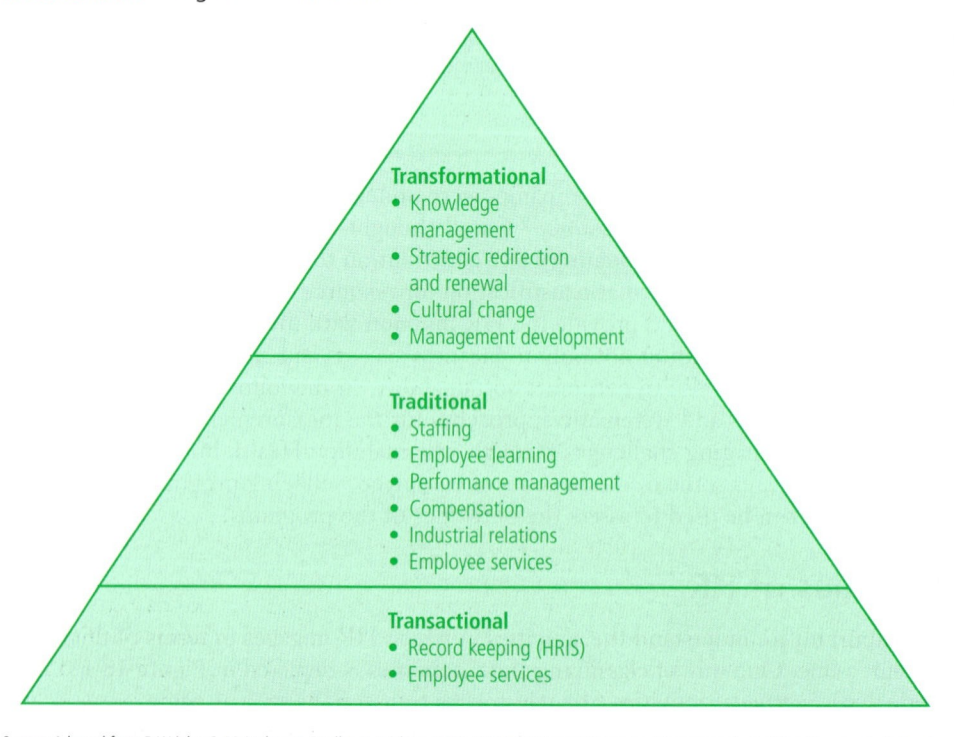

Transformational
- Knowledge management
- Strategic redirection and renewal
- Cultural change
- Management development

Traditional
- Staffing
- Employee learning
- Performance management
- Compensation
- Industrial relations
- Employee services

Transactional
- Record keeping (HRIS)
- Employee services

Source: Adapted from P. Wright, G. McMahan, S. Snell & B. Gerhart, 1998, *Strategic Human Resource Management: Building Human Capital and Organizational Capability*, Technical Report, Cornell University, Ithaca, NY.

To do this, however, requires HR managers to:

1 develop a strategy for the HR function
2 assess the current effectiveness of the HR function
3 restructure, redesign and reengineer or outsource HR processes to improve efficiency and effectiveness.

The first of these three steps was discussed in detail in Chapter 2 Strategic human resource management. The following sections discuss steps two and three.

HR metrics

In an environment of radical corporate transformation, many HR professionals and functions are reinventing themselves, through improved services at a lower cost and through stronger links with business. Human resource professionals have realised the need to become more responsive—providing value creation, sustainability and efficient services to both their external and internal customers.[32] Several authors have argued that there is a need to develop better understanding of strategy and its implications for HR and of the relationships between HR practices and organisational performance.[33] The development of a more strategic role for HR practitioners has led to numerous suggestions to improve understanding of the contribution and effectiveness of the HR function.[34]

Human resource professionals need to adopt a system of **HR metrics**, or measurements, for human performance that will enable effective decisions to be made regarding the HR function and value creation in organisations. As discussed in Chapter 2 Strategic human resource management, the strategic decision-making process for the HR function requires that decision makers have a good sense of the effectiveness of the current HR function. This information provides the foundation for decisions regarding which processes, systems and skills of the HR employees need improvement. Diagnosis of the effectiveness of the HR function provides critical information for its strategic management. Therefore, we suggest that metrics—that show a connection between HR practices and key organisational outcomes—are essential.[35]

HR metrics
measurements for human performance that enable effective decisions to be made regarding the HR function and value creation in organisations.

In addition, having good measures of the HR function's effectiveness markets the function and provides accountability.

Marketing the function

Evaluation is a sign to other managers that the HR function really cares about the organisation as a whole and is trying to support operations, production, marketing and other functions of the company. Information regarding cost savings and benefits is useful to prove to internal customers that HR practices contribute to the bottom line. Such information is also useful for gaining additional business for the HR function.

Providing accountability

Evaluation helps determine whether the HR function is meeting its objectives and using its budget effectively.

Effective measurement of the HR function should enable it to move from an area limited to subjective and intuitive measures only, to a function that uses objective measures to create and manage HR practices for the organisation, customers and employees. Such a transformative process elevates the HR function to an equal footing with other functional areas of the organisation and develops long-term support within the organisation for HR activities that are evidence-based and objectively evaluated.[36]

Approaches for evaluating effectiveness

There are two broad approaches for evaluating the effectiveness of HR practices: the audit approach and the analytic approach. The 'audit approach' uses traditional evaluation of HR programs, by reviewing the outcomes of those activities. Companies using the 'analytic approach' may select from an array of possible tools available for measuring HR effectiveness. These include human resource accounting, utility analysis, HR activity indices, the balanced scorecard and causal chain analysis. This is not an exhaustive list.[37] Each tool may be useful for different purposes or circumstances; each has advantages and disadvantages and not every measurement tool is equally effective and appropriate for all situations.[38]

The audit approach

The audit approach focuses on reviewing the various outcomes of HR functional activities. Both key indicators and customer satisfaction measures are typically collected. The **audit approach** is an assessment of HR effectiveness that involves reviewing customer satisfaction or key indicators (e.g. turnover rate, or average days to fill a position) related to an HR activity (for example, staffing). Table 18.1 opposite lists examples of key indicators and customer satisfaction measures for staffing, equal employment opportunity, compensation, learning and development, performance management, occupational health and safety, industrial relations and succession planning. The development of human resource information systems has made it much easier to collect, store and analyse the functional key indicators than in the past. (See Chapter 7 Human resource planning and human resource information systems.)

In Chapter 2 Strategic human resource management, we discussed how HR functions can become much more customer-oriented as part of the strategic management process. If, in fact, the function desires to be more customer-focused, then one important source of effectiveness data can be the customers. In the same way in which firms often survey their customers to determine how effectively the customers feel they are being served, the HR function can survey its internal customers.

One important internal customer, or stakeholder, is the employees of the firm (also see Chapter 15 Ethics and human resource management). Employees often have both direct contact with the HR function (through activities such as payroll administration) and indirect contact with the function (through their involvement in activities such as receiving performance appraisals, pay increases and training programs). Many organisations use their regular employee attitude survey as a way to assess the employees as users—customers of the HR programs and practices.[39] However, the problem with assessing effectiveness only from the employees' perspective is that often they are responding not from the standpoint of 'the good of the firm', but, rather, from their own individual perspective. For example, employees notoriously and consistently express dissatisfaction with pay levels. Who does not want more money? To simply increase pay across the board, however, would put the firm at a serious labour-cost disadvantage.

Thus, many firms have used surveys of senior executives as a better means of assessing the effectiveness of the HR function. The top-level line executives can see how the systems and practices are impacting both employees and the overall effectiveness of the firm from a strategic standpoint. This can also be useful for determining how well HR employees' perceptions of their function's effectiveness

---

Audit approach
type of assessment of HR effectiveness that involves reviewing customer satisfaction or key indicators (for example, turnover rate, or average days to fill a position) related to an HR activity (for example, staffing).

TABLE 18.1 Examples of key indicators and customer satisfaction measures for HR functions

Key indicators	Customer satisfaction measures
Staffing	
Average days taken to fill open requisitions	Anticipation of personnel needs
Ratio of acceptances to offers made	Timeliness of referring qualified workers to line supervisors
Ratio of minority/women applicants to representation in local labour market	Treatment of applicants
Per capita requirement costs	Skill in handling terminations
Average years of experience/education of recruits per job family	Adaptability to changing labour market conditions
Equal employment opportunity	
Ratio of EEO grievances to employee population	Resolution of EEO grievances
Minority representation by EEO categories	Day-to-day assistance provided by HR department in implementing affirmative action plan
Minority turnover rate	Aggressive recruitment to identify qualified women and minority applicants
Managing work–life balance and diversity	
Availability work–life programs	Employee usage of work–life programs
	Employee satisfaction with work–life programs
Compensation	
Per capita (average) merit increases	Fairness of existing job evaluation system in assigning grades and salaries
Ratio of recommendations for reclassification to number of employees	Competitiveness in local labour market
Percentage of overtime hours to straight time	Relationship between pay and performance
Ratio of average salary offers to average salary in community	Employee satisfaction with pay
Employee learning and development	
Percentage of employees participating in training programs per job family	Extent to which training programs meet the needs of employees and the company
Training dollars per employee	Communication to employees about available training opportunities
	Quality of introduction/orientation programs
Performance management	
Distribution of performance appraisal ratings	Assistance in identifying management potential
Appropriate psychometric properties of appraisal forms	Organisational development activities provided by HR department
Succession planning	
Ratio of promotions to number of employees	Extent to which promotions are made from within
Ratio of open requisitions filled internally to those filled externally	Assistance/counselling provided to employees in career planning
Occupational health and safety	
Frequency/severity ratio of accidents	Assistance to line managers in organising safety programs
Safety-related expenses per $1000 of payroll	Assistance to line managers in identifying potential safety hazards
Plant security losses per square metre (e.g. fires or burglaries)	Assistance to line managers in providing a good working environment (lighting, cleanliness, heating etc.)
Industrial relations	
Ratio of grievances by pay plan to number of employees	Assistance provided to line managers in handling grievances
Frequency and duration of work stoppages	Efforts to promote a spirit of cooperation in plant
Percentage of grievances settled	Efforts to monitor the industrial relations climate in plant
Overall effectiveness	
Ratio of HR staff to employee population	Accuracy and clarity of information provided to managers and employees
Turnover rate	Competence and expertise of staff
Absenteeism rate	Working relationship between organisations and HR department
Ratio of per capita revenues to per capita cost	
Net income per employee	

Source: Adapted from A.S. Tsui & L.R. Gomez-Mejia, 'Evaluating HR effectiveness', in L. Dyer (ed), 1998, *Human Resource Management: Evolving Roles and Responsibilities*, Bureau of National Affairs, Washington, DC, pp. 187–227.

align with the views of their line colleagues. For example, a study of 14 firms revealed that HR executives and line executives agreed on the relative effectiveness of HR's delivery of services such as staffing and training systems (that is, which were most and least effectively delivered), but not on the absolute level of effectiveness. Ratings by HR executives of HR's effectiveness in different roles also diverged significantly from line executives. In addition, line executives viewed HR as being significantly less effective with regard to HR's actual contributions to the firm's overall effectiveness.[40]

The analytic approach

Analytic approach
type of assessment of HR effectiveness that involves determining the impact of, or the financial costs and benefits of, a program or practice.

The **analytic approach** is a type of assessment of HR effectiveness that involves determining the impact, or the financial costs and benefits, of a program or practice. It focuses on either: (1) determining whether the introduction of a HR program or practice (for example, a recruitment program, training program or new compensation system) has the intended effect; or (2) estimating the financial costs and benefits resulting from a HR practice. Evaluating a HR program is one strategy for determining whether the program works. Typically, in an overall evaluation of effectiveness, we are interested in determining the degree of change associated with the program.

Cost–benefit analysis can be applied to determine the economic benefits of HR programs and practices using accounting methods. For example, an annual survey of 100 Australian organisations conducted since 1997 has shown that the costs of recruitment have risen steadily, with a median recruitment cost of $1917 per new recruit in 2000, which reflects an increase of 12.5 per cent from 1999. The survey also showed that the major cost factor in recruitment is the costs associated with the HR, and other, employees administering the process.[41] While this may be interesting information, a cost–benefit analysis can provide more value overall. Determining the economic benefits of HR programs and practices involves determining the related costs and benefits. Using this strategy, we are not concerned with how much change occurred, but rather with the dollar value (costs versus benefits) of the program. Cost information for HR programs or practices is important for several reasons. To use training programs as an example, cost information is important in order to:

1 understand total expenditures for training, including direct and indirect costs
2 compare the costs of alternative training programs
3 evaluate the proportion of money spent on the program's development, administration and evaluation, as well as to compare monies spent on training for different groups of employees (for example, production workers versus clerical workers)
4 control costs.[42]

Determining costs

In this section, we use the example of a training program to show how to determine the return on investment.

Training program costs include direct and indirect costs.[43] Direct costs include salaries and benefits for all employees involved in the training program, including: trainees, instructors, consultants and employees who design the program; program material and supplies; equipment or classroom rentals or purchases; and travel costs. Indirect costs are not related directly to the design, development or delivery of the training program. They include: general office supplies, facilities, equipment and related expenses; travel and expenses not directly billed to one program; salaries for managers and staff not related to any one training program; and administrative and staff support salaries.

One method for comparing costs of alternative training programs is the resource requirements model.[44] This model compares equipment, facilities, personnel and materials costs across different stages of the training process (program design, implementation, needs assessment, development and evaluation). Use of the resource requirements model can help determine overall differences in costs between training programs. Also, costs incurred at different stages of the training process can be compared across programs.

Determining benefits

To identify the potential benefits of training, the company must review the original reasons that the program was conducted. For example, a training program may have been conducted in order to reduce production costs or overtime costs or to increase the amount of repeat business. A number of methods may be helpful in identifying the benefits of a training program:

1. Technical, academic and practitioner literature summarises the benefits that have been shown to relate to a specific training program.
2. Pilot programs assess the benefits on a small group of trainees before a company commits more resources.
3. Observance of successful job performers can help a company determine what successful job performers do differently from unsuccessful job performers.[45]

Making the analysis

A cost–benefit analysis is best explained by an example. Let us examine a wood plant that produced panels for use as building materials. The plant employed 300 workers, 48 supervisors, seven shift superintendents and a plant manager. The business had three problems. First, 2 per cent of the wood panels produced each day were rejected because of poor quality. Second, the production area was experiencing poor housekeeping, such as improperly stacked finished panels that would fall on employees. Third, the number of preventable accidents was higher than the industry average. To correct these problems, supervisors were trained in performance management and interpersonal skills related to quality problems and poor work habits of employees and in rewarding employees for performance improvement. The supervisors, shift superintendents and plant manager attended a training program. The program sessions were conducted in a hotel close to the plant. The training program was purchased from a consultant and used a videotape. Also, the instructor for the program was a consultant. Costs were determined as shown in Table 18.2 overleaf.

Benefits of the training program were identified by considering why the program was conducted (quality of panels, housekeeping and accidents). Table 18.3 page 671 shows how benefits were determined.

It is important to recognise that a range of methods, some quite sophisticated, are available for determining the dollar value of HR programs, such as those for employee training.[46] Table 18.4 page 672 lists examples of various types of cost–benefit analyses that are done.

Human resource accounting attempts to place a dollar value on human resources as if they were physical resources (for example, plant and equipment) or financial resources (for example, cash). Efforts to measure the costs associated with HR activities are not new. Human resource managers have been using HR accounting[47] and financial efficiency measures since the 1970s. This measurement tool involves systems for calculating costs of HR programs and HR functions, with a variety of dollar- or time-based ratios for activities such as staffing, compensation and employee development. These measures are typically expressed as 'input–output' ratios, such as

Human resource accounting attempts to place a dollar value on human resources as if they were physical resources (for example, plant and equipment) or financial resources (for example, cash).

TABLE 18.2 — Training program costs

Direct costs	$
Instructor	0
In-house instructor (12 days @ $125 per day)	1 500
Fringe benefits (25 per cent of salary)	375
Travel expenses	0
Materials ($60 × 56 trainees)	3 360
Classroom space and audiovisual equipment (12 days @ $50 per day)	600
Refreshments ($4 per day × 3 days × 56 trainees)	672
Total direct costs	6 507

Indirect costs	$
Training management	0
Clerical and administrative salaries	750
Fringe benefits (25 per cent of salary)	187
Postage, shipping and telephone	0
Pre- and post-training learning materials ($4 × 56 trainees)	224
Total indirect costs	1 161

Development costs	$
Fee for program purchase	3 600
Instructor training	
Registration fee	1 400
Travel and lodging	975
Salary	625
Benefits (25 per cent of salary)	156
Total development costs	6 756

Overhead costs	$
General organisational support, top management time (10 per cent of direct, indirect and development costs)	1 443
Total overhead costs	1 443

Compensation for trainees	$
Trainees' salaries and benefits (based on time away from job)	16 969
Total training costs	32 836
Cost per trainee	587

time taken to fill employee vacancies, employee turnover rates and costs.[48] However, measuring the costs of HR is not enough to provide a 'real' understanding of the contribution and effectiveness of the HR function. A focus solely on cost may lead managers to assume that cutting costs will solve all problems. Understanding costs may be useful as a starting point for measurement. However, these measures do not enable a company to create value through HR practices. For example, time taken to fill employee vacancies can be reduced but effective recruitment and selection are complex processes, and any organisation that intends to compete through people must take the utmost care with how it conducts these processes (see Chapter 8 Recruitment and selection). To be effective, HR metrics must 'assess strategic value and effectiveness, not just efficiency'.[49]

TABLE 18.3 Determination of training benefits

Operational results area	How measured	Results before training	Results after training	Differences (+ or –)	Expressed in $
Quality of panels	Percentage rejected	2 per cent rejected—1440 panels per day	1.5 per cent rejected—1080 panels per day	0.5 per cent —360 panels	$720 per day $172 800 per year
Housekeeping	Visual inspection using 20-item checklist	10 defects (average)	2 defects (average)	8 defects	Not measurable in $
Preventable accidents	Number of accidents	24 per year	16 per year	8 per year	
	Direct cost of accidents	$144 000 per year	$96 000 per year	$48 000 per year	$48 000 per year

$$\text{ROI} = \frac{\text{Return}}{\text{Investment}} = \frac{\text{Operational results}}{\text{Training costs}} = \frac{\$220\,800}{\$32\,836} = 6.7$$

Total savings: $220 800

Source: Adapted from D.G. Robinson & J. Robinson, 1989, 'Training for impact', *Training and Development*, August, pp. 30–42.

Utility analysis assesses the dollar value of HRM activities such as training programs based on estimates of the difference in job performance between trained and untrained employees, the number of individuals trained, the length of time a training program is expected to influence performance and a measure of the variability in job performance in the untrained group of employees.[50] It requires assessments of variables such as knowledge, skills and performance, which are then transformed into dollar values and offset with estimated costs.[51] Utility analysis can also be used to estimate the financial impact of employee behaviours (for example, absenteeism, turnover, job performance and substance abuse). These methods require the use of a pre-test/post-test design with a comparison group. Other types of economic analysis evaluate training programs as they benefit the firm or the government using direct and indirect costs, government incentives paid for training, wage increases received by trainees as a result of completion of training programs, tax rates and discount rates.[52] Utility analysis provides a wide array of possible approaches for estimating the possible returns on HR program investments. Utility analysis is a rigorous measurement technique but has been criticised because its complexity and numerous assumptions may reduce its credibility and usefulness when applied to HR programs.[53]

To provide another example, wellness programs are a popular HR program for reducing health-care costs through reducing employees' risk of heart disease and cancer. One research project examined four different types of wellness programs. Part of the evaluation involved determining the costs and benefits associated with the four programs over a three-year period.[54] A different type of wellness program was implemented at each site. Site A instituted a program involving raising employees' awareness of health risks (that is, distributing news articles, and providing blood pressure testing and health education classes). Site B set up a physical fitness facility for employees. Site C raised awareness of health risks and followed up with employees who had identified health risks. Site D provided health education and follow-up counselling and promoted physical competition and health-related events. Table 18.5 overleaf shows the effectiveness and cost-effectiveness of the site C and site D wellness models.

Utility analysis
an assessment of the dollar value of HRM activities such as training, based on the difference in job performance between trained and untrained employees, the number of individuals trained, the length of time training is expected to influence performance, and the variability in job performance among untrained employees.

TABLE 18.4 Types of cost-benefits analysis

Human resource accounting
- Capitalisation of salary
- Net present value of expected wage payments
- Returns on human assets and human investments

Utility analysis
- Turnover costs
- Absenteeism and sick-leave costs
- Gains from selection programs
- Impact of positive employee attitudes
- Financial gains of training programs

Source: Based on A.S. Tsui & L.R. Gomez-Mejia, 'Evaluating human resource effectiveness', in L. Dyer (ed), 1988, *Human Resource Management: Evolving Roles and Responsibilities*, Bureau of National Affairs, Washington, DC, pp. 187–227.

TABLE 18.5 Effectiveness and cost effectiveness of two wellness programs for four cardiovascular disease risk factors

	Site C	Site D
Annual direct program costs, per employee per year	$30.96	$38.57
Percentage of cardiovascular disease risks[a] for which risk was moderately reduced or relapse prevented	48%	51%
Percentage of preceding entry per annual $1 spent per employee	1.55%	1.32%
Amount spent per 1 per cent of risks reduced or relapse prevented	$0.65	$0.76

[a] High blood pressure, overweight, smoking and lack of exercise.

Source: J.C. Erfurt, A. Foote & M.A. Heirich, 1992, 'The cost-effectiveness of worksite wellness programs', *Personnel Psychology*, 45, p. 22.

A good example of the level of sophistication that can be required for cost–benefit analysis is shown in Table 18.6 opposite. This table shows the types of information needed to determine the dollar value of replacing a middle-level manager in a professional services firm.[55]

In this example, direct and indirect dollar costs have been calculated for each of the processes prior to exit and on replacement with the new recruit, producing a conservative figure that represents the turnover cost to the organisation. In measuring the turnover costs, the analysis was divided into three areas: separation costs, replacement costs and training costs.[56] The analysis is consistent with contemporary studies that have applied the same methodology in other industries such as hospitality and tourism.[57] Data were obtained through analysis of budgets; interviews with senior executives, training managers, recruitment coordinators and administration personnel within the organisation; and exit interviews.[58]

Return on investment (ROI) assigning a value to the benefits achieved by an HR activity and dividing that value by the costs associated with the activity.

Utility analysis, and specific measures such as **return on investment (ROI)** for HR activities, which assign a value to the benefits achieved by a HR activity and divides that value by the costs associated with the activity,[59] can be considerably useful. However, an underlying assumption is that accurate assessments of benefits and costs can be calculated; for some areas of HRM, such as expatriate assignments, this may be very difficult. Reports indicate that relatively few organisations gather comprehensive financial efficiency or ROI measures for international HRM activities. For example, with regard to expatriate ROI, 'there is no universal understanding of the meaning of ROI, and there are few mechanisms in place for measuring it accurately'.[60]

TABLE 18.6 Example of components identified in determining the dollar value of employee turnover

	Cost $	% Each subdivision	% Total turnover costs
Separation costs:			
Exit interviews	794.89	6.60	
Administration	62.20	0.50	
Lost productivity	11 154.21	92.80	
Subtotal	12 011.30		16.07
Replacement costs:			
Preparation of job descriptions	62.20	0.10	
Review resumés and interview applicants	1 108.95	3.10	
Agency and related costs	15 760.00	44.70	
Pre-employment practices	196.65	0.50	
Orientation	269.75	0.70	
Lost productivity	17 846.75	50.60	
Subtotal	35 244.30		47.16
Training costs	27 482.40	100	36.77
Total	74 738.00		100

Source: J. Abbott, H. De Cieri & R.D. Iverson, 1998, 'Costing turnover: implications of work/family conflict at management level', *Asia Pacific Journal of Human Resources*, 36 (1), p. 38. © Sage Publications, 1998. Reprinted by permission.

The analytic approach is more demanding than the audit approach because tools such as human resource accounting and utility analysis require the detailed use of statistics and finance. However, it is well recognised by academics and practitioners in the accounting and management fields that, in the new economy, organisations increasingly derive value from intangible assets and, thus, traditional corporate measurement systems must include measurement of these intangible assets.[61] Scholars in the field of strategic HRM have noted the importance of understanding the *value of human capital*, defined as the collective value of the assembled workforce, or 'intellectual capital'—discussed in Chapter 11 Learning and development.[62] Indeed, more employers are now prepared to pay a premium for superior talent.

Efforts to identify and measure 'human capital' and 'intellectual capital' are faced with numerous challenges, because these are not easy assets to measure.[63] However, a focus only on easy to measure assets and on short-term results with positive financial outcomes to appease shareholders will have negative long-term implications.[64] A focus on performance indicators beyond financial outcomes is increasingly advocated in many industries and organisations, as we discussed in the earlier section on corporate sustainability. Therefore, many companies have moved beyond human resource accounting and utility analysis to measure the effectiveness of HR. For instance, Westpac Banking Corporation New Zealand introduced a work–life program based firmly on the principles of respect for diversity. The program included a range of policies, such as school holiday programs, study and parental leave, unpaid leave for career breaks and graduated return to work. This work–life program resulted in savings on recruitment and retraining costs so that the bank's investment in these policies has more than been repaid. 'Less quantifiably, the bank has retained good staff, so it is not only number crunching. It needs to be a win-win situation', McKenzie says. 'You have customers, staff and stakeholders. But it's no good investing a whole lot of money in an area if shareholders will suffer.'[65]

HR Activity Index
measures the association between a collection of HR activities and changes in organisational outcomes such as profits and shareholder value creation.

A popular tool for measurement of HR effectiveness is a **HR Activity Index**, which measures the association between a collection of HR activities and changes in organisational outcomes such as profits and shareholder value creation.[66] These HR activity indices have been applied in many companies and the focus has tended to be on specific HR activities, testing for relationships with specific actions and performance outcomes. For example, the consulting firm Watson Wyatt conducted a study of HR practices in 405 companies and identified a correlation between human capital and shareholder value. Based on its research, the consulting firm has created a 'Human Capital Index', which rates how much a company's HR practices affect the financial performance of the company. This index identifies HR practices in five key areas that, the consultants suggest, will lead to an increase in shareholder value. The five areas are: (1) recruiting excellence; (2) a collegial flexible workplace; (3) communications integrity; (4) clear rewards and accountability; and (5) prudent use of resources.[67] Another example of HR indices is evident regarding research that measures the relationship between high-performance work systems (HPWS) and organisational performance. As discussed in several chapters of this book, the development of effective HR systems can bring substantial successes to an organisation.[68]

However, there are several criticisms of HR activity indices. First, many measure only whether HR practices exist in a company; they do not ask how the HR practices are implemented, or whether the HR practices are managed well. Second, they typically use one description for an entire company; that is, they ask one HR manager to report on the existence of a particular HR practice. However, in many companies, HR practices will vary across business units and locations, so one description may not be an accurate representation.[69] It should also be noted that the Watson Wyatt Index and much of the research in this area is based on large, public companies; it may not be applicable to small firms. Several researchers have pointed out that the research results for this approach should be treated with caution, as the causal mechanisms and direction of relationships may be unclear. This lack of clarity may lead to incorrect conclusions or actions.[70]

The *balanced scorecard* (which was introduced in Chapter 1 Human resource management in Australia) is a measurement tool that managers can use to obtain an indication of the performance of a company based on the degree to which stakeholder needs are satisfied. The balanced scorecard enables managers to look at the company from the perspective of internal and external customers, employees and shareholders, by measuring how the organisation or the HR function meets objectives in four areas: (1) customers; (2) financial markets; (3) internal processes; and (4) learning and growth.[71] Numerous companies have adapted the balanced scorecard to develop their own HR scorecard.[72] An example is the Melbourne Market Authority, a government business enterprise that operates a market complex for cut flowers and fresh produce, including 2300 businesses that together turn over more than $1300 million a year. In late 1999 the authority undertook a strategic review and developed a new corporate plan, including the adoption of the 'balanced scorecard' to implement its new strategy. As part of this new approach, all employees were required to develop and apply competencies that support the goals identified in the balanced scorecard. This was implemented in December 2000 and, in less than three months, financial performance had improved 7.5 per cent and other qualitative improvements were observable, such as improved communication flows and attentiveness to the needs of various internal and external customer groups.[73]

A vast array of HR measures can be categorised into the balanced scorecard and a key benefit is that this approach is well known to many managers.[74] There is also potential for flexibility, as computer software can allow users to explore HR metrics to support their own analysis questions. A potential concern with the balanced scorecard, however, is that naïve users may misinterpret or misanalyse the information.[75]

Causal chain analysis measures the links between HR activities or employee behaviours and attitudes, and business processes or outcomes, to draw a chain of causal relationships between employees, customers and profit. Hence, this is sometimes referred to as an 'employee–customer–profit' chain.[76] A well-known example is that of the Sears Department Stores in the United States, which analysed the links between HR practices (such as the use of empowered teams), employees' attitudes (such as job satisfaction and organisational commitment), employees' on-the-job behaviours, customer perceptions of service, customer retention, and revenue growth.[77] Such an approach has been adopted in Australian companies such as Foster's and Westpac Bank. While causal chains provide tangible measurement of the links between people and business outcomes, they can require a substantial investment of effort and resources and a strong understanding of the underlying connections and areas for investment.[78]

The development and spreading use of the various measurement tools reflects the emergence of **human capital management**, a management approach that aims to capture all efforts related to people in an organisation. While human capital management includes HRM, it is intended to serve as more than a new label for the HR function. Human capital management focuses on measuring the effectiveness of HR activities, with an emphasis on enhancing the fit between those activities and the organisational strategic goals. Human capital management measurement systems can guide managers to improve organisational performance through better management of people.[79] Human capital management refers to an 'organisation-wide business development goal, rather than a limited human resources function'.[80] As Professor Roger Collins suggests in the quote on page 684, HR professionals need to establish credibility with other managers and move outside the silo structure of the HR function. Some researchers view human capital management as offering an alignment between the individual and organisation that offers the 'key to successful management in the future'.[81]

'Managing challenges through HR innovation: Lead v Lag indicators: educating analyst' indicates HR faces the opportunity and challenge of measuring the intangibles in their organisation and then effectively communicating this to the analysts.

As Table 18.7 illustrates, six attributes have been identified as essential in an effective human capital measurement system. It also shows that five human capital management factors that have been shown to consistently predict business results. These factors can be measured through an employee survey and, by using statistical techniques, each of these factors can be linked to alternative business outcomes.[82]

> **Causal chain analysis**
> measures the links between HR activities or employee behaviours and attitudes, and business processes or outcomes.

> **Human capital management**
> a management approach that aims to capture all efforts related to people in an organisation; while human capital management includes HRM, it focuses on measuring the effectiveness of HR activities, with an emphasis on enhancing the fit between those activities and the organisational strategic goals.

Improving HR effectiveness

Once a strategic direction has been established and HR's effectiveness has been evaluated, leaders of the HR function can explore how to improve its effectiveness in contributing to the firm's competitiveness. Returning briefly to Figure 18.1 on page 664, which depicted the different activities of the HR function, often the improvement focuses on two aspects of the pyramid. First, within each activity, HR needs to improve both the efficiency and effectiveness in performing each of the activities. Second, there is often a push to eliminate as much of the transactional work as possible (and some of the traditional work) to free the time and resources in order to focus more on the higher-value-added transformational work. Redesign of the structure (reporting relationships) and processes (through outsourcing and information technology) enables the function to achieve these goals simultaneously. Figure 18.2 overleaf depicts this process.

LEAD v LAG INDICATORS: EDUCATING ANALYST

There has been a multitude of studies demonstrating the strong link between intangible assets and long-term company performance. But this research is yet to gain any significant traction in both the analyst community and companies themselves.

This presents an opportunity for HR professionals, who need to step up and point out that intangibles matter and present their value in a numerical fashion, according to Ammentorp. 'It's a new chance for the HR professionals to step up. It's about pushing the agenda and showing HR does deserve a seat at the leadership table because it offers critical input into the strategic and financial success of the organisation.'

Given that information around good people management, employee engagement, leadership and culture are not readily available, analysts have extreme difficulty rating stocks on non-financial metrics, according to IXP3 Human Capital's Potgieter. 'Analysts are, however, increasingly rating stocks on non-financial metrics', he says.

Recently an analyst published a rating on one of the large banks based on human capital metrics, in particular staff turnover, according to Potgieter. Given that analysts are now rating on human capital metrics, this in turn means that HR directors will increasingly need to be prepared to provide metrics to analysts (or internal investor relations staff) in a short time frame.

'HR directors will increasingly be called upon to produce HR metrics as the demand for this information increases from both analysts and shareholders alike', he says. 'HR analysts will need to start tracking these metrics and put in place systems that will enable the metrics to be produced as and when they are required.'

Automated systems and dashboards are critical systems that deliver reporting in the format that it is available on demand, Potgieter adds. HR directors will also increasingly be asked to attend Annual General Meetings to field questions from analysts and shareholders, he predicts.

'In many organisations, there will also be a requirement to add additional skills to the traditional HR team. HR directors will need individuals with IT, financial and HR skills to implement, monitor and control systems required to collate this information', Potgieter says.

Source: C. Donaldson, 'Lead v lag indicators: educating analyst', *Human Resources,* 25 July, p. 13. www.humanresourcesmagazine.com.au

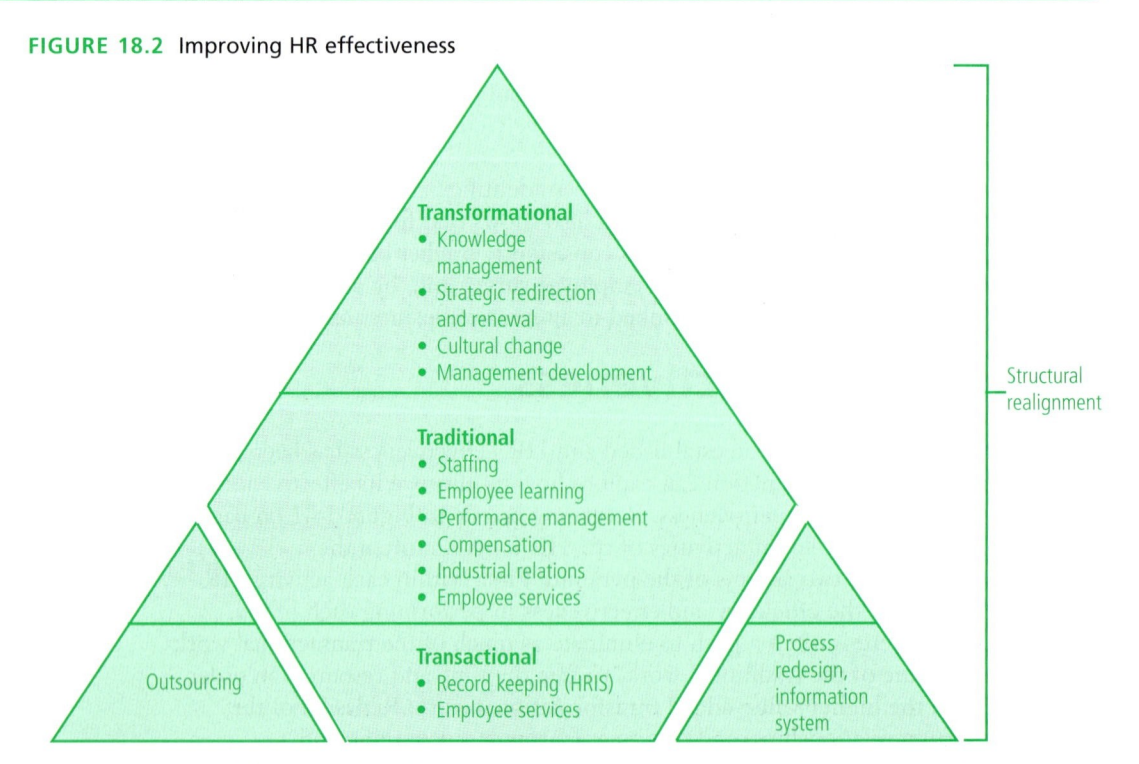

MANAGING CHALLENGES THROUGH HR INNOVATION

FIGURE 18.2 Improving HR effectiveness

Transformational
- Knowledge management
- Strategic redirection and renewal
- Cultural change
- Management development

Traditional
- Staffing
- Employee learning
- Performance management
- Compensation
- Industrial relations
- Employee services

Transactional
- Record keeping (HRIS)
- Employee services

Outsourcing

Process redesign, information system

Structural realignment

Source: Adapted from P. Wright, G. McMahon, S. Snell & B. Gerhart, 1998, *Strategic Human Resource Management: Building Human Capital and Organizational Capability,* Technical Report, Cornell University, Ithaca, NY.

TABLE 18.7 Human capital management

Human resource accounting

Essential attributes of human capital measurement

1. **Descriptive.** At a minimum, a measurement system should produce summary statistics that provide a clear and succinct summary for each issue of interest. Descriptive data tend to focus on the occurrence of a phenomenon, its frequency or its intensity. For example, descriptive statistics can help an organisation monitor the degree to which an important 'best practice' is (or is not) actually being implemented throughout the organisation.
2. **Credible.** A measurement system must be designed to provide the credible and unbiased insights needed to improve business results. Typically, any system designed primarily for the purpose of self-justification is quickly seen as suspect and is given little credence by senior executives. Many ROI initiatives, for example, fall into this category.
3. **Predictive.** A measurement system must produce statistics that help an organisation predict where it is headed. Predictive measures are those that have been linked to the organisation's desired business results.
4. **Detailed.** The information produced by a measurement system must be sufficiently detailed and disaggregated to provide insights into where action should be taken. For example, many types of information must be available across departments or business units in order to allow for a possible intervention to be targeted on those areas where it might be most successful.
5. **Actionable.** A measurement system should focus on those issues over which an organisation can exert influence. Other items, however interesting they may be, are unhelpful in enabling action to drive business results.
6. **Cost-effective.** As important as a powerful measurement system is to a well-managed business, it must be cost effective if it is to be sustainable.

Key human capital measures

1. **Leadership/managerial practices**, which include managers' and leaders' communication, performance feedback, supervisory skills, demonstration of key organisational values, efforts and ability to instil confidence.
2. **Workforce optimisation**, which includes an organisation's success in optimising the performance of its workforce through the establishment of essential processes for getting work done, provision of good working conditions, strong recruiting decisions and an emphasis on accountability.
3. **Learning capacity**, which includes an organisation's overall ability to learn, innovate and continually improve.
4. **Knowledge accessibility**, which includes an organisation's 'collaborativeness' and its capacity for making knowledge and ideas widely available to employees.
5. **Employee engagement**, which includes an organisation's capacity to engage, retain and optimise the value of its employees.

The best way to measure these factors within an organisation is through a thoughtfully constructed survey of employees. Note that such a survey varies considerably from the typical employee satisfaction survey.

By using statistical techniques, each of the five human capital categories, as well as their specific components, can be linked to a variety of alternative measures of business outcomes. Such linkages provide senior executives with a clear prioritisation—a roadmap of sorts—of the human capital management initiatives that will generate the greatest improvement in business results.

Source: Based on L. Bassi & D. McMurrer, 2004, 'Improving your return on people: next generation measurement systems', *Human Resources*, 22 September, pp. 14–15. Reproduced by permission of *Human Resources* magazine (www.human resourcesmagazine.com.au).

'Managing challenges through attracting and retaining people: Recruitment innovation: talent pipelines and supply chains' discusses ways in which processes can be used to make recruitment and selection more effective.

Restructuring to improve HR effectiveness

Traditional HR functions were structured around the basic HR subfunctions, such as staffing, training, compensation, appraisal and employee relations. Each of these areas had a director who reported to the director or general manager of HR, who often reported to a director of finance and administration. However, for the HR function to

RECRUITMENT INNOVATION: TALENT PIPELINES AND SUPPLY CHAINS

With the pending mass exodus of senior knowledge workers due to the retirement of the baby boomer generation, it has become essential for recruitment departments to move from being isolated, reactive and administrative to become aggressive, proactive parts of the organisation that are integrated and aligned with top priorities of the business. By developing innovative, sophisticated forecasting and planning tools, combined with the principles of Supply Chain Management (SCM) for talent, this transformation can occur within a surprising time frame.

Talent or Labour Supply Chains may represent the most promising solution to workforce planning so far devised. Whether in the energy sector, or in healthcare, the talent supply chain is built using process mapping, modelling and process engineering. At Valero Energy, the world's twelfth largest company by revenue, a Labour Supply Chain (LSC) model instantly scales recruiting supply channels. Valero's LSC system provides the technology and departmental business infrastructure to rapidly adapt and scale recruiting supply channels and targets to meet changing business conditions, objectives and competitive threats.

Valero's system design was patterned after Dell's 'just-in-Time' supply chain model taught at the University of Texas. The talent acquisition steps are modelled into six processes. The supplier interaction is modelled into three processes and the customer interaction is modelled into four processes. The processes are then mapped directly to talent acquisition and talent management software systems.

According to the *Harvard Business Review*, 'The holy grails of supply chain management are high speed and low cost.' Not surprisingly these principles above are adhered to by those most respected for the sophistication of their supply chains, including Wal-Mart, Amazon.com and Dell computers. However, the supply chains in these companies aren't just fast and cost effective. They are also:

- **Agile:** They respond quickly to sudden changes in supply or demand. They handle unexpected disruptions smoothly and cost efficiently.
- **Adaptable:** They evolve over time as economic progress, political shifts, demographic trends, and technological advances reshape markets.
- **Aligned:** They align the interests of all participating firms with their own (business interests). As each player maximises its own interests, it optimises the chain's performance as well.

These characteristics are similar to those required by recruiting organisations: cost effectiveness, high quality, customer service focused and scaleable. Add to this agile, adaptable and aligned, and it describes not only the makings of an effective staffing infrastructure model, but quite possibly the perfect staffing model for the globally competitive 21st century.

The continuous supply of talent is today even more valuable than the continuous supply of product and raw materials. The talent supply chain, then, must be continuously monitored, tuned and repaired to achieve bottom line business objectives. The supply chain model itself enables levels of analysis and metrics impossible with current off the shelf talent acquisition systems.

Nonetheless, the same level of metrics and analytics available to Wal-Mart and Dell for SCM are now available for talent acquisition, delivery and management, but the tools must, in most cases, be custom configured and built into the talent acquisition platform.

Source: Extract from A. Schweyer & D. Hilbert, 2006, 'Recruitment innovation: talent pipelines and supply chains', *Human Resources*, Issue 111, 22 August, p. 10. www.humanresourcesmagazine.com.au

truly contribute strategically to firm effectiveness, the senior HR person must be part of the top management team (reporting directly to the chief executive officer) and there must be a different structural arrangement within the function itself.

A recent generic structure for the HR function is depicted in Figure 18.3 opposite. As we see, the HR function effectively is divided into three divisions: the centres for expertise, the field generalists and the service centre.[83] The centres for expertise usually consist of the functional specialists in the traditional areas of HR such as recruitment, selection, training and compensation. These individuals ideally act as consultants in the development of state-of-the-art systems and processes for use in the organisation. The field generalists consist of the HR generalists who are assigned to a business unit within the firm. These individuals usually have dual reporting

FIGURE 18.3 Old and new structures for the HR organisation

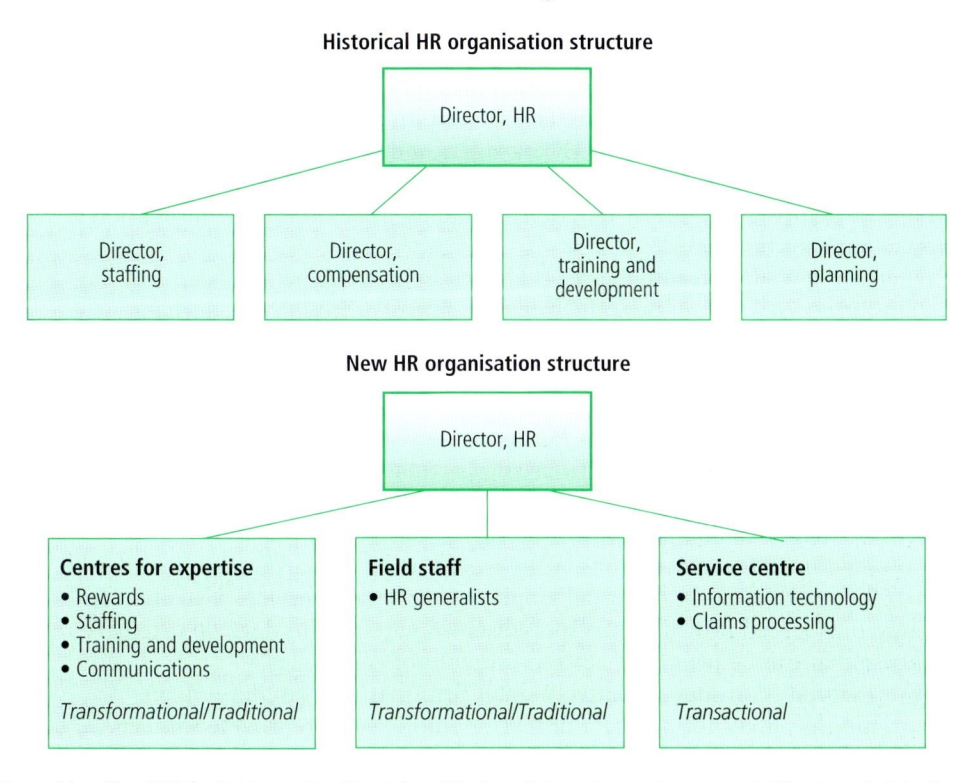

Historical HR organisation structure

- Director, HR
  - Director, staffing
  - Director, compensation
  - Director, training and development
  - Director, planning

New HR organisation structure

- Director, HR
  - **Centres for expertise**
    - Rewards
    - Staffing
    - Training and development
    - Communications

    Transformational/Traditional
  - **Field staff**
    - HR generalists

    Transformational/Traditional
  - **Service centre**
    - Information technology
    - Claims processing

    Transactional

Source: Adapted from P. Wright, G. McMahon, S. Snell & B. Gerhart, 1998, *Strategic Human Resource Management: Building Human Capital and Organizational Capability*, Technical Report, Cornell University, Ithaca, NY.

relationships to both the head of the line business and the head of HR (although the line business tends to take priority). They ideally take responsibility for helping the line executives in their business by strategically addressing people issues and they ensure that the HR systems enable the business to execute its strategy. Finally, the service centre consists of individuals who ensure that the transactional activities are delivered throughout the organisation. These service centres often leverage information technology to deliver employee services efficiently. For example, organisations such as Telstra have created call-in service centres so that employees can dial a central number where service-centre employees are available to answer their questions and process their requests and transactions.

Such structural arrangements improve service delivery through specialisation. Centres for expertise employees can develop current functional skills without being distracted by transactional activities and generalists can focus on learning the business environment without having to maintain expertise in functional specialisations. Finally, service centre employees can focus on efficient delivery of basic services across business units.

Outsourcing to improve HR effectiveness

Restructuring the internal HR function and redesigning the processes represent internal approaches to improving the effectiveness of the HR function. A survey of 100 firms across Australia, conducted annually since 1997, has identified numerous changes taking place in the HR function, including increases in HR staffing levels, professional qualifications and specialisation.[84] In 2000, the ratio of employees to HR employees was 50 to six, showing an increase in HR staffing levels over the previous four years. This finding is interesting as it contrasts with the overwhelming trend suggested by other studies, in Australia and overseas, of outsourcing the HR function.[85] The survey also found that HR employees are increasing their professional profiles, with more HR managers and professionals employed and decreasing numbers of clerical and administrative HR roles. This may also reflect some restructuring of the HR function, including outsourcing or automation of more administrative tasks.[86]

Increasingly, HR executives are seeking to improve the effectiveness of the systems, processes and services the function delivers through outsourcing. *Outsourcing* entails contracting with an outside vendor to provide a product or service to the firm, as opposed to producing the product using employees within the firm.[87]

Why would a firm outsource a HR activity or service? Usually this is done for one of two reasons: either the outsourcing partner can provide the service more cheaply than it would cost to do it internally or the partner can provide it more effectively than it can be performed internally. Early on, firms resorted to outsourcing for efficiency reasons. Why would using an outsourced provider be more efficient than having internal employees provide a service? Usually it is because outsourced providers are specialists who are able to develop extensive expertise that can be leveraged across a number of companies.[88]

For example, consider a relatively small firm that seeks to develop an expatriation program for a small number of employees. To provide this service to employees, the HR function would need to have a knowledge of a wide range of areas related to international transfers, such as visa requirements, international taxation issues and host country conditions for housing. It could be much more efficient to outsource these areas to consultants who can provide this specialist knowledge and related services (see Chapter 16 International human resource management, for more details of expatriate management issues).

Now consider the aspect of effectiveness. The outsourced provider works for a number of firms and specialises in expatriate services; thus, its employees develop state-of-the-art knowledge of running expatriate services. They can learn unique innovations from one company and transfer that learning to a new company. In addition, employees can be more easily and efficiently trained, because all of them will be trained in the same processes and procedures. Finally, due to the experience in providing expatriate services on a constant basis, the firm is able to develop a capability to perform these services that could never be developed by individual employees in one small firm spending part of their time on these services.

A survey that reported in 1999, examined 20 Australian organisations that had already outsourced part or all of their HR function.[89] The reasons given by these organisations for outsourcing HR are shown in Table 18.8. Although these figures are based on a small sample only, the reasons for outsourcing are quite varied.

What kinds of services are being outsourced? Firms primarily outsource transactional activities and services of HR, such as payroll. However, a number of traditional and some transformational activities have been outsourced as well. (This has also been discussed in Chapter 7 Human resource planning and human resource information systems, in some detail.) While outsourcing may be an effective HR strategy in some circumstances, it may not be universally appropriate. It is important to analyse outsourcing proposals both in financial terms and in terms of employee outcomes, such as job satisfaction and job performance.

TABLE 18.8 Why do organisations outsource HR function?

Why outsource?	(n = 20) % responses
Achieve economies of scale	40
Achieve cost savings	35
Overcome a lack of in-house specialist expertise and backup in:	
• information technology	10
• recruitment	10
• industrial relations	10
• job sizing	5
• executive pay	5
State government policy	20
Department portfolio restructuring	15
Increase quality and standard of HR service delivery	15
Improve service to HR clients	15
Standardise processes	15
Increase the range of services to HR clients	10
Achieve greater productivity/efficiencies	10
Enable management to focus on core business and not be distracted by non-core activities	10
Reduce duplication of resources	10
Redirect resources away from support to capability	5
Implement recommendations from an external review	5
Implement recommendations from an internal review	5
Achieve predictable services and costs	5
Achieve guaranteed standards	5
Reduce 'empires'	5
Utilise savings to provide services in other areas and fund other government priorities	5
Respond to market changes	5

Source: L. Norman, 1999, 'HR goes out to save money', *HRMonthly*, August, p. 27. *HRMonthly* is published for the Australian Human Resources Institute. www.ahri.com.au

Improving HR effectiveness through process redesign

In addition to structural arrangements, process redesign enables the HR function to deliver HR services more efficiently and effectively. Process redesign often uses information technology, but information technology applications are not a requirement. Thus, we will discuss the general issue of process reengineering and then explore information technology applications that have aided HR in process redesign.

Reengineering is a complete review and redesign of critical work processes to make them more efficient and improve the quality of the end product or service. Reengineering is especially critical to ensuring that the benefits of new technology can be realised. Applying new technology to an inefficient process will not improve efficiency or effectiveness. Instead, it will increase product or service costs related to the introduction of the new technology.

Reengineering
review and redesign of work processes to make them more efficient and improve the quality of the end product or service.

Reengineering can be used to review the HR department functions and processes, or it can be used to review specific HR practices such as work design or the performance management system. The reengineering process involves the four steps shown in Figure 18.4 below: (1) identify the process to be reengineered; (2) understand the process; (3) redesign the process; and (4) implement the new process.[90]

Identifying the process

Managers who control the process or are responsible for functions within the process (sometimes called 'process owners') should be identified and asked to be part of the reengineering team. Team members should include employees involved in the process (to provide expertise) and those outside the process, as well as internal or external customers who see the outcome of the process.

Understanding the process

Several things need to be considered when evaluating a process:

- Can employers combine jobs?
- Can employers provide employees with more autonomy? Can employers build decision making and control into the process through streamlining the process?
- Are all the steps in the process necessary?
- Are data redundancy, unnecessary checks and controls built into the process?
- How many special cases and exceptions have to be dealt with?
- Are the steps in the process arranged in their natural order?
- What is the desired outcome? Are all of the tasks necessary? What is the value of the process?

Various techniques are used to understand processes. Data-flow diagrams are useful to show the flow of data among departments. Figure 18.5 opposite shows a data-flow diagram for payroll data. This figure shows the steps in producing employee salary payments (pay slips). Information about the employee and department are sent to the general account. The pay slip is issued based on information generated from the general accounting ledger. Data–entity relationship diagrams show the types of data used within a business function and the relationship among the different types of data. In scenario analysis, simulations of 'real-world' issues are presented to data end-users. The end-users are asked to indicate how an information system could help address their particular situations and what data should be maintained to deal with

FIGURE 18.4 The reengineering process

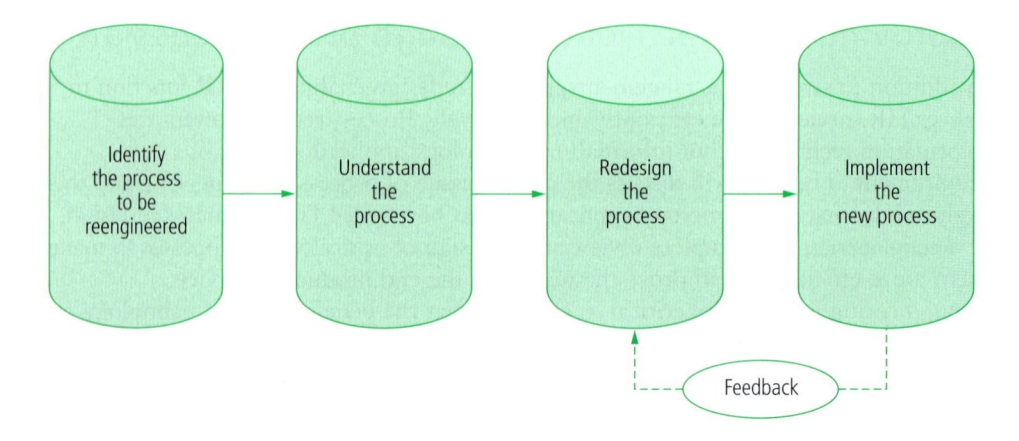

FIGURE 18.5 A data-flow diagram for payroll data

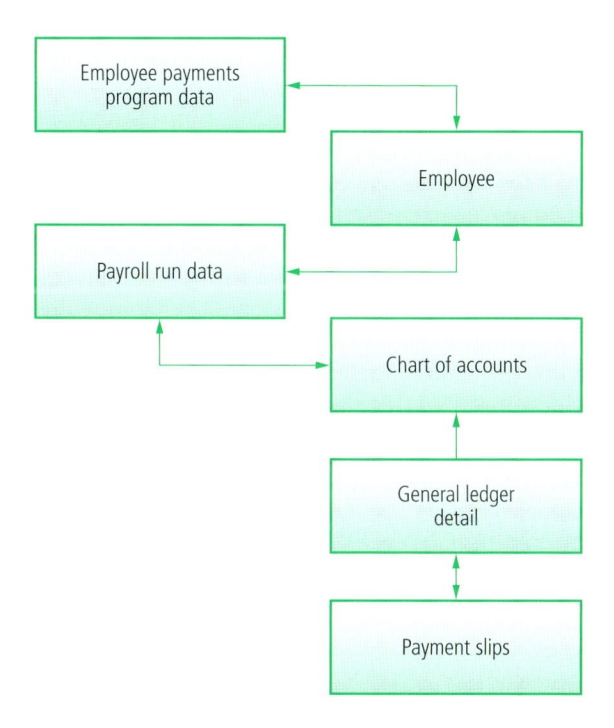

```
Employee payments
program data  ──────────┐
                        ↓
                   ┌─────────┐
                   │Employee │
                   └─────────┘
                        ↑
Payroll run data ←──────┤
      │                 │
      └──→ ┌────────────────┐
           │Chart of accounts│
           └────────────────┘
                   ↑
           ┌────────────────┐
           │ General ledger │
           │    detail      │
           └────────────────┘
                   ↑
           ┌────────────────┐
           │ Payment slips  │
           └────────────────┘
```

those situations. Surveys and focus groups collect information about the data collected, used and stored in a functional area, as well as information about time and information-processing requirements. Users may be asked to evaluate the importance, frequency and criticality of automating specific tasks within a functional area. For example, how critical is it to have an applicant-tracking system that maintains data on applicants' previous work experience? Cost–benefit analyses compare the costs of completing tasks with and without an automated system or software application. For example, the analysis should include the costs in terms of people, time, materials and dollars; the anticipated costs of software and hardware; and labour, time and material expenses.[91]

Redesigning the process
During the redesign phase, the team develops models, tests them, chooses a prototype and determines how to integrate the prototype into the organisation.

Implementing the process
The company tries out the process by testing it in a limited, controlled setting before expanding its use companywide.

Improving HR effectiveness through new technologies

Several new and emerging technologies can help improve the effectiveness of the HR function. New technologies are current applications of knowledge, procedures and equipment that have not been used previously. New technology usually involves automation—that is, replacing human labour with equipment, information processing or some combination of the two. Human resource information systems were discussed in detail in Chapter 7 Human resource planning and human resource information systems.

There is evidence that new technology is related to improvements in productivity. Improvements in productivity have been credited largely to downsizing, restructuring and reengineering. In some cases technology has replaced human capital.[92] However, new technology has allowed companies to find more effective, not simply more efficient, ways of operating.[93] Technology requires companies to have appropriately skilled and motivated people and streamlined work processes. A user friendly intranet site is essential as are knowledgeable call centre staff who are able to access an online knowledge base and employee data.[94]

A United States technology company, Novell, had a high employee turnover rate of around 30 per cent, and a high induction cost for new employees (each costing US$3224). Novell found that every time a new employee joined the company, 17 different information systems had to be updated. Novell used its software and technology to solve this problem, reducing the individual induction cost to US$124. In the process, they developed a HR software program that they claim has also led to an increase of 15 per cent in employee productivity. The program includes immediate access to an office, network account, email, telephone, computer, business cards, badge, security access to appropriate buildings, pagers, mobile phones and so on. Employees also receive immediate access to service and information based on their role. When employees arrive, leave or are transferred, their files are changed instantaneously. The program is also being used in some universities to manage student enrolments.[95]

MANAGING PEOPLE

THE FUTURE OF HR

Sir Winston Churchill was once reported as saying: 'The future will be kind to me, as I intend to write it'. Some people might accuse Churchill of being pretentious. For them it would be difficult, if not impossible, to imagine that one person could shape destiny. For others, Churchill's ambition could be an inspiration—for them the challenge of creating or shaping the future is more certain than predicting it. Underlying these positions is the reality that, individually and collectively, we all have a view about our ability to shape outcomes and the future.

At the risk of being contentious, there seems to be little evidence that the HR occupational group has exercised much influence over its own destiny. Whether it is legislation, government policy, professional standards, occupational image and reputation, or impact on management education and practice, we would be hard pressed to present tangible evidence of our direct and lasting impact. There are at least several reasons for this; reasons that must be acknowledged and overcome if we are to change the status quo.

First, HR people have weak occupational socialisation—we lack strong identity and aspirations. In comparison to lawyers, doctors, dentists, engineers and accountants, we have few recognised standards of entry, educational preparation and practice, few rites of passage and a professional body weakened by a chequered history of achievement and influence.

Second, there are multiple entry points into our occupational group. While this brings the benefits of diversity, it also makes it difficult to build a strong occupational identity that encompasses who we are, what we do and how we add value.

Third, it may be that our origins as service providers and administrators, rather than direct bottom line contributors (compared with our counterparts in sales and production), have conditioned us to be more passive in our role and influence or indeed less ambitious.

Whatever the origins and current status, we have to think and act as though our views are both worthy and important; we have to think and act as though we can impact the objectives, dynamics and performance of our organisations.

So in the future, what is possible and desirable? Let me present four options for your consideration.

First, the financial performance of our organisations is necessary but not sufficient. Despite the best efforts of their advocates, triple bottom lines and balanced scorecards are still the exception rather than the rule. The magnitude of our influence in this world is largely determined by our credibility among the prevailing power brokers. Our credibility will be enhanced among these individuals and groups by demonstrating that we not only understand our organisation's business model and how it adds value to our customers and shareholders, but also how the management and leadership of people contribute to the success of that business model. On one hand we have never had better and more compelling evidence to suggest that people practices impact financial performance and longer-term success, while on the other hand, many HR people, when asked to articulate their organisation's business model and strategy, struggle to provide an accurate and comprehensive understanding of these issues. Until we are able to present and gain unqualified acceptance for the business case for HR, our ability to influence other agendas will always be limited. So our future must include a dimension that acknowledges that the occupational group must become more corporate and commercially savvy.

A second feature of the future will be that our relative numbers will decrease as managers and members take more responsibility for people management and leadership. The pathway to this future is for HR professionals to work less on themselves and more on their partners. There are limited returns to be gained from developing ourselves if this is in isolation from working on our relationships with managers, members and external service providers. So the future will see us working more on collective learning and development than on competency development within the occupational group; on developing organisation-wide HR capability rather than functional competence.

Third, if in our future we are to be more significant and influential, if we are to unlock value, we will have to understand some of the fundamental changes that are taking place in our organisations. For example, the traditional functional silos are being de-emphasised to enhance integration for customers/clients. Implicit in these developments is the need to integrate the thinking, discussions, roles and contributions of marketing, sales, finance, IT and HR.

Such integration opens up opportunities, for example, for us to add value by integrating our corporate product and employment brands as sources of higher performance and competitive advantage. So our future may well lie in creating new hybrid occupational categories rather than strengthening our existing functional thinking and practice.

Human resources (HR) plus marketing could focus on reputation as well as brand creation and migration, while HR plus finance could open up opportunities to produce more robust cost–benefit analyses and causal linkages between practices and processes as well as performance. So a significant future may require that we weaken our traditional occupational identity and professional zeal in order to enhance our impact. To achieve such outcomes, we need to plan and be prepared to take part in interdisciplinary and cross-functional conferences and education.

Fourth, given the increasing investment that we are required to make in career preparation and continuing education, and given the pervasive nature of work, the boundaries between learning, work and our personal lives will become more diffuse. If these trends are to be positive, rather than counterproductive, then the world of work will have to undergo fundamental change. Our organisations will have to become communities; our use of the term employee will have to give way to the concept of member; and our organisations will have to encompass wider definitions of success.

Such definitions of success will more adequately recognise that organisations are embedded in and dependant on the communities that they seek to serve. In the same way in which environmentalism has gained momentum over the past two decades, this very term will have to be expanded to encompass the psychological and sociological impact of work and organisational life on the quality of our lives and society. Such developments open up opportunities to shape the role and contributions of our organisations in the years ahead.

So how can we meet the challenge of writing the future? In every occupational group there is a pro-change constituency that is concerned about the future; what we lack are the forums to debate and resolve some of these issues. These issues, however, are too important to leave to others. We each carry a responsibility for writing our future: our own and that of our organisation. This calls for reflection, discussion, debate, resolution and action. When will you take up this challenge?

Source: Based on R. Collins, 2004, 'Will the future of HR wither away?' *Human Resources,* 4 May. www.humanresourcesmagazine.com.au

QUESTIONS

1 What challenges does this article suggest for the HR function and HR professionals in the future?
2 What opportunities does this article suggest for the HR function and HR professionals in the future?

HRM spotlight: 'A puppet, a lie and the HR guy' provides a further view about the future of HR.

A PUPPET, A LIE AND THE HR GUY

Pinnocchio was heading for trouble. His unscrupulous new friends, Fox and Cat, had plans for the puppet who believed their story—that money trees do in fact grow in the field of miracles—no hard work required. These intriguing characters belong in a book—not on your payroll, in your brand or on your board.

The spotlight is harsh: investors, analysts and regulators are keeping a closer eye than ever on corporate ethics. Ethics are heavily influenced by good governance. Yet good governance cannot be achieved without ethics—at both the organisational and the operational levels. This co-dependent relationship needs policies and values which promote and deliver good corporate citizenship, as people committed to making ethical decisions and who act in accordance with them.

Directors should be looking to achieve three key objectives through governance: creating and maintaining a culture of compliance; minimising contradictory incentives and opportunities for non-compliant behaviour; maximising the capacity to detect and respond to non-compliant behaviour through appropriate internal controls.

The Cole Inquiry has generated much of the current debate and attention around ethical conduct and corporate culture. It has turned the spotlight on these issues and placed the limelight at the top end of town. Yet, many organisations in Australia are still not aware that, since 1999, Australia's federal criminal code contains a section that requires a Board of Directors to establish a corporate culture that shows zero tolerance for corruption and which actively encourages compliance.

This legislation mirrors the widely used US legislation that was first introduced in 1977 and was updated when the US and Australia, along with many other countries, signed up to the OECD convention on combating bribery of foreign public officials in international business transactions in 1997.

This year the OECD issued a report critical of Australia's efforts in this area. It noted that there has never been a case on matters in Australia despite the world focus on the lack of good governance in business. This report, along with the Cole Inquiry coverage, will surely be the genesis for change.

The evidence overwhelmingly shows those organisations with strong, constructive cultures outperform weaker and less adaptable organisations. These strong commercial advantages and imperatives for developing an ethical culture and promoting ethical conduct across the organisation are recognised by the best run companies in Australia and around the globe.

… So how do you know if your organisation's culture is protecting people or putting them at risk? Some questions:

- Does your organisation's culture support ethical behaviour at all levels?
- Are current HR policies supporting ethical behaviour?
- How often do executive leaders engage the organisation in a discussion about the value of ethics?
- Is your organisation pursuing transparency—open organisations create strong ethical branding?
- Do you have the basics in place such as training on ethical expectations built into your onboarding process?
- Like cultures that emphasise safety, do you use routine events like opening a meeting to share a story to demonstrate ethics is distinguishing your brand in the market?
- Does your organisation report on ethical performance standards?

… Now, more than ever, CEOs understand that it (is) their absolute responsibility to lead an ethical and profitable organisation. They need to clearly express the ethics, branding and business performance equation and connect their people to this. With the talent shortage upon us, companies that don't bother to take a proactive stance will be in a weaker hiring and retention position.

Source: Extract from L. Barry & F. O'Toole, 2006, 'A puppet, a lie and the HR guy', *Human Resources,* Issue 107, 27 June, p. 10.

CHAPTER SUMMARY

The roles required of the HR function have changed as people have become recognised as a true source of competitive advantage. This has required a transformation of the HR function from focusing solely on transactional activities to an increasing involvement in strategic activities. In fact, according to a recent study, 64 per cent of HR executives said that their HR function is in a process of transformation.[96] It is the strategic management of the HR function that will determine whether HR will transform itself into a true strategic partner or simply disappear.

In this chapter, we have emphasised that the HR function must deliver transactional, traditional and transformational services and activities to the firm, and it must be both efficient and effective. Human resource executives must strategically manage the HR function in the same way in which the firm must be strategically managed. This requires HR professionals to develop measures of the function's performance through customer surveys and analytical methods. These measures can form the basis for planning ways in which to improve performance. Human resource performance can increase through new structures for the function, through using reengineering and information technology, and through outsourcing. Each of these strategies may be appropriate in some circumstances, but each requires careful planning, attention to detail in implementation, and ongoing evaluation. Multiple performance outcomes should be considered, including financial terms and social terms (such as job satisfaction), if the HR function and the organisation are to achieve both efficiency (cost savings) and effectiveness (value enhancement).

WEB EXERCISES

A Visit the Business for Social Responsibility website at www.bsr.org and view the latest issue of *Leading Perspectives*, an e-magazine presenting commentary on corporate social responsibility and articles analysing current developments and future trends that impact communities, policy makers and businesses alike.

Question
What role might human resource practices play in improving an organisation's performance in corporate social responsibility (or sustainability)?

B Hewlett-Packard (HP) is one of the world's largest computer companies and a producer of test and measurement instruments. It is well known for its printers, which set the standard for technology, performance and reliability. The company also manufactures medical electronic equipment, instruments and systems for chemical analysis, hand-held calculators and electronic components. Hewlett-Packard is consistently recognised as one of the best companies to work for. Visit its website at www.hp.com. Select 'Australia' from the list of locations. Click on 'Company Information' and 'About HP'. Review HP's corporate objectives (click on 'Corporate Objectives and the HP Way') and the company's commitment to human resource management (click on 'HP's People').

Question
1 What are HP's corporate objectives?
2 Which human resource practices help HP reach its corporate objectives?

C The Body Shop has built a reputation as an organisation that endeavours to achieve the triple bottom line: positive results not only in financial terms but also with regard to social and environmental outcomes. The Body Shop in Australia has conducted annual social and environmental audits to assess its performance in these areas. Visit www.thebodyshop.com.au and view the results of the social audit.

Question
1 What role might human resource practices play in improving an organisation's performance in a social audit?
2 Should other organisations follow the example of The Body Shop and introduce auditing of the 'triple bottom line'?

DISCUSSION QUESTIONS

1. Why do you think that few companies take the time to determine the effectiveness of HR practices?
2. Should a company be concerned about evaluating HR practices? Why?
3. What might people working in the HR function gain by evaluating the function? What might employees gain by an evaluation of the HR function?
4. A retail electronics-store chain recently invested a large amount of money to train sales staff to improve customer service. The skills emphasised in the training program include how to greet customers, determine their needs and demonstrate product conveniences. The company wants to know whether the program is effective. What outcomes should it measure? What type of evaluation design should it use?
5. If you were required to demonstrate that a specific HRM activity in your organisation was contributing to sustainable competitive advantage, what types of evidence would you collect and how would you present this evidence?
6. What are the advantages and disadvantages of the balanced scorecard for measuring the HR contribution?
7. Outline the steps you would follow to develop and manage a strategy for outsourcing a HR function or activity. What are the implications of outsourcing human resource activities for HRM?
8. Identify and discuss the major issues in managing the new HR organisation structure depicted in Figure 18.3 on page 679.

HUMAN RESOURCE MANAGEMENT IN AUSTRALIA

CSC Australia had a lot riding on its award-winning 'goal alignment initiative'. It was the crucial first step in the company making a major change of direction from a cost efficiency model to a bold new customer centric model.

The executive team envisioned gaining significant competitive advantage from the strategy when it launched last year. But everything depended on the staff of more than 3500 being willing and able to change their approach and to implement it. They would have to 'engage in becoming customer-intimate in a way that was real, meaningful and compelling'.

CSC Australia (part of a multinational employing 80 000 people) provides consulting, systems integration, labour supply and other services from some 50 locations around the country. Its new customer intimate model is defined in five core areas: meaningful relationships with customers, delivering business outcomes to them, reliable service, being easy to do business with and bringing CSC's global experience to the table.

From the start, IIR advocated using a novel and participative approach—including a sailing boat of sorts. 'About 200 facilitators were trained from around the company, and the regular briefings for employees took a pictorial approach, using a sailing boat metaphor', says vice-president of HR Trish Butler, who is in her sixth year with CSC. 'Employees discovered the messages in an interactive way through questioning, then we asked which elements of the strategy they thought their particular job contributed to. They went away with a piece of paper with three areas written on it, for them to use when goal-setting with their manager.' In 90 minutes employees gained a practical understanding of the new direction in customer intimacy and a strong sense of how individual actions could make a difference.

In phase two, line managers were trained in setting a business context for their team and demonstrating the link between the corporate strategy, their business plan and their teams' work. Goals for the coming year were set. The content was delivered by external consultants, with a member of the HR team opening and closing each session.

Managers were trained in goal-setting and interpreting what the strategy meant for them.

'They were taught to think about the multiple stakeholders guiding their teams, the customers they were supporting, the directives they were getting from CSC Australia, and globally—how to integrate all those messages and work with their people to set goals', says Butler.

In October, CSC had its first customer service week. 'We asked for nominations of people thought to be exemplars of customer service relationships, and we got 270 nominees—a very satisfying response. It was a huge response. It was a huge job to select at state level and then at national level.'

Surveys about workplace culture and climate have been the main instruments for measuring the effectiveness of the initiatives. 'We asked specifically around the area of people's personal goals, and whether they felt they were more connected to company strategy and contributing to it. The response was positive. We have also had dramatic increases in our financial outcomes.'

One of the financial metrics is 'day sales outstanding' [DSO]—how long it takes to collect the cash. If customers are questioning bills or aren't happy with them, the DSO blows out. 'That's continued to trend down', says Butler. 'The measures seem to be stacking up to say that this approach is having a good business impact.'

Now it's perseverance that's important. 'The employees have to see that we're doing this for a second year and we're going to do it for a third—that it's not the latest fad and we're serious about it. We're into the second phase, to align our goals around a model based on customers, teams, business units, with our customers the highest priority.'

Employees are aligning their goals to 'value delivery teams' structured according to the supply chain for each customer. 'Instead of following the usual structure along a line of service or product, we're shifting that around and challenging the paradigms that have existed within the organization.'

Source: [no author], 2006, 'Customer service centred', HR Monthly, November, p. 2

QUESTIONS

1 What were the major aspects of the goal alignment initiative at CSC?
2 Identify the major strengths of the goal alignment initiative.
3 Visit the www.au.country.csc.com/en/ and read about some of the work CSC is doing. Consider the way in which the technology provided by CSC is changing the way work is organised and done.

ENDNOTES

CHAPTER 1 NOTES

1   P.M. Wright & G.C. McMahan, 1992, 'Theoretical perspectives for strategic human resource management', *Journal of Management*, 18, pp. 295–320.

2   P. Boxall & J. Purcell, 2000, 'Strategic human resource management: where have we come from and where should we be going?', *International Journal of Management Reviews*, 2 (2), pp. 183–203; C.C. Cooper & R.J. Burke (eds), 2003, *The new world of work: Challenges and opportunities*, Blackwell, Oxford, U.K; M.A. Hitt, B.W. Keats & S.M. DeMarie, 1998, 'Navigating in the new competitive landscape: Building strategic flexibility and competitive advantage in the 21st century', *Academy of Management Executive* 12 (4), pp. 22–42; J. Paauwe, 2004, *HRM and Performance—Achieving Long Term Viability*, Oxford University Press, Oxford, U.K; M.V. Roehling, W.R. Boswell, P. Caligiuri, D. Feldman, M.E. Graham, J. Guthrie, M. Motohiro & J.W. Tansky, 2005, 'The future of HR management: Research needs and directions', *Human Resource Management*, 44 (2), pp. 207–16; P.M. Wright, T.M. Gardner & L.M. Moynihan, 2003, 'The impact of HR practices on the performance of business units', *Human Resource Management Journal*, 13 (3), p. 21–36.

3   C T. Kulik & H.T.J. Bainbridge, 2006, 'HR and the line: The distribution of HR activities in Australian organizations', *Asia Pacific Journal of Human Resources*, 44, pp. 240–56; G. Currie & S. Procter, 2001, 'Exploring the relationship between HR and middle managers', *Human Resource Management Journal*, 11 (3), pp. 53–69; A Thornhill & M.N.K. Saunders, 1998, 'What if line managers don't realise they're responsible for HR? Lessons from an organization experiencing rapid change', *Personnel Review*, 27(6), p. 460–76; C. Donaldson, 2006, Topping up on talent, *Human Resources*, 21 March 2006, p. 14.

4   P.F. Boxall & P.J. Dowling, 'Human resource management and the industrial relations tradition', *Labour & Industry* 3, 1990, pp. 195–214; G.R. Ferris, W.A. Hochwarter, M.R. Buckley, G. Harrell-Cook & D.D. Frink, 'Human resources management: Some new directions', *Journal of Management*, 25 (3), 1999, pp. 385–421; D. Guest, 1987, 'Human resource management and industrial relations', *Journal of Management Studies* 24 (5), pp. 503–22.

5   P. Boxall & J. Purcell, J, 2000, 'Strategic human resource management: where have we come from and where should we be going?', *International Journal of Management Reviews*, 2 (2), pp. 183–203; P.M. Wright & G.C. McMahan, 1992, 'Theoretical perspectives for strategic human resource management', *Journal of Management* 18 (2), pp. 295–320; M.C. Galang, W. Elsik & G.S. Russ, 1999, 'Legitimacy in human resources management', *Human Relations* 50, 1999, pp. 1403–26; G.S. McMahan, M. Virick & P.M. Wright, 'Alternative theoretical perspectives for strategic human resource management revisited: Progress, problems, and prospects', in P.M. Wright, L.D. Dyer, J.W. Boudreau & G.T. Milkovich (eds), 1999, *Strategic Human Resource Management in the Twenty-First Century*, JAI Press, Greenwich, CT, pp. 99–122; P.M. Wright, B.B. Dunford & S.A. Snell, 2001, 'Human resources and the resource based view of the firm', *Journal of Management*, 27, pp. 701–21.

6   R. Miles & C. Snow, 1984, 'Designing strategic human resource systems', *Organizational Dynamics*, 13, pp. 36–52.

7   R.S. Schuler & S.E. Jackson, 1997, 'Linking competitive strategies with human resource management practises', *Academy of Management Executive*, 1 (3), pp. 207–19; S.E. Jackson, R.S. Schuler & J.C. Rivero, 1989, 'Organizational characteristics as predictors of personnel practices', *Personnel Psychology*, 42 (2), pp. 727–86.

8   C. Sheehan, P. Holland & H. De Cieri, 2006, 'What really explains the relationship between HRM and organizational performance?', Paper presented at Academy of Management Annual Meetings, Atlanta, GA, August 11–16; P. Cappelli & H. Singh, 1992, 'Integrating strategic human resources and strategic management', in D. Lewin, O.S. Mitchell & P.D. Sherer (eds), *Research frontiers in industrial relations and human resources*, Madison WI, Industrial Relations Research Association; P.M. Wright, B.B. Dunford & S.A. Snell, 2001, 'Human resources and the resource based view of the firm', *Journal of Management*, 27, pp. 701–21.

9   P. Boxall & J. Purcell, 2003, *Strategy and human resource management*, Basingstoke, U.K., Palgrave Macmillan; P.M. Wright, B.B. Dunford & S.A. Snell, 2001, 'Human resources and the resource based view of the firm', *Journal of Management*, 27, pp. 701–21.

10   P.F. Boxall, 1996, 'The strategic HRM debate and the resource-based view of the firm', *Human Resource Management Journal*, 2 (3), pp. 60–79; P.M. Wright, G.C. McMahan & A. McWilliams, 1994, 'Human resources and sustained competitive advantage: A resource-based perspective', *International Journal of Human Resource Management* 5 (2), pp. 301–26; P.M. Wright, B.B. Dunford & S.A. Snell, 2001, Human resources and the resource based view of the firm, *Journal of Management*, 27, pp. 701–21.

11   Ferris, Hochwarter, Buckley, Harrell-Cook & Frink.

12   G.R. Ferris & T.A. Judge, 1991, P'ersonnel/human resource management: A political influence perspective', *Journal of Management*, 17, pp. 447–88, at p. 450.

13   M.T. Royle, A.T. Hall, W.A. Hochwarter, P.L. Perrewé & G.R. Ferris, 2005, 'The interactive effects of accountability and job self-efficacy on organizational citizenship behavior and political behavior', *Organizational Analysis*, 13, pp. 53–71.

14   M. Novicevic & M. Harvey, 2001, 'The changing role of the corporate HR function in global organizations of the twenty-first century', *International Journal of Human Resource Management*, 12, pp. 1251–68.

15   P.S. Budhwar, 2000, 'Evaluating levels of strategic integration and devolvement of human resource management in the UK'. *Personnel Review*, 29, pp. 141–61; E. Farndale, 2005, 'HR department professionalism: A comparison between the UK and other European countries', *International Journal of Human Resource Management*, 16, pp. 660–75.

16   M.C. Galang & G.R. Ferris, 1997, 'Human resource department power and influence through symbolic action', *Human Relations*, 50, pp. 1403–26; C. Sheehan, P. Holland & H. De Cieri, 2006, 'What really explains the relationship between HRM and organizational performance?', Paper presented at Academy of Management Annual Meetings, Atlanta, GA, August 11–16.

17   P.F. Boxall, 1993, 'The significance of human resource management: A reconsideration of the evidence', *International Journal of Human Resource Management* 4 (3), pp. 645–65; M. Beer, B. Spector, P.R. Lawrence, D.Q. Mills & R.E. Walton, 1984, *Managing Human Assets*, Free Press, New York; J. Guest, Storey (ed.), 1995, *Human Resource Management: A Critical Text*, Routledge, London.

18   Boxall & Dowling.

19   C. Sheehan, P. Holland & H. De Cieri, 2006, 'Current developments in HRM in Australian organizations', *Asia Pacific Journal of Human Resources* 44 (2), pp. 132–52; C. Fisher & P.J. Dowling, 1999, 'Support for an HR approach in Australia: The perspective of senior HR managers', *Asia Pacific Journal of Human Resources*, 37 (1), pp. 1–19; C. Fisher, P.J. Dowling & J. Garnham, 1999, 'The impact of changes to the human resource function in Australia', *International Journal of Human Resource Management*, 10 (3), pp. 501–14; J. Storey, 1992, 'The HRM phenomenon', in J. Storey (ed.), *Developments in the Management of Human Resources: An Analytical Review*, Blackwell, Oxford, pp. 23–37.

20   C. Sheehan, P. Holland & H. De Cieri, 2006, 'Current developments in HRM in Australian organizations', *Asia Pacific Journal of Human Resources*, 44 (2), pp. 132–52; B.E. Becker & M.A. Huselid, 1999, 'Overview: Strategic human resource management in five leading firms'. *Human Resource Management*, 38(4), pp. 287–301. S. Peck, 'Exploring the link between organizational strategy and the employment relationship: The role of human resources policies', *Journal of Management Studies* 31 (5), 1994, pp. 715–36; M.A. Sheppeck

Endnotes

& J. Militello, 2000, 'Strategic HR configurations and organizational performance', *Human Resource Management*, 39(1), pp. 5–16.

21 Boxall & Dowling; K. Legge, 1995, *Human Resource Management: Rhetorics and Realities*, MacMillan, London.

22 J. Storey & K. Sisson, 1993, *Managing Human Resources and Industrial Relations*, Open University Press, Buckingham, UK; Cooper & Burke, (eds) 2003.

23 P. Howes, 1997, 'Company benchmarks on the basis of size', *HR Monthly*, November, p. 20.

24 SHRM–BNA Survey No. 60, *Human Resources Activities, Budgets, and Staffs: 1994–95*, bulletin to management, Bureau of National Affairs Policy and Practise Series, 29 June 1995, Bureau of National Affairs, Washington, DC.

25 C. Sheehan, P. Holland & H. De Cieri, 2006, 'Current developments in HRM in Australian organizations', *Asia Pacific Journal of Human Resources*, 44 (2), pp. 132–52; C. Sheehan, P. Holland & H. De Cieri, 2006. 'What really explains the relationship between HRM and organizational performance?', Paper presented at Academy of Management Annual Meetings, Atlanta, GA, August 11–16; C. Fisher, P.J. Dowling & J. Garnham, 1999, 'The impact of changes to the human resource function in Australia', *International Journal of Human Resource Management*, 10 (3), pp. 501–14, B.E. Becker & M.A. Huselid, 1999, 'Overview: Strategic human resource management in five leading firms', *Human Resource Management*, 38(4), pp. 287–301.

26 D. Ulrich, 1997, *HR Champions*, Harvard Business School Press, Boston.

27 G.R. Ferris & T.A. Judge, 1991, 'Personnel/human resource management: A political influence perspective', *Journal of Management*, 17, pp. 447–88, at p. 450.

28 R.W. Beatty, J.R. Ewing & C.G. Tharp, 2003, 'HR's role in corporate governance: present and prospective', *Human Resource Management*, 42, pp. 257–69.

29 S. Greengard, 1998,'Building a self-service culture that works', *Workforce*, July, pp. 60–4; A. Kidman, 2004, 'Riding the self-service wave'. *Human Resources*, 30 June, p. 14–15.

30 S.L. Robinson, M.S. Kraatz & D.M. Rousseau, 1994, 'Changing Obligations and the Psychological Contract: A Longitudinal Study', *Academy of Management Journal*, 37 (1), pp. 137–52; D.M. Rousseau, 1995, *Psychological Contracts in Organizations: Understanding Written and Unwritten Agreements*, Sage Publications, Thousand Oaks; D.M. Rousseau, 2004, 'Research Edge: Psychological Contracts in the Workplace: Understanding the Ties That Motivate', *The Academy of Management Executive*, 18 (1), pp. 120–7.

31 Towers Perrin, 1992, *Priorities for Competitive Advantage: An IBM Study Conducted by Towers Perrin*.

32 C. Sheehan, P. Holland & H. De Cieri, 2006, 'Current developments in HRM in Australian organizations', *Asia Pacific Journal of Human Resources* 44 (2), pp. 132–52; C. Sheehan, P. Holland & H. De Cieri, 2006, 'What really explains the relationship between HRM and organizational performance?', Paper presented at Academy of Management Annual Meetings, Atlanta, GA, August 11–16; P. McGraw, 2002, 'The HR function in local and overseas firms: Evidence from the PricewaterhouseCoopers-Cranfield HR Project', *Asia Pacific Journal of Human Resources*, 40(2), pp. 205–27.

33 A. Sherry, 2000, 'HR departments must keep the customers happy', *Business Review Weekly*, 20 April, p. 46.

34 R. Roberts & P. Hirsch, 2005, 'Evolution and revolution in the twenty-first century: Rules for organizations and managing human resources', *Human Resource Management*, 44 (2), pp. 171–6; D. Ulrich, 1998, 'A new mandate for human resources', *Harvard Business Review*, January–February, pp. 124–34.

35 Towers Perrin, p. 6.

36 N. Way, 2000, 'Talent war', *Business Review Weekly*, 18 August, p. 64.

37 Australian Bureau of Statistics, 2006, *Population Projections, Australia 2004–2101*, catalogue no. 3222.0, Australian Government Publishing Service, Canberra.

38 Australian Bureau of Statistics, 2006, *Year Book Australia 2006*, catalogue no. 1301.0, Australian Bureau of Statistics: Canberra; Australian Bureau of Statistics, 2006, *Population Projections, Australia 2004–2101*, catalogue no. 3222.0, Australian Government Publishing Service, Canberra; Australian Bureau of Statistics, 2006, *Labour Force, Australia*, catalogue no. 6203.0, Australian Government Printing Service, Canberra; Australian Bureau of Statistics, 1999, *Labour Force Projections, Australia 1999–2016*, catalogue no. 6260.0, Australian Government Printing Service, Canberra.

39 Australian Bureau of Statistics, 2006, *Population Projections, Australia 2004–2101*, catalogue no. 3222.0, Australian Government Publishing Service, Canberra; Australian Bureau of Statistics, 2006, *Australian Social Trends 2006*, catalogue no. 4102.0, Australian Government Publishing Service, Canberra.

40 Department of Employment and Workplace Relations, 2006, *Workforce tomorrow. Adapting to a more diverse Australian labour market*. Australian Government: Canberra; Department of Employment and Workplace Relations, 2006, *Australian Jobs 2006*, Australian Government: Canberra; K. Munk, 2003, 'The older worker: everyone's future', *Journal of Occupational Health and Safety—Australia and New Zealand*, 19 (5), pp. 437–46; Australian Bureau of Statistics, 2003, *Population by Age and Sex, Australian States and Territories*, catalogue no. 3201.0, Australian Bureau of Statistics: Canberra; Australian Bureau of Statistics, 1999, *Year Book Australia 1999 Special Article—Older Australians*, catalogue no. 1301.0, Australian Bureau of Statistics: Canberra.

41 Australian Bureau of Statistics, 2006, *Year Book Australia 2006*, catalogue no. 1301.0, Australian Bureau of Statistics: Canberra; Australian Bureau of Statistics, 2003, *Population by Age and Sex, Australian States and Territories*, catalogue no. 3201.0, Australian Bureau of Statistics: Canberra.

42 L.C. Hartmann, 1998, 'The impact of trends in labour force participation in Australia', in M. Patrickson & L.C. Hartmann (eds), *Managing an Ageing Workforce*, Woodslane, Warriewood, NSW, pp. 3–25; Australian Bureau of Statistics, 2006, *Year Book Australia 2006*, catalogue no. 1301.0, Australian Bureau of Statistics: Canberra.

43 Australian Bureau of Statistics, 2006, *Year Book Australia 2006*, catalogue no. 1301.0, Australian Bureau of Statistics: Canberra.

44 Australian Bureau of Statistics, 2004, *Labour Force, Australia, Detailed*, May, catalogue no.6291.0.55.001, Australian Bureau of Statistics: Canberra.

45 Australian Bureau of Statistics, 2004, *Year Book Australia 2004*, catalogue no. 1301.0, Australian Bureau of Statistics: Canberra; A. Preston & J. Burgess, 2003, 'Women's work in Australia: Trends, issues and prospects', *Australian Journal of Labour Economics*, 6 (4), pp. 497–518.

46 Australian Bureau of Statistics, 2004, *Year Book Australia*; Australian Bureau of Statistics, 1999, *Labour Force, Australia*; D. Beck & E. Davis, 2005, 'EEO in senior management: Women executives in Westpac', *Asia Pacific Journal of Human Resources*, 43 (2), pp. 273–88.

47 I. Wilkinson & C. Cheung, 1999, 'Multicultural marketing in Australia: Synergy in diversity', *Journal of International Marketing* 7 (3), pp. 106–25.

48 Human Rights and Equal Opportunity Commission, 1997, *Bringing Them Home: Report of the National Inquiry into the Separation of Aboriginal and Torres Strait Islander Children from their Families*, Human Rights and Equal Opportunity Commission, Sydney.

49 M. Schaper, 1999, 'Australia's Aboriginal small business owners: Challenges for the future', *Journal of Small Business Management* 37 (3), pp. 88–93.

50 Australian Bureau of Statistics, 2004, *Year Book Australia 2004*, catalogue no. 1301.0, Australian Bureau of Statistics, Canberra.

51 Wilkinson & Cheung.

52 K Betts, 2003, 'Immigration policy under the Howard Government', *Australian Journal of Social Issues*, 38 (2), pp. 169–92; L Boreham, G. Stokes & R. Hall (eds), 2004, *The Politics of Australian Society: Political Issues for the New Century*, (2nd ed) Frenchs Forrest, NSW, Pearson Longman; P. Oslington, 1998, 'Australian immigration

policy and unemployment', *Australian Journal of Labour Economics*, 2 (2), pp. 91–104; Australian Bureau of Statistics, 1994, *Australian Social Trends 1994*, catalogue no. 4102.0, Australian Government Publishing Service, Canberra; Department of Immigration and Multicultural Affairs, 1998, *Australian Immigration: The Facts*, Australian Government Publishing Service, Canberra.

53 Australian Bureau of Statistics, 2006, *Year Book Australia 2006*, catalogue no. 1301.0, Australian Bureau of Statistics, Canberra.

54 Australian Bureau of Statistics, 2006, *Year Book Australia 2006*, catalogue no. 1301.0, Australian Bureau of Statistics: Canberra.

55 Federal Race Discrimination Commissioner, 1997, *Face the Facts*, Australian Government Publishing Service, Canberra.

56 Australian Bureau of Statistics, 1999, *Labour Force, Australia*.

57 Drake International, *Generation Y. Attracting, engaging and leading a new generation at work*, White Paper, 3 (1).

58 C.C. Cooper & R.J. Burke (eds), 2003, *The new world of work: Challenges and opportunities.* Blackwell, Oxford, U.K; B. Wooldridge & J. Wester, 1991, 'The turbulent environment of public personnel administration: Responding to the challenge of the changing workplace of the twenty-first century', *Public Personnel Management* 20, pp. 207–24; J. Laabs, 1998, 'The new loyalty: Grasp it, earn it, keep it', *Workforce*, November, pp. 34–9.

59 I.S. Fulmer, B. Gerhart & K.S. Scott, 2003, 'Are the 100 Best better? An empirical investigation of the relationship between being a "great place to work" and firm performance', *Personnel Psychology*, 56 (4), pp. 965–93; Anonymous, 1986,'Employee dissatisfaction on rise in last 10 years, new report says', *Employee Relations Weekly*, Bureau of National Affairs, Washington, DC.

60 T.H. Cox & S. Blake, 1991, 'Managing cultural diversity: Implications for organizational competitiveness', *Academy of Management Executive*, 5, pp. 45–56; B. Harrington & J.B. James, 2006, 'The standards for excellence in work-life integration: From changing policies to changing organizations', in M. Pitt-Catsouphes, E.E. Kossek & S. Sweet (eds), *The Work and Family Handbook: Multidisciplinary Perspectives and Approaches*, pp.665–84, Lawrence Erlbaum Associates, New Jersey USA; E.E. Kossek & S.A. Lobel (eds), 1996, *Managing Diversity: Human Resource Strategies for Transforming the Workplace*, Blackwell, Cambridge, MA.

61 D.A. Avery & P. McKay, 2006, 'Target practice: An organizational impression management approach to attracting minority and female job applicants', *Personnel Psychology*, 59, pp. 157–87; E. Friday & S.S. Friday, 2003, 'Managing Diversity Using a Strategic Planned Change Approach', *Journal of Management Development*, 22, pp. 863–80; M. Loden & J.B. Rosener, 1991, *Workforce America! Managing Employee Diversity as a Vital Resource*, Business One Irwin, Homewood, IL; A. Sheridan & L. Conway, 2001, 'Workplace flexibility: reconciling the needs of employers and employees', *Women in Management Review*, 16 (1), pp, 5–11.

62 Public Service and Merit Protection Commission, 1999, *State of the Service 1998–99*, Commonwealth of Australia, Canberra.

63 Public Service and Merit Protection Commission.

64 M. London, 1996, 'Redeployment and continuous learning in the 21st century: Hard lessons and positive examples from the downsizing era', *Academy of Management Executive*, 10 (4), pp. 67–79; A. Sheridan & L. Conway, 2001, 'Workplace flexibility: reconciling the needs of employers and employees', *Women in Management Review*, 16 (1), pp. 5–11.

65 Australian Bureau of Statistics, 2000, *Australia Now—A Statistical Profile. Industry Overview*, Australian Government Printing Service, Canberra.

66 Australian Bureau of Statistics, 2000, *Australia Now—A Statistical Profile. Industry Overview*; J. Walsh, 1997, 'Employment systems in transition? A comparative analysis of Britain and Australia', *Work, Employment and Society* 11 (1), pp. 1–25.

67 Australian Bureau of Statistics, 2006, *Year Book Australia 2006*, catalogue no. 1301.0, Australian Bureau of Statistics, Canberra.

68 Australian Bureau of Statistics, 2006, *Year Book Australia 2006*, catalogue no. 1301.0, Australian Bureau of Statistics, Canberra.

69 R. Batt, 2002, 'Managing customer services: Human resource practices, quit rates, and sales growth', *Academy of Management Journal*, 45, pp. 587–98; M. Korczynski, 2002, *Human resource management in service work*, London, Palgrave; B. Schneider & D.E. Bowen, 1993, 'The service organization: Human resource management is crucial', *Organizational Dynamics*, spring, pp. 39–52; B. Schneider, S.K. Gunnabon & K. Niles-Jolly, 1994, 'Creating the culture and climate of success', *Organizational Dynamics*, summer, pp. 17–29; R. Batt, 2000, Strategic segmentation in front-line services: matching customers, employees and human resource systems, *The International Journal of Human Resource Management*, 11 (3), pp. 540–61.

70 US Department of Labor, *BLS Releases New 1996–2006 Employment Projections*, www.bls.gov/new.release/ecopro.nws.htm; P.F. Drucker, 1999, 'Knowledge-worker productivity: the biggest challenge', *California Management Review*, 41 (2), pp. 79–94; G. Tovstiga, 1999, 'Profiling the knowledge worker in the knowledge intensive organization: emerging roles', *International Journal of Technology Management*, 18, pp. 14–28.

71 A. Saveri, 1991, 'The realignment of workers and work in the 1990s', in J.M. Kummerow (ed.), *New Directions in Career Planning and the Workplace*, Consulting Psychologists Press, Palo Alto, CA, pp. 117–53; M. Korczynski, 2002, *Human resource management in service work*, London, Palgrave.

72 Department of Employment and Workplace Relations, 2006, *Workforce tomorrow. Adapting to a more diverse Australian labour market*, Australian Government, Canberra; Department of Employment, Education, Training and Youth Affairs, 1998, *Skills in Australia. Trends and Shortages*, Analytical Series no. 98/5, Australian Government Publishing Service, Canberra; Department of Employment and Workplace Relations, 2006, *Australian Jobs 2006*, Australian Government, Canberra.

73 Australian Bureau of Statistics, 2006, *Year Book Australia 2006*, catalogue no. 1301.0, Australian Bureau of Statistics, Canberra.

74 A. Van den Heuvel & M. Wooden, 1997, 'Self-employed contractors and job satisfaction', *Journal of Small Business Management* 35 (3), pp. 11–20; A. Kalleberg, 2000, 'Nonstandard employment relations: Part-time, temporary and contract work', *Annual Review of Sociology*, 26, pp. 341–65; M. Mallon & J. Duberley, 2000, 'Managers and professionals in the contingent workforce', *Human Resource Management Journal*, 10 (1), pp. 33–47; S.P. Matusik & C.W.L. Hill, 1998, 'The utilization of contingent work, knowledge creation, and competitive advantage' *Academy of Management Review*, 23 (4), pp. 680–97; R.J. Paul & J.B. Townsend, 1998, 'Managing the contingent workforce—Gaining the advantages, avoiding the pitfalls', *Employee Responsibilities and Rights Journal*, 11 (4), pp. 239–52.

75 Australian Bureau of Statistics, 2006, *Year Book Australia 2006*, catalogue no. 1301.0, Australian Bureau of Statistics, Canberra; G. Murtough & M. Waite, 2001, 'A new estimate of casual employment?: Reply', *Australian Bulletin of Labour*, 27 (2), pp. 109–17.

76 J. Burgess & J. Connell, 2006, 'Temporary work and human resource management: Issues, challenges and responses', *Personnel Review*, 35 (2), pp. 125–40; P. Brotherton, 1995, 'Stuff to suit', *HR Magazine*, December, pp. 50–5; Kalleberg, 2000; Matusik & Hill, 1998; K. Purcell & J. Purcell, 1998, 'In-sourcing, outsourcing, and the growth of contingent labour as evidence of flexible employment strategies', *European Journal of Work and Organizational Psychology*, 7 (1), pp. 39–59.

77 M. Lindorff, 2000, 'Home-based telework and telecommuting in Australia: more myth than modern work form', *Asia Pacific Journal of Human Resources*, 38 (1), pp. 1–11.

78 M. Lindorff, 2000.

79 www.workchoices.gov.au; B. Creighton & A. Stewart, 2000, *Labour Law: An Introduction*, (3rd edn) The Federation Press, Sydney; A. Chapman, 2000, 'Industrial legislation in 1999', *The Journal of Industrial Relations* 42 (1), pp. 29–40; R. Morris, D. Mortimer & P. Leece (eds), 1999, *Workplace Reform and Enterprise Bargaining: Issues, Trends and Cases*, 2nd edn, Harcourt Brace, Sydney; Public Service and Merit Protection Commission, 1999, *Workplace Diversity Report, 1998–99*, Commonwealth of Australia, Canberra.

80 P. Holding, 2000, 'Injury, dismissal and discrimination', *Law Institute Journal*, April 18, p. 60.
81 M. Pastin, 1986, *The Hard Problems of Management: Gaining the Ethics Edge*, Jossey-Bass, San Francisco; T.L. Beauchamp & N. E. Bowie (eds), 2004, *Ethical Theory and Business*. Pearson Education, New York.
82 L. Carey, 1999, 'Ethical dimensions of a strategic approach to HRM: An Australian perspective', *Asia Pacific Journal of Human Resources*, 37 (3), pp. 53–68.
83 C. Lee, 1986, 'Ethics training: Facing the tough questions', *Training*, 31 March, pp. 33, 38–41. Pastin.
84 Reputex, 2005, 'Australia & New Zealand: Most socially responsible companies announced', Media release, Reputex, Melbourne, www.reputex.com.au, accessed 28 February 2007; Anonymous, 2002, 'The good reputation index', *The Age*, 28 October, special supplement.
85 Reputex, 2005, 'Australia & New Zealand: Most socially responsible companies announced', Media release, Reputex, Melbourne, www.reputex.com.au, accessed 28 February 2007; Anonymous, 'The good reputation index'.
86 G.F. Cavanaugh, D. Moberg & M. Velasquez, 1981, 'The ethics of organizational politics', *Academy of Management Review* 6, pp. 363–74.
87 W.H. Braun & M. Warner, 2002, 'Strategic human resource management in western multinationals in China', *Personnel Review*, 31, pp. 553–79; P. Deng, 2004, 'Outward investment by Chinese MNCs: Motivations and implications', *Business Horizons*, 47 (3), pp. 8–16.
88 K.S. Law, D.K. Tse & N. Zhou, 2003, 'Does human resource management matter in a transitional economy? China as an example'. *Journal of International Business Studies*, 34, pp. 255–65; I.K. McDaniels & J. Waterman, 2000, 'WTO: A done deal?', *The China Business Review*, 27 (6), pp. 22–7.
89 J.P. Burns, 1999, 'The People's Republic of China at 50: National political reform', *The China Quarterly*, 159, pp. 580–94; J. Story, 2003, *China: The race to market*, Pearson Education, London.
90 W. Zhao & X. Zhou, 2004, 'Chinese organizations in transition: Changing promotion patterns in the reform era', *Organization Science*, 15, pp. 186–99;C.J. Zhu & P.J. Dowling, 2002, 'Staffing practices in transition: Some empirical evidence from China', *International Journal of Human Resource Management*, 13, pp. 569–87.
91 M. Warner, 1995, *The management of human resources in Chinese industry*, St Martin's Press, New York.
92 www.china.org.cn; L. Dai, 2005, 'Foreign direct investment reaches over US$60 billion', *People's Daily (renmin ribao)*, Overseas edition, 29 September, p. 2.
93 P. Deng, 2004, 'Outward investment by Chinese MNCs: Motivations and implications' *Business Horizons*, 47 (3). pp. 8–16; H. Liu & K. Li, 2002, 'Strategic implications of emerging Chinese multinationals: The Haier case study', *European Management Journal*, 20(6), pp. 699–706; X. Liu, T. Buck, & C. Shu, 2005, 'Chinese economic development, The next stage: Outward FDI?' *International Business Review*, 14, pp. 97–115.
94 L. Dai, 2005, 'Foreign direct investment reaches over US$60 billion', *People's Daily (renmin ribao)*, Overseas edition, 29 September, p. 2.
95 D. Aalund, 1998, 'What's the Euro?', *The Wall Street Journal*, 28 September, p. R6; G. Sheridan, 2004, May 3, 'Bigger the better—Europe—A worldwide special report—Australia and the EU', *The Australian*, p. T08.
96 H. De Cieri, 2006, in press. 'Transnational firms and cultural diversity', In P. Boxall, J. Purcell & P. Wright (eds), *Handbook of human resource management*, Oxford University, Oxford; A. Fish & J. Wood, 1997, 'Cross-cultural management competence in Australian business enterprises', *Asia Pacific Journal of Human Resources*, 35 (1), pp. 37–52. Manpower, 2006, *Confronting the coming talent crunch: what's next?* A Manpower White Paper. Manpower Services, Sydney; K. Roberts, E.E. Kossek & C. Ozeki, 'Managing the global workforce: Challenges and strategies', *Academy of Management Executive* 12 (4), 1988, pp. 93–106.

97 P.J. Dowling & D.E. Welch, 2004, *International Human Resource Management*, 4th edn, International Thomson, London.
98 P. Sparrow, H. Harris & C. Brewster, 2003, *Globalising human resource management*, Routledge, London.
99 Cendant Mobility, 2002, *2002 worldwide benchmark study: New approaches to global mobility*, Cendant Mobility Services Corporation, Bethesda, MD; GMAC Global Relocation Services, 2003, National Foreign Trade Council, & SHRM Global Forum, *Global relocation trends 2002 survey report*, GMAC Global Relocation Services, New Jersey; H. De Cieri & M. Fenwick, 2006, *An exploratory framework for global mobility risk management*, Competitive paper presented at the Academy of International Business Annual Conference, Beijing China, June 23–26.
100 H. Harris and C. Brewster, 2003, 'Alternatives to traditional international assignments', In W. Mayrhofer, G. Stahl & T. Kuhlmann (eds) *Innovative Anstatze im Internationalen Personalmanagement (Innovating HRM)*, München/Mering, Hampp Verlag; D.E. Welch & M. Fenwick, 2003, 'Virtual assignments: A new possibility for international human resource management', in R. Wiesner & B. Millett (eds), *Human resource management: Challenges and future directions*, John Wiley & Sons, Milton, Queensland, pp. 279–91.
101 P. Davidson & E. Kinzel, 'Supporting the expatriate: A survey of Australian management practice', *Asia Pacific Journal of Human Resources*, 33 (3), 1995, pp. 105–16; M. Lazarova & P. Caligiuri, 2001, 'Retaining repatriates: The role of organizational support practices', *Journal of World Business*, 36(4), pp. 389–401; S.A.Y. Poelmans (ed.), 2005, *Work and Family: An International Research Perspective*, Lawrence Erlbaum Associates, New Jersey USA.
102 D.E. Welch, M.S. Fenwick & H. De Cieri, 1994, 'Staff transfers as a control strategy', *International Journal of Human Resource Management*, 5 (2), pp. 474–89.
103 P. Evans & T.S. Wurster, 1998, 'Strategy and the new economics of information', *Harvard Business Review*, 75, pp. 70–83; J. Seely-Brown & P. Duguid, 2000, 'Balancing act: How to capture knowledge without killing it", *Harvard Business Review* 78(3), pp. 73–80. K.E. Sveiby, 2001, 'A knowledge-based theory of the firm to guide in strategy formulation', *Journal of Intellectual Capital*, 2, pp. 344–58.
104 C.C. Cooper & R.J. Burke (eds), 2003, *The new world of work: Challenges and opportunities*, Blackwell, Oxford, U.K; D. De Long & P. Seeman, 2000, 'Confronting conceptual confusion and conflict in knowledge management', *Organizational Dynamics*, 29, pp. 33–44; P.F. Drucker, 1999, 'Knowledge-worker productivity: the biggest challenge', *California Management Review*, 41 (2), pp. 79–94; R.M. Grant, 1996, 'Toward a knowledge-based theory of the firm', *Strategic Management Journal*, 17, 109–22; I. Nonaka & H Takeuchi, 1995, *The knowledge creating company*, Oxford University Press, New York; W. Orlikowski, 2002, 'Knowing in practice: enacting a collective capability in distributed organizing', *Organization Science*, 13, pp. 249–73.
105 M. Considine, S. Marginson, P. Sheehan, (with the assistance of M. Kumnick), 2001, *The comparative performance of Australia as a knowledge nation*, Report to the Chifley Research Centre, Chifley Research Centre, Melbourne; Y. Doz, J. Santos & P. Williamson, 2001, *From global to metanational: How companies win in the knowledge economy*, Harvard Business School Press, Boston.
106 M. Considine, S. Marginson, P. Sheehan, (with the assistance of M. Kumnick), 2001.
107 *The Australian Government's innovation report, 2003-04*. Canberra: Australian Government Publishing Service; M. Vaile, 2000, *Australia and the knowledge economy*, Speech by the Australian Minister for Trade, 31 October, Economist Intelligence Unit, Canberra.
108 M. Considine, S. Marginson, P. Sheehan, (with the assistance of M. Kumnick), 2001, p.4.
109 K.E. Sveiby, 1997, *The new organizational wealth: Managing and measuring knowledge-based assets*. Berrett-Koehler, San Francisco; K.E. Sveiby, 2001, 'A knowledge-based theory of the firm to guide in strategy formulation', *Journal of Intellectual Capital*, 2, pp. 344–58; also see J. Schapper, J. Wolfram Cox, & H. De Cieri, 2003, *Cubism and organizational analysis: Revisiting representation in the age of the knowledge

economy, Paper presented in the Organization and Management Theory Division, Academy of Management Annual Meetings, Seattle WA, August 1–6.

110 M. Dodgson, 1993, 'Organizational learning: A review of some literatures', *Organization Studies*, 14, pp. 375–94.

111 S. Brint, 2001, 'Professionals and the "knowledge economy": Rethinking the theory of postindustrial society', *Current Sociology*, 29(4), pp. 101–32; P. Brown & S. Williams, 2004, *The mismanagement of talent—employability and jobs in the knowledge economy*, Oxford University Press, Oxford, UK.

112 P. Thompson, C. Warhurst & G. Callaghan, 2001, 'Ignorant theory and knowledgeable workers: Interrogating the connections between knowledge, skills and services', *The Journal of Management Studies*, 38 (7), pp. 923–42.

113 J.A. Neal & C.L. Tromley, 1995, 'From incremental change to retrofit: Creating high performance work systems', *Academy of Management Executive*, 9, pp. 42–54.

114 A. Varma, R.W. Beatty, C.F. Schneier & D.O. Ulrich, 1999, 'High performance work systems: Exciting discovery or passing fad?', *Human Resource Planning*, 22 (1), pp. 26–37.

115 P. Choate & P. Linger, 1986, *The High-Flex Society*, Knopf, New York; P.B. Doeringer, 1991, *Turbulence in the American Workplace*, Oxford University Press, New York; S. Hutchinson, P. Purcell & N. Kinnie, 2000, 'Evolving high commitment management and the experience of the RAC call centre', *Human Resource Management Journal* 10 (1), pp. 63–76.

116 K. Miller, 1989, *Retraining the American Work Force*, Addison-Wesley, Reading, MA; S. Frenkel, M. Korczynski, L. Donoghue & K. Shire, 1995, 'Re-constituting work: Trends towards knowledge work and info-normative control', *Work, Employment and Society*, 9 (4), pp. 773–96; S. Frenkel, M. Tam, M. Korczynski & K. Shire, 1998, 'Beyond bureaucracy? Work organization in call centres', *International Journal of Human Resource Management* 9 (6), pp. 957–79; R.M. Hodgetts, F. Luthans & J.W. Slocum, 1999, 'Strategy and HRM initiatives for the '00s environment', *Organizational Dynamics*, 28 (7), pp. 7–21; D. Lepak & S.A. Snell, 1998, 'Virtual HR: Strategic human resource management in the 21st century', *Human Resource Management Review*, 8 (3), pp. 215–34; P.R. Sparrow & K. Daniels, 1999, 'Human resource management and the virtual organization: Mapping the future research issues', in C.L. Cooper & D.M. Rousseau, *Trends in Organizational Behaviour*, John Wiley & Sons, Chichester, UK, pp. 45–61.

117 S. Deery, R. Iverson & J. Walsh, 2002, 'Work Relationships in Telephone Call Centers: Understanding Emotional Exhaustion and Employee Withdrawal', *Journal of Management Studies*, 39 (4), pp. 471–96; D. Knights & D. McCabe, 1998, 'What happens when the phone goes wild?': Staff, Stress and Spaces for escape in a BPR Telephone Banking Work Regime', *Journal of Management Studies*, 35 (2), pp. 163–94.

118 B.L. Kirkman & B. Rosen, 1999, 'Beyond self-management: Antecedents and consequences of team empowerment', *Academy of Management Journal* 42 (1), pp. 58–74.

119 J.L. Cordery, 1995, 'Work redesign: Rhetoric vs reality', *Asia Pacific Journal of Human Resources*, 33 (2), pp. 3–19.

120 T.J. Atchison, 1991, 'The employment relationship: Untied or re-tied', *Academy of Management Executive* 5, pp. 52–62.

121 D. McCann & C. Margerison, 1989, 'Managing high performance teams', *Training and Development Journal*, November, pp. 52–60; S. Sheman, 1996, 'Secrets of HP's 'muddled' team', *Fortune*, 18 March, pp. 116–20.

122 T. Peters, 1988, 'Restoring American competitiveness: Looking for new models of organizations', *The Executive* 2, pp. 103–10.

123 M.J. Kavanaugh, H.G. Guetal & S.I. Tannenbaum, 1990, *Human Resource Information Systems: Development and Application*, PWS-Kent, Boston; S. Liff, 1997, 'Constructing HR information systems', *Human Resource Management Journal* 7 (2), pp. 18–31; D. Loh & H. De Cieri, 2005, 'An actor network study of human resource information systems: The interplay between vendors and clients', in H. De Cieri & C. Costa (eds), 2005, *Proceedings of the Inaugural Australian Centre for Research in Employment and Work (ACREW) Conference*. Melbourne, Australia June 24–25. (CD-ROM).

124 R.N. Ashkenas, 1994, 'Beyond the fads: How leaders drive change with results', *Human Resource Planning* 17, pp. 25–44.

125 M.A. Huselid, 1995, 'The impact of human resource management practises on turnover, productivity, and corporate financial performance', *Academy of Management Journal* 38, pp. 635–72.

126 B. Becker & M.A. Huselid, 1998, 'High performance work systems and firm performance: A synthesis of research and managerial implications', in G.R. Ferris (ed.), *Research in Personnel and Human Resource Management*, 16, JAI Press, Greenwich, CT, pp. 53–101; P.M. Wright, T.M. Gardner & L.M. Moynihan, 2003, 'The impact of HR practices on the performance of business units', *Human Resource Management Journal*, 13 (3), pp. 21–36.

127 B. Becker & B. Gerhart, 1996, 'The impact of human resource management on organizational performance: Progress and prospects', *Academy of Management Journal*, 39, pp. 779–801.

128 R. Noe, J. Hollenbeck, B. Gerhart & P. Wright, 2006, *Human resource management. Gaining a competitive advantage*, (5th edn), McGraw-Hill/Irwin, New York, p. 12.

129 J.L. Cummings & J.P. Doh, 2000, 'Identifying who matters: Mapping key players in multiple environments', *California Management Review* 42 (2), pp. 83–104; D. Ulrich, 1989, 'Assessing human resource effectiveness: Stakeholder, utility and relationship approaches', *Human Resource Planning*, 12 (4), pp. 301–15.

130 Global Reporting Initiative, 2002, *Sustainability Reporting Guidelines*, Global Reporting Initiative: Boston MA, http://www.globalreporting.org/guidelines/, accessed October 10, 2004; M. Greenwood & H. De Cieri, 2006, in press, 'Stakeholder theory and the ethicality of human resource management', in A. Pinnington, R. Macklin & T. Campbell (eds), *Ethics in human resource management and employment relations*, Oxford University Press, Oxford; M. van Marrewijk, 2003, 'Concepts and definitions of CSR and corporate sustainability: between agency and communion', *Journal of Business Ethics*, 44, pp. 95–105.

131 J.R. Jablonski, 1991, *Implementing Total Quality Management: An Overview*, Pfeiffer & Company, San Diego.

132 R.L. Dodson, 1991, 'Speeding the way to total quality', *Training and Development Journal*, June, pp. 35–42.

133 Bureau of Business Practises, 1992, *Profile of ISO 9000*, Allyn & Bacon, Boston; 'ISO 9000 International Standards for Quality Assurance', *Design Matters*, July 1995, http//www.best.com/~ISO9000/att/ISONet.html/.

134 Australian Quality Council Ltd.

135 http://www.sai-global.com/AWARDS/ accessed 1 August 2006.

136 http://www.sai-global.com/AWARDS/ accessed 1 August 2006.

137 J. Main, 1991, 'Is the Baldrige overblown?', *Fortune*, 1 July, pp. 62–4.

138 Australian Quality Council Ltd.

139 R.S. Kaplan & D.P. Norton, 1992, 'The balanced scorecard—measures that drive performance', *Harvard Business Review*, January–February, pp. 71–9; R.S. Kaplan & D.P. Norton, 1993, 'Putting the balanced scorecard to work', *Harvard Business Review*, September–October, pp. 134–47; R.S. Kaplan & D.P. Norton, 1996, 'Using the balanced scorecard as a strategic management system', *Harvard Business Review*, January–February, pp. 75–85; A.K. Yeung & B. Berman, 1997, 'Adding value through human resources: Reorienting human resource measurement to drive business performance', *Human Resource Management* 36, pp. 321–35.

140 D. Ulrich, 1997, 'Measuring human resources: An overview of practise and a prescription for results', *Human Resource Management*, 36, pp. 303–20.

141 P. Holland, C. Sheehan & H. De Cieri, 2006, 'Talent quest', *Monash Business Review*, 2 (2), pp. 15–17; P. Holland, C. Sheehan & H. De Cieri, 2006, 'Attracting and retaining talent. Exploring human resources management trends in Australia', in H. De Cieri, A. Bardoel, R. Barrett, D. Buttigieg, A. Rainnie & K. McLean (eds), *Socially*

responsive, socially responsible approaches to employment and work. Proceedings of the ACREW/KCL Conference, Prato Italy, July 1–4.

142 R.E. Herman & J.L. Gioia, 2001, 'Helping your organization become an employer of choice'. *Employment Relations Today,* 28(2), pp. 63–78; R.E. Herman & J.L. Gioia, 2000, *How to Become an Employer of Choice,* Oakhill Press, Winchester, VA.

143 C. Fox, 2003, 'Best Employers Are Real Stars', *Australian Financial Review,* March 14, p. 11.

144 W.A. Kahn, 1990, 'Psychological conditions of personal engagement and disengagement at work', *Academy of Management Journal,*33, pp. 692–724; F. Luthans & S.J. Peterson, 2002, 'Employee engagement and manager self-efficacy', *Journal of Management Development,* 21 (5/6), pp. 376–87; D.R. May, R.L. Gilson & L.M. Harter, 2004, 'The psychological conditions of meaningfulness, safety and availability and the engagement of the human spirit at work', *Journal of Occupational and Organizational Psychology,* 77, pp. 11–37.

145 M. Greenwood & H. De Cieri, 2006, in press), 'Stakeholder theory and the ethicality of human resource management', in A. Pinnington, R. Macklin & T. Campbell (eds), *Ethics in human resource management and employment relations,* Oxford University Press, Oxford.

146 C. Fox, 2003, 'Best Employers Are Real Stars', *Australian Financial Review,* 14 March 2003, p. 11.

147 ™The People Practices Inventory is a trademark of Hewitt Associates LLC; www.hewitt.com.

148 http://was7.hewitt.com/bestemployers/anz/2005list.htm; S. Doran, 2006, ?We have ways of making you stay', *Sydney Morning Herald,* 26 August, p.1.

149 W.F. Cascio, 1991, *Costing Human Resources: The Financial Impact of Behavior in Organizations,* 3rd edn, PWS-Kent, Boston.

CHAPTER 2 NOTES

1 J. Barney, 1991, 'Firm resources and sustained competitive advantage', *Journal of Management,* 17, pp. 99–120.

2 L. Dyer, 'Strategic human resource management and planning', in K. Rowland and G. Ferris (eds), 1985, *Research in Personnel and Human Resources Management,* JAI Press, Greenwich, CT, pp. 1–30.

3 J. Quinn, 1980, *Strategies for Change: Logical Incrementalism,* Richard D. Irwin, Homewood, IL.

4 M. Porter, 1980, *Competitive Strategy: Techniques for Analyzing Industries and Competitors,* Free Press, New York.

5 R. Miles and C. Snow, 1978, *Organizational Strategy, Structure, and Process,* McGraw-Hill, New York.

6 P. Wright and G. McMahan, 1992,'Theoretical perspectives for strategic human resource management', *Journal of Management,* 18, pp. 295–320.

7 S. Snell and J. Dean, 1992, 'Integrated manufacturing and human resource management: a human capital perspective', *Academy of Management Journal,* 35, pp. 467–504.

8 P. Boxall and J. Purcell, 2003, *Strategy and Human Resource Management,* Palgrave, Macmillan, Hampshire, pp. 71–88.

9 J. Butler, G. Ferris and N. Napier, 1991, *Strategy and Human Resource Management,* Southwestern, Cincinnati, OH.

10 F. Biddle and J. Helyar, 1998, 'Behind Boeing's woes: Chunky assembly line, price war with Airbus', *The Wall Street Journal,* 24 April, pp. A1, A16.

11 K. Martell and S. Carroll, 1995, 'How strategic is HRM?', *Human Resource Management,* 34, pp. 253–67.

12 R. Kramar, 2006, *Cranfield-PricewaterhouseCoopers Survey on International Strategic Human Resource Management,* Macquarie University, North Ryde, New South Wales, pp. 7–8.

13 K. Golden and V. Ramanujam, 1985, 'Between a dream and a nightmare: on the integration of the human resource function and the strategic business planning process', *Human Resource Management,* 24, pp. 429–51.

14 Kramar, 2006.
15 Kramar, 2006, p. 8.
16 Kramar, 2006, p. 10.

17 C. Sheehan, P. Holland & H. De Cieri, *Current Development in HRM in Australian Organisations.*

18 C. Hill and G. Jones, 1989, *Strategic Management Theory: An Integrated Approach,* Houghton Mifflin, Boston.

19 L.C. Hartmann, 1998, 'The impact of trends in labour force participation in Australia', in M. Patrickson and L.C. Hartmann (eds), *Managing an Ageing Workforce,* Woodslane, Warriewood, New South Wales, pp. 22–3.

20 R. Kramar, 'Managing diversity', in Patrickson and Hartmann (eds), 1998, pp. 121–35.

21 A. Sherry, 2000, 'HR Department must keep the customers happy', *Business Review Weekly,* 20 April, p. 46.

22 P. Wright, G. McMahan and A. McWilliams, 1994, 'Human resources and sustained competitive advantage: A resource-based perspective', *International Journal of Human Resource Management,* 5, pp. 301–26.

23 P. Buller, 1988, 'Successful partnerships: HR and strategic planning at eight top firms', *Organizational Dynamics,* 17, pp. 27–42.

24 M. Hitt, R. Hoskisson and J. Harrison, 1991, 'Strategic competitiveness in the 1990s: challenges and opportunities for U.S. executives', *The Executive,* 5, May, pp. 7–22.

25 C. Fox, 2002, 'Not just the numbers', *Australian Financial Review,* Boss, October; Watson Wyatt Worldwide, 2003, 'Watson Wyatt's Human Capital Index', *2002/2003 Survey Report*; 2003, 'People Power: Agenda 2003', *Australian Financial Review,* Boss, February, p. 38.

26 Watson Wyatt Worldwide, 2003.

27 P. Wright, G. McMahan, B. McCormick and S. Sherman, 1996, 'Strategy, core competence, and HR involvement as determinants of HR effectiveness and refinery performance', paper presented at the 1996 International Federation of Scholarly Associations in Management, Paris, France.

28 N. Bennett, D. Ketchen and E. Schultz, 1995, 'Antecedents and consequences of human resource integration with strategic decision making', paper presented at the 1995 Academy of Management Meeting, Vancouver, BC, Canada.

29 J.E. Delery and D.H. Doty, 1996, 'Modes of theorizing in strategic human resource management: tests of universalistic, contingency, and configurational performance predictions', *Academy of Management Journal,* 39 (4), pp. 802–35; J. Pfeffer, 1995, 'Producing sustainable competitive advantage through effective people management', *Academy of Management Executive,* 9 (1), pp. 55–72; A.K. Yeung and B. Berman, 1997, 'Adding value through human resources: reorienting human resource management to drive business performance', *Human Resource Management,* 36 (3), pp. 321–35.

30 P. Ruzek, 1997, 'Leadership and excellence in the human resources industry', *HRMonthly,* December, pp. 17–20.

31 P. Ruzek, 1997, pp. 17–20.

32 Craig Donaldson, 2004, 'Main roads WA: dynamic HR', *Human Resources,* issue 55(5), May, THC Press, Chatswood, pp. 10–11.

33 K. Golden and V. Ramanujam, 1985; R. Kramar, 1992, 'Strategic human resource management: are the promises fulfilled?', *Asia Pacific Journal of Human Resources,* 30 (1), pp. 1–15.

34 J. Galbraith and R. Kazanjian, 1986, *Strategy Implementation: Structure, Systems, and Process,* West Publishing, St Paul, MN.

35 B. Schneider and A. Konz, 1989, 'Strategic job analysis', *Human Resource Management,* 27, pp. 51–64.

36 P. Wright and S. Snell, 1991, 'Toward an integrative view of strategic human resource management', *Human Resource Management Review,* 1, pp. 203–25.

37 S. Snell, 1992, 'Control Theory in strategic human resource management: The mediating effect of administrative information', *Academy of Management Journal,* 35, pp. 292–327.

38 R. Schuler, 'Personnel and human resource management choices and organizational strategy', in R. Schuler, S. Youngblood and V. Huber (eds), 1988, *Readings in Personnel and Human Resource Management,* 3rd edn, West Publishing, St Paul, MN.

39 J. Dean and S. Snell, 1991, 'Integrated manufacturing and job design: moderating effects of organizational inertia', *Academy of Management Journal*, 34, pp. 776–804.
40 E. Lawler, 1992, *The Ultimate Advantage: Creating the High-Involvement Organization*, Jossey-Bass, San Francisco.
41 J. Olian and S. Rynes, 1984, 'Organizational staffing: integrating practice with strategy', *Industrial Relations*, 23, pp. 170–83.
42 G. Smith, 1992, 'Quality: small and midsize companies seize the challenge—not a moment too soon', *Business Week*, 30 November, pp. 66–75.
43 J. Kerr and E. Jackofsky, 1989, 'Aligning managers with strategies: Management development versus selection', *Strategic Management Journal*, 10, pp. 157–70.
44 J. Kerr, 1988, 'Strategic control through performance appraisal and rewards', *Human Resource Planning*, 11, pp. 215–23.
45 Snell, 1992.
46 B. Gerhart and G. Milkovich, 'Employee compensation: research and practice', in M.D. Dunnette and L.M. Hough (eds), 1991, *Handbook of Industrial and Organizational Psychology*, vol. 2, 2nd edn, Consulting Psychologists Press, Palo Alto, CA, pp. 481–569.
47 D. Balkin and L. Gomez-Mejia, 1987, 'Toward a contingency theory of compensation strategy', *Strategic Management Journal*, 8, pp. 169–82.
48 Donaldson 'Ironing out industrial relations', *Human Resources*, 21 March 2006, p16.
49 S. Cronshaw and R. Alexander, 1986, 'One answer to the demand for accountability: selection utility as an investment decision', *Organizational Behavior and Human Decision Processes*, 35, pp. 102–18.
50 P. MacDuffie, 1995, 'Human resource bundles and manufacturing performance: organizational logic and flexible production systems in the world auto industry', *Industrial and Labor Relations Review*, 48, pp. 197–221; P. McGraw, 1995, 'A hard drive to the top', *U.S. News and World Report*, 118, pp. 43–4.
51 M. Huselid, 1995, 'The impact of human resource management practices on turnover, productivity, and corporate financial performance', *Academy of Management Journal*, 38, pp. 635–72.
52 D.P. Lepak and S. A. Snell, 1999, 'The human resource architecture: towards a theory of human capital allocation and development', *Academy of Management Review*, 24 (1), January, pp. 31–48.
53 Lepak and Snell, 1999, pp. 31–48
54 M. Porter, 1985, *Competitive Advantage*, Free Press, New York.
55 R. Schuler and S. Jackson, 1987, 'Linking competitive strategies with human resource management practices', *Academy of Management Executive*, 1, pp. 207–19.
56 R. Miles and C. Snow, 1984, 'Designing strategic human resource management systems', *Organizational Dynamics*, 13 (1), pp. 36–52.
57 J. Arthur, 1992, 'The link between business strategy and industrial relations systems in American steel mini mills', *Industrial and Labor Relations Review*, 45, pp. 488–506.
58 D. Dunphy and D. Stace, 1990, *Under New Management*, McGraw-Hill, Roseville, New South Wales, pp. 131–3.
59 Dunphy and Stace, 1990, p. 119.
60 Dunphy and Stace, 1990, pp. 204–6.
61 BridgeNews, 2001, 'Yoyo Yahoo wants a new leader', *The Australian*, 9 March.
62 P.J. Gollan, 2003, 'People power', *HRMonthly*, December, p. 14.
63 A. Thompson and A. Strickland, 1986, *Strategy Formulation and Implementation: Tasks of the General Manager*, 3rd edn, BPI, Plano, TX.
64 G. Fairclough, 1998, 'Business bulletin', *The Wall Street Journal*, 5 March, p. A1; G. Fairclough, 1997, 'Business bulletin', *The Wall Street Journal*, 2 October, p. A1.
65 P. Sebastian, 2000, 'Business bulletin', *The Wall Street Journal*, 19 October.
66 H. Vines, 1999, 'Mergers and acquisitions drive need for new leadership awareness', *HRMonthly*, August, pp. 16–22.
67 Janine Ogier, 2002, 'Moving Targets', *HRMonthly*, February, pp. 20–21.
68 ACIRRT, 1999, *Australia at Work: Just Managing?*, Prentice-Hall, Sydney, p. 52.
69 P. Cleary, 1997, 'How the axe fell on 3.3 million', *The Sydney Morning Herald*, 20 October, p. 1.
70 ACIRRT, 1999, pp. 149–50.
71 J.S. Champy, 1995, *Reengineering Management: The Mandate for New Leadership*, Harper Business, New York.
72 S. Pearlstein, 1994, 'Corporate cutback yet to pay off', *Washington Post*, 4 January, p. B6.
73 K. Cameron, 1994, 'Guest editor's note: investigating organizational downsizing—fundamental issues', *Human Resource Management*, 33, pp. 183–8.
74 M. Berry, 2000, 'No productivity boost from downsizing: new research', *Benchmarking, Information Australia*, Melbourne, 13 April, pp. 1–2.
75 C.R. Littler, R. Dunford, T. Bramble and A. Hede, 1997, 'The dynamics of downsizing in Australia and New Zealand', *Asia Pacific Journal of Human Resources*, 35 (1), pp. 65–79; Berry, 2000, pp. 1–2.
76 J. Lopez, 1993, 'Managing: early-retirement offers lead to renewed hiring', *The Wall Street Journal*, 26 January, p. B1.
77 A. Church, 1995, 'Organizational downsizing: what is the role of the practitioner?', *The Industrial–Organizational Psychologist*, 33 (1), pp. 63–74.
78 N. Templin, 1992, 'A decisive response to crisis brought Ford enhanced productivity', *The Wall Street Journal*, 15 December, p. A1.
79 Quinn, 1980.
80 H. Mintzberg, 1978, 'Patterns in strategy formulation', *Management Science*, 24, pp. 934–48.
81 R. Pascale, 1984, 'Perspectives on strategy: the real story behind Honda's success', *California Management Review*, 26, pp. 47–72.
82 R. Pascale, 1984, 'Perspectives on strategy: the real story behind Honda's success', *California Management Review*, 26, pp. 47–72.
83 Templin, 1992.
84 P. Senge, 1990, *The Fifth Discipline*, Doubleday, New York.
85 T. Stewart, 1992, 'Brace for Japan's hot new strategy', *Fortune*, 21 September, pp. 62–76.
86 V. Alee, 1998, 'Creating value in the knowledge economy', *HRMonthly*, April, pp. 12–17.
87 C. Snow and S. Snell, 1992, Staffing as Strategy, vol. 4 of *Personnel Selection*, Jossey-Bass, San Francisco.
88 T. Batten, 1992, 'Education key to prosperity—report', *Houston Chronicle*, 7 September, p. 1B.
89 P. Wright, 1991, 'Human resources as a competitive weapon', *Applied Advances in Strategic Management*, 2, pp. 91–122.
90 G. McMahan, University of Texas at Arlington, personal communications.
91 J. Purcell, 1991, 'The Meaning of Strategy in Human Resource Management' in J. Storey (ed), *New Perspectives on Human Resource Management*, Routledge, London, pp. 67–91.
92 J. Purcell, 1991, 'The Meaning of Strategy in Human Resource Management' in J. Storey (ed), *New Perspectives on Human Resource Management*, Routledge, London, pp. 67–91.
93 G. McMahan and R. Woodman, 1992, 'The current practice of organization development within the firm: a survey of large industrial corporations', *Group and Organization Studies*, 17, pp. 117–34.
94 D. Ulrich, 1997, *HR Champions, Harvard Business School Press*, Boston; D. Ulrich, M.R. Losey and G. Lake (eds), 1997, Tomorrow's HR Management, John Wiley and Sons, New York.
95 Ulrich, 1997, pp. 1–51.
96 R. Kramar, 2006, *Cranet-Macquarie survey on international strategic human resource management.* p. 9.
97 D. Wightman and J. Werner, 'From personnel manager to HR consultant—the Auschain experience', in O'Neill and Kramar (eds), 1999, pp. 17–26; G. Andrewartha, 'The future role of human resource management', in O'Neill and Kramar (eds), 1999, pp 1–16; Sherry, 2000.
98 D. Ulrich and A. Yeung, 1989, 'A shared mindset', *HR Magazine*, March, pp. 38–45.
99 G. Jones and P. Wright, 1992, 'An economic approach to

conceptualizing the utility of human resource management practices', *Research in Personnel/Human Resources*, 10, pp. 271–99.
100   Craig Donaldson, 2003, 'Earning a place at the strategy table', *Human Resources*, 27 August, THC Press, Chatswood, p. 12.
101   Australasian Centre for Human Resource Management, unpublished data, 2000, Cranfield-PricewaterhouseCoopers Survey on Strategic International Human Resource Management.
102   R. Schuler and J. Walker, 1990, 'Human resources strategy: focusing on issues and actions', *Organizational Dynamics*, Summer, pp. 5–19.
103   1998, 'Successful change requires HR's skills, survey shows', *HRMonthly*, February, p. 9.
104   C. Tebbel, 1999, 'Selling the concept of strategic HR', *HRMonthly*, July, pp. 18–19.
105   R. Kramar, 2006, *Cranet-Macquarie survey on international strategic human resource management*. p. 9.
106   Tebbel, 1999, pp. 17–19.
107   S. Inglis and P. Davidson, cited in Tebbel, 1999, p. 17.

CHAPTER 3 NOTES

1   For a still relevant and very readable general account of the nature of labour law in the British context see O. Kahn-Freund, 1972, *Labour and the Law*, Stevens, London and for the historical background to the development of labour law from the Industrial Revolution onwards see E. Thompson, 1968, *The Making of the English Working Class*, Penguin, London.
2   See C, Parker, 2002, *The Open Corporation—Effective Self-regulation and Democracy*, Cambridge University Press, Cambridge for an interesting discussion of broadly defined corporate regulation and the parameters of the regulation debate generally. Another perspective which is quite different but equally engaging is to be found in N. Gunningham & R. Johnstone, 1999, *Regulating Workplace Health and Safety: Systems and Sanctions*, Oxford University Press, Oxford, which in spite of its title has much to say about the wider regulation debate.
3   For a more detailed treatment of the law of employment, the leading books in the area are B. Creighton & A. Stewart, 2005, *Labour Law—An Introduction*, Federation Press, Sydney; J. Macken, P. O'Grady, C. Sappideen & G Warburton,2002, *Law of Employment*, Law Book Company, Sydney; R. Owens & J. Riley, 2006, *The Law of Work*, Oxford University Press, South Melbourne and M. Pittard & R. Naughton, 2003, *Australian Labour Law—Cases and Materials*, Butterworths, Sydney.
4   See the collection of papers in S. Deery & R. Mitchell, 1999, *Employment Relations: Individualisation and Union Exclusion*, Federation Press, Sydney.
5   See R. Callus & R. Lansbury (eds), 2002, *Working Futures—The Changing Nature of Work and Employment Relations in Australia*, Federation Press and J. Conaghan, R. Fischl & K. Klare, (eds), 2002, *Labour Law in an Era of Globalization—Transformative Practices and Possibilities*, Oxford University Press, Oxford. One very potentially important source of possible future developments in Australia could come from the European Union via the United Kingdom which in the past has proved to be the most fertile nursery for many Australian laws.
6   See the High Court of Australia decision in *Hollis v Vabu P/L* (2001) 181 ALR 263.
7   See United States of America, Switzerland and Canada.
8   See G. Williams, 1998, *Labour Law and the Constitution*, Federation Press, Sydney.
9   Known in the Constitution as the conciliation and arbitration power which provided the Commonwealth Parliament with power to legislate with respect to 'conciliation and arbitration for the prevention and settlement of industrial disputes extending beyond the limits of any one state'.
10   See in particular the discussion of the now infamous White Australia Policy and trade union attitudes in M. Hearn & H. Knowles, 1996, *One Big Union—A History of the Australian Workers Union 1886–1994*, Cambridge University Press, Melbourne.

11   Other powers of relevance include defence, territories and the power to legislate with respect to the employees of the Commonwealth itself, this latter power being pretty much a dead letter in recent times.
12   The classic account remains J. La Nauze, 1972, *The Making of the Australian Constitution*, Melbourne University Press, Melbourne.
13   For a thorough discussion of the challenge and its outcomes see A. Stewart & G. Williams, 2007, *WorkChoices—What the High Court Said*, The Federation Press, Annandale.
14   That is indirectly using the machinery of conciliation and arbitration to settle interstate industrial disputes.
15   See *Burwood Cinema Ltd v Australian Theatrical and Amusement Employees' Association* (1925) 35 CLR 528 and *Metal Trades Employers Association v Amalgamated Engineering Union* (1935) 54 CLR 387.
16   Sometimes also called enterprise agreements or even enterprise bargaining agreements. Under s 321 of the *Workplace Relations Act 1996*, they are called workplace agreements. This new term encompasses both the existing Australian Workplace Agreements which are individual as well as various kinds of collective union and non-union agreements. See ss 326–331.
17   While the applicable awards and agreements lay down the enforceable minima in respect of wages and conditions, employers are, of course free to pay above these minima and in certain industries this happens almost as a matter of course to attract and retain staff.
18   Although some state acts allow for this as well.
19   See ss 19–60 of the *Workplace Relations Act 1996*.
20   See ss 61–126 of the *Workplace Relations Act 1996*.
21   The wage components of the standard are to be found in ss 176–200 of the *Workplace Relations Act 1996*.
22   Beyond our discussion here but of more than passing relevance is the relationship between the contract of employment and the industrial award. See *Byrne and Frew v Australian Airlines Ltd* (1995)185 CLR 410.
23   See the *Workplace Relations Legislation Amendment (Independent Contractors) Act 2006*.
24   See the High Court of Australia decision in *Hollis v Vabu P/L* (2001) 181 ALR 263.
25   A very useful web address is www.austlii.edu.au which covers all Australian states as well as federal statute law and case decisions. It is generally admirably up to date.
26   The issues are set out clearly in C. Burton, 1988, *Refining Merit*, Australian Government Publishing Service, Canberra.
27   There is a vast literature in this area. Some interesting reading is to be found in R. Delbridge & J. Lowe, 1997, 'Managing human resources for business success: a review of the issues', 8 *International Journal of Human Resource Management*, 857–73; L. Dickens, 1999, 'Beyond the business case', 9 *Human Resource Management Journal*, 9–19 and C. Edwards & O. Robinson, 2004, 'Evaluating the Business Case for Part-time Working Amongst Qualified Nurses', 42 *British Journal of Industrial Relations*, 167–83.
28   See principally *Plessy v Ferguson* 163 US 537 (1896).
29   The most famous of these is *Brown v Board of Education of Topeka, Kansas* 347 US 483 (1954). An excellent account of this case and its effects by one of the people involved is to be found in C. Ogletree, 2004, *All Deliberate Speed—Reflections on the First Half Century of Brown v Board of Education* ,Norton, New York.
30   For an excellent history of these concepts see E. Kelly & F. Dobbin, 1998, 'How affirmative action became diversity management: employer response to antidiscrimination law, 1961 to 1996', 41 *American Behavioral Scientist* 960–89. The original use of the concept is to be found in R. Thomas, 1990, 'From affirmative action to affirming diversity', *Harvard Business Review* March–April, 107–17.
31   See L. Barmes with S. Ashtiany, 2003, 'The Diversity Approach to Achieving Equality: Potential and Pitfalls', 32 *Industrial Law Journal*, 274–96. For a local perspective see M. Patrickson & P. O'Brien (eds), 2001, *Managing Diversity: an Asian and Pacific Focus*, John Wiley and Sons, Brisbane.
32   The standard work is C. Ronalds & R. Pepper, 2004, *Discrimination Law and Practice*, Federation Press, Sydney. Another

excellent book from a British perspective is S. Fredman, 2002, *Discrimination Law*, Oxford University Press, Oxford.
33   The federal acts are the *Racial Discrimination Act 1975*, *Sex Discrimination Act 1984*, *Disability Discrimination Act 1992* and the *Age Discrimination Act 2004*. The state acts are *Anti-Discrimination Act 1977* (NSW), *Anti-Discrimination Act 1991* (Qld), *Equal Opportunity Act 1984* (SA), *Racial Vilification Act 1996* (SA), *Anti-Discrimination Act 1998* (Tas), *Equal Opportunity Act 1995* (Vic), *Racial and Religious Tolerance Act 2001* (Vic), *Equal Opportunity Act 1984* (WA), *Criminal Code* Chapter XI—*Racist Harassment and Incitement to Racial Hatred 1990* (WA), *Discrimination Act 1991* (ACT) and the *Anti-Discrimination Act 1992* (NT).
34   See *O'Callaghan v Loder* [1983] 3 NSWLR 89.
35   Including the author!
36   See *Hill v Water Resources Commission* (1985) EOC 92-127.
37   See *Horne v Press Clough Joint Venture and MEWU* (1994) EOC 92-556 AND 92-591.
38   See s 659 of the *Workplace Relations Act 1996*.
39   The best treatment of this issue and the wider discrimination field remains M. Thornton, 1990, *The Liberal Promise: Anti-Discrimination Legislation in Australia*, Oxford University Press, Melbourne. See especially pp. 33–43 for a discussion of the shortcomings of the anti-discrimination individual rights based approach.
40   See the approaches taken in some recent books on these issues: B. Pocock, 2003, *The Work/Life Collision*, Federation Press, Sydney, B. Pocock, 2006, *The Labour Market Ate My Babies: Work, Children and a Sustainable Future*, Federation Press, Sydney and A. Summers, 2003, *The End of Equality—Work ,Babies, and Women's Choices in 21st Century Australia*, Random House, Sydney.
41   For a thoughtful perspective on some of these issues from beyond the HRM context see I. Watson, J. Buchanan, I. Campbell & C. Briggs, 2003, *Fragmented Futures: New Challenges in Working Life*, Federation Press, Sydney.
42   At a federal level, these laws have been almost always under review and debate since their introduction in 1994.
43   The reader is reminded here of the general references on labour law appearing in endnote 3 above for more detail on this very complex area.
44   See s 635 of the *Workplace Relations Act 1996*.
45   See s 649 of the *Workplace Relations Act 1996*.
46   See the extensive exceptions in ss 638 and 643 of the *Workplace Relations Act 1996*.
47   See s 660 of the *Workplace Relations Act 1996*.
48   See *Health and Morals of Apprentices Act 1802* (UK).
49   See N. Gunningham & R. Johnstone, 1999, above. The leading books in the area are R. Johnstone, 2004, *Occupational Health and Safety Law and Policy—Text and Materials*, Law Book Co, Sydney and P. Bohle & M. Quinlan, 2000, *Managing Occupational Health and Safety—A Multidisciplinary Approach*, Macmillan, Melbourne.
50   In 2005 the NSW government announced the establishment of a five year statutory review of the *Occupational Health and Safety Act 2000* and the absolute obligation currently placed on those parties in default (e.g. employers) is clearly under scrutiny. One of the aims of the review is to consider

CHAPTER 4 NOTES

1   S. Clarke, 2003, 'The contemporary workforce: implications for organisational safety culture', *Personnel Review*, 32 (1), pp. 40–57; M.C. Barth & W. McNaught, 1991, 'The impact of future demographic shifts on the employment of older workers', *Human Resource Management*, 30 (1), pp. 31–44; J. Pfeffer, 1994, *Competitive Advantage Through People*, Harvard Business School Press, Boston.
2   P. Huuhtanen, 1988, 'The aging worker in a changing work environment', *Scandinavian Journal of Work Environment Health*, 14 (1), pp. 21–3.
3   C. Mayhew & C.L. Peterson (eds), 1999, *Occupational Health and Safety in Australia: Industry, Public Sector and Small Business*, Allen and Unwin, St Leonards.
4   V. Blewett & A. Shaw, 1995a, 'Benchmarking OHS: a tool for best practice', *Journal of Occupational Health and Safety—Australia and New Zealand*, 11 (3), pp. 237–42; H. De Cieri, 1995, 'Occupational health and safety' in G.L. O'Neill & R. Kramar (eds), *Australian Human Resources Management: Current Trends in Management Practice*, Pitman, Melbourne, pp. 281–301; M. Quinlan (ed.), 1993, *Work and Health: The Origins, Management and Regulation of Occupational Illness*, Macmillan, South Melbourne.
5   Australian Safety and Compensation Council, 2006, *Compendium of Workers' Compensation Statistics, Australia, 2003–04*, Canberra, Australian Government.
6   T. Theorell, G. Ahlberg-Hulten, F. Sigala, A. Perski & M. Soderholm, 1990,'A psychosocial and biomedical comparison in six contrasting service occupations', *Work and Stress*, 4 (1), pp. 51–63; C. Peterson, 2003, 'Stress among health care workers', *Journal of Occupational Health and Safety—Australia and New Zealand*, 19 (1), pp. 49–58; 2003, 'Tackling the crisis of fear in the workplace—occupational health and safety: a special advertising report', *The Australian*, 20 August, p. 24.
7   Cox, 1987, in G. Mendelson, 1990, 'Occupational stress part 1: an overview', *Journal of Occupational Health and Safety—Australia and New Zealand*, 6 (3), p. 176.
8   G. Mendelson, 1990, 'Occupational stress part 1: an overview', *Journal of Occupational Health and Safety—Australia and New Zealand*, 6 (3), pp. 175–80, at p. 176.
9   C.A. Heaney, B.A. Israel, S.J. Schurman, E.A. Baker, J.S. House & M. Hugentobler, 1993, 'Industrial relations, worksite stress reduction and employee wellbeing: a participatory action research investigation', *Journal of Organizational Behavior*, 14 (5), pp. 495–510.
10   Mendelson, 1990.
11   A. Hepworth, M. Priest & A.l Day, 2003, 'Drug tests in the office: you may be next', *Australian Financial Review*, 3 October, p. 1.
12   A. Hepworth, M. Priest & A.l Day, 2003, 'Drug tests in the office: you may be next', *Australian Financial Review*, 3 October, p. 1.
13   A. Hepworth, M. Priest & A.l Day, 2003, 'Drug tests in the office: you may be next', *Australian Financial Review*, 3 October, p. 1.
14   Australian Safety and Compensation Council, 2006, *Compendium of Workers' Compensation Statistics, Australia, 2003–04*, Canberra, Australian Government.
15   J. Ellis, 2004, 'Where's the outrage over workplace deaths?', *The Age*, 28 April, p. 12.
16   Australian Safety and Compensation Council, 2006, *Compendium of Workers' Compensation Statistics, Australia, 2003–04*, Canberra, Australian Government; it should be noted that the 2003–04 data are preliminary, and are the most recent data available at the time of preparing this chapter.
17   Australian Safety and Compensation Council, 2006, *Compendium of Workers' Compensation Statistics, Australia, 2003–04*, Canberra, Australian Government.
18   CCH Australia, 2004a, *Managing Occupational Health and Safety: Basic Legal Requirements*, CCH Australia, North Ryde.
19   A. Casey (ed.), 2004, *OHS legal guide*, CCH Australia, North Ryde.
20   Casey, 2004.
21   Casey, 2004.
22   Casey, 2004.
23   N. Gunningham, 1996, 'From compliance to best practice in OHS: the roles of specification, performance and systems-based standards', *Australian Journal of Labour Law*, 9 (3), pp. 221–46; K. Turner, 1989, 'Safety, discipline and the manager: building a "higher class of men"', *Sociology*, 23 (4), pp. 611–28.
24   E.A. Emmett, 1992, 'New directions for occupational health and safety in Australia', *Journal of Occupational Health and Safety—Australia and New Zealand*, 8 (4), pp. 293–308.
25   Emmett, 1992.
26   CCH Australia, 2004b, *Occupational Health and Safety: Legislative Overview*, CCH Australia, North Ryde.
27   Lord Alfred Robens, 1972, *Report of the Committee on Safety and Health at Work 1970–72*, Her Majesty's Stationery Office, London,

Endnotes

Comnd 5034, (Robens Report) in R. Johnstone, 1999, 'Improving worker safety: reflections on the legal regulation of OHS in the 20th century', *Journal of Occupational Health and Safety—Australia and New Zealand*, 15 (5), pp. 521–526. Also see R. Johnstone, 2004, *Occupational Health and Safety Law and Policy—Text and Materials*, Law Book Co, Sydney.

28   Industry Commission, 1995, *Work Health and Safety*, Industry Commission, Melbourne, p. 356 in Johnstone, 1999, p. 522.
29   Robens, 1972 in Johnstone, 1999, p. 522.
30   C. Tolhurst, 2001, 'Room for smarter approaches', *Australian Financial Review*, 15 August, p. 8.
31   Casey, 2004; B. Creighton & A. Stewart, 2000, *Labour Law: An Introduction*, 3rd edn, The Federation Press, Sydney; M.J. Pittard, 2000, *Australian Labour Law*, 4th edn, Butterworths, Sydney; S. Jamieson & M. Westcott, 2001, 'Occupational Health and Safety Act 2000: a story of reform in New South Wales', *Australian Journal of Labour Law*, 14 (2), pp. 177–89; Mayhew & Peterson, 1999.
32   See www.comlaw.gov.au.
33   P. Robinson, 2004, 'Safety group replaced', *The Age*, 18 May, p. 8.
34   See www.ascc.gov.au.
35   See www.ascc.gov.au.
36   See www.ascc.gov.au.
37   Johnstone, 1999.
38   A. Brooks, 2001, 'Systems standard and performance standard regulation of occupational health and safety: a comparison of the European and Australian approaches', *The Journal of Industrial Relations*, 43 (4), pp. 361–86; CCH Australia, 2004a, b.
39   A. Brooks, 2001.
40   See CCH, 2004a for detailed coverage of each of these Acts. Also see http://www.nla.gov.au/oz/law.html.
41   Casey, 2004.
42   'Victorian OHS revamp: report', 2004, *Human Resources*, 54, 21 April, pp. 1, 6.
43   K. Barrymore, 2005. Tougher work safety laws. *Financial Review*, 4 February, p. 80.
44   Casey, 2004; CCH Australia, 2004b.
45   Casey, 2004.
46   Casey, 2004; T. Driscoll, R. Mitchell, J. Mandryk, S. Healey, L. Hendrie & B. Hull, 2003, 'Coverage of work-related fatalities in Australia by compensation and occupational health and safety agencies', *Occupational and Environmental Medicine*, 60, pp. 195–200.
47   Workplace Relations Ministers Council, 2001, Comparative Performance Monitoring, Third Report, Australian and New Zealand Occupational Health and Safety and Workers Compensation Schemes.
48   K. Purse, 2002, 'Workers compensation-based employment security for injured workers: a review of legislation and enforcement', *Journal of Occupational Health and Safety—Australia and New Zealand*, 18 (1), pp. 61–6; also see R. Baril, D. Berthelette & P. Massicotte, 2003, 'Early return to work of injured workers: multidimensional patterns of individual and organizational factors', *Safety Science*, 41, pp. 277–300.
49   Casey, 2004.
50   CCH Australia, 2004b.
51   Casey, 2004.
52   Quinlan, 1993; R. Loudoun & B. Harley, 2001, 'Industrial relations decentralisation and the growth of 12-hour shifts in Australia', *The Journal of Industrial Relations*, 43 (4), pp. 402–21, at p. 415.
53   Loudoun & Harley, 2001.
54   Loudoun & Harley, 2001, p. 415.
55   J. Roughton, 1992, 'Managing a safety program through job hazard analysis', *Professional Safety*, 37, pp. 28–31.
56   'Older workers' have been variously defined as 55 years and over (Australian Bureau of Statistics, 1996, *Labour Force Australia*, cat. no. 6203.0, ABS, Canberra, March), between 50 and 80 years of age (R.J. Paul & J. B. Townsend, 1993, 'Managing the older worker—don't just rinse away the gray', *Academy of Management Executive*, 7 (3),

pp. 67–74), and as 40-plus years (K. Munk, 2003, 'The older worker: everyone's future', *Journal of Occupational Health and Safety—Australia and New Zealand*, 19 (5), pp. 437–45).
57   Australian Bureau of Statistics, 1999, *Year Book Australia 1999 Special Article—Older Australians*, cat. no. 1301.0, ABS, Canberra.
58   Barth & McNaught, 1991; also see K. Munk, 2003. The older worker: everyone's future. *Journal of Occupational Health and Safety – Australia and New Zealand*, 19, p. 437–46.
59   Australian Bureau of Statistics, 1999, *Year Book Australia 1999 Special Article—Older Australians*, cat. no. 1301.0, ABS, Canberra.
60   Australian Bureau of Statistics, 1996, *Labour Force Australia*, cat. no. 6203.0, ABS, Canberra, March; Munk, 2003.
61   Australian Bureau of Statistics, 1996, catalogue no. 6203.0.
62   Australian Bureau of Statistics, 1999, catalogue no. 1301.0; Barth & McNaught, 1991.
63   C.E. Schwoerer & D.R. May, 1996, 'Age and work outcomes: the moderating effects of self-efficacy and tool design effectiveness', *Journal of Organizational Behavior*, 17, pp. 469–87; see Munk, 2003, for a detailed review of issues for older workers in Australia.
64   H. De Cieri, 1998, 'Occupational health and safety issues', *Managing an Aging Workforce*, M. Patrickson & L Hartmann (eds), Woodslane, Sydney.
65   Barth & McNaught, 1991; L. Bennington & P. Tharenou, 1996, 'Older workers: myths, evidence and implications for Australian managers', *Asia Pacific Journal of Human Resources*, 34 (3), pp. 63–76; L.M. Finkelstein, M.J. Burke & N.S. Raju, 1995, 'Age discrimination in simulated employment contexts: an integrative analysis', *Journal of Applied Psychology*, 80 (6), pp. 652–63.
66   M. London, 1996, 'Redeployment and continuous learning in the 21st century: hard lessons and positive examples from the downsizing era', *Academy of Management Executive*, 10 (4), pp. 67–79; M. Patrickson & L. Hartmann, 1996a, 'Australian gender differences in preferences for early retirement', *International Employment Relations Review*, 2 (1), pp. 1–19; Paul & Townsend, 1993.
67   R.D. Iverson & P.J. Erwin, 1997, 'Predicting occupational injury: the role of affectivity', *Journal of Occupational and Organizational Psychology*, 70, pp. 113–28; J. Reason & D. Lucas, 1984, 'Absent-mindedness in shops: its incidence, correlates and consequences', *British Journal of Clinical Psychology*, 23, pp. 121–31; S.R. Rhodes, 1983, 'Age-related differences in work attitudes and behaviour: a review and conceptual analysis', *Psychological Bulletin*, 93 (2), pp. 328–67.
68   K.L. Ringenbach & R.R. Jacobs, 1995, 'Injuries and aging workers', *Journal of Safety Research*, 26 (3), pp. 169–76.
69   Munk, 2003.
70   C. James & A. Brownlea, 1994, 'Work-related injury: managing the impact', *Asia Pacific Journal of Human Resources*, 32 (3), pp. 80–96.
71   A. Chapman, J.A. Mandryk, M.S. Frommer, B.V. Edye & D.A. Ferguson, 1990, 'Chronic perceived work stress and blood pressure among Australian government employees', *Scandinavian Journal of Work and Environmental Health*, 16, pp. 258–69.
72   Schwoerer & May, 1996.
73   Rhodes, 1983.
74   Hollis et al., 1994 in Bennington & Tharenou, 1996.
75   M.I. Härmä, T. Hakola & J. Laitinen, 1992, 'Relation of age and circadian adjustment to night work', *Scandinavian Journal of Work and Environment and Health*, 18, pp. 116–18.
76   M.J. Smith, M.J. Colligan & D.L. Tasto, 1982, 'Health and safety consequences of shiftwork in the food processing industry', *Ergonomics*, 25 (2), pp. 133–44.
77   Smith et al., 1982.
78   D. R. Biggins & T. H. Fair, 1988, 'Occupational health and the democratisation of work part 1: challenges for management', *Journal of Occupational Health Safety—Australia and New Zealand*, 4 (3), pp. 307–12; V. Blewett & A. Shaw, 1995b, 'Enterprise bargaining— supporting or hindering OHS best practice', *Journal of Occupational Health Safety—Australia and New Zealand*, 11 (2), pp. 139–44.
79   Clarke, 2003; M. MacIntosh, R. Gough, J. Teicher, A. Smith & W. Mortensen, 1996, *The Impact of Workplace Reform on Occupational*

Health and Safety: A Study of Five Workplaces, working paper series, National Key Centre in Industrial Relations, Monash University, Clayton.
80   CCH Australia, 2004b.
81   A. Wyatt & M. Oxenburgh (eds), 2004, *Managing Occupational Health and Safety*, CCH Australia Ltd, North Ryde.
82   CCH Australia, 2004a.
83   S. Cox & T. Cox, 1991, 'The structure of employee attitudes to safety: a European example', *Work and Stress*, 5 (2), pp. 93–106; D.M. DeJoy, B.S. Schaffer, M.G. Wilson, R.K. Vandenberg. & M.M. Butts, 2004, 'Creating safer workplaces: assessing the determinants and role of safety climate', *Journal of Safety Research*, 35, pp. 81–90; C.A. Heaney, B.A. Israel, S.J. Schurman, E.A. Baker, J.S. House & M. Hugentobler, 1993, 'Industrial relations, worksite stress reduction and employee wellbeing: a participatory action research investigation', *Journal of Organizational Behavior*, 14 (5), pp. 495–510; D.A. Hofmann & A. Stetzer, 1996, 'A cross-level investigation of factors influencing unsafe behaviors and accidents', *Personnel Psychology*, 49, pp. 307–39.
84   F. Guldenmund, 2000, 'The nature of safety culture: a review of theory and research', *Safety Science*, 34, pp. 215–57.
85   A. Cheyne, A. Oliver, J.M. Tomas & S. Cox, 2002, 'The architecture of employee attitudes to safety in the manufacturing sector', *Personnel Review*, 31 (6), pp. 649–70, at p. 651.
86   Cheyne et al., 2002; M.D. Cooper, 2000, 'Towards a model of safety culture', *Safety Science*, 36, pp. 111–36; Guldenmund, 2000.
87   Advisory Committee for Safety in Nuclear Installations, 1993, p. 23 in J. Harvey, H. Bolam, D. Gregory & G. Erdos, 2001, 'The effectiveness of training to change safety culture and attitudes within a highly regulated environment', *Personnel Review*, 30 (6), pp. 615–36, at p. 616.
88   I.R. Coyle, S.D. Sleeman & N. Adams, 1995, 'Safety climate', *Journal of Safety Research*, 26 (4), pp. 247–54; M. Janssens, J.M. Brett & F.J. Smith, 1995, 'Confirmatory cross-cultural research: testing the viability of a corporation-wide safety policy', *Academy of Management Journal*, 38 (2), pp. 364–82; M. Patrickson & L. Hartmann, 1996, 'Older women: retailing utilises a neglected workforce resource', *Asia Pacific Journal of Human Resources*, 34 (2), pp. 88–98.
89   See C. Gallagher, E. Underhill & M. Rimmer, 2001, *Occupational Health and Safety Management Systems: A Review of Their Effectiveness in Securing Healthy and Safe Workplaces*, AusInfo, Canberra.
90   Gallagher, Underhill & Rimmer, 2001.
91   Wyatt & Oxenburgh, 2004.
92   Gallagher, Underhill & Rimmer, 2001.
93   Wyatt & Oxenburgh, 2004.
94   CCH Australia, 2004a.
95   Gallagher, Underhill & Rimmer, 2001.
96   Casey, 2004.
97   Mayhew & Peterson, 1999; Quinlan, 1993.
98   R.G. Hallock & D.A. Weaver, 1990, 'Controlling losses and enhancing management systems with TOR analysis', *Professional Safety*, 35, pp. 24–6.
99   M. MacIntosh, 1994, 'From regulation of self-management in occupational health and safety: A study of the impact of workplace reform in a medium sized manufacturing plant', *International Journal of Employment Studies*, 2 (2), pp. 305–26; Mayhew & Peterson, 1999; Wyatt & Oxenburgh, 2004.
100 Blewett & Shaw, 1995b; Mayhew & Peterson, 1999.
101 Blewett & Shaw, 1995a; De Cieri, 1995; B. Hocking, 1991, 'Cost–benefit analyses of occupational health and safety in Telecom', *Journal of Occupational Health and Safety—Australia and New Zealand*, 7 (3), pp. 209–13.
102 Mayhew & Peterson, 1999; Quinlan, 1993.
103 Casey, 2004.
104 Casey, 2004.
105 Victorian Government web site for OHS: www.worksafe.vic.gov.au.
106 The National Safety Council of Australia web site is www.safetynews.com/default.asp.

107 For example, S. Clarke, 1998, 'Organisational factors affecting the incident reporting of train drivers', *Work and Stress*, 12, pp. 6–16; Hofmann & Stetzer, 1996.
108 R. Hechanova-Alampay & T.A. Beehr, 2001, 'Empowerment, span of control and safety performance in work teams after workforce reduction', *Journal of Occupational Health Psychology*, 6 (4), pp. 275–82.
109 J.P. Womack, 1996, 'The psychology of lean production', *Applied Psychology: An International Review*, 45, pp. 119–22.
110 Hechanova-Alampay & Beehr, 2001.
111 Clarke, 2003.
112 Ringenbach & Jacobs, 1995.
113 London, 1996; Munk, 2003.
114 London, 1996; Paul & Townsend, 1993; Ringenbach & Jacobs, 1995.
115 D.M. Eichar, S. Norland, E.M. Brady & R.H. Fortinsky, 1991, 'The job satisfaction of older workers', *Journal of Organizational Behavior*, 12 (7), pp. 609–20.
116 Eichar et al., 1991, pp. 609.
117 Schwoerer & May, 1996.
118 J. Barling, C. Loughlin & E.K. Kelloway, 2002, 'Development and test of a model linking safety-specific transformational leadership and occupational safety', *Journal of Applied Psychology*, 87 (3), pp. 488–96; D. Zohar, 2002, 'The effect of leadership dimensions, safety climate and assigned priorities on minor injuries in workgroups', *Journal of Organizational Behavior*, 23, pp. 75–92.
119 R. Sinclair, R. Smith, M. Colligan, M. Prince, T. Nguyen & L. Stayner, 2003, 'Evaluation of a safety training program in three food service companies', *Journal of Safety Research*, 34, pp. 547–58.
120 R. Wolfe, D. Parker & N. Napier, 1994, 'Employee health management and organizational performance', *Journal of Applied Behavioral Science*, 30 (1), p. 23.
121 G. Pfeiffer, 1986, 'Health risk and occupational category', *Employee Assistance Quarterly*, 1 (3), pp. 25–34; Ringenbach & Jacobs, 1995.
122 S. Billing, 2003, 'Time and time again', *HRMonthly*, November, pp. 41–2; S. Stephan, 2001, 'Improving the safety culture of the Australian mining industry', *Journal of Occupational Health and Safety—Australia and New Zealand*, 17 (3), pp. 237–49.
123 Paul & Townsend, 1993.
124 Huuhtanen, 1988.
125 B.L. Friedman, 1992, 'Job prospects for older workers', *Journal of Aging and Social Policy*, 4 (3/4), pp. 53–72, at p. 70.
126 London, 1996.
127 Friedman, 1992.
128 Clarke, 2003.
129 Clarke, 2003, p. 52.
130 Paul & Townsend, 1993.
131 M.A. Huselid, S.E. Jackson & R.S. Schuler, 1997, 'Technical and strategic human resource management effectiveness as determinants of firm performance', *Academy of Management Journal*, 40 (1), pp. 171–88.
132 C. Mayhew, 2002a, 'OHS challenges in Australian small business: old problems and emerging risks', *Safety Science Monitor*, 6 (1), pp. 26–37.
133 C. Mayhew, 2002a; C. Mayhew, 2000, 'OHS in Australian "micro" small businesses: evidence from nine research studies', *Journal of Occupational Health and Safety—Australia and New Zealand*, 16 (4), pp. 297–305.
134 C. Mayhew & M. Quinlan, 'The effects of outsourcing on occupational health and safety: a comparative study of factory-based workers and outworkers in the Australian clothing industry', 1999, *International Journal of Health Services*, 29 (1), pp. 83–107.
135 C. Mayhew, 2002a; C. Mayhew, 2002b, 'Getting the message across to small business about occupational violence and hold-up prevention: a pilot study', *Journal of Occupational Health and Safety—Australia and New Zealand*, 18 (3), pp. 223–30.
136 C. Mayhew, 2002a.
137 Australian Bureau of Statistics, 1999, *Characteristics of Small Business 1999*, catalogue no. 8127.0, ABS, Canberra.

138 Australian Bureau of Statistics, 1999, catalogue no. 8127.0.
139 C. Mayhew & C. Young, 1999, 'The impact of an intensive mailed OHS information campaign on small business cabinetmakers', *Journal of Occupational Health and Safety—Australia and New Zealand*, 15 (1), pp. 47–52.
140 S. Cowley, D. Else & A. LaMontagne, 2004, 'Increasing the adoption of OHS risk controls in small business: can social marketing help to achieve change?', *Journal of Occupational Health and Safety—Australia and New Zealand*, 20 (1), pp. 69–77.
141 N. Weinreich, 1999 in Cowley, Else & LaMontagne, 2004.
142 Mayhew, Young, Ferris & Harnett, 1997 in Mayhew, 2002a.
143 Mayhew, 2002a.
144 For a copy of the *Managing safety in your workplace: a step-by-step guide*, available in CD-ROM or booklet, contact WorkSafe Victoria www.worksafe.vic.gov.au; also see D. Gray, 2003, 'Speak up on work safety', *The Age*, 16 June, p. 6.
145 Blewett & Shaw, 1995a; De Cieri, 1995; Quinlan, 1993.
146 H. Rivzi, 1997, 'Toying with workers', *Multinational Monitor*, 17 (4), multinationalmonitor.org/hyper/mm0496.03.html.
147 E.A. Emmett, 1995a, 'Strategy and coordination framework for an enhanced Australian role in the improvement of occupational health and safety in the Asia–Pacific region', *Journal of Occupational Health and Safety—Australia and New Zealand*, 11 (2), pp. 115–24; E.A. Emmett, 1995b, 'Regulatory reform in occupational health and safety in Australia', *Journal of Occupational Health and Safety—Australia and New Zealand*, 11 (6), pp. 607–16.
148 See, for example, *World Population Prospects: The 2002 Revision*, United Nations, New York, 2003, unstats.un.org/unsd/cdb, viewed 29 August 2004.
149 Emmett, 1995a.
150 M. Warner, 1996, 'Chinese enterprise reform, human resources and the 1994 labour law', *International Journal of Human Resource Management*, 7 (4), pp. 779–96; C.J. Zhu, 1997, 'Human resource development in China during the transition to a new economic system', *Asia Pacific Journal of Human Resources*, 35 (2), pp. 19–44.
151 Gunningham, 1996.
152 A. Hopkins, 1994, 'Compliance with what? The fundamental regulatory question', *British Journal of Criminology*, 34 (4), pp. 431–43.
153 Emmett, 1995b.
154 Quinlan, 1993.
155 W.K. Poon, 1995, 'Human resource management in Hong Kong' in L.F. Moore & P.D. Jennings (eds), *Human Resource Management on the Pacific Rim: Institutions, Practices and Attitudes*, de Gruyter, Berlin, pp. 91–117; Rivzi, 1997; Zhu, 1997.
156 Asia Monitor Resource Center, 1997, 'The Hong Kong Takeover of South China', *Multinational Monitor*, 18 (6), www.essential.org/monitor/hyper/mm0697.06.html.
157 M. Chen & A. Chan, 2003, 'Employee and Union Inputs Into Occupational Health and Safety Measures in Chinese Factories', *Social Science and Medicine*.
158 Janssens, Brett & Smith, 1995.
159 Blewett & Shaw, 1995a; De Cieri, 1995; Quinlan, 1993.

CHAPTER 5 NOTES

1 I. Campbell and P. Brosnan, 1999, 'Labour market deregulation in Australia: the slow combustion approach to workplace change', *International Review of Applied Economics*, 13 (3), pp. 353–94.
2 S. Machin, 1996, 'Wage inequality in the UK', *Oxford Review of Economic Policy*, 12 (1), pp. 47–64.
3 R. Morris, D. Mortimer and P. Leece, 1999, *Workplace Reform and Enterprise Bargaining*, 2nd edn, Harcourt Brace, Sydney.
4 B. Dabscheck, 1995, *The Struggle for Australian Industrial Relations*, Oxford University Press, South Melbourne.
5 Business Council Bulletin, May–June 1985, cited in Dabscheck, 1995.
6 S. Deery, D. Plowman, J. Walsh and M. Brown, 2001, *Industrial Relations: A Contemporary Analysis*, 2nd edn, Irwin/McGraw-Hill, North Ryde, New South Wales.

7 Business Council of Australia (BCA), 1989, *Enterprise-Based Bargaining: A Better Way of Working*, Business Council of Australia, Melbourne.
8 B. Kelty, 'Together for tomorrow', in *Australian Council of Trade Unions, ACTU: Together for Tomorrow*, 1991, Australian Council of Trade Unions, Melbourne, p. 1.
9 C. Briggs, 1999, 'The transition and decline of the ACTU during the 1990s: from a "governing institution" to a "servicing" organisation', *New Zealand Journal of Industrial Relations*, 24 (3), pp. 257–89.
10 Australian Industrial Law Reports: 33 AILR 118.
11 P. Waring, 1999, 'The rise of individualism in Australian industrial relations', *New Zealand Journal of Industrial Relations*, 24 (3), pp. 291–318.
12 Australian Industrial Relations Commission, 1993, *Review of Wage Fixing Principles*, print K9700, Australian Industrial Relations Commission, Melbourne, October.
13 *Workplace Relations Act 1996*, (section 3(d)).
14 For a recent discussion, see B. Van Gramberg, J. Teicher & G. Griffin, 2000, 'Industrial relations in 1999: workplace relations legalism and individualism', *Asia Pacific Journal of Human Resources*, 38 (1), pp. 4–22.
15 A. Ferner and R. Hyman, 1992, *Industrial Relations in the New Europe*, Blackwell Business, Oxford, p. xxxiii.
16 G. Giudice, 1999, 'Keynote address', *Industrial Relations Society of Australia, 1999 National Convention*, Fremantle, Western Australia, 22 October.
17 Australian Industrial Relations Commission, 2004, *Annual Report of the Australian Industrial Relations Commission, 2002/2003*, Australian Industrial Relations Commission, Melbourne.
18 Australian Bureau of Statistics (ABS), 2001, *2001 Labour Statistics in Brief*, Australia, catalogue no. 6104.0, Australian Bureau of Statistics, Canberra.
19 Hon Kevin Andrews MP, Minister for Employment and Workplace Relations, Minister Assisting the Prime Minister for the Public Service, 7 December 2006. Media Release, 'Latest Strike Data Exposes Same Old Labor Policy', http://mediacentre.dewr.gov.au/mediacentre/MinisterAndrews/Releases/LatestStrikeDataExposesSameOldLaborPolicy.htm. accessed 1 January 2007.
20 Justice J. Guidice, 2006 'The impact of workchoices—some preliminary observations' *Australian Labour Law Association's third biennial conference*, Brisbane, Friday 22 September, 2006, available at http://www.airc.gov.au/about_the_commission/speeches/GiudiceJ_ALLA_Conference_220906.htm, accessed 15 December 2006.
21 B. Van Gramberg, 'Exploring avenues for the growth of alternative dispute resolution in Australian workplaces', in I. McAndrew and A. Geare (eds), 2002, *Proceeding Conference of the Association of Industrial Relations Academics of Australia and New Zealand*, Queenstown, New Zealand, 6–8 February, pp. 525–36.
22 J.H. Wooten, 1970, 'The role of the tribunals', *Journal of Industrial Relations*, 12 (2), p. 134.
23 Australian Bureau of Statistics (ABS), 2006. *Labour Force, Australia: Spreadsheets*, catalogue no. 6202.0.55.001, April quarter, Australian Bureau of Statistics, Canberra.
24 Australian Centre for Industrial Relations Research and Training (ACIRRT), 1999, *Australia at Work*, Australian Centre for Industrial Relations Research and Training, Sydney.
25 Campbell and Brosnan, 1999.
26 J. Burgess, J. Lee and M. O'Brien, 2004, 'The Australian Labour Market in 2003', *Journal of Industrial Relations*, 46 (2), pp. 141–59.
27 Burgess et al., 2004.
28 L. Kaye, 1999, 'Strategic human resources management in Australia: the human cost', *International Journal of Manpower*, 20 (8), pp. 577–87.
29 P. Barnes, R. Johnson, A. Kulys and S. Hook, 1999, *Productivity and the Structure of Employment*, Productivity Commission, Melbourne.
30 Australian Bureau of Statistics (ABS), 2002, *Employment Services 2000/2001*, catalogue no. 8558.0. Australian Bureau of Statistics, Canberra.

31 I. Ross, 1999, 'The future of award regulation', speech to ACIRRT Conference, Sydney, 16 July.
32 Campbell and Brosnan, 1999.
33 M. Emmott and S. Hutchinson, 'Employment flexibility: threat or promise?', in P. Sparrow and M. Marchington (eds), 1998, *Human Resource Management: The New Agenda*, Financial Times/Pitmans, London, pp. 229–44; J. Teicher and B. van Gramberg, 1999, 'A brave new world of workplace relations: a review of the ministerial implementation discussion paper and other documents', *International Employment Relations Review*, 5 (1), pp. 75–87.
34 Office of the Employment Advocate, 2004, AWA Statistics, 2004, viewed 12 January 2005, www.oea.gov.au.
35 Office of the Employment Advocate, 2007, 'Workplace Agreement Statistics' http://www.oea.gov.au/graphics.asp?showdoc=/news/researchStatistics.aspsd
36 McIlwain, P. 2005, Submission to Senate Employment, Workplace Relations and Education References Committee Inquiry into Workplace Agreements, http://www.oea.gov.au/docs/News/senate_submission_050926.pdf accessed 18 December 2006.
37 P. Reith, 1999, 'Workplace relations—the reform debate', keynote address to the National Key Centre in Industrial Relations, Monash University, Melbourne, 30 November.
38 Watts and Mitchell, 2004.
39 Australian Bureau of Statistics (ABS), 2000, *Employee Earnings and Hours*, catalogue no. 6306.3, Australian Government Publishing Service, Canberra.
40 A. Roan, T. Bramble and G. Lafferty, 2001, 'Australian workplace agreements in practice: the 'hard' and 'soft' dimensions', *Journal of Industrial Relations*, 43 (4), pp. 387–401.
41 Roan, Bramble & Lafferty, 2001, pp. 387–401.
42 N. Wailes, 1999, 'The importance of small differences: the effects of research design on the comparative study of industrial relations reform in Australia and New Zealand', paper presented to AIRAANZ '99, University of South Australia, Adelaide, 4–6 February.
43 Australian Bureau of Statistics (ABS), 2001a, *Employee Earnings and Hours, Australia*, catalogue no. 6303.0, Australian Government Publishing Service, Canberra.
44 M. Bray, D. Macdonald, S. Le Quex and P. Waring, 2001, 'The representation gap in Australian workplaces', *Proceedings of the 15th AIRAANZ Conference*, Wollongong, New South Wales, 31 January–3 February, p. 44.
45 Australian Bureau of Statistics (ABS), 2004, *Australian Labour Market Statistics*, Feature Article: Trade Union Membership, catalogue no. 6105.0, Australian Government Publishing Service, Canberra.
46 Australian Bureau of Statistics (ABS), 2005, Catalogue no. 6105.0, August. Australian Government Publishing Service, Canberra.
47 P. Dyer, 2004 'Reform Backlash—Rush to Sign Up for Unions' *Sunday Telegraph*, 13 November, p. 42.
48 Hon Kevin Andrews, Minister for Employment and Workplace Relations 2006, 'Union Density continues downward slide' Media Release, 28 March, http://mediacentre.dewr.gov.au/mediacentre/AllReleases/2006/March/UnionDensityContinuesDownwardSlide.htm accessed 18 December 2006.
49 A. Barnes, 2006 'Trade Unionism in 2005' *Journal of Industrial Relations*, 48, (3), pp. 369–383.
50 Waring, 1999.
51 Australian Bureau of Statistics (ABS), 2000, *Employee Earnings and Hours*, catalogue no. 6306.3, Australian Government Publishing Service, Canberra.
52 Construction, Forestry and Mining Employees Union (CFMEU), 1993, *Future Directions or a Dead End? Enterprise Bargaining and Deregulation of the Australian Labour Market*, Construction, Forestry and Mining Employees Union, Melbourne, July, pp. 4–5.
53 P. K. Sett, 2004, 'Human Resource Management and Firm Level Restructuring: The South Asian Drama' *Research and Practice in Human Resource Management*, 12 (1), 1–33.
54 Bray, Macdonald, Le Quex and Waring, 2001.
55 Waring, 1999.
56 B. Townley, 1994, *Reframing Human Resource Management: Power, Ethics and the Subject at Work*, Sage Publications, London.
57 Briggs, 1999.
58 M. Cranston, 2000, 'The terminal decline of Australian trade union membership', *IPA Review*, 52 (4), pp. 26–8.
59 Cranston, 2000, pp. 26–8.
60 Australian Bureau of Statistics (ABS), 2003, *Year Book Australia 2002*, 'The Labour Force'. Australian Bureau of Statistics, Canberra.
61 ACIRRT, 1999.
62 Teicher & Van Gramberg, 1999.
63 Briggs, 1999.
64 R. Cooper, 2004, 'Unionism in 2003', *Journal of Industrial Relations*, 46 (2), pp. 2213–225.
65 C. Wright, 1995, *The Management of Labour: A History of Australian Employees*, Oxford University Press, Melbourne.
66 M. Bray & P. Waring, 2006, 'The rise of managerial prerogative under the Howard Government' *Journal of Industrial Relations*, 32 (1), pp. 45–61.
67 Waring, 1999.
68 R. Loudoun and B. Harley, 2001, 'Industrial relations decentralisation and the growth of 12-hour shifts in Australia', *Journal of Industrial Relations*, 43 (4), pp. 402–21.
69 J. Teicher & B. Van Gramberg, 'Privatising local government: the Victorian experience', in P. Fairbrother, M. Paddon and J. Teicher (eds), 2002, *Privatisation and Globalisation: Australian Studies*, Federation Press, Sydney, pp. 183–208; M. Paddon, 1999, 'The impact of changes in government policy and forms of service delivery on the employment of and services to women—a case study of local government childcare provision in Victoria', unpublished report, Public Sector Research Centre, University of New South Wales, January; J. Walsh and J. O'Flynn, 1999, 'Managing through contracts: the employment effects of compulsory competitive tendering in Australian local government', *Working Paper in Human Resource Management, Employee Relations and Organisation Studies no. 3*, Department of Management, University of Melbourne, Melbourne.
70 For example, R. Milne and M. McGee, 1992, 'Compulsory competitive tendering in the NHS: a new look at some old estimates', Fiscal Studies, 13 (3), pp. 96–111; J. Quiggin, 1996, *Great Expectations: Microeconomic Reform and Australia*, Allen and Unwin, St Leonards, New South Wales.
71 For example, ACIRRT, 1999; S.J. Procter, M. Rowlinson, L. McArdle, J. Hassard and P. Forrester, 1994, 'Flexibility, politics and strategy: in defence of the model of the flexible firm', *Work, Employment and Society*, 8 (2), pp. 221–42.
72 Kaye, 1999.
73 J. Purcell, 1996, 'The end of institutional industrial relations in Britain: lessons for Australia', *11th Foenander Lecture in Industrial Relations*, University of Melbourne, 19 September.
74 D. P. Skarlicki, & R. Folger, 1997, 'Retaliation in the Workplace: The Roles of Distributive, Procedural, and International Justice' *Journal of Applied Psychology* 82 (3), pp. 434–443.
75 P. Cappelli, 1999, *The New Deal at Work*, Harvard Business School Press, Boston.
76 Cappelli, 1999.
77 B. Ryan, 1997, 'A review of managerial impacts on council structures', paper presented at the CPMP Conference, Hobart, 17–19 April.
78 J. Dore, 1998, 'Revising our expectations of local government', *Australian Journal of Public Administration*, 57 (3), pp. 92–9.

CHAPTER 6 NOTES

1 J. Galbraith and R. Kazanjian, 1986, *Strategy Implementation: Structure, Systems, and Process*, West Publishing, St Paul, MN.
2 S. Brint, 2001, 'Professionals and the "knowledge economy": rethinking the theory of postindustrial society', *Current Sociology*, 49 (4), pp. 101–32; B. Burchell, D. Lapido and F. Wilkinson (eds), 2002, *Job

Endnotes

Insecurity and Work Intensification, Routledge, London; C.C. Cooper and R.J. Burke (eds), 2003, *The New World of Work: Challenges and Opportunities*, Blackwell, Oxford, UK; S.K Parker, T.D. Wall and J.L Cordery, 2001, 'Future work design research and practice: towards an elaborated model of work design', *Journal of Occupational and Organizational Psychology*, 71, pp. 413–40; P. Thompson, C. Warhurst and G. Callaghan, 2001, 'Ignorant theory and knowledgeable workers: interrogating the connections between knowledge, skills and services', *The Journal of Management Studies*, 38 (7), pp. 923–42.

3 B. Burchell, D. Lapido and F. Wilkinson (eds), 2002; J. Mead and D. James, 2003, 'Jobs for a new age', *Business Review Weekly*, 18 September, p. 66.

4 D. Ilgen and J. Hollenbeck, 1991, 'The structure of work: job design and roles', in M. Dunnette and L. Hough (eds), *Handbook of Industrial and Organizational Psychology*, 2nd edn, Consulting Psychologists Press, Palo Alto, CA, pp. 165–208.

5 R. Harvey, 1991, 'Job analysis', in Dunnette and Hough (eds), pp. 71–164; M. Brannick and E. Levine, 2002, *Job Analysis: Methods, Research, and Applications for Human Resource Management in the New Millennium*, Sage, Thousand Oaks.

6 R. Griffin, 1982, *Task Design: An Integrative Approach*, Scott-Foresman, Glenview, IL.

7 B. Brocka and M.S. Brocka, 1992, *Quality Management: Implementing the Best Ideas of the Masters*, Business One Irwin, Homewood, IL.

8 R. Pritchard, D. Jones, P. Roth, K. Stuebing and S. Ekeberg, 1988, 'Effects of group feedback, goal setting, and incentives on organizational productivity', *Journal of Applied Psychology*, 73, pp. 337–60.

9 D. Bowen and E. Lawler, 1992, 'Total quality-oriented human resources management', *Organizational Dynamics*, 20 (4), pp. 29–41.

10 B. Burchell, D. Lapido and F. Wilkinson (eds), 2002; W. Tuohy, 2003, 'Are men becoming the new part-timers?' *The Age*, July 12, p. 5.

11 M. Fefer, 'Bill Gates' next challenge', 1992, *Fortune*, 14 December, pp. 30–41.

12 E. McCormick, 1976, 'Job and task analysis', in M. Dunnette (ed), *Handbook of Industrial and Organizational Psychology*, Rand McNally, Chicago, pp. 651–96; M. Brannick and E. Levine, 2002.

13 E. Primoff and S. Fine, 1988, 'A history of job analysis', in S. Gael (ed), *The Job Analysis Handbook for Business, Industry, and Government*, Wiley, New York, pp. 14–29.

14 W. Cascio, 1991, *Applied Psychology in Personnel Management*, 4th edn, Prentice-Hall, Englewood Cliffs, NJ.

15 Brannick and Levine, 2002; P. Wright and K. Wexley, 1985, 'How to choose the kind of job analysis you really need', *Personnel*, May, pp. 51–5.

16 J. Walker, 1992, *Human Resource Strategy*, McGraw-Hill, New York.

17 R. Gatewood and H. Feild, 1990, *Human Resource Selection*, 2nd edn, Dryden, Hinsdale, IL.

18 I. Goldstein, 1993, *Training in Organizations*, 3rd edn, Brooks/Cole, Pacific Grove, CA; I. Grugulis, 2003, 'Putting skills to work: learning and employment at the start of the century', *Human Resource Management Journal*, 13 (2), pp. 3–12.

19 K. Murphy and J. Cleveland, 1991, *Performance Appraisal: An Organizational Perspective*, Allyn and Bacon, Boston.

20 R. Harvey, L. Friedman, M. Hakel and E. Cornelius, 1988, 'Dimensionality of the job element inventory, JEI: a simplified worker-oriented job-analysis questionnaire', *Journal of Applied Psychology*, 73, pp. 639–46.

21 F. Green and D. James, 2003, 'Assessing skills and autonomy: the job holder versus the line manager', *Human Resource Management Journal*, 13 (1), pp. 63–77.

22 R. Cerabona, 2001, 'Working at home: the new office', *Canberra Times*, 5 August, p. 11; M. Lindorff, 2000, 'Home-based telework and telecommuting in Australia: more myth than modern work form', *Asia Pacific Journal of Human Resources*, 38 (1), pp. 1–11.

23 A. Turner, 2003, 'Home alone', *The Age*, Computer section, 30 September, p. 5.

24 A. O'Reilly, 1973, 'Skill requirements: supervisor–subordinate conflict', *Personnel Psychology*, 26, pp. 75–80.

25 J. Hazel, J. Madden and R. Christal, 1964, 'Agreement between worker–supervisor descriptions of the worker's job', *Journal of Industrial Psychology*, 2, pp. 71–9.

26 K. Wexley and S. Silverman, 1978, 'An examination of differences between managerial effectiveness and response patterns on a structured job-analysis questionnaire', *Journal of Applied Psychology*, 63, pp. 646–9.

27 P. Conley and P. Sackett, 1988, 'Effects of using high- versus low-performing job incumbents as sources of job-analysis information', *Journal of Applied Psychology*, 72, pp. 434–7.

28 W. Mullins and W. Kimbrough, 1988, 'Group composition as a determinant of job-analysis outcomes', *Journal of Applied Psychology*, 73, pp. 657–64.

29 N. Hauenstein and R. Foti, 1989, 'From laboratory to practise: neglected issues in implementing frame-of-reference rater training', *Personnel Psychology*, 42, pp. 359–78.

30 N. Schmitt and S. Cohen, 1989, 'Internal analysis of task ratings by job incumbents', *Journal of Applied Psychology*, 74, pp. 96–104.

31 F. Landy and J. Vasey, 1991, 'Job analysis: the composition of SME samples', *Personnel Psychology*, 44, pp. 27–50.

32 E. McCormick and R. Jeanneret, 1988, 'The position analysis questionnaire', in Gael (ed), pp. 880–901; P.R. Jeanneret and M.H. Strong, 2003, 'Linking O*NET job analysis information to job requirement predictors: an O*NET application', *Personnel Psychology*, 56, pp. 465–92.

33 *PAQ Newsletter*, 1989, August.

34 E. Primhoff, 1975, *How to Prepare and Conduct Job Element Examinations*, United States Government Printing Office, Washington DC.

35 E. Fleishman and M. Reilly, 1992, *Handbook of Human Abilities: Definitions, Measurements and Job Task Requirements*, Management Research Institute, Inc, Potomac, MD.

36 E. Fleishman and M. Mumford, 1988, 'Ability requirements scales', in Gael (ed), pp. 917–35.

37 R. Christal, 1974, *The United States Air Force Occupational Research Project*, AFHRL-TR-73-75, Air Force Human Resources Laboratory, Occupational Research Division, Lackland AFB, TX.

38 M.K. Lindell, C.S. Clause, C.J. Brandt and R.S. Landis, 1998, 'Relationship between organizational context and job analysis ratings', *Journal of Applied Psychology*, 83, pp. 769–76.

39 F.P. Morgeson and M.A. Campion, 1997, 'Social and cognitive sources of potential inaccuracy in job analysis', *Journal of Applied Psychology*, 82, pp. 627–55.

40 N. O'Malley, 'Musical chairs for adults', 2000, *The Sydney Morning Herald*, 30 August, p. 3; A. Kalleberg, 2000, 'Nonstandard employment relations: part-time, temporary and contract work', *Annual Review of Sociology*, 26, pp. 341–65; M. Mallon and J. Duberley, 2000, 'Managers and professionals in the contingent workforce', *Human Resource Management Journal*, 10 (1), pp. 33–47; S.P. Matusik and C.W.L. Hill, 1998, 'The utilization of contingent work, knowledge creation, and competitive advantage', *Academy of Management Review*, 23 (4), pp. 680–97; R.J. Paul and J.B. Townsend, 1998, 'Managing the contingent workforce—gaining the advantages, avoiding the pitfalls', *Employee Responsibilities and Rights Journal*, 11 (4), pp. 239–52.

41 K. Cameron, S. Freeman and A. Mishra, 1991, 'Best practices in white collar downsizing: managing contradictions', *The Executive*, 5, pp. 57–73.

42 See Parker et al., 2001.

43 M. Campion and P. Thayer, 1985, 'Development and field evaluation of an interdisciplinary measure of job design', *Journal of Applied Psychology*, 70, pp. 29–34.

44 R. Griffin and G. McMahan, 1993, 'Motivation through job design', in J. Greenberg (ed), *OB: The State of the Science*, Lawrence Erlbaum Associates, Hillsdale, NJ.

45   M. Campion, 1989, 'Ability requirement implications of job design: an interdisciplinary perspective', *Personnel Psychology*, 42, pp. 1–24.
46   F. Herzberg, 1987, 'One more time: how do you motivate employees?', *Harvard Business Review*, 65, pp. 109–20.
47   R. Hackman and G. Oldham, 1980, *Work Redesign*, Addison-Wesley, Boston.
48   B.L. Kirkman and B. Rosen, 1999, 'Beyond self-management: antecedents and consequences of team empowerment', *Academy of Management Journal*, 42 (1), pp. 58–74; J.L. Cordery, 1995, 'Work redesign: rhetoric vs reality', *Asia Pacific Journal of Human Resources*, 33 (2), pp. 3–19.
49   F. Taylor, 1967, *The Principles of Scientific Management*, W.W. Norton, New York, (originally published in 1911 by Harper and Brothers).
50   D. May and C. Schwoerer, 1994, 'Employee health by design: using employee involvement teams in ergonomic job redesign', *Personnel Psychology*, 47, pp. 861–86.
51   W. Howell, 'Human factors in the workplace', in Dunnette and Hough (eds), 1991, pp. 209–70; visit The University of Queensland, Australia, web site to view the key centre for human factors and applied cognitive psychology information at www.humanfactors.uq.edu.au/.
52   M. Campion and C. McClelland, 1991, 'Interdisciplinary examination of the costs and benefits of enlarged jobs: a job-design quasi-experiment', *Journal of Applied Psychology*, 76, pp. 186–98.
53   M. Campion and C. Berger, 1990, 'Conceptual integration and empirical test of job design and compensation relationships', *Personnel Psychology*, 43, pp. 525–53.
54   D.P. Lepak and S. Snell, S, 1999, 'The human resource architecture: towards a theory of human capital allocation and development', *Academy of Management Journal*, 24 (1), pp. 31–48; D.P. Lepak and S.A. Snell, 2002, 'Examining the human resource architecture: the relationships among human capital, employment and human resource configurations', *Journal of Management*, 28, pp. 517–43.
55   Lepak and Snell, 2002, at p. 519; also see J. Barney, 1991, 'Firms resources and sustained competitive advantage', *Journal of Management*, 17, pp. 99–129.
56   Lepak and Snell, 2002, at p. 519.
57   Lepak and Snell, 2002.
58   P.F. Drucker, 1999, 'Knowledge-worker productivity: the biggest challenge', *California Management Review*, 41 (2), pp. 79–94; S. Frenkel, M. Korczynski, L. Donoghue and K. Shire, K, 1995, 'Re-constituting work: trends towards knowledge work and info-normative control', *Work, Employment and Society*, 9 (4), pp. 773–96; H. Scarborough, 1999, 'Knowledge as work: conflicts in the management of knowledge workers', *Technology Analysis and Strategic Management*, 11 (1), pp. 5–16.
59   W.C. Kim and R. Mauborgne ,1999, 'Strategy, value innovation, and the knowledge economy', *Sloan Management Review*, 40 (3), at p. 52.
60   See, for example, P. Evans and T.S. Wurster, 1998, 'Strategy and the new economics of information', *Harvard Business Review*, 75, pp. 70–83; J. Seely-Brown and P. Duguid, 2000, 'Balancing act: how to capture knowledge without killing it', *Harvard Business Review*, 78 (3), pp. 73–80; K.E. Sveiby, 2001, 'A knowledge-based theory of the firm to guide in strategy formulation', *Journal of Intellectual Capital*, 2, pp. 344–58.
61   P.F. Drucker, 1999, 'Knowledge-worker productivity: the biggest challenge', *California Management Review*, 41 (2), pp. 79–94.
62   Lepak and Snell, 2002.
63   Lepak and Snell, 2002.
64   Lepak and Snell, 2002.
65   R.R. Batt, 1999, 'Work organization, technology, and performance in customer service sales', *Industrial and Labor Relations Review*, 52, pp. 539–64.
66   Datamonitor, 1998, *Call centres in Europe*, Datamonitor, London; ACTU, 2003, 'Summary of key issues in call centre week of action', October, ACTU, Australia, see the Union Network International web site at www.union-network.org; D. Crowe and E. Connors, 2004, 'Alcoa software jobs go offshore', *The Australian Financial Review*, May 4, p. 31.
67   Nancarrow, 2004, 'Out of India', *The Sunday Age*, 29 February, p. 8.
68   Nancarrow, 2004, p. 8.
69   A.R. Hochschild, 1983, *The Managed Heart: Commercialization of Human Feeling*, University of California Press, Berkeley, CA, p. 7.
70   A.R. Hochschild, 1983; Also see G. Callaghan and P. Thompson, 2002, 'We recruit attitude: the selection and shaping of routine call centre labour', *Journal of Management Studies*, 39, pp. 233–53; D.S. Pugh, 2001, 'Service with a smile: emotional contagion in the service encounter', *Academy of Management Journal*, 44, pp. 1018–1027.
71   S.J. Deery and N. Kinnie, 2002, 'Call centres and beyond: a thematic evaluation', *Human Resource Management Journal*, 12 (4), pp. 7–8.
72   P. Bain and P. Taylor, 2000, 'Entrapped by the electronic panopticon? Worker resistance in the call centre', *New Technology, Work and Employment*, 15 (1), pp. 2–18; Deery and Kinnie, 2002.
73   D. Holman, 2002, 'Employee wellbeing in call centres', *Human Resource Management Journal*, 12 (4), pp. 35–50.
74   S.J. Deery, R.D. Iverson and J. Walsh, 2002, 'Work relationships in call telephone centres: understanding emotional exhaustion and employee withdrawal', *Journal of Management Studies*, 39, pp. 471–96.
75   See D. Holman, 2002.
76   G.S. Alder, 1998, 'Ethical issues in electronic performance monitoring: a consideration of deontological and teleological perspectives', *Journal of Business Ethics*, 17 (7), pp. 729–43; also see Chapter 15: Ethics and human resource management.
77   S. Frenkel, M. Korczynski, K. Shire and M. Tam, 1999, *On the front line: Organization of Work in the Information Economy*, Cornell University Press, Ithaca, NY.
78   Batt, 1999.
79   M. Workman and W. Bommer, 2004, 'Redesigning computer call centre work: a longitudinal field experiment', *Journal of Organizational Behavior*, 25, pp. 317–34.
80   Workman and Bommer, 2004.
81   Lepak and Snell, 2002.
82   W. Taylor, 2004, 'The pump action guns keep firing out the ideas', *The Age*, My Career, 3 July, p. 12.

CHAPTER 7 NOTES

1   J.B. Barney & P.M. Wright, 1998, 'On becoming a strategic partner: the role of human resources in gaining competitive advantage', *Human Resource Management*, 37 (1), pp. 31–46; P. Cappelli & H. Singh, 1992, 'Integrating strategic human resources and strategic management', in D. Lewin, O.S. Mitchell & P.D. Sherer, (eds), *Research Frontiers in Industrial Relations and Human Resources*, Industrial Relations Research Association, Madison, WI; L. Dyer, 1983, 'Bringing human resources into the strategy formulation process', *Human Resource Management*, 22 (3), pp. 257–71; J. Storey, R.S. Schuler & S.E. Jackson, 2000, 'HRM and its link with strategic management', in J. Storey (ed) *Human Resource Management: A Critical Text*, 2nd edn, International Thomson, London, pp. 3–25.
2   S. Briggs & W. Keogh, 1999, 'Integrating human resource strategy and strategic planning to achieve business excellence', *Total Quality Management*, 10 (4 and 5), pp. 447–53; C.R. Greer, D.L. Jackson & J. Fiorito, 1989, 'Adapting human resource planning in a changing business environment', *Human Resource Management*, 28 (1), pp. 105–23; M.A. Huselid, 1993, 'The impact of environmental volatility on human resource planning and strategic human resource management', *Human Resource Planning*, 16 (3), pp. 35–50; D.E. Hussey, 1996, *Business Driven Human Resource Management*, John Wiley and Sons, Chicester, United Kingdom; R.W. Rowden, 1999, 'Potential roles of the human resource professional in the strategic planning process', *S.A.M. Advanced Management Journal*, 64 (3),   pp. 22–7.
3   S. Rothwell, 1995, 'Human resource planning', in J. Storey (ed), *Human Resource Management: A Critical Text*, Routledge, London, pp. 167–202.
4   D.W. Jarrell, 1993, *Human Resource Planning: A Business Planning Approach*, Prentice-Hall, Englewood Cliffs, NJ.

Endnotes

5   K.S. Cameron, S.J. Freeman & A.K. Mishra, 1993, 'Downsizing and redesigning organizations', in G. Huber & W. Glick (eds), *Organizational Change and Redesign*, Oxford University Press, New York.

6   C.R. Littler, R. Dunford, T. Bramble & A. Hede, 1997, 'The dynamics of downsizing in Australia and New Zealand', *Asia Pacific Journal of Human Resources*, 35 (1), pp. 65–79; M. London, 1996, 'Redeployment and continuous learning in the 21st century: hard lessons and positive examples from the downsizing era', *Academy of Management Executive*, 10 (4), pp. 67–79; L. Ryan & K.A. Macky, 1998, 'Downsizing organizations: uses, outcomes and strategies', *Asia Pacific Journal of Human Resources*, 36 (2), pp. 29–45.

7   Media Release, 2003, 'Commonwealth Bank launches new "which new bank" customer service vision', Commonwealth Bank of Australia, 19 September.

8   Australian Bureau of Statistics, 2006, *Year Book 2006*, catalogue no. 1301.0, Australian Government Publishing Service.

9   Australian Bureau of Statistics, 2003, *Labour Force Australia*, catalogue no. 6203.0, Australian Government Publishing Service.

10 P. Dawkins, C.R. Littler, M.R. Valenzuela & B. Jensen, 1999, 'The contours of restructuring and downsizing in Australia', Melbourne Institute of Applied Economic and Social Research, University of Melbourne, Melbourne; M. Magnet, 1994, 'The productivity payoff arrives', *Fortune*, 27 July, pp. 79–84.

11 T. Watkins, 2001, 'Defence force seeks help for staff on redundancy "shock"', *The Dominion*, 16 August, p. 2.

12 J.E. Gutknecht & J.B. Keys, 1993, 'Mergers, acquisitions and takeovers: maintaining morale of survivors and protecting employees', *Academy of Management Executive*, 7 (3), pp. 26–36; B. Kane, 2000, 'Downsizing, TQM, re-engineering, learning organizations and HRM strategy', *Asia Pacific Journal of Human Resources*, 38 (1), pp. 26–49.

13 M.L. Marks & P.H. Mirvis, 2000, 'Managing mergers, acquisitions, and alliances: creating an effective transition structure', *Organizational Dynamics*, Winter, pp. 35–46.

14 Marks & Mirvis, 2000.

15 Marks & Mirvis, 2000.

16 Gutknecht & Keys, 1993; N. Hubbard & J. Purcell, 2001, 'Managing employee expectations during acquisitions', *Human Resource Management Journal*, 11 (2), pp. 17–33; Marks & Mirvis, 2000.

17 Marks & Mirvis, 2000.

18 Gutknecht & Keys, 1993; Hubbard & Purcell, 2001; Marks & Mirvis, 2000.

19 Gutknecht & Keys, 1993.

20 L. Bannister, 2004, 'Assessing acquisitions: an IAG case study', *Human Resources*, 24 March, pp. 12–13.

21 Dawkins, Littler, Valenzuela & Jensen; M.F.R. Kets de Vries & A. Balazs, 1997, 'The downside of downsizing', *Human Relations*, 50 (1), pp. 11–50; K.P. DeMeuse, P.A. Vanderheiden & T.J. Bergmann, 1994, 'Announced layoffs: their effect on corporate financial performance', *Human Resource Management*, 33, pp. 509–30.

22 W.R Cascio, 1993, 'Downsizing: What do we know? What have we learned?', *Academy of Management Executive*, 7, pp. 95–104.

23 C. Rance, 2001, 'Should I stay or should I go?', *The Age*, 16 August, p. 9.

24 R. Folger & D.P. Skarlicki, 1998, 'When tough times make tough bosses: managerial distancing as a function of layoff blame', *Academy of Management Journal*, 41, pp. 79–87.

25 J. Larkin, 2001, 'A word in your ear', *Far Eastern Economic Review*, 13 September, p. 37.

26 H. De Cieri & M. Olekalns, 2001, 'Managing diversity in Australia', in M. Patrickson & P. O'Brien, (eds), *Managing Diversity in the Asia–Pacific*, Jacaranda Wiley, Brisbane, pp. 21–36; M. Patrickson & L. Hartmann, (eds), 1998, *Managing an Ageing Workforce*, Woodslane, Warriewood, New South Wales.

27 S. Kim & D. Feldman, 1998, 'Healthy, wealthy, or wise: predicting actual acceptances of early retirement incentives at three points in time', *Personnel Psychology*, 51, pp. 623–42.

28 P. Wechsler, 1998, 'ATandT managers rush out the door', *Business Week*, 15 June, p. 53. Also see L.C. Hartmann, 'The impact of trends in labour force participation in Australia', in Patrickson & Hartmann (eds), pp. 3–25.

29 A. Gripper, 1996, 'Temporary successes', *The Sydney Morning Herald*, 20 February, p. 13.

30 A. Gripper, 1996.

31 S. Caudron, 1994, 'Contingent work force spurs HR planning', *Personnel Journal*, July, pp. 52–9.

32 G. Flynn, 1995, 'Contingent staffing requires serious strategy', *Personnel Journal*, April, pp. 50–8.

33 C. Rance, 1994,'Keys to successful contracting', *The Age*, 19 February, Employment section, p. 3.

34 C.R. Greer, S.A. Youngblood & D.A. Gray, 1999, 'Human resource management outsourcing: the make or buy decision', *Academy of Management Executive*, 13 (3), pp. 85–96.

35 J.B. Quinn, 1999, 'Strategic outsourcing: leveraging knowledge capabilities', *Sloan Management Review*, Summer, pp. 9–21; K. Nicholas, 2004, 'Cost pressures force more Telstra Jobs offshore', *Australian Financial Review*, 16 February, p. 1.

36 D. Crowe, 2003, 'Qantas outsourcing deals may not go far enough', *Australian Financial Review*, May 19, p. 52.

37 K. Nicholas & M. Priest, 2004, 'Offshore brings the best back home', *Australian Financial Review*, April 30, p. 80.

38 N. Tabakoff, 1999, 'The go-between', *Business Review Weekly*, 8 October, p. 82.

39 R.A. Bettis, S.P. Bradley & G. Hamel, 1992, 'Outsourcing and industrial decline', *Academy of Management Executive*, 6, pp. 7–22.

40 J. Kessler, J. Coyle-Shapiro & J. Purcell, 1999, 'Outsourcing and the employee perspective', *Human Resource Management Journal*, 9 (2), pp. 5–20; B.S. Klaas, J. McClendon & T.W. Gainey, 1999, 'HR outsourcing and its impact: the role of transaction costs', *Personnel Psychology*, 52 (1), pp. 113–36.

41 M. Bryan, 2004, 'US outsourcers export jobs', *Australian Financial Review*, June 4, p. 76.

42 Huselid, 1993; R.L. Kane & S. Stanton, 1991, 'Human resource planning: Where are we now?', *Asia Pacific HRM*, 29 (2), pp. 5–20; Rothwell, 1995.

43 K.A. Kovach & C.E. Cathcart, 1999, 'Human resource information systems (HRIS): providing a business with rapid data access, information exchange and strategic advantage', *Public Personnel Management*, 28 (2), pp. 275–82; S. Liff, 1997, 'Constructing HR information systems', *Human Resource Management Journal*, 7 (2), pp. 18–31; A.S. Targowski & S.P. Deshpande, 2001, 'The utility and selection of an HRIS', *Advances in Competitiveness Review*, 9 (1), pp. 42–56.

44 D. Loh, H. De Cieri & J. Wolfram Cox, 2001, 'An actor-network perspective on human resource information systems in organisations', paper presented at the Australian and New Zealand Academy of Management annual conference, Auckland New Zealand, 5–7 December; D. Lepak & S.A. Snell, 1998, 'Virtual HR: strategic human resource management in the 21st century', *Human Resource Management Review*, 8 (3), pp. 215–34; F. Niederman, 1999, 'Global information systems and human resource management', *Journal of Global Information Management*, 7 (2), 1999, pp. 33–9.

45 Lepak & Snell, 1998; P.R. Sparrow & K. Daniels, 1999, 'Human resource management and the virtual organization: mapping the future research issues', in C.L. Cooper & D.M. Rousseau (eds), *Trends in Organizational Behavior*, John Wiley and Sons, Chichester, United Kingdom, 1999, pp. 6, 45–61.

46 Kovach & Cathcart, 1999.

47 D.E. Guessford, A.B. Boynton, R. Laudeman & J.P. Giusti, 1993, 'Tracking job skills improves performance', *Personnel Journal*, 72 (6), p. 109; Kovach & Cathcart, 1999.

48 Kovach & Cathcart, 1999.

49 Niederman, 1999.

50 J. Macy, 2004, 'Data disarray' *HRMonthly*, September, pp. 36–8.

51 J. Macy, 2004, 'Data disarray' *HRMonthly*, September, pp. 36–8.

52 R. McLeod, 1998, *Management Information Systems*, 7th edn, Prentice-Hall, Englewood Cliffs, NJ; G.M. Williams & J. Jamrog,

1996, 'Information technology and HR', *Human Resource Planning*, 5 (6), pp. 1–8.
53   B.A. Barry, 1989, 'Trends in human resource management', *HRM Australia*, 21 (3), pp. 19–24; M. Kavanagh, H.G. Guetal & S. Tannenbaum, 1990, *Human Resource Information Systems: Development and Application*, PWS-Kent, Boston.
54   Barry 1989; Kavanagh, Guetal & Tannenbaum, 1990; Kovach & Cathcart, 1999; McLeod, 1998.
55   E.W. Rogers & P.M. Wright, 1998 'Measuring organizational performance in strategic human resource management: problems, prospects, and performance information markets', *Human Resource Management Review*, 8 (3), pp. 311–31; A. Yeung & B. Berman, 1997, 'Adding value through human resources: reorienting human resource measurement to drive business performance', *Human Resource Management*, 36 (3), pp. 321–55.
56   R. Broderick & J.W. Boudreau, 1992, 'Human resource management, information technology, and the competitive edge', *Academy of Management Executive*, 6, pp. 7–17; Targowski & Deshpande, 2001.
57   J. Macy, 2004, 'Data disarray' *HRMonthly*, September, pp. 36–8.
58   Anonymous, 2000, 'Employee intranet self-service boom', *The Age*, 12 October, 'HR in the 21st century' supplement, p. 4.
59   M. Finch, 2005. Power to the masses with MSS and ESS. *Human Resources*, 9 August, pp. 24–5.
60   A. Kidman, 2004, 'Riding the self-service wave', *Human Resources*, 30 June, pp. 14–15.
61   A. Kidman, 2004, 14–15.
62   K. Sunderland, 2001, 'Portal power', *HRMonthly*, August, pp. 18–26.
63   Sunderland, 2001.
64   B.C. Marney, 1999, 'HRIS: the union of human resources and technology', *HR Banker*, July, pp. 6–8; S.E. O'Connell, 1995, 'New technologies bring new tools, new rules', *HR Magazine*, December, pp. 43–8; S.E. O'Connell, 1996, 'The virtual workplace moves at warp speed', *HR Magazine*, March, pp. 51–7; Peoplesoft, 2001, *The eBusiness Imperative for HRMS*, PeopleSoft white paper series, September.
65   R. Phaneuf, 2000, 'Plug employees in with online benefits', *Risk Management*, July, pp. 47–9; S. Greengard, 1995, 'Catch the wave as HR goes online', *Personnel Journal*, July, pp. 54–68; A. Doran, 1995, 'The Internet: the new tool for the HR professional', *The Review*, August–September, pp. 32–5.
66   S. Greengard, 1996, 'Home, home on the web', *Personnel Journal*, March, pp. 26–33.
67   Australian Bureau of Statistics, *2001 Census Basic Community Profile and Snapshot*.
68   PeopleSoft, 2001; P. Yelland, 2000, 'Human resources takes a global road', *The Sydney Morning Herald*, 15 August, p. 4; T.L. Hunter, 1992, 'How client/server is reshaping the HRIS', *Personnel Journal*, July, pp. 38–46; B. Busbin, 1995, 'The hidden costs of client/server', *The Review*, August–September, pp. 21–4.
69   A.L. Lederer, 1993, 'Emerging technology and the buy–wait dilemma: sorting fact from fantasy', *The Review*, June–July, pp. 16–19.
70   Kovach & Cathcart, 1999.
71   J. Clark & R. Koonce, 1995, 'Meetings go high-tech', *Training and Development*, November, pp. 32–8; A.M. Townsend, M.E. Whitman & A.R. Hendrickson, 1995, 'Computer support adds power to group processes', *HR Magazine*, September, pp. 87–91.
72   B. Ziegler, 1995, 'Internet software poses big threat to Notes, IBM's stake in Lotus', *The Wall Street Journal*, 7 November, pp. A1, A8.
73   A. Thompson & R. Turner, 2000, 'People portals', *Australian Financial Review*, 9 October, p. 40.
74   Sunderland, 2001.
75   Kovach & Cathcart, 1999; PeopleSoft, 2001; Targowski & Deshpande, 2001.
76   Kovach & Cathcart, 1999; PeopleSoft, 2001.
77   Targowski & Deshpande, 2001; Kavanagh, Guetal & Tannenbaum, 1990.
78   J. Macy, 2004, 'Data disarray' *HRMonthly*, September, pp. 36–8.
79   B. Cullen, 2001, 'E-recruiting is driving HR systems integration', *Strategic Finance*, July, pp. 22–6; L. Stevens, 1993, 'Resume scanning simplifies tracking', *Personnel Journal*, April, pp. 77–9.
80   E. Wilson, 1999, 'People management joins the Net', *Australian Financial Review*, 1 October, p. 74.
81   G. Bylinsky, 1991, 'How companies spy on employees', *Fortune*, 4 November, pp. 131–40; E.R. Eddy, D.L. Stone & E.F. Stone-Romero, 1999, 'The effects of information management policies on reactions to human resource information systems: an integration of privacy and procedural justice perspectives', *Personnel Psychology*, 52 (2), pp. 335–58; H. Zampetakis, 2000, 'Net aim to cut churn rate at call centres', *Australian Financial Review*, 17 May, p. 38.
82   S. Frenkel, M. Tam, M. Korczynski & K. Shire, 1998, 'Beyond bureaucracy? Work organization in call centres', *International Journal of Human Resource Management*, 9 (6), pp. 957–79; S. Hutchinson, P. Purcell & N. Kinnie, 2000, 'Evolving high commitment management and the experience of the RAC call centre', *Human Resource Management Journal*, 10 (1), pp. 63–76.
83   Frenkel, S., Korczynski, M., Shire, K. & Tam, M., 1999, *On the Front Line: Organizatoin of Work in the Information Economy*, Cornell University Press, Ithaca, NY.
84   Sunderland, 2001.
85   www.peoplesoft.com.
86   Sunderland, 2001.
87   Kovach & Cathcart, 1999; Targowski & Deshpande, 2001; S.E. Forrer & Z.B. Leibowitz, 1991, *Using Computers in Human Resources*, Jossey-Bass, San Francisco.
88   Kovach & Cathcart, 1999; Targowski & Deshpande, 2001.
89   PeopleSoft, 2001.
90   F.H. Wagner, 1991, 'The nuts and bolts of computer-assisted job evaluation', *The Review*, October–November, pp. 16–22.
91   D. Neiger, 2000, 'Putting the HRIS into SMEs', *HRMonthly*, November, pp. 38–9.

CHAPTER 8 NOTES
1   A.E. Barber, 1998, *Recruiting Employees*, Sage, Thousand Oaks, CA.
2   M. Sachdev, 2000, 'E-cru itment in the new economy', *HRMonthly*, July, pp. 34–5.
3   J.A. Breaugh, 1992, *Recruitment: Science and Practise*, PWS-Kent, Boston.
4   C.K. Stevens, 1998, 'Antecedents of interview interactions, interviewers' ratings, and applicants' reactions', *Personnel Psychology*, 51, pp. 55–85.
5   A.E. Barber, J.R. Hollenbeck, S.L. Tower & J.M. Phillips, 1994, 'The effects of interview focus on recruitment effectiveness: A field experiment', *Journal of Applied Psychology*, 79, pp. 886–96.
6   J.D. Olian & S.L. Rynes, 1984, 'Organizational staffing: Integrating practice with strategy', *Industrial Relations*, 23, pp. 170–83.
7   G.T. Milkovich & J.M. Newman, 1990, *Compensation*, Richard D. Irwin, Homewood, IL.
8   K. Clark, 1997, 'Reasons to worry about rising wages', *Fortune*, 7 July, pp. 31–2.
9   S.L. Rynes & A.E. Barber, 1990, 'Applicant attraction strategies: An organizational perspective', *Academy of Management Review*, 15, pp. 286–310.
10   Breaugh, 1992.
11   C. Fox, 2000,'Tech talent: The rank truth', *Australian Financial Review*, 15 June, p. 74.
12   Fox, 2000.
13   M.A. Conrad & S.D. Ashworth, 1986, 'Recruiting source effectiveness: A meta-analysis and re-examination of two rival hypotheses', paper presented at the annual meeting of the Society of Industrial/Organizational Psychology, Chicago.
14   Breaugh, 1992.
15   Breaugh, 1992.

Endnotes

16   R.S. Schuler & S.E. Jackson, 1987, 'Linking competitive strategies with human resource management practices', *Academy of Management Executive*, 1, pp. 207–19.
17   C.R. Williams, C.E. Labig & T.H. Stone, 1994, 'Recruitment sources and posthire outcomes for job applicants and new hires: a test of two hypotheses', *Journal of Applied Psychology*, 78, pp. 163–72.
18   A. Halcrow, 1988, 'Employers are your best recruiters', *Personnel Journal*, 67, pp. 42–9.
19   Breaugh, 1992.
20   P.A. Hausdorf & D. Duncan, 2004, 'Firm size and Internet recruiting in Canada: a preliminary investigation', *Journal of Small Business Management*, 42 (3), pp. 325–34; also see C. Donaldson, 2002, 'Cap Gemini Ernst & Young: winning the web recruitment race', *Human Resources*, July, pp. 13–14.
21   F. Lievens & M.M. Harris, 2003, 'Research on Internet recruiting and testing: current status and future directions', in C.L. Cooper & I.T. Robertson (eds), *International Review of Industrial and Organizational Psychology*, 18, pp. 131–65.
22   See S. Hinton, 2003, 'Rhetoric and reality of e-recruitment: has the Internet really revolutionised the recruitment process?' in Weisner & Millett (eds), 2003, *Human Resource Management: Challenges and Future Directions*, John Wiley Ltd, Brisbane.
23   Hinton, 2003.
24   V. Porzsolt, 2002, 'Leaping the digital divide', *HRMonthly*, October, pp. 34–5.
25   Lievens & Harris, 2003.
26   See www.thebodyshop.com.au/infopage.cfm?pageID=35, the web site of The Body Shop Australia. Web site accessed 28 February 2007.
27   Anonymous, 2003, 'More than 45_000 jobs at the click of a mouse', *The Weekend Australian*, CareerOne, 2 August, p. 6.
28   D. Brown, 2004, 'Unwanted online jobseekers swamp HR staff', *Canadian HR Reporter*, 5 April, pp. 1, 2.
29   Gutmacher, 2000, cited in Lievens & Harris, 2003.
30   Lievens & Harris, 2003.
31   Lievens & Harris, 2003.
32   K.O. Magnusen & K.G. Kroeck, 1995, 'Video conferencing maximizes recruiting', *HR Magazine*, August, pp. 70–2.
33   R. Epstein & G. Singh, 2003, 'Internet recruiting effectiveness: evidence from a biomedical device', *Journal of Human Resources Development and Management*, 3 (3), p. 216.
34   L. Tingle, 2004, Job Network fiasco exposed, *Australian Financial Review*, 18 February, p. 1.
35   See http://www.workplace.gov.au/workplace/Category/SchemesInitiatives/JobNetwork/, the web site for the Australian Government Job Network. Web site accessed 28 February 2007.
36   L. Tingle & C. Murphy, 2003, 'Work still cut out for job network', *Australian Financial Review*, 1 August, p. 3.
37   A. Crabb, J. Szego & C. Milburn, 2003, 'Jobless lost in matrix as job search system splutters along', *The Age*, 19 July, p. 6.
38   See the Westpac web site for a list of the external recruitment services they utilise: www.westpac.com.au.
39   D. Meagher, 2000, 'Getting a head', *Australian Financial Review*, 14 August, p. 10. This article quotes Ms Ann Sherry, when she was head of Group HR at Westpac. Ms Sherry is now CEO at Westpac New Zealand.
40   J. Reingold, 1997, 'Casting for a different set of characters', *Business Week*, 8 December, pp. 38–9.
41   J. Greenwald, 1984, 'Invasion of the body snatchers', *Time*, 23 April, p. 41.
42   P. Smith, 1995, 'Sources used by employers when hiring college grads', *Personnel Journal*, February, p. 25.
43   J.W. Boudreau & S.L. Rynes, 1985, 'Role of recruitment in staffing utility analysis', *Journal of Applied Psychology*, 70, pp. 354–66.
44   See Graduate Careers Council of Australia, 2005, *The Grad Files*, Graduate Careers Council of Australia, Parkville, Victoria, Australia, (Table 2), www.gradlink.edu.au, viewed 15 September 2006.
45   See Graduate Careers Council of Australia, 2005.
46   See Graduate Careers Council of Australia, 2005.

47   P. Somerville, 2004, 'Educated? Only to a degree', *HRMonthly*, July, p. 15.
48   R. Hawk, 1967, *The Recruitment Function*, American Management Association, New York.
49   C.K. Stevens, 1997, 'Effects of pre-interview beliefs on applicants' reactions to campus interviews', *Academy of Management Journal*, 40, pp. 947–66.
50   C.D. Fisher, D.R. Ilgen & W.D. Hoyer, 1979, 'Source credibility, information favorability, and job offer acceptance', *Academy of Management Journal*, 22, pp. 94–103; G.N. Powell, 1991, 'Applicant reactions to the initial employment interview: Exploring theoretical and methodological issues', *Personnel Psychology*, 44, pp. 67–83; N. Schmitt & B.W. Coyle, 1976, 'Applicant decisions in the employment interview', *Journal of Applied Psychology*, 61, pp. 184–92.
51   M.S. Taylor & T.J. Bergman, 1984, 'Organizational recruitment activities and applicants' reactions at different stages of the recruitment process', *Personnel Psychology*, 40, pp. 261–85; Fisher, Ilgen & Hoyer, 1979.
52   L.M. Graves & G.N. Powell, 1995, 'The effect of sex similarity on recruiters' evaluations of actual applicants: a test of the similarity–attraction paradigm', *Personnel Psychology*, 48, pp. 85–98.
53   R.D. Bretz & T.A. Judge, 1998, 'Realistic job previews: a test of the adverse self-selection hypothesis', *Journal of Applied Psychology*, 83, pp. 330–7.
54   J.P. Wanous, 1980, *Organizational Entry: Recruitment, Selection and Socialization of Newcomers*, Addison-Wesley, Reading, MA.
55   P. Hom, R.W. Griffeth, L.E. Palich & J.S. Bracket, 1998, 'An exploratory investigation into theoretical mechanisms underlying realistic job previews', *Personnel Psychology*, 51, pp. 421–51.
56   G.M. McEvoy & W.F. Cascio, 1985, 'Strategies for reducing employee turnover: A meta-analysis', *Journal of Applied Psychology*, 70, pp. 342–53; S.L. Premack & J.P. Wanous, 1985, 'A meta-analysis of realistic job preview experiments', *Journal of Applied Psychology*, 70, pp. 706–19.
57   P.G. Irving & J.P. Meyer, 1995, 'Re-examination of the met-expectations hypothesis: a longitudinal analysis', *Journal of Applied Psychology*, 79, pp. 937–49.
58   R.W. Waiters, 1985, 'It's time we become pros', *Journal of College Placement*, 12, pp. 30–3; Barber, 1998.
59   S.L. Rynes, R.D. Bretz & B. Gerhart, 1991, 'The importance of recruitment in job choice: A different way of looking', *Personnel Psychology*, 44, pp. 487–522.
60   C. Donaldson, 2002, 'IBM's guide to innovative recruitment', *Human Resources*, August, pp. 19–21.
61   D. Sears, 2003, *Successful Talent Strategies: Achieving Superior Business Results Through Market-focused Staffing*, Amacon, New York.
62   J.C. Nunnally, 1978, *Psychometric Theory*, McGraw-Hill, New York.
63   B. Schneider, 'An interactionist perspective on organizational effectiveness', in K.S. Cameron & D.A. Whetton (eds), 1983, *Organizational Effectiveness: A Comparison of Multiple Models*, Academic Press, Orlando, FL, pp. 27–54.
64   N. Schmitt, R.Z. Gooding, R.A. Noe & M. Kirsch, 1984, 'Meta-analysis of validity studies published between 1964 and 1982 and the investigation of study characteristics', *Personnel Psychology*, 37, pp. 407–22.
65   J. Cohen, 1977, *Statistical Power Analysis for the Behavioral Sciences*, Academic Press, New York.
66   C.H. Lawshe, 1985, 'Inferences from personnel tests and their validity', *Journal of Applied Psychology*, 70, pp. 237–8.
67   D.D. Robinson, 1981, 'Content-oriented personnel selection in a small business setting', *Personnel Psychology*, 34, pp. 77–87.
68   C.H. Lawshe, 1975, 'A quantitative approach to content validity', *Personnel Psychology*, 28, pp. 563–75.
69   P.R. Sackett, 1987, 'Assessment centers and content validity: some neglected issues', *Personnel Psychology*, 40, pp. 13–25.
70   F.L. Schmidt & J.E. Hunter, 1980, 'The future of criterion-related validity', *Personnel Psychology*, 33, pp. 41–60; F.L. Schmidt, J.E.

Hunter & K. Pearlman, 1982, 'Task differences as moderators of aptitude test validity: a red herring', *Journal of Applied Psychology*, 66, pp. 166–85; R.L. Gutenberg, R.D. Arvey, H.G. Osburn & R.P. Jeanneret, 1983, 'Moderating effects of decision-making/information processing dimensions on test validities', *Journal of Applied Psychology*, 68, pp. 600–8.

71 F.L. Schmidt, J.G. Berner & J.E. Hunter, 1974, 'Racial differences in validity of employment tests: reality or illusion', Journal of Applied Psychology, 58, pp. 5–6.

72 Society for Industrial and Organizational Psychology, 1987, *Principles for the Validation and Use of Personnel Selection Procedures*, University of Maryland Press, College Park, MD.

73 J.W. Boudreau, 'Utility analysis for decisions in human resource management', in M.D. Dunnette & L.M. Hough (eds), 1991, *Handbook of Industrial and Organizational Psychology*, 2nd edn, Consulting Psychologists Press, Palo Alto, CA.

74 R.L. Dipboye, 1991, *Selection Interviews: Process Perspectives*, South-Western, Cincinnati, OH.

75 L. Di Milia, 2004, 'Australian management selection practices: Closing the gap between research findings and practice', *Asia Pacific Journal of Human Resources*, 42, pp. 214–28.

76 J.E. Hunter & R.H. Hunter, 1984, 'Validity and utility of alternative predictors of job performance', *Psychological Bulletin*, 96, pp. 72–98; L.M. Graves & R.J. Karren, 1996, 'The employee selection interview: a fresh look at an old problem', *Human Resource Management*, 35 (2), pp. 163–80.

77 R. Pingitore, B.L. Dugoni, R.S. Tindale & B. Spring, 1994, 'Bias against overweight job applicants in a simulated interview', *Journal of Applied Psychology*, 79, pp. 909–17.

78 M.A. McDaniel, D.L. Whetzel, F.L. Schmidt & S.D. Maurer, 1994, 'The validity of employment interviews: a comprehensive review and meta-analysis', *Journal of Applied Psychology*, 79, pp. 599–616; A.I. Huffcutt & W.A. Arthur, 1994, 'Hunter and Hunter (1984) revisited: interview validity for entry-level jobs', *Journal of Applied Psychology*, 79, pp. 184–90; Graves & Karren, 1996.

79 J. Solomon, 1989, 'The new job interview: show thyself', *The Wall Street Journal*, 4 December, p. B4.

80 M.A. Campion, J.E. Campion & J.P. Hudson, 1994, 'Structured interviewing: A note of incremental validity and alternative question types', *Journal of Applied Psychology*, 79, pp. 998–1002; E.D. Pulakos & N. Schmitt, 1995, 'Experience-based and situational interview questions: studies of validity', *Personnel Psychology*, 48, pp. 289–308.

81 S. Greengard, 1995, 'Are you well armed to screen applicants?', *Personnel Journal*, December, pp. 84–95.

82 G. Stasser & W. Titus, 1987, 'Effects of information load and percentage of shared information on the dissemination of unshared information during group discussion', *Journal of Personality and Social Psychology*, 53, pp. 81–93; also see J. Sullivan, 2004, 'How many turkeys do you hire?', *Human Resources*, 25 February, pp. 22–3.

83 T. Libby, 1986, 'Surviving the group interview', *Forbes*, 24 March, p. 190; Dipboye, 1991, p. 210.

84 L. Di Milia, 2004, 'Australian management selection practices: Closing the gap between research findings and practice', *Asia Pacific Journal of Human Resources*, 42, pp. 214–28.

85 Hunter & Hunter, 1984.

86 Hunter & Hunter, 1984; R.R. Reilly & G.T. Chao, 1982, 'Validity and fairness of some alternative employee selection procedures', *Personnel Psychology*, 35, pp. 1–62.

87 F.A. Mael & B.E. Ashforth, 1995, 'Loyal from day one: biodata, organizational identification, and turnover among newcomers', *Personnel Psychology*, 48, pp. 309–33.

88 T.W. Dougherty, D.B. Turban & J.C. Callender, 1994, 'Confirming first impressions in the employment interview: a field study of interviewer behavior', *Journal of Applied Psychology*, 79, pp. 659–65.

89 D. Hovenden, 2004, 'Uncovering articulate incompetents', *Human Resources*, 11 February, pp. 12–13.

90 P. Yelland, 1999, 'The writing's on the wall', *The Sydney Morning Herald*, 23 November, p. 6.

91 L. Bennington & R. Wein, 2002, 'Aiding and abetting employer discrimination: the job applicant's role', *Employee Responsibilities and Rights Journal*, 14 (1), pp. 3–16; A. Lam & B.H. Kleiner, 2001, 'Criminal background checks of prospective employees: why and how should it be done?', *Managerial Law*, 43 (1/2), pp. 132–7.

92 J.R. Hollenbeck, D.R. Ilgen & S.M. Crampton, 1992, 'Lower-back disability in occupational settings: a human resource management view', *Personnel Psychology*, 42, pp. 247–78.

93 J. Hogan, 1991, 'Structure of physical performance in occupational tasks', *Journal of Applied Psychology*, 76, pp. 495–507.

94 B.R. Blakely, M.A. Quinones, M.S. Crawford & I.A. Jago, 1994, 'The validity of isometric strength tests', *Personnel Psychology*, 47, pp. 247–74.

95 J. Hogan, 'Physical abilities', in M.D. Dunnette & L.M. Hough (eds), 1991, *Handbook of Industrial and Organizational Psychology*, 2nd edn, Consulting Psychologists Press, Palo Alto, CA.

96 Nunnally, 1978.

97 M.J. Ree, J.A. Earles & M.S. Teachout, 1994, 'Predicting job performance: Not much more than g', *Journal of Applied Psychology*, 79, pp. 518–24.

98 L.S. Gottfredson, 1986, 'The g factor in employment', *Journal of Vocational Behavior*, 29, pp. 293–6; Hunter & Hunter, 1984; Gutenberg, Arvey, Osburn & Jeanneret, 1983; Schmidt, Berner & Hunter, 1974.

99 M.R. Barrick & M.K. Mount, 1991, 'The big five personality dimensions and job performance: a meta-analysis', *Personnel Psychology*, 44, pp. 1–26; L.M. Hough, N.K. Eaton, M.D. Dunnette, J.D. Camp & R.A. McCloy, 1990, 'Criterion-related validities of personality constructs and the effect of response distortion on test validities', *Journal of Applied Psychology*, 75, pp. 467–76.

100 W.S. Dunn, M.K. Mount, M.R. Barrick & D.S. Ones, 1995, 'Relative importance of personality and general mental ability on managers' judgments of applicant qualifications', *Journal of Applied Psychology*, 80, pp. 500–509; O. Behling, 1998, 'Employee selection: will intelligence and conscientiousness do the job?', *Academy of Management Executive*, 12 (1), pp. 77–86.

101 L. Smith, 1994, 'Stamina: who has it, why you need it and how you get it', *Fortune*, 28 November.

102 P.M. Wright, K.M. Kacmar, G.C. McMahan & K. Deleeuw, 1995, 'P = f(M x A): cognitive ability as a moderator of the relationship between personality and job performance', *Journal of Management*, 21, pp. 1129–39.

103 Schmidt & Hunter, 1998, cited in S.L. Rynes, K.G. Brown & A.E. Colbert, 2002, 'Seven common misconceptions about human resource practices: research findings versus practitioner beliefs', *Academy of Management Executive*, 16 (9), pp. 92–103.

104 J.F. Salgado, 2003, 'Predicting job performance using FFM and non-FFM personality measures', *Journal of Occupational and Organizational Psychology*, 76, pp. 323–46.

105 M.K. Mount, M.R. Barrick & J.P. Strauss, 1994, 'Validity of observer ratings of the big five personality factors', *Journal of Applied Psychology*, 79, pp. 272–80.

106 M.R. Barrick, G.L. Stewart, M.J. Neubert & M.K. Mount, 1998, 'Relating member ability and personality to work team processes and team effectiveness', *Journal of Applied Psychology*, 83, pp. 377–91; J.L. LePine, J.R. Hollenbeck, D.R. Ilgen & J. Hedlund, 1997, 'Effects of individual differences on the performance of hierarchical decision making teams: Much more than g', *Journal of Applied Psychology*, 82, pp. 803–11.

107 Mount, Barrick & Strauss, 1994.

108 J.G. Rosse, M.D. Stecher, J.L. Miller & R.A. Levin, 1998, 'The impact of response distortion on pre-employment personality testing and hiring decisions', *Journal of Applied Psychology*, 83, pp. 634–44.

109 P. Yelland, 2001, 'Testing times ahead for online job-seekers', *The Sydney Morning Herald*, 7 October, p. 4.

110 P. Yelland, 2001.

111 P.F. Wernimont & J.P. Campbell, 1968, 'Signs, samples and criteria', *Journal of Applied Psychology*, 46, pp. 417–19.

112 Hunter & Hunter, 1984; W. Cascio & N. Phillips, 1979, 'Performance testing: A rose among thorns?', *Journal of Applied*

Psychology, 32, pp. 751–66; F.L. Schmidt, A. Greenthol, J.E. Hunter, J. Berner & F. Seaton, 1977, 'Job sample vs. paper-and-pencil trade and technical tests: adverse impact and examiner attitudes', *Personnel Psychology*, 30, pp. 187–97.
113   Hunter & Hunter, 1984.
114   F.L. Schmidt & J.E. Hunter, 1998, 'The validity and utility of selection methods in personnel psychology: Practical and theoretical implications of 85 years of research findings', *Psychological Bulletin*, 124, pp. 262–74.
115   D.S. Ones, C. Viswesvaran & F.L. Schmidt, 1993, 'Comprehensive meta-analysis of integrity test validities: Findings and implications for personnel selection and theories of job performance', *Journal of Applied Psychology*, 78, pp. 679–703.
116   H.J. Bernardin & D.K. Cooke, 1993, 'Validity of an honesty test in predicting theft among convenience store employees', *Academy of Management Journal*, 36, pp. 1097–1106.
117   D.S. Ones & C. Viswesvaran, 1998, 'Gender, age, and race differences on overt integrity tests: results across four large-scale job applicant data sets', *Journal of Applied Psychology*, 83, pp. 35–42.
118   M.R. Cunningham, D.T. Wong & A.P. Barbee, 1994, 'Self-presentation dynamics on overt integrity tests: experimental studies of the Reid report', *Journal of Applied Psychology*, 79, pp. 643–58.
119   M. Freudenheim, 1988, 'Workers' substance abuse increasing, survey says', *The New York Times*, 13 December, p. 2; J.P. Guthrie & J.D. Olian, 1989, 'Drug and alcohol testing programs: the influence of organizational context and objectives', paper presented at the Fourth Annual Conference of the Society for Industrial/Organizational Psychology, Boston.
120   P. Holland, A. Pyman & J. Teicher, 2005, 'Negotiating the contested terrain of drug testing in the Australian workplace', *Journal of Industrial Relations*, 47, pp. 326–38.
121   K.R. Murphy, G.C. Thornton & D.H. Reynolds, 1990, 'College students' attitudes toward drug testing programs', *Personnel Psychology*, 43, pp. 615–31.
122   [Anonymous] 2004, 'HR drags ageing workforce chain', *Human Resources*, 25 February, pp. 1, 9.
123   [Anonymous] 2004, 'HR drags ageing workforce chain', *Human Resources*, 25 February, pp. 1, 9.

CHAPTER 9 NOTES
1   B. Schneider & J. Rentsch, 'Managing climates and cultures: a futures perspective', in J. Hage (ed), 1988, *Futures of Organizations*, Lexington Press, Lexington, MA, pp. 181–203; S.E. Jackson, 'Stepping into the future: guidelines for action', in S. Jackson and Associates (eds), 1992, *Diversity in the Workplace: Human Resource Initiatives*, Guilford Press, New York, pp. 13–36.
2   E.E. Kossek & S.A. Lobel, 'Introduction: transforming human resource systems to manage diversity—an introduction and orienting framework', in E.E. Kossek & S.A. Lobel (eds), 1996, *Managing Diversity: Human Resource Strategies for Transforming the Workplace*, Blackwell, Cambridge, MA, pp. 1–20; R.M. Kanter, 1993, *Men and Women of the Corporation*, Harper, New York.
3   M. Loden & J.B. Rosener, 1991, *Workforce America! Managing Employee Diversity as a Vital Resource*, Business One Irwin, Homewood, IL; S.E. Jackson, K. May & K. Whitney, 'Diversity in decision making teams', in R.A. Guo & E. Salas (eds), 1995, *Team Decision Making Effectiveness in Organizations*, Jossey-Bass, San Francisco, pp. 204–61.
4   J.A. Gilbert, B.A. Stead & J.M. Ivancevich, 1999, 'Diversity management: a new organizational paradigm', *Journal of Business Ethics*, August, pp. 61–76.
5   S. Nkomo & T. Cox, 'Diverse identities in organisations', in S.R. Clegg, C. Hardy & W.R. Nord (eds), 1999, *Managing Organizations: Current Issues*, Sage Publications, London, pp. 88–106.
6   R.R. Thomas Jr. 1991, *Beyond Race and Gender: Unleashing the Power of your Total Workforce*, Amacon, New York.
7   International Labour Office (ILO), 1987, *Equal Opportunity: Trends and Perspectives*, Women at Work series, no. 2, International Labour Office, Geneva.

8   Loden & Rosener, 1991; Jackson, May & Whitney, in R.A. Guo & E.Salas (eds), 1995.
9   C. Chen, 1992, 'The diversity paradox', *Personnel Journal*, January, pp. 32–5.
10   A. Price, 1997, *Human Resource Management in a Business Context*, International Thomson Business Press, London.
11   F. Krautil, 'Managing diversity in Esso Australia', in E.M. Davis & C. Harris (eds), 1995, *Making the Link*, no. 6, Affirmative Action Agency and the Labour Management Studies Foundation, Sydney, pp. 22–8.
12   Public Service Merit Protection Commission. 1997, 'Towards a more diverse workforce in APS', *The Public Service Commissioner's Annual Report 1996–7 on Equal Employment Opportunity*, Australian Government Publishing Service, Canberra.
13   Public Service Merit Protection Commission, 1997.
14   Australian Human Resources Institute (AHRI), 2002, *Report Card: AHRI's Workforce Diversity Survey 2001*.
15   J. Bourke, 2006, 'Moving Ahead on Diversity and Equality: Results from the 2005 Australasian Diversity and Equity Survey', *Making the Link*, 17, (eds) E.M. Davis & V. Pratt, CCH Australia Ltd, pp. 52–5.
16   Bourke, 2006.
17   U. Drewniak, 2004, 'Inside age diversity at Deutsche Bank', *Human Resources*, 5 May, p. 12. Reproduced by permission of *Human Resources* magazine, (www.humanresourcesmagazine.com.au), Australia's leading fortnightly publication dedicated to the HR profession.
18   Loden & Rosener, 1991; Thomas Jr, 1991; M. Loden & R.H. Loeser, 1991, 'Working diversity: managing the difference', *The Bureaucrat*, Spring, pp. 21–5.
19   Australian Bureau of Statistics, *Population Projections*, Catalogue No. 3220.0, p. 2.
20   Loden & Rosener, 1991; Thomas Jr, 1991.
21   American Association of Retired Persons (AARP), 1995, *The Aging Workforce: Managing an Aging Workforce*, AARP, Washington, DC.
22   Thomas Jr, 1991; J.O. Rodgers, 1993, *Implementing a Diversity Strategy*, Limra's Market Facts, May–June.
23   R. Kramar, 2000, *Cranfield-PricewaterhouseCoopers Survey on International Strategic Human Resource Management*, Macquarie University, North Ryde, New South Wales, p. 12; 2000, 'Growing concern as global economy takes more jobs overseas', *Human Resources*, 1 (3), pp. 1–2; 1999, 'War for talented workers hots up', *HRMonthly*, October, pp. 30–1.
24   H. Vines, 1999, 'Diversity differences at work', *HRMonthly*, May, pp. 23–6; 2000, 'Growing concern as global economy takes more jobs overseas'; 1999, 'War for talented workers hots up'.
25   M. Patrickson, 'Introduction to diversity', in M. Patrickson & P. O'Brien (eds), 2002, *Managing Diversity: An Asian and Pacific Focus*, John Wiley & Sons, Milton, pp. 1–20.
26   Loden & Rosener, 1991; Thomas Jr, 1991.
27   C. Rance, 2003, 'Managing a global workforce', *HRMonthly*, August, pp. 34–6. *HRMonthly* is published for the Australian Human Resources Institute, www.ahri.com.au.
28   Industry Task Force on Leadership and Management Skills, 1995, *Enterprising Nation*, Australian Government Publishing Service, Canberra.
29   C. Burton, 'Managing for diversity: report to Karpin', in Davis & Harris (eds), 1995, pp. 66–71.
30   Edith Cowan University, 1996, 'Effective organisations: gender issues in management', curriculum materials for *Enterprising Nation*, Australian Government Publishing Service, Canberra.
31   2006, *EOWA Australian Census of Women in Leadership*, EOWA, Sydney.
32   S. Lambert et al., 1993, *Added Benefits*, University of Chicago, Chicago.
33   T.H. Cox & S. Blake, 1991,'Managing cultural diversity: implications for organizational competitiveness', *Academy of Management Executive*, 5 (3), pp. 45–56.
34   Australian Bureau of Statistics (ABS), 1991, *Projections of the Populations of Australia, States and Territories, Series D Projections*,

catalogue no. 3220.0, Australian Government Publishing Service, Canberra.
35 J. Storey, 1992, *Developments in the Management of Human Resources*, Blackwell, Oxford.
36 R. Kramar, 1997, 'Developing and implementing work and family policies: the implications for human resource policies', *Asia Pacific Journal of Human Resources*, 35 (3), pp. 1–19; R. Squirchuk & J. Bourke, 'Gender equity: from equal opportunity in employment to family-friendly policies and beyond', in L. Haas, P. Hwang & G. Russell (eds), 1999, *Organizational Change and Gender Equity: International Perspectives on Parents at the Workplace*, Sage, Thousand Oaks, CA, pp. 117–32.
37 G. Russell & L. Bowman, 2000, *Work and Family: Current Thinking, Research and Practice*, Commonwealth of Australia, Canberra, p. 33.
38 Westpac, 2002, *First Social Impact Report*, Westpac Banking Corporation, p. 8.
39 Thomas Jr, 1991.
40 P. Saul, 1996, 'Managing the organization as a community of contributors', *Asia Pacific Journal of Human Resources*, 34 (3), pp. 19–36.
41 Work and Family Unit, 2001, *ACCI National Work and Family Awards 2001*, Commonwealth of Australia, Canberra, p. 14.
42 Krautil, in Davis & Harris (eds), 1995.
43 K. Spearritt & J. Teicher, 1995, 'From equal employment opportunity to diversity: Australia's response to workforce diversity', working paper no. 38, National Key Centre in Industrial Relations, Monash University, Melbourne.
44 P. Hall, 1996, *Affirmative Action and Managing Diversity*, monograph no. 5, Australian Government Publishing Service, Canberra.
45 J. Gillespie, 1995, 'How to be heard by business—a customer centred and cost benefit approach to diversity policies', *Recruiting, Developing and Retaining the Corporate Woman*, IBC Conference, Sydney 30–31 October.
46 J. Gillespie, 'Profiting from diversity: the Westpac experience', in G. O'Neill & R. Kramar (eds), 1999, *Australian Human Resources Management*, Business and Professional Publishing, Warriewood, New South Wales.
47 R. Kramar, 2004, 'Does Australia Really Have Diversity Management', in *Making the Link*, 15, eds E.M. Davis & V. Pratt (eds), CCH Australia Ltd. N. Purcell, 2003, 'An ageless workforce—opportunities for business', An Ageless Workforce—Opportunities for Business Symposium, 27 August. I. Atlas, 2003, 'Australia's changing workforce—challenges and opportunities: employers perspective—Westpac', Executive Breakfast, Department of Employment and Workplace Relations, 1 October.
48 Krautil, in Davis & Harris (eds), 1995.
49 Work and Family Unit, 2001, pp. 22–3.
50 P. Migliorino, G. Miltenyi & H. Robertson, 1994, *Best Practice in Managing a Culturally Diverse Workplace—A Manager's Manual*, Australian Government Publishing Service, Canberra.
51 Migliorino, Miltenyi & Robertson, 1994, p. 81.
52 P. Galagan, 1993, 'Leading diversity', *Training and Development Journal*, April.
53 S. Overell, 1996, 'IPD says diversity is next step for equality', *People Management*, 2 (24), December, pp. 12–13.
54 Regulatory Review of the Affirmative Action (Equal Employment Opportunity for Women) Act 1986, 1998, *Unfinished Business*, Australian Government Publishing Service, Canberra.
55 D.A. Thomas & R.J. Ely, 1996, 'Making difference matter: a new paradigm for managing diversity', *Harvard Business Review*, September–October, pp. 79–90.
56 Kossek & Lobel, 1996.
57 Kossek & Lobel, 1996.
58 D. Sousa, 1996, 'Beyond affirmative action: the perils of managing diversity', *Chief Executive*, 119, December, pp. 42–8; D. Sousa, 1997, 'The diversity trap', *Forbes*, 159 (2), 27 January, p. 83;

Equal Opportunities Review, 1996, 'Proportion of women directors doubles', *EOR*, 65, January–February, pp. 5–6; J. Gordon, 1995, 'Different from what?: diversity as a performance issue', *Training*, 32 (5), May, pp. 25–34; W. Beaver, 1995, 'Let's stop diversity training and start managing for diversity', *Industrial Management*, 37 (4), July–August, pp. 7–9.
59 Beaver, 1995.
60 Beaver, 1995.
61 Kanter, 1993; J. Pfeffer, 'Organizational demography', in L.L. Cummings & B.M. Staw (eds), 1983, *Research in Organizational Behavior*, vol 5, JAI Press, Greenwich CT, pp. 299–357.
62 D. Sousa, 1996.
63 Thomas Jr, 1991.
64 A. Morrison, M. Ruddeman & M. Hughes-James, 1993, *Making Diversity Happen: Controversies and Solutions*, Center for Creative Leadership, Greensborough, NC.
65 T. Cox, 1993, *Cultural Diversity in Organizations: Theory, Research and Practice*, Berrett-Koehler, San Francisco.
66 Kossek & Lobel, 1996.
67 R. Kramar, 'Managing diversity', in G. O'Neill & R. Kramar (eds), 1999, *Australian Human Resources Management*, vol. 2, Woodslane, Warriewood, New South Wales, pp. 193–206; R. Kramar, 'Equal employment opportunities', in M. Warner et al. (eds), 1996, *International Encyclopaedia of Business and Management*, Routledge, London, pp. 1269–77.
68 H. MacDonald, 1993, 'The diversity industry', *The New Republic*, 5, July, pp. 22–5.
69 M.V. Hermon, 1996, 'Building a shared understanding and commitment to managing diversity', *Journal of Business Communication*, 33 (4), October, pp. 427–42.
70 A. Morrison, 1992, *The New Leader's Guidelines on Leadership Diversity in America*, Jossey-Bass, San Francisco.
71 Hermon, 1996, p. 436.
72 Cox, 1993.
73 P.L. McLeod & S.A. Lobel, 1992, 'The effects of ethnic diversity on idea generation in small groups', *Academy of Best Management Paper Proceedings*, pp. 227–31; W.E. Watson, K. Kumar & L.K. Michaelson, 1993, 'Cultural diversity's impact on interaction process and performance: comparing homogeneous and diverse task groups', *Academy of Management Journal*, 36, pp. 590–602.
74 C.J. Nemeth & J. Wachter, 1983, 'Creative problem solving as a result of majority versus minority influence', *European Journal of Social Psychology*, 13, pp. 45–55; T. Cox & C. Smolinski, 1994, *Managing Diversity and Glass Ceiling Initiatives as National Economic Imperatives*, research report prepared for the Glass Ceiling Commission, United States Department of Labor, Washington, DC.
75 Cox, 1993; P. Wright, S. Ferris, J. Hiller & M. Kroll, 1995, 'Competitiveness through management diversity: effects on stock price valuation', *Academy of Management Journal*, 38 (1), pp. 272–87.
76 J. Stevens, 1995, 'Weighing up the evidence on managing diversity', *Personnel Management*, 1 (13), 29 June, p. 61.
77 Kossek & Lobel, 1996.
78 Kramar, 'Equal employment opportunities', in Warner et al. (eds), 1996.
79 G. Robinson & K. Dechant, 1997, 'Building a business case for diversity', *Academy of Management Executive*, 11 (3), August, pp. 21–31.
80 Kramar, 1997.
81 C.A. O'Reilly, D.F. Caldwell & W.P. Barnett, 1989, 'Work group demography, social integration, and turnover', *Administrative Science Quarterly*, 34, pp. 21–37.
82 S.E. Jackson, J.F. Brett, V.I. Sessa, D.M. Cooper, J.A. Julin & K. Peyronnin, 1991, 'Some differences make a difference: individual dissimilarity and group heterogeneity as correlates of recruitment, promotions and turnover', *Journal of Applied Psychology*, 76, pp. 675–89; G.W. Wagner, J. Pfeffer & C.A. O'Reilly, 1984, 'Organisational demography and turnover in top management groups', *Administrative Science Quarterly*, 29, pp. 74–92; F.J. Milliken & L.L. Martins,

Endnotes

1996,'Searching for common threads: understanding the multiple effects of diversity in organizational groups', *Academy of Management Review*, 21 (2), pp. 402–33.
83   A.S. Tsui, T.D. Egan & C.A. O'Reilly, 1992, 'Being different: relational demography and organisational attachment', *Administrative Science Quarterly*, 37, pp. 549–79.
84   Milliken & Martins, 1996; A.S. Tsui & C.A. O'Reilly, 1989, 'Beyond simple demographic effects: the importance of relational demography and superior–subordinate dyads', *Academy of Management Journal*, 32, pp. 402–23.
85   O'Reilly, Caldwell & Barnett, 1989.
86   Kanter, 1993, p. 291; Spearritt & Teicher, 1995, p. 28.
87   C.M. Solomon, 1991, 'Are white males being left out?', *Personnel Journal*, November, pp. 88–94.
88   Kanter, 1993.
89   P. Galagan, 1993.
90   Thomas Jr, 1991.
91   L. Mulvena, 1999, 'Characteristics of organisations with family-friendly policies and practices', master of organisational psychology thesis, Macquarie University, cited in Russell & Bowman, 2000.
92   Haas, Hwang & Russell (eds), 1999.
93   Russell & Bowman, 2000.
94   Morehead et al., 1997, *Change at Work: The 1995 Australian Workplace Industrial Relations Survey (AWIRS 95)*, Longman, South Melbourne, pp. 288–90.
95   P. Sheldrake & P. Saul, 'First line managers: a study of the changing role and skills of first line managers', in Industry Task Force on Leadership and Management Skills, 1995, *Industry Task Force on Leadership and Management Skills* (report also known as the Karpin Report), Australian Government Publishing Service, Canberra, pp. 665–712.
96   Australian Council of Trade Unions (ACTU), 1999, *Employment Security and Working Hours: A National Survey of Current Workplace Issues*, Australian Council of Trade Unions, Canberra; Australian Bureau of Statistics, 1994, 1995–2011 Labour Force Projections: Australia, catalogue no. 6260.0, Australian Government Publishing Service, Canberra.
97   ACIRRT, 1999, *Australia at Work: Just Managing?*, Prentice-Hall, Sydney; Affirmative Action Agency, 1996, *Best Practice in Affirmative Action: Case Studies*, Australian Government Publishing Service, Canberra; ACTU, 1999; Australian Bureau of Statistics, 1994.
98   P. Reith, 1999, 'Delivering on work and family: the *Workplace Relations Act 1996*', *Australian Bulletin of Labour*, 25 (3).
99   C. Kilmartin, 1996, 'Are Australian workplaces family friendly?', *Family Matters*, 44, Winter, pp. 36–7.
100 A.A. Johnson, 1995, 'The business case for work-family programs', *Journal of Accountancy*, August, pp. 53–7.
101 A.A. Johnson, 1999, 'Strategic meal planning: work/life initiatives for building strong organizations', paper presented at the Conference on Integrated Health, Disability and Work/Life Initiatives, 25 February, New York.
102 Families and Work Institute, 1993, *An evaluation of Johnson and Johnson's Work–Family Initiative*, Families at Work Institute, New York, NY.
103 Kramar, 1997.
104 Work and Family Unit, 2001, pp. 6–7.
105 A. Horin, 2000, 'Going for the juggler', *The Sydney Morning Herald*, 24 June, p. 6S.
106 D. Edgar, 1999, 'The future of work and family', *Australian Bulletin of Labour*, 25 (3).
107 2004, 'Business slated over work/family', *Human Resources*, September, THC Press, Chatswood, pp. 1, 7.
108 Graeme Russell, 'Men: working through life, living through work', in E. Davis and V. Pratt (eds), 2003, *Making the Link*, no. 14, CCH Australia Ltd, Sydney, pp. 52–63.
109 Affirmative Action Agency, 1996.
110 Q. Bryce, 'Advocating quality child care', in E.M. Davis & V. Pratt (eds), 1997, *Making the Link*, no. 8, Macquarie University, Sydney, p. 25.
111 Australian Bureau of Statistics, 1994.
112 L.C. Hartmann, 'The impact of trends in labour-force participation in Australia', in M. Patrickson & L.C. Hartmann (eds), 1998, *Managing an Ageing Workforce*, Woodslane, Warriewood, New South Wales, pp. 3–25.
113 R. Kramar, 'Managing diversity', in Patrickson & Hartmann (eds), 1998, pp. 121–35.
114 Vines, 1999, p. 25.
115 H. MacKay, 1997, *Generations: Baby Boomers, their Parents and their Children*, Macmillan, Sydney.
116 C. Gill, 2000, 'Talent wins', *HRMonthly*, April, pp. 34–5.
117 J. Pfeffer, 1998, *The Human Equation*, Harvard Business School Press, Boston, pp. 64–98.
118 ACIRRT, 1999.
119 ACIRRT, 1999; Kramar, 'Managing diversity', in O'Neill & Kramar (eds), 1999, pp. 193–206; Kramar 'Equal employment opportunities', in M. Warner et al. (eds), 1996.
120 P. Saul, 1996, pp. 19–36.
121 ACIRRT, 1999.
122 D. Ulrich, M.R. Losey & G. Lake (eds), 1997, *Tomorrow's HR Management*, John Wiley and Sons, New York.
123 Wright, Ferris, Hiller & Kroll, 1995.
124 R. Kramar, 1996, *The Business Case for a Family Friendly Workplace*, NSW Department of Industrial Relations, Sydney; J. Gillespie, 'Profiting from diversity: the Westpac experience', in O'Neill *and* Kramar (eds), 1999, pp. 207–16.
125 Equal Opportunities Review, 1996.
126 Cox & Smolinski, 1994.
127 S. Youngblood & K. Chambers-Cook, 1984, 'Childcare assistance can improve employee attitudes and behavior', *Personnel Administrator*, February, pp. 93–5; I. Bruegal & D. Perrons, 'Where do the costs of unequal treatment fall? An analysis of the incidence of the costs of unequal pay and sex discrimination in the United Kingdom', in J. Humphries & J. Rubery (eds), 1995, *The Economics of Equal Opportunity*, Equal Opportunities Commission, Manchester, United Kingdom.

CHAPTER 10 NOTES

1   R. Kramar, 2006, *Cranet-Macquarie Survey on International Strategic Human Resource Management*, Macquarie University, North Ryde, New South Wales, p. 18.
2   C. Lee, 1996, 'Performance appraisal: can we manage away the curse?', *Training*, May, pp. 44–9.
3   J.A. Siegal, '86 Your Appraisal Process?' *HR Magazine*, October 2000, pp. 199–202.
4   H. Scotts, 'Planning and managing employee performance', in G. O'Neill and R. Kramar, (eds) 1999, *Australian Human Resources Management*, vol. 2, Woodslane Pty Ltd, Warriewood, New South Wales, pp. 56–7.
5   R. Wainwright, 2001, 'Crash verdict: Qantas to blame', *The Sydney Morning Herald*, 25 April, p. 1.
6   W. Cascio, 1996, 'Managing for maximum performance', *HRMonthly*, September, pp. 10–13.
7   Scotts, in O'Neill and Kramar, 1999, pp. 54–5.
8   K. Murphy and J. Cleveland, 1991, *Performance Appraisal: An Organizational Perspective*, Allyn and Bacon, Boston.
9   J.E. Hunter, J.L. Schmidt and M.K. Judiesch, 1990, 'Individual differences in output variability as a function of job complexity', *Journal of Applied Psychology*, vol 75, no 1, pp. 28–42.
10   C. Wallace & J. Hetherington, 2003, *The Complete Guide to Call and Contact Centre Management*, Penguin Group Australia Ltd, Melbourne, pp. 156–9.
11   Scotts, in O'Neill and Kramar, 1999, pp. 48–60
12   F. Simons, 2000, 'Can we talk?', *Australian Financial Review, Boss*, 10 April, p. 50

13   Unpublished Cranet-e data, 2000, European Centre for Human Resource Management, Cranfield, United Kingdom.
14   A. Nankervis & P. Leece, 1997, 'Performance appraisal: two steps forward, one step back?', *Asia Pacific Journal of Human Resources*, 35 (2), pp. 80–92; Kramar, 2000.
15   Commerce Clearing House, 1985, *Performance Appraisal: What Three Companies Are Doing*, Commerce Clearing House, Chicago
16   J. Cleveland, K. Murphy & R. Williams, 1989, 'Multiple uses of performance appraisal: prevalence and correlates', *Journal of Applied Psychology*, 74, pp. 130–5
17   F. Donhoe and G. Southey, 1996, 'Design strategy for a manager's performance management process in QIDC', *Asia Pacific Journal of Human Resources*, 34 (2), pp. 99–109
18   Anonymous, 2006, 'Coaching needing supervision', *Human Resources* Magazine, p. 1.
19   M. Beer, 'Note on performance appraisal', in M. Beer & B. Spector (eds), 1985, *Readings in Human Resource Management*, Free Press, New York.
20   J. Milliman, S. Nason, C. Zhu & H. de Cieri, 2002, 'An exploratory assessment of the purposes of performance appraisals in North and Central America and the Pacific Rim', *Asia Pacific Journal of Human Resources*, vol 40, no. 1, pp. 108, 112–15.
21   Milliman et al, 2002; C. Zhu & P. Dowling, 2000, 'Managing people during economic transition: the development of HR practices in China', *Asia Pacific Journal of Human Resources*, vol 38, no 2, pp. 90–93.
22   Beer, in Beer & Spector (eds), 1985; Kramar, 2000; Nankervis & Leece, 1997.
23   Unpublished Cranet-e data, 2000.
24   L. Gettler, 1999, 'Appraisal seldom pays: research', *The Age*, 14 October, p. 5.
25   C. Longenecker, 1987, 'Behind the mask: the politics of employee appraisal', *Academy of Management Executive*, 1, p. 183.
26   J. Milliman et al., 2002, pp. 108–9, 112–15.
27   C. Zhu & P. Dowling, 2000, pp. 93–5.
28   M. Beer, 1981, 'Performance appraisal: dilemmas and possibilities', *Organizational Dynamics*, Winter, p. 27.
29   R.S. Schuler, 1981, 'Taking the pain out of the performance appraisal interview', *Supervisory Management*, August, pp. 8–13.
30   A. Wherrett, 2003, 'Measuring leadership behaviour: the role of HR', *Human Resources*, June, p. 8. Reproduced by permission of *Human Resources* magazine, (www.humanresourcesmagazine.com.au), Australia's leading fortnightly publication dedicated to the HR profession.
31   C.E. Schneier, D.G. Shaw & R.W. Beatty, 1991, 'Performance measurement and management: a tool for strategic execution', *Human Resource Management*, 30, pp. 279–301.
32   E. Sexton, 1997, 'BHP: new yardsticks to gee up employees', *The Sydney Morning Herald*, 9 June, p. 39.
33   R.S. Kaplan & D.P. Norton, 1996, 'Using the balanced scorecard as a strategic management system', *Harvard Business Review*, January–February, pp. 75–85.
34   C. Birch, 1998, 'Balanced scorecard points to wins for small firms', *Australian CPA*, 68 (6), July, pp. 43–5.
35   R. Schuler & S. Jackson, 1987, 'Linking competitive strategies with human resource practices', *Academy of Management Executive*, 1, pp. 207–19.
36   L. King, J. Hunter & F. Schmidt, 1980, 'Halo in a multidimensional forced-choice performance evaluation scale', *Journal of Applied Psychology*, 65, pp. 507–16.
37   B.R. Nathan, A.M. Mohrman & J. Milliman, 1991, 'Interpersonal relations as a context for the effects of appraisal interviews on performance and satisfaction: a longitudinal study', *Academy of Management Journal*, 34, pp. 352–69; M.S. Taylor, K.B. Tracy, M.K. Renard, J.K. Harrison & S.J. Carroll, 1995, 'Due process in performance appraisal: a quasi-experiment in procedural justice', *Administrative Science Quarterly*, 40, pp. 495–523; J.M. Werner & M.C. Bolino, 1997, 'Explaining U.S. Courts of Appeals' decisions involving performance appraisal: accuracy, fairness, and validation', *Personnel Psychology*, 50, pp. 1–24.
38   L. Parker, 2003, 'Performance anxiety', *HRMonthly*, December, pp. 21–2.
39   E. Davis, 1999, 'Overcoming obstacles to good performance management', *HRMonthly*, February, pp. 15–16.
40   Albermarle Paper Company versus Moody, 1975, 10 FEP 1181.
41   F. Blanz & E. Ghiselli, 1973, 'The mixed standard scale: a new rating system', *Personnel Psychology*, 25, pp. 185–99; K. Murphy & J. Constans, 1987, 'Behavioral anchors as a source of bias in rating', *Journal of Applied Psychology*, 72, pp. 573–7.
42   P. Smith & L. Kendall, 1963, 'Retranslation of expectations: an approach to the construction of unambiguous anchors for rating scales', *Journal of Applied Psychology*, 47, pp. 149–55.
43   Murphy & Constans, 1987; M. Piotrowski, J. Barnes-Farrel & F. Esrig, 1989, 'Behaviorally anchored bias: a replication and extension of Murphy and Constans', *Journal of Applied Psychology*, 74, pp. 823–6.
44   U. Wiersma & G. Latham, 1986, 'The practicality of behavioral observation scales, behavioral expectation scales, and trait scales', *Personnel Psychology*, 39, pp. 619–28.
45   G. Latham & K. Wexley, 1981, *Increased Productivity Through Performance Appraisal*, Addison-Wesley, Boston.
46   Wiersma & Latham, 1986.
47   D.C. Anderson, C. Crowell, J. Sucec, K. Gilligan & M. Wikoff, 1983, 'Behavior management of client contacts in a real estate brokerage: getting agents to sell more', *Journal of Organizational Behavior Management*, 4, pp. 67–96.
48   D.C. Anderson, C. Crowell, S. Sponsel, M. Clarke & J. Spence, 1983, 'Behavior management in the public accommodations industry: a three-project demonstration', *Journal of Organizational Behavior Management*, 4, pp. 33–65.
49   J. Komaki, R. Collins & P. Penn, 1982, 'The role of performance antecedents and consequences in work motivation', *Journal of Applied Psychology*, 67, pp. 334–40.
50   Latham & Wexley, 1981.
51   R. Reilly, S. Henry & J.W. Smither, 'An examination of the effects of using behavior checklists on the construct validity of assessment centre dimensions', *Personnel Psychology*, 43, pp. 71–84.
52   H.J. Bernardin & J.E.A. Russell, 1998, *Human Resource Management*, Irwin McGraw-Hill, Boston, p. 152.
53   Bernardin & Russell, 1998, p. 154.
54   S. Snell, 1992, 'Control theory in strategic human resource management: the mediating effect of administrative information', *Academy of Management Journal*, 35, pp. 292–327.
55   T. Patten Jr, 1982, *A Manager's Guide to Performance Appraisal*, Free Press, New York.
56   Scotts, in O'Neill & Kramar, 1999, pp. 43–61; M. O'Donnell & R. O'Donnell, 1983, 'MBO—is it passe?', *Hospital and Health Services Administration*, 28 (5), pp. 46–58; T. Poister & G. Streib, 1989, 'Management tools in government: trends over the past decade', *Public Administration Review*, 49, pp. 240–8.
57   D. McGregor, 1957, 'An uneasy look at performance appraisal', *Harvard Business Review*, 35 (3), pp. 89–94.
58   E. Locke & G. Latham, 1990, *A Theory of Goal Setting and Task Performance*, Prentice-Hall, Englewood Cliffs, NJ.
59   S. Carroll & H. Tosi, 1973, *Management by Objectives*, Macmillan, New York.
60   G. Odiorne, 1986, *MBO II: A System of Managerial Leadership for the 80s*, Pitman, Belmont, CA.
61   R. Rodgers & J. Hunter, 1991, 'Impact of management by objectives on organizational productivity', *Journal of Applied Psychology*, 76, pp. 322–6.
62   K. Helliker, 1995, 'Pressure at Pier 1: beating sales numbers of year earlier is a storewide obsession', *The Wall Street Journal*, 7 December, pp. B1, B2.
63   R. Pritchard, S. Jones, P. Roth, K. Stuebing & S. Ekeberg, 1989, 'The evaluation of an integrated approach to measuring organizational productivity', *Personnel Psychology*, 42, pp. 69–115.
64   E. Pritchard et al., 1989.

Endnotes

65 P. Wright, J. George, S. Farnsworth & G. McMahan, 1993, 'Productivity and extra-role behavior: the effects of goals and incentives on spontaneous helping', *Journal of Applied Psychology*, 78 (3), pp. 374–81.
66 Latham & Wexley, 1981.
67 Gary P. Latham, J. Almost, S. Mann & C. Moore, 2005, 'New Developments in Performance Management', *Organizational Dynamics*, vol 34, No. 1, pp. 77–87.
68 R.L. Cardy, 'Performance appraisal in a quality context: a new look at an old problem', in J.W. Smither (ed), 1998, *Performance Appraisal: State of the Art in Practice*, Jossey-Bass, San Francisco, pp. 132–62.
69 E.C. Huge, 1990, *Total Quality: An Executive's Guide for the 1990s*, Richard D. Irwin, Homewood, IL (see Chapter 5, 'Measuring and rewarding performance', pp. 70–88); W.E. Deming, 1986, *Out of Crisis*, MIT Center for Advanced Engineering Study, Cambridge, MA.
70 M. Caroselli, 1991, *Total Quality Transformations*, Human Resource Development Press, Amherst, MA; Huge, 1990.
71 J.D. Cryer & R.B. Miller, 1991, *Statistics for Business: Data Analysis and Modeling*, PWS-Kent, Boston; C. Carter, 1992, 'Seven basic quality tools', *HR Magazine*, January, pp. 81–3; D.K. Denton, 1995, 'Process mapping trims cycle time', *HR Magazine*, February, pp. 56–61.
72 D.E. Bowen & E.E. Lawler III, 1992, 'Total quality-oriented human resource management', *Organizational Dynamics*, 21, pp. 29–41.
73 R. Kramar, P. McGraw & R. Schuler, 1997, *Human Resource Management in Australia*, Addison-Wesley Longman, Sydney, p. 379.
74 Scotts, in O'Neill & Kramar, 1999, p. 46.
75 J. Hunt & J. Wallace, 1997, 'A competency-based approach to assessing managerial performance in the Australian context', *Asia Pacific Journal of Human Resources*, 35 (2), pp. 52–4.
76 A. Gonczi, P. Hager & I. Oliver, 1990, 'Establishing competency-based standards in the professions', *Research Paper No. 8*, AGPS, Canberra.
77 Scotts, in O'Neill & Kramar, 1999, p. 54.
78 V. Dulewicz & M. Higgs, 1999, *Emotional Intelligence Questionnaire: User Guide*, NFER-Nelson, Windsor.
79 M. Freeman, 2000, 'Putting the bite into feedback', *HRMonthly*, June, pp. 42–3.
80 L.M. Spencer & S.M. Spencer, 1993, *Competence at Work: Models for Superior Performance*, John Wiley and Sons, New York, p. 266.
81 Kramar, 2006, p. 18; Nankervis & Leece, 1997, p. 88; CCH Australia Ltd, 1995, *Australian and New Zealand Human Resources Management*, CCH Australia, North Ryde, New South Wales.
82 R. Heneman, K. Wexley & M. Moore, 1987, 'Performance rating accuracy: a critical review', *Journal of Business Research*, 15, pp. 431–48.
83 T. Becker & R. Klimoski, 1989, 'A field study of the relationship between the organizational feedback environment and performance', *Personnel Psychology*, 42, pp. 343–58.
84 L. Axline, 1991, 'Performance biased evaluations', *Supervisory Management*, November, p. 3.
85 K. Wexley & R. Klimoski, 'Performance appraisal: an update', in K. Rowland & G. Ferris (eds), 1984, *Research in Personnel and Human Resource Management*, vol. 2, JAI Press, Greenwich, CT.
86 C.A. Norman & R. Zawacki, 1991, 'Team appraisals—team approach', *Personnel Journal*, 70, pp. 101–4.
87 F. Landy & J. Farr, 1983, *The Measurement of Work Performance: Methods, Theory, and Applications*, Academic Press, New York.
88 G. McEvoy & P. Buller, 1987, 'User acceptance of peer appraisals in an industrial setting', *Personnel Psychology*, 40, pp. 785–97.
89 D. Antonioni, 1994, 'The effects of feedback accountability on upward appraisal ratings', *Personnel Psychology*, 47, pp. 349–56.
90 Murphy & Cleveland, 1991.
91 J. Bernardin & L. Klatt, 1985, 'Managerial appraisal systems: has practice caught up with the state of the art?', *Public Personnel Administrator*, November, pp. 79–86.
92 R. Steel & N. Ovalle,, 1984 'Self-appraisal based on supervisor feedback', *Personnel Psychology*, 37, pp. 667–85; L.E. Atwater, 'The advantages and pitfalls of self-assessment in organizations', in Smither (ed), 1998, pp. 331–65.
93 Bureau of Labor Statistics, 1997, *Employment and Earnings*, United States Department of Labor, Washington, DC.
94 E. Gummerson, 1987, 'Lip services—a neglected area of service marketing', *Journal of Services Marketing*, 1, pp. 1–29.
95 H.J. Bernardin, C.M. Hagan, J.S. Kane & P. Villanova, 'Effective performance management: a focus on precision, customers, and situational constraints', in Smither (ed), 1998, pp. 3–48.
96 R. Hoffman, 1995, 'Ten reasons you should be using 360-degree feedback', *HR Magazine*, April, pp. 82–4.
97 G.N. Mclean, 1996, '360-degree feedback: does it belong in the practitioner's toolkit?', paper presented at the 1996 American Society for Training and Development Conference and Exposition, June.
98 S. Sherman, 1995, 'How tomorrow's best leaders are learning their stuff', *Fortune*, 27 November, pp. 90–104; W.W. Tornow, M. London and Associates, 1998, *Maximizing the Value of 360-Degree Feedback*, Jossey-Bass, San Francisco; D.A. Waldman, L.E. Atwater & D. Antonioni, 1988, 'Has 360-degree feedback gone amok?', *Academy of Management Executive*, 12, pp. 86–94.
99 Kramar, 2006.
100 A. Tversky & D. Kahneman, 1973, 'Availability: a heuristic for judging frequency and probability', *Cognitive Psychology*, 5, pp. 207–32.
101 K. Wexley & W. Nemeroff, 1974, 'Effects of racial prejudice, race of applicants, and biographical similarity on interviewer evaluations of job applicants', *Journal of Social and Behavioral Sciences*, 20, pp. 66–78.
102 D. Smith, 1986, 'Training programs for performance appraisal: a review', *Academy of Management Review*, 11, pp. 22–40.
103 G. Latham, K. Wexley & E. Pursell, 1975, 'Training managers to minimize rating errors in the observation of behavior', *Journal of Applied Psychology*, 60, pp. 550–5.
104 J. Bernardin & E. Pence, 1980, 'Effects of rater training: creating new response sets and decreasing accuracy', *Journal of Applied Psychology*, 65, pp. 60–6.
105 E. Pulakos, 1984, 'A comparison of rater training programs: error training and accuracy training', *Journal of Applied Psychology*, 69, pp. 581–8.
106 W. Borman, 'Job behavior, performance, and effectiveness', in M.D. Dunnette & L.M. Hough (eds), 1991, *Handbook of Industrial and Organizational Psychology*, vol. 2, 2nd edn, Consulting Psychologists Press, Palo Alto, CA, pp. 271–326.
107 S.W.J. Kozlowski, G.T. Chao & R.F. Morrison, 'Games raters play: politics, strategies, and impression management in performance appraisal', in Smither (ed), 1998, pp. 163–205.
108 J. Hor, 2004, *Work alert*, Issue 2, 12 March, CCH Australia Ltd, North Ryde, p. 2. Reproduced with kind permission of CCH Australia Limited from Work Alert. For more information see www.cch.com.au.
109 K. Wexley, V. Singh & G. Yukl, 1973, 'Subordinate participation in three types of appraisal interviews', *Journal of Applied Psychology*, 58, pp. 54–7; K. Wexley, 'Appraisal interview', in R.A. Berk (ed), 1986, *Performance Assessment*, Johns Hopkins University Press, Baltimore, MD, pp. 167–85.
110 D. Cederblom, 1982, 'The performance appraisal interview: a review, implications, and suggestions', *Academy of Management Review*, 7, pp. 219–27; B.D. Cawley, L.M. Keeping & P.E. Levy, 1998, 'Participation in the performance appraisal process and employee reactions: a meta-analytic review of field investigations', *Journal of Applied Psychology*, 83 (3), pp. 615–63.
111 W. Giles & K. Mossholder, 1990, 'Employee reactions to contextual and session components of performance appraisal', *Journal of Applied Psychology*, 75, pp. 371–7.
112 P.S. Kirkbride & S.F. Y. Tang, 1989, 'Personnel management in Hong Kong: a review of current issues', *Asia Pacific Human Resource Management*, vol 27, no. 2, pp. 43–57; C. M. Vance, S.R. McClaine, D.M. Boje & H.D. Stage, 1992, 'An examination of the transferability of traditional performance appraisal principles across cultural boundaries', *Management International Review*, 32, pp. 312–26.
113 Locke & Latham, 1990.

114 H. Klein, S. Snell & K. Wexley, 1987, 'A systems model of the performance appraisal interview process', *Industrial Relations*, 26, pp. 267–80.
115 M. London & E.M. Mone, 'Managing marginal performance in organizations striving for excellence', in A.K. Korman (ed) 1993, *Human Resource Dilemmas in Work Organizations: Strategies for Resolution*, Guilford Press, New York, pp. 95–124.
116 W. Bennis & B. Nanus, 1985, *Leaders*, Harper and Row, New York.
117 W.G. Dyer, 1995, *Teambuilding: Current Issues and New Alternatives*, Addison-Wesley, Reading, MA.
118 R. Kramar, 'Discrimination and the development of personnel management', in G. Palmer (ed) 1988, *Australian Personnel Management: A Reader*, Macmillan, Melbourne, pp. 304–28.
119 J. Hor, 2004, *Work Alert*, issue 2, 12 March, CCH Australia Ltd, North Ryde, p 2.
120 S.E. Forrer & Z.B. Leibowitz, 1991, *Using Computers in Human Resources*, Jossey-Bass, San Francisco; G. Bylinsky, 1991, 'How companies spy on employees', *Fortune*, 4 November, pp. 131–40; T.L. Griffith, 1993, 'Teaching Big Brother to be a team player: computer monitoring and quality', *Academy of Management Executive*, pp. 73–80
121 M. Bryan, 2000, 'Every step you take, every move you make …', *Australian Financial Review*, 4 March, p. 27.
122 Danielle Townsend, 2003, 'Rank and File', *HRMonthly*, February, pp. 17–18. *HRMonthly* is published for the Australian Human Resources Institute, www.ahri.com.au.

CHAPTER 11 NOTES
1 A. Smith, 2006, 'The development of employer training in Australia', *Education + Training*, 48(4), pp. 252–61.
2 P. McLagan, 1989, *Models for HRD practice*, ASTD Press, St Paul, Minnesota.
3 W.J. Rothwell, E.S. Sanders, & J.G. Soper, 1999, *ASTD models for workplace learning and performance: roles, competencies and outputs*, ASTD, Alexandria, VA.
4 Australian Bureau of Statistics, 1990a, *Employer Training Expenditure Australia*, July to September 1989. AGPS, Canberra.
5 J. Teicher, 1995, 'The training guarantee: a good idea gone wrong?', in F. Ferrier and C. Selby-Smith (eds) *The Economics of Education and Training*, AGPS, Canberra, pp. 105–12.
6 Australian Bureau of Statistics, 2003, *Employer Training Expenditure and Practices*, AGPS, Canberra.
7 Australian Bureau of Statistics, 1998, *Training and Education Experience Australia*, AGPS, Canberra.
8 Australian Bureau of Statistics, 2002, *Training and Education Experience Australia*, AGPS, Canberra.
9 Australian Bureau of Statistics, 2003, *Employer Training Expenditure and Practices*, AGPS, Canberra.
10 R. Hall, J. Buchanan & G. Considine, 2002, 'You value what you pay for': enhancing employers' contributions to skill formation and use', a discussion paper for the Dusseldorp Skills Forum, Sydney.
11 E. Keep & J. Payne, 2002, 'Policy interventions for a vibrant work based route—or when policy hits reality's fan (again)' in K. Evans, P Hodkinson, & L. Unwin, *Working to learn: transforming learning in the workplace*, Kogan Page, London.
12 National Centre for Vocational Education Research, 2005, *Students and Courses—Summary*, NCVER, Adelaide.
13 C. Down, 2002, *Qualitative impact of training packages on vocational education and training*, Australian National Training Authority, Brisbane.
14 National Centre for Vocational Education Research, 2005, *Students and Courses—Summary*, NCVER, Adelaide.
15 National Centre for Vocational Education Research, 2006, *Apprentices and Trainees—June quarter 2006 Summary*, NCVER, Adelaide.
16 R. Noe, 1999, *Employee Training and Development*, Irwin McGraw-Hill, Burr Ridge, IL.
17 I.L. Goldstein, E.P. Braverman & H. Goldstein, 'Needs assessment', in K.N. Wexley (ed), 1991, *Developing Human Resources*, Bureau of National Affairs, Washington, DC, pp. 5.35–5.75.
18 J.Z. Rouillier & I.L. Goldstein, 1991, 'Determinants of the climate for transfer of training', paper presented at Society of Industrial/Organizational Psychology meetings, St Louis, MO; J.S. Russell, J.R. Terborg & M.L. Powers, 1985, 'Organizational performance and organizational level training and support', *Personnel Psychology*, 38, pp. 849–63; H. Baumgartel, G.J. Sullivan & L.E. Dunn, 1978, 'How organizational climate and personality affect the pay-off from advanced management training sessions', *Kansas Business Review*, 5, pp. 1–10.
19 A.P. Carnevale, L.J. Gainer & J. Villet, 1990, *Training in America*, Jossey-Bass, San Francisco; L.J. Gainer, 1989, 'Making the Competitive Connection: Strategic Management and Training', *Training and Development*, September, pp. s1–s30.
20 Carnevale, Gainer and Villet, 1990.
21 Deakin University, 'The Coles Institute—an Australian first', www.deakin.edu.au/deakin_events/April 1999/coles.htm, viewed 04/02/05; C. Richards, 1999, 'New era of corporate learning begins', *The Age*, 14 April, p. 5.
22 P. Vincent, 2001, 'Degrees of freedom', *The Sydney Morning Herald*, 21 March, p. 5.
23 Australian Bureau of Statistics, 2001–02.
24 B. Gerber, 1989, 'How to buy training programs', *Training*, June, pp. 59–68.
25 R. Zemke & J. Armstrong, 1997, 'How long does it take? The sequel', *Training*, May, pp. 69–79.
26 G. Rummler, 1996, 'In search of the holy performance grail', *Training and Development*, April, pp. 26–31; D.G. Langdon, 1997, 'Selecting interventions', *Performance Improvement*, 36, pp. 11–15.
27 R.F. Mager & P. Pipe, 1984, *Analyzing Performance Problems: Or You Really Oughta Wanna*, 2nd edn, Pittman Learning, Belmont, CA; A.P. Carnevale, L.J. Gainer & A.S. Meltzer, 1990, *Workplace Basics Training Manual*, Jossey-Bass, San Francisco; Rummler, 1996.
28 C.E. Schneier, J.P. Guthrie & J.D. Olian, 1988, 'A practical approach to conducting and using training needs assessment', *Public Personnel Management*, Summer, pp. 191–205.
29 V.J. Marsick & K.E. Watkins, 1990, *Informal and Incidental Learning in the Workplace*, Rouledge, London.
30 M. Knowles, 1970, *The Modern Practice of Adult Learning: Anadragogy Versus Pedagogy*, Association, New York.
31 P. E. Doolittle & W.G. Camp, 1999, 'Constructivism: The Career and Technical Education Perspective', *Journal of Vocational and Technical Education*, 16(1), pp. 23–46.
32 Doolittle & Camp.
33 S. Billett, 2001, *Learning in the Workplace: Strategies for Effective Practice*, Allen and Unwin, Sydney.
34 Billett, 2001, p. 21.
35 J. Lave & E. Wenger, 1991, *Situated Learning: Legitimate Peripheral Participation*, Cambridge University Press, UK.
36 A. Bockarie, 2002, 'The Potential of Vygotsky's Contributions to Our Understanding of Cognitive Apprenticeship as a Process of Development in Adult Vocational and Technical Education', *Journal of Vocational and Technical Education*, 19(1).
37 E. Smith, 2002, 'The Relationship Between Organisational Context and Novice Workers' Learning', *International Journal of Training & Development*, 6(4), pp. 254–62.
38 E. Wenger, 1998, *Communities of Practice: Learning, Meaning and Identity*, Cambridge University Press, UK.
39 E. Smith, 2002, 'The Relationship Between Organisational Context and Novice Workers' Learning', *International Journal of Training & Development*, 6(4), pp. 254–62.
40 C.E. Schneier, 1974, 'Training and development programs: what learning theory and research have to offer', *Personnel Journal*, April, pp. 288–93; M. Knowles, 'Adult learning', in R.L. Craig (ed), 1987, *Training and Development Handbook*, 3rd edn, McGraw-Hill, New York, pp. 168–79; R. Zemke & S. Zemke, 1981, '30 things we know for sure

Endnotes

about adult learning', *Training*, June, pp. 45–52; B.J. Smith & B.L. Delahaye, 1987, *How To Be an Effective Trainer*, 2nd edn, John Wiley, New York.

41   B. Mager, 1984, *Preparing Instructional Objectives*, 2nd edn, Lake Publishing, Belmont, CA; Smith and Delahaye, 1987.

42   K.A. Smith-Jentsch, F.G. Jentsch, S.C. Payne & E. Salas, 1996, 'Can pre-training experiences explain individual differences in learning?', *Journal of Applied Psychology*, 81, pp. 110–16.

43   J.K. Ford, D.A. Weissbein, S.M. Guly & E. Salas, 1998, 'Relationship of goal orientation, metacognitive activity and practice strategies with learning outcomes and transfer', *Journal of Applied Psychology*, 83, pp. 218–33.

44   J.C. Naylor & G.D. Briggs, 1963, 'The effects of task complexity and task organization on the relative efficiency of part and whole training methods', *Journal of Experimental Psychology*, 65, pp. 217–24.

45   W. McGehee & P.W. Thayer, 1961, *Training in Business and Industry*, Wiley, New York.

46   R.M. Mager, 1988, *Making Instruction Work*, David Lake, Belmont, CA.

47   R.M. Gagne & K.L. Medsker, 1996, *The Condition of Learning*, Harcourt Brace, Fort Worth, TX.

48   P.J. Decker & B.R. Nathan, 1985, *Behavior Modeling Training: Principles and Applications*, Praeger, New York.

49   Smith & Delahaye, 1987; M. Van Wart, N.J. Cayer & S. Cook, 1993, *Handbook of Training and Development for the Public Sector*, Jossey-Bass, San Francisco.

50   J.B. Tracey, S.I. Tannenbaum & M.J. Kavanaugh, 1995, 'Applying trained skills on the job: the importance of the work environment', *Journal of Applied Psychology*, 80, pp. 239–52; P.E. Tesluk, J.L. Farr, J.E. Mathieu & R.J. Vance, 1995, 'Generalization of employee involvement training to the job setting: Individual and situational effects', *Personnel Psychology*, 48, pp. 607–32; J.K. Ford, M.A. Quinones, D.J. Sego & J.S. Sorra, 1992, 'Factors affecting the opportunity to perform trained tasks on the job', *Personnel Psychology*, 45, pp. 511–27.

51   Australian National Training Authority (ANTA), 2000, 'Kmart Australia—The Key to Success', www.anta.gov.au, viewed 2001.

52   J.M. Cusimano, 1996, 'Managers as facilitators', *Training and Development*, 50, pp. 31–3.

53   C.M. Petrini (ed), 1990, 'Bringing it back to work', *Training and Development Journal*, December, pp. 15–21.

54   Ford, Quinones, Sego & Sorra, 1992.

55   Ford, Quinones, Sego & Sorra, 1992; M.A. Quinones, J.K. Ford, D.J. Sego & E.M. Smith, 1995–96, 'The effects of individual and transfer environment characteristics on the opportunity to perform trained tasks', *Training Research Journal*, 1, pp. 29–48.

56   G. Stevens & E. Stevens, 1996, 'The truth about EPSS', *Training and Development*, 50, pp. 59–61.

57   R.D. Marx, 1982, 'Relapse prevention for managerial training: A model for maintenance of behavior change', *Academy of Management Review*, 7, pp. 433–41; G.P. Latham & C.A. Frayne, 1989, 'Self-management training for increasing job attendance: A follow-up and replication', *Journal of Applied Psychology*, 74, pp. 411–16.

58   Australian Bureau of Statistics, 2001–02.

59   Scott, 2000.

60   Anonymous, 1995, 'Top training facilities', *Training*, March, special section H; U. Gupta, 1996, 'TV seminars and CD-ROMs train workers', *The Wall Street Journal*, 3 January, pp. B1, B6.

61   C. Lee, 1991, 'Who gets trained in what?', *Training*, October, pp. 47–59; W. Hannum, 1990, *The Application of Emerging Training Technology*, University Associates, San Diego, CA; B. Filipczak, 1991, 'Make room for training', *Training*, October, pp. 76–82; Carnevale, Gainer & Meltzer, 1990.

62   Lee, 1991; Carnevale, Gainer & Meltzer, 1990.

63   R.B. Cohn, 1996, 'How to choose a video producer', *Training*, July, pp. 58–61.

64   W.J. Rothwell & H.C. Kanzanas, 1990, 'Planned OJT is productive OJT', *Training and Development Journal*, October, pp. 53–6.

65   M. Flanagan, 2000, 'Current status of realistic anaesthesia patient simulators', discussion paper, Southern Health Care Network Simulation Centre, Melbourne.

66   M.W. McCall Jr & M.M. Lombardo, 1982, 'Using simulation for leadership and management research', *Management Science*, 28, pp. 533–49.

67   N. Adams, 1995, 'Lessons from the virtual world', *Training*, June, pp. 45–8.

68   A. Richter, 1990, 'Board games for managers', *Training and Development Journal*, July, pp. 95–7.

69   M. Hequet, 1995, 'Games that teach', Training, July, pp. 53–8.

70   G.P. Latham & L.M. Saari, 1979, 'Application of social learning theory to training supervisors through behavior modeling', *Journal of Applied Psychology*, 64, pp. 239–466.

71   Hannum, 1990.

72   F. Stewart, 2000, 'Qantas flies into cyberspace', *The Australian*, 29 November, p. 40.

73   R.J. Wagner, T.T. Baldwin & C.C. Rowland, 1991, 'Outdoor training: Revolution or fad?', *Training and Development Journal*, March, pp. 51–7; C.J. Cantoni, 1995, 'Learning the ropes of teamwork', *The Wall Street Journal*, 2 October, p. A14.

74   P.F. Buller, J.R. Cragun & G.M. McEvoy, 1991, 'Getting the most out of outdoor training', *Training and Development Journal*, March, pp. 58–61.

75   C. Clements, R.J. Wagner & C.C. Roland, 1995, 'The ins and outs of experiential training', *Training and Development*, February, pp. 52–6.

76   Clements, Wagner & Roland, 1995.

77   P. Froiland, 1994, 'Action learning', *Training*, January, pp. 27–34.

78   R.L. Oser, A. McCallum, E. Salas & B.B. Morgan Jr, 1989, *Toward a Definition of Teamwork: An Analysis of Critical Team Behaviors*, technical report 89–004, Naval Training Research Center, Orlando, FL.

79   Froiland, 1994.

80   K. Kraiger, J.K. Ford & E. Salas, 1993, 'Application of cognitive, skill-based, and affective theories of learning outcomes to new methods of training evaluation', *Journal of Applied Psychology*, 78, pp. 311–28; J.J. Phillips, 1996a, 'ROI: the search for best practices', *Training and Development*, February, pp. 42–7; D.L. Kirkpatrick, 'Evaluation of training', in R.L. Craig (ed), 1976, *Training and Development Handbook*, 2nd edn, McGraw-Hill, New York, pp. 18.1–18.27.

81   J.J. Phillips, 1996b, 'Was it the training?', *Training and Development*, March, pp. 28–32; Phillips, 1996a.

82   D.A. Grove & C. Ostroff, 'Program evaluation', in Wexley (ed), 1991, pp. 5.185–5.220.

83   J. Komaki, K.D. Bardwick & L.R. Scott, 1978, 'A behavioral approach to occupational safety: pinpointing and reinforcing safe performance in a food manufacturing plant', *Journal of Applied Psychology*, 63, pp. 434–45.

84   A.P. Carnevale & E.R. Schulz, 1990, 'Return on investment: accounting for training', *Training and Development Journal*, July, pp. s1–s32; P.R. Sackett & E.J. Mullen, 1993, 'Beyond Formal Experimental Design: Toward an Expanded View of the Training Evaluation Process', *Personnel Psychology*, 46, pp. 613–27; S.I. Tannenbaum & S.B. Woods, 1992, 'Determining a strategy for evaluating training: operating within organizational constraints', *Human Resource Planning*, 15, pp. 63–81; R.D. Arvey, S.E. Maxwell & E. Salas, 1992, 'The relative power of training evaluation designs under different cost configurations', *Journal of Applied Psychology*, 77, pp. 155–60.

85   Grove & Ostroff, in Wexley (ed), 1991.

86   D.C. Feldman, 1976, 'A contingency theory of socialization', *Administrative Science Quarterly*, 21, pp. 433–52; D.C. Feldman, 1980, 'A socialization process that helps new recruits succeed', *Personnel*, 57, pp. 11–23; J.P. Wanous, A.E. Reichers & S.D. Malik, 1984, 'Organizational socialization and group development: toward an integrative perspective', *Academy of Management Review*, 9, pp. 670–83; C.L. Adkins, 1995, 'Previous work experience and organizational socialization: a longitudinal examination', *Academy of Management Journal*, 38, pp. 839–62; E.W. Morrison, 1993, 'Longitudinal study of

the effects of information seeking on newcomer socialization', *Journal of Applied Psychology*, 78, pp. 173–83.
87 G.M. McEnvoy & W.F. Cascio, 1985, 'Strategies for reducing employee turnover: A meta-analysis', *Journal of Applied Psychology*, 70, pp. 342–53.
88 M.R. Louis, 1980, 'Surprise and sense making: what newcomers experience in entering unfamiliar organizational settings', *Administrative Science Quarterly*, 25, pp. 226–51.
89 R.F. Morrison & T.M. Brantner, 1992, 'What enhances or inhibits learning a new job? A basic career issue', *Journal of Applied Psychology*, 77, pp. 926–40.
90 D.A. Major, S.W.J. Kozlowski, G.T. Chao & P.D. Gardner, 1995, 'A longitudinal investigation of newcomer expectations, early socialization outcomes, and the moderating effect of role development factors', *Journal of Applied Psychology*, 80, pp. 418–31.
91 D.C. Feldman, 1988, *Managing Careers in Organizations*, Scott-Foresman, Glenview, IL.
92 Feldman, 1988; D. Reed-Mendenhall & C.W. Millard, 1980, 'Orientation: a training and development tool', *Personnel Administrator*, 25 (8), pp. 42–4; M.R. Louis, B.Z. Posner & G.H. Powell, 1983, 'The availability and helpfulness of socialization practises', *Personnel Psychology*, 36, pp. 857–66; C. Ostroff & S.W.J. Kozlowski Jr, 1992, 'Organizational socialization as a learning process: the role of information acquisition', *Personnel Psychology*, 45, pp. 849–74; D.R. France & R.L. Jarvis, 1996, 'Quick starts for new employees', *Training and Development*, October, pp. 47–50.

CHAPTER 12 NOTES

1 M. London, 1989, *Managing the Training Enterprise*, Jossey-Bass, San Francisco; Holland, P. & De Cieri, H. (Eds.) 2006. *Contemporary issues in human resource development*, Pearson Education, Sydney.
2 R.W. Pace, P.C. Smith & G.E. Mills, 1991, *Human Resource Development*, Prentice-Hall, Englewood Cliffs, NJ; W. Fitzgerald, 1992, 'Training versus development', *Training and Development Journal*, May, pp. 81–4; R.A. Noe, S.L. Wilk, E.J. Mullen & J.E. Wanek, 'Employee development: issues in construct definition and investigation of antecedents', in J.K. Ford (ed) 1997, *Improving Training Effectiveness in Work Organizations*, Lawrence Erlbaum, Mahwah, NJ, pp. 153–89; M. Watkins, 2004, 'Transition traps: common pitfalls for new managers', *Human Resources*, 8 September, pp. 10–11.
3 J.H. Greenhaus & G.A. Callanan, 1994, Career Management, 2nd edn, Dryden Press, Fort Worth, TX.
4 H. De Cieri & P.J. Dowling, 'Human resource management for engineers', in D.A. Samson (ed), 2000, Management for Engineers, 3rd edn, Pearson, Melbourne.
5 D.T. Hall, 1996, 'Protean careers of the 21st century', Academy of Management Executive, 11, pp. 8–16; D.T. Hall & J.E. Moss, 1998, 'The new protean career contract: helping organizations and employees adapt', *Organizational Dynamics*, Winter, pp. 22–37.
6 D.M. Rousseau, 1996, 'Changing the deal while keeping the people', *Academy of Management Executive*, 11, pp. 50–61; D.M. Rousseau and J.M. Parks, 'The contracts of individuals and organizations', in L.L. Cummings & B.M. Staw (eds), 1992, *Research in Organizational Behavior*, vol. 15, JAI Press, Greenwich, CT, pp. 1–47; also see J.A. Coyle-Shapiro, L.M. Shore, M.S. Taylor & L.E. Tetrick (eds), 2004, *The Employment Relationship: Examining Psychological and Contextual Perspectives*, Oxford University Press, New York; L.J. Millward & P.M. Brewerton, 2000, 'Psychological contracts: employee relations for the twenty-first century?', in C.L. Cooper and I.T. Robertson (eds), *International Review of Industrial and Organizational Psychology*, John Wiley and Sons Ltd, New York, pp. 1–61.
7 P. Sellers, 1994, 'Don't call me a slacker', *Fortune*, 12 December, pp. 181–96.
8 M.B. Arthur, P.H. Claman & R.J. DeFillippi, 1995, 'Intelligent enterprise, intelligent careers', *Academy of Management Executive*, 9, pp. 7–20.

9 K.R. Brousseau, M.J. Driver, K. Eneroth & R. Larsson, 1996, 'Career pandemonium: realigning organizations and individuals', *Academy of Management Executive*, 11, pp. 52–66.
10 M.B. Arthur, 1994, 'The boundaryless career: a new perspective of organizational inquiry', *Journal of Organizational Behavior*, 15, pp. 295–309; P.H. Mirvis & D.T. Hall, 1994, 'Psychological success and the boundaryless career', *Journal of Organizational Behavior*, 15, pp. 365–80; L.T. Eby, M. Butts & A. Lockwood, 2003, 'Predictors of success in the era of the boundaryless career', *Journal of Organizational Behavior*, 24, pp. 689–708; M.A. Peiperl, M.B. Arthur, R. Goffee & T. Morris (eds), 2000, *Career Frontiers: New Conceptions of Working Lives*, pp. 2–45, Oxford University Press, London.
11 P. Holland & H. De Cieri, (Eds.) 2006. *Contemporary issues in human resource development*, Pearson Education, Sydney.
12 J. Gilley & S. Eggland, 1989. *Principles of human resource development*, Addison-Wesley, Reading, MA, p.5.
13 M. McCracken & M. Wallace, 2000, 'Exploring strategic maturity in HRD – rhetoric, aspiration or reality?', *Journal of European Industrial Training*, 24 (8), pp. 425–67.
14 T.R. Athey & M.S. Orth, 1999, 'Emerging competency methods for the future', *Human Resource Management*, 38 (3), pp. 215–28; P. Cappelli & A.C. Crocker-Hefter, 1996, 'Distinctive human resources are a firm's core competencies', *Organizational Dynamics*, 28 (2), pp. 7–21.
15 O. Nordhaug, 1998, 'Competence specificities in organisations', *International Studies of Management and Organization*, 28 (1), pp. 8–29; J. Sandberg, 2000, 'Understanding human competence a work: an interpretative approach', *Academy of Management Journal*, 43, pp. 9–25.
16 R.J. Campbell, 'HR development strategies', in K.N. Wexley (ed), 1991, *Developing Human Resources*, Bureau of National Affairs, Washington, DC, pp. 5.1–5.34; M.A. Sheppeck & C.A. Rhodes, 1988, 'Management development: revised thinking in light of new events of strategic importance', *Human Resource Planning*, 11, pp. 159–72; B. Keys & J. Wolf, 1988, 'Management education: current issues and emerging trends', *Journal of Management*, 14, pp. 205–29; L.M. Saari, T.R. Johnson, S.D. McLaughlin & D. Zimmerle, 1988, 'A survey of management training and education practises in U.S. companies', *Personnel Psychology*, 41, pp. 731–44.
17 T. Russell, 2004, 'More business acumen: MBAs', *Human Resources*, 19 October, pp. 12–14.
18 E. Blass, 2005, 'The rise and rise of the corporate university', *Journal of European Industrial Training*, 29 (1), pp. 58–74; S. Taylor & R. Paton, 2002, *Corporate universities—Historical development, conceptual analysis and relations with public-sector higher education*, The Observatory on Borderless Higher Education: London; P. Holland & A. Pyman, 2006, 'The emergence of the corporate university', in P. Holland & H. De Cieri, (Eds.) 2006, *Contemporary issues in human resource development*, Pearson Education, Sydney.
19 S. Shaw, 2005, 'The corporate university: Global or local phenomenon?', *Journal of European Industrial Training*, 29 (1), pp 21–39.
20 J. Reingold, 1997, 'Corporate America goes to school', *Business Week*, 20 October, pp. 66–72.
21 T.A. Stewart, 1991, 'GE keeps those ideas coming', *Fortune*, 12 August, pp. 41–9.
22 G.P. Hollenbeck, 1991, 'What did you learn in school? Studies of a university executive program', *Human Resource Planning*, 14, pp. 247–60.
23 A. Howard & D.W. Bray, 1988, *Managerial Lives in Transition: Advancing Age and Changing Times*, Guilford, New York; J. Bolt, 1989, *Executive Development*, Harper Business, New York; J.R. Hinrichs & G.P. Hollenbeck, 'Leadership development', in Wexley (ed), 1991, pp. 5.221–5.237.
24 S.K. Hirsch, 1992, *MBTI® Team Member's Guide*, Consulting Psychologists Press, Palo Alto, CA; A.L. Hammer, 1993, *Introduction to Type and Careers*, Consulting Psychologists Press, Palo Alto, CA, 1993.
25 Thorne & H. Gough, 1991, *Portraits of Type*, Consulting Psychologists Press, Palo Alto, CA.

Endnotes

26   D. Druckman & R.A. Bjork (eds), 1991, *In the Mind's Eye: Enhancing Human Performance*, National Academy Press, Washington, DC; M.H. McCaulley, 'The Myers-Briggs Type Indicator® and leadership', in K.E. Clark & M.B. Clark (eds), 1990, *Measures of Leadership*, Leadership Library of America, West Orange, NJ, pp. 381–418; statement is fully supported and well-documented in Myers, McCaulley, Quenk & Hammer, 1998, *MBTI Manual*, 3rd edn.

27   G.C. Thornton III & W.C. Byham, 1982, *Assessment Centers and Managerial Performance*, Academic Press, New York; L.F. Schoenfeldt & J.A. Steger, 'Identification and development of management talent', in K.M. Rowland & G. Ferris (eds), 1989, *Research in Personnel and Human Resource Management*, vol. 7, JAI Press, Greenwich, CT, pp. 151–81.

28   Thornton and Byham, 1982.

29   B.B. Gaugler, D.B. Rosenthal, G.C. Thornton III & C. Bentson, 1987, 'Metaanalysis of assessment center validity', *Journal of Applied Psychology*, 72, pp. 493–511; D.W. Bray, R.J. Campbell & D.L. Grant, 1974, *Formative Years in Business: A Long-Term AT&T Study of Managerial Lives*, Wiley, New York.

30   R.G. Jones & M.D. Whitmore, 1995, 'Evaluating developmental assessment centers as interventions', *Personnel Psychology*, 48, pp. 377–88.

31   C.D. McCauley & M.M. Lombardo, 'Benchmarks®: an instrument for diagnosing managerial strengths and weaknesses', in Clark and Clark (eds), 1990, pp. 535–45.

32   C.D. McCauley, M.M. Lombardo & C.J. Usher, 1989, 'Diagnosing management development needs: an instrument based on how managers develop', *Journal of Management*, 15, pp. 389–403.

33   S.B. Silverman, 'Individual development through performance appraisal', in Wexley (ed), 1991, pp. 5.120–5.151.

34   M. London & J.W. Smither, 1995, 'Can multi-source feedback change perceptions of goal accomplishment, self-evaluations and performance related outcomes?', *Personnel Psychology*, 48, pp. 803–39; J.S. Lublin, 1994, 'Turning the tables: underlings evaluate bosses', *The Wall Street Journal*, 4 October, pp. B1, B14; B. O'Reilly, 1994, '360 feedback can change your life', *Fortune*, 17 October, pp. 93–100; J.F. Milliman, R.A. Zawacki, C. Norman, L. Powell & J. Kirksey, 1994, 'Companies evaluate employees from all perspectives', *Personnel Journal*, November, pp. 99–103.

35   Center for Creative Leadership, 1992, *Skillscope for Managers: Development Planning Guide*, Center for Creative Leadership, Greensboro, NC; G. Yukl & R. Lepsinger, 1995, '360 feedback', *Training*, December, pp. 45–50.

36   L. Atwater, P. Roush & A. Fischthal, 1995, 'The influence of upward feedback on self- and follower ratings of leadership', *Personnel Psychology*, 48, pp. 35–59; J.F. Hazucha, S.A. Hezlett & R.J. Schneider, 1993, 'The impact of 360-degree feedback on management skill development', *Human Resource Management*, 32, pp. 325–51; J.W. Smither, M. London, N. Vasilopoulos, R.R. Reilly, R.E. Millsap & N. Salvemini, 1995, 'An examination of the effects of an upward feedback program over time', *Personnel Psychology*, 48, pp. 1–34.

37   D. Bracken, 1994, 'Straight talk about multirater feedback', *Training and Development*, September, pp. 44–51.

38   M.W. McCall Jr, M.M. Lombardo & A.M. Morrison, 1988, *Lessons of Experience*, Lexington Books, Lexington, MA.

39   R.S. Snell, 1990, 'Congenial ways of learning: so near yet so far', *Journal of Management Development*, 9, pp. 17–23.

40   McCall, Lombardo & Morrison, 1988; M.W. McCall Jr, 1988, 'Developing executives through work experiences', *Human Resource Planning*, 11, pp. 1–11; M.N. Ruderman, P.J. Ohlott & C.D. McCauley, 'Assessing opportunities for leadership development', in Clark and Clark (eds), 1990, pp. 547–62; C.D. McCauley, L.J. Eastman & P.J. Ohlott, 1995, 'Linking management selection and development through stretch assignments', *Human Resource Management*, 34, pp. 93–115.

41   C.D. McCauley, M.N. Ruderman, P.J. Ohlott & J.E. Morrow, 1994, 'Assessing the developmental components of managerial jobs', *Journal of Applied Psychology*, 79, pp. 544–60.

42   M. London, 1985, *Developing Managers*, Jossey-Bass, San Francisco; M.A. Campion, L. Cheraskin & M.J. Stevens, 1994, 'Career-related antecedents and outcomes of job rotation', *Academy of Management Journal*, 37, pp. 1518–42; London, 1989.

43   D.C. Feldman, 1988, *Managing Careers in Organizations*, Scott-Foresman, Glenview, IL.

44   J.M. Brett, L.K. Stroh & A.H. Reilly, 'Job transfer', in C.L. Cooper & I.T. Robinson (eds), 1992, *International Review of Industrial and Organizational Psychology: 1992*, John Wiley and Sons, Chichester, United Kingdom; D.C. Feldman & J.M. Brett, 1983, 'Coping with new jobs: a comparative study of new hires and job changers', *Academy of Management Journal*, 26, pp. 258–72.

45   R.A. Noe, B.D. Steffy & A.E. Barber, 1988, 'An investigation of the factors influencing employees' willingness to accept mobility opportunities', *Personnel Psychology*, 41, pp. 559–80; S. Gould & L.E. Penley, 1984, 'A study of the correlates of willingness to relocate', *Academy of Management Journal*, 28, pp. 472–8; J. Landau & T.H. Hammer, 1986, 'Clerical employees' perceptions of intraorganizational career opportunities', *Academy of Management Journal*, 29, pp. 385–405; R.P. Duncan & C.C. Perruci, 1976, 'Dual occupation families and migration', *American Sociological Review*, 41, pp. 252–61; J.M. Brett & A.H. Reilly, 1988, 'On the road again: predicting the job transfer decision', *Journal of Applied Psychology*, 73, pp. 614–20.

46   D.T. Hall & L.A. Isabella, 1985, 'Downward moves and career development', *Organizational Dynamics*, 14, pp. 5–23.

47   H.D. Dewirst, 'Career patterns: mobility, specialization, and related career issues', in R.F. Morrison & J. Adams (eds) 1991, *Contemporary Career Development Issues*, Lawrence Erlbaum, Hillsdale, NJ, pp. 73–108.

48   J.M. Brett, 1992, 'Job transfer and well-being', *Journal of Applied Psychology*, 67, pp. 450–63; F.J. Minor, L.A. Slade & R.A. Myers, 'Career transitions in changing times', in Morrison & Adams (eds), 1991, pp. 109–20; C.C. Pinder & K.G. Schroeder, 1987, 'Time to proficiency following job transfers', *Academy of Management Journal*, 30, pp. 336–53; G. Flynn, 1996, 'Heck no—we won't go!', *Personnel Journal*, March, pp. 37–43.

49   K. Marshall, 2001a, 'World of work shrinks as the risks expand', *Australian Financial Review*, 24 October, p. 9; [Anonymous] 2002, 'Expat programs cut to save on costs', *Human Resources*, June, p. 4.

50   C.J. Bachler, 1995, 'Workers take leave of job stress', *Personnel Journal*, January, pp. 38–48.

51   D.B. Turban & T.W. Dougherty, 1994, 'Role of protege personality in receipt of mentoring and career success', *Academy of Management Journal*, 37, pp. 688–702; E.A. Fagenson, 1992, 'Mentoring who needs it? A comparison of proteges and nonproteges' needs for power, achievement, affiliation, and autonomy', *Journal of Vocational Behavior*, 41, pp. 48–60.

52   A.H. Geiger, 1992, 'Measures for mentors', *Training and Development Journal*, February, pp. 65–7; L.C. Ehrich & B. Hansford, 1999, 'Mentoring: Pros and cons for HRM', *Asia Pacific Journal of Human Resources*, 37 (3), pp. 92–107.

53   K.E. Kram, 1985, *Mentoring at Work: Developmental Relationships in Organizational Life*, Scott-Foresman, Glenview, IL; L.L. Phillips-Jones, 1983, 'Establishing a formalized mentoring program', *Training and Development Journal*, February, pp. 38–42; K. Kram, 1983, 'Phases of the mentoring relationship', *Academy of Management Journal*, 26, pp. 608–25; G.T. Chao, P.M. Walz & P.D. Gardner, 1992, 'Formal and informal mentorships: a comparison of mentoring functions and contrasts with nonmentored counterparts', *Personnel Psychology*, 45, pp. 619–36.

54   G.F. Dreher & R.A. Ash, 1990, 'A comparative study of mentoring among men and women in managerial, professional, and technical positions', *Journal of Applied Psychology*, 75, pp. 539–46; J.L. Wilbur, 1987, 'Does mentoring breed success?', *Training and Development Journal*, November, pp. 38–41; R.A. Noe, 'Mentoring relationships for employee development', in J.W. Jones, B.D. Steffy & D.W. Bray (eds), 1991, *Applying Psychology in Business: The Handbook for Managers and Human Resource Professionals*, Lexington Books, Lexington, MA, pp. 475–82; M.M. Fagh & K. Ayers Jr, 1985, 'Police mentors', *FBI Law Enforcement Bulletin*, January, pp. 8–13; Kram, 1983; R.A. Noe, 1988, 'An investigation of the determinants of successful

assigned mentoring relationships', *Personnel Psychology*, 41, pp. 457–79; B.J. Tepper, 1995, 'Upward maintenance tactics in supervisory mentoring and nonmentoring relationships', *Academy of Management Journal*, 38, pp. 1191–205; B.R. Ragins and T.A. Scandura, 1994, 'Gender differences in expected outcomes of mentoring relationships', *Academy of Management Journal*, 37, pp. 957–71.
55 Kaye & B. Jackson, 1995, 'Mentoring: a group guide', *Training and Development*, April, pp. 23–7.
56 D.B. Peterson & M.D. Hicks, 1996, *Leader as Coach*, Personnel Decisions, Minneapolis, MN.
57 R. Zemke, 1996, 'The corporate coach', *Training*, December, pp. 24–8.
58 K. Marshall, 2001b, 'KPMG links staff's ambitions with its goals', *Australian Financial Review*, 24 October, p. 12.
59 Marshall, 2001b.
60 D.T. Jaffe & C.D. Scott, 'Career development for empowerment in a changing work world', in J.M. Kummerow (ed) 1991, *New Directions in Career Planning and the Workplace*, Consulting Psychologists Press, Palo Alto, CA, pp. 33–60; L. Summers, 1994, 'A logical approach to development planning', *Training and Development*, November, pp. 22–31; D.B. Peterson & M.D. Hicks, 1995, *Development First*, Personnel Decisions, Minneapolis, MN.
61 T. Russell, 2004, 'Taking the lead in leadership', *Human Resources*, 16 November, pp. 14–15.
62 Rio Tinto, 2005, *2005 Sustainable Development Review. Global commitment with local solutions*, www.riotinto.com.se, accessed 30 September 2006.
63 C.B. Derr, C. Jones & E.L. Toomey, 1988, 'Managing high-potential employees: current practises in thirty-three U.S. corporations', *Human Resource Management*, 27, pp. 273–90.
64 H.S. Feild & S.G. Harris, 1991, 'Entry-level, fast-track management development programs: developmental tactics and perceived program effectiveness', *Human Resource Planning*, 14, pp. 261–73.
65 Feild & Harris, 1991.
66 Derr, Jones & Toomey, 1988; K.M. Nowack, 1994, 'The secrets of succession', *Training and Development*, November, pp. 49–54; J.S. Lublin, 1996, 'An overseas stint can be a ticket to the top', *The Wall Street Journal*, 29 January, pp. B1, B2.
67 [Anonymous] 2002, Streamlining succession management through psychometrics, *Human Resources*, June, pp. 24–5.
68 Derr, Jones & Toomey, 1988; Nowack, 1994; Lublin, 1996.
69 M.W. McCall Jr & M.M. Lombardo, 1983, *Off the Track: Why and How Successful Executives Get Derailed*, technical report no. 21, Center for Creative Leadership, Greensboro, NC; E.V. Veslor & J.B. Leslie, 1995, 'Why executives derail: perspectives across time and cultures', *Academy of Management Executive*, 9, pp. 62–72.
70 L.W. Hellervik, J.F. Hazucha & R.J. Schneider, 'Behavior change: models, methods, and a review of evidence', in M.D. Dunnette & L.M. Hough (eds), 1992, *Handbook of Industrial and Organizational Psychology*, 2nd edn, Consulting Psychologists Press, Palo Alto, CA, vol. 3, pp. 823–99.
71 D.B. Peterson, 1990, 'Measuring and evaluating change in executive and managerial development', paper presented at the annual conference of the Society for Industrial and Organizational Psychology, Miami.

CHAPTER 13 NOTES
1 J.S. Adams, 1965, 'Inequity in social exchange', in L. Berkowitz (ed), *Advances in Experimental Social Psychology*, Academic Press, New York; P.S. Goodman, 1974, 'An examination of referents used in the evaluation of pay', *Organizational Behavior and Human Performance*, 12, pp. 170–95.
2 J.B. Miner, 1980, *Theories of Organizational Behavior*, Dryden Press, Hinsdale, IL.
3 E. Jacques, 1961, *Equitable Payment*, Heinemann, London.
4 M. Armstrong, 1994, *Employee Reward*, IPD, London.
5 Steve Lohr, 1992, 'Ford and Chrysler outpace Japanese in reducing costs', *The New York Times*, 18 June, p. D1.
6 B. Gerhart & G.T. Milkovich, 1990, 'Organizational differences in managerial compensation and financial performance', *Academy of Management Journal*, 33, pp. 663–91; E.L. Groshen, 1988, 'Why do wages vary among employers?', *Economic Review*, 24, pp. 19–38.
7 G.A. Akerlof, 1984, 'Gift exchange and efficiency-wage theory, four views', *American Economic Review*, 74, pp. 79–83; J.L. Yellen, 1984, 'Efficiency wage models of unemployment', *American Economic Review*, 74, pp. 200–5.
8 S.L. Rynes & G.T. Milkovich, 1986. 'Wage surveys, dispelling some myths about the 'market wage', *Personnel Psychology*, 39, pp. 71–90.
9 B. Gerhart & G.T. Milkovich, 1991, 'Employee compensation, research and practise', in M.D. Dunnette & L.M. Hough (eds), *Handbook of Industrial and Organizational Psychology*, 2nd edn, Consulting Psychologists Press, Palo Alto, CA, pp. 481–569; J. Martocchio, 2001, *Strategic Compensation: A Human Resource Management Approach*, Prentice-Hall, Englewood Cliffs, NJ.
10 G.T. Milkovich & J. Newman, 1990, *Compensation*, BPI/Irwin, Homewood, IL.
11 Armstrong, 1994.
12 M. Armstrong & H. Murlis, 1994, *Reward Management*, 3rd edn, Kogan Page/IPD, London.
13 B. Gerhart, G.T. Milkovich & B. Murray, 1992, 'Pay, performance, and participation', in D. Lewin, O.S. Mitchell & P.D. Sherer (eds), *Research Frontiers in Industrial Relations and Human Resources*, IRRA, Madison, WI.
14 C.H. Fay, 1989, 'External pay relationships', in L.R. Gomez-Mejia (ed), *Compensation and Benefits*, Bureau of National Affairs, Washington, DC.
15 J.P. Pfeffer & A. Davis-Blake, 1987, 'Understanding organizational wage structures: A resource dependence approach', *Academy of Management Journal*, 30, pp. 437–55.
16 H.Z. Levine, 1992, 'The view from the board: The state of compensation and benefits today', *Compensation and Benefits Review*, March, p. 24.
17 C.M. Solomon, 1995, 'Global compensation, learn the ABCs', *Personnel Journal*, July, p. 70; R.A. Swaak, 1995, 'Expatriate management: The search for best practices', *Compensation and Benefits Review*, March–April, p. 21. For more details on this issue of international compensations see P.J. Dowling, D.E. Welch & R.S. Schuler, 1999, *International Human Resource Management: Managing People in a Multinational Context*, South-Western Publishing, Cincinnati, OH.
18 Runzheimer International, *1997–1998 Survey of Geographic Pay Differential Policies and Practices*, Runzheimer International, Rochester, WI, 1997.
19 E.E. Lawler III, 1981, *Pay and Organizational Development*, Addison Wesley, Reading, MA.
20 R. Folger & M.A. Konovsky, 1989, 'Effects of procedural and distributive justice on reactions to pay raise decisions', *Academy of Management Journal*, 32, pp. 115–30; Gerhart, Milkovich & Murray, 1992; J. Greenberg, 1986, 'Determinants of perceived fairness of performance evaluations', *Journal of Applied Psychology*, 71, pp. 340–2; H.G. Heneman III, 1985, 'Pay satisfaction', *Research in Personnel and Human Resource Management*, 3, pp. 115–39.
21 J. Greenberg, 1990, 'Employee theft as a reaction to underpayment of inequity: The hidden cost of pay cuts', *Journal of Applied Psychology*, 75, pp. 561–8.
22 Adams, 1965; C.J. Berger, C.A. Olson & J.W. Boudreau, 1983, 'The effect of unionism on job satisfaction: the role of work-related values and perceived rewards', *Organizational Behavior and Human Performance*, 32, pp. 284–324; P. Cappelli & P.D. Sherer, 1990, 'Assessing worker attitudes under a two-tier wage plan', *Industrial and Labor Relations Review*, 43, pp. 225–44; R.W. Rice, S.M. Phillips and D.B. McFarlin, 1990, 'Multiple discrepancies and pay satisfaction', *Journal of Applied Psychology*, 75, pp. 386–93.
23 Cappelli & Sherer 1990.

Endnotes

24 J. Mathews, 1994, *Catching the Wave: Workplace Reform in Australia*, Allen and Unwin, Sydney.
25 S.E. Gross, 1997, 'When jobs become team roles, what do you pay for?', *Compensation and Benefits Review*, January–February, pp. 48–51.
26 G. Paulin & F. Cook, 1997, 'What should be done about executive compensation?', *ACA Journal*, Autumn, pp. 20–35.
27 G. Cornish & G. Adams, 1993, 'Trends in remuneration: the concept of "total quality pay"', *Asia Pacific Journal of Human Resources*, 31 (2), pp. 75–86.
28 Cornish & Adams, 1993; Armstrong, 1994.
29 This section draws freely on B. Gerhart & R.D. Bretz, 1994, 'Employee compensation', in W. Karwowski and G. Salvendy (eds), *Organization and Management of Advanced Manufacturing*, Wiley, New York, pp. 81–101.
30 R.M. Kanter, 1989, *When Giants Learn to Dance*, Simon and Schuster, New York; E.E. Lawler III, 1990, Strategic Pay, Jossey-Bass, San Francisco; Anonymous, 1990, 'Farewell, fast track', *Business Week*, 10 December, pp. 192–200.
31 Transfield Defence Systems Industrial Agreement, 1994, Tenix Defence Systems, Williamstown, Australia, pp. 22–3.
32 M. Rimmer & C. Verevis, 1990, *Award Restructuring: Progress at the Workplace*, Monograph no. 22, University of New South Wales, Sydney.
33 L. Still & D. Mortimer, 1993, 'The effectiveness of award restructuring and the training levy in providing a more educated workforce: A comparative study', in D. Mortimer, P. Leece and R. Morris (eds), *Workplace Reform and Enterprise Bargaining: Issues, Cases, Trends*, Harcourt Brace, Sydney, pp. 37–54; J. Sloan, 1993,'Wage fixing under Accord Mark VII and the role of national wage principles', *Australian Bulletin of Labour*, 19 (3), pp. 218–40.
34 Lawler, 1990; G. Ledford, 1991, '3 cases on skill-based pay: An overview', *Compensation and Benefits Review*, March–April, pp. 11–23; G.E. Ledford, 1995, 'Paying for the skills, knowledge, competencies of knowledge workers', *Compensation and Benefits Review*, July–August, p. 55.
35 Ledford, 1991.
36 P.S. Adler, 1988, 'Managing flexible automation', *California Management Review*, 30 (3), pp. 34–56; T. Cummings & M. Blumberg, 1987, 'Advanced manufacturing technology and work design', in T.D. Wall, C.W. Clegg & N.J. Kemp (eds), *The Human Side of Advanced Manufacturing Technology*, John Wiley and Sons, Chichester, United Kingdom; Y.P. Gupta, 1989, 'Human aspects of flexible manufacturing systems', *Production and Inventory Management Journal*, 30 (2), pp. 30–6; R.E. Walton & G.I. Susman, 1987, 'People policies for the new machines', *Harvard Business Review*, 87 (2), pp. 98–106; J.P. Womack, D.T. Jones & D. Roos, 1990, *The Machine That Changed the World*, Macmillan, New York, p. 56.
37 T.D. Wall, J.M. Corbett, R. Martin, C.W. Clegg & P.R. Jackson, 1990, 'Advanced manufacturing technology, work design, and performance: a change study', *Journal of Applied Psychology*, 75, pp. 691–7.
37 Womack, Jones & Roos, 1990.
39 Lawler, 1990
40 Lawler, 1990; Gerhart & Milkovich, 1991.
41 B.C. Murray & B. Gerhart, 1998, 'An empirical analysis of a skill-based pay program and plant performance outcomes', *Academy of Management Journal*, 41 (1), pp. 68–78.
42 Murray & Gerhart, 1998; N. Gupta, D. Jenkins & W. Curington, 1986, 'Paying for knowledge: myths and realities', *National Productivity Review*, Spring, pp. 107–23.
43 World Bank, 1995, *World Development Report 1995: Workers in an Integrating World*, Oxford University Press, New York.
44 OECD, 1997, *Education at a Glance—OECD Indicators 1997*, OECD, Paris.
45 C. Sparks and M. Greiner, 1997, 'U.S. and foreign productivity and labor costs', *Monthly Labor Review*, February, pp. 26–35.
46 E. Faltermayer, 1991, 'U.S. companies come back home', *Fortune*, 30 December, pp. 106ff.
47 Faltermayer, 1991.
48 J. Shields, J. O'Donnell & J. O'Brien, 2003, *The Buck Stops Here: Private Sector Executive Remuneration in Australia*, A report prepared for the Labour Council of New South Wales.
49 G.L. O'Neill & M. Iob, 1999, 'Determinants of executive remuneration in Australian organisations: an exploratory study', *Asia Pacific Journal of Human Resources*, 37 (1), pp. 65–75.
50 T. Perrin, 1997, 'Pay rates around the world', *Australian Financial Review*, 10 May, p. 2.
51 Shields, O'Donnell & O'Brien, 2003.
52 D.M. Cowherd & D.I. Levine, 1992, 'Product quality and pay equity between lower-level employees and top management: an investigation of distributive justice theory', *Administrative Science Quarterly*, 37, pp. 302–20.
53 See for example C. Young, 1998, 'Trends in executive compensation', *Journal of Business Strategy*, 19 (2), March–April, pp. 21–5, and G. O'Neill, 2000, 'Lies, damned lies, statistics … and CEO pay', *HRMonthly*, February, pp. 30–1.
54 P.J. Holland, P.J. Dowling & P.A. Innes, 2001, 'CEO compensation in Australia: is there a relationship between principles, policies and practices?', *Asia Pacific Journal of Human Resources* 39 (3), pp. 41–58.
55 G.L. O'Neill, 1999a, *Executive Remuneration in Australia: An Overview of Trends and Issues—A White Paper*, AHRI/Hay Group, New South Wales.
56 Ernst and Young, 1999, 'Best Practice in the disclosure of directors and executives remuneration', *Corporate Governance Series*, April.
57 M. Bloom & G.T. Milkovich, 1999, 'Strategic perspective on international compensation and reward systems', in P.M. Wright, L.D. Dyer, J.W. Boudreau & G.T. Milkovich (ed), *Strategic Human Resource Management in the Twenty-First Century*, JAI Press, Stanford, CA, pp. 283–304; O'Neill, 1999.
58 O'Neill, 1999a; G.L. O'Neill, 1999b, 'Issues in the design and structure of executive remuneration', in G. O'Neill & R. Kramar (eds), *Australian Human Resource Management*, vol. 2, Woodslane, Warriewood, New South Wales, pp. 155–70.
59 B. Hall & J. Liebman, 1998, 'Are CEOs really paid like bureaucrats?', *The Quarterly Journal of Economics*, 113 (3), pp. 653–91.
60 D.E. Strachan & L.G. Myslewski, 1997, 'Linking CEO compensation to organizational performance', *Association Management*, 49 (4), pp. 63–70.
61 A. Rappaport, 1999, 'New thinking in how to link executive pay with performance', *Harvard Business Review*, 77 (2), pp. 91–102.
62 L. Gomez-Mejia and D. Balkin, 1992, *Compensation, Organizational Strategy, and Firms' Performance*, South-Western Publishing, Cincinnati, OH; O'Neill, 1999a.
63 Young, 1998.
64 R.S. Kaplan & D. Norton, 1993, 'Putting the balanced scorecard to work', *Harvard Business Review*, 71 (3), pp. 134–47; R.S. Kaplan & D. Norton, 1996, 'Using the balanced scorecard as a strategic management system', *Harvard Business Review*, 74 (1), pp. 75–85.
65 P. Rolph, 1999, 'The balanced scorecard: Get smart and get control', *Chief Executive*, July–August, pp. 52–6.
66 R.I. Wise, 1997, 'The balanced scorecard approach to strategy management—the public manager', *The New Bureaucrat*, 26 (3), pp. 47–50.
67 D. Brown & M. Armstrong, 1999, *Paying for Contribution: Real Performance-Related Pay Strategies*, Kogan Page, London.
68 Kaplan & Norton, 1996.
69 P. Kelly, 1992, *The End of Certainty: The Story of the 1980s*, Allen and Unwin, Sydney, p. 7.
70 S. Deery, D. Plowman & J. Walsh, 1997, *Industrial Relations: A Contemporary Analysis*, 2nd edn, McGraw-Hill, Sydney.
71 M. Gardner & G. Palmer, 1997, *Employment Relations and Human Resource Management in Australia*, 2nd edn, Macmillan, Melbourne.
72 J. Quiggan, 1996, *Great Expectations: Micro-Economic Reform and Australia*, Allen and Unwin, St Leonards, New South Wales.

73   M. Horridge, 1988, 'Tariffs in Australia: theory, history and effects', *Australian Economic Review*, University of Melbourne Press, 2nd quarter, pp. 61–73.
74   Quiggan, 1996. p. 20.
75   J. Hill, W. Howard & R. Lansbury, 1982, *Industrial Relations—An Australian Introduction*, Longman Cheshire, Melbourne.
76   Hill, Howard & Lansbury, 1982.
77   S. Deery & D. Plowman, 1991, *Industrial Relations*, 3rd edn, McGraw-Hill, Sydney.
78   Gardner & Palmer, 1997.
79   See for example M. Costa & M. Duffy, 1991, *Labour, prosperity and the nineties: beyond the bonsai economy*, The Federation Press, Leichhardt, New South Wales; Quiggan, 1996.
80   K. Anderson & R. Garnaut, 1986, *The Political Economy of Manufacturing Protection: Experiences of ASEAN and Australia*, Allen and Unwin, Sydney.
81   M. Rimmer & G. Zappala, 1988, 'Labour market flexibility and the second tier', *Australian Bulletin of Labour*, 14 (4), pp. 564–91; Quiggan, 1996.
82   T. Keenoy & D. Kelly, 1996, *The Employment Relationship in Australia*, Harcourt Brace, Sydney.
83   For further discussion, see P. Forsyth, 1992, *Micro-Economic Reform in Australia*, Allen and Unwin, Sydney; and J. Niland, 1991, 'Transforming industrial relations teaching and research: international trends', in R. Lansbury (ed), *ACIRRT Monograph No. 4*, University of Sydney, Sydney, pp. 41–7.
84   See for example J. Atkinson, 1984, 'Manpower strategies for flexible organisations', *Personnel Management*, August, pp. 28–31; M. Piore and C. Sabel, 1984, *The Second Industrial Divide: Possibilities for Prosperity*, Basic Books, New York; Rimmer & Zappala, 1988; J. Mathews, 1989, *Tools of Change: New Technology and the Democratisations of Work*, Pluto Press, Sydney.
85   Rimmer & Zappala, 1988.
86   Australian Conciliation and Arbitration Commission, 1988, 1988 National Wage Case, Decision, print H4000, Australian Conciliation and Arbitration Commission, Melbourne.
87   J.J. Macken,1989, *Award Restructuring*, The Federation Press, Leichhardt, New South Wales; C. Fox, W. Howard, & M. Pittard, 1995, *Industrial Relations in Australia: Development*, Law and Operations, Longman, Melbourne.
88   Australian Conciliation and Arbitration Commission, 1988; Rimmer & Verevis, 1990.
89   J. Mathews, 1990, 'An Australian model of award restructuring', working paper no. 84, School of Industrial Relations and Organisational Behaviour, University of New South Wales, Sydney; Still & Mortimer, 1993.
90   E. Davis & R. Lansbury, 1988, 'Industrial relations in Australia', in G. Bamber and R. Lansbury (eds), *International and Comparative Employment Relations*, Allen and Unwin, Sydney, pp. 110–43.
91   R. Curtain & J. Mathews, 'Two models of awards restructuring in Australia', *Labour and Industry*, 3 (1), 1990, pp. 58–75.
92   See Still & Mortimer, 1993; Fox, Howard & Pittard, 1995.
93   Davis & Lansbury, 1988.
94   Davis & Lansbury, 1988; Mathews, 1990.
95   S. Charlesworth, 1997, 'Enterprise bargaining and women workers: the seven perils of flexibility', *Labour and Industry*, 8 (2), pp. 101–15.
96   Fox, Howard & Pittard, 1995.
97   Introduced by the AIRC in June 1993 to replace the Enterprise Bargaining Principle. Its essential difference was the incorporation of technical features associated with the traditional award systems.
98   D. Clark, 1997, *Student Economic Brief*, AFR Books, Melbourne, pp. 31–2.
99   Davis & Lansbury, 1988.
100 Fox, Howard & Pittard, 1995.
101 R. May, 2006, 'The British Fair Pay Commission and the Proposed Australian Fair Pay Commission', *Journal of Australian Political Economy*, 56, pp. 92–104.
102 See K. Andrews, 2005, 'Building better workplaces', Speech at the National Press Club, Canberra, 31 May. K. Andrews, 2006, *WorkChoices: A New Workplace Relations System*, in J. Teicher, R. Lambert & A. O'Rourke, (Eds), *The New Industrial Relations Agenda*, Pearson, Sydney.

CHAPTER 14 NOTES

1   Portions of this chapter have been adapted from the following literature reviews: B. Gerhart & S.L. Rynes, 2003, *Compensation: Theory, Evidence, and Strategic Implications*, Sage, Thousand Oaks, CA; B. Gerhart & G.T. Milkovich, 1992, 'Employee compensation: research and practice', in M.D. Dunnette & L.M. Hough (eds), *Handbook of Industrial and Organizational Psychology*, vol. 3, 2nd edn, Consulting Psychologists Press, Palo Alto; B. Gerhart, G.T. Milkovich & B. Murray, 1992, 'Pay, performance, and participation', in D. Lewin, O.S. Mitchell & P.D. Sherer (eds), *Research Frontiers in Industrial Relations and Human Resources*, Industrial Relations Research Association, Madison, WI; B. Gerhart & R.D. Bretz, 'Employee compensation', in W. Karwowski & G. Salvendy (eds), 1994, *Organization and Management of Advanced Manufacturing*, John Wiley and Sons, New York.
2   B. Gerhardt, 2000, 'Compensation Strategy and Organisatin performance', in S.L.Rynes & B. Gerhart (eds), *Compensation in Organisations: Current Research and Practice*, Jossey-Bass, San Francisco, pp. 151–94; B. Gerhart & G.T. Milkovich, 1990, 'Organizational differences in managerial compensation and financial performance', *Academy of Management Journal*, 33, pp. 663–91.
3   C. Rance, 2003, 'Pay gains', *HRMonthly*, September, p. 32.
4   G. O'Neill, 2003, 'Practice: rewarding strategies', *HRMonthly*, September, p. 33.
5   R. Kramar, 2006, *Cranet-Macquarie survey on international strategic human resource management*, Centre for Australasian Human Resource Management, Macquarie University, North Ryde, NSW; R. Kramar, 2000, *Cranfield-Pricewaterhouse survey on international human resource management*, Macquarie University, North Ryde, NSW; R. Kramar & N. Lake, 1997, *Cranfield-Pricewaterhouse survey on international strategic human resource management*, Macquarie University, North Ryde, NSW.
6   P. Sheldon & A. Junor, 2006, 'Australian HRM and the Workplace Relations Amendment (Work Choices) Act 2005', *Asia Pacific Journal of Human Resources*, vol 44, no 2, August, p. 165.
7   V.M. Gibson, 1995, 'The new employee reward system', *Management Review*, 84 (2), pp. 13–18; Heneman, R.L., Ledford, G.E., Jr., & Gresham, M.T., 2000, 'The changing nature of work and its effect on compensation design and delivery', in S.L. Rynes & B. Grehart (eds), *Compensations in organisations* (pp. 195–240), Jossey-Bass, San Francisco.
8   T. Amabile, 1988, 'A Model of creativity and innovation in organizations', in B.M Staw & L.L. Cummings (eds), *Research in organizational behaviour*, p. 10. JAI Press, Greenwich, CT; M. Beer & G. Rogers, 1995, 'Do incentives work? The perceptions of a worldwide sample of senior executives', *Human Resource Planning*, 26(3), pp. 30–44. (1998); *The Economist*, 348, 8083, 59–60; A. Kohn, 1993, 'Why incentive plans cannot work', *Harvard Business Review*, 71 (5), p. 54; H. Meyer, 1975, 'The pay-of-performance dilemma', *Organisation Dynamics*, 3, pp. 39–50; J. Pheffer, 1998, 'Six dangerous myths about pay', *Harvard Business Review*, 76(3), pp. 108–119; J.D. Shaw, N. Gupta & J.E. Delery, 2002, 'Pay dispersion and work force performance: Moderating effects if incentives and interdependence', *Strategic Management Journal*, 23, pp. 491–512.
9   G. O'Neill, 1994, 'AIC Case Study: Performance Management and Performance Reward as Organisation Change Strategies', in M. Patrickson and G. Bamber (eds), *Strategic Management of Organisational Change*', Longman and Cheshire, Melbourne.
10 E. Deci & R. Ryan, 1985, *Intrinsic Motivation and Self-Determination in Human Behavior*, Plenum, New York; A. Kohn, 1993, 'Why incentive plans cannot work', *Harvard Business Review*, September–October.

Endnotes

11 C. Wright, 1995, *The Management of Labour: A History or Australian Employers*, Oxford University Press, Melbourne.

12 S.L. Rynes, B. Gerhart & L. Parks, 'Personnel Psychology: Performance Evaluation and Compensation,' *Annual Review of Psychology* (2005), R. Eisenberger & J. Cameron, 1996, 'Detrimental effects of reward: reality or myth?', *American Psychologist*, 51 (11), pp. 1153–66.

13 S.L. Rynes, B .Gerhart & L. Parks, 'Personnel Psychology: Performance Evaluation and Compensation,' *Annual Review of Psychology*, 2005, R. Eisenberger & J. Cameron, 1996, 'Detrimental effects of reward: reality or myth?', *American Psychologist*, 51 (11), pp. 1153–66.

14 R.A. Lambert & D.F. Larcker, 'Executive compensation, corporate decision making, and shareholder wealth', in F. Foulkes (ed) 1989, *Executive Compensation*, Harvard Business School Press, Boston, pp. 287–309.

15 L.R. Gomez-Mejia, H. Tosi & T. Hinkin, 1987, 'Managerial control, performance, and executive compensation', *Academy of Management Journal*, 30, pp. 51–70; H.L. Tosi Jr & L.R. Gomez-Mejia, 1989, 'The decoupling of CEO pay and performance: an agency theory perspective', *Administrative Science Quarterly*, 34, pp. 169–89.

16 K.M. Eisenhardt, 1989, 'Agency theory: an assessment and review', *Academy of Management Review*, 14, pp. 57–74.

17 M.T. Bloom & G.T.Milcovich, 'Relationships among Risk, Incentive Pay, and Organisational Performance', *Academy of Management Journal*, 41, 1998, pp. 283–97; R.E. Hoskisson, M.A. Hitt & C.W.L. Hill, 1993, 'Managerial incentives and investment in RandD in large multiproduct firms', *Organizational Science*, 4, pp. 325–41.

18 Eisenhardt, 1989.

19 Eisenhardt, 1989; E.J. Conlon & J.M. Parks, 1990, 'Effects of monitoring and tradition on compensation arrangements: an experiment with principal–agent dyads', *Academy of Management Journal*, 33, pp. 603–22; K.M. Eisenhardt, 1988, 'Agency- and institutional-theory explanations: the case of retail sales compensation', *Academy of Management Journal*, 31, pp. 488–511; Gerhart & Milkovich, 'Employee compensation', in Dunnette and Hough (eds), 1992.

20 G.T. Milkovich, J. Hannon & B. Gerhart, 1991, 'The effects of research and development intensity on managerial compensation in large organizations', *Journal of High Technology Management Research*, 2, pp. 133–50.

21 A. Maslow, 1954, *Motivation and Personality*, Harper and Row, New York.

22 F. Herzberg, B. Mausner & B. Snyderman, 1959, *The Motivation to Work*, John Wiley, New York.

23 D.C. McClelland, 1961, *The Achieving Society*, Van Nostrand Reinhold, New York.

24 D.C. McClelland & D.H. Burnham, 1976, 'Power is the great motivator', *Harvard Business Review*, March–April, pp. 100–10.

25 P. Robinson, 2001, 'Cancel the pay rise—we need quality time', *The Sydney Morning Herald*, 5 October, p. 3.

26 A. Horin, 2003, 'Discovering what works on the shopfloor', *The Sydney Morning Herald*, 26–28 December.

27 B. Gerhart & G.T. Milcovich, 'Employee Compensation'; Gerhart & Rynes, 'Compensation: Theory, Evidence and Strategic Implications'; G.T. Milkovich & A.K. Wigdor, 1991, *Pay for Performance*, National Academy Press, Washington, DC; Gerhart & Milkovich, in Dunnette and Hough (eds), 1992.

28 C. Trevor, B. Gerhart & J.W. Boudreau, '1997, Voluntary turnover and job performance: curvilinearity and the moderating influences of salary growth and promotions', *Journal of Applied Psychology*, 82, pp. 44–61.

29 R.D. Bretz, R.A. Ash & G.F. Dreher, 1989, 'Do people make the place? An examination of the attraction–selection–attrition hypothesis', *Personnel Psychology*, 42, pp. 561–81; T.A. Judge & R.D. Bretz, 1992, 'Effect of values on job choice decisions', *Journal of Applied Psychology*, 77, pp. 261–71; D.M. Cable & T.A. Judge, 1994, 'Pay performances and job search decisions: a person–organization fit perspective', *Personnel Psychology*, 47, pp. 317–48.

30 R. Anderson, 1999, 'Beyond the colour of your money', *HRMonthly*, November, p. 32.

31 D. Cullen, 2000, 'Get with the program', *The Sydney Morning Herald*, 29 April, p. 127.

32 R. Kramar, 2006, *Cranet-Macquarie Survey on International Strategic Human Resource Management*, Macquarie University, North Ryde, New South Wales, pp. 22–3.

33 Gerhart & Milkovich, 'Employee Compensation'; Gerhart & Rynes, *Compensation: Theory, Evidence and Strategic Implications*; A. Majchrzak, 1988, *The Human Side of Factory Automation*, Jossey-Bass, San Francisco; E.E. Lawler III, 1990, *Strategic Pay*, Jossey-Bass, San Francisco; Gerhart & Milkovich, in Dunnette & Hough (eds), 1992.

34 S. Long, 2000, 'Ordinary workers moving to performance related pay', *Australian Financial Review*, 24 March, p. 23.

35 Milcovich & Wigdor, *Pay for Performance*; Rynes, Gerhart & Parks, 'Personnel Psychology: Performance, Evaluation and Compensation'; R.D. Bretz, G.T. Milkovich & W. Read, 1992, 'The current state of performance appraisal research and practice', *Journal of Management*, 18, pp. 321–52.

36 Bretz, Milkovich & Read, 1992.

37 Bretz, Milkovich & Read, 1992.

38 W.E. Deming, 1986, *Out of the Crisis*, Center for Advanced Engineering Study, Massachusetts Institute of Technology, Cambridge, MA, p. 110.

39 Deming, 1986.

40 Deming, 1986.

41 Trevor, Gerhart & Boudreau, 1997.

42 R. Folger & M.A. Konovsky, 1989, 'Effects of procedural and distributive justice on reactions to pay raise decisions', *Academy of Management Journal*, 32, pp. 115–30; J. Greenberg, 1986, 'Determinants of perceived fairness of performance evaluations', *Journal of Applied Psychology*, 71, pp. 340–2.

43 E.E. Lawler III, 'Pay for performance: a strategic analysis', in L.R. Gomez-Mejia (ed), 1989, *Compensation and Benefits*, Bureau of National Affairs, Washington, DC; A.M. Konrad & J. Pfeffer, 1990, 'Do you get what you deserve? Factors affecting the relationship between productivity and pay', *Administrative Science Quarterly*, 35, pp. 258–85; J.L. Medoff & K.G. Abraham, 1981, 'Are those paid more really more productive? The case of experience', *Journal of Human Resources*, 16, pp. 186–216; K.S. Teel, 1986, 'Are merit raises really based on merit?', *Personnel Journal*, 65 (3), pp. 88–95.

44 B. Gerhart & S. Rynes, 1991, 'Determinants and consequences of salary negotiations by graduating male and female MBAs', *Journal of Applied Psychology*, pp. 256–62.

45 E.A. Locke, D.B. Feren, V.M. McCaleb, K.N. Shaw & A.T. Denny, 'The relative effectiveness of four methods of motivating employee performance', in K.D. Duncan, M.M. Gruenberg & D. Wallis (eds), 1980, *Changes in Working Life*, John Wiley, New York, pp. 363–88.

46 Gerhart & Milkovich, in Dunnette & Hough (eds), 1992.

47 F. Simons, 2000, 'A piece of the action', *Australian Financial Review*, 10 July, p. 51.

48 This idea has been referred to as the 'share economy'. See M.L. Weitzman, 1985, 'The simple macroeconomics of profit sharing', *American Economic Review*, 75, pp. 937–53. For supportive empirical evidence, see the following studies: J. Chelius & R.S. Smith, 1990, 'Profit sharing and employment stability', *Industrial and Labour Relations Review*, 43, pp. 256S–73S; B. Gerhart & L.O. Trevor, 1995, 'Employment stability under different managerial compensation systems', working paper, Cornell University, Center for Advanced Human Resource Studies, New York; D.L. Kruse, 1991,'Profit sharing and employment variability: microeconomic evidence on the Weitzman theory', *Industrial and Labor Relations Review*, 44, pp. 437–53.

49 Gerhart & Milkovich, in Dunnette & Hough (eds), 1992; M.L. Weitzman & D.L. Kruse, 'Profit sharing and productivity', in A.S. Blinder (ed), 1990, *Paying for Productivity*, Brookings Institution, Washington, DC; D.L. Kruse, 1993, *Profit Sharing: Does It Make a Difference?*, Upjohn Institute, Kalamazoo, MI.

50 American Management Association, 1991, *CompFlash*, April, p. 3. General Motors' Saturn division has also scaled back its reliance on profit sharing because of lower-than-expected profits.
51 American Management Association, 1991, p. 3.
52 1990, 'Executive compensation: taking stock', *Personnel*, 67, December, pp. 7–8; 1991, 'Another day, another dollar needs another look', *Personnel*, 68, January, pp. 9–13.
53 L. Gettler, 2000, '#2 Cisco Systems', *The Sydney Morning Herald*, 16 August, p. 8.
54 P. Cleary & F. Buffini, 2000, 'Employee share schemes may get tax break', *Australian Financial Review*, 29 August, p. 1.
55 Gerhart & Milkovich, 1990.
56 2000, 'Share schemes need addressing', *Australian Financial Review*, 16 May, p. 18.
57 1995, *EBRI Databook on Employee Benefits*, Employee Benefit Research Institute, Washington, DC; see www.nceo.org, National Center for Employee Ownership web site.
58 D. Jones & T. Kato, 1995, 'The productivity effects of employee stock ownership plans and bonuses: evidence from Japanese panel data', *American Economic Review*, 185 (3), June, pp. 391–414.
59 Simons, 2000.
60 'Share schemes need addressing', 2000.
61 M.A. Conte & J. Svejnar, 'The performance effects of employee ownership plans', in Blinder (ed), 1990, pp. 245–94.
62 Conte and Svejnar in Blinder (ed), 1990, pp. 245–94; T.H. Hammer, 'New developments in profit sharing, gainsharing, and employee ownership', in J.P. Campbell, R.J. Campbell and Associates (eds), 1988, *Productivity in Organizations*, Jossey-Bass, San Francisco; K.J. Klein, 1987, 'Employee stock ownership and employee attitudes: a test of three models', *Journal of Applied Psychology*, 72, pp. 319–32.
63 J.L. Pierce, S. Rubenfeld & S. Morgan, 1991, 'Employee ownership: a conceptual model of process and effects', *Academy of Management Review*, 16, pp. 121–44.
64 One study found that the value of shares was reduced annually by an amount roughly equal to 2.2 per cent of pretax profits (Anonymous, 1991, 'Unseen apples and small carrots', *The Economist*, 13 April, p. 75).
65 L. Hatcher & T.L. Ross, 1991, 'From individual incentives to an organization-wide gainsharing plan: effects on teamwork and product quality', *Journal of Organizational Behavior*, 12, pp. 169–83; R.T. Kaufman, 1992, 'The effects of improshare on productivity', *Industrial and Labor Relations Review*, 45, pp. 311–22; M.H. Schuster, 1984, 'The Scanlon plan: a longitudinal analysis', *Journal of Applied Behavioral Science*, 20, pp. 23–8; J.A. Wagner III, P. Rubin & T.J. Callahan, 1988, 'Incentive payment and nonmanagerial productivity: an interrupted time series analysis of magnitude and trend', *Organizational Behavior and Human Decision Processes*, 42, pp. 47–74; M.M. Petty, B. Singleton & D.W. Connell, 1992, 'An experimental evaluation of an organizational incentive plan in the electric utility industry', *Journal of Applied Psychology*, 77, pp. 427–36; J.L. McAdams, 1995, 'Employee involvement and performance reward plans', *Compensation and Benefits Review*, March–April, p. 45; W.N. Cooke, 1994, 'Employee participation programs, group-based incentives, and company performance: a union–nonunion comparison', *Industrial and Labor Relations Review*, 47, pp. 594–609.
66 P. Carey, 'Gainsharing: a metal industry case study', in G. O'Neill & R. Kramar (eds), 1997, *Australian Human Resource Management*, vol. 1, Business and Professional Publishing, Warriewood, New South Wales, pp. 179–90; T.L. Ross & R.A. Ross, 'Gainsharing: sharing improved performance', in M.L. Rock and L.A. Berger (eds), 1991, *The Compensation Handbook*, 3rd edn, McGraw-Hill, New York.
67 T.M. Welbourne & L.R. Gomez-Mejia, 'Team incentives in the workplace', in Rock & Berger (eds), 1991.
68 R.S. Kaplan & D.P. Norton, 1996, 'Using the balanced scorecard as a strategic management system', *Harvard Business Review*, January–February, pp. 75–85.
69 G. O'Neill, 'Issues in the design and structure of executive remuneration', in G. O'Neill & R. Kramar (eds) 1999, *Australian Human Resources Management*, vol. 2, Business and Professional Publishing, Warriewood, New South Wales, pp. 155–69.
70 O'Neill in O'Neill & Kramar (eds), 1999; C. Fox, 2000, 'Push for global pay standards', *Australian Financial Review*, 13 April, p. 70.
71 A. Ferguson and K. De Clercq, 1999, 'Boss cocky', *Business Review Weekly*, 5 November, p. 60; M.C. Jensen & K.J. Murphy, 1990a, 'Performance pay and top-management incentives', *Journal of Political Economy*, 98, pp. 225–64.
72 I. Weinberg, 1995, 'What is reasonable executive compensation?', *Journal of Compensation and Benefits*, 11 (1), pp. 17–23; Jensen and Murphy, 1990a.
73 G.L. O'Neill & M. Iob, 1999, 'Determinants of executive remuneration in Australian organizations: an exploratory study', *Asia Pacific Journal of Human Resources*, 37 (1), p. 73.
74 M.C. Jensen & K.J. Murphy, 1990b,'CEO incentives—it's not how much you pay, but how', *Harvard Business Review*, 68, May–June, pp. 138–53.
75 L. Gomez-Meija & R.M. Wiseman, 1997, 'Reframing executive compensation: An assessment and outlook', *Journal of Management*, vol 23, no3, pp. 291–374.
76 M.J. Jensen & W.H.Meckling 1976, 'Theory of the firm: Managerial behaviour, agency costs and ownership structure', *Journal of Financial Economics*, vol 3, pp. 305–60; L. Bebchuk & J. Fried 2004, *Pay without performance: The unfulfilled Promise of executive compensation*, Harvard University press, Cambridge MA.
77 Gerhart & Milkovich, 1990.
78 Kramar, 2006.
79 Kramar, 2000; Ferguson & De Clercq, 1999.
80 G. O'Neill, 2000, 'Lies, damned lies, statistics … and CEO pay', *HRMonthly*, February, pp. 30–1.
81 C. Lacy, 2000, 'Shareholder versus executive pay', *Australian Financial Review*, 31 August 2000, p. 12.
82 G. O'Neill, in G. O'Neill & R. Kramar (eds), 1999, p. 166.
83 'Executive Salaries', 2004, The Australian Financial Review, pp S10-S11.
84 2004, 'Exec pay challenging', *HRMonthly*, July, p. 7.
85 J. Cutcher-Gershenfeld, 1991, 'The impact on economic performance of a transformation in workplace relations', *Industrial and Labor Relations Review*, 44, pp. 241–60; I. Goll, 1991, 'Environment, corporate ideology, and involvement programs', *Industrial Relations*, 30, pp. 138–49.
86 L.R. Gomez-Mejia & D.B. Balkin, 1992, *Compensation, Organizational Strategy, and Firm Performance*, South-Western, Cincinnati, OH; G.D. Jenkins & E.E. Lawler III, 1981, 'Impact of employee participation in pay plan development', *Organizational Behavior and Human Performance*, 28, pp. 111–28.
87 D.I. Levine & L.D. Tyson, 'Participation, productivity, and the firm's environment', in Blinder (ed), 1990.
88 T. Welbourne, D. Balkin & L. Gomez-Mejia, 1995, 'Gainsharing and mutual monitoring: a combined agency–organizational justice interpretation', *Academy of Management Journal*, 38, pp. 881–99.
89 Westbourne, Balkin & Gomez-Mejia, 1995.
90 A.S. Blinder, Introduction, in Blinder (ed), 1990, pp. 1–13.
91 M. Beer & M.D. Cannon, 2004, 'Response to comments: Promise and Peril in implementing pay-for performance', *Human Resource Management*, Spring 2004, vol 43. no 1,pp. 43–8.
92 J. Baron, 2004, 'Promise and Peril in implementing pay-for-performance' by M. Beer and M.D. Cannon, *Human Resource Management*, Spring, vol 43, no 1, pp. 21–7
93 Hammer, in Campbell & Campbell and Associates (eds), 1988; Milkovich and Wigdor, 1991; D.J.B. Mitchell, D. Lewin & E.E. Lawler III, 'Alternative pay systems, firm performance and productivity', in Blinder (ed), 1990.
94 Kaufman, 1992; Schuster, 1984; Wagner, Rubin & Callahan, 1988.
95 C.R. Gowen III & S.A. Jennings, 1991, 'The effects of changes in participation and group size on gainsharing success: a case study', *Journal of Organizational Behavior Management*, 11, pp. 147–69.

96 T. Kocham, L. Hatcher, T.L. Ross & D. Collins, 1991, 'Attributions for participation and nonparticipation in gainsharing-plan involvement systems', *Group and Organization Studies*, 16, pp. 25–43; Mitchell, Lewin & Lawler, in Blinder (ed), 1990.

97 M. Beer & M. D. Cannon, 2004 'Promise and Peril in implementing pay-for-performance', Human Resource Management, vol 43, no1, Spring, p1-20

98 M. Beer & Mark D. Cannon, 2004, 'Response to comments: 'Promise and Peril in implementing pay-for-performance', *Human Resource Management*, Spring 2004, vol 43. no 1,pp. 43–8.

99 Kochan, 2004; R.B. McKersie & L.C.Hunter, 1973, *Pay, Productivity and Collective Bargaining*, McGraw-Hill, New York; M. Beer & N. Katz, 2003, 'Do incentives work? The perceptions of a worldwide sample of senior executives', *Human Resource Planning*, vol 26, no 3, pp. 30–44.

100 A.J. Baker, 1993, 'Stock options—a perk that built Silicon Valley', *The Wall Street Journal*, 23 June, p. A20.

CHAPTER 15 NOTES

1 See for example Beauchamp & Bowie, 2004, *Ethical Theory and Business* (7th edn), Prentice Hall, Englewood Cliffs, New Jersey.

2 J. Collier, 1998, 'Theorising the ethical organization', *Business Ethics Quarterly*, 8 (3), pp. 621–54.

3 T.L. Beauchamp & N.E. Bowie, 2004, *Ethical Theory and Business* (7th edn), Prentice Hall, Englewood Cliffs, New Jersey.

4 Beauchamp & Bowie, 2004.

5 A. Etzioni, 1990, *The Moral Dimension Towards a New Economics*, The Free Press, New York; R. Gray, D. Owen & C Adams, 1996, *Accounting and Accountability: Changes and Challenges in Corporate Social and Environmental Reporting*, Prentice Hall, London; and K. Legge, 1996, *Human Resource Management: Rhetorics and Reality*, Macmillan, London.

6 Etzioni, 1990.

7 T. Wilcox & D. Lowry, 2000, 'Beyond resourcefulness: casual workers and the human-centered organisation', *Business and Professional Ethics Journal*, 19 (3 and 4), pp. 29–53.

8 K. Kamoche, 2001, *Understanding Human Resource Management*, Open University Press, Buckingham, p. 18.

9 A. Crane & D. Matten, 2004, *Business Ethics*, Oxford University Press, Oxford, p. 19.

10 Crane & Matten, 2004.

11 N. Klein, 2000, *No Logo No Space No Choice No Jobs: Taking Aim at the Brand Bullies*, Flamingo, London.

12 Australian Council of Social Service (ACOSS), 2003, *Hidden Unemployment in Australia*, Australian Council for Social Service, Sydney.

13 I. Watson, J. Buchanan, I. Campbell & C. Briggs, 2003, *Fragmented Futures: New Challenges in Working Life*, Federation Press, Sydney.

14 H.J. Van Buren III, 2003, 'Boundaryless careers and employability obligations', *Business Ethics Quarterly*, 13 (2), pp. 131–50 (see p. 131).

15 D. Winstanley & J. Woodall, 2000a, *Ethical Issues in Contemporary Human Resource Management*, MacMillan Business, Basingstoke.

16 J. Woodall & D. Douglas, 2000, 'Winning hearts and minds: ethical issues in human resource development' in D. Winstanley & J. Woodall 2000a, (eds), *Ethical Issues in Contemporary Human Resource Management*, MacMillan Business, Basingstoke, pp. 116–36 (see p. 116).

17 C. Wiley, 1998, 'Re-examining perceived ethics issues and ethics roles among employment managers', *Journal of Business Ethics*, 17, pp. 147–61 (see pp. 148–9).

18 For some, the centrality of ethics in HRM is interpreted as a requirement that HR managers and HR departments engender ethical compliance among their employees. According to A.R. Nankervis, R.L. Compton & M. Baird, 2002, *Strategic Human Resource Management*, 4th edn, Nelson Thomson Learning, South Melbourne, ethics in HRM can be defined as 'the contribution to the design of right values and behaviours in the social and operational context' (p. 29) and 'the HRM role needs to monitor and maintain behavioural norms within an organisation' (p. 30). In contrast, this author explicitly rejects this notion of HRM as the ethical police officer of the organisation ensuring that managers and workers behave themselves.

19 D. Winstanley, J. Woodall & E. Heery, 1996, 'Business ethics and human resource management themes and issues', *Personnel Review*, 25 (6), pp. 5–12 (see p. 7).

20 Wiley, 1998, p. 149.

21 Australian Human Resources Institute (AHRI), 2004, 'AHRI awards for excellence in people management assessment criteria', AHRI, www.awards.ahri.com.au/assets/criteria.pdf, viewed 9/11/2004.

22 M. G. Velasquez, 1998, *Business Ethics: Concepts and Cases*, Prentice Hall, Upper Saddle River, New Jersey.

23 L.P. Hartman, 1998, *Perspectives in Business Ethics*, McGraw-Hill, Chicago, 1998.

24 N. Davis, 1991, 'Contemporary deontology' in P. Singer (ed), *A Companion to Ethics*, Blackwell Reference, Oxford, pp. 205–18.

25 Davis in Singer, 1991.

26 Davis in Singer 1991.

27 J. Rawls, 1972, *A Theory of Justice*, Oxford University Press, Oxford.

28 Beauchamp & Bowie, 2004.

29 Hartman, 1998.

30 P. Pettit, 1991, 'Consequentialism' in P. Singer (ed), *A Companion to Ethics*, Blackwell Reference, Oxford.

31 R.C. Solomon, 2002, 'Business ethics and virtue' in R. Frederick (ed), *A Companion to Business Ethics*, Blackwell Publishers, Malden, Massachusetts.

32 Beauchamp & Bowie, 2004.

33 Rawls, 1972.

34 Beauchamp & Bowie, 2004.

35 These criticisms are based on Beauchamp & Bowie, 2004, and R. Frederick, 2002, 'An outline of ethical relativism and ethical absolutism', in Frederick, pp. 65–80, but are typical of arguments from a large number of writers.

36 Frederick in Frederick, 2002.

37 F.N. Brady & C.P. Dunn, 1995, 'Business meta-ethics: an analysis of two theories', *Business Ethics Quarterly*, 5 (3), pp. 385–98.

38 Brady & Dunn, 1995.

39 Bowie, 1999.

40 K. Goodpaster, 2002, 'Teaching and learning ethics by the case method', in N.E. Bowie (ed), *The Blackwell Guide to Business Ethics*, Blackwell, Oxford.

41 Goodpaster in Bowie, 2002, p. 126.

42 Goodpaster in Bowie, 2002.

43 Freeman, 1984.

44 W.M. Evan & R.E. Freeman, 1998, 'A stakeholder theory of the modern corporation: Kantian capitalism', in Beauchamp and Bowie, 2004, p. 58.

45 Evan & Freeman, 1998 in Beauchamp and Bowie, 2004, p. 58.

46 R.A. Phillips, 1997, 'Stakeholder theory and a principle of fairness', *Business Ethics Quarterly*, 7 (1), pp. 51–66.

47 Beauchamp & Bowie, 2004.

48 Beauchamp & Bowie, 2004, p. 29.

49 Beauchamp & Bowie, 2004, pp. 30–1.

50 For example R. Duska, 2002, 'Employee rights' and J.B. Ciulla, 2002, 'Business ethics and work: questions for the twenty-first century' in Frederick provide an analysis of such texts.

51 Many examples of this exist and have been documented. See, for example, Klein, 2000.

52 For more detail of such issues, see P.J. Dowling & D.E. Welch, 2004, *International Human Resource Management*, 4th edn, International Thomson, London.

53 J.R. Rowan, 2000, 'The moral foundation of employee rights', *Journal of Business Ethics*, 24 (4), pp. 355–61.

54 N.E. Bowie, 1998, 'A Kantian theory of meaningful work', *Journal of Business Ethics*, 17 (9–10), pp. 1083–92.

55 Van Buren III, 2003.

56 Bowie, 1998.
57 Bowie, 1998, p. 1083.
58 Van Buren III, 2003. Employability is defined by the ILO as having 'the skills, knowledge and competencies that enhance a worker's ability to secure and retain a job, progress at work and cope with change, secure another job if she/he so wishes, and enter more easily into the labour market at different periods of the life-cycle', *Learning and Training for Work in the Knowledge Society*, International Labour Organization.
59 Rowan, 2000.
60 According to Rousseau & Parks, mutual obligations are the essence of the 'psychological contract' between employers and employees. D.M. Rousseau & J.M. Parks, 1992, 'The contracts of individuals and organisations', *Research in Organizational Behavior*, 15, pp. 1–47.
61 S. Bok, 'Whistleblowing and professional responsibility', in N.E. Bowie (ed) *Ethical Theory and Business*, 6th edn, Prentice Hall, Englewood Cliffs, New Jersey, 2001.
62 R. Duska, 2004, in Beauchamp & Bowie, 2004.
63 R.A. Larmer, 1992, 'Whistleblowing and employee loyalty', *Journal of Business Ethics*, 11 (2), p. 125.
64 Rosseau & Parks, 1992.
65 Beauchamp & Bowie, 2004.
66 The opposite of this is true in HRM texts that assume that ethics in HRM is about controlling the behaviour of the employee. However, as noted earlier, this pseudo-ethical debate has been rejected as being a manifestation of the 'problem'.
67 Crane & Matten, 2004, switch sides on their 'employee and employer rights list' without acknowledgment of doing so.
68 Beauchamp & Bowie, 2004.
69 Crane & Matten, 2004.
70 S. Aryee, P.S. Budhwar & Z.X. Chen, 2002, 'Trust as a mediator of the relationship between organizational justice and work outcomes: test of a social exchange model', *Journal of Organizational Behavior*, 23 (3), pp. 267–85.
71 B. Erdogan, M.L. Kraimer & R.C. Liden, 2001, 'Procedural justice as a two-dimensional construct: an examination in the performance appraisal context', *The Journal of Applied Behavioral Science*, 37 (Jun), pp. 205–22.
72 M.R. Greenwood & J.A. Simmons, 2004, 'Towards ethical human resource management', *Business and Professional Ethics Journal*, 23 (3).
73 D. Winstanley & J. Woodall, 2000b, 'The ethical dimensions of human resource management', *Human Resource Management Journal*, 10 (2), pp. 5–20.
74 L. Harris, 2002, 'Achieving a balance in human resourcing between employee rights and care for individual', *Business and Professional Ethics Journal*, 21 (2), pp. 45–60.
75 Ciulla in Frederick, 2002.
76 Ciulla in Frederick, 2002, p. 272.
77 M.R. Greenwood, 2002, 'Ethics and HRM: a review and conceptual analysis', *Journal of Business Ethics*, 36 (3), pp. 261–79; Winstanley & Woodall, 2000a.
78 Wilcox & Lowry, 2002, p. 29.
79 L. Kohlberg, 1969, 'Stage and sequence: the cognitive-developmental approach to socialization', in D. A. Goslin (ed), *Handbook of Socialization Theory*, Rand McNally, Chicago.
80 K.L. Trevino, 1992, 'Moral reasoning and business ethics: implications for research, education, and management', *Journal of Business Ethics*, 11 (5/6), p. 445–60.
81 N. Bowie, 2000, 'A Kantian theory of leadership', *Leadership and Organization Development Journal*, 21 (4), pp. 185–93 (see p. 191).
82 R. Macklin, 2003, 'The Efficacy of Agnes Heller's Moral Philosophy for HRMs', paper presented at the Society for Business Ethics, Seattle, Washington, 31 July–3 August.
83 Bowie, 2000.
84 Macklin, 2003.
85 Macklin, 2003, p. 6.
86 D. Foote & I Robinson, 1999, 'The role of the human resources manager: strategist or conscience of the organisation?', *Business Ethics: A European Review*, 8 (2), pp. 26, 88–98.
87 D. Ardagh, 2003, 'Professionalisation of a Practice: Human Resource Management as a Test Case', Paper presented at the Proceedings of the Hawaii International Conference on Business, Honolulu, Hawaii, 18–21 June.
88 The Australian Human Resource Institute (AHRI) published a code of ethics and professional conduct for its members in August 2006. It is available at http://www.ahri.com.au/upload/AHRICode_FINAL290806.doc. The equivalent body in the United States, the Society for Human Resource Management, does have a code which is accessible at www.shrm.org/chapters/resources/codeofconduct.asp
89 Membership of AHRI is entirely voluntary and the body has no capacity to register/deregister HR officers.
90 Wiley, 1998, p. 147.
91 Foote & Robinson, 1999.
92 Foote & Robinson, 1999, p. 96.
93 M.R. Greenwood & J. Simmons, 2004.
94 Wilcox & Lowry, 2000.
95 Klein, 2000.
96 Wilcox & Lowry, 2000.
97 Wilcox & Lowry, 2000, p. 32.
98 T. Claydon & M. Doyle, 1996, 'Trusting me, trusting you? The ethics of employee empowerment', *Personnel Review*, 25 (6), pp. 13–25.
99 M.R. Greenwood, 2002, p. 272.
100 K. Legge, *Human Resource Management: Rhetorics and Reality*, Macmillan, London, 1995.
101 J. Gandz & F. G. Bird, 1996, 'The ethics of empowerment', *Journal of Business Ethics*, 15 (4), pp. 383–92.
102 Ciulla in Frederick, 2002.
103 Wilcox & Lowry, 2000, p. 33.
104 Greenwood & Simmons, 2004.
105 This analysis draws from A. J. Walsh, 2001, 'Are market norms and intrinsic value mutually exclusive?', *Australasian Journal of Philosophy*, 79 (4), pp. 523–43.
106 D. Guest & N. Conway, 1999, 'Peering into the Black Hole: the downside of the new employment relations in the UK', *British Journal of Industrial Relations*, 37 (September), pp. 367–89.
107 Guest & Conway, 1999.
108 Legge, 1995.
109 Ciulla in Frederick, 2000.
110 Burgess & Campbell, 1998 and Van Gramberg et al., 2000.
111 AHRI, 2006a, *By-Law 1 Code of ethics & professional conduct*, Australian Institute of Human Resource Management, Melbourne: http://www.ahri.com.au/upload/AHRICode_FINAL290806.doc.
112 AHRI, 2006b, *By-Law 4 AHRI Membership Accreditation*, Australian Institute of Human Resource Management, Melbourne: http://www.ahri.com.au/upload/Profess_Grades_110806_wcb.pdf.
113 AHRI, 2006a, p. 1.

CHAPTER 16 NOTES

1 This chapter is adapted from the opening chapters of the following books with the permission of the publisher, Thomson Learning, UK: P. J. Dowling, D.E. Welch & R.S. Schuler, 1998, *International Human Resource Management: Managing People in a Multinational Context*, 3rd edn, South–Western, Cincinnati); P. J. Dowling and D.E. Welch, 2004, *International Human Resource Management: Managing People in a Multinational Context*, 4th edn, Thomson Learning, London; and P.J. Dowling, M. Festing & A.D. Engle, 2008, *International Human Resource Management: Managing People in a Multinational Context*, 5th edn, Thomson Learning, London.
2 H. De Cieri & P.J. Dowling, 'Strategic Human Resource Management in Multinational Enterprises: Theoretical and Empirical Developments', in P. Wright et al (eds) *Research and Theory in SHRM: An agenda for the 21st century*, JAI Press, Greenwich, CT.
3 For examples of this approach, see N. Adler, 1997, *International Dimensions of Organizational Behaviour*, 3rd edn, South-Western, Cincinnatti, Ohio; and A. Phatak, 1997, *International Management: Concept & Cases*, South-Western, Cincinnati, Ohio. See also the Special

Issue on Asia-Pacific HRM, *International Journal of Human Resource Management*, 2000, 11(2).

4   See for example, C. Brewster & A. Hegewisch, 1994, *Policy and Practice in European Human Resource Management—The Price Waterhouse Cranfield Survey*, Routledge, London.

5   See P. Dowling & R. Schuler, 1990, *International Dimensions of Human Resource Management*, 1st edn, PWS-Kent, Boston, MA; P. Dowling, R. Schuler & D. Welch, 1994, *International Dimensions of Human Resource Management*, 2nd edn, Wadsworth, Belmont, CA; P. J. Dowling, D.E. Welch & R.S. Schuler, 1998, *International Human Resource Management: Managing People in a Multinational Context*, 3rd edn, South–Western, Cincinnati.

6   T.M. Welbourne & H. De Cieri, 2001, 'How New Venture Initial Public Offerings Benefit from International Operations', *International Journal of Human Resource Management*, 12(4), pp. 652–68.

7   P. Morgan, 1986, 'International Human Resource Management: Fact or Fiction', *Personnel Administrator*, 31(9), pp. 437.

8   See H. De Cieri, S.L. McGaughey, & P.J. Dowling, 1996, 'Relocation' in *International Encyclopaedia of Business and Management*, ed. M. Warner, vol. 5, Routledge, London, pp. 4300–10, for further discussion of this point.

9   For an example of the way in which the term is being used, see M.G. Harvey, M.M. Novicevic and C. Speier, 2000, 'Strategic Global Human Resource Management: The Role of Inpatriate Managers', *Human Resource Management Review*, 10(2), pp. 153–75.

10 Curiously, the Reference Guide also states that the word inpatriate 'can also be used for U.S. expatriates returning to an assignment in the U.S.'. This is a contradiction of the first part of the definition of an inpatriate being a 'Foreign manager in the U.S.' and is illogical. U.S. expatriates returning to the U.S. are PCNs and cannot also be classed as 'Foreign managers in the U.S.'—perhaps they are 'repatriates', but they are not inpatriates. As defined, this term is only of use in the United States.

11 G. Stahl & I. Bjorkman (eds.), 2006, *Handbook of Research in International Human Resource Management*, Edward Elgar, Cheltenham, UK, p. 1.

12 P.J. Dowling, 1988, 'International and Domestic Personnel/Human Resource Management: Similarities and Differences,' in *Readings in Personnel and Human Resource Management*, 3rd edn, R.S. Schuler, S.A. Youngblood, & V.L. Huber (eds), West Publishing, St. Paul, Minn.8792.

13 See D.L. Pinney, 1982, 'Structuring an Expatriate Tax Reimbursement Program', Personnel Administrator, 27(7), pp. 1925; and M. Gajek & M.M. Sabo, 1986, 'The bottom line: What HR managers need to know about the new expatriate regulations', Personnel Adminstrator, 31(2) pp. ??.

14 For up-to-date information on the FCPA see the U.S. Department of Justice website: www.usdoj.gov/criminal/fraud/fcpa.html.

15 P. Morgan, 'International Human Resource Management'.

16 R.D. Robinson, 1978, *International Business Management: A Guide to Decision Making*, 2nd edn, Dryden, Hinsdale, Ill.

17 Although less common in the United States, the use of private boarding schools is common in countries (particularly European countries) which have a colonial tradition where both colonial administrators and business people would often undertake long assignments overseas and expect to leave their children at a boarding school in their home-country. This is especially true of Britain which also has a strong cultural tradition of the middle and upper classes sending their children to private boarding schools (curiously described by the British as 'public' schools, even though they are all private institutions which charge fees) even if the parents were working in Britain.

18 See 'Terrorism', Chapter 4 in T.M. Gladwin & I. Walter, 1980, *Multinationals Under Fire: Lessons in the Management of Conflict*, John Wiley, New York; M. Harvey, 1993, 'A survey of corporate programs for managing terrorist threats', *Journal of International Business Studies*, 24(3), pp. 465–78. For an excellent website on Terrorism see the following site at Columbia University: www.columbia.edu/cu/lweb/indiv/lehman/guides/terrorism.html

19 For the latest information on epidemic and pandemic crises see the World Health Organization web site at: www.who.int/csr/en/

20 G. Lee & M. Warner, 2005, 'Epidemics, labour markets and unemployment: the impact of SARS on human resource management in the Hong Kong service sector' *International Journal of Human Resource Management*, 16(5), pp. 752–71.

21 M. Erez & P.C. Earley, 1993, *Culture, Self-Identity and Work*, Oxford University Press, Oxford.

22 J.E. Harris & R.T. Moran, 1979, *Managing Cultural Differences*, Gulf, Houston.

23 R.S. Bhagat & S.J. McQuaid, 1982, 'Role of Subjective Culture in Organizations: A Review and Directions for Future Research', *Journal of Applied Psychology*, 67, pp. 653–85.

24 See J.W. Berry, 1980, 'Introduction to methodology', in *Handbook of Cross-Cultural Psychology*, Vol. 2: Methodology, H.C. Triandis & J.W. Berry (eds), Allyn & Bacon, Boston; H. De Cieri, & P.J. Dowling, 1995, 'Cross-cultural issues in organizational behaviour', in *Trends in Organizational Behaviour*, vol. 2, C.L. Cooper & D.M. Rousseau (eds), John Wiley & Sons, Chicester, U.K., pp. 127–45; and M.B. Teagarden & M.A. Von Glinow, 1997, 'Human resource management in cross-cultural contexts: Emic practices versus etic philosophies', *Management International Review*, 37 (1, Special Issue), pp. 7–20.

25 See H. Triandis & R. Brislin, 1984, 'Cross-Cultural Psychology', *American Psychologist*, vol. 39, pp. 1006–16.

26 See G. Hofstede, 1983, 'The cultural relativity of organizational practices and theories,' *Journal of International Business Studies*, 14(2), pp. 75-89.

27 T.S. Kuhn, 1962, *The Structure of Scientific Revolution*, 2nd edn, University of Chicago Press, Chicago, Ill.

28 J. D. Child, 1981, 'Culture, contingency and capitalism in the cross-national study of organizations,' in *Research in Organizational Behavior*, vol. 3, L.L. Cummings & B.M. Staw (eds), JAI Publishers Greenwich, Conn.

29 See D.A. Ricks, 1993, *Blunders in International Business*, Blackwell, Cambridge, MA for a comprehensive collection of mistakes made by multinational firms which paid insufficient attention to their cultural environment in their international business operations. For further literature on this topic see the following: P.S. Kirkbride & S.F.Y. Tang, 1994, 'From Kyoto to Kowloon: Cultural barriers to the transference of quality circles from Japan to Hong Kong', *Asia Pacific Journal of Human Resources*, 32(2), pp. 100–11; M. Tayeb, 1994, 'Organizations and national culture: Methodology considered', *Organisation Studies*, 15(3), pp. 429–46; and P. Sparrow, R.S. Schuler, & S.E. Jackson, 1994, 'Convergence or divergence: human resource practices and policies for competitive advantage worldwide', *International Journal of Human Resource Management*, 5(2), pp. 267–99; M. Morishima, 1995, 'Embedding HRM in a social context', *British Journal of Industrial Relations*, 33(4), pp. 617–43; and J.E. Delery & D.H. Doty, 1996, 'Modes of theorizing in strategic human resource management: tests of universalistic, contingency, and configurational performance predictions,' *Academy of Management Journal*, 39, pp. 802–35.

30 S.P. Huntington, 1996, 'The West: Unique, Not Universal', *Foreign Affairs*, November/December, pp. 2846.

31 C. Brewster, 'Comparing HRM policies and practices across geographical borders'. In G.Stahl & I. Bjorkman (eds), 2006, *Handbook of Research in International Human Resource Management*, Edward Elgar, Cheltenham, UK.

32 R.L. Tung, 1993, 'Managing cross-national and intra-national diversity', *Human Resource Management*, 32(4), pp. 461–77.

33 T. Wyatt, 1989, 'Understanding Unfamiliar Personnel Problems in Cross-Cultural Work Encounters', *Asia Pacific HRM*, 27(4), p. 5.

34 G. Hofstede, 1980, *Culture's Consequences: International Differences in Work-Related Values*, Sage, Newbury Park, CA.

35 There is a voluminous literature on Hofstede's work. An excellent website which summarises some of this work can be found at: geert-hofstede.international-business-center.com/index.shtml. For a

recent article on Hofstede's work see: F. Chiang, 2005, 'A critical examination of Hofstede's thesis and its application to international reward management', *International Journal of Human Resource Management*, 16(9), pp. 1545–63.
36   B. McSweeney, 'Hofstede's Model of National Cultural Differences and Their Consequences: A triumph of faith—A Failure of analysis', *Human Relations*, 55(1), pp. 89–118.
37   M.H. Hoppe, 2004, 'Retrospective on Culture's Consequences', *Academy of Management Executive*, 18(1), pp. 73–93.
38   B. Gerhart & M. Fang, 2005, 'National culture and human resource management: assumptions and evidence', *International Journal of Human Resource Management*, 16(6), pp. 971–86.
39   K. Leung, RS Bhagat, NR Buchan, M. Erez & CB Gibson, 2005, 'Culture and international business: recent advances and their implications for future research', *Journal of International Business Studies*, 36(4), pp. 35778.
40   M.E. Porter, 1986, 'Changing Patterns of International Competition', *California Management Review*, 28(2), pp. 9–40.
41   M.E. Porter, 1985, *Competitive Advantage: Creating and Sustaining Superior Performance*, The Free Press, New York.
42   A. Laurent, 1986, 'The Cross-Cultural Puzzle of International Human Resource Management', *Human Resource Management*, vol. 25, pp. 91102.
43   Ibid., p, 100.
44   This section is based on the World Investment Report, 2005, *TNCs and the Internationalisation of R&D. United Nations Conference on Trade and Development*, (UNCTAD), September.
45   It should be noted that while News Corporation was an Australian company when this data was collected, the company has since shifted its headquarters to the United States and in future would be shown as a U.S. company.
46   S. Tamer Cavusgil, 1993, *Internationalising Business Education: Meeting the Challenge*, Michigan State University Press, East Lansing, MI.
47   See C. Bartlett & S. Ghoshal, 1992, *Transnational management: Text, cases, and readings in cross border management*, Irwin, Boston, MA; and V. Pucik, 1997, 'Human resources in the future: An obstacle or a champion of globalization?', *Human Resource Management*, 36, pp. 163–7.
48   H. De Cieri and P.J. Dowling, 1999, 'Strategic Human Resource Management in Multinational Enterprises: theoretical and empirical developments,' in P.M. Wright et al. (eds), *Research in Personnel and Human Resource Management: Strategic Human Resources in the 21st Century*, Supplement 4, JAI Press, Stamford, CT.
49   S. Taylor, S. Beechler & N. Napier, 1996, 'Towards an integrative model of strategic international human resource management', *Academy of Management Review*, 21, pp. 959–85.
50   Taylor et al, ibid; K. Kamoche, 1997, 'Knowledge creation and learning in international HRM', *International Journal of Human Resource Management*, 8, pp. 213–22.
51   D. Welch, 2000, 'Determinants of International Human Resource Management Approaches and Activities'; M. Harvey, M.M. Novicevis & C. Speier, 2000, 'An Innovative Global Management Staffing System: A Competency-based Perspective', *Human Resource Management*, 39(4), pp. 381–94.
52   B. Becker & B. Gerhart, 'The Impact of Human Resource Management on Organizational Performance: Progress and Prospects', *Academy of Management Journal*, 39(4), pp. 779–801; L. Dyer and T. Reeves, 1995, 'Human Resource Strategies and Firm Performance: What do we know and where do we need to go?', *International Journal of Human Resource Management*, 6(3), pp. 656–70.
53   M. Festing, 1997, 'International Human Resource Management Strategies in Multinational Corporations: Theoretical Assumptions and Empirical Evidence from German Firms', *Management International Review*, 37(Special issue No.1) pp. 43–63; and S.J. Kobrin, 1994, 'Is There a Relationship between a Geocentric Mind-set and Multinational Strategy?', *Journal of International Business Studies*, 25, pp. 493–511.
54   P.M. Caligiuri & L.K. Stroh, 1995, 'Multinational Corporate Management Strategies and International Human Resource Practices: Bringing IHRM to the Bottom Line', *International Journal of Human Resource Management*, 6, pp. 494–507; R.B. Peterson, J. Sargent, N.K. Napier & W.S. Shim, 1996, 'Corporate Expatriate HRM Policies, Internationalisation, and Performance in the World's Largest MNCs', *Management International Review*, 36, pp. 215–30; P. Sparrow, R.S. Schuler & S.E. Jackson, 1994, 'Convergence or Divergence: Human Resource Practices and Policies for Competitive Advantage Worldwide', *International Journal of Human Resource Management*, 5, pp. 267–99.
55   R.L. Desatnick & M.L. Bennett, 1978, *Human Resource Management in the Multinational Company*, Nichols, New York.

CHAPTER 17 NOTES

1   M.L. Schmit & S.P. Allscheid, 1995, 'Employee attitudes and customer satisfaction: Making theoretical and empirical connections', *Personnel Psychology*, 48, pp. 521–36.
2   F. Reichheld, 1996, *The Loyalty Effect*, Harvard Business School Press, Cambridge, MA.
3   J.P. MacDuffie, 1995, 'Human resource bundles and manufacturing performance: Organizational logic and flexible production systems in the world auto industry', *Industrial and Labor Relations Review*, 48, pp. 197–221; also see ; P. Boselie, G. Dietz & C. Boon, 2005, 'Commonalities and contradictions in HRM and performance research', *Human Resource Management Journal*, 15 (3), pp. 67–94; D. Guest, 2002, 'Human resource management, corporate performance and employee wellbeing: building the worker into HRM', *Journal of Industrial Relations*, 44 (3), pp. 335–58.
4   F.D. Frank, R.P. Finnegan & C.P. Taylor, 2004, 'The Race for Talent: Retaining and Engaging Workers in the 21st Century', *HR Human Resource Planning*, 27 (3), pp. 12–25; P. Holland, C. Sheehan & H. De Cieri, 2006, 'Attracting and retaining talent. Exploring human resources management trends in Australia', in H. De Cieri, A. Bardoel, R. Barrett, D. Buttigieg, A. Rainnie & K. McLean (eds.) *Socially responsive, socially responsible approaches to employment and work*. Proceedings of the ACREW/KCL Conference, Prato Italy, July 1–4; Manpower, 2006; *Confronting the coming talent crunch: what's next? A Manpower White Paper*. Manpower Services: Sydney, Australia.
5   A. Rucci, S.P. Kirn & R.T. Quinn, 1999, 'The employee–customer–profit chain at Sears', *Harvard Business Review*, 76 (1), pp. 82–97.
6   B. Cross & T. Travaglione, 2004, 'The times they are a-changing: Who will stay and who will go in a downsizing organization?', *Personnel Review* 33, pp. 275–90.
7   J.D. Shaw, J.E. Delery, C.D. Jenkins & N. Gupta, 1998, 'An organizational-level analysis of voluntary turnover', *Academy of Management Journal*, 41, pp. 511–25.
8   L. Gooch & F. Leyden, 2004, '600 jobs go at Kodak's Coburg plant', *The Age*, 17 September, pp. 1, 4.
9   M. Skulley, 2006, 'Ford set to axe 640 jobs as sales slip', *Australian Financial Review*, 4 November, p. 6.
10   J.M. Nowakowski & D.E. Conlon, 2005, 'Organizational justice: Looking back, looking forward', *International Journal of Conflict Management*, 16, pp. 4–29.
11   N.D. Cole & G.P. Latham, 1997, 'Effects of training in procedural justice on perceptions of disciplinary fairness by unionized employees and disciplinary subject matter experts', *Journal of Applied Psychology*, 82, pp. 699–705.
12   D.P. Skarlicki & R. Folger, 1997, 'Retaliation in the workplace: the roles of distributive, procedural, and interactional justice', *Journal of Applied Psychology*, 82, pp. 434–43.
13   S. Lee & B.H. Kleiner, 2003, 'Electronic surveillance in the workplace', *Management Research News*, 26 (2–4), pp. 72–81; D.R. Nolan, 2003, 'Privacy and profitability in the technological workplace', Journal of Labor Research, XXIV (2), pp. 207–30; A.M. Townsend & J.T. Bennett, 2003, 'Privacy, technology, and conflict: emerging issues and actions in workplace privacy', *Journal of Labor Research*, XXIV (2), pp. 196–206.

Endnotes

14 R.G. Boehmer, 1992, 'Artificial monitoring and surveillance of employees: the fine line dividing the prudently managed enterprise from the modern sweatshop', *DePaul Law Review*, 41, pp. 739–819; D. van den Broek, 2002, 'Monitoring and surveillance in call centres: some responses from Australian workers', *Labour and Industry*, 12 (3), pp. 43–58.

15 L.M. Andersson & C.M. Pearson, 1999, 'Tit for tat? The spiralling effect of incivility in the workplace', *The Academy of Management Review*, 24 (3), pp. 452–71; P.M. Glendinning, 2001, 'Workplace bullying: curing the cancer of the American workplace', *Public Personnel Management*, 30 (3), pp. 269–86; D. Salin, 2003, 'Ways of explaining workplace bullying: a review of enabling, motivating and precipitating structures and processes in the work environment', *Human Relations*, 56 (1), pp. 1213–32; B.J. Tepper, 2000, 'Consequences of abusive supervision', *Academy of Management Journal*, 43 (2), pp. 178–90.

16 D. Utatao, 2001, cited in Anonymous, 'Bullying costs Australian workplaces A$12bn', *Human Resources*, 1 (10), pp. 1, 9.

17 Anonymous, 2001, 'Bullying costs Australian workplaces A$12bn', *Human Resources*, 1 (10), pp. 1, 9.

18 C. Mayhew & D. Grewal, 2003, 'Occupational violence/bullying in the maritime industry: a pilot study', *Journal of Occupational Health and Safety—Australia and New Zealand*, 19 (5), pp. 457–63; P. McCarthy, C. Mayhew, M. Barker & M. Sheehan, 2003, 'Bullying and occupational violence in tertiary education: risk factors, perpetrators and prevention', *Journal of Occupational Health and Safety—Australia and New Zealand*, 19 (4), 319–26.

19 D. Kelly, 2005. Review of workplace bullying: strengthening approaches to a complex phenomenon. *Journal of Occupational Health and Safety—Australia and New Zealand*, 21, pp. 551–64.

20 D. Salin, 2003; D. Swanwick, 2004, 'How to beat the workplace bully', *Management*, June, pp. 45–6; A. See, 2002, 'Workplace bullying: prosecution risks rise', *Human Resources*, August, p. 6.

21 C. Oleson, 2004, 'Negotiating and teaching workplace drug testing: a labor perspective', *Labor Studies Journal*, 28 (4), pp. 67–86.

22 E.F. Ferraro, 2000, 'Is drug testing good policy?', *Security Management*, 44, pp. 1, 166.

23 M.T. French, M.C. Roebuck & P.K. Alexandre, 2004, 'To test or not to test: do workplace drug testing programs discourage employee drug use?', *Social Science Research*, 33, pp. 45–63, at p. 45; also see P. Holland, A. Pyman & J. Teicher, 2005, 'Negotiating the contested terrain of drug testing in the Australian workplace', *Journal of Industrial Relations*, 47, pp. 326–38.

24 C. Oleson, 2004, p. 77.

25 French et al., 2004; P. Holland & M. Wickham, 2002, 'Drug testing in the workplace: unraveling the issues', *Journal of Occupational Health and Safety—Australia and New Zealand*, 18 (1), pp. 55–9; G.H. Seijts, D.P. Skarlicki & S.W. Gilliland, 2003, 'Canadian and American reactions to drug and alcohol testing programs in the workplace', *Employee Responsibilities and Rights Journal*, 15 (4), pp. 191–208.

26 A. Kirk & D. Brown, 2001, 'A comparison of internal and external providers of EAPs in Australia', *Journal of Occupational Health and Safety—Australia and New Zealand*, 17 (6), pp. 579–85; J. Smith, 1992, 'EAPs evolve to health plan gatekeeper', Employee Benefit Plan Review, 46, pp. 18–19; T. Treadgold, 1999, 'Someone to watch over you', *Business Review Weekly*, 29 March, p. 37.

27 J. Burns, 2004, 'Employers happy to assist', *Human Resources*, 28 July, pp. 12–13.

28 J. Burns, 2004, 'Employers happy to assist', *Human Resources*, 28 July, pp. 12–13.

29 M. Date, 1999, 'As they like it', *The Sydney Morning Herald*, 18 August, p. 4.

30 G.C. Parliman & E.L. Edwards, 1992, 'Employee assistance programs: an employer's guide to emerging liability issues', *Employee Relations Law Journal*, 17, pp. 593–601.

31 S.H. Milne, T.C. Blum & P.M. Roman, 1994, 'Factors influencing employees' propensity to use an employee assistance program', *Personnel Psychology*, 47, pp. 123–45.

32 C.R. Littler, R. Dunford, T. Bramble & A. Hede, 1997, 'The dynamics of downsizing in Australia and New Zealand', *Asia Pacific Journal of Human Resources*, 35 (1), pp. 65–79; L. Ryan & K.A. Macky, 1998, 'Downsizing organizations: uses, outcomes and strategies', *Asia Pacific Journal of Human Resources*, 36 (2), pp. 29–45; B. Kane, 2000, 'Downsizing, TQM, re-engineering, learning organizations and HRM strategy', *Asia Pacific Journal of Human Resources*, 38 (1), pp. 26–49.

33 C. Richards, 2000, 'Retrenchment: What is the next move?', *The Age*, 29 April, p. 24.

34 Richards, 2000.

35 L. Wood & J. Koutsoukis, 2000, 'Telstra plan to axe 16 000', *The Age*, 9 March, p. 1.

36 C. Dwyer, 2000, 'Cushioning the blow of letting employees go', *Australian Financial Review*, 23 June, p. 74; also see H. De Witte, J. Vandoorne, R. Verlinden & N. De Cuyper, 2005, 'Outplacement and re-employment measures during organizational restructuring in Belgium: Overview of the literature and results of qualitative research', *Journal of European Industrial Training*, 29 (2/3), pp. 148–64.

37 N. Way, 2000a, 'In the money, but out of work', *Business Review Weekly*, 7 April, p. 13.

38 Richards, 2000; J. Flint, 1999, '"Kind" managers try to help axed staff', *The West Australian*, 28 July, p. 44.

39 Richards, 2000.

40 L. Gettler, 2000, 'Welcome to the Planet of the Aged', *The Age*, 9 September, p. 5.

41 [Anonymous] 2002, 'Best practice outplacement', *Human Resources*, January, pp. 12–14.

42 S. Branch, 1998, 'You hired 'em, but can you keep 'em?', *Fortune*, 9 November, pp. 247–50.

43 J.L. Price, 2001, 'Reflections on the determinants of voluntary turnover', *International Journal of Manpower*, 22, pp. 600–24.

44 P. Boxall, K. Macky. & E. Rasmussen, 2003, 'Labour turnover and retention in New Zealand: The causes and consequences of leaving and staying with employers', *Asia Pacific Journal of Human Resources*, 41 (2), pp. 196–214.

45 N. Way, 2000b, 'The resignation push-pull', *Business Review Weekly*, 18 August, p. 25.

46 N. Way, 2000b.

47 D.W. Baruch, 1944, 'Why they terminate', *Journal of Consulting Psychology*, 8, pp. 35–46; J.G. Rosse, 1988, 'Relations among lateness, absence and turnover: is there a progression of withdrawal?', *Human Relations*, 41, pp. 517–31; P.W. Hom & A.J. Kinicki, 2001, 'Toward a greater understanding of how dissatisfaction drives employee turnover', *Academy of Management Journal*, 44 (5), pp. 975–87.

48 C. Hulin, 'Adaptation, persistence and commitment in organizations', in M.D. Dunnette & L.M. Hough (eds), 1991, *Handbook of Industrial and Organizational Psychology*, 2nd edn, Consulting Psychologists Press, Palo Alto, CA, pp. 443–50.

49 C. Hulin, M. Roznowski & D. Hachiya, 1985, 'Alternative opportunities and withdrawal decisions', *Psychological Bulletin*, 97, pp. 233–50.

50 C.E. Labig & I.B. Helburn, 1986, 'Union and management policy influences on grievance initiation', *Journal of Labor Research*, 7, pp. 269–84.

51 C. Schreisheim, 1978, 'Job satisfaction, attitudes towards unions, and voting in a union representation election', *Journal of Applied Psychology*, 63, pp. 548–52.

52 M.P. Miceli & J.P. Near, 1985, 'Characteristics of organizational climate and perceived wrongdoing associated with whistle-blowing decisions', *Personnel Psychology*, 38, pp. 525–44; J.P. Near & M.P. Miceli, 1995, 'Effective whistle-blowing', *Academy of Management Review*, 20, pp. 679–708; R.L. Sims & J.P. Keenan, 1998, 'Predictors of external whistle-blowing: Organizational and intrapersonal variables', *Journal of Business Ethics*, 17, pp. 411–21.

53 S. Trudgett, 2000, 'Resignation of women managers: dispelling the myths', *Asia Pacific Journal of Human Resources*, 38 (1), pp. 67–83.

54 R.D. Hackett & R.M. Guion, 1985, 'A re-evaluation of the job satisfaction–absenteeism relation', *Organizational Behavior and Human Decision Processes*, 35, pp. 340–81.

55 P. Cappelli, 2000, 'A market-driven approach to retaining talent', Harvard Business Review, 78 (1), pp. 103–11; M. McCoy, 2000, 'Balance: the myths of time', *Australian Financial Review*, 28 January, p. 8.

56 B. Donaghy, 1999, 'Classic sickies', *The Sydney Morning Herald*, 20 November, p. 1.

57 F. Cumming, 1999, 'Only one in nine days off is genuine', *The Sun-Herald*, 21 March, p. 37.

58 J.G. Rosse & H.E. Miller, 'Relationship between absenteeism and other employee behaviors', in P.S. Goodman & R.S. Atkin (eds), 1984, *New Approaches to Understanding, Measuring, and Managing Employee Absence*, Jossey-Bass, San Francisco.

59 R. Kanungo, 1982, *Work Alienation*, Praeger, New York.

60 R.T. Mowday, R.M. Steers & L.W. Porter, 1979, 'The measurement of organizational commitment', *Journal of Vocational Behavior*, 14, pp. 224–47; R. Zeffane, 1994, 'Patterns of organizational commitment and perceived management style: a comparison of public and private sector employees', *Human Relations*, 47, pp. 977–1010.

61 N.T. Feather & K.A. Rauter, 2004, 'Organizational citizenship behaviours in relation to job status, job insecurity, organizational commitment and identification, job satisfaction and work values', *Journal of Occupational and Organizational Psychology*, 77, pp. 81–94; L.M. Saari & T.A. Judge, 2004, 'Employee attitudes and job satisfaction', *Human Resource Management*, 43, pp. 395–407.

62 B. Benkhoff, 1997, 'Ignoring commitment is costly: new approaches establish the missing link between commitment and performance', *Human Relations*, 50, pp. 701–26; R.D. Iverson, 1996, 'Employee acceptance of organizational change: the role of organizational commitment', *International Journal of Human Resource Management*, 7 (1), pp. 121–48; J. Laabs, 1998, 'The new loyalty: grasp it, earn it, keep it', *Workforce*, November, pp. 34–9.

63 E.A. Locke, 'The nature and causes of job dissatisfaction', in M.D. Dunnette (ed), 1996, *Handbook of Industrial and Organizational Psychology*, Rand McNally, Chicago, pp. 901–69; also see L.M. Saari & T.A. Judge, 2004, 'Employee attitudes and job satisfaction', *Human Resource Management*, 43, pp. 395–407.

64 J.W. Thibaut & H.H. Kelly, 1959, *The Social Psychology of Groups*, Wiley, New York.

65 J.S. Adams & W.B. Rosenbaum, 1962, 'The relationship between worker productivity to cognitive dissonance about wage inequities', *Journal of Applied Psychology*, 46, pp. 161–4.

66 D. Watson, L.A. Clark & A. Tellegen, 1988, 'Development and validation of brief measures of positive and negative affect: the PANAS scales', *Journal of Personality and Social Psychology*, 54, pp. 1063–70.

67 T.A. Judge, E.A. Locke, C.C. Durham & A.N. Kluger, 1998, 'Dispositional effects on job and life satisfaction: the role of core evaluations', *Journal of Applied Psychology*, 83, pp. 17–34.

68 B.M. Staw, N.E. Bell & J.A. Clausen, 1986, 'The dispositional approach to job attitudes: a lifetime longitudinal test', *Administrative Science Quarterly*, 31, pp. 56–78; B.M. Staw & J. Ross, 1985, 'Stability in the midst of change: a dispositional approach to job attitudes', *Journal of Applied Psychology*, 70, pp. 469–80.

69 R.P. Steel & J.R. Rentsch, 1997, 'The dispositional model of job attitudes revisited: findings of a 10-year study', *Journal of Applied Psychology*, 82, pp. 873–9.

70 T.A. Judge, 1993, 'Does affective disposition moderate the relationship between job satisfaction and voluntary turnover?', *Journal of Applied Psychology*, 78, pp. 395–401.

71 R.D. Arvey, T.J. Bouchard, N.L. Segal & L.M. Abraham, 1989, 'Job satisfaction: genetic and environmental components', *Journal of Applied Psychology*, 74, pp. 187–93.

72 S.L. Hershberger, P. Lichenstein & S.S. Knox, 1994, 'Genetic and environmental influences on perceptions of organizational climate', *Journal of Applied Psychology*, 79, pp. 24–33.

73 S. Long, 2000, 'Work-related mental health problems on the rise', *Australian Financial Review*, 10 January, p. 31.

74 http://www.betterhealth.vic.gov.au/bhcv2/bhcarticles.nsf/pages/Work-related_stress, accessed November 1, 2006; R. Moodie & C. Borthwick, 1999, 'All worked up: it's enough to make you sick', *Australian Financial Review*, 6 August, p. 3.

75 Moodie & Borthwick, 1999.

76 B.A. Gerhart, 1987, 'How important are dispositional factors as determinants of job satisfaction? Implications for job design and other personnel programs', *Journal of Applied Psychology*, 72, pp. 493–502.

77 E.F. Stone & H.G. Gueutal, 1985, 'An empirical derivation of the dimensions along which characteristics of jobs are perceived', *Academy of Management Journal*, 28, pp. 376–96.

78 L.W. Porter & R.M. Steers, 1973, 'Organizational, work and personal factors in employee absenteeism and turnover', *Psychological Bulletin*, 80, pp. 151–76.

79 S. Melamed, I. Ben-Avi, J. Luz & M.S. Green, 1995, 'Objective and subjective work monotony: effects on job satisfaction, psychological distress, and absenteeism in blue collar workers', *Journal of Applied Psychology*, 80, pp. 29–42.

80 G.R. Oldham, A. Cummings, L.J. Mischel, J.M. Schmidtke & J. Zhou, 1995, 'Listen while you work? quasi-experimental relations between personal-stereo headset use and employee work responses', *Journal of Applied Psychology*, 80, pp. 547–64.

81 Locke, in Dunnette (ed), 1996.

82 G.P. Latham & C. C. Pinder, 2005, 'Work motivation theory and research at the dawn of the twenty-first century', *Annual Review of Psychology*, 56, pp. 485–516; L.M. Saari & T.A. Judge, 2004, 'Employee attitudes and job satisfaction', *Human Resource Management*. 43, pp. 395–407.

83 M. Mallon & T. Kearney, 2001, 'Team development at Fisher and Paykel: the introduction of "everyday work teams"', *Asia Pacific Journal of Human Resources*, 39 (1), pp. 93–106.

84 J.R. Hackman & G.R. Oldham, 1976, 'Motivation through the design of work', *Organizational Behavior and Human Performance*, 16, pp. 250–79.

85 Cappelli, 2000.

86 D.R. Ilgen & J.R. Hollenbeck, 'The structure of work: job design and roles', in Dunnette & Hough (eds), *Handbook of Industrial and Organisational Psychology*, 2e Vol 2, Consulting Psychologists Press, Palo Alto, California, 1991, pp. 165–208.

87 J.A. Breaugh & J.P. Colihan, 1994, 'Measuring facets of job ambiguity: construct validity evidence', *Journal of Applied Psychology*, 79, pp. 191–201.

88 M.A. Shaffer & D.A. Harrison, 1998, 'Expatriates' psychological withdrawal from interpersonal assignments: work, non-work, and family influences', *Personnel Psychology*, 51, pp. 87–118.

89 P.M. Caligiuri, M.M. Hyland, A.S. Bross & A. Joshi, 1998, 'Testing a theoretical model for examining the relationship between family adjustment and expatriates' work adjustment', *Journal of Applied Psychology*, 83, pp. 598–614.

90 T.J. Newton & R.S. Keenan, 1987, 'Role stress re-examined: an investigation of role stress predictors', *Organizational Behavior and Human Decision Processes*, 40, pp. 346–68; Ryan & Macky, 1998.

91 I. Dayal & J.M. Thomas, 1968, 'Operation KPE: developing a new organization', *Journal of Applied Behavioral Sciences*, 4, pp. 473–506.

92 B.M. Meglino, E.C. Ravlin & C.L. Adkins, 1989, 'A work values approach to corporate culture: a field test of the value congruence process and its relationship to individual outcomes', *Journal of Applied Psychology*, 74, pp. 424–33; also see F. StinglHamber & C. Vandenberghe, 2003, 'Organization and supervisors as sources of support and targets of commitment: a longitudinal study', *Journal of Organizational Behavior*, 24, pp. 251–70.

93 G.C. Ganster, M.R. Fusilier & B.T. Mayes, 1986, 'Role of social support in the experience of stress at work', *Journal of Applied Psychology*, 71, pp. 102–11; also see D.G. Allen, L.M. Shore & R.W. Griffeth, 2003, 'The role of perceived organizational support and supportive human resource practices in the turnover process', *Journal of Management*, 29 (1), pp. 99–118.

Endnotes

94 M.A. Donovan, F. Drasgow & L.J. Munson, 1998, 'The perceptions of fair interpersonal treatment scale: development and validation of a measure of interpersonal treatment in the workplace', *Journal of Applied Psychology*, 83, pp. 683–92; T. Simons & Q. Roberson, 2003, 'Why managers should care about fairness: the effects of aggregate justice perceptions on organizational outcomes', *Journal of Applied Psychology*, 88 (3), pp. 432–43.
95 R.T. Keller, 1989, 'A test of the path–goal theory of leadership with need for clarity as a moderator in research and development organizations', *Journal of Applied Psychology*, 74, pp. 208–12.
96 Anonymous, 1999, 'Shares "sickie cure"', *Northern Territory News*, 26 July, p. 27.
97 Cappelli, 2000.
98 W. Brockbank, 1999, 'If HR really were strategically proactive: present and future directions in HR's contribution to competitive advantage', *Human Resource Management*, 38, pp. 337–52; Cappelli, 2000; F.D. Frank, R.P. Finnegan & C.P. Taylor, 2004, 'The Race for Talent: Retaining and Engaging Workers in the 21st Century', *HR Human Resource Planning*, 27 (3), pp. 12–25; P. Holland, C. Sheehan & H. De Cieri, 2006, 'Attracting and retaining talent. Exploring human resources management trends in Australia', in H. De Cieri, A. Bardoel, R. Barrett, D. Buttigieg, A. Rainnie & K. McLean (eds), *Socially responsive, socially responsible approaches to employment and work*. Proceedings of the ACREW/KCL Conference, Prato Italy, July 1-4.
99 R. Elsdon & S. Iyer, 1999, 'Creating value and enhancing retention through employee development: the Sun Microsystems experience', *Human Resource Planning*, 22, p. 39; also see N. Williams, 2004, 'Resourceful thinking: the Volvo approach to retention', *Human Resources*, 24 March, pp. 14–16. Courtesy of *Personnel Today*.
100 Date, 1999.
101 E.M. Garger, 1999, 'Holding on to high performers: a strategic approach to retention', *Compensation and Benefits Management*, 15 (4), pp. 10–17.
102 Cappelli, 2000, p. 104.
103 Cappelli, 2000; also see C. Smith, M. Daskalaki, T. Elger & D. Brown, 2004, 'Labor turnover and management retention strategies in new manufacturing plants', *International Journal of Human Resource Management*, 15 (2), pp. 371–96.
104 B.E. Becker & M.A. Huselid, 'High performance work systems and firm performance: a synthesis of research and managerial implications', in G.R. Ferris (ed) 1998, *Research in Personnel and Human Resources Management*, vol. 16, JAI Press, Greenwich, CT, pp. 53–101.
105 Anonymous, 2004, 'Departing management taking the bottom line with them', *Human Resources Magazine*, 22 July, p. 8.
106 Anonymous, 2004.
107 The Hudson Report, 2004, cited in Anonymous, 2004.
108 N. Way, 2000c, 'Talent war', *Business Review Weekly*, 18 August, p. 64.
109 N. Way, 2000c.
110 Garger, 1999.
111 J.D. Olian, C.C. Durham, A.L. Kristof, K.G. Brown, R.M. Pierce & L. Kunder, 1998, 'Designing management training and development for competitive advantage: lessons from the best', *Human Resource Planning*, 21, pp. 20–31.
112 Elsdon & Iyer, 1999, p. 41.
113 H.G. Heneman & D.S. Schwab, 1985, 'Pay satisfaction: its multidimensional nature and measurement', *International Journal of Applied Psychology*, 20, pp. 129–41.
114 T. Judge & T. Welbourne, 1994, 'A confirmatory investigation of the dimensionality of the pay satisfaction questionnaire', *Journal of Applied Psychology*, 79, pp. 461–6.
115 A.O. Hirshman, 1970, *Exit, Voice and Loyalty*, Harvard University Press, Cambridge, MA.
116 D. Farrell, 1983, 'Exit, voice, loyalty and neglect as responses to job dissatisfaction: a multidimensional scaling study', *Academy of Management Journal*, 26, pp. 596–607; J. Zhou & J. George, 2001, 'When job dissatisfaction leads to creativity: encouraging the expression of voice', *Academy of Management Journal*, 44 (4), pp. 682–96.
117 D.G. Spencer, 1986, 'Employee voice and employee retention', *Academy of Management Journal*, 29, pp. 488–502.
118 M.D. Fottler, M.A. Crawford, J.B. Quintana & J.B. White, 1995, 'Evaluating nurse turnover: comparing attitude surveys and exit interviews', *Hospital and Health Services Administration*, 40 (2), pp. 278–89.
119 R.A. Giacolone, S.B. Knouse & A. Montagliani, 1997, 'Motivation for and prevention of honest responding in exit interviews and surveys', *The Journal of Psychology*, 131 (4), pp. 438–48.
120 Fottler, Crawford, Quintana & White, 1995.
121 J. Lefkowitz & M.L. Katz, 1969, 'Validity of exit interviews', *Personnel Psychology*, 22 (4), pp. 445–55.
122 J. Hinrichs, 1975, 'Measurement of reasons for resignation of professionals: questionnaire versus company and consultant exit interviews', *Journal of Applied Psychology*, 60 (14), pp. 530–2.
123 Giacolone, Knouse & Montagliani, 1997.
124 D.C. Feldman & B.S. Klaas, 1999, 'The impact of exit questionnaire procedures on departing employees' self-disclosure', *Journal of Managerial Issues*, 11 (1), pp. 13–25; R.A. Giacolone, C.L. Jurkiewicz & S.B. Knouse, 2003, 'Exit surveys as assessments of organizational ethicality', *Public Personnel Management*, 32 (3), pp. 397–410.
125 Elsdon & Iyer, 1999, pp. 39–47.

CHAPTER 18 NOTES
1 D. Townsend, 2001, 'For what it's worth', *HRMonthly*, July, pp. 20–6.
2 D. Townsend, 2001.
3 B.E. Becker & M.A. Huselid, 'High performance work systems and firm performance: a synthesis of research and managerial implications', in G.R. Ferris (ed), 1998, *Research in Personnel and Human Resources Management*, 16, JAI Press, Greenwich, CT, pp. 53–101.
4 K.L. Zellars & J. Fiorito, 1999, 'Evaluations of organizational effectiveness among HR managers: cues and implications', *Journal of Managerial Issues*, XI (1), pp. 37–55
5 C.M. Daily, D.R. Dalton & A.A. Cannella Jr, 2003, 'Corporate governance: decades of dialogue and data', *Academy of Management Review*, 28 (3), pp. 371–82; also see *Academy of Management Review*, 28 (3), (special topic forum on corporate governance).
6 Global Reporting Initiative, 2002, *Sustainability Reporting Guidelines, Global Reporting Initiative*, Boston MA, www.globalreporting.org/guidelines/, viewed 10 October 2004, p. 2.
7 W. Norman & C. MacDonald, 2004, 'Getting to the bottom of "triple bottom line"', *Business Ethics Quarterly*, 14 (2), pp. 243–62.
8 M. van Marrewijk, 2003, 'Concepts and definitions of CSR and corporate sustainability: between agency and communion', *Journal of Business Ethics*, 44, pp. 95–105.
9 C.A. Hemingway & P.W. Maclagan, 2004, 'Managers' personal values as drivers of corporate social responsibility', *Journal of Business Ethics*, 50, pp. 33–44; K. Splevins, 2004, 'Good deeds', *The Sydney Morning Herald*, 21 July, p. 4.
10 Global Reporting Initiative, 2002.
11 C. Ryan, 2003, 'The reputation wars', *Australian Financial Review*, 14 November, p. 24.
12 Telstra, 2003, Corporate Social Responsibility Report, www.telstra.com, viewed 21 August 2004.
13 National Australia Bank Ltd, 2004, ASX Announcement, 10 December, www.nabgroup.com, viewed 12 December 2004; also see M. Merz, 2004, 'Profit fall hits NAB very hard', *Daily Telegraph*, 11 December, p. 82.
14 Splevins, 2004.
15 B. Ramasamy & H.W. Ting, 2004, 'A comparative analysis of corporate social responsibility awareness', *Journal of Corporate Citizenship*, 13, pp. 109–123; P. Sagar & A. Singla, 2004, 'Trust and corporate social responsibility: lessons from India', *Journal of Communication Management*, 8 (3), pp. 282–90; R. Welford, 2004,

'Corporate social responsibility in Europe and Asia', *Journal of Corporate Citizenship*, 13, pp. 31–47.

16 N. Sarbutts, 2003, 'Can SMEs "do" CSR? A practitioner's view of the ways small- and medium-sized enterprises are able to manage reputation through corporate social responsibility', *Journal of Communication Management*, 7 (4), pp. 340–47.

17 L. Gettler, 2004, 'Forget the spin—corporate social responsibility is a hellhole of contradictions and conflicting interests', *The Age*, 4 August, p. 6; J. Snider, R.P. Hill & D. Martin, 2003, 'Corporate social responsibility in the 21st century: a view from the world's most successful firms', *Journal of Business Ethics*, 48, pp. 175–87; H. Trinca, 2004, 'Corporate social responsibility moves onto the front page', *Australian Financial Review*, 31 July, p. 20; D. Wheeler, B. Colbert, & R.E. Freeman, 2003, 'Focusing on value: reconciling corporate social responsibility, sustainability and a stakeholder approach in a network world', *Journal of General Management*, 28 (3), pp. 1–28.

18 Norman & MacDonald, 2004.

19 R.W. Beatty, J.R. Ewing & C.G. Tharp, 2003, 'HR's role in corporate governance: present and prospective', *Human Resource Management*, 42, pp. 257–69.

20 P.J. Dowling & D.E. Welch, 2004, International Human Resource Management, 4th edn, *International Thomson*, London; A.B. Carroll, 2004, 'Managing ethically with global stakeholders: a present and future challenge', *Academy of Management Executive*, 18 (2), pp. 114–20.

21 R.P. Hill, D. Stephens & I. Smith, 2003, 'Corporate social responsibility: an examination of individual firm behavior', *Business and Society Review*, 108 (3), pp. 339–64.

22 J. Thomson, 2001, 'Test of virtue', *Business Review Weekly*, 27 July, p. 60.

23 Thomson, 2001.

24 Ryan, C. 2003; Thomson, 2001.

25 Ryan, 2003; see Global Reporting Initiative, 2002.

26 Global Reporting Initiative, 2002.

27 Anonymous, 2004, 'Becoming socially responsible', Probono Australia web site, www.probonoaustralia.com.au/new/home.asp?a=1andc=32andd=2, viewed 21 August 2004.

28 R. Kramar, 2004, 'Corporate social responsibility ….. a challenge for HR?', *Human Resources*, 24 February.

29 Anonymous, 2004, 'Boards struggle with non-financials', *Human Resources*, 17 November.

30 B.E. Becker, M.A. Huselid & D. Ulrich, 2001, *The HR Scorecard: Linking People, Strategy, and Performance*, Harvard Business School Press, Boston; E.W. Rogers & P.M. Wright, 1998, 'Measuring organisational performance in strategic human resource management: problems, prospects, and performance information markets', *Human Resource Management Review*, 8 (3), pp. 311–31; A.K. Yeung & B. Berman, 1997, 'Adding value through human resources: reorienting human resource measurement to drive business performance', *Human Resource Management*, 36, pp. 321–35.

31 T. Evans, 2001, 'Influencing performance', *HRMonthly*, August, pp. 14–17.

32 Rogers & Wright, 1998.

33 B. Becker & B. Gerhart, 1996, 'The impact of human resource management on organizational performance: progress and prospects', *Academy of Management Journal*, 39 (4), pp. 779–801; L.D. Dyer & T. Reeves, 1995, 'Human resource strategies and firm performance: what do we know and where do we go?', *International Journal of Human Resource Management*, 6 (3), pp. 656–70; Watson Wyatt Worldwide, 2001, 'Human Capital Index', *Human Capital as a Lead Indicator of Shareholder Value*, Watson Wyatt Worldwide, Washington DC.

34 A.S. Bargerstock, 2000, 'The HRM effectiveness audit: a tool for managing accountability in HRM', *Public Personnel Management*, 29 (40), pp. 517–27; K.L. Zellars & J. Fiorito, 1999; Ramlall, 2003, 'Measuring human resource management's effectiveness in improving performance', *Human Resource Management*, 42, pp. 52–62.

35 H. De Cieri & J.W. Boudreau, 2003, 'Global human resource metrics', in J. Scott, J. Edwards & N. Raju (eds), *The Human Resources Program Evaluation Handbook*, Sage, Thousand Oaks, CA, pp. 493–513; J.J. Jamrog & M.H. Overholt, 2004, 'Measuring HR and organizational effectiveness', *Employment Relations Today*, Summer, pp. 33–45.

36 J.W. Boudreau & P.M. Ramstad, 1997, 'Measuring intellectual capital: learning from financial history', *Human Resource Management*, 36 (3), pp. 343–56; T.E. Murphy & S. Zandvakili, 2000, 'Data- and metrics-driven approach to human resource practices: using customers, employees and financial metrics', *Human Resource Management*, 39 (1), pp. 93–105.

37 For a detailed discussion of the growing array of alternative measurement tools available to organisational decision makers, see J.W. Boudreau & P.M. Ramstad, 2002a, 'Strategic I/O psychology and the role of utility analysis models', in W. Borman, D. Ilgen & R. Klimoski (eds), *Handbook of Psychology*, vol. 12, *Industrial and Organizational Psychology*, Chapter 9, pp. 193–221, Wiley, New York.

38 J.W. Boudreau & P.M. Ramstad, 2002b, *Strategic HRM Measurement in the 21st Century: From Justifying HR to Strategic Talent Leadership* (CAHRS working paper 02–15), Cornell University, Ithaca, NY.

39 D. Ulrich, 1997, 'Measuring human resources: an overview of practice and a prescription for results', *Human Resource Management*, 36 (3), pp. 303–20.

40 P.M. Wright, G.C. McMahan, S.A. Snell & B. Gerhart, 2001, 'Comparing line and HR executives' perceptions of HR effectiveness: services, roles, and contributions', *Human Resource Management*, 40 (2), pp. 111–23.

41 K. Barrett & A. Ellerby, 2001, 'The rising cost of HR', *HRMonthly*, June, pp. 26–7.

42 A.P. Carnevale & E.R. Schulz, 1990, 'Return on investment: accounting for training', *Training and Development Journal*, July, pp. S1–S32.

43 Carnevale & Schulz, 1990; G. Kearsley, 1982, *Costs, Benefits, and Productivity in Training Systems*, Addison-Wesley, Boston.

44 D.G. Robinson & J. Robinson, 1989, 'Training for impact', *Training and Development Journal*, August, pp. 30–42.

45 Robinson & Robinson, 1989.

46 N. Bontis, N.C. Dragonetti, K. Jacobsen & G. Roos, 1999, 'The knowledge toolbox: a review of the tools available to measure and manage intangible resources', *European Management Journal*, 17 (4), pp. 391–402; T. Stewart, 1997, *Intellectual Capital*, Doubleday, New York; N. Bontis, 2001, 'Assessing knowledge assets: a review of the models used to measure intellectual capital', *International Journal of Management Reviews*, 3 (1), pp. 41–60.

47 E.G. Flamholtz, 1999, *Human Resource Accounting*, 3rd edn, Kluwer, Boston, MA.

48 J.W. Boudreau & P.M. Ramstad, 2002b.

49 R.J. Grossman, 2000, 'Measuring up: appropriate metrics help HR prove its worth', *HR Magazine*, January, pp. 25–8.

50 J.E. Mathieu & R.L. Leonard, 1987, 'Applying utility analysis to a training program in supervisory skills: a time based approach', *Academy of Management Journal*, 30, pp. 316–35; F.L. Schmidt, J.E. Hunter & K. Pearlman, 1982, 'Assessing the economic impact of personnel programs on work-force productivity', *Personnel Psychology*, 35, pp. 333–47; J.W. Boudreau 1983, 'Economic considerations in estimating the utility of human resource productivity programs', *Personnel Psychology*, 36, pp. 551–76.

51 J.W. Boudreau, 1991, 'Utility analysis for decisions in human resource management', in M.D. Dunnette & L.M. Hough (eds), *Handbook of Industrial and Organizational Psychology*, vol. 2, pp. 621–745, Consulting Psychologists Press, Palo Alto, CA; Boudreau & Ramstad, 2002a, in Borman, Ilgen and Klimoski (eds).

52 U.E. Gattiker, 1995, 'Firm and taxpayer returns from training of semiskilled employees', *Academy of Management Journal*, 38, pp. 1151–73.

53 Boudreau & Ramstad, 2002a, in Borman, Ilgen & Klimoski (eds).

54 J.C. Erfurt, A. Foote & M.A. Heirich, 1992, 'The cost-effectiveness of worksite wellness programs', *Personnel Psychology*, 15, p. 22.

Endnotes

55 J. Abbott, H. De Cieri & R.D. Iverson, 1998, 'Costing turnover: implications of work/family conflict at management level', *Asia Pacific Journal of Human Resources*, 36 (1), pp. 25–43.

56 W. Cascio, 1991, *Costing Human Resources*, PWS-Kent, Boston.

57 M.A. Deery & R.D. Iverson, 'Enhancing productivity: intervention strategies for employee turnover', in N. Johns (ed), 1996, *Productivity Management in Hospitality and Tourism*, Cassell, London, pp. 68–95.

58 Abbott, De Cieri & Iverson, 1998.

59 Grossman, 2000.

60 2002, *Global Relocation Trends 2001 Survey Report*, February, sponsored by GMAC Global Relocation Services, National Foreign Trade Council (NFTC), and SHRM Global Forum, p. 9.

61 Boudreau and Ramstad, 1997; J.W. Boudreau & P.M. Ramstad, 'Human resource metrics: can measures be strategic?', in P.M. Wright, L.D. Dyer, J.W. Boudreau & G.T. Milkovich (eds), 1999, *Research in Personnel and Human Resources Management: Strategic Human Resources Management in the Twenty-First Century*, Supplement 4, JAI Press, Stamford, CT, pp. 75–98; D. Stamps, 2000, 'Measuring minds', *Training*, May, pp. 1–7.

62 N. Bontis, N.C. Dragonetti, K. Jacobsen & G. Roos, 1999; T. Stewart, 1997; N. Bontis, 2001.

63 J. Pfeffer, 1997, 'Pitfalls on the road to measurement: the dangerous liaison of human resources with the ideas of accounting and finance', *Human Resource Management*, 36, pp. 357–65.

64 D.P. Lepak & S. Snell, 1999, 'The human resource architecture: towards a theory of human capital allocation and development', *Academy of Management Journal*, 24 (1), pp. 31–48.

65 T. Elliott, 2004, 'Bank balance brings a return on investment', *The Australian*, 8 March, pTO6.

66 B. Becker & M. Huselid, 1998, 'High performance work systems and firm performance: a synthesis of research and managerial implications', *Research in Personnel and Human Resource Management*, 16, pp. 53–101; P. Cappelli & D. Neumark , 2001, 'Do 'high-performance' work practices improve establishment-level outcomes?', *Industrial and Labor Relations Review*, 54, pp. 737–75.

67 Grossman, 2000; Watson Wyatt Worldwide, 2001.

68 For example, see A.P. Bartel, 2004, 'Human resource management and organizational performance: evidence from retail banking', *Industrial and Labor Relations Review*, 57 (2), pp. 181–203; Becker & Huselid, in G.R. Ferris (ed), 1998; P.M. Wright, T.M. Gardner & L.M. Moynihan, 2003, 'The impact of HR practices on the performance of business units', *Human Resource Management Journal*, 13 (3), pp. 21–36.

69 Boudreau & Ramstad, 2002b.

70 Boudreau & Ramstad, 2002a, in Borman, Ilgen & Klimoski (eds); Wright, Gardner & Moynihan, 2003.

71 R.S. Kaplan & D.P. Norton, 1992, 'The balanced scorecard—measures that drive performance', *Harvard Business Review*, January–February, pp. 71–9; R.S. Kaplan & D.P. Norton, 1993, 'Putting the balanced scorecard to work', *Harvard Business Review*, September–October, pp. 134–47; R.S. Kaplan & D.P. Norton, 1996, 'Using the balanced scorecard as a strategic management system', *Harvard Business Review*, January–February, pp. 75–85; also see R.W. Beatty, M.A. Huselid & C.E. Schneier, 2003, 'New HR metrics: scoring on the business scorecard', *Organizational Dynamics*, 32 (2), pp. 107–121.

72 Becker, Huselid & Ulrich, 2001.

73 Smith & Nunn, 2001, 'Bearing fruit', *HRMonthly*, May, pp. 42–3.

74 Boudreau & Ramstad, 2002a, in Borman, Ilgen and Klimoski (eds).

75 Boudreau & Ramstad, 2002b.

76 Boudreau & Ramstad, 2002b. A. Rucci, S.P. Kirn & R.T. Quinn, 1998, 'The employee– customer–profit chain at Sears', *Harvard Business Review*, 76 (1), pp. 82–97.

77 A. Rucci, S.P. Kirn and R.T. Quinn, 1998, 'The employee-customer-profit chain at Sears', *Harvard Business Review*, 76 (1), pp. 82–97.

78 Boudreau & Ramstad, 2002b.

79 J.C. Hayton, 2003, 'Strategic human capital management in SMEs: an empirical study of entrepreneurial performance' *Human Resource Management*, 42 (4), pp. 375–91; J. W. Walker, 2001, 'Human capital: beyond HR?', *Human Resource Planning*, 24 (2), pp. 4–5.

80 R. Finn, 2003, 'Human-capital management (HCM): a three letter acronym too far for HR or the way to get the people agenda on to that of the board?', *Human Resource Management International Digest*, 11 (5), pp. 2–4.

81 M. van Marrewijk & J. Timmers, 2003, 'Human capital management: new possibilities in people management', *Journal of Business Ethics*, 44 (2/3), pp. 171–84.

82 L.Bassi & D. McMurrer, 2004, 'Improving your return on people: next generation measurement systems', *Human Resources*, 22 September, pp. 14–15.

83 P. Wright, G. McMahan, S. Snell & B. Gerhart, 1998, *Strategic Human Resource Management: Building Human Capital and Organizational Capability*, technical report, Cornell University, Ithaca, NY.

84 Barrett & Ellerby, 2001.

85 C.R. Greer, S.A. Youngblood & D.A. Gray, 1999, 'Human resource management outsourcing: the make or buy decision', *Academy of Management Executive*, 13 (3), pp. 85–96; C.R. Littler, R. Dunford, T. Bramble & A. Hede, 1997, 'The dynamics of downsizing in Australia and New Zealand', *Asia Pacific Journal of Human Resources*, 35 (1), pp. 65–79; L. Norman, 1999, 'HR goes out to save money', *HRMonthly*, August, pp. 26–7.

86 Barrett & Ellerby, 2001.

87 I. Kessler, J. Coyle-Shapiro & J. Purcell, 1999, 'Outsourcing and the employee perspective', *Human Resource Management Journal*, 9 (2), pp. 5–20; B.S. Klaas, J. McClendon & T.W. Gainey, 1999, 'HR outsourcing and its impact: the role of transaction costs', *Personnel Psychology*, 52 (1), pp. 113–36; J.B. Quinn, 1999, 'Strategic outsourcing: leveraging knowledge capabilities', *Sloan Management Review*, Summer, pp. 9–21.

88 Greer, Youngblood and Gray, 1999.

89 Norman, 1999.

90 T.B. Kinni, 1994, 'A reengineering primer', *Quality Digest*, January, pp. 26–30; 1994, 'Reengineering is helping health of hospitals and its patients', *Total Quality Newsletter*, February, p. 5; R. Recardo, 1994, 'Process reengineering in a finance division', *Journal for Quality and Participation*, June, pp. 70–3.

91 L. Quillen, 1989, 'Human resource computerization: a dollar and cents approach', *Personnel Journal*, July, pp. 74–7.

92 D. Lepak & S.A. Snell, 1998, 'Virtual HR: strategic human resource management in the 21st century', *Human Resource Management Review*, 8 (3), pp. 215–34; P.R. Sparrow & K. Daniels, 'Human resource management and the virtual organization: mapping the future research issues', in C.L. Cooper & D.M. Rousseau (eds), 1999, *Trends in Organizational Behaviour*, vol. 6, John Wiley and Sons, Chichester, UK, pp. 45–61.

93 S. Greengard, 1994, 'New technology is HR's route to reengineering', *Personnel Journal*, July, pp. 32c–32o; K.A. Kovach & C.E. Cathcart, 1999, 'Human Resource Information Systems (HRIS): providing a business with rapid data access, information exchange and strategic advantage', *Public Personnel Management*, 28 (2), pp. 275–82.

94 K. Mcrae, 2003, 'HR Shared Services—a growing trend', *Human Resources*, 3 December.

95 R. Birchfield, 2001, 'Cutting employee turnover costs', *Management*, 1 October, p. 33, Profile Publishing Limited, Auckland.

96 S. Csoka & B. Hackett, 1998, *Transforming the HR Function for Global Business Success*, report 1209–1999.

(Reference to each term indicated by the chapter number in brackets)

360-degree feedback system a performance appraisal process for managers that includes evaluations from a wide range of people who interact with the manager. The process includes self-evaluations as well as evaluations from the manager's boss, subordinates, peers and customers. (12)

Ability an enduring capability that an individual possesses. (6)

Acceptability refers to whether the people who use the performance measure accept it. (10)

Acquisition also often referred to as a takeover; the process through which one company takes over the controlling interest of another company. (7)

Action plan a written document that includes the steps that the trainee and manager will take to ensure that training transfers to the job. (12)

Administrative expert a role performed by HR practitioners, aiming to build an efficient infrastructure by ensuring efficient performance of organisational processes. (1)

Affirmative action programs associated with the provision of quotas and other forms of reparation to compensate for past injustices suffered by a class or group of persons. This has most famously occurred in the United States in the case of African American people. (3)

Agent in agency theory, a manager or one who acts on behalf of an owner (principal); in HR management, may refer to an employee. (14)

Analytic approach type of assessment of HR effectiveness that involves determining the impact of, or the financial costs and benefits of, a program or practice. (18)

Anticipatory socialisation socialisation that occurs before an individual joins a company. Includes expectations about the company, job, working conditions and interpersonal relationships. (11)

Appraisal politics refer to evaluators purposefully distorting a rating to achieve personal or company goals. (10)

Assessment collecting information and providing feedback to employees about their behaviour, communication style or skills. (12)

Assessment centre a process in which multiple raters evaluate employees' performance on a number of exercises. (8, 12)

Audit approach type of assessment of HR effectiveness that involves reviewing customer satisfaction or key indicators (e.g. turnover rate, or average days to fill a position) related to an HR activity (e.g. staffing). (18)

Auditing (of OHS) a systematic examination against established criteria, conducted regularly to identify deviations from the OHS management system and determine whether these deviations can compromise health, safety and productivity. (4)

Australian Industrial Relations Commission (AIRC) the federal industrial tribunal established to implement section 51(xxxv) of the Australian Constitution, which empowers the Australian Government to legislate for the prevention and settlement of interstate industrial disputes. (5)

Australian workplace agreements (AWAs) agreements negotiated directly between an employer and employee(s), and intro-duced under the *Workplace Relations Act 1996 (Cwlth)*. (5)

Award restructuring (or the Structural Efficiency Principle) a reform of the Australian wages system aimed at developing a more highly-skilled workplace; for example, by the reduction of job classifications, the establishment of skill-related career paths linked to pay scales, and multi-skilling to enhance workforce flexibility. (13)

Awards written determinations created by federal or state industrial tribunals, specifying the minimum terms and conditions of employment, such as hours of work, minimum pay and types of leave allowable. (3, 5)

Balanced scorecard a means of performance measurement that gives managers a chance to look at their company from the perspectives of internal and external customers, employees and shareholders. (1)

Benchmarks® an instrument designed to measure the factors that are important in order to be a successful manager. (12)

Blended learning the use of multiple presentation methods within the same training program. (11)

Call centre also called customer service centre. An organisation (or organisational segment) dedicated to service and/or sales, in which employees interact by telephone or computer with customers to provide a service or to sell a product. (1)

Career management system used in an organisation to identify employees' development needs and to enable employees to progress through a sequence of positions, developing their knowledge, skills and abilities. (12)

Career support coaching, protection, sponsorship and providing challenging assignments, exposure and visibility. (12)

Careers a sequence of positions held within an occupation. (12)

Causal chain analysis measures the links between HR activities or employee behaviours and attitudes, and business processes or outcomes. (18)

Centralisation degree to which decision-making authority resides at the top of the organisational chart. (6)

Change agent a role performed by HR practitioners, aiming to develop the organisation by managing transformation and change. (1)

733

Glossary

Coach a peer or manager who works with an employee to motivate him or her, help in skills development and provide reinforcement and feedback. (12)

Cognitive moral development refers to the development of moral judgment, the formation of a system of values or moral ideas from organised patterns of thought. (15)

Collectivism the tendency to emphasise the interests and wellbeing of the group over those of each individual. (15)

Commodification the action of turning something or someone into, or treating something or someone as, a mere commodity. (15)

Compa-ratio an index of the correspondence between actual and intended pay. (13)

Compensable factors the characteristics of jobs that an organisation values and chooses to pay for. (13)

Concentration strategy a strategy focusing on increasing market share, reducing costs or creating and maintaining a market niche for products and services. (2)

Conciliation and arbitration system a system whereby industrial parties are encouraged to sort out their differences by means of conciliation (with the assistance of the industrial tribunal). However, when this fails to produce a negotiated outcome, the tribunal may impose a binding decision—that is, arbitration. Sometimes this system is called compulsory conciliation and arbitration because the industrial parties must come to conciliation if the other party (or the tribunal) calls for this to happen, and any decision is binding on the parties. (3)

Concurrent validation a criterion-related validity study in which a test is administered to all the people currently in a job and then incumbents' scores are correlated with existing measures of their performance on the job. (8)

Consequences the type of incentives that employees receive for performing well. (11)

Constitution a set of rules and principles by which a body (e.g. nation or sports club) may be governed and power relations defined. (3)

Content validation a test-validation strategy performed by demonstrating that the items, questions or problems posed by a test are a representative sample of the kinds of situations or problems that occur on the job. (8)

Contingent workforce temporary, part-time and self-employed workers who are not considered full-time employees. (1, 6)

Convergence hypothesis the hypothesis that management practices around the world would converge, based on two assumptions. First, that there were principles of sound management that held regardless of national environments. Second, that the universality of sound management practices would lead to societies becoming more and more alike in the future. (16)

Corporate governance the way in which decisions are made about the deployment of an organisation's resources and the resolution of conflicts among an organisation's stakeholders. (18)

Corporate social responsibility (CSR) (and corporate sustainability) the continuing, voluntary commitment by companies to establish and maintain a systematic approach to the management of environmental, social, economic and governance issues. This requires companies and managers to behave in ethical ways and to contribute to economic development while improving quality of life for employees, their families, the local community and society in general. (18)

Corporatism a formal cooperative agreement between the government and the union movement ensuring union involvement in the reform process. (5)

Correlation coefficient a statistic that measures the degree to which two sets of numbers are related to each other. (8)

Culture a distinct way of life shared by members of a group or society, with common values, attitudes and behaviours that are transmitted over time in a gradual, yet dynamic, process. (16)

Culture shock a phenomenon experienced by people who move across cultures. People, in effect, experience a shock reaction to new cultural experiences that cause psychological disorientation because they misunderstand or do not recognise important cues. (16)

Decentralisation (of industrial relations) lowering of the centre of industrial relations activity from the AIRC to the level of individual workplaces. (5)

Delayer reduce the number of job levels within an organisation. (13)

Deontological theory an ethical theory based on the specific principle that actions have inherent rightness or wrongness dependent on whether they correspond to a duty but independent of their consequences. (15)

Departmentation the degree to which work units are grouped, based on functional similarity or similarity of work flow. (6)

Deregulation (of the labour market) refers to the repeal of laws and regulations that created universal standards of employment. (5)

Development (also employee development) the acquisition of knowledge, skills and behaviours that improve an employee's ability to meet changes in job requirements and in client and customer demands. (12)

Direct applicants people who apply for a job vacancy without prompting from the organisation. (8)

Direct discrimination when someone is treated less favourably on the basis of a particular characteristic (e.g. gender) than someone with a different characteristic in circumstances that are materially the same. (3)

Distributed work, telework and telecommuting work done outside of the traditional work environment, including at home, while travelling, or anywhere an employee can interact with managers, peers, customers, products or processes using technology. (1)

Distributive justice (also distributive fairness) the perception that rewards are distributed in relation to contribution. (13, 15, 17)

Divergence hypothesis in opposition to the convergence hypothesis, the notion that societies and management practices around the world will remain, or become more, dissimilar. (16)

Diversity enlargement a technique aimed at increasing the representation of groups with particular personal characteristics, such as ethnic or gender backgrounds. (9)

Diversity management (or managing diversity) is a process of managing people's similarities and differences; it is built on a set of values that recognises that the differences between people are a potential strength for the organisation. This process of management creates an environment that allows all employees to contribute to organisational goals and experience personal growth. (9)

Diversity management program a management process that seeks to achieve its goals and competitive advantage by systematically managing the different needs of individual employees. (9)

Diversity training is designed to change employee attitudes about diversity and/or develop skills needed in order to work with a diverse workforce. (9)

Downsizing the planned elimination of large numbers of personnel, designed to enhance organisational effectiveness. (2, 7)

Downward move a job change involving a reduction in an employee's level of responsibility and authority. (12)

Duty of care the requirement for everything reasonably practicable to be done to protect the health and safety of the workplace. (4)

Economic rationalist frameworks general term for neo-liberal or neo-classical economic systems within Western society. (15)

E-recruitment a method of Internet recruitment that involves the recruiter searching online for job candidates. However, the term is often used to refer to the general process of Internet recruitment. (8)

Emic (also see etic) culture-specific aspects of concepts or behaviour. (15, 16)

Emotional labour jobs in which employees are required to adhere to rules regarding the expression of emotions. This is often evident in front-line customer service jobs. (6)

Employee assistance programs (EAPs) employer programs that attempt to ameliorate problems encountered by workers who are drug dependent, alcoholic or psychologically troubled. (17)

Employee champion a role performed by HR practitioners, aiming to increase employee commitment and capability by listening and responding to employees' concerns. (1)

Employee engagement harnessing of employees to their work roles, including cognitive, physical and emotional engagement. (1)

Employee learning (training) a planned effort to facilitate the learning of job-related knowledge, skills and behaviour by employees. (2)

Employee self-service systems (ESS) enable employees to directly enter their personal data into the HRIS and to directly access information, such as leave entitlements or pay details.

Employee stock ownership plan (ESOP) an employee ownership plan that provides employers certain tax and financial advantages when stock is granted to employees. (14)

Employee survey research a process of monitoring employees' job satisfaction and organisational and other important job atti-tudes using questionnaires, interviews or focus groups. (17)

Employee voice an individual's formal opportunity to complain about his or her work situation. (17)

Employer associations are organisations that offer a range of services to employers, including industrial relations advice, trade information and financial assistance. (5)

Employer of choice an approach to attracting, retaining and motivating employees, based on financial success and factors such as an organisation's reputation, organisational leadership, work environment, support structures and facilities, recognition of employees for their efforts, and availability of a range of opportunities for progression. (1)

Enterprise agreements negotiated between employers and employees, in conjunction with awards, as the primary instruments to regulate employment conditions. (5)

Enterprise bargaining (also referred to as workplace bargaining) direct negotiations between an employer (or enterprise) and its employees (or their representatives) with a view to deciding terms and conditions of employment. (5)

Equal employment opportunity (EEO) the government's attempt to ensure that all individuals have an equal opportunity for employment, regardless of characteristics such as race, colour, religion, gender or national origin. (3, 9)

Ergonomics the interface between individuals' physiological characteristics and the physical work environment. (6)

Ethical pluralism the idea that moral reasoning in applied situations is often based on a variety of ethical principles accepting a pluralistic approach to ethical decision making. Supporters suggest that moral insight is more important than adherence to ethical dogma. (15)

Ethical relativism the concept that there is not a single ethical truth but that ethical beliefs are contingency based (some forms hold that whatever a culture thinks is right or wrong is really right or wrong for the members of that culture). (15)

Ethical theory specific reflections on the nature and justification of right actions in a manner that introduces clarity, substance and precision of argument. (15)

Ethicality of HRM refers to the ethical endowment or quality of HRM—that is, the extent to which HRM possesses such qualities. (15)

Ethics general term commonly used to refer to both moral beliefs and ethical theory. (15)

Ethnocentrism the assumption that one's own cultural approach is superior to any other. An ethnocentric approach to international staffing typically results in all key management positions being held by PCNs. Also, international HRM activities are typically developed and administered by PCNs. (16)

Etic (also see emic) culture-common aspects of concepts or behaviour. (15, 16)

Expatriates employees sent by his or her company in one country to work in a different country. (16)

Expatriate failure (also premature termination) the premature return of an expatriate from an international assignment. (16)

Expectancy theory says that the attractiveness of any job is a function of valence, instrumentality and expectancy. (14)

External analysis consists of examining the organisation's operating environment to identify strategic opportunities and threats. (2)

External growth strategy an emphasis on acquiring vendors and suppliers or buying businesses that allows a company to expand into new markets. (2)

External labour market people outside the firm who are actively seeking employment. (1)

Family-friendly programs HR policies such as flexible hours, part-time work, job sharing, telecommuting or working from home, use of employee sick days to attend to family commitments, employee assistance programs and relocation services. (9)

Feedback information that employees receive while they are performing, concerning how well they are meeting objectives. (11)

Flexible work arrangements variations to standard work; may involve flexible work hours, telework, provision of various leave types, and 'family-friendly' practices such as child-care or elder-care assistance. (6)

Forecasting the attempts to determine the supply of and demand for various types of human resources to predict areas within the organisation where there will be future labour shortages or surpluses (7).

Formal education programs include off-site and on-site programs that are designed specifically for the company's employees, short courses that are offered by consultants or universities, executive programs, and university programs in which participants actually live at the university while taking classes. (12)

Frame of reference a standard point that serves as a comparison for other points and, thus, provides meaning. (17)

Freedom of association the right to join or not to join a trade union. (5)

Gainsharing a form of group compensation based on group or plant performance (rather than organisation-wide profits) that does not become part of the employee's base salary. (14)

Generalisability the degree to which the validity of a selection method established in one context extends to other contexts. (8)

Global industry an industry in which a firm's competitive position in one country is significantly influenced by its position in other countries. (16)

Global knowledge economy increasing knowledge-intensity of production, and globalisation of economies, communications and cultures. (1)

Goals what an organisation hopes to achieve in the medium- to long-term future. (2)

'Hard' HRM performance-oriented HRM where employees are viewed instrumentally as a means to achieve an organisation's economic goals. (15)

Hazards circumstances, procedures or environments that expose individuals to possible injury, illness, damage or loss. (4)

High commitment HRM a management approach that emphasises employee engagement, participation in decision making, and systemic relationships between technical, social and other organisational elements. (15)

High involvement work processes (also see high commitment HRM) a management approach that emphasises employee engagement, participation in decision making, and systemic relationships between technical, social and other organisational elements. (6)

High-performance work systems (HPWS) work systems that maximise the fit between the company's social system (employees) and its technology (including information, technology and work). (1)

Host country the country in which the parent-country organisation seeks to locate or has already located a facility. (16)

Host-country nationals (HCNs) employees born and raised in a host country. (16)

HR Activity Index measures the association between a collection of HR activities and changes in organisational outcomes such as profits and shareholder value creation. (18)

HR metrics measurements for human performance that enable effective decisions to be made regarding the HR function and value creation in organisations. (18)

Human capital the knowledge, skills, abilities and other characteristics (KSAOs) of individuals. (6, 15)

Human capital management a management approach that aims to capture all efforts related to people in an organisation; while human capital management includes HRM, it focuses on measuring the effectiveness of HR activities, with an emphasis on enhancing the fit between those activities and the organisational strategic goals. (1)

Human resource accounting attempts to place a dollar value on human resources as if they were physical resources (e.g. plant and equipment) or financial resources (e.g. cash). (18)

Human resource development (HRD) especially in the sense developed by the ASTD in the USA, refers to a wide range of organisational strategies, policies, plans, practices and organised activities that aim to improve personal growth and/or performance, in order to improve the job, the individual, and/or the organisation. It forms a major part of the entire human resource management systems of organisations. (11, 12)

Human resource information system (HRIS) a system to acquire, store, manipulate, analyse, retrieve and distribute information related to a company's human resources. (1, 7)

Human resource management (HRM) the policies, practices and systems that influence employees' behaviour, attitudes and performance. (1)

Human resource planning (HRP) (also workforce planning) the process through which organisational goals are translated into HR goals concerning staffing levels and allocation. Human resource planning involves forecasting HR needs for an organisation and planning the necessary steps to meet these needs. (7)

Human resource policies organisational decisions that affect the practices and systems that, in turn, influence employees' behaviour, attitudes and performances. (8)

Human rights the right of people, particularly vulnerable people, to moral protection. (15)

Imaging a process for scanning documents, storing them electronically, and retrieving them. (7)

In-basket a simulation of the administrative tasks of a manager's job. (12)

Indirect discrimination when a compulsory requirement is attached to a job (which has nothing to do with the real performance of the job), which would prevent substantial proportions of particular groups from being able to comply, and the individual in question cannot comply. (3)

Input instructions that tell employees what, how and when to perform; also the support they are given to help them perform. (11)

Intellectual capital includes basic skills (skills needed for an employee to perform his or her job), advanced skills (such as how to use technology to share information with other employees), an understanding of the customer or manufacturing system, and self-motivated creativity. (11)

Interactional justice (also interpersonal fairness) refers to the quality of interpersonal treatment in processes. (15)

Internal analysis the process of examining an organisation's strengths and weaknesses. (2)

Internal growth strategy a focus on new market and product development, innovation and joint ventures. (2)

Internal labour force labour force of current employees. (1)

International HRM (IHRM) the field of study related to the interplay among human resource activities, types of employees, and countries of operation. (16)

Internet recruitment any method of attracting job applicants that relies on the Internet. (8)

Interview situation in which employees may be asked questions about their work and personal experiences, strengths and weaknesses, and career plans. (12)

Involuntary turnover reflects a separation initiated by the organisation, often when the individual would prefer to stay a member of the organisation. (17)

ISO 9000 a series of quality assurance standards developed by the International Organization for Standardization in Switzerland. ISO 9000 certification is a requirement for doing business in many countries and regions, including Australia, the European community, Iceland, Liechtenstein, Norway, Switzerland, Japan, South America and Africa. (1)

Job analysis the process of getting detailed information about jobs. (2, 6)

Job boards Internet websites that provide listings of job opportunities and applicants' resumés. (8)

Job description a list of the tasks, duties and responsibilities (TDRs) that a job entails. (6)

Job design the process of defining the way work will be performed and the tasks that will be required in a given job. (2)

Job enlargement adding challenges or new responsibilities to an employee's current job. (12)

Job enrichment ways in which to add complexity and meaningfulness to a person's work. (17)

Job evaluation an administrative procedure used to measure job worth. (13)

Job experiences the relationships, problems, demands, tasks and other features that employees face in their jobs. (12)

Job involvement the degree to which people identify themselves with their jobs. (17)

Job redesign changing the tasks or the way work is performed in an existing job. (6)

Glossary

Job rotation the process of systematically moving a single individual from one job to another over the course of time. The job assignments may be in various functional areas of the company or movement between jobs in a single functional area or department. (12, 17)

Job satisfaction a pleasurable feeling that results from the perception that a person's job fulfils or allows for the fulfilment of that person's important job values. (17)

Job specification a list of the knowledge, skills, abilities and other characteristics (KSAOs) that an individual must have to perform a job. (6)

Job structure the relative pay of jobs in an organisation. (13)

Job withdrawal a set of behaviours that dissatisfied individuals enact to avoid the work situation. (17)

Justice ethics based on the duty to treat all parties fairly and to distribute risks and benefits equitably. 'Justice' is used broadly to cover both these principles and the specific rules derived from these principles. (15)

Key jobs benchmark jobs, used in pay surveys, that have relatively stable content and are common to many organisations. (13)

Knowledge actual or procedural information that is necessary for successfully performing a task. (6)

Knowledge management processes, techniques, systems and structures that aim to improve the creation, sharing and use of knowledge. (1, 11)

Knowledge work usually involves the research and development of new products and/or services; is performed by knowledge workers. (1, 6)

Knowledge workers highly-skilled employees whose work utilises theoretical and analytical knowledge that is acquired via formal education. (1, 6)

Leaderless group discussion a team of five to seven employees assigned a problem to solve together within a certain time period. (12)

Learning and development (also employee development) the acquisition of knowledge, skills and behaviours that improve an employee's ability to meet changes in job requirements and in client and customer demands (11, 12)

Learning organisation an organisation whose employees are continuously attempting to learn new things and apply what they learn to improve product or service quality. (11)

Managerialist view looks at organisational behaviour and theory from the exclusive point of view of managers, the functional agents of an administered society. (15)

Managing diversity (or diversity management) is a process of managing people's similarities and differences; it is built on a set of values that recognises that the differences between people are a potential strength for the organisation; this process of management creates an environment that allows all employees to contribute to organisational goals and experience personal growth. This concept originated from the human-rights oriented civil rights/anti-discrimination approach that came out of the civil rights movement of 45-odd years ago. (3)

Marginal employees those employees who are performing at a bare-minimum level due to a lack of ability and/or motivation to perform well. (10)

Mentor an experienced, productive senior employee who helps develop a less-experienced employee. (12)

Merger the union of two or more commercial interests or corporations, usually of similar size. (7)

Merit increase grid a grid that combines an employee's performance rating with that employee's position in a pay range to determine the size and frequency of his or her pay increases. (14)

Minimum wage the lowest amount that employers are legally allowed to pay. (13)

Mission a statement of the organisation's reason for being; it usually specifies the customers served, the needs satisfied and/or the values received by the customers, and the technology used. (2)

Moral insight the capacity of an individual to determine whether a person or action is moral in terms of being right, good, virtuous and/or just. (15)

Multidomestic industry an industry in which competition in each country is essentially independent of competition in other countries. (16)

Multinational enterprise (MNE) an enterprise that conducts trans-actions in or between two countries, with a system of decision making that permits influence over resources and capabilities, where the transactions are subject to influence by factors external to the parent country of the enterprise. (16)

Myers-Briggs Type Indicator® Instrument (MBTI® Instrument) a personality assessment used for team building and leadership development that identifies employees' preferences for directing and receiving energy, information gathering, decision making and lifestyle. (12)

Needs assessment the process used to determine if training is necessary. (11)

Negative affectivity a dispositional dimension that reflects pervasive individual differences in satisfaction with any and all aspects of life. (17)

Neo-classical (or neo-liberal) paradigm the view, often in economics, that human behaviour is driven by the relationship between scarce means and alternative ends, such that individuals act in a rational self-serving manner to maximise their own utility. (15)

Neo-liberal policies economic policies including the adoption of free-market principles rather than government regulation, an emphasis on managerial prerogative and a decrease in the role and influence of the AIRC. (5)

Non-key jobs unique to organisations, and cannot be directly valued or compared through the use of market surveys. (13)

Occupational health and safety (OHS) the physical, physiological and psychosocial conditions of an organisation's workforce, related to aspects of work and the work context. (4)

Offshoring the movement of jobs to other countries, usually to take advantage of lower costs. (6)

OHS management system organisational policy and programs that cover the planning, implementation, evaluation and improvement of OHS in an organisation. (4)

OHS policy a written statement approved by top management, typically accompanied by a set of OHS programs, rules and instructions, that identifies OHS accountabilities and sets out the ways in which OHS compliance will be met. (4)

OHS program a plan designed for policy implementation that identifies the OHS procedures, practices and people necessary to reach policy objectives. (4)

Older workers variously defined as 55 years of age and over, between 50 and 80 years of age, and as 40-plus years of age. (2, 4)

Organisation(al) structure the relatively stable and formal network of vertical and horizontal interconnections among jobs that constitute the organisation. (6)

Organisational commitment the degree to which an employee identifies with the organisation and is willing to put forth effort on its behalf. (17)

Organisational justice reflects individual or group perceptions of fairness within an organisation and behavioural reactions to such perceptions. (15)

Organisational redesign restructuring or delayering of the organisation, with elimination of functions, layers and work processes (often a type of downsizing strategy). (7)

Organisational socialisation the process by which new employees are transformed into effective members of a company. (11)

Outplacement counselling refers to counselling that tries to help displaced employees manage the transition from one job to another. (17)

Output a job's performance standards. (11)

Outsourcing an organisation's use of an outside organisation for a broad set of services. (1)

Parent country (also known as the home country) the country in which a company's corporate headquarters is located. (16)

Parent-country nationals (PCNs) employees who were born and live in a parent country. (16)

Pay grades jobs of similar worth or content grouped together for pay administration purposes. (13)

Pay level the average pay, including wages, salaries and bonuses, of jobs in an organisation. (13)

Pay-policy line a mathematical expression that describes the relationship between a job's pay and its job evaluation points. (13)

Pay structure the relative pay of different jobs (job structure) and how much they are paid (pay level). (13)

Performance appraisal process that allows for assessing progress towards the achievement of the desired goals or other performance standards. (10)

Performance feedback the process of providing employees with information regarding their performance effectiveness. (10)

Performance feedback process a process whereby the defined expected performance information and the measured performance information is fed back to the employee. (10)

Performance management the process through which managers ensure that employees' activities and outputs are congruent with the organisation's goals. (2, 10)

Performance planning and evaluation (PPE) systems systems that seek to tie the formal performance appraisal process to the company's strategies by specifying at the beginning of the evaluation period the types and level of performance that must be accomplished to achieve the strategy. (10)

Person characteristics an employee's knowledge, skills, abilities and attitudes. (11)

Pluralism an approach that sees society as comprising a diversity of interest groups with divergent social interests and, as such, this approach accepts conflict between employer and employee as usual. (5, 15)

Predictive validation a criterion-related validity study that seeks to establish an empirical relationship between applicants' test scores and their eventual performance on the job. (8)

Principal in agency theory, the owner of a business; in HR management, may refer to a manager. (14)

Procedural justice (also procedural fairness) a concept of justice focusing on the methods used to determine the outcomes received. (13, 15, 17)

Procurement situations where a vendor is contracted to perform activities that an organisation has not performed before. (7)

Profit sharing a group compensation plan in which payments are based on a measure of organisation performance (profits) and do not become part of an employee's base salary. (14)

Promotion advancement into a position with greater challenge, more responsibilities, and more authority than the employee's previous job. (12)

Protean career a career that is frequently changing due to both changes in the person's interests, abilities and values, and changes in the work environment. (12)

Glossary

Psychological contract the expectations that employers and employees have about each other. (1, 12)

Psychological success the feeling of pride and accomplishment that comes from achieving life goals. (12)

Psychosocial support serving as a friend and role model, providing positive regard and acceptance, and creating an outlet for a protégé to talk about their anxieties and fears. (12)

Range spread the distance between the minimum and maximum amounts in a pay grade. (13)

Realistic job preview accurate information about the attractive and unattractive aspects of a job, working conditions, company and location, to ensure that potential employees develop appropriate expectations. (8)

Recruitment any practice or activity carried out by the organisation with the primary purpose of identifying and attracting potential employees. (2, 8)

Redundancy dismissal based on the elimination of jobs due to organisational restructuring or technological change, which leads to certain jobs or skills being no longer required. (5)

Reengineering review and redesign of work processes to make them more efficient and improve the quality of the end product or service. (18)

Referrals people who are prompted to apply for a job by someone within the organisation. (8)

Reinforcement theory claims that a response followed by a reward is more likely to reoccur in the future. (14)

Relational psychological contracts expectations between employers and employees that tend to focus on open-ended relationships with emotional involvement as well as economic exchange. (15)

Relationship recruitment a recruitment method that relies on Internet tools to learn about the interests of individuals who visit a company's website, then the individual is approached regarding a job opportunity. (8)

Reliability the consistency of the performance measure; the degree to which a performance measure is free from random error. One important type of reliability is inter-rater reliability: the consistency among the individuals who evaluate the employee's performance. (8, 10)

Repatriation the preparation of expatriates for return to the parent company and country from a foreign assignment. (16)

Reputation Index (published between 2000 and 2003) took into account the views of stakeholders and experts, including consumers, investors, employees and activists, about the reputation of companies taken in *Business Review Weekly*'s (*BRW*) list of Australia's top 1000 companies. The model has since been further developed as RepuTex Ratings. (1)

Return on investment (ROI) assigning a value to the benefits achieved by an HR activity and dividing that value by the costs associated with the activity. (18)

Rights and duties of employees suggests that employees are seen to have rights and duties that not only encompass basic human rights and duties but also take into account the particular demands of the work setting. (15)

Risk the potential outcome of injury, illness, damage or loss resulting from a hazard. (4)

Risk management the process of identifying all hazards in the work or workplace, followed by an assessment of the associated risks and the implementation of effective measures to control those risks. (4)

Role ambiguity the level of uncertainty about what an organisation expects from an employee in terms of what to do and how to do it. (17)

Role analysis technique a method that enables a role occupant and other members of the role occupant's role-set to specify and examine their expectations for a role occupant. (17)

Role behaviours behaviours required of an individual in his or her role as a job holder in a social/work environment. (2)

Role conflict recognition of incompatible or contradictory demands by the person occupying a role. (17)

Role overload a state in which too many expectations or demands are placed on a person. (17)

Role play a participant taking the part or role of a manager or other employee. (12)

Sabbatical a leave of absence from the company to renew or develop skills. (12)

Safety awareness programs employer programs that attempt to instil symbolic and substantive changes in the organisation's emphasis on safety. (4)

Safety climate the attitudes, beliefs, perceptions and values that employers and employees share in relation to safety, and it is a subset of culture. (4)

Safety culture results from individual and group values, attitudes, perceptions, competencies and behaviours that determine the commitment to, and the style and effectiveness of, an organisation's OHS management. (4)

Selection the process by which an organisation attempts to identify applicants with the necessary knowledge, skills, abilities and other characteristics that will help it achieve its goals. (2)

Selection interview a dialogue initiated by one or more persons to gather information and evaluate the qualifications of an applicant for employment. (8)

Self-service giving employees control of HR transactions. (1)

Sexual harassment behaviour of a sexual nature that is neither welcome nor solicited. (3)

Shared services the standardisation of common administrative functions and transactional processes within an organisation. (18)

Skill an individual's level of proficiency at performing a particular task. (6)

Skill-based pay pay based on the skills employees acquire and are capable of using. (13)

Social marketing the use of commercial marketing strategies to promote behavioural change that will improve the health or wellbeing of the target group, such as a workforce, or of society in general. (4)

'Soft' HRM commitment-oriented HRM that emphasises mutuality—mutual goal, mutual influences, mutual benefits—between employees and the organisation. (15)

Specificity the extent to which the performance measure gives specific guidance to employees about what is expected of them and how they can meet these expectations. (10)

Stakeholder theory a theory of the firm that holds that the organisation has a moral relationship with a number of non-owner stakeholders based on the notion that these stakeholders have a stake or claim in the firm. (15)

State a generic term covering not simply the government of the day, but all the other apparatus as well (including bureaucracy, judiciary etc.). (3)

Stock option an employee ownership plan that gives employees the opportunity to buy the company's stock at a previously fixed price. (14)

Strategic business partner a role performed by HR practitioners, aiming to execute organisational strategy by aligning HR processes with the organisational strategy. (1)

Strategic choice the organisation's strategy; the ways in which an organisation will attempt to fulfil its mission and achieve its long-term goals. (2)

Strategic congruence the extent to which the performance management system elicits job performance that is congruent with the organisation's strategy, goals and culture. (10)

Strategic human resource management (SHRM) the pattern of planned HR deployments and activities intended to enable an organisation to achieve its goals. (1, 2)

Strategy formulation the process of deciding on a strategic direction by defining a company's mission and goals, its external opportunities and threats, and its internal strengths. (2)

Strategy implementation the process of devising structures and allocating resources to enact the strategy a company has chosen. (2)

Stress response an individual's emotional and/or physiological response to events perceived or evaluated as a threat to his or her wellbeing. (4)

Strike employees' refusal to work until their demands (e.g. for improved work conditions) are met by their employer. (5)

Structural Efficiency Principle (or award restructuring) a reform of the Australian wages system aimed at developing a more highly-skilled workplace; for example, by the reduction of job classifications, the establishment of skill-related career paths linked to pay scales and multi-skilling to enhance workforce flexibility. (13)

Subjectivism the view that individuals are the sole authority over their ethical principles. (15)

Succession planning the identification and tracking of high-potential employees capable of filling higher-level managerial positions. (7, 12)

Sustainability report a company report presenting information on the economic, environmental and social dimensions of its activities, products and services. (It is synonymous with social report, citizenship report, triple bottom line report, corporate social responsibility report.) Where it includes governance issues, it may be referred to as a quadruple bottom line report. (18)

SWOT analysis involves identifying the organisation's strengths and weaknesses and the opportunities and threats in its external operating environment. (2)

Systemic change a program of organisational cultural change involving all staff (often a type of downsizing strategy). (7)

Talent management a long-term and integrated approach to managing employees—by attracting them into the organisations, and providing development and engagement opportunities utilising a sophisticated system of HR practices. (1)

Teleological theory an outcome-based ethical theory that considers the rightness or wrongness of our acts to be determined by a comparative assessment of their consequences. (15)

Telework (telecommuting, also distributed work) work done outside of the traditional work environment, including at home, while travelling, or anywhere an employee can interact with managers, peers, customers, products or processes using technology. (6)

Third-country nationals (TCNs) employees born in a country other than a parent or host country. (16)

Total quality management (TQM) a cooperative form of doing business that relies on the talents and capabilities of both labour and management to continually improve quality and productivity. (1)

Training focuses on the development of the skills of the workforce and although it may be job orientated, training is related promiarily to meeting the skills of the organisation (11)

Transactional psychological contracts expectations between employers and employees that are focused on a specific economic exchange with little flexibility and narrowly defined terms. (15)

Transfer the movement of an employee to a different job assignment in a different area of the company. (12)

Transfer of training refers to the use of knowledge, skills and behaviours learned in training on the job. (11)

Transitional matrices matrices showing the proportion or number of employees in different job categories at different times (7).

Glossary

Triple bottom line the combination of economic, social and environmental performance indicators for an organisation. (18)

Unfair dismissal generally refers to a situation where regard for a fair procedure (i.e. the right to hear of the transgression and be given the opportunity to defend oneself) has been ignored, or where a transgression itself does not reasonably suggest dismissal is an appropriate management response. (3)

Unions collections of workers who have joined together in order to better their terms and conditions of employment. (5)

Unitarism assumes that all parties in an organisation share similar goals and interests and, as such, does not acknowledge the potential for conflict between employer and employee. (1, 15)

Universalism (or absolutism) the belief that there is a single truth. In ethics, universalism implies a single perspective as to what is right and wrong and it is in contrast to relativism. (15)

Upward feedback a performance appraisal process for managers, which involves collecting subordinates' evaluations of managers' behaviours or skills.

Utilitarianism an ethical theory that defines an action as right if it maximises the common or collective good. (15)

Utility the degree to which the information provided by selection methods enhances the effectiveness of selecting personnel in real organisations. (8)

Utility analysis an assessment of the dollar value of HRM activities such as training, based on the difference in job performance between trained and untrained employees, the number of individuals trained, the length of time training is expected to influence performance, and the variability in job performance among untrained employees. (18)

Validity (often referred to as content validity) the extent to which a performance measure assesses all the relevant—and only the relevant—aspects of job performance. (8, 10)

Veil of ignorance a conceptual device that requires each person to put him or herself in the original position, that is, to imagine he or she is ignorant of his of her particular characteristics such as race, gender, intelligence and family background. (15)

Virtue ethics focuses on the person who performs the action rather than the principles or the outcome of an action. Virtue ethics is concerned with the character or character traits of the actor as expressed in his or her actions. (15)

Vocational education and training. VET is a more externally focused concept than training. Like training, it is concerned with meeting the skills needs of the organisation but VET is essentially focused on meeting the skills needs of individuals so that they can find employment in the labour market. This involves gaining nationally recognised qualifications that may or may not meet the needs of the employing organisation. (11, 12)

Vocational rehabilitation occupational reintegration, or return-to-work, for injured workers. (4)

Voluntary turnover reflects a separation initiated by the individual, often when the organisation would prefer that the person stay a member of the organisation. (17)

Whistleblowing reporting outside an organisation on activities, within an organisation, that have the potential to cause serious harm to the public. (15)

Work intensification employees working longer hours and working harder than ever before. (4, 6)

WorkChoices the collective name for a series of amendments made to labour law by the Australian Federal Government in 2005 (3)

Work-flow design the process of analysing the tasks necessary for the production of a product or service, prior to allocating and assigning these tasks to a particular job category or person. (6)

Workforce reduction a type of downsizing strategy, using a cost-cutting approach emphasising short-term results and redundancies. (7)

Workplace agreement a written agreement between an employer and an employee/s (or a union) that is lodged with a government agency (5, 14)

Workplace bullying repeated and persistent negative acts by one employee, or a group of employees, against others, which create a hostile work environment. (17)

INDEX

3M, diversity management 318
360-degree feedback 458–9
457 visas *see* skilled temporary migrants

abilities 190
Able Management Consultants (AMC) 524
Aborigines *see* Indigenous Australians
ABS *see* Australian Bureau of Statistics
absenteeism 381, 632
  and older workers 127
absolutism (ethical theory) 569
acceptability
  measures
    performance management 354–5
Accord, The 152, 517
accountability
  human resource management 665
accumulation effect 539
acquisitions, related to downsizing 226–7
action learning 430
action plans
  transfer of training 421
  career planning 468–70
Active Recruitment
  and WorkChoices 95
activity index 674
ACTU
  Future Strategies: Unions Working Together for a Fairer Australia 165
  unions@work 165
  work and family test case 330
administration
  role of HR professionals 10, 13
  outsourcing 13
administrative linkage
  HRM and strategy formulation 59
adventure learning 428–9
advertisements, recruitment 264
affective outcomes
  training programs 431
affirmative action 101
Affirmative Action (Equal Opportunity for Women) Act 1986 (Cwlth) 101, 308
AFPC *see* Australian Fair Pay Commission
age diversity
  Deutsche Bank 315
ageing workforce 16
  see also older workers
agency theory 532–4
agents (agency theory) 532

AHRI *see* Australian Human Resources Institute
AIRC *see* Australian Industrial Relations Commission
Airflite 262
Albermarle v Moody 422 US 405, 412–413 (1975) 356
Alcoa
  unions global fight against 164
  work and family initiatives 329
alcohol abuse in the workplace 118
  testing policies 586–7
allowable matters 154–5, 156
AMC *see* Able Management Consultants
Amcor
  health and wellbeing strategies 129
  HR initiatives 342
American Express 3–4
AMP
  employee assistance program 628
  retention strategies 640
analytic approach
  evaluating HRM 668–75
anti-discrimination, laws 99–100
anticipatory socialisation 433–4
ANZ Bank
  offshoring 167
  organisational change 212–14
  performance management 213
  talent management 213
  IT centre, Bangalore 230
ANZ DL 348
  performance targets related to strategic plan 348
appraisal politics 378–9
apprenticeship 403–4
APRA *see* Australian Prudential Regulation Authority
Aruspex 217–18
AS Tools 352
ASCC *see* Australian Safety and Compensation Council
Asia, GDP growth 86
Asia-Pacific region, occupational health and safety 138–41
assessment *see* employees, assessment
assessment centres 291, 364–5, 455–6
  defined 291, 455
Atlas, Ilana 187
attribute approach
  performance measurement 358–60

audit approach
  evaluating HRM 666–8
auditing
  occupational health and safety 132–4
Australia
  economic structure 20–1
  anti-discrimination legislation 99–100
  absenteeism 381
  employee share ownership schemes 543
  executive pay 492, 510–12
    governance 512
    share options 514
  industrial relations 150–9
  labour force 15–20, 22–3
    skill deficiencies 21–2
    competitiveness 507–9
  learning and development 397
  occupational health and safety
    statistics 117–19
    legislation 119–23
    enforcement authorities 123–4
    complementary regulation 124–5
    codes of practice 125
    national standards 125
    regulations 125
    related to industrial relations 125
  performance management
    legal issues 384–6
  rewards
    government regulation 515–20
  training, in organisations 399–402
  vocational education and training 402–4
  turnover 631
  wage determination 515–17
    reconstruction 517
  workforce 15–20, 22–3
    skill deficiencies 21–2
  workplace health 131
    stress 635
Australia. Constitution 93
Australian and New Zealand Direct Line (ANZ DL) *see* ANZ DL
Australian Bureau of Statistics (ABS)
  Training Expenditure Surveys (TES) 399, 400
  Survey of Education and Training Experience (SET) 400–1
  Employer Training Practices Survey (TPS) 401
  Training Expenditure and Practices surveys 402
Australian Business Excellence Awards 35–6
Australian Business Limited 241
Australian Capital Territory, occupational health and safety 122
Australian Fair Pay and Conditions Standard 154

743

Index

Australian Fair Pay Commission (AFPC) 95, 519–20
Australian Human Resources Institute (AHRI)
  remuneration and benefits survey 483–5
Australian Industrial Relations Commission (AIRC) 150–1, 156–9
  wage determination 516–17
Australian Kitchen Industries
  blended learning 424
Australian Prudential Regulation Authority (APRA)
  and appointments 386
Australian Qualifications Framework 403
Australian Quality Awards *see* Australian Business Excellence Awards
Australian Safety and Compensation Council (ASCC) 120–1
Australian Taxation Office
  health and wellbeing program 141–2
Australian Workplace Agreements (AWAs) 71–2, 94–5, 153, 160–2
  Commonwealth Bank 161
Australian Workplace Safety Standards Act 2005 (Cwlth) 120
automatisation 417
autonomy, in job design 200
AVON, passport program 452
award restructuring 491, 518
  delayering 504
awards 94, 151, 154–5
AWAs *see* Australian Workplace Agreements

B2E systems 249
Babcock & Brown 210
Bahl, Siddharth 206
Baker's Delight, and WorkChoices 94–5
balanced scorecard 36–7, 352
  organisational performance 514
  performance pay systems 545–7
  related to executive pay 550–1
  measure of HR performance 674
banding, job levels 504
banking industry, offshoring jobs 167, 623
BARS *see* behaviourally anchored rating scales
BASF Australia 243
Bashinsky, Alec 29
Bass, Laurie 341
Batson, Robyn 349
Beaconsfield mine 145–7
behaviour-based contracts 533–4
behaviour change
  response to dissatisfaction 631–2
behaviour modelling 427–8
behavioural approach
  performance measurement 360–5
behavioural competency 107
behavioural observation scales (BOS) 361, 363

behavioural perspective
  human resource management 6
behaviourally anchored rating scales (BARS) 361–3
benchmark jobs 493
benchmarks® 456–7
benefits (employees) *see* rewards
benefits (of HR), determination 669
Bentham, Jeremy 568
Berger, Yossi 113–14, 117
BHP Billiton
  performance benchmarks 352
biographical data, use in selection 288
biological approach
  job design 198–9, 200–1
blended learning 424–5
  defined 425
Bluescope Steel
  graduate recruitment 272
Boeing
  strategic management failure 58
  team training 429–30
bonus envy 513
Boral, fitness program 129
BOS *see* behavioural observation scales
Briggs, Michael 235
Brooks, Duncan 142
BT (British Telecom)
  diversity management 321
Buckman Labs, knowledge workers 82
Bunker, George M. 337–8
business competence, as an HR skill 84
business games 427
business long-stay 333
business to employees systems 249

call centres 30, 204, 206–7
  monitoring of calls 346
Canadian Imperial Bank of Commerce 82
CaPeR system 388–9
CAPTure (software program) 217–18
career development 189
  software applications 246
career management 466–70
  staff retention 642–4
career patterns 448–9
career support 465
careers
  defined 447
  related to, learning and development 447–9
Carter, Jacky 188
case studies 427
Catalyst Recruitment 334–5
causal chain analysis 675
cause-and-effect diagrams 369
centralisation
  organisation structure 183–4

Certified Workplace Agreements 518
change agent
  role of HR professionals 10
China
  market potential 25–6
  labour law reform 140
  multinational enterprises 26
    sending staff overseas 205
  skilled labour shortage 233
  use of performance management 350
  and world economy 608
Cisco Systems, share options scheme 542
CityWatcher.com
  use of RFID chips 581
Civil Rights Act 1964 (US) 97
classroom instruction 423
client-server architecture 236–8
co-workers
  affect on job satisfaction 638–9
coaching 466, 478–9
cognitive ability tests 288–9
cognitive moral development 577
cognitive outcomes
  training programs 430
Coles
  corporate university 407
  customer service training 416–17
Coles Institute 407
collectivism, suppression 581–2
Collins, Roger 3, 208–9, 664, 675
commodification
  defined 580
  of labour 580–1
Commonwealth Bank
  and AWAs 161
communication
  importance
    during mergers 77
    performance-based pay 552
communities of practice 413–15
companies, changes in structure 31
company directors
  risks and rewards 556
Company Law review Act 1998 (Cwlth)
  and disclosure of executive packages 551
comparative approach
  performance measurement 356–8
compensable factors 493
compensation *see* rewards
competencies 372–3
competency-based pay 504–5, 507
competitive advantage
  role of HRM 80–2
  utilising labour markets 219
  effect of diversity management 312–13
competitiveness, enhancement 82
concentration strategies 75–6

744

Conciliation and Arbitration Act 1904 (Cwlth) 150
conciliation and arbitration system 92
concurrent validation
　compared with predictive validation 280–2
　defined 280
conditions of employment, machinery 93–5
consequences, defined 409
consequentialism 568
Constantinides, Kristian 262
Constitution 93
contaminated job performance measures 353–4
content validity *see* validity
contingent workforce 197
　defined 22
　growth 22–3
　Google 299
contract work 204
　office cleaning 521–2
contracts of employment 95–6
contrast error
　performance measurement 377
control charts 370
convergence hypothesis 601–2
corporate culture 686
　Virgin Blue 53–4
corporate governance 659
corporate social responsibility (CSR) 659, 660–3
　Yue Yuen Industrial (Holdings) 661
　implications for HRM 662–3
corporate sustainability *see* sustainability
corporate universities 407–8
corporatism 166
correlation coefficients 276–8
corruption 578
cost-benefit analysis
　economic benefits of HR programs 668
cost strategies 72
　related to employee skills 74
costs (of HR), determination 668–9
Crazy John's 533
Crimes (Industrial Manslaughter) Amendment Act 2003 (ACT) 119
criterion-related validation 279–82
critical incidents 360–1
CSR *see* corprate social resonsibility
cross-training 429
cultural audits 316, 324
　Esso 316–17, 319
cultural awareness 602–3
cultural diversity 303–4
cultural environment
　and international HRM 600–2
culture shock 601
Culture's Consequences (Hofstede) 603

customers
　source of performance data 376–7

data fields 238
data files 238
data-flow diagrams 682–3
DEC *see* Digital Equipment Corporation
decentralisation (of IR) 151–2
　as future challenge 166–7
decision support systems 234
Declaration of Philadelphia 306
Defence Housing Authority (DHA)
　performance management 388–9
delayering 504
Deloitte
　organisational change 29
　graduate recruitment 272
Deming, W. Edwards
　on meeting customer needs 33
　on merit pay 537–8
demotions 463–4
deontology 567–8
departmentalisation 183–4
deregulation
　labour market 151–2
　as future challenge 166–9
Deutsche Bank
　diversity management 310
　age diversity 315
DHA *see* Defence Housing Authority
differentiation strategies 72
　related to employee skills 74
Digital Equipment Corporation (DEC) 317
　performance assessment 375
Diment, David 141–2
direct applicants 263–4
direct discrimination 99–100
directional strategies 75–80
directors *see* company directors
distributed work 23
distributional errors
　performance measurement 378
distributive justice 488, 569, 576
　and job satisfaction 637
divergence hypothesis 602
diversity
　understanding of the concept 321–3
　case study 337–8
diversity enlargement 323
diversity management 136, 304–5
　programs 3-07–8, 306, 307–8
　defined 304
　model 305–8
　Deutsche Bank 310
　effect on competitive advantage 312–13
　initiatives 315–20
　　at 3M 318
　　BT (British Telecom) 321

　　issues 321–8
　　advisory panels 324–5
　　business case 325–6
　　demonstrating organisational improvements 325
　　contradictory evidence 326
　　attitudinal issues 327–8
　　future directions 330–4
　　related to
　　　equal employment opportunity 308–10
　　　organisational performance 310–14
　　　organisational change 313–14
　　added value 333–4
Diversity Research Network 337–8
diversity sensitivity 323–4
diversity training 323–4
Diversity@work 338
divisional structures 184–6
Donaldson, Craig 43–4
downshifting 70, 566
downsizing 77–80, 225–8
　defined 225
　problems 227–8
downward moves (demotions) 463–4
Drake International, *Making Diversity Work for your Organisation and Australia's Future* 337
drug abuse in the workplace 118
drug tests
　in the workplace 586–7
　in recruitment 292
　involuntary termination 626–7
Du Pont Fibers Division
　profit sharing 541–2
duty of care 120

e-learning 428
e-recruitment 265
early retirement programs 228
Eastman Kodak
　executive pay 551
economic rationalist frameworks 564
economy, structure 20–1
Edsall, Judy 388, 389
education and training
　Victoria 450
　see also formal education; training; vocational education and training
EEO *see* equal employment opportunity
electronic monitoring 387–8, 624–5
　global positioning systems 240, 387–8
　legal issues 241
electronic performance support systems (EPSS) 402
Ella Baché, and WorkChoices 95
emails, monitoring 387
emergent strategies 80, 81–2

745

Index

emic 601
  defined 570
emotional labour 205–6
employability, right to 573
employee assistance programs 627–8
employee benefits *see* employees, benefits
employee champion
  role of HR professionals 10
employee engagement, defined 37
employee self-service systems 235, 237, 249
employee share ownership schemes (ESOPs) 543
employee survey research 646, 646–7
employee values 18–20
employee voice 650
employees
  as an asset 34
  attracting 37–8
  benefits 71
  databases 244–5
  assessment 452–7
  attitude to HR function 666
  development 70–1
    dimension of HRM 41
    defined 71
    and performance management 348–50
    staff retention 642
    see also learning and development
  fitness programs 129
  health and wellbeing 131
  international assignments 615–17
    strategies 589–90
  learning and development *see* learning and development
  obligations 575
  participation in decision-making
    rewards management 501
    performance-based pay 552
  recruitment *see* recruitment
  retention *see* retention
  selection *see* selection (employees)
  poaching 110–11, 257–8
  productivity, related to stress 116
  as a resource 489–90
  rights 572–5
  skills
    requirements 30
    related to, strategic types 73–5
  stress
    reduction 116
    see also stress response
  termination *see* involuntary turnover
  turnover *see* turnover
employer associations, defined 150
employer of choice, defined 37
employer prerogative 165–6
Employer Training Practices Survey (ABS) 401

employment
  changing nature 159–62
  see also workforce; and, entries beginning with the word workplace
employment agencies 267
employment brands 188
employment relations
  changes 565
  justice and fairness 575–6
encounter phase
  organisational socialisation 434–5
enterprise agreements 153
Enterprise Awards Principle 518
enterprise bargaining 153, 156–9, 518–19
Enterprise Bargaining Principle 518–19
enterprise learning 441–2
Enterprising Nation (Karpin) 312–13
EPSS *see* electronic performance support systems
equal employment opportunity (EEO) 305
  defined 96
  laws 96–102
  and equal employment diversity management 308–10
Equal Opportunity for Women in the Workplace Amendment Act 1999 (Cwlth) 101, 308–9, 322
equity theory 486–8
ergonomics 200
Ericsson
  performance management 388–9
ESOPs *see* employee share ownership schemes
ESS systems 235, 237, 249
Esso
  cultural audits 316–17, 319
  parental leave 322–3
ethical pluralism 570
  and stakeholder concept 571
ethical principals 567–71
ethical relativism 569–70
ethical theory 564
ethics 23–4, 564–84, 686
  defined 564
ethnicity, workforce 17–18
ethnocentrism 607
etic 601
  defined 570
executive education 451–2
executive pay 492, 509–15, 547–51, 559–60
  design and structure 512–15
  governance 512
  trends 512–15
  related to performance 544, 547, 548–9
  disclosure 551
exit interviews 650
expatriate assignments 464

expatriates 593–4
  failure 598
expectancy theory 530–2
  related to merit pay 539
expert systems 234–5
external analysis 61–2
external equity pay comparisons 487
external growth strategies 76–7
external labour market, defined 15

F-JASs *see* Fleishman Job Analysis Surveys
Fairfax *see* John Fairfax Holding
fairness
  rewards management 486–8
  in the employment relationship 575–6
family-friendly programs 328
Farrell, Bill 43–4
FDI *see* foreign direct investment
FedEx
  people service profit philosophy 619–20
feedback *see* performance feedback; training, feedback
Fisher and Paykel
  team building 636
Fleishman Job Analysis Surveys (F-JASs) 194–5
  abilities included 196
flexible work arrangements, defined 179
Florida, Richard 555
Fonterra Co-operative Group
  international assignment strategy 589–90
forced distribution
  performance measurement 356
Ford Australia, redundancies 623–4
forecasting 220–4, 242
foreign assignments *see* international assignments
Foreign Corrupt Practices Act 1977 (US) 573, 596
foreign direct investment (FDI)
  in China 25, 26
  by China 26
formal education 451–2
  programs, defined 451
frames of reference 633
freedom of association 162
Fujitsu Australia, ESS system 235
functional structures 184, 186
Future Strategies: Unions Working Together for a Fairer Australia (ACTU) 165

gainsharing 544–5
gender issues, workforce 16–17
generalisability (selection processes) 283–4
generations X and Y 18, 177–8
Georgiou, Chris 438–9
GEOs *see* global executive officers
Gill, Matthew 145, 146

global executive officers (GEOs) 63
Global Human Capital Study (IBM) 43–4
global industries 603–4
global knowledge economy 28
global markets 25–6
global positioning systems 240
Global Reporting Initiative 662
global workforce 26–7
globalisation 24–7
   impact on HR strategies 27
   Woods Bagot 313
   related to pay structures 500
   economies 564–5
goals
   strategic management 61
   human resource planning 224–31
   career planning 468
Gold Coast City Council 354–5
Google
   staff retention 3
   recruitment 298–300
graduate recruitment 267–8, 272, 599
   Google 299
graphic rating scales
   performance measurement 358
group-building methods 428–30
group incentives 545
groupware 239
guerilla recruiting 257–8
guest workers 333

halo and horns errors
   performance measurement 378
hands-on learning 425–8
hard HRM 579
Harrison v Department of TAFE (1992) 385
Harvard framework of HRM 7–8
hazards
   defined 115
   evaluation 133
   identification 133
HBA Health Insurance 331
HCNs see host-country nationals
Headtrax 387–8
health hazards 115
health-promotion programs 135–6, 663
   Victoria Police 142–3
   cost-benefit analysis 671–2
HECS 178
Hertz, diversity in recruitment 332
Herzberg, Frederick, two-factor theory 199
Hewitt Associates
   Best Employers awards 38
Hewlett–Packard (HP) 317
high commitment HRM 579–80
high involvement work processes 207
high performance cultures 392

high-performance work systems 29
   HRM practices 32
Highfield, Bruce 53–4
Hofstede, Geert, *Culture's Consequences* 603
home country see parent country
homosocial reproduction 327
honesty tests 291–2
Honeywell
   Management Practices Index 317
Hopper & Others v Virgin Blue Airlines (2006) 107–8
host country, defined 592
host-country nationals (HCNs) 592
hot-desk workers 197
Howie, Luke 98
HP see Hewlett–Packard
HR activity index 674
HR metrics 665
HRIS see human resource information systems
HRM see human resource management
HRP see human resource planning
human capital 580
   defined 190, 580
   management 43–4, 64, 675
     defined 5
   pool 82
   types 203
   rating by investors 341–2
   measurement 673
Human Capital Index (Watson Wyatt) 674
human resource accounting 669–70, 677
human resource departments, roles and activities 9–14
human resource development (HRD) 397, 449
human resource information systems (HRIS) 32, 232–5
   defined 232
   software applications for HRM 240–9
   human resource planning 242–6
human resource management (HRM) 4–6
   behavioural perspective 6
   conceptual foundations 7–9
   competitive challenges 24–41
   compared with international HRM 594–607
   activities 663–5
   accountability 665
   customer satisfaction
     key indicators 667
   defined 4
   dimensions 39–41
   and decline in union membership 163

duality of role 577–9
effectiveness
   measurement 659–66
   evaluation 666–75
   improving 675–84
ethical behaviour
   impact of organisational culture 579
   political-influence perspective 7
innovation 28–32, 66
   linkage with strategic management 57–8
importance of job analysis 188–9
organisation structure 208–10
   as locus of employment ethics 565–7
ethicality 576–7
marketing the function 665
metrics 665
functions, outsourcing 679–81
future prospects 684–6
practices
   related to, strategy implementation 68–72
   options 69
process redesign 681–3
related to
   innovation 548
   sustainability 659–63
resource-based view 6–7
return on investment 672
restructuring functions 677–9
role 46, 48–50, 149
   in strategy formulation 58–60
   in strategic competitive advantage 80–2
   transformation 657–8
theoretical perspectives 6–7
use of information technology 235–40
as a strategic tool 579
use of new technologies 683–4
within
   the enterprise 579–80
   society 580–2
human resource managers see human resource professionals
human resource planning (HRP) 189, 217–51
   defined 219
   strategic approach 219–20
   program implementation and evaluation 231–2
   software applications 242–4
human resource policies 260–1
human resource professionals
   responsibilities 9–14
   skills required 14–15
   shortage 483–4
   role in remuneration policy 559–60
   duality of role 577–9
   moral development 577

Index

IBM
  Global Human Capital Study 43–4
    diversity strategy 303–4
    blended learning 425
Ilhan, John 533
ILO *see* International Labour Organisation
image advertising 261
imaging 239
implementation strategies 82–3
in-basket exercises 455
incentives 71
Independent Contractors Act 2006 (Cwlth) 151
index of transnationality 605–6
India
  call centres 206
  skilled labour shortage 233
  and world economy 608
Indigenous Australians
  in the workforce 17
  employment and training, Qantas 451
indirect discrimination 99–100
individual incentives 540
induction *see* orientation programs
industrial disputes
  resolution processes 157, 173–4
  see also strikes
industrial relations 150–71
  Australia 150–9
  future challenges 166–9
Industrial Relations Reform Act 1993 (Cwlth) 518
information technology
  impact on skill requirements 30
  use in human resource management 235–40
  use in recruitment management 266
  outsourcing 353
innovation
  and human resource management (HRM) 548
  in recruitment 678
inpatriates 593–4
input
  defined 409
  related to performance and learning 409
instructional design process 404–10
integration competence, as HR skill 85
integrative linkage
  HRM and strategy formulation 60
intellectual capital *see* human capital
intended strategies 80–1
inter-active voice technology 236
interactional justice 576
  involuntary turnover 624
interactive video 428
internal analysis 62
internal equity pay comparisons 487
internal growth strategies 76

internal promotion
  effect on
    job characteristics 260
    recruit characteristics 263
internal workforce, defined 15
international assignments 615–17
  strategies 589–90
  risk exposure 598
international human resource management (IHRM) 589–90, 591–613
  defined 591
  scope 591–4
  compared with domestic HRM 594–607
  involvement in employees' personal lives 597
  strategic view 607–11
International Labour Organisation (ILO)
  and equal treatment for men and women 306
international mobility 589–90
international projects, costing 247
international transfers 464
Internet
  misuse 104–5, 387
  use in human resource management 236
  use in recruitment 264–5
interpersonal relationships 464–6
interviews
  staff selection 286–7
  staff assessment 455
intranets 239–40
involuntary turnover 622–9
  defined 622
  principles of justice 624–5
Islam, in the workplace 98
ISO 9000 35

Jardine Matheson
  international recruitment 610–11
JDI *see* Job Descriptive Index
Jenkins, Adrian 475
job analysis 69–70, 187–97
  defined 69, 180
  dynamic elements 195–7
  contemporary organisational context 203–7
  importance
    to HR managers 188–9
    to line managers 189–90
  information
    nature 190–1
    sources 191–2
  methods 192–5
  ratings
    compared with performance 192
    supervisors compared with incumbents 192
job-based pay structures 502–7

job boards 265
job customisation 636–7
job descriptions 190
  sample 191
Job Descriptive Index (JDI) 644
job design 69–70, 197–202
  approaches 198
    biological approach 198–9, 200–1
    mechanistic approach 198, 200
    motivational approach 198, 199–200
    perceptual motor approach 199, 201
    trade-offs 201–2
  defined 69, 197
  related to OHS 135
  implications of organisational structure 186–7
  outcomes 201–2
  contemporary organisational context 203–7
job dissatisfaction
  symptoms 630–3
  sources 634–40
job enlargement 200, 461
job enrichment 200, 636
job evaluation 189, 488, 493–4
  software applications 247
  conflicts with pay surveys 498–9
job experiences 459–64
job involvement 633
Job Network 267
job-performance tests 290
job previews, realism 273
job redesign, defined 197
job rotation 461–2, 636
job satisfaction 633
  measurement 644–5
  monitoring 646–51
job specifications 190
job structure 493–4
  defined 486
job withdrawal 630–3
John Fairfax Holdings
  executive pay 549
Jung, Carl 453
justice, in the employment relationship 575–6
justice ethics 569
Kant, Immanuel 567, 580
Karpin, David, *Enterprising Nation* 312–13
Kazama v Qantas Airways (2005) PR969209 108
Kearney, A.T. 261
key jobs 493
Kmart Australia
  management support for training 420–1
Knight, Minna 241
knowledge, job requirement 190
knowledge economy 28–9

knowledge management 28
knowledge work, defined 21, 203
knowledge workers 203–4
   defined 28, 203
   employment level 555
   competition for 641
Kochan, Thomas 337–8
Kodak
   closure of Coburg plant 622–3
KPMG Australia
   career management system 466–7
KSAOs (knowledge, skills, abilities and other characteristics) 190
   transferability 204
Kunnen, Hans 341–2

labour
   costs
      commodification 580
         instability of country differences 507–8
      demand for 222–4
   markets
      and competitive advantage 219
   supply 222–4
   supply chains 678
labour force *see* workforce
labour-market competition
   effect on pay levels 489
Lafferty, George 191
lag indicators 65
   use by analysts 676
Laker, John 386
Langhorne, Jo 475–6
laser disc technology 239
Law of effect (Thorndike) 530
lead indicators
   company value 65
   labour demand 222
   use by analysts 676
lead-the-market pay strategies 261
leaderless group discussions 455
leadership, development 470
learning 70–1, 189
   in the workplace 410–13
   components 414–15
   environments 415–22
learning and development 189, 396–439, 447
   software applications 246
   Sing Tel Optus 395–6
   defined 396, 447
   OPSM 438–9
   MECWA 445–6
   related to careers 447–9
   approaches 449–66
   managers with dysfunctional behaviours 473–5
   see also employees, development
Leasing Centre, and WorkChoices 95

legality (selection processes) 286
legislation 23
LG Electronics 205
Lion Nathan
   use of IT in recruitment 266
   talent retention 642
Lovett, Penny 331

Main Roads WA 65
Making Diversity Work for your Organisation and Australia's Future, Drake International 337
managed decentralisation 152
management by objectives (MBO) 365–6
management of change
   as HR competency 84–5
Management Practices Index (Honeywell) 317
managerial initiatives
   diversity management 317–20
managerialist view 581
managers
   work changes 31
   source of performance information 374
   support for training 420–1
   as assessors 456
   performance pay 547–8
   attitude to international operations 607
managing diversity 97
marginal employees
   performance management 382–3, 384–5
   defined 383
market pay surveys 490–3
   related to pay structure 495–6
   conflict with job evaluation 498–9
market pressures
   effect on pay levels 488–9
marketing HRM 665
Marriott Corporation
   customer satisfaction surveys 376
Masnick, Julie 266
MBO *see* management by objectives
MBTI® instrument 453–5
McFarlane, John 212–13
meaningful work
   employee right 573
means-based approach
   performance measurement 372–4
measurement
   in employee selection 275–8
   employee performance 351–5
mechanistic approach
   job design 198, 200–1
MECWA, learning and development 445–6
Melbourne Market Authority
   use of balanced scorecard 674
mentoring 464–6, 475–6

mergers
   related to downsizing 226–7
merit increase grids 536–7
merit pay 535–9
   criticisms 537–9
Mill, John Stuart 568
minimum wage 515–17
   defined 516
mission statements 61, 62
mixed standard scales
   performance measurement 359–60
MNCs (multinational corporations) *see* multinational enterprises
MNEs *see* multinational enterprises
Monash medical Centre
   anaesthetic patient simulator 426
monotony at work 635
moral development
   human resource managers 577
moral insight 570
motivational approach
   job design 198, 199–200
Motorola
   Pager Robotic Assembly 427
Mudginberri dispute 166
multidomestic industries 603–4
multinational enterprises (MNEs)
   approaches to global mobility 26–7
   Chinese 26
   sending staff overseas 205
   in the global economy 564–5
   rights of employees 573
   defined 591
   reliance on home-country market 605
Murphy, Peter 88
Myer–Briggs Type Indicator® Personality Instrument 453–5

NAB *see* National Australia Bank
National Australia Bank (NAB)
   corporate renewal 654–5
   corporate social responsibility 660
National Health Survey 131
National Occupational Health and Safety Commission Act 1985 (Cwlth) 120
needs assessments
   defined 405
   use in designing training systems 405–6
negative affectivity 634
neo-classical paradigm 564
neo-liberal paradigm 564
neo-liberal policies 155
   defined 150
networks 236–8
New South Wales
   occupational health and safety 122, 138
   Police Service 355

Index

New Zealand Defence Force
   redundancies 226
Nicholson, Kylie 303–4
non-key jobs 493
non-standard employment 159–60, 169
   growth 226
   see also temporary workers
Northern Territory, occupational health and safety 122
Novell
   use of technology 684
NSW Independent Pricing and Regulatory Tribunal 479

obesity 141–3
OBM *see* organisational behaviour modification
Occupational Health and Safety Act 1989 (ACT) 122
Occupational Health and Safety Act 2000 (NSW) 122, 138
Occupational health and Safety Act 2004 (Vic) 123
Occupational Health and Safety (Commonwealth Employment) Act 1991 (Cwlth) 119
occupational health and safety (OHS) 106–7, 114–43
   auditing 132–4
   Asia-Pacific region 138–41
   Australia
      statistics 117–19
      legislation 119–23
      enforcement authorities 123–4
      complementary regulation 124–5
      codes of practice 125
      national standards 125
      regulations 125
      related to industrial relations 125
   defined 115
   management 128–34
   HRM strategies 134–7
   management systems 130
      elements 131–2
   as part of integrated HRM strategy 117
   policies 130
   programs 130
   training and development for managers 135–6
   small businesses 137–8
   strategies, evaluation 141
   work-related illness 582–3
Occupational Health, Safety and Welfare Act 1986 (SA) 122
Occupational Safety and Health Act 1984 (WA) 123
Occupational Safety and Health Legislation Amendment Act 1995 (WA) 123

offshoring 204–5, 226
   banking industry 167, 623
   defined 204
   problems 507–9
   Qantas 574
   management 612–13
OHS *see* occupational health and safety
OJT *see* on-the-job training
older workers 16, 63
   occupational health and safety 126–8, 136
   early retirement programs 228
   prejudice against 334–5
O'Loughlin, Helen 250–1
on-the-job training (OJT) 426
one-way linkage, HRM and strategy formulation 59–60
operational initiatives, diversity management 320
OPSM
   learning and development 438–9
organisation structure 183–4
   defined 180
   configurations 184–7
   related to job design 186–7
   Westpac 187
   HR 208–10
organisational analysis
   design of training systems 406
   design of training schemes 407–8
organisational behaviour modification (OBM) 363–4
organisational change 29
   related to linkage between HR and business strategies 74–5
   ANZ Bank 212–14
   and diversity management 313–14
organisational commitment 633
organisational justice 576
organisational performance
   effect of diversity management 310–14
organisational redesign, defined 225
organisational socialisation 433–5
   encounter phase 434–5
   settling-in phase 435
organisational strategies
   defined 80
   evaluation and control 80–2
   diversity management 315–17
   formulation 56–7
      role of HRM 58–60, 61–6
   implementation 56–7
      role of HRM 66–8
      related to choice of HR practices 68–72
   international operations 607–11
   related to
      training 408–9
      rewards strategy 554–5

organisational structure *see* organisation structure
orientation programs 435, 437
   content 436
   effectiveness criteria 436
   staff retention 642
Oticon, knowledge workers 82
outcome-oriented contracts 533–4
outplacement counselling 628–9
   defined 629
output
   defined 409
   related to performance and learning 409
outsourcing 208–9, 230–1, 574
   HR administration 13
   jobs 79
   information technology 353
   HR functions 679–81
   defined 680
overseas assignments *see* international assignments
overtime 231
paired comparisons
   performance measurement 357
PAQs *see* position analysis questionnaires
parent country, defined 593
parent-country nationals (PCNs), defined 592
Pareto charts 369
pay
   grades 496–8
   influence on
      employees 530–4
      labour force composition 534–5
      job satisfaction 639–40
   levels 488–500
      defined 486
   ranges 491
   spread 496
   structures 71, 486, 494–8
      defined 486
      effect of globalisation 500
      related to geographic regions 500
      job based 502–7
   systems
      related to training 435
   see also skill-based pay systems
pay-policy lines 495, 496
Pay Satisfaction Questionnaire (PSQ) 644–5
PayConnect Solutions 235
payroll, software applications 32, 246–7
PCNs *see* parent-country nationals
peers, source of performance information 375
PeopleSoft 245
Pepsico, acquisitions 57–8
perceptual motor approach, job design 198, 201

750

performance appraisal 342–3
  in management development 57–9
  defined 344
  strategic purpose 348
  developmental purposes 349–50
  administrative uses 350, 351
performance-based pay 528–57
  teachers 531
  programs 535–47
  participation by employees 552
  process issues 553
performance-based reward systems 527–8
performance feedback 379–83
  defined 344, 379
  criteria for effectiveness 380–3
  frequency 380
  focus 382
  related to training 409
performance hurdles 544
performance management 71, 189, 342–90
  ANZ Bank 213
  software applications 245
  defined 343
  organisational model 344–7
  purposes 347–51
  strategic purpose 347–8
  developmental purpose 348–50
  administrative purpose 350–1
  use of technology 387–8
performance measurement
  criteria 351–5
  approaches 355–74
  information sources 374–7
  rater errors 377–9
  organisations 513–14
performance planning and evaluation (PPE) systems, defined 345
performance-related pay see performance-based pay
person analysis
  design of training systems 406, 408–10
person characteristics 409
person-job match 636–7
personal dispositions 634–5
personality inventories 289–90
physical ability tests 288
physical job withdrawal 632
Piaget, Jean 412
Pier 1 Imports, MBO 366
Pilkington, Ross 113
planning for the future 88–9
Plummer, John 334
pluralism
  defined 153, 570
  suppression 581–2
political-influence perspective
  human resource management 7
portals 240

Porter, Michael
  on competitive advantage 72–3
  on patterns of international competition 603–4
Portman Ritz–Carlton Hotel, Shanghai
  best employer award 228
  recruitment 293
position analysis questionnaires (PAQs) 193–4
post-test only evaluation 432
PPE systems see performance planning and evaluation (PPE) systems
pre-test/post-test evaluation 432
predictive validation
  compared with concurrent validation 280–2
  defined 280
Prices and Incomes Accord 152, 517
PricewaterhouseCoopers 77, 102
principals (agency theory) 532
Privacy Amendment (Private Sector) Act 2000 (Cwlth) 265
private employment agencies 267
procedural justice 488, 576
  involuntary turnover 624
process-flow analysis 369
process redesign
  human resource management 681–3
product-market competition
  effect on pay levels 488–9
productivity measurement and evaluation system 181, 366–7
profit sharing 540, 541–2
ProMES technique 181, 366–7
promote-from-within policies see internal promotion
promotions 462, 463–4
protean careers 448
PSQ see Pay Satisfaction Questionnaire
psychological contracts 448, 565
  defined 13
psychological job withdrawal 632–3
psychological success 448
psychosocial support 465
public employment agencies 267

Qantas
  education and training
    anti-discrimination case 108
    Indigenous Australians 451
  offshoring 574
Qantas College Online 428
Qantas Flight Catering 319–20
QIDC see Queensland Industry Development Corporation
quality approach
  performance measurement 368–72
Queensland, occupational health and safety 122

Queensland Industry Development Corporation (QIDC)
  performance management 348–9

Randolph, Marcus 46
ranking
  performance measurement 356
raters
  performance measurement errors 377–9
Rawls, John 569
realistic job previews 273
reality checks 467
Rebel Sport
  blended learning 424
recognition-based reward systems see performance-based reward systems
recruiters 270–4
  functional area 271
  traits 271
  realism 272–3
  impact 273–4
recruiting culture 298–300
recruitment 70, 259–74
  defined 259
  emerging strategies 261
  graduates 267–8, 272, 599
    Google 299
  laws 102–3
  software applications 244, 245
  software packages 250–1
  human resource policies 260–1
  Portman Ritz-Carlton Hotel, Shanghai 293
  innovations 678
  sources 261–8
    evaluation 268–70
  see also selection (employees)
Recruitment Process Outsourcing (RPO) 294–5
redundancy 159
reengineering 681–3
references, use in selection 287–8
referrals (recruitment) 263–4
reinforcement theory 530
relational databases 238–9
relational psychological contracts 565
relationship recruitment 265
reliability
  measurement, defined 275, 354
  MBTI® instrument 455
  staff performance 354
  staff selection 275–9
  standards 278–9
repatriation 597
reputation index 24, 662
resource-based view
  human resource management 6–7

751

Index

Restructuring and Efficiency Principle 517–18
results approach
   performance measurement 365–8
retention 37–8, 39, 472, 651–2
   inducements 3–4
   Australia 43
   related to, induction schemes 437
   management 640–51
   talented staff 641, 643
return on investment (ROI) 89
   ESS systems 237
   graduate recruitment 272
   performance-based reward systems 527–8
   HR activities 672
   training programs 431, 434
      determination 433
rewards 41
   human resources information systems 32
   Google 299–300
   costs, monitoring 499–500
   government regulation 515–20
   effect on labour force composition 534–5
   management 137, 485–522
      software applications 248
      communication 501–2
      importance of process 501–2
      participation of employees 501
      related to, organisational strategy 554–5
   related to
      strategic management 71, 85
      performance management 350
      performance 409
      job satisfaction 639–40
   see also pay
RFID chips 581
Rich, Christina 102
rights ethics 571
risk
   management 130
   defined 133
   exposure, international assignments 598
Robens, Alfred, Baron Robens 120, 121, 125
ROI *see* return on investment
role
   ambiguity 637
   source of dissatisfaction 637–8
role analysis technique 637–8
role behaviours 74
role conflict 637
role overload 637
role plays 455
Royal, Carol 341
RPO *see* Recruitment Process Outsourcing
Russell, Teresa 141–2
Russell, Todd 146–7

SA Water Corporation 331
sabbatical leave 464
safety climate 130
safety culture 130
Safety Management Achievement Program 134
Safety MAP 134
St George Bank 48–50
   merger with Advance Bank 77
   offshoring 167
   blended learning 425
   enterprise learning 441–2
salaries
   planning
      software applications 247
   surveys
      software applications 247
S.C. Johnson 316
scientific management 200
Sears Department Stores
   executive pay 550–1
   causal chain analysis 675
selection (employees) 70, 189, 275–93
   laws 102–3
   interviews 286–7
   methods
      standards 275–86
      types 286–92
self assessment 375–6, 467
self-management skills 422
self-managing work teams *see* work teams
self selection 263
self service, defined 13
Sensis
   performance management 387
SET *see* Survey of Education and Training Experience
settling-in phase
   organisational socialisation 435
sexual harassment 100–1
Seymour, Jane 91
share options 542–3
Shaw Contracting 352
Shell
   social responsibility 660
shiftwork, and older workers 127–8
SHRM *see* strategic human resource management
Siemens
   virtual teaming 595
similar to me error
   performance measurement 377
simulations 426–7
Sing Tel Optus
   learning and development policy 395–6
skill-based outcomes
   training programs 430

skill-based pay 504–7
   defined 505
skill-based pay systems 435
skill deficiencies *see* skilled labour, shortage
skill variety 199
skilled labour
   shortage 21–2, 262
      China 233
      India 233
      minerals industry 404
skilled temporary migrants 333
skills, job requirement 190
small businesses
   occupational health and safety 137–8
social learning, principles 414
social marketing 138
socialisation *see* organisational socialisation
socially responsible investment (SRI) 660–3
   assessment 662
soft HRM 580
South Australia, occupational health and safety 122
South Blackwater mine 586–7
specificity
   measures
      performance management 355
SRI *see* socially responsible investment
staff *see* employees
stakeholder theory 571
State, defined 92
STEP *see* Support Through Education Program
Stewart, Andrew 91
stock ownership 540
Stockland, coaching 478
strategic business partner
   role of HR professionals 10
strategic choice 57–8, 63
strategic competitive advantage 80–2
strategic congruence
   measurement criteria 351–2
strategic decision-making, role of HR professionals 8–9
strategic human resource management (SHRM) 4, 54–87, 579
   defined 4, 56
   professional competencies 83–5
strategic human resources planning 221
strategic management
   defined 55–6
   components 56–7
   linkage with HRM 57–8
strategic planning, human resources management 224–31
strategic types 72–80
   related to HR needs 73–5
strategies *see* organisational strategies
stress 115, 635

stress response 115
strikes 157
structural configurations 184–7
Structural Efficiency Principle 491, 518
structural HRM strategies
  occupational health and safety 134–5
structural realignment 675, 676
  see also human resource management (HRM), functions
subjectivism 570
subordinates
  source of performance data 375
succession planning 242, 471–3, 474
  examples 243
    AMCOR 342
Sullivan, John 257
supervisors
  affect on job satisfaction 638–9
support networks 421
Support Through Education Program (STEP) 445–6
survey-feedback interventions 646–51
Survey of Education and Training Experience (ABS) 400–1
Sussan (fashion retailer)
  performance management. 349
sustainability 32–3, 341–2
  3M policies 318
  related to HRM 659–63
  measurement 660–3
sustainability reports 660
SWOT analysis 62–4
systemic change 225

talent
  international recruitment 610–11
  competition for 640–1
  retention 641, 643
  supply chains 678
talent management 73, 253–4
  defined 5
  ANZ Bank 213
task analysis
  inventories 194
  design of training systems 406, 410
  questionnaire 411
task identity 199
tasks
  complexity, and job satisfaction 635
  source of dissatisfaction 635–7
Tasmania, occupational health and safety 123
TCNs see third-country nationals
teachers, performance-based pay 531
teams see work teams
telecommuting 23
teleological theory 568
telework 23, 191–2
  defined 179

Telstra
  cost-cutting program 163
  executive pay 549
  corporate social responsibility 660
temporary migrants 333
temporary workers 229–30
  recruited from overseas 333
termination see involuntary turnover
termination of employment, laws 103–5
TES see Training Expenditure Surveys
third-country nationals (TCNs), defined 592
Thorndike, E.L.
  Law of effect 530
Thoughtware Australia 319
time series evaluation 432–3
TMP worldwide
  employee retention survey 39
total quality management (TQM) 33–7
  related to staff development 71
Towers Perrin Workplace Index 75
TQM see total quality management
trade unions see unions
traditional activities 663–4, 676
traineeships 403–4
training 396
  diversity sensitivity 323–4
  objectives 415–16
  feedback 418
  methods, selection 422–30
  outcomes, identification 430–1
  programs
    administration 418–19
    audiovisual techniques 423–4
    presentation methods 423–5
    evaluation 430–3
    return on investment 431, 433
  systems design 404–10
  resources 408
  transfer 419–20
  action plans 421
Training Expenditure and Practices surveys (ABS) 422
Training Expenditure Surveys (ABS) 399, 400
Training Guarantee Scheme 399
training programs, return on investment 434
transaction processing 234
transactional activities 663, 664, 676
transactional psychological contracts 565
transfer of training 419–20
  action plans 421
transfers (jobs) 462–3
transformational activities 664, 676
transitional matrices 223–4
transnational index 605–6
transportable talent 268

triple bottom line 659
true scores (measurement devices) 275–6
trust gap 511
turnover, management 168–9, 622–40
two-factor theory (Herzberg) 199
two-way linkage, HRM and strategy formulation 60

UNCTAD see United Nations Conference on Trade and Development
unemployment level 168–9
unfair dismissal 91, 104–5, 155, 168
  hearings in AIRC 157
  and performance management 384–5
unions
  defined 150
  membership 162–5
  global cooperation 164
unions@work 165
Unisys
  international assignment strategy 589–90
unitarism 581
  defined 9
United Nations Conference on Trade and Development (UNCTAD) 605–6
universalism 569
universities, graduate placement 267–8
upward feedback 458
utilitarianism 568
utility analysis 671
utility (selection processes) 284–6

validity
  measurement, defined 279, 352
  MBTI® instrument 455
  staff selection 279–83
  staff performance 352–4
veil of ignorance 569
VET see vocational education and training
Victoria
  occupational health and safety 123
  education and training 450
Victoria. Department of Human Services 243
Victoria. Police
  health promotion program 142–3
Virgin Blue 60
  corporate culture 53–4
  anti-discrimination case 107–8
virtual reality 427
virtual teaming 595
virtue ethics 568–9
Visy, graduate recruitment 272
vocational education and training (VET) 397–8
  Australia 402–4
  defined 451
vocational rehabilitation 124

Index

voluntary turnover 630–40
  defined 630
  law firms 631
Vygotsky, Lev 412

wage drift 487
wages, machinery 93–5
war for talent 640
Ward, Peter 331
Watson Wyatt
  Human Capital Index 674
Webb, Brant 146
wellness programs *see* health-promotion programs
Western Australia, occupational health and safety 123
Westpac Banking Corporation
  organisation structure 187
  human resources information system 250–1
  diversity management 314, 317, 319
  health maintenance and stress management 635
  work-life program 673
Whirlpool Corporation
  customer satisfaction surveys 376
whistleblowing 575, 632
women
  in the workforce 16–17, 164
  in senior positions 472
Woo, Nam K. 205
Woods Bagot 313
work, analysis and design 179–211
work-flow analysis 181–3
work-flow design, defined 181
Work Health Act 1986 (NT) 122
work inputs, analysis 182–3
work intensification, defined 115, 179
work-life balance 328–30
work-life program, Westpac 673
work outputs, analysis 181

work processes, analysis 181–2
work redesign 189
work-related illness 582–3
  older workers 127
work-related injuries, older workers 127
work-related stress 115
work-sample tests 290–1
work teams 30–1
  performance management 384
  training 429–30
  awards 545
  related to job satisfaction 636
WorkChoices 34, 94–5, 154–5
  and AWAs 71–2, 160
  defined 92
  effect on young workers 170–1
  and performance assessment 385–6
  and performance-based pay 529
workers compensation and rehabilitation 124
workforce
  planning *see* human resource planning
  characteristics 15–20
  composition 15–16
  ageing 16
  gender issues 16–17
  ethnic diversity 17–18
  skill deficiencies 21–2
  global 26–7
  reduction 225
  dynamics analysis 242–4
  profile analysis 242
  changes 331–2
workplace agreements 153, 154
  see also Australian Workplace Agreements
Workplace Amendment (Work Choices) Act 2005 (Cwlth) *see* WorkChoices
workplace bargaining 153, 156–9
workplace bullying 625–6, 626–7
workplace deaths 113
workplace diversity programs 20
workplace harassment 91

workplace health
  stress 115, 635
  Australia 131
workplace health and safety *see* occupational health and safety
Workplace Health and Safety Act 1995 (Qld) 122
Workplace Health and Safety Act 1995 (Tas) 123
Workplace Health and Safety Amendment Act 2002 (Tas) 123
Workplace Health and Safety and Other Acts Amendment Act 2003 (Qld) 122
Workplace Relations Act 1996 (Cwlth) 92, 94, 151, 153–4, 565
  2005 amendments *see* WorkChoices
  and occupational health and safety 125
  allowable matters 154–5
  unfair dismissal 155, 157
  dispute resolution 157–8
  and union membership 162
  and management prerogative 166
  and flexible employment 332–3
  wage determination 519
workplace romances
  organisational policies 563
workplace stress 635
workplace surveillance
  NSW 110, 241
  involuntary turnover 624–5
Workplace Surveillance Act 2005 (NSW) 110, 241
WorkSafe Victoria 113
World Wide Web *see* Internet
WRA *see Workplace Relations Act 1996* (Cwlth)

Yen, Melossa 88–9
Young, Mary 221
young workers 170–1
Yue Yuen Industrial (Holdings)
  social responsibility 661